The Genesis Documents

Undergirding the Truth of Genesis and the Ancient Faith of the Church

By

Michael J. Gladieux

Book Cover: Artwork by Kevin Hughes
Artist-Oil Painter
Landscapes, Streetscapes, and Still Life
Website: kevinhughespaintings.com

The Genesis Documents

Undergirding the Truth of Genesis and the Ancient Faith of the Church
By
Michael J. Gladieux

Copyright © 2017 by Michael J. Gladieux.
All rights reserved.
Registration #: TXu 2-063-279
Registration Effective Date: July 26, 2017

Except for the use of brief quotations in printed reviews, no part of this book may be reproduced in any form without the prior permission of the author, Michael J. Gladieux, Ann Arbor, Michigan.

Unless otherwise specifically noted, all Scripture references are taken from the NASB translation:
    Scripture taken from the New American Standard Bible ®,
    © Copyright 1960, 1962, 1963, 1968, 1971, 1972, 1973, 1975, 1977, 1995 by The Lockman Foundation. Used by permission.

Publishing Services:	Sellbox.com
ISBN (paperback)	978-1547068876
First Printing:	07-12-2017
Final Printing:	12-05-2020
	This includes the additions suggested by The Kolbe Institute.
	This printing comes from the following MS Word Document:
	Genesis Documents 20201205 Copyrighted Proofed Published
	File size: 4701 KB
	Date-time stamp: December 5, 2020, 7:15 AM
Second Edition:	10-11-2022
	This includes the chapter "Biblical Archeology and the Pentateuch"
	This printing comes from the following MS Word Document:
	Genesis Documents 2nd Edition
	File Size: 24,278 KB
	Date-time stamp: 10-11-2022, 10:03 AM
	And from the following PDF Document:
	Genesis Documents 2nd Edition
	File Size: 9017 KB
	Date-time stamp: 10-11-2022, 10:04 AM

Dedication of this Book

I am dedicating this book to my late mother-in-law Cornelia Anne Harris who went home and wept bitterly after she heard the priest teach from the pulpit that the Deluge of Noah was just an old myth.

I am also dedicating this book to Sister Frances Marie, my first-grade teacher who was a Sister of St. Agnes, and who wept copiously when they replaced our traditional catechism with a modern one that downplayed the stories of Adam, Eve, Cain, and Abel. How was she to teach us, she asked?

God counts the tears of women.[a]

People today can hardly remember how the Church used to view Truth and the Faith. These proscriptions reveal the perverse ideas sprouting in the Church 115 years ago.

From *Lamentabili Sane* by Pope Pius X, 1907 (see: http://www.papalencyclicals.net/pius10/p10lamen.htm)

With truly lamentable results, our age, **casting aside all restraint in its search for the ultimate causes of things**, frequently pursues novelties so ardently that **it rejects the legacy of the human race**. Thus it falls into very serious errors, which are even more serious when they concern sacred authority, the interpretation of Sacred Scripture, and the principal mysteries of Faith . . . Therefore, after a very diligent investigation and consultation with the Reverend Consultors, the Most Eminent and Reverend Lord Cardinals, the General Inquisitors in matters of faith and morals have judged the following propositions to be condemned and proscribed. In fact, by this general decree, they are condemned and proscribed. [Selected from 65 proscriptions in all.] [Bold mine.]

5. Since the deposit of Faith contains only revealed truths, the Church has no right to pass judgment on the assertions of the human sciences.
9. They display excessive simplicity or ignorance who believe that God is really the author of the Sacred Scriptures.
11. Divine inspiration does not extend to all of Sacred Scriptures so that it renders its parts, each and every one, free from every error.
12. If he wishes to apply himself usefully to biblical studies, the exegete must first put aside all preconceived opinions about the supernatural origin of Sacred Scripture and interpret it the same as any other merely human document.
57. The Church has shown that she is hostile to the progress of the natural and theological sciences.
58. Truth is no more immutable than man himself, since it evolved with him, in him, and through him.
63. The Church shows that she is incapable of effectively maintaining evangelical ethics since she obstinately clings to immutable doctrines which cannot be reconciled with modern progress.
64. Scientific progress demands that the concepts of Christian doctrine concerning God, creation, revelation, the Person of the Incarnate Word, and Redemption be re-adjusted.
65. Modern Catholicism can be reconciled with true science only if it is transformed into a non-dogmatic Christianity, that is to say, into a broad and liberal Protestantism.

The following Thursday, the fourth day of the same month and year, all these matters were accurately reported to our Most Holy Lord, Pope Pius X. His Holiness approved and confirmed the decree of the Most Eminent Fathers and ordered that each and every one of the above-listed propositions be held by all as condemned and proscribed.

PETER PALOMBELLI, Notary of the Holy Roman and Universal Inquisition

---

[a] A quotation from the movie *A Stranger Among Us*, so asserted because "women understand the world more deeply than men do." This is because "they are more sensitive than men" and so "they weep more over its abuses." This might be based in the Babylonian Talmud, perhaps being loosely taken from Baba Mezi'a 59: "One should be heedful of wronging his wife, for since her tears are frequent she is quickly hurt."

Acknowledgments

Thank you, Abba Father and Jesus my Lord for assigning this work to me and for seeing me through to its completion.

> What does this mean? Here is what I am saying: The Lord took an eager young child who had been interested in math and science all of his life, who had always believed that the theories of origins that he was taught were utterly true, but who had left that love behind in college, and who was thinking of "getting back into" his childhood fascination. He showed him the foolishness of his childhood ideas, led him to the truth of His precious word instead, and walked him through the complex maize of science and archeology—all of the topics that impacted His book of Genesis, showed him the roadblocks to faith in the full truth of Genesis, explained to him how (historically) a tragic lie that Genesis was not completely true had come upon western civilization, and led him to write this book. It is a work that has been inspired by the Lord God from its very beginning and through to its final end. All honor for successful thoughts and insights belongs to Him alone. All foolish errors were introduced by me, of course, in my imperfection. Again, thank You, Abba Father, and my Lord Jesus.

I would like to thank Mr. Kevin Hughes for his careful work in calculating the chronology of the Old Testament from the creation to the Exodus, and for the many discussions that he has had with me on chronology. His insights have been most helpful. I also want to acknowledge his careful review of my initial manuscript, his careful correction of several errors, and his encouragement at various steps along the way. Finally, he has graced this work by the presence of his lovely artistic work. The cover of the book is his work as are the chronological charts.

I want to thank Dr. Marsha Daigle-Williamson (now promoted to glory) for her careful and expert review of my writing, and for her correction of many technical errors in the notes and format. She has also been a source of encouragement for me along the way.

I would like to thank Dan Robelen, pastor of Dexter Gospel Church in Dexter, Michigan, for his careful review of certain sections of this work and for his discussions about the content and style. His insights and suggestions were most helpful and encouraging.

I would like to thank Dr. Jack Hughes, teacher, author, and pastor of Crossing Church in Crestwood, Kentucky, who has offered careful and thoughtful comments on style and approach that have helped make my final product to be much better.

Thank you to my sweet wife Martha who has patiently endured my absent-mindedness and distractedness over the period of several years as I put this work together.

I would like to thank my friend Dr. George Hoffman for his helpful suggestions about the explanations that I offer in the area of archeology.

I would like to thank Carole Monica C. Burnett, Ph. D, Editor, Fathers of the Church and Fathers of the Church Mediaeval Continuation, and other members of her staff for help in tracking down and obtaining the English translation of certain ancient works.

Thank you to brothers and sisters of the Kolbe Institute for many helpful suggestions.

Thank you especially to John Wynne for his careful review of my chapter on the Mosaic authorship of the Pentateuch.

Thank you to many other precious brothers and sisters whose prayers have sustained me along the way.

Table of Contents

Preface to the Second Edition	v
Preface	vi
Introduction – The Father Answers	viii
The Ancient Faith	**2**

The Origin of the Ancient Faith: 2; The Fathers of the Faith: 3; The Ancient Faith and Origins—Issues: 6; Augustinian Understanding of the Creation Account: 13; Origen: 23; Augustine on Eden and on Allegory: 32; Concluding Perspective on Augustine and Origen: 34; Quotations from other Fathers: 35; A Short Digression on Ancient and Modern Cosmological Concepts: 53; One Perspective from Judaism: 79; Opposite Quotations from the Fathers: 80; Summary of the Ancient Faith about Genesis: 88; Relevance of Creation Belief for Today: 90; Restating the Purpose of this Work: 92; Introductory Thoughts on the Authorship of Genesis: 93

Biblical Archeology and the Pentateuch — **96**

Part 1—The Traditional Church Doctrine on the Authorship of the Pentateuch and Joshua: 96; Part 2—Rationalism and Scholarly Skepticism/Unbelief in Biblical Archeology Today: 104; Philosophical and Historical Roots: 105; Specific Examples of Scholarly Skepticism about the History of Israel: 114; Overview of Scholarly Thinking on Chronology: 120; Examples of Scholarly Thinking—The Conquest of Canaan: 121; Overview of Scholarly Thinking on Epigraphy: 123; Summary of Scholarly Challenges to Biblical Truth: 125; Part 3—Response: Moses Wrote the Pentateuch and it is Historically Reliable: 126; The Basis for the Exodus Date—Biblical Chronology: 126; The Chronology of the Sojourn in Egypt: 135; Evidence for the Sojourn in Egypt: 138; Evidence for the Exodus: 141; The Conquest of Canaan: 144; Summary of the Information that we Have Uncovered thus Far: 152; An Alphabetic Script at the Time of the Exodus: 153; A Broader Perspective on the Origins of the Hebrew Script: 164; Unified Chronology of the Time of Joseph: 167; The Development of the proto-Sinaitic Script: 168; Issues Surrounding the Mosaic Authorship of Genesis: 170; Conclusion: How I Will Move Forward in this Work: 171

The Genesis Documents — **173**

Introduction to an Archeological Find: 173; The Earliest Development of Writing: 174; A Few Basic Facts about Ancient Middle Eastern Writing: 177; One Key Discovery—Archeological Evidence for the Sacrifice of Noah: 178; Ancient Middle Eastern Writing and Genesis: 179; Fundamental Thesis on the Authorship of Genesis: 180; Detailed Description of Babylonian Writing Techniques and their Connection to Genesis: 180; The Original Authors of Genesis: 188; Statement of our Hypothesis as Derived from Wiseman: 191; Implications for the JEPD Theory: 192; How our Hypothesis Relates to the Reading of Genesis: 194; Carrying Forward our Purpose in this Work—Genesis is Historically Accurate: 196

The Creation — **198**

Archeological Considerations: 198; Connections Between the Pre-Deluge Tablets: 201; Other Creation Accounts: 202; Commentary and Theological Considerations: 206; Christian Revelation and our Approach to

Understanding Genesis: 206; Day 1: 209; A Brief Survey of Radiometric Dating Results: 215; Reaction of the Scientific Community to Radiocarbon Test Results—One Instance: 217; The Divine Purpose of Creation: 219; More Details on the Roles within the Trinity: 223; Day 2: 229; The Fathers' Ideas and Modern Theories of Origins: 234; Day 3: 236; Observations from Geology: 237; Day 4: 240; A Critique of Modern Cosmology: 241; Comparing Creation to Naturalistic Theories—The Big Bang: 241; Creation and the Cosmic Configuration: 244; Celestial Mechanics: 246; Historical Overview of Cosmological Thought: 247; Day 5: 250; A Critique of Biological Evolution: 253; Genetics and the Future of Biological Life Forms on Earth: 257; Philosophical Bias in Scientific Theories: 261; Day 6: 263; The Creation of Man: 266; Made in His Image and Likeness: 272; Day 7: 295; Concluding Observations about the Creation Account: 296

Adam 299

Archeological Considerations: 299; Relation to the Creation Account and Introductory Remarks: 299; Textual and Theological Considerations: 305; The Creation of Adam: 311; Two Insights from Genetics: 314; The Garden of Eden: 316; The Nature of God from His Interaction with Adam and Eve: 319; Meditation on the Spiritual State of Adam and Eve and our State: 320; The Two Special Trees in Eden: 322; The Creation of Eve: 327; Meditation on Human Nature: 330; Allegorical Meaning of the Creation of Woman: 331; How Human Life Would Have Progressed on Earth if Adam and Eve Had Not Sinned: 334; Details about the Ages to Come: 338: An Interpretation Based on the Documentary Hypothesis: 340; Answers to All of the Issues that Plagued Augustine: 346; An Explanation of the Human Condition from Scientific Naturalism: 349; The Temptation and Fall: 352; The True Nature of Sin: 363; The Nature of Salvation: 369; A Reply to Origen on Universal Salvation: 370; Perspectives on the Fall and the Promise of a Savior: 372; God's Special Concern for Women: 376; Life Outside of Eden: 381; The Civilization of Cain and his Descendants: 386; The Beginning of the Patriarchal Line: 388; The Signature of Adam: 391; The Importance of Adam's Story: 392

Noah 395

Archeological Considerations: 395; Theological Considerations: 396; The Corruption of Mankind on the Earth: 400; An Interpretation of the Nephilim from the Documentary Hypothesis: 401; Another Interpretation of the Nephilim in Genesis 6:1–4: 403; Conclusion to the Account of Noah: 412

Interlude: Creation Theory 413

Overview of the Originally Created Earth: 413; Geological Indications of a Universal Flood as Described in Genesis: 420

The Deluge 421

Archeological Considerations: 421; Historical Considerations: 422; The Building of the Ark: 424; Other Accounts of the Flood: 428; Description of the Deluge—Psalm 29: 431; The Ark Touches Down: 436; Events Immediately after the Flood—The Promise to Noah: 439; Crawford's Archeological Evidence for the Sacrifice of Noah: 439; Original Sin and the Birth of the Messiah: 441; Mary and the Hypostatic Union: 447; God Re-establishes Mankind after the Deluge: 453; Life after the Deluge: 456; Estimated Post-Flood Population Projection: 459; Concluding Remarks on the Flood Account: 462

Lyrical Verses on the Tower of Babel — 464
Babel — 465
Archeological Considerations: 465; Historical Considerations: 465; Introduction and Overview of Shem's Account: 466; The Table of Nations: 471; Chronological Matrix—Adam to Exodus: 474; Babel: 474; The Development of Human Civilization after the Flood and after Babel: 477; Other Events after Babel: 478; The Creation of the Genesis Documents: 481; Scattering Details: 482; Theological Considerations and Perspectives: 484; The Patriarchal Library at the Beginning of Historical Times: 486; Summary and Perspective on the First Eleven Chapters of Genesis: 487

Terah the Father of Abraham — 488
Archeological Considerations: 488; Historical Considerations: 489; The Nuzi Tablets: 491

Abraham and Isaac — 493
Archeological Considerations: 493; The Contents of Isaac's Story: 493; The Signature of Isaac: 506

Jacob — 508
Archeological Considerations: 508; The Contents of Jacob's Story: 509; The Conclusion of Jacob's Account: 519

The Sons of Jacob — 520
Archeological Considerations: 520; The narratives: 521; Moses: 525; Moses Edited the Account of Jacob: 526; Moses Providentially Called and Chosen by God: 527; From Jacob to the Exodus: 527; The Population Growth of Israel in Egypt: 528; The Genesis Documents: 531; Concluding Thoughts: 532

Summary and Final Conclusion — 534
What we have Discovered: 534; Genesis and the Spirit of the Age—The Modern Controversy: 538; A Brief Personal Story: 541; The Unavoidable Choice that Stands Before us: 541

Appendix I – Old Testament Chronology — 542
Time from the Abrahamic Covenant to the Exodus: 542; Time from the Abrahamic Covenant to Entering Egypt: 543; Time from Entering Egypt to the Exodus: 543; Linking the Biblical Chronology to Known Historical dates: 543

Appendix II – The Modern Theory of Origins — 545
Cosmological Perspective: 545; Developments on Earth: 546; Focus on the Advent of Man: 547

Appendix III – The Documentary Hypothesis — 548

End Notes — 549
The Ancient Faith: 549; Biblical Archeology and the Pentateuch: 557; The Genesis Documents: 560; The Creation: 560; Adam: 569; Noah: 570; Interlude: Creation Theory: 571; The Deluge: 571; Babel: 574; Terah the Father of Abraham: 574; Abraham and Isaac: 575; Jacob: 575; The Sons of Jacob: 575; Summary and Conclusion: 575; Appendix II – The Modern Theory of Origins: 575

Preface to the Second Edition

When I first wrote this book I considered that the most significant challenges to the truth of Genesis came from the scientific (actually, the pseudo-scientific) theories that abound in our culture today. Thus, Evolution, the Big Bang, and various geological theories that purport to explain how the surface of the earth came to be as it is today. These theories are all naturalistic, and as such they deny the supernatural account of origins that is put forth in the Sacred Scriptures. They actually present people with an alternate world view of how origins happened—one that excludes God. Therefore I focused on showing that those theories are not science, and there is no reason to accept them as true. Indeed, the entire world view from within which they operate is a fantasy.

But I did not discuss the archeological theories that undergird another set of objections to the truth of Genesis, theories that deny the truth of the entire Pentateuch and much that is to be found in the Old Testament historical books. While these theories and their claims do not focus primarily on Genesis, the objections that they raise do impact Genesis, for it is part of the Pentateuch, and it is the first historical book of the Old Testament. These theories are bound up in a view of mankind and of human history that denies the working of God in the calling, formation, and history of the nation of Israel. Such ideas are rooted in a view of history and of human nature that completely denies the supernatural.

Therefore in the second edition I have included another chapter on "Biblical Archeology and the Pentateuch" in which I review /discuss in some detail the basic fallacies of these theories, and show the weightlessness of their claims. This gives us a firm foundation from which we can assert the truth and historical accuracy of the Pentateuch, which is bound up with the Mosaic authorship of those books. That is, showing that Moses wrote the Pentateuch and asserting its historical reliability are linked together. The Biblical archeology that shows these truths is very convincing when we see it laid out in front of us, and the weakness of ideas and theories to the contrary is quite obvious.

<u>Why? WHY? **WHY?**</u>:
But any thoughtful reader must ask why. Why have so many academic disciplines developed along lines of thinking that express an anti-Biblical perspective? 600 years ago the culture and society of Europe was founded on Christian/Biblical principles. What happened in the intervening centuries, and how did it happen? **This is a vital question, but one that is not very often asked**. Surely it must be in the back of any thoughtful mind that contemplates the present intellectual elan.

During the last 4-5 centuries a new paradigm has been inserted into the intellectual mind. It has engaged our culture in a determined flight from God and His revelation, a flight viewed by those who are caught up in it as an exercise in freedom, as the casting off at last of the constraints of a more primitive and ignorant age of man, as the dawning of a "new age" of intellectual and spiritual awakening that will at last unlock the total human potential. It is an exercise in radical disbelief/skepticism toward Christianity and all things supernatural, but it expresses an insanely optimistic faith in the potential of man and his capabilities.

How did this arise? From what pit of hell did it spring? This illusion is the common source of the pseudo-scientific ideas that oppose the Sacred Scriptures, whether they are biological, cosmological, geological, archeological, historical, psychological, or from whatever discipline. To shed some light onto this centuries-long trend I have included an overview of the history and development of thought in Europe, to expose its roots so that we can see the common source of the deceptive, anti-Biblical theories that are rampant in our culture today.

Preface

This is a commentary on Genesis, the first book of the Bible. Genesis means origins. It is the ancient story of how this world, humanity, and the nations of the earth came to be.

Why would anyone today undertake to write a commentary on Genesis? Think of the obstacles and problems that they must confront! If Genesis were true, as the universal faith of the ancients held, then consider what such a belief would mean in the midst of the huge mountain of knowledge that has accumulated in the last two to three centuries. We now "understand" that the universe has come into its present state via the outworking of natural processes that have been going on for billions of years. We now "understand" that life arose through a gradual complexification of species that has been going on for more than several hundred million years. The earth itself is over "four billion years" old, and the major geological features on the earth—such as the continents and the oceans—were formed by geological processes that have been operating from deep within the earth for most of that time. If Genesis were true then all of these theories would necessarily be condemned as false—and we now understand them to be "proven scientifically" to be true.

That is not all. The very text of Genesis has been carefully explained as having arisen from the cumulative effort of primitive ancient people who worked over many centuries, adding to it and gradually massaging it into its present form. Their input into the book, especially those sections that deal with "origins," was taken largely from the creation myths that were so widely prevalent among many ancient civilizations in the Middle East in the two or three millennia before Jesus walked on earth. How could a book that was put together from such sources, in such a hodge-podge manner, that was rooted in the primitive cultures that existed back when men were so unknowledgeable, actually have anything to say to us in the twenty-first century? What could it add to our enormous and impressive body of wisdom about mankind and its origins?

Anyone who ever thought of writing a commentary on Genesis would inevitably have to address all such issues in some manner. It would be an overwhelming and bewildering task. How could anyone have the breadth of scholarship to even begin such a task, and how could the final product in any way consider all of the issues?

This book is going to do exactly that. I never meant to write such a book. But over three decades ago I was confronted with the conflict between secular theories of origins and the claims of Genesis. I sought an explanation—a resolution—to that conflict, and I was given one. It was an answer to a prayer whose broad implications I have only come to understand over many years. I am going to share with you the encounter with God that began my quest, and the outworking of that quest. I will not attempt to disprove any of the modern perspectives on origins by intricately investigating them, but I will confront them directly and I will cast doubt on them. I will show the basic philosophical bias from which they have sprung. In fact, they are scientifically and intellectually bankrupt, as can be easily seen. I will present to you extremely powerful evidence for the truth of Genesis—inherent in the book itself—recognizing that to accept that evidence will topple the many theories that people naively hold sacred and foolishly consider to be true in our day. I ask only that you follow my logical presentation with an open mind and read to the end.

This book is a carefully organized, logical, and reasonable explanation of the book of Genesis—and it is a defense of its historical accuracy. Certainly, I present many simple and logical reasons for the position that I take, especially reasons for believing that the accounts of Genesis should be taken as true in their entirety. The reasons, as we shall see, are inherent in the book of Genesis itself—reasons that are rooted in a few simple observations that have arisen because of archeological discoveries in the past century.

But as always in the history of Christianity, the acceptance of God's word and our belief in it must ultimately rest in our own choices. It is the sovereign determination of God that each person must choose, either to receive His truth and believe Him or to reject His word. In that case the person will, inevitably, decide to place his or her trust in some other source of knowledge, in some other person or belief system. In our day and age many competing ideologies clamor for our attention and demand our adherence to their tenants. These are often in direct contradiction to the Ancient Faith and the Scriptures.

For this reason I recognize that whatever I say, and however carefully I present these arguments for the truth of Genesis, it will always resolve according to a choice that each person has made in their hearts: Do I accept and believe that God is true, or do I trust in the ideas and theories of men? For the issue when you read this book is not whether or not what I say is true. It is whether God is true. If you are inclined to believe that the Bible is true—that it is the inspired, infallible, inerrant Word of God, which is what all of the men of old firmly believed—then you will welcome this book as a very helpful and insightful work that undergirds the Ancient Faith of the Church and the truth of Genesis. If you are inclined to trust in some of the many and varied theories about origins that are prevalent in our society today, then this work probably will not convince you.

Let me put this differently: The world in which we live today is corrupt and disintegrating on basically every level, and it has discarded the Christian faith and its world view. In this work I am saying that, although our age has abandoned the Ancient Faith and has immersed itself in intellectual theories and ideas that contradict it at every point, still the Ancient Faith is—and always has been—true. As you read, consider carefully the reasons that I advance on behalf of the Ancient Faith. Observe also the utter absurdity of the modern theories of origins, their inadequacy and bankruptcy, and be willing to question them and the naturalistic premises upon which they stand—the world view from which they have sprung.

Therefore I start this work with the following prayer, and I ask you to pray it along with me as we begin:

>**Abba Father and Lord Jesus Christ, I know that You have spoken to us clearly in Your word, which is a lamp to our feet and a light to our path. I want to trust what You have to say to us—and to me in particular. I choose now to trust in You and in Your word in Scripture. I trust first of all that You have spoken to mankind in a clear and understandable way, and that Your word is so written that we—that I—can understand it. I accept Your Word as true because of Who You are: Creator and Savior of mankind; because of the kind of person You are: Faithful and Wise. You could never be wrong about any subject, and You would never lie or deceive Your people about anything. Please clearly show me, as I consider the thoughts in this work, how I should understand Your word in Genesis; and please show me clearly what You are saying to me and to all mankind in and through the first book in Your holy Bible. Thank You Lord!**

Amen! Now let us begin our exposition.

Introduction – The Father Answers

This book certainly would be called a commentary on Genesis by many. It definitely does comment on the book, including the first eleven chapters of the book—those very chapters that have come to be viewed as mythical, allegorical, or in some way not fully historical. But this book is really a history book. It uses the chapters of Genesis to tell the story of the origins of the world, of life, and in particular of human life. We claim that Genesis consists of an accurate and faithful history of these things—that it tells the story of God's creation of man, of our fall, and of His continuing plan to bring salvation to us.

History is very important. In ancient Israel the recounting of history was considered to be a prophetic role. The reason is that when we tell history we must decide what events to include in our history and how we interpret those events; that is, what meaning and significance we attach to the past. This task can only be accurately carried out with the explicit guidance and enlightenment of the Spirit of God. Thus the telling of history must be seen as a prophetic function. This is especially important today because history is being told in ways that cannot be reconciled with the Scriptures. We are told that earth and its inhabitants were millions and billions of years in the making, originating from the long-term outworking of naturalistic processes. This removes from the human race the fundamental purpose and meaning of life, distances us from the One Who created us, and makes society and individuals prey to our basest instincts. In this book I bring forth new archeological evidence for the accuracy of the traditional biblical world view.

How did I ever come to even think about or consider these issues? I want to begin this book by explaining to you how I got started in these subjects, for there was a question I posed to the Lord, and there was a most unexpected answer to that question. The initial question arose as I was sitting at my desk at work. I was a computer programmer and a system design specialist for the University of Michigan in Ann Arbor, Michigan. I worked at the Administrative Services Building on the corner of Hoover and Greene Street.

In those days, perhaps around 1980 or so, we were granted a fifteen-minute break from 10:00 AM to 10:15 AM each morning. I would read the *Detroit Free Press* during my break and it always had an interview with someone famous. One day it was with Isaac Asimov, and it was a discussion about his new book *In the Beginning*. I began to read it with great relish for he was one of my favorite authors. By this time I was a "born again" Christian who "knew" that the Bible was true. In the midst of the interview the reporter asked Isaac what his book and its ideas had to do with the book of Genesis. He said this: "Nothing. I don't see why some people can't feel secure unless they think there is an old man with a white beard up there that has everything under control."

This remark, from a childhood "icon" with whom I had always felt a kind of kinship, was like a dagger in my gut. I did not expect it at all. I turned to the heavenly Father and I said to Him earnestly, "Father, there has to be an apologetic for this. It has to be simple, straightforward, and clear—and I need to know it." I immediately felt a kind of interior peace, and I put down the paper and returned to my work. In order to understand what I was asking the Lord for in that prayer I need to share with you something about how I grew up and what my basic attitudes were toward such things as "origins."

I was born into a devout Roman Catholic family in New Haven, Indiana. I attended St. John the Baptist Catholic Church and their associated grade school. I went to Central Catholic High School in Fort Wayne, Indiana. I eventually went to Notre Dame in South Bend, Indiana. But before I ever entered school there were some important events that affected me in my youngest years. I was born into a family of seven children. There were five children in the space of ten years, then a ten-year gap, then I came along, and then my youngest brother. My brother Chuck was ten years older than I was. When I was about 2½ years old, my brother was helping my Mom do the dishes after dinner. He would wipe and put away the dishes while she actually washed them. They always had really interesting conversations and I would commonly sit on a kitchen chair and listen to them. This one evening my brother was saying, "Sister told us today that there was no end to the stars. They just keep going on and on forever." I was utterly caught up in that concept. I went to bed that night and imagined in my mind—kind of like the Starship Enterprise going through space. I pictured going through space, and the stars whipping by, and there being no end. It was inconceivable! I would imagine, what if I came to the end, then what would be there? A wall of some kind? Was it hard or soft? I imagined it to be soft. What was on the other side of the wall? The idea of infinity was beyond my ability to grasp, but it fascinated me. This fascination continued throughout my youth.

I was taught by the Sisters of Saint Agnes. In second grade Sister Francis De Sales told us, "Now you can read, so here is your library card. You can use it to check out a book from the public library anytime you want." I walked past the library on the way home, so that afternoon I stopped and asked for some books on Astronomy. I found and checked out five books on that topic and carried them home with my lunch bag. When I got home I immediately opened them and began to read—well, I tried to read. I could understand absolutely nothing at all. I was frustrated and very disappointed. I thought I could read! I kept returning to those books but eventually, before I ran past the two-week limit, I returned them. Totally deflated, I turned instead to comic books, which I found on a rack in the Dan Purvis Rexall drug store in New Haven. But I turned around and lo, there was a different rack of paper-back books. There were several with pictures of galaxies and stars on the cover. They said things like "The Expanding Universe" and "The Big Bang." I bought them and I read them. Yes I could understand them quite clearly. This was the period of time in my life during which I became familiar with Isaac Asimov.

In fourth grade Sister Luella told us about the various books of the Bible. She started in the first book. She said to us, "Boys and girls, today we are going to study the book of Genesis. In the book of Genesis God tells us how He made everything. We need to know that, and we could never have figured it out on our own." When the kids all went out for recess I stayed behind and asked her, "Sister, what about the Big Bang Theory? That tells us how everything came to be." She looked down at me, for she was quite tall and must have been in her sixties, and she said kindly, "Mike, I don't know about those theories, but I know the Bible is God's word and so it must be true." I totally believed her and left, but this idea came into my mind, "So—they're both true. They just say the same thing but in different ways." That was the exact idea that I had in my mind when I asked the Father, "Father, there has to be an apologetic for this. It has to be simple, straightforward, and clear, and I need to know it." I still thought what I had imagined back in fourth grade, but I had been waiting for a long time to understand exactly **how** the two ideas fit together. Now it was time for an answer. That is exactly what I was asking for from the Father as I sat at my desk. My question to Him was a direct continuation of the conversation that I had with Sister Luella almost thirty years before. I can explain this now and in retrospect, but I did not consciously realize that when I asked the question.

That night as I left the Administrative Services building in Ann Arbor I was not thinking of the *Detroit Free Press* and that interview with Isaac Asimov, nor was I thinking about the question that I had posed to the Father as a result of reading the newspaper article. To my right were the railroad tracks. I turned right and crossed them and entered a large parking lot behind the band building. On the windshield of my car was a tract that said on its front page "Have you been Brainwashed?" There was one on every windshield, which made me angry, and my inclination was to toss that junk right onto the street and drive home. I felt a tap on my right shoulder—the Holy Spirit saying, "Read it." So I stood there in the parking lot next to my car and opened that little tract and began to read.

I cannot even recall exactly what was in it, except that it pointed out in simple terms that the theory of evolution and the Big Bang Theory were not likely to be true. As I read that tract I suddenly "saw" that the theories that I had so diligently read about, and that I had utterly believed, were not true at all. It was not a logical argument, although there surely was a kind of logic to all that they said. No, it was a spiritual revelation. It was definitely a supernatural insight that God the Father granted to me as I read that simple tract.

St. Ignatius of Loyola speaks at length about such things in his writing on the discerning of spirits. He gives an example. Suppose that a man were looking at and admiring a rose, and as he looked he was greatly impressed with its intricate beauty and color. He goes away very pleased and feeling good because of the insight he had with the rose. That is very nice, but not at all supernatural. But suppose that, as he looked at that rose, he passed in his thoughts from the rose to the Trinity, and suppose that he had a mystical insight into the wisdom of God, His careful planning of the creation, and His place in all things for him—and suppose that the revelation he was granted changed his life and drew him closer to God, with results that lasted for the rest of the time he was on earth. Such an event could not be other than the Holy Spirit, for only He can draw us to God in that way, and only He can transform our inner man so that we long for and seek after God in an on-going and continual way.

The revelation that I was granted at that moment has changed my life. I was drawn by that special insight into a deeper revelation of God and of His nearness to me. My life of prayer was deepened, and I began to rise up earlier to seek Him. I fell in love with Him, and this has remained in my life to this day. At the time that revelation happened, I did not connect it with the question that I had asked the Father earlier in the day as I sat at my desk. I certainly did not connect it with the discussion that I had with Sister Luella in the fourth grade many years before. I was just ecstatic. I was so happy and so glad, for a reason that I could not assign to any earthly cause, but which came into me from God. I jumped into my car and drove home. I ran in the back door, caught up my wife into my arms and tried to explain to her that "they are not science and they are not true." I couldn't fully explain it to her, but I knew it was so. I laughed. She laughed with me and hugged me. Then she jumped back to the stove where our dinner was burning, and I sat down at the kitchen table and held that tract in my hand and looked at it.

"Lord, I have to meet the man who put this on my windshield." I said this out loud, for I had never in my life thought the thoughts that were in that pamphlet, and I had never in my life spoken with someone who thought like what was explained in that little booklet. I was starving for conversation and personal dialogue, for the exchange of ideas, and for direct thoughts and answers to the various questions I had. I couldn't explain then what had happened to me, but I would now say the following things in partial explanation of it:
- I went through a paradigm shift in my thinking.
- I had the Spirit of the Age and its presumptions ripped from my mind.
- I was granted a mindset—a point of view—that was "like" what people had before the scientific naturalism of our day became prevalent in society—not that I took up ancient thinking completely, but I became detached from the current ideas of origins.

None of these are completely adequate, but all of them are true—as far as they go.

The next day I left work at lunch time to go to the Intramural Building, which was down the street from the Administrative Services Building, and which was where I and many of my coworkers went to exercise. We played paddleball, a game like racquetball, which was a great way to work out when you spent the day at a desk job like we all did. As I was walking down Hoover Street toward the railroad tracks a man came up to me and shook my hand and gave me a tract—exactly like the one I had read the day before! He was a stranger and I had never seen him before. He said, "Here let me give you this." I looked at the booklet, put it in my shirt pocket, and said, "I have one of these and I have read it. I need to talk to you." We stood there and talked for quite a while. He explained to me that there were many scientists who thought this way and who wrote about what they thought. I asked where I could get their books. He told me about the Institute for Creation Research and their catalogue. I asked how I could get it. He said to me, "Give me your name and address and I'll send it to them and they'll mail you their catalogue of books." I did exactly that. As he started to walk on, toward the corner of Hoover and Green, the opposite way that I was going, I realized that when he left then I had no one with whom to discuss this subject—I knew no one who thought this way about things. I grabbed him and said, "Wait! What if you don't give them my name?" He looked at me kind of funny and said, "Man, you're a live one. I'll give them your name." And I said, "You'd better!" Then he walked away, and I continued on to the Intramural Building. But it was too late to exercise, so I turned around and went back to work.

In a couple of weeks I got a catalogue from the Institute for Creation Research, and I chose and ordered a half dozen books. When they came I devoured them and ordered more. I devoured those as well. I became convinced—not that I was not already certain—that this was basically the right way to look at the world around me. I had indeed grown up brainwashed. As years wore on I seldom felt any need to share with others my new-found understanding of things. It was a lovely little thing that God had given to me for my benefit and I reveled in it quietly. Eventually I turned to the book of Genesis to read it. I had read it before, always with the sense of the Holy Spirit "hovering" over it, but with no true understanding of it. I had come to believe that the true meaning of Genesis was hidden from me in a mystery of some kind. But this time there was a holy light on the book as I read it. I read the first three chapters with that holy light resting upon them and I understood everything very clearly. The book said exactly what it meant, and it meant exactly what it said. The truth of Genesis had been hiding from me in plain sight!

This was not the end of my dealing with the Lord on this matter. Soon after I had read Genesis, with the holy light on the pages and the inner conviction about the truth of that book, I spoke to the Lord and said, "Well, everybody ought to think this same way about Genesis." By "this way" I meant the way that I now thought as I read the book. "Why would anyone ever think other about it?" At that point the Lord reminded me of where I had come from. He recalled to my mind an incident at work from a few years before.

I had been listening to a Walkman with ear plugs and heard on the news about a guy who said that Genesis was true and that the world was only a few thousand years old. I took off my ear plugs and turned off the radio. I sat at my desk and considered what he had said. He must be a fervent Christian, because no one would dare to think such a thing unless he was very committed. But he was so wrong! I turned to the Lord and said, "Lord I know he is my brother, so I love him. But WHY does he have to be such an **IDIOT**!" I said it with much emphasis, and at that time the Lord said nothing to me in return. Now He recalled that moment to my mind. Of course! Just a little while ago I had thought in a way diametrically opposed to what I now thought. It had seemed so utterly obvious, so clearly and certainly right. When I had asked the Father for an "apologetic," what I had in mind was nothing like the answer He had given to me. Now my mind was in a totally different place. I saw myself and the change that had come upon me. I began to think about what it was before that had made me so certain that I was right. Now I knew what I believed. I believed God and His word. What did I believe before? I had put my faith in the theories and ideas of men. I was convinced that the modern theories of origins were scientifically proven and that they were true.

I thought about this for a long time. I considered how a person can be "certain" about a fact or an assertion even when it is not true. I thought about the power and persuasive force of our modern culture. I also thought about what Christians must have believed about Genesis in previous ages. I said to the Lord, "If I went back a few centuries, to the ancient times, I am sure that every Christian would have believed about Genesis even as I do, right?" He said nothing to me in reply, but books and articles began to trickle into my possession that said all kinds of things about what "the Fathers" said and believed about Genesis. It seemed bewildering and confusing, but at that same time the Lord led me to a very simple understanding of how Genesis was written, of how He originally inspired the book. This is a vital missing insight in the Church today. This insight is the subject of this book.

All of this that I am relating happened decades ago. After I retired I felt the Lord leading me to write a book on Genesis, which follows my revelation. I make three points:
- The universal Ancient Faith of the Church was that Genesis is true—not merely in a metaphorical way, or in a spiritual way, or in an allegorical way, but plainly true.
- Certain archeological insights reveal how each section of Genesis was first written. I explain the insights and show how that understanding of the composition of the book is overwhelmingly confirmed simply by reading the book. The evidence is simple, straightforward, and clear. In Egypt at the time of the Exodus Moses edited the various "sections" and combined them to produce the present book of Genesis.
- Finally, as my initial spiritual revelation in the parking lot indicated, the theories of origins that we call "scientifically true" are not science and they are not true, and this age of the world is greatly deceived by their claims.

The above three points are the subject of this book. Now just a bit more on these points.

It is not the purpose of this book to directly address scientific theories because this is a work on the Bible and its historicity. But I do mention the assertions of those theories in summary form, I show why they are illogical and surely not true, and I refer the reader to scientific works with alternative perspectives on the subjects that they address. I highlight this fact: The assertions of those theories, including the timing and chronology that they assert for the past, are not science. If the book of Genesis contains accurate historical information, then such theories cannot be accepted as fact. Those theories raise many questions but offer few or no true answers to how things originated in the unknowable past. I admit that no certain explanation can be adduced to many questions, but the biblical view is by far the most clear, consistent, and coherent. This answer is not widely accepted by people because it is set squarely in the context of a super-naturalistic world view, which is foreign to people in our culture.

The most important idea that I present in this book is the explanation of exactly how the book of Genesis was written. Our understanding of the composition of Genesis stands in contrast to the JEPD Theory or Documentary Hypothesis. We show that Genesis was written not by unknown people but by holy men of old who "spoke as they were carried along by the Holy Spirit" (1 Peter 2:21). It was not adapted from pagan mythology but was directly inspired by God. We will identify the men who were the original authors of the book of Genesis. This is vital because it gives us a concrete understanding of what it means to say that Genesis was "inspired by God." It tells us exactly who the persons were that God inspired—men who were directly involved in the events that are related.

The diverse accounts that comprise Genesis were accumulated by the patriarchs over many centuries and finally carried into Egypt. At the time of the Exodus Moses read the accounts and, under divine leading and inspiration, put them together to form the book of Genesis as we now have it. Our theory of how Genesis was written is actually quite simple to explain, and the basis for it is not just a single special archeological discovery but thousands of discoveries that together make up a broad-based understanding of the style of ancient Middle Eastern writing. The proof of our theory is that, when we examine Genesis section-by-section, each section displays overwhelming evidence of having been written by the author that we named. Therefore the entire book of Genesis testifies to the correctness of our hypothesis. The evidence from the text of Genesis itself is the simple, straightforward, and clear proof of the rightness of our theory. The conclusion of our theory is also immediate: Genesis is true because it is made up of the personal first-hand accounts of people who were there—men who were directly involved in the events described. This undergirds the Ancient Faith as regards Genesis.

This is the apologetic that the Lord has given to me: "My book is true. My honor and My name are wrapped up in this book. All discussions about the origin of things have to be settled by reference to My book, for it alone gives men the correct perspective on—and the actual truth about—the distant and unseen past of mankind." Christians have always done apologetics by standing upon the Bible, and I did ask the Father for an apologetic. Thus the reasoning of this book is: Describe the Ancient Faith; show how Genesis was written; show how that idea is overwhelmingly confirmed by the text of the book; deduce that Genesis must be true—and that the Ancient Faith must also be true.

The Ancient Faith

The Origin of the Ancient Faith:
The Ancient Faith—the faith that was delivered once and for all to the saints—the faith that sprang from that initial gushing forth of the Holy Spirit upon the 120 disciples in the upper room. We all aspire to fill our hearts with and to uphold this faith steadfastly. This is the core of beliefs that was confirmed to the Apostles and those first believers on that glorious day. This is what Jesus referred to before He ascended when He said, "And behold, I am sending forth the promise of My Father upon you; but you are to stay in the city until you are clothed with power from on high" (Luke 24:49). And again, "But the Helper, the Holy Spirit, whom the Father will send in My name, He will teach you all things, and bring to your remembrance all that I said to you" (John 14:26). And again, "But when He, the Spirit of truth, comes, He will guide you into all the truth" (John 16:13). And again, "I will ask the Father, and He will give you another Helper, that He may be with you forever" (John 14:16). The initial set of beliefs that came from Jesus—this is the Ancient Faith.

This faith was on the earth long before the medieval corruptions that afflicted the Roman Church. It was on the earth before the birth of Jan Hus, before John Wycliffe, and before anyone ever heard of the Protestant Reformation. The Ancient Faith was present before 1054 when the great schism split the Roman branch of Christianity from the Greek Orthodox Church. Long before the advent of these landmark historical events that gave rise to the names and categories that we now use to identify Christians, this faith burned in the hearts of holy men of old and flowed from the tips of their pens into the classic Christian writings that have inspired centuries of faithful men and women.

Continuity of the Ancient Faith:
This is the faith of all of the Fathers of the Church and of the centuries of holy men and women that followed in their footsteps. The Ancient Faith has always been with us and has endured and weathered all worldly and ecclesiastical storms. The Holy Spirit has not allowed the truth that He once inspired in the hearts and minds of His chosen to fade or to die. This is the faith that we seek to portray before our eyes in this chapter—especially as it touches on the foundational beliefs of the Church regarding the book of Genesis, the origin of the world, the origin of man, the purpose for which God created humans, the meaning of sin and the fall, and our understanding of the salvation that the promised "Seed of the woman" would finally bring to us.

The Ancient Faith included a set of beliefs about Jesus as well as a certain perspective on the existing Jewish Scriptures. The faith was expressed in a clear but mystical way within the Old Testament, but it could only be understood with the guidance of the Holy Spirit. Thus a certain "spiritual" understanding of the Old Testament Scriptures was a foundational part of the Ancient Faith. The spiritual understanding of the Scriptures was explained to some extent by Jesus while He was on the earth, and was revealed more completely to the Church by the indwelling Holy Spirit. That understanding was written into the New Testament Scriptures where it was elaborated on more completely. This understanding of the total body of scriptural truth was clearly taught by the holy men of old and was carried forward throughout the centuries by successive generations of new believers. This is the Ancient Faith. It has never left the Church.

The Fathers of the Faith:

A study of the ancient writers is vital because the faith that originally came from Jesus and the Apostles will be reflected in the beliefs of those who lived immediately after the time of Apostles. We will see that faith clearly reflected in the generations of persecuted believers who lived for and who died for Jesus Christ, and we will see it displayed also in the carefully constructed treatises of those believers—leaders of Christian thinking who shaped and faithfully expressed the Christian world view—who arose in the following generations and centuries. Such faith can be clearly seen in the body of writings of those Christian thinkers from apostolic times onward.

In this work we are concerned with the Ancient Faith as it applies to the understanding of Genesis, especially to the first chapters of that book. In order to show clearly what that faith is, I will draw from a large body of works by Christian teachers and Fathers of the Church going back as early as records exist. I want to include the writings from the earliest thinkers of the, from the three centuries of persecution that the Church weathered at the first. I also want to include the writings of the holy disciples of the next thousand years of Christianity—the age of Christendom.

In the fourteenth century a series of difficult tragedies befell the Church, both in the east and in the west. In the Latin Church the centuries of corruption gave rise to the turmoil of the reformation as Wycliffe, Hus, and others arose to challenge the foundations of the established order. In the far east Christianity had spread throughout Asia to the Pacific Ocean, and in Africa it had spread south at least as far as the equator. A series of tragic events reduced those distant branches of the Church to a small remnant of believers. Those events completed their destruction of Christian centers in the fourteenth century.[1] About a century later related forces razed Constantinople. Therefore our survey of the Ancient Faith will end in the fourteenth century.

It was my original intention to give a representative sample of the perspectives of early thinkers on creation, but as I read it was clear that certain basic attitudes were universal and common to all. I continued to explore and found that the pattern was never broken. For this reason I amplified my search to include every work I could find on Genesis and origins and to also include many works that merely mentioned a fact or two offhandedly. The result is a picture of the heart and mind of earlier centuries of Christians as it relates to the subject of creation. This is revealed clearly not only in their major formal treatises on the subject, but also in many other works that they wrote. This is more than I started out to accomplish, but it serves very well as an introduction to the thesis of this book, which is: "How was Genesis written and how true is the book?" The answer is "Genesis is completely true." The importance of this issue is emphasized by noting that it was the universal faith of all previous centuries of Christians. That is the Ancient Faith.

Here is the body of men and their works that I will draw on in this work. This compilation of ancient writers and their works attempts to include all writings that address the issue of creation or that discuss the first chapters of Genesis, but it also includes a small number of tangentially related works—works that touch on various issues that are related to the central topics raised in Genesis. I am trying to cover the writings from the first fourteen centuries of the Church. If I have omitted any, which seems inevitable because there are so many, it is only because I did not discover them, not because I chose to ignore them.

Christian Writer	Work	
Clement of Rome (died c99)	*Epistle of Clement*	
Barnabas (c100)	*Epistle*	
Papias (c70-c130)	*Fragments of his Works*	
Mathetes (c130)	*Epistle to Diognetus*	
Hermas (xx-c150)	*Shephard*	
St Justin Martyr (100-165)	*Hortatory Address to the Greeks*	
	Dialogue with Trypho	
	Apology 1	
	Apology 2	
	On the Resurrection	
Tatian (c120-c180)	*Address to the Greeks*	
Theophilus of Antioch (xxx-c184)	*To Autolycus*	
Athenagoras of Athens (133-190)	*On the Resurrection of the Dead*	
	A Plea for the Christians	
Clement of Alexandria (c150-c215)	*The Miscellanies (Stromata)*	
	The Instructor	
	An Exhortation to the Greeks	
Julius Africanus (c160-c240)	*Five Books of Chronography*	
Cyprian of Carthage (c200-258)	*On Mortality*	
	On the Dress of Virgins	
Irenaeus of Lyons (1xx-202)	*Demonstration of the Apostolic Teaching*	
	Against Heresies	
	Fragments of Lost Writings	
Hippolytus of Rome (170-235)	*Chronicle*	Not Available
	Refutation of all Heresies	
	Exegetical Fragments	
	Against Plato	Not in English
	Against Noetus	
	Against Beron and Helix	
	Commentary on Daniel	
	The Apostolic Tradition	
Tertullian (c155-c240)	*Apology*	
	On the Flesh of Christ	
	On the Prescription of Heretics	
	Against Hermogenes	
	On Idolatry	
	On the Resurrection of the Flesh	
	The Soul's Testimony	
	A Treatise on the Soul	
	On the Apparel of Women	
	On the Veiling of Virgins	
Minucius Felix (xxx-250)	*Octavius*	
Origen (184-253)	*Against Celsus*	
	Homilies on Genesis	
	On First Principles	
Dionysius of Alexandria (c200-264)	*From the Books on Nature against the Epicureans*	
Victorinus of Pettau (xxx-c304)	*On the Creation of the World*	
Methodius of Olympus (260-312)	*The Banquet of the Ten Virgins*	
	Discourse on the Resurrection	
	Extracts from the Work on Things Created	
Lactantius (c250-c325)	*Divine Institutes*	
	Epitome of the Divine Institutes	
Gregory the Illuminator (c257-c331)	*The Teaching of Saint Gregory: An Early Armenian Catechism*	
Eusebius of Caesarea (c275-339)	*Chronicle*	Not in English
	Ecclesiastical History	
	Preparation for the Gospel	
Aphrahat (c280-c345)	*The Demonstrations*	
Athanasius the Great (296-373)	*On the Incarnation*	
	Against the Heathen	
Eusebius of Emesa (c300-c360)	*Commentary on Genesis*	Not in English
Macarius the Great (c300-391)	*Fifty Spiritual Homilies*	
Ephrem the Syrian (306-373)	*Commentary on Genesis*	
	Hymns on Paradise	
	Select Poems	
Hilary of Poitiers (c310-c367)	*Commentary on Matthew*	

Author	Work	
Epiphanius of Salamis (c310-403)	Tractatus Mysteriorum	Not in English
	Panarion	
	Ancoratus	
Cyril of Jerusalem (c313-386)	Catechetical Lectures	
Didymus the Blind (c313-398)	Commentary on Genesis	
Basil of Caesarea (329-379)	Hexameron	
	On the Origin of Man	
Gregory of Nazianzus (c329-390)	Five Theological Orations	
	Poems and Songs	
Gregory of Nyssa (c335-c395)	The Making of Man	
	Apologia to his Brother Peter on the Hexameron	Not in English
	The Life of Moses	
	Against Eunomius	
Ambrose of Milan (c340-397)	Hexameron	
	Book on Paradise	
	Book on Cain and Abel	
	On the Decease of his Brother Satyrus	Not in English
	On Noah	Not in English
Firmicus Maternus (c346)	The Error of the Pagan Religions	
Tyconius (Before 400)	Book of Rules	
Gaudentius of Brescia (died c410)	Tractatus	Not in English
Paulus Orosius (c375-c418)	Seven Books of History against the Pagans	
Jerome (c347-420)	Hebrew Questions on Genesis	
	Against Jovian	Not in English
	On the Epistle to Titus	
	Chronicon	
St. John Chrysostom (349-407)	Homilies on Genesis	
	On the Creation of the World	Not in English
Severian of Gabala (3xx-c409)	Homilies on Creation and the Fall	
Theodore of Mopsuestia (350-428)	Commentary on Genesis	Not in English
St Augustine (354-430)	The Literal Meaning of Genesis	
	Unfinished Literal Commentary on Genesis	
	City of God	
	Confessions	
	On Christian Doctrine	
	On Genesis against Manichees	
	Responses to Miscellaneous Questions	
	Revisions/Retractions	
John Cassian (c360-435)	Conferences	
Sulpicius Severus (c363-c425)	Sacred History	
	The First Dialogue	
Cyril of Alexandria (c376-444)	Glaphyra on Genesis	
	Letters	
Nemesius of Emesa (c390)	Of the Nature of Man	
Panodorus of Alexandria (c400)	Antiochian Chronography	Not in English
Theodoret of Cyrus (c393-c463)	Questions on Genesis	
Jacob of Sarug (c451–521)	Homilies on Genesis	
	Homily on the Creation of Adam and the Resurrection of the Dead	
	Homily on the Tower of Babel	
Severus of Antioch (c459-xxx)	Hymns	
Fulgentius of Ruspe (c465-c527)	To Peter on the Faith	
Fulgentius the Mythographer (6th Century)	On the Ages of the World and of Man	
Gregory of Tours (538-594)	The History of the Franks	
Isidore of Seville (c560-636)	Chronica Majora	
	On the Nature of Things	
Isaac the Syrian (of Nineveh) (c613-c700)	Ascetical Homilies	
Anastasius of Sinai (died after 700)	Hexameron	
	The Creation of Man	Not in English
	Questions and Answers	
Jacob of Edessa (c640-708)	Hexameron	Not in English
Venerable Bede (c672-735)	On the Nature of Things	
	On Times	
	Commentary on 1 Peter	
	On Genesis	
John Damascene (c675-749)	On the Orthodox Faith	
	The Fount of Knowledge	

George the Monk Synkellos (died after 810)	*Chronicle*	
Moses bar Kepha (born c813 in Ninevah)	*Hexameron*	Not in English
Symeon the New Theologian (949-1022)	*The First-Created Man*	
Marianus Scotus (1028-1082)	*Chronicle*	Not in English
Theophylact of Ochrid (c1055-1107)	*Explanation of the New Testament*	
Commentary on 1 Peter	Not in English	
Peter Abelard (1079-1141)	*Hexameron*	
Bernard of Clairvaux (1090-1153)	*The Sentences of Bernard of Clairvaux*	
Hugh of St. Victor (1096-1141)	*On the Three Days*	
	Sentences on Divinity	
Peter Lombard (1096-1160)	*The Sentences*	
Robert Grosseteste (c1175-1253)	*Hexameron*	
Bonaventure (1221-1274)	*Breviloquium*	
Thomas Aquinas (1225-1274)	*Summa Theologica*	
	Summa Contra Gentiles	
	Comments on the Sentences of Peter Lombard	
	Questions On the Power of God	
Roger Bacon (c1219-c1292)	*Opus Majus*	
Gregory of Palamas (1296-1359)	*Homilies*	
	The One Hundred and Fifty Chapters	

The summary results of our lengthy overview of the thoughts of these ancient writers on creation can be found on page 88.

The Ancient Faith and Origins—Issues:

Why we are Doing this Lengthy Historical Survey:

The purpose of this work is not to convince unbelievers to convert to Christianity; rather, it is to induce believers to acknowledge the full scope of Christian revelation. It is to lead us all to a clear understanding of what the Church has always held in regard to creation. The reason why I want men and women to understand this is because the Ancient Faith as regards origins has been greatly eroded and we no longer realize what the Christians of ages past believed—what they understood Genesis to be saying—about creation. The accurate understanding of the Ancient Faith on origins has been obscured in the Church today. This historical error must be corrected. That is why I am doing this survey.

As a result of our deception we no longer feel the need to assert or defend the Ancient Faith as regards origins. That precious set of truths, foundational as it is to the total body of faith, is unknown and untaught today. Almost all Christians would claim that what our Lord taught about any given area of the faith was fully true. Almost all would also accept that what He taught was passed on to His Apostles and to the early Church as well. Most would also assert that today we should continue to teach such beliefs in our churches. I want to show us what the Church believed universally about origins during the first 1400 years of its existence. It is my claim that the Church has abandoned the completeness of these truths, and I want to encourage us to reclaim them fully once again. In fact, these truths are extremely important to us in this day. Most Christian theology is rooted in the first three chapters of Genesis. The entire Christian world view is at stake in this matter.

Looking at the Ancient Faith:

The Ancient Faith emerged from the faith of Israel and rested upon an understanding of their Scriptures. The truth and divine inspiration of the Old Testament was the foundation of Judaism, but a new or "spiritual" understanding of the Old Testament was integral to the Ancient Faith; that is, a Holy-Spirit-inspired understanding of the Old Testament that was new and exciting became the conscious faith of the Church. Think of what it meant to see the events of the life of Jesus unfold before your eyes, and then to look into the

Old Testament books—books that had been written centuries before and which Jewish people had always considered to be divinely inspired—and see in them clear pictures of what Jesus said and did, and clear pictures of Who He was; that is, descriptions of Him that had been written centuries before New Testament times!

This exciting new set of insights into the existing Jewish holy books was the intellectual and spiritual foundation of the Ancient Faith of the Church. We take these things for granted today but in the first century they formed the stunning biblical proof for the faith.

The Ancient Faith saw the truths of Christianity foretold in the Old Testament Scriptures and revealed in the person and work of Jesus—but this understanding of the Scriptures had to be revealed to each person. Ironically, the faith was rejected by many Jews, even as was Jesus Himself. However even this rejection was clearly foretold in the ancient writings—and the divine purpose in allowing it was also foretold.

Jesus began the application of the Old Testament Scriptures to His own person and to the works that He came to accomplish. This revelation was continued and completed by the Holy Spirit when He descended upon the 120 disciples in the upper room on the feast of Pentecost, and as He has continued to inspire the Church since that time. We need examples to make what I am saying concrete.

When speaking to the religious leaders of Israel about the fact that they were going to reject Him Jesus quoted a verse as applying to Him in that situation (see Matthew 21:42):
> THE STONE WHICH THE BUILDERS REJECTED,
> THIS BECAME THE CHIEF CORNER *stone*;
> THIS CAME ABOUT FROM THE LORD,
> AND IT IS MARVELOUS IN OUR EYES (PSALM 118:22–23)

In Acts 4:11 Peter quoted this verse to the elders of Israel again and applied it to Jesus and to the fact that they had rejected Him just as had been written by David—and just as Jesus had explained to them even while they were doing the rejecting! This is an example of how the Old Testament predicted the rejection of the Messiah.

Why would the Messiah be rejected? The Old Testament also explains this to us:
> He was despised and forsaken of men, A man of sorrows and acquainted with grief. And like one from whom men hide their face He was despised, and we did not esteem Him. Surely our griefs He Himself bore, and our sorrows He carried. Yet we ourselves esteemed Him stricken, Smitten of God, and afflicted. But He was pierced through for our transgressions, He was crushed for our iniquities. The chastening for our well-being *fell* upon Him, and by His scourging we are healed. All of us like sheep have gone astray, each of us has turned to his own way; but the LORD has caused the iniquity of us all to fall on Him. He was oppressed and He was afflicted, yet He did not open His mouth. Like a lamb that is led to slaughter, and like a sheep that is silent before its shearers, so He did not open His mouth. By oppression and judgment He was taken away; and as for His generation, who considered that He was cut off out of the land of the living for the transgression of my people, to whom the stroke *was due*? (Isaiah 53:3–8)

Thus He would be rejected because His death was necessary in order to pay for the sin of mankind. It was divinely planned for our sakes. God would allow it because someone had to pay the penalty for the sins of mankind and no one on earth was able to pay that terrible price (see Psalm 49:5–9ff). The rejection of the Messiah, his unfair treatment at the hands of the people of His generation, and His being put to death unjustly; all were part of the plan of God to redeem mankind by sacrificing His own Son for our sins.

Sometimes the spiritual understanding of a passage that Jesus fulfilled involved seeing more in that passage than would have been clear at first glance. This type of Scripture interpretation is sometimes used in prophetic texts and is called "allegorical." That is, it sees more in an Old Testament passage than what is literally stated in the words. The allegorical understanding of Scripture did not undermine the basic historical method of understanding it; rather it was founded squarely upon the basic historical truth of the Old Testament. The two methods of understanding Scripture were deeply intermingled with each other and reinforced each other. Thus sometimes a passage had merely a literal historical meaning, sometimes it had only an allegorical meaning, and sometimes it had both meanings and they were intertwined in the passage and reinforced each other. The passage about the "stone that the builders rejected" in the example above was allegorically interpreted, but the passage from Isaiah was utterly literal in every way.

There are hundreds of examples of allegorical interpretation. It is written:
> Now the LORD said to Moses and Aaron in the land of Egypt, "This month shall be the beginning of months for you; it is to be the first month of the year to you. Speak to all the congregation of Israel, saying, 'On the tenth of this month they are each one to take a lamb for themselves, according to their fathers' households, a lamb for each household. Now if the household is too small for a lamb, then he and his neighbor nearest to his house are to take one according to the number of persons *in them*; according to what each man should eat, you are to divide the lamb. Your lamb shall be an unblemished male a year old; you may take it from the sheep or from the goats. You shall keep it until the fourteenth day of the same month, then the whole assembly of the congregation of Israel is to kill it at twilight. Moreover, they shall take some of the blood and put it on the two doorposts and on the lintel of the houses in which they eat it." (Exodus 12:1–7)

But these instructions for choosing, testing, and killing the Passover lamb, and for sprinkling its blood, all of which the Lord gave Moses at the time of the Exodus also apply to the death of Jesus. He is our Passover Lamb, chosen for us by the Father. He presented Himself to the nation of Israel four days before Passover in AD 33. He weathered the opposition and critical examination of every sect of the Jews and the Gentiles during the four days leading up to His death. He died on the cross at the time when the Jews were sacrificing their Passover lambs by following these instructions which had been given 1,500 years before. His blood protects us from the eternal death of sin. He is THE Passover Lamb.

Therefore the Passover ceremony was designed by the Lord God centuries beforehand in such a manner that it would prefigure the saving act that was to be accomplished for us in the fullness of time through the death of Jesus Christ the Son of God.

Jesus also employed the allegorical method of interpreting Scripture in His ministry. He often spoke in parables and made various allegorical connections between Himself, His work, and passages in the Old Testament. This became the heritage of the Church in the New Testament. In the examples shown, and in **hundreds** of other passages of the Old Testament Scriptures, the ancient writers and Church leaders saw direct references to the personal activity of Jesus the Son of God, allegorical references to Him in stories and events from Old Testament times, and prophetic statements that foretold realities about Him and the events of His life. Although the Jewish rabbis did interpret their own Scriptures allegorically, they did not see in them all of the connections to the Messiah that we do today. This "spiritual" understanding of the Old Testament texts was and still is uniquely the inheritance of the Christian Church granted to us by the Holy Spirit.

The early Church read these things—verses written in the Old Testament Scriptures long before Jesus walked on the earth. They watched as they came to pass in His life and in the response that many of the leaders and people of Israel made to Him. They saw His rejection by them, His unjust punishment and death at their hand, and they saw also the eternal sovereign plan of God revealed in those events. They saw the eternal purpose of God in allowing these things to happen because that divine purpose had been stated beforehand in the Old Testament Scriptures.

Finally the disciples saw the divine confirmation of Jesus' identity in His resurrection, which He had predicted beforehand! Therefore the Old Testament Scriptures had to be divinely inspired. And they all had to be completely true, because God would never lie or make a mistake. Thus Christian revelation reaffirmed and undergirded the faith of the Jewish people in their Scriptures—even though many Jews rejected Jesus. There are hundreds of passages and events in the Old Testament whose full truth and proper meaning are only now revealed to mankind. Clearly only God could write such a book, so the Bible is His holy word and Jesus is the promised Messiah, the Son of God, and God incarnate.

Jesus Himself passed the "spiritual" understanding of the Scriptures on to the Church. As He spoke to the two disciples on the road to Emmaus:
> And He said to them, "O foolish men and slow of heart to believe in all that the prophets have spoken! Was it not necessary for the Christ to suffer these things and to enter into His glory?" Then beginning with Moses and with all the prophets, He explained to them the things concerning Himself in all the Scriptures. (Luke 24:25–27)

Thus their hearts were "burning within them" as He explained those very things that I have listed for us in these examples, and many more like them. This was the glory and inspiration that accompanied the Ancient Faith as it sprang afresh from Judaism in the first century—and it definitely involved many passages in the book of Genesis.

Later Jesus spoke to all of His disciples and commissioned them.
> Now He said to them, "These are My words which I spoke to you while I was still with you, that all things which are written about Me in the Law of Moses and the Prophets and the Psalms must be fulfilled." **Then He opened their minds to understand the Scriptures**, and He said to them, "Thus it is written, that the Christ would suffer and rise again from the dead the third day, and that repentance for forgiveness of sins would be proclaimed in His name to all the nations, beginning from Jerusalem. You are witnesses of these things (emphasis added). (Luke 24:44–48)

Thus a unique revelation about the Old Testament Scriptures was the biblical insight that undergirded the Ancient Faith of the Church. These insights were to continue in the Church when the Holy Spirit was sent. The Spirit would lead the disciples into all truth and teach them everything (John 16:13), would recall to their minds all that Jesus had said (John 14:26), and would never leave them (John 14:16).

The Fathers often speak of the "spiritual" understanding of the Scriptures, and they say that we can correctly understand the Scriptures only when we think about them in the way that the Church teaches. When they say these things they are talking about this glorious set of insights that were granted to the Church by Jesus Himself or by the Holy Spirit, and which were understood by the Church to have been given to us directly by God from the beginning. This is the Ancient Faith.

The reason that we are interested today in the understanding of Scripture that was held by the ancients is not primarily because they were smarter or more insightful than we are, although they did have marvelous spiritual gifts. The primary reason that we are concerned with their view of Scripture is that they lived nearer to the time of Jesus and the Apostles, and so they probably held a view that was received from them. They were the spiritual successors of the Apostles, and by understanding what they believed and how they thought, we gain clear insight into what Jesus and the Apostles thought; that is, what the Holy Spirit communicated to them at Pentecost when the Church was born. The Holy Spirit continued to reveal such things to the later generations of believers.

> But the Helper, the Holy Spirit, whom the Father will send in My name, He will teach you all things, and bring to your remembrance all that I said to you. (John 14:26)

If we can see clearly what those generations of believers thought, and if they agree on a certain point of faith, then we can be confident that we have grasped the Ancient Faith—the Apostolic Faith—the faith that was delivered once and for all to the Church. If we see that same faith in the writings of holy men in the centuries that follow then we can be sure that the same Holy Spirit that Jesus gave to the Church at Pentecost, and that He promised would abide with us forever, was still inspiring the same faith in those later generations of believers. Thus studying the faith of the earlier centuries of believers will give us an insight into the Ancient Faith.

The Ancient Faith and Genesis:
What does this have to do with Genesis? It is written:

> Let us make man in our image and after our likeness" (Genesis 1:26)

In this passage in the Genesis account of creation, and throughout the creation account, the early Church saw Jesus working with the Father to create all things. This particular passage was seen as a clear reference to the deliberation between the Father and Son before they acted with the Holy Spirit to create Adam and Eve. Thus Jesus existed before the world was created and was involved with God the Father throughout the creation, for "apart from Him was not anything made that has been made" (John 1:3). The Jews did not see this. It was revealed to believers by the Holy Spirit. It was one aspect of the insightful gift that He gave to the early Church, the exciting truth of the Ancient Faith.

It is written:

> Now the LORD appeared to him [Abraham] by the oaks of Mamre, while he was sitting at the tent door in the heat of the day. When he lifted up his eyes and looked, behold, three men were standing opposite him; and when he saw *them*, he ran from the tent door to meet them and bowed himself to the earth . . . [after eating with Abraham] . . . the men turned away from there and went toward Sodom, while Abraham was still standing before the LORD. Abraham came near and said, "Will You indeed sweep away the righteous with the wicked?" (Genesis 18:1–2, 22–23)

This is the account of the announcement to Abraham of the destruction of Sodom and Gomorrah. The Lord and two angels appeared to Abraham on their way to look into the many outrages that had come to their attention regarding those wicked cities. We know that one of those three angels, whom Abraham addressed as the Lord, was Jesus the Son of God. There are many similar passages throughout the Old Testament where the Lord, or the "Angel of the Lord," appears to and interacts with people. These were seen as clear references to the pre-incarnate activity of Jesus in Old Testament times.

Undergirding all biblical interpretation, including how we look at Genesis, is the uniform belief that the Scriptures were inspired by God, that He is faithful and all knowing, and that the only way to look at the Bible is that it is utterly true. That includes Genesis.

Interpretation Issues Unique to Genesis:

The early parts of Genesis are, by their very nature, difficult to comprehend and very far removed from our human experience. The creation of all things—the formation of the plethora of different objects that make up this world of ours—boggles our minds. It is a subject that exceeds our capacity for complete understanding. Therefore as we try to grasp the meaning of the words in Genesis, and as we attempt to correlate them with other verses that touch on the subject of the ultimate origin of all things, we must realize that we are dealing with an issue that is beyond our human ability. We must trust God, Who alone knows and understands the mysteries surrounding this subject—Who alone was able to complete such a mighty work. This raises issues about how we are to understand His words. Are they speaking directly about material reality? Are they crafted to explain to us what we can never understand, and so are metaphorical or allegorical in some way? Are the words filled with figures of speech or poetic forms?

Also, the accounts of Genesis seem to state that at its beginning this world functioned differently than it now functions, and that God modified it because of the sin of our first parents and the sins of later generations. In two different places in Genesis the Lord God changed this world significantly: After Adam and Eve first fell, and when the tragedy of the great Deluge was brought upon the world at the time of Noah. Therefore the words of Genesis in its early chapters describe conditions on this earth that are strikingly different from what we see around us now. The only certain truth about those early times that we can glean is from the Bible, so how we interpret it on these subjects is very important.

In our attempt to interpret Genesis correctly it would be helpful if we could determine the genre of the Genesis narratives; that is, if we could understand the ancient times within which the Genesis narratives arose so we could know more fully how to understand the accounts. The early Fathers did not have this luxury when they attempted to interpret Genesis, so any such insights would give us a tremendous advantage over them. In this work we will show that Genesis was written by people who were directly involved in the events at the very beginning of the human race and at other critical times in the early history of man. Thus, they were eye witnesses and their stories are fully reliable. This sets the genre of Genesis (it is "personal narratives") and will guide us as we interpret it. Our view of the genre of Genesis undergirds the implicit understanding of the Fathers.

Finally, a complete picture of the early years of the creation and of mankind cannot be gleaned only from the Genesis account but must include testimony from a large number of other verses scattered throughout the Bible. That is, the Lord God inspired holy men throughout the ages with specific insights into the origin of things. We cannot ignore or omit these important inspired additions to the origins picture. All these words must be fit together and be brought to bear in a coordinated, consistent way to arrive at the full story that God is revealing to us about the origin of all things. In addressing these issues we must recall that the Holy Spirit inspired the Bible, including Genesis, and He has led the Church in understanding the Scriptures—especially in finding His own mind as we study them. His leading in past times is a clear guide for us today. Whatever we eventually understand—if it is under His leading—should agree with what He revealed to the holy men of old—and what was understood by people throughout the ages. For this reason we are beginning by looking first at what the holy men of old thought about Genesis.

Allegorical and Literal Interpretation of Genesis:

For some the issue of literal vs allegorical interpretation has been a foundational point in how they think about Genesis. This has also raised questions in some minds about how the Fathers understood Genesis: Was it understood literally, as the description of events that actually happened in the unseen past—or was it to be understood allegorically with the actual events of the past therefore remaining a shrouded mystery? As we have seen in our previous discussion, these two methods of interpretation are not opposed to one another but can be and often are intertwined with each other. After a careful survey of the ancient writers we will see that, with no exceptions, they one and all believed in a combination of literal and allegorical interpretation of Genesis, but none of them ever rejected the literal interpretation of the text.

The "allegorical vs literal" understanding of Genesis was often addressed by Augustine. We will see his ideas as we go along. As an introduction to his thinking, here is what he says on the allegorical interpretation of a passage as being completely compatible with the literal understanding of it, and that both of them can be, and often should be, held to.

> Although we hold with complete faith to the resurrection of Lazarus in accordance with the gospel account, yet I have no doubt that there is an allegorical meaning as well. When deeds are allegorized they do not do away with faith in the actual thing; such is the case when Paul explains that the two sons of Abraham are an allegory of the two covenants. Did Abraham not exist, then, or did he not have two sons?[2]

The allegorical and literal interpretation of Genesis is an issue that we will see often as we become familiar with the comments of the ancients on that book. It is the express goal of this work to expound a literal understanding of Genesis and to show that such a view accords with and greatly enhances our faith, and thus is in accord with the "rule of faith." We do not reject the allegorical interpretations, but we show that they fit together with the literal understandings, are intertwined with them inextricably, and support and enhance them. Both together constitute the "spiritual" understanding of the Scriptures.

There is a basic principle for interpreting passages in the Bible as "only allegorical" or as also "to be taken literally:" If the literal meaning "makes sense," or if it does not violate reason or necessity, then assert the literal meaning. Pope Leo XIII explains:

> But he [i.e., the one who interprets the Bible] must not on that account consider that it is forbidden, when just cause exists, to push inquiry and exposition beyond what the Fathers have done; provided he carefully observes the rule so wisely laid down by St. Augustine–not to depart from the literal and obvious sense, except only where reason makes it untenable or necessity requires. (*Providentissimus Deus*, Section 15)

This seems like a fine rule but it is very difficult to apply, for what does it mean to say a passage, when interpreted literally, is "untenable according to reason," or is required to be taken non-literally because of "necessity?" The meaning of these phrases cannot be gleaned by studying early interpreters. Thus some think it is "unreasonable" to assert that Paradise was actually a physical location on this earth. Some think that is actually quite fine. Some believe that it is necessary to say the tree of life and the tree of the knowledge of good and evil were not actual trees, but others assert they were physical trees in the garden, because that is what the Scriptures say, etc.

I think that the major underlying reason for this disparity is that, although all agreed that the text of Genesis was inspired by God, there was not a clear understanding of what that meant; that is, just exactly *how* did God inspire Moses when he wrote Genesis?

This is a foundational question that this book will address and which we will answer. Thus the basic approach to interpreting Genesis will be settled once we understand exactly how the process of inspiration transpired. The most desirable way to interpret Genesis, or any Bible passage, is almost always the literal way. I think that all agree on that, but now we can tell for the first time exactly how and to what degree to apply all of these ideas to texts in Genesis because we will see how God inspired it.

The Bible of the Fathers:
As we delve into the Fathers and their comments on Genesis we must remember that the ancients usually worked from the Greek translation of the Hebrew Scriptures that we call the Septuagint or the LXX[3], and Augustine used a Latin text called the Vetus Latina since he was not fluent in either Hebrew or Greek. In those translations significant differences from the Hebrew Scriptures that we are so used to can be found. One striking example is in the genealogies of the LXX, which differ systematically from those in the Hebrew Bible.

Hebrew Bible or Masoretic Text	**Septuagint or LXX**
Adam was 130 when he begat Seth	Adam was 230 when he begat Seth
(In both manuscripts Adam lived a total of 930 years)	
Seth was 105 when he begat Enosh	Seth was 205 when he begat Enosh
(In both manuscripts Seth lived a total of 912 years)	

Many of the genealogical records in the LXX add 100 years to the age of the patriarchs when they begot the next generation. This is a common but not a universal divergence between the two versions of Genesis. The result of this difference is to increase times between successive generations of the patriarchs and thus to push the calculated date of the creation back about 1,500 years. Thus the date of creation according to the LXX was about 5500 BC, instead of 4000 BC.[b] There are other translation differences in the LXX and Vetus, which we will point out if and when they impact our studies.

Introduction to the Fathers on Genesis:
In the pages that follow I want to explain the thinking that characterized the holy men of old as they read Genesis—to explain the mindset that they had as they approached the book, the basic attitudes that they held to, and why they held them. In this way we can see their faith and reasoning as they explain the book to us.

I want to begin with two very influential and brilliant figures: Origen (184-253) and Augustine (354-430). Both lived and wrote in North Africa. Sandwiched between them was another North African thinker who clearly was influenced by Origen and who influenced Augustine: Didymus the Blind (c. 313–398). These three men held unique perspectives on Genesis. We will look at their thinking in some detail, and then we will turn to the rest of the Fathers and give exhaustive examples of their views on the book. We will focus mainly on the creation account because it determines our world view, but we will also consider the story of Adam and Eve in the Garden of Eden (Chapters 2–3), the Deluge, and Babel.

Augustinian Understanding of the Creation Account:[4]

Go to page 88 to skip over this detailed record of the ancient beliefs on Genesis

Of all the Fathers Augustine thought most deeply about the total biblical creation scenario, and his ideas are the most difficult to grasp. I will include many and varied quotations from him to give the reader a more complete picture of his complex and multifaceted thoughts.

---

[b] I have found no good explanation for how or why this divergence exists. It is a pattern, not a copy error.

Augustine clearly believed that the Genesis creation account was given to us by God to show us how the creation of all things happened. In his book *The Literal Meaning of Genesis* He undertakes a strenuous and detailed analysis of the creation account in his efforts to explain exactly how that historical event took place. In doing so he also refers to other Scriptures that relate to the creation and seeks to fit them all together consistently so as to form a complete picture of what happened. Augustine's effort to understand all of the Scriptures relating to the creation is a painstaking and intricate work—the most careful work of any ancient writer. I want to present the result of his work in outline form here.

Because of the enormous influence Augustine has had in the Church, and because of the complicated theory he has espoused and the confusion it has engendered, I think it is needful to state in simple words the incredibly abstruse idea that Augustine proposes as the actual literal way to understand the creation account in Genesis. Then I want to help us understand where such an idea came from. I state his view as follows:

> God created everything together simultaneously in an instant in eternity, in one great "Day," and then He showed it to us in stages, unfolding it before us in the creation account as being developed and perfected in six days. Each day of the account shows us another aspect of the instantly completed creation, so that we mortals can understand what He did in that instant.

There are several foundational concepts that undergird the thinking of Augustine as he tries to explain the creation account in this way. I want to trace them for us, referring to one who preceded him by a few decades. That person is Didymus the Blind, a leader of the Coptic Church in Alexandria. I want to focus on a portion of his thinking on Genesis in which he explains for us quite clearly about the six days of creation.

According to Didymus, the acts of the six days were accomplished instantaneously, and were presented to us as if they had been accomplished sequentially. The actions may actually have been executed by the First Cause at once. The various steps were intrinsically intertwined, and the basis for their logical connections was locked up in the fundamental nature of the things that the Lord God was creating, reflecting their essential, logically interconnected interrelationships. That is to say, the things created had causal and logical dependencies between themselves. The totality of their unified, completed creation can be expressed through the "perfect number" six. Thus they are presented to us sequentially, as having happened over six days, even though their creation was actually accomplished simultaneously and instantaneously. Didymus explains,

> In the beginning of the book we said that as an efficacious being God has only to wish for what He wishes to exist. In His case, you see, it is out of the question that action should precede effect, as is the case with human endeavor, where only after action does the work come into being, and after the building process the house; the house does not exist during the building process, nor the ship during the shipbuilding, since the actions themselves require time. God, on the other hand, acts outside of time in bringing into being what he wishes; the outcome is definitely not a consequence [By this he means it did not happen over time, even though it was an effect of what God wished.]. It was therefore simultaneously that he wished the lights to come into existence, and they were; and simultaneously he wanted the water to be gathered together into a single mass, and his command was executed; and in saying *Let a firmament be made,* it came into existence. Hence, in consequence of this thought . . . [This ellipsis is not mine, but is in the translation. Something was missing in the document.] we should think of the six *days* not as though cited as part of a chronological presentation but as a rational basis peculiar to God's creation and the force of the number. Six, in fact, is the first of the perfect numbers; they say that perfect numbers are those composed of their own parts, and there are only four between 1 and 1000. So the first is 6, half of which is 3, a third 2, a sixth 1, and when added together they total 6. The same is true of 28.[5]

From here Didymus goes into a somewhat extended explanation of "perfect" numbers.

Here are some concepts in the thinking of Didymus that are imbedded in his comments.
- He says that in the case of the Lord God, because of His infinite power and because He summoned all matter into existence from nothing by His will, it is impossible that matter could resist His wish even for a moment. Therefore the commands of the creation were carried out instantly. This is a very common theme among the Fathers. (But most Fathers allowed that God spread His works over six days anyway, because that is what His word says—and perhaps, as some opine, as a model for frail human beings who would work for six days and then need to rest. Therefore God took six days to accomplish what He could have done instantly, and rested on the seventh day which He did not need to do, but which He did to set for us an example. This is reflected in the Sabbath commandment in Exodus 20:11.)
- The number six, being a "perfect" number, was a mystical touchpoint for some of the interpreters of Scripture—not many, but Didymus and Augustine were among them.[6] [see note]

As Didymus proceeds through his commentary on Genesis he usually gives a literal and an allegorical sense for each passage that he comments on. He comments on creation as above and then later returns to the same idea and states that his explanation was the literal understanding of the six days. Then he elucidates their anagogical sense. By anagogical he means the spiritual or mystical interpretation that might also be seen as an allusion to or a prefiguring of the person and work of Jesus Christ.

> To make a remark further regarding what was said about the text properly mentioning six *days*, not hours or months or years: saying months or years would imply slowness, and hours would be incomprehensible, since the person unable to grasp *day* would not understand "hour," either. Having given a perfect number, therefore, it was only right and proper to adopt *days* . . .

> While this is what we have to say in clarifying the literal sense, the anagogical sense would be as follows. It was said before that the phrase *Let there be light* should be applied to the Savior, not that he was brought into being from what did not exist, but by comparison with those to whom he gives light. In the case of those given light, some receive less light, others more, and in addition to them there are some that are in the dark of night. Accordingly, today as well the thoughts of the Son prove to be lights, as the intent of the text in hand can logically be understood. He is adapted to the measure of each one, to the more elevated being the Sun of justice, while to the less developed he provides in appropriate measure the light of the Spirit in the manner of the moon. Those illuminated in the night, on the other hand, would be everyone who, though mature, is necessarily subject to the needs of the body. The person who is mature, even though being such, nevertheless has a body and so needs nourishment and is subject to the other needs of the body.[7]

In his view, for the Lord God to express the creation in terms of months or years would imply that it took a long time, which is contrary to his original discussion about the "fully efficacious" nature of God, which implies an instantaneous outworking of His commands. To speak using a scale of "hours" would be, in his way of thinking, incomprehensible to humans. Thus God expresses his completed work as having taken place during the "perfect number" of days; that is, in six days. Then Didymus goes on into an extended mystical meditation on Jesus as the light of mankind.[c]

---

[c] The commentary by Didymus is fragmented and is missing his ideas for chapter 2 of Genesis, but from his comments on the fall in Genesis 3 it seems that he did not believe Paradise was a physical place on this earth, but that it was perhaps in the spiritual plane. Thus Augustine's remarks about taking Genesis 2 literally (see below) might be addressed, in part, to the followers of Didymus, for their correction.

Augustine was influenced by Didymus and adopted his way of thinking about creation. The challenge for Augustine was to unite the philosophical concept of "simultaneous creation" with the Genesis narrative and to show how the account from Moses actually should be understood as saying this to the astute reader. This is all the more difficult because, as is clear from many statements of Augustine, he believes without any doubt in the total, absolute truth of every word of the Bible. The task of uniting this philosophical concept with the text of Genesis is what Augustine is about in his commentary. Realizing this is the key to understanding what he is doing in *The Literal Meaning of Genesis*.

Now let us turn to Augustine with a quotation on the "six days" from the *City of God* to introduce his theory of the creation. Augustine claims that the company of the angels is the light that God created on the first day.

> Clearly, then, if the angels are included among the works of God on those six days, they are the light which was given the name *day,* and, to stress the unity of that day, it was called not "the first day" but rather *one day.* Nor is the second a different day, or the third, or the rest. Rather the very same one day is repeated up to the number six or seven on account of the seven phases of knowledge, namely, the six of the works that God created and the seventh of God's rest. For when God said, *Let there be light* (Gen 1:3), and light was created, if the creation of the angels is rightly understood to be included in this light, then they were surely created as participants in the eternal light which is itself the immutable wisdom of God, by which all things were made, and which we call the only-begotten Son of God. Thus the angels, illumined by the light that created them, themselves became light and were called *day* by virtue of their participation in the immutable light and day which is the Word of God, by which both they and everything else were created. For *the true light that enlightens everyone coming into this world* (John 1:9) also enlightens every pure angel, so that he is light not in himself but in God.[8]

Thus there was a spiritual and intelligent creation that God made first. This is signified by the statement "let there be light" followed by the statement "and there was light." This signifies the creation of the companies of angels, who subsequently observed the rest of the creation. Augustine states that the fashioning of heaven was done first in the Eternal Word then in the knowledge of the angels, then in itself in the physical creation. These three steps in the creation also apply to the specific steps of creation that follow, including the waters and dry lands, the trees and plants, the heavenly lights, and the animated beings in the waters and on the earth.

This approach rests on the idea that the angels understand things differently than we do, not "by understanding them through the things that have been made" (Romans 1:20) as human beings do and thus by reaching a progressively better understanding as time goes on. Rather they have constantly enjoyed the eternity of the Word in holy contemplation ever since they were formed out of light by Him. The angels learned about the creation directly from God when He produced in them first of all the knowledge of each of the various creatures that He intended to make.[9]

Therefore when we read in the creation account "And God said, let it be made . . ." we should understand that Scripture is turning its gaze back to the eternity of God's Word. When we read "and thus it was made" we should understand that the idea of the thing about to be created is being produced in the mind of the angels. When we then hear it repeated that "God made . . ." then we are to understand the physical creation as being enacted in space and time. And when we read "and God saw that it was good" we are to understand that God in His courtesy took pleasure in what had been made, because it had been His pleasure that it should be made when "the Spirit of God was hovering over the waters."[10]

Before we continue to examine this tortuous way of understanding the straightforward account of the creation that appears in Genesis chapter one, let us step back a bit and answer a question that must be in your mind: Why would Augustine continue such an arcane approach to interpreting the creation account? Could it be simply that he was "influenced" by thinkers in Alexandria such as Didymus? The question is made more difficult to answer because we see him going through lengthy arguments in support of his position in various passages in *The Literal Meaning of Genesis*, and we could be inclined to see these arguments as the reason why he adopts this point of view. But often these are his defense of a position that he has taken for various other reasons.

Augustine is aware that the explanation he offers is extraordinary.[11] He realizes that it is difficult to understand. At the end of Book VII of his *Literal Interpretation*, where he is considering when God created the soul of Adam—an extremely complex consideration because of his assertion that God created all things simultaneously in one great Day—Augustine considers the possibility of holding to the position that it was created when it was breathed into the body of Adam after that body had been formed. Then he relates the problems that would arise if one were to hold to such a (simple and straightforward) position. It would compel you to also hold that both the man and the woman had been created on the sixth day, and then he lists the problems that would have to be dealt with if you hold that position. He lists seven reasons—all rooted in the assumption that all of the Scriptures are perfectly true—that have led him to his unique conclusion.[12]

I will list these seven reasons in their details and deal with each of them completely in the commentary. The most important of them are rooted in a fundamentally flawed translation of the Hebrew Scriptures into the Greek. But there are other issues that are perfectly handled by the clearer understanding of the Scriptures that results from our insights from archeology, which are the central theme of this work.

Augustine explains that it was from all evidence of all the Scriptures that He concluded that God created all things simultaneously at once, some already in their established natures and some in their pre-established causes. This is why he was compelled, in his thinking, to adopt this abstruse position. It was, ultimately, because he believed firmly, as did all "but unbelievers and the ungodly" (his words), in the perfect truth of Scripture. This unshakeable faith led him to his conclusions.[13] But how and why was he so led? Let us return to the creation account as Augustine constructed it:

Making of light: (This light is the intelligent creation, the company of the angels)
Verse 3:   God said, let there be light
     (Spoken to the eternal Word)
    And there was light
     (Actual enactment of the command, but this happened not in space
     and time. This was the creation of the angels in the spiritual realm.)
This light is actually a term for the intelligent creation—the company of the angels—the created intellectual light. The reason that there is no repetition here, no "and it was so," is that in the very act of being created angels came to the knowledge of the fact of their existence. After that God showed His holy angels—the intelligent creation—each step of His physical creation as He determined to create it. When the angels knew the thing that was actually made then that was evening. The angels then referred this knowledge of the thing made to the praise of God and this is what is meant by the next morning.[14]

Here is the unfolding of the rest of the creation work as Augustine envisions it from the creation account:

Making of the firmament:
    Verse 6:   God said, let there be a firmament,   and it was so
                  (Spoken in the eternal Word)   (In the mind of the angels)
    Verse 7:   And God made the firmament
                  (Actual creation in space and time by Jesus)

Gathering the waters to make the dry land appear:
    Verse 9:   God said, let the waters be gathered   and it was so
                  (Spoken in the eternal Word)   (In the angels)
    Verse 9:   And the waters were gathered together
                  (Actual enactment in space and time by Jesus)

Creation of vegetation:
    Verse 11:   God said, let the earth bring forth trees etc.   and it was so
                   (Spoken in the eternal Word)   (In the angels)
    Verse 12:   And the earth brought forth trees etc.
                   (Actual enactment in time by Jesus)

    . . . etc.

Creation of man:
    Verse 26:   God said, let us make man etc.
                   (Spoken in the eternal Word)
    Verse 27:   And God made man etc.
                   (Actual enactment in time by Jesus and the Father together)

Augustine is careful to consider every jot and tittle of the scriptural text as he comments on the creation of man in this scenario. He notes that there is no statement "and it was so" after the creation of man. Man, like the angels, became aware of himself as soon as he was created. Thus there was no "and it was so" for man, just as there was no such statement for the creation of the angels; that is, for the creation of light.

> Well, it is this principle that is being kept to in the making of man. God, you see, has just said, *Let us make man to our image and likeness* etc.; and then it does not say, *and thus it was made*, but leads straight into, *and God made man to the image of God,* precisely because human nature too is intellectual like that light [the angels], and that is why being made is the same thing for it as recognizing the Word of God by whom it is being made.[15]

As he considers this scenario Augustine ponders why there is no "and God saw that it was good" after the creation of man, but does not come up with a certain reason.[16]

In developing this idea Augustine also explains that when things were created in the one "Day" in eternity some were created in their "causes" or in their "potentialities," but not in actual fact. The unfolding of their realities in time happened after the one "Day." Mortal humans have no way of fully understanding that "Day," or even the six days as they are unfolded for us. In asserting his view Augustine allows that another explanation might possibly be found for the creation account that is better than what he offers.

> And thus throughout all those days there is just the one day [one day of creation, "the day which the Lord has made"], which is not to be understood after the manner of these days that we see measured and counted by the circuit of the sun, but in a different kind of mode.[17]

> Now clearly, in this earth-bound condition of ours we mortals can have no experiential perception of that day, or those days which were named and numbered by the repetition of it. So . . . let us suppose . . . that these seven days [of a normal week] . . . represent those first seven in some fashion, though they are not at all like them, but very, very dissimilar.[18]

> I am certainly not insisting on this one [way of looking at things] in such a way as to contend that nothing else preferable can be found.[19]

Here is an example of the conundrum that Augustine faced in his work, one text that stands out as the most repeated scriptural reference in Augustine, one mistranslated verse from Sirach 18:1: *He created all things simultaneously together.* He repeatedly returns to this verse in his ruminations and concludes from it that the Lord must have brought forth the entire creation in an instant and then unfolded it according to the time-bound course of how things grow and develop. I wonder if Didymus saw this verse and was led astray by a mistranslation of it as well!

> The creator, after all, about whom scripture told this story of how he completed and finished his works in six days, is the same as the one about whom it is written elsewhere, and assuredly without there being any contradiction, that *he created all things simultaneously together* (Sir 18:1). And consequently, the one who made all things simultaneously together also made simultaneously these six or seven days, or rather this one day six or seven times repeated. So then, what need was there for the six days to be recounted so distinctly and methodically? It was for the sake of those who cannot arrive at an understanding of the text, "he created all things together simultaneously," unless scripture accompanies them more slowly, step by step, to the goal to which it is leading them.[20]

This verse (Sirach 18:1) is one of the seven reasons that Augustine gives for adopting his view on the creation account. As I said, we will deal with all of them in the commentary.

Thus it was his understanding that there was just one "Day" of creation. All things were actually created simultaneously and were revealed to the angels in their instantaneous understanding, but were explained to mankind—because of our human limitations—as being spread over a period of six days. It might be faithful to his concept to explain that God created everything at once then presented that creation event to us in the Genesis narrative six times, and each time He revealed to us another aspect of the work that He accomplished instantaneously during that one great "Day." Thus the events of the "Day" were shown to mankind as spread over six days to help us understand it. I reiterate that this extraordinary point of view was the result of three convergent ideas:

- All of the Scriptures are absolutely true. This was the universal belief of all of the Fathers and doctors of the Church. Augustine thought very deeply about the Scriptures that related to creation. He arrived at his conclusions from considering the unified testimony that they presented when they were all taken together.
- God accomplishes whatever He wishes for instantaneously because He is a "fully efficacious" being.
- Augustine was working with scriptural texts that had a series of serious errors in them, and though he knew of the Hebrew Scriptures[21] he did not refer to them or read from them because he did not know how to read Hebrew.

Undergirding this point of view was the widely-held opinion of the Fathers that the events of creation were uniquely God's work, supernatural in character, and were not amenable to the investigative efforts of human beings. Thus the concept that God had to unveil the truths of the creation in six successive stages was not foreign to their basic attitude. An attendant issue with the Fathers was how the angels fit into the creation account. When Augustine formulated his explanation it also offered an answer to that question.

I said that Augustine makes several arguments for this approach to understanding the creation account not because they are foundational to his position but because, once he has adopted this unusual position, he then feels that he must defend it and work out all of the difficult consequences to understanding the text of Genesis like this. For example consider his dismay at this passage that explains the human speech that Adam recited when he originally saw Eve: *This is now flesh of my flesh and bone of my bones, etc.* As Augustine observes, this human speech, which is reported to have happened in the midst of those instantaneous acts of creation, must have taken some time to be uttered. Augustine says that at this point in chapter two, when God describes in more detail the making of the woman from the side of the man, we are not in the one great "Day" of creation, but in the time of man when events happen sequentially, one after another.

But earlier it had been theorized that the creation of man, as part of day six, happened during the one great "Day" in eternity.

> Well, but on the sixth day it was not that the male was made, and the woman was made later with the onset of time; but *He made them*, it says, *male and female He made them and blessed them*. So how, then, with the man already placed in Paradise, was the woman made for him? . . . But none of this could have been done except over intervals of time. And so it follows that none of it was done in the way that all things were created simultaneously.

> However easy, after all, a human being may think it is for God to have done all this simultaneously with the rest, we know with absolute certainty that the words of a human being can only be uttered aloud over intervals of time. When we hear the man's words, therefore, when he was giving names either to the animals or to the woman, or when he also went on to say, *For this reason a man shall leave his father and mother and be joined to his wife; and they shall be two in one flesh* (Genesis 2:24), whatever the syllables this was uttered with, not even any two of them could have been spoken simultaneously; how much less, then, could all of this have happened all together with all the things that were created simultaneously! And this would mean that those "all things" were not after all created simultaneously at the absolute starting point of the ages, but that they were made over successive intervals of time, and that that day originally established was of a material, not a spiritual nature, and was making morning and evening by heaven knows what kind of circling round of light, or by its emission and contraction.

> But taking into consideration everything that has been discussed above in the preceding books, we have concluded more probably and reasonably that it was a spiritual day which was sublimely instituted at the beginning [that is, the company of the angels], and that the day was called a kind of wise light, whose presence was vouchsafed to the simultaneous creation through six stages of knowledge arranged in due order; and that this opinion chimes in with the words of scripture, because it says later on, *When the day was made God made heaven and earth, and all the greenery of the field before it was upon the earth, and all the hay of the field before it sprang up* (Genesis 2:4-5); and is also supported by what is written elsewhere: *The one who lives forever created all things simultaneously* (Sir 18:1). So there can be no doubt that this account of the man being molded from the mud of the earth, and a wife being formed for him from his side, does not belong to the creating of all things simultaneously and God resting when they were complete, but to that divine work which is continuing now through the ages as they unroll, at which *he is working until now* (Jn 5:17).[22]

> So when it says, *He still cast up from the earth every tree that had a beautiful look about it*, He makes it perfectly clear that He was now casting up trees from the earth quite differently from the way the earth then on the third day produced grass for fodder . . . Then, of course, it was done potentially, causally, in the work involved in creating all things together simultaneously, from which He rested on the seventh day when they were completed; whereas now it was being done visibly in the work belonging to the march of time.[23]

Augustine goes on to argue for various positions in support of and as foundational to the problems that he notices. But those arguments are best understood not as the basis of his position but rather as the necessary defense of his position—which position he has adopted for the seven reasons that he himself listed—which reasons we shall consider. All of the intricate considerations that Augustine goes through, as when he asks how Adam could have uttered those words in Eden, show how Augustine thinks about the truth of the creation account and the plain history that he believes it is relating.

In the midst of his account of the six days Augustine states that both the "creation in six days" and the "simultaneous creation of all things" are true, but those original six days were of a different character from the days that we experience today.

> Indeed, though, both statements are true: both that the things mentioned were made "before and after" in the course of the six days, and that they were all made simultaneously, because each passage of scripture, both the one telling the story of God's works through these days, and the one saying that he made all things simultaneously, are speaking the truth. And they are both true with one truth, because they were both written under the inspiration of the one *Spirit of truth* (John 16:13).[24]

> God made them in One Day ("The day that the Lord has made") and also in six days. Both are true. Now these ordinary seven days, which are unfolded and folded up again by the rotation of light from the heavenly bodies, bear a kind of shadowy resemblance to those primordial days; and accordingly they serve to remind us to investigate those days in which the created spiritual light was presented with all the works of God through the perfection of the number six.[25]

Like Didymus, Augustine asserts that this interpretation of the creation is not intended to be taken metaphorically. Rather it is his understanding of the actual way that the events happened in the distant past. He has sought to understand exactly how the world was made as revealed in the Scriptures, and this is what He believes they are telling us.[26] And, like Didymus, Augustine accords mystical significance to the perfect number six.

With all of these contorted ideas and extraordinary thoughts Augustine still affirmed the creation of the world as being less than 6,000 years in the past. Thus he excoriates the philosophers who claim that the human race has always existed. He states:

> These people are also led astray by certain wholly fallacious writings which cover, so they tell us, many thousands of years in their recording of history. On the basis of Sacred Scripture, however, we calculate that not even six thousand years have passed since the origin of humankind.[27]

And he again reiterates this later on in his arguments, for those who ask "why, after an eternity of time, did God at one point choose to create mankind?" It is a good question!

> And I would want to give this same response with regard to the first creation of man for the sake of those who are similarly troubled as to why man was not created during the innumerable and infinite ages of the past but instead was created so recently that it turns out, according to Sacred Scripture, that he came into existence less than six thousand years ago. If this brief span of time disturbs them because the years since man's creation, as recorded in our authorities, seem so very short to them, they should take note that nothing which has any limit lasts all that long and that, compared to unending eternity, all the finite expanses of time must be reckoned not just as very little but as nothing at all. As a consequence, even if we said not that five thousand or six thousand but that sixty thousand or six hundred thousand years had passed since God created man—or sixty or six hundred or six hundred thousand times that number, or even if we multiplied this total by itself again and again until we no longer had a name for the number—it would still be possible to ask why he did not create man before that.[28]

He then goes on to disavow the idea that there are innumerable worlds or that this world was destroyed at regular intervals and then arose again. Then he presents the origin of the *City of God* as descending from Seth, the son of Adam, and contrasts it with the city of man which started with the murderer Cain. He then defends the long lives of the men in the early days before the Flood, asserts that that those were years as we understand them (not especially short), that there were giants in the past, that the Flood account is accurate, and that other attacks against the historical accuracy of Genesis are rubbish.

The attempt of Augustine to explain the creation account in detail by carefully analyzing it and by trying to include in his explanation other Scriptures that relate to the creation is truly a superb effort. It is too bad that he was sometimes reasoning from inaccurate or misleading translations! He is the only ancient commentator to attempt this level of in-depth analysis and explanation of the Genesis text. Other writers took the text as given, assumed it was true as written, and did not attempt to dissect it in such minute detail. Of course, that approach is also a fine way to handle Scripture. However, as we comment on the creation account we will try to do something like what Augustine did, but we will use the correct Bible texts as the basis for what we do, and we will have the advantage of certain archeological findings to support us as well.

In pondering the creation of all things that God accomplished, and the beginning of time that accompanied that first moment of creation, Augustine says:

> But there could not have been any time that had passed [before the creation in Genesis 1:1], because there was no created being to provide the change and motion of which time is a function [Like Aristotle, Augustine thinks that time is connected to the movement or change of things]. Thus, if change and movement were created when the world was made, the world was made with time, and this seems to hold good in the very order of the first six or seven days. For both the morning and the evening of these days are enumerated until, on the sixth day, all that God made during those days is completed, and, on the seventh day, God's rest is presented in a great mystery. But what kind of days these are it is extremely difficult, or even impossible, to conceive, let alone to put into words. We note, of course, that the days known to us have evenings and mornings only because of the setting and rising of the sun; but those first three days passed without the sun, which was made, we are told, on the fourth day. Scripture narrates that, at the first, light was made by the Word of God, and that God separated the light from the darkness and called the light day and the darkness night. But what kind of light it was, and by what alternating motion it made evening and morning, and what sort of evening and morning these were, are all things far removed from our senses. Nor is it possible for us to understand how it was so, but we must still believe it without the least hesitation.[29]

Thus he asserts that human minds cannot grasp the nature of those six days, nor can we ever, by any art or science that we might devise, peer within them and thus come to understand the way in which God operated to accomplish the creation of all things. The creation is properly the work and the understanding of God alone, accomplished by Him during the six days of awe—days during which He laid the foundation of the universe.

This is a fair presentation of Augustine's views on the creation account in chapter one of Genesis. His views on the Garden of Eden are classic and will be expressed when we comment on chapters two and three of Genesis.

Awe before the Lord at His supernatural works of creation was widely held and expressed by the early commentators on Genesis. There are also other concepts imbedded in the thinking of Didymus, Augustine, and many of the early writers—ideas about the nature of God, about how He dwells in eternity unlike us, about the spiritual realities in general, about how angels come to know or understand things, etc. These ideas are not actually rooted in the Scriptures but are philosophical or metaphysical concepts that have been applied to understanding Scripture and to understanding the nature of God, angels, and the creation. I will also address these ideas in my commentary, for they are foundational to the extraordinary view of creation that we see presented in a few of the writings of the Fathers—the above being an excellent example of what I am talking about.

Origen:

Who was Origen? He was an early writer and apologist for the faith who spent much of his life in North Africa. Here are a few details about this extraordinary man.

> [I]t seems that the following assertions about Origen's youth can be accepted as quite probably factual, based on their harmony with Origen's later achievements. Origen's education in the Scriptures was begun quite early and may have been supervised by his father. His broad knowledge of the Bible demonstrated in his commentaries and homilies gives evidence of a mind that has lived in the Bible for years. He also received the standard education for a boy in that day. We may reasonably assume that he progressed exceptionally well in both these educational endeavors. He may also have shown some ascetic tendencies in his youth since Egypt was the seedbed of Christian asceticism and Origen displayed tendencies in this direction later.[30]

In his zeal Origen self-castrated himself because he took literally the words of Jesus:[31]

> For there are eunuchs who were born that way from their mother's womb; and there are eunuchs who were made eunuchs by men; and there are *also* eunuchs who made themselves eunuchs for the sake of the kingdom of heaven. He who is able to accept *this*, let him accept *it*. (Matthew 19:12)

For this reason his ordination to the priesthood was challenged at one point in his life, for priests were not to have mutilated bodies according to Church thinking.

Origen's father had been martyred for the faith when he was a youth and he desired the same. Thus he was a very ardent follower of Jesus. In AD 249 when Decius became emperor an edict was issued demanding that all people offer sacrifices to the gods. At that time Origen was imprisoned in Caesarea and tortured, but he was not killed. The persecutions continued until around 253 when Valerian came to power and a brief peace ensued. Origen probably died early in the reign of Valerian.[32]

Origen was a controversial interpreter even in his own day, and the head of the school at Alexandria, one Demetrius (Pope Demetrius I of Alexandria), opposed his teachings, especially his allegorical interpretation of certain early chapters of Genesis. However, only fragments of his Genesis commentary are preserved.[33] Origen was extremely influential both in his own time and for centuries after, and even today he continues to be a source of significant influence and controversy. Perhaps his most inflammatory teaching was the doctrine of universal salvation; that is, he claimed that all intelligent creatures must be saved in the end.[34] Origen greatly loved and promoted the allegorical interpretation of the Scriptures. This is very important to one who seeks to know how he understood the creation of all things. He was a brilliant and devoted follower of our Lord. We must approach him with the utmost respect and honor. I will carefully outline his teachings on the creation, as much as have been preserved from his huge volume of writings.

The loud dissent against the error of universal salvation and other points of his teaching echoed through the centuries. One Sulpicius Severus (c 363-c425) a Christian writer of Aquitania, relates a riotous incident that he personally witnessed over Origen's assertion of universal salvation. Two partisan groups were reading his works.

> When this passage and others like it were produced by the bishops, the animosity of the two parties led to dissension. When episcopal authority proved incapable of repressing this, an unfortunate thing occurred: the prefect was called in to direct the discipline of the Church. In terror, the brothers dispersed and the monks scattered and fled. Edicts were issued, preventing their remaining permanently in any place. One thing disturbed me greatly: the attitude of Jerome, a man eminently Catholic and very skilled in the sacred law. He was thought at first to be a follower of Origen; now he is eminent for having condemned the whole corpus of his

writings. When outstanding and very learned men were reported to disagree in this dispute, I certainly should not venture to give rash judgment about anyone. What is in question may be a simple error—and this is my opinion—or else, as others think, a genuine heresy. In any event the strenuous measures repeatedly taken by the bishops were unable to repress it. Surely, it could not have had so wide a spread unless dissension had served to increase it.[35]

But Origen was a staunch defender of Christianity, a brilliant thinker, and a voluminous writer. In answering Celsus, a third-century detractor of Christian beliefs and writings, Origen fought back, but not in the way some wanted him to:

In the next place, as it is his object to slander our Scriptures, he ridicules the following statement: "And God caused a deep sleep to fall upon Adam, and he slept: and He took one of his ribs, and closed up the flesh instead thereof. And the rib, which He had taken from the man, made He a woman," and so on; without quoting the words, which would give the hearer the impression that they are spoken with a figurative meaning. He would not even have it appear that the words were used allegorically, although he says afterwards, that "the more modest among Jews and Christians are ashamed of these things, and endeavor to give them somehow an allegorical signification.". . . [and just as you Celsus take some of your verses to have a deeper meaning, why do you assert that the verse] regarding the woman who was taken from the side of the man (after he had been buried in deep slumber), and was formed by God, appears to you to be related without any rational meaning and secret signification?[36]

Origen goes on to argue that the account of the serpent and the fall must be understood allegorically. Speaking of the larger account of Paradise including the two trees in Eden he continues: "and the other statements which follow, which might of themselves lead a candid reader to see that all these things had not inappropriately an allegorical meaning;" that is, he intends by this, **only** an allegorical meaning.[37]

Yet Origen argues for the historical accuracy of the dimensions of the ark of Noah, the historicity of the Deluge, and even the historical accuracy of the details about the dove and the raven. Then he excoriates Celsus for suggesting that Moses copied from other accounts of the Deluge, such as from the Greeks, in composing his record of Genesis. Thus he sees the account of the Flood as completely historical.[38]

He discusses some issues raised by Celsus about the wells dug by the patriarchs (see Genesis 21:25, 30 where Abraham dug a well, and Genesis 26:18–21 where Isaac dug wells) and he notes that "Scripture frequently makes use of the histories of real events in order to present to view more important truths, which are but obscurely intimated; and of this kind are the narratives relating to the wells."[39] Additionally he relates examples of similar allegorical interpretations that Paul makes in discussing the incident with Ishmael and Isaac, who were born from Hagar and Sarah, in Galatians 4:21-24. Therefore he sees other stories in Genesis as having a basis in history and also having an allegorical meaning that is derived from the historical facts.[40]

From these examples and from many more instances that Origen presents to us in his writing *Against Celsus* we can see that Origen interpreted the Bible as follows:
- Some passages in the Old Testament are purely allegorical and do not provide us with historical knowledge about the events that they relate.
- Some Old Testament passages are purely historical and do not provide us with any allegorical meaning beyond the straightforward history that they relate.
- Some Old Testament passages relate real historical events but also contain allegorical meanings beyond but in addition to the events that they relate.

Thus we can say that some of the events in the early chapters of Genesis were thought of as being merely allegorical by Origen—basically, chapters two and three which talk about Adam and Eve in the Garden of Eden. One can look in *Against Celsus* Book 4 Section 38 and beyond for many examples. In general we can assert that Origen did believe in the inspiration and the integrity of Scripture, and that he asserted a three-fold sense in the holy writings: A literal sense, a moral sense, and an allegorical sense.

There is only one extant work of Origen that can be adduced in order to glean a little of his understanding of the creation account, and that is his first homily on Genesis. Let us look at this work and summarize what he says. Origen begins with this key statement:

> IN THE BEGINNING GOD MADE HEAVEN AND EARTH. What is the beginning of all things except our Lord and "Savior of all," Jesus Christ "the firstborn of every creature"? In this beginning, therefore, that is, in his Word, "God made heaven and earth" as the evangelist John also says in the beginning of his Gospel: "In the beginning was the Word, and the Word was with God, and the Word was God. The same was in the beginning with God. All things were made by him and without him nothing was made." Scripture is not speaking here of any temporal beginning, but it says that the heaven and the earth and all things which were made were made "in the beginning," that is, in the Savior.[41]

Thus he asserts that the initial beginning of the creation was accomplished not in time but in eternity, in the Son of God, Jesus Christ. This is clarified a bit later.

> According to the letter [That is, understanding literally what is written] God calls both the light day and the darkness night. But let us see according to the spiritual meaning why it is that when God, in that beginning which we discussed above, "made heaven and earth," and said, "let there be light" and "divided between the light and the darkness and called the light day and the darkness night," and the text said that "there was evening and there was morning," it did not say: "the first day," but said, "one day." It is because there was not yet time before the world existed. But time begins to exist with the following days. For the second day and the third and fourth and all the rest begin to designate time.[42]

Therefore the first act of creation was in an eternal day, but subsequent acts take place according to the temporal sequence of things. Finally, one more important statement:

> "And God said: 'Let there be a firmament in the midst of the water and let it divide water from water.' And it was so done. And God made the firmament." Although God had already previously made heaven, now he makes the firmament. For he made heaven first, about which he says, "heaven is my throne." But after that he makes the firmament, that is, the corporeal heaven. For every corporeal object is, without doubt, firm and solid; and it is this which "divides the water which is above heaven from the water which is below heaven." For since everything which God was to make would consist of spirit and body, for that reason heaven, that is, all spiritual substance upon which God rests as upon a kind of throne or seat, is said to be made in the beginning. But this heaven, that is, the firmament, is corporeal.[43]

Thus the first "heaven" was a spiritual heaven made in eternity in the one "day," and the firmament is the corporeal heaven made on the second day. In our commentary we will see that in the Hebrew text the word translated "firmament" does not imply a solid thing. The Hebrew word actually means "a stretched-out thinness;" that is, something like the space of the sky. The ancient understanding of the open space that we see when we look at the sky as a solid dome is the result of a peculiarity of the Greek LXX translation and of the deficiency of ancient cosmology. People did not understand that opposing forces held the heavenly objects in place and prevented them from falling down. They assumed therefore that a solid dome was placed there by God to support the heavens.

In one quotation above we also see something that will often be evident within Origen's commentary on the creation. He says "according to the letter," and then gives a very brief literal interpretation of the text; then he follows up with a much more extended discussion of the allegorical meaning of the text. It is almost as if he sees the literal meaning as so obvious as to not need to be dwelt on, while the allegorical meaning is in need of extensive explanation. Thus he sees the text as literally and allegorically true.

Thus after the dry land appears, which God calls earth, He commands the earth to bear vegetation.
> But let us see from the following words what those fruits are which God orders the earth, on which he himself bestowed this name, to produce. "And God saw," the text says, "that it was good, and God said: 'Let the earth bring forth vegetation producing seed according to its kind and likeness, and the fruit tree bearing fruit whose seed is within it according to its likeness on the earth.' And it was so done." According to the letter, the fruits are clearly those which "the earth," not "the dry land" produces. But again let us also relate the meaning to ourselves.[44]

After this simple statement about the "letter" Origen spends considerable time exhorting his readers to "bear fruit" in their walk with the Lord.

Origen does not give a statement about the literal meaning of the lights in the sky, but likens them to the Lord Jesus (the sun), the Church (the moon, which shines by light that is reflected from the sun), and the holy men and women of old (the stars).

Origen talks of the creatures in the sea:
> And God said: "Let the waters bring forth creeping creatures having life and birds flying over the earth in the firmament of heaven." And it was so done. According to the letter "creeping creatures" and "birds" are brought forth by the waters at the command of God and we recognize by whom these things which we see have been made. But let us see how these same things come to be in . . . our mind or heart.[45]

Origen also sees the "great whales" allegorically:
> I think impious thoughts and abominable understandings which are against God are indicated in those great whales.[46]

When he considers how this allegorical understanding could be acceptable since God pronounces all of His works as "good," including these sea creatures, he continues with a line of reasoning that we find elsewhere in his works.
> Those things which are opposed to the saints are good for them because they can overcome them and when they have overcome them they become more glorious with God. Indeed when the devil requested that power be given to him against Job, the adversary, by attacking him, was the cause of double glory for Job after his victory. What is shown from the fact that he received double those things which he lost in the present is that he will, without doubt, also receive in the same manner in the heavenly places. And the Apostle says that "No one is crowned except the one who has striven lawfully." And indeed, how will there be a contest if there not be one who resists? How great the beauty and splendor is of light would not be discerned unless the darkness of night intervened. Why are some praised for purity unless because others are condemned for immodesty? Why are strong men magnified unless weak and cowardly men exist? If you use what is bitter then what is sweet is rendered more praiseworthy. If you consider what is dark, the things which are bright will appear more pleasing to you. And, to put it briefly, from the consideration of evil things the glory of good things is indicated more brilliantly. For this reason, therefore, the Scripture says this about everything: "And God saw that they were good."[47]

These considerations are a fundamental reason why Origen sees the eventual universal salvation of all—for all things are ordered by God to the benefit of the saints (Romans 8:32) and thus, after playing their perverse and contrary part in the glorification of His people, all of creation, including the fallen angels, will be brought to final salvation. This is a foundational aspect of his mistaken argument for universal salvation in *Principles*.

Origen continues:
> "And God said: 'Let the earth bring forth the living creature according to its kind, four-footed creatures and creeping creatures and beasts of the earth according to their kind.' And it was so done. And God made the beasts of the earth according to their kind and all the creeping creatures of the earth according to their kind. And God saw that they were good." There is certainly no question about the literal meaning. For they are clearly said to have been created by God, whether animals or four-footed creatures or beasts or serpents upon the earth. But it is not unprofitable to relate these words to those which we explained above in a spiritual sense.[48]

One of the uncertainties of Origen's interpretations, lost with his missing manuscripts, is how he explained the account of man in Paradise. But after considering the literal and allegorical understanding of the creation, and how it all relates to man in some way, he comments on the creation of man in Genesis 1. He says that he has already considered the way that created things apply to man allegorically, and now he wants to talk about what sort of a living being man might be. I think in this part of his commentary he is speaking literally; that is, he is giving his literal understanding about the creation of man. He talks at great length about the way in which we are "His image and likeness."

> I see, however, something indeed even more distinguished in the condition of man, which I do not find said elsewhere: "And God made man, according to the image of God he made him." We find this attributed neither to heaven nor earth nor the sun or moon. We do not understand, however, this man indeed whom Scripture says was made "according to the image of God" to be corporeal. For the form of the body does not contain the image of God, nor is the corporeal man said to be "made," but "formed," as is written in the words which follow. For the text says: "And God formed man," that is fashioned, "from the slime of the earth." But it is our inner man, invisible, incorporeal, incorruptible, and immortal which is made "according to the image of God." For it is in such qualities as these that the image of God is more correctly understood. But if anyone suppose that this man who is made "according to the image and likeness of God" is made of flesh, he will appear to represent God himself as made of flesh and in human form. It is most clearly impious to think this about God.[49]

And he then stresses that the "image" in which we are made is actually Jesus the Word:
> Therefore, what other image of God is there according to the likeness of whose image man is made, except our Savior who is "the firstborn of every creature?" about whom it is written that he is "the brightness of the eternal light and the express figure of God's substance,"? who also says about himself: "I am in the Father, and the Father in me," and "He who has seen me has also seen the Father" For just as one who sees an image of someone sees him whose image it is, so also one sees God through the Word of God which is the image of God. And thus what he said will be true: "He who has seen me has also seen the Father." Man, therefore, is made according to the likeness of his image and for this reason our Savior, who is the image of God, moved with compassion for man who had been made according to his likeness, seeing him, his own image having been laid aside, to have put on the image of the evil one, he himself moved with compassion, assumed the image of man and came to him [in the incarnation].[50]

Finally, as to the timing of the creation of man, Origen notes that God created us both male and female and says:
> It seems to be worth inquiring in this passage according to the letter how, when the woman was not yet made, the Scripture says, "Male and female he made them." Perhaps, as I think, it is because of the blessing with which he blessed them saying, "Increase and multiply and fill the earth." Anticipating what was to be, the text says, "Male and female he made them," since, indeed, man could not otherwise increase and multiply except with the female. Therefore, that there might be no doubt about his blessing that is to come, the text says, "Male and female he made them." For in this manner man, seeing the consequence of increasing and multiplying to be from the fact that the female was joined to him, could cherish a more certain hope in the divine blessing. For if the Scripture had said: "Increase and multiply and fill the earth and have dominion over it," not adding this, "Male and female he made them," doubtless he would have disbelieved the divine blessing.[51]

Here Origen asserts again that this inquiry into man is meant to be a literal interpretation of the text. But he says, that "the woman was not yet made" evidently because the "let us make man" is in verse twenty-six, but the fact that this also includes the woman is not mentioned until verse twenty-seven. And he also speaks about the "blessing that is to come" for the same reason. Then Origen concludes his discussion of the creation of man by asserting that he has spent time on the literal understanding of this passage.[52]

Finally Origen mentions the "historical" interpretation which explains to us that God gave us only vegetation to eat at the first. The permission to eat flesh was only given after the Flood. Initially we all were vegetarians.[53]

Because Origen's commentary on the creation has some information about the creation of man, we can see that he did believe that we were created on the sixth day. But we know that he does not hold to the literal understanding of chapter two of Genesis, and his homilies do not comment on that part, but skip directly to the account of the Flood.

Thus we can say that Origen seems to hold to the six days of creation being historical, but the details of what he thought about Paradise are left shrouded in mystery. If the story of Eden is not literally true, but is an allegorical representation of what happened, then what is his view of how it actually happened? And how did the fall happen? We cannot tell. Origen does give a kind of general overview of the creation account.

> Concerning, then, the creation of the world, [can other] portions of Scripture . . . give us more information regarding it, than the account which Moses has transmitted respecting its origin? And although it comprehends matters of profounder significance than the mere historical narrative appears to indicate, and contains very many things that are to be spiritually understood, and employs the letter, as a kind of veil, in treating of profound and mystical subjects; nevertheless the language of the narrator shows that all visible things were created at a certain time.[54]

Origen also comments on the Garden of Eden in off-hand ways in some homilies. When the Lord God spoke to Jacob as he was going "down" into Egypt to see his son Joseph He said that He would go with him into Egypt and would make a great nation out of him. Origen comments on what it means to "be with him in Egypt," and in the struggles which that entails. In the process of that comment he mentions the early Genesis account.

> Let us consider, therefore, whether there may be depicted in this statement a figure . . . of the first-formed man who descends to the struggles of this world after he was cast out of the delights of Paradise. The struggle with the serpent was set before him when it is said: "You shall watch for his head and he shall watch for your heel." and again, when it is said to the woman: "I will put enmity between you and him, and between your seed and his seed." Nevertheless, God does not desert those placed in this struggle, but is always with them. He is pleased with Abel; he reproaches Cain; he is present with Enoch, when he is invoked; he commands Noah to construct an ark of salvation in the flood; he leads Abraham "from the house of his father" and "from his kinsmen"; he blesses Isaac and Jacob; he leads the sons of Israel out of Egypt. He writes the Law of the letter through Moses; he completes what was lacking through the prophets. This is what it means to be with them in Egypt.[55]

When I say that Origen sees the story of Eden as an "allegorical representation" of what actually happened we can immediately surmise that he must have thought the historical event was nothing like what is depicted in the story of Eden. But from these references it appears that he thought that the story was like a veil that overlaid the actual historical event, but that was not necessarily very far from what actually happened. Nevertheless, from these considerations alone we cannot tell for certain what his mind was.

Deducing the Doctrine of Origen from that of Didymus:

Didymus, who was deeply influenced by Origen, in the third chapter of his *Commentary on Genesis*, gives us a hint of the allegorical thinking of his mentor. Didymus says, in commenting on Genesis 3:7ff,

> It would in fact be worthwhile for those adopting a factual approach to explain without absurdity how *they stitched together for themselves aprons from fig leaves,* how *they heard the sound of the Lord as he strolled* when they had committed deeds unworthy of it, why he was *strolling in the evening,* and finally how *they hid themselves* under the tree and what idea they had of God. In my view, in fact, it would not be possible for them to maintain a thread of factuality in all this worthy of an explanation deriving from the Holy Spirit.[56]

The sarcastic way of speaking by which Didymus dismisses the straightforward literal meaning of this passage is reminiscent of Origen in several of his comments. Didymus, who was also from North Africa, was deeply influenced by his predecessor Origen.

Didymus then goes on to explain how we ought to understand this account correctly. The "stitching together" of the leaves is seen as fabricating a flimsy excuse to God for their disobedience as conscience comes upon them to convict them. Leaves were in contrast to the "bearing of fruit" that God wishes for His people. This was exemplified by the time when Jesus cursed the fig tree and said that it would not again ever bear fruit; not because it was deficient, but as a way of referring to the nation of Israel that had rejected Him. The Lord God does not "stroll" in the garden because He is pure spirit and cannot walk in a literal sense. Instead His "strolling" is sign that they had distanced themselves from Him who normally is always "at the right hand" of the righteous (Psalm 16:6). This happened "in the evening" because sin removes us from the clear light of the day of His righteousness. And Adam and Eve "hid from God" in that they abandoned a pure understanding of Him because of their sin. Thus they were distanced from Him.

The name "Lord God" that is used in this account instead of just "God" as in the creation account is one indicator that it is as Lord that we are personally accountable to Him and as Lord that He will judge us, not just as creator. Thus Didymus takes into account the change in the name of God that happens as we move into Genesis chapter two. "They heard the sound" of God walking, not as He stomped along on the ground but stomped in their thinking, for nothing is hidden from God. Their nakedness was the loss of virtue, for virtue is a covering for us before the Lord God. Adam imputed his sin to his wife Eve but allegorically the Church's sin was imputed to Jesus Who "became sin for us." When it is written that "the Lord God said" we must understand that the words were formed in the mind of the person or persons involved, in accord with the fact that God is a spirit.

By the time Didymus gets to the curses on Eve and on Adam he begins to take some words literally again. He eventually explains that, although some things are treated in an allegorical sense there is no need that all things be so treated. Thus he moves in and out of the allegorical and literal interpretation methods. The clothing of skins was an allegorical statement, and in fact Adam and Eve did not even have material bodies in the garden because it was a spiritual place not on earth at all! Didymus actually sees all of these events as having taken place simultaneously in some spiritual realm. Adam and Eve were expelled from that realm just as the fallen angels were when they sinned.[57]

In this statement I believe that we see the key position of Didymus, and also of Origen—that the Garden of Eden was in a spiritual plane, and when Adam fell our first parents were expelled to live on the earth—in a way, perhaps, that recalls the fall of Lucifer and his expulsion out of heaven (Isaiah 14:12). Therefore the events of Eden were "extra-earthly" and did not take place the way that earthly events happened. In this way the events in chapter 2 and 3 of Genesis can be viewed as having taken place in eternity, in an instant, just as did the creation account of chapter 1. Thus the passage of time as we commonly experience it begins with the expulsion of Adam and Eve from Paradise.

From his commentary we see that Didymus did in fact believe that Adam and Eve were two actual people, that they did willfully sin against God, and they fell from grace. Thus the account is of something that really happened, but not on this earth. They began their existence in a realm that was spiritual in nature and not at all on this earth. the account of the garden is partially to be taken literally and partially allegorically. The true earthly history of man begins with chapter four and their life outside of Eden. We might reasonably infer that this also represents the thinking of Origen, although his personal commentary on Genesis has been lost. This explains how Origen could allegorize the account of Eden but still keep the biblical chronology for the creation account. Although Augustine was greatly influenced by Didymus and Origen, we will observe that he totally rejected this "spiritualization" of the account of Adam and Eve in the garden.

Again I want to draw your attention to the simple fact that preconceptions in the mind of Didymus (and I assume also in the mind of Origen) were behind their assessment that some of the "facts" presented to us in chapter two of Genesis about the Garden of Eden were not according to "common sense" and thus could not be taken literally. However, other Fathers had no such difficulties. It was a subjective determination that each made on their own. But Origen and his teachings on Genesis were greatly abhorred by some, both in his day and in the centuries that followed. Eventually the literal interpretation of Paradise became the standard. In this work, once we see how Genesis was originally written down, it will be almost impossible for anyone to take a "spiritualized" view of Eden.

Here are further quotations from the works of Origen that indicate his thinking. However, because many of his works have not been well preserved it seems that a fully accurate reconstruction of his detailed theories might prove to be quite impossible. Nevertheless, his belief in the nature of God and the creation of all things is stated in some detail. He states his firm belief in the following because they were, according to his understanding, delivered to the Church by the Apostles.

> [T]he Scriptures were written by the Spirit of God, and have a meaning, not such only as is apparent at first sight, but also another, which escapes the notice of most. For those words which are written are the forms of certain mysteries, and the images of divine things. Respecting which there is one opinion throughout the whole Church, that the whole law is indeed spiritual; but that the spiritual meaning which the law conveys is not known to all, but to those only on whom the grace of the Holy Spirit is bestowed in the word of wisdom and knowledge.[58]
>
> The particular points clearly delivered in the teaching of the apostles are as follow:
> *First*, That there is one God, who created and arranged all things, and who, when nothing existed, called all things into being—God from the first creation and foundation of the world—the God of all just men, of Adam, Abel, Seth, Enos, Enoch, Noe [i.e., Noah], Shem, Abraham, Isaac, Jacob, the twelve patriarchs, Moses, and the prophets; and that this God in the last days, as He had announced beforehand by His prophets, sent our Lord Jesus Christ to call in the first place Israel to Himself, and in the second place the Gentiles, after the unfaithfulness of the people of Israel . . . *Secondly*, That Jesus Christ Himself, who came (into the world), was born of the Father before all creatures; that, after He had been the servant of the Father in the creation of all things—"For by Him were all things made"—He in the last times, divesting Himself (of His glory), became a man.[59]

> This also is a part of the Church's teaching, that the world was made and took its beginning at a certain time, and is to be destroyed on account of its wickedness.[60]

From his statement about Adam, Abel, Seth, etc. it is evident that Origen believed that whatever happened in Eden, Adam, Eve, and their descendants were actual people. Origen saw the genealogies of Genesis as being reliable. He believed that they allowed us to determine the length of time from the creation of all things. In response to those who asserted that the world must be eternal for one reason or another he states,

> Such is the objection which they are accustomed to make to our statement that this world had its beginning at a certain time, and that, agreeably to our belief in Scripture, we can calculate the years of its past duration.[61]

And finally, in his writing *Against Celsus* Origen argues explicitly for the recent creation of all things, gives a broad scriptural limit on how old the world is, and defends the truth of the account of the Flood in the time of Noah.

> After these statements, Celsus, from a secret desire to cast discredit upon the Mosaic account of the creation, which teaches that **the world is not yet ten thousand years old**, but very much under that, while concealing his wish, intimates his agreement with those who hold that the world is uncreated. For, maintaining that there have been, from all eternity, many conflagrations and many deluges, and that the flood which lately took place in the time of Deucalion [i.e., Noah] is comparatively modern, he clearly demonstrates to those who are able to understand him that, in his opinion, the world was uncreated. But let this assailant of the Christian faith tell us by what arguments he was compelled to accept the statement that there have been many conflagrations and many cataclysms, and that the flood which occurred in the time of Deucalion . . . [was merely] more recent than any others. (emphasis added)[62]

<u>Origen on the Deluge</u>:
Before I leave Origen I want to relate a summary of his second homily on Genesis, his discourse on the Deluge of Noah. In this commentary we see Origen following his usual pattern of giving first the literal understanding of a passage, then the spiritual. He clearly distinguishes three forms of commentary in this homily: literal, allegorical, and moral.

> As we begin to speak about the ark which was constructed by Noah at God's command, let us see first of all what is related about it literally, and, proposing the questions which many are in the habit of presenting, let us search out also their solutions from the traditions which have been handed down to us by the forefathers. When we have laid foundations of this kind, we can ascend from the historical account to the mystical and allegorical understanding of the spiritual meaning and, if these contain anything secret, we can explain it as the Lord reveals knowledge of his word to us.[63]

Origen follows with a thorough explanation of his understanding of the configuration of the ark—its dimensions and its form. Then he inserts a fascinating detail about the three decks in the ark:

> It has indeed been handed down to us, and not without probability, that the lower parts, which we said above were built double, which also separately are called double-decked, the upper parts which are called triple-decked excepted, were made double for this reason: since all the animals spent a whole year in the ark, and of course, it was necessary that food be provided that whole year and not only food, but also that places be prepared for wastes so that neither the animals themselves, nor especially the men, be plagued by the stench of excrement. They hand down, therefore, that the lower region itself, which is at the bottom, was given over and set aside for necessities of this kind. But the region above and contiguous to this one was allotted to storing food.[64]

Thus he says that the lower chambers were built with a double compartment so that the excrement from the animals might drop down and not accumulate. This also helped to lessen the bad odor that would necessarily follow. Some modern commentators have hypothesized just such an arrangement as logical and reasonable. Origen says that he received this as "handed down" from reliable sources. Here are a few more details that he says were "handed down" to him:

> But above all, the abode for men was located at the highest point . . . But they also hand down that the door which is said to have been made in the side was at that place so that it might have the lower areas, which the text called double-decked, below it and the upper areas, which the text called triple-decked, may be called upper from the location of the door and all the animals brought in thence might be separated with the appropriate distinction to their own places whatever they were, as we said above. But the protection of the door itself is no longer performed by human methods. For how, after it is closed and there was no human outside the ark, could the door be coated with pitch on the outside, unless it was without doubt the work of divine power lest the waters gain entrance by an access which a human hand might not secure? For this reason, therefore, Scripture, although it had said about all other things, that Noah made the ark and brought in the animals and his sons and their wives, did not say of the door that Noah closed the door of the ark, but Scripture says that "The Lord God closed the door of the ark from without, and so the flood occurred." It should be observed, however, that after the flood Noah is not said to have opened the door, but the "window," when he sent forth "a raven to see whether the water had ceased upon the earth."[65]

So it appears that the door of the ark was at a middle level, neither the highest deck nor the lowest. The door had to be shut from without by another than the family of Noah, so it is most logical that the Scriptures say that the Lord shut them in. But because Noah was "shut in" he did not send out the birds by that sealed door but by an upper window.

After this careful literal commentary on the text Origen begins his spiritual interpretation by drawing a connection between the time of Noah and the time of the return of Jesus,[66] then continuing for a few pages. Finally Origen concludes his commentary with a short discourse on the moral implications of the account of the Flood. He introduces it with:

> For the literal meaning which preceded is placed first as a kind of foundation at the lower levels. This mystical interpretation was second, being higher and loftier. Let us attempt, if we can, to add a moral exposition as the third level, granting that even this text itself appears to contain a mystery not different from this very exposition we are undertaking in that it neither said "with two decks" only and was silent, nor "with three decks" alone and ceased, but when it had said "with two decks," it added also "with three decks." For "with three decks" denotes this threefold exposition.[67]

Origen then follows with a few moral insights and concludes his homily on the Flood. We can see a clear example of his Bible scholarship from this homily, showing his use of the literal, allegorical, and moral interpretation of a passage.

Augustine on Eden and on Allegory:

From Origen's account of the creation, as short as it is, we see a clear connection that flowed from Origen through Didymus the Blind, and on to Augustine. The idea of one "day" in eternity when some or all things were created is a clear connection. Didymus followed Origen's pattern of commentating on Genesis—first a short literal interpretation, then an extended allegorical discourse. Thus we are seeing a kind of "North African" connection. With his extensive influence Origen affected the opinions of Christians for many centuries. This may help explain what we read in Augustine as he argues against a purely allegorical interpretation of Genesis. Here is what Augustine says specifically about the Genesis account of Paradise and of Adam and Eve in the garden:

> I am well aware that many people have said many things about Paradise. There are, however, three generally held opinions about this topic; one held by those who think Paradise should only be understood in the literal material sense, another by those for whom only the spiritual sense is true, the third by those who take Paradise in each way, differently though in the material, differently in the spiritual sense. So then, in a word, I admit that it is the third opinion which I favor. This is the line on which I have here and now undertaken to talk about Paradise (to the extent that the Lord sees fit to help me); that the man made out of mud—which of course is a human body—is to be understood as having been placed in a bodily Paradise; and so Adam himself, even if he stands

> for something else in the way the apostle said he is the form of the one to come is still to be taken as a human being set before us in his own proper nature, who lived a definite number of years and after producing a numerous progeny died just as other human beings die, though he was not born of parents like others but was made from the earth, as was required at the beginning of the line; and so the Paradise too, in which God placed him, is to be understood as quite simply a particular place on earth, where the man of earth would live.[68]

It is clear that Augustine intends to take up the challenge of Origen and Didymus to give a clear, reasonable, God-honoring, literal interpretation of Genesis—including Eden. This gives us another insight into what Augustine is about in his literal commentary on Genesis—he is responding to Origen and to Didymus about the earthly historicity of Eden.

Augustine addressed the fact that many things discussed in Genesis were beyond our human experience, as opposed to other accounts in the Bible of more familiar things. But he insisted on the literal meaning of the passages anyway, lest our overall faith in the truth of Scripture be tainted by our rejection of the first things. This comment might also give us a glimmer of how Origen understood the account of Paradise in Genesis chapter two as becoming historical only once Adam had been forced out of Paradise. Thus we should see that in the following comment Augustine is addressing the beliefs of Origen and Didymus on this subject—the beliefs that they expressed in their long-lost accounts on Genesis chapter two.

> But there [in the books of kingdoms] things are being said with which ordinary human life has made us quite familiar, and so it is not difficult, indeed it is the obvious thing to do, to take them first in their literal sense, and then to chisel out from them what future realities the actual events described may figuratively stand for. Here on the other hand, because things are being said which do not meet the gaze of eyes fixed on the ordinary course of nature, some people think they should not be understood in their proper sense, but just figuratively, and they suggest that history, that is, the account of events that actually happened, begins from the moment when Adam and Eve, turned out of Paradise, came together and had children as though forsooth we are quite familiar with people living as many years as they did, or with things like Enoch being taken, or a very old and barren woman giving birth, and other things of that sort![69]

Augustine directly addressed comments to Christian believers who had problems with understanding these things literally. I do think that Augustine, who was converted from the Manichean heresy, had a special desire to speak to any of those who might have been following him from that sect into Christianity. Perhaps he was addressing these comments to such younger brothers and sisters, as well as to the people who had been influenced by the writings of Origen. These remarks of Augustine do give us a kind of pastoral guideline for dealing with believers in our churches who express a serious difficulty with faith in the literal meaning of Genesis. Today the cultural forces that command our intellectual attention have created an atmosphere where belief in Genesis is most difficult for some. Patient explanation is the best response, and then allowing everyone time, under God's leading, to feel their way along with these issues.

> But as for these people of ours, who have faith in these divine books and are not prepared to have Paradise understood according to the proper literal sense—as a most delightful place, that is, shady with groves of fruit trees and extensive too and rendered fertile by a huge spring—when they can see so many large tracts of grassland turn into woods without any human labor, just by the hidden work of God, I only wonder how they can believe that the man himself was made in a way they have never seen. Or if he too is to be understood figuratively, who was it who begot Cain and Abel and Seth? Or did they also only exist in figure, not also as real human beings born of human beings?
>
> So then they should pay very close attention to where this assumption of theirs is leading them, and try hard with us to take all these primordial events of the narrative as actually having happened in the way described. Is there anyone, after all, who would not support them as they turned their minds

> next to working out what lessons these things have for us in their figurative meaning, whether about spiritual natures and experiences or even about events to come in the future?
>
> Certainly, if the bodily things mentioned here could not in any way at all be taken in a bodily sense that accorded with truth, what other course would we have but to understand them as spoken figuratively, rather than impiously to find fault with holy scripture? On the other hand, if these things understood in a bodily sense, far from being an embarrassment to the divine narrative, actually lend it more solid support, nobody I imagine will be so disloyally obstinate as to insist on remaining wedded to his old opinion that they can only be taken figuratively, when he sees them, on being expounded in their proper sense, to be in accordance with the rule of faith.[70] [The "rule of faith;" that is, they fit nicely into the understanding of the truth that the Holy Spirit inspired in the church from the beginning, and enhance the truth of that original faith.]

Augustine explains how he originally responded to the heresy of the Manichees after his initial conversion, and how his response to the situation matured over the years. This is an example of the "allegorical vs literal" interpretation of Genesis.

> I too, you see, shortly after my conversion wrote two volumes against the Manichees who do not just go wrong by taking these books of the Old Testament in a way that is not correct, but who blaspheme by rejecting them outright with detestation. So my aim was to confute their ravings as quickly as possible, and also to prod them into looking for the Christian and evangelical faith in the writings which they hate. Now at that time it had not yet dawned on me how everything in them could be taken in its proper literal sense; it seemed to me rather that this was scarcely possible, if at all, and anyhow extremely difficult. So in order not to be held back, I explained with what brevity and clarity I could muster what those things, for which I was not able to find a suitable literal meaning, stood for in a figurative sense; I did not want them to be put off by being faced with reams of obscure discussion, and so be reluctant to take these volumes in their hands. Bearing in mind, however, what I really wanted but could not manage, that everything should first of all be understood in its proper, not its figurative sense, and not altogether despairing of the possibility that it could so be understood, this is what I put near the beginning of the second volume.
>
> > Certainly (I say) whoever wishes to take everything that is said quite literally, that is, to understand it not otherwise than the text actually reads, and in so doing can avoid any blasphemy, and can set it all out in accordance with the Catholic faith, not only should one not begrudge him this, one should hold him to be a remarkable and most praiseworthy understander.[71]

Concluding Perspective on Augustine and Origen:

In *The Literal Meaning of Genesis*, written over two decades after his commentary on Genesis directed to the Manichees, Augustine attempts to be just such an admirable "understander" of the first chapters of the book. One of the issues that he must address is just when the creation accounts of Genesis chapter 1 and that of chapter 2 transition from "events that take place in eternity, in an instant of time," to events that happen on earth and in time as we experience it. If one thinks that the creation of chapter 1 was instantaneous and in eternity then it is logical to understand the more detailed account of the creation of man in chapter two as also an event that happened in eternity. But Augustine does not want to understand the account of Eden in that way!

We will see this issue as critical to the thinking of Augustine: How could the creation in chapter 1 have taken place instantaneously in eternity and that of chapter 2 have taken place in normal human time? This is a problem because the creation of man and woman in chapter 2 is an expanded account of some of the events of the sixth day as explained in chapter 1. Of course, the entire issue would be simply resolved if one could just view both creation accounts as happening during the normal passage of time as we experience it, rather than cutting over from eternity to earthly time at some point.

This gives us a good picture of the approach of Origen and Augustine to interpreting Genesis. It also helps us to understand the reactions to the style of Origen, both from others in his own times and from people in later years. Finally it helps us to understand the tension that Augustine and later writers felt as they sought to comprehend the first two chapters of Genesis, and especially to determine how they fit together seamlessly. We will address these issues in our commentary.

Quotations from Other Fathers:
The writings of the earliest Fathers refer to the creation briefly and do not contain any in-depth commentary on the book. It might have been that the more extensive works had to wait for the time of peace that descended on the Church at the conversion of the emperor Constantine. Early references to the creation are found as incidental writings that had a different purpose; for example, they were apologetic in nature, they were discussions of theological issues that touched on Genesis lightly, they were pleas for a more equitable treatment of Christians at the hands of the hostile Roman government, or they were explanations of Christian faith and practice that were directed to various governmental magistrates or to philosophical opponents.

But certain themes are found commonly: only God is uncreated substance, the Father the Son and the Holy Spirit; God's commands were instantaneously carried out because He willed all things into existence and His will causes their continued being; the duration of the creation event was six days; the universe was not formed from properties that are inherent in the natural realm, but was formed by the action of an extra-natural being who caused it to exist and who formed its various structures by His commands.

Clement of Rome (died c. 99) exhorted the Corinthians at the time when envy and strife were tearing them apart. As was common in apostolic times he drew from examples of the earliest record of human history to call them from envy to virtuous actions.
> And God had respect to Abel and to his offerings, but Cain and his sacrifices He did not regard. And Cain was deeply grieved, and his countenance fell. And God said to Cain, Why art thou grieved, and why is thy countenance fallen? If thou offerest rightly, but dost not divide rightly, hast thou not sinned? Be at peace: thine offering returns to thyself, and thou shalt again possess it. And Cain said to Abel his brother; Let us go into the field. And it came to pass, while they were in the field, that Cain rose up against Abel his brother, and slew him. Ye see, brethren, how envy and jealousy led to the murder of a brother . . . Let us [rather] steadfastly contemplate those who have perfectly ministered to His excellent glory. Let us take, for instance, Enoch, who, being found righteous in obedience, was translated, and death was never known to happen to him. Noah, being found faithful, preached regeneration to the world through his ministry; and the Lord saved by him the animals which, with one accord, entered into the ark.[72]

Speaking of the end of all lawlessness and sin that the Lord God will make in due time, **Barnabas** (c. 100) in his epistle says:
> Of the Sabbath He speaketh in the beginning of the creation; *And God made the works of His hands in six days, and He ended on the seventh day, and rested on it, and He hallowed it.* Give heed, children, what this meaneth; *He ended in six days.* He meaneth this, that in six thousand years the Lord shall bring all things to an end; for the day with Him signifyeth a thousand years; and this He himself beareth me witness, saying; *Behold, the day of the Lord shall be as a thousand years.* Therefore, children, in six days, that is in six thousand years, everything shall come to an end. *And He rested on the seventh day.* This He meaneth; when His Son shall come, and shall abolish the time of the Lawless One, and shall judge the ungodly, and shall change the sun and the moon and the stars, then shall he truly rest on the seventh day. (Chapter 15, verses 3–5, trans. J. B. Lightfoot)

Papias (c. 70-c. 130), taught by John the Beloved disciple, left some fragments. Here is a mysterious allegorical reference to the creation that is attributed to him:

> [We can take] occasion from Papias of Hierapolis, the illustrious, a disciple of the apostle who leaned on the bosom of Christ, and Clemens, and Pantaenus the priest of [the Church] of the Alexandrians, and the wise Ammonius, the ancient and first expositors, who agreed with each other, who understood the work of the six days as referring to Christ and the whole Church.[73]

Mathetes (c. 130), a designation that means simply "a disciple," may have been an associate or catechumen of St. Paul. In his epistle to Diognetus he states

> When you have read and carefully listened to these things, you shall know what God bestows on such as rightly love Him, being made (as ye are) a paradise of delight, presenting in yourselves a tree bearing all kinds of produce and flourishing well, being adorned with various fruits. For in this place [i.e., in Paradise] the tree of knowledge and the tree of life have been planted; but it is not the tree of knowledge that destroys—it is disobedience that proves destructive. Nor truly are those words without significance which are written, how God from the beginning planted the tree of life in the midst of Paradise, revealing through knowledge the way to life, and when those who were first formed did not use this (knowledge) properly, they were, through the fraud of the Serpent, stripped naked [or deprived of it]. For neither can life exist without knowledge, nor is knowledge secure without life. Wherefore both were planted close together. The Apostle, perceiving the force (of this conjunction), and blaming that knowledge which, without true doctrine, is admitted to influence life, declares, "Knowledge puffeth up, but love edifieth."[74]

The Shephard of Hermes (died c. 150) in his sections on the commandments says:

> FIRST Of all, believe that there is one God who created and finished all things, and made all things out of nothing. He alone is able to contain the whole but Himself cannot be contained.[75]

St. Justin Martyr (100-165) in his second *Apology* made this remark about the Flood:

> The fire of judgment would descend and utterly dissolve all things, even as formerly the flood left no one but him only with his family who is by us called Noah, and by you Deucalion, from whom again such vast numbers have sprung, some of them evil and others good.[76]

Speaking about the creation he said this:

> His Son, who alone is properly called Son, the Word, who was with Him [God, the Father] and was begotten before all things, when in the beginning He [God, the Father] created and arranged all things through Him [the Son], is called the Christ, because He was anointed and because God the Father arranged all things of the creation through Him.[77]

Justin also refers to the continuity of the faith as received from those before him.

> But we have learned from tradition that God has no need of the material gifts of men . . . We have been taught, are convinced, and do believe, that He approves of only those who imitate His inherent virtues . . . We have also been instructed that God, in the beginning, created in His goodness everything out of shapeless matter.[78]

Thus the truths that he was explaining were received from believers who preceded him. The correct understanding of the Scriptures was inherited from the Apostles.

Tatian (c. 120-c. 180) said the following:

> Our God did not begin to be in time: He alone is without beginning, and He Himself is the beginning of all things.[79]

> God was in the beginning; but the beginning, we have been taught, is the power of the Logos. For the Lord of the universe, who is Himself the necessary ground of all being, inasmuch as no creature was yet in existence, was alone; but inasmuch as He was all power, Himself the necessary ground of things visible and invisible, with Him were all things; with Him, by Logos-power, the Logos Himself also, who was in Him, subsists . . . But He [the Logos] came into being by participation, not by abscission; for what is cut off is separated from the original substance . . . Matter is not, like God, without beginning, nor, as having no beginning, is of equal power with God; it is begotten, and not produced by any other being, but brought into existence by the Framer of all things alone.[80]

> The case stands thus: we can see that the whole structure of the world, and the whole creation, has been produced from matter, and the matter itself brought into existence by God; so that on the one hand it may be regarded as rude and unformed before it was separated into parts, and on the other as arranged in beauty and order after the separation was made. Therefore in that separation the heavens were made of matter, and the stars that are in them; and the earth and all that is upon it has a similar constitution: so that there is a common origin of all things . . . And these things severally it is possible for him to perceive who does not conceitedly reject those most divine explanations which in the course of time have been consigned to writing, and make those who study them great lovers of God.[81]

He speaks of the lost glory of Paradise:
> The demons were driven forth to another abode; the first created human beings were expelled from their place: the one, indeed, were cast down from heaven; but the other were driven from earth, yet not out of this earth, but from a more excellent order of things than exists here now. And now it behoves us, yearning after that pristine state, to put aside everything that proves a hindrance.[82]

Theophilus of Antioch (died c. 184) speaks of the inspiration of the men who wrote the holy Scriptures and of the divine truth of what they wrote—especially on the creation of all things.
> But men of God carrying in them a holy spirit and becoming prophets, being inspired and made wise by God, became God-taught, and holy, and righteous. Wherefore they were also deemed worthy of receiving this reward, that they should become instruments of God, and contain the wisdom that is from Him, through which wisdom they uttered both what regarded the creation of the world and all other things.[83]

> And first, they taught us with one consent that God made all things out of nothing; for nothing was coeval with God: but He being His own place, and wanting nothing, and existing before the ages, willed to make man by whom He might be known; for him, therefore, He prepared the world. For he that is created is also needy; but he that is uncreated stands in need of nothing. God, then, having His own Word internal within His own bowels, begat Him, emitting Him along with His own wisdom before all things. He had this Word as a helper in the things that were created by Him, and by Him He made all things.[84]

After describing the particulars of the six days of creation Theophilus says,
> Of this six days' work no man can give a worthy explanation and description of all its parts, not though he had ten thousand tongues and ten thousand mouths; nay, though he were to live ten thousand years, sojourning in this life, not even so could he utter anything worthy of these things, on account of the exceeding greatness and riches of the wisdom of God which there is in the six days' work above narrated.[85]

After speaking of the "six days of awe" he speaks of the creation of man and of Paradise.
> For when God said, "Let Us make man in Our image, after Our likeness," He first intimates the dignity of man. For God having made all things by His Word, and having reckoned them all mere bye-works, reckons the creation of man to be the only work worthy of His own hands. Moreover, God is found, as if needing help, to say, "Let Us make man in Our image, after Our likeness." But to no one else than to His own Word and wisdom did He say, "Let Us make."[86]

> You will say, then, to me: "You said that God ought not to be contained in a place, and how do you now say that He walked in Paradise?" Hear what I say. The God and Father, indeed, of all cannot be contained, and is not found in a place, for there is no place of His rest; but His Word, through whom He made all things, being His power and His wisdom, assuming the person of the Father and Lord of all, went to the garden in the person of God, and conversed with Adam . . . The Word, then, being God, and being naturally produced from God, whenever the Father of the universe wills, He sends Him to any place; and He, coming, is both heard and seen, being sent by Him, and is found in a place.[87]

> Man, therefore, God made on the sixth day, and made known this creation after the seventh day, when also He made Paradise, that he might be in a better and distinctly superior place.[88]

> By the expressions, therefore, "out of the ground," and "eastwards," the holy writing clearly teaches us that Paradise is under this heaven, under which the east and the earth are.[89]

So after personally working with the Father to make man, Jesus walked and talked to Adam and Eve in the garden. Why does Theophilus say that the garden was planted by God *after* the seventh day? Perhaps because the word speaks of planting the garden after it relates the six days of creation. Thus he assumes that it was a later work, rather than a backward reference giving more details to a work previously done. And he asserts that, by the plain reading of the text, Eden must have been on this earth. This is not an inconsequential assertion. People had never seen Eden and so assuming it was on this earth presented a possible problem. But most assumed either that it had never been discovered, being hidden by the Lord God, or that it had been destroyed by the Flood when "the world that then was perished."

Finally, Theophilus has extended sections on the chronology of the ancient times, which he asserts in contrast to the chronologies of other peoples, and then concludes:
> All the years from the creation of the world amount to a total of 5698 years, and the odd months and days.[90]

Julius Africanus (c. 160-c. 240) who wrote a chronology of the world, "a most accurate and labored performance"[91] according to Eusebius, calculated the creation date as follows:
> For the Jews, deriving their origin from them as descendants of Abraham, having been taught a modest mind, and one such as becomes men, together with the truth by the spirit of Moses, have handed down to us, by their extant Hebrew histories, the number of 5500 years as the period up to the advent of the Word of salvation, that was announced to the world in the time of the sway of the Caesars.[92]
>
> The period, then, to the advent of the Lord from Adam and the creation is 5531 years, from which epoch to the 250th Olympiad there are 192 years, as has been shown above.[93]

Remember that he, like almost all of the Fathers, was working from the Greek LXX. In his history Eusebius relates how Africanus pursued his research for this work, and why it was greatly prized by the Church.
> He [Africanus] says that he had gone to Alexandria, on account of the great celebrity of Heraclas, the same that we have already shown was advanced to the episcopate there, and who was, also, very eminent for his skill in philosophical studies, and the other sciences of the Greeks.[94]

Minucius Felix (died 250) in recording an extensive debate between one Marcus and one Octavius, explains the Christian position:
> It is clear as daylight that God, the Author of all, has neither a beginning nor an end. While giving birth to all things He has given to Himself eternal life; before creating this world He has been a world unto Himself; by His word He calls into existence all things that are, disposes them according to His wisdom, and perfects them by His goodness.[95]

Cyprian of Carthage (c. 200–258) in his treatise on mortality speaks of the desire that some had to be martyred for their faith but who were not granted that gift. He reminds them that God knows the hearts of all beforehand. He cites the sin of Cain as an example.
> But perchance someone may object, and say, "It is this, then, that saddens me in the present mortality, that I, who had been prepared for confession, and had devoted myself to the endurance of suffering with my whole heart and with abundant courage, am deprived of martyrdom, in that I am anticipated by death." In the first place, martyrdom is not in your power, but in the condescension of God; neither can you say that you have lost what you do not know whether you would deserve to receive. Then, besides, God the searcher of the reins and heart, and the investigator and knower of secret things, sees you, and praises and approves you; and He who sees that your virtue was ready in you, will give you a reward for your virtue. Had Cain, when he offered his gift to God, already slain his brother? And yet God, foreseeing the fratricide conceived in his mind, anticipated its condemnation. As in that case the evil thought and mischievous intention were foreseen by a

> foreseeing God, so also in God's servants, among whom confession is purposed and martyrdom conceived in the mind, the intention dedicated to good is crowned by God the judge.[96]

Encouraging his flock about the immortal life that awaits us and the glory that it will bring Cyprian refers to Enoch and his translation as an example:

> Thus, moreover, we find that Enoch also was translated, who pleased God, as in Genesis the Holy Scripture bears witness, and says, "And Enoch pleased God; and afterwards he was not found, because God translated him." To have been pleasing in the sight of God was thus to have merited to be translated from this contagion of the world.[97]

Irenaeus of Lyons (died 202) in his youth was acquainted with Polycarp who was the bishop of Smyrna and a direct disciple of John. Irenaeus met an old friend at Rome who had been taken in by the Valentinian heresy. This may be what spurred him to write his exhaustive work *Against Heresies*. In it he relates events at the beginning of the world.

> For in as many days as this world was made, in so many thousand years shall it be concluded. And for this reason the Scripture says: "Thus the heaven and the earth were finished, and all their adornment. And God brought to a conclusion upon the sixth day the works that He had made; and God rested upon the seventh day from all His works." This is an account of the things formerly created, as also it is a prophecy of what is to come. For the day of the Lord is as a thousand years; and in six days created things were completed: it is evident, therefore, that they will come to an end at the sixth thousand year.[98]

> [I]mmediately after Adam had transgressed, as the Scripture relates, He pronounced no curse against Adam personally, but against the ground, in reference to his works, as a certain person among the ancients has observed: "God did indeed transfer the curse to the earth that it might not remain in man." But man received, as the punishment of his transgression, the toilsome task of tilling the earth, and to eat bread in the sweat of his face, and to return to the dust from whence he was taken. Similarly also did the woman [receive] toil, and labor, and groans.[99]

> Men therefore shall see God, that they may live, being made immortal by that sight, and attaining even unto God; which, as I have already said, was declared figuratively by the prophets, that God should be seen by men who bear His Spirit [in them], and do always wait patiently for His coming.[100]

Irenaeus held that man was created in the image of God both in his body and his soul.

> Now God shall be glorified in His handiwork, fitting it so as to be conformable to, and modelled after, His own Son. For by the hands of the Father, that is, by the Son and the Holy Spirit, man, and not (merely) a part of man, was made in the likeness of God. Now the soul and the spirit are certainly a *part* of the man, but certainly not *the* man; for the perfect man consists in the commingling and the union of the soul receiving the spirit of the Father, and the admixture of that fleshly nature which was moulded after the image of God . . . For if any one take away the substance of flesh, that is, of the handiwork (of God), and understand that which is purely spiritual, such then would not be a spiritual man, but would be the spirit of a man, or the Spirit of God. But when the spirit here blended with the soul is united to (God's) handiwork, the man is rendered spiritual and perfect because of the outpouring of the Spirit, and this is he who was made in the image and likeness of God. But if the Spirit be wanting to the soul, he who is such is indeed of an animal nature, and being left carnal, shall be an imperfect being, possessing indeed the image (of God) in his formation (*in plasmate*), but not receiving the similitude through the Spirit; and thus is this being imperfect. Thus also, if any one take away the image and set aside the handiwork, he cannot then understand this as being a man, but as either some part of a man, as I have already said, or as something else than a man. For that flesh which has been moulded is not a perfect man in itself, but the body of a man, and part of a man. Neither is the soul itself, considered apart by itself, the man; but it is the soul of a man, and part of a man. Neither is the spirit a man, for it is called the spirit, and not a man; but the commingling and union of all these constitutes the perfect man.[101]

In his work *The Demonstration of the Apostolic Preaching*, he presents the main points of the Christian faith. He explains that the faith had been handed down in the Church by the succession of bishops and was substantially the same in all parts of the world. Possibly our *Apostle's Creed* is derived from this work.

For it is necessary that things that are made should have the beginning of their making from some great cause; and the beginning of all things is God. For He Himself was not made by any, and by Him all things were made.[102]

And, since God is rational, therefore by (the) Word He created the things that were made; and God is Spirit, and by (the) Spirit He adorned all things.[103]

But man He formed with His own hands . . . And that he might become living, He breathed on his face the breath of life . . . Moreover, he was free and self-controlled. . . And this great created world, prepared by God before the formation of man, was given to man as his place . . . And there were in this place also with (their) tasks the servants of that God who formed all things . . . Now the servants were angels.[104]

Now, having made man lord of all earth and of all things in it, He secretly appointed him lord also of those who were servants in it. They however were in their perfection; but the lord, that is, the man, was (but) small; for he was a child; and it was necessary that he should grow and thus come to his perfection. [Then God prepared a lovely place for man to grow and to come to his perfection, a place that Irenaeus **possibly** believed was a region not on this earth.] And so fair and good was this Paradise, that the Word of God continually resorted thither, and walked and talked with the man, figuring the things that should be in the future, (namely) that He should dwell with him and talk with him, and should be with men, teaching them righteousness.[105]

But, lest man should conceive thoughts too high, and be exalted and uplifted, as though he had no lord, because of the authority and freedom granted to him . . . a law was given to him by God, in order that he might perceive that he had as lord the Lord of all.[106]

Hippolytus of Rome (170-235) said:

GEN. 1:5. And it was evening, and it was morning, one day.

HIPPOLYTUS. He did not say "night and day," but "one day," with reference to the name of the light. He did not say the "first day;" for if he had said the "first" day, he would also have had to say that the "second" day was made. But it was right to speak not of the "first day," but of "one day," in order that by saying "one," he might show that it returns on its orbit, and, while it remains one, makes up the week.

GEN. 1:6. And God said, let there be a firmament in the midst of the water.

HIPPOLYTUS. On the first day God made what He made out of nothing. But on the other days He did not make out of nothing, but out of what He had made on the first day, by molding it according to His pleasure.[107]

God, subsisting alone, and having nothing contemporaneous with Himself, determined to create the world. And conceiving the world in mind, and willing and uttering the word, He made it; and straightway it appeared, formed as it had pleased Him.[108]

And in *Noah's* time there occurred a flood throughout the entire world, which neither Egyptians, nor Chaldeans, nor Greeks recollect . . . This *Noah*, inasmuch as he was a most religious and God-loving man, alone, with wife and children, and the three wives of these, escaped the flood that ensued. And he owed his preservation to an ark.[109]

And in like manner *God commanded*, that from earth should arise reptiles and beasts, as well males and females of all sorts of animals; for so the nature of the things produced admitted. For as many things as He willed, God made from time to time. These things He created through *the* Logos, it not being possible for things to be generated otherwise than as they were produced.[110]

For the word, "Let us make," is about the man that was to be; and then comes the word, "God made man of the dust of the ground," so that the narrative is of one and the same man. For then He says, "Let him be made," and now He "makes him," and the narrative tells "how" He makes him.[111]

Sometimes the Fathers reveal their attitude toward Genesis in their comments on other books. In his commentary on Daniel Hippolytus said:

But that we may not leave our subject at this point undemonstrated, we are obliged to discuss the matter of the times, of which a man should not speak hastily, because they are a light to him. For as the times are noted from the foundation of the world, and reckoned from Adam, they set clearly before us the matter with which our inquiry deals. For the first appearance of our Lord in the flesh took place in Bethlehem, under Augustus, in the year 5500; and He suffered in the thirty-third year. And 6,000 years must needs be accomplished, in order that the Sabbath may come, the rest, the holy day "on which God rested from all His works." For the Sabbath is the type and emblem of the future kingdom of the saints, when they "shall reign with Christ," when He comes from heaven, as John says in his Apocalypse: for "a day with the Lord is as a thousand years." Since, then, in six days God made all things, it follows that 6,000 years must be fulfilled. And they are not yet fulfilled, as John says: "five are fallen; one is," that is, the sixth; "the other is not yet come."[112]

Tertullian (c. 155-c. 240) explains the beginning of human life in the womb. He states that a baby can live if born seven months after conception.

> But inasmuch as birth is also completed with the seventh month, I more readily recognize in this number than in the eighth the honour of a numerical agreement with the sabbatical period; so that the month in which God's image is sometimes produced in a human birth, shall in its number tally with the day on which God's creation was completed and hallowed. Human nativity has sometimes been allowed to be premature, and yet to occur in fit and perfect accordance with an *hebdomad* sevenfold number, as an auspice of our resurrection, and rest, and kingdom. The *ogdoad*, or eightfold number, therefore, is not concerned in our formation; for in the time it represents there will be no more marriage.[113]

Thus he asserts that there will be 6,000 years of history until the kingdom is established as the seventh thousand-year period. This parallels with the six days of creation and the fact that the seventh day was hallowed as a day of rest. After the seventh thousand is completed, in the time of the *ogdoad* or eighth millennium, the eternal state will be inaugurated, and we will be as the angels when there will be no more marriage or birth.

He also speaks of the creation from nothing.

> The object of our worship is the One God, He who by His commanding word, His arranging wisdom, His mighty power, brought forth from nothing this entire mass of our world, with all its array of elements, bodies, spirits, for the glory of His majesty; whence also the Greeks have bestowed on it the name of Κόσμος [cosmos].[114]

Many ancients believed that human history on earth would last 6,000 years, to be followed by a thousand-year millennium. This they saw as paralleling the six-day creation which is followed by a day of rest. Thus, one day for each 1,000 years of earth history. If anyone believed this it would seem to me that they implicitly believed in a six-day creation and that the earth was a few thousand years old, in accordance with the genealogies of Genesis. However, in this work I will not attempt to identify and quote from all such people.[115] [see note]

Clement of Alexandria (c. 150-c. 215) speaks of the days of creation as he discusses the commandments, specifically as he discusses the Sabbath commandment.

> And the fourth word [i.e., commandment] is that which intimates that the world was created by God, and that He gave us the seventh day as a rest, on account of the trouble that there is in life. For God is incapable of weariness, and suffering, and want. But we who bear flesh need rest.[116]

Clement goes on to observe that the creation was concluded in six days and follows up in his discussion with an additional explanation of the seventh day rest of God.

> God's resting is not, then, as some conceive, that He ceased from doing. For, being good, if He should ever cease from doing good, then would He cease from being God, which is a sacrilege even to say. The resting is, therefore, the ordering that the order of created things should be preserved inviolate, [i.e., the command that they should continue to exist as He had made them.] and that each of the creatures should cease from the ancient disorder. [i. e., they should no longer partake of the initial "formless and void" state.] For the creations on the different days followed in a most important succession; so that all things brought into existence might have honor from priority, created together in thought, but not being of equal worth. Nor was the creation of each signified by

> the voice, inasmuch as the creative work is said to have made them at once. For something must needs have been created first, from which came those that were second, all things being originated together from one essence by one power. For the will of God was one, in one identity. And how could creation take place in time, seeing time was born along with the things which exist.[117]

In his *Stromata* Clement argues that Moses is more ancient than the pagan myths with their heroes and gods. He is dazzlingly well-read, quotes from many and sundry of their works, and repeatedly refers to the biblical chronology according to the LXX. He says,

> From Adam to the deluge are comprised two thousand one hundred and forty-eight years, four days. From Shem to Abraham, a thousand two hundred and fifty years. From Isaac to the division of the land, six hundred and sixteen years. Then from the judges to Samuel, four hundred and sixty-three years, seven months. And after the judges there were five hundred and seventy-two years, six months, ten days of kings. After which periods, there were two hundred and thirty-five years of the Persian monarchy. Then of the Macedonian, till the death of Antony, three hundred and twelve years and eighteen days. After which time, the empire of the Romans, till the death of Commodus, lasted for two hundred and twenty-two years.[118]

Thus he clearly believes that the biblical chronologies tell us when the world was created. Because Commodus died in AD 192, Clement placed Jesus at approximately 5626 years after the creation. In relating these things he is consciously following and expanding on what Tatian said in his *Address to the Greeks*.[119]

Theophilus of Antioch (died c. 184) summarized the creation as follows:
> For the heavens are His work, the earth is His creation, the sea is His handiwork; man is His formation and His image; sun, moon, and stars are His elements, made for signs, and seasons, and days, and years, that they may serve and be slaves to man; and all things God has made out of things that were not into things that are, in order that through His works His greatness may be known and understood.[120]

The early Christians often wrote to the existing magistrates asking for just and equitable treatment and freedom from persecution based on lies or misunderstandings. In making this case **Athenagoras of Athens** (133–190) wrote:
> That we are not atheists, therefore, seeing that we acknowledge one God, uncreated, eternal, invisible, impassible, incomprehensible, illimitable, who is apprehended by the understanding only and the reason, who is encompassed by light, and beauty, and spirit, and power ineffable, by whom the universe has been created through His Logos, and set in order, and is kept in being—I have sufficiently demonstrated.[121]

Pope Dionysius of Alexandria (c. 200-264), first to be accorded the title "The Great," wrote with passion against the Epicureans. Does their assertion about the nature of the world and its random generation sound like what we are being told today?
> Is the universe one coherent whole, as it seems to be in our own judgment . . . or is it indeed something manifold and infinite, as has been the opinion of certain others who, with a variety of mad speculations and fanciful usages of terms, have sought to divide and resolve the essential matter of the universe, and lay down the position that it is infinite and unoriginated, and without the sway of providence? For there are those who, giving the name of atoms to certain imperishable and most minute bodies which are supposed to be infinite in number, and positing also the existence of a certain vacant space of an unlimited vastness, allege that these atoms, as they are borne along casually in the void, and clash all fortuitously against each other in an unregulated whirl, and become comingled one with another in a multitude of forms, enter into combination with each other, and thus gradually form this world and all objects in it; yea, they construct infinite worlds.[122]

Thus our modern ideas, and the terminology that was adopted to express them, have been taken from the ancient Greeks and their philosophical constructions. Dionysius argues:
> How shall we bear with these men who assert that all those wise, and consequently also noble, constructions [in the universe] are only the works of common chance—those objects, I mean, of

> which each taken by itself as it is made, and the whole system collectively, were seen to be good by Him by whose command they came into existence. For, as it is said, "God saw everything that He had made, and behold, it was very good." But truly these men do not reflect on the analogies of small familial things which might come under their observation at any time, and from which they might learn that no object of any utility, and fitted to be serviceable, is made without design or by mere chance, but is wrought by skill of hand and is contrived so as to meet its proper use.[123]

He argues further and reveals the claims of the atheistic philosophers:

> And, again [they assert], there are some bodies made up of atoms of a definite kind and a certain common figure, while there are others made up of diverse atoms diversely disposed. But who, then is the sagacious discriminator that brings certain atoms into collection and separates others; and marshals some in such a wise as to form the sun, and others in such way as to originate the moon?[124]

Do not present theories of origins claim these exact things, but in greater detail? Is it not exactly the claim of modern theories that they explain just how random processes in fact have generated this cosmos of ours? It has happened by the working of processes that operate under the physical laws that have been discovered in the last few centuries. Surely their bold claims must be checked out! We definitely will do that in this work.

Victorinus of Pettau (died c. 304) wrote a summary of the Genesis creation account with a meditation on each of the days in the account and assigned allegorical significance to each day.

> To me, as I meditate and consider in my mind concerning the creation of this world in which we are kept enclosed, even such is the rapidity of that creation; as is contained in the book of Moses, which he wrote about its creation, and which is called Genesis. God produced that entire mass for the adornment of His majesty in six days . . . This sixth day is called *parasceve*, that is to say, the preparation of the kingdom. For He perfected Adam, whom *He made* after His image and likeness. But for this reason He completed His works before He created angels and fashioned man, lest perchance they should falsely assert that they had been His helpers. On this day also, on account of the passion of the Lord Jesus Christ, we make either a station to God, or a fast.[125]

The sixth day of the week was the day that Adam and Eve were created, with Eve being formed from the side of Adam while he slept. The sixth day was also the day when our Lord was crucified and when His side was pierced with the spear as He slept the sleep of death. John sees great significance in this, for the Church is the bride of Christ and was also born from His side on that sixth day (John 19:33–35). The early Church saw deep allegorical meaning in such facts, and fasting on that day was common. This may also illuminate the seemingly abstruse quotation of Papias, for the sixth day is called both the sacrificial day for the Passover and the preparation day for the kingdom. This way of using allegory when reading and interpreting the Scriptures was widespread in the early centuries of the Church. It was built upon that initial insight into the Scriptures that the Holy Spirit gave to the Church at Pentecost.

Methodius of Olympus (260–312) discourses on the glory of virginity, chastity, and the begetting of new human life. In his discussion about this and related topics be begins in Genesis and the creation account of man and woman. He asserts it is to be understood both literally and allegorically—both as an historical fact and as referring to Christ and to the Church, and as prefiguring the on-going generation of the human race throughout the ages—until the total number of people predetermined by God have been born. He sees the "perfect" number six as mystically related to the creation, the Trinity, and man.

> Moreover, it is evident that the creation of the world was accomplished in harmony with this number, God having made heaven and earth, and the things which are in them, in six days; the word of creative power containing the number six, in accordance with which the Trinity is the maker of bodies.[126]

> Let us begin with Genesis, that we may give its place of antiquity and supremacy to this scripture. Now the sentence and ordinance of God respecting the begetting of children is confessedly being fulfilled to this day, the Creator still fashioning man . . . and the predestined number of men shall be fulfilled; then from henceforth shall men abstain from the generation of children. But at present man must cooperate in the forming of the image of God, while the world exists and is still being formed; for it is said, "Increase and multiply." And we must not be offended at the ordinance of the Creator, from which, moreover, we ourselves have our being. For the casting of seed into the furrows of the matrix is the beginning of the generation of men, so that bone taken from bone, and flesh from flesh, by an invisible power, are fashioned into another man. And in this way we must consider that the saying is fulfilled, "This is now bone of my bone, and flesh of my flesh" . . . And perhaps there will be room for some to argue plausibly among those who are wanting in discrimination and judgment, that this fleshly garment of the soul [i.e., the body], being planted by men, is shaped spontaneously apart from the sentence of God. If, however, he should teach that the immortal being of the soul also is sown along with the mortal body, he will not be believed; for the Almighty alone breathes into man the undying and un-decaying part, as also it is He alone who is Creator of the invisible and indestructible. For, He says, He "breathed into his nostrils the breath of life; and man became a living soul."[127]

Thus we beget, but God breathes the soul into each person and forms us in our mother's womb. This is an excellent example of the intertwined use of both historical-literal and allegorical interpretation of the Genesis account. In the midst of many Scripture verses that are applied allegorically to understand sexuality, chastity, virginity, and procreation, the ten virgins whom he uses as speakers to relate his thoughts speak of the creation account in its various aspects, on numerology, on the Book of Revelation, etc.

Methodius explains the complementary roles of the Father and the Son in the creation:
> We said there are two kinds of formative power in what we have now acknowledged; the one which works by itself what it chooses, not out of things which already exist, by its bare will, without delay, as soon as it wills. This is the power of the Father. The other which adorns and embellishes, by imitation of the former, the things which already exist. This is the power of the Son, the almighty and powerful hand of the Father, by which, after creating matter not out of things which were already in existence, He adorns it.[128]

Lactantius (died c. 325) speaks of the events of Genesis:
> Plato and many others of the philosophers, since they were ignorant of the origin of all things, and of that primal period at which the world was made, said that many thousands of ages had passed since this beautiful arrangement of the world was completed; and in this they perhaps followed the Chaldeans, who, as Cicero has related in his first book respecting divination, foolishly say that they possess, comprised in their memorials four hundred and seventy thousand years; in which matter, because they thought that they could not be convicted, they believed that they were at liberty to speak falsely. But we, whom the Holy Scriptures instruct to the knowledge of the truth, know the beginning and the end of the world, respecting which we will now speak in the end of our work, since we have explained respecting the beginning in the second book. Therefore let the philosophers, who enumerate thousands of ages from the beginning of the world, know that the six thousandth year is not yet completed, and that when this number is completed the consummation must take place, and the condition of human affairs be remodeled for the better, the proof of which must first be related, that the matter itself may be plain. God completed the world and this admirable work of nature in the space of six days, as is contained in the secrets of Holy Scripture, and consecrated the seventh day, on which He had rested from His works.[129]

> But afterwards God, when He saw the earth filled with wickedness and crimes, determined to destroy mankind with a deluge; but, however, for renewing the multitude, He chose one man, who, when all were corrupted, stood forth pre-eminent, as a remarkable example of righteousness. He, when six hundred years old, built an ark, as God had commanded him, in which he himself was saved, together with his wife and three sons, and as many daughters-in-law, when the water had covered all the loftiest mountains.[130]

Eusebius of Caesarea (c. 275-339) produced a large work including the *Demonstration* and the *Preparation for the Gospel* in which he surveys the religious and moral thoughts and practices of the pagan nations. Then he explains the doctrines that Christians hold. He explains the foundational Jewish thought from which the Christians take their beliefs.

> Their system [the Hebrews] then sets forth the first principle of theology by beginning from the power which made and organized the universe . . . by aid of the Holy Ghost, under whose inspiration Moses commenced his doctrine of God in the following manner: "In the beginning God created the heaven and the earth" . . . Then he says: "God said, let there be light, and there was light." And again: "God said, let there be a firmament, and it was so" . . . The scriptures then, by saying in these places "God said" represents the divine command, and that God willed all things to be made, not, however, that we need suppose Him to speak with a voice and words.[131]

Eusebius goes on to explain the creation of all things including man and his placement in Paradise. This, Eusebius states, is foundational to all religion. He then explains the "second principle of creation" the Word of God and the Wisdom of God, begotten but not made, through Whom God made all things. He includes two very interesting quotations from Philo of Alexandria on the Word. Philo is quoted as follows:

> Why as if speaking of another God does He say, "In the image of God I made man," and not in the image of Himself? With consummate beauty and wisdom is this oracle expressed. For nothing mortal could be made in the likeness of the Most-High God and the Father of the universe, but in the likeness of the second God, who is the Word of the former."[132]

> If therefore anyone wishes to escape the difficulties which present themselves in the questions thus raised, let him say freely that nothing material is so strong as to be able to support the weight of the world. But the eternal Word of the everlasting God is the most strong and firm support of the universe. He it is who, being extended from the middle to the ends and from the extremities to the middle, runs the full length of nature's invincible course, bringing all the parts together and binding them fast. For the Father who begat Him made Him an indissoluble bond of the universe.[133]

The first quotation appears only in Eusebius. The second is from *Noah's Husbandry*, book 2.

Aphrahat (c. 280-c. 345) was a Persian Sage of which little is known. In his work is a tone of authority so he must have been a recognized teacher in his day. Aphrahat reviews the age when each of the patriarchs was born and then summarizes the ancient chronology:

> From Adam up until Noah entered the ark there were one thousand, six hundred and fifty-one years, as it is written in the Book of Generations. And from when Noah came out of the ark up to [the] time when God established a covenant with Abraham there were three hundred and eighty-seven years, as it is written in the Book of Generations. From the promise to Abraham to when Jacob went to Egypt were two hundred and five years, and the Israelites were in Egypt for two hundred and twenty-five years. From the promise to Abraham to when the people came out from Egypt were four hundred and thirty years, as Paul, the apostle, testified: *"The Law which came four hundred and thirty years after the covenant (which was ratified in a previous time by God) was unable to remove it and bring an end to the promise."*[134]

Aphrahat then continues with the Old Testament chronology from the Exodus to the time when Solomon began to build his temple. He continues through the kings of Israel up to and through the time of the captivity in Babylon, and then to the return from the captivity and all the way to Jesus.[135] He then has extended sections of praise and thanksgiving to the Lord for sending us a redeemer. Aphrahat completed his work during a time of persecution by Shapur, King of Persia.[136] This was about AD 345.

Ephrem the Syrian (306-373) wrote a vigorous rebuttal of certain heretical claims made by Bardaisan, Marcion, and Mani who asserted that the basic substance of this world had always existed. They held that God merely arranged things to be as they now are, and that the creation account was therefore to be understood allegorically in certain places.

The claim of the heretics that Ephrem countered was that the fundamental elements of wind, earth, fire, and water had existed from the beginning and that God had fashioned all things from them. Such thinking was blasphemous and led men to idolatry.

> The reason that Moses wrote (this book) [that is, Genesis] is as follows: The Creator had been manifest to the mind of the first generations, even up until the (generation of) the Tower [the Tower of Babel]. The fact that creatures were created was also publicly taught . . . among the sons of Shem . . . [But in Egypt men] became estranged from these noble commandments . . . and they considered substances, which had come into being out of nothing, to be self-existent beings, and they called created things that had been made out of something "gods."[137]

Ephrem than explains the proper way to understand the writing of Genesis. He asserts that the account of chapter two was added to give additional details not mentioned in the first chapter of the writing of Moses.

> [At that time Moses] wrote about the work of the six days that were created by means of a Mediator who was of the same nature and equal in skill to the Maker. And after (Moses) said, "This is the book of the generations of heaven and earth," he turned back and recounted those things that he had left out and not written about in his first account. He spoke of the origin of the house of Adam and of their dwelling in Paradise, of the coming of the serpent, of his deceit, of their rashness concerning the tree which had been forbidden them, and of their being cast out from there as punishment.[138]

In commenting on Genesis 1 he states emphatically,

> *In the beginning God created the heavens and the earth*, that is, the substance of the heavens and the substance of the earth. So let no one think that there is anything allegorical in the works of the six days. No one can rightly say that the things that pertain to these days were symbolic, nor can one say that they were meaningless names or that other things were symbolized for us by their names. Rather, let us know in just what manner heaven and earth were created in the beginning. They were truly heaven and earth. There was no other thing signified by the names "heaven" and "earth." The rest of the works and things made that followed were not meaningless significations either, for the substances of their natures correspond to what their names signify . . . Therefore, it is evident that heaven and earth came to be from nothing because neither water nor wind had yet been created, nor had fire, light or darkness been given their natures, for they were younger than heaven and earth. These things were created things that came after heaven and earth and they were not self-subsistent beings . . . [Moses] did not write about everything for us, for he did not record for us the day on which the spiritual beings were created . . . After (Moses) spoke of heaven and earth, of the darkness, the abyss and the wind that came to be at the beginning of the first night, he then turned to speak about the light that came to be at the dawn of the first day. At the end of the twelve hours of that night, the light was created . . . For Nisan was the first month; in it the number of the hours of day and night were equal. The light remained a length of twelve hours so that each day might also obtain its (own) hours just as the darkness had obtained a measured length of time. Although the light and clouds were created in the twinkling of an eye, the day and the night of the first day were each completed in twelve hours.[139]

Ephrem asserts that the works of the six days were enacted "in the twinkling of an eye." In his opinion the creation took place during the first month of the year, which was the month of Nisan. That month happens near the equinox when the days and the nights are of nearly the same duration, about twelve hours each.

Ephrem was a father who was well acquainted with Hebrew, who commented from the Jewish Scriptures rather than the Septuagint, and who was deeply influenced by Jewish traditions and ideas. In his poetical works he speaks allegorically about Paradise. He sees it as the place where Adam was placed in the beginning and also the place where the redeemed will reside in eternity. Thus he sees it as existing outside of space and time. This is an idea borrowed from ancient Jewish sources. Because the Revelation of John was not available to Ephrem (it was not translated into Syriac until the late 400's or the early 500's) his idea of the afterlife was not fully informed by all the Scriptures.[140] [see note]

Ephrem may have had a spiritual revelation or vison of the glorious afterlife that spurred him to write his hymns.

> With the eye of my mind I gazed upon Paradise; the summit of every mountain is lower than its summit. The crest of the flood reached only to its foothills.[141]

Thus he viewed Paradise as a very high mountain. How could it be in the spiritual plane but still have been touched in any way by the Flood? The images that he conveys to us by his words cannot be taken literally, he asserts. Rather the words he uses to describe Paradise are used metaphorically. The Garden is, like the Lord God Himself, totally beyond the ability of our earth-bound mind and imagination to understand or describe. Words can never suffice to actually communicate its glories.

> Do not let your intellect be disturbed by mere names. For Paradise has simply clothed itself in terms that are akin to you; it is not because it is impoverished that it has put on your imagery; rather, your nature is too weak to be able to attain to its greatness, and its beauties are much diminished by being depicted in the pale colors with which you are familiar. For feeble eyes cannot gaze upon the dazzling sight of its celestial beauties.[142]

Here are a few more details that he presents to us, both historical (considering the origin of man) and eschatological (considering the final state of man).

> When Adam sinned God cast him forth from Paradise, but in His grace He granted him the low ground beyond it, settling him in the valley below the foothills of Paradise.[143]

> The children of light dwell on the heights of Paradise, and beyond the abyss they espy the rich man; he too, as he raises his eyes to Lazarus, and calls out to Abraham, to have pity on him. But Abraham, that man so full of pity, who even had pity on Sodom, has no pity yonder for him who showed no pity. The Abyss severs any love which might act as a mediary, thus preventing the love of the just from being bound to the wicked.[144]

God dwells at the very summit of the mountain which is Paradise, and the tree of life is standing on the topmost peak.

> As for that part of the Garden, my beloved, which is situated so gloriously at the summit of that height where dwells the Glory [the Shekinah Glory], not even its symbol can be depicted in man's thought, for what mind has the sensitivity to gaze upon it, or the faculties to explore it, or the capacity to attain to that Garden whose riches are beyond comprehension.[145]

Halfway up the mountain is the tree of knowledge which, if Adam should pass its test, he would only then be granted access to the summit of the mountain and the tree of life.

> In the midst of Paradise God had planted the Tree of Knowledge to separate off, above and below, sanctuary [the lower reaches of the mountain originally granted to Adam] from the Holy of Holies [the summit of the mountain where God and the Tree of Life were to be found].[146]

> The Tree was to him like a gate; its fruit was a veil covering that hidden Tabernacle. Adam snatched that fruit, casting aside the commandment. When he beheld that Glory within, shining forth with its rays, he fled outside; he ran off and took refuge among the modest fig trees.[147]

These lovely meditations on the glory of the afterlife and the Paradise of God that awaits the faithful are very edifying. They are allegorical in nature, but the exposition that Ephrem wrote against the heretics was a literal rendering of Genesis. He employed ether style, as appropriate to his purpose.

Hilary of Poitiers (c. 310-c. 367) was a bishop of that city in France. He is sometimes referred to as the "Hammer of the Arians" for his strong stand against that heresy. In his commentaries on the parable about the master of the house who set out to hire workers for his vineyard at various times throughout the day (see Matthew 20:1–14), he makes a comment that reveals his understanding of the age of the earth.

> In the first hour, signified by the morning, we should recognize the covenant established with Noah, then with Abraham at the third hour, with Moses at the sixth hour, and at the ninth hour with David and the prophets. If we count the number of covenants established with humanity through individuals,

> so there are enumerated in the marketplace those who went out. At the eleventh hour the Lord shows the time of His advent in the body. His birth from Mary, which had been determined to take place during the present age out of all ages, pertains to that eleventh hour of the day. In fact, when one divides all 6,000 years [here he assumes 6,000 years of life on earth before the judgment and entrance into the kingdom] by the number 500 [twelve hours in a day, 500 years to each hour], the time of his birth in the flesh is computed according to a counting of the whole divided by elevens.[148]

He says that Jesus was born at the eleventh hour according to the LXX chronology, or about 5,500 years after the creation of the world. Hilary may be referring implicitly to the chronology of Hippolytus. We saw it in his commentary on Daniel, even though we have not found his actual *Chronicle* in English. In ancient times the chronology of Hippolytus was a widely known and accepted work.

Cyril of Jerusalem (c. 313-386) delivered a series of catechetical lectures in 347 or 348 in the churches constructed over the holy sites of the crucifixion and the resurrection. He explains the reason Jesus came to save us to his catechumens.

> If then thou inquire the reason of Christ's coming, go back to the first book of the scriptures. In six days God made the world; but the world was for man. The sun, however resplendent with bright beams, was made to give light to man. And all living creatures were made to serve us. Herbs and trees were created for our enjoyment. All the works were good, but of those none was an image of God, save only man. The sun was fashioned by His mere command; man by God's hands. *Let us make man in Our image, after Our likeness.* The wooden image of an earthly king is honored; how much more, then, the rational image of God.[149]

Basil of Caesarea (329-379) eventually became the bishop of that city. He was the older brother of Gregory of Nyssa and a close friend and associate of Gregory of Nazianzus. He actively encouraged social justice on behalf of the poor and was deeply interested in personal spirituality and morality. With the two Gregory's he also stood firmly against the Arians. He wrote extensively in all of these matters. Discussing the several meanings of the opening verse of Genesis "in the beginning God created," Basil invites his readers to calculate the first moment of creation, although he does not actually do so in his works.

> In fact, it is even possible for you to learn when the formation of this world began, if only going back from the present to the past you would strive to discover the first day of the generation of the world. You will in this way find from what moment the first movement of time came; then, too, that the heavens and the earth were laid down, first, like the foundation stones and groundwork; and, next, that there was some systematic reason directing the orderly arrangement of visible things.[150]

He then continues with a detailed day-by-day description of the work of the six days.

Gregory of Nazianzus (329-390) was known as **Gregory the Theologian** after his death because of his clear exposition of the doctrine of God. He clearly defended the vital truth that all three persons of the Trinity shared the same uncreated substance. This was held when Eunomius and other neo-Arians were claiming that only the Father was "absolute reality" ("I am Who am"), that the Son was a perfect image that He had begotten but not of His own substance, and that the Holy Spirit was the first creation of the Son.

The Gregory's, Basil of Caesarea, Cyril of Alexandria, and Athanasius the Great held forth the Ancient Faith that The Word was fully God, uncreated substance, and begotten from before all ages, and without compromising His full divinity He became fully man. In His one person was a fully human and fully divine being. In the Nicene Creed we see the result of these battles recorded for later generations:

> I believe in one Lord Jesus Christ, the Only Begotten Son of God, born of the Father before all ages. God from God, Light from Light, true God from true God, begotten, not made, one in being with the Father; through Him all things were made . . . I believe in the Holy Spirit, the Lord, the giver of life,

> who proceeds from the Father [and the Son],[151] who with the Father and the Son is adored and glorified, who has spoken through the prophets.

These precious truths inform our understanding of many verses of the Bible, preserving for us the faith that was delivered once and for all to the saints.

The attacks against these precious truths were sustained for many centuries but the Holy Spirit enlisted an army of holy men to defend, preserve, and elucidate the Ancient Faith. Today we are in a centuries-long battle for the true understanding of creation. Was it a six-day-long supernatural action on the part of God, or was it possibly a lengthy event that stretched over many eons in which the Lord God worked through natural processes to bring about the world that we see around us? Inextricably bound up with this question is another: How was the book of Genesis written down? Did Moses write it, or did other unknown men assemble it over many centuries? These are the issues we are considering in this book. Let us now return to the testimony of the ancients on these things.

Gregory of Nazianzus held the office of Archbishop of Constantinople until late in his life when he resigned and returned to Cappadocia. In those later years he wrote poems. He explains why he wrote his poetry late in his career, the final expression of the struggles that characterized his life.

> Seeing many write in this present life words without measure smoothly rolling,
> who pass most time in drudgeries producing only a hollow logorrhea,
> and how they write so brazenly things clogged full of idiocies,
> as sand fills the sea or fruit-flies Egypt: I've found this to be the single sweetest council, that,
> pitching out all other word, one hold on only to those inspired by God,
> as a calm anchor to those who flee the storm.
> For if the Scriptures provide such a handle—the Spirit—it's for you the wisest course
> that you should be a citadel from all vain words, for those who've started poorly.
> Why, friend, not write words free of doubt, in place of nether-stretching thoughts?
> And, seeing this is impossible in a world so fragmented into sects,
> where all find grounds for their own straying in those writings they've set above themselves,
> I took this other literary road, which, whether good or not, is dear to me:
> to put my own afflictions into verse.[152]

It is clear that the opposition and personal attacks that Gregory endured in his doctrinal struggles had worn down the great champion of the faith.

Gregory mentions his views on the creation in a few passing verses of his poetry.

> Come, then, and I will speak of the beloved mysteries of God,
> whatever virginity has revealed in these last times.
> Once it was, when black night concealed all things.
> There was then no beloved morning light; nor had the sun made its fiery way from the east.
> The crescent moon, night's glory, did not show. But all things were jumbled with each other
> uselessly wandering locked together in the murky chains of first-born chaos.
> But you, O blessed Christ, obedient to the counsels of the great Father,
> distinguished all things beautifully throughout the world.
> Now indeed the original light appeared, so that all his works might rejoice, being full of light . . .
> The Father, then, beholding and knowing all this arrangement,
> was pleased in the likeminded works of his Son, the Lord.[153]

> A "when" was [that is, the moment when time began], and it then was that the mind's high
> Word fixed fast the world which formerly was not, at the bidding of the mighty Father's mind.
> He spoke, and just what he wanted was accomplished.
> And when everything, the earth, and the sky, and the sea, made up a world,
> he sought, again, for one who'd discern his wisdom, mother of all things,
> and to be, for things on earth, a king in divine likeness . . .

> Wherefore it pleases me to form a species out of both [both spirit and animal],
> midway between mortals and immortals: thinking man, who shall delight in my works . . .
>
> Having said this, then, he took up a portion of new-formed earth
> and with immortal hands set up my shape, to which he then imparted his own life. For into it he shot spirit, an influx of the unseen Godhead.
> And from dirt and breath he made a man, image of the immortal: for mind's lordly nature is in both.
> And so I feel an attachment to this life, through what's earth in me,
> but inwardly long for another, through the part that's divine.
> Such was the conjoining of the original man. Since then, however, bodies derive from flesh,
> and the soul is mixed in imperceptibly, falling from without into the moulding of dust.
> He who mixes them knows how he first breathed in, and fastened his image to earth;
> unless someone, coming to the aid of my words, and following
> after others, should boldly add this doctrine:
> that the first body, after it was blended with us from the soil,
> later became the human stream, and never leaves off
> producing from time-to-time new human beings from the first-formed root;
> and the soul breathed out from God thereafter enters newborn into human patterns,
> having out of the first seed been partitioned into many,
> though keeping an ever-constant form in mortal parts.[154]

Because he sees the souls of subsequent people as coming from the "first seed" and as "partitioned into many" Gregory might allow that all souls were created together in some primitive form at the beginning, and that each is then uniquely prepared by God to go into the bodies of the subsequent generations of human beings. This is not the position of the Church today. We hold that each individual human soul is created by God from nothing.

Gregory of Nyssa (c. 335-c. 395) was the younger brother of Basil the Great and was a bishop of Nyssa in central Turkey. Gregory had the highest respect for his brother as a person and as a theologian. We have no English translation of his *Apology to his brother Peter on the Hexameron*, but we have a clear description of his opinion of what his brother Basil wrote.

> For he alone has worthily considered the creation of God who truly was created after God, and whose soul was fashioned in the image of Him who created him—Basil, our common father [i.e., their father in the faith] and teacher—who by his own speculation made the sublime ordering of the universe generally intelligible, making the world as established by God in the true Wisdom known to those who by means of His understanding are led to such contemplation: but we, who fall short even of worthily admiring him, yet intend to add to the great writer's speculations that which is lacking in them, not so as to interpolate his work by insertion . . . but so that the glory of the teacher [that is, his brother Basil] may not seem to be failing among his disciples.[155]

This gives us a picture of his attitude toward the account of the six days and also places his own work *On the Making of Man* in proper context; that is, it was written to supplement the work of his brother on the six days by commenting on the creation of man as given in Genesis 2. Speaking of the special dignity of man in the creation Gregory says,

> But it is right that we should not leave this point without consideration, that while the world, great as it is, and its parts, are laid out as an elemental foundation for the formation of the universe, the creation is, so to say, made off-hand by the divine power, existing at once on His command, while counsel precedes the making of man.[156]

Considering the majesty and perfection of God Gregory struggles to find a way in which we could ever be "in His image." But finally he states his opinion of what it means.

> What therefore will you perhaps say is the definition of the image? How is the incorporeal likened to the body? how is the temporal like the eternal? that which is mutable by change like to the immutable? that which is subject to passion and corruption to the impassible and incorruptible? That which constantly dwells with evil, and grows up with it, to that which is absolutely free from evil . . . How then is man, this mortal, passible, short-lived being, the image of that nature which is immortal, pure, and everlasting?[157]

> God is in His own nature all that our mind can conceive as good—rather, transcending all good that we can conceive of or comprehend. He creates man for no other reason than that He is good; and being such, and having this as His reason for entering upon the creation of our nature, He would not exhibit the power of His goodness in an imperfect form, giving our nature some one of the things at His disposal, and grudging it a share in another: but the perfect form of goodness is here to be seen by His both bringing man into being from nothing, and fully supplying him with all good gifts. But since the list of individual good gifts is a long one, it is out of the question to apprehend it numerically. The language of scripture therefore expresses it concisely as a comprehensive phrase, in saying that man was made "in the image of God."[158]

Gregory also states his opinion that, if Adam had not sinned, there would have been no sex. He sees the final state of glory—in which we are like the angels of God who neither marry nor are given in marriage—as a return to the state that Adam and Eve had in Paradise. This implies that he understood the original state of Adam and Eve to be the same as our final state of glory, or at least very much like it. Just as myriads of angels were created in great numbers by a method that we cannot imagine, so by that same method God would have increased our numbers without the need for procreation. Thus God, in His foreknowledge of the fall, created the sexual capacity in mankind.[159]

Athanasius of Alexandria, also known as **Athanasius the Great** (296-373), composed an explanation of the Christian world view for unbelievers to read. He concludes:

> For the providence over all things belongs naturally to Him by Whom they were made; and who is this save the Word of God, concerning Whom in another psalm he says: "By the Word of the Lord were the heavens made, and all the host of them by the Breath of His mouth" [Psalm 33:6]; For He tells us that all things were made in Him and through Him. Wherefore He also persuades us and says, He spake and they were made, He commanded and they were created" [Psalm 148:5] as the illustrious Moses also at the beginning of his account of Creation confirms what we say by his narrative, saying: and God said, "let us make man in our image and after our likeness" [Genesis 1:26]: for also when He was carrying out the creation of the heaven and earth and all things, the Father said to Him, "Let the heaven be made," and "let the waters be gathered together and let the dry land appear," and "let the earth bring forth herb" and "every green thing" [Genesis 1:6–11]: so that one must convict Jews also of not genuinely attending to the Scriptures. For one might ask them to whom was God speaking, to use the imperative mood? If He were commanding and addressing the things He was creating, the utterance would be redundant, for they were not yet in being, but were about to be made; but no one speaks to what does not exist, nor addresses to what is not yet made a command to be made. For if God were giving a command to the things that were to be, He must have said, "Be made, heaven, and be made, earth, and come forth, green herb, and be created, O man." But in fact He did not do so; but He gives the command thus: "Let us make man," and "let the green herb come forth." By which God is proved to be speaking about them to some one at hand: it follows then that some one was with Him to Whom He spoke when He made all things. Who then could it be, save His Word? For to whom could God be said to speak, except His Word? Or who was with Him when He made all created Existence, except His Wisdom, which says: "When He was making the heaven and the earth I was present with Him" [Proverbs 8:22–30]? But in the mention of heaven and earth, all created things in heaven and earth are included as well. But being present with Him as His Wisdom and His Word, looking at the Father He fashioned the Universe, and organised it and gave it order; and, as He is the power of the Father, He gave all things strength to be, as the Saviour says: "What things soever I see the Father doing, I also do in like manner." And His holy disciples teach that all things were made "through Him and unto Him;" and, being the good Offspring of Him that is good, and true Son, He is the Father's Power and Wisdom and Word, not being so by participation, nor as if these qualities were imparted to Him from without, as they are to those who partake of Him and are made wise by Him, and receive power and reason in Him; but He is the very Wisdom, very Word, and very own Power of the Father, very Light, very Truth, very Righteousness, very Virtue, and in truth His express Image, and Brightness, and Resemblance. And to sum all up, He is the wholly perfect Fruit of the Father, and is alone the Son, and unchanging Image of the Father.[160]

Thus the account of the creation in Genesis clearly shows us the coordinated work of the Father and the Son as they together created all things.

Having explained the creation by the Father and the Son, Athanasius proceeds to the Incarnation, which he explains is dependent upon the creation. He rejects the idea that God was merely a mechanic, forming things out of preexisting material, but that He was the One Who summoned all things from nothing. When we fell into sin, He Himself set about to redeem us. The mighty work of redeeming man could only be accomplished by the One Who had created us in the beginning.[161]

Macarius the Great (c. 300-391) meditates on the state of Adam before the fall.
> So long as the Word of God was with him, and the commandment, everything was his. The Word Himself was to him an inheritance; He was his clothing, and a glory that was his defense; He was his instruction . . . As in the case of the prophets, the Spirit wrought in them and taught them, and was within them, and appeared to them outwardly, so with Adam. The Spirit, when it pleased him, was with him, and taught him, and suggested "speak thus," and he said it. For the Word was all things to him, and so long as he abode in the commandment he was a friend of God.[162]

He then talks about the effects of the fall on Adam.
> Adam, on transgressing the commandment, suffered a twofold disaster. He lost the pure and lovely possession of his nature, which was after the image and the likeness of God; and he lost also that very image in which was laid up for him according to promise all the heavenly inheritance.[163]

He answers a question as to whether Satan knows our thoughts and intentions. Macarius observes that, as we know our neighbors by associating with them for twenty years or so, in the same way Satan, who is six thousand years old, knows us very well.[164] Thus he implicitly asserts that creation, according to the LXX, was about that far in the past. However, Macarius did not attribute to Satan knowledge of all our heart's workings.

Thus we see that the Ancient Faith of the Church is not just revealed in formal treatises on Genesis. In the meditations of pious souls, in the defense of the faith against various and sundry topics seemingly unrelated to the origin of things, and in hymns and various forms of worship we see the consistent point of view of the holy ones of old.

Ambrose of Milan (c. 340-397) was also dealing with certain philosophers who claimed that the natural realm had always existed. Thus he voiced repeated denunciations of that idea. He had recourse to Moses as his authority.
> "In the beginning" he said. What a good arrangement that he should first assert what these men are accustomed to deny, that they may realize, too, that there was a beginning to the world, lest men be of the opinion that the world was without a beginning. For this reason David, too, in speaking of "heaven, earth, and sea," says: "Thou hast made all things in wisdom." He (Moses) gave, therefore, a beginning to the world; he gave also to the creature infirmity, lest we believe him to be without a beginning, uncreated, and still partaking in the divine essence. And fittingly he added "He created" lest it be thought there was a delay in creation. Furthermore, men would see how incomparable the Creator was who completed such a great work in the briefest moment of His creative act, so much so that the effect of His will anticipated the perception of time. No one saw Him in the act of creation; they saw only the created work before them. Where, therefore, was there a delay, since you may read: "For He spoke and they were made; He commanded and they were created?" He who in a momentary exercise of His will completed such a majestic work employed no art or skill so that those things which were not were so quickly brought into existence; the will did not outrun the creation, nor the creation the will.[165]

> Addressing the Romans, he [Paul] says concerning the Father: "For from Him and through Him and unto Him are all things." "From Him" means the beginning and origin of the substance of the

> universe, that is, by His will and power. For all things began by His will . . . As long as He wishes all things remain and endure . . . In the beginning of time, therefore, God created heaven and earth. Time proceeds from this world, not before this world.[166]

As we read the Fathers comments on the nature of this world we see that their cosmology is deficient, but their comments on the scriptural text are brilliant, partaking of an eternal truth like that of the Scriptures themselves. In this work I retain the comments of the Fathers on Genesis, but I don't accept all of their cosmology; in fact, I don't totally accept ours either!

> On the nature and position of the earth there should be no need to enter into any discussion . . . It is sufficient for our information to state what the text of holy scripture establishes, namely, that, "He hangeth the earth upon nothing" [Job 26:7].[167]

Ambrose then proceeds to dismiss questions about whether the earth is hanging in air, water, or whatever, and how it stays in place. There are many different opinions, he says, (I am omitting these) and then he quotes what God said to Job: "Where were you when I laid the foundation of the earth? Tell me if thou hast understanding" (Job 38:4ff). He concludes:

> The earth therefore is not suspended in the middle of the universe like a balance hung in an equilibrium, but the majesty of God holds it together by the law of His own will, so that what is steadfast should prevail over the void and the unstable . . . Let others hold approvingly that the earth never will fall because it keeps its position in the midst of the world in accordance with nature. They maintain that it is from necessity that the earth remains in its place and is not inclined in another direction, as long as it does not move contrary to nature but in accordance with it . . . However . . . I believe that all things depend on His will, which is the foundation of the universe and because of which the world endures up to the present.[168]

A Short Digression on Ancient and Modern Cosmological Concepts:

The questions reviewed briefly by Ambrose would be asked differently today. The earth is "kept in place" by the perfect balance between gravity and centrifugal force as it orbits the sun. Centrifugal force is the result of its tendency to continue in a straight line once it is in motion, and gravity is the universal attraction between all bodies in the universe. But then, what exactly causes gravitational attraction; or even, why do bodies in motion tend to continue in motion in the same direction and at the same velocity? Why does matter exhibit such properties? In the end the answer Ambrose gives would be the same; that is, ultimately something about our world is incomprehensible. It is the power of God that upholds all things, and it is His wisdom that created the world with its perfectly balanced properties. Ultimately this is beyond man's ability to understand. We will discuss these mysterious forces and others that hold our cosmos together in our comments on "Day 4" in the section "A Critique of Modern Cosmology."

When I refer above to "ancient cosmology" I do **not** mean imagining the earth is not round. The Greek philosopher Demosthenes measured the circumference of the earth at about 25,000 miles, and that experiment was repeated by Thomas Aquinas. Thus some of the ancients knew that the earth was round, although some might not have known of these experiments or might not have accepted them as valid. But that is not what I am referring to when I speak of ancient cosmology. I am referring to the forces of the natural realm.

Today we take the view that what keeps the celestial objects in place—what prevents their falling to the earth—is the counterbalancing of opposing forces. One force is gravity and the other is centrifugal force. Gravity is the universal tendency of a body to attract other bodies towards itself, and centrifugal force arises when a body in motion naturally seeks to continue in motion in the same direction and at the same velocity unless forced to change by an external constraint. As celestial bodies move they tend to keep moving at the same velocity and in the same direction (because of their inertia), but gravity draws them towards other bodies. As a result they move in elliptical paths through space.

The ancients did not take the view that counterbalanced forces like I have just described were keeping celestial objects from falling to earth. Thus they often imagined that some kind of structure had to be supporting the heavens above the earth. This remained true whether they thought the earth was round or whether they had some other idea about it. Our basic Newtonian understanding of the cosmos was **not** part of their world. This in turn influenced how the ancients interpreted the creation account in Genesis and how they understood the "firmament" that Genesis describes. We will discuss this when we comment on Genesis chapter 1. For now, I reiterate simply that I accept the Genesis account as completely accurate and as not at all implicated in any misunderstandings of the nature of our world, whether held to by the ancients or by us today. Theological and spiritual considerations drawn from Genesis are true, as are whatever details it provides us about the material realm. The Bible is the inspired, infallible, inerrant Word of God, is eternally true, and rises above every limitation of human culture, all human systems of thought, all human philosophies, and all human ideologies.

Today, although we have described gravitational force mathematically, and although we have described other forces that hold our world together (electromagnetic force, which underlies chemical bonding; nuclear force and the weak interactive force, which operate at the nuclear level)—although we can describe these forces mathematically and work with them in our theories—we cannot explain what they are. We cannot explain how the sun, which is millions of miles distant from the earth, draws the earth towards itself. The forces are a reality—the reality that holds the world together—but we have never been able to identify their fundamental nature. That remains shrouded in mystery. Similarly, we can describe inertia, which all bodies exhibit, as a basic aspect of material objects. But what is it? Why do all physical objects exhibit a tendency to remain at rest or to remain in motion? This is the basis for centrifugal force, yet this fundamental aspect of reality is as opaque to us as it was to the ancients.[169] The balance between these tendencies in matter is what holds the universe together. It is what results in the world's orderly and consistent functioning. Someone must have thought this up and put it in place. The creation account tells us Who did that, and Scripture hints at how He did it. Thus we will also look at various ideas about the dynamic forces that order the cosmos when we comment on the creation.

Returning to Ambrose and his ideas about the creation of land animals, he echoes the universal sentiment of the ancients in his understanding of their manner of reproduction.
> The Word of God permeates every creature in the constitution of the world. Hence, as God has ordained, all kinds of living creatures were produced from the earth. In compliance with a fixed law they all succeeded each other from age to age according to their aspect and kind . . . What was once enjoined became in nature a habit for all time.[170]

No kind of living thing ever changes or evolves into any other kind of living thing. This is the teaching of Scripture as universally understood by the Fathers.

In speaking of Paradise Ambrose uses an extended metaphorical approach. He notes that Paul was "caught up into Paradise" but could not tell whether he was in the body or not, and he could not speak of it. Thus Ambrose says that he is unable to declare the position of Paradise or to speak of it definitively. He says that Paradise was a spiritual state where Adam and Eve were, a land of fertility and delight where their soul found pleasure. The river that irrigated it was Jesus and the four branches into which it split were the four cardinal virtues: prudence, temperance, fortitude, and justice. The entire interpretation is developed along such lines.[171] When he interprets Paradise in this way, including the creation of Eve, the temptation, and the fall, Ambrose is also compelled to allegorize the animals that were in Paradise.

> The beasts of the field and the birds of the air which were brought to Adam [for him to name] are our irrational senses, because beasts and animals represent the diverse emotions of the body, whether of the more violent kind or even of the more temperate.[172]

Ambrose then observes that God placed man in dominion over these "animals" and that people failed to keep such impulses in check. This is an insightful use of the analogy, but his extended allegory breaks down with some of his other comments on the subject.

Firmicus Maternus (c. 346), an aristocratic Sicilian and Christian apologist, wrote this:

> For after long ages, in the last reaches of time, that is, almost at the end of the week of centuries, the word of God commingled itself with human flesh, to save mankind, to conquer death, to link the frailty of the human body with divine immortality.[173]

With the phrase the "week of centuries" Firmicus, like Tertullian, is referring to the belief that Jesus was born in the midst of the 6th millennium, near the end of the ages of the world, which were to extend for a total of 6,000 years before the great judgment and the establishment of the kingdom of God.

Tyconius (around 400) was a North African scholar and a member of the Donatist party. He wrote a *Book of Rules* for discovering the meaning of Scripture.

> Temporal quantity, in scripture, often has mystic significance through the rhetorical figure of synecdoche . . . [where] either a part represents the whole or a whole represents the part . . . [as one of his examples he says] The world's age is six days, i.e., six thousand years. In what is left of the sixth day the Lord was born, suffered, and rose again.[174]

Paulus Orosius (c. 375- c. 418) was born in Bracara, Portugal. He knew Augustine and wrote his own most famous work as a supplement to Augustine's *City*. Orosius' work is a history of tragedy throughout the ages of mankind. He begins his history with an overall chronology of the world.

> Now from Adam, the first man, to the king Ninus [an early king of Assyria], so-called the "Great," when Abraham was born, 3,184 years passed, which have been omitted or unknown by all historians. But from Ninus or Abraham to Caesar Augustus, that is, to the birth of Christ, which was in the forty-second year of the Caesar's rule, when the gates of Janus were closed [that is, a time of peace, for they were opened so that Janus might accompany troops to war], for peace had been made with the Parthians and wars had ceased in the whole world, 2,015 years have passed, in which between the performers and the writers the fruits of labors and occupations of all were wasted. Therefore, the subject itself demands that I touch upon briefly a few accounts from these books which, when speaking of the origin of the world, have lent credence to past events by the prediction of the future and the proof of subsequent happenings, not that we may seem to press their authority upon anyone, but because it is worthwhile to recall the general opinion which is common to all of us.[175]

After a brief overview of the geography of the world Orosius speaks of the fall of man and the degeneration of the Flood. The universal Deluge, he notes, is recognized even by a few pagans, for they have noticed the shellfish and snails on distant mountains.[176] He then continues on with his history of the wars and conflicts throughout the ages of the world. To the ancients the creation of Genesis was not "prehistory," just the first events of the history of mankind—events that were only related to us accurately by the Scriptures.

Epiphanius of Salamis (c. 310-403) reacted against the allegorizing of Origen because he had interpreted Paradise as not being on this earth but rather in a spiritual plane. Epiphanius asserted the literal meaning of the entire creation account of Genesis:

> But if Paradise is not on the earth and the things which have been written in Genesis are not literal but are being allegorized, nothing of the following speaks truth, but all things are being allegorized. "In the beginning," for it says, "God made heaven and earth:" and it is not being allegorized, but visible. And firmament, it says, and sea, both crops and trees and plants, pastures, animals, fish, birds, all things which are seen, which have come to be in truth, and he made man to exist in truth. Therefore, he placed this one whom he formed in Paradise, having made the same man according to his image, according to the image of God.[177]

In his *Panarion* or "against heresies," which he calls the "savage beasts" of paganism, he treats of eighty different pagan sects in three volumes. Epiphanius begins with a review of human history on earth.

> For at the beginning Adam was brought to life on the sixth day, after being formed from earth and infused with (God's breath). He was not begun on the fifth day and completed on the sixth; the idea of those who say this is a mistaken one. He was unspoiled and innocent . . . and after 930 years of life he died.[178]

Epiphanius continues relating the story of human beginnings as a way of introducing the various heresies that crept in as history unfolded. He includes a few chronological markers along the way. It was 2262 years from Adam to the Deluge,[179] and it was 3332 years from Adam to Terah.[180] Thus, based on the genealogies, the world is thousands of years old.

Jerome (c. 347-407) was a father of the Church who learned the language and customs of the Jews, and who also passed this knowledge on to others. Jerome wrote a careful explanation of Hebrew words that cleared up many misunderstandings that people had from deficiencies in previous translations. His comments on Genesis are insightful.

> *In the beginning, God made heaven and earth* . . . most people think that in the Hebrew is contained *In the Son, God made heaven and earth*, which the facts of the matter itself prove to be mistaken. For both the Septuagint, and Symmachus and Theodotion, translated it as *In the Beginning*; and in the Hebrew Bible is written *bresith* [Hebrew: beginning, first-fruits, best, chief] . . . So the verse can be applied to Christ more in respect of its intention than following its literal translation: to Christ who is proved to be founder of heaven and earth both at the very front of Genesis, which is the head of all the books, and also at the beginning of John the Evangelist's works . . . But this should be known, this book is called *bresith*, because they [the Jews] have this custom of giving names to scrolls from their opening words.[181]

Thus we realize the interpretation of Genesis 1:1 given by many Fathers, who understood it to mean "in the beginning; that is, in His Son," is better seen as a secondary reading.

> *And the Spirit of God moved over the waters.* In place of what is written in our codices as moved, the Hebrew has *merefeth*, which we can render as "was brooding over" or "was keeping warm," in likeness of a bird giving life to its eggs with warmth. Consequently we understand that this is said not about the spirit of the world, as some suppose, but about the Holy Spirit.[182]

This explains why some ancient interpreters held that this was not the Holy Spirit. Today it seems very obvious to us that this should be understood as the Holy Spirit and that all three persons of the Trinity were active in the creation from its beginning.

> *So when the sons of God saw the daughters of men, that they were comely.* The Hebrew word *eloim* is of common number; for both "God" and "gods" are designated in the same way. For this reason Aquila dared to say "sons of the gods," in the plural, understanding "gods" as holy ones or angels . . . *Moreover there were giants in the earth in those days; and after these things, as the sons of God were accustomed to go into the daughters of men, so they would breed with them* . . . In the Hebrew, it has the following: *Falling ones* (that is, *annaphelim*) were on the earth in those days . . . the name *falling ones* is indeed fitting both for angels and for the offspring of holy ones.[183]

Jerome has a reference to the chronology of the world in his commentary on Titus. He is commenting on Titus 1:2 where Paul says: *In the hope of eternal life, which God, who cannot lie, promised long ages ago* [lit., *before times eternal*].

> But I do not think that the following point should be silently passed over: How did the "God who does not lie" promise eternal life "before the eternal ages?" According to the history of Genesis the world was created by Him. Through the alternation of nights and days [referring to the phrase "it was evening and morning . . ." in the creation account], and also of months and years, time was created . . . Before the time of this world, then, one should believe that there was a certain eternity of ages in which the Father was always with the Son and the Holy Spirit.
>
> And thus I would say that God's time alone is an entire *eternity*; or rather, time is incalculable, since He himself is infinite, who being prior to times transcends all time. But a thousand years of our world are not yet fulfilled [Lit.: **six thousand years** of our world are not yet fulfilled; Latin: "***sex milia necdum nostri orbis implementer anni***"[184]; perhaps this is a misprint or a translation error, for "a thousand" seems to make no sense.], and what great prior eternities, how much time, what great beginnings of ages must one think have existed in which angels, thrones, dominions, and other powers served God. And they existed at God's command, apart from the alternations and measure of time! And so, before all this time, which neither worlds dare to utter, nor mind to comprehend, nor hidden thought to reach, God the Father of his own wisdom promised that his own Word, both his own very wisdom itself and the life of those who would believe, would come into the world.[185]

Thus Jerome meditates on the phrase "before times eternal" and observes "six thousand years of our world," which was preceded by an unknown length of time in which God created the angels and they served him, and before that the incomprehensible eternal ages when only God existed. During that incomprehensible time the Father promised eternal life to believers—a life which would come in and through His Son. Jerome notes that this decision of the Trinity (like the decision that the Son would be "the Lamb slain") was made before the angels were created. This is why the "princes of this world (the demonic hosts)" did not understand the mystery of the cross (1 Corinthians 2:6–8). Such foundational Trinitarian decisions preceded the creation of the angels. This comment by Jerome indicates that he saw the course of history for this world as still less than six thousand years in his day.[186]

It is also likely, from these and similar comments by Paul, that he was made privy to some of the Trinitarian decisions that determined the course of the world. For example, see also Hebrews 1:2 where Paul notes that the Father and the Son "planned the ages". This is one reason why we might think that Paul was the author of Hebrews. Consider Ephesians 1:3–4 in the same light. Paul says that "He chose us before the foundation of the world" and "He predestined us". There are many such references to the period "before the ages" in the writings of Paul. They are a characteristic of his, indicating a special privilege he was shown. How many inspired writers were "caught up to the third heaven" (2 Corinthians 12:2) and had such mysteries revealed to them? In Revelation John relates holy mysteries both past and future, but nothing of the world-planning Father-Son council before all ages.[187]

There was a puzzling problem in the LXX with the ages of the patriarchs before the Flood. The ages were such that Methuselah would not have died until fourteen years after the Deluge. Jerome remarks on this and on the consternation that it caused among many, then he explains how the Hebrew text completely clears up the problem.[188] This discussion shows how seriously all of the Fathers took the ages of the patriarchs that are recorded in Genesis. They saw the genealogical information as completely true and reliable.

In Jerome we see the beginning of the use of Hebrew scholarship in the study of the Old Testament books, a benefit that is well developed in our day. Eventually Jerome would continue and translate the entire Old Testament into Latin from Hebrew. That translation, called the Vulgate, was the standard in the Catholic Church for well over a millennium.

Nemesius of Emesa (c. 350-400?) was a convert to Christianity later in his life. He had been provincial governor of Cappadocia between 383 and 389 and knew Gregory of Nazianzus in the later years of Gregory's life. Gregory reports that Nemesius was a philosopher at heart and longed to leave his governorship and devote himself to his true avocation. In about 390 Nestorius did leave his office and became a Christian. Since he had been a governor, he advanced rapidly in the Church, became a bishop in Emesa, and wrote his philosophical work by AD 400. His one work, written while he was still a relatively young believer, seems because of its abrupt ending, to be a kind of "rough draft" that was never fully completed.

> The Jews say that man was created at first neither avowedly mortal nor yet immortal, but rather in a state poised between the two, in the sense that, if he gave himself up to his bodily passions he should be subject to all the changes of the body, but if he put the good of his soul foremost, he should be deemed worthy of immortality. For if God had made man mortal from the first, he would not have appointed dying as the penalty of his offense, seeing that no one would condemn to mortality someone who was already mortal. If, to take the other case, God had made man immortal, he would not have subjected him to the need of nourishment. No immortal being is dependent upon bodily food.[189]

> Only man's body, though mortal, is immortalized. This privilege of the body is for the soul's sake. So, likewise, the soul's privilege is on account of the body. For it is only man, among the rational beings, that has this unique privilege, of claiming forgiveness by repenting. Neither demons nor angels repent and are forgiven. In this fact, most particularly, God shows himself both just and merciful, and is so acknowledged. As for angels, seeing that there is no compulsion drawing them to sin, and that they are by nature exempt from bodily passions, needs, and pleasures, there is plain reason why they cannot claim pardon by repenting. Man, on the other hand, is not only rational but a living organism. The wants and passions of a living creature often distract his consideration. Afterwards, when he comes to his senses again, and, fleeing lust, returns to the way of virtues, he obtains both justice and mercy in pardon.[190]

Sulpicius Severus (c. 355-c. 420) was a native of Aquitaine and a priest who wrote about the life of Saint Martin. He also produced two books on chronology. He explains why he wrote his chronicles.

> I have taken on the task of briefly condensing the events that have been disclosed in the Sacred Scriptures, starting from the beginning of the world, and, having divided the periods, speaking selectively about events right up to our own time. Many people who were desperate to learn about divine things through reading matter in an abridged form were eagerly demanding this work from me. Consequently, I did not spare myself the hard work of enclosing in two books all the events that have been written out in multiple volumes.[191]

> God established the world nearly six thousand years ago, as we will explain in the course of the volume. Nevertheless, those who have published their investigations of the length of time agree little about this among themselves.[192]

> Noah left the ark. That event, I calculate, took place 2,242 years after the beginning of the world.[193]

> Abraham was the son of Terah, born 1070 years after the flood.[194]

In this way he proceeds up to his own time. His chronological data is based on the LXX, and that explains why he arrives at the dates we are seeing. The divergent final numbers that he notes have been arrived at by various investigators continued to be a subject of concern for many centuries. In the 1200's Roger Bacon will still comment on it and propose a solution.

Cyril of Alexandria (c. 376-444) in his expansive work *Glaphyra on Genesis* looks at the books of Moses through the lens of the redemptive works of Jesus, for Moses carefully lays the groundwork for understanding the human condition and for appreciating the promise of God that is addressed to those who find themselves in the predicament of sin.

Now we shall first present the literal events [of the creation and fall] in a helpful way, making them suitably clear. Then, refashioning the narrative by bringing it out of type and shadow, we shall explain it with reference to the mystery of Christ, having him as the goal, since it is true that Christ is the end of the law and the prophets.[195]

Commenting on the inscrutable nature of the creative works of God he says:

Now the God of all, being a Master Craftsman by his own all-effecting power, that is, by the Son, with respect to everything whatsoever that was made declares, "all things came into being through him, and not one thing came to be without him." In the beginning he formed heaven and earth before all else, and called them into being, though nothing then existed . . . That our faculties are insignificant or as absolutely nothing in comparison with God, he himself clearly states, "For my purposes are not like your purposes, neither are my ways like your ways. For as the heaven is far from the earth, so is my way far from your ways, and your thoughts from my thinking." Let it be allowed, then, that extraordinariness and incomprehensibility are the touchstone concerning these things. For God creates as he himself knows how and as only he is able.[196]

Then he briefly reviews the works of the six days and states:

What seemed good to him he brought about instantaneously and incomprehensibly. Respecting each of the things that were made, its Maker was the Word, and its origin was solely a command.[197]

He then explains the special place of man, the one for whom creation was fashioned.

[He] introduced last of all, the one on account of whom those other things had been brought into existence, namely man. For it was necessary that the Maker of all things, being in nature good, or rather that which he is being goodness itself, should be known by us. The earth had to be filled with those who knew how to give him glory and, as it is written, from the beauty of created things the glory of the one who had made them was to be viewed . . . Now he had made all the rest of creation instantaneously, merely by speaking, forming it by his own word as God. However . . . God honored the making of this masterpiece with his own deliberation and personal involvement. Having sculpted man out of the soil he made him into a rational creature and, in order that he might replicate the rationality of his own nature, he immediately implanted within him an immortal, life-giving Spirit.[198]

Cyril then explains the glories of Paradise and the exalted position in which God had created man. But it was necessary that man realize His place before God.

But then it was absolutely necessary for the man who had come into such glory and delight to understand clearly that God held a position over him as his King and Lord. Lest man should fall by the considerable prosperity that was readily available to him, possibly even wishing to be freed from the authority and supremacy of him who ruled, God immediately issued a law and accompanied it with the threat of punishment should it be transgressed.[199]

And the condition of corruption into which Adam fell was passed on to his descendants.

For when the author of sin deceived Adam in the beginning, he made him to be guilty of the charge of carelessness, and so it came about that he was brought down to death. Then the punishment passed upon all men, this condition coming forth just as things grow out of a root.[200]

After considering the wretched state to which man had fallen, Cyril asks why God even created him in the first place. But then he recalls the providential wisdom and glory of God.

What then? I imagine one might say that if man was going to fall into such a woeful condition, would it not reasonably be considered much better for him not to exist? . . . I would say that it is extremely dangerous and approaches the point of complete madness, or rather even greatly surpasses it, not to honor the divine purposes as being just, or to suppose that the Supreme Being either perhaps had no regard for what was proper, or that he failed utterly in what was best and profitable for us humans.[201]

Then, having laid the foundation, Cyril returns to the doctrine of Jesus Christ which God in His infinite wisdom and foreknowledge had determined before the creation.

For God understood that, as soon as he had brought man into being, he would fall into corruption. Nor was he ignorant of the manner in which this could be cured. The divine Paul, by the foreknowledge of the Spirit, testifies unambiguously to the antiquity of salvation through Christ. For thus he wrote to his own disciple, Timothy, "So do not be ashamed of giving testimony to our Lord or of me his prisoner, but join with me in suffering for the gospel, relying on the power of God, who saved us and called us with a holy calling. This was not according to our works, but according to his

> own purpose and grace which was given us in Christ Jesus before all ages, and which has been revealed in the last ages through the appearing of our Savior Jesus Christ" . . . And the Only-Begotten Word of God voluntarily came down into our estate, not that he might be ruled over by death along with us, since he himself is the one who makes all things alive, but that having manifested that nature which was subject to corruption, he might transform it into life.[202]

In this way Cyril testifies clearly to the common view of the ancients on the creation with its direct implications for understanding the Incarnation and the gospel message. Cyril's work is notable in the clarity and completeness of its presentation of the overall plan of salvation. Cyril adds this astute observation:

> I for my part hold this wonderful restoration to be a work of divine power and authority, one that is able to bring things into existence out of that which does not exist, and which summons those things which are, to all intents and purposes, deprived of excellence and wholeness, and brings them back to a good estate.[203]

That is, only the Creator could bring about the redemption of His creatures after their tragic fall. That work of restoration is of the same magnitude and glory as the work of creation.

Both the creation and the redemption are uniquely and only the work of God Himself. Thus their truth is embedded in inscrutable mysteries and must be received by faith. For no man can understand how a sinless person was born of woman after the fall, much less how any person could be both fully God and fully man. And no man can understand how God by His will summoned the primordial substance of the universe into existence and formed it into the world that we see around us. We do not even understand what it means to exist, much less the nature of the One Who, by His own self, must necessarily exist and Who called forth all.

Theodoret of Cyrus (c. 393-c. 463) was bishop of Cyrus, a city about 65 miles northeast of Antioch. He wrote a lengthy series of questions and answers on the Octateuch. He explains his attitude toward the Scriptures and his reason for writing his lengthy work.

> Some inquire [into the scriptures] irreverently, believing they find holy Scripture wanting: in some cases, not teaching right doctrine, in others, giving conflicting instructions. In contrast, others, longing to find an answer for their question, search because they love learning. Accordingly, it is my intention to stop the blasphemous mouths of the former, please God, by demonstrating the consistency of holy Scripture and the excellence of its teaching, and also, to the extent possible, provide the latter with solutions to their difficulties.[204]

Theodoret speaks of the creation of man as a joint effort between the Father and the Son.

> When he [God] was on the point of creating [man] . . . he gave a riddling indication of both the identity of [his] substance and the numerical distinction of [his] persons. With "God said" he indicated the divine nature held in common, and adding "let us make," he revealed the numerical distinction of persons. Likewise by saying "image" in the singular he brought out the identity of nature. He did not say "images," but "image." Yet, when he said "our" he indicated the numerical distinction of the hypostases.[205]

Theodoret discusses the ways in which we are "in His image" and yet the ways in which God must, by His divine nature, always exceed what we can be. We build structures out of existing material with effort and over a length of time. In contrast

> The God of the universe creates both from the existent and the non-existent, and, without effort or lapse of time, puts his intention into effect as soon as he wills it.[206]

When speaking of the long lives of the early men he gives this reason:

> [They lived that long] so that the race could grow in numbers thanks to the longer life-span.[207]

In the many questions about Genesis and in his answers, Theodoret affirms that God did indeed create **all** things from nothing—including the waters of the great deep—and that He accomplished all of His creative acts during the six days.[208]

Jacob of Sarug (451-521) was a bishop in the Church of the East who wrote many lyrical commentaries on the Bible. He has been called the "flute of the Spirit" by his admirers. He comments on the six days of creation in his verses on Genesis.

I then began to reflect, "Before this action that occurred [God creating the world], what was there?" for it is not written that there was nothing.
Before the signal [Syriac; *remza*: sign, gesture, nod; something effected quickly and effortlessly] which established the ages from nothing, what did a place devoid of any creature look like?
Before there was either light or darkness, what color was that light of Existence [Syriac; *ituta*: meaning being or existence and always referring to God as the Being or the Self-Existent One]?[209]

There came that first impetus from the Self-Existent One, and the signal went forth and made nothing into something.
It was at this point that Moses began to speak: "In the beginning God created the heavens and the earth."
From that signal and thereafter the scribe began to write down what came to be during the six days of creation.[210]

[Referring to the creation of the angels and the heavenly powers] This account of the captains of the powers and of the hosts was not spoken of in that account of the (first) six days.
Only about those corporeal, solid, and visible things did Moses record how they came to be from nothing.[211]

So too did God "cut" the world out of nothing, to begin from that and, without toil, to establish creation.
And with one signal He created a world with nothing fashioned in it, then in six days He established and set in order what He had fashioned.
It was not that God's might was lacking that He prolonged the time, so that it took six days for all of creation to be perfected.
Rather, what creation needed was an orderly arrangement, so that by being created one thing at a time it might be prepared properly.
These preparations necessitated such patient deliberateness, so that each creation might provide an occasion for its companion to be made.[212]

When creating the heavens and the earth He is 'Creator',
whereas when fashioning various created things He is 'Maker'.
He created creation with a signal [that is, with a nod; quickly and effortlessly]
    and His hidden power established it,
    and from that he began to make beautiful things in six days.
Before everything He was self-existent with no need for created things
    and His Existence has no name except "He is."
When He condescended and created things from nothing
    He received the name 'Creator' because He created.
Then when He began to make those beautiful things that came to be
    He consented to be called 'Maker' as well.
He is 'Maker' when He makes a thing from another thing,
    but 'Creator' when He creates from nothing.[213]

Fulgentius of Ruspe (c. 465-c. 527), bishop of that Tunisian city, was recognized for his virtue. The Arians banished him to Sardinia for his stand against them. He gave advice to a younger believer named Peter before he journeyed to Jerusalem lest his tender faith be corrupted. He explains that the Father, the Son, and the Spirit each partake together of uncreated substance, yet are distinct persons.

All of this is demonstrated for us in the strongest fashion at the very beginning of the Holy Scriptures, when God says, "Let us make human beings in our likeness." When, using the singular number, he says "image," he shows that the nature is one, in whose image the human being was made. But, when he says "our" in the plural, he shows that the very same God in whose image the human being was made is not one person. For, if in that one essence of Father, Son, and Holy Spirit, there were one person, "to our image" would not have been spoken but "in my image." Nor would he have said, "let us make," but, "I shall make." If, in reality, in those three persons three substances were to be understood or believed, "to our image" would not have been said; rather, "to our images"; for there could not be one image of three unequal natures. But, while the human being is said to be made according to the one image of the one God, the divinity of the Holy Trinity in one essence is announced.[214]

In speaking of the creation of the many beings that God has made Fulgentius says,
> First of all, believe that every nature which is not God the Trinity (which alone is the true and eternal God) has been created out of nothing by the true and eternal God . . . This God . . . has given to all natures which he made that they are good; not however, so good as the Creator of all good things who not only is good to the greatest degree but is also the greatest and unchangeable good . . . These things, in their very diversity, commend the goodness and omnipotence of the Creator even more. For, unless he were omnipotent he would not have made the greatest and the least of these things with one and the same ease . . . Neither are these corporeal beings of one nature with God, in each of whom He has placed individual brute and irrational spirits by which the same corporeal beings are given life and senses . . . which, although it is recognized that he implanted in these bodies what is necessary for life and gave them the capability of sensing, still, he granted these same souls no light of understanding by which they could either know or love their creator . . . [And] even of those spirits of which there can be no doubt that they are rational and intelligent . . . at times they do not know something, at others, they do know; sometimes they will, at others they do not will; sometimes they are wise, at other times foolish; sometimes, from being just, they become wicked, at other times, having been wicked, they become just . . . [The Creator] has given them [angels and men] the ability to know and love Him in such a way as to have it or to lose it [that is, the knowledge and love of God]. But if anyone of his own will were to lose it, from then on, he would not be able to regain it on his own initiative . . . Angels and human beings, because of the fact that they have been created as rational, have received from God in the very creation of a spiritual nature, the gift of eternity and happiness.[215]

Speaking of the initial state of Adam and Eve before the fall he says,
> Hold most firmly and never doubt that the first human beings, i.e., Adam and his woman, were good, righteous, and created without sin, with free will by which they could have, if they were willing, always served and obeyed God with a humble and good will . . . [A]nd they did sin, not out of any necessity, but by their own will; and, by that sin, human nature was so changed for the worse that, through that sin, death obtained the rule not only in the first human beings themselves but also that the dominion of sin and death would pass on to all human beings.[216]

Speaking of the nature of the final state of glory he quotes Paul and says:
> "That which is corruptible must clothe itself with incorruptibility, and that which is mortal must clothe itself with immortality" [1 Corinthians 15:53]. The masculine and feminine sexes will remain, just as the same bodies were created; and their glory will vary according to the diversity of their good works.[217]

Thus he draws a direct connection between the original creation of human beings as both male and female and their final state of glory.

Fulgentius the Mythographer, also from ancient times near the 6th century, who likely was not the same person as the Fulgentius above, produced a work *On the Ages of the World and of Man*. In this work he employs a literary style that was not uncommon in the ancient times: he has twenty-two sections in his work and in the first section he uses no words that have in them the letter "A;" in the second section he uses no word that contains the letter "B," etc. This makes for a somewhat clumsy writing style. Referring to the numerical values assigned to the letters of the alphabet he says:
> Thus with our letters, if you count them as far as the last one, z, the total comes to five hundred, whence twelve times five hundred gives the age of the existing world.[218]

Thus he asserts, in agreement with the LXX, that the world was about 6000 years old in his day. Of course, he gives no reason for making his calculation in this way, but he does reveal his view that the genealogies of Genesis can be used to calculate the age of the world. In this obtuse calculation he might also be referring to the chronology of Hippolytus as he describes it in his commentary on Daniel, even as Hilary of Poitiers referred to it in his commentary on the gospel of Matthew.

Some of these examples that I present are from people who have theological views that differ from ours substantially in various ways. Their views, which they base on Scripture (especially Genesis), are varied, but their belief in the truth of Genesis does not waver at all. How they built their theological speculations on the Genesis accounts may vary, but their starting point was always the absolute truth of all Scripture, including Genesis. They all approached Genesis with the conviction that it was explaining to them how and when the world began and how and when the human race began.

Gregory of Tours (538-594) lived in the basin of the Loire river in France. This was the southernmost area of Frankish colonization, on the border of the barbarians. His work *History of the Franks* is important because it details the disintegration of the Roman empire and the birth of the nation of France. He relates the chronology of the earliest years of mankind as well, but does not bother to compute it himself. He borrows it from those who went before him. By approvingly relating the results of their work he testifies to his confidence in the genealogies of Genesis. He says:

> As to the reckoning of this world, the chronicles of Eusebius, bishop of Caesarea, and of Jerome the priest, speak clearly, and they reveal the plan of the whole succession of years. Orosius too, searching into these matters very carefully, collects the whole number of years from the beginning of the world down to his own time.[219] (Preface, book 1, pp. 6–7)

Gregory explains the "anger of the Lord" that brought the Flood at the time of Noah.

> Noah, who was most faithful and especially belonged to him [God] and bore the stamp of his image, he saved in the ark, with his wife and those of his three sons, that they might restore posterity. Here the heretics upbraid us because the holy Scripture says that the Lord was angry. Let them know therefore that our God is not angry like a man; for he is aroused in order to inspire fear; he drives away to summon back; he is angry in order to amend. Furthermore I have no doubt that the ark typified the mother church. For passing amidst the waves and rocks of this world it protects us in its motherly arms from threatening ills, and guards us with its holy embrace and protection.
>
> Now from Adam to Noah are ten generations, namely: Adam, Seth, Enos, Cainan, Malalehel, Jareth, Enoch, Mattusalam, Lamech, Noah. In these ten generations 2242 years are included.[220]

Isidore of Seville (c. 560-636), in his *Chronica Maiora*, gives a careful chronology of the world based in the genealogies of Genesis: [Note that he is using the LXX.]
1. God created everything in six days. On the first day he fashioned light; on the second, the firmament of heaven; on the third, the land and the sea; on the fourth, the stars; on the fifth, the fish and the birds; on the sixth, the animals and the beasts of burden and finally the first man, Adam, in his image.
2. Adam, at age 230, bore Seth . . . The first age [before the deluge] came to an end in the year 2242 . . . The second age [from the Deluge to the birth of Abraham, 942 years in all] came to an end in the year 3184 . . . The third age of the world [from Abraham to David, 940 years in all] came to an end in the year 4125 . . . The fourth age of the world [from David to the migration to Babylon, 485 years] ended in the year 4610 . . . The fifth age [from migration to Babylon to the birth of Jesus Christ, 587 years in all] came to an end in the year 5155.[221]

Isaac the Syrian (c. 613-c. 700) was ordained bishop of Nineveh but withdrew from that post after just five months to live a life of solitude. Despite his ascetic life he emerged as an authoritative theologian. His writings on the ascetic life reflect the deep spirituality of his own life with God. Here are a few brief insights into his spiritual battles:

> They say that the holy angels take on the likeness of saints, venerable and good men, and they manifest these likenesses to the soul in the dreams of sleep, when her thoughts wander, to bring her joy and exceeding gladness; and during the day the angels continually stir these likenesses in

> the contemplation of their thoughts . . . So it is also in prolonged warfare. He who is accustomed to meditate on that which is evil will be deluded by the demons by a likeness of evil. For the demons assume a likeness and manifest to the soul phantasies that frighten her.[222]

Let us look at some advice that he offers to those embroiled in such spiritual warfare. Do not presume to enter into debate with the demons, for they are older and wiser than we are. Rather, turn to God in supplication, beseeching Him to deliver you from their filth.

> The man who does not contradict the thoughts sowed in us by the enemy, but severs any conversation with them by means of his supplication to God, may have this fact as a sign that his mind has found the wisdom and power that is of grace, and that his true knowledge has freed him of many labors. This man, by discovering the short path that he has come upon, has cut off the many distracted windings of the long way. For we do not have strength to gainsay at all times every thought that opposes us, so that they may be silenced; and it often happens that they inflict a severe wound upon us which remains unhealed for a long time. Do you think to lecture those who are 6,000 years old? And this will itself be a weapon in their hands with which they will smite you, greatly surpassing your wisdom and your prudence. Yet even if you conquer them, the filth of such thoughts will pollute your mind and their stench will linger long in your nostrils. By the first method, however, you will be free of all this and of fear; for there is no helper like God.[223]

In this we see wise advice for us in our daily struggles with the enemy. At the same time we also see that Isaac thought our enemy to be about 6,000 years old, for he was created when the world was made. This reveals to us the world view of that wise saint of old.

Anastasius of Sinai (died after 700) was abbot of Saint Catherine's Monastery at Mount Sinai. He considers various notions about the nature of Paradise. Then he says:

> "Similar," as one exegete says, "to what was the state of human beings, midway between corruption and incorruption, such was, and still is, Paradise." Perhaps those who held this last view have spoken well . . . However one should be aware that some have also proposed the following theory: just as Scripture is accustomed of speaking of two Jerusalems, an earthly and a heavenly . . . so of two Paradises, one spiritual . . . [and] another perceptible to the senses . . . The reason is that if we talk of the snake and the waters [that is, the rivers of Paradise] as spiritual things we undo and turn topsy-turvy Holy Scripture.[224]

Many of the ancients considered the original state of Adam and Eve to be not fully immortal but also not truly mortal. They hung in the midst, awaiting their decision to obey or not.

Anastasius wrote a commentary on the six days, describing it as a "spiritual anagogy" [a rising upward or ascent: As a method of interpretation it sees allusions to spiritual realities in ordinary, mundane words.] He takes the literal meaning of the creation account as the starting point for an extensive comparison with the new creation in Christ. He showed courage in writing an allegorical interpretation of the six days because "Origenism" had been twice condemned—first by the Second Council of Constantinople in 553, and then again forcefully by the third in 680–681. He explains his approach by quoting from Paul.

> Indeed, if all creation arose for man and Paul raises Adam and Eve to Christ and the church when he says: *This mystery is great, but I am speaking about Christ and the Church*, then he is saying, undeniably, that all creation, having arisen for man and his mate, refers to Christ and his Church.[225]

However he in no way discards the literal meaning of the text, but comments briefly on that meaning and then follows extensively with a rhapsody of allegory. He explains:

> We do not seek, however, to annul the literal meaning. Rather, we seek the meaning that the Holy Spirit, in its great goodness and love for humanity, mystically encrypted within the literal. Toward this end we will examine the text first in a bodily or physical sense.[226]

> Remember me, oh reader, as one who said that we are not destroying the literal meaning, but are pursuing its unwritten anagogy. We are students of Paul, who said: *The letter kills*. So it killed the Jews. On account of this, after examining the literal meaning, we search for the Spirit. Its shadow can be seen between the words, but its fulfillment is Christ.[227] [see note]

Here is one example of his thinking as he reflects on Genesis 1:2, *the earth was formless and void and darkness was upon the face of the deep*.

> Through his words, Moses brought to life a portrait of the earthly cosmos. It was something murky: always in twilight, deep, depressed, misty, and bearing darkness everywhere. The earth itself, as if overpowered and strangled by darkness and the shadow of death, was in the nether regions of the underworld. It was choked by the waters that lay upon it; it was darkened by the darkness of the deep. And when the breath of the wind was borne mightily upon the water, the currents rocked and beat the earth below . . . This therefore is the literal description, according to Moses, of the earth.[228]

> The mundane earth, human nature, lay surrounded by such terrors. Then time's fulfillment arrived: when human nature was to rise from the subterranean depth of pleasures and be freed from the choking waters, and when the waves against her were to be calmed; when the evil winds were to fall silent, the darkness of ignorance was to move on and the light of divine understanding was to be ignited. God cried out and said: "Let there be light." He meant Christ, *the true light*, who illuminates *every person coming into the world*. *Let there be*: through birth let him come openly. That is, let Him be formed and receive a body. Moses wanted to point out to you that the Incarnation of the Word was more important than all else. On account of the Incarnation everything came into being. Without it, all things are pointless, accomplishing nothing . . . When did he resolve upon this creation [that is, upon the new creation rooted in the Incarnation]? Not when he began to bring forth the spiritual things, but the imperceptible. For he understood that these perceptible things—not the spiritual—would suffer miserably and be ruined by the approaching sin of Adam. In his love for humanity, he anticipated the onslaught of this suffering and prepared the doctor before the injury and the pain.[229]

Anastasius refers to the birth of Christ as being in the 5th millennium from Adam, about 5,500 years after Adam.[230] In this he shows his faith in the genealogies of Genesis and the age of the earth that they give to us. However he and many commentators fall short in explaining Eden and the story of Adam and Eve. They lapse into metaphorical interpretations which are, in my opinion, confusing and impossible to understand. One major point of this work will be to explain simply and clearly the relationship between the creation story in Genesis 1:1–2:4 and the account of the creation of Adam and Eve as given later on in chapter 2. I will follow Augustine in viewing the story of Adam and Eve as having happened on this earth. It is true history, the story of the beginning of the human race on earth.

The Venerable Bede (c. 672-735) gives us the complete chronology of the world from the creation to the time of Christ. He was one of the earliest to use the Masoretic text for his computations. He explains:

> In common parlance, *the day is the presence of the sun above the earth*. And properly speaking it comprises 24 hours. The *Chaldeans* and the *Persians* reckon the day *between two sunrises*, the *Egyptians* between two *sunsets*, the *Romans from midnight* to midnight, the *Umbrians* and *Athenians from noon to noon*. Moses called the period from morning to morning a single day . . . Time is distributed into the six ages of the world. *The first age, from Adam to Noah,* contains . . . one thousand six hundred fifty-six years. This age perished completely *in the Flood . . . The second age from Noah to Abraham . . .* two hundred ninety-two years . . . *The third* age . . . nine hundred forty-two years . . . *The fourth age . . .* four hundred seventy-three years . . . *The fifth age . . .* five hundred eighty-nine years. . . [for a total of 3952 years] *The sixth Age, which is unfolding now,* has no fixed sequence of generations or times, but . . . will end in the death of the whole world-age.[231]

In commenting on how the Lord God summoned all things into existence Bede says:

> By introducing the creation of the world in the first sentence, Holy Scripture appropriately displays at once the eternity and omnipotence of God the creator. For by asserting that God created the world at the beginning of time, Scripture signifies that he indeed existed eternally before time. And when it tells that he created heaven and earth in the very beginning of creation, by such great swiftness of work it declares that he, for whom to have willed is to have done, is omnipotent . . .

God, whose ability to complete his work is unlimited, he who, as it is written, *has done all things whatsoever he would,* had no need of a delay of time . . . Hence it is well said that *In the beginning God created heaven and earth* . . . with such great swiftness of divine power that the first moment of the infant world had not yet passed.[232]

By this he asserts that the matter that comprises heaven and earth was created instantly by God. Bede was influenced by Augustine as can be seen from the above and also in the way he introduces how all things were made:

The divine power, which created and governs all existing things, can be understood in four different ways: First, that *all these things were not made but are eternal in* the dispensation of the *Word of God, who,* as the Apostle testifies, *predestined us* for his kingdom *before the times of the world.* Second, that the elements *of the world* were made all at the same time in unformed matter, when he who lives eternally *created everything at once.* Third, that the same matter is formed into a heavenly and an earthly creation, *partly from existing causes, and partly from causes not yet existing,* but each thing coming into existence by the distinct workings of the first six days. Fourth, that the temporal constitution of the whole world is brought about in the natural course of things by *the seeds* and *primordial causes* of this same creation, wherein the Father and the Son work right up to the present, and God even *feeds the ravens'* and clothes *the lilies. At the very beginning of creation, heaven, earth, the angels, air, and water were made* from nothing. Indeed, light was made on the first day and it was made from nothing. *On the second, the firmament* was made in the midst of the waters . . . *On the sixth, the rest of the animals* were made from the earth, *and man* was created, in the flesh of course from the earth, but in the soul from nothing. He was placed in Paradise, which *God had planted from the beginning.* On the seventh God rested, not from the governance of creation, since *in him we live, and move, and are,* but from the creation of new material.[233]

St. John Damascene (c. 675-749) in his landmark work *The Fount of Knowledge*, states for us the nature of God and the creation, and gives his high and holy view of Paradise.

Now because the good and transcendentally good God was not content Himself, but by a superabundance of goodness saw fit that there should be some things to benefit by and participate in His goodness, He brings all things from nothing into being and creates them, both visible and invisible.

Our God . . . Himself "made heaven and earth, and all things that are in them." . . . [Some] from no pre-existing matter . . . others . . . He made from those things that had their existence directly from Him. For by the command of the Creator these last were made . . .

It [Eden] was situated in the east and was higher than all the rest of the earth. It was temperate in climate and bright with the softest and purest of air. It was luxuriant with ever-blooming plants, filled with fragrance, flooded with light, and surpassing all conception of sensible fairness and beauty. In truth, it was a divine place and a worthy habitation for God in His image. And in it no brute beasts dwelt, but only man, the handiwork of God . . . Some have imagined Paradise to have been material, while others have imagined it to have been spiritual. However, it seems to me that, just as man was created both sensitive and intellectual, so did this most sacred domain of his have the twofold aspect of being perceptible both to the senses and to the mind. For, while in his body he dwelt in this most sacred and superbly beautiful place, as we have related, spiritually he resided in a loftier and far more beautiful place. There he had the indwelling God as a dwelling place and wore Him as a glorious garment. He was wrapped about with His grace, and, like some one of the angels, he rejoiced in the enjoyment of that one most sweet fruit which is the contemplation of God, and by this he was nourished.[234]

In this last comment on Eden we see how John Damascene addressed the issue of the Garden of Eden: Did it exist on a spiritual plane or was it on the earth? Did the events described in chapters 2 and 3 of Genesis take place in eternity or during the passage of time as we experience it? He tried to merge the two ideas as he approached this issue, while holding that Eden was actually on this earth.

George the Monk Synkellos (died about 810) was a Byzantine chronographer of highest repute. [Synkellos: an ecclesiastical office in the Eastern Rite churches; the archbishop's closest advisor and also his likely successor.] He was awarded this post because of his tireless crusade against heretics and the physical abuse that he suffered for that. His history of the world is outstanding within a long tradition of such works in the Byzantine Church, and is notable for its scope, accuracy, and wealth of source material. After he died in 810 his unfinished work was completed by Theophanes Confessor. Their joint effort has been dubbed the "greatest achievement of Byzantine historical scholarship."[235] He works from the LXX and states his basic chronological position at the very beginning of his work.

> "In the beginning God created the heaven and the earth." It is the beginning of the whole chronological process in the visible creation subject to time, when the heaven and the earth were brought through immeasurable goodness from non-being into being by God the Father through the only-begotten Son and Holy Spirit, the holy consubstantial Trinity, the source of life. This is the holy first-created day of the first month called Nisan by the Hebrews and the divinely inspired scriptures, [from Exodus 12:2: "This month shall be . . . the first month of the year to you."] corresponding to the 25th of the Roman month of March, and the 29th of the seventh Egyptian month. This fact is acknowledged by all our holy fathers and teachers and the holy catholic and apostolic Church . . . Concerning this issue, I have made every effort to arrange the chronology presented here with tables and explanations . . . claiming . . . that in AM [*anno mundi*] 5501 our Lord and God was made incarnate from the Holy Virgin.[236]

The chronology of the creation is fully biblical, but George the Monk also quotes extensively from pseudepigrapha [e.g., *The Life of Adam, Jubilees, Enoch*], which sources he refers to in order to explain the origin of certain aberrant ideas about the early life of Adam and Eve. He dismisses these sources as untrustworthy, as do we.

> But there are some who carry on arguments without restraint, either out of feigned intellectual curiosity or stung by vainglory. And with divine texts in hand they attempt to show that our forefather Adam was not immediately placed into Paradise by God; or else that he entered into Paradise before the forming of the woman and conferred names on the beasts and the birds of the sky, which, as they insist, would not be the work of one day for the infirmity and capacity of the human being.[237]

> [Then he quotes from the *Life of Adam* which asserts that he entered Paradise on the 46th day, and also makes many other extensive and detailed assertions about the early life of man.][238]

> For this reason I have been compelled also to make a statement about this matter in turn, to the extent that among other historians who have composed either Jewish antiquities or Christian histories there has been discussion of this matter on the basis of *Little Genesis* and the so-called *Life of Adam* (even if it appears not to be authoritative). I do this lest those who investigate these matters fall into even more absurd notions.[239]

Thus we see that he was careful to consider all sources of information about the early years of mankind and to sift through them and retain only what was authoritative.

George also quotes extensively from various ancient pagan accounts of the earliest years of mankind, but tends to dismiss them as unreliable because they are inconsistent with the Holy Bible. We will skip all such fanciful details.

Another source that he quotes is Eusebius and his chronological studies. Eusebius carefully computed ancient dates from the Hebrew Bible, the LXX, and the Samaritan Bible. Thus, although we have not found an English translation of the *Chronicle* by Eusebius we can give these numbers from the calculations of Eusebius:

Years from Adam to Abraham according to the LXX:	3184
Years from Adam to Abraham according to Hebrew Bible:	1948
Years from Adam to Abraham according to Samaritan Bible:	2249[240]

Thus we can see that the study of ancient chronology, as an inseparable part of the study of origins, was very important throughout Christianity in ancient times.

As we read the extensive quotes that George the Monk gives from the pseudepigrapha it is clear that some strange ideas that various early Fathers express—those discussed by him and others as well—might have had their origin in those works. It seems possible that in the early centuries, before the canon of Scripture was universally agreed upon, various commentators could have indiscriminately taken ideas from those books and mentioned them in their commentaries on Genesis. In this way certain aberrant ideas were brought into the Church and remained in circulation for many years.

Symeon the New Theologian (949-1022) speaks of the creation days.
> God, in the beginning, before He planted Paradise and gave it over to the first-created ones, in five days set in order the earth and what is on it, and the heaven and what is in it. And on the sixth day he created Adam and placed him as lord and king of the whole visible creation. Then there was not yet Paradise.[241]

Thus Symeon seems to assert that the creation of Paradise, planted lovingly by God, took place after the seven days. He continues and explains his view.
> For after He had created everything else, and made man also, and rested on the seventh day from all the works which He had begun to do, He planted Paradise in Eden, in the East, as a royal dwelling, and He led into it as king the man whom He had made . . . [God planted Paradise after He had made everything else] because He, as the Foreknower of everything, arranged the whole creation in order and in an orderly sequence, and He assigned seven days that they might be an image of the ages which were subsequently to pass in time. But Paradise He planted after those seven days, that it might be an image of the future age.[242]

Thus Symeon asserts a numerological-allegorical understanding of the creation. Perhaps he was influenced by one of the pseudepigrapha when he said Eden was planted after the seven days. He also explains the state of Adam and the creation before the fall.
> Adam was made with a body that was incorrupt, although material and not yet spiritual, and was placed by the Creator God as an immortal king over an incorrupt world, not only over Paradise, but also over the whole of creation that was under the heavens.[243]

Thus Adam and Eve were in a blessed state of being, but not in their final state of glory. They were waiting for the time when God would grant them their spiritual bodies.

Symeon also meditates on how human life on earth would have progressed if Adam and Eve had not fallen into sin.
> Imagine how many [people] there would have been if all those born from the creation of the world had not died! And what kind of life they would have lived, being immortal and incorrupt, strangers to sin, sorrows, cares, and difficult necessities! And how, prospering in the keeping of the commandments and the good ordering of the dispositions of the heart, in time they would have ascended into the most perfect glory, and being changed, would have drawn near to God; and the soul of each one would have become light-bearing by reason of the illuminations which would have been poured out upon it from the Divinity! And this sensuous and crudely material body would have become as it were immaterial and spiritual, above all senses; and the joy and rejoicing with which we then would have been filled by fellowship with one another, in truth would have been unutterable and beyond human thought.[244]

Eventually all men would have ascended into glory with God to fulfill their God-ordained destiny to be before Him in love as His beloved (Ephesians 1:4).

Peter Abelard (1079-1141) was a French scholastic of widespread fame. Here are a few points that he makes in his commentary on the six days:
- The work of the six days eludes our understanding as do parts of Ezekiel (the sections about the wheels and the section about the temple) and the Song of Songs. The difficulty of the Genesis creation is reflected in the rarity of interpretations which have been given for it throughout the ages.[245]

- By "heaven and earth" Moses designates the basic material from which all physical things were formed, but not the angels. The work of the first day was a creation from nothing, and later work was a forming of what was first created.[246]
- He explicitly states that what we are as human was not animal previously, nor did any animal previously exist in any species other than its own.[247]
- In speaking of the creative commands of God, he asserts that these were given by the Father "in His Word." He explains that in the Hebrew the creative commands are literally, "be," and their fulfillment was, "it was." Therefore they should be understood as having been enacted instantly.[248]
- Peter Abelard has an unusual view of cosmology and does not rightly understand the firmament. He thinks that the objects above the firmament are kept there by a solid structure. Although we do not know what holds the heavens in place, we know that it is not a solid structure. In describing the "waters above the firmament" he notes that some have claimed that those waters fell during the Deluge as the rains fell for forty days. He rejects that idea because in Psalm 148:4–5 it says, "let the waters above the heavens praise the name of the Lord," and he interprets this to mean that they must still be there. Thus the Flood of Noah must be attributed only to atmospheric precipitation and the opening of the springs of the great abyss.[249]

On the timing of the first days of the creation, explaining how long they were and how the waters were gathered above the firmament on the second day, he says this:

> But if anyone should ask how much time passed before they were established, wishing to know what the first day was before the second, he should bear in mind that those six days in which the world was completed ought not to be measured according to those which we now have according to the illumination of the sun, especially since the sun had not yet been created on those first three days. When therefore we reckon days in these works of God and we say that *there was morning and evening one day*, we do not interpret day or evening or morning according to our days as we now know them, but we distinguish one day from another according to the differentiation of works, in other words the first of God's works which he had previously achieved is called the first day.[250]

That is, the division between the first few days was not the rising or setting of the sun, as it is now, but was established according to the works that God did. A certain set of works constituted the first day, and another set of works is the second day, etc. This does not yet answer the question of "how much time passed."

> In fact it was necessary for heaven and earth, that is, matter for what was to come, to be prepared in the elements before it was formed in the works that follow. Accordingly (the prophet) calls the first creation of matter in the elements the first day.[251]

Thus, as he mentioned earlier, the first day was distinguished as a work of creation "*ex nihilo.*" The matter that was created then was so designed by God that it could properly support the many varied structures into which it would be formed in the days to follow. Now, after this interlude, he finally gets to the timing of the first days.

> But so that we may return to what was interrupted, not omitted—let the reader know that we inserted this—when he hears one day or another named by the prophet, he should not understand those intervals of time that we now take for our days, but trace the difference among days back to the difference among works, however long the delay in their sequence or their production. Let no one therefore marvel when he hears that on the second day waters are set over heavens already in existence, as if there were some delay between their existence and their establishment, since in fact they were established there straight away after they came into existence. And so, when it is now said, *Let there be a firmament* or *He divided the waters which were*, etc., that founding or dividing of theirs is so to be understood, that without delay after they came into existence they were established.[252]

Thus he returns to the assertion that the creative acts were carried out instantly. This is what determines the timing of the six days. In all of these thoughts Peter Abelard is very similar to Augustine.

One interesting point that is unique to Peter Abelard: He says that man was created in the image of God, but woman was in man's likeness. This is because of 1 Corinthians 11:7 which says that man is in the image of God, and thus he should not cover his head, but woman, because she does cover her head, must not be in His image. Rather she is in the likeness of God.[253] In this way he distinguishes and contrasts "image" and "likeness."

Bernard of Clairvaux (1090-1153) was a medieval luminary who became a counselor to ecclesiastical and secular leaders. He composed works of theology and spirituality that inspired many. He explains,
> There are three trees of life. The first is that material tree that God made from the earth in the beginning when He planted it in the middle of paradise. Adam was expelled from paradise so that after his sin he could not touch its fruit. The second is the Lord Jesus Christ who, by taking on human form, was "planted" in the middle of his church, just as the tree of life was planted in the middle of paradise. Whoever has worthily eaten of his fruit will live forever. The third tree is the tree of life that is planted in the invisible paradise, and that is the wisdom of God. Its fruit is the food of the blessed angels . . . There are three paradises. One is earthly, and its inhabitant was the earthly Adam. The second is spiritual. It is the church of the saints which the celestial Adam founded . . . The third is the celestial paradise, which is the kingdom of God, eternal life, and the land of those who truly live. God dwells in this paradise . . . Now let us proceed to draw a comparison. Most assuredly that tree of life which was in the earthly paradise could support the life of the body without any difficulty. But the tree of life in the spiritual paradise—that is, the Lord Jesus Christ—promises eternal life to those who eat his flesh and drink his blood. The third tree of life not only restores one's original well-being, but adds to it greater strength. It not only repairs what had perished, but adds what had been lacking.[254]

Hugh of St. Victor (1096–1141) was a philosopher and theologian who served as head of the monastery of St. Victor in Paris. He wrote on the immensity, multiplicity, magnitude, and beauty of the creation as a way of coming to know and appreciate the glory of God.
> Diligently hear and consider the things that I am going to say. What kind of power (*potentia*) was it that made something to be when there was nothing? What understanding (*sensus*) could comprehend what power (*virtus*) is involved in making something from nothing, even to make one thing, however tiny?[255]

He summarizes the previous ideas of creation as put forth by Augustine and others.
> Different people have offered different opinions about the creation of the world. Some say that God created the whole world from nothing and at once, (that is), at the same time and moment, both complete in all its parts and perfect in forms in exactly the same state as it is now. But others say that God created it successively over the course of six days; to the things that were at first formless God afterwards gave forms.[256]

> A question arises when it is said in this verse: *God rested from all his work*. Why is it that the Truth says in the Gospel: *My Father is working until now, and I am working*. But one must see that there are four works of God: the work of creation, the work of disposition, the work of enlargement, and the work of administration. The work of creation was what was done in the beginning, so that what did not exist came into existence; and about this it is said: *In the beginning God created the heaven and the Earth*. The work of disposition is what was done in the six days, so that what was in existence came into a better existence; and about this it is said: *God rested on the seventh day from all his work that He had accomplished*. The work of enlargement is completed in the six ages, so that what was less becomes more; and about this it is said: *My Father is working until now*, and so on. The work of administration occurs when God maintains the enlarged existences in the good lest they fail.[257]

He then takes the position that God created the world in six days, gives reasons why that position seemed most reasonable to him, and responds to a few of the reasons Augustine gave for his position on the instantaneous creation of all things. He summarizes:
> Therefore it is clear that the world was perfected successively in six days, namely, it was first formless and afterward formed. But as to why God completed his work within a span of six days, this was already discussed above, namely, on account of the perfection of that number.[258]

In describing the works of the second day he discusses the question of how to understand the firmament. The ancients almost had to imagine it as something with solidity because they did not think that opposing forces were keeping the heavens suspended—the forces of gravity, centrifugal force, etc., standing in opposition and maintaining heavenly stability.
> There are various opinions about this firmament. Some say that the firmament is moved and driven with such a great force that within twenty-four hours it is moved from point to point, that is, from the east to the west and back again into the east. They say that all the stars are fixed in this firmament except the seven planets . . . But it seems to us that the firmament is immobile, while the whole company (*chorus*) of stars is moved.[259]

He then concludes with an observation that the six days as described by Moses focus on this creation and this temporal existence, but our hope is beyond this earthly life.
> One must note that the Jews honor the seventh day, but we honor that eighth day. Thus their feast and joy are within the number seven because only temporal goods are promised to them and they only hope for the goods of this present life, all of which extends within the number seven. But God does not promise us temporal goods but eternal goods, not the goods of this life but of the future. And thus it is demanded of us to observe not the seventh day but the eighth day, which follows right after the number seven.[260]

We often think of the Middle Ages as a time when Europe was completely Christian and gross heresies had been laid to rest. But that is not the case. In the 1100's and 1200's the Albigensian heresy sprang up in Albi of France. From what we can see from our perspective, it taught that there were two principles from which the universe developed, the good god of light (presumably Jesus) and the wicked god of darkness (the god of the Old Testament and the Devil). Material reality and our bodies were evil and the soul must escape from this realm. Thus there was no resurrection. Salvation came by being spiritual and good enough. Otherwise a person was reincarnated again, perhaps as an animal and perhaps as another human. The Albigensians attracted people by their great asceticism and condemned the institutional Church as too wealthy and as corrupt.

The Fourth Council of the Lateran, called "The Great Council," which convened about AD 1215, issued this statement of belief, perhaps in response to the Albigenses.
> We firmly believe and simply confess that there is only one true God, eternal and immeasurable, almighty, unchangeable, incomprehensible, and ineffable, Father, Son and holy Spirit, three persons but one absolutely simple essence, substance, or nature. The Father is from none, the Son from the Father alone, and the holy Spirit from both equally, eternally without beginning or end; the Father generating, the Son being born, and the holy Spirit proceeding; consubstantial and coequal, co-omnipotent and coeternal; one principle of all things, creator of all things invisible and visible, spiritual and corporeal; who by his almighty power at the beginning of time created from nothing both spiritual and corporeal creatures, that is to say angelic and earthly, and then created human beings composed as it were of both spirit and body in common. The devil and other demons were created by God naturally good, but they became evil by their own doing. Man, however, sinned at the prompting of the devil.

The phrases "one principle of all things, creator of all things invisible and visible, spiritual and corporeal; who by his almighty power at the beginning of time created from nothing both spiritual and corporeal creatures, that is to say angelic and earthly, and then created human beings composed as it were of both spirit and body in common" were perhaps the only conciliar statement about creation (other than the condemnation of "Origenism") that ever was issued against a heresy. This is because throughout the history of the Church, no matter what other errors arose, every Christian maintained the core beliefs about creation. This is what our survey about the creation is revealing.

The phrase "at the beginning of time" was understood by many of the ancients to mean "instantaneously, at that first indivisible moment of time." Thus this was asserting that God created instantaneously, as all of the Fathers had said.

Peter Lombard (c. 1096-1160) was commended to Bernard of Clairvaux in Paris in 1136. He studied there, became a "celebrated theologian," and was appointed Bishop of Paris in 1159. He composed his master work *The Sentences*, which were commented on by many Scholastics for centuries to come. He was known as the Master of the Sentences. He explains why he wrote them, because he found himself in the midst of a spiritual battle. Probably the Albigenses as described above were a part of what concerned him. Peter Lombard frequently quoted the earlier Fathers as a signpost of the orthodox way.

> Desiring to contribute something out of our poverty and indigence along with the poor woman into the Lord's treasury, to scale the heights, we have presumed to perform a work that is beyond our strength.[261]

> Burning for this, to fortify "our faith against the errors of carnal and natural men" [Augustine, *De Trinitate*, 3, pref.] with the shield of the tower of David . . . we likewise are eager to hand on the knowledge of the Church's mysteries according to our own understanding.[262]

As Peter observed the confusion that surrounded the faith He quoted Hilary of Poitiers.

> Yet we do not doubt "that every utterance of human speech has always been exposed to the danger of calumny and contradiction by the envious. For when the sentiments of the will do not agree, the ideas of the mind are also lacking in agreement, so that even though every statement perfectly conforms to the standard of truth, still . . . the error of impiety struggles against the truth which it either does not understand or with which it is dissatisfied, and the envy of the will results. How *the God of this age is at work in the sons of disobedience* [Ephesians 2:2], who do not subject their will to reason and who have no eagerness for learning, but rather seek to adapt the words of truth to those things which they idly imagine: they chase after the system not of what is true, but what pleases them [Hillary of Poitiers, *De Trinitate*, 10.1–2]."[263]

And he consciously took comfort and guidance in the understanding of the Fathers.

> And so, to overthrow their assembly, which is also hateful to God, and to shut their mouths lest this virus of wickedness be able to contaminate others, and wishing to place the light of truth on a lampstand, with God's help and with much labor we have compiled this volume, divided into four books, from testimonies of the truth that have been established forever. In this book you will find the examples and teaching of our forefathers; in it, through a sincere profession of our Lord's faith . . . wherever our voice sounds forth even a little, it will not depart from the boundaries set by our fathers.[264]

How is God known or recognized through the creation?

> For, just as Ambrose says, "so that God, who is invisible by nature, could be known even by visible things, He performed a work which has manifested the craftsman by its visibility, so that what is unsure could be known by what is sure, and He might be believed to be God of all things who did what was impossible for man to do."[265]

Thus the creation is a work that only God could do and that reflects to us His nature. He then quotes Augustine.

> For as Augustine says in the book *On the City of God*, "The greatest philosophers saw that no body was God, and therefore, seeking God, they rose beyond all material things. They also saw that whatever is changeable is not the most high God and the principle of all things, and therefore they transcended every soul and changeable spirit. Then they perceived that whatever is changeable

can only derive from what exists unchangeably and simply. Therefore they understood both that he had made all of these things, and that he could have been made by no one" [Augustine, *De Civitate Dei*, 8, 6].[266]

When Peter Lombard wrote his *Sentences* he could not have imagined that they would "become the standard work for the training of theologians for many centuries to come . . . [nor could he have foreseen] the monopoly which the *Sentences* would enjoy in the professional training of theologians in medieval and early modern universities."[267] Almost every medieval theologian of note wrote a commentary on the *Sentences*.[268] Because of the enormous and lasting impact of this work, and because it consciously incorporates the thoughts of many Fathers who went before, I am listing a number of its conclusions.

Peter Lombard begins his second volume of *Sentences* with a lengthy exposition on the angels. Although this is not the subject of the creation account in Genesis, it still forms an excellent supplement by giving us a picture of the broader creation of God. I restate here a number of points that Peter Lombard makes about the spiritual realm because the nature of that realm, and its relationship with physical reality, is a great mystery.

1. To "create" is to make something from nothing, and to "make" is to fashion something from that which previously existed. Only God can create.
2. God created because He is good. That is why we exist.
3. If we say that human beings replace the ranks of the fallen angels, we must not understand that as implying that if they had not defected then we would not have been created. We were created in our own right by God.
4. All creatures, corporeal and spiritual, began with the creation of the world in time. [Thus he did not see the angels as having been created and as existing for some period before the creation of this world.]
5. The angels were created in the heavens, the empyrean, which is above the firmament.
6. All angels were created from the same spiritual substance, but with differences in their "fineness of essence," their "perspicacity of wisdom," and their "aptitude of choice." [This is most probably how he understands the different ranks or hierarchies of angels.]
7. The wicked angels were created as good initially, but fell by their own choice.
8. The initial state in which the angels were created was eventually perfected in the case of the good angels, who are now in full blessedness.
9. The fallen angels dwell neither in the empyrean realm nor on earth but in the cloudy atmosphere awaiting their judgment.
10. There is a hierarchy of rule among the fallen angels, just as among the good angels.
11. All bodies, created by God initially, as they come forth visibly, take their forms according to seeds that the creator assigned to them. By virtue of the rules of their origin, embedded in these invisible seeds which are in the physical creation, each body assumes its proper size and form. Angels have bodies which are subtle enough to know of these invisible seeds, and the evil angels use this knowledge to magnify their power before us and to deceive us.
12. Some hold that all angels have bodies, but the bodies of the fallen angels were changed for the worse when they fell. Others hold that they assume a body in order to perform a task and then set it aside when the task is completed.
13. God certainly appeared to men in bodily form in the past.
14. God has never appeared to mortals in the form by which He is God.[269]

Here are a few points from Peter Lombard's views on the six days:
1. God created the physical realm as explained in the Genesis account. The initial creation was before any day, and the work of formation followed. The works of formation were not enacted simultaneously (all at the same instant) as held by some Fathers, but at intervals of time over the course of six days.
2. The view that the works of formation were spread over six days was the view of most Fathers and seems to accord more with the Scripture in Genesis.
3. The chaotic and confused material realm was called "earth" and "water." "Heaven" he takes to be the angelic nature.
4. "Darkness" is not something proper, but is the absence of light.

5. The "light" that God made could have been both spiritual and material, but it probably refers to a kind of material light and was not another creation from nothing.
6. "Day" in Scripture is understood in different ways, but the "day" where it says in Scripture: *And it became evening and morning, the first day*, is to be understood as twenty-four hours. Thus evening was made first, then day, and that completed twenty-four hours, a natural day.
7. The statement "God said" is not to be taken as if God spoke in time nor by a sound, but rather in His Word through Whom He made all things. Thus He spoke outside of time, in eternity, but the forming of all things happened in time.
8. The entire creation is the cooperative work of the Trinity, of all three persons together.
9. There is confusion about the nature of the firmament. What is its shape? Is it fixed? If so, then how do the stars move in a circle? If it moves, why is it called a firmament? [These confusing matters are the direct result of the inadequate cosmology of the ancients, as we have noted.][270]

In speaking of the creation of man Peter Lombard says:
1. The expression *Let us make man in our image and likeness* indicates the plurality of persons speaking and the unity of their substance.
2. After a lengthy discussion of the various opinions, he asserts that men and women were created in the image and likeness of God in respect to their mind by which they excel irrational creatures. In His image, according to memory, intelligence and love; in His likeness, according to innocence and justice. [From this it seems to me that man still retains the image of God but lost his likeness to Him in the fall.]
3. *God formed man from the mud of the ground* refers to the making of our body. *God breathed in His face the breath of life* refers to the creation of the soul. God did not do this by using hands to form or by using cheeks to blow, for God is spirit and is not composed of limbs.
4. The breath from which God made the soul of Adam was not from His own substance but was from nothing.
5. However God created the soul of Adam, He creates our souls in the body, for he creates them by infusing them and at the same time that He infuses them.
6. Adam was made fully mature.
7. Paradise was on this earth, a corporeal place, planted during the third day when God commanded the vegetation to sprout. But it was also a spiritual state.
8. The tree of life and the tree of the knowledge of good and evil were in Paradise, and the second was also created good. It received its name because it was the matter of the temptation.
9. Eve derived her body from Adam—a testimony to the unity of human nature—but not her soul.
10. The Catholic Church asserts that souls are not made simultaneously, or from one another, but they are created when they are infused into bodies. Thus they did not exist from the beginning among other intellectual natures, were not created all at once, and are not inseminated with the body through coition, but are created individually by God from nothing.
11. The state of man as regards death: He was mortal and immortal in his body before the fall, for he had the power to die and also the power to not die; he was mortal and dead after the fall, for he had the power to die but not the power to not die; he will be immortal and unable to die in the resurrection, for he will have the power to not die and no power to die.
12. Sex was designed by God, from the beginning, as His way to make more human beings, but it became a matter of lust and was thus polluted after the fall.
13. If we had not sinned we would have been taken eventually into God's presence in heaven without dying.[271]

This is a summary of the foundational text for instruction in advanced theology that was in use throughout the Church for over seven centuries. **Why did we ever stop using it?**

Robert Grosseteste (c. 1175-1253) was a British intellectual and an Oxford scholar who wrote a commentary on the six days. He refers liberally to the writings and opinions of those who went before him and is careful to explain Augustine's position throughout, as well as the more common position that the creation happened over a period of six days of time as we experience it. His approach is to give the literal interpretation of the text of Genesis and then to follow up with an allegorical and a moral interpretation. Here are a few of his thoughts.

Over the deep . . . was darkness, since there was yet no light to light up their darkness. And the spirit, that is, the good will of the Lord, stirred over these waters, in order to draw them out into visible forms. And for this to come to be, God, by his first word, made physical light from these waters, giving light to the darkness of the waters that we have mentioned, as far as [that is, all the way down to] the earth. And he divided up the period of a day, that is, twenty-four hours of the equinox [he asserts that the creation happened in the Jewish month Nisan, at the vernal equinox] in such way that for half of the day the earth where people dwell should have light, while for the other half the light should be put beneath it, and made day and night; which, taken together, form one day of nature.[272]

We could ask Jerome, Bede and Basil and those who follow them, whether the light came to be in an instant; and likewise, whether the firmament was made all at once, and whether the same is true of the gathering of the waters in one place, and the drawing out from the earth of things that grow in the earth . . . [was it] the whole day in which each of the works was performed, or a lesser time? And I think that to this question these authorities would answer that the light which made the first three days was made in an instant, all at once. When this was done the period of the first day had its beginning, and there was no moment of that day that was prior to the perfection of that light. They would also reply that the sun was made all at once, that is to say, at the first instant of the fourth day. That instant was the beginning of the fourth day and the end of the third day. The sun was not either perfect or begun at any moment on the third day, but it nevertheless was perfect in carrying out its movement for the whole period of the fourth day. This is clear from the details of the text.[273]

The translation of the Seventy has it as follows: "Let the earth bring forth the herb of food, such as may seed according to its kind and likeness; and fruit bearing trees that bear fruit, whose own seed is in it itself according to its kind upon the earth." As one may gather from Basil, by these words is indicated the order of the production of an herb to its completion. This order existed naturally in the establishment of the first plants only if they arose all at once and not successively. Nowadays this occurs successively, through moments of time.[274]

According to those who say that the first three days were days of time, we have to distinguish two senses of "time." In the one way "time" means the extent of duration that passes from future expectation, through the present, to the past. This must necessarily have existed even when there were no stars, provided that some change, either in bodies or in spirits, preceded the establishment of the luminaries. [This refers to the idea, from Aristotle, that time is associated with motion or change in something.] But "times" also means, as Augustine says, the times "that come to be through the stars: not only the extent of duration, but the interweaving of affections in this heaven." These times—i.e., the measurements that are distinct and determinate and which mark out durations—were first made by the stars as they ran in their ordered motions.[275]

But when the human being by sin abandoned and threw off its obedience towards God, it was just for the natural ordering that was subject to the human being to feel a rebellion against it through that disobedience. Through this justice the flesh came to rebel against the spirit, and the things outside that lack reason came to revolt against the human being. It is not that the human being lost its natural power of dominion, i.e., the power of reason to command. But this power was weakened and vitiated by sin, and so irrational things, at the fall of the human being, were made worse and less able to obey the command of reason.[276]

There follows: "And God rested on the seventh day from all his work which he had done." . . . God did not establish any new species or nature after the six days. Hence on the seventh day he rested and ceased from establishing new species or natures. But He did not cease from conserving and fostering and governing the natures or species he had made . . . In *Genesis* . . . it is very clearly stated that God finished all his works. What is written there, that he rested, is to be understood as meaning that he rested from the creation of new creatures, not from governing them.[277]

Thus Robert explains the thinking of the earlier Fathers while he gives his own interpretation of the six days of creation as well.

Bonaventure (1221-1274), a luminary in the Franciscan movement and one of the leading scholars in the history of Roman Catholicism wrote this on the creation:

> Now that we have presented a summary review of the Trinity of God, we need to say a few things about the creation of the world. Concisely put, we should maintain the following belief concerning this: namely, that the entire world machine was brought into existence in time and from nothing by one First Principle, unique and supreme, whose power, though immeasurable, has arranged all things in measure, number, and weight.[278]

> We must now consider corporeal nature with relation to its production, its being, and its operation. With regard to its production, we must hold specifically that physical nature was brought into existence over the course of six days in the following manner. In the beginning, before any day, God created heaven and earth. Then, on the first day, the light was formed; on the second, the firmament was established in the midst of the waters; on the third, the waters were separated from the land and gathered together into one place; on the fourth, the heavens were adorned with lights; on the fifth, the air and the waters were filled with birds and fishes; on the sixth, the land was furnished with animals and human beings. On the seventh day God rested, not from activity and work, since he continues to work to this very hour, but from the production of any new species. For God made all things then (during the six days of the Genesis account) – either in their prototypes, as is the case with those that propagate themselves, or in a seminal reason, as with other things that come into existence in a different way.[279]

> Now God could have done all of these things simultaneously, but preferred to accomplish them over a succession of times. First of all, this would serve as a clear and distinct manifestation of God's power, wisdom, and goodness. Secondly, there was a fitting correspondence between these operations and having various 'days' or times. Finally, the primal production of the world ought to contain the seeds of all things that would later be accomplished, as a prefiguration of future ages; thus, these seven days would contain seminally, as it were, the division of all times to come, as we have already explained above through the succession of the seven ages of history. That is why, to the six days of work was added a seventh day of rest: a day to which no dusk is ascribed (in Scripture) – not that this day was not followed by night, but because it was to prefigure the repose of souls that shall have no end. Now, if from another point of view, it is said that all things were made at once, this is simply considering the work of the seven days from the perspective of the angels. At any rate, the first manner of speaking is more in keeping with the Scripture and with the authority of the saints, both those before and after Saint Augustine.[280]

In his writings we see the move of later scholarship away from the idea of Augustine that all things were created in an instant in eternity to the belief that the scriptural description should be understood in its most natural way; that is, "six days" means simply six days.

Finally it is clear that Bonaventure considered the book of creation as a necessary logical prerequisite to our understanding of the work of restoration or redemption.

> The First Principle reveals itself to our minds through the Scriptures and through creatures. In the book of creation it manifests itself as the effective Principle, and in the book of Scripture as the restorative Principle. Now, the restorative Principle cannot be known unless the effective Principle is also known. Thus it follows that Holy Scripture, even though it is concerned mainly with the works of restoration, must necessarily also deal with the works of creation, insofar as they lead to the knowledge of the first effective and recreating Principle.[281]

Thomas Aquinas (1225-1274), in his discussion of questions *On the Power of God*, also reviews the faith of the Fathers on the six days of creation. In his philosophical defense of the faith he asserts the following, among many other additional things:

- God created all things from nothing in an instant because of His infinite power, and He continues to uphold them in existence. He explains that "to create" as stated in Genesis 1:1 means to make out of nothing. He asserts that it is contrary to or above nature for something to come out of nothing, but God is more powerful than nature and He demonstrates His superior power by making out of nothing.[282]

- In considering "whether matter was created all at once or by degrees" Aquinas notes that Augustine asserts that the six days of creation are not days as such but were a six-fold manifestation of the creation to the angelic mind, as we have explained, and that the actual creation was an instantaneous event where all things were made together, either in their actual perfect existence or in their first causes.

Aquinas states that according to other holy men these days denote order of time and succession in the production of things. Thus in their opinion there was order not only of nature but also of time and duration in the works of the six days. Thus the other Fathers assert that the works of the six days were produced not simultaneously but by degrees. This was not because of a lack of power on the part of God, but was directed to a manifestation of His wisdom in the production of all things because He first conferred on all things an imperfect being and afterwards perfected them. Thus the world was brought by stages from nothingness to ultimate perfection in six days. The account of the creation shows that all things derived their being from God and that He is the Author of their perfection.

In either case the various creative decrees of God were all enacted instantaneously.

Aquinas notes that Augustine's explanation is more subtle and is a better defense of the Scripture against the ridicule of unbelievers; but the second, which is maintained by the other saints, is easier to grasp and more in keeping with the surface meaning of the text. Aquinas asserts that neither approach is contrary to the faith.[283]

Roger Bacon (c. 1219-c. 1292) was one of the early scientists. He discusses natural and moral philosophy and explains the proper uses of mathematics and astronomy in the area of sacred things. One important application is in the determination of the proper chronology of the world from its creation—that is, from Adam—through the Deluge and to Christ. In view of the divergent dates that had been calculated, precision could only be achieved by correcting and coordinating the various calendars via mathematics and astronomy. He wrote his greatest work, *Opus Majus*, at the request of Pope Clement IV.

> For the whole course of history is traced through times and generations and ages from the beginning of the world to Christ the Lord, and all things have been set in order on his account, that no other legislator might be expected, but that he alone may be the savior of the world by his own law; that the error of the Jews regarding their expectation of the Messiah may be removed; likewise the error of the Saracens regarding Mahomet, who followed Christ . . . [Also the error of many others who have made spurious claims. He then speaks of the various calendars and the widely varying ways that they function and the need to coordinate them all to fit the Latin calendar and the dates that we have regarding the arrival of Christ] . . . Since, therefore, there are contained in scripture years lunar and years solar as well as those of the Greeks and Latins and the like, and we wish to reduce all the calendars to solar years and to the years of the Latins, which are the years of Christ, it is necessary for us in sacred history to know the differences of these calendars, and also to know what is peculiar to each and how they may be equalized, and how we can draw the greater from the less and the converse, and extract any information desired from anyone of them. But this cannot be done, as Scripture requires, except by means of canons, tables, and other astronomical means. But years are computed from the beginning of the world, according to the Hebrew and according to the translation of the Seventy; but they disagree internally, and all authors of history and chronicles and sacred writers in this matter contradict one another in turn, not only in the matter of the whole time from the beginning to Christ, but also in regard to particular ages. But this diversity cannot be cleared away except through a sure source. No science can in this matter discover nor has it the ability to ponder on the means of settling such an important question except astronomy.[284]

Thus it is clear that the medieval scholars were convinced that the genealogies of Genesis were the key to setting the precise chronology of the world, and that the various calendrical systems had to be synchronized in order to clear up the discrepancies that historians had encountered in their chronological calculations. We can see, from the different years and dates calculated by the ancients, the divergent results to which Roger Bacon is referring.

The task of computing accurately the exact date of the creation was considered to be a very important and worthy pursuit. Many attempted it, as we have seen. Every scholar knew that the genealogies of Genesis provided us with the basic means for determining the date of the creation, but there were two Scriptures: the LXX and the Masoretic text. Once one accepted that the Masoretic text was the authoritative text for Genesis and its genealogies were to be used then it became vital for the clear time frame of the Bible to be connected to a past event of secular history. Then the chronology of the whole world, both our times and the ancient ages that predated secular history, could be determined.

Dating time from the creation was common for various bodies of believers. The Greek Orthodox recognized the Byzantine Calendar and took the creation date to be 5501 BC. The Jewish people took 3761 BC as the date of the creation. These are still used today by each of these religious groups. The secular event that the biblical genealogy was tied to could be the time of the construction of the temple of King Solomon, for example, for this was 480 years after the Exodus (1 Kings 6:1), and the genealogies from the creation to when Jacob entered Egypt were in Genesis. Most people believed that the Jews were in Egypt for either 215 years or for 430 years. Thus if the date of the construction of the temple of King Solomon could be determined by secular history then current and ancient times could be joined to form a complete chronology of the world starting from creation. Scholars continued to work on this problem until at least into the 1600's.[285] [see note]

Gregory of Palamas (1296-1359) was a great luminary and teacher in the Orthodox Church. He wrote a major treatise called *The Fifty Chapters* which detailed his views on natural and theological science. We will consider his explanation of how human beings come to "understand" or "know," and the limitations that must attend our knowledge. Gregory briefly reviews the speculations of the Greek philosophers that were reviving in his day. These speculations, and all knowledge that might be derived from them, must always partake of the limitations inherent in our human nature. First Gregory observes that the senses gather data for us about the physical world. Then he continues:

> The imaginative faculty of the soul, which in turn appropriates these sense impressions from the senses, completely separates not the senses themselves but what we have called the images in them from the bodies and their forms. And it holds them stored there like treasures, bringing them forward interiorly for it use, one after another, each in its own time . . . This imaginative faculty of the soul in the rational animal constitutes an intermediary between the mind and the senses. For when the mind beholds and dwells upon the images received within itself from the senses as separated from bodies and already incorporeal, it formulates thoughts in various ways by distinctions, analyses, and syntheses. This happens in different ways: with and without passion and somewhere between passion and *apatheia*, both with and without error. And these are the situations from which are born most virtues and vices, as well as both good and evil opinions . . . It is a great wonder and worthy of consideration, how beauty or ugliness, wealth or poverty, honour or dishonour, and, in a word, either the intelligible light that grants eternal life or the intelligible darkness of chastisement becomes fixed in the soul through transitory and sensible things.[286]

So all knowledge from the philosophers partakes of the limitations of our humanity. Our data is limited, and our interpretation of that data has a "spin" placed on it that derives from the predispositions and prejudices of each person.

Gregory then poses the crucial question that must follow on these considerations and immediately gives the answer, showing the vital and precious nature of divine revelation.

> Where can we learn anything certain and free from deceit about God, about the world as a whole, about our own selves? Is it not from the teaching of the Spirit? For this teaching has taught us that God alone is true being, eternal being and immutable being, that he neither received being out of non-being nor returns to non-being, and that He is trihypostatic and omnipotent. In six days he brought forth beings from non-being by a word, or rather as Moses says, he established everything at once, for we heard him say, "In the beginning God created heaven and earth"; not absolutely void nor without any intermediary bodies at all, for the earth was mixed with water and each was pregnant with air, and with plants and animals according to their species, while the heaven was pregnant with the various lights and fires in which he established the universe. In this way then God created heaven and earth in the beginning as a sort of all-containing receptacle of matter, bearing all things in potency. Thereby, he rightly drives off those who wrongly hold that matter preexisted of itself.[287]

In his *Homilies* Gregory explains his thinking again so that we can understand clearly.

> So then "In the beginning God created heaven and earth", as matter able to endure anything and strong enough to bear everything, rightly thereby dealing a blow from a distance to those who falsely hold that matter existed independently beforehand. Then He developed and embellished it. In six days He assigned to each of His creatures which made up His world its own due order.[288]

Thus the primordial matter that God willed into existence had latent within it the potential to be formed into the various structures that God planned to exist in His world. This is what he meant by the phrases "pregnant with" and "an all-containing receptacle." The primordial matter was also suitable for what God was going to build from it and was strong enough to endure under the demands that would be placed upon it. Gregory continues to the creation of man, explaining our unique place in this marvelous world that God has made.

> At the creation first one thing was brought into existence, then another, and so on in turn. Last of all came man (Gen. 1:26), who was worthy of God's greater honour and consideration both before and after his creation. All the visible world was made before him for his sake . . . A divine Counsel concerning him preceded him, and he was created by God's hand and in His image. He did not take his whole being from matter or from the visible world, like other living creatures did, but only his body. His soul he took from the heavenly realms, from God Himself when He breathed life into him in a way that defies description (Gen. 2:7). Man was a great wonder surpassing all else, towering above everything, superior to all. Man was capable of knowing God, as well as receiving Him and declaring Him, and was most certainly the highest achievement of the Creator's sublime majesty. He had paradise for his home, specially planted by God (Gen. 2:8ff). There it was his lot to have sight of God, speak to Him face-to-face, and receive a council and commandment from Him concerning the fasting appropriate to that place (Gen. 2:16–17) [Fasting: That is, do not eat from one tree].[289]

As the centuries wore on the unwavering faith in the truth of Genesis remained and men formulated substantial and varied theories upon that faith: the nature of God, the nature of man, the nature of this world, etc. Many brilliant and holy men wrote in defense of the Ancient Faith as it was assaulted from diverse speculative platforms. Many times they returned to Genesis and the creation account to lay the foundation for their defense.

One Perspective from Judaism:

It is beyond the scope of this work to consider in any detail the beliefs of the Jewish holy men of ancient times, but it is certainly the assertion of Christians through the ages that our faith is an outgrowth of Judaism and that it is a proper development upon the faith of ancient Israel. Therefore I quote from the writings of Saadia ben Joseph Goah, a tenth-century Egyptian-born scholar and founder of Hebrew linguistics and theology. It gives us a taste of his thinking. In preparing to investigate the creation of all things he says:

> This treatise starts out with the preliminary observation that whoever ventures into it is seeking light on something that has never been beheld with human eyes nor has been perceived by the senses, but which he is nevertheless anxious to ascertain by rational deduction. The problem I have reference to is: "How did all things come into being in our time?" Now the principle object of his investigation is something so subtle and fine that the senses are unable to grasp it. He therefore endeavors to attain it intellectually . . . When, then, we reach the conclusion that all things were created out of nothing, although our senses have never experienced anything like it, it is not meet for us to reject that conclusion or to say frivolously: "How can we acquiesce in anything like that of which we have never seen?" For our investigation was from the very start of such a nature as to yield for us something the like of which we have not seen.[290]
>
> And now that I have made this preliminary observation perfectly clear, I say that our Lord, exalted be He, made it known to us that all things were created and that He had created them out of nothing. Thus the scripture says: *In the beginning God created the heaven and the earth* (Genesis 1:1). It says also: *I am the Lord, that maketh all things; that stretched forth the heavens alone; that spreadeth abroad the earth by Myself* (Isaiah 44:24).[291]
>
> Or perhaps some thoughtful person will think to himself and ask: "How can something be derived from nothing?" Our answer is that if mortal creatures had been in a position to conceive of how such a thing could come about, it would not have been necessary for our reason to attribute it exclusively to the eternal Creator, since each one of us would have been able to comprehend something of this nature. However, our reason has decided to ascribe this act exclusively to the Creator, precisely because there is no way whereby a mere creature could conceive of how such an event could have taken place . . . Now perhaps someone will say: "How can it be acceptable to reason that the world has been in existence only 4693 years?" We reply thereunto that since we acknowledge that the world has been created, it must have had a beginning. Dost thou not see, even if we mortal creatures had been living in the hundredth year of creation, would we have been astonished at that fact or denied it? All the less can we deny it at this age in which we live.[292]

The author does not go into a detailed commentary on Genesis, but these preliminary remarks and thoughts are remarkably similar to those of the early Fathers, especially in their remarks about the "six days of awe" which cannot be understood by any man, and in his clear belief that the genealogies of Genesis tell us when the world was made.

In the quotations that I have given I have reported on the thoughts and attitudes of every Christian thinker that I could find in the first 1400 years of Christianity. In these quotations I have neither omitted anything nor slanted their beliefs. Although their surely must be many more ancient writers who expressed their views on Genesis and the origin of the world, these must give us a full, fair, and reasonable picture of the Ancient Faith—the faith that came from Jesus and the Apostles, and the faith that the Holy Spirit continued to inspire in the hearts and minds of holy men and women throughout the centuries.

Opposite Quotations from the Fathers:
I have sometimes run across quotes taken from works of the Fathers that are asserted to uphold an interpretation of Genesis that might be made to go along with certain current theories about the origin of man or the universe. Now I want to respond to several such quotes. They seem to imply that some of the Fathers of the Church, usually Augustine or Origen, agreed in principle with modern theories of origins, or at least could reasonably be interpreted to agree with them. Here are some examples.

From Augustine:
> There is knowledge to be had, after all, about the earth, about the sky, about the other elements of this world, about the movements and revolutions or even the magnitude and distances of the constellations, about the predictable eclipses of moon and sun, about the cycles of years and seasons, about the nature of animals, fruits, stones and everything else of this kind. And it

> frequently happens that even non-Christians will have knowledge of this sort in a way that they can substantiate with scientific arguments or experiments. Now it is quite disgraceful and disastrous, something to be on one's guard against at all costs, that they should ever hear Christians spouting what they claim our Christian literature has to say on these topics, and talking such nonsense that they can scarcely contain their laughter when they see them to be *toto caelo* [by the total extent of the heavens], as the saying goes, wide of the mark.[293]

This warning by Augustine about not asserting things that we think the Bible says, but that it does not say, because we are ignorant about our own books or because we have a distorted or mistaken understanding of them, has been quoted by some to quiet any who assert the truth of the Bible even in the face of modern theories of origins, which claim to be fully scientific and true. This passage, when quoted today, has a powerful effect on people because of the enormous respect that we have been taught to place in these theories.

Certainly science and scientific knowledge has grown in the past few centuries, giving us medical cures, technological advances, and many other engineering marvels that have transformed our lives. This inevitably lends great weight to any assertion that claims to be "scientifically" derived and proven. Therefore in our day this quotation has the effect of quelling any Christian voice that might raise itself to contradict these "scientific" theories.

Augustine then goes on and states his approach to understanding Genesis, in view of this situation that can be a scandal to the faithful and an occasion for the mocking and derision of Christians by unbelievers. We must understand, as we talk of these things, that there have always been and there will always be some unbelievers who mock Christians and Christian beliefs. This hurts, but we must bear it patiently. So Augustine then continues by explaining his approach to interpreting Genesis:

> It is in order to take account of this state of things that I have, to the best of my ability, winkled out and presented a great variety of possible meanings to the words of the book of Genesis which have been darkly expressed in order to put us through our paces. I have avoided affirming anything hastily in a way that would rule out any alternative explanation that may be a better one, so leaving everyone free to choose whichever they can grasp most readily in their turn, and when they cannot understand, let them give honor to God's scripture, keeping fear for themselves.[294]

This certainly makes it sound as if Christians should proceed only with care and timidity if we claim anything to be true on the basis of our Scriptures. This quotation, when taken by itself, tends to lessen our confidence in the reliability of Scripture as a whole, enhances our fear of and respect for scientific theories, and makes us reluctant to assert anything on the basis of the book Genesis.

But Augustine asserts the following things in his works, as we have seen:
> The Lord God willed this entire world into existence. It had a supernatural origin, not an origin from itself.
> There was a worldwide universal Flood that destroyed all of mankind except for those in the ark with Noah.
> The earth was less than 6,000 years old in his day.
> The early patriarchal ages were over 900 years, as Genesis asserts.

He says these things in direct argument with and contradiction to the contrary claims of many secular thinkers of his day. He makes these claims because he believes in the absolute accuracy of the Scriptures, and he believes this because they were inspired by God Who cannot lie or be mistaken. Thus we must use that first quotation most carefully, for it might have the effect of reducing Christian faith to being dependent on the theories of men rather than on the Word of God. When the above quotation is given it would also be equitable and fair to include these words of Augustine that follow it.

> Some of the weaker brothers and sisters, however, are in danger of going astray more seriously when they hear these godless people holding forth expertly and fluently on the "music of the spheres," or on any questions you care to mention about the elements of this cosmos. They wilt and lose heart, putting these pundits before themselves, and while regarding them as great authorities, they turn back with a weary distaste to the books of salutary godliness, and can scarcely bring themselves to touch the volumes they should be devouring with delight–shrinking from the roughness of the husks of the wheat and eagerly eyeing the flowers of the thistles. After all, they have no time to *be still* (Ps 46: 11), and to *see how sweet is the Lord* (Ps 34:8), nor are they *hungry on the sabbath* (Mt 12: 1); and that is why they are too lazy to use the authority they have received from the Lord to pluck the ears of wheat and go on rubbing them in their hands until they come to what they can eat.[295]

By "plucking the ears of wheat" and "rubbing them . . . until they come to something they can eat" Augustine is referring to making the effort to dig into the Bible and to find out the deep and nourishing truths in it that await the diligent student. These truths must be clearly and forcibly proclaimed to men, for they are our faith. It is only the foolish and thoughtless assertions of the unlearned that must not be put forth as biblical truth.

Then Augustine continues:
> Someone is going to say, "What about you, with all this rubbing of corn in this essay, how much grain have you extracted? What have you winnowed? Why is practically everything hidden still in a heap of questions? Affirm some of the many meanings you have argued can be understood."
>
> To which I reply that I have happily reached this very food: namely that I have learned that we should not hesitate to give the answers that have to be given, in line with the faith, to people who make every effort to discredit the books our salvation depends on. So we should show that whatever they have been able to demonstrate from reliable sources about the world of nature is not contrary to our literature, while whatever they may have produced from any of their volumes that is contrary to this literature of ours, that is, to the Catholic faith, we must either show with some ease, or else believe without any hesitation, to be entirely false. And we should so hold onto our mediator, *in whom are stored up all the treasures of wisdom and of knowledge* (Col 2:3), that we are neither seduced by the chatter of false philosophy, nor frightened out of our wits by the superstitions of false religion.[296]

Is this not a much more balanced approach to the study of our Scriptures? Does it not affirm their absolute accuracy and reliability? The first quotation, given without context, has the very effect that Augustine warned against: It causes believers to "wilt and lose heart."

Brothers and sisters do not be conformed to this age but be transformed by the renewal of your mind! The Bible is true. The Bible is the Word of God and it is true. The Fathers did apologetics as often in their writings as they did any activity. Far from discouraging it, they kept insisting that is was vital to the faith. Apologetics was always done by using the Word of God as the foundation of all truth. The effect of causing believers to "wilt and lose heart" is that apologetics is discouraged. If that happens then how can we "give an answer for the hope that we have" (1 Peter 3:15)?

Here is another quotation from Augustine that has been lifted out and presented to readers:
> [T]he world was made with time, and this seems to hold good in the very order of the first six or seven days. For both the morning and the evening of these days are enumerated until, on the sixth day, all that God made during those days is completed, and, on the seventh day, God's rest is presented in a great mystery. But what kind of days these are it is extremely difficult, or even impossible, to conceive, let alone to put into words.[297]

Now when this quotation is given by itself it would seem that Augustine, because he is not able to describe the exact nature of the "six days of awe" that the Lord God unfolded before us, is here allowing that they might be of any nature whatsoever, and thus he is allowing for the possibility of a kind of modern "day-age" theory to explain them. But we know that Augustine asserted that the creation happened in a single instant, that it was a supernatural act of God, and that it took place less than 6,000 years before his time. This quotation is part of a larger statement that he makes in the *City* that agrees perfectly with what we have so carefully explained:

> Again, if the holy and utterly truthful Scriptures say that *in the beginning God made heaven and earth* precisely to make us understand that nothing whatsoever was made prior to this (for if God had made something prior to everything else that he made, that is what Scripture would have said that he made in the beginning), it is beyond doubt that the world was not made in time but with time. For what happens in time happens both after some time and before some time, after the time that has passed and before the time that is to come. But there could not have been any time that had passed, because there was no created being to provide the change and motion of which time is a function. Thus, if change and movement were created when the world was made, the world was made with time, and this seems to hold good in the very order of the first six or seven days. For both the morning and the evening of these days are enumerated until, on the sixth day, all that God made during those days is completed, and, on the seventh day, God's rest is presented in a great mystery. But what kind of days these are it is extremely difficult, or even impossible, to conceive, let alone to put into words.[298]

Thus Augustine asserts again the absolute truthfulness and reliability of the Scriptures and then notes, as is his understanding from Aristotle, that time does not pass unless there is motion, and motion cannot exist before there is something to move, and thus time began when God called forth the world from nothing, as it says, *In the beginning God made heaven and earth*. Of course the six days are of a mysterious nature, for he cannot imagine how things passed during those days any more than we can. But that does not imply that they can be extended to long periods of time. Such thinking utterly opposes the thoughts of Augustine, of the Fathers, and of all Christian thinkers through all the past ages of the Church.

Augustine continues in his *City*:
> We note, of course, that the days known to us have evenings and mornings only because of the setting and rising of the sun; but those first three days passed without the sun, which was made, we are told, on the fourth day. Scripture narrates that, at the first, light was made by the Word of God, and that "God separated the light from the darkness and called the light day and the darkness night." But what kind of light it was, and by what alternating motion it made evening and morning, and what sort of evening and morning these were, are all things far removed from our senses. Nor is it possible for us to understand how it was so, but we must still believe it without the least hesitation.[299]

Augustine says this because, as we have noted, he asserts both that all things were made together simultaneously, and because they were made in six days. This truly is a great mystery, as he asserts, and as we all can agree. But long periods of time cannot be imputed to those six days. If there are things in the creation account that we cannot come to understand, then we still must believe them without hesitation. The Fathers all asserted the absolute truthfulness of the Scriptures and used them as the basis for their rebuttal of aberrant ideas and points of view. Such rebuttals were called "apologetics."

From Origen:
> For who that has understanding will suppose that the first, and second, and third day, and the evening and the morning, existed without a sun, and moon, and stars? and that the first day was, as it were, also without a sky? And who is so foolish as to suppose that God, after the manner of a husbandman, planted a Paradise in Eden, towards the east, and placed in it a tree of life, visible and palpable, so that one tasting of the fruit by the bodily teeth obtained life? and again, that one was a partaker of good and evil by masticating what was taken from the tree? And if God is said to walk in the Paradise in the evening, and Adam to hide himself under a tree, I do not suppose that any one doubts that these things figuratively indicate certain mysteries, the history having taken place in appearance, and not literally.[300]

One who reads this quotation might imagine, from our perspective today, that Origen held to a view of Genesis that allows for the first three days to be interpreted as long periods of time. But we saw clearly that such was not the case and that, whatever his unknown view on the first three days was, and whatever allegorical interpretation he had for them, it certainly did not involve long periods of time. He took them in a way that preserved the chronology but that saw the events as partially shrouded in the words of Genesis—events that took only a short time to enact, but whose true nature was in some manner hidden by but indicated in those words. We know he thought the firmament was made on the second day, and that the dry land separated from the waters and that vegetation sprouted on the third day.

Didymus, influenced by Origen, said that the first three days, although they passed without the heavenly lights, still exhibited the same duration of seventy-two hours. Augustine was familiar with Origen, surely read his *Commentary on Genesis,* and said that the days were mysterious because they must have had some different and unimaginable progression from day to night. So perhaps Origen's idea was that the progression of day and night was not that of an ordinary day, as Augustine said. Because his works are not fully preserved we cannot know what his understanding was—only that it was not long periods of time. As we noted about the details of his thinking on the creation of man and woman in Genesis chapter 2, it was probably not very far from the words of the text, as inferred from his other quotations referring to those accounts.

In all of my readings I have run across only one thought that is rightly considered as being ***possibly*** in conformity with modern theories of origins, and I share that with you now.

> It is well known that man has some things in common with the inanimate creatures, and shares life with the plant and animal creation, while partaking intelligence with all in common with all beings endowed with reason. With inanimate things he shares a material body mingled of the four elements. With plants he shares not only this but also the faculties of nutriment and generation. With irrational animals he shares all these things, and, in addition, a range of voluntary movements, together with the faculties of appetite, anger, feeling, and respiration. All these things man and the irrational animals have in common, if not everywhere on equal terms. Finally, by being rational, man shares with the incorporeal rational intelligences the prerogative of applying, to whatever he will, reason, understanding, and judgment . . . It follows from these considerations that man's being is on the boundary between the intelligible order and the phenomenal order. . . We may see herein the best proof that the whole universe is the creation of one God. For not only has He united all particular things in making them members of one order of reality, but he has made them fit together each to each . . . **Again, when the Creator passed in turn from the creation of plants to that of animals, we may suppose that he did not, so to say, leap from one order to the next, and suddenly make creatures endowed with the powers of locomotion and sensation. Rather, he advanced towards this end by slow degrees and seemly moderation . . . After the *pinna* [animals that are fixed to the bed of the sea, as if with roots] and such like creatures, God next made the animals with but a very limited range of movement, yet able to move themselves from one place to another. Such are most of the shell-fish, and earthworms. Next he endowed particular species with more of this or that faculty, such as sentience or locomotion, until he reached the highest types of animal. By that, I mean those animals, which possess all the senses, and are capable of unrestricted movement. And when God passed from the irrational animals to create a rational living creature, man, he did not introduce this living creature abruptly, but led up to it, by the development, in certain animals, of instinctive intelligence, of devices and clever tricks for self-preservation, which make them appear almost rational. Only after them did he bring forth man, the truly rational living creature . . .** The foregoing considerations justify the Mosaic story of creation when it makes man the last to be created. For, not only was it logical that, if all other creatures were made for his sake, they should be provided in

> advance for him to use, and that, then, he, the intended user, should be created when all was ready, but there was another reason besides. God created both an intelligible and a phenomenal order, and required some one creature to link these two together, in such a way that the entire universe should form one agreeable unity, unbroken by internal incoherences. [emphasis mine][301]

This lengthy passage by **Nemesius** uses "gradualistic" wording to expound on the order of the creation as related in Genesis, and especially to explain the overall unity of creation. It is the only instance of such thinking that I found in any ancient Christian writer; that is, thinking in which incremental changes are assumed in the creation account. As noted, Nemesius was a philosopher at heart. He explains things in accordance with his careful philosophical speculations, but not taking into account the theological or scriptural effect of the position that he is advocating. Notice that Nemesius does not say that the simple life forms are transformed into more sophisticated ones over long periods. But God does create incrementally more "advanced" life forms in successive acts of creation.

The compelling nature of this explanation comes not from his assertion that things were formed gradually, each incrementally different from its predecessor, but from his simple observation of the facts of the world around us. These observations speak eloquently of the interconnectedness of all things, the unity of creation, and the marvelous way that the diverse variety of things fit together. This is an observed fact not dependent on how the created order came to be. The observation that in this multifaceted array of things we are on the boundary between the phenomenal order and the intelligible order is also an observed fact, no matter how things were formed. The concluding observation that the Mosaic account reflects a certain logical progression is also noted by the Fathers.

The part of Nemesius' explanation that I bolded is what sounds "evolutionary." From our perspective many centuries later we might tend to see his account as claiming that the creation took eons to complete. He certainly sees the creation as a sequence of divinely-guided incremental steps, a process that by stages arrived at successively more capable and skillful life forms, and that eventually produced human beings. It might be thought of as an example of "theistic evolution," to use our terminology. But it is not at all clear that he envisioned many eons of time in his theory. He probably did not, and might even have held to a six-day-long scenario in which the creative commands, instead of being enacted all at once, were carried out quickly but incrementally. We know little about Nemesius. This one work, apparently never completed, is all that we have to go on.

Brothers and sisters, I am well aware that many want desperately to synchronize our Scriptures with the modern theories of origins, for they believe that both have to be true. Living in our culture exposes us to a constant barrage of "millions and billions of years" and of "the evolution of all things" and of "the gradual unfolding of the universe." Thus I encourage you to expose your minds to other ideas. Read material from authors who think about these things biblically.

Soon after I started this book I ran across a work by a Greek Orthodox monk that is most encouraging. The book is *Genesis, Creation, and Early Man* by Fr. Seraphim Rose. The book is very large, over 1,100 pages. But if you can, read his personal story (pages 1–88), and then the next 500 pages. It emphasizes in a firm and undeniable way the heart and mind of the Fathers. This testimony is from a man who was immersed in patristic thinking for many decades of his life.

Brothers and sisters, if you think that you must take a modern synthetic view of Genesis, please do not try to drag into your position any of the Fathers of the Church, for it is utterly unfair to them. You must decide to stand on your own if you take such a position. Here are the consequences:
1. You must deny the truth of the Scriptures.
2. You must disagree with the universal belief of all holy men and women in the first thirteen centuries and more of Christianity as to how to understand Genesis.
3. You must discard the Christian world view.
4. You must give up the foundation of much Christian theology and belief: What is the nature of man; what is the purpose and meaning of our life on this earth; what is the meaning and purpose of sexuality; what is the meaning of the fall and sin; what is the nature of the salvation that Christ earned for us as God's response to the fall; what is the nature of our final state of glory with the Lord God. All of these Christian doctrines will have to be re-thought and revised to fit into your new world view.

Instead of doing this I advocate that we all, in the midst of this dark and godless age, do the exact opposite and draw together around the Ancient Faith. At this time in history it is most important for all churches to do this. Today we all must stand with the Fathers. For the darkness of this age is very much a consequence of the repudiation of Genesis, the loss of a Christian understanding of the nature of mankind, the meaning of sex, and the purpose of human life on this earth.

In grappling with this subject we are not merely confronting a different "point of view," we are dealing with an entirely different world view. We are not merely encountering people who think differently on this subject, we are encountering an opposing spirit. This is not just the clash of ideas; it is spiritual warfare. The only reference of certain truth to which we can appeal in this struggle is the Word of God. This is—and this must be—our one and only certain source of truth. "Thy word is truth" (John 17:17).

This is a very serious matter. And it is confusing and counter-productive to present out-of-context quotations from the ancient writers in an attempt to portray them as agreeable to a certain modern viewpoint. It is a misrepresentation of the history of Christian belief. A simple truth lies at the heart of this issue: No man can serve two masters. You cannot believe in the Word of God and also in the vain philosophies of men. You cannot serve divine wisdom and the wisdom of this world and of the "great thinkers" of this age. You must choose whom you are going to follow and whom you are going to trust. So choose! Again, I advocate standing with the Fathers instead of trying to make them agree with the various modern theories that are floating around.

In this work I have made every effort to cut through all of the divergent ideas and give a completely accurate and faithful picture of the Ancient Faith of the Church toward creation. The reason I actually obtained each and every work on that list at the beginning of this chapter was so that I could see first-hand what they said and what their reasons were for their beliefs. In this way I have tried to understand the heart and mind of the ancients, not just their words. Most writers were simple and straightforward in their beliefs and thinking, but some were more challenging to understand. In the case of those authors I made the effort to read them carefully, perhaps several times if necessary, and to think about their words and ideas. The quotations that I have given are, in accord with my best efforts, a completely balanced, accurate, and faithful presentation of their thought.

In ancient times Christian thinkers had only one source of knowledge about the origin of things, and that was the Bible. In their times Christianity had rebuked and rejected all alternative philosophical notions about origins, and the one place they all went for such information was Scripture. When they approached Genesis they saw it as **the** source of knowledge about where we had come from, and as given to us by God. I know because when God showed me that the present theories are not science and are not true, then I saw the Bible in just that way. It became precious to me in a way it had never been.

In the past it was possible for men to think that the Bible was speaking figuratively about some matters of origins, depending on what they saw as "reasonable" or as "necessary from common sense," but they all saw it as the one-and-only authoritative source of wisdom on the subject of origins. Thus they interpreted it accordingly. An idea like the day-age theory was never conceived of by reading the Bible. It came about by bringing a second source of information into consideration and by trying to marry that source to the Bible. That is a modern phenomenon and cannot be found in the ancient writers.

If this study of the ancients on Genesis says anything, it testifies loudly to the profound impact the scientific/technological revolution has had on the hearts and minds of people in the past two centuries or so. Our world view has been turned upside down! In the midst of this turmoil we must realize that God's word is still the only certain truth. If we hold to that truth then we must see what is transpiring in our culture as nothing other than a pervasive and long-lived deception. It is the attempt to discredit the Word of God by exalting and asserting the truth of various "scientific" human ideas and beliefs.

Throughout this work I continue to emphasize the idea of how we have been lied to in the past century or two about the origins of the world and of mankind. I keep insisting that our perspective has been skewed by the inundation of our minds by human notions portrayed as scientific fact. If this seems difficult to accept, then consider what is going on in our country right now in regard to sexuality. We are being flooded with the idea that sex is a "right" that all possess, to be exercised according to one's personal choice, and that no one else—not even God, if He exists—has the right to tell us what to do or not to do. In a decade or two our children will live in a world where homosexuality is a normal and valid lifestyle—where statements about its being sin are considered narrow-minded and even hateful. This will be the perception with which they grow up, whether their parents like it or not. In fact, this is being promulgated even while I write this book.

We all know this and we must acknowledge the power of our anti-Christian culture as it tries to sell this concept to the next generation. The issue of human origins has already been lost by the Church in the broader society, and very soon the one about the meaning of sexuality will be lost. And why will that happen? Because men have been sold on the lie that humans have evolved by chance from the basic elements of the universe, rather than being created by God in His image and His likeness, as male and female. In the Church we must regain the truth of our origins—the Ancient Faith—the truth of the Bible.

What is lost when Genesis is eclipsed is the basic understanding of what it means to be human, what it means to be created in His image and likeness. This is not actually the gospel, but precedes it in the thinking of all people. It is foundational for understanding what is "normative" for human beings, how and why we all consistently fall short, and what can be done to correct the deficiency. People who have lost their connection to God as their Creator have lost the most foundational truth that connects them to their own human nature. They are floundering under a confusion of identity. That is why any society that rejects God as Creator descends into the perversions that Paul describes (Romans 1:18ff).

The coming of the Son of Man will be as it was in the days of Noah [and] as it was in the days of Lot (Luke 17:26–30). Today in our culture we are in a situation that is similar to that of Noah and Lot. Jesus also posed a question to us: When the Son of Man comes, will He find [the] faith on the earth (Luke 18:8)? Jesus did not answer His own question. The way that we handle the issue of origins will determine that answer.

Summary of the Ancient Faith about Genesis:
The Scriptures are inspired by God and thus are totally free from error. This truth flows directly from the nature of God, Who cannot lie or make a mistake, and Who is faithful. Only God is uncreated substance. The physical universe was brought into existence by an act of His will. All things were configured (or formed) by words of command that He spoke out. This was accomplished by the Father and the Son working together, but it also involved the activity of the Holy Spirit. We are shown their interactive effort in the account of the "six days." The world was not formed by the action of natural processes, or as the result of tendencies or properties that were inherent in the natural order, but by the supernatural action of God.

Again: the world was produced by an act of God Who, as the only uncreated substance, willed into existence matter or the basic material of the universe. Then He spoke verbal commands to form the various structures of the world. The created realm, which owes its very existence to Him, could not resist His will or His words and thus the steps of creation were accomplished instantaneously and effortlessly. God is not part of the natural realm. He is supernatural—outside of and above this world. Basil teaches us:
> It is right that any one beginning to narrate the formation of the world should begin with the good order which reigns in visible things. I am about to speak of the creation of heaven and earth, which was not spontaneous, as some have imagined, but drew its origin from God. What ear is worthy to hear such a tale? How earnestly the soul should prepare itself to receive such high lessons.[302]

Because the actions of God, either by His will or by His word of command, did not take a long time to be fulfilled—because created matter could not resist Him—the Fathers were not concerned about how the Lord God could accomplish His creative acts in so short a time as a day, but rather why the commands would have taken as much time as a day. They all asserted that they were carried out in an instant. **As a result of attitudes such as these no ancient writer ever hinted that the world was as much as ten thousand years old**. In other words the ancients believed that the genealogies of Genesis were accurate.

When an ancient writer was confronted with a pagan historical claim that the world was older than that, or with a philosophical theory saying that the world was eternal, that writer immediately spoke against the assertion and had recourse to Moses as proof that it was spurious. These attitudes and responses were universal.

All ancients without exception believed that God created this world out of nothing, and that the Genesis account was a fully accurate account of exactly how and when He did it. The Biblical/Christian world view is immediately set by these few observations. Here it is:
> **Only God is uncreated substance. He called the world forth from nothing and He upholds it. Thus the world is a supernatural phenomenon, created by the direct acts of God. His works were enacted instantaneously. The sequence of events that gave rise to the world lasted six days and took place a few thousand years ago as indicated by the genealogies of Genesis.**

This is the Ancient Faith as it touches on Genesis and the subject of origins.

All writers believed that the Flood of Noah was universal in extent. It completely covered the entire world and resulted in the death of every living thing except for the people and the animals that were in the ark with Noah. The Deluge was brought on by God because of the overwhelming wickedness of the people at the time of Noah. It was His judgment on mankind because of our sin. There were no exceptions to this belief.

From these simple statements about the universal perspective of the ancient writers we see that attitudes then were diametrically opposite to the prevailing attitudes of our day. The ancients had a supernatural mentality as they dealt with the issues of creation and Genesis; that is, a power from outside of the natural realm caused this world to exist and formed it to be what we now see around us. They believed that Genesis accurately explained to us exactly how and when this supernatural act of God took place.

As the centuries wore on and Christian thinkers formulated the theological-philosophical systems of thought so prevalent in the Middle Ages, these ideas were not discarded but rather became the foundational concepts of their theologies. All later thinkers believed in the six-day creation account and the young age of the earth as historical fact. I found not even one exception to this, not even a hint of an exception. This is the Ancient Faith.

No Church council ever explicitly defined the six-day creation account or the young age of the earth as articles of faith, but this was not because they did not see them as true or as important. Rather it was because no one ever challenged them. The early Church fought a centuries-long battle for orthodox Christology and made many careful pronouncements in that area of belief. By contrast, in our day we are in the midst of a centuries-long battle for the foundational truth of creation. Wake up, Church!

Our culture is buried in the pseudo-scientific philosophy of "scientific naturalism" and the attendant belief that the universe sprang up from properties that are inherent in matter and that this process took billions of years to work itself out. The Fathers believed all that they believed because that is what the Bible says, and they believed that the Bible was true—that it was the inspired, infallible, inerrant Word of God. This is how all of them understood Genesis. This is the Ancient Faith as it relates to the book of Genesis. Men who accept the billions-of-years idea believe it because they are trusting in the wisdom of man and the pseudo-scientific theories that they have proposed. Which of the two is the most reliable basis on which to rest our faith?

The belief in biblical inerrancy seems to have stayed in the Church until sometime in the nineteenth century when modern theories of origins became prevalent. In the Roman Catholic Church the evidence indicates that the ancient beliefs were still in place at the end of the reign of Pope Leo XIII, or the early twentieth century.

Pope Leo XIII definitely understood what was coming upon the Church. In his encyclical *Providentissimus Deus* (November 18, 1893) Leo wrote strongly on the truth of Scripture and stressed the importance of the unified testimony of the Fathers on matters of faith and morals. In referring to the teachings of St. Irenaeus and many other Fathers, as reiterated by both the Council of Trent (section b: *Decree on the Bible, and the Manner of Interpreting Sacred Scripture*) and the First Vatican Council (chapter 2: *Revelation*), he forcefully states that it is never permitted to interpret Holy Scripture against the teaching of the Church or against the unanimous agreement of the Fathers (Section 14.33). He reiterates:
> [T]he Holy Fathers, We say, are of supreme authority, whenever they all interpret in one and the same manner any text of the Bible, as pertaining to the doctrine of faith or morals; for their unanimity clearly evinces that such interpretation has come down from the Apostles as a matter of Catholic faith. (Section 14)

We have seen that all the Fathers interpreted Genesis as fully true, accurate history. That should settle definitively the Catholic view on the issue. Pope Leo then goes on to state:

> But he [a teacher or expositor of the scriptures] must not on that account consider that it is forbidden, when just cause exists, to push inquiry and exposition beyond what the Fathers have done; provided he carefully observes the rule so wisely laid down by St. Augustine–not to depart from the literal and obvious sense, except only where reason makes it untenable or necessity requires; a rule to which it is the more necessary to adhere strictly in these times, when the thirst for novelty and unrestrained freedom of thought make the danger of error most real and proximate. Neither should those passages be neglected which the Fathers have understood in an allegorical or figurative sense, more especially when such interpretation is justified by the literal, and when it rests on the authority of many. For this method of interpretation has been received by the Church from the Apostles, and has been approved by her own practice. (Section 15)

The principles here laid down will apply to cognate sciences, and especially to History. It is a lamentable fact that there are many who with great labor carry out and publish investigations on the monuments of antiquity, the manners and institutions of nations, and other illustrative subjects, and whose chief purpose in all this is too often to find mistakes in the sacred writings and so to shake and weaken their authority. Some of these writers display not only extreme hostility, but the greatest unfairness; in their eyes a profane book or ancient document is accepted without hesitation, whilst the Scripture, if they only find in it a suspicion of error, is set down with the slightest possible discussion as quite untrustworthy.

> . . . But it is absolutely wrong and forbidden [in responding to the attacks he outlined above], either to narrow inspiration to certain parts only of Holy Scripture, or to admit that the sacred writer has erred. For the system of those who, in order to rid themselves of these difficulties, do not hesitate to concede that divine inspiration regards the things of faith and morals, and nothing beyond, because (as they wrongly think) in a question of the truth or falsehood of a passage, we should consider not so much what God has said as the reason and purpose which He had in mind in saying it–this system cannot be tolerated. For all the books which the Church receives as sacred and canonical, [sic] are written wholly and entirely, with all their parts, at the dictation of the Holy Ghost; and so far is it from being possible that any error can co-exist with inspiration, that inspiration not only is essentially incompatible with error, but excludes and rejects it as absolutely and necessarily as it is impossible that God Himself, the supreme Truth, can utter that which is not true. This is the ancient and unchanging faith of the Church, solemnly defined in the Councils of Florence and of Trent, and finally confirmed and more expressly formulated by the Council of the Vatican. (Section 20)[303] [see note on papal writings]

Relevance of Creation Belief for Today:

I referred to the fact that a wave of deception about sexuality is sweeping over our land. In Christian thought the issue of origins is deeply intermingled with our understanding of human nature and the purpose of sexuality. In the same Pope's encyclical on Christian marriage (*Arcanum Divinae*, February 10, 1880) he reiterates the consistent teaching of the Church relating to the divine institution of marriage. Pope Leo XIII obviously realized, even back then, that marriage was under attack.

> The true origin of marriage, venerable brothers, is well known to all. Though revilers of the Christian faith refuse to acknowledge the never–interrupted doctrine of the Church on this subject, and have long striven to destroy the testimony of all nations and of all times, they have nevertheless failed not only to quench the powerful light of truth, but even to lessen it. We record what is to all known, and cannot be doubted by any, that God, on the sixth day of creation, having made man from the slime of the earth, and having breathed into his face the breath of life, gave him a companion, whom He miraculously took from the side of Adam when he was locked in sleep. God thus, in His most far-reaching foresight, decreed that this husband and wife should be the natural beginning of the human race, from whom it might be propagated and preserved by an unfailing fruitfulness throughout all futurity of time. And this union of man and woman, that it might answer more fittingly to the infinite wise counsels of God, even from the beginning manifested chiefly two most excellent properties– deeply sealed, as it were, and signed upon it–namely, unity and perpetuity. From the Gospel we see clearly that this doctrine was declared and openly confirmed by the divine authority of Jesus Christ.

> He bore witness to the Jews and to His Apostles [Matthew 19:4–9; Mark 10:2–9] that marriage, from its institution, should exist between two only, that is, between one man and one woman; that of two they are made, so to say, one flesh; and that the marriage bond is by the will of God so closely and strongly made fast that no man may dissolve it or render it asunder. (*Arcanum Divinae*, Section 5)

Thus it is that he bears testimony to the constant faith of the Church that marriage was established by God on the sixth day, and that this truth was clearly confirmed by Jesus Christ Himself. This has always been the teaching and belief of the Church. Thus the most basic truths about human nature, sexuality, and the purpose of God in creating us are rooted inextricably in our understanding of Genesis. This is the Ancient Faith as it touches upon Genesis, and that faith is deeply relevant to us and to our situation today.

Three times in Romans chapter one Paul links the rejection of God as creator to sexual and societal chaos. Paul describes the inexcusable decision of men who, knowing God and seeing His eternal power and Godhead, refuse to acknowledge Him as God. Instead they turn to images of corruptible man and various animals. Then he says:

> **Therefore** God gave them over in the lusts of their hearts to impurity, so that their bodies would be dishonored among them. For they exchanged the truth of God for a lie, and worshiped and served the creature rather than the Creator, who is blessed forever. Amen. (Romans 1:24–25)

Again he reiterates:

> **For this reason** God gave them over to degrading passions; for their women exchanged the natural function for that which is unnatural, and in the same way also the men abandoned the natural function of the woman and burned in their desire toward one another, men with men committing indecent acts and receiving in their own persons the due penalty of their error. (Romans 1:26–27)

Again he states:

> And **just as they did not see fit to acknowledge God any longer, God gave them over** to a depraved mind, to do those things which are not proper. (Romans 1:28)

The result of rejecting God as creator—the result of refusing to acknowledge Him for Who He is—inevitably will be a descent into sexual depravity. God created us for Himself, and acknowledging Him as creator is the most fundamental fact about Him. To deny that truth, or to blur its real meaning, leads to the severing of our basic connection with Him and exposes us to the influence of social and moral degradation and chaos. We can expect to see various sexual disorders appear in the society that thusly rejects Him.

There is something in our humanity that requires a solid connection to the One Who made us—that is left fluttering helplessly in an existential void when we are cut off from Him. The inevitable result of that severing is the loss of human purpose and dignity in society. Thus the chaos does not manifest itself only in sexual disorder. Such cultures will suffer from a crisis of meaninglessness—human life has no purpose. Paul continues with a litany of interpersonal problems that afflict a culture that rejects the Creator. Goodness is eclipsed by mean-spirited self-centeredness and the principles of social justice are undermined.

> [B]eing filled with all unrighteousness, wickedness, greed, evil; full of envy, murder, strife, deceit, malice; *they are* gossips, slanderers, haters of God, insolent, arrogant, boastful, inventors of evil, disobedient to parents, without understanding, untrustworthy, unloving, unmerciful; and although they know the ordinance of God, that those who practice such things are worthy of death, they not only do the same, but also give hearty approval to those who practice them. (Romans 1:29–32)

The tragic consequences that Paul describes as following upon the rejection of God as the creator should be viewed not as the vindictive response of a petulant God Whom we have dared to cross, but as the destruction of our humanity that results inevitably from our decision to distance ourselves from Him and from the truth that He is our creator. In order to prevent this slide into depravity the Lord God would have to extend a special grace to us to hold us back from our downward descent.

Paul indicates that God normally refrains from this and instead "gives us up" to our sad decisions and allows human society to follow its natural course—the adopting of various disordered lifestyles. In our confused society we have names for this degeneration. We call it "sexual liberation," "gay liberation," "women's liberation," and various other forms of "liberation." But all of these so-called liberation movements distance us from the pattern of life that God established when He made us, and undermine the norms of righteousness and godliness that uphold every healthy society.

These connections were outlined by Basil of Caesarea centuries ago.
> Why are the nations handed over to a reprobate mind, and why do they do what is improper (Romans 1:28)? Is it not because they said, "There is no God?" Why have they fallen into dishonorable passions, as the females among them have changed the natural usage into what is unnatural, while the males commit unseemly acts with males (Romans 1:26)? Is it not because they have exchanged the glory of the incorruptible God for the likeness of cattle and four-footed beasts and reptiles (Romans 1:23)? Therefore he is a fool, truly deprived of his mind and wisdom, who says, "there is no God."[304]

What was universally evident to the earlier generations of believers has become opaque to many of us today, no doubt because of the influence of the pseudo-scientific theories of origins that have permeated our culture. These have filled our minds and left us with little room for a credulous response to the Word of God in Genesis. I say this because when the Lord showed me that the present theories of origins were not science and that they were not true it opened my eyes to the understanding of Genesis. It was not long after that revelation that I opened the Bible and read the first chapters of Genesis. The clear and simple statements contained therein—the straightforward and obvious truth of those verses—leapt from the page into my mind and my spirit. We must be transformed by the renewal of our minds and be set free from the domination of the spirit of this age. Then we can again appropriate the Ancient Faith and stand with all the holy men of old.

Many sweet and edifying forms of Christian worship and expression have emerged in our culture in the past fifty years or more. All are precious. But whatever movement we are involved in today we must realize that ultimately Christian revelation and Christian truth are inextricably bound up with the faith that has been understood and expressed in all of the past centuries, and with the faith of ancient Israel. That connection is made in and through the Bible. If the Bible is not true then Christians are left to be cast adrift in a sea of turbulent anti-Christian philosophies and ideologies. Any movement, no matter how kind or lovely it is, if left in such an environment, will be overwhelmed and perish. Truth is firmly rooted in God's word, and only there. "Thy word is truth" (John 17:17). It is our only connection to the fundamental Christian truths and to our Christian roots.

Restating the Purpose of this Work:
We also must realize that how we understand or interpret Genesis is inextricably bound up with how we think it came to be written. The truth of Genesis is intertwined with how we understand it to have been put into writing, and that is the central topic of this book.

At this point I want to restate the purpose of this book and the issues that it addresses.
1. We intend to set before our readers a clear picture of what the faith of the Church toward Genesis has been throughout the ages; that is, we want to clearly present to you the Ancient Faith toward origins. This we have already done.

2. We will present to you a clear picture of how Genesis was written. This picture of the composition of Genesis will completely confirm the Ancient Faith about the book and will undergird and even deepen that ancient understanding of Genesis.
3. We will explain how the present theories of origins came to be viewed as utterly true, and why they are not science and are not actually true.

The most important contribution to these issues that this work offers is an enlightening and clear understanding of how Genesis was written—who wrote it and how did they do it? The Bible must always be our certain source of truth in combatting error. When we come to understand *how* Genesis was inspired by God, then its reliability will be undergirded in our thinking. Then doing apologetics will come back into vogue.

Introductory Thoughts on the Authorship of Genesis:

Who wrote Genesis and how did they write it? This has been a burning issue in the last few centuries. It cries out for a logical and reasonable answer. The understanding that people bring to this issue will deeply influence how they interpret the book. A theory like the JEPD Theory asserts that Genesis was written over a long period of time and by many different unknown authors. Over many centuries pagan myths were sifted through by the ancient Hebrews and purified, redacted, and combined together to form the early chapters of Genesis. The final synthesis that produced the book in its present form was completed just a few centuries before Jesus was born. While some parts of the book of Genesis may go back to Moses and his time, others do not. It is a patchwork theory for the composition of Genesis. That theory does not agree with the ancients at all.[d]

The Fathers and early commentators were unanimous in their belief that Moses wrote Genesis. Their writings are peppered with phrases like "in the book of Moses it says," and "Moses tells us," and "according to Moses," and "but Moses was God's spokesman and he explains." There are so many such statements and they are so numerous as to be universally stated and assumed by all early thinkers.

But on the question of exactly how Moses wrote the book of Genesis there are scarcely any carefully developed ideas. This is very important because Genesis differs strikingly from the other four books of the Pentateuch. Those final four books relate events in which Moses was the central figure, and he easily could have written them from his personal experience. But the events in the book of Genesis preceded his birth by many years— by from several centuries to two millennia or more. If he wrote Genesis, then how did he obtain the information which he relates to us in that book?

The Fathers did not delve into this issue, perhaps because they lacked the tools with which to investigate this question. In modern times this vacuum in scholarship has been filled in by theories like the JEPD Theory, which I outlined above. There are many statements in the works of the Fathers to the effect that God inspired Moses in the writing of Genesis, or that He spoke to him while he was on the mountain with Him, but there is no detailed explanation about how that divine inspiration happened. Some hinted that perhaps God revealed to Moses the events at the beginning of human history just as He showed John the consummation of all things. Augustine wrote this:

> Of all visible things the greatest is the world; of all invisible things the greatest is God. But we *see* that the world exists, while we *believe* that God exists, we believe that God made the world, and we base our belief on no one more safely than on God himself. Where did we hear him say so? Nowhere better,

---

[d] See Appendix III for a brief outline of this theory.

as yet, than in the Holy Scriptures, where his prophet said, *In the beginning God made heaven and earth* (Gen 1:1). Was his prophet there when God made heaven and earth? Of course not, but the wisdom of God, through which all things were made, was there, and this wisdom also transfers itself to holy souls, and makes them friends of God and prophets, and tells them inwardly and soundlessly of God's works.[305]

Severian of Gabala opines:
> While the story is a composition of Moses the lawgiver and is a revelation of the Holy Spirit, it describes the creation performed by the power of God and revealed to Moses by the charism of inspiration; it is not as a historian that Moses said this but as an inspired author. In fact, he told what he had not seen and described what took place when he was not an eyewitness . . . For example, no prophet was present–Isaiah, to cite one–when this happened in the case of Moses; but since the spirit of Moses was in him, it was inspired composition for the events to be revealed to him.[306]

By comparison, we know that John the beloved was not personally involved in the events that he describes in Revelation. Rather God showed them to him in a series of visions. But if the Lord actually inspired Moses by showing him the first things just as He showed John the last things then there is no hint of that within the text of Genesis. Here is what I mean: In the Book of Revelation John states that he was present with God and was being shown the things of which he wrote. "I heard behind me a loud voice like *the sound* of a trumpet, saying," and "The One who holds the seven stars in His right hand . . . says this," and "the first voice which I had heard, like *the sound* of a trumpet speaking with me, said, 'Come up here, and I will show you what must take place after these things,'" and "he carried me away in the Spirit to a great and high mountain, and showed me," and "he carried me away in the Spirit into a wilderness; and I saw a woman sitting on a scarlet beast." In these and many more ways it is clear from the text of Revelation that John was "made present" to the events of the book and was being shown those events through a series of supernatural visions, revelations, or locutions.

But there are no such statements in Genesis. If the Lord showed past things to Moses in visions then Moses wrote in a way that gives no hint of such revelations. The events of Genesis are related to us as simple stories that are told to us in a matter-of-fact way, not as revealed visions. For this reason—from the way that the text is presented to us—it appears that Moses wrote Genesis, not from specific divine revelations that the Lord gave to him during his life, but from other sources that he had available to him in Egypt.

Of course Moses wrote the book under the prompting of the Holy Spirit, and he wrote it with the careful guidance of the Holy Spirit; but it appears as if he had sources from which he was working, and that he edited them and produced Genesis from them with the leading of the Holy Spirit. A Pontifical Biblical Commission ruling of 1906 allows this view.[307]

<u>Ideas about the Sources that Moses Had:</u>
Then we might ask if those sources were written sources or oral sources. At one point in time it was not believed that writing was widely known to the ancients. But today we know from archeology that writing was known and widely used for at least two millennia before the time of Moses. Archeology shows that those subjects dealt with in Genesis—the creation and the Deluge—were commonly written down by ancient people. This was almost certainly because they considered such topics to be of utmost importance and to be foundational to their view of themselves. Societies rested upon such ideas.

Because the events of Genesis are of the same nature, dealing with the origin of man and the world, we should assume that the records from which Moses derived the biblical accounts were also written down and were not merely entrusted to oral transmission. Thus we can expect that Moses wrote Genesis using written records that he had available to him, and we will show this to be so. He must have edited those records—**The Genesis Documents**—and selected exactly what was needed and wanted by the Lord God, following His leading as he put together the book that we now have.

Thus Moses had various source documents from which to work as he compiled Genesis. Where did those documents come from, who wrote them, and how did those men come to know of the events of which they wrote? **The answer to these questions is the central topic of this work and will be taken up in the next two chapters.**

A Broader Archeological Issue:
The Mosaic authorship of Genesis is bound up with a broader issue: The Mosaic authorship of the entire Pentateuch. Therefore, in the next chapter we will look at scholarly objections to the Mosaic authorship and historical accuracy of the first five Biblical books. We will give sound reasons for believing that Moses wrote them, and that Exodus, Leviticus, Numbers, and Deuteronomy—in which Moses was the central figure—are fully historical. As part of our investigations we will explain how/when writing developed in ancient times; that is, how the tools for writing complex works developed and became available to Moses. That will lay a foundation for considering the unique issues surrounding the Mosaic authorship of Genesis.

In chapter three we will focus on Genesis. Names, geography, and other internal evidence indicate that much of Genesis was first written in ancient Babylonia. Those extinct cultures, which flourished for over two millennia, were the seed bed for the text of Genesis. Thus we must look at how the scribes of ancient Mesopotamia wrote documents. We must uncover the unique writing techniques that were known and used in those ancient times—methods which continued to be widely used until a few centuries before Jesus walked the earth.

As we examine in some detail the writing methods and techniques of the scribes of ancient Mesopotamia we will gain an understanding of what the sources of Genesis—**The Genesis Documents**—were, how they came to be written down, and who wrote them. This will help us identify the genre of the writings and evaluate their accuracy/historical reliability.

Scholars classify the genre of ancient texts as historical/mythical/legendary depending on how true they think the texts are. Works that are fully true and factual are designated as historical; works that relate some truth but are subject to fanciful descriptions, details and exaggerations are designated as mythical; writings that have little or no truth value at all are designated as legendary. Scholarly opinions about Genesis assign to it the genre of "myth." However in previous times the Church assigned to Genesis the genre of "history" and asserted that it was true. In this work we will again give strong reasons for maintaining that Genesis is history and that it is true. The techniques and tools that we will use were not available to the Fathers, but they will lead to conclusions that are identical to theirs. Thus,

Our findings will confirm the Ancient Faith of the Church that Genesis truly is the inspired, infallible, inerrant Word of God—preserved for us from the beginning of human history—relating to us the true story of the creation of all things, the beginning of the human race, our fall into sin, and the promise by God of a redeemer. These findings will also confirm the universal conviction of all ancient Christians that at every stage of its writing the book of Genesis was transmitted to us, as was all divine wisdom, when "Holy men of God spoke *as they were* moved by the Holy Ghost" (2 Peter 1:21), and not by multiple unknown men. Therefore Genesis is completely "God breathed" (2 Timothy 3:16), as is all of Scripture.

Biblical Archeology and the Pentateuch

Underreported but significant archeological finds in the Middle East and Egypt have brought to light many aspects about the life and times of those people and cultures. Such discoveries relate directly to the contents of Old Testament books. In particular, our understanding of the first five books of the Bible—their historical reliability in particular—has been greatly bolstered. The reliability of the Old Testament as a whole has also been positively impacted.

This chapter will explain these finds in the context of the overall scholarly climate now present in historical and archeological studies (and, indeed, in all domains of thought). This chapter has three major sections.
1. The traditional Church doctrine on the authorship of the Pentateuch and Joshua.
2. The scholarly unbelief and skepticism that dominate Biblical Archeology today. The discussion includes a brief explanation of how the skepticism has arisen—the roots of the thinking that undergird it—and examples of how this skepticism is manifested in various scholars of our day, both unbelieving and believing scholars.
3. The abundant archeological evidence for the Mosaic authorship of the Pentateuch and the historical accuracy and reliability of the early books of the Bible, including a further discussion and evaluation of scholarly thinking to the contrary.

Part 1—The Traditional Church Doctrine on the Authorship of the Pentateuch and Joshua:
The traditional understanding about the authorship of the books of the Bible comes primarily from the Bible itself, and secondarily from Christian and Jewish tradition. The books of the Pentateuch have universally been attributed to Moses, both by the Jews and by Christians. The book of Joshua has usually been attributed to Joshua. As we consider this, and since we know that many times scribes were employed to write on behalf of others, I believe we would be within the bounds of traditional wisdom if we allowed that both Moses and Joshua employed one or more scribes to write their respective books partially, but under their close supervision, but that they still wrote much of their books with their own hands.

Based on tradition and the straightforward meaning of the text, it is reasonable to begin our study with the assumption that these books were written directly by Moses and Joshua, or by those designated by them, and that the books were written very close in time to when the events took place and represent eyewitness accounts. Given the linkage with reported events to eyewitnesses, it is reasonable to view the books as trustworthy and true, meaning that all of the reported events are accurately reported. This starting point is reasonable, not only for the Christian faithful, but also for any historian or archeologist who wants to discover the truth and allows for the possibility that the Old Testament books are what they claim to be—an accurate historical account of God's interaction with His chosen people. To dismiss the accounts in the writings of Moses and Joshua as unhistorical from the start involves an anti-supernatural bias (to be discussed further in Part 2) and, as we will see, actually requires a very poor interpretation of archeological evidence.

Having stated the traditional belief about the authorship of the early books of the Bible, let us look at the internal evidence of the Scriptures themselves to understand why this view about their authorship was so universally held, for the text of the early books has much to say about how and when they were written down. In this section we will consider Exodus, Leviticus, Numbers, and Deuteronomy for Moses, plus the book of Joshua. Genesis is a special case, and we will consider it separately.

One simple observation to begin with is that the Bible asserts there was writing at the time of Moses, and that he indeed wrote down what was happening during the desert wanderings. Based on the following, it is clear that Moses wrote at the command of the Lord.

> Then the LORD said to Moses, "**Write this in a [lit.: the] book** as a memorial and recite it to Joshua, that I will utterly blot out the memory of Amalek from under heaven." (Exodus 17:14) [bold mine]

> Then He said to Moses, "Come up to the LORD, you and Aaron, Nadab and Abihu and seventy of the elders of Israel, and you shall worship at a distance. Moses alone, however, shall come near to the LORD, but they shall not come near, nor shall the people come up with him." Then Moses came and recounted to the people all the words of the LORD and all the ordinances; and all the people answered with one voice and said, "All the words which the LORD has spoken we will do!" **Moses wrote down all the words of the LORD.** . . Then he took the book of the covenant and read it in the hearing of the people. . . Then Moses went up with Aaron, Nadab and Abihu, and seventy of the elders of Israel, and they saw the God of Israel; and under His feet there appeared to be a pavement of sapphire, as clear as the sky itself. Yet He did not stretch out His hand against the nobles of the sons of Israel; and they saw God, and they ate and drank. (Exodus 24:1–4, 7, 9–11) [Bold mine]

> The LORD said to Moses, "**Write down [lit.: for yourself] these words**, for in accordance with these words I have made a covenant with you and with Israel." So he was there with the LORD forty days and forty nights; he did not eat bread or drink water. And he [Moses; or He, the Lord] wrote on the tablets the words of the covenant, the Ten Commandments. (Exodus 34:27–28) [bold mine]

The precise timeframe for the writing of the last four books of the Pentateuch is:

Timeframe for the writing of the Books of Exodus, Leviticus, Numbers, and Deuteronomy
Exodus: Begins perhaps several months before the first Passover, before leaving Egypt
Ends on the first day of the first month of the year after leaving Egypt
Leviticus: Begins on the first day of the first month of the year after leaving Egypt
Ends on the first day of the second month of the year after leaving Egypt
Numbers: Begins on the first day of the second month of the year after leaving Egypt
Ends on the first day of the eleventh month of the fortieth year after leaving Egypt
Deuteronomy: Begins on the first day of the eleventh month of the fortieth year after leaving Egypt
Ends on the first day of the twelfth month of the fortieth year after leaving Egypt
*********** Moses dies, and Israel mourns for Moses for one month ***********
Joshua: Begins on the first day of the first month of the forty-first year after leaving Egypt. On the tenth of the first month of the forty-first year Israel crossed the Jordan into Canaan. After being circumcised and celebrating the Passover the manna ceased.

Events Described in the Book of Exodus:
Israel left Egypt on the fifteenth of Nisan, the first month of the year (Exodus 12:1–51). The Lord delivered Israel from Pharaoh at the Red Sea (Exodus 14:1–31), gave quail and manna for the people to eat (Exodus 16:1–35), and provided water from the rock at Rephidim (Exodus 17:1–7). During this time the Lord directly guided Israel and commanded them where to go (Exodus 17:1). The Israelites arrived at the wilderness of Sinai in the third month (Exodus 19:1). The Lord then said to them through Moses:

> You yourselves have seen what I did to the Egyptians, and *how* I bore you on eagles' wings, [i.e., by My supernatural power] and brought you to Myself. Now then, if you will indeed obey My voice and keep My covenant, then you shall be My own possession among all the peoples, for all the earth is Mine; and you shall be to Me a kingdom of priests and a holy nation. (Exodus 19:4–6)

> At this time and place the Lord made a covenant with Israel. (Exodus 24:1–8)

God commanded Moses to make the tabernacle so that He could dwell among the people (Exodus 25:8). At that time the Lord gave Moses detailed instructions on how to construct the tabernacle and all of the holy things associated with it. Moses must have written the detailed and complex instructions down because the artisans followed all of them perfectly.

> So the sons of Israel did all the work according to all that the LORD had commanded Moses. And Moses examined all the work and behold, they had done it; just as the LORD had commanded, this they had done. So Moses blessed them. (Exodus 39:42–43)

But because of the sin of Israel with the golden calf, God moved His tabernacle outside of the camp (Exodus 33:1–8), lest He destroy them. Only Moses could go into the tent, which they called the "tent of meeting," to speak to the Lord face to face (Exodus 33:1–11). God commanded Moses to set up the tabernacle on the first day of the first month of the year immediately after the Exodus from Egypt (Exodus 40:1). Then the glory of the Lord filled the tent, and from that time on the Lord guided Israel and spoke to Moses and the Israelites throughout the entire time of the desert wanderings.

> Then the cloud covered the tent of meeting, and the glory of the LORD filled the tabernacle. Moses was not able to enter the tent of meeting because the cloud had settled on it, and the glory of the LORD filled the tabernacle. Throughout all their journeys whenever the cloud was taken up from over the tabernacle, the sons of Israel would set out; but if the cloud was not taken up, then they did not set out until the day when it was taken up. For throughout all their journeys, the cloud of the LORD was on the tabernacle by day, and there was fire in it by night, in the sight of all the house of Israel. (Exodus 40:34–38)

When God spoke to Moses He spoke to him directly. He spoke to him from above the mercy seat, from between the Cherubim. This explanatory detail is related a bit later on in the book of Numbers.

> Now when Moses went into the tent of meeting to speak with Him, he heard the voice speaking to him from above the mercy seat that was on the ark of the testimony, from between the two cherubim, so He spoke to him. (Numbers 7:89)

Thus the events of the book of Exodus conclude on the first day of Nisan in the year after Israel left Egypt, on the day the tabernacle was erected so that God could dwell with them.

Events Described in the Book of Leviticus:
It appears that at this time Moses began to write Leviticus.

> Then the LORD called to Moses and spoke to him from the tent of meeting, saying. . . (Leviticus 1:1)

This formula for how God spoke to Moses is repeated many times in Leviticus. In that book Moses records the ceremonial laws and ordinances that the Lord gave to Israel while they were still at Sinai. Thus it appears that Leviticus begins on the first day of the first month of the second year after Israel left Egypt, picking up exactly where the book of Exodus ends. All of Leviticus takes place in that one month, or perhaps in a little bit longer, ending before they left Sinai on the 20th day of the second month (see Numbers 10:11). During that time God established the statutes, ordinances, laws, and commandments between Himself and Israel. Leviticus ends with:

> These are the statutes and ordinances and laws which the LORD established between Himself and the sons of Israel through Moses **at Mount Sinai**. (Leviticus 26:46)

> These are the commandments which the LORD commanded Moses for the sons of Israel **at Mount Sinai**. (Leviticus 27:34) [bold mine]

Events Described in the Book of Numbers:
Numbers begins one month after Levitus begins, on the first day of the second month.

> Then the LORD spoke to Moses in the wilderness of Sinai, in the tent of meeting, on the first of the second month, in the second year after they had come out of the land of Egypt. (Numbers 1:1)

It is likely that Leviticus ended at the end of the first month of the second year, and then Moses began to write Numbers. Numbers begins at Sinai, but continues on, detailing the journeys of Israel through the desert until just before they enter the promised land.

From the beginning of Numbers until Numbers 10:11, the Lord commanded Moses to take a census of Israel. Thus the book recounts details about the census data. Then the Lord explained the order of the tribes as they would move on their journey through the desert. The camp was to be alerted to movements using two silver trumpets. Then they left Sinai.
> Now in the second year, in the second month, on the twentieth of the month, the cloud was lifted from over the tabernacle of the testimony; and the sons of Israel set out on their journeys from the wilderness of Sinai. Then the cloud settled down in the wilderness of Paran. So they moved out **for the first time** according to the commandment of the LORD through Moses. (Numbers 10:11–13) [bold mine]

Numbers describes the travels of the nation to the wilderness of Paran, where the people tragically fell away from the Lord and were unable to enter the promised land. At that time the judgment of the Lord was pronounced upon them.
> The LORD spoke to Moses and Aaron, saying, "How long *shall I bear* with this evil congregation who are grumbling against Me? I have heard the complaints of the sons of Israel, which they are making against Me. Say to them, 'As I live,' says the LORD, 'just as you have spoken in My hearing, so I will surely do to you; your corpses will fall in this wilderness, even all your numbered men, according to your complete number from twenty years old and upward, who have grumbled against Me. Surely you shall not come into the land in which I swore to settle you, except Caleb the son of Jephunneh and Joshua the son of Nun. Your children, however, whom you said would become a prey—I will bring them in, and they will know the land which you have rejected. But as for you, your corpses will fall in this wilderness. Your sons shall be shepherds for forty years in the wilderness, and they will suffer *for* your unfaithfulness, until your corpses lie in the wilderness. According to the number of days which you spied out the land, forty days, for every day you shall bear your guilt a year, *even* forty years, and you will know My opposition. I, the LORD, have spoken, surely this I will do to all this evil congregation who are gathered together against Me. In this wilderness they shall be destroyed, and there they will die.'"
>
> As for the men whom Moses sent to spy out the land and who returned and made all the congregation grumble against him by bringing out a bad report concerning the land, even those men who brought out the very bad report of the land died by a plague before the LORD. But Joshua the son of Nun and Caleb the son of Jephunneh remained alive out of those men who went to spy out the land. (Numbers 14:26–35)

From that time until chapter 21 the Israelites continue to wander in the desert. Very little of those many years of wandering are recorded for us until they arrive at:
> . . . The land of Moab, at the top of Pisgah which overlooks the wasteland. (Numbers 21:20)

Then the Lord had Moses take a second census (Numbers 26).
> These are those who were numbered by Moses and Eleazar the priest, who numbered the sons of Israel in the plains of Moab by the Jordan at Jericho. But among these there was not a man of those who were numbered by Moses and Aaron the priest, who numbered the sons of Israel in the wilderness of Sinai. For the LORD had said of them, "They shall surely die in the wilderness." **And not a man was left of them, except Caleb the son of Jephunneh and Joshua the son of Nun**. (Numbers 26:63–65) [Bold mine]

Moses was not allowed to enter the promised land either, because he had dishonored the Lord at the waters of Meribah.
> Then the LORD said to Moses, "Go up to this mountain of Abarim, and see the land which I have given to the sons of Israel. When you have seen it, you too will be gathered to your people, as Aaron your brother was; for in the wilderness of Zin, during the strife of the congregation, you rebelled against My command to treat Me as holy before their eyes at the water." (These are the waters of Meribah of Kadesh in the wilderness of Zin.) (Numbers 27:12–14)

At that time the Lord reiterated to the new generation of Israel the solemn feasts that were to be observed when they entered the promised land. And the book of Numbers ends with:
> These are the commandments and the ordinances which the LORD commanded to the sons of Israel through Moses in the plains of Moab by the Jordan *opposite* Jericho. (Numbers 36:13)

All of these writings are in third person narrative with Moses written into the stories. These detailed accounts surely were written down at the time that the events which they record happened. Moses must have personally written many of them, although it is possible that he also employed one or more scribes to write for him, but under his careful supervision. This was not an uncommon practice, and he was clearly busy with many responsibilities. But it seems inconceivable that the accounts were written down decades or centuries later. Because the Israelites had writing, and because it was widespread among them, they would have written down such important and detailed instructions, which came directly from the Lord, at the time they first received them.

The Book of Deuteronomy:
Deuteronomy has passages that are written in third person narrative with Moses written into the story, but very many passages are written in the first person. Clearly this book, or almost all of it, was written by Moses at the end of the forty years of wandering, while they were in the land of Moab across the Jordan from Jericho, before the Conquest. It was begun sometime after they arrived at Moab, after other events in Numbers that were recorded as happening there, on the first day of the eleventh month of the fortieth year.

> These are the words which Moses spoke to all Israel across the Jordan in the wilderness. . . In the fortieth year, on the first *day* of the eleventh month, Moses spoke to the children of Israel, according to all that the LORD had commanded him *to give* to them, after he had defeated Sihon the king of the Amorites, who lived in Heshbon, and Og the king of Bashan, who lived in Ashtaroth and Edrei. Across the Jordan in the land of Moab, Moses undertook to expound this law. (Deuteronomy 1:1, 3–5)

After reiterating the Law the Lord had given to them in great detail, Moses said:

> It came about, when Moses finished writing the words of this law in a book until they were complete, that Moses commanded the Levites who carried the ark of the covenant of the LORD, saying, "Take this book of the law and place it beside the ark of the covenant of the LORD your God, that it may remain there as a witness against you. For I know your rebellion and your stubbornness; behold, while I am still alive with you today, you have been rebellious against the LORD; how much more, then, after my death? Assemble to me all the elders of your tribes and your officers, that I may speak these words in their hearing and call the heavens and the earth to witness against them. For I know that after my death you will act corruptly and turn from the way which I have commanded you; and evil will befall you in the latter days, for you will do that which is evil in the sight of the LORD, provoking Him to anger with the work of your hands." (Deuteronomy 31:24–29)

This book began on the first day of the eleventh month of the fortieth year after the sons of Israel had come out of Egypt. Then Moses went up to view the promised land and died there, and the people mourned for him for one month. The account of his death, and the mourning of the people for him for one month, was written either by Joshua or an appointed scribe. Other than that section, Moses wrote the entire book of Deuteronomy. He wrote, as asserted repeatedly, within in the space of about one month while in Moab opposite from Jericho. One month later, after mourning for Moses, Johua began to lead the people.

Special Passages in the Books of Moses:
Some passages in Exodus, Leviticus, and Numbers imply that at a later time Moses returned and added further explanatory comments to those books. He must have done that during the month that he was writing Deuteronomy. Here are some examples of Moses reflecting on the events of the previous forty years, explaining how they worked out over many years:

> And throughout all their journeys whenever the cloud was taken up from over the tabernacle, the sons of Israel would set out; but if the cloud was not taken up, then they did not set out until the day when it was taken up. For throughout all their journeys, the cloud of the LORD was on the tabernacle by day, and there was fire in it by night, in the sight of all the house of Israel. (Exodus 40:36–38)

> Now on the day that the tabernacle was erected the cloud covered the tabernacle, the tent of the testimony, and in the evening it was like the appearance of fire over the tabernacle, until morning . . . Whenever the cloud was lifted from over the tent, afterward the sons of Israel would then set out; and in the place where the cloud settled down, there the sons of Israel would camp. At the command of the LORD the sons of Israel would set out, and at the command of the Lord they would camp; as long as the cloud settled over the tabernacle, they remained camped. Even when the cloud lingered over the tabernacle for many days, the sons of Israel would keep the LORD'S charge and not set out. . . Whether it was two days or a month or a year that the cloud lingered over the tabernacle, staying above it, the sons of Israel remained camped and did not set out; but when it was lifted, they did set out. At the command of the LORD they camped, and at the command of the LORD they set out; they kept the LORD'S charge, according to the command of the LORD through Moses. (Numbers 9:15, 17–19, 22–23)

God wanted these things to be recorded for our instruction. (1 Corinthians 10:11).

The Book of Joshua:
After Moses died Joshua took command and the Lord began to speak to him regularly and to encourage him.

> Only be strong and very courageous; be careful to do according to all the law which Moses My servant commanded you; do not turn from it to the right or to the left, so that you may have success wherever you go. This book of the law shall not depart from your mouth, but you shall meditate on it day and night, so that you may be careful to do according to all that is written in it; for then you will make your way prosperous, and then you will have success. (Joshua 1:7–8)

Joshua would experience success not because of superior numbers or more clever battle strategy, but because the Lord was with him, if he just paid attention to the law of the Lord that had been given to him in the book of Moses. A large part of that involved placing the book of the law always before him and heeding what it said. That implies that the books of Moses had already been written down. Thus Moses wrote them.

Joshua led the people across the Jordan on the tenth day of the first month of the new year. There they were circumcised and celebrated their first Passover in the land which the Lord was to give them. And the manna ceased at that time.

> Now the people came up from the Jordan on the tenth of the first month and camped at Gilgal on the eastern edge of Jericho. (Joshua 4:19)

> While the sons of Israel camped at Gilgal they observed the Passover on the evening of the fourteenth day of the month on the desert plains of Jericho. On the day after the Passover, on that very day, they ate some of the produce of the land, unleavened cakes and parched *grain*. The manna ceased on the day after they had eaten some of the produce of the land, so that the sons of Israel no longer had manna, but they ate some of the yield of the land of Canaan during that year. (Joshua 5:10–12)

The following passage also indicates that Moses had written the law down and that Joshua had that book when they first entered the promised land.

> Then afterward he [Joshua] read all the words of the law, the blessing and the curse, according to all that is written in the book of the law. There was not a word of all that Moses had commanded which Joshua did not read before all the assembly of Israel with the women and the little ones and the strangers who were living among them. (Joshua 8:34,35)

Later Additions to the Books of Moses and Joshua:
There are passages in the books of Moses and Joshua that imply, by their very content, that they were written at some later date. Here are examples of what I am referring to:

> So Moses the servant of the LORD died there in the land of Moab, according to the word of the LORD. And He buried him in the valley in the land of Moab, opposite Beth-peor; **but no man knows his burial place to this day. . . Since that time no prophet has risen in Israel like Moses**, whom the LORD knew face to face, for all the signs and wonders which the LORD sent him to perform in the land of Egypt against Pharaoh, all his servants, and all his land, and for all the mighty power and for all the great terror which Moses performed in the sight of all Israel. (Deuteronomy 34:5,6; 10–12) [bold mine]

Moses did not write the account of his own death, yet it could have been written by Joshua or another contemporary of Moses. But "no man knows his burial place to this day" indicates that a significant period of time had passed since the death of Moses. Likewise, the phrase "since that time no prophet has arisen like Moses" indicates that a significant time period had passed without the "prophet like Moses" arising. This is significant because Moses himself predicted that God would send such a man. God told him as much.

> The LORD your God will raise up for you a prophet like me from among you, from your countrymen, you shall listen to him. This is according to all that you asked of the LORD your God in Horeb on the day of the assembly, saying, "Let me not hear again the voice of the LORD my God, let me not see this great fire anymore, or I will die." The LORD said to me, "They have spoken well. I will raise up a prophet from among their countrymen like you, and I will put My words in his mouth, and he shall speak to them all that I command him. It shall come about that whoever will not listen to My words which he shall speak in My name, I Myself will require *it* of him." (Deuteronomy 18:15–19)

When verse ten was written he had not yet appeared. When he did, they crucified Him.

From Joshua:

> Now it came about when all the kings of the Amorites who *were* beyond the Jordan to the west, and all the kings of the Canaanites who *were* by the sea, heard how the LORD had dried up the waters of the Jordan before the sons of Israel until they had crossed, that their hearts melted, and there was no spirit in them any longer because of the sons of Israel. (Joshua 5:1)

The heart attitude of his enemies would have been difficult for Joshua to know this at this time in the Conquest, after they had just crossed the Jordan. It might be a later addition.

> Is it not written in the book of Jashar? And the sun stopped in the middle of the sky and did not hasten to go *down* for about a whole day. **There was no day like that before it or after it,** when the LORD listened to the voice of a man; for the LORD fought for Israel. (Joshua 10:13–14)

This also must have been written at a later time, reflecting on that awesome event.

> Israel served the LORD all the days of Joshua **and all the days of the elders who survived Joshua, and had known all the deeds of the LORD which He had done for Israel.** (Joshua 24:31)

This verse was written long after the death of Joshua, reflecting on the next generations of Israelites that followed him. It is a significant statement because the next book (Judges) picks up after the death of Joshua. It begins with Israel listening to the Lord, then records major times of falling away by the people, and the judgments of God resulting from those unfaithful deeds. The above last verse in Joshua and the first verse in the book of Judges serve to connect the two books. So Judges follows Joshua and builds upon it.

> Now it came about after the death of Joshua that the sons of Israel inquired of the LORD, saying, "Who shall go up first for us against the Canaanites, to fight against them?" (Judges 1:1)

Tradition (the Jewish Talmud) attributes Judges to Samuel. It is not written in chronological order, and it contains events from many parts of Israel, spread over several hundred years. Because writing was widely known, it is reasonable to hypothesize that local records were being kept that detailed the successes and the failures of the people. Near the time of the solidification of the nation of Israel, as the time of the monarchy approached, Samuel must have collected and written down those stories to teach his people about faithfulness to the Lord God. At that time he might also have added some insightful and inspired comments to the books of Moses and Joshua. Notice the similarity between Joshua 24:29–33 and Judges 2:6–10, possibly indicating a common authorship for that particular passage.

Clearly I am speculating that the one who added the later comments to the books of Moses and Joshua was the prophet Samuel, but he is an excellent traditionally held prospect.

Summary of the Writing of the Books of the Law, with Implications:
The books of the Law were being written continuously as the events that they record were taking place. These observations are summarized by the following simple diagram.

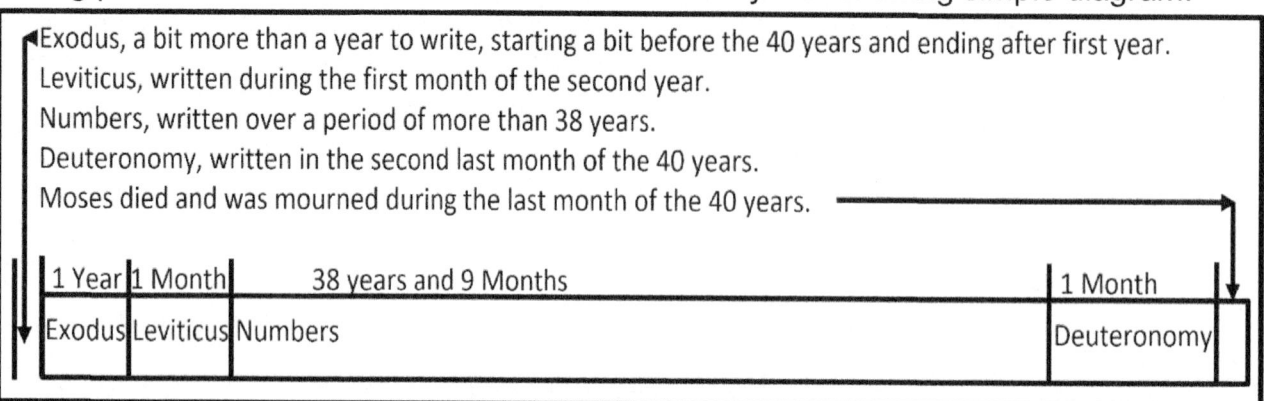

There are direct implications about the trustworthiness and historical reliability of these books that follow from these observations.
- The events that are recorded in these books are first-hand accounts written by the people who went through the events themselves.
- The records of the events were made very close to the time that the events took place. The accounts were written continuously throughout the desert wanderings.
- Also, the entire nation of Israel went through those events and were witnesses to the stories as they were being written down at that time.
- Those events are referred to repeatedly in the later books of the Old Testament. They are foundational to the nation of Israel. The backward reference to the events of these books begins immediately in the book of Joshua, while many of those who participated in the events were still alive, and continues throughout the centuries.

Conclusion: The events recorded in the four books of the Law are surely true. They are as historically reliable as any written account could ever be.

The few later additions to these books by Moses or by a later editor (perhaps Samuel, as we have hypothesized) as they reflected on the events recorded therein do not in any way detract from the accuracy and historical reliability of the books.

The complete accuracy and historical reliability of these books (and all of the Biblical books) is the unbroken unanimous belief of the People of God, both during Old Testament times and during the Church Age. The reasons for these beliefs are not difficult to understand: The internal consistency and reasonableness of the testimony that they bear, along with the uniform logic that they exhibit as the foundational accounts of God's workings to save His people by establishing the nation of Israel, His chosen people; the way that they blend into the rest of the history of Israel and give it meaning; the way that the Old Testament lays the foundation for the advent of Jesus Christ and the final salvation of all mankind in the New Testament; the continuous developing story of God's wonderful plan to save us that is exhibited throughout the total Biblical account. This is the Ancient Faith.

In our day we see that a foundation has been laid that utterly rejects the totality of Christian revelation, which has posited another worldview to replace it—a worldview that opposes and is contrary to the Ancient Faith.

Part 2—Rationalism and Scholarly Skepticism/Unbelief in Biblical Archeology Today:

Various ideas, theories, and supposed "facts" about the history of Israel and Judah and the origin of the Hebrew people have arisen in the last few centuries which present a direct challenge to the traditional authorship and truthfulness of the Old Testament. This, in turn, challenges the Ancient Faith of the Church. A Christian scholar and academic comments on the atmosphere in academia that is widely prevalent today:

> There is a great battle for the Bible going on . . . in universities throughout the world. They are taking pot shots at the Bible at record speed. In 2016 I finished a degree . . . from the University of Toronto—my PhD in Syro-Palestinian archeology with a first minor in Egyptian Language and a second minor in ancient Near Eastern languages. While I was in my course work there . . . I heard things about the Bible that shocked me in classes from professors. . . And the things I heard for me were like fingernails on the chalkboard. . . [T]he challenge that we have is that when we send our children . . . off to colleges and universities, they are going to get ears full of this. And the pressure will be on them to accept it and embrace it. And the idea is this: If a professor at a secular university . . . who is against the Bible, can go after the history in the Bible and "prove" to his students or her students that it's full of errors, or causes problems with history as we know it, if they can convince [them] that it's not accurate in some way, or that it can't be verified and thus [they] can't trust it, then what happens is [their] faith and trust in the spiritual message and in the moral message—in the relational message—it all of a sudden is eroded. And this is the attack. One of the most acute attacks is on the Israelites and everything related especially to the . . . sojourn . . . in Egypt.[308]

For those faithful who believe that there must be a harmony between faith and reason, the question that emerges is whether this sort of "scholarship" is based upon sound evidence and reason, or if something else is at work in the form of an attack on truth that must deny the best explanation of the evidence.

The present-day attack on the reliability of the Scriptures has a very long history, going back several centuries. Pope Leo XIII expressed his deepest concern over this in 1893 in his encyclical *Providentissimus Deus*.

> It must be clearly understood whom we have to oppose and contend against, and what are their tactics . . . We have to meet the Rationalists, true children and inheritors of the older heretics, who, trusting in their turn to their own way of thinking, have rejected even the scraps and remnants of Christian belief which had been handed down to them. They deny that there is any such thing as revelation or inspiration or Holy Scripture at all; they see, instead, only the forgeries and the falsehoods of men; they set down the Scripture narratives as stupid fables and lying stories: the prophecies and the oracles of God are to them either predictions made up after the event or forecasts formed by the light of nature; the miracles and the wonders of God's power are not what they are said to be, but the startling effects of natural law, or else mere tricks and myths; and the Apostolic Gospels and writings are not the work of the Apostles at all. These detestable errors, whereby they think they destroy the truth of the divine Books, are obtruded on the world as the peremptory pronouncements of a certain newly-invented "free science;" a science, however, which is so far from final that they are perpetually modifying and supplementing it. And there are some of them who, notwithstanding their impious opinions and utterances about God, and Christ, the Gospels and the rest of Holy Scripture, would faro be considered both theologians and Christians and men of the Gospel, and who attempt to disguise by such honorable names their rashness and their pride. To them we must add not a few professors of other sciences who approve their views and give them assistance, and are urged to attack the Bible by a similar intolerance of revelation. And it is deplorable to see these attacks growing every day more numerous and more severe.[309]

If we are to understand Pope Leo's warning, we must understand who the rationalists are to whom he refers. We will see that the difficult situation which came upon the Church over a century and a quarter ago, which Pope Leo XIII was addressing, has not diminished today. In fact, it has broadened in scope and is attacking and undermining every aspect of Christian Faith and Christian practice. Pope Saint Pius X called this attack Modernism, the summation of all heresies, and Pope Saint John Paul II told us "we are now living in the final confrontation between the Church and the anti-Church, between the gospel and the anti-gospel."

Thus we must address this issue directly, and because it has deep historical roots we must ask how the Christian culture of Europe come to such a state. We need to understand the nature of the ideas that are coming against the Faith, which means understanding how they developed historically in Christian Europe. I want to give a summary perspective on European thought over the past 400 years. I will do this in order to lay bare the basic presuppositions, the underlying assumptions, upon which modern ideas and thought systems are based—the deep roots from which spring the continuous stream of direct attacks against the faith that, by this time, have been in full bloom for at least two centuries.

Philosophical and Historical Roots:
Let me give a very down to earth example of what we are dealing with. When we built our home thirty years ago we designed and planted an area in front of our house. It had many lovely flowers and small plants in it, and a kind of ivy that surrounded the plants and that served as ground cover for all of the bare places between the various flowers. Over time the ivy, which was a more aggressive plant, completely took over the planting area. When we tried to cut it back, it regrew with a vengeance. No matter how we chopped or pruned, the ivy always returned. It had established an underlying root system that was a continuous source of new ivy growth, new growth that also tended to smother out all the other plants.

Likewise, what we are dealing with today, and what has been a continual issue for over two centuries, is not a grouping of disconnected ideas, but a kind of foul bouquet of ideas that spring from a common root system, a philosophy that forms an interrelated family of ideas that are fundamentally opposed to the Faith and that continually bring forth theories and ideologies contrary to the Faith. It is not enough to prune the leaves; that is, to address the various ideas or movements that arise individually. We need to identify and address the root causes from which they keep springing, the erroneous presuppositions upon which they are based. The foundation, the root system for these errors—which by now is firmly established in our culture—was laid in the 1600's, centuries before they came to full flower.

Around that time several important developments were shaking Europe and Christianity. The geocentric view of the world, which placed mankind at the center of God's loving acts and elevated him to the center of the Creator's concern, was being challenged. The result was the shaking of an important pillar of the Christian worldview and the most thorough cultural earthquake in history, as a foundational underlying concept of European culture was called into question. The protestant reformation had divided the Church, covering the claims of Christianity with doubt in the eyes of many intellectuals. The ancient Greek philosophers had been reintroduced into Europe, and their pagan ideas were circulating as well.

Into this atmosphere of intellectual doubt and uncertainty Renee Descartes was born and raised. He is known for his famous statement "I think, therefore I am," his response to the burning question of the day, "what do we actually know for sure to be true?"[310] Descartes sought to discover and elucidate a universal methodology for attaining knowledge, based somewhat upon mathematical methods, but applicable to all areas of understanding and investigation, which would be the key to establishing certain truth in each and every area.

Descartes wrote several important works that left a lasting impression on western thought. All of them, in some sense, were an attempt to place human life and thought on a footing that was solid, that was certainly true. His first work, *Le Monde*, was not published until after his death, likely because he knew it would not be accepted by the Church. Some later works, such as *A Discourse on Method*, were published in his lifetime. Simply stated, the idea or thesis of *Le Monde* was this: Imagine a world where God never works a miracle. He calls forth the primeval substance into existence, then it develops by itself—in accordance with the laws of matter inherent within it—into all the structures and systems that comprise the cosmos. In that world God never works a miracle, He never intervenes in any way.

In *A Discourse on Method*, and in several successive works as well, Descartes proposed the methodology by which, in his imaginary world, (and in the real world) we might come to understand how the diverse structures and systems arose without the direct action of God. His methodology, a kind of universal mathematics, could be applied to any area of study to yield the most reliable and true insights. Descartes referred to this methodology as his "admirable science." He formulated it from a special dream that he had been given at the age of 23 by the "Spirit of Wisdom," as he named his revelator. Jacques Maritan comments:

> In place of a specific plurality of *human* sciences . . . we have one single knowledge: science, Science with a capital 'S,' Science such as the modern world was to worship it; Science in the pure state, radiating from unique and unparalleled geometric clarity, and that Science is the human mind. The idea of mathematical Gnosis, the idea of universal method, the idealistic conception of knowledge, all that fused in one identical apperception—such, it seems to me, is the primordial vision which assigned to Descartes his destiny, on that November night when the Spirit of Wisdom, as he says in his diary, descended upon him to take possession of him, and to open to him the treasure of all the sciences.
>
> The understanding becomes an absolute, and this absolute understanding is man himself.[311]

Descartes proposed that over long periods of time, and little-by-little, all developed without divine intervention, but rather in accordance with the principles of operation that guided matter itself. He proposed that we can discover these developmental paths, which are the ultimate and only sure truths. There is no knowledge that cannot be thus uncovered, and the human mind can know these things by careful investigation. So besides knowing that he existed, he also asserted that absolute truth about the world around us was attainable, but only by this methodology. No other path to knowledge could be trusted, for we cannot know for certain, by any other methodology, that what we arrive at is true. Maritan notes that for Descartes,

> Human reason is Reason in itself, Reason in its pure state. A universal rule and measure, all things must be adjusted to its level. It is no longer measured, it measures, it subjugates the object . . . There are self-evident ideas; they are clear and distinct ideas, the ideas of what Descartes called simple natures. To know is to reduce everything to these clear and distinct ideas, to break up the object into these atoms of evidence . . . [They are, because his methology is somewhat mathematical] the elements of a mechanical reconstruction of reality . . .
>
> [In the Medieval Christian conception of knowledge] the whole movement of intelligence was holy, consecrated, because it was orientated toward God. Philosophy itself was Christian, secular knowledge was Christian. As a matter of fact, philosophy by its very object is quite distinct from faith and from theology. It is strictly of the natural and rational order.[312]
>
> With Descartes, everything changes. This distinction achieved in coherence and dynamic solidarity becomes separation, isolation—and soon even opposition. Philosophy is sufficient absolutely and unto itself alone in the soul; not only is its object of the natural order, but to all intents and purposes it demands that its subject as such be cut off from all supernatural life, cut off from itself as Christian. Hence is explained the absurd myth from which we are still suffering, of a man presumably in the state of pure nature in order to philosophize, who crowns himself with grace in order to merit heaven . . . **The Cartesian revolution has been a process of secularization of wisdom** . . . From the world of matter, which is beneath thought, thought must drive out absolutely all obscurity. Above it, it must acknowledge the obscurity of things divine; but woe to it if it tries to venture there.[313] [bold mine]

This was the birth of Rationalism as a philosophy, as a method of inquiry. Only trust what we can directly observe and fully comprehend. Only trust as true what can be reduced to clear and distinct ideas that are beyond doubt, using the approach of mathematics as a guide. For the rationalist, **there is no truth which the human mind cannot either know directly or to which it cannot reason logically from what is known directly, as clear and distinct ideas**. This elevates man and his intellect to the pinnacle of truth and implicitly destroys revelation as a source of truth. This is because man cannot fully comprehend the supernatural, miracles, and fulfilled prophecies and, therefore, the reality of these concepts must be rejected under rationalist philosophy (even, as in our case, if volumes of historical and archeological evidence support the miraculous Biblical accounts). All truth is attained in and through this universal mathematic, through its universally applicable methodology.

> With regard to what is inferior to man, to the world of corporeal nature, Cartesian intellect claims to understand everything exposed to the core, through the substance, through the essence itself. Matter lies naked before it as before the angels. The mathematical knowledge of nature, for Descartes, is [a knowledge which answers] questions bearing upon the first principles of things. This knowledge is, for him, the revelation of the very essence of things. These are analyzed exhaustively by geometric extension and local movement. The whole of physics, that is, the whole of the philosophy of nature, is nothing but geometry.
>
> Thus Cartesian evidence goes straight to mechanicism. It mechanizes nature, it does violence to it; it annihilates everything which causes things to symbolize with the spirit, to partake of the genius of the Creator, to speak to us. The universe becomes dumb.[314]

Here are some obvious repercussions that must follow from the thinking of Descartes:
1. Divine revelation must be rejected as a source of true knowledge.
2. The area of "origins," with which the book of Genesis deals, must be removed from the area of divine revelation—from historical theology—and considered to be within the domain of natural science; that is, something to be reasoned to by mankind and explained through a non-supernatural process (Darwinian evolution to explain life, Lyell's gradualism to explain geology, the Big Bang to explain the cosmos, etc.) Thus not Genesis, but only reason, can be trusted as a source of such knowledge.
3. Miracles cannot be proven or reasoned to; thus they never happen. Thus Biblical stories relating the miracles of God cannot be taken at face value. In general, we must separate faith and reason and rely only on (anti-supernatural) reason.

Anyone can see that such ideas are contrary to the Christian Faith, which has always been based on a supernaturalistic worldview. But these basic principles of investigation soon became intrenched in most academic disciplines after Descartes died in 1650. They became the unspoken assumptions, determining the basic methodology by which the disciplines operated. Thus most areas of study have long-held roots that are anti-Biblical, anti-Christian, and that extend back to Descartes. Therefore they continue to produce ideas and theories which contradict the Christian Gospel, and which can be used as a platform from which to attack, undermine, and discredit the Bible and the Faith. These presuppositions are not often spoken of today because they are part of the present secular worldview, the presumed "surely true" things which all people "know" before any discussion begins. We might refer to them as the thoughts of the "zeitgeist," or the "the spirit of this age."

The "enlightenment" which developed at that time and afterward was essentially a revolt against the authority of the philosophical, intellectual, and religious traditions that had been the foundation of Christian Europe for many centuries, championed as the emergence of a new kind of "freedom" that encompassed most areas of life; the intellectual, social, religious, political, historical, etc. More comments by Maritan:

> The cultural significance of rationalism thus becomes clearly apparent to us. It *implies* an anthro-

> pocentric naturalism of wisdom; and what optimism! It is a doctrine of necessary progress, of salvation by science and by reason [Today: "follow the science."]; I mean, temporal and worldly salvation of humanity by reason alone, which, thanks to the principles of Descartes, will lead man to felicity, to "that highest degree of wisdom in which the sovereign good of human life consists" (he wrote *it* himself in the preface to the French translation of the *Principles*)—in giving man full mastery over nature and over his nature; and, as the Hegelians were to add two centuries later, over his history. As if reason by itself alone was capable of making men act reasonably and of securing the good of peoples! There is no worse delusion.
>
> On the balance-sheet we should inscribe: Rupture of the impulse which was directing all the labor of human science towards the eternal, toward conversation with the three divine Persons—upsetting of the elan of knowledge.[315]

As time passed, area after area of thought came under the sway of rationalist attitudes. This re-thinking of history, politics, religion, philosophy, etc. did not arise because of new information that had been discovered in any of these areas of thought. Instead it arose from reconsideration of these areas of investigation from a perspective that was hostile to and that systematically excluded God and Christian revelation. It arose from considerations that proceeded from anti-Biblical assumptions about the nature of truth and of reality, about how to investigate and come to the truth, about the nature of mankind, about the nature of society, about how to understand the past, about the meaning of human existence, etc.

For example, new attitudes and ideas emerged that affected how people thought about government and the history of mankind. In his landmark work *Leviathan* Thomas Hobbes asserted that there is nothing other than the universe and anything not part of it is nothing and nowhere. (This is exactly what Carl Sagan said in the Cosmos TV series: "The universe is all there is, and all there ever was.") For Hobbes "good" and "evil" were terms relative to the person, describing what he or she liked or disliked; wanted or hated. Mankind from the beginning was in a constant state of struggle with others. Social contracts were made to alleviate this struggle by allowing people to each achieve some of their desired ends, and to thus arrive at some kind of peace and coexistence. To achieve these ends, all power and authority was to be surrendered to the state. These assertions were embodied in a totally materialistic view of history and government.

Other thinkers followed suit. Thus Locke asserted that the basic function of government was (merely) to further and protect the wealth and prosperity of its citizens. That proved to be a very "this-world" kind of thinking, omitting the Divine purpose for life on earth, and opening the way for immoral practices such as abortion.

Rationalism was brought openly into Biblical studies by Spinoza. In his *Theologico-Political Treatise* he stated that, in interpreting Sacred Scripture we should accept nothing that we ourselves do not clearly perceive (Descartes' clear and distinct idea concept). He said the Church promoted miracles to advance its own position of influence and control in society, which was harmful. It's supposed "light from on high" was actually the enemy of truth because it was contrary to reason, which is the highest function of our humanity. Thus religion was a bastion of prejudice against reason. The fixed order of nature does not permit miracles, so those passages of Scripture that assert them must be seen as spurious. Many of the passages of scripture had been corrupted over time—used and promulgated by organized religion for its own ends, made up to control people. Such ideas relate directly to the attacks on Scripture that we see going on around us today.

Of course, the idea of God as the explanation for the cosmos that we see around us was contradicted by Spinoza, who was both a rationalist and a pantheist, one who viewed the material universe as all that exists. Spinoza believed that the Christian God, if He existed, could not be known through reason, which is the only basis for certain and true knowledge. God, if He exists, is to be identified with the universe itself, which has always existed and is the sum total of all that is, the sum total also of all that we can know.

Having severed their connection to the commandments of God and the Church, philosophers began to speculate on many areas of thought, writing on history, sociology, government, etc. They imagined that society had developed from a more primitive state over time, that man was inherently good (not fallen), and that the basic flaws in men and in human society were the result of problems in the family and in the government, which robbed man of his essential freedom to be himself and to prosper. Families and societies must be "fixed" in order to allow for man to blossom forth. In these ideas the Church, the family, patriotism, and other traditional social constructs began to be viewed with deep suspicion. Philosophers were deconstructing Christian civilization piece by piece, and replacing it with a chaotic babel of ideas that were without foundation—but all of which asserted that reason alone held the answers to all the questions, issues, and problems that mankind faced.

More specific attacks against the Scriptures ensued. Minor variations in gospel accounts were taken to mean that the gospels were in error. Simple reconciliations of these differing accounts that went back to the time of the Fathers were dismissed. Rather, it was asserted that the gospels could not have been written by eyewitnesses. The Apostles invented the idea that Jesus was the Messiah. They had contrived the New Testament accounts to make it seem as if He had fulfilled prophecy. In general, if revelation ever occurred it did not go beyond what we could know by reason anyway, and in places where it seemed to it was corrupted. In fact, the "Jesus" that the Church preached was nothing like Who He really was. He did not think of Himself as divine, He did not teach the Trinity or other spiritual mysteries, and He died with the cry of despair on His lips, thinking that He had been a failure.

Jesus was merely a simple Middle Eastern peasant who was trying to gain some kind of political advantage for oppressed people. His failed mission was hijacked by the early Church out of a love for Jesus or a love for power, and was re-presented as a supernatural "thing" with vast and eternal spiritual import. It is important to note that such attacks were not isolated; they constituted the mainstream of biblical scholarship by the early 1800's, especially in liberal Protestant circles, expressed through the works of Reimarus, Strauss, and other negative critics.

The Old Testament also came under attack as men questioned the Mosaic authorship of the Pentateuch. Surely the accounts of the Creation, Deluge, Exodus, and Conquest could not be historical. This was the beginning of the hypothesis that many different documents had been intermingled to create these ancient texts. This undermined their credibility because they were seen as having been written many centuries after-the-fact, and as having been originally based on centuries-old oral traditions. Scholars began to cut up the text of the Scriptures into smaller units that were studied in isolation from their total context, dating them according to their various theories about how they had first been written down and later assembled. As this rationalist deconstruction occurred, one consequence was that the many hundreds of Old Testament prophecies fulfilled by Jesus came to be dismissed as inauthentic by the negative critics—jimmied by the New Testament authors to fit His life.

The idea that one could isolate passages in the Old Testament and date them to various eras gave rise to the belief—built upon the philosophy of Hegel, and eventually taking form as the so-called Documentary Hypothesis—that religious practices and tenets had evolved over time, and that this development could be traced out by studying it in the isolated fragments of Biblical texts, arranged according to the dates that had been assigned to their composition. This idea was not compatible with the fact that God was working throughout the history of His chosen people, speaking to them, revealing Himself to them, and directing their national life—that Israel's religion was given by God. Again, this flowed from a godless naturalistic view of history (especially the history of Israel), of the Scriptures, and of human life in general. These ideas were the direct outflow of Descartes' philosophy when extended to theology and the Sacred Scriptures.

Although no new information about the past, about the Scriptures, etc. had been brought forth, myriads of new theories were expounded, which came forth in a multitude of published works over a period of several centuries. The sheer volume was difficult to respond to and to refute. **What was new was the attitude of radical skepticism toward the supernatural that was expressed in them**. They established a climate of doubt and unbelief as the "spirit of the age" became ever more firmly entrenched in scholarly thinking. Comprehensive doubt and incredulity developed toward Christianity, the Faith, and the overall Biblical testimony about Jesus. Surely, the negative critic assumed, the real historical person of Jesus cannot be anything like what has been presented to us in the Scriptures. Thus began the quest for the "historical Jesus," which is still an ongoing movement today.

Discounting the historicity of the Old Testament, which levied further doubt upon the reliability of the New Testament, went along with casting the idea of salvation from sin by God in a jaundiced light. Such an idea simply did not fit in the new paradigm. "No God will save us; we must save ourselves." This new conception of "salvation" could only be implemented through proper application of our own resources, abilities, and powers. Our own reason, which is the key to all knowledge, must be leveraged to its fullest. Maritan observes,

> To delude oneself with the thought that the idealistic ruminating of physics and mathematics *is* enough to force the gates to the kingdom of God, [enough] to introduce man to wisdom and to freedom, [enough] to transform him into a fire of love burning for all eternity, *is* psychological childishness and metaphysical humbug. Man becomes spiritualized only by joining with a spiritual and eternal living One. There is only one spiritual life which does not mislead—that which the Holy Spirit bestows. Rationalism is the death of spirituality.[316]

Up to this point (by the early 1800's) the rationalist philosophy had not become firmly established in the natural sciences, yet control of this influential domain was an absolute necessity in order for the new worldview to gain complete credibility. Following upon the ideas in *Le Monde*, Charles Lyell published his *Principles of Geology* in the 1830's. He claimed that natural processes like those we observe today had formed the strata and geologic features of the earth over millions of years. This contradicted the historicity of Genesis, especially the account of the Deluge. In the same philosophical vein, Darwin's *The Origin of Species* in 1859, claimed that all living things had arisen not by the creative power of God but naturalistically, over many millions of years, by gradual development and complexification—from a single cell to human beings. With these two publications natural science quickly came under the rationalist and anti-supernaturalistic worldview that was initially posited by Descartes. In the first half of the 20th century, the Big Bang cosmology would complete the rationalist take-over of origins science, but by that time, Darwin (building explicitly upon Lyell) had already won the day.

I must point out that Darwin's *Origin of Species* was immediately accepted and acclaimed in his day, **even though there was no proof at all for his claims**. Once again, his work did not stem from scientifically verified evidence, but from a point of view of radical skepticism and purely naturalistic assumptions, plus a series of unproven conjectures based thereon. Yet, it was acclaimed and promoted as "sure and certain scientific truth" because it fit in with and fortified the rationalist ideas of Descartes. Charles Lyell's work on Geology falls into the exact same category. **To this day the actual scientific proof of these works has not been offered**. But the world view that they represent and undergird is alive and well in our culture; indeed. it has dominated and taken over the intellectual centers of our day.

Therefore Mr. John Wynne names this comprehensive false view of reality the **Cartesian-Darwinian Narrative**—the fantastic philosophical notion, now imbedded in almost all academic disciplines, that the world and all that is in it can be and must be viewed, understood, and explained only as the outworking of natural processes operating under the known present physical laws. These processes can and must be investigated and understood by human reason and only by human reason, which is the ultimate and final arbiter of truth.

This "spirit" has blanketed the earth today. No ideas are exempt from the dark cloud that it casts, no domain of knowledge is unaffected. The consequent futility of our existence, the loss of purpose and meaning in our daily lives, the hopelessness, the immersion in sensuality such as aberrant sexuality and drugs, the broken families, the insane political movements and ideologies that have arisen to demand allegiance from lost men and women, the loss of understanding of what it means to be a human being, the confusion within the Church as to the validity of its own gospel message, the utter despair and the senseless violence that is rampant—these are the heritage that Rationalism, the Cartesian-Darwinian Narrative, and the "Enlightenment" have bequeathed to the human race. We are a people bereft of our soul, standing on the edge of a precipice overlooking an utterly black bottomless pit, about to hurl ourselves headlong into nothingness.

Let me explain. St Theresa of Lisieux (the Little Flower) talked of the Church as God's garden, and of personal souls in it as His individual flowers. She was blessed, by her own testimony, to have been born into a fertile place—within a family of deep faith in God and of devotion to Him. This happened within a Church that was still, in the late 1800's, not overwhelmed with the spirit of skepticism that surrounds us now. No such faith-filled environment exists today in the Catholic Church. The faithful are barraged with claims that "Genesis is just a kind of complex myth," "the gospels cannot be trusted to give us an accurate portrait of Jesus," "Paul did not write all the epistles attributed to him," "Moses did not write the Pentateuch," and so forth.

In our present-day environment a precious "Little Flower" has no chance to bloom or to grow into a beautiful blossom for Our Lord. The environment of the Christian Faith has been fundamentally eradicated. The best that can grow is a small, deformed, stunted flower that has almost no fragrance to it. This situation is so bad, it has so penetrated the Church, that her leaders—including her evangelists and revivalists—often do not even recognize what has happened—what has been lost. The Ancient Faith is choked out by the weeds of Rationalism. Unbelief is now so entrenched that it is mistaken for a kind of intellectual objectivity and for a deep and humble form of honesty. The darkness of our godless culture has forced its way into the highest chambers of the Church, where it is firmly established. The basic cause of this tragic situation—THE ROOT CAUSE—is the rejection of the Bible as the inspired, infallible, inerrant Word of God. People no longer trust His Word, and so do not actually, do not truly, do not really know Him—Who He is, or what He is actually like.

Speaking bluntly, the "faith" that we profess today is not at all the Faith that the Church held throughout the ages. The martyrs who shed their blood, the desert monks who retired to their distant monasteries to escape the world, the popes, the bishops, the theologians, the nuns, the virgins, the Fathers and Doctors, were all—every one of them—foolish enough and "primitive" enough to actually believe that the Bible was true, that it was the inspired, infallible, inerrant Word of God. They based their lives and their deaths on that faith. We do not believe that today. We are much too sophisticated. We are much too worldly.

Let me be even more specific in my explanation. No one can read the creation account in Genesis chapter 1 in the straightforward, obvious sense and imagine that God is speaking to them and saying that this world is billions of years old and that it came to be via an (essentially) endless or infinite series of natural causes that He somehow willed and was working through. Everyone who reads that text realizes that God is saying (in conjunction with the genealogies a few chapters later) that He created the world in just six days (144 hours) and that He performed that series of supernatural actions a few thousand years ago. This is utterly clear, as is fully verified by the unanimous testimony of all Christians (and Jews) from ages past. If that is not true, then a foul seed of confusion is planted in the heart and mind of the reader. God is tricky, reasons the confused reader. You cannot be sure what He means when He speaks to you. Maybe the collection of Scriptures isn't any more than the merger of multiple views of God held by many ancient cultures. Therefore, God is a mysterious and distant Being. You can't know Who He really is or what He is really like. Did He really create millions of years of struggle and death? Is that the "very good" creation that He made? Then what "very good" hope do we have for the future? A dark cloud begins to grow within the heart and mind of the reader. And faith—true faith, Biblical faith—is stunted. This is the battle we are in today. WAKE UP, CHURCH. We cannot ignore this and hope it will go away. This is our battle.

This is a very brief overview of the "Spirit of the age" in which we are living. What I have listed is a small subset of the avalanche of anti-Christian and anti-Biblical works that have been published in the last few centuries, all stemming, at least indirectly, from the ideas of Descartes in the early 1600's. Clearly this broad, multi-faceted attack on Christian truth, coming from so many areas of thought, bursting forth suddenly and continuing for over four centuries, was not planned or executed by anyone on this earth. We are in the midst of a gigantic, sustained, demonic assault on the Church and on the Gospel. When the ancient materialist philosophy of Epicurus and others was soundly rejected by the early Church, the father of lies needed another philosophy that achieved the same end, but through an indirect route. Rationalism—when applied to all areas of thought—is at the root of the present assault.

This simple overview elucidates the words of Pope Leo XIII as quoted from *Providentissimus Deus*, and gives what Pope Pius X and Pope John Paul II said tangible substance. This summary puts the present issues that we are facing into broader historical perspective. It helps us understand and evaluate the thinking of modern scholars, places academic trends into perspective, and helps us to see the underlying reasons for the claims and ideas that are so widely propagated. It will also help us to evaluate how reliable such assertions are. Finally, it brings us back to our work in this book—to the Bible, in particular to the Pentateuch, and ultimately to the book of Genesis, with which we are most directly concerned.

Summary: Observations on the Value and Errors of Rationalistic/Naturalistic Thinking:

From the Biblical perspective, we must realize that thinking along Rationalistic lines; that is, thinking that looks for only non-supernatural reasons for how or why things happen, will be adequate and successful almost all of the time. This is the direct consequence of what the Bible says about the creation of this world.

> Thus the heavens and the earth were completed, and all their hosts. By the seventh day God completed His work which He had done, and He rested on the seventh day from all His work which He had done. Genesis (2:1,2)

The supernatural work of creating the world and all that is in it was completed at the end of the sixth day. From that that on time our Lord began "upholding all things by the word of His power" (Hebrews 1:3). From the seventh day onward, the created realm began to function according to the created natures of its various parts, and this implies that normally the world does not exhibit supernatural intervention in its operation. Therefore, "natural" causes, or causes that proceed from the nature of the physical realm itself, are adequate to explain how the world around us works—most of the time.

This simple observation is why "scientific" explanations for the world around us tend to be very successful. This is why "science," or "human reason" can explain how many things around us work. It is the basis for the present technological and medical establishment and it wide-spread success. God has so created His world that it works well on its own, and He does not normally need to intervene in its daily operation.

But Rationalism has not been satisfied to stop there. The assertion is that **everything** has a naturalistic explanation. Yet, the Bible claims to be the historical record of God's work in the affairs of man and the world. It is explicitly the account of how the Lord has been at work to create, judge, and redeem mankind. If we apply the Rationalistic/Naturalistic assumptions to our study of Sacred Scripture then we are approaching that study with a bias against what the Bible claims to be. This is because God is not a natural cause. He is not part of the natural realm. He is supernatural. He is transcendent. The failure to not accept this "line of demarcation" has resulted in removing areas of study from the realm of revelation and insisting that they belong instead in the realm of natural philosophy.

In particular, the following scholarly disciplines have been adversely affected:
- The study of the ultimate origins of all things—of the world, of life, and of human life in particular. This has relegated the book of Genesis to a non-historical status. It is merely an ancient myth, put together by primitive people who were not as wise or knowledgeable about the world as we are today.
- The study of the origin of the nation of Israel, which is God's chosen nation: Thus, the Exodus, the Conquest, and the entire providential care for and guidance of the nation are denied because of the supernatural elements contained therein. This is an explicit denial of the validity of the Christian hope of salvation and eternal life.
- The nature of mankind as "created by God in His image and likeness" is replaced with the idea that we developed gradually along naturalistic lines over many years, even over many millions of years, without divine intervention. Thus, human culture also developed in this random way. Thus the meaning and purpose of human life is re-defined. Ancient unknowable "pre-history" is re-imagined, the purpose/role of government is re-imagined, the present way we ought to behave is re-imagined, and finally the ultimate purpose and goal of humanity is re-imagined.

In other words, an entirely new worldview has come into existence, one that is opposed to the Christian and Biblical worldview. This is what we have just explained briefly.

<u>Our Response to the Barrage of Rationalist Ideas</u>:
We cannot respond to all the aberrant ideas that have burst upon all domains of thought in the centuries since Descartes. But having briefly explained the roots of Rationalism and its influence, **we will definitely show that the modern attack against Genesis and the Pentateuch clearly incorporates rationalist thinking and, as a result, demands that the books must be unhistorical, even before the evidence is fairly considered.** In Part 3 we will show that the archeological evidence, when freed from an anti-supernatural bias, all but destroys the skepticism that still dominates the field.

In particular, I want to focus on the many people/theories that have arisen to attack the credibility of the Sacred Scriptures. These will not focus on broad philosophical concepts (as in the previous discussion of Descartes and his minions), but on ideas that are rooted directly and immediately in present-day scholarly writing and theories. While the scholarly methods are presented as the product of sound reasoning and as the "near-consensus of modern critics", their clear connection to Rationalism will be obvious, the destructive effect of their naturalistic methodology will be apparent, and the theoretical models which they construct (from naturalistic assumptions) to explain history will be seen as utterly futile.

Specific Examples of Scholarly Skepticism about the History of Israel:
What we are about to look at is not pretty. To use the analogy of the Church as God's lovely garden, and of souls as His individual flowers: The beliefs and thoughts of modern scholars are either weeds growing where flowers used to be—and where they are still supposed to be, but where they have been choaked out completely—or they are flowers that are stunted and misshapen in their growth. Let us examine God's garden.

Foundational point: How one understands the accuracy of the Pentateuch has a direct and immediate impact on how he or she thinks about the historical accuracy of the entire Old Testament. Here is why.

Many have observed that belief in Genesis is directly opposed by belief in various theories of origins and gradualist ideas that have captured our culture—Biological Evolution, Lyell's Geology, The Big Bang, etc. But we might not realize the connection between belief in the Pentateuch and acceptance of the rest of the Old Testament books as historically reliable. Yet, the early history of Israel—its patriarchal stories and its birth as a nation—and the stories about its ongoing life in the Promised Land, are a continuous, developing story. If one denies early Israelite history—that is; Abraham, the Sojourn, the Exodus, the Conquest of Canaan—then the other Old Testament books; the Prophets, Kings, Chronicles, etc. are also subject to dismissal. The entire history of the chosen people is called into question because the Biblical narrative is a unified whole, expressing the overall Biblical world view. The truthfulness of the Pentateuch is foundational to the reliability of the entire Old Testament and to the total corpus of Christian revelation. If the Lord our God did not miraculously deliver the Hebrews from slavery in Egypt and give them Canaan as a divine inheritance, then salvation history and His intention to save us becomes murky, at best. In the minds of many, the foundation of the Christian faith is destroyed, for the very nature of God as a faithful, good, forgiving, saving Being is undermined.

In this section I want to explain the basic issues around which these discussions revolve. In presenting this material I must come into disagreement with certain scholars, and I must expose their ideas as mistaken, even as containing a certain bias against God and against His Holy Scriptures. But I want to make it clear as I begin that I am not judging anyone to be evil or sinister. Scholars who hold to ideas contrary to the faith can be kind, sweet, men and women who believe that they are fair and objective in what they are saying. Most are brilliant, and many are self-professed Christians. They are certainly no worse than I am. So when I disagree with them I am not setting myself against them or above them. But they have been "caught up" in the spirt of the age.

This is not a battle against flesh and blood. We must recognize who our real enemy is, and that he can and does deceive even the most erudite. The Word of God says that "they will go on deceiving and being deceived." What some see as objective I see as anti-Christian bias against the supernatural, but something that is so established in our culture that it has become accepted as normal and true. This is the nature of deception.

The worldview of the Cartesian-Darwinian Narrative now dominates all domains of thought— it is a comprehensive view of reality. Therefore Biblical scholars think and write from within an assumed geological and anthropological framework that is firmly rooted in a non-Biblical way of looking at the world. Here is a quote from the introductory remarks of a well-known twentieth century work on Jericho.

> The importance of Jericho stretches far back beyond this time [the time of Joshua] when rich civilisations in the [Fertile] Crescent and hungry nomads in the interior met in the age-long struggle of the Desert and the Sown [i.e., the inhabited and cultivated areas]. It has long been recognised that the very origins of civilisation are to be sought in the Fertile Crescent. **These origins lie in the first steps towards settled life which is the characteristic of the Neolithic Period. For hundreds of thousands of years, primitive man had lived on wild foods, as a hunter and food gatherer.** As such, he was a nomad, following the supplies of wild food, with the seasonal growth of wild fruits and the movements of wild animals. Any one area could hold only a limited population, so settled life of groups of men was impossible. The revolutionary step forward was the discovery that wild grains could be cultivated and made more productive, and wild animals herded and their products made constantly available. With this discovery, the growth of fixed settlements became possible. The transition is that from the Palaeolithic and succeeding Mesolithic stage to the Neolithic. From this, all civilization is derived. It is in the inception of this revolution that Jericho takes a great place.[317] [bold mine]

These remarks show clearly the assumed ancient history of mankind and our development into "civilized" societies over untold hundreds of thousands of years of gradual evolution— evolution of both our human species and of our human cultures. *How the author interprets what she finds in her archeological digs is always fitted into this overarching worldview.* The ideas that we see expressed by scholars today also fall within that same worldview, even if they do not explicitly state as much in their writings. This worldview has never been proven, but it is assumed by virtually all archeologists without question.

With that simple observation in mind, let us begin by giving an example of how scholars are led to reject the Old Testament revelation about the history of Israel. I will refer to such scholars as "incredulous" scholars and will allow them to speak for themselves, to explain their thinking in their own words. We will concentrate on present-day scholarship/ideas; that is, I will not review the broader chaotic history of theories that have risen and fallen since early in the nineteenth century. Many authors include an historical summary of such theories in their book to serve as a kind of prelude to their own theories and ideas.[318] [See note for reference]

If someone rejects the picture of the birth of Israel that is presented to us in the Exodus and in the Conquest of Johsua, then how do they imagine that Israel became a nation? What actually happened that gave birth to Israel and Judah? What follows is the thinking that guides scholars as they construct their picture of these historical events, in their own words.

> Given the fact that we are almost totally dependent on the biblical account and that **this account itself raises serious credibility problems**, what approach can a reasonably cautious historian take in dealing with the origins of Israel and Judah? Is it possible to employ the Genesis-Joshua materials for historical reconstruction in any responsible fashion? Basically three options present themselves, all three of which will be found represented among current textbooks on Israelite and Judean history.[319] [My bold. The supernatural elements are the "credibility problems."]

The authors (Miller and Hayes) list three possible approaches: take the account as it stands (including the supernatural elements in the Creation, the Exodus, the Conquest of Canaan, etc.); totally reject that part of the account; take some kind of compromise position.[320]

The authors then choose the most common approach taken, a kind of compromise, and give a thoughtful analysis of how scholars work within that approach.

> The third option is to develop an alternate hypothesis for the origins of Israel and Judah which is based to some degree on the biblical material, yet which does not follow the biblical account exactly (perhaps not even closely) . . . Analysis of recent treatments of early Israelite and Judean history reveals that four factors generally contribute to the shaping of such compromise positions.
> 1. One factor, of course, is the historian's threshold of credibility. It is tempting, for example, to try to follow the general story line of the biblical account, but to begin the story at some point later than creation, to reduce what appear to be unrealistically large numbers, to make selective adjustments in the biblical chronology, and to offer naturalistic explanations for the miracles. Even very biblically conservative historians sometimes avoid the issue of whether the world really was created in just seven days and only six thousand years ago, for example, by beginning their treatment of Israelite history with Abraham.[321]
> 2. A second factor is the evidence from ancient nonbiblical documents and archaeology . . . the various hypotheses reviewed above which sought to correlate the biblical account with the nonbiblical data usually involved a compromise approach. That is, the correlations proposed usually called for some significant adjustments in the biblical account. The patriarchs became Amorites rather than Arameans for the Amorite hypothesis. The date of the exodus was lowered from the fifteenth to the thirteenth century in order to correlate it with the Ramesside period in Egypt and the Transjordanian occupational gap. In order to correlate the Israelite conquest with the Late Bronze Age [i.e., 1250 BC to 1000 BC] city destructions in Palestine, it was necessary . . . to adjust the biblical chronology [etc.].[322]
> 3. A third factor is the results of literary-critical analysis of the biblical materials. Literary critics distinguish . . . between the individual compositional units of Genesis-II Kings, on the one hand, and the overall, composite account, on the other. Often the compositional units—the songs, genealogies, stories, and such that have been incorporated into the larger account—appear to be rather old, have a more authentic ring than the compilers' editorial comments, and seem to conflict with the compilers' historical assumptions and claims.[323]
> 4. Finally, historians consciously or unconsciously tend to rely on models. Two such models, one derived from an assumed Middle Eastern cultural pattern, and the other from the social sciences, have been widely influential among biblical historians in recent years.[324]

This gives us a good foundation for understanding the approach taken by the "incredulous" scholars, but it is definitely worthwhile to look at the two models put forth by scholars. This will help us to understand more concretely what they are referring to, so we can more easily interpret what they say in their writings. Miller and Hayes briefly explain each type of model.

> The first of these may be referred to as the "nomadic model." Those who utilize this model **assume** that the Arabian Desert has been, through the ages, a constant source of nomads who infringe

> from time to time upon the surrounding cultivated areas seeking territory and grazing lands for their flocks. Accordingly, the ancestors of Israel and Judah are believed to have entered Palestine as nomadic groups, gradually settling in unoccupied areas and establishing relationships with the indigenous population. Instead of an initial conquest, therefore, this view postulates a long period of infiltration and settlement during which the newcomers and the settled populations interacted, absorbing and being absorbed. This period of gradual settlement by various and diverse groups would have been followed by a period of consolidation and eventual dominance of the newcomers over the native population.[325] [bolding mine]

The second type of model projects a kind of Hegelian/Marxist dialectic into ancient Canaanite culture.

> The second model seeks to understand the origins of Israel in terms of internal developments within . . . Palestine itself. Proponents of this view, while admitting that some of the ancestors may have entered the land from the outside, insist that essentially Israel was the product of a socio-economic and political upheaval within the Land of Canaan—a revolt of marginal and oppressed elements within the heterogeneous population of the land directed against the economical and political structures of the Canaanite city-states and their monarchical, feudalistic governments.[326]

Note that little or no historical or archeological proof for either model exists, but scholars seek to find hints that support their theories (or models) within the text of Scripture or in the fragments of archeological finds. This is cogently brought home when the authors of their volume explain their own approach to reconstructing the history of the Hebrews. To understand their basic attitude toward the truth of the early Biblical books: They reject the scenario presented in Genesis through Joshua as "an artificial and theologically influenced literary construct." So it is not historical, but sections of it might be useful to them.[327] (In the Church we might hear such writings referred to as a kind of "complex myth.")

> The approach taken in this volume with regard to the question of Israelite and Judean origins can perhaps be described as an extremely cautious and eclectic compromise position, determined to a certain degree by all four of the factors mentioned above, plus a considerable amount of **intuitive speculation**. Admittedly, this is not very satisfying from a methodological standpoint. In our opinion, however, this is the best one can do, given the nature of the limited evidence at hand . . . we are cautious about saying anything. **The evidence, or lack of evidence, is such that a confident treatment of the origins of Israel and Judah in terms of critical historiography is, in our opinion, simply impossible. This is one of those places where the historian must be willing to concede that anything said is largely guesswork**.[328] [bolding mine]

Here are a few observations about this revealing analysis of the current scholarly theories and models that they have presented to explain the origin of the nation of Israel.

1. The objection to the historical accuracy of the Biblical record begins with the total rejection of Genesis through Joshua. This is done supposedly, the authors state, because the Biblical account "raises serious credibility problems." As we move in this work through the Biblical account, please note the overall consistency of the narrative, its clarity, and its internal logic. The "credibility problems" stem from the supernatural interventions that are recorded therein and that, presumably, have been disproven by evolutionary science and evidence from other domains. This *a priori* objection is only and exactly a bias against the supernatural and a misplaced trust that experts in other fields have actually shown Biblical claims to be untrue.

   It is the mindset of scientific naturalism that finds the early books of the Bible to be "incredible." This observation applies not only to Genesis, but to all of the Biblical books through and including Joshua. This is a clear and unmistakable example of the underlying rationalistic assumptions that are guiding scholars as they study the Scriptures, and there is an unbroken line of such reasoning that extends all the way back to Spinoza and Descartes.

2. The scholarly objections to the Biblical account as it stands are rooted not only in a simple statement of unbelief, but in assertions made from within alternate models or theoretical reconstructions of the past. Thus once the Biblical record has been dismissed, in the whole or in part, what replaces it is the theoretical and unprovable ideas and reconstructions of scholars. It is a universally observed fact that, once the Biblical (supernaturalistic) account of the past is rejected then is it necessary, it is obligatory, to supply another naturalistic, rationalistic, explanation for the past to replace the Biblical account. Because the scholars are very learned, their models or their "theoretical constructions" can seem very convincing, especially if they are presented to a listener who has not performed an independent and objective study—such as a young and impressionable college student who is taking their class.

3. The data that is available to the scholar is fragmented and sparce. It is not possible to confidently reconstruct the distant past from what archeology has discovered. This frank admission that the authors make reveals the shaky basis of all models and theories that might be put forth, especially when the historical accuracy of the Scriptural accounts is rejected a priori. This is openly admitted to by the authors, and it reveals the shaky basis of all models and theories that might be put forth to replace the historical accounts in Sacred Scripture. Our authors are not the only ones to frankly discuss this shortcoming in the data from archeology. Early last century the great English luminary Sir Alan Henderson Gardiner made the same observation.

    This observation about the fragmented and sparce evidence that is available to the archeologist is widely known and referred to. Many "facts" have been uncovered, but when scholars begin to formulate broader scenarios about past civilizations they are going beyond what they "know." They are expressing in some way their preconceived notions or their own personal beliefs. Interpreting the "facts" and connecting them to make broad assertions about ancient cultures—the stories found in archeological texts—is a dubious practice. They reflect the preconceptions (biases) of the person who makes them—and Biblical scholars who have rejected the earliest Biblical record are definitely biased against the supernatural—against any divine intervention in history. This is the zeitgeist.

What this means is that scholars start from the various archeological finds that they have, and move on to construct broader scenarios about the past. They "tell stories" about past times and places and peoples, weaving together the details of their finds, seeking to form a cogent "model" or reconstruction of the past. The stories always sound plausible, even compelling, but the above observations should alert the reader that all claims of "proof" about the distant past, claims that dismiss the Biblical record and put forward an alternate historical narrative, are based more on certain preconceived beliefs than on good science.

Their methodology is suspect because of their underlying rationalistic assumptions. The authors quoted above state this openly as they begin their work. The evidence needed for a complete and accurate exposition is not available.

The fragmented nature of the data that archeologists have uncovered, the effect on their "models" or "hypothetical reconstructions," and the need to invent a rationalistic story to explain the evidence cannot be overstated. I want to list more references to this important fact. These are taken from *Israel in Egypt—Evidence for the Authenticity of the Exodus Tradition* by James K. Hoffmeier. Reinforcing the problem that Miller and Hayes described, he summarizes the "minimalist" trend of dismissing the Biblical text.

> The recent discussions on the origins of Israel have grown out of the demise of the conquest model and the rise of more archaeological, sociological, and anthropological approaches toward reconstructing Israel's early history. While there seems to be something of a school developing that believes the Israelites were indigenous to Canaan, there is little evidence to support this assertion. Despite the current movement towards minimalist and reductionist [i.e., unbelieving] readings of the biblical text and the elevation of the newer approaches, Siegfried Herrmann has argued for more traditional, text-based methods to answer the problems of Israel's origins.[329]

Dr. Hoffmeier is a more credulous scholar, and he is clearly critical of the approaches that are commonly being developed to explain the origin and history of the nation of Israel.

In his discussion of various approaches/theories Dr. Hoffmeier makes it clear that competing ideas have multiplied, and that no model is evidence-based or compelling. **This confusion is common in other fields, such as paleoanthropology (the study of human evolution), and serves as a marker that the field has taken a wrong turn, that it is built upon an incorrect foundation that does not lead to the discovery of truth.** We will examine this in detail later.

We will now explain a few concrete assumptions/conclusions that are in error, but which nonetheless now dominate the fields of archeology and ancient history. One fallacy of such theories is the assumption that the Exodus, if it happened, fell around 1250 BC, some two centuries later than the date suggested by the Biblical text (this will be discussed further below). Because of the mistaken date for the Exodus scholars have looked for archeological support for the Conquest and entry into the Promised Land around 1210 BC. Due to the underlying chronological error, the sought-for evidence is not found, and the entire notion of the Conquest is sometimes called into doubt. A related fallacy is the failure to understand the level of the destruction of Canaan described in Joshua and this, in turn, overstates the expected evidence for the Conquest. (The Bible describes the complete destruction of about a dozen cities. The other cities were conquered, their inhabitants were killed, and they were then utilized and lived in by the Israelites. Also, many indigenous peoples living outside the cities were not eradicated, but remained in the land of Canaan and lived side-by-side with the Hebrews for centuries.) We will also look at this in detail later.

Obviously, if there is no evidence of an Exodus in 1250 BC and no evidence of a subsequent Conquest, the Sojourn in Egypt must also be called into question. Dr. Hoffmeier makes this observation and notes that the Sojourn, the Exodus, and the Conquest of Canaan are so linked that rejection of one leads also to dismissal of the others.[330] Indeed, as we have noted, this "domino effect" extends to all of the early (history) books of the Old Testament because they are all linked together and all follow logically one after the other, forming a continuous connected historical narrative.

In all of his discussions Hoffmeier brings up various theories or models of the skeptical and shows how diverse, contradictory, or flimsy their assertions are—lacking any basis in solid evidence. Then he explains the general historical reasonableness of the Biblical account.

As an example, he asserts that Semitic people commonly migrated into Egypt for reasons of drought and hunger throughout most of the second millennium BC,[331] consistent with the Biblical Sojourn of the Hebrews. Of special importance are the recent excavations at Tell El-Daba (Avaris) in the area of the eastern Nile delta where the Israelites would have lived, but some other data also supports the Biblical account of the Sojourn. Dr. Hoffmeier also investigates the background in Egypt that supports the historicity of the Joseph story. He seeks to undergird the basic historicity of the Biblical account, advancing facts to support it by showing that it reasonably fits within the culture and times of the second millennium BC.[332] Finally, he presents evidence that demonstrates the reasonableness of the Moses story.[333]

This gives us, **in general terms**, some insight into the varied state of Middle Eastern and Egyptian archeology today. The initial hopes that certain knowledge of the distant past would be forth coming were deceptive. Instead chaos and confusion reign because the methods were built upon an unsound foundation, the often-hidden foundation of Rationalism. From this base, critics mount attacks on the truth of the Bible. Even so, the more objective writers (those less impacted by Rationalism) such as Hoffmeier present sufficient background information to support the belief that the Sojourn, the Exodus, and the Conquest had some historical basis, thus undergirding the Biblical account in general terms. However, in Part 3, I will present specific detailed evidence for all three events (Sojourn, Exodus, Conquest) that explicitly supports the historical accuracy of the Biblical narrative.

However, first I want to focus more on scholarly thinking in a few key areas of archeology.

Overview of Scholarly Thinking on Chronology:

I have introduced the common (but I believe false) assumption among scholars that the Exodus, if it occurred, was around 1250 BC.[334] Let us now explain where this assumption comes from and how it is linked to the presumed reigns of prominent Egyptian pharaohs.

One argument for a 1250 date for the Exodus is called the Transjordanian Occupational Gap Theory. Numbers 20ff and Judges 11 assert that the Hebrews were forced to fight against the Edomite, Moabite, and Amorite kings who lived in that area east of the Jordan. But a surface survey by archeologists indicates there was a gap in the "sedentary occupation" of those areas between 1900 BC and 1300 BC. That is, no settled indigenous people lived in those areas that might have challenged the Hebrews as they passed by their lands. Thus an Exodus date before 1300 BC seems likely.

This issue is part of an on-going technical debate among archeologists and is based on a negative finding—the absence (or apparent absence) of evidence for a population that was settled in fixed and permanent towns, and on the assumption that the opposition described in the Bible actually requires such settled populations; that is, might the Israelites have been opposed by the named people groups even if they were not inhabiting permanent towns? This is a negative argument based on a theory—an unproven and possibly irrelevant theory.

Another argument for a 13th century Exodus came from William F. Albright who noted that a number of cities in Canaan had been destroyed, and the dates for their destruction was in the late 1200's BC. But the destruction of some of these cities were later redated and/or their destruction reasonably assigned to other causes. Recall that in Joshua Jericho, Ai, and Hazor were destroyed initially, and 8-10 more cities afterwards. The goal of the Conquest was to destroy all pagan shrines but to take all wells, vineyards, cities, etc. intact to possess and dwell in them. This set of supposed reasons has therefore lost its convincing force.

But by far the most direct reason for dating the Exodus to around 1250 BC comes from one key verse in the Bible.
    And they [Hebrew slaves] built for Pharaoh storage cities, Pithom and Ramesses." (Exodus 1:11)
The city Pithom is not known, but archeologists have excavated the city of Ramesses (Pi-Ramesses) very thoroughly. It is located in the eastern part of the Nile delta, in the area of Egypt that would have been ancient Goshen. The city existed for only a short time,

for less than 200 years. The city was built by Ramesses II, and it is the **majority opinion of scholars that he reigned** from (approximately) 1279 BC to 1213 BC. Therefore a date for the Exodus of around 1250 BC seems right.

If Ramesses II did not reign from these dates—if he reigned in a different time frame—then the date of the Exodus must also change; or if he is not actually the Pharaoh of the Exodus, then the date of the Exodus would change as well. All this has direct Biblical implications, because one major reason for discounting the historicity of the Pentateuch is that, once a date of 1250 BC is set for the Exodus, scholars make a few devastating observations:
1. There is little or no archeological evidence for a Semitic people living in Egypt in 1250 BC or in the time period immediately preceding that date. (no Sojourn)
2. There is little or no archeological evidence for the devastating effects of the Exodus upon Egypt, as described in the Bible, at any time around 1250 BC. (no Exodus)
3. There is little or no evidence for Israel entering Canaan forty years later. (no Conquest)

These tragic realities are reflected in the remarks of believing scholars as they attempt to defend the (at least partial) historicity of the Sojourn, the Exodus, and the Conquest. But these voices are few compared to the negative critics.

Conclusion of Negative Critics: The books of Exodus through Joshua are not historically reliable. The Bible, at least those five Old Testament books, are not accurate. They are a fanciful tale. Many scholars would compare them to *The Iliad and The Odyssey*. They are a great epic story—the Hebrew Epic—and they may contain a few historical facts, but they are not history.

The chronological reasonings presented thus far give insight into how Archeologists reason through the fragments and details of their finds to reconstruct the past. Chronology is an important factor in these reasonings—it is vital to piecing things together correctly, to making accurate connections in the past. Many of the above ideas are presently being debated by scholars. These are technical and on-going discussions. But because such chronological assertions about ancient times come from "models" or "theoretical formulations" that scholars construct on insufficient data and personal inclination, nothing is settled in these debates.

In Part 3 we will present evidence for a different date for the Exodus.

Examples of Scholarly Thinking—The Conquest of Canaan:
Here is an example of how a "less skeptical" scholar thinks about the Conquest of Canaan.[335] Although he is "less skeptical," the total accuracy of the Biblical account is not supported. Events like the Exodus or the Conquest of Canaan might be referred to as "themes," as if their existence is relegated to the pages of the Biblical text only, rather than their being an actual historical occurrence. A number of examples of archeological finds that match the Biblical account are referred to. But he still accepts the prevailing idea that the Exodus happened around 1250 BC, so the connections to other ancient events, which is always dependent upon linking them via chronology, makes the connection weak or invalid.

Again, little attempt is made to defend the full historical truth of the Scriptures. Along the way, attempts are made to correlate the supernatural events of the Bible with phenomena that can be explained as natural happenings—perhaps happenings providentially guided by God. These explanations are clearly contrived, and they in no way undergird or support the Biblical account, substituting natural explanations that are absurd for the supernatural explanations of the Bible. The author I am referring to is the renowned K. A. Kitchen.

1. He opines the crossing of the Jordan as recorded in Joshua would be the result of the banks of the Jordan that collapsed and stopped the flow of the river.[336]
2. He notes that the use of spies, as described in Joshua, was common back into the 18th century and later.[337] He supplies a lot of such background information. This is interesting, but does not specifically undergird the Biblical account.
3. But the divine intervention by the Lord in Israel's Battles is compared to the claims made in ancient times by pagan kings. Any "special phenomena" were readily interpreted to be the helping hand of their particular deity, as he explains. This is how ancient people saw the world around them and, as is implied by the author, this is not the way we see the world today—and we are correct, of course, and in this way the Biblical narrative is stripped of its supernatural elements. They are explained away.[338]
4. The death of Korah and the other rebels is explained away as the collapse of a crust that covered a deep mass of liquid ooze. Moses, who was familiar with the desert and its dangerous mudflats, orchestrated this miracle.[339] In general, supernatural explanations are not accepted at face value, but instead they must be reinterpreted in naturalistic terms.
5. When dealing with the archeological background for the Conquest of Canaan, the author gives several reasons why we do not see evidence like what might be expected from the Biblical text.[340] The author is clearly looking at finds from the 13th century and into the early 12th century. In many ways, he is appealing to the fact the archeological data is fragmented, partial, and inconclusive. That is why evidence for the Conquest is partial or is almost entirely missing.

   Dr. Kitchen does point out that the plan was to fully destroy the pagan altars and places of worship (Deuteronomy 12:2–3), but to occupy and benefit from the cities, houses, vineyards wells, etc. which the previous inhabitants had constructed (Deuteronomy 6:10–11). Therefore we should not expect to always find evidence of cities totally destroyed. This is an excellent point.
6. Because of his later Exodus date, Kitchen gives a shortened chronology for Judges and 1 Samuel 1–7, for the period from Joshua to Saul and the kingdom.[341] This is because no matter when the Exodus occurred, the dates for the reigns of Hebrew kings are chronologically fixed. So if the Exodus is placed at a later date, then the period of the judges, which fits between the Conquest and kings, must be shorter.

Dr. Kitchen gives a good overall picture of Israel as a people of conquest, then as a set of tribal groupings occupying the land along with many of the previous people groups still also in place. Then the nation finally attained a greater sense of national cohesiveness with the establishment of the monarchy. This is a helpful picture of the development of the nation of Israel. He also has a section at the end which debunks the various models of occupation that Miller and Hayes described for us earlier. I appreciate his detailed explanations that show the unreasonableness of these two views of how the nation of Israel came to be. In this way Dr. Kitchen performs a wonderful service for the Church and for the Faith. He is an eminent scholar who takes a date of around 1250 BC for the Exodus and does his best to defend it.

Nevertheless, as I read his work I am also struck by the loss of faith in the Biblical record that it engenders. There is faith, but not the full confidence that was the universal characteristic of ages past. The acts of God on behalf of His people are stripped out. Too many miracles are explained away, too weak are the supporting archeological connections, still too bound to "models" of societal development to allow the Divine workings with the nation to be fully seen. He writes as a believer, but his reconstruction of the nation of Israel, his historical model of their development, allows the naturalistic worldview to displace the supernatural.

When I read the account of the Conquest of Canaan in Joshuah, I am touched and thrilled at the faithfulness of the Lord God. In his dying words Joshuah encourages his people.
> For the LORD has driven out great and strong nations from before you; and as for you, no man has stood before you to this day. One of your men puts to flight a thousand, for the LORD your God is He who fights for you, **just as He promised you** . . . Now behold, today I am going the way of all the earth, and **you know in all your hearts and in all your souls** that not one word of all the good words which the LORD your God spoke concerning you has failed; **all have been fulfilled for you, not one of them has failed**. (Joshua 23:9–10, 14)

I am thrilled and touched because this is a love letter bequeathed to the human race by our heavenly Father, and the basic approach of scholarly work today, including that of Kitchen, is to examine it detail by detail, dissect it from beginning to end, tear it apart and reassemble it in a different way, and finally to leave (at least a portion of) the grace and love in the letter obscured by doubts and rationalistic sophistry. This is a tragedy that in no way serves the Church or enhances the Faith. This is the legacy of Rationalism in Biblical Studies today. Rationalism leaves little or no room for the God of the Bible, even with believers.

Once again, the "story" that Kitchen tells seems plausible as he relates it. He is a brilliant scholar. He brings many facts to bear on the narrative that he presents to us. But we must realize that what he says proceeds from his own inclinations as well as from the facts; in truth, probably more from his desire to preserve the Faith in some measure, but to still stay faithful to and rooted in the rationalistic presuppositions that have become the foundation of his discipline, as acknowledged by, and referred to implicitly by almost all scholars today.

Overview of Scholarly Thinking on Epigraphy:

Epigraphy is the study of ancient inscriptions and writings, and their interpretation. This is a vital aspect of archeology, especially in Egypt and the Middle East where thousands of hieroglyphic and cuneiform inscriptions have been discovered.

The most important development in human history might well have been the invention of an alphabetic script. The standard understanding of how and when this happened is that the Phoenicians, who lived in Lebanon north of Israel, first invented and used alphabetic scripts around 1050 BC. The Phoenicians were expert sailors, and their writings are found scattered about the Mediterranean, so they must have invented alphabetic writing. Several other alphabetic scripts then developed in Canaan—the Hebrew alphabet, the Arabic and the Aramaic alphabets, etc. They are all similar to each other, all clearly related Semitic scripts. This development was long after Moses.

Why was the invention of an alphabetic script such an important development? To explain this I want to digress a bit into ancient scripts. The oldest type of writing was pictographic writing, composed of pictographs, which are pictorial symbols for a word or phrase.[342] Then hieroglyphics and cuneiform writing developed, composed of many hundreds of symbols designating words, parts of words, and determinatives. The latter help direct readers in understanding/interpreting other symbols, thus reducing possible ambiguities in writings.

Finally came alphabetic scripts composed of relatively few symbols (letters) each of which represents one of the (relatively few) sounds that comprise one spoken language. There are only a few different sounds that make up any given spoken language, so an alphabet has just a few symbols or letters in it. The earliest alphabets only had symbols or letters for consonants, not for vowels, so they were **consonantal alphabets**. Hebrew has just 22 letters in it, each representing a consonant that is pronounced in the Hebrew language.

Here is an explanation of the power of an alphabetic script:
1. any pronounceable word can be written down quickly and easily.
2. Because there are relatively few symbols or letters, the script is easier to learn—easier to write with and easier to read.

So alphabetic scripts represent a huge advancement over other scripts.

Here are a few examples to drive home this point. I will give examples of alphabetic scripts and also of our decimal numbering system because both of these writing techniques are vital to the advanced technological culture in which we are living. They are the bedrock of our culture, and we rarely think about them. We take their presence for granted.

For instance, how could we do advanced mathematics or computer calculations if we used Roman numerals instead of our decimal number system? Thanks to the Hindus who gave us this numbering system around AD 800! In a similar vein, how can complex, intricate, detailed, abstract ideas, expressed within a flowing narrative, be easily put into writing if we are using a script that is object-based rather than one based on phonetics and on the relatively few sounds that we can and do make when we speak?

Examples:
> **The mass of a hydrogen atom is 1.6727 * 10^{-30} grams, or .00000000000000000000000000016727 grams.**

Imagine trying to express even such a basic fact in Roman numerals.

> **Extrapolation of the expansion of the universe backwards in time using general relativity will produce, at some time on the past, a singularity with infinite density and temperature. At that point the laws of physics as we know them cannot hold, and so we cannot predict what the singularity was like. That mysterious time is referred to as the Plank epoch. After the short time (of the plank epoch) the cosmos entered into a time when the laws of physics with which we are familiar began to hold sway; that is, general relativity and the laws governing subnuclear interactions. In the first 10^{-43} seconds of the Big Bang the universe was filled homogeneously and isotropically with high energy density and huge . . .**

Could one write this or other even more technical passages in cuneiform or hieroglyphics? Also, could one write Shakespear's plays or sonnets?

Whatever we think and feel we must be able to speak, or else communication cannot take place. For culture to develop, what we speak and feel we also must be able to write down quickly, easily, and accurately so that many others can see it and read it. Besides the ideas expressed in a narrative, the smooth flow of the ideas—the artistic nature of how the facts, the ideas, and the sentiments are expressed—call forth demands from the written script that object-based scripts cannot deliver.

These observations have major implications for the Mosaic authorship of the Pentateuch and for its historical reliability. Here is why: The Pentateuch, **especially the last four books**, make up a complex, artistic work with many details expressed within a flowing narrative. It would have been extremely difficult, if not utterly impossible, for such a work to have been written down in a non-alphabetic script—in either cuneiform or hieroglyphics. It is asserted by scholars that Moses did not have an alphabetic script at his disposal.

Thus, if the Hebrews did not have an alphabetic script available to them at the time of the Exodus, then the Pentateuch must have been transmitted by the Hebrews for at least several centuries in oral, rather than in written form. But oral traditions are "known" to be more historically unreliable, "known" to be very prone to exaggeration when recited over and over for many generations, for many years or centuries. These considerations add fuel to the scholarly suspicion that the stories in the Pentateuch are greatly embellished versions of more mundane and less supernatural events because they are not eyewitness accounts. As I mentioned before, they are seen as the Hebrew Epic Tale, as a great literary work, but not as reliable history. This is because it is believed Moses did not have alphabetic writing.

In addition, the writings of Moses in the Pentateuch presuppose a broader literate population, one that is widely schooled in reading and writing. We noted this above.
> You shall teach them to your sons . . . and you shall write them on the doorposts of your house and your gates. (Deuteronomy 11:19–20)

But it is "judged" that hieroglyphics (and cuneiform) were sufficiently complex, and difficult writing methods that only the very highly educated possessed the ability to read and write.

Therefore, the picture of reading and writing that is portrayed in the Pentateuch simply is not possible for the Jews of 1250 BC. Therefore, the Pentateuch was not written by Moses, and it is not an historically reliable document.

This completes my brief overview of scholarly work/opinions in the area of Old Testament archeology and Biblical studies that attack their credibility. Let us characterize the basic objections to the historicity/accuracy/reliability of the Pentateuch.

Summary of Scholarly Challenges to Biblical Truth:
In the overview of the distant past of Egypt, the Middle East, and the Hebrew people that is presented to us by scholars today, we can identify two basic claims against the Mosaic authorship of the Pentateuch and its historical accuracy:
1. There is little or no archeological evidence for a Semitic people living in Egypt at or near to 1250 BC, nor of their leaving the country suddenly at that time, nor of their entering and conquering Canaan about forty years later.
2. There was no alphabetic script in which Moses might have written the Pentateuch. Therefore it was transmitted orally for centuries and is historically unreliable. This is reinforced by the claim that reading and writing were not widely known among the Hebrews at the time of the Exodus.

These are the claims of skeptical scholars that we must answer if we are to show that the Pentateuch is a reliable historical document.

In archeology today we are in a situation that, in many ways, is analogous to the time of Descartes. In his day men were wondering what, if anything, can mankind know for sure to be true? What single thing can we "hang our hat on" in the area of Egyptian and Middle Eastern archeology? This is a serious situation because Biblical Archeology is being used at this time as a foundation for attacks against the credibility of the Sacred Scriptures.

The field of Biblical Archeology is in chaos today. As we have pointed out, the methodology being used in this field of study is based on rationalistic principles, and that is a key reason for the chaos—and it is a key reason for the anti-Christian theories that keep springing forth from those who work in that field.

Part 3—Response: Moses Wrote the Pentateuch and it is Historically Reliable:[343] [see note]

Introductory Observation:

At the time of Descartes the skepticism of the age kept men from seeking their firm truthful foundation in the Word of God. Still today the practice is to separate faith and reason and to discount faith as a part of, or as a guide to, an accurate understanding of the world. But:

> Everyone who hears these words of Mine and acts on them may be compared to a wise man who built his house on the rock. (Matthew 7:24)

In this work I intend to put forth a view of Egyptian and Middle Eastern archeology that is based on the firm belief that the Bible is accurate. From that foundation I will construct a scenario for ancient Egypt and Canaan that includes the Sojourn in Egypt, the Exodus, and the Conquest of Canaan—and which, by its reasonableness and consistency, undergirds the total reliability and complete accuracy of the Biblical narrative on these subjects.

I am able to present this because a small number of scholars have dared to challenge the timeline that is traditionally accepted for the Exodus and for parts of Egyptian chronology. They have then been able to assemble mountains of evidence that collaborates the Biblical accounts of the Sojourn, the Exodus, and the Conquest of Canaan. We will follow their ideas and their thinking. But we will also quote "incredulous" scholars and their ideas as we progress through our reasoning.

I want to begin by making an important observation about the discussion of these topics. There is a direct relationship between the Mosaic authorship of the Pentateuch and the historical reliability of those books. The basic approach in scholarship when denying the truth of any Biblical book is to first question its Patriarchal or Apostolic authorship, then to date its creation or writing to a somewhat later period of time, and thereby attack its basic credibility. Therefore the Mosaic authorship of the Pentateuch and its historical accuracy are linked together in the academic discussions of our time.

This issue is more than a fringe issue. It stands at the center of our Christian faith. Jesus, the Incarnate Word of God, the Creator of the universe, spoke directly to this point:

> If you believed Moses, you would believe Me, for he wrote about Me. If you do not believe his writings, how will you believe My words? (John 5:46–47)

> For Moses said, 'HONOR YOUR FATHER AND YOUR MOTHER'. (Mark 7:10)

Our Lord believed that Moses wrote the Pentateuch. He cannot be wrong. This assertion was the understanding of the Jews throughout their history and the understanding of all the Fathers and Doctors throughout the history of Christianity. We have always believed God commanded Moses to write the Pentateuch and that He inspired him as he wrote it.

> Then the LORD said to Moses, "Write this in a book [lit.: the book] as a memorial and recite it to Joshua, that I will utterly blot out the memory of Amalek from under heaven." (Exodus 17:14)

We also reiterate how vital chronology is to the study of ancient times. We cannot link two past events together accurately unless we know the times when they happened. Therefore chronology is the basis for an accurate reconstruction of the past.

The Basis for the Exodus Date—Biblical Chronology:

The chronology of the reigns of the Hebrew kings has been worked out in conjunction with a broader Middle Eastern and Assyrian chronology to a very high level of certainty. This well-known fact is most important. At this point I want to explain what the Bible says about the date of the Exodus, which relies on the accuracy of the chronology of the Hebrew kings.[344]

In the midst of much chaos, how did the chronology of the Hebrew kings become a solidly worked-out historical fact? For centuries this was a mysterious subject, seemingly fraught with inconsistencies. Then a man named Edwin R. Thiele found the key that resolved all of the seeming contradictions and harmonized Biblical and other Middle East chronologies. He explains the long-standing issue that confronted scholars.

> For more than two thousand years Hebrew chronology has been a serious problem for Old Testament scholars. Every effort to weave the chronological data of the kings of Israel and Judah into some sort of harmonious scheme seemed doomed to failure. The numbers for the one kingdom could not, it seemed, be made to agree with the numbers of the other. The data concerning the synchronisms appeared in hopeless contradiction with the data as to the lengths of reign. Dates established by the biblical numbers seemed to be constantly out of line with the dates of Israel's neighbors.[345]

The author goes on to explain:

> Thirty years after the publication of my solution to the problem of the mysterious numbers of the Hebrew kings comes a need for a new edition. Confused and erroneous as these numbers seemed to be, they have proven themselves to be remarkably accurate. The basic factors that brought about the solution stand out today more clearly than ever.[346]

Thus a long-standing chronological difficulty was solved and has stood the test of time. In the introduction to Thiele's work his mentor Professor William A. Irwin of the University of Chicago, explains the importance of Dr. Thiele's chronology to historical studies.

> It has been well said that chronology is the one sure basis of accurate historical knowledge. History, it is true, is much more than tables of dates and lists of events; these are merely annals, but history must set all in a coherent and meaningful structure of change and development. Nonetheless, to the extent that the historian is deprived of accurate dating, his results grow proportionately vague and uncertain. They become, one might say, a collection of mental antiquities, interesting and possibly beautiful, but nothing more than curios until touched by magic like that of the trained museologist who arranges his disparate pieces in a cultural sequence.[347]

Thus Dr. Thiele's work, first published in 1951 as his doctoral thesis, has become a classic in the field of Biblical chronology. From his work we will use two pieces of information.

First: In Judah, the reigns of kings were reckoned on a Tishri-to-Tishri year. Tishri was an early fall month in the Hebrew lunar calendar, falling around September or October. So if a king assumed the throne in May, for example, the first year of his reign would not begin until Tishri 1 of that year. The time from May until Tishri 1 would be considered to be "the beginning of the reign" of the king. To say that a king reigned five years in all would mean that his reign spanned a total of five Tishri 1's. Even if he died on Tishri 1 of the fifth year, it would still be reckoned as a year of his reign, and not as part of the reign of his successor.

Second: According to Thiele's chronology the first year of Rehoboam's reign was 930 BC; that is, the first year of his reign was reckoned from Tishri 1 of the year 930 BC. Because his father Solomon reigned for forty years (that is, for a total of forty Tishri 1's), the first year of Solomon's reign began on Tishri 1, 970 BC. This verse tells us the exact year of the Exodus:

> Now it came about in the four hundred and eightieth year after the sons of Israel came out of the land of Egypt, in the fourth year of Solomon's reign over Israel, in the month of Ziv which is the second month, that he began to build the house of the LORD. (1 Kings 6:1)

From this information we can determine the year in which the month Ziv of the fourth year of Solomon's reign fell. Here is a table of the first four regnal years of Solomon:

Beginning of regnal year:	Regnal year ends day before:	Regnal Year:
Tishri 1, 970 BC	Tishri 1, 969 BC	1
Tishri 1, 969 BC	Tishri 1, 968 BC	2
Tishri 1, 968 BC	Tishri 1, 967 BC	3
Tishri 1, 967 BC	Tishri 1, 966 BC	4 ←

The month Ziv is in the spring or early summer. The month Ziv of the fourth year of the reign of Solomon was in 966 BC. Thus the Exodus was 480 years earlier, in 1446 BC.

The Exodus happened on Nisan 15, so there was a part of a year—from 15 to 45 days—in 966 that preceded the dates in the month Ziv. If that partial year was reckoned as another year, which sometimes was done, then the Exodus would be one year later, or in 1447 BC. Clearly this date (whichever we choose) cannot be reconciled with Ramesses II being the pharaoh of the Exodus. We must reconcile that claim, which is also based on the Bible.

Besides Exodus 1:11, which asserts the Hebrews built the city of Pi-Ramesses for pharaoh, there is another Biblical reference connecting the Hebrews to the city Pi-Ramesses and the land of Goshen. In Genesis, in chapter 47, when Jacob and his family are entering Egypt at the time of the famine, it is repeatedly stated that they were to settle in the best of the land, in the land of Goshen. But it is also stated that they would settle in the land of Ramesses.
> So Joseph settled his father and his brothers and gave them a possession in the land of Egypt, in the best of the land, in the land of Rameses, as Pharaoh had ordered. (Genesis 47:11).

How could Ramesses be pharaoh at the time of Joseph and also at the time of the Exodus? These events are separated by centuries. What we are seeing here is an anachronism, a place that has been renamed to a more modern or up-to-date name, likely because its old name had become obscure and meaningless to those who were reading the text of the Bible, to the Jews of Old Testament times. The name of the city where the family of Jacob settled had a different name at the time of the famine, but it passed out of usage at some point in Old Testament times, so the Hebrew scribes substituted the then-current name of the place into the text of the Bible. Both cities were in the same location, in the land of Goshen, in the best part of the land of Egypt, but the new name was more meaningful and understandable.

An example from our own country is the name of the city founded by the Pilgrims. Surely they founded New York. That is the present name of the city. But when they founded it the name was New Amsterdam. Yet today we can easily say that the Pilgrims founded the city of New York, even though it did not receive that name until the Dutch ceded it to the British in 1664. The statement refers to the name the city had at the time of the writing, not to the name it had many years earlier. Thus using Exodus 1:11 to set the date of the Exodus was a mistake from the beginning, and the date must be determined another way.

There are a few other examples of anachronisms in the Old Testament, no doubt arising from the need to update ancient place names. A few examples: Genesis 14:14 says that "Abram pursued them unto Dan." But Dan (the northern most area of the promised land) was not called by that name at the time of Abram. Thus this is a later update to that ancient place name, whatever it was called at the time of Abram. In Genesis 21:34 it is said that "Abraham sojourned in the land of the Philistines for many days." **If** the present scholarly opinion is correct that the Philistines did not live in that area at that early date, then this is another example of an anachronism, an update to an ancient place name that had become obsolete at some point in the history of Israel. The same could be conjectured about the reference to "Philistines" in chapter 26 of Genesis.

One question that arises is, when scholars chose 1250 BC as the date of the Exodus then how did they get around that clear and obvious chronological statement? They said that 480 years was an editorial comment based on the fact that there were 12 generations from the Exodus to Solomon and the Hebrews had reckoned 40 years to a generation. Because there actually are more like 20-25 years in a generation, the actual time period was more like 240-300 years, which agrees approximately with 1250 BC. Considering the importance of chronology in general, and the precision of Old Testament chronology in particular, it is clear that such an attempt to dismiss this clear chronological statement is not acceptable.

I want to give an example revealing more clearly the reasoning by which one scholar rejects this straightforward chronological statement in the Bible.

> The figure [480] resolves into twelve units of forty years, the latter figure being commonly used in the Old Testament to represent a generation; further, the succession of High Priests from Aaron to the return from the Exile can be divided into two sections, one bridging the time between the Exodus and the first temple, and the other extending from the building of the first temple to the Exile, each section consisting of twelve generations; and the sum of the lengths of the reigns of Judah's kings from the fourth year of Solomon to the destruction of Jerusalem by Nebuchadnezzar, as given in the books of Kings, with the addition of fifty years for the Exile, yields another period of 480 years between the building of the first temple and the founding of the second, which exactly balances the 480 years between the Exodus and the building of the first temple. For these reasons the figure is held to be artificial and unreliable.[348]

The scholar that reasoned in this way is not the author of the book referenced, but someone whom he is quoting. The author of the book goes on to refute this reasoning. But I want to examine the presuppositions that underlie this kind of thinking.

1. The scholar who is quoted here believes that the Book of 1 Kings was written at a date long after the time of the events that it describes, after returning from the captivity in Babylon, and at least as late as when the second temple was being built or after it had been built. Thus he considers it to be historically unreliable.
2. The person believes that the writer of 1 Kings had a special religious motive in mind as he wrote, a motive that led him to write about history in a cavalier way, distorting the facts in order to emphasize a certain theological point.
3. The person reinterprets a book that appears to be written in the genre of history as a religiously motivated text with questionable historical content—as a pious fraud.
4. The person stretches to find a repetitious numerical pattern in the succession of the high priests and in the duration of times in order to substantiate his reasoning.

These attitudes certainly undergird the remarks made by the one who wrote this opinion, and they impute motives to the writer of the 1 Kings, as if the scholar could read his mind. Such attitudes were commonly expressed by enlightenment authors for over two centuries before this scholar wrote. They were not based on new information, as we mentioned. They were simply expressing new attitudes toward the Scriptures, attitudes of radical skepticism that proceeded directly from rationalist presuppositions.

Lest the reader think that such scholarship is just cavalier, or is the product of wicked minds, let me give another illuminating quote that elucidates this thinking.

> In interpreting the Old Testament record, it is necessary to remember how it is composed. From the period of the Patriarchs onwards, the earlier books of the Old Testament are true history, but it is a traditional history, a record of tribal events transmitted verbally. In the actual form that we know, the books of the Pentateuch are quite late, perhaps not earlier than the seventh century B.C. But the authors certainly had earlier documents as their sources, some of them perhaps as early as the twelfth century B.C. Behind these lie the traditional history, passed on from generation to generation. The earlier written records were themselves compilations, as a **critical analysis can show**, with sources in the traditional history of more than one tribe or group, and the final form carries on the process. **At each stage, the aim of the editor was to produce a continuous narrative, with the supreme aim of showing the relationship of the Israelites to their god Yahweh and his guidance of their destiny.** As regards pure history, such a compilation has two main limitations. Traditional, verbal, history is incomplete, striking events alone being remembered, and its chronological framework is very loose, for it must be remembered that the Israelites had no fixed calendar. A generation is at best a vague term, and when events of past generations are recorded, some may be combined, others, believed to be very ancient, antedated. Secondly, in the process of compilation, a record from one source may be made subsequent to that from another, whereas they are in fact contemporary, and thus an inflated chronology is produced, while, when the overriding purpose is a religious one, great events which are taken as evidence of Yahweh's providing for his chosen people are believed to have affected the history of all groups, whereas they formed part of the history of one group only.

> **Therefore, in attempting to reconcile literary and archaeological evidence, we may take it in the first place that chronology based on the Biblical record cannot be taken literally. Almost any adjustment is possible according to what one wishes to adjust it to.**[349] [bold mine]

The idea that the Biblical record was composed over many centuries by a series of unknown people has never been proven. Of course that would undermine Biblical truth. Such a claim cannot be proven in any way—including the (supposed) critical analysis that underlies it. Note the presumption that this person also can read the mind and motives of the "editor." These erroneous statements reflect a bias rooted in an anti-supernaturalistic worldview.

These ideas are based exactly on the "new presuppositions" that writers worked from as a result of the "enlightenment," which are themselves expressions of rationalist assumptions going back to Descartes. **There is no evidence** for any of the assertions that these authors make. In these examples the authors are leaning on rationalist assumptions and conclusions of scholars from the school of "higher criticism," who are themselves simply reading their original anti-supernaturalistic bias into their scholarship. One area of study feeds into and supports another as the Cartesian-Darwinian Narrative spreads and reinforces itself, creating a comprehensive worldview. Modern scholarship is immersed in these attitudes. And the result of their thinking in this instance is to discount Biblical chronology. With this kind of thinking and scholarship, it is most important to take note of the widely accepted accuracy of the total chronology of the Kings of Israel and Judah. It contradicts this thinking, exposing the bias in the reasons and causes that are cited when people express these ideas.

I see the chronology of Thiele as a gift to believers from God at this time.

There is another less exact but important Biblical chronological clue that reinforces 1446 BC as the date of the Exodus. In the book of Judges Jephthah sent messengers to the sons of Ammon saying,
> While Israel lived in Heshbon and its villages, and in Aroer and its villages, and in all the cities that are on the banks of the Arnon, **three hundred years**, why did you not recover them in that time? (Judges 11:26) [bold mine]

This was spoken, reasoning from the chronology of Thiele, around 1100 BC. About 300 years earlier Joshuah had established the children of Israel along the banks of the Arnon (Joshua 12:1–2, 13:9, 16). Thus the approximate time for the Conquest of Canaan was about 300 years earlier; i.e., around 1400 BC. The 1210 BC date for the Conquest is impossible because it is two centuries later than this date, but the 1406 BC date fits perfectly.

But as an example of the chaos that plagues ancient chronology, the dates for the reign of Ramesses II are also questioned by scholars today. For instance, Egyptologist Dr. David Rohl proposes a date in the **900's BC** for the reign of Ramesses II.[350] He dates the beginning of his reign to the late 900's BC, not to the 1279 BC date that most scholars accept. Of course, the many scholars who hold to the 1279 BC date for the beginning of the reign of Ramesses II have reasons for their position, as we have noted. But Dr. Rohl proposes a disparity of more than three centuries in the chronology of Egypt! I want to look briefly at the reasoning by which he arrives at his assertion. We will follow Dr. Rohl as he begins with a key text from the Old Testament:
> When the kingdom of Rehoboam was established and strong, he and all Israel with him forsook the law of the LORD. And it came about in King Rehoboam's fifth year, because they had been unfaithful to the LORD, that **Shishak** king of Egypt came up against Jerusalem with 1,200 chariots and 60,000 horsemen . . . [He] took the treasures of the house of the LORD and the treasures of the king's palace. He took everything; he even took the golden shields which Solomon had made. (2 Chronicles 12:1–2, 9) [bolding mine]

The question is, who is the Egyptian Pharaoh referred to as "Shishak," and how does his identity impact the date of the Exodus? Traditionally he has been identified with Shoshenk I. This was first determined by Champollion, a child prodigy in the field of philology. He was the French scholar who first deciphered Egyptian hieroglyphs and who first translated the Rosetta stone. He became a founding figure in Egyptology. How did Champollion conclude that Shashak was the Egyptian pharaoh Shoshenk I?

Once Champollion found the key to hieroglyphs he traveled to Egypt to test out his discovery. Among the ruins of the Temple of Amun-Re at Karnak in Thebes he found a scene of a military campaign into Canaan led by Pharaoh Shoshenk I. Among the names of the people and places that Shoshenk I had conquered was the name "Iuda ha Malkuth," which Champollion identified as "Judah the Kingdom." Therefore he connected Shoshenk I with Shishak of the above passage. But the translation of "Iuda ha Malkuth" was soon corrected to "Yad ha-Melek," which means "Hand of the King," a completely different meaning.

That error, and the identification of Shishak with Shoshenk I, has never been corrected by scholars even to this day! (The two names are similar, after all.) But Dr. Rohl points out that the campaign waged by Shoshenk I, as derived from the many place names that his inscription mentions, does not even come close to matching the towns of Judah that were fortified by Rehoboam against a possible Egyptian attack. Here is what the Bible says about the fortifications that Rehoboam made as a defense against Egypt:

> Rehoboam lived in Jerusalem and built cities for defense in Judah. Thus he built Bethlehem, Etam, Tekoa, Beth-zur, Soco, Adullam, Gath, Mareshah, Ziph, Adoraim, Lachish, Azekah, Zorah, Aijalon and Hebron, which are fortified cities in Judah and in Benjamin. He also strengthened the fortresses and put officers in them and stores of food, oil and wine. *He put* shields and spears in every city and strengthened them greatly.
> (2 Chronicles 11:5–12)

These fortified cities are shown as dots on the map of Judah to the right. Also shown are those cities mentioned in Shoshenk I's campaign list, in the path that he followed as he pillaged Canaan. Clearly, they are not at all the same cities. We see that Shoshenk carefully circumvented Judah, missing all but one of the fortified cities. Here is what David Rohl so cogently observes:

> [Let us carefully consider] the matter of Rehoboam's fortified strongholds captured by Shishak on his way to Jerusalem. If we compare the list in 2 Chronicles 11 with Shoshenk's campaign list, do we find those strongholds? No, we do not. Of the fifteen fortresses strengthened by Rehoboam to resist attack from the southwest only one – Aijalon - appears in Shoshenk's list. And that one is directly on the route crossing the hill country north of Jerusalem and the Judean border, used by Shoshenk to reach the Jordan valley. So the next question is: why, if the two campaigns represent the same historical event, does Shoshenk not mention the other fourteen fortresses of Rehoboam among the one hundred and fifty places listed at Karnak? . . .

> Which brings me to the next point. If Jerusalem was such a big prize and the target of Shoshenk's military campaign, how come it does not appear in the Shoshenk campaign relief either? . . . The relief at this point is perfectly preserved. Jerusalem is not included in the campaign list . . .
>
> It is absolutely clear from the Shoshenk campaign relief that his focus is the region north of Judah and then, subsequently, the Negeb desert region south of Judah. The one area he does not invade is the Kingdom of Judah, and he does not plunder its capital city either. Shoshenk's main interest lies in the hill country controlled by the Northern Kingdom of Israel, the Jordan valley, the Jezreel valley and the Sharon plain bordering the Mediterranean coast . . .
>
> To summarize, Shoshenk I did not campaign against the Southern Kingdom of Judah where Egypt's enemy, Rehoboam, ruled in the biblical story. Instead Shoshenk marched into the Northern Kingdom of Israel where his ally, Jeroboam, ruled. This is in complete contradiction to the story of Shishak. While the biblical Shishak defeats Judah and no mention is made of a campaign against Israel, Shoshenk avoids entering Judah and heads up into the territory of Israel. Moreover, Shishak plundered Jerusalem and Shoshenk does not even mention this important prize in his list of defeated/subject cities. Don't let anyone tell you that Jerusalem was not listed because it handed over a ransom and was not therefore officially subjugated. That is not how these triumph reliefs worked. Any city plundered or subjugated or forced to pay tribute, gets listed.[351]

This surely indicates that Shoshenk I was not the Shishak of the Chronicles passage. Dr. Rohl also points out that **a major part of the chronology of the kings of Egypt, those with their reigns after Shoshenk I and going into the New Kingdom, are determined by the identification of Shoshenk I with Shishak of the Bible**. Ramesses II is a pharaoh of the New Kingdom. Thus the date commonly assigned to his reign by modern scholars is linked to the confusion regarding Shishak and Shoshenk I. Since Ramesses II is (I believe wrongly) equated to the pharaoh of the Exodus by most scholars, the assumed but errant dates of his reign result in errant dates of around 1250 BC for the Exodus. But as Dr. Rohl observes, the chronology of the Kings of Judah as worked out by Edwin R. Thiele is a solid rock on which to build a correct date for the Exodus.

Because the chronology of the reigns of the kings of Israel and Judah has been definitively worked out, and thus is a firm foundation on which to base the chronology of other events, it is good technique to connect an ancient event with the reign of a Hebrew king, if possible, in order to give that event an accurate chronological context. Such a luxury is not available in the archeology of ancient Egypt. Shoshenk I was in the "Third Intermediate Period," so his reign came just before the New Kingdom, when Ramesses II reigned. That is why, once the chronology of Shoshenk I has been determined, the chronology of many subsequent kings can also be established. This also implies that an extended section of Egyptian chronology has been in error because of the mistaken identification of Shoshenk I with the Shishak of the Bible. Dr. Rohl is seeking to correct a long-standing chronological error.

A Modified Chronology of the Reign of Ramesses II:
When did Ramesses II reign in Egypt? What chronological evidence can we muster? The Bible and Egyptian hieroglyphs imply that the time of the Exodus was much earlier than when Ramesses II reigned. Also, a large granite slab called the Israel Stella, discovered in the late 1890's by Sir William Matthew Flinders Petrie (called the father of Egyptian Archeology), refers to the nation of Israel as a significant Canaanite entity. It was engraved by Merneptah, the thirteenth son and immediate successor of Ramesses II. The hieroglyphs are his campaign register, listing the nations that he conquered or subjugated. Prominent among his list of conquered nations is Israel, "Israel is laid waste, his seed is no more." This is the typical exaggeration and boasting found on such war campaign registers. Israel was not totally destroyed. But it must have existed as a nation at that time.

But if Ramesses II was the pharaoh of the Exodus, then how could his son be referring to Israel as a major established entity on this stella? The Israel Stella implies that the Exodus happened long before the reign of Ramesses II—or, alternately, that his reign followed the Exodus by many years.[352] Of course, there is great controversy and scholarly debate rages over the right way to understand and interpret the stella.[353]

Another discovery that has much more recently come to light is a block fragment from a statue that is dated to even earlier in Egyptian history, and that has the name "I-a-shra-i-l" on it. Just how much earlier has not yet been determined for certain. This is in the Egyptian Museum in Berlin. It was found in 1913, but has been ignored until recently. These two references to "Israel" imply the Hebrews left Egypt well before Ramesses was born.[354]

In fact, Dr. Rohl asserts that Ramesses II was the Shishak of 2 Chronicles 12. He uses this to redate his reign to begin in 943 BC. We noted that Shishak sounds a lot like Shoshenk. That was why Champollion first made the connection and identified them as the same person, and that may very well be why the identification continues to hang on even today.

But Ramesses II was called by other titles and names, which Dr. Rohl explains were like nicknames. One of his other names, common throughout broad areas of Egypt and the Middle East, was *Sysw*. Looking back into the past when Proto-Hebrew was the written script, he notes that the names Sysw and Shishak would have been **written** identically, resulting in confusing the names when the books of Moses were rediscovered. People who read the text forgot the correct pronunciation of the Hebrew word written as SYSW.

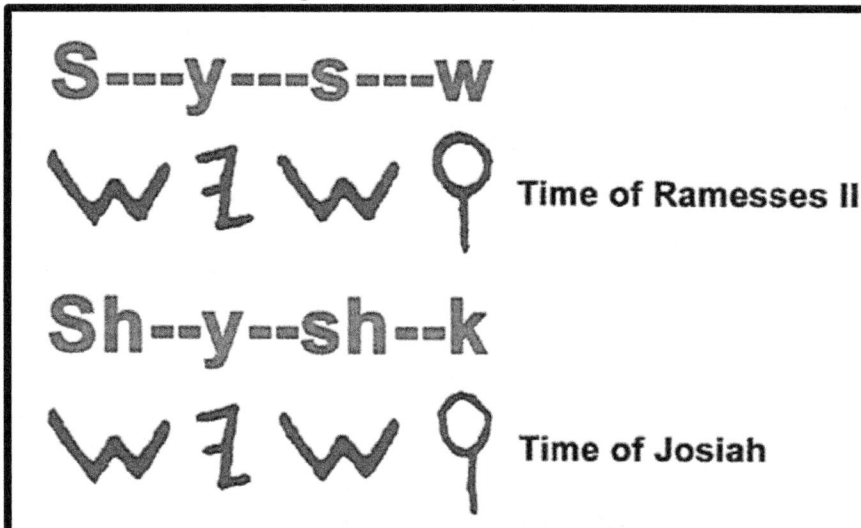

The second line has the nickname "*Sysw*" as it would have been written in "Proto-Hebrew" at the time of Rehoboam.

The fourth line is how the Biblical name "Shishak" would have been written in "Proto-Hebrew" at the time of Josiah when the book of Moses was rediscovered in the temple.

The two scripts are clearly indistinguishable![355]

Dr. Rohl closes his discussion of Shishak with this fascinating insight from a colleague:
> Biblical scholar Peter van der Veen of Johannes Gutenberg University, Mainz, brought to my attention the fact that the name Shy-shak can be interpreted as a combination of two Hebrew words. *Shy* (or *shay)* was the word used (in Psalm 68:29) to describe the gifts or tribute brought to the Temple of Solomon by visiting kings. In other words this was the word for the temple treasure. *Shak,* on the other hand, may derive from the Semitic verb *shakak* which has the meaning 'to ride over the spoils' or simply 'to plunder'. If you put these two Hebrew words together you get "plunderer of the treasure of the Temple of Solomon". What better nickname for Ramesses the Great, who seems to have been the true plunderer of Solomon's treasure in 925 BC![356]

I am not claiming that the extended story or "narrative" that Dr. Rohl is putting forward is accepted by all scholars. It surely is not. It certainly uses several archeological discoveries and interprets them to give some basis to his story. Of course, those who tell another and different story either interpret his facts differently, or fill in the gaps to tell their story in their own different way. However, this revised chronology—for a part of ancient Egypt—is one of the foundations upon which we can construct significant archeological evidence to support the historical accuracy of the Pentateuch. That is one major reason to give it credence. It also reveals the shaky nature of the chronology that scholars have accepted for Egypt.

Astronomical Confirmation of this Drastic Chronological Revision:
Also, there is an astronomical check that provides strong reason for accepting the revised chronology to which Dr. Rohl has reasoned. Astronomical methods employ the lunar calendars that were universally used by the ancients, and leverage upon the fact that lunar months are either 29 or 30 days long, depending on the fact that the lunar orbit is 29.53 days long and on when a new moon was observed at sunset, which was how a new month was reckoned.

Records of ancient times exist and can be compared to astronomically calculated months. Sequences of 29- or 30-day months can be compared to determine the exact year or years that had such a sequence of 29- and 30-day months. Such a sequence exists in ancient records for the final kings of the 12th dynasty and the first few kings of the 13th dynasty of Egypt. When this test was applied to the previous assumed chronology no match of even 60% could be attained. But the revised chronology matched between 97% and 100%! This is a very strong indication that it is correct. For our records and going forward, I present the old and new dates for the reigns of a few of the pharaohs of the 12th and 13th dynasties.

Dates for the Reigns of Pharaohs of the 12th Dynasty and the start of the 13th Dynasty

Pharaoh	Old Chronology	New Chronology	Years Shifted
Amenemhat I	1937-1908 BC	1803-1774 BC	134-134 years
Senuseret I	1917-1872 BC	1774-1730 BC	143-142 years
Amenemhat II	1875-1840 BC	1745-1712 BC	130-128 years
Senuseret II	1842-1836 BC	1716-1698 BC	126-138 years
Senuseret III	1836-1817 BC	1698-1658 BC	138-159 years
Amenemhat III	1817-1772 BC	1678-1631 BC	139-141 years
Amenemhat IV	1772-1763 BC	1633-1626 BC	139-137 years
Sobekneferu	1763-1759 BC	1627-1624 BC	136-135 years
[End of the 12th Dynasty, beginning of the 13th Dynasty]			
Sobekhotep I	1758-1755 BC	1624-1621 BC	134-134 years[357]

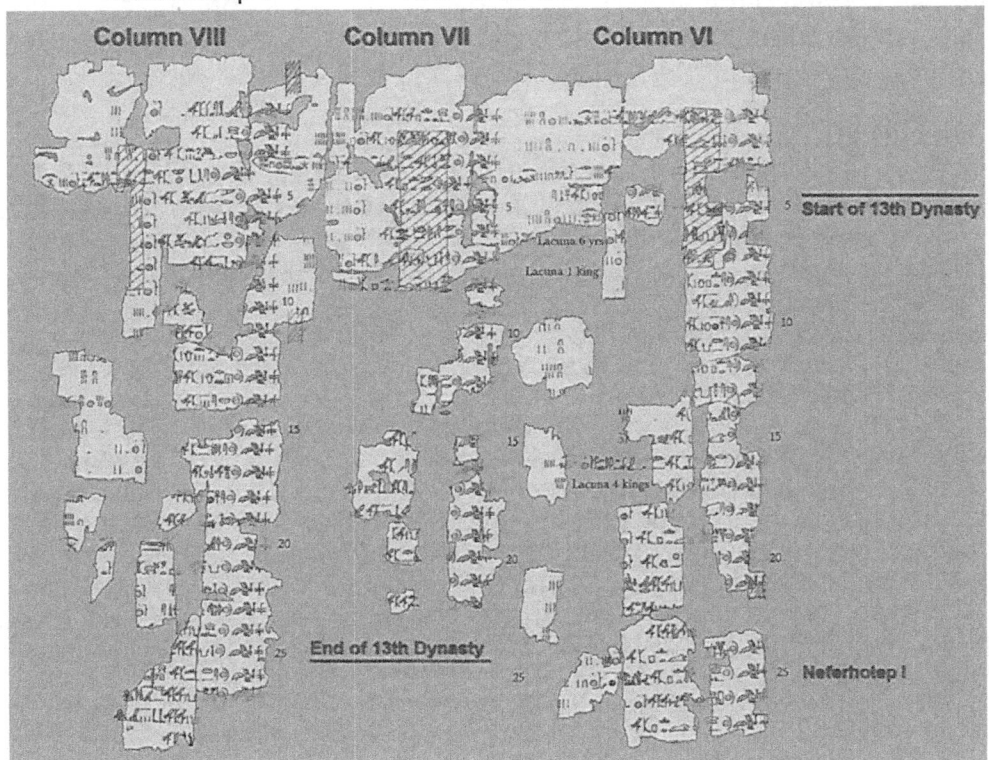

The shifting of dates in these chronologies is not consistent throughout the reigns of all the pharaohs. Date shifts range from 126 to 159 years, thus varying by 33 years. Why is there such uncertainty if the astronomical data gave an exact year?

The 39 lunar dates to which the astronomical calculations are being compared are from the reigns of Senuseret III and Amenemhat III. The reign or coregency of the other pharaohs must be interpolated from data about those ancient pharaohs taken from a certain papyrus record. To the left is what that record looks like—not very intact!

> The kings of the Egyptian 13th Dynasty are listed in a papyrus from the 19th Dynasty which is today called the 'Royal Canon of Turin' (because it is housed in the Egyptian Museum of Turin). The document actually gives the names and reign lengths of the pharaohs from mythological or pre-dynastic times right through to the beginning of the 18th Dynasty (which is the beginning of the New Kingdom), so it is an extremely valuable source for the chronology of the era we are interested in. . . . a bit of the 13th dynasty in Column VI is preserved.[358]

This has greatly affected the determination of the dates above, causing scholars to estimate or guess at figures.

> We find that Neferhotep I is listed as the twenty-seventh ruler of the dynasty (according to Kim Ryholt's analysis) with a reign length of 11 years 1 month. Working backwards, most of the names of his twenty-six predecessors are fairly easily read (with the exception of six rulers lost in lacunae in the document from which the scribe was copying). Unfortunately, nearly all the reign lengths are lost in the damaged sections of the papyrus. However, scholars are aware that the reigns in this era were very short, few extending beyond three years. So we can assign roughly three-and-a-half years to each, giving us an approximate date for the start of the dynasty of 1626 BC and, in that same year, the end of the 12th Dynasty.[359]

Not to mention the fact that this record is dated to the 19th dynasty, which is five or six centuries after the 12th and 13th dynasties. Obviously, even though the astronomical technique (likely) yields an excellent and firm point of reference, the fragmentary nature of the archeological data as a whole still leaves uncertainty in the total chronology. Yet this fragmentary document is often given more credence and authority in chronological matters than the Biblical record!

We are used to the exact and complete records of the reigns of the kings of Israel and Judah as given in the books of Kings and Chronicles. This is what parts of Egyptian chronology are based on. This is why it is important to connect Egyptian dates to Middle Eastern and Biblical events, whose chronology is known "for certain," in order to date much of ancient Egypt.

The conclusions of the scholars that we discuss in this work are greatly influenced by their bias/worldview; either they accept the supernatural origin of the world, of humanity, and of God's chosen people, or they must look for (and even demand) some other (naturalistic) explanation for all of these events to replace the Biblical account. As a consequence, the total Biblical record is often demoted to lower reliability in their minds. They thus look to archeology and its tentative and fragmented data on which to base their conclusions.

The Chronology of the Sojourn in Egypt:

Once we set the date of the Exodus we can also set the chronology for the Sojourn of the Hebrews in Egypt. So when did the Israelites enter Egypt? Knowing that the Exodus was in 1446 BC we can then ask the question in an equivalent way: How long was the Sojourn in Egypt? The Bible speaks to this, but in a way that has often confused people. I want to go through the reasoning. The apostle Paul says:

> Now the **promises** were spoken to Abraham and to his seed. He does not say, "And to seeds," as *referring* to many, but *rather* to one, "And to your seed," that is, Christ. What I am saying is this: **the Law, which came four hundred and thirty years later**, does not invalidate a covenant previously ratified by God, so as to nullify the promise. For if the inheritance is based on law, it is no longer based on a promise; **but God has granted it to Abraham by means of a promise**. (Galatians 3:16–18) [bold mine] [430 years from the promise to Sinai and the Law.]

The promise made to Abraham to which Paul refers is recorded in Genesis 12, 13, and 15.

> Now the LORD said to Abram: "Go forth from your country, and from your relatives and from your father's house to the land which I will show you. And I will make you a great nation, and I will bless you, and make your name great; and so you shall be a blessing; and I will bless those who bless you, and the one who curses you I will curse. And in you all the families of the earth will be blessed." (Genesis 12:1–4) [This is the promise made to Abraham (Abram).]
> The promise (covenant) is reiterated in other words in Genesis 13:14–18. Then in Genesis 15, Abram said, "O Lord GOD, what will You give me, since I am childless, and the heir of my house

> is Eliezer of Damascus?" And Abram said, "Since You have given no offspring to me, one born in my house is my heir." Then behold, the word of the LORD came to him, saying, "This man will not be your heir; but one who will come forth from your own body, he shall be your heir." And He took him outside and said, "Now look toward the heavens, and count the stars, if you are able to count them." And He said to him, "So shall your descendants be." Then he believed in the LORD; and He reckoned it to him as righteousness. And He said to him, "I am the LORD who brought you out of Ur of the Chaldeans, to give you this land to possess it." (Genesis 15–7) [Here, when the Lord God showed him the heavens, is where and when Abram believed God.]
>
> He said, "O Lord GOD, how may I know that I will possess it?" [Abram is asking for an official contract, something to ratify the agreement or promise that God made.] So He said to him, "Bring Me a three-year old heifer, and a three-year old female goat, and a three-year old ram, and a turtledove, and a young pigeon." Then he brought all these to Him and cut them in two, and laid each half opposite the other; but he did not cut the birds. The birds of prey came down upon the carcasses, and Abram drove them away.
>
> Now when the sun was going down, a deep sleep fell upon Abram; and behold, terror and great darkness fell upon him. *God* said to Abram, "Know for certain that your descendants will be strangers in a land that is not theirs, where they will be enslaved and oppressed four hundred years. But I will also judge the nation whom they will serve, and afterward they will come out with many possessions. As for you, you shall go to your fathers in peace; you will be buried at a good old age. Then in the fourth generation they will return here, for the iniquity of the Amorite is not yet complete."
>
> It came about when the sun had set, that it was very dark, and behold, *there appeared* a smoking oven and a flaming torch which passed between these pieces. On that day the Lord made a covenant with Abram, saying,
>> "To your descendants I have given this land, from the river of Egypt as far as the great river, the river Euphrates:
>
> the Kenite and the Kenizzite and the Kadmonite and the Hittite and the Perizzite and the Rephaim. (Genesis 15: 8–21) [This is where God formally ratified His promise to Abram via a covenant.]

The promise was made as soon as Abraham departed from his family in Haran. Then 25 years after he left Haran Isaac was born. At some point Isaac was weaned, likely around age five. At that time Ismael so mocked Isaac that Sarah demanded that he and Hagar, his mother, be cast out of the household. Ismael's mocking began the oppression of which the Lord had spoken to Abraham. It was 430 years from God's promise to the giving of the Law on Sanai, and 430 - 25 - 5 = 400 years of oppression that came upon the descendants [seed] of Abraham. This happened as they were sojourning in (or passing through) various lands that were not their own, not their home, not their promised inheritance. Abram was 75 when he left Ur, Isaac was born 25 years later when he was 100, Jacob was born when Isaac was 60, and Jacob was 130 when he entered Egypt. 25 + 60 + 130 = 215 years in Canaan. This leaves 215 years for the Sojourn in Egypt.

This seems reasonable enough in itself, but there is another verse that brings confusion into this discussion.
> Now the time that the sons of Israel lived in Egypt was four hundred and thirty years. And at the end of four hundred and thirty years, to the very day, all the hosts of the LORD went out from the land of Egypt. (Exodus 12:40, NASB)

This makes it seem as if the 430 years was all spent in the land of Egypt, not divided up between Egypt and various places in the Middle East while the patriarchs wandered there. How can/should we reconcile the verses in Galatians and in Exodus?

The King James translates Exodus 12:40 as follows:
> Now the sojourning of the children of Israel, who dwelt in Egypt, *was* four hundred and thirty years. And it came to pass at the end of the four hundred and thirty years, even the selfsame day it came to pass, that all the hosts of the LORD went out from the land of Egypt. (Exodus 12:40, KJV)

This account says that the children of Israel sojourned for a total of 430 years. The Sojourn of the Hebrews began in Canaan. We know this because when Jacob stood before pharaoh as they entered into Egypt at the time of the famine this was their conversation:
> Then Joseph brought his father Jacob and presented him to Pharaoh; and Jacob blessed Pharaoh. Pharaoh said to Jacob, "How many years have you lived?" So Jacob said to Pharaoh, "The years of my sojourning are one hundred and thirty; few and unpleasant have been the years of my life, nor have they attained the years that my fathers lived during the days of their sojourning." (Genesis 47:7–9)

Thus the sojourning began earlier in the life of Jacob, while he was still living in Canaan, and it followed the sojourning of Isaac and Abraham as well. So the sojourning began in the land of Canaan. This agrees with Galatians. So is this just a translation issue?

No, it is also an issue of the correct text. Looking at other texts of Genesis—other than the Masoretic text—we see the following for Exodus 12:40:
> They (the Israelites) left Egypt in the month of Zanthicus, on the fifteenth day of the lunar month; four hundred and thirty years after our forefather Abraham came into Canaan two hundred and fifteen years only after Jacob entered Egypt. [Josephus: *Antiquities of the Jews,* Chapter XV:2]

> And the sojourning of the children of Israel - that is which they sojourned in the land of Egypt and in the land of Canaan - was four hundred and thirty years. [Exodus 12:40, *Septuagint* version]

> Now the sojourning of the children of Israel and of their fathers when they had dwelt in the land of Canaan and in Egypt was four hundred and thirty years. [Exodus 12:40, Samaritan *Pentateuch*]

> It therefore seems that the words 'and in the land of Canaan' have somehow dropped out of the Qumran and subsequent Masoretic editions at some stage during the process of copying. The *Septuagint* was presumably translated from an original Hebrew text of the Torah during the third century BC (when seventy Jewish scholars were commissioned to write a Greek translation of the Old Testament for Ptolemy II's new library in Alexandria c. 270 BC). Josephus wrote his *Antiquities of the Jews* in the first century AD, while the Samaritan *Pentateuch* comes from several centuries earlier. The Qumran fragmentary papyrus of Exodus dates either to the second half of the third century BC or as late as 25 BC (depending on expert opinion), suggesting that the omission occurred sometime in the third century BC or later.[360]

For these reasons I think that 430 years in Egypt **and** Canaan is the correct understanding of the time of the Israelite's sojourning. 215 of that was in Canaan, and 215 was in Egypt. Thus the date when Jacob and his family entered Egypt was 1446 + 215 = 1661 BC. As we will see when we comment on Genesis, Joseph preceded his father and the rest of his family into Egypt by many years. He was sold into slavery in Egypt in 1713 BC. This gives the chronology of the Sojourn of the Hebrews in Egypt.

In this work I develop a Biblical chronology for events going back to the creation. It is not precise in that it can be off by a few years. But it includes a chronology for the time of the Sojourn and the Exodus. Dr. Rohl's chronology for the Egyptian pharaohs of the 12th/13th dynasties fits my dates nicely. I will develop a coordinated chronology using two reigns:
Senuseret III = 1698-1658 BC [This is the pharaoh whose dreams Joseph interpreted.]
Amenemhat III = 1678-1631 BC [co-regent with Senuseret III for 20 years]

How vital is this date to this work? In our work we will construct a basic chronology of the Old Testament from creation to the Exodus. If we are off by a few years it will not affect what we are about, so I choose 1446 BC as the date of the Exodus. 1445 or 1447 BC would have done just as well for us. But two centuries off? That is a significant length of time.

Scholars have asserted that there is little or no support for the Biblical account of the Sojourn in Egypt, the Exodus, or the Conquest of Canaan when 1250 BC is chosen for the date of the Exodus. That is definitely not the case when we choose 1446 BC as our Exodus date.

Evidence for the Sojourn in Egypt:

Once we assign 1446 BC as the date for the Exodus then abundant archeological evidence for the Sojourn can be found. Again, the Sojourn lasted for a total of 215 years, so it began in 1661 BC (Joseph 1682 BC) and ended with the Exodus in 1446 BC.

Because the Bible says that Jacob and his family settled in the land of Goshen, which is the Eastern part of the Nile delta, we must look there for the signs of their culture. We pointed out that the reference to Ramesses II in the Bible is an anachronism. The location where the Hebrew slaves built a city for pharaoh at the time of the Exodus was located at the same place but was called by another name. That would mean that Pi-Ramesses had been built near to or on top of some other more ancient city. One such city has been found there, built centuries earlier. It is called Avaris. The Sojourn was contemporary with Avaris, not with Pi-Ramesses, which was built centuries after the Jews had left Egypt.

Here is a short overview of ancient Eastern Nile delta history based on the work of Austrian archeologist Manfred Bietak and his team of workers.

> The entire area of the two cities - one Middle Bronze Age [Avaris] and the other Late Bronze Age [Ramesses] - had been surveyed by the Austrians (back in the 1960s) using eight hundred and fifty drill-cores to establish the topographical layout (and, in particular, the location of the Pelusiac branch of the Nile). Then, over the last decade, a much more detailed ground-penetrating radar project was undertaken, by both the Germans (at Pi Ramesse) and Austrians (at Avaris), to reveal a vast city complex.[361]

> It was at this spot that the Pelusiac branch split into two channels, hence the original name of the town - *Rowaty* ('Mouth of the Two Ways'). Many centuries later, the royal city of Ramesses II was built in the triangle of land between these two branches of the river, north of the old city of Avaris. Ramesside texts actually mention Avaris as the southern quarter of Pi Ramesse.[362]

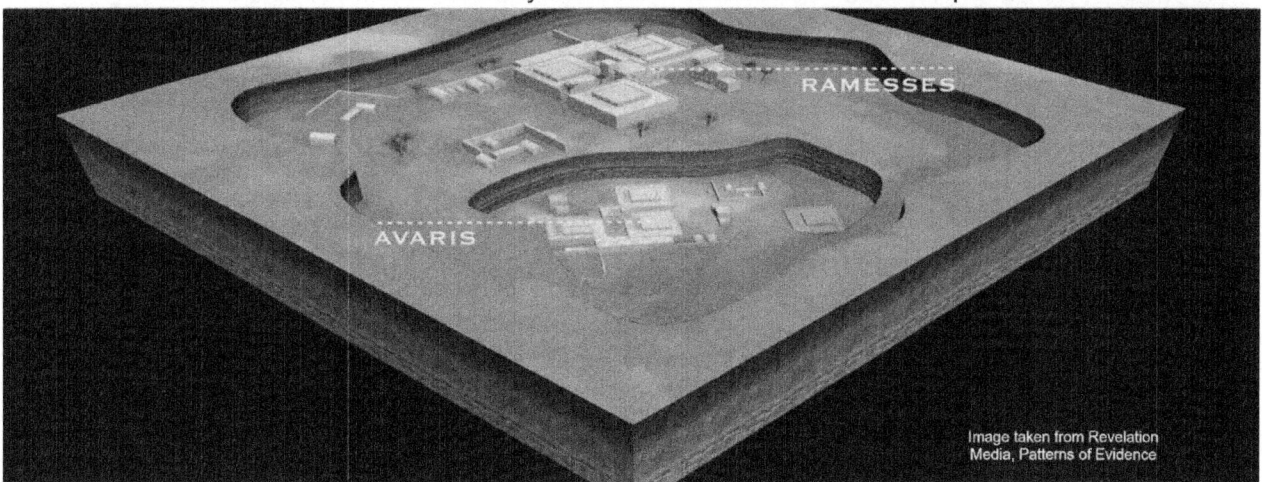

Image taken from Revelation Media, Patterns of Evidence

The arrival of Jacob and his family is clearly marked in the digs.

> Towards the end of the 12th Dynasty, the old, abandoned settlement of Khety's Rowaty witnessed the arrival of Semitic peoples from the north-east. The new village rapidly expanded into a town and then, within a couple of centuries, it became a huge city of over a square mile. This demographic change, marked by the arrival of these Asiatics as observed in the archaeology, began at the very moment we have placed the arrival of Jacob and his tribe in the land of Goshen. At about the same time, the name of the city was changed to *Ha(t)ware(t)* (pronounced Hawara or Haware, Greek Auaris, modern Avaris) which means the 'Office of the Region' because it became the northern headquarters of the government - most likely represented by the presence of the vizier [presumably Joseph] for at least part of the year.[363]

> Time then to see what we can learn about these Proto-Israelites from archaeology. As I said, the city of Avaris began life as a small village towards the end of the 12th Dynasty when the

'Mittelsaal Haus' [central hall/house] of Jacob was erected in Area F. At about the same time, houses began to be built a couple of hundred yards to the south-east on the turtleback ridge (now known as Tell A) that would eventually become the heart of the Asiatic city of Avaris.[364]

Avaris had a mixed population of Egyptians, Semites, and even some Greeks. It included 25,000 to 30,000 Semitic people. Avaris was surrounded by dozens of other settlements which together would have made up a large and expanding population of Semitic people. But this was in 1450 BC and the decades that followed, not in 1250 BC.[365]

The Bible says the Hebrews "filled the land." Indeed, other settlements of Semitic people have been found in various Egyptian cities. One example is Kahun, which is further south, further up the Nile River. It had also developed a large Semitic population by 1450 BC.[366]

Back to Avaris: Much later, probably by more than a century, archeology indicates that the outlook of the Semitic population of Avaris changed for the worse.

> According to the archaeological evidence at Tell ed-Daba, conditions then began to deteriorate, with skeletal remains in the graves showing signs of malnutrition (Harris lines in the bones.) Anthropological studies show that adults were dying in their early thirties. Strangely, there were far more burials of infants and young children (50%) than normal (25%) for this sort of ancient civic society. Moreover, there were more females than males in the adult grave population. For every three females there were only two males. Where had the adult males gone?

> The Bible provides the answer. The opening chapter in the Book of Exodus tells us that the Egyptians first enslaved the Israelites, then culled the male infants because the slave population was getting too large, and Pharaoh perceived this as a threat. Obviously, in archaeological terms, this would mean an increase in infant burials and a skew in the adult population in favor of females.[367]

More specific details about Avaris from around 1450 BC:[368]
- A Semitic population with their distinct culture had lived at Avaris for centuries.
- One modest Semitic dwelling had an elaborate Egyptian structure built on top of it. It must have belonged to a man of prestige. The elaborate superstructure had 12 pillars in it, and in the garden or courtyard surrounding it were 12 tombs.
- One of the tombs was in the shape of a pyramid, which is significant because that shape of tomb was normally reserved for pharaohs, but this man was not a pharaoh because inside of the pyramid was a statue of a man with red hair and pale, yellow, skin. That was how Egyptians depicted northerners. The statue had a throw stick across the shoulder, a unique symbol of office made for an official from Asia. The statue itself was twice as high as normal, indicating again his great importance.[369]
- On the back of this man we can see the faintest remains of paint-colored stripes from a multi-colored coat. The statue as been broken and cast down, but here is shown an artist's reconstruction with an enhanced photo of the coat on that statue. Here is the description of the find from the Austrian archeological mission at Tell el-Daba:
  > Of special interest was the discovery of fragments of a smashed tomb statue. The head, parts of the cloak and the seat were found in tomb p/19-Nr. 1. Other fragments, such as a joining shoulder and the left foot were discovered in nearby tombs. The statue was made of limestone and originally was larger than life. It portrayed a seated man wearing a striped cloak and a red, mushroom shaped hairstyle. Such hairstyles are found on various Egyptian depictions of Asiatics in the Middle Kingdom. The skin color of the man is shown as yellow. In the right hand he is holding a throw stick which is resting against his right shoulder. Egyptian Middle Kingdom images showing people as Asiatics most commonly show these as conquered enemies. This man, on the other hand, held a position of power, on a local level. He reached this position, however, by maintaining - even emphasizing - what for the Egyptians constituted an 'Asiatic'.[370] [this note directs to the website for the Australian archeological team.]

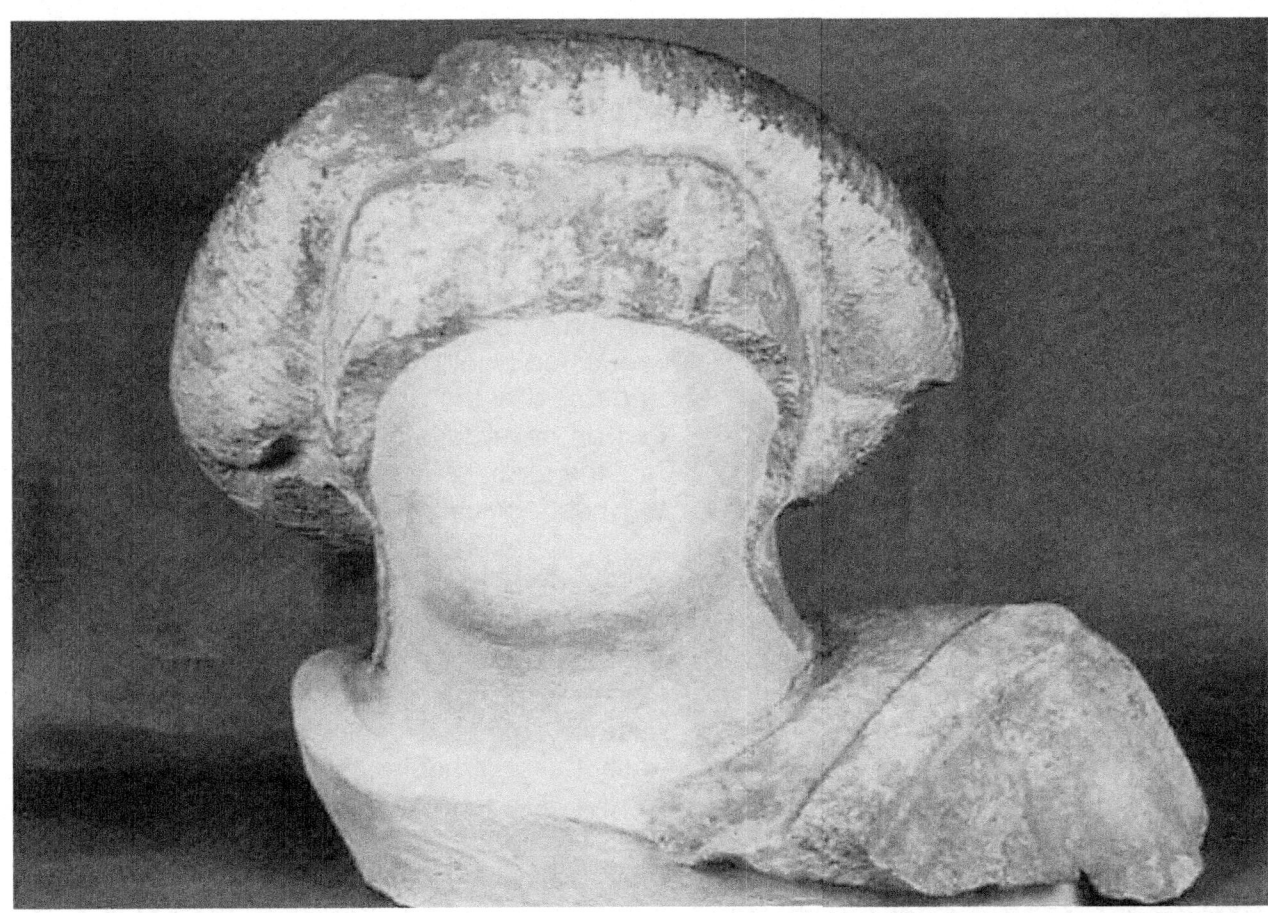

Above is a picture from the web site of the reconstructed statue found at Avaris. Below is a slightly enhanced photo of the shoulder showing the faint stripes of its colorful coat Finally, see the artistic reconstruction of the statue on the next page. It appears to be a statue of Joseph. From its composition we can tell it was carved in the royal workshop at Hawara. That was the workshop of Amenemhat III. The chronology of David Rohl indicates that Joseph served as the vizier of Egypt under that pharaoh.

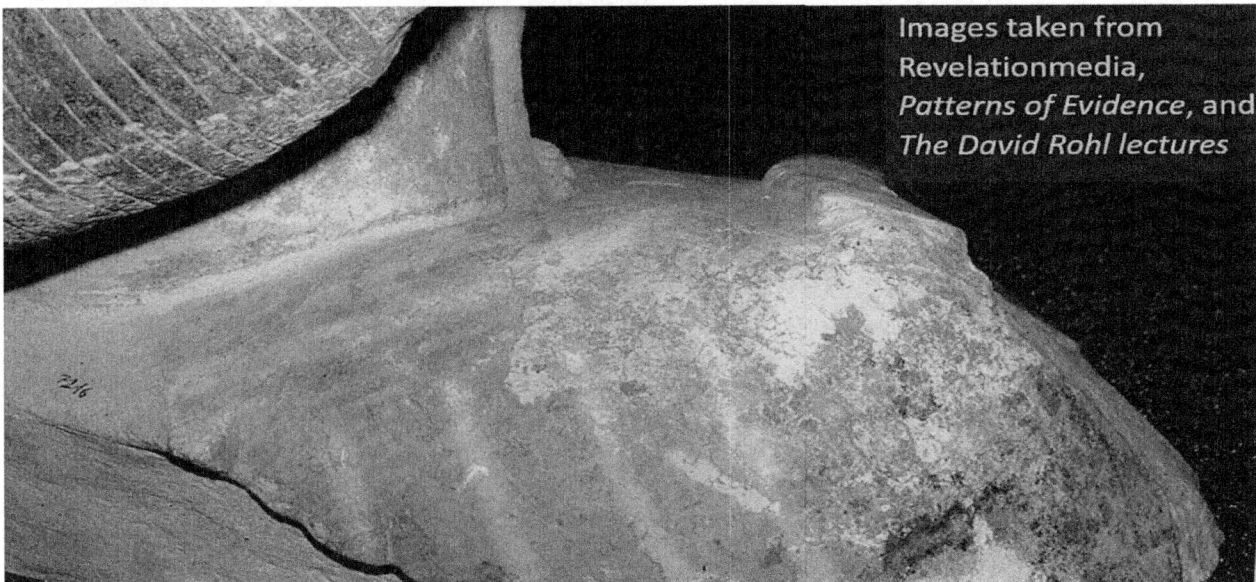

Images taken from Revelationmedia, *Patterns of Evidence,* and *The David Rohl lectures*

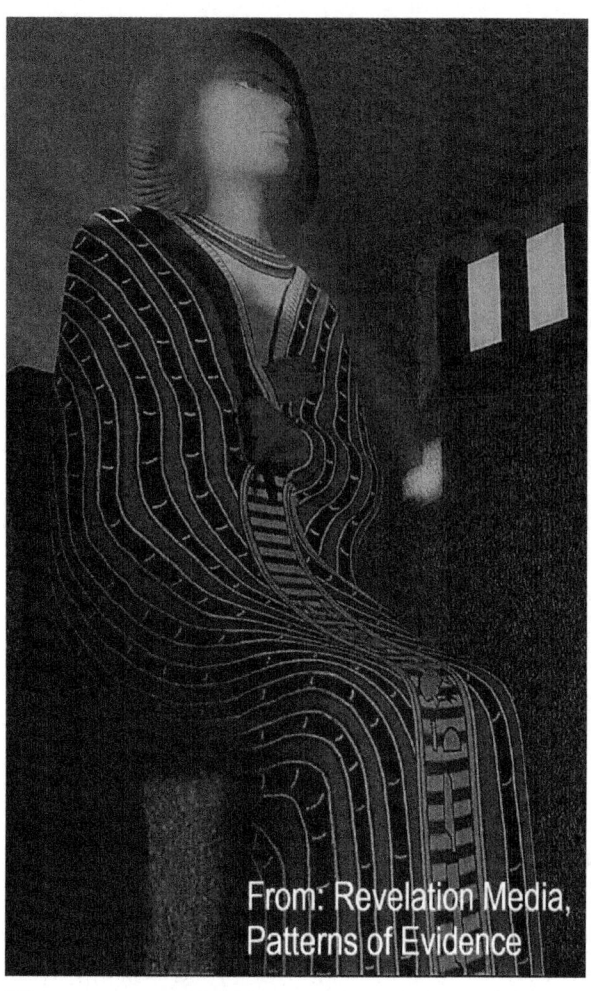
From: Revelation Media, Patterns of Evidence

- Finally, in the account in Scripture Joseph commanded his descendants to carry his bones with them when at last the Lord God visited them and took them to the land that He had promised to their forefathers. The tomb had been raided, as we notice from the fact that the statue lies broken in pieces, but no grave robber would have taken bones. Only those treating Joseph's body with the reverence that he had requested would have taken the bones. Thus it appears that the body of Joseph was removed, just as he requested, and buried in Israel. In fact the body of Joseph is claimed to be buried at Shechem in Israel, where there is a shrine.
- One further point about the tombs found at Avaris; The Egyptian graves were hastily filled with bodies, while in the Semitic quarter we see signs of a sudden mass abandonment. Because of the careful and elaborate burial customs of the Egyptians, in contrast to the hasty burial of bodies thrown together in Avaris graves, it appears as if they must have been facing a plague, or dealing with some kind of a quite contagious disease. This is very much like what we would expect as the result of the judgments of the Exodus.[371]

There was a similar sudden unexplained departure of the entire Semitic population at Kahun around the same time. The sudden departure of Semites from Kahun used to be a mystery.

> A further question remains to be answered—why did the inhabitants of this first occupation at Kahun [first observed many decades ago by Sir William Matthews Petrie] leave their homes? . . . There are different opinions . . . The quantity, range, and types of articles left behind may indeed suggest that the departure was sudden and unpremeditated.[372]

One reason why that sudden departure used to be such a mystery is that the date of the departure was thought to be long before the Hebrews were living in Egypt. But with our new chronology, and with a 1446 BC Exodus date, this event becomes much easier to explain because it looks like the departure of the Jews at time of the Exodus.

Evidence for the Exodus:

When the Exodus judgments fell on Egypt they would have left the nation weakened and in a desperate state. Are there archeological records reporting such an occurrence? Yes, an ancient Egyptian Papyrus, *The Admonitions of an Egyptian Sage*, written by an otherwise unknown person named Ipuwer. The document is addressed to his majesty the pharaoh and describes circumstances that sound like what would have prevailed in Egypt as a result of the Exodus judgments. Here are some statements from the *Admonitions*: [In **bold**][373]

- **Behold, Egypt is fallen to the pouring of water, and he who poured water on the ground seizes the mighty in misery.**[374] In Exodus 4:9 Our Lord, speaking to Moses, gives him three signs to validate himself to the elders of Israel, to show that he has been sent to them from the Lord God.

But if they will not believe even these two signs or heed what you say, then you shall take some water from the Nile and pour it on the dry ground; and the water which you take from the Nile will become blood on the dry ground. (Exodus 4:9)

- **The river is blood! As you drink of it, you lose your humanity and thirst for water.**[375]

    Then the LORD said to Moses, "Pharaoh's heart is stubborn; he refuses to let the people go. Go to Pharaoh in the morning as he is going out to the water, and station yourself to meet him on the bank of the Nile; and you shall take in your hand the staff that was turned into a serpent. You shall say to him, 'The LORD, the God of the Hebrews, sent me to you, saying, "Let My people go, that they may serve Me in the wilderness. But behold, you have not listened until now." Thus says the LORD, "By this you shall know that I am the LORD: behold, I will strike the water that is in the Nile with the staff that is in my hand, and it will be turned to blood. The fish that are in the Nile will die, and the Nile will become foul, and the Egyptians will find difficulty in drinking water from the Nile."'" Then the LORD said to Moses, "Say to Aaron, 'Take your staff and stretch out your hand over the waters of Egypt, over their rivers, over their streams, and over their pools, and over all their reservoirs of water, that they may become blood; and there will be blood throughout all the land of Egypt, both in *vessels of* wood and in *vessels of* stone.'" So Moses and Aaron did even as the LORD had commanded. And he lifted up the staff and struck the water that *was* in the Nile, in the sight of Pharaoh and in the sight of his servants, and all the water that *was* in the Nile was turned to blood. The fish that were in the Nile died, and the Nile became foul, so that the Egyptians could not drink water from the Nile. And the blood was through all the land of Egypt. (Exodus 7:14–21)

- **Gone is the grain of abundance . . . Food supplies are running short . . . Nobles hunger and suffer . . . Upper Egypt has become a wasteland . . . Grain is lacking on every side . . . Women say, "Oh that we had something to eat."**[376]

    And all the livestock of Egypt died; but of the livestock of the sons of Israel, not one died . . . Now the flax and the barley were ruined, for the barley was in the ear and the flax was in bud . . . Locusts came up over all the land of Egypt and settled in all the territory of Egypt; *they were* very numerous. There had never been so *many* locusts, nor would there be so *many* again. For they covered the surface of the whole land, so that the land was darkened; and they ate every plant of the land and all the fruit of the trees that the hail had left. Thus nothing green was left on tree or plant of the field through all the land of Egypt. Exodus (9:6, 31; 10:14, 15)

- **Behold, plague sweeps the land; blood is everywhere with no shortage of the dead . . . Children are dashed against the walls. The funeral shroud calls out to you before you come near . . . Woe is me for the grief of this time . . . He who buries his brother in the ground is everywhere . . . Wailing is throughout the land, mingled with lamentations.**[377]

    Now it came about at midnight that the LORD struck all the firstborn in the land of Egypt, from the firstborn of Pharaoh who sat on his throne to the firstborn of the captive who was in the dungeon, and all the firstborn of cattle. Pharaoh arose in the night, he and all his servants and all the Egyptians, and there was a great cry in Egypt, for there was no home where there was not someone dead. (Exodus 12:29, 30)

    This reflects what we saw at Avaris: bodies were thrown hastily in graves, contrary to Egyptian custom, and the homes of the Semitic population suddenly abandoned.

- **There is fire in their hearts! If only he had perceived their nature in the first generation! Then he would have smitten the evil — stretched out his arm against it. He would have destroyed their seed and their heritage.**[378]

    This must reflect the author's anguish at what the Hebrews were doing to Egypt at that dark and difficult time. The Exodus was a tragedy for the nation of Egypt.

<u>Good Evidence—But Scholars Doubt:</u>
Dr. Rohl is very impressed by this ancient document and its parallels to the Exodus.

   Now, you may think, like me, that this is all pretty remarkable stuff and that there are indeed clear parallels between the biblical story and the 'Admonitions' of Ipuwer ... but most Egyptologists dismiss such conclusions with disdain. They argue that the 'Admonitions of an Egyptian Sage' is nothing more than a literary device or a piece of imaginative prose designed to give a flavor of what life would be like if Pharaoh did not maintain order in the land. For them it cannot reflect any actual event in Egyptian history.[379]

An example of scholarly disagreement can be found in Miriam Lichtheim, renowned translator of Egyptian documents, who gives a lengthy introduction to the *Admonitions* before translating it. Expounding at great length and agreeing with many other scholars, she calls the writing in the *Admonitions* a complete fantasy.

> Ever since [Sir Alan Henderson] Gardiner's pioneering edition of this difficult text, his view of the Admonitions as the work of a Twelfth Dynasty author who laments the alleged calamities of the First Intermediate Period has held sway. It is, however, **contradictory and untenable**. Gardiner maintained on the one hand that "the pessimism of Ipuwer was intended to be understood as the direct and natural response to a real national calamity" . . . I submit that there is strong inherent reason why this cannot be so. . . [She compares it to compositions with politico-propagandistic aims expressed through the poetic elaboration of the topos "national distress" and concludes] the Admonitions . . . reveals itself as a **composition of the same genre and character**, which differs only in being longer, more ambitious, more repetitious, and more extreme in its use of **hyperbole**. Its very verbosity and repetitiveness mark it as a latecomer in which the most comprehensive treatment of the theme "national distress" is attempted, in short, as a work of the late Middle Kingdom and of **purely literary inspiration**. The unhistorical character of the whole genre was recognized by S. Luria in an article that did not receive the attention it deserved. . . Luria also made the telling point that the description of chaos in the Admonitions is **inherently contradictory, hence historically impossible: On the one hand the land is said to suffer from total want; on the other hand the poor are described as having become rich, of wearing fine clothes, and generally of disposing of all that once belonged to their masters**. In sum, the Admonitions of Ipuwer . . . **does not derive from any . . . historical situation**. It is the last, fullest, most exaggerated, and hence least successful, composition on the theme "order versus chaos."[380] [bold mine]

Even though the Exodus explicitly says:

> Now the sons of Israel had done according to the word of Moses, for they had requested from the Egyptians articles of silver and articles of gold, and clothing; and the LORD had given the people favor in the sight of the Egyptians, so that they let them have their request. Thus they plundered the Egyptians. (Exodus 12:35, 36)

On this particular point the *Admonitions* has these corresponding remarks:

> **The slave takes what he finds . . . What belongs to the palace has been striped . . . Gold, lapis lazuli, silver, and turquois are strung on the necks of female slaves . . . See how the poor of the land have become rich whilst the man of property is a pauper.**[381]

Dr. Rohl records an interview with Dr. Maarten Raven, curator of the Leiden Museum in the Netherlands where the Admonitions is kept. Some of Dr. Raven's remarks:

> Ipuwer? We don't know who he was, but he was obviously somebody in a position to address his majesty the king. There is only one copy of this specific text and that is here in the Leiden Museum. It's a very, very vivid report - or would-be report - of what happens to Egypt when the central power falls away.
>
> I see **no connection between the papyrus of Ipuwer and the stories of the Plagues of Egypt**. It is, in a way - a very indirect way - an eyewitness report of a historical period. It pretends to be such a report, but in fact it isn't. . . **All the time we have to convince ourselves that this person can't have seen all this. He imagined it.** Or he had received this information from other similar propagandistic literature. . . Yes. It's very fantastic. **But he hasn't seen it - he just imagined it. . .**
>
> **Don't confuse this with the message of the Bible - the Ten Plagues.** That's quite a different story. Whether this happened or not is irrelevant. It's a beautiful literary document and, again yes, God was angry and punished the Egyptians. But **this is just a literary cliché. . .**
>
> **It's out of the question that this papyrus can refer to one and the same event.** Conventional chronology has it that the Exodus took place somewhere during the Ramesside period in Egypt - maybe around 1200 BC - whereas with our papyrus, when you look at the grammar and literary figures, etc., there's no question that it was composed in the Middle Kingdom and that is six, seven, eight hundred years earlier.[382] [bold mine]

Actually, the Middle Kingdom in Egypt continued as late as the 15th century if we accept Dr. Rohl's chronology. His remark on this points to a recurring theme in scholarly unbelief.

> So, when it comes down to the nitty gritty of why Raven cannot accept any parallels with the biblical account, it appears to rest on the chronological issue once more. **The reason why the account of Ipuwer could not possibly be an Egyptian account of the Exodus is because it is much too early in history.** But that is only the case if you have the Exodus set in your mind as having occurred in the time of Ramesses II or his immediate successors. So the Ramesses Exodus Theory gets in the way of an obvious parallel once again.[383]

Chronology is a huge factor in the rejection of this clear evidence for the Exodus (as is an underlying anti-supernaturalism). Poor chronology will be seen as a recurring reason for much of the skepticism that is so common in scholarly circles. However, because Ms. Lichtheim dated this to the late Middle Kingdom, and Dr Rohl's new chronology places the 1400's BC during the Middle Kingdom, the date of this composition now matches the Exodus timeframe, so only an anti-supernatural bias would refuse to see the confirmation of Biblical details from archeology.

The Conquest of Canaan:

We are looking for archeological collaboration in the time frame of 1406 BC, Middle Bronze Age II, not 1210 BC. As we noted, only three Canaanite cities were initially destroyed by Joshua. These were Jericho, Ai, and Hazor. But, as we shall see, others were destroyed at other times in the Conquest. The Israelites were commanded by God to destroy all pagan shrines, and the cities were "infested" with them. But most cities, orchards, wells, herds, fields, etc. were to be taken over as part of the divine inheritance that the He was giving to His people—blessings that they would enter into even though they had not worked for them.

We will begin with the city of Jericho, which was excavated by Sellin and Watzinger (in the early 1900's), then by John Garstang (in the 1930's), and finally and most exhaustively by Kathleen M. Kenyon (in the 1950's). We will look at the opinions of Garstang and Kenyon, which are based on excavations that fell about 25 years apart. Then we will also look at the evaluation of their finds made by another scholar about 25 years after Kenyon completed her excavation notes. We will only briefly mention the finds from the previous excavation of Sellin and Watzinger, for each successive dig was more elaborate than the previous.

Let us begin with a summary of Professor Garstang's four-year excavation effort appearing in a *London Illustrated News* article. His examination of evidence pointed to at least four periods of occupation for the ancient city of Jericho. The Scriptures record the destruction of the fourth and last period of occupation, which Professor Garstang refers to as "City IV." He explains that Biblical event and its date, as verified from his archeological finds:

> The palace, the store-rooms, like the house-rooms against the city wall, bear witness to a general conflagration which completed the destruction of the city. Below the black masses of charcoal and white ash, . . . waist-deep in most rooms, were found the objects which represent the culture and life of the inhabitants of Jericho at the time when the city fell. Especially important in this connection was the recovery from the top-most strata of numerous fragments of painted vases and Cypriote wares, which by reason of their distinctive features can be closely dated. These, in the now agreed opinion of experienced archaeologists, range in date from 1600-1400 B.C., and they include portions of a number of vessels which correspond piece by piece, detail by detail, with objects from the dated tombs of the fifteenth century B.C.. . .. Further, during the whole routine of these excavations, lasting now four years, in the course of which my wife has methodically washed, and I have examined, more than 100,000 specimens or fragments, not a single piece has been found, to my knowledge, within the walled city of the Bronze Age that should be attributed to a later age than that of Amenhetep III [At that time, Amenhetep III was believed to have reigned from 1410-1375 B.C. However the chronology of Egyptian kings can be changed, as we noted.], whose scarabs give the last date also among the tomb deposits.

> Life within the city and the use of the tombs both ceased suddenly, after a continuous history of a thousand years, about 1400 B.C.; and this is the round date to which, on independent evidence we had already assigned the final disaster to the city walls. It is thus established that the Bronze Age city of Jericho perished by earthquake and fire about 1400 B.C.[384]

In his book Professor Garstang notes that much of what he found, which was also mentioned in the Biblical account, could not have been known unless the author had been there to see it, for it would have been covered over soon after, only recoverable by careful excavation.

> We have compared our archeological results with the indications of the Bible narrative, both as regards the features of the Fourth City as well as the manner and date of its destruction; and we also have tested the implied setting of the narrative in the scheme of Egyptian history based upon that date, without finding any radical discrepancy. On the contrary much of the detail convinces us not only that the fall of the Fourth City is that described in the Book of Joshua, but that the narrative embodies the tradition of an eye-witness.

Ms. Kenyon does not agree with Professor Garstang. Let us look into her excavation notes and see why that is so, for she also records many details that fit the Biblical account.

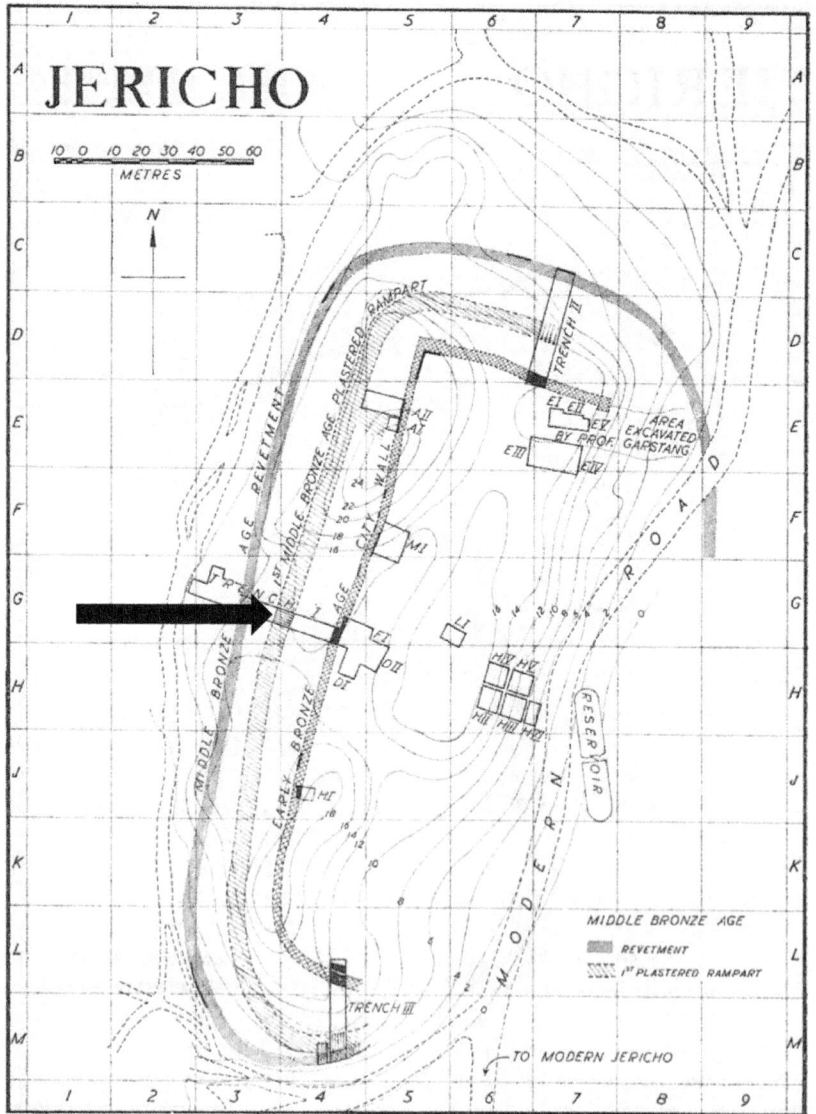

Both Ms. Kenyon and Professor Garstang note that the city was occupied multiple times over a long period of time. The City of Jericho that Joshua destroyed they call "City IV." It seems as if Jericho during the time of Joshua was an extremely well-fortified city, which possessed an outer wall composed of 15 feet of large stones cemented together, and on top of that yet another mud wall 10 feet high. Inside of that outer wall was a steep rampart of slick plaster which would have been very difficult to climb.

> The excellence and slipperiness of the surface in Trench I [black arrow] emphasizes what a very difficult obstacle it would have been to storm.[385]

On top of that was yet another 25-foot-high wall of mud that was 10 feet thick. (Labeled as "Early Bronze Age City Wall" in Sketch.)

Although not shown, the walls also extended on the east and enclosed a spring of water that nourished the city.

(For reference, here is Kenyon's sketch of Middle Bronze Age Jericho.[386])

- **MB IIB [Middle Bronze Age IIB] Jericho was apparently destroyed by an earthquake, with its strong defensive wall (which stood at the top of a sloping plastered rampart) falling outwards and down the slope, tumbling over the stone revetment wall at the base of the glacis.**[387]

    Ms. Kenyon's notes describe it as follows:
    > A heavy fill of fallen red bricks piling nearly to the top of the revetment. These probably came from the wall on the summit of the bank [and/or] . . . the brickwork above the revetment.[388]

    > So the people shouted, and *priests* blew the trumpets; and when the people heard the sound of the trumpet, the people shouted with a great shout and the wall fell down flat, so that the people went up into the city, every man straight ahead, and they took the city. They utterly destroyed everything in the city, both man and woman, young and old, and ox and sheep and donkey, with the edge of the sword. (Joshua 6:20–21)

    My observation: Joshua and the Israelites knew what an earthquake was. In the time of Uzziah a major earthquake is recorded (Amos 1:1). If this destruction had been the result of an earthquake then Joshuah would have said so. Such an event would have destroyed other near-by cities as well. But that did not happen. What happened was not an earthquake. It was a miraculous divine intervention, specifically at Jericho.

- **MB IIB City IV was destroyed by a massive conflagration, leaving an ash layer several feet thick. Again, Kenyon vividly describes what she had found, making it clear that the walls had fallen down *before* the fire.**[389]

    Ms. Kenyon's notes explain:
    > The destruction was complete. Walls and floors were blackened or reddened by fire, and every room was filled with fallen bricks, timbers, and household utensils; in most rooms the fallen debris was heavily burnt, but the collapse of the walls of the eastern rooms seems to have taken place before they were affected by the fire.

    > The destruction was followed by a period of abandonment, for which the stratigraphical evidence is very striking. Above the destruction debris was a layer of wash, up to 1 m. thick. It cuts right down to the surviving tops of the walls and the debris packed between them, on a line sloping steeply down to the east. It is made up of powdery streaks of burnt material, red, white, black, brown, and blue. It quite clearly represents a wash down the side of the mound of the gradual erosion of the top of the burnt buildings. Its thickness showed that the process was a prolonged one, the product of successive winter rains. It is this level that is called 'The Streak' in the reports of the 1930-6 excavations. and it was found over a large part of the Middle Bronze Age buildings in this area.[390]

    So the entire city was thus destroyed—totally destroyed.
    > They burned the city with fire, and all that was in it. Only the silver and gold, and articles of bronze and iron, they put into the treasury of the house of the LORD. (Joshua 6:24)

- **Storage jars in Jericho's MB IIB houses were found to be full of charred grain.**[391]

    This indicates that it was in the springtime, soon after the harvest of the barley. The people of Jericho had stored food from the spring harvest in anticipation of a siege.
    > On the tenth day of the first month [Nisan, so around April] the people went up from the Jordan [they had crossed on dry land behind the Ark] and camped at Gilgal on the eastern border of Jericho. [They attacked Jericho after Passover, Nisan 14–15.] (Joshua 4:19)

- **The siege had not lasted long because the food stores were not depleted.**[392]
    > So he [Joshua] had the ark of the LORD taken around the city, circling *it* once; then they came into the camp and spent the night in the camp . . . Thus the second day they marched around the city once and returned to the camp; they did so for six days . . . Then on the seventh day they rose early at the dawning of the day and marched around the city in the same manner seven times; only on that day they marched around the city seven times. At the seventh time, when the priests blew the trumpets, Joshua said to the people, "Shout! For the LORD has given you the city. (Joshua 6:11, 14–16)

This is unusual because normally a city would be under siege for an extended period before it fell. This was a unique situation, as described in the Bible. Also, we might ask ourselves why the Israelites did not take some of the grain, since there was so much stored there. It was because according to Joshua 6:17 the city and all that was in it was "devoted to the Lord." The grain was burned in the fire with the rest of the city, even though it would have been very useful, for they had been migrating and the manna had just ceased (see Joshua 5:11–12).

- **Also, drawings by the earlier archeologists show one section of the wall that had not collapsed.** This surely must be where Rahab the harlot lived with her family.

    Excavations of the northern part of Tell es-Sultan (ancient Jericho) by Sellin and Watzinger revealed something rather remarkable. Here houses had been constructed between the upper wall of the citadel and the lower wall resting on top of the stone revetment. These were not the dwellings of the wealthy citizens of Jericho but rather the houses of the poor. It was definitely the seedy side of town. The streets between the houses consisted of steps descending down the slope between the walls. The houses had shops on the ground floors and living quarters above, suggesting that this was the town market district. But, even more remarkably, some houses here were actually built into the lower mud brick wall standing above the revetment. These looked directly out onto the mountains, affording easy escape from the city . . . and photographs from the German excavations show that the outer wall here had not collapsed during the earthquake which had destroyed the rest of Jericho and brought the walls 'a tumbling down' elsewhere.

    . . . Here were houses that corresponded exactly to the story of Rahab the 'harlot' of Jericho who lived within the wall—the scarlet woman who had harbored the Israelite spies sent by Joshua before lowering them down from her window in the wall for their escape across the fields to the nearby hills (Joshua 2:1–24). The medieval Jewish commentator Rashi claimed that, far from being a harlot, Rahab was a food seller, while Josephus calls her an innkeeper. [The Hebrew word means harlot, but it derives from a word meaning well-fed, thus *implying* wanton.][393]

    After protecting the spies from the searchers sent by the king of Jericho, Rahab said:
    Now therefore, please swear to me by the LORD, since I have dealt kindly with you, that you also will deal kindly with my father's household, and give me a pledge of truth, and spare my father and my mother and my brothers and my sisters, with all who belong to them, and deliver our lives from death." So the men said to her, "Our life for yours if you do not tell this business of ours; and it shall come about when the LORD gives us the land that we will deal kindly and faithfully with you." (Joshua 2:12–14)

    Joshua said to the two men who had spied out the land, "Go into the harlot's house and bring the woman and all she has out of there, as you have sworn to her." So the young men who were spies went in and brought out Rahab and her father and her mother and her brothers and all she had; they also brought out all her relatives and placed them outside the camp of Israel. (Joshua 6:22–23)

    Rahab the harlot and her father's household and all she had, Joshua spared; and she has lived in the midst of Israel to this day, for she hid the messengers whom Joshua sent to spy out Jericho. (Joshua 6:25)

We also mention a find at another city that the Bible says was totally destroyed by Israel. At Hazor a burn layer was found dated to the same time as the destruction at Jericho, and in its palace was found a cuneiform tablet with the name Jabin on it (see Joshua 11).[394]

Once the towns of the hill country were subdued or destroyed, Joshua marched his troops up to Hazor, 'foremost of the kingdoms' as the Bible calls it. Here the same pattern of evidence can be witnessed. The vast Middle Bronze Age lower town was burned and destroyed, but then reoccupied again some years later. The upper citadel was also burned to the ground . . . but from the ruined palace came the fragment of a small cuneiform tablet bearing the name of the king of Hazor who lived in that palace. He was called Yabni-Addu. The current excavator of the site, Professor Amnon Ben-Tor, agrees that this is identical to the name Jabin, mentioned in the Conquest narrative as the king of Hazor killed by Joshua during the taking and sack of the city.[395]

The role "King of Canaan" which Jabin filled (Joshua 11:1ff), and the description "head of all those kingdoms" (Joshua 11:10) as applied to Hazor, were only true in very early times. This indicates that this section of Joshua comes from the 1400's, not some later date.

> This Jabin is referred to as the 'King of Canaan' with the obvious conclusion that he was the greatest ruler in the region. As Yohanan Aharoni [Israeli archeologist and inspector in Galilee for the Department of Antiquities.] notes, the only time that the city of Hazor was the 'head of all those kingdoms' in Canaan was in the Middle Bronze IIB and not in the Late Bronze IIB when Gaza, under the control of the New Kingdom pharaohs, was the political hub of the region.[396]

We have referred to the fact that Jericho, Hazor, and Ai are prominently mentioned in the text of Joshua as being fully destroyed. But other cities are also said to have been utterly destroyed, or at least all of their inhabitants killed, at the same time. Some have not been identified by archeology, but many have. Here is a list of those that have been identified, showing the claims made in the Bible compared with the finds of archeologists—assuming a 1406 BC date for the Conquest of Canaan, so the finds should be dated around 1400 BC, near to or right after the destruction of Jericho and Hazor:

City-Biblical Reference	Archeological Find
Bethel (Destroyed; Judges 1:22–26)	destroyed about 1400 BC
Debir (Captured; Joshua 15:1–17)	destroyed about 1400 BC
Lachish (No survivors; Joshua 10:31–32)	destroyed about 1400 BC
Hebron (Utterly destroyed; Joshua 10:36–37)	destroyed about 1400 BC
Hormah (Utterly destroyed; Judges 1:16–17)	destroyed about 1400 BC
Dan [Leshem] (No survivors; Joshua 19:47–48; Judges 18:27)	destroyed about 1400 BC[397]

Thus the archeological remains of many cities in Canaan match the account of the Conquest as it is described in Joshua and in parts of Judges; that is, as long we use the date of 1406 BC for the Conquest.

But Scholars Debate:
However, Ms. Kenyon maintains that the uncovered destruction cannot be identified with the Biblical Conquest of Jericho because she dates the event to around 1550 BC, which is at least three centuries too early for the Conquest if you subscribe to a 1250 BC Exodus, and still a century too early if you choose a 1446 BC date. How can she ignore or dismiss Garstang's dating evidence from the pottery and scarabs? She says:

> In the excavations of the 1930's, a number of tombs were found which contained Late Bronze as well as Middle Bronze objects. At the time when Professor Garstang was reporting on these tombs, knowledge of the pottery of the earlier part of the Late Bronze Age was very inadequate. With the subsequent publication of a number of excavations, notably that of Megiddo, it has very much increased.
>
> His conclusion that these tombs show continuous occupation therefore requires revision, for a whole century or more of pottery is lacking in them. Moreover, our further examination of the tombs shows how unreliable stratification by absolute level within the tombs can be, owing to the habit of mounding up earlier materials round the edge when later burials are put in. The occurrence of Late Bronze Age objects at the same absolute level as Middle Bronze Age ones does not therefore indicate an overlap of forms. Moreover, the other dating criterion used, scarabs of the period for which the pottery seems to indicate a gap, is not safe, for scarabs are the sort of thing liable to be heirlooms.
>
> A review of the finds made in these tombs suggests that, as with the tombs found in the more recent excavations, the main use ceased at the end of the Middle Bronze Age, early in the sixteenth century B.C.[398]

Ms. Kenyon also claims that a more careful dating of the debris from the destruction shows that not all of it comes from the same time periods, that the broken walls might not all have existed during the same periods of Jericho's history—some too early, some too late to be matched to the Biblical events.

She says there is no solid evidence for the Biblical event, likely because of erosion.

> It is a sad fact that of the town walls of the Late Bronze Age within which period the attack by the Israelites must fall by any dating, not a trace remains. The erosion which has destroyed much of the defences has already been described . . . The excavation of Jericho, therefore, has thrown no light on the walls of Jericho of which the destruction is so vividly described in the Book of Joshua . . . As concerns the date of the destruction of Jericho by the Israelites, all that can be said is that the latest Bronze Age occupation should, in my view, be dated to the third quarter of the fourteenth century B.C. This is a date which suits neither the school of scholars which would date the entry of the Israelites into Palestine to c. 1400 B.C. nor the school which prefers a date of c. 1260 B.C.[399]

On the point of erosion—that much has been lost or obscured thereby, Kitchen agrees with Kenyon. He also accepts her chronology and thus most of her conclusions as well.

> It [Jericho] was obviously very prosperous in the Middle Bronze Age (early second millennium), as the spectacular finds from that period's tombs bear witness. But only traces of this survive on the town mound itself . . . But this all perished violently, including by fire, at roughly 1550 or soon after. And for about 200 years the ruins lay barren . . . During that interval a great deal of the former Middle Bronze township was entirely removed by erosion . . . If 200 years of erosion sufficed to remove most of later Middle Bronze Jericho, it is almost a miracle that anything on the mound has survived at all from the 400 years of erosion between 1275 and the time of Ahab (875-853), when we hear report of Jericho's rebuilding (1 Kings 16:34) in Iron II - double the length of time that largely cleared away the Middle Bronze town.[400]

In this way he argues for a possible 1250 BC Exodus and a correspondingly later date for the Conquest. Thus he claims that the absence of supporting archeological evidence is due to a number of factors, with erosion being one of the primary factors in this case.

So: Garstang produced an emphatic dating for the fall of Jericho at around 1400 BC. **Then:** 25 years later Ms. Kenyon gave an emphatic dating of around 1550 BC. **But:** 25 years after Kenyon, Professor John J. Bimson carefully reconsidered the foundations of Ms. Kenyon's thinking (along with the ideas of a number of other scholars) including the dating via pottery and the dating via the assumed connections with the Egyptians and their expulsion of the Hyksos from Egypt. He points out underlying their dating is the **theory** that the Canaanite cites were Hyksos cities, that they had moved into the Middle East after leaving Egypt, and that they were destroyed in a war of retribution by the Egyptians. He shows that to be an untenable theory, and again argues exhaustively for a date for the destruction of Jericho that falls in the latter half of the 1400's BC! Thus he says, pointing out the previous errors in the underlying assumptions of Kenyon, and the faulty conclusions she drew from them:

1. The MB II B-C cities of Palestine were not strongholds of the Hyksos, and their fortification-systems should not be described as Hyksos. [Hyksos: Oppressors of Egypt for centuries.]
2. Thus the destruction of these cities has nothing to do with an Egyptian war of retaliation against the Hyksos; Egyptian action against the Hyksos probably never extended beyond Sharuhen, in the south of Palestine. [Hyksos: Finally driven out of Egypt forever.]
3. The destruction of the MB II cities has been incorrectly dated, because of its association with a hypothetical Egyptian offensive against the Hyksos throughout Palestine. Their destruction should be dated not to the 16th century BC but to the 15th. Consequently the appearance of bichrome ware [the key distinctive pottery that was used to date the city and its destruction] and the beginning of the LBA must also be redated. [LBA: Late Bronze Age. This means the end of the MBA, or Middle Bronze Age, must be extended to over a century later than previously thought, for the MBA immediately preceded the LBA.]
4. The destruction of the MB II cities was the work of the Israelite tribes which left Egypt during the first half of the 15th century BC.[401] [It was not the Egyptians pursuing the Hyksos.]

Clearly the interpretation of what has been found at Jericho differs widely among scholars, and the points to be made are detailed and technical. Many scholars assert that Ms. Kenyon misdated the excavation site and that it should be dated to around 1400 BC, which would fit perfectly with a 1446 BC date for the Exodus. Many scholars also claim that the dates for the Middle Bronze Age are uniformly off and that they need to be adjusted. That is why Kenyon misdated the destruction of Jericho. This is another issue of chronology.

One observation about the many scholarly objections to connecting events to the Bible: It seems that chronology is almost always a large factor in such a discussion. So to conclude: A chronological indicator matching the destruction of Jericho to the time of Joshua can be found in the tombs of Jericho from the end of the Middle Bronze Age. Kenyon notes:
> Of the other seventeen Middle Bronze Age tombs dealt with in this volume . . . six contained multiple simultaneous burials. . . On the evidence of the pottery and the other finds, these six tombs were all contemporary. There must clearly be a reason why they are in such noticeable contrast to the other tombs. It does not seem probable that it is a case of retainers or family being killed to accompany the head of the household . . . [for] no one body is treated as more important than the rest. Moreover, no evidence has been found of violent death. The alternative is that many members of a number of families died simultaneously. Since the pottery indicates that this group of tombs belongs to the very end of the Middle Bronze Age, it might be tempting to associate the mass burials with the final destruction of the Middle Bronze Age town, probably to be ascribed to an Egyptian raid in the campaign which drove the Hyksos out of Egypt at the beginning of the 18th dynasty, and therefore to be dated to c. 1580-1560 BC. [Note that this **assumed** invasion of Canaan by Egypt to "drive out the hated Hyksos" in c. 1580 BC to 1560 BC is just that—an assumption with no evidential basis, as Bimson notes above in point 3. This is one reason why Kenyon misdated the fall of Jericho.] But this [ascribing it to the Egyptian invasion] is unlikely on two grounds. In the first place, the skeletons, as we have noted, show no signs of injuries. In the second, survivors of the destruction of the town by fire would be unlikely to bury the dead with such an elaborate equipment, and the furnishings of the houses must have been destroyed in the fire. **It is therefore probable that disease was responsible for the death of entire families.** This may have taken place very shortly before the final destruction of the town. On this evidence from the tell, the site was then completely abandoned for a considerable period, and therefore no subsequent burials were made in the tombs.[402] [Bold mine]

Now consider this account of the sin of the sons of Israel while they were camped at Shittim, directly across from Jericho, a short time before beginning the conquest of the city. The Lord had just protected Israel from the attempt by Balak to get Balaam to curse the Sons of Israel. Then the sons of Israel sinned against the Lord God.
> While Israel remained at Shittim, the people began to play the harlot with the daughters of Moab. For they invited the people to the sacrifices of their gods, and the people ate and bowed down to their gods. So Israel joined themselves to Baal of Peor, and the LORD was angry against Israel. The LORD said to Moses, "Take all the leaders of the people and execute them in broad daylight before the LORD, so that the fierce anger of the LORD may turn away from Israel. So Moses said to the judges of Israel, "Each of you slay his men who have joined themselves to Baal of Peor."
>
> Then behold, one of the sons of Israel came and brought to his relatives a Midianite woman, in the sight of Moses and in the sight of all the congregation of the sons of Israel, while they were weeping at the doorway of the tent of meeting. When Phinehas the son of Eleazar, the son of Aaron the priest, saw it, he arose from the midst of the congregation and took a spear in his hand, and he went after the man of Israel into the tent and pierced both of them through, the man of Israel and the woman, through the body. So the plague on the sons of Israel was checked. Those who died by the plague were 24,000. (Numbers 25:1–9)

This plague, which was inflicted upon Israel shortly before the assault on Jericho, must have overflowed into the city of Jericho and resulted in the deaths of many of the residents of the city. If this striking "coincidence" is accurately interpreted, then the sons of Israel were indeed responsible for the destruction of the city of Jericho, which followed shortly after the burials from the plague took place. Therefore, the date for that final destruction was 1406 BC, after which time the city, although inhabited for many centuries, lay desolate as the Bible indicates because of the curse that Joshua placed on it (see Joshua 6:26).

One of the dating factors not mentioned by Bimson and others, but which is clearly important, is the result of radiocarbon dating. C^{14} dating was conceived of in the late 1940's by Willard F. Libby, a University of Chicago professor of Physical Chemistry. He first published his work "Radiocarbon Dating" in 1952, for which he won the Nobel prize in 1960. The technique was still quite new at the time that Ms. Kenyon used it to date her specimens. Her Middle Bronze Age radiocarbon measurements were made in the 1950's. Her notes indicate:

> Fifty-five radiocarbon determinations have been made of material from various levels at Jericho ranging in age from the Mesolithic (Natufian) to the Bronze Age . . . There have nevertheless been great improvements in methodology since the mid 1950's when the first dates were obtained. Some of these original determinations may therefore be less dependable than those made more recently.[403]

There is a known anomaly that recurs for radiocarbon dating. We must look briefly at that.

Correcting C^{14} Chronology:
In his lectures Dr. Douglas Petrovich has pointed out a serious anomaly in the C^{14} results from before 1,400 BC. C^{14} dates are too early by 120-140 years for events that lie before 1,400 BC, an anomaly now known to all experienced researchers in the field.

Although the chronology of many ancient sites seems well worked out, Manfred Bietak, the Austrian archeologist who was the principle at the Avaris dig, notes a serious discrepancy between the C^{14} dates for Tell el-Daba and the results from stratigraphy. Referring to the recently published C^{14} results he notes:

> The results have just been published (Kutschera et at. 2012) but . . . the radiocarbon results from Tell el-Dab'a [Avaris] show an average offset of 120 years (Figure 8.2). The dates are too high . . . As a matter of fact, offsets of samples from Ancient Egypt, also apart from Tell el-Dab'a, are an old problem of radiocarbon research (S. Bonani et al., 2001).[404]

Bietak argues strongly and convincingly against those who would redate the strata based on the C^{14} data, pointing out the wide range of archeological data that it contradicts.

> In addition to the ceramic assessment and its seriation, which add to the accuracy of stratigraphic excavation over vast expanses, other criteria for compiling evidence for individual settlement phases were also employed, such as follow-up of architectural units and their relationship to adjacent buildings. This also spawned the observation that there are phases in which specific building material and specific house types were introduced for the first time. The discovery of emergency graves surfacing at the end of a specific phase *(Gj1-3)* late in the 13th Dynasty and in two different excavation areas was an observation which confirmed the ceramic and architectural connection of the two stratigraphies. As a result, the stratigraphy and the dating of the phases of Tell el-Dab'a is highly reliable and was confirmed repeatedly by site-to-site comparisons with other excavations (Bietak et al. 2008; Bader 2009).[405]

Because Bietak collaborates his results with other widely scattered digs even stretching into the Levant, he casts significant doubt on the reliability of Kenyon's C^{14} numbers.[406]

Dr. Petrovich points out that this anomaly is well known and widespread in both Egypt and in the Middle East, that it begins to show up for dates before 1400 BC, and that it becomes more pronounced (up to several hundred years) as we move further back in time.[407] These considerations lead us to re-evaluate the C^{14} dates for Jericho, lowering them by about 140 years. If we do that then the chronology for the destruction of Jericho changes as follows:

> Possible C^{14} dates fell between 1601-1566 BC or, equally likely, 1561-1524 BC. If we reduce these dates by 140 years we get date ranges of 1561-1426 BC or, equally likely, 1421-1384 BC. These fit very well with the Biblical date for the destruction of Jerico at 1406 BC.[408]

I know of no naturalistic explanation for the sudden chronological anomaly around 1400 BC. Apparently Dr. Petrovich also knows of no such explanation. But the phenomenon is widely known and must be considered when interpreting radiometric dating results.

Summary of the Information that we Have Uncovered thus Far:

Let us now recap what we have discovered thus far as it relates to the Sojourn, the Exodus, and the Conquest of Canaan. The string of archeological finds that we have reviewed thus far present striking support and collaboration for the accuracy of the Biblical accounts of the origin and establishment of the Hebrew nation. The total picture that these finds present to us can be expressed as follows:

> **The Hebrews entered Egypt and lived there for centuries, spreading throughout the land, and becoming very numerous. They left Egypt during a series of trying and catastrophic circumstances, entered the Land of Canaan 40 years later, and conquered the indigenous people there, destroying many of their fortified cities. They tore down their pagan shrines and took up residence as the dominant people group in Canaan. They did not completely eradicate all of the indigenous people, but lived beside them for many centuries as their national identity solidified. This is how the nation of Israel came into existence.**

This matches the Biblical scenario perfectly. The amazing circumstances that resulted in the deliverance of the Jews from bondage in Egypt and the birth of the nation of Israel were accomplished by the sovereign will of the God of Abraham, Isaac, and Jacob, as recorded in the Sacred Scriptures. The origin of the nation of Israel cannot be adequately explained only in naturalistic terms. There was a strong supernatural element in the formation of the nation. The Bible gives to us the broader scenario, while archeology can only allow us to peek at discrete events along the way.

Of course, the reasonableness of this scenario, or the reasonableness of various key parts of it, can be bandied about by archeologists as they attempt to piece together the broader picture of the distant past of Egypt and the Middle East. We can watch these discussions as they progress through the decades—through the generations of scholars—but the nature of the data that they have—fragmented, partial, open to various interpretations—can never disprove the clear and simple facts we have seen, which undergird the Biblical narrative.

Scholars can ask many questions about the details of the Biblical account, and can attempt to uncover more information about the historical setting in which the Biblical events actually might have happened. For instance, what were the conditions like at the time of Joseph, at the time of Moses, while the Israelites were wandering in the desert, while they were in the process of establishing themselves in the Promised Land, etc.? These investigations can shed light on the circumstances that prevailed as the Biblical events unfolded. But the scholars are servants of the Word, not the final word on exactly what happened. The Lord has not given that kind of ultimate knowledge into the hands of men. We are and will always be dependent upon His revelation—not just for the total picture, but for the correct way to understand and interpret that picture. The telling of history is a prophetic function.

The telling of history is a prophetic function because the Lord God is in charge of human history. Human development and human history are under His sovereign control. They are not merely the product of social forces or human will. Thus the correct understanding of history is, and can only be understood, if/when we understand and consider His sovereign will and His purposes for the human race. This is a matter of revelation. It can never be discovered by any merely human activity or investigation. The scholarship that we have looked into in this chapter has sometimes proceeded without regard for the Divine purpose for human beings. The mind of God, Who created humans for His high and holy purposes, is revealed only in His holy word, in the Sacred Scriptures. The meaning of human life on this earth, the purpose of our existence, is central to the understanding of all history.

An Alphabetic Script at the Time of the Exodus:

We have answered the objection that there is little or no archeological evidence for the Sojourn, the Exodus, and the Conquest of Canaan. But the second objection to the Mosaic authorship of the Pentateuch, and therefore to its historical reliability, is that there was no alphabetic script in which Moses might have written the Pentateuch, especially the last four books. Therefore it had to have been transmitted orally for centuries and is historically unreliable. This is reinforced by the claim that reading and writing were not widely known among the Hebrews at the time of the Exodus.

We observed that consonantal alphabetic scripts emerged in the ancient Middle East in the 11th century BC, with the Phoenicians seemingly inventing the first and oldest such alphabet.

It is difficult to understand how such an idea still prevails because in 1904/1905 Sir William Matthew Flinders Petrie, known as the father of Egyptian archeology, discovered a script in the Sinai Peninsula (named **proto-Sinaitic**) that was alphabetic, consonantal, and dated to about 1500 BC. He found them at the turquoise mines at Serabit el Khadim.

> Here we have the result, at a date some five centuries before the oldest Phoenician writing that is known . . . It finally *disproves* the hypothesis that the early Israelites, . . . could not have used writing.[409]

Thus it predates all Middle Eastern alphabetic scripts by many centuries. It was clearly the progenitor of alphabetic writing. Additionally, he noted the script was unquestionably Semitic in form—a Semitic script from which all Semitic scripts developed, and from which alphabetic writing must therefore have developed.

It is the opinion of scholars that this script could support a work as artistic and detailed as the last four books of the Pentateuch. In other words, if the Hebrews knew and used this script then the proto-Sinaitic script would be the earliest form of Hebrew, what we might call proto-Hebrew, and Moses could have used it to write down the Pentateuch.

After Petrie discovered the scripts they were examined by another luminary in Egyptian archeology, Sir Alan Henderson Gardiner. He showed that the scripts had been created by reforming Egyptian hieroglyphics.[410] This implies the person who invented the script was Semitic but also knew Egyptian Hieroglyphics. He was a Semite who was educated in the writing of Egypt, and he lived in Egypt before 1500 BC. Could he perhaps have been a Phoenician who worked the mines at Serabit el Khadim for the Egyptians?

Other instances of the same ancient script have been found in Egypt; at Lahun in central Egypt, at Wadi el-Hol in southern Egypt, and at Bir Nasb also in the Sinai Peninsula.[411] The implications of these additional finds are clear: The Semitic scripts were not invented in Canaan at all, but had to have originated in Egypt, then were imported into the Middle East. **The only Semitic people in Egypt at those early times were the Hebrews.** Thus, the archeological trail for the invention of alphabetic writing, the earliest Semitic scripts, leads to the Hebrews. Only one modern scholar has dared to follow that controversial trail.

This is the historical background for the work of a modern Egyptologist and epigrapher Dr. Douglas Petrovich. His new discoveries, constructed upon older existing finds, have shown that Hebrew is the world's oldest alphabet. Dr. Petrovich is also the author of the book *The World's Oldest Alphabet—Hebrew as the Language of the Proto-Consonantal Script*. His distinct contribution has been the translating of the proto-Sinaitic inscriptions. This has given us a spectacular insight into the life of the Hebrews as they dwelt in Egypt. We will look at a few of the inscriptions from Serabit el Khadim and their most revealing translations.

Translating Inscriptions Written Near the Time of the Exodus:
There were two distinctive features at Serabit: The turquoise mines, which the Egyptians worked by using both paid and slave laborers; the temple of Hathor, the "Mistress of Serabit," a major goddess in the Egyptian pantheon of gods. The idolatry of the Israelites before the time of the Exodus makes her an important factor in these inscriptions.

We will look at four inscriptions from around the time of the Exodus.

Inscription Sinai 349 [412]

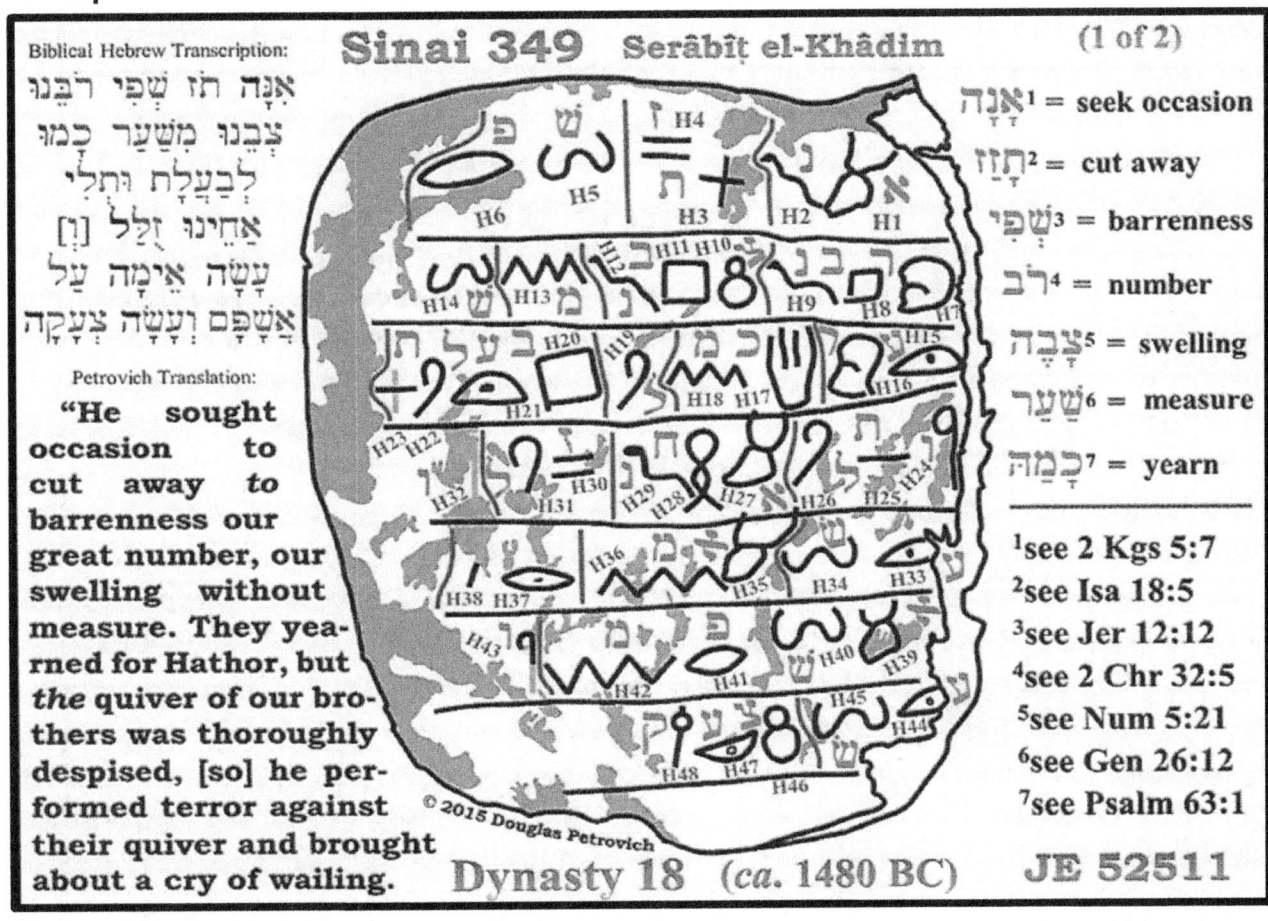

Translation:
> He sought occasion to cut away to barrenness our great number, our swelling without measure. They yearned for Hathor [Goddess of music, love, sexuality, maternal care. The Hebrews were calling out to a pagan deity!], but the quiver of our brothers was thoroughly despised, [so] he performed terror against their quiver and brought about a cry of wailing. [Note: "quiver" refers to the sons and daughters a person has.]

Dr. Petrovich comments on this inscription, found at the turquoise mines at Serabit el-Khadim. (We know that slaves were commonly used by the Egyptians to work those mines.)
> The text of Sinai 349 presents a clearly defined "he vs. us" juxtaposition. Considering that a Hebrew who worked the turquoise mines in Sinai undoubtedly authored the inscription, the reference to "our (= us)" suggests that he considered himself as a member of the first-person-plural entity spoken of throughout the text, and that the Hebrew people are to be identified with that entity. The referent of the "he" in Sinai 349 is less explicit, but the contextual events of biblical history may shed light on this question. [That is, "he" would have been pharaoh!]

Hathor was often portrayed in Egyptian art as a cow or as a woman wearing a headdress of cow horns with the disk of the sun. Here we see worship of this deity by the Hebrews and their asking her/it for deliverance. This makes the incident with Aaron and the golden calf all the more poignant. "This is your god, O Israel, who brought you up from the land of Egypt" (Exodus 32:4). The plagues of the Exodus were God showing His supremacy over the gods of Egypt, wooing the people from their idolatry. The reversion to pagan worship was described by the Lord to Moses as "corrupting themselves, turning aside from the way which I commanded them" (Exodus 32:7–8). God took the people out of Egypt, but it was more difficult to take Egypt out of the people.

Inscription Sinai 357 [413]

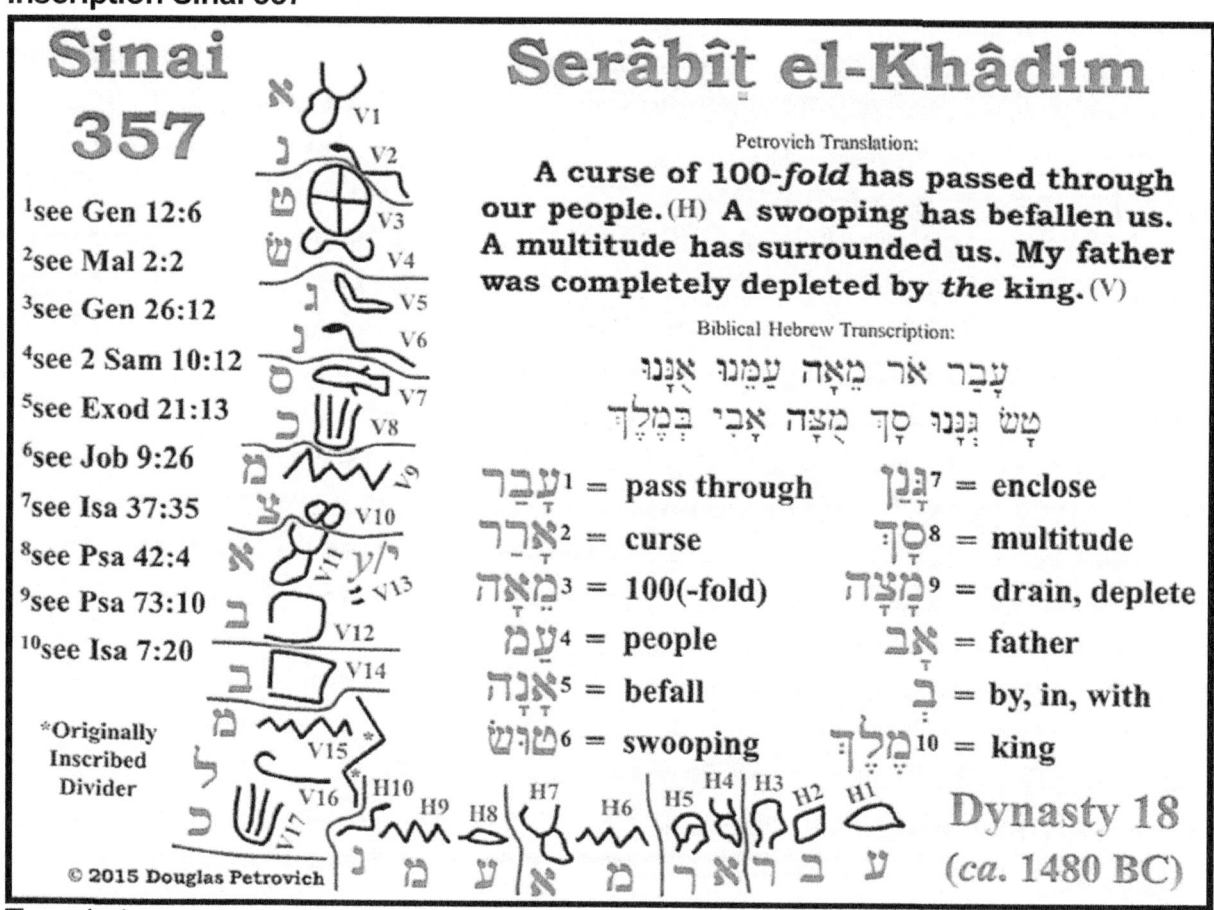

Translation:
> A curse of 100-fold has passed through our people. A swooping has befallen us.
> A multitude has surrounded us. My father was completely depleted by the king.

Here are a few of Dr. Petrovich's comments:
> Sinai 357 is another in the trend of New Kingdom inscriptions with a highly pessimistic tone. The writer of Sinai 349 lamented how "he," probably referring to the Egyptian king, sought occasion to cut away the Hebrews' great number, their swelling without measure. This matches well chronologically and descriptively with the account of the royally-sponsored edict in Exodus 1 to slaughter all newborn male Hebrews. Sinai 357 most likely records similar hardships that the Israelites were experiencing before the exodus, but this time with an explicit reference to the king as the culprit behind the evil deeds.
>
> A swooping (see Job 9:26—where an eagle swoops down on its prey with swiftness and stealth) has befallen them.

"Swooping" indicates the unexpected and sudden nature of what befell the Hebrews.

Inscription Sinai 375a [414]

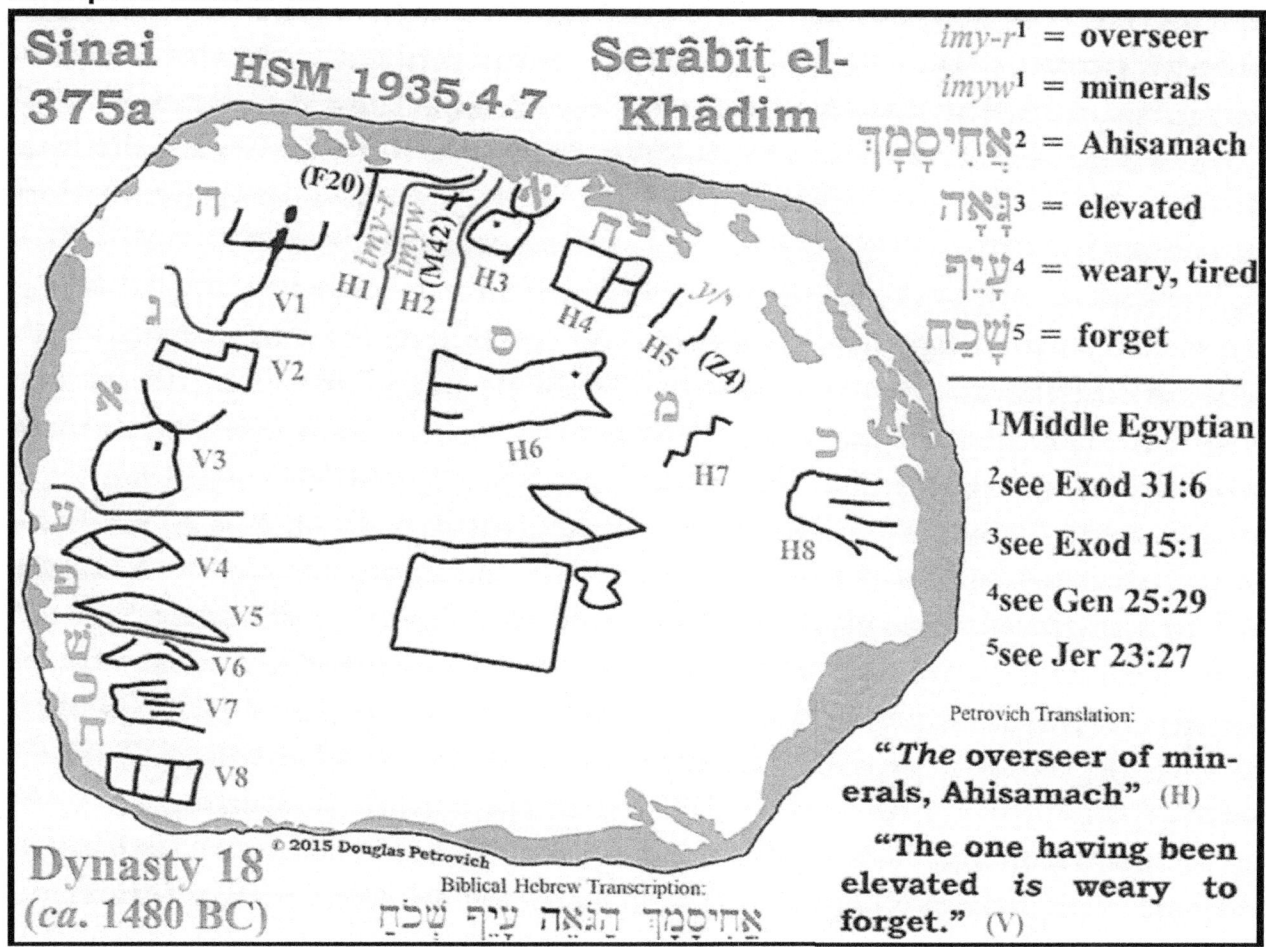

Translation:
> The overseer of minerals, Ahisamach. The one having been elevated is weary to forget.

The one elevated to a position as overseer of minerals would be a skilled worker in brass and other metals. He was probably weary because of the long oppression levied on him and his people. Ahisamach is named in the book of Exodus. He is the father of a skilled craftsman named Oholiab, whom God appointed to do work on the tent of meeting.

> And behold, I Myself have appointed with him Oholiab, the son of Ahisamach, of the tribe of Dan; and in the hearts of all who are skillful I have put skill, that they may make all that I have commanded you: the tent of meeting, and the ark of testimony, and the mercy seat upon it, and all the furniture of the tent, the table also and its utensils, and the pure *gold* lampstand with all its utensils, and the altar of incense, the altar of burnt offering also with all its utensils, and the laver and its stand, the woven garments as well, and the holy garments for Aaron the priest, and the garments of his sons, *with which* to carry on their priesthood; the anointing oil also, and the fragrant incense for the holy place, they are to make *them* according to all that I have commanded you. (Exodus 31:6-9)

This makes sense because such skills were passed on from father to son. The person named in Sinai 375a, Ahisamach, is the father of the biblical artisan Oholiab. This gives us a key connection to the biblical text.

The final inscription from the period just before the Exodus is dated by Dr. Petrovich to the actual year of the Exodus.

Inscription Sinai 361 [415]

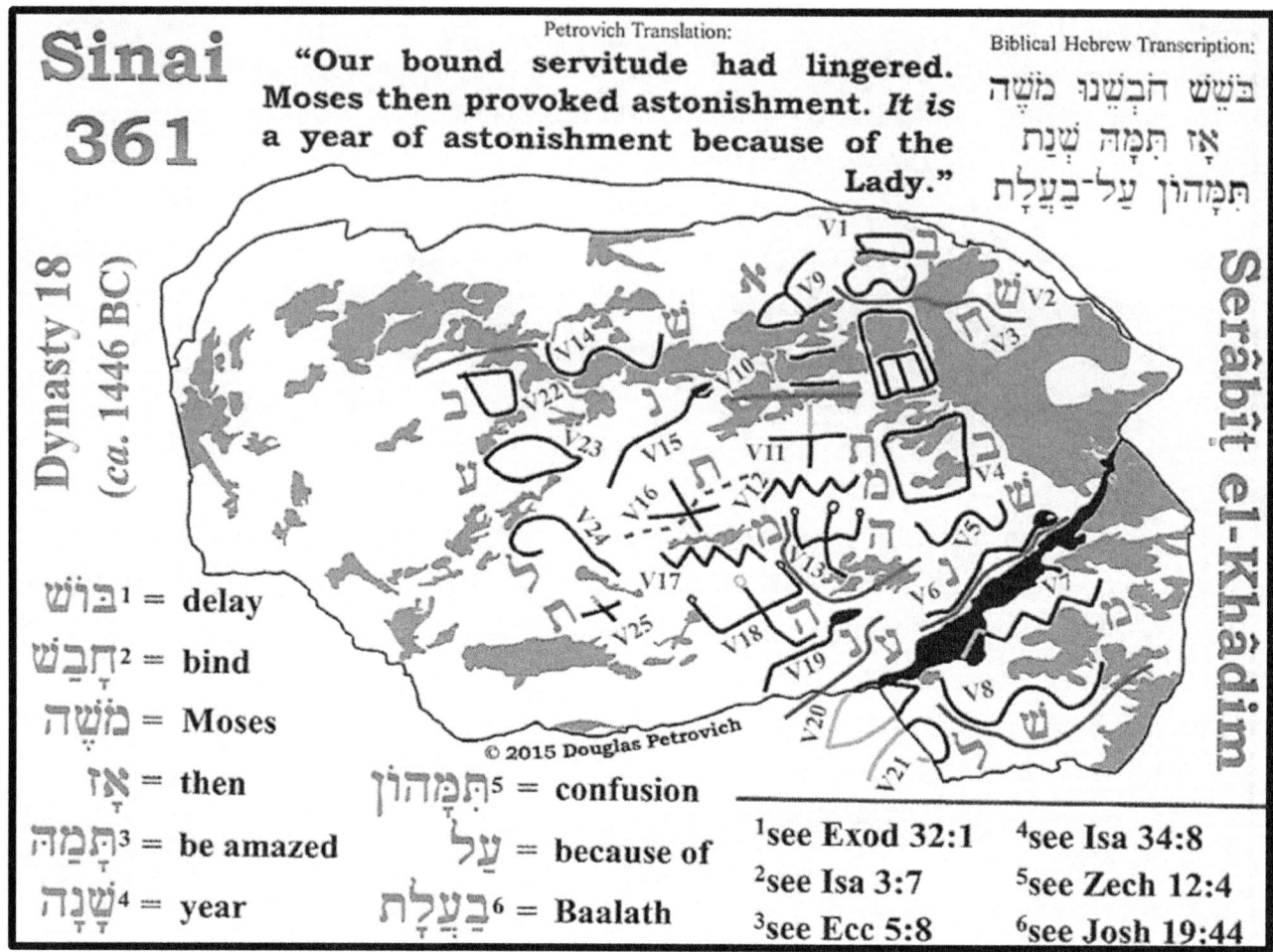

Translation:
> Our bound servitude had lingered. Moses then provoked astonishment. It is a year of astonishment because of the Lady.

His fascinating comments on this text:

> Just as with virtually all of the Hebrew inscriptions of the New Kingdom, Sinai 361 expresses pessimism and exasperation. The first statement the author makes is that the bound servitude of his people had lingered. The word expressing this action also is used of the saddling of donkeys, or the harnessing of animals, accentuating the instrument with which the animal is forced to obey the wishes of the enforcer. When the word is used of humans, the idea of forcing a person into servitude is connoted (Isaiah 3:7). Therefore, the writer was communicating that the Hebrew people had endured bound servitude under compulsion, although there is no indication that the servitude had ceased at the time of writing . . .

> As for the significance of attributing this as "a year of astonishment," the author of Sinai 361 may have been . . . explaining that Moses' provoking of astonishment was not merely a momentary event, but one in which this astonishment continued throughout the year. The point was not that this astonishment had lasted 12 full months, or that it began on the first day of the calendar year, but that the year was filled with astonishing events. This commentary would fit well with the events of the plagues reported in the Bible, which undoubtedly continued over a period of months, caused amazement, and brought despair to the Egyptians who endured these events (Exodus 10:7).

> The author evidently had hoped or expected that the Hebrews' bound servitude would have ceased,

which was not the case. This failed freedom from forced labor brought him disappointment and despair. Given the relationship between the first and second statements in the inscription, the author evidently connected the continued servitude with Moses' provoking of astonishment, which transpired at the time that the servitude lingered, meaning that perhaps there was hope that Moses would have brought an end to it. This would fit well with the biblical narrative.

Again we see the Hebrews connecting the events surrounding the Exodus with a pagan deity, referred to here as "the Lady" (probably Hathor). The Lord God was delivering them, but they did not fully realize what was happening or Who their deliverer was. Thus in His commandments God begins with:

> I am the Lord your God who brought you out of the land of Egypt, out of the house of slavery. (Exodus 20:2)

It is also worth noting that the Exodus portrays the Hebrews as crying for help in their deep affliction, but that it does not explicitly say they cried only to the Lord God. They surely must have cried out to Him, but it appears that they called out to other "gods" as well. But the One Who heard their cries was not Hathor or any other "god," but the God of their fathers.

> Now it came about in *the course of* those many days [while Moses was in Midian] that the king of Egypt died. And the sons of Israel sighed because of the bondage, and they cried out; and their cry for help because of *their* bondage rose up to God. So God heard their groaning; and God remembered His covenant with Abraham, Isaac, and Jacob. God saw the sons of Israel, and God took notice *of them*. (Exodus 2:23–25)

Also, consider these scriptures:

> Our fathers in Egypt did not understand Your wonders [i.e., wonderful acts] . . . Nevertheless, He saved them for the sake of His name, that He might make His power known . . . They made a calf in Horeb and worshiped a molten image. (Psalm 106:7, 8, 19)

> Did you present Me with sacrifices and grain offerings in the wilderness for forty years, O house of Israel? You also carried along Sikkuth [Saturn, or a shrine of your Moloch] your king and Kiyyun [or stands of], your images, the star of your gods which you made for yourselves. Therefore, I will make you go into exile beyond Damascus," says the LORD, whose name is the God of hosts. (Amos 5:25–26)

The idolatry that the sons of Israel had adopted in Egypt (and possibly also in Canaan) wasn't easy for them to shake off. It stuck with them and resulted in their downfall centuries later. In contrast, the patriarchs Abraham, Isaac, and Jacob were monotheistic and faithful.

Translating Inscriptions Written Near the Time of Joseph:

The next inscriptions—Sinai 115 and Sinai 405—were written over two centuries before the Exodus. They are from a set of early inscriptions written by an individual whose name is inscribed above some of them in Egyptian—Hebeded. These inscriptions are the earliest known examples of proto-Sinaitic. They are distinguished by the fact that some of them are signed, and some are also dated. Some of these inscriptions also have a distinctive picture of Hebeded riding a donkey with two attendants, probably sons, walking before and after him. They also reveal that Hebeded was the leader of several mining expeditions to Serabit. We mention four of his inscriptions, but will look at just two in greater detail:

Sinai 115	Dated to the 18th year of Amenemhat III, the latest dated inscription by Hebeded, has a picture of him riding on a donkey.
Sinai 85	Dated to the 4th year of Amenemhat III, the earliest dated inscription.
Sinai 112	Same picture—a man with two sons, but younger. This is one that is signed Hebeded, and one of the sons is named. He is "Kekbi."
Sinai 405	Same picture, and very well preserved because it was providentially buried in the sand. Thus, more details are revealed in this stela.

Dr Petrovich and Sir Alan Henderson Gardiner comment on this group of inscriptions:

Inscription Sinai 115 [416]

Translation:
    Six Levantines: Hebrews of Bethel, the Beloved.

Paraphrasing Dr. Petrovich's explanation: [Note: Levant = the Middle East.]
    The person who inscribed the word "Levant" (*Retjanu*) wrote it as *etjanu*, leaving off the "R," which is how Asiatic people spoke/wrote the word. This is a further indication that the author was Semitic. The word translated as "Bethel" is actually "earth-god house" or "house of the earth-god." Remember that when Jacob fled from Esau to Padam-Aram he slept and had the dream of God speaking to him. He named that place "Bethel," or "house of God." God appeared to Jacob (Genesis 35:1) and told him to go live at Bethel after the treachery of his sons at Shechem. Jacob then renamed the place "El-Bethel," or "God of Bethel." The place was sacred to Jacob and his family, a place where Joseph had lived with them before he was sold into slavery. Joseph would have re-called it with love and with longing, as would members of his Egyptian family if he told them of it. Bethel—the house of God on earth; Bethel, the beloved.

The 18th year of Amenemhat III is a relative date. In order to translate this into an absolute date I will refer to the chronology of Dr. Rohl for the kings of the 12th Dynasty. He assigns a date of 1664 BC to the 18th year of this king. (See below, where I coordinate Dr. Rohl's dates and my chronology.) 1664 BC was three years before Jacob entered Egypt. Joseph was acting as vizier for the king and was 66 years old. The famine was in the land.

Note on the chronology of the kings of the 12th Dynasty of Egypt: We have already seen that the chronology of the kings of Egypt has many uncertainties in it. The ideas of Dr. Rohl resulted in variations in that chronology of from 100 to 300 years or more, depending on a variety of factors. Besides that major uncertainty in the broader chronology of the Egyptian kings, the 12th Dynasty is also fraught with its own unique uncertainties.

> From a chronological point of view, the Twelfth Dynasty raises questions which affect the determination of both the absolute and relative chronology of the period, namely the duration of the entire dynasty and the duration of each kingdom. . . Over the years, many debates among scholars have been held on the topic.[417]

The 12th Dynasty has a "Low Chronology" and a "High Chronology" for its kings, reflecting issues with when it began. It also has a "Short Chronology" and a "Long Chronology," and these assign either 177 or 213 total years to the dynasty. Therefore the absolute dates I assign to these reigns are subject to at least minor adjustment, even after the work of Dr. Rohl to determine the broader chronology of the Egyptian kings.

Inscription Sinai 405 [418]

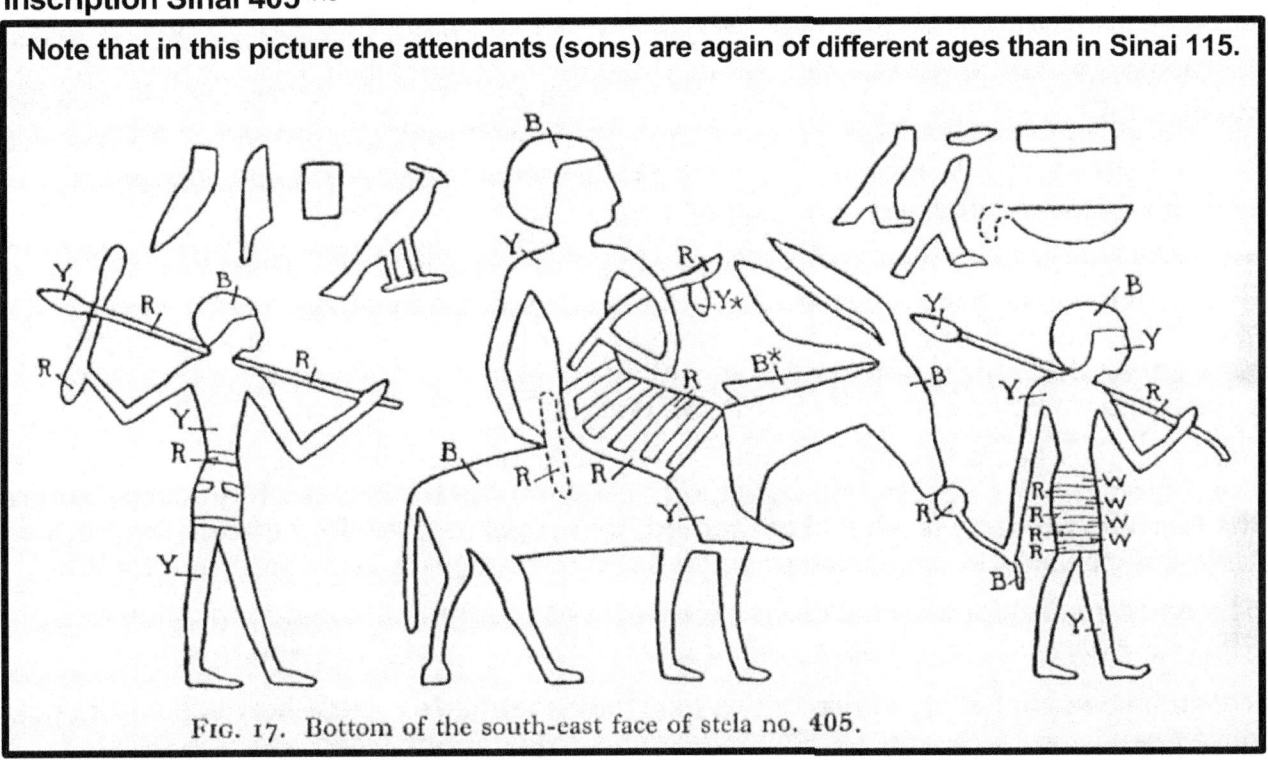

FIG. 17. Bottom of the south-east face of stela no. 405.

Gardiner comments on this stela:

> [At the bottom of the south-east face of stela Sinai 405] is a representation in relief of a man riding on a donkey. The animal is led by a man carrying a spear over his left shoulder, and is followed by yet another man armed also with a spear and a throwing stick. The man on the donkey holds an adze in his left hand, and a short stick (for urging the donkey?) in his right. The man leading the donkey is called '*Shekam*', the man behind the donkey '*Apim*', and as the bodies of all three are painted yellow, they were therefore Semites. The stela, having probably been buried deep in sand and, after its transfer to the present position, disguised by the wall, the colours (yellow, black, red, and white) were well preserved at the time of discovery in 1935. The details of the colouring are shown by the accompanying figure (fig. 17).

With the many details that these multiple inscriptions by Hebeded give us, we are in a position to make an educated guess at who he was—a Hebrew who recalled Bethel with longing and with love, who led multiple mining expeditions to Serabit (and thus was a person of status in Egypt), who had several sons whom he took with him on his mining trips. In these details, one clue (the son Shekam) points to a biblical person—Manessa, the oldest son of Joseph.

Facts about Manessa: Joshuah 17:1-2 lists seven sons of Manessa; Machir, Abiezer, Helek, Asriel, Shechem, Hepher, and Shemida. 1 Chronicles 7:14 says his concubine bore him Machir and Asriel. Presumably, his wife bore him the other five sons. The third son of Manessa by his wife was "Shechem," and **this Hebrew name is a transliteration of the Egyptian name "Shekam" found on Sinai 405, as noted by several scholars.** Other named sons (Kekbi, Apim) cannot be linguistically identified as one of Manessa's sons.

My guess: Hebeded = Manessa, the first-born son of Joseph. I assume he was born when Joseph was 31. He held a place of status in Egypt, for Joseph was second to Pharaoh.

This also gives us a hint as to who invented the proto-Sinaitic script. Joseph, in his role as vizier under Pharaoh Amenemhat III, was a Semite who had to know hieroglyphics in order to carry out his job of administering the land of Egypt to prepare for and manage the famine. He must have invented the script and taught it to his sons. These earliest inscriptions were the work of Manessa. The earliest of these inscriptions, Sinai 85, was written in the 4th year of Amenemhat III, or in 1678 BC. Thus the script must have been invented a short time before that date—perhaps around 1680 to 1700 BC. As noted, this time estimate for the invention of the proto-Sinaitic script might need to be adjusted slightly because of the uncertainties in the chronology of the kings of the 12th dynasty.

The later inscriptions' translations give us clear extra-Biblical confirmation of the major events that immediately preceded the Exodus and that made it the powerful event that it was. They confirm that the Hebrews were in Egypt, they were in severe bondage there before their deliverance, and they were writing about it; they had an alphabetic script and were using it; they were widely learned in reading/writing.

We have often heard that the judgments of the Exodus were aimed at or directed against the Egyptian Gods. Seeing how steeped in idolatry the Hebrews in Egypt were before the Exodus, we can see why. God wanted His people to know for certain Who He was, how very powerful He was. Hathor could not deliver them, but He could, and He did.

The early inscriptions' translations give us a peek into the time and family of Joseph. They also allow us to estimate when the script was invented and who invented it.

These first examples of the use of this early alphabet make it clear how this script could have been used by Moses. Dr. Rohl makes the obvious connection:
> The actual Ten Commandments of Moses, composed atop Mount Sinai, must have been written in Proto-Hebrew which, in reality, was none other than the Proto-Sinaitic script we came across at Serabit el-Khadim. [Dr. Rohl believes that the path that Moses led the Israelites on at the Exodus took them near to Serabit el-Khadim and the turquois mines there, where they picked up the Hebrew slaves that were working the mines.] Now that we know that the Exodus took place in the Middle Bronze Age, rather than at the end of the Late Bronze Age [i.e., in 1446 BC, not 1250 BC], it becomes obvious that the Decalogue ('ten words') of the Mosaic law were composed of the Egyptian hieroglyphic signs that Joseph and his kin had borrowed to write their Semitic alphabet. This then evolved into what scholars call Proto-Canaanite (which, in reality, included Late Bronze Age Proto-Hebrew); and from this came Iron Age Phoenician and Hebrew . . . and, of course, the Greek and Roman alphabets of the Classical era.[419]

Proto-Sinaitic Inscriptions in Canaan:
Dr. Rohl mentions "proto-Canaanite" inscriptions, which are very old inscriptions found in the land of Canaan. These were always assumed to be early forms of Phoenician writing since the Phoenicians were thought to have invented the alphabetic script. But now it is mandatory to see these as early Hebrew inscriptions.

The oldest proto-Canaanite scripts have been found in Israel, at Shechem, Gezer, and Lachish. [420] They have been tentatively dated to 1700 BC to 1500 BC. A few somewhat later inscriptions have been tentatively dated to 1300 BC to 1100 BC. As far as I know, none of these proto-Canaanite inscriptions have ever been translated. But recently two inscriptions have been found and translated.

One: A "Curse Tablet" on Mount Ebal:
A small "defixio" or "curse tablet" was discovered by researchers with the Associates for Biblical Research. This discovery was made public in March of 2022.[421]

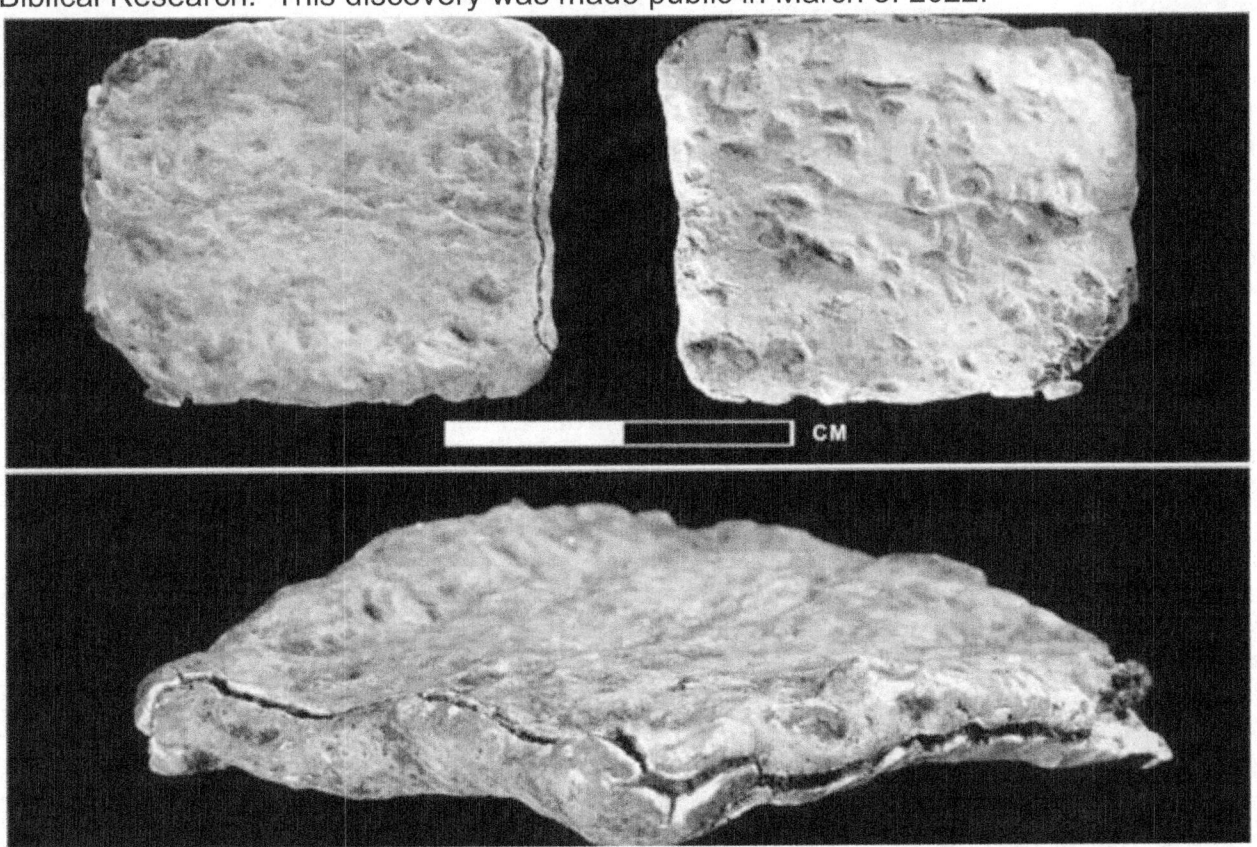

The small "curse tablet" was found on Mount Ebal in the altar that Joshua built soon after the Hebrews entered Canaan at the time of the Conquest. Moses commanded Joshua: "place the blessing on Mount Gerizim and the curse on Mount Ebal" (Deuteronomy 11:29) after the people enter the land. The blessings would accrue if they obeyed the Lord and walked in His ways, and the curses would fall if they did not. Joshua obeyed Moses.

> Then Joshua built an altar to the Lord, the God of Israel, in Mount Ebal, just as Moses the servant of the Lord had commanded . . . All Israel with their elders and officers and their judges were standing on both sides of the ark. . . Half of them *stood* in front of Mount Gerizim and half of them in front of Mount Ebal, just as Moses the servant of the Lord had given command. (Joshua 8:30-33)

The defixio was found in the altar on Mount Ebal. It had writing in it. It says:

> Cursed, cursed, cursed. Cursed by the God YHW. You will die cursed. Cursed you will surely die. Cursed by YHW. Cursed, cursed, cursed.

This is dated to the Middle Bronze Age II, the same time as the destruction of the Canaanite cities Jericho, Ai, etc. According to the Bible, Joshua performed this action early in the Conquest, right after the destruction of Ai. The writing must be Hebrew because the name YHW appears in it. The form of the writing is like that in the proto-Sinaitic inscriptions.

The Researchers for Biblical Archeology named the script "proto-alphabetic." Here is the name of God as written in the "proto-alphabetic"

The divine name YHW from Mt. Ebal in proto-alphabetic script

Drawing by Gershon Galil

This find proves that the Hebrews carried the proto-Sinaitic script into Canaan at the time of the Conquest. Joshua obeyed Moses and "placed the curse (defixio) on Mount Ebal." So the other early proto-Canaanite inscriptions are early Hebrew, not early Phoenician.

Two: An Inscription of a Piece of Pottery:
A proto-Canaanite inscription was found in 2018 by a team of excavators from the Austrian Archeological Institute in the burn layer of Lachish. Dr. Petrovich has translated it.[422]

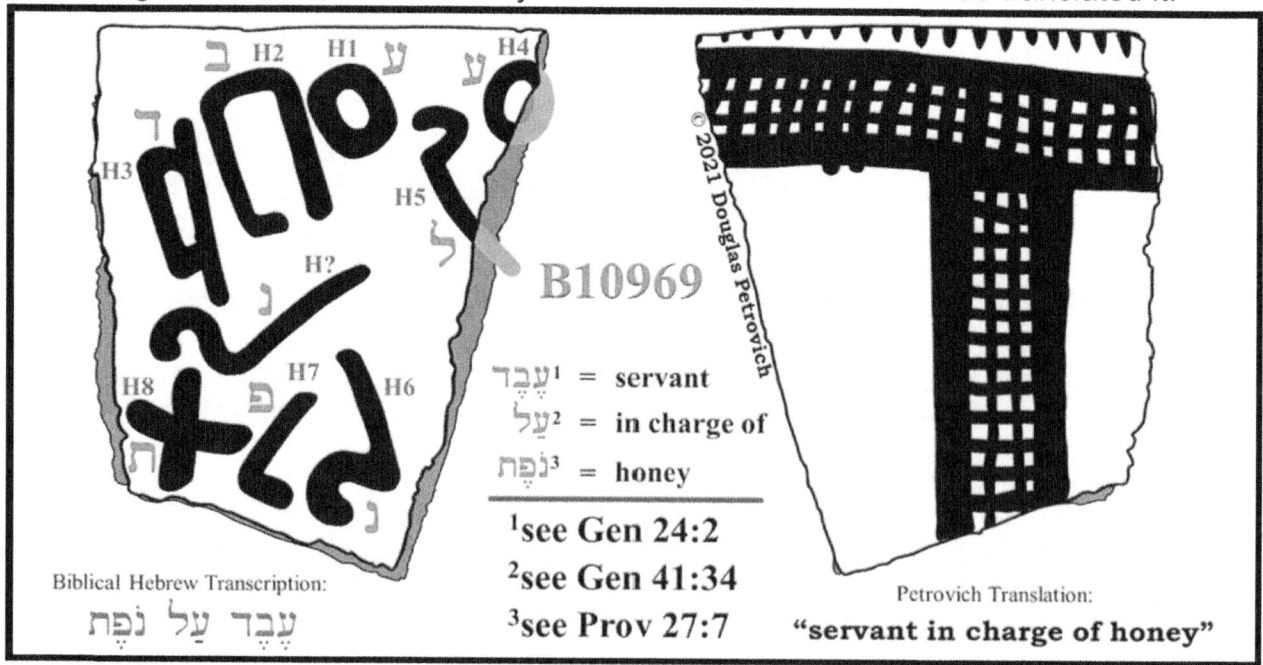

Again, this is the early Hebrew script, proto-Sinaitic. Because it was found in the burn layer at Lachish, it is dated to the Middle Bronze Age II. It must have been dropped by a Hebrew after the destruction of Lachish. Thus, Lachish was destroyed by the Hebrews.

But all Middle Bronze Age II cities were destroyed during the same time period. They all have the same relative time for their destruction. Thus, all were destroyed the Hebrews. If the Conquest happened at the later date of ~1210 BC then the MB II would have to extend until that late date, which is impossible. Thus, the date of the Conquest is the earlier date, 1406 BC, in accord with the biblical chronology. Also, the end of the MB II cannot have been in 1550 BC, like Kenyon claimed, but must be extended until 1400 BC like Garstang originally asserted, and as Bimson reiterated. This find undergirds all the biblical chronological assertions that we made about the timing of the Exodus/Conquest. The key was the identifying of the proto-Sinaitic inscriptions as early Hebrew, and then the translation of those inscriptions and of similar ones in Canaan. The following illustrates the chronological implications of this find:

> **The Conquest has two possible dates. Which is correct?**
>
> **And when did MB II end?** |1406 BC   1210 BC
>
> 1550 BC   1400 BC
>
> **Pottery shows the Hebrews destroyed Lachish. The only possible time, the only overlapping time, is 1406 BC.**

A Boader Perspective on the Origins of the Hebrew Script:
At this point, I want to back up a bit and form a hypothetical scenario to explain exactly how and when this alphabetic script was invented, and how it happened that many Hebrews were versed in this script. I also want to talk about the unique roles that Joseph and Moses each played in the development of this script. As with all archeological scenarios, models, or "hypothetical constructs," this is not totally founded on facts, as is the existence of the above inscriptions, but it is still very instructive. (Of course, some will surely argue with Dr. Petrovich about the translation of various of the above scripts. But few things from ancient times are completely free from controversy and scholarly dispute.)

Another way to explain this: In what we see above, Dr. Petrovich is not trying to put forth a broad scenario about the past. He is looking deeply at one narrow subject—the remnants of the proto-Sinaitic script as it is found in and around ancient Egypt. There still is some subjectivity in what he is doing, but not as much as if he were trying to interpret diverse findings and then weave them into a broader scenario. That is what I want to do next, as many archeologists do. But one observation about my scenario; the Bible does give us a broad scenario on the history of the world and on the nation of Israel. What I am about to put together fits in with the Bible, and that gives it a greater likelihood of being accurate.

The ruling pharaohs at the time of Joseph, according to the revised chronology of David Rohl, as explained above, were Senuseret III and his son Amenemhat III.
- This is the revised chronology that Dr. Rohl puts forth once he demonstrates that Ramesses II ruled in the 10th century not in the 13th century.
- Senuseret III was the pharaoh who elevated Joseph to vizier in Egypt because he had wisely interpreted his dreams. His son continued to carry out his policies.
- I will move the reigns of Dr. Rohl's kings three years into the past to make them dovetail perfectly with my Biblical chronology.[423] Remember, we noted that the Egyptian chronology was a bit uncertain, inexact, and estimated.

> Senuseret II = 1719-1701 BC (instead of 1716-1698)
> Senuseret III = 1701-1661 BC (instead of 1698-1658)
> Amenemhat III = 1681-1634 BC (instead of 1678-1631)

Let us look at the chronology of the family of Jacob so that we can see how Dr. Rohl's chronology connects with it.

The Flexible Chronology of the Family of Jacob:
Scripture delineates the chronology of the birth of each of the patriarchs, thus giving us a firm timeline from the Creation, the Deluge, the Sojourn, and through to the Exodus. But many smaller events within that framework are not specified. One such ambiguity is seen in the chronology of the family life of Jacob. He was born in 1791 BC and died in 1644 BC. He spent 20 years in Padan Aram building his family. He entered Egypt in 1661 BC at the age of 130. But at what age did he leave for Padan Aram? Analysis of the passages from Genesis 28 (see commentary) indicate that he was between (about) age 40 at a minimum and age 63 at most. Therefore we must choose or set the age for his departure. How we do this will determine the year in which Joseph (at age 17) is sold into slavery in Egypt, how old he is when Jacob enters Egypt, how many years are available for the small family of Jacob to develop into 70 total members when he enters Egypt, and how long Joseph has to prepare for the famine in Egypt before Jacob arrives. These developments must be given sufficient time. With this in mind, I choose/set:

Jacob: Leave for Padan Aram at age 47 (1744 BC); so Joseph: Enter Egypt in 1713 BC.
Joseph will have 30 years to prepare for the famine, from age 30 to age 60. Jacob will enter the land of Egypt when Joseph is 69, after seven years of plenty and two years of famine.

Two dates tie Biblical chronology to Dr. Rohl's: In 1713 BC (the date I choose/set), at 17, Joseph is sold into slavery. In 1661 BC (fixed date) Jacob enters Egypt. **It was the second year of the famine.** Thereafter Avaris began to have a population that included Asiatic (i.e., Semitic) people, as we saw earlier. But because that time period also overlapped the reign of Amenemhat III, it was also the time of (possibly) the worst famine in the history of Egypt. The following scenario utilizes Dr. Rohl's insights and historical connections.[424]

A Few Facts of History and Climate:
The Nile waters rose each year in late June and peaked in September, flooding the land with life-giving water and a fresh deposit of black silt to fertilize the land. The waters of the Nile were measured during the reign of Amenemhat III at the fortresses of Semna and Kumma hundreds of miles upstream. The records of these measurements are preserved still today. The fortresses were on each side of a narrow gorge in the Nile, and that is the place where the measurements were made—on the sides of the cliff walls of the gorge.

In the 3rd-19th years of the king—for 17 years straight—the water levels rose to 14 feet higher than normal. This modest rise in the flood level of the Nile would have eventually brought agricultural prosperity to the nation—a time of plenty. The Bible says the last seven of these years were **very** prosperous. That is when Joseph collected and stored grain for pharaoh.

> Now Joseph was thirty years old when he stood before Pharaoh, king of Egypt. And Joseph went out from the presence of Pharaoh and went through all the land of Egypt. [This project must have taken many years (over 20) to implement, to make preparations.] During the seven years of plenty the land brought forth abundantly. So he gathered all the food of *these* seven years which occurred in the land of Egypt and placed the food in the cities; he placed in every city the food from its own surrounding fields. Thus Joseph stored up grain in great abundance like the sand of the sea, until he stopped measuring *it*, for it was beyond measure. (Genesis 41:46–49)

Joseph was wise enough, from the interpretation of pharaoh's dreams with which he had been gifted, to prepare for and harness the years of plenty when they came along. But Joseph was also wise enough to instigate another engineering project, one not explained in the Bible. To understand that project we must understand the cause of the years of famine that followed. The records of Semna and Kumma show that in the next 12 years the water level of the Nile was even higher—so high that the Nile would have completely flooded Egypt and caused widespread destruction. It would also have prevented the people from planting their crops because the land would have been under water during the times of planting. This would have resulted in a terrible famine instead of plenty.

This might be hinted at in the dreams that pharaoh had, as interpreted by Joseph.
> So Pharaoh spoke to Joseph, "In my dream, behold, I was standing on the bank of the Nile; and behold, seven cows, fat and sleek came up out of the Nile, and they grazed in the marsh grass. Lo, seven other cows came up after them, poor and very ugly and gaunt, such as I had never seen for ugliness in all the land of Egypt; and the lean and ugly cows ate up the first seven fat cows. Yet when they had devoured them, it could not be detected that they had devoured them, for they were just as ugly as before. Then I awoke. (Genesis 41:17–21)

Why were the cows coming up from out of the Nile? Because the Nile was the cause, both of the years of plenty and of the years of famine. Pharaoh's second dream was:
> I saw also in my dream, and behold, seven ears, full and good, came up on a single stalk; and lo, seven ears, withered, thin, *and* scorched by the east wind, sprouted up after them; and the thin ears swallowed the seven good ears. (Genesis 41:21–24)

Here is how Dr. Rohl analyzes the dreams, garnering the total picture of what they meant:
> A combination of excess water coming from the southern reaches of the Nile and a severe heat brought by east winds suggests to me that we have here a northward shift in the climate zones. This brought tropical rains to Ethiopia, normally associated with the equatorial zone, and a northward movement of the Arabian desert zone into Canaan, producing hot winds from across the rift valley of the Jordan. This turned the already marginal pasturelands of the southern highlands of Judah and the northern Negeb into inhospitable desert.[425]

In other words, the jet stream shifted, and all Egypt and all of the Middle East suddenly was afflicted by devastating climatic changes. Famine was everywhere—in Egypt because of too much river water, and in other places because of too little rainfall. A certain verse in Genesis makes more sense with this understanding.
> Then Joseph said to his brothers, "Please come closer to me." And they came closer. And he said, "I am your brother Joseph, whom you sold into Egypt. Now do not be grieved or angry with yourselves, because you sold me here, for God sent me before you to preserve life. For the famine *has been* in the land these two years, and **there are still five years in which there will be neither plowing nor harvesting**. God sent me before you to preserve for you a remnant in the earth, and to keep you alive by a great deliverance. (Genesis 45:4–7) [my bold]

Why would a famine prevent both plowing and reaping? What kind of situation had arisen that caused this catastrophe? Certainly a severe, annual, overflowing of the Nile would prevent both sowing and reaping. Also, as in other places of the account, Joseph expresses his faith perspective that the hand of the Lord was in the events. In fact, his having been sold into Egypt by his brothers, as hard-hearted as it was, turned out by the grace of the Lord God to be an opportunity to preserve the family of Jacob.

This set the stage for the account of Genesis.
> When the famine was *spread* over all the face of the earth, then Joseph opened all the storehouses, and sold to the Egyptians; and the famine was severe in the land of Egypt. *The people of* all the earth came to Egypt to buy grain from Joseph, because the famine was severe in all the earth. (Genesis 41: 56, 57)

Archeologists have found abundant remains of these many storehouses.[426]

Joseph took additional action to alleviate the famine. After all, the devastatingly high level of the Nile water lasted for 12 years, not just for seven. That brings us to the engineering project that was undertaken to alleviate the problem for all time. This is not in the Bible.

> As if guided by some remarkable premonition, a massive project was begun to construct a long canal (or perhaps widen and deepen an existing prehistoric river offshoot), branching away from the Nile at Asyut and flowing northwards all the way to a natural break in the western desert escarpment where is disgorged into Fayum basin, there to form a huge reservoir called Lake Moeris in the classical literature. At the point where this waterway reached the westwards break in the desert ridge the *ha toer* dam was constructed, with sluice gates to control the water, which could either be directed into Lake Moeris during the inundation or redirected back into the Nile to flow northwards into the delta during the dry season.[427]

This allowed water to be diverted out of or into the Nile and, in general made the nation less dependent on the whims of the weather and the unpredictable levels of the Nile that resulted from weather or climate changes. This canal, called the Canal of Joseph, or *Bahr Yussef*, is still in existence in Egypt today.

> It seems clear that the great canal was excavated to divert a large part of the floodwaters from the Nile into Fayum basin, thus preventing the worst of the high waters from reaching Lower Egypt and the delta. This was the solution which the Egyptian state came up with to alleviate the cause of famine, and there can be little doubt that it would have made a considerable difference to the fortunes of Lower Egypt in this period of crisis. Though this huge engineering project to divert the floodwaters is not mentioned in the Book of Genesis, the building of the canal and the storage of grain were actions which saved Egypt from the worst of the famine. And the name of that canal? Well, it has always been known simply as the Bahr Yussef - the 'Waterway of Joseph'.[428]

The massive engineering projects that Joseph undertook to prepare for the coming famine (and to insulate Egypt from any such successive famines) took many years to plan, design, and implement. All the Bible says is that "Joseph . . . went throughout the land of Egypt" (Genesis 41:46). Clearly such huge undertakings could have consumed his time and his attention for 30 or more years. Pharaoh gave him his signet ring and gold necklace, and made him second only to himself in order to assure he had the authority to complete it.

Amenemhat III was so impressed by this engineering marvel, revealed as a solution to a devastating flood by a dream and a divine interpretation, that he built his Hawara pyramid on the desert plateau overlooking the channel and also erected two huge statues of himself at the mouth of the canal, at the location where it emptied into the lake.

Unified Chronology of the Time of Joseph:
I set out to produce a unified chronology of the archeological events as Dr. Rohl pieces them together, the dated inscriptions of Dr. Petrovich, and the Biblical chronology that I develop in this book.[429] Here it is, with the dates for Senuseret II, Senuseret III, and Amenemhat III adjusted back into the past by three years.

My unified chronology utilizes us these important chronological facts and connections:
1. Joseph was 17 when he was sold into slavery (Genesis 37:2). In my calculations in this work I choose/set this this date to be 1713 BC. This is not a fixed date, as I have explained (not one determined by the text of Genesis) but one chosen by me from within a certain flexible framework. It must be set to this value once I assume that Jacob departed for Padan Aram in 1744 BC at age 47.
2. Joseph was 30 when he stood before pharaoh to interpret his dreams (Genesis 41: 46), necessarily in 1700 BC once his date of entrance into Egypt is set to 1713.
3. Jacob entered Egypt in 1661 BC, which was also the second year of the famine.
4. The one key unifying fact: The 2nd year of the famine (1661 BC) is also the 21st year of Amenemhat III. This connects us to the chronology of the Egyptian kings.

Putting this information together, here is the table of the unified chronology.

Year	Event	Joseph's age
1713	Joseph is sold into slavery.	Joseph is 17
1702	Joseph interprets the dreams of Pharaoh's baker and his cupbearer.	Joseph is 28
1701	Senuseret II dies. Senuseret III begins to reign. Joseph is still in prison.	Joseph is 29
1700	Joseph interprets the dreams of pharaoh Senuseret III and receives a wife.	Joseph is 30

Note: Genesis 41:13—the use of "he" in referring to pharaoh (while speaking to Senuseret III) implies the "pharaoh" who hanged and/or restored the two servants was not the same person to whom the cupbearer was speaking. ("He" restored me to my office, but "he" hanged him.) Grammatically, the "he" referred to could not be the then-current pharaoh. It was his father.

Year	Event	Joseph's age
1699	Manessa is born	Joseph is 31
1699-1670	Joseph "goes through all the land of Egypt"	Joseph is 31-60
1690	Joseph invents proto-Sinaitic script. (estimated, + or – 9 years)	Joseph is 31-49
1681	1st year of Amenemhat III He continues his father's policies.	Joseph is 49
1679	3rd year of Amenemhat III High waters of the Nile river begin, so Abundant grain, but storage bins not yet ready and waterway not completed. Joseph's preparations take time!	Joseph is 51
1678	4th year of Amenemhat III Sinai 85, earliest inscription, Manessa 21.	Joseph is 52
1669	13th year of Amenemhat III Abundance, beginning of grain storage.	Joseph is 61
1664	18th year of Amenemhat III Sinai 115, latest inscription, Manessa 35.	Joseph is 66
1663	19th year of Amenemhat III High waters and abundance, last year.	Joseph is 67
1662	20th year of Amenemhat III VERY high waters and famine begins. First year of famine, people live off stored grain, waterway not ready yet.	Joseph is 68
1661	21st year of Amenemhat III (Senuseret III dies) Jacob enters Egypt when the famine has been in the land for two years.	Joseph is 69
1656	26th year of Amenemhat III Seventh and last year of the famine.	Joseph is 74
1655	27th year of Amenemhat III First year the waterway is completed. No famine in Egypt, Nile is controlled.	Joseph is 75
1651	31st year of Amenemhat III 12th year of VERY high Nile water.	Joseph is 79
1650	32nd year of Amenemhat III Nile returns to normal levels.	Joseph is 80
1644	Jacob dies at 147 years of age	Joseph is 86
1620	Joseph dies	Joseph is 110

The Development of the proto-Sinaitic Script:

Here are some facts that we have uncovered thus far about this earliest alphabetic script, plus a few pieces of new information, and detailed steps explaining how the development of proto-Sinaitic might have happened, and the roles of Joseph and Moses in it:

- It was invented in Egypt before 1678 BC, at the time of Amenemhat III and Joseph.
- The script is a very early form of alphabetic writing and is Semitic in form. It is a kind of proto-Semitic/proto-alphabetic script, the earliest known alphabetic or Semitic script.
- The characters of the script were formed from recharacterized hieroglyphic symbols, so the person who invented it had to have been a Semite who knew hieroglyphics.
- The only known Semitic people in Egypt at that time were Joseph and his family. In order to fulfill the charge pharaoh had given him to prepare for the coming famine Joseph had to be familiar with Egyptian hieroglyphics.
- Thus: Joseph invented the script—a stroke of genius (**actually, divine inspiration**), while charged by Pharoah Amenemhat III with the administration of the land of Egypt when he was preparing for the famine.
- At the same time Joseph's first-born son Manessa was leading mining expeditions to Serabit el Khadim and often took two of his sons with him. He left inscriptions at Serabit, signing some as "Hebeded." The inscriptions also identify one of his sons as "Shekam," the exact Egyptian equivalent of the Hebrew name Shechem.

- Therefore we can reasonably identify Hebeded with Manessa. He is the one who wrote the earliest inscriptions.
- Therefore, Joseph must have taught the script to his sons Ephraim and Manessa.
- After he entered Egypt in 1661 BC Jacob adopted Ephraim and Manessa as his own. This was about 25 years after the invention of the proto-Sinaitic script. The two sons learned the Semitic ways of Jacob's family, and the family learned their proto-Semitic script. That gave the Hebrews a skill that greatly benefitted them while they were living and prospering in the land of Egypt in the following centuries.
- When the Hebrews left Egypt the use of the script left with them. No proto-Sinaitic inscriptions dated after 1446 BC have been found in Egypt.
- At the time of the Exodus Moses used the proto-Sinaitic script to write a monumental literary work. He used it to write the Pentateuch. It was the first time in history that a work of that complexity, with a flowing script, had been produced. It demonstrated the true capability inherent in alphabetic scripts.

In Canaan:
- The script was carried into Canaan by the Hebrews when they entered Canaan at the time of the Conquest. This has been confirmed by the two recent examples of the script that have been found (and translated) in Canaan.
- Joseph Naveh (an eminent epigrapher of the 20th century) asserts that, of all the Semitic scripts in Canaan, Old Hebrew is most like proto-Sinaitic.[430]
- The oldest Phoenician inscriptions are found on the sarcophagus of "king Ahiram,"[431] dated to near the time of the reign of Solomon.
- The oldest scripts in Canaan are found in Israel, not in Phoenicia (Lebanon).[432]
- Thus, Phoenician developed from Old Hebrew, not the other way around. In fact, the time of Solomon, when Hiram of Lebanon (Phoenicia) was working with him to supply materials for the temple, would have been when the Phoenicians learned alphabetic writing from the Hebrews. (~946 BC?, see 1 Kings 9:11). This identifies the archeological person known as "Ahiram" with king Hiram of the Bible.
- The proto-Canaanite scripts found in the Middle East are not ancient Phoenician, but are ancient Hebrew. Old Hebrew, Phoenician, proto-Canaanite, and all other Semitic scripts are to be identified with, or developed from, the proto-Sinaitic script that the Hebrews brought into the land of Cannan at the time of the Conquest.

I believe that the Lord inspired Joseph to invent the alphabetic script so that, when Moses came along his holy word could be written down and read by His chosen people—not just by a few educated scribes and/or priests, but by many Hebrews, so that the heads of the Jewish households could "write these words on the doorposts of their gates and teach them to their children" as God commanded them to do. **God's revelation to man in the Scriptures is complex enough that it demands an alphabetic script, so God inspired its invention.**

When Moses came along he did something with the script that no one had ever done before. He used it to write a book. He used it to write a large, literary work—the Pentateuch. He was well educated in all the learning of Egypt and had the training necessary for such a monumental and unprecedented task, extending the function of the script to far beyond anything that his enslaved compatriots had ever imagined.

> [The Israelites] had taken the Egyptian symbols and adapted them for writing their names and a few simple phrases in their own language. But it took the multilingual skills of an educated Hebrew prince of Egypt to turn these simple first scratchings into a functional script, capable of transmitting complex ideas and a flowing narrative. **The Ten Commandments and the Laws**

> **of Moses were written in Proto-Sinaitic.** The prophet of Yahweh – master of both the Egyptian and Mesopotamian epic literature – was not only the founding father of Judaism, Christianity and, through the Koranic traditions, Islam, but also the progenitor of the Hebrew, Canaanite, Phoenician, Greek, and therefore, modern western alphabetic scripts.[433] [bold mine]

Moses was the first person to utilize the full capabilities of an alphabetic script. He took what had been used to write simple phrases or short notes, and wrote a landmark literary work. He exercised fully the potential that was inherent in such a tool, and he was the first person in history to do so. **It was another instance of divine inspiration.**

We take alphabetic writing for granted. The power to communicate in writing that it grants to us is an eons-old inherited gift whose absence we cannot even imagine. But the word of our God, if it is to be written down, requires just such a tool. **The Bible, God's revelation to mankind in written form, requires more than cuneiform or hieroglyphics or any similar method of written communication can deliver.** That is why God inspired His servants to invent alphabetic scripts, and why he showed us how to make full use of that tool. God's revelation to man demands an alphabetic script! And He carefully arranged events so that His people, when the written word was before them, would have the ability to read it.

God wanted this ability not just for a few highly educated people, but for all of His sons and daughters. I mean, He wants that for all of us today. I think this skill was gifted to the human race for that primary purpose—so we could read His word. Other beneficial uses have also been made of alphabetic writing, but that was its first and primary purpose.

Issues Surrounding the Mosaic Authorship of Genesis:

We noted: Given the full context and timeframe of each book, the early Biblical books seem to have been written sequentially, each after the previous book. This is true for Leviticus, which begins immediately after Exodus ends; with Numbers, which appears to begin immediately after Leviticus; with Deuteronomy, which appears to have been written as soon as Numbers ended; with Joshua, which takes up as soon as Deuteronomy ends and the period of grieving for Moses was ended; and with Judges, which seems to pick up after Joshua.

The book of Genesis is unique because at the time of Moses all events recorded in Genesis were more than two centuries in the past, and some were millennia in the past. Thus neither Moses nor any of his approximate contemporaries were possible eyewitnesses to any of those events. Therefore we have to ask and consider how Moses wrote the book of Genesis. I am not referring so much to whether he had the necessary linguistic skills and tools to write it, for we have already shown that to be the case. Rather, I am asking how he obtained the information in that book. How did he come to know about what is written therein?

First of all, there is textual evidence that Moses and the Hebrews of his day knew about the patriarchs and what happened in their lives many centuries before. Consider these verses:

> Then Moses said to God, "Behold, I am going to the sons of Israel, and I will say to them, 'The God of your fathers has sent me to you.' Now they may say to me, 'What is His name?' What shall I say to them?" God said to Moses, "I AM WHO I AM"; and He said, "Thus you shall say to the sons of Israel, 'I AM has sent me to you.'" God, furthermore, said to Moses, "Thus you shall say to the sons of Israel, 'The LORD, the God of your fathers, the God of Abraham, the God of Isaac, and the God of Jacob, has sent me to you.' This is My name forever, and this is My memorial-name to all generations. (Exodus 3:13–15)

> God spoke further to Moses and said to him, "I am the LORD; and I appeared to Abraham, Isaac, and Jacob, as God Almighty, but *by* My name, LORD [YHWH], I did not make Myself known to them. (Exodus 6:2)

The last quotation from Exodus six could be, and preferably should be translated as a question: "But by My name, Lord [YHWH] did I not make Myself known to them [to the patriarchs]?"[434] God's question implies they knew Him by that name, and that Moses should realize that.

These verses imply the sons of Israel knew the name YHWH and knew it had been revealed by God to Abraham, Isaac, and Jacob. The last statement, asked of Moses, implies that he also knew the name of the God of Abraham, Isaac, and Jacob—and that he realized the patriarchs knew it. Thus when he went to the sons of Israel saying that "God has sent me to you to deliver you because He has heard your cry," they were already familiar with the God of Abraham, Isaac, and Jacob, and they already knew that his name was YHWH, and they knew that the patriarchs knew His name. All of that was common knowledge to the Hebrews. They knew the stories of Genesis. This implies that there was either a written or an oral tradition that the sons of Israel had received and kept about their forefathers.

The issue of where Moses obtained the information that he records in Genesis has been a question in the Church from the beginning. The Fathers and Doctors assumed that he was shown those facts supernaturally by God. But they had no tools with which to study or investigate this issue. We do today. And the idea that perhaps Moses had sources from which he might have drawn has been broached in the Church more recently. It was first presented before the Pontifical Biblical Commission in 1906.

> **Q3:** Can it be granted, without prejudice to the Mosaic authenticity . . . that [he] . . . made use of sources . . . written documents or oral traditions, from which, . . . under . . . divine inspiration, he [drew when he wrote the Book of Genesis?]
> **Response:** Yes.[435]

If the sources of information about the patriarchs, which Moses and the sons of Israel had recourse to, were in written form—if they were very ancient indeed, from before the Sojourn in Egypt—then those documents had to have been written in cuneiform. That was the only form of writing that existed in ancient Babylonia from which they had come. From the point of view of literary complexity, this is reasonable because, unlike the last four books of the Pentateuch, the stories of Genesis have a simpler literary structure that could easily have been written in cuneiform, like **The Gilgamesh Epic**, a classic of Babylonian cuneiform.

As to when Genesis was written: It appears that the beginning of Exodus was written as a follow-up to the last part of the book of Genesis. The book of Exodus begins as follows:

> Now these are the names of the sons of Israel who came to Egypt with Jacob; they came each one with his household: Reuben, Simeon, Levi and Judah; Issachar, Zebulun and Benjamin; Dan and Naphtali, Gad and Asher. All the persons who came from the loins of Jacob were seventy in number, but Joseph was *already* in Egypt. Joseph died, and all his brothers and all that generation. But the sons of Israel were fruitful and increased greatly, and multiplied, and became exceedingly mighty, so that the land was filled with them.
>
> Now a new king arose over Egypt, who did not know Joseph. (Exodus 1:1–8)

These verses set the stage for explaining how the sons of Israel who had entered Egypt centuries before finally came to be oppressed by the Egyptians. It connects to Genesis, and it prepares for the explanation of the oppression, which led to deliverance by the Lord God at the Exodus, which led to the desert wanderings, which led to the Conquest of the land of Canaan. It is a transition from very ancient times to the time of the Exodus.

My guess: Moses knew the events related in Genesis, had organized and edited them, and had already written Genesis before he wrote the rest of the Pentateuch.

Conclusion: How I Will Move Forward in this Work:

I will make use of the foundation that we have uncovered in this chapter: I assume that the Exodus happened in 1446 BC, in accordance with the clear chronology of Scripture. I assume that Moses wrote the Pentateuch; in fact, he wrote it in the proto-Sinaitic script.

(Because he was intimately involved in the last four books of the Pentateuch, I assume that they are historically accurate, as Christians have always believed.) I will assume that the length of the Sojourn in Egypt was 215 years. I must take a position on this in order to establish a chronology for the earliest times: the Creation, the Deluge, Babel, and the lives of the patriarchs before and leading up to the Sojourn in Egypt. This is a general overall chronology, which can be off by a few years here and there, but which gives us a broad chronological framework for the most ancient times of which Genesis speaks.

One other chronological issue that affects the events in Genesis: We have already noted that the Septuagint has a different chronology for the periods from creation to the flood and from the flood to Abraham. The Septuagint inserts an extra 100 years between many of the generations of the early patriarchs. If we accept that chronology then it pushes back the flood by hundreds of years and it pushes back the time of the creation by over 1500 years. These differences are not scribal errors, and I have never heard a good explanation of why or how the textual variations happened. I have considered this, and I have no indication about how to resolve this matter. Therefore I have decided to continue using the text that we have received from the Masoretic source and from the Vulgate, the text with which we are most familiar in the Latin branch of Christianity. This has been used by and approved by the Latin branch of Christianity for many centuries.

Based on the understanding that Moses could have written Genesis by using certain written sources at his disposal, and based on the archeological evidence already presented in this chapter—and that which will be presented in the next chapter—the following is the position I am taking in this book regarding the narratives that Moses presents to us in Genesis:

We realize that oral traditions have been generally considered to be of less reliability than written records. In this work we hold, and will demonstrate, that there were not oral but written records from which Moses drew when he wrote the Book of Genesis. Those records were first written in the Middle East and were written in cuneiform. Moses used the proto-Sinaitic script that was widely known by many of his Israelite countrymen, the script first invented by Joseph, which he had taught to them two or more centuries earlier, to write the first five books of the Pentateuch. He wrote the last four books from his own personal experience, for he was intimately involved in the events that they portray. He wrote Genesis by using, referring to, and editing a set of written documents that he had in his possession. I call these documents:

The Genesis Documents

These were known to Moses and the Hebrews. They were written in cuneiform. The purpose of the next chapter is to show you, the reader, what they were and who first wrote them. When we discover what those documents were and who wrote them, it will give us with every possible literary/textual reason to believe Genesis is true.

Believing that Genesis is true—believing that the Ancient Faith is actually true—is a thought that will shake the very foundations of academia today, because it contradicts the Cartesian-Darwinian Narrative, which is the basis of the current worldview in almost all fields of study.

George Orwell is credited with a saying that is directly applicable to the situation that we will face in the Church when we recapture the truth of Genesis—a revolutionary idea.

In times of universal deceit speaking the truth becomes a revolutionary act.

I am not looking to begin a revolution. I seek a **resolution** to the dilemma that has plagued the Church for centuries. And I seek a **restoration** of the Ancient Faith that came down to us from Jesus and the Apostles, a faith that has been cast aside in deference to specious human wisdom. And I seek a **renewal** of the Church which is certain to follow in the wake of such a wise and blessed return to complete confidence in our God and His holy Word.

The Genesis Documents

Introduction to an Archeological Find:
It is a lamentable corollary of the proliferation of knowledge that in any area of learning, as time progresses and as the understanding in that area expands, the scholarship for that subject becomes more ingrown and focused on its own problems—to the ignoring of its implications for other areas of learning. But cross-pollination between disciplines, whenever it can be productively conducted, is a tremendous benefit to both of the areas involved in that sharing. We know that the area of archeology has greatly enhanced the study of the sacred Scriptures in the past. In this work I want to introduce to the study of Scripture another important archeological discovery. This truth does not depend on one dig or one special find, but flows from a broad understanding of how ancient Babylonian scribes wrote their documents; that is, the formal structure of their cuneiform tablets.

This information has come to light from the discovery and study of tens of thousands of ancient records scattered over many centuries and many ancient archeological digs. Up to this time biblical scholarship has missed or ignored the implications of this somewhat technical piece of information, even though it is well known among the archeologists who deal with it regularly, and even though it is quite straightforward and easy to grasp —even for those who are not immersed in such studies. Once we understand certain simple facts about how the scribes of ancient Mesopotamia wrote their documents, we will find a direct application of that information to Genesis, because the structure of the Book of Genesis clearly displays the same ancient writing techniques and styles.

Before delving into ancient writing I want to explain how we happened to stumble across this truth. To explain this I want to begin by identifying two men, a father and his son, who were instrumental in bringing to light the connection between ancient writing styles and the book of Genesis, for this will introduce us to understanding a mystery that has been with the Church for several centuries: the mystery of the composition of the book of Genesis.

The father first noticed the structure of ancient Middle Eastern writing when he was an officer in the British Air Force and was in the Middle East on assignment. His name was P. J. Wiseman (1888–1948), and it was his special privilege to be personally present when many of the archeological sites were being excavated. He was an enthusiastic amateur archeologist fascinated by the findings at the sites and was able to discuss those findings with professional archeologists at the dig sites. He noticed certain striking literary patterns in the writing on the tablets, and saw in them a connection to the book of Genesis. Though he was an amateur archeologist, he published a book on this subject in 1936 entitled *New Discoveries in Babylonia about Genesis*. In the midst of the war it lapsed into obscurity.

His son Donald John Wiseman (October 25, 1918, to February 10, 2010) inherited his father's passion for the archeology of the Middle East and pursued it vigorously. He studied at Dulwich College and King's College London, where he won the McCaul Hebrew prize. He read Oriental Languages at Wadham College, Oxford, studying Hebrew under Godfrey Driver and Akkadian under Oliver Gurney. He was professor of Assyriology at the University of London from 1961 through 1982. Upon his retirement, he was made an honorary member of the School of Oriental and African Studies and elected a fellow of King's College London. He served as chairman of Tyndale House from 1957 to 1986 and as president of the Society for Old Testament Studies. He had a variety of roles with the Universities and Colleges Christian Fellowship, including two terms as president, in 1965–1966 and 1973–1974. He was chairman of the Scripture Gift Mission from 1978 to 1992, and served for a time on the New International Version Committee on Bible Translation. Donald Wiseman was a devout Christian and his work was motivated by his Christian conviction that the Bible was accurate, reliable, and deeply relevant to life today. Wiseman worked for four years at the British Museum deciphering cuneiform tablets excavated by Leonard Woolley at Alalakh in Syria. He also made several trips to Nimrud in modern-day Iraq, compiling a catalogue of the cuneiform tablets unearthed there. He served at different times as director, chairman, and president of the British School of Archaeology in Iraq, and as editor of the school's journal, *Iraq*. He was also a trustee of the British School of Archaeology in Jerusalem, and a founding member of the British Institute in Amman for Archaeology and History.

He attained many other academic honors and distinctions, and eventually published an edited and updated form of his father's book entitled **Ancient Records and the Structure of Genesis**. I base my approach in this book on the archeological material in that work of Donald Wiseman, which has been largely unknown or ignored by biblical scholars.

The Earliest Development of Writing:
How/when/why did writing develop? Philosophers have been seeking a satisfactory answer to that question for centuries, but without success. The ideas and theories put forth have changed as the world view of scholars has changed.

> Not so long ago, it used to be thought that mankind was indebted to Adam himself for the discovery of writing. According to Blaise de Vigenere [*Traite des chiffres et secretes manieres d'ecrire*, Paris, 1586] or Clement Duret [*Tresor de l'histoire des langues*, Koln, 1613] who wrote at the end of the sixteenth and the beginning of the seventeenth century, a natural script existed from the beginning of the world, one Adam had deciphered by means of the animals that Yahweh presented to him, by giving each its name. Half a century later, John Wilkins saw a very differrent reason for the appearance of writing. [*Essay towards Real Character and a Philosophical Language*, London, 1668] According to him, only at a mature age, after he had been taught by experience that writing was a necessity, did Adam come to invent the Hebrew alphabet. Finally, at the end of the eighteenth century, Edmund Fry arrogated as his own the old and very popular thesis that it was the angel Raphael who revealed to Adam, not one, but two scripts of the Chaldean alphabets [*Pantagraphia*, London, 1799].

> These fantastic ideas are no longer current today, and we realize that the oldest known script was a gift neither from god nor nature, but was a human invention. We attribute the invention to the Sumerians and place it chronologically in the course of the second half of the fourth millennium B.C., between 3400 and 3300. Geographically, we situate the discovery in southern Mesopotamia, a region that today is in the south of Iraq.[436]

From this and similar statements we can see that early ideas about writing have fallen by the way to be replaced with ideas that fit the spirit of our present age—ideas which themselves will be discarded with disdain when present ways of thinking pass out of vogue. Of course theories about the origin of writing are bound up with theories about the origin of human speech and theories about the origin of mankind itself. Here are a few such thoughts:

> It is now generally accepted that our remote ancestors were akin to the ape family, although it is not true to say that they were apes. But at some time roughly computed as a million years ago, they came down from the trees and learned to walk upright. In evolution there is something called *specialization,* which means that the body concentrates on developing one particular part. Our ancestors "specialized" in the enlargement of the brain. . .

The process by which Man learned to express himself in speech must have been a long one, and we can only guess how it happened... If one takes the religious viewpoint it was indeed God-given, in that all things come from God; but the process by which it was acquired, over scores of thousands of years, was a slow one. The art of writing came only at the end of the long period during which speech was developed...

One fact is certain, that the art of passing on information and ideas by word of mouth developed with the increasing capacity of Man's brain... However, countless thousands of years ago, when our primitive ancestors began to speak, they probably began by imitating the sounds of other animals...

For the origins of speech one must depend on theories rather than known facts. In comparatively recent times objects have been given the names of the men who made or used them, and perhaps this happened in ancient times... However, it is most probable that the earliest words were related to animal sounds and gestures. It is also very likely that speech did not begin to develop quickly until men began to live in permanent settlements, where they saw more of each other than when they were wandering hunters, and where they needed to communicate ideas to each other somehow.

This would explain why the art of writing, which is only a way of making speech permanent and capable of being transmitted far beyond the range of the human voice, appears to have begun in Egypt and Mesopotamia... The apparent reason for this is that in these favored regions men first learned to live together in permanent settlements.[437]

Based on such theories/ideas, let us briefly outline a modern theory of how writing developed. The process is imagined as having progressed through three stages, starting with pictures, and ending with a "true writing system."[438]

1. The first stage, pictographic writing, employed "pictograms" (pictures, pictographs) or signs that limited themselves to reproducing concrete and real objects, sketched with greater or lesser regard for the details of what the object actually looked like. A written system of this type was independent of any spoken language, potentially employed a huge number of symbols, and was a kind of "mnemonic device" rather than a true writing system.

A pictogram is a written character that symbolizes an object without indicating how to pronounce it. Instead it conveys the meaning or idea of its intended object because it resembles the object. Pictographic writing is a form of writing using pictograms to convey meaning. Thus it is definitely not an alphabetic form of writing. Another type of writing—cuneiform—eventually superseded it.

"A conservative estimate is that the pictographic forms of writing which have been found may be dated from 3300 to 2800 BC; thereafter cuneiform writing came into use."[439] Other scholars estimate pictographic to have begun before 3400 BC. "There are some that even continue to think along the lines of Edward Chiera [*They Wrote on Clay*, Chicago, 1938; also, M. W. Green, *Visible Language*, 1981, p. 346.] for whom a pictographic stage not surviving in our sources would have preceded the first written marks from Mesopotamia... [because the highly sophisticated signs that we have found] imply the existence of an earlier writing stage that was more primitive and purely pictographic."[440] Such thinking presumes the earlier writing was on wood or some other perishable medium, and for that reason no trace has been preserved for us.

2. Eventually "pictograms" changed to "logograms," or spoken words and sounds of a language. This was accompanied by the invention of phonetization where the writing of things changed into the writing of words, and the writing system was by its nature tied to one spoken language. Characters still preserved a pictographic significance, referring to a real object, but at the same time also assumed a phonetic value. This transition was facilitated by the schematization and increasingly abstract stylization of the written signs. This led to the birth of cuneiform writing as pictograms became replaced by unrecognizable abstract signs representing ideas—ideograms. Each ideogram represented a certain number of words that were conceptually related.
3. The third and final stage was reached due to the bilingualism that characterized the cultures of ancient Mesopotamia, where writing was first developed. The need arose to put into writing a second language, a Semitic language, Akkadian, using the very same signs that the Sumerians had used for their speech. This led to the coupling of script to speech, and "true writing" was born.

So one modern theory goes. This relegates pictographic "writing" to a kind of "pre-writing" status and identifies cuneiform as the earliest true writing. Those who consider pictographic writing to be "true writing" hold to a somewhat different theory or explanation. Indeed, the basic presuppositions of such thinking are exposed and forcefully rejected by some, who observe that such theories are fatally slanted, conditioned by our cultural and philosophical bias.

> [such ideas; that is, judging some forms of writing as more "primitive" than our own] are part of a teleological vision that . . . places our alphabet, regarded as the best of all writing systems, as the final point of a process of perfecting and progress. Naturally this view leads to the general application of the aspect that we attribute to our own alphabet, namely the ability to express the sounds of the language, to all known graphic systems. From this perspective we are forced to accept the existence of only one true script, a unique script that would have developed in linear fashion, and which showed awkward and imperfect beginnings before it manifested itself fully in the alphabet. In other words, the history of the scripts that preceded the alphabet is conceived of only in a way that leads to the latter. The description of the initial phases of writing is only done for the purpose of revealing the alphabet's beginnings. Furthermore, if by definition a beginning is identical to a first appearance in historical time, it is also characterized as the elementary or the primitive in a logical order. The pictographic thesis is the perfect example of such a beginning. . . "Blatant ethnocentrism!"
>
> We see [from such an arrogant and self-centered perspective] that primitiveness is not a fact given by history but, the contrary, the result of a reconstruction. Similarly, we see that the history of writing, as it exists now, was fashioned along a unitary scheme, which was developed *a posteriori*. There is nothing in the present state of knowledge that allows us to state that the oldest scripts are also the most primitive ones, that they are nothing but simplistic outlines and inept attempts. The "theory of stages" of the development of writing must be abandoned.[441]

So we must recognize the limitations of our present theories as well as their myopic nature because our present world view has infected our thinking. But the lack of agreement about how/when/why writing first developed does not invalidate the many discoveries that have been made, and which give us a fragmented but informative picture of what ancient writing methods were, as well as a glimpse at the cultures that produced such writing.

I will hold that writing was given to us by the Lord God—that it did not develop because of human cleverness or from some kind of cultural necessity. It was, from the beginning, part of God's divine plan for humanity—fulfilling a vital function vis-à-vis His self-revelation to us. It was required so that we could understand His plan and purposes for us. That is why naturalistic theories that attempt to explain its origin and purpose fail and/or fall short.

A Few Basic Facts about Ancient Middle Eastern Writing:

The discovery and deciphering of many thousands of tablets with cuneiform writing from the various ancient cities of Egypt and the Middle East (Nippur, Ur, Ebla, etc.) resulting from the archeological digs in the nineteenth and twentieth centuries have painted a vivid picture of the ancient civilization shared by people of the Babylonian, Mesopotamian, and adjacent Middle Eastern areas. That civilization can be traced via its artifacts and written records back to well before 3000 BC, indicating that this area of the world was the cradle of the most ancient civilizations of mankind. Those civilizations seem to have sprung up full blown with art, religion, architecture, commerce, schooling and education, government and law—without signs of a more primitive culture preceding them; that is, both the cultures and their associated writing systems do not seem to have any predecessors. This sudden appearance undercuts most naturalistic theories of origins of the cultures and their writing.

Our understanding of these ancient peoples is based, more than anything else, upon the deciphering of the clay and stone tablets that have been discovered. It is important for our purposes that we delve into certain technical details about the materials used when producing those written records—the style of the writing involved and the methods used by the ancients to collect and access them—which, we will hold, were widely used in their daily lives.

Ancient Records and the Structure of Genesis, Central pictorial insert

Most of the inscriptions recovered in ancient Mesopotamia show the style of writing known as cuneiform or wedge-shaped writing. The Scribes used a reed stylus to form the various wedge shapes. They wrote on clay tablets which were made from the silt and mud of that area. Clay tablets could be dried and preserved for centuries, and they could also be re-wetted to make additions if necessary.

Writing became very prevalent within the ancient civilizations of the Middle East and was commonly used in normal daily communications. Investigators have found letters concerning daily family matters written by a wife to her husband while he was traveling on business, and from a son to his father while he was away. As the discoveries indicate:

> Excavations on almost any town or city site in southern Iraq will turn up at least a few tablets, and if one digs in a town of the Old Babylonian period it seems that one can find a few tablets in almost every house. Small private libraries existed at all periods. . . the agents of Ashurbanipal reported to him on the contents of several private libraries which they were sending to him from Babylonia.[442]

Ironically, this same author asserts that literacy was not very widespread in Mesopotamia because scribal arts and crafts required extensive training![443]

However on the tablets we see preserved legal and governmental records, religious writings, and many other kinds of writings. large libraries of clay or stone tablets have been unearthed, and schools for teaching reading, writing, and mathematics have also been discovered with the lessons for the pupils still intact. Quite a few writings date to centuries before Abraham was born. This is the literary milieu in which Genesis was originally written. It seems to have declined and died out with the imposition of the Greek culture.

> From the time of Alexander the Great onwards [343 BC] the use of cuneiform script is increasingly restricted, being superseded by Aramaic; a few legal and literary texts were still written in cuneiform as late as 40 BC, and the last astronomical text is datable to 75 AD.[444]

One Key Discovery—Archeological Evidence for the Sacrifice of Noah:

Proto-Sumerian inscriptions were found on a stone in the Ahora Gorge on Mt. Ararat by Edward E. Crawford in 1983. The fact that the inscriptions are less stylized than the proto-Sumerian pictographs found to the south and in Mesopotamia, plus the irregular size and manner in which the pictographs are arranged in relation to each other, indicate that the Ahora inscriptions are older. Crawford was able to translate the pictographs on the stone, and his translation has been checked by other scholars. It reads as follows:

> Reading counterclockwise and primarily from right to left, following the direction of the foot:
> God's sacrificial offering of the ox (and possibly of sheep and other animals) [is or gives rise to] the covenant of the bright bow [or the rainbow]: let man and woman go forth and procreate. (Or: go forth and procreate.)[445]

The inscription on this stone is similar to the text of Genesis describing the covenant that the Lord God made with Noah after the flood. It appears that this stone was inscribed by Noah when he offered sacrifices to God after the Flood, but before he left Ararat. The Bible explains that the Lord accepted Noah's sacrifices (8:20–22), established the covenant of the rainbow with him and his sons (9:9–17), and gave them the command to go forth and multiply (9:1, 9:7). Therefore this discovery is an important verification of the Deluge account in Genesis.

Below is a schematic picture of the stone that Crawford discovered on Mount Ararat, which he called the "Ahora Covenant Inscription." Because this was published in "Research and Exploration," a peer-reviewed journal of "National Geographic," the translation was verified by multiple scholars and is very likely to be accurate.[446]

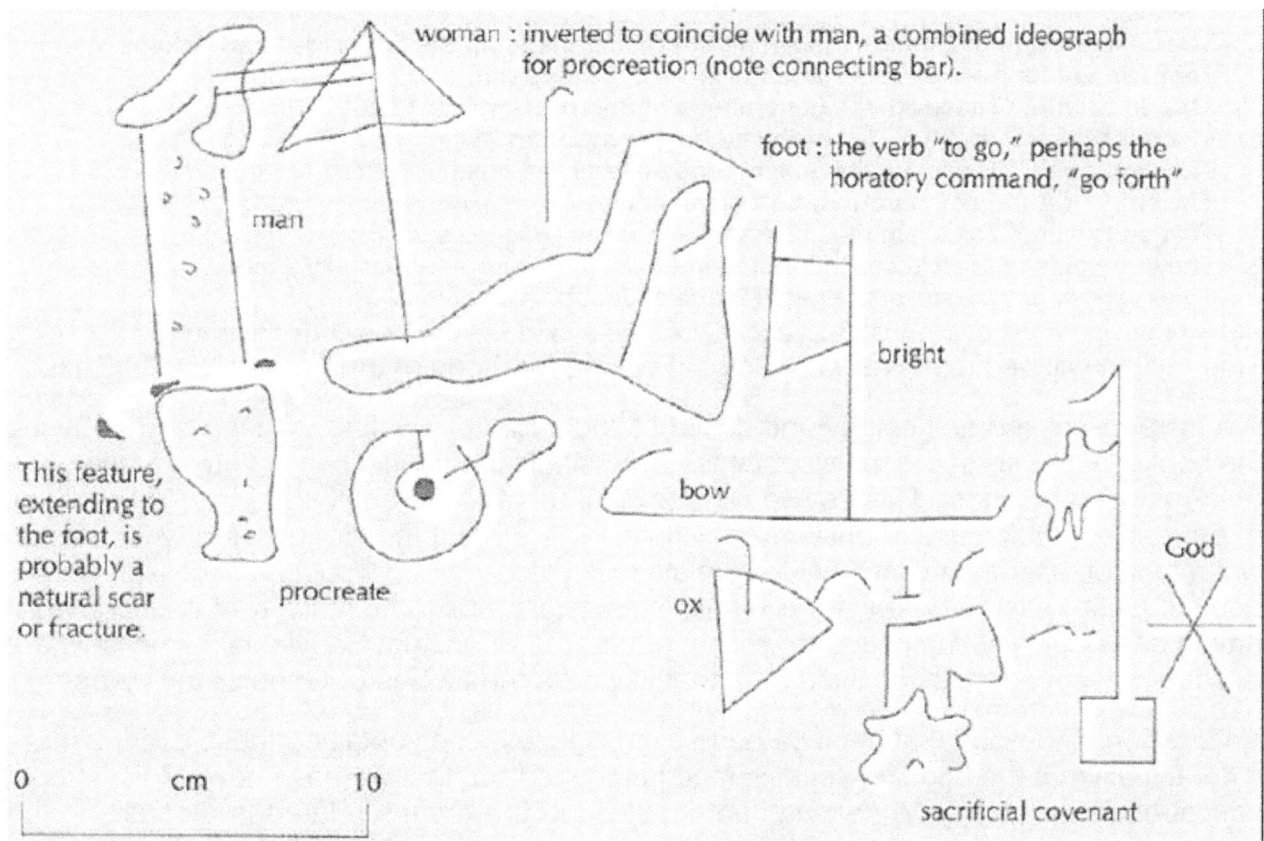

Noah must have inscribed this stone soon after he disembarked from the arc using the writing techniques from before the Deluge. This is our only remnant of pre-Deluge writing.

Crawford's discovery implies that there was writing before the Deluge, and that it was pictographic in nature. This will be important as we discuss Genesis in this work.

Ancient Middle Eastern Writing and Genesis:

<u>Preliminary Observations about the Structure of Genesis:</u>

From a cursory reading of Genesis we see that the overall structure is delineated by the recurrence of the phrase "these are the generations of." The word for "generations" in Greek is "*genesis*", the word from which the book derives its name. Thus these usages are not completely arbitrary, but in some way reflect the basic purpose and nature of the book of Genesis. So I present this preliminary outline of the book of Genesis using some of the occurrences of this phrase to demarcate the sections in my outline.

1. **The story of the creation of the whole world.**
   This ends with: "These are the generations of the heavens and the earth" (Genesis 2:4).
2. **The story of Adam and Eve; their creation, temptation, fall, the judgments of God, their children Cain and Able, Cain's family to the seventh generation, and the birth of the next two generations in the Godly line, Seth and Enosh.**
   This ends with: "This is the book of the generations of Adam" (Genesis 5:1).
3. **The genealogy from Adam to Noah, plus a short description of the tragic situation in human society at the time of Noah, just before the great Deluge.**
   This ends with: "These are the records of the generations of Noah" (Genesis 6:9).
4. **The building of the ark, the gathering of the animals, the Deluge, God's covenant with Noah after the Flood, the story of Canaan, and the blessing of Japheth and Shem by Noah.**
   This ends with: "These are the generations of the sons of Noah, Shem, Ham, and Japheth" (Genesis 10:1).
5. **The descendants of Japheth, Ham, and Shem that made up the languages and nations after the confusion of tongues at Babel, and the story of Babel itself.**
   This ends with: "These are the generations of Shem" (Genesis 11:10).
6. **The genealogy from Shem to Terah and his sons Abram, Nahor, and Haran.**
   This ends with: "These are the generations of Terah" (Genesis 11:27).
7. **The story of Abraham, Sarah, Isaac, and Ishmael.**
   This ends with: "These are the generations of Isaac" (Genesis 25:19).
8. **The story of Isaac, Rebecca, and their sons Esau and Jacob—especially Jacob.**
   This ends with: "These are the generations of Jacob" (Genesis 37:2).
9. **Stories about the descendants of Jacob, extending into Egypt. This ends the book.**

This outline will be helpful as we study the writing methods of the ancient Middle East.

We have discussed archeology and ancient Middle Eastern writing, and we have outlined the book of Genesis showing its contents. But what is the connection between the two? A quick glance at Genesis tells us (we will see) that most of the book, the first eight sections of our outline, took place in ancient Babylonia. Therefore if the stories were written down when or soon after the events that they relate took place—which would be necessary for the book of Genesis to be historically accurate in its details—then the majority of the book must have been originally committed to writing in the area of ancient Babylonia. That is where Abraham, Isaac, and Jacob lived, and that is where the stories of Genesis took place.

An additional question that must be addressed is how Moses obtained those documents—if he actually put the book of Genesis together in the form that we have now. This is most critical because clearly Moses was not involved in the events related in Genesis in the same way that he was in the events of the other four books of the Pentateuch. He could only have written Genesis (edited it, to be more precise) by using such documents. This leads us to the basic thesis of this work, which we will state and show to be true.

Fundamental Thesis on the Authorship of Genesis:

Our Thesis: There is a direct connection between the ancient Middle Eastern writings we have been looking at and the book of Genesis. There are techniques and literary devices in Genesis that parallel the literary styles of ancient Babylonia. They point unerringly to how and where the book of Genesis was first composed, and they show us how Moses came into possession of the original writings, from which he wrote Genesis. Dr. Wiseman, who first observed the striking similarity between Genesis and the Babylonian writings, explains his basic insight and its connection to the Mosaic authorship of Genesis.

> The proposed solution to the problem of the composition of Genesis . . . is the result of applying the findings which archaeological research has presented to us in recent years. During this period the writer has spent several years in "the land that was Babylonia" (modern south Iraq), visiting the various excavations at the ancient sites, and in constant touch with the latest discoveries. In this environment of ancient things Genesis was carefully reexamined, not for the purpose of discovering a new solution to its composition, but solely to illustrate the geography and archaeology of the country in relation to it.
>
> While engaged in these studies the key to its literary composition became increasingly clear, for Genesis was permitted the rare privilege of being allowed to speak for itself in the light of all the knowledge we now possess of the methods of writing practiced in patriarchal times. It would seem that the key to its composition has previously remained unrecognized, and therefore unused. While prevailing theories have been unable to unlock the door to its literary structure, it is submitted that the following explanation does:
>
> ***The book of Genesis was originally written on tablets in the ancient script of the time by the patriarchs who were intimately concerned with the events related, and whose names are clearly stated. Moreover, Moses, the compiler and editor of the book, as we now have it, plainly directs attention to the source of his information.***[447]

We will explain why Dr. Wiseman asserts this. We will look in detail at the techniques of ancient Middle Eastern scribes and compare what we find with the book of Genesis.

Detailed Description of Babylonian Writing Techniques and their Connection to Genesis:

To understand how the ancients wrote and why they invented their unique methods, we must consider the practical issues to be faced by a civilization that keeps its records on clay or stone tablets. They faced problems both similar to and divergent from what we have to deal with today, simply because they wrote on that medium.

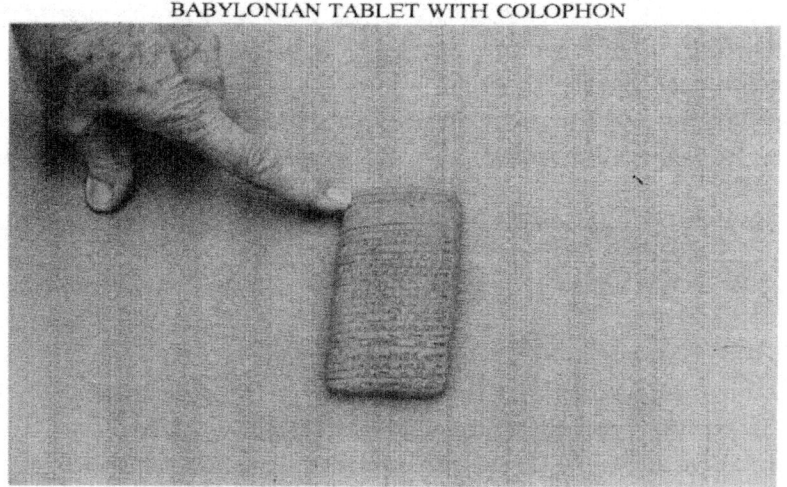

BABYLONIAN TABLET WITH COLOPHON

At the place where the finger is pointing is a colophon making it clear that this is a continuation of a series of tablets. Similar evidence of a colophon is found in the Genesis records.

How and where did they [the ancients] sign and date their letters and other tablets? Seeing that clay tablets cannot be stitched, as can pieces of parchment or the pages of a book, what means were used to connect tablets together and preserve their proper sequence when more than one tablet was necessary to contain a piece of writing? These problems are rarely referred to in popular books on excavation and the student must turn to technical works, the contents of which are largely printed in cuneiform, in order to obtain an adequate answer to them.[448]

The indexing data such as the title of the document, who owned (i.e., who wrote) the document, the date and time of its writing, its sequence within the series of tablets that made up the total document (if it required more than one tablet to hold it) were saved in an area called the "**colophon**." Above is what the tablets actually looked like.[449] The text above the clear band near the top is the colophon, the area of the tablet that contains the identifying data and the indexing data for the tablet.

Therefore the common practice of the ancient scribes was this: When a scribe wrote on a tablet he usually impressed the owner's seal on the clay in the colophon of the document. This seal could be from a cylinder or a precious stone and often included the owner's name in cuneiform. Sometimes the name of the owner was written on the tablet by the scribe separately. When a document or a connected series of documents was too large for one tablet, then the series of tablets that contained the document had to be identified, linked together, and kept in proper sequence. This was achieved by the use of "titles," "catch-lines," and "numbers." The title was taken from the first words of the first tablet and then repeated on each subsequent tablet, followed by the number for that tablet. As an additional safety measure it was also common to use "catch-lines" where the first few words of the next tablet were written at the end of the previous tablet.

Thus these literary aids and clues were part of the group of identifying lines at the end of each tablet, a section of the tablet called the colophon. This section identified the original owner of the tablet, the scribe who wrote it for him, the group or series of tablets to which it belonged, the title of the series, and sometimes the original library from which it was taken, when/if the scribal transcription was not the original composition of the document. The connection to the book of Genesis rests on the following observed fact:

> We find that some of these ancient literary usages are still embedded in the present English text [of Genesis]. Just as the scribes of Nineveh 2,500 years ago, when copying tablets which had been written a thousand years earlier, ended the tablet with a short statement indicating from which library the original text had come, we suggest that the compiler of Genesis has done precisely the same thing.[450]

More on Colophons:
Before we look at Genesis let us explain the colophon and its usages in more detail. The colophon was the key area of a tablet that identified its source and characteristics. Established techniques for maintaining libraries of documents that had been written on tablets were widely used throughout the Middle East for many centuries. The colophon was the area of the tablet that was employed for organizing documents in these libraries.

> The ancient Mesopotamian scribe, when copying literary, scientific, or historical texts frequently appended a colophon to his copy. This practice occurred in all periods, but was much more common in the Neo-Assyrian [approximately 934 BC through 610 BC] and Neo-Babylonian [626 BC through 539 BC] periods. In the early periods, the colophon tended to be very simple and contained only a date, the number of lines in the composition, or the scribe's name. In the later periods the colophon tended to be longer, and usually contained a great deal more information.[451]

The scribes were careful when transcribing the contents of tablets, with checks contained within the process of copying. This was expressed by a phrase in the colophon which, when translated meant "according to its original, written, checked, and copied."[452] This assured the accuracy of the copied contents of the tablet. But the colophons themselves were not part of the contents of the document, strictly speaking, and when creating them the scribes gave free play to their imagination and creativity.[453] Still the demands of the task, which was the management of large libraries of documents, often required a variety of information in the colophon in order that other scribes might be able to search for and find the document and then identify its attributes, just as we do in our libraries today. Here is a description of the information stores—the large libraries—which existed:

> In the first millennium BCE Mesopotamian scribes used to add highly developed colophons to their works, especially when writing scholarly texts, for example, on medicine, divination or astral sciences. This kind of postscript, often located at the end of the text, provides modern historians with a plethora of information relative to the scribe who wrote the text, the place where he composed it, the content of the composition, the original document copied (if any), and the owner of the tablet. Other writing practices are particularly remarkable, such as noting long compositions on series of dozens of numbered tablets, in the same way as we number the pages of a book. These practices reflect a very specific context of that time: that of the creation, enrichment, management and maintenance of large libraries.[454]

The colophon itself was highly developed and could contain a variety of indexing data.
> Maximally, a colophon might contain all of the following information:
> 1. The catch-line
> 2. The name of the series and number of the tablet
> 3. The number of lines on the tablet
> 4. The source of the copy
> 5. The name of the owner of the tablet
> 6. The name of the scribe making the copy
> 7. The reason for making the copy
> 8. The curse or blessing
> 9. The date
> 10. Disposition of the copy
>
> Minimally, the colophon might contain only one of the above categories.[455]

Of these fields, the ones that appear in Genesis are the name of the owner of the tablet, the catch-line, the date, and the title. By the "owner" of a document we mean the person who was responsible for originally writing it, the one who was the source or authority for the information that the document contains. The "date" is the date when he (the original owner) wrote the document. A catch-line is an identifying phrase that is repeated in two consecutive tablets in order to connect them; that is, to identify that they follow one after the other in the sequence of tablets, because the information that is being conveyed is too lengthy or extensive to fit on one tablet. Titles are from the first line of a document.

Ownership Lines in Genesis:
With this information about colophons before us we have the tools necessary to determine the fundamental source documents of Genesis, for the traces of the colophons from those ancient writings are still evident in the text of the book. The basic structure of Genesis is delineated by the repetitive phrase "these are the generations of." This phrase occurs eleven times in the book. The word translated as "generations" is the Hebrew word *"toledot."* The meaning of this word and its common usages are vital at this point, so we must look at that Hebrew word before we go further. Here are the eleven usages of the phrase "these are the generations [*toledot*] of" in Genesis:

    2:4   These are the ***generations*** of the heavens and the earth
    5:1   This is the book of the ***generations*** of Adam
    6:9   These are the ***generations*** of Noah
    10:1   These are the ***generations*** of the sons of Noah

11:10 These are the ***generations*** of Shem
11:27 These are the ***generations*** of Terah
25:12 These are the ***generations*** of Ishmael
25:19 These are the ***generations*** of Isaac
36:1 These are the ***generations*** of Esau
36:9 These are the ***generations*** of Esau
37:2 These are the ***generations*** of Jacob

The Meaning of *Toledot* and its Connection to Babylonian Literary Techniques:
Throughout the Bible the most common usage for the word "*toledot*" is to introduce a genealogical list, a count, or other information about a person's descendants. It is used this way in many places in the Bible. Here are some examples:

Exodus 6:16   These are the names of the sons of Levi according to their ***generations***: Gershon and Kohath and Merari; and the length of Levi's life was one hundred and thirty-seven years.

What follows this in the biblical text of Exodus is a list of the descendants of Levi.

Numbers 1:20-21   Now the sons of Reuben, Israel's firstborn, their ***genealogical registration*** by their families, by their fathers' households, according to the number of names, head by head, every male from twenty years old and upward, whoever *was able to* go out to war, their numbered men of the tribe of Reuben *were* 46,500.

Here "genealogical registration" is the Hebrew word "*toledot*." And what follows is a numerical count of Reuben's descendants.

1 Chronicles 1:29-31   These are their ***genealogies***: the firstborn of Ishmael *was* Nebaioth, then Kedar, Adbeel, Mibsam, Mishma, Dumah, Massa, Hadad, Tema, Jetur, Naphish and Kedemah; these *were* the sons of Ishmael.

And what follows here and in many places in Chronicles is a list of descendants for the person, going down through the generations.

These examples are also similar to three of the instances where the key phrase "these are the generations of." (where *toledot* is translated as *generations*) is used in the book of Genesis. In these passages the phrase is followed by a list of descendants:

25:12 These are the generations of Ishmael
36:1 These are the generations of Esau
36:9 These are the generations of Esau

The other eight usages of the word "*toledot*" in the phrase "these are the generations of" in Genesis do not conform to this pattern. There is no mention of the descendants of the person named, or else the genealogy is mixed with other narrative stories. In these passages the word has a slightly different meaning and usage. In these instances we should understand the word "*toledot*" as meaning "personal history" or "family history," and we should see the phrase "these are the generations of" as being an ownership line that names the person who wrote the tablet. Let us look at this other meaning.

The Hebrew scholar Friedrich Wilhelm Gesenius (1796-1843) defines "*toledot*" as follows:
Genealogy, pedigree. As a very large portion of the most ancient Oriental history consists of genealogies, it means—**history, properly of families**. Gen 6:9, "this is the history of Noah." And thus it is also applied to the origin of other things. Gen. 2:4, "this is the origin of the heavens and the earth."

The *Enhanced Strong's Lexicon*[456] says it means "**descendants, results, proceedings, generations, genealogies,**" or (metaphorically) "the begetting or account of heaven." The *Theological Wordbook of the Old Testament*[457] says it means "**descendants, results, or proceedings.**" *Brown Driver's Brigg's Lexicon*[458] describes it as indicating an account of **men and their descendants, their successive generations, their families, etc**. Finally, the *Hebrew Wordbook of the Old Testament*[459] says it means "**descendants, proceedings, or results.**" This can be seen repeated in all modern lexicons and biblical wordbooks. Thus *toledot* refers to not only a genealogical listing but to the results or proceedings of men and their families. It is used even today as the equivalent of our word "history."

> To this day the Rabbis who are immersed in biblical Hebrew use the word "*toledot*" as the equivalent of the ordinary word "history." The Hebrew collections of Jewish traditions about the life of Jesus is called *toledot Jesu* and this the Jews always translate *History of Jesus*.[460]

So the *toledot* of a person can be understood as the history of or about the person who is named, or the history written by him from his experience, especially the history of his origins and of the proceedings of his family. The English equivalent of the phrase as used in these passages would be: "These are the historical origins of . . ." or "These are the family history of . . ." This appears to be the proper understanding of the word in the remaining eight passages. When used in this way the word comes at the end of the person's history, not at the beginning as in the genealogical lists. When we see the word used in this way we must look at the text that precedes it to understand the passage to which it refers. Here is the only biblical example of this usage outside of Genesis:

> Numbers 3:1 Now these are *the records of* the **generations** of Aaron and Moses at the time when the LORD spoke with Moses on Mount Sinai.
> No genealogical lists follow for Moses and Aaron. This is because in this case the reference points backward to the narrative that preceded it, which was written by Moses and Aaron, and which gives instructions for how the tribes of Israel should set up their camp. (see Numbers 2)

The remaining eight occurrences of "*toledot*" in Genesis (2:4, 5:1, 6:9, 10:1, 11:10, 11:27, 25:19, 37:2) are examples of this type of pattern and usage, and so the preceding text of Genesis is, in each instance, a personal/family historical account written by the one whose name appears in the "generations" line. Thus the book of Genesis is composed of a series of personal and family histories, each ending with the words "these are the generations of . . ." followed by the name of the person whose account we have just read.

This usage follows the ancient pattern of the ownership line in the colophon of the clay tablets of Mesopotamia. **Thus the authors (owners) of those accounts, after the first one which has no name, are: Adam, Noah, the sons of Noah, Shem, Terah, Isaac, and Jacob.**

Catch-Lines in Genesis:
There is another repeated pattern contained in the documents of Genesis which also indicates their ancient origin as clay tablets. The "catch-lines" that were commonly used to connect tablet to tablet in a series are still in evidence in the text of Genesis. The following phrases appear to be "catch-lines," not only because they are repeated in adjacent sections, as if to connect adjacent sections when they had been written on tablets, but because the phrases are near to the ownership lines—part of the colophon. Here are the phrases that appear to be "catch-lines" in Genesis:

1:1	God created the heavens and the earth
2:4	Lord God made the heavens and the earth
2:4	When they were created
5:2	When they were created
6:10	Shem, Ham, and Japheth
10:1	Shem, Ham, and Japheth
10:32	After the flood
11:10	After the flood
11:26	Abram, Nahor, and Haran
11:27	Abram, Nahor, and Haran
25:12	Abraham's son
25:19	Abraham's son
36:1	Who is Edom
36:8	Who is Edom
36:9	Father of the Edomites (lit., Father Edom)
36:43	Father of the Edomites (lit., Father Edom)

> The very striking repetition of these phrases exactly where the tablets begin and end will best be appreciated by those scholars acquainted with the methods of the scribes in Babylonia, for those were the arrangements then in use to link the tablets together. I submit that the repetition of these words and phrases precisely in those verses attached to the colophon, "These are the origins of" cannot be mere coincidence. They have remained buried in the text of Genesis, their significance apparently unnoticed.[461]

These repeated phrases have long been a source of puzzlement to Bible scholars, and many a theory has been spawned in the attempt to explain them. The secret to the composition of Genesis is inextricably linked to correctly understanding the significance of such repetitious phrases as these. It is a little-known fact that the use of "catch-lines" in this way was widespread in ancient Middle Eastern scribal communities.

> Often the tablet with a colophon is part of a series. That is, it is one tablet from a multi-tablet composition. When this is the case, the colophon usually begins with the first line of the following tablet. This "catch-line" is usually quoted in full, but occasionally, when the line is relatively long, only part of it is quoted.[462]

The first instance of a pair of catch-lines is in the prior tablet and then it is repeated near the beginning of the next tablet in order to connect the tablets. A repeated phrase is less likely to be a catch-line if it appears in the middle or near the end of the next tablet.

All the repetitious phrases identified by Wiseman satisfy the "proximity to the beginning of the account" criterion admirably. That is, the second in each pair of "catch-lines" is always near to the beginning of the account in which it appears. When taken together the phrases in Wiseman's list of catch-lines establish the overall unity of the Genesis account from 1:1 through 37:1. They show that each author had the previous sections before him and that he was consciously appending his narrative to the preceding section.

In formulating past theories it has been proposed that these were remnants of a clumsy attempt to patch together multiple diverse ancient mythical accounts by the redactor who assembled the book of Genesis into its final form. However the explanation offered here assumes no such patchwork attempt but is an insight based directly on the nature of the writings themselves. Our explanation springs from an understanding of the writing styles in ancient Mesopotamia. It also grants to us a significant insight into the nature of a major portion of Genesis; from 1:1 through 37:2. Thus with this understanding of the connecting phrases as identified above we can arrive at the following simple conclusions about the bulk of the Genesis account (1:1 through 37:2):

- Adam had in his possession the first unnamed account when he wrote his story. He consciously linked his history to it as a continuation of it. This is seen from the connecting "catch-lines" in 1:1 and 2:4, "God created the heavens and the earth." and "Lord God made the heavens and the earth."
- Likewise, the "catch-lines" in 2:4 and 5:2 show that Noah was consciously connecting his account to the previous writing, which he must have possessed. This is shown because "when they were created" appears in both verses.
- In this way we can see that each of the persons named as authors were in possession of the previous accounts and made a clear statement in their writing to connect what they were writing to a previous account.
- Therefore Genesis 1:1 through 37:2 was a cumulative work written by the succession of authors named in the signature lines. It was a carefully accumulated history that was passed on throughout the ages. It was consciously appended to by each of the successive authors. This basic insight is important to understanding the historical context within which the book arose, as our commentary will show, and knowing how the book of Genesis was written down is vital to interpreting it correctly.

Titling in Genesis:
Additionally the text of Genesis has remnants of titling in a manner that was common with the scribes of ancient Mesopotamia:

> On cuneiform tablets the "title" was taken from the commencing words of the record. In a similar manner the Hebrews called the first five books of the Bible by titles taken from their opening words. Thus they called
>
> Genesis $b^e resit$, the Hebrew for "in the beginning";
> Exodus was called $w^e'elleh\ s^e mot$ ("Now these are the words");
> Leviticus is called $wayyiqra'$ ("and he called");
> Numbers, $b^e midbar$ ("in the wilderness");
> Deuteronomy, $hadd^e barim$. ("the words");
>
> These are the titles given to the first five books of Moses in the Hebrew Bible.
>
> This practice was carried out in the ancient Near East in the following manner. When two or more tablets form a series, they were identified together because the first few words of the first tablet were repeated in the colophon (or title page) of the subsequent tablets, somewhat similar to the way in which the name of a chapter is repeated at the head of each page of a modern book. Where pages of a book were not bound together as they are now, the advantage of this would be obvious. By the repetition of such words as we have listed, the whole of the Genesis tablets were connected together.[463]

Thus titling, beginning with Genesis and extending throughout the Pentateuch, also shows the use of the techniques of the scribes of ancient Mesopotamia.

Date Lines in Genesis:
Here is an explanation of how dates were embedded into the ancient writings:

> In addition, some of these tablets show evidence of "dating." After a tablet had been written and the name impressed on it, it was customary in Babylonia to insert the date on which it was written. In the earliest times this was done in a very simple fashion, for it was not until later that tablets were dated with the year of the reigning king. It was the custom to do it in the following way: "The year in which the throne of Nabu was made," "Year Sumu-el the king built the wall of Sippar," "Year of the canal Tutu-hengal" (presumably the year the canal was cut), "Year Samsuiluna made a throne of gold," and "Year in which canal Hammurabi was dug."[464]

In Genesis 25:11 it says, "and Isaac dwelt by Beer-lahai-roi." This tells us when Isaac wrote (or completed writing) his tablet. Genesis 36:8 "and Esau dwelt in Mount Seir" tells us the time when the genealogical list was written. Genesis 37:1, "And Jacob dwelt in the land wherein his father was a stranger, in the land of Canaan," is an example of a date line telling us when Jacob completed his account. Genesis 2:3, "He rested from all His work which God had created and made" is another date line.

When we say a line is a "date line" we allow that it can also provide information to us as a normal informational statement. Thus Esau really did dwell in Mount Seir, and it was at that time—while he dwelt in Mount Seir—that he wrote the preceding genealogical record of his family. Likewise "in the day that God created man" in 5:1 is a date line. The phrase "Terah lived seventy years and begat Abram, Nahor, and Haran" in 11:26 is likely giving us the date when Terah wrote his tablet—when he was seventy years old—not when he gave birth to his three sons.[465] These phrases, scattered throughout the accounts, give us hints as to when various sections of the text were written. We will mention these clues as we comment on the text.

The identification of date lines can be subjective. Not every time-phrase is speaking about when the account was written. Not every such phrase is what we have identified as a "date line." The likelihood that any given time-phrase is a date line, rather than just a designation of when some event within the account was taking place, increases with its proximity to the signature line. A time designation that falls within one or two lines of the signature is much more likely to indicate when the account was written; that is, when the signature was appended to the account, which would coincide with the time the account was written—or at least when it was completed—if it was not all written at one time. In general, dates are identified by reading a document and judging reasonably.

Thus the structure of Genesis is similar to that of the ancient Middle Eastern tablets that have been found, where the name of the person who owned the record was written in the colophon of the record, with the use of "catch-lines," "titles," and "dating." Thus Genesis is composed of historical records written by and written about the people who lived in those times. The fact that the ancient tablet structure of Genesis is still evident in the book testifies to both the ancient date of its original writing and to the reverence that Moses had for those records as he combined them to form the book of Genesis. He carefully preserved the documents with little or no modifications, but adhered to the literary style that was common for centuries before his time, when written records were preserved on tablets with cuneiform writing. Therefore the book of Genesis is a series of historical accounts from ancient times written by the men who lived in those times.

Let us look once again at the formula "this is the **book** of the generations of Adam" that is found in Genesis (5:1), which indicates that Adam could write:
> Here the word *seper,* translated "book," means "written narrative," or as F. Delitzsch translates it, "finished writing." Moreover, the Septuagint Version renders chapter 2:4: "This is the *book* of the origins of the heavens and the earth." The "books" of that time were tablets; the word simply means "record." The earliest records of Genesis, therefore, claim to have been written down, and not as is often imagined, passed on to Moses by word of mouth.[466]

I reiterate: The repeated use of the phrase "these are the generations [**family history**] of" was intentional on the author's part. Moses intentionally wrote in this way. He included these key phrases for a reason—to identify his original sources. This is like what authors do today as they write books, making liberal use of end notes to identify/credit sources.

> In this way Moses clearly indicates the source of the information available to him and names the persons who originally possessed the tablets from which he gained his knowledge. These are not arbitrarily invented divisions; they are stated by the author to be the framework of the book.[467]

Moses followed established scribal techniques when he converted the ancient records about origins from tablets to papyrus. The documents themselves conformed to the ancient scribal usage, and Moses preserved that information for his readers. The data we now have about ancient Mesopotamian scribal techniques, with name lines, catch-lines, dates, and titles shows us this. This information was not available to the men who formulated previous theories about the authorship of Genesis, e.g., the JEPD Theory.

Emphasizing a few Facts about Mesopotamian Writing, Useful in this Work Later On:
In the Old Babylonian era (c. 2000 BC–c. 1600 BC) colophons were less widespread but were still found in specific contexts. In that earlier period they are less systematic, codified, and informative than in later times, but they do contain dates, proper names, and catch-lines, as is well documented.[468] Thus these scribal practices go back at least as far as 2000 BC, were known during Old Testament times, but diminished before the time of Christ. Akkadian, an ancient Semitic language, was widely spoken in Mesopotamia in the centuries surrounding the time of Abraham, and Cuneiform writing did not disappear until around the time of Jesus.[469] Thus it seems likely that Abraham spoke an ancient Semitic language—perhaps some type of proto-Hebrew—which continued to be used in an evolving form past the time of the Exodus and even through Old Testament times. Ideograms continued to be mixed with cuneiform writing for centuries, so the transition from the older pictographic form of writing to cuneiform was a gradual change.[470]

The Original Authors of Genesis:

Archeology has Revealed to us the Original Authors of Genesis:
Archeology attests that when Abraham left Ur of the Chaldees, whatever family records he carried with him would have been written in cuneiform on clay tablets. Those tablets came into the possession of Moses centuries later, and he used them to write Genesis. The book can be divided into nine sections whose original authors we can now identify.

1:1-2:4	This is the book of the origin of the heavens and the earth. It is the only tablet with no personal signature because no human could know from first-hand experience the information that it contains. Wiseman holds it was written by Adam as the Lord explained it to him because it is written in the third person. But all accounts are in the third person. We hold that God wrote it and gave it to Adam, setting "person mode" for all accounts. The date in 2:3 indicates that God wrote it as He rested from His work of the six days; that is, on the seventh day.
2:5-5:2	This is the history of Adam, his personal first-hand story.
5:3-6:9a	This is the history of Noah, his personal and family records.
6:9b-10:1	This is the history of the sons of Noah.
10:2-11:10a	This is the history of Shem.
11:10b-11:27a	This is the history of Terah.
11:27b-25:19a	This is the history of Isaac, including some history of Ishmael. He conveyed his personal stories and family genealogy to Isaac when they reunited to bury Abraham. Isaac inserted it into his account as part of his broader family history.

25:19b-37:2a	This is the history of Jacob, including some of Esau's history as well. It is inserted after Jacob and Esau came together to bury Isaac. Jacob knew the early genealogy of Esau (36:1-8) from their childhood times with Isaac and Rebekah. The second genealogy (36:9-30) includes the family of Esau from when he dwelt in Edom, plus the family of Seir the Horite. Jacob got this information when the brothers came together to bury Isaac. The next section (36:31–43) is a later insert by Moses from the time of the Exodus. We will discuss this in detail when we comment on that section of Genesis.
37:2b-50:26	This section contains Egyptian cultural markers. It was written by the descendants of Jacob while they were living in the land of Goshen. Thus it was not originally written on clay tablets but on papyrus. Moses included it in the Genesis account because it is an important part of the family history of Israel, bridging from Jacob's time to the time of the Exodus.

Note: This assertion is based on two simple facts; (1) the Hebrew word for generations, *toledot*, means family history; (2) the literary style of Genesis reflects the ancient Babylonian practice of placing the owners name at the end of his writing, so the "generation" lines are signatures. Thus the authors of sections 2-8 are: Adam, Noah, The sons of Noah, Shem, Terah, Isaac, and Jacob. This identifies for us the original source documents for most of Genesis and the names their authors.

Additional supporting facts from the book of Genesis itself:
- In no instance is an event recorded which the person or person's named as the owner or writer of that section could not have written by personal knowledge or could not have easily obtained from another person. We will see this explicitly as we comment on each section in detail. The content of each narrative is just what would be expected if it were the family history of the named author.
- The history recorded in each section ceases in all instances before the death of the person named as the owner of the section. In most cases it continues until near the death of the owner of the section. Also, each account is in chronological order. We will see these facts as we comment on the individual sections.

It cannot be mere coincidence that the events recorded in each section so fit with the lifespan of the person named as its owner. Anyone writing even a century after the time of those named owners would never have written in that way. Therefore each section of Genesis bears the marks of having been written by the person named; i.e., by one who was personally acquainted with the events that are recorded. The precious details of the creation of the world and of mankind were not simply committed to memory, but were written down and preserved. Writing is now known to have been widespread in those days, and no story could be more important than the creation of all things. And the simple observation that these sections of Genesis were written by the persons named in the "signature" lines lends an enormous weight of authority to the contents of the sections.

Therefore the various pagan accounts of the creation that were written around the time of the patriarchs or centuries later must be seen as diluted corruptions of the original account. The influence of mankind's descent into idolatry and its loss of contact with God is what caused those stories to be distorted with grotesque and/or mythological details, or stripped of much of their content, so that what remained was merely a small fraction of the original account that we see in Genesis. Therefore the majesty of the Lord God and the story of His glorious work of creation were essentially lost to the members of those civilizations. (Paraphrased from *Ancient Records and the structure of Genesis*, pages 69–70 and 73)

An Important Observation about Scriptural Writings—Third-Person Narrative Mode:
This is not about Babylonian writing techniques, but is an observation about writing styles in general. In third-person mode, the characters in the narrative are referred to by the one who is relating the story (the narrator) as "he," "she," "it," or "they," not as "we" or "I" (first-person), or as "you" (second-person). This implies that the narrator is not one of the persons being talked about in the account, but is merely the one who is relating the story to us.

But in Scripture it is common for stories to be written in third-person narrative mode **and** to include the narrator as a participant. Perhaps the Lord inspired His word to be written down in this way because it is such an effective method for engaging the reader in the story.

In the following passage from the gospel of John the disciple "whom Jesus loved" is John.
> There was reclining on Jesus' bosom one of His disciples, whom Jesus loved. So Simon Peter gestured to **him**, and said to **him**, "Tell *us* who it is of whom He is speaking." **He**, leaning back thus on Jesus' bosom, said to Him, "Lord, who is it?" Jesus then answered, "That is the one for whom I shall dip the morsel and give it to him." (John 13: 23–25)

Samuel relates his first experience of the Lord speaking to him in the temple.
> It happened at that time as . . . Samuel was lying down in the temple of the LORD where the ark of God *was*, that the LORD called Samuel; and **he** said, "Here I am." Then **he** ran to Eli and said, "Here I am, for you called me." But he said, "I did not call, lie down again." So **he** went and lay down. (1 Samuel 3:2–5)

In the book of Joshua the author writes as follows about himself in third-person mode:
> Now it came about when Joshua was by Jericho, that **he** lifted up **his** eyes and looked, and behold, a man was standing opposite him with his sword drawn in his hand, and Joshua went to him and said to him, "Are you for us or for our adversaries?" He said, "No; rather I indeed come now *as* captain of the host of the LORD." And Joshua fell on his face to the earth, and bowed down, and said to him, "What has my lord to say to his servant?" (Joshua 5:13–14)

This literary technique was also employed by the Lord God Himself. Even though very few passages of Scripture are the direct writing of God, there are some. One example is in Exodus where Moses tells us about the tablets of the law that he carried down from the mountain. In these tablets the Lord is writing in third-person mode. Moses explains:
> The tablets were God's work, and the writing was God's writing engraved on the tablets. (Exodus 32:16)

Yet written on these tablets, as a part of the commandment to keep holy the Sabbath day, is the following summary account of the creation:
> For in six days the LORD made the heavens and the earth, the sea and all that is in them, and rested on the seventh day; therefore the LORD blessed the sabbath day and made it holy. (Exodus 20:11)

Note that the Lord does not say, "For in six days **"I"** made the heavens . . . etc."

In these instances we see the Scriptures using the third-person narrative mode, but with the narrator written into the account. The example of how the Lord wrote His summary of the creation account in Exodus is especially noteworthy because the complete account of the creation in Genesis 1:1ff is written in the same style—in the third-person narrative—with the Lord Himself written into the account. This style of writing sets the tone for all the accounts of Genesis, for we find no first-person pronouns in any of those personal stories. This precedent may also explain why this style of writing is sprinkled throughout Scripture.

We should also add that the use of third person narrative with the author included in the account was common in ancient literature other than the Bible. In Caesar's *Conquest of Gaul* we find the same technique used by Julius Caesar as he relates his strategies.

> About the middle of March a startling announcement reached Caesar. The Helvetii had actually begun to move; and their hordes would soon be streaming over the Roman Province. . . Caesar instantly left Rome, and, hurrying northward ninety miles a day, crossed the Alps, took command of the Provincial legion, ordered a fresh levy, and reached Geneva at the end of a week. He immediately destroyed the bridge by which the Helvetii intended to cross the river. They sent ambassadors to say that they only wanted to use the road through the Province, and would do no mischief. Would Caesar give them permission? Caesar had no intention of granting their request; but, as he wanted to gain time for his levies to assemble, he told the ambassadors that he would think over what they had said, and give them an answer on the 9th of the following month. [date was 58 BC][471]

This work, written by Caesar himself, is generally considered to be a "propaganda piece" which he wrote in an attempt to justify his military and political campaign.

Statement of our Hypothesis as Derived from Wiseman:

The book of Genesis is internally organized according to eight sections each of which is terminated by the phrase "these are the generations of." These sections were written by the person or person whose name appears after that phrase, the first section being unique. The authors of the first thirty-six chapters of Genesis are as follows:

The Lord God	1:1 through 2:4a
Adam	2:4b through 5:1a
Noah	5:1b through 6:9a
The Sons of Noah	6:9b through 10:1a
Shem	10:1b through 11:10a
Terah	11:10b through 11:27a
Isaac	11:27b through 25:19a
Jacob	25:19b through 37:2a

These sections of Genesis were originally written on clay tablets in the land of ancient Mesopotamia and were accumulated and kept as sections of a continuously developing story of the human race. This full collection of tablets was carried into Egypt by Jacob at the time of the famine when his son Joseph was coregent in Egypt.

Note that this final assertion, explaining how the tablets were passed along through successive generations and were finally carried into the land of Egypt where Moses had access to them, again is based on two simple facts: (1) obviously, family histories were meant to be passed on to the next generation of the patriarchal line; (2) the presence of the catch-lines, which gives clear textual evidence that each author had the previous account before him as he wrote his own, directly implies that the accounts were in fact being passed on, and that each successive author was pointedly connecting his account to the accounts that preceded his, thus consciously creating a cumulative history of mankind going back to Adam and the creation of the world.

This fact, in conjunction with the two simple facts that identified the original source documents of Genesis and their authors, is the foundation of our view of how the information in Genesis was originally written down, and how those documents came to Moses. They are also the reason we assert that the book is accurate and not an allegory or myth. It is the family history of those who lived through the formative events at the beginning of the human race. Thus Genesis is true.

The last fourteen chapters of Genesis were written by the sons of Jacob—not on clay tablets, but on papyrus, after the family entered Egypt and the sons were living in the land of Goshen. Two centuries later Moses read those writings, edited them, and put them together to create the book of Genesis that we now have. I name the documents which Moses used to write Genesis, "**The Genesis Documents**."

The scribal techniques that Moses employed as he edited Genesis remained in general use and were clearly understood for a millennium after his time. Thus contemporaries of Moses, and those who followed him until late in Old Testament times, would have had knowledge of the techniques he used, and would have clearly understood the meaning of key phrases and usages in Genesis. The techniques and styles of the literary methods that the patriarchs used when they wrote their accounts, and the same techniques that Moses understood and employed when he edited those ancient accounts and wrote the book of Genesis, were continuously understood and widely used from at least as early as 2000 BC, and until a few centuries before Jesus. As empires collapsed and new powers rose to replace them the knowledge of that art was lost—buried under the sands of the Middle East where it remained for over 2,000 years. It has only recently been rediscovered.

Implications for the JEPD Theory:
Let us pause and consider what we are saying: The importance of the mountains of information assembled in the twentieth century from these archeological finds cannot be overstated. These considerations have profound implications for how we think about the book of Genesis. When the proponents of the higher critical school proposed their theories of how Genesis came to be, they were in the dark about these facts and knew nothing of the ancient Middle Eastern civilizations or of their writing methods. The Old Testament was the only primal historical document that they had.

At the time their theories were proposed people doubted that writing had even been in existence as far back as the time of David in 1000 BC—much less did they realize that many thousands of documents on clay tablets lay buried in the Middle East, that those documents were collected together by the use of repetitious "catch-lines," that they were all carefully identified by author and library, that they were titled for identification, and that they were dated by the methods and techniques we have described.

Scholars were entirely in the dark about the scribal practices of ancient civilizations! Thus their analysis of the text of Genesis was conducted without knowledge of the style, special words, or phrases used by the ancients in their writing—and without an understanding of their culture or language. How could they accurately estimate the age of the book, identify its authors, and effectively describe how it was composed? How could they accurately determine the genre of the book of Genesis while missing this information?[e]

> When this is understood, it is not surprising to read in J. Wellhausen's account of the inception and growth of this literary analysis, about "conjectures," or of the way successive critics scrapped not only the conclusions but the principles on which their predecessors had based their theories. Thus the "two document theory" was contradicted by the "supplementary hypothesis," and this in its turn was displaced by the "crystallization hypothesis." Like men groping in the dark, advanced scholars wove together their intermixture of short-lived theories. At last Wellhausen wrote of "inconsistency," "reaction," "had really gone too far," "the fragmentary hypothesis was now superseded," this fragmentary theory "remained dominant till Hupfeld denied" and "his (Hupfeld's) assumption was corrected by Noldeck."[472]

---

[e] See Appendix III for a short statement of the documentary hypothesis.

We have seen how anti-supernaturalistic assumptions twisted archeological theories about the Pentateuch and the origin of alphabetic scripts. The particular situation relating to the authorship of Genesis was not helped by the assumption of evolution that was so prevalent by that time. If mankind had evolved from a more primitive life form, then human civilization also must have developed from a more primitive state in the distant past.

> Although nothing was known at this time, apart from Genesis, of early civilizations, these scholars assumed that the times must be excessively crude, yet they committed the fallacy of subjecting Genesis to a type of contemporary literary analysis, just as if it were a piece of modern writing.
>
> **This lack of knowledge regarding early history made it possible for the critics to assume that civilization was primitive, and writing almost unknown to the patriarchs. So unenlightened were most of the workers at this time, it was imagined that the wedge-shaped writing which had been found, was only a form of pottery decoration.** Until the mounds of Babylonia gave up their tens of thousands of tablets, and these, together with the inscriptions from the land of Egypt, had been deciphered, it was customary for commentators on Genesis to write a special introduction which defensively suggested that writing was sufficiently prevalent to enable Moses to write! Thus the conservative *Speakers' Commentary* issued in 1871 says on page two: "The first question then which naturally occurs is, was the art of writing known so early as Moses? and especially was it known to the Egyptians and the Jews?"[473] [bold mine]

With nothing concrete to base their theories on, scholars seized on subtle details:

> Some critics affirm that they can detect differences of phraseology and style in the book. They say that they are able to disjoin and isolate not only verses but phrases, and to distribute them among writers respectively called "Priestly," "Jehovist," "Elohist," etc. They assert their ability to discover where and when an editor or redactor has amended or added a single word. It is significant that, although they claim to know the literary style of these writers, they do not know their names or when or where they lived. In fact, this is the theory that presently holds the field: instead of merely one "Priestly" and one "Jehovist" writer, the book was composed by a school of writers, and their composition was spread over a considerable period. They add that the writings of this group were subjected to the scrutiny of several editors who endeavored to harmonize the narratives, and that the efforts of these editors received the attention of a final editor who scrutinized their work and gave the book the form it now possesses. They were forced to introduce this final editor. The admission is, however, fatal to their theory, for he would most certainly have been capable of eliminating any discrepancies or repetition had he seen them to exist. The least we can assume is that a Hebrew literary editor would have been as capable of detecting a discrepancy as the average modern scholar. According to this analysis the chapter becomes a tangle in which the products of "schools of writers" have been worked in alternately, yet the result is a continuous narrative.[474]

Because we note many "duplicate phrases" in Genesis, and there once was no explanation for this, scholars asserted that there must have been two or more accounts folded together to create what we now have as the finished form of the book. But we see that these repetitions are exactly what the ancient scribes inserted in the succession of the tablets in order to tie together the total document. They indicate to us that the entire Genesis account was accumulated over generations and was intended by its writers to be read and understood as a unified account of human history. The tablets were added to by each generation of patriarchs and passed on to the next as a cumulative history.

> Many theologians do not seem to realize that this charge of "repetition" could be brought against nearly every piece of ancient writing. It is characteristic of the style of the time and is evidence of their ancient character. In this connection Professor Arno Poebel in his work on cuneiform *Historical Texts*, issued by the University of Pennsylvania in 1914 (in commenting on some ancient Sumerian tablets found at Nippur), writes: "the readers of the Bible, moreover, will recognize the quaint principle of partial repetition or paraphrase."[475]

The idea that Genesis is a clumsy patchwork assembled by an unknown redactor who left useless repetitive phrases scattered throughout his finished product shaped Bible commentaries. The Jerusalem Bible, in its "Introduction to the Pentateuch," speaks from this basic attitude. Assuming oral traditions were the basic sources for Genesis, it says:

> [F]or many centuries all five of the books were attributed to Moses as the sole or principal author. However, modern study of the texts has revealed a variety of styles, a lack of sequence and such repetitions and variations in narrative that it is impossible to ascribe the whole group to a single author; four distinct literary "traditions" can be identified and stand side by side in the Pentateuch. Two of these go back to the time when Israel became a nation–a period dominated by the figure of Moses: the conditions of earlier times converging on him and the **memories** [emphasis is mine; they assume that there were no written records] of what happened under his leadership together made up the national epic . . . The Mosaic religion set its enduring seal on the faith and practice of the nation [of Israel], and the Mosaic law remained its standard; the modifications required by changing conditions over some seven centuries were presented as interpretations of the mind of Moses and invested themselves with his authority.[476]

By this reasoning hundreds of Old Testament references to Moses and his writings in the Pentateuch would have to be dismissed or reinterpreted in a radical way.

Other imagined problems include explanatory insertions that appear to have been made at a later date and certain supposed irregularities in the stories of the text. These will be dealt with as we comment on the text of Genesis in detail. The most important lesson that we can take away from this analysis of past theories and their foibles is this:

> **When we do not have enough information to lead us to clear and reasonable conclusions we should be careful to say simply, "I just do not know." Whenever we attempt to reconstruct the distant past we are in uncertain waters. I will encounter the same issue in this book and will have to account for that fact in various situations.**

The insights we have provided contradict these previous theoretical attempts to explain how Genesis was written. But there is also an important positive implication for how we understand Genesis once we assert that it was written by the authors that are named.

Before we understood how Genesis had been written, when we imagined that God had inspired a later person to write it—Moses in the traditional view of its authorship—then it was reasonable to think of the various descriptions of how the Lord interacted with men as being metaphorical or an ancient way of speaking about something that was distant and not clearly understood. But when we see that the stories are first-hand accounts then the implication for how we understand the description of divine interaction with men is different. Adam and the following patriarchs are actually describing for us how God dealt personally with them. It was direct and intimate, as one person to another. This is an important revelation to us of what God is like, and it affects how we interpret Genesis and the accounts that are in the book. We will deal with this in detail in the commentary.

How our Hypothesis Relates to the Reading of Genesis:

The signature lines with the names attached—Adam, Noah, etc.—are verified from the text of Genesis simply by reading the book; that is, each section that is asserted to have been written by the person whose name appears in the "generations" line should contain only information that he could have known personally. This will be verified from reading the text of Genesis, which confirms this assertion. In general, all of the assertions that we make about the book of Genesis in this work can be verified simply by sitting down and reading the book. They are not difficult to understand or to verify.

Observations from the Old Testament:
If the scribal practices of ancient Mesopotamia were known in Old Testament times then how does that book, which references Moses and his books so often, refer to Genesis? The Old Testament mentions Moses by name over 700 times. Many of the references are in the books attributed to him but almost all the references are in the book of Joshua or in later books. Although these books reiterate many times the commands that God gave to Israel through Moses, and attribute the laws and directives in the last four books of the Pentateuch to Moses, they never once attribute the book of Genesis to Moses. The many references to the actions and the leading of Moses, hundreds in number, spread throughout the books of the Old Testament, are one overwhelming reason why we must ascribe the Pentateuch to him.

But the fact that no statement was ever made asserting that Moses wrote the book of Genesis is also significant. All of the Old Testament books were written before 400 BC, and therefore all were written while the children of Israel—and all of the nations of the Middle East—were still familiar with the writing methods that we see reflected in Genesis. Thus they would have realized that Moses was explicitly directing their attention to those authors whose works he was quoting as he wrote. But while this argument from omission is consistent with the idea that Moses did not author Genesis in the same way that he authored the rest of the Pentateuch, it is an argument from omission and is not conclusive. It is also consistent with the idea that the scribal techniques that we see in Genesis continued to be known and understood throughout Old Testament times, and that Israel understood the book of Genesis accordingly.

Observations from the New Testament:
There are eighty references to Moses by name in the New Testament. Once again it is never stated that Moses wrote Genesis. The following is as close to such a reference as can be seen in the New Testament. This is from the time after the resurrection when Jesus appeared to the men on the way to Emmaus:
> Then beginning with Moses and with all the prophets, He explained to them the things concerning Himself in all the Scriptures. (Luke 24:27)

Does this mean starting with Genesis, as if Moses wrote that book? There is a similar message of Jesus recorded a bit later in Luke:
> These are My words which I spoke to you while I was still with you, that all things which are written about Me in the Law of Moses and the Prophets and the Psalms must be fulfilled. Then He opened their minds to understand the Scriptures, and He said to them, "Thus it is written that the Christ would suffer and rise again from the dead the third day and that repentance for forgiveness of sins would be proclaimed in His name to all the nations, beginning from Jerusalem. You are witnesses of these things." (Luke 24:44)

In this second message Jesus explicitly narrows the meaning of His reference to Moses. It is "the Law of Moses," which would refer to the last four books of the Pentateuch only. In fact, our Lord draws a clear distinction between "the Law of Moses" and the traditions handed down from the fathers, which would be the accounts of Genesis:
> For this reason Moses has given you circumcision (not because it is from Moses, but from the fathers), and on *the* Sabbath you circumcise a man. (John 7:22)

Also, when Jesus responded to the Pharisees with His teaching about divorce he said:
> And He answered and said, "Have you not read that He who created *them* from the beginning MADE THEM MALE AND FEMALE, and said, 'FOR THIS REASON A MAN SHALL LEAVE HIS FATHER AND MOTHER AND BE JOINED TO HIS WIFE, AND THE TWO SHALL BECOME ONE FLESH'? So they are no longer two, but one flesh. What therefore God has joined together, let no man separate." They said to

> Him, "Why then did Moses command to GIVE HER A CERTIFICATE OF DIVORCE AND SEND *her* AWAY?" He said to them, "Because of your hardness of heart Moses permitted you to divorce your wives; but from the beginning it has not been this way. (Matthew 19:4–8)

In this discussion Jesus refers to Moses, as do the Jewish leaders, but He does not say that the statement about being made "male and female" was written by Moses. Again, these are further indications, albeit from omission, that Moses edited earlier accounts, and from them he created for us the present book of Genesis. All of these observations are merely consistent with the thesis that Moses did not actually write Genesis himself.

Understanding What It Means to Say that Genesis Was Inspired by God:
The assertions that we are making about the authorship of Genesis are most important because when we assert that Genesis was "inspired by God," we ought to have some idea of exactly who was inspired. It was not only Moses, although he was guided by the Holy Spirit to put Genesis together. But initially it was the various ancient writers whose records he was carefully assembling and editing to construct Genesis. The inspired men of old were the ones who actually heard God speak, who witnessed His actions, and who lived through the enactment of His decrees. Those men were Adam, Noah, the sons of Noah, Shem, Terah, Isaac, Jacob, and the sons of Jacob.

Those men were each inspired by God to write down their account of the events which they had witnessed and participated in. Each was guided by the Lord to write exactly what He wanted them to write. Moses was the editor or redactor who, under the leading of the Holy Spirit, finally put their accounts together for us. It is not likely or even plausible that such accounts are speaking anthropomorphically or allegorically because the patriarchs were recounting their life stories. There was no reason to write in figures of speech. Such literary devices came into vogue at later dates for other types of writing. The patriarchs precede such forms of expression and their purpose in writing precludes the use of such literary styles. The genre is "personal family history," the most surely accurate, reliable type of narrative. What could be more certain than a person telling us the history of his family from his own personal experience and from that of his other family members?

Carrying Forward our Purpose in this Work—Genesis is Historically Accurate:
In the chapters to come we will comment on Genesis from the perspective that the book is the personal accounts of men who lived through those events. We will observe and note the following overwhelming supportive evidences for the Wiseman hypothesis, as we have adapted it, from within the text of Genesis:

- Each section of Genesis is composed of material that would easily and naturally be known to the person whose name appears at the end of that section. In many cases the information reaches until near the time of the author's death. This is supportive of the chronology and patriarchal ages recorded in Genesis. No later writer could have contrived to write the accounts of Genesis in this way.
- The chronologies of Genesis are consistent with the hypothesis that the accounts were written by persons who knew of each other and who passed the tablets on to the next generation. If the genealogies of Genesis had large gaps in them, as some have suggested, then the succession of the patriarchs would have been interrupted and the continuity of the overall account would have been broken. Thus the genealogies of Genesis correctly delineate for us the chronology of the

events described. There is noticeable internal evidence for the continuity of the total account. This fact is supported by the documentation of the "catch-lines" that have been identified. The conclusion that they lead to is that the overall Genesis account was consciously accumulated and appended to by the patriarchs through the centuries and is a unified work of many men over that stretch of time.
- Each individual account is in chronological order.
- The consistency of the accounts of Genesis, even to the minutest detail of history and geography, testifies to their historical and geographical authenticity and to the fact that the persons who wrote them must have had first-hand knowledge.
- In several instances this approach to understanding Genesis clarifies the text and helps us to understand certain ambiguous or difficult verses. It points us to the answers to certain hard questions that the Fathers had as they read Genesis.
- This view of the composition of Genesis addresses the peculiar issues raised by the proponents of the JEPD Theory of how Genesis was written, while providing us with a more traditional way of viewing the text and its meaning. The questions posed by the supporters of the JEPD Theory include:
  - The change in the name of God between chapter 1 and the following chapters: This is explained as the change in authorship and perspective from God to Adam and later men.
  - Repetitious phrases within the text indicating that Genesis may have arisen by patching together multiple ancient accounts—and that the final result was a bit clumsy: This has been accounted for by explaining the use of catch-lines in ancient writings.
  - Doubly or triply occurring statements (hinting at multiple accounts intermingled): These appear only in the section written by the three sons of Noah, Shem, Ham, and Japheth.
  - Additionally, we will select two texts from Genesis and compare the JEPD approach to interpreting that passage to the approach of The Genesis Documents. We will compare the understanding of the text of Genesis that they each arrive at and compare both views with the views of the Fathers. The Wiseman Hypothesis will provide us with a view of the authorship and interpretation of Genesis that accords totally with the Ancient Faith, which better elucidates the text and its meaning, and which connects it nicely with other logically or thematically related biblical texts. It enhances the total corpus of the Christian Faith.
- Understanding that the book of Genesis is a series of personal accounts written by men who were directly knowledgeable about the events leads us to conclude that the accounts of Genesis are fully historical and accurate. This is the view of Genesis that all previous centuries of the Church had. Thus this understanding of the composition of Genesis undergirds the truth of Genesis and the Ancient Faith of the Church regarding Genesis.

It is impossible to accurately understand and interpret an ancient document unless we have an idea of how it came to be written and why the author or authors bothered to put it into writing. The Wiseman Hypothesis, as we have adapted and expanded it in this work, provides us with the first clear understanding of how, when, and why the accounts of Genesis were first put down in writing. It is confirmed fully by the text of Genesis itself.

These facts will become clear as we move through the text of Genesis and comment on it, section by section. As we do this I will also provide liberal quotations from the Fathers, showing us their thoughts on various topics that are raised by Genesis—and I will share my own thoughts on those topics as well. All this will result in a commentary on Genesis that is insightful, faithful to the actual meaning of the text, and faithful to the traditional beliefs and attitudes of Christian thinkers throughout the Church age.

The Creation

Here is the beginning and the end of the text of the first set of tablets:

<u>1</u> ¹ In the beginning God created the heavens and the earth. ² The earth was formless and void, and darkness was over the surface of the deep, and the Spirit of God was moving over the surface of the waters . . .

<u>2</u> ¹ Thus the heavens and the earth were completed, and all their hosts. ² By the seventh day God completed His work which He had done, and He rested on the seventh day from all His work which He had done. ³ Then God blessed the seventh day and sanctified it, because in it He rested from all His work which God had created and made. ⁴ᵃ This is the account [lit., the generations] of the heavens and the earth.

<u>Archeological Considerations</u>:
From the content of this tablet we see that no human could have written it from their own personal experience. Significantly this tablet is the only one that does not have a name. Here are the archeological comments on this piece of writing.

> Naturally the wording is simple, but the truth conveyed is profound. Human as the language is, it is still the best medium God could use to communicate with man. It is God teaching Adam, in a simple yet faultless way, how the earth and the things which he could see on and around it had been created. The Lord God talked with Adam in the Garden. This tablet purports to be a simple record of what God said and did. Adam is told just as much as his mind could understand. The details and processes are not fully revealed. Had they been, how could he and later ages have understood them? We would claim, then, that this first section of Genesis is the most ancient piece of writing. It is a record of what God told Adam. It is not an *impersonal* general account. It is God teaching the first man the elemental things about the universe, at the very dawn of human language.[477]

Imagine God giving this to the first human and explaining to him from this tablet exactly how he came to be and his place in the grand plan of the creation. The human being is intelligent enough to understand but has no knowledge of anything outside of himself as yet. This explanation of archeology fits the insights of the Fathers that the creation of things was a subject that, by its nature, could only be understood by the Lord God. The Lord God explained it to Adam in a way that was accurate, as far as it went, and that was perfectly suited to his level of comprehension at that early time.

> Here we get back also to the very inauguration of written history. For it may have been written before even the sun and moon had been given names. Let us note the simplicity with which the facts are presented. There is a type of repetition and simplicity rarely recurring in Scripture. "Let there be *lights* in the firmament . . . and God made two *great lights,* the *greater light* to rule the day and the *lesser light* to rule the night."

> We know that long before the time of the Flood men worshipped the sun and the moon and had given them names. Had this first chapter of Genesis been written even as late as Abraham's day, instead of the simple expression "greater light" we should have had the Babylonian word for the sun, *samas*. It is used in the legal tablet (containing the names of thirteen witnesses) in my personal possession. Moreover, *samas* was the name of the sun god worshipped by the Babylonians. In his laws, Hammurabi depicts himself in the attitude of receiving his laws from this *samas*. When Abraham left Ur, the moon god was the chief object of worship in that city. The great tower built in the center of the city (at least 250 years before the time of Abraham) was surmounted by a temple dedicated to this moon god. Names for the sun and moon have been among the oldest words known in any language, yet this document was written before names had been given to the "greater and lesser lights."[478]

The narrative of the first tablet does not name the celestial objects and that is significant. Archeologists who are familiar with the parallel narratives from antiquity notice this striking fact which we might overlook. God named some things that He created, but some others He left unnamed, granting to people the prerogative of naming them. All ancient cultures gave names to the sun and the moon. Because this narrative does not name those celestial objects, its writing must have preceded all such ancient cultures. It is truly from the very dawn of human history. But Wiseman has other insightful comments.

> This earliest of all documents is written in a most exceptional way. It is recording the words of God used in telling Adam the story of Creation. Observe the method employed in writing this narrative. "And God *said* . . . And God *called.*" What God called the components of the universe is placed on record. "And God called the light *day* and the darkness called He *night* . . . And God called the firmament *heaven:* and God called the dry land *earth* and the gathering together of waters called He *seas.*" It is written in the style of someone recording precisely what Adam heard when the narrative was told to him.
>
> Further it is written on a very personal note. It is far removed from the style of a vision. There is no "I saw," "I beheld," "I heard." It is direct speech, "And God said, Behold I have given you every herb yielding seed which is upon the face of all the earth, and every tree in which is the fruit of a tree yielding seed which is upon the face of all the earth, and every tree in which is the fruit of a tree yielding seed to you, and it shall be for meat." These words were spoken to the first man. It is not a vague and general account. All the reader needs to do is to realize its unique features and to compare it with the Babylonian versions.[479]

The contents of this tablet were directed to Adam personally. They were crafted so as to be fully understandable at his level, and yet to be accurate. Many gifted men and women today can write on a technical subject in such a way that those who are not immersed in their area of expertise can understand them, while at the same time remaining fully true to the subject matter without portraying it in a misleading or distorted way. This is what the Lord is doing as He explains to Adam the origin of all things. Looking at the creation account in this way accords with the viewpoint of the Fathers, that the creation was and is beyond the ability of Human beings to comprehend. It is proper to God alone.

> This first chapter is so ancient that it does not contain mythical or legendary matter; these elements are entirely absent. It bears the markings of having been written before myth and legend had time to grow, and not as is often stated, at a later date when it had to be stripped of the mythical and legendary elements inherent in every other account of Creation extant. This account is so original that it does not bear a trace of any system of philosophy. Yet it is so profound that it is capable of correcting philosophical systems. It is so ancient that it contains nothing that is merely nationalistic; neither Babylonian, Egyptian, nor Jewish modes of thought find a place in it, for it was written before clans, nations, or philosophies originated. Surely, we must regard it as the original, of which the other extant accounts are merely corrupted copies. Others incorporate their national philosophies in crude polytheistic and mythological form. This is pure. Genesis 1 is as primitive as the first human. It is the threshold of written history.[480]

These comments from archeology summarize the unique nature of this account of the creation. These insightful remarks indicate to us from yet another perspective the very ancient nature of this writing. Before nations and cultures had arisen, before men could devise their philosophies, before it could be tainted by human devices of any type, this account of the creation was written.

The name line, or ownership line (if we can even call it that), of the first tablet is:
> This is the account [lit., the generations] of the heavens and the earth. (Genesis 2:4a)

The date for the writing of this account is given in Genesis 2:3, just before the name. It was when "He rested from all His work which God had created and made," as Dr. Wiseman explains. Thus it must have been written on the seventh day, before the day ended, and before God could record the end of that day. The early date of this writing implies that Adam could read—and therefore that he also must have been able to write—even from the earliest times. The Lord God gave this account to Adam as an instructional tool, to explain to him how he had come into consciousness, how he fit into the broader creation, and what His relationship was to God—vital, foundational information for man to know.

This reminds me of a question I asked the priest in religion class in fourth grade: "When God first created Adam and Eve how could they talk, read, write, or understand anything? How could they function?" He said: "Mike, they had infused knowledge." In modern computer lingo, those units came preloaded with lots of useful software! Thus I suggest that this tablet was written first of all. It is the first writing in history. God also wrote other passages of Scripture. He wrote the ten commandments on tablets of stone with His own finger (Exodus 31:18). We often see Scripture as the inspired Word of God but expressed through the medium of His chosen writer. But in this tablet we are reading words that are straight from the Lord—not expressed through any human intermediary. That is another reason why it contains no trace of any human culture.

The first man, created directly from the dust of the ground, must have been instilled with certain human capabilities. This is how Adam could read this account. Today children imbibe such skills from their elders or from formal education. But in the beginning it could not have been thus. The Lord God gave this tablet to Adam—but He also gives it to all men. He addresses it to us as well. When we look at this piece of writing in this way then it makes us carefully consider what the Lord is saying to the human race through it. He is describing for us how He made all things. He wants us to understand this. Creation is His defining work. He and only He is the creator. It is His foundational work—a work by which we come to know who He is and what He means to us. It defines Him to us, just as the redemption, accomplished much later in history, defines Him to us.

In this tablet God tells us that He is *'elohiym* the awesome creator of all things, and that He wants us to know Him and to understand Who He is and Who He was from before all times and all ages. Throughout the history of the Jewish people and the Church this has been read and believed. Could He have written it in such a way that they all failed to understand Him correctly? I think we should assume that He communicates through this writing in such a way that we can both understand Him and be accurately informed as to how He accomplished His work. The communication is crafted to match the limits that our human state imposes on our understanding. The creation is important because we are part of it and because it is the key work that identifies Him to us. Who is He? He is the One Who summoned all things into existence. It is because of the importance of this truth that He wrote it down with His own hand and delivered it to man at the very beginning of the creation—so that mankind would understand it right from the start.

The account of the creation that we are about to study did not arise by the action of man, nor from any human culture. God Himself wrote it and has given it to us. This agrees completely with the Ancient Faith of the Church. This is in perfect harmony with the faith and the implicit understanding of the holy men of old. They did not know that God wrote it personally, but they knew it was His perfect word directed to them and to all men.

Connections Between the Pre-Deluge Tablets:

The "Ahora Covenant Stone" implies the four pre-Deluge accounts had to be pictographic. Those accounts must have been translated at some later date by Noah and/or Shem—probably after the confusion of tongues at Babel as civilizations arose, and as cuneiform became the script of choice. In this way they could be read by the later patriarchs. We will discuss this later on, in the chapter "Babel."

Here are some key connections between the first three accounts, from Dr. Wiseman.
1:1--In the beginning **God created the heavens and the earth**. (catch phrase)
2:3—He rested from all His work which He had created and made (date line)
2:4—These are the generations of the heavens and the earth (end of God's account)
2:4—<u>when they were created</u> (catch phrase)
2:4—**In the day the Lord God made earth and heaven**. (catch phrase)
5:1—This is the book of the generations of Adam (end of Adam's account)
5:2—in the day <u>when they were created</u>. (catch phrase)

The **bold** phrases connect God's account and Adam's account. The <u>underlined</u> phrases connect Adam's account and Noah's account. So we see that the first three accounts were consciously connected together. Adam had the first account, written by the Lord, when he began to write his own. Also, Noah had Adam's story when he wrote his account.

There is also a reference in Noah's account to what Adam reports. Noah says his name as given to him by his father Lamech was prophetic, indicating that he would "comfort us concerning our work and the toil of our hands because of the ground that the Lord has cursed" (Genesis 5:29). This is a reference to the curse described in Adam's account. It shows that Lamech had read Adam's record. Thus the accounts were being passed on to successive generations.

The phrase "in the day the Lord God made earth and heaven" is likely also a date, but it cannot be taken as the time when Adam wrote his account because it is too far from his signature line. I take it to be the time he wrote the first section of his account, the story of the creation of the first pair and of their placement in the garden of Eden. It is an internal date. As we will see, Adam's account can be divided into 5 sections. This can be taken as the date when Adam wrote the first section, the date when he began his account. This line also makes his account flow naturally from the Lord's account because it indicates that he and his wife were created when everything else was created by God. This is the time when the creation of the man and the woman took place according to Adam.

The phrase from Genesis 2:3, coming directly before the signature line, is the date of the writing of the Lord's account.

From these facts and inferences we will formulate the following hypothesis, the details of which will be more fully developed in the following sections of the commentary:
- The first account, the story of the creation of all things, was written by the Lord God during the creation week. The contents of this tablet, the fact that it is unnamed, the lack of cultural indicators within it, and the need make Himself known to man from the earliest moment of our creation, all agree nicely with the assertion that God wrote this account. In fact, the date line indicates it was written on the seventh day, "when He rested from all His work which He had created and made."

- The second tablet consists of five separate episodes by Adam. The first episode is Adam and Eve's creation and placement in the Garden of Eden. It is stated by Adam to have occurred during the six days of creation. He probably wrote that first section early on in his new life. The four subsequent episodes stretch over the many later centuries of Adam's life. We will look at these in the chapter "Adam."
- The third tablet consists of two parts: The family genealogical register which was kept throughout the generations by Noah's ancestors, and which stretches from Adam to him, plus his personal account of the conditions that immediately preceded the Deluge.

Other Creation Accounts:

The Genesis account of the creation is certainly not the only one that we have in hand. There are many ancient accounts that have been preserved in part or perhaps totally from ancient peoples scattered around the world. It is worth our time to briefly examine some of these in order to compare them to the Genesis account, which we believe is the only one that was actually given to us directly by the Creator Himself. While we are comparing the Genesis account with other creation stories we can also glance at the modern theories of origins that have arisen in the context of our own culture. Because we are immersed in our culture and deeply imbedded in the viewpoints that characterize it, we tend to grant high credibility to such accounts. They speak to us in a language and with a style that is familiar to us—touching subconscious spots in our psyche—appealing to our affinity for technobabble and our innate respect for science-speak.

We can compare our text to the Babylonian account of creation since its origins were geographically near to this account. The *Enûma Eliš* can be summarized this way:

> This is set before the height of heaven was named and the earth beneath did not bear a name . . . and no field was formed, no marsh was seen . . . when none of the gods had been called into being . . . and no destinies were ordained, then were created the gods in the midst of heaven. [Then is described the anguish and wars and tribulations between the gods when Ummu-Hubur made invincible weapons and monster-serpents and other terrible monsters.] Then Marduk asked the gods to "make his fate preeminent and proclaim it" if he could just conquer Tiamat (another name for Ummu-Hubur) their mother who was waging war against them. The gods got drunk at a feast and there decreed for Marduk the fate that he had requested. He succeeded in his struggle against her when with a spear he burst her belly, severed her inward parts, pierced her heart, and cut off her life. Then he stood on her hinder parts and with a club he smashed her skull. He split her up like a flat fish into two halves. One half he established as a covering for heaven. Marduk made the stars of the Zodiac and ordained the year and its months. He appointed the moon god. He created man to serve the gods of heaven and to build their shrines. He created man for this service in order to appease the anger of the other gods toward himself. Thus our lot is to serve the gods.

This is a greatly condensed and abbreviated summary of the creation myth of Babylon, which has innumerable bloody and murderous episodes in it that I have passed over.

We can easily see that as man fell into the darkness of separation from the Lord because of sin, the knowledge of God was lost and/or distorted. The majesty and glory that is appropriate to Him became muddied, and grotesque myths were concocted. The version presented here was found in the library of the Assyrian king Ashurbanipal and dates back to the seventh century BC. It is estimated to have been originally composed sometime between 1500 and 1700 BC, and then copied once or several times before a copy was placed in the king's library.

An earlier creation tablet from Ebla, dated as early as 2300 BC, is called the "Lugo Tablet" because it ascribes creation to one called Lugo (or Lugal); i.e., "the great one." After it was unearthed it was publicly unveiled in Ann Arbor, Michigan, in 1975, and reads thus:

> There was no heaven,
> > Lugo formed it.
> There was no earth,
> > Lugo formed it.
> There was no sun,
> > Lugo formed it.
> There was no moon,
> > Lugo formed it.

This is much closer to the Genesis account, but it still lacks the detail and cohesiveness of the Genesis account. Also it calls the celestial objects by name rather than describing them as "the greater light" and "the lesser light." (Picture of the tablet below)[481]

CREATION TABLET AT EBLA

One of the most important finds at Ebla was a creation tablet ascribing the great works of creation to one great being, "Lugal". It was earlier than the Babylonian creation epic.

Here are a number of creation stories from various indigenous American peoples. They were scattered far from the Middle East, and they are dated to much more recent times because native American civilizations are less ancient than those from the Middle East.

The Maya people of South America have this creation story:[482]
The god Hurakan, the mighty wind, passed over the universe, still wrapped in gloom. He called out "Earth," and the solid land appeared. Then the chief gods took counsel among themselves as to what should next be made and they created the animals. Then they tried to make man but had to make several attempts before finally succeeding.

The ancient Mexican idea of creation:[483]
Before ever were years or days, the world lay in darkness. All things lacked order, and water covered the slime and ooze that was the initial state of the earth. (This picture is found in many native American creation-stories. Most American Indian peoples believed that the earth had been created from the slime which arose above the primeval waters. The sky is masculine in their stories, and the earth is feminine and births many things, according to how or with what the sky impregnates her.)

Toltec Legend of the Creation: (predecessors of the Aztecs)[484]
The Toltecs credited a certain "Lord of All Existence" with the creation of the universe, the stars, mountains, and animals. At the same time he made the first man and woman, from whom all the inhabitants of the earth are descended.

Aztec Creation Myth:[485]
In the beginning there was nothing and the dual god/goddess (male/female, good/evil, chaos order) Ometeotl created itself. It gave birth to the four directions. As they began to create, their works were eaten by the dragon/serpent Cipactli who carried the universe. The gods killed it and pulled its body in four directions. Its head became the heavens; its tail the underworld; its middle body the earth; its eyes became caves and fountains. Flowers, plants and trees came from its hair; rivers from its mouth; hills and valleys from its nose; its shoulder became the mountains. This extensive myth pictures the passage of several ages. During the second age men were created. During the fourth age the water came down and flooded the whole earth leaving it in darkness. The age we are in now is the fifth age.

Inca Story of Creation:[486]
Pachacamac was the sun god. He rose out of Lake Titicaca and married Pachamama the beautiful moon. They ruled all things together and had children. Pachacamac made the first humans from stones from a huge mountain. They were not adept at anything so the gods sent their children to teach them weaving, farming, and other basic life skills.

Comanche Creation Story:[487]
One day the Great Spirit gathered the dust from the four winds and created the Comanche people who were powerful as a mighty whirlwind. But he also made a demon that tormented people and who could appear in many forms. He still harms them every chance he gets.

Arikara (a tribe from North Dakota) Creation Story:[488]
The Great Sky Spirit, whose other name is the Great Mystery, was the lord who made all things. The sky existed and beneath it was an endless body of water where two ducks eternally swam. The Great Sky Spirit made two brothers and they commanded the ducks to swim to the bottom of the great water and bring up some earth. From this they made the plains and hills and mountains. They taught two spiders how to reproduce and the spiders produced plants, animals . . . and men. But they also produced a race of evil giants, so the Great Sky Spirit destroyed them by a great flood, but saved mankind because he loved us.

All of these fragmentary stories and many more from peoples scattered throughout the world can reveal a glimmer of the truth and majesty of the biblical account. In some the original story of creation was not completely forgotten, but others retained no real light.[f] It is not reasonable to theorize that a coherent and intact account of the creation such as is found in Genesis came later than and was derived from primitive pagan accounts. It is much better to see the Genesis account as prior to the others and as connected to the actual historical event that it describes. The other accounts are much later and are removed from the actual historical event. The story that they tell is fragmented, jumbled, and missing the ring of reality. In order for this obvious fact to make sense the Genesis account must be older than the others, and that is exactly what our hypothesis states. It is the account written at the time of the creation—accurate and complete. It did not arise in a milieu where many mythical accounts were circulating. The milieu arose at a time later than the biblical account and as a result of the events that Genesis describes; that is, as a result of the Flood and the scattering of the peoples at Babel.

---

[f] Maria Leach, *The Beginning: Creation Myths Around the World* documents the chaos of pagan creation myths from peoples around the world. People often lost all knowledge of the One Who created mankind and the purpose for which He did so. How then could they worship "in spirit and in truth" (John 4:24)?

The current scientific naturalistic theories of origins can also be compared to the biblical account of creation just as the *Enûma Eliš* and other creation stories were.

> In the beginning there was nothing at all. But a quantum fluctuation in nothingness produced a singularity of enormous density. This happened for no reason at all. The singularity then began to expand, along with the space that contained it, for no reason at all. In this way the universe created itself. [For a more extensive rendition of this modern myth see Appendix II.]

This explanation, current among some scientists today, has a few problems. The goal of modern cosmological theories is to explain how the universe came to be as we now see it, but without God, simply as the outworking of natural processes operating under the laws of physics. The above explanation violates two foundational scientific laws: If nothingness "fluxed" into something (a singularity that contained all matter), then the law of the conservation of matter and energy was violated; and if that compact singularity began to expand then that violated the law of gravity—because that singularity would be the deepest black hole possible, and black holes draw all nearby matter into them while allowing nothing to leave the gravitational well in which they themselves are immersed. This explanation also is flawed because it offers mankind no reason for existing. We are an accident of improbability. This does not satisfy our need as humans for meaning and purpose. It is spiritually stultifying.

All of the above accounts of creation arose out of various diverse human cultures and civilizations. All of them bear the marks of the cultures out of which they arose. The mythological accounts are from primitive tribal cultures that knew little of the vast world that they inhabited. They wrote with the simple and narrow purpose of exalting their own culture and the god that they themselves had, in their ignorance, invented from their own imaginations.

The scientific attempts to explain the origin of this world arose from the midst of a culture that had rejected all belief in the divine origin of the world, and had futilely attempted to explain such awesome events as the extended outworking of processes that they had studied and come to understand, all the while believing that their human concepts could actually explain the incomprehensible works of the One Who summoned all things from nothing and Who assembled them according to His plans and purposes. The account that is recorded for us in Genesis is the account written by the One Who actually made everything. The Genesis account is the Truth (John 17:17).

These comparisons highlight two fundamental principles which we should observe when thinking about origins:
- First: We should see the Genesis account of origins as pre-eminent and prior to pagan accounts, rather than derived from them. They are corruptions of the true account, which our Lord has carefully preserved for us in pure form in the Bible.
- Second: When dealing with scientific theories of origins, we should see them as merely the best guesses of the brightest minds of our culture, not as proven fact. The cosmos as we can observe it extends for over thirteen billion light years in every direction, and there is no end in sight. It is beyond reason to accept that a human being actually has the wisdom to deduce how it originally came to be. No one even knows how big it is![489 see note] We might ask for a bit more humility from those who make such grandiose claims. We should believe God, not question His word; and we should question human claims of "fact" instead of gullibly believing them.

Commentary and Theological Considerations:
Christian Revelation and our Approach to Understanding Genesis:
Given the origin of the first tablet we must approach it with great reverence, according to it the highest respect and honor. There are two considerations that we must remember when reading the creation account. First, it is dealing with a subject that is inherently beyond human understanding—a subject that is proper to God alone. Second, the Lord chose to communicate to us in human language about this subject. Thus we should assume that our Lord intended that we understand what He says about it.

When the ancients read Genesis they assumed that they were reading the Word of God and that He directly and clearly spoke to them through those words. We will assume the same. We will not assume that His thoughts are so high that His words do not actually communicate to us accurate and understandable ideas; that is, He did not speak to us with the expectation that we could not understand Him. That implies that we can understand what His words mean, even if we cannot understand the details of how they were enacted. He wants us to understand and to believe. This is the only reliable source of information about the creation that we possess.

> With great gratitude let us accept what is related [by Moses], not stepping out of our own limitations, and not testing what is above us as the enemies of truth did when, wishing to comprehend everything with their minds, they did not realize that human nature cannot comprehend the creation of God.[490]

When we fail to understand perfectly the details of how things took place it is because the acts of creation are uniquely the work of God and are intrinsically beyond our human capabilities. He is the creator, and we are His creatures. Therefore our understanding must be "in part." But as far as His explanation goes, we assume that He spoke to us in such a way that we can understand what He says and that His words express, to the limits of the human capability, a true impression of what He wanted to tell us—and what He wanted to tell us is what actually happened. Things that are far beyond our human comprehension He did not tell us about. He is not trying to be abstruse in the word that He gives to us, and we need not be trained philosophers or scientists to understand.

> You see, when God formed human beings in the beginning, he used to speak to them personally, in a way that was possible for human beings to understand him! This was the way, for example, that he came to Adam, the way he upbraided Cain, the way he conversed with Noah, the way he accepted Abraham's hospitality. And even when all human-kind fell into evil ways, the creator of all did not abandon the human race. Instead, when they then proved unworthy of his converse with them, he wanted to renew his love for them; he sent them letters as you do to people far away from you, and this drew all humankind back again to him. It was God who sent them letters, Moses who delivered them. What do the letters say? "In the beginning God made heaven and earth."[491]

In this commentary we will assume that a simple reading of the text of Genesis, with the understanding of it that can be gleaned by comparison with other texts of Scripture, will communicate to us the accurate truth about the origin of all things.

Because the creation of all things, the creation of humanity, the early sin-free times in the Garden of Eden, the Flood, etc. are intrinsically beyond our personal experience, and because they are speaking of things which we cannot directly handle or see, we must realize the nature of the journey on which we are embarking. The Fathers knew that this subject was awesome and mysterious, and therefore it was inevitable that while on it we would encounter things that we would be tempted to call unreasonable. We must resist that temptation. Remember what the Jewish scholar Saadia ben Joseph Gaon said:

> This treatise starts out with the preliminary observation that whoever ventures into it is seeking light on something that has never been beheld with human eyes nor has been perceived by the senses . . . When, then, we reach the conclusion that all things were created out of nothing, although our senses have never experienced anything like it, it is not meet for us to reject that conclusion or to say frivolously: "How can we acquiesce in anything like that of which we have never seen?"[492]

This wisdom applies to the creation and to various later events in Genesis as well.

If we can perceive a few logical causal connections from His word then that is wonderful. But humility demands that we always carefully limit our definitive assertions to those things that He told us. Thus if we hypothesize further than that, then we must acknowledge that what we are saying is speculative. In reading about the creation we are standing on the narrow boundary between the impenetrable mystery of that which properly belongs to God alone, and the gracious revelation that He has chosen to grant to us about how He made us and how He made all things. Thus we shall believe what He says because He has told us, but we will not go further, unless perhaps with some cautious speculation, because we are entering ground that is by nature beyond our ken.

This account of the origin of the universe cannot be accommodated to current scientific theories. But these are not new. Similar ideas were put forth by philosophers and discarded by the Fathers of the Church in the first centuries of the Christian era. Basil explains:

> Those who were too ignorant to rise to a knowledge of a God, could not allow that an intelligent cause presided at the birth of the Universe; a primary error that involved them in sad consequences. Some had recourse to material principles and attributed the origin of the Universe to the elements of the world. Others imagined that atoms, and indivisible bodies, molecules and ducts, form, by their union, the nature of the visible world. Atoms reuniting or separating, produce births and deaths, and the most durable bodies only owe their consistency to the strength of their mutual adhesion: a true spider's web woven by these writers who give to heaven, to earth, and to sea so weak an origin and so little consistency! It is because they knew not how to say "In the beginning God created the heaven and the earth." Deceived by their inherent atheism it appeared to them that nothing governed or ruled the universe, and that all was given up to chance. To guard us against this error the writer on the creation, from the very first words, enlightens our understanding with the name of God; "In the beginning God created."[493]

When scientists found that small particles of various types did make up the universe the name they gave them, in accord with the nomenclature of the ancients, was "atoms." Now we understand that these fundamental building blocks of matter are themselves composed of smaller particles (electrons, neutrons and protons) which are themselves sub-dividable into yet smaller sub-nuclear particles, which themselves are theorized to be built of even smaller objects that we call strings. Thus the hottest topic of study and speculation in particle physics today is String Theory. A foundational driving concept in all of the work today is the idea—the hope—that the universe can and will explained as the outworking of processes that flow from the nature of matter and that operate without God. This is the faith and the hope of the modern pseudo-scientific philosophers.

However we must understand that what we are reading about is a supernatural event that can never be explained as the outworking of natural causes operating under the known physical laws. Seeing Genesis in that way is the pit in which I once was trapped. It is our cultural inclination to take this attitude and to fall into this trap. This is because of the scientifically oriented culture in which we have been raised. The six days of creation, "the six days of awe," were uniquely the work of God alone. The creation of all things is an act that only God could perform. Man cannot peer within the six days of miraculous works by any art or science that he can devise. All that we can know about the six days and the early times of man is what God has chosen to reveal to us in His word.

I want to recall one personal experience that highlights what I am saying about how we read and understand Genesis. For years I was totally immersed in the secular theories of origins. It never occurred to me that they would affect my understanding of Genesis. That may sound a bit naïve but that was the way I thought. Then something happened that made me realize that those theories were not science and were not true! After that I returned to Genesis and read it. As I read I realized that I understood it quite clearly, and that it meant exactly what it said. I had been reading it with a veil over my eyes before that time, but I hadn't even known that I had such a veil. I had been attempting subconsciously to reconcile Genesis with secular theories, but it cannot be done. I was amazed at how clear Genesis was. Its meaning had been hiding from me in plain sight!

A plain reading of Genesis is certainly the way the Fathers approached it. We also must read it in this way, or we will never understand it. Of course we might make theological deductions from the text in various ways. And we can explain how it can be more fully understood by drawing out the spiritual and allegorical meanings that it has when it is read in the light of the New Testament. But under all such ideas the text has a literal historical sense that is its foundational meaning. Any "deeper" understandings will flow from and enhance the literal meaning. In approaching Genesis this way we will come to perceive a certain internal logic to its words, a logic that is enhanced by comparing it with other Scriptures. As a result of New Testament revelation we will see that the creation account speaks of Jesus and His role in the creation and also of the Holy Spirit and His role.

We will, of course, always use the "rule of faith" as our guide in all interpretations; that is, the faith once received from the Apostles by the action of the Holy Spirit that Jesus promised to send upon the Church (John 16:13, John 14:26), as it is expressed perfectly in and through the sacred Scriptures and was proclaimed by the Church from the beginning. The rule of faith injects the unique revelation that the Holy Spirit brought to the Church at Pentecost, and which He still grants to believers today. Thus the literal understanding of Genesis surely means that we will see the Son of God acting in the account of the creation, for by Him and through Him are all things.[494] The Jews did not understand this, but we see that it was in the pages of their holy documents from the beginning. Thus for Christians the literal meaning of Genesis is a spiritually discerned understanding. This insight has been with the Church since the earliest days, even since the Apostles.

In this commentary we will try to elucidate the literal historical meaning of the text of Genesis in light of this ancient insight given to the Church; that is, we will try to explain the historical events that this book is talking about, as well as spiritual insights that are deduced by comparison with related New and Old Testament texts. In this we follow in the path of Augustine who, more deeply than any other ancient commentator, tried to understand the spiritually discerned historical meaning that this book is conveying to us.

Augustine thought that every word of Genesis—every word of Scripture from whatever book—was inspired by God and thus was free from all error. Because his attempt to accurately comprehend the meaning of Genesis resulted in many penetrating insights, questions, and problems, we will quote from his works in this commentary more than from any other ancient writer. We will try to understand the text as he did, by reconstructing the historical scenario that the creation account is revealing to us.

From our perspective we have a tremendous advantage over the Fathers. Most of them were working from the LXX rather than the Masoretic text. Thus errors in the translation sometimes misled them. We take for granted that we have easy access to translations of the Scriptures, Bible dictionaries, concordances, cross references, archeological finds, maps, study guides, and instantaneous electronically based word studies. We are not wedded to the ancient cosmology which many ancients implicitly accepted.

But we will not make the mistake of gullibly accepting the present cosmological theories as fact either. The Fathers were devout and believing souls, possessed brilliant minds, and present us with many thoughtful and inspired meditations on the Scriptures. We can learn an immense amount from them, but we also have certain advantages over them, for we have methods and techniques for studying and investigating the Word that were unheard of in their day.

For convenience I will also include an alternative text of Genesis in those instances where it differs significantly from the Hebrew text, so we can see what the Fathers were using.

The basic scenario that we will assume in our reading of the creation account is that the Father is the preeminent creator and that He released the power of the Holy Spirit at the beginning. The Holy Spirit is the power of God. The Father issues the decree to create at each stage of the process. Each command is a divine authorization for the Son to create. The Son uses the power of the Holy Spirit to actuate the command of the Father. The Son is the Artist who fashions all things that we see around us. This is the dynamic of the interrelationships of the Trinity that stands behind the creation of all things and that we will see as we study the creation account in Genesis.

Day 1:
Genesis 1:1—In the beginning God created the heavens and the earth.

The word for God (*'elohiym*) is plural, hinting at a mysterious plurality of persons in God, and the verb for create (*bara*) is singular, showing the unity of God's being. So a unified action of all three persons of the Trinity is involved in the creation. Only God is uncreated substance. All else was summoned by Him from non-being by the free choice of His will and not because of any lack or necessity on His part. He created all things, and because of His will they existed and were created. (Revelation 4:11). In a special way the Father created through and by His Son who already was with God in the beginning before any other of the works of God came to be, and through Whom all things came into being (John 1:2–3). The entire creation is preeminently the work of the Father. But the Son participates in all that the Father does by using the power of the Holy Spirit that the Father grants to Him.

Revelation 4:11 says that "by Your will all things *are* and were created." Thus the on-going existence of all things is also the work of the Father. But if Jesus stopped "upholding the universe by the word of His power" (Hebrews 1:3) then all things would revert back into chaos, because "in Him all things are held together" (Colossians 1:17). From these two verses we can see that the continued existence of things is also dependent on the Son. The Father and the Son work together in creating and in upholding all things.

<u>In the Beginning</u>:
What is this "beginning" referring to? There was the beginning from before all ages in which the Father eternally begot His son. The Son partakes of the uncreated essence of the Father and thus is properly called God. But the beginning in this verse refers to the calling into existence of the created order; that is, of material substance that does not partake of the eternal essence of the Trinity. The Hebrew word used for "beginning" is the same word used in Proverbs 8:22, "The Lord possessed Me in the *beginning* of His way, before His works of old," which refers to the beginning before all beginnings.

But the beginning to which our verse refers—as to how this beginning came about—we can assume, from the fact that no verbal command is issued, that it was accomplished without any word being spoken by God, but merely by the act of His will, as indicated in Revelation 4:11, "Because of Your will all things existed and were created." Therefore this beginning is the original moment when the order of material things began. It was the agreed-upon work of all three persons of the Trinity, but enacted by the Father.

This verse reveals God creating in a way that contrasts to the other statements in this chapter. In those statements He says, "Let there be . . ." but here He creates without a word of bidding. Why is that so? Why doesn't He say, "Let there be heaven and earth?" In the other steps of creation God is speaking to His Son, the eternal Word, bidding Him to form various parts of the creation from material that already exists, and then the Son responds by so doing. At this time there is nothing in existence other than the Lord. This is creation *ex nihilo*. The Father is preeminently the One Who creates out of nothing, so He would be commanding Himself.

The initial work of creation was internal to the Trinity. It was a willing that took place "from everlasting . . . before the first dust of the world" (Proverbs 8:23, 26) when only "the Word was with God" (John 1:1). Thus a wordless willing is logical because before substance was called into being there was nothing about which God could command, nothing to which His word of bidding might direct His Son. The initial creative act brought into existence the first substance that was not a part of the divine essence.

This initial act of creating, which brought forth the first "formless and void" substance, was not accomplished by speaking a word but by an act of will that proceeded from the Father. Genesis 1:1 tells us why there is something rather than nothing at all. God, who is outside of the material realm and who by His very nature must be, willed into existence the contingent substance that makes up the world that we now inhabit. This calling forth of the primeval substance of the universe happened the moment before time began and was the beginning of the existence of matter and space as well. We can see this as the Father enacting a decision to create that was made in the eternal councils of the Trinity.

Because God is uncreated substance, and because the very existence of this realm or order of things is dependent on His decision, it is inconceivable that the act of creating could take any time. Created substance cannot resist His will. The initial creation was an instantaneous event. It happened at an indivisible instant before time began.
> Or, perhaps, the words "In the beginning he created," were used because of the instantaneous and timeless act of creation, since the beginning is something immeasurable and indivisible. As the beginning of the road is not yet the road, and the beginning of the house, not yet the house, so also, the beginning of time is not yet time, on the contrary, not even the least part of

it. And, if anyone should say contentiously that the beginning is time, let him know that he will be dividing it into parts of time. And these parts are beginning and middle and end. But, it is entirely ridiculous to think of the beginning of a beginning. Moreover, he who divides the beginning will make two instead of one, or rather, many and unlimited beginnings, since the part which is divided is always cut into other parts. In order, therefore, that we may be taught that the world came into existence instantaneously at the will of God, it is said: "In the beginning he created." Other interpreters of this, giving the meaning more clearly, have said: "God made summarily," that is, immediately and in a moment. Such, then, to mention a few from the many points, is the explanation concerning the beginning.[495]

Psalm 148:2 says, "praise Him all His angels" and then asserts, "For He commanded and they were created" (148:5), referring to the angels as well as the heavens, the sun, and the moon. So the creation of God extends beyond the material objects that are properly investigated by physics and the other natural sciences, and also includes the realm of spiritual things. Thus Genesis 1:1 might also be seen as being embedded within that broader reality. Not that this verse speaks of those spiritual realities. Although the broader biblical revelation tells us that the angels were part of the picture, in this verse they are present only in the background. God speaks to Job about this moment and says:

> Where were you when I laid the foundation of the earth? Tell *Me*, if you have understanding. Who set its measurements? Since you know. Or who stretched the line on it? On what were its bases sunk? Or who laid its cornerstone, when the morning stars sang together and all the sons of God shouted for joy? (Job 38:4–7)

Lateran IV teaches that the angels and all material substance was created at one instant.[496] They were likely created at the moment the heavens were called into being because they dwell there. While God created our physical world the "morning stars" sang together and the "sons of God" shouted for joy. This was often pondered by the Fathers, leading to various opinions: How/when did the creation of the angels fit into this creation account?

Thus Basil comments on the totality of created things as extending beyond the physical, opining that angels, as of a higher spiritual realm, were created before this world:

> In fact, there did exist something, as it seems, **even before this world**, which our mind can attain by contemplation, but which has been left uninvestigated because it is not adapted to those who are beginners and as yet infants in understanding. This was a certain condition older than the birth of the world and proper to the supramundane powers, one beyond time, everlasting, without beginning or end. In it the Creator and Producer of all things perfected the works of His art, a spiritual light befitting the blessedness of those who love the Lord, rational and invisible natures, and the whole orderly arrangement of spiritual creatures which surpass our understanding and of which it is impossible even to discover the names. These fill completely the essence of the invisible world, as Paul teaches us when he says: "For in him were created all things," whether visible or invisible, "whether Thrones, or Dominations, or Principalities, or Powers," or Forces, or hosts of Angels, or sovereign Archangels. When at length it was necessary that this world also be added to what already existed, primarily as a place of training and a school for the souls of men, then it was created a fit dwelling place for all things in general which are subject to birth and destruction . . . **[It is] not because he is testifying that according to seniority it [this world, this creation] was first of all that exists, [that] he [Moses] says that in the beginning it was created, but he is describing the existence of these visible and sensible creatures after that of the invisible.** [bolding mine][497]

He also notes that this world was created as a "school for the souls of men"—a place of training and preparation for man—not as our final dwelling. Since one third of the angels rebelled with Lucifer when he fell (Revelation 12:4), it is worthwhile to note that God in His wisdom did not make angels privy to all the divine counsels before the creation. These will be revealed by God successively throughout the centuries as His divine plans unfold within the pages of human history. The holy angels long to gain a glimpse into these.

> As to this salvation, the prophets who prophesied of the grace that *would come* to you made careful searches and inquiries, seeking to know what person or time the Spirit of Christ within them was indicating as He predicted the sufferings of Christ and the glories to follow. It was revealed to them that they were not serving themselves, but you, in these things which now have been announced to you through those who preached the gospel to you by the Holy Spirit sent from heaven—things into which angels long to look. (1 Peter 1:10–12)

> To bring to light the administration of the mystery which for ages has been hidden in God who created all things; so that the manifold wisdom of God might now be made known through the church to the rulers and the authorities in the heavenly *places*. (Ephesians 3:9–10)

In speaking of the fallen angels and their knowledge of the crucifixion Paul says:

> Yet we do speak wisdom among those who are mature; a wisdom, however, not of this age nor of the rulers of this age who are passing away; but we speak God's wisdom in a mystery, the hidden *wisdom* which none of the rulers of this age has understood; for if they had understood it they would not have crucified the Lord of glory. (1 Corinthians 2:8)

The "rulers of this age" are not human potentates but Satan and his minions, the "prince of the power of the air" (Ephesians 2:2). How wise of our Lord to refuse them access to His plans for redeeming men! Paul notes that they would never have worked to fulfill the destiny of Jesus to be sacrificed as the "Lamb foreordained from before the foundation of the world" if they had understood the mystery of the cross—the plan of God from before all ages to redeem unto Himself a people cleansed by the blood of His beloved Son.

God knew that some of the angels would fall away and that they would deceive mankind into falling captive to them as well. Therefore He did not reveal all of His plans to them—His plans about how He would purchase us back from their dark power and use their very envy and pride to bring His plan to perfection. The fall of certain of the angels, and their influence in the affairs of men, is vital to explaining the tragic twist that continually inserts itself into human history. It is comforting to know that the Holy One has so determined His purposes that He would not allow us to be swept away in their evil plans. They are more cunning than we, are but they are not wiser than God. This perspective offers us a host of reasons why we should trust God and His word, "a lamp for our feet and a light for our path" (Psalm 119:105).

<u>Fear of the Lord—Awe before Him</u>:
The Fathers saw the "six days of awe" as containing an impenetrable mystery that only God can know. That is, the creation of all things is beyond our human comprehension. We have no experience of it, and no way of comprehending all that was really going on. We can only know what God tells us. I want to restore this sense of awe at His majesty to our twenty-first century minds. That means removing some of our preconceptions about the world around us. The idea that this creation truly has a supernatural origin must mean that we take such a perspective as this. At the root of all reality we must realize that existence itself is a mystery. I also want to reemphasize that God has told us what He did and how He did it because He wants us to understand and to be in awe of Him. We should accept what He tells us as true because He would not lie to us or deceive us. He chose to speak to us about this subject because He wanted us to know Him and to understand something of who he is through this account of creation.

God Created:

The plural Hebrew word for God (*'elohiym*) is used throughout the creation account to refer to God. In light of the New Testament we see this as referring to the action of the Trinity of persons in the creation events. But the word for create in 1:1 is *bara'*, a singular, (used only with God as the subject) meaning shape, fashion, or create. Together these indicate, even in the first verse of the Bible, a plurality of persons but a unity of being in God. The Ancient Faith states this was creation from non-being because God is Almighty and needed nothing else to create. He called forth a primordial substance from non-being by an act of His will, then fashioned all material objects from that substance.

The word *bara'* is used two other times in the creation account, always to introduce a new realm of being in God's creation. It is used in 1:21 to refer to the creation of animal life—everything which moves and possesses the breath of life. It is used in 1:27 to speak of the creation of man, who possesses an immortal soul and is in the very image of God. This shows us an additional distinction in the creation of God: Plant life can be viewed as complex biochemical formations, but not as life in the same way as animals and men; animals are not merely complex chemical machines, for they have awareness and they respond with consciousness to their environment; and mankind is aware and also is designed to fellowship with God because of the immortal soul that is a part of his basic constitution. Therefore, the creation acts of days five and six differ in that they involve something more than just the reconfiguring of the initial primordial substance. In all other descriptions of what God is doing during the six days we will understand Him to be reconfiguring the basic material that He called into existence "in the beginning" to form the structures we see in the world about us—the stars, the oceans, the continents, etc.

The Heaven(s) and the Earth:

The Hebrew word for heavens is *shamayim* and is plural. The singular of this word does not appear in the Bible, but sometimes this plural word is translated as "heavens" and sometimes as "heaven." In the LXX account of the creation the Greek word was translated as heaven in the singular. Thus some Fathers insisted that there is only one heaven. But others allowed for several. Here we might ask what is being referred to by heaven or heavens. We can understand this phrase as referring to the physical heaven that we can observe with our senses, both in and above earth's atmosphere, and in and above the starry heights. But at this time these parts of the creation have not yet been formed and so we should realize that "heavens" refers to the initial unformed substance that would eventually be made into what we now see around us as the atmospheric and the starry heavens. Because of the other Scriptures that reveal to us a broader reality in Scripture this sometimes refers to the spiritual realm which is understood as the dwelling place of God and of the holy angels, a spiritual reality. However in this Scripture verse the context indicates that it refers to the physical realities, but not yet fully formed.

In our modern cosmologies we have called this "space" or the "ether." It would seem to be necessary, since God created it, that it is not "nothing" or "empty." Space is something.

The word for earth is *'erets* in Hebrew and can refer to the whole earth as opposed to just a part of the earth, the earth as opposed to the heavens, or the inhabited earth. Here the combination of the words "heaven and earth" should be seen as referring to the entire realm of physical things in their primordial unformed state.

<u>The Permanent Endurance of Creation</u>:
The holiest name of God, by which He revealed Himself to the patriarchs and to Moses at the burning bush, is translated as "I am" or "I am who am" or "I am that I am." God is who or what must exist. This is because it is His nature to be. He is the only thing that is not a contingent being. It is His nature to exist. He always has existed and always will. Unlike all created substance, He is unique unto Himself, the foundation of all existence. He is the reason why there is something rather than nothing at all. He is the answer to the conundrum of the cosmological theories: How/why did things come into existence? It was by the Father's will that all things are and were created (Revelation 4:11).

In contrast, this creation was not necessary. It was contingent upon His free choice to make it. Therefore, can He or will He eventually revoke His decision and let it fall back into nothingness? Many Scriptures indicate that this initial act of God's will, the choice He made to create, will never be revoked.

> He commanded and they were created [sun, moon, angels, etc.]. He has also established them forever and ever. He has made a decree which will not pass away. (Psalm 148:5–6)

> A generation goes and a generation comes, but the earth remains forever. (Ecclesiastes 1:4)

> Like the earth which He has founded forever. (Psalm 78:69)

> He established the earth upon its foundations, so that it will not totter forever and ever. (Psalm 104:5)

> and those who lead the many to righteousness [are] like the stars forever and ever. (Daniel 12:3)

Therefore, it seems that this act of "willing forth" the universe from nothing is irrevocable.

However, the fundamental nature of the world is predicted to change at some future time that has not been specified. For the "form of this world is passing away" (1 Corinthians 7:31), and also, "heaven and earth will pass away, but My words will never pass away" (Matthew 24:35). Thus a radical and fundamental transformation is in the future, one that will produce new heavens and a new earth that will be a perfectly suited dwelling for the redeemed—that will be in accordance with their glorified state. Those immersed in the study of "this world only" can be deceived about the ultimate destiny of things.

> Doubtless, their superfluous worldly wisdom will one day make their condemnation more grave because, while they are so keenly aware of vain matters, they have been blinded to the comprehension of the truth. They who measure the distances of the stars and register both those in the north, which are always shining above the horizon, and those which lie about the south pole visible to the eye of man there, but unknown to us; who also divide the northern zone and the zodiac into numberless spaces; who carefully observe the rising of the stars, their fixed positions, their descent, their recurrence, and the length of time in which each of the wandering stars completes its orbit; these men have not found one means from all this either to understand that God is the Creator of everything and the just Judge who gives the deserved reward for the actions of our life, or to acknowledge the idea of a consummation of all things consequent upon the doctrine of judgment, namely that it is necessary for the world to be changed if truly the state of the souls is to change to another form of life. As the present life has a nature akin to this world, so also the future existence of our souls will receive a lot consistent with its state.[498]

As we will note as we go on, the formation of the objects in this world can change from age to age, but the basic existence of which they all partake is established forever. The subsequent acts of creation will form this basic substance into the various objects that we see in the world around us. From the Scripture verses quoted it is also apparent that the earth, sun, moon, and stars will continue to exist in some form, however things are refashioned in subsequent ages. These observations are confirmed from scientific evidence for the permanent nature of the basic substance of the creation. The first law of thermodynamics states that the sum total of all matter and energy in the universe is constant. Thus, even if something is burned up its substance is merely transformed into other matter or into energy. Even if matter is "dissolved" by a nuclear reaction it merely changes partly into energy. At the sub-nuclear level it seems as if the basic substance always remains, but its outward form can be altered or transformed in various ways. All these observations are consistent with the idea that the initial decision of God to create this world will never be revoked. But the form of things can and will radically change.

When God laid the foundation of the earth did it contain radioactive material in it? The crust of the earth might not have had anything in it that was decaying at that time. The sin of Adam introduced corruption and death into this creation (Romans 8:19–21). It is a widespread fact that radiometric measurements of the crust of the earth show it to be several billion years old. But it is also a fact that other radiometric measurements show that its age is only a matter of thousands of years, and that the crust of the earth was formed very quickly, not over eons of time. There is also strong evidence that the rate of radioactive decay was much higher at some time in the past, probably during the Deluge.[499] This mixture of readings is not widely known, yet it has been documented for decades by scientists. It does not make sense if we interpret the reading from a purely naturalistic point of view, but the biblical account of creation explains it plausibly.

Here is a simple way to look at it that I am proposing. It is likely that when God cursed the ground after Adam's sin then radioactive decay began, proceeding at accelerated rates at various times, up to and during the Deluge. Present "mixed data" readings are a result of that event and of the fact that most scientists assume that what we see today is the outworking of the present physical laws continuously operating without interruption. But earth's creation and the curses that followed upon the fall were not accomplished by the working out of natural processes. They were divine interventions in history.

A Brief Survey of Radiometric Dating Results:
There are a variety of radiometric dating techniques that scientists employ to estimate the ages of rocks and fossils. One well known method is carbon 14 dating, a technique that was developed by Willard Libby in the late 1940's. He won the Nobel Prize in Chemistry in 1960 for his work. How does carbon 14 dating work?

As long as a biological organism is alive it interacts with the atmosphere to maintain the same tiny percent of C-14 in itself as is circulating the earth's atmosphere, about 1 C-14 atom per 1 trillion total carbon atoms. But once an organism dies its interchange with the atmosphere of the earth stops. As the C-14 atoms which it contained decay into nitrogen 14 they are not replaced, and the percent of C-14 in that organism gradually decreases.

Every 5730 years half of the C-14 atoms change into nitrogen. Thus if we measure the percentage of C-14 atoms in an object that used to be a living organism we can tell how long it has been dead. For example, if a fossil, a piece of coal, a diamond, oil from an oil well, or any other carbon-based substance is tested and is found to have just 1 C-14 atom per 2 trillion total atoms of carbon then that indicates it is about 5730 years old, since half of its C-14 atoms have changed into nitrogen. Here are a few examples:

Amount of C-14 per Total Carbon Content	Age of Material in years
1 C-14 atom per 4 trillion total carbon atoms	11,460
1 C-14 atom per 8 trillion total carbon atoms	17,190
1 C-14 atom per 32 trillion total carbon atoms	28,650
1 C-14 atom per 256 trillion total carbon atoms	45,840

Therefore, a substance that has only 1 C-14 atom per 1024 trillion total carbon atoms would be about 57,300 years old, and that is the lower limit that our instruments can measure. In just 1 million years the entire earth, if it started out as 100% C-14, would decay into nitrogen. So this method can be used for dates less than 60,000 years, and no organic or organically based substance more than 60,000 years old can have detectable amounts of C-14 in it. In other words, such old substances should be "carbon dead." In particular, since evolution requires many millions of years, so that all fossils taken from the fossil record are many millions of years old, they should have no measurable amounts of C-14 in them. And no rock formation from the geological column should have measurable C-14.

In the last few decades much C-14 testing has been performed on materials that have an organic base such as coal, diamonds, marble, natural gas, fossil wood, etc. Following are a few of the results of those measurements.
1. A survey of articles from reputable journals showed seventy-eight different types of carbon-based substances that were assumed to be "carbon dead," (because they all were from the fossil record or the geologic column, and were presumed to be millions of years old) but which had measurable amounts of C-14 in them.[500]
2. In a pointed test of this by geologists, 10 samples of coal and 7 samples of diamonds from three continents were all found to have measurable amounts of C-14 in them.[501]
3. Twenty dinosaur bones from different regions and strata, each supposedly millions of years old, were tested and found to have measurable amounts of C-14 in them.

There are far too many similar results even to refer to here. Two researchers in the field summarized these recent findings as follows:
> "It is remarkable, but essentially everything in the fossil record contains measurable amounts of carbon-14. This seems contrary to popular wisdom, but it is widely recognized within the carbon-14 community. Taken at face value, this suggests that the entire fossil record is less than 100,000 years old. Many will be offended by this idea—but like it or not, this is what the carbon-14 dating appears to be showing."[502]

Such results show conclusively that the standard dates given for the fossil record and for the geologic strata in which they are found are not even close to accurate. Specimens with ages in the millions or billions of years have measurable amounts of C-14 in them!

In addition to these results some ingenuous tests have been performed with other radiometric dating techniques, which are able to give measurements in the range of millions and billions of years. The age of volcanic rock is often measured by the Potassium-Argon method, giving very old ages for lava flows. As a check, this technique was also used to measure the age of historic lava flows. It still gave old ages. Some examples:
1. Volcanic rock from the 1980 Mount St. Helens volcano was 350,000 years old.[503]
2. Rocks from the Mt. Ngauruhoe eruption that were less than 100 years old tested out as up to 3.5 million years old.[504]
3. Rocks from Hawaii eruptions in 1800-1801 tested out as 275,000 years old and 1.6 million years old in two different Potassium-Argon dating procedures.[505]

4. New Zealand volcano eruptions from 1949, from 1954, and from 1975 tested out to be between 275,000 years old and 3.5 million years old. The same flow was also tested using a Lead-Lead method and measured to be 3.9 billion years old.[506]

Thus the large ages given by other radiometric dating methods are clearly unreliable for proving that the age of the geologic column, the fossils contained within it, and the earth itself, are many millions or billions of years old. One simple explanation for this disparity in results is that radioactive decay rates were higher in the past. Another hypothesis is that some of the daughter elements produced by the decay process were present when the sample was laid down initially, and are not just the result of radioactive decay in place. And there are other imponderables. Such mixed results would be expected if we view the rock layers as having been disturbed and/or intermingled by the Flood and if we look at decay as having begun after the curse, and as having proceeded at uneven rates in the past.

To understand what we are observing in the world today we must take into account the supernatural acts of God in the past as they are faithfully recorded in His word. These have been followed by various "secondary causes," which we now know as the physical laws, operating for many years. Thus "natural history" is a combination of explicitly divine acts and "normal" or "natural" physical processes. This brings to our attention a third important principle for understanding origins:

- The universe, the earth, human life, and all life had a supernatural origin, not an origin from the outworking of natural processes. To understand the world as it now is we must take this into account. No naturalistic explanation of all radiometric data will ever be possible. They must be understood as the outworking of first causes (God's direct actions as He explains them to us in His holy word) followed by secondary causes (the physical laws that science has discovered). Even then our understanding will always be partial and incomplete. The ultimate origin of all things is shrouded in an impenetrable mystery knowable only to the Creator Himself.

The world around us is decaying at many levels: nations and cultures are rising and falling; Ideologies and political movements come and go; people are born and die; Buildings and structures wear out and crumble; Mountains and lakes grow and subside; materials of various kinds decay radioactively at various rates; even protons (probably) decay with a half-life of about 10^{32} years—and they are necessary to all atomic forms and thus to all material substances. Thus the form of this universe is limited in its lasting power. Only the underlying sub-nuclear substance is permanent. At a proper future moment the Lord will reconstitute this creation in a way that will grant all its structures permanence. The new heaven and the new earth will endure forever (Revelation 21:1, Isaiah 66:22).

Reaction of the Scientific Community to Radiocarbon Test Results—One Instance:
On April 9, 2012, a group of ten scientists were invited to give a presentation in August of that year at the Asia Oceania Geoscience Society. Their abstract dealt with the C-14 dating of dinosaur bones. They explain that carbonized wood and dinosaur bone fragments from a site in Texas showed measurable amounts of C-14, indicating that the ages of the objects were less than 50,000 years. Testing of dinosaur fragments from the Carnegie Museum of Natural History showed similar results. These test results are part of a more expansive group of tests performed on carboniferous materials that were thought (or assumed) to be many millions of years old, but all of which test out to be less than 50,000 years old.[507]

Their presentation was rescinded and deleted from the AOGC website. The lab that did the testing also contacted the scientists and notified them that they would not accept any further samples from them for C-14 testing. One of the ten scientists in the group was a chemist named Hugh Miller of the International Paleo-chronology Group. Here are copies of the correspondence that he received from the AOGC and the radiocarbon laboratory at the University of Georgia.[508]

From the AOGC Conference leadership:

AOGS Society T03SS0141H
AOGS Secretariat Office
C/o Meeting Matters International
Tel: (65) 6472 3108 Fax: (65) 6472 3208
Add: #06-23, ONE COMMONWEALTH
1 Commonwealth Lane, Singapore 149544
Email: info@asiaoceania.org

Hugh Miller, Consulting Chemist
Paleo Group, USA
Email: hugoc14@aol.com

Dear Mr. Miller,

Presentation: BG02-D3-PM2-Leo2-005: A Comparison of δ13C & pMC Values for Ten Cretaceous-jurassic Dinosaur Bones from Texas to Alaska, USA, China and Europe

As a result of comments from attendees at the recent AOGS-AGU (WPGM) meeting in Singapore we have examined your abstract which was delivered in session BG-02.

The interpretation which you present in your abstract is that the age of various dinosaurs, previously interpreted as being Mesozoic in age, are less than ~50,000 years. Your report that these ages were calculated using C-14 methods. There is obviously an error in these data. The abstract was apparently not reviewed properly and was accepted in error. For this reason we have exercised our authority as program chairs and rescinded the abstract. The abstract will no longer appear on the AOGS web site.

Program Chairs,
Minhan Dai, Xiamen University
Peter Swart, University of Miami

From the radiocarbon laboratory at the University of Georgia:

> **Jeff Speakman**
>
> From: Jeff Speakman
> Sent: Monday, July 21, 2014 12:28 PM
> To: 'HugoC14@aol.com'
> Subject: Radiocarbon Dating
>
> Dear Mr. Miller,
>
> I have recently become aware of the work that you and your team have been conducting with respect to radiocarbon dating of bone. The scientists at CAIS and I are dismayed by the claims that you and your team have made with respect to the age of the Earth and the validity of biological evolution. Consequently, we are no longer able to provide radiocarbon services in support of your anti-scientific agenda. I have instructed the Radiocarbon Laboratory to return your recent samples to you and to not accept any future samples for analysis.
>
> Sincerely,
> Jeff Speakman
>
> Jeff Speakman, Ph.D.
> Director, Center for Applied Isotope Studies
> University of Georgia
> 120 Riverbend Rd.
> Athens GA 30602-4702

It is clear that if the crust of the earth and the fossils that are embedded in it are found to be merely thousands of years old then evolution cannot be the explanation for how the life forms around us arose. This pulls the foundation out from under the Cartesian-Darwinian view of the world because such "scientific" explanations are necessary to substantiate and prove its basic assertion that "God never works a miracle." Such an anti-supernaturalistic world view must provide a natural-cause explanation for everything, and gradual evolution over millions of years is the only possible naturalistic explanation for the origin of life.

I am certain that the scientists who put forth evolution as the explanation for how life began are confident that it is true. Therefore, although Hugh Miller and his colleagues invited the other scientists to check their work, they did not do so. There was no need. They had to be wrong. Thus objective inquiry was stifled. A "cancel culture" was effectively installed in academia and certain concepts and results were peremptorily dismissed. The accuracy of millions of books and journal articles was hanging in the balance. The reputations and the careers of thousands of highly respected men and women were on the line. An entire world view—an entire world, along with the people who lived in it—was in jeopardy.

The Divine Purpose of Creation:
The Bible also tells us how God planned the world before He made it, and in doing so it offers us an insight into the purposes of God in creating us. The Father and the Son made the ages of the world together (Hebrews 1:3). At that time, the Father predestined us to be before Him in love as His sons (Ephesians 1:5). He foresaw that we would fall into sin and determined to sacrifice His only begotten Son for us at that time, for He is the Lamb foreordained from before the foundation of the world (1 Peter 1:20). In other words, He did not choose to create until the decision had been made to redeem us. God would not have created us if it would have necessarily resulted in our eternal damnation.

The Necessity of the Cross:

The cross of Jesus was such a difficult and strenuous thing for Him to go through. Was it really necessary? Couldn't God have simply decreed that mankind be forgiven? For no judge sits above Him, and His decisions are final. Couldn't He have simply decreed that we should be forgiven and cleansed of our sin? It would seem, as these thoughts indicate, that He could have done just that. Thus the cross was not necessary. No one and no thing compelled God to save us through the cross of Jesus Christ. Because God is God, the Most High One, the cross was not necessary. But . . .

If God had merely decreed our forgiveness, or if He had declared it through some way of lesser pain and sorrow, then the deeply serious nature of sin would not have been so clearly displayed. The seriousness of our relationship with Him, the catastrophic nature of the breach in that loving bond, the meaning of human life and of the purpose that He had when He created us, would have been understated. Because of the depth of His love for us, because of the hurt that sin inflicted upon Him, because of the precious way that He treasures us, this single awesome act was necessary. It was the only way for Him to redeem us that faithfully expressed all of these realities.[509] Thus, divine justice could only be fully satisfied by this redemptive act—overcoming selfishness by selfless love.

Because of the cross we see the supreme love that He has for mankind. We truly have been created in His image and likeness. We truly are His beloved sons and daughters. We are members of His family as surely as is His Eternal Word, the Only Begotten God. Only the cross could speak of this. Therefore the role of Jesus in history as the Lamb of God Who takes away the sins of the world is a window into the heart of God that shows us His goodness and His love for us, and that reveals to us as nothing else could just Who He is and what place we have in His heart and in His plans.

The wounds of Jesus by which He purchased us back for Himself are clearly displayed to all in heaven (Revelation 5:6) for the Lamb is standing as if slain; that is, still bearing the marks of His slaughter. The mystics say that the sight of His wounds is the greatest of consolations to the saints in heaven. And the light of the New Jerusalem is Jesus the Lamb (Revelation 21:23). It is not Jesus the Word of God or Jesus the Good Shephard that is its light, but Jesus the Lamb is the One Who enlightens that eternal holy city.

Thus, because of His love for us; because of His nature of perfect goodness and love; because of the place that He had destined for us before Him as His beloved daughters and sons; because of all these things, the cross was infinitely appropriate. The Love of God constrained Him to choose the cross as the means of redeeming us. The steadfast lovingkindness of the Father demanded that He openly give all that He had. The love of the Son compelled such a giving of His own life for us.

Thus because God is God Almighty the cross was not necessary or forced upon Him. But because God is Abba, the cross was necessary as the completely fit expression of His love for us and of our predestined place in His family. Love is not love unless it is freely given. The sacrifice of Jesus was perfect love, given freely by Him and by the Father.

The Cross was Foreordained:

An absolute prerequisite for the creation was the Father's decision to sacrifice His only begotten Son for us, and the Son's willingness to allow Himself to be sacrificed. This truth of their incomprehensible love preceded the act of creation. It is the first and foundational love of all existence, and it is also the underlying principle that governs all of our human relationships. This is because we were created in His image and likeness and are destined to share in the life and the relationships of the Trinity forever.

> By this the love of God was manifested in us that God has sent His only begotten Son into the world so that we might live through Him. In this is love, not that we loved God, but that He loved us and sent His Son *to be* the propitiation for our sins. Beloved, if God so loved us, we also ought to love one another. No one has seen God at any time; if we love one another, God abides in us, and His love is perfected in us. By this we know that we abide in Him, and He in us, because He has given us of His Spirit. We have seen and testify that the Father has sent the Son *to be* the Savior of the world. (1 John 4:9–14)

The revelation of the Lord God as generous, selfless, self-sacrificing love is diametrically opposed to the carnal, selfish, vicious gods of the pagan myths. His purity of motive, the wisdom, majesty, and power that is forever manifested in His acts of creation, His beauty—all of these attributes are why He is worthy of honor and glory and power (Revelation 4:11). This foundational truth gives us the eternal purpose for our existence and also shows us how to conduct our lives while on this earth.

Jesus asked the Father to give those whom He was about to redeem a place with Him so that we could behold His glory, the glory that He had with the Father before the worlds were formed (John 17:24). What we live in a partial way on this earth, which is merely a place of preparation for eternity, will be perfected in us when we see Him face to face (1 Corinthians 13:12). The shadows of eternity amidst which we live in this life will give way to the realities that can never pass away. We are being prepared for this weight of glory. This is a powerful motivation for us to live in a good, upright, and loving way.

> See how great a love the Father has bestowed on us, that we would be called children of God; and *such* we are. For this reason the world does not know us, because it did not know Him. Beloved, now we are children of God, and it has not appeared as yet what we will be. We know that when He appears, we will be like Him, because we will see Him just as He is. And everyone who has this hope *fixed* on Him purifies himself, just as He is pure. (1 John 3:1–3)

When the predestined number of people have been born and prepared for life with God then this world will be reconstituted into its permanent state. It will no longer be a place of preparation, but the eternal place where we will dwell with the Lord God forever.

Genesis 1:2a—The earth was formless and void and darkness was over the surface of the deep

The words "formless and void" indicate material that is a jumble, both disordered and chaotic. Imagine a bunch of cut trees lying about in a large open area, but which would someday be a made into a building. There is no discernable order or purpose to them when you see them scattered around in the open field. The original substance was of this nature. There was no light, but everything was dark. The "deep" is used to refer to the waters of a deep ocean or of a subterranean basin. The first state of things was not very appealing. It was not livable at all.

Returning to the Hebrew word *bara'*, it can mean to create or to form. By saying that the initial state of the creation was "formless and void" it is immediately implied that the first act of creation was not to form or shape anything. Because it resulted in something that was formless and void the word in this instance must refer to creating out of nothing.

<u>Meditation on "Formless and Void":</u>
Matter that is "formless and void" is something we have no experience with. We always assume that matter, when it exists, possesses the properties that we have discovered in our investigations into physics. That is, we see the physical laws as part of matter at all times. But at this initial moment a certain type of basic "primordial substance" is called into being by God, and it is not necessary to assume that it is obeying the physical laws that we normally associate with matter—not when it is described as "formless and void." The physical laws (gravity, momentum, conservation of matter and energy, Boyle's laws governing gases, etc.) were not in effect. God had just made something out of nothing! But I assume that this primordial substance had within itself the potential to support and become all of the structures that God would form from it. However at this initial moment of the creation it had not **necessarily** been actuated or endowed with any specific qualities.

Creation violated of the law of conservation of matter and energy, the very first law of thermodynamics. Eventually God will establish the ordinances that govern the physical realm. This is part of His work of the six days. Thus at the end of that time the creation will be complete; that is, the various structures will all be in place, the physical laws will be set in operation, and the entire created realm will be functioning in an orderly and "very good" way. In general, the physical laws are in effect because of the decree of the Lord, not because matter has an inherent nature to behave in a certain way. The nature of matter that we observe and the physical laws that it now follows, were not **necessarily** part of its initial existence. God infused the current laws into matter at some point during the six days; or we can equivalently say that He overrode them during the six days and only allowed them to take effect after the six days of creation were completed.

Genesis 1:2b—And the Spirit of God was moving over the surface of the waters

Jerome has explained that, according to the Hebrew meaning of *moving*, we understand "brooding" or "keeping warm" as a mother bird over her young.[510] Thus "spirit" (Heb. *ruwach*) cannot refer to a wind, but must be personal; that is, the Holy Spirit. He was dispatched at the beginning of the creation when the Father called the primordial substance into existence, and He was waiting for the word of God's command when He would transform the newly-created chaotic substance into the orderly cosmos that we see around us. He was "brooding," quivering, full of energy, waiting to impart this to the creation, which seems at this point to be a stagnant chaos. The phrase "surface of the waters" implies that there was a great primeval store of water that God called into existence at first. It is not clear from this first verse whether there was any solid material intermixed with that water.

Genesis 1:3—Then God said, "Let there be light"; and there was light.

This is the first verbal statement of the creation account. Let us use it to establish the order of the roles within the Trinity during the creation. It is written, "For God who said, 'Light shall shine out of darkness,' is the One who has shone in our hearts to give the light of the knowledge of the glory of God" (2 Corinthians 4:6). Thus we should see this command (and thus all of the creative commands) as coming from the Father. The Holy Spirit was hovering over the deep waiting for this command. But to whom was the command of the Father directed? We assume that He was speaking to someone, and only His Son was there with Him, so the Word heard the command and carried it out, bringing forth light.

More Details on the Roles within the Trinity:
When God sent His Son to earth a new revelation about the Trinity was granted to us. We can use that New Testament information to explain the roles within the Trinity during the creation. This insight will make the logic of the creation scenario much clearer.

Jesus explains a key fact about the Holy Spirit.
> When the Helper comes, whom I will send to you from the Father, *that is* the Spirit of truth **who proceeds from the Father**, He will testify about Me. (John 15:27)

The Holy Spirit proceeds from, or comes forth from, the Father. At the beginning of things we see Him brooding over the primordial unformed substance. He was dispatched by the Father with the initial act of creation, as the Father willed the primordial substance to be.
> And Jesus returned to Galilee in the power of the Spirit. (Luke 4:14)
> but you will receive power when the Holy Spirit has come upon you. (Acts 1:8)

The power to carry out the actions of God comes by and through the Holy Spirit, whether the Father or the Son carries out that action. The Holy Spirit is the power of God.

John also gives us foundational information about the Son.
> All things came into being through Him, and apart from Him nothing came into being. (John 1:3)

Therefore the Son is working with the Father throughout the entire creation.
> Then I was beside Him, *as* a master workman and I was daily His delight. Rejoicing always before Him, rejoicing in the world, His earth, and *having* my delight in the sons of men. (Proverbs 8:30–31)

So Jesus was like a master craftsman in the work that He did. He was enjoying the Father's creation and especially the earth and the area where human beings are.

We can use these ideas to make some general observations about the creation scenario. The Father creates *ex nihilo* and the Son "forms," "molds," or "makes" the various structures that are created. He works at the bidding of the Father. As the creation proceeds the part that the Son plays becomes more and more evident. A repeated phrase "it was so" is the Hebrew word *ken* meaning "thus" or "just so." It first appears in verse 7 and accompanies the completion of a creative effort. It can be viewed as an affirmation by the Son that He has done the bidding of the Father. The Father gives His approval by saying "it is good."

So God spoke. There are three questions that come to mind about this verse. First, in what way do we understand the assertion that God spoke? Does He have a mouth and lungs with which to send sound out into the air? Was there air to carry the sound? The Fathers often asked questions of this sort. This is the type of question that one would ask if he believed that every word of the Bible was true and was communicating to us objective historical facts. The ancients pointed out that such a view of God was not in accord with His spiritual nature and must be seen as a way of accommodating His account to our human perspective and understanding. That certainly makes sense.

But I have experienced times when the Lord spoke to me. For instance I asked Him why I always got angry in certain situations. He said to me, "You're a proud man, Mike." The words were sent to me in my inner man. I knew for certain that they would never have been heard by someone else if they had been next to me. I perceived them in English, the only language that I know, and they were very definitely from Jesus in heaven. I could even say that the tone of His voice was like silver bells—very sweet and kind, and yet masculine. So I assume that when the Father spoke at the time of the creation as recorded in the account of the six days, His words were sent to the Son without lungs or mouth or air, in a way that was independent of any language, in a way appropriate to the demands of the task to which they are directed, and with divine power that resulted in the fulfillment of what they had commanded. The command was directed to the Son and the divine power for completing the command was the Holy Spirit.

So God was speaking to His Son. Augustine explains:
> It is by the Word, always adhering to the Father that God eternally says everything, not with the sound of a voice or with thoughts running through the time which sound takes, but with the light, co-eternal with Himself, of the Wisdom He has begotten . . . Accordingly where scripture states "God said let it be made," we should understand an incorporeal utterance of God in the substance of His co-eternal Word, calling back to Himself the imperfection of the [initial formless and void] creation, so that it should not be formless, but should be formed, each element on the particular lines that follow in due order.[511]

The complete instantaneous response of the physical realm to the creative commands of God was the common point of view of the Fathers.
> You see, this is God's way: created things are governed by his will. "The water under heaven was gathered together into its masses, and the dry land appeared." Just as in the case of the light, when darkness was everywhere, he ordered the creation of the light, and caused a division between the light and the darkness, so as to assign one to the day and the other to the night.[512]

Likewise in speaking of the third day when vegetation was created instantly:
> According to the text, the Lord gave directions and at once the earth went into labor and adorned itself with its own crop of seeds.[513]

Psalm 33:9: "For He spoke, and it was done. He commanded, and it stood fast."

Basil explains that God's way of relating the creation forces us to consider the Son Who was working with the Father in all that was transpiring. It induces us to realize His role.
> [L]et us first inquire how God speaks. Is it in our manner? Or, is the image of the objects first formed in His intellect, then, after they have been pictured in His mind, does He make them known by selecting from substances the distinguishing marks characteristic of each? Finally, handing over the concepts to the vocal organs for their service, does He thus manifest His hidden thought by striking the air with the articulate movement of the voice? Surely it is fantastic to say that God needs such a roundabout way for the manifestation of His thoughts. Or, is it not more in conformity with true religion to say that the divine will joined with the first impulse of His intelligence is the Word of God? ***The Scripture delineates Him in detail in order that it may show that God wished the creation not only to be accomplished, but also to be brought to this birth through some co-worker.*** It could have related everything fully as it began, "In the beginning God created the heavens and the earth," then, "He created light," next, "He created the firmament." But, now, introducing God as commanding and speaking, it indicates silently Him to whom He gives the command and to whom He speaks, not because it begrudges us the knowledge, but that it might inflame us to a desire by the very means by which it suggests some traces and indications of the mystery . . . By these means Scripture leads us on to the idea of the Only-begotten in a certain orderly way. And surely, for an incorporeal nature there was no need for vocal speech, since the thoughts themselves could be communicated to His Co-worker. ***So, what need was there of speech for those who are able by the thought itself to share their plans with others? . . . [T]herefore, this way of speaking has been wisely and skillfully employed so as to rouse our mind to an inquiry of the Person to whom these words are directed*** [emphasis added].[514]

Once we have considered how we might understand that "God spoke," the next questions that present themselves are "why" and "how" it could be that light was created before the heavenly luminaries? The first of these two questions asks "why". This was understood in various ways and from various perspectives by the Fathers. One answer was given by

Chrysostom. He said that this was so that man might understand that the gift of light was from God and that it could never be attributed to any created thing—including the sun or the moon—which pagan peoples were inclined to worship. Instead these were created after the fact and appointed to rule over the day and the night.[515]

However, Aquinas looked at the release of light at such an early stage of the creation as being most appropriate. It was the divine action that dealt with the most basic type of "formlessness" that was inherent in the primordial substance. For light is one quality that is most fundamentally proper to all physical bodies, thus it was first instilled in matter.

> Mention is made of several kinds of formlessness, in regard to the corporeal creature. One is where we read that "the earth was void and empty" and another where it is said that "darkness was upon the face of the deep." Now it seems to be required, for two reasons, that the formlessness of darkness should be removed first of all by the production of light. In the first place because light is a quality of the first body . . . and thus by means of light it was fitting that the world should first receive its form. The second reason is because light is a common quality. For light is common to terrestrial and celestial bodies. But as in knowledge we proceed from general principles, so do we in work of every kind . . . It was fitting, then, as an evidence of the Divine wisdom, that among the works of distinction the production of light should take first place, since light is a form of the primary body, and because it is [the] more common quality.[516]

He lists those two reasons why light was appropriately created first of all and then adds:

> Basil, indeed, adds a third reason: that all other things are made manifest by light. And there is yet a fourth . . .; that day cannot be unless light exists, which was made therefore on the first day.[517]

As we consider the connection in the divine economy of the world between light and the celestial bodies that now produce it, we should observe that in the final consummation of all things the sun and the moon will have different roles. Thus consider these passages, for day cannot be without light, but both can exist with neither sun nor moon:

> No longer will you have the sun for light by day, nor for brightness will the moon give you light; but you will have the LORD for an everlasting light, and your God for your glory. Your sun will no longer set, nor will your moon wane; for you will have the LORD for an everlasting light, and the days of your mourning will be over. (Isaiah 60:19–20)

> And the city has no need of the sun or of the moon to shine on it, for the glory of God has illumined it, and its lamp *is* the Lamb. The nations will walk by its light, and the kings of the earth will bring their glory into it. In the daytime (for there will be no night there) its gates will never be closed; (Revelation 21:23–25)

> And there will no longer be *any* night; and they will not have need of the light of a lamp nor the light of the sun, because the Lord God will illumine them; and they will reign forever and ever. (Revelation 22:5)

So the present function of the sun and moon will not continue. Light was created before they existed and will continue after they no longer serve as governing luminaries. The new creation will be brought into existence by the Son by reconstituting things at some future date—when the full purpose of this place of preparation has been realized.

The "how" of this question ("how" was light made before the luminaries of the heavens) can be answered by first asking if this command involved an additional creation of substance, something over and above the original dark, formless, and void primordial material from the initial moment of creation. After all, light is quite the opposite of a formless and void substance, but it is not reasonable to think that there was a second *ex nihilo* creation.

Therefore I think that God brought forth the light from that original substance. Physics tells us that all energy of every type including light can be converted from material mass by the famous formula $E=mc^2$. Thus in bringing forth the initial light God **might** have caused some of the physical material to be converted to energy and suddenly, without calling into existence any more substance, there was light—if that relativistic law of convertibility was in effect at that early time in the creation, when matter was still "formless and void."

The ancients definitely did not think of this. We also do not know for certain that this is what happened, but can see this as a possible way of understanding this verse. And it does seem that, after the initial creative decision, no further material substance should be formed. At this time we can perceive that God was transforming a stagnant world into an energized world; one full of dynamic forces that could actuate it. This would be a massive reversal of the Law of Entropy—the second law of thermodynamics—which states that all things are running down, dying back, and moving inevitably toward an eventual stagnant end. Stagnation was the initial state of the formless matter, but God injected energy into the world by this word of command. Thus conversion of matter into energy makes sense.

This energy surely came from the Spirit of God that was "hovering" or "shaking" or "fluttering" over the primordial deep and which was pregnant with divine power. Thus the Father issued this command and the Son carried it out by the Holy Spirit that had been dispatched at the very beginning. This gives a possible insight into how there could be light before the heavenly bodies came into existence.

The initial emanation of light was still undirected, unbridled, and scattered about in all directions. It was a wonderful type of energy, bright and boundless in power, but it still could not be used constructively. It had to be properly channeled and harnessed to its tasks. It seems that from the time that the Lord injected this initial measure of light and energy into the creation it has been following the Law of Entropy; that is, the creation has been running down.

So the light was created before the heavenly luminaries in this way. And once we see the logical pattern according to which the creation unfolded we also know better than to worship the luminaries, as if the present light and warmth that is so vital to life on earth had originally come from them. This is how and why the light came before the sun, as much as we from our human vantage point can comprehend.

Finally, I will reassert at this time that the Father spoke these words to the Son and then the Son released the light. He did this by the power of the Holy Spirit which at this time was present above the deep after having been sent forth by the Father along with the initial choice to create. We will continue to observe that the commands of creation are issued by the Father and are enacted by the Son.

The order that God follows in His creative acts will be first to energize His creation, then to direct and channel that energy in a constructive way, and then to fashion the various structures that we see around us that need, use, or continue to produce energy.

On the Divine Origin of this Account:
Another question that applies to this command and to the entire six day creation account is this: How and when did the creation facts become known to men? There was no one present to see or record these events. Only the Lord Himself was in a position to know these things. The action of creating all things is appropriate to God and only to God. It

is the foundational work that identifies Him to mankind. Thus He must have told human beings the information that is recorded here.

Surely the knowledge of His creative acts would be something that God would want men to know right from the beginning. Thus He must have told Adam about the six days at the beginning of the creation. This is what the archeological considerations behind the first tablet of Genesis indicate as well. It was written by God on the seventh day and given to Adam early on—likely soon after He was made and before the fall. Thus the assumed date line "and He rested on the seventh day from all the work He had done" (Genesis 2:3), indicating when this account was written, is most reasonable.

Let me say this in a different way: The account we are reading did not arise from within any human culture. It precedes all other written records. It bears no marks of being the work of some human. It is not the product of the medieval cosmology that was inherited from the Greeks. It is not the outgrowth of a primitive Middle Eastern tribal society of Semitic people. It did not arise out of the pagan milieu of ancient Mesopotamia. It is much more ancient than any of those cultures and any of their writings or ideas. It was written by the Lord God during the creation of the world and given by Him to Adam, the first man, and has been providentially preserved through the centuries and passed on to us today. This is the account from the hand of God describing for us how He created us and how He created the whole world. He gave it to the first man early on.

Genesis 1:4a—God saw that the light was good

God approved of what had been done. It pleased Him and was in accord with His good pleasure. The Father was pleased with the way that the Son and the Holy Spirit carried out His command. God pronounced things as "good" before He began to separate the light from the darkness. The light He saw as good. In the subsequent steps of creation God will incorporate the light energy into the formation of the structures of the universe. It is vital to all created things. That is one reason why He sees it as good.

But the light must be directed in order to accomplish its tasks. Unbridled and undirected energy is not constructive. At least it is not usefully constructive for most purposes. It must be harnessed. I speak in this way for lack of a better vocabulary. I might say it like this: God was determining the laws of physics that energy was to obey in this world that we are so familiar with. That is what I am saying when I speak of God directing or bridling or harnessing the energy. We cannot assume, at that early time in the universe, that the present physical laws were operational.

Genesis 1:4b—And God separated the light from the darkness.

Darkness is not something that God created, but is only the absence of light. God said that the light was good, but He never said that the darkness was good. The Lord God did not create the darkness. It is the emptiness or lack that results when light is directed somewhere else. Such is the case also with sin. God did not create it, but rather it is the absence of, or even perhaps the denial or contradiction of, all that is good.

God separated the light from the darkness in a way that we cannot visualize. But this separation, this directing of the light "not here, but there" was a necessary prerequisite to making it useful, to harnessing light to functionality. This made the boundless energy available and useable. From the viewpoint of modern physics we can say that God is establishing the laws that govern the creation. We take these for granted but they had to be established by divine decree. The orderly operation of the cosmos that we assume as a constant was not there in the beginning when the elements were "formless and void."

The operation of the world before the current regular ordinances were in place is not easily visualized. This is why we cannot understand exactly "how" God carried out this early step in the creation. Because of our exposure to physics we easily imagine that the physical laws that we have recently discovered, are and always were, inherent in matter—that the natural realm always possessed these properties. But order like this had to be created, had to be willed and intentionally made by God. The natural realm is not self-existent, and it also is not self-ordered or self-regulated. The transition from a state of non-being to a state of existence, then from a state of chaos to a state of order, is what this creation account is describing for us. St. John Chrysostom says:
> What is meant by "He separated?" He gave each its own place and defined its appropriate time. And when this had been done, he then gave each its proper name. The text goes on, you see: "God called the light day, and the darkness night."[518]

Augustine philosophizes more deeply about this act of separating, hypothesizes about the puzzle of dividing of the light from the darkness, and further speculates about the timing of the creation and of how God is explaining it to us:
> But how was there made evening and morning? Or did God take as long to make the light and to divide between the light and the darkness as it takes for a day of daylight to last, that is, excluding the night? . . . Or were all things in fact completed by God as in a craftsman's thought-out design, not in a stretch of time, but in that very power which made to abide in a timeless state even those things which we perceive as not abiding, but as passing away in time?[519]

Yes, there surely must have been a timeless state that preceded the creation of the material world, but in these verses God is not speaking about the eternal plan that He had in that unknown timeless beforehand, but about the implementation of that plan in space and time. The separation of light from darkness must have involved the withdrawal of the light from some part of His newly created substance. Light can be directed—toward one thing and away from another thing. This is what He did in those earliest moments of time. This was connected to, but prior to, making the energy useful and able to fulfill its role in creation.

Today, although we understand that the scattering of light is normal, we also know that it can be directed in a contained beam of light called a laser. Such perfectly coordinated light rays adhere to each other and move together in one direction. It is true that we still cannot visualize how this separation was enacted, nor can we be sure what God is describing when He says this, but we are closer to understanding it now than Augustine was in his day. We can understand that transforming such a stagnant substance was a necessary first step in the creation—but transforming it into some randomly energized substance still was not the full answer. That energy had to be constructively contained and directed since eventually it would be applied to everything in the creation and thus it would become a vital component in their functioning. Beyond this, we must just accept and believe what God tells us. This is what Augustine himself says in the face of such a great mystery. In speaking about the alternation of day and night during the first three days, even before the sun was in existence he says:

But what kind of light it was, and by what alternating motion it made evening and morning, and what sort of evening and morning these were, are all things far removed from our senses. Nor is it possible for us to understand how it was so, but we must still believe it without the least hesitation.[520]

Genesis 1:5a—God called the light day and the darkness He called night.

God did not name everything that He made, but those things to which God gave names are worthy of note. He gave names to the light and the darkness, calling them day and night. Remember that in the new creation there will be no night, but only one eternal unfading day. So are "day" and "light" the same thing? Are "night" and "darkness" the same thing? Not really, for "day" is that period of time **on earth** when it is bathed in light, and "night" is that period of time **on earth** when it is in darkness. For there is a light that is not "day" and there is a darkness that is not "night." The two terms "day" and "night" relate directly to the earth in its states of being. Therefore these terms are more specific than the terms "light" and "darkness." The two chief heavenly luminaries were appointed to rule over the day and the night, not over the light and the darkness. Their function is related to the earth and to life on the earth. The time that is being described in the days of creation is earth time. We might call it "earth standard time."

Genesis 1:5b—And there was evening and there was morning, one day.

With this statement the first of the six days is concluded. In making this statement God is defining for us the meaning of "day," for God did not say "the first day" as He does later on; that is, "second day," "third day," etc. Rather "day" is being defined. It is the alternation of darkness and light that is produced by one rotation of the earth on its axis. Each day starts with a time of darkness—with night—because the initial state of the creation was darkness. God did not define the meaning of "day" until He had named "evening" and "morning" (or "night" and "day") as two states that the earth would be in. These terms are used to relate light and darkness to the earth, i.e., they incorporate earth-related concepts. Today the Jewish people still reckon the end of one day and the beginning of the next as happening at sundown—so first darkness, then light. That is why their weekly Sabbath observation begins at sunset on Friday and extends to sunset on Saturday.

Augustine noticed the double use of the word "day," both for that state of the earth when it was in the light, and for that period of time encompassing the passage through one period of earthly darkness and the subsequent period of earthly light.

> The term "day" is not now being used in the same way as when it is said *and God called the light day*, but in the same way as when we say, for example, there are thirty days in a month. Here, you see, we are including nights in the term "day," whereas in the previous verse day was being distinguished from night.[521]

God uses the two concepts where the light as pertaining to the earth is called "day," and the darkness as pertaining to the earth is called "night," to define the meaning of the term "day" as it will used in the rest of the creation narrative when He enumerates the days. A "day" is one rotation of the earth on its axis—24 hours.

Day 2:
Genesis 1:6a—Then God said, "Let there be an expanse in the midst of the waters …"

LXX—And God said: "let a *solid structure* be made in the midst of the water …"

["Vetus" will be used for Augustine's translation of the Vetus Latina and "LXX" for the Septuagint.]
[Also, places where such an alternative translation differs from the Masoretic text will be *italicized*.]

This verse has caused consternation because we do not know what the "expanse" actually is. The ancient Jewish understanding of the word translated as "expanse" (*raqiya`*) was of an extended solid surface like a vault or dome. And the LXX translates this as "solid structure." These concepts reflect the cosmological view of the people of those times, which they imputed to the Scriptures when they read them, and which they wrote down when they translated the Masoretic text into the LXX. However, the Hebrew word actually means a kind of "stretched out thinness." Thus it corresponds to the atmosphere of the earth and/or the starry heavens—to what we call "space." Numerous verses of Scripture speak of God "stretching out the heavens" at the creation. Here are a few:[522 see note]

> He who sits above the circle of the earth, and its inhabitants are like grasshoppers, Who stretches out the heavens like a curtain and spreads them out like a tent (Isaiah 40:22)

> Thus says the LORD, your Redeemer, and the one who formed you from the womb, "I, the LORD, am the maker of all things, stretching out the heavens by Myself" (Isaiah 44:24)

> That you have forgotten the LORD your Maker, who stretched out the heavens and laid the foundations of the earth (Isaiah 51:13)

> *It is* He who made the earth by His power, who established the world by His wisdom; and by His understanding He has stretched out the heavens. (Jeremiah 10:12)

This meaning of *raqiya`* as an expanse or a "stretched out thinness" may reflect the fact of this stretching out. An interesting detail: We know from General Relativity that a stretching of space itself (not just a stretching of the atmosphere, but of the fabric of space itself) would result in a time dilation that would cause time to pass much more rapidly in the universe than on the earth. Thus certain cosmic processes that we have observed and that seem to have been continuing for more than a few thousand years might have been going on, when measured by cosmic time, for hundreds of thousands or for millions of years—while on earth just a few moments of time would have elapsed.

The time frame of the creation account, measured as it is by the rotation of the earth—measured by what we have referred to as "earth standard time"—would in such a case correspond to elapsed cosmic times that are longer. This insight is speculative, like the one about converting matter to energy via the formula $E=mc^2$, because the physical laws were not necessarily functioning during the six days the same way they do now. Also such a relativistic time dilation would only come into effect in "stretching out" the vast reaches of intergalactic space, not in the formation of the atmosphere around the earth, which is what this verse is referring to. The intergalactic "stretching" will be on the fourth day.

raqiya`: What is the firmament, or the expanse—what we call space? It cannot be empty, for electromagnetic and gravitational waves are transmitted through it. Waves, as opposed to particles, are propagated as vibrations in a conducting medium. This is how sound is propagated within the medium of air. So space must have texture, must be composed of something. In 19th century physics it was called (a)ether, and now, in the age of relativity, it is referred to as the gravitational field. If we think this way then space is endowed with physical qualities. It is strong and firm enough to hold the celestial bodies. As God said to Job, it is "strong [mighty, firm, hard] as a molten [to cast, pour out, be firmly established] mirror" (Job 37:18). Yet it is flexible/permeable enough to allow bodies to move through it and to allow for the transmission of light. The composition of space is a mystery. Some modern theories propose that "empty" space is filled with "Planck particles" that are only 10^{-20} times the size of electrons, but which are the heaviest particles existing in the natural realm. Thus the matrix that transmits gravitational and electromagnetic waves and that contains/upholds the celestial bodies is a kind of super-particle vacuum.[523] Whatever fanciful theory we accept, it is certain that space is not empty, that it consists of a conducting and supporting medium of some sort, and that it thus must be detectable and measurable. This is the "expanse" that the Lord created, which He stretched out on the fourth day. This is the stary heaven, the huge cosmos that we see above us. Above and beyond this is the heaven of God.

The second thing about verse 1:6a that we need to understand is the phrase "in the midst of the waters." The second half of verse six, and verses seven and eight, explain it.

Genesis 1:6b—And let it separate the waters from the waters.

LXX—and let it be dividing between water and water." *And thus it was made.*

Genesis 1:7—God made the expanse and separated the waters which were below the expanse from the waters which were above the expanse; and it was so.

LXX—And God made a *solid structure* and divided between the water which was below the *solid structure* and the water that was above the *solid structure*.

Genesis 1:8—God called the expanse heaven. And there was evening and there was morning, a second day.

LXX—And God called the *solid structure* heaven. *And God saw that it was good.* **And there was made evening and there was made morning, a second day.**

These verses tell us that God created a separating expanse (we call this heaven, or the heavens) within the waters and moved some of the waters above the expanse and left some below it. The purpose of the expanse was to separate waters from waters. Augustine asks:
> Were the waters the same above the structure as these visible ones below the structure? . . . [B]ecause it seems to be referring to that water over which the Spirit was being borne, . . . are we to suppose that . . . the lower water is the basic "body material," while the higher is the basic "soul material" [by this he means heavenly or celestial material]?[524]

The waters above the expanse will be used to create the heavenly objects and the waters below the expanse will be used to create the earthly structures.

This creation command of day two tells us how the atmospheric area around the earth was created. We are not given specific details, but we are told that it opened up as the result of a divine action. The unique nature of the atmosphere of the earth, distinct from that of all other planets, is what allows for life on earth. While creating this open area the Lord providentially determined that it would be so constituted as to perfectly sustain life on our planet. There is no naturalistic explanation for how earth's atmosphere came to be. The waters above the atmosphere appear to be gone today, perhaps because they were used by God in the creation of the heavenly structures as described on day four.

Up to this point the Bible presents us with this picture of the initial stages of the creation: God first made the basic or primordial substance of the universe. This was made up of water and (maybe) solids. If the "deep" of the earliest time of creation was spherically configured then it must have been many light years in diameter in order to comprise the total substance of what now exists. Then God transformed some of that substance into light and directed or contained the light (by the constraints placed on it as He established certain of the physical laws) so as to make it constructively useful.

Then God separated the huge mass of water by opening up an expanse within it and by moving most of the water above the expanse to be used for making the celestial objects. A smaller amount He kept on the surface of the earth to fashion into earthly things or to remain suspended above the atmosphere. The creative commands were spoken by the Father but were carried out by the Son by using the power of the Holy Spirit. Hippolytus comments on the expanse:

> As the excessive volume of water bore along over the face of the earth, the earth was by reason thereof "invisible" and "formless." When the Lord of all designed to make the invisible visible, He fixed then a third part of the waters in the midst; and another third part He set by itself on high, raising it together with the firmament by His own power; and the remaining third He left beneath, for the use and benefit of men.[525]

Hippolytus can speak of "one-third" and "one-third" because the ancients had no idea at all of the enormous size of the heavens that they were viewing from the earth. Yet his basic idea and explanation is sound. Only the percentages are off. Since we understand today just how large the creation is, we might ask ourselves why the Lord God made such a huge universe. If we are His only creation, then why is the universe so enormous? Here is a perspective on that question as explained from the psalms:

> The heavens are telling of the glory of God. And their expanse is declaring the work of His hands. (Psalm 19:1)

The enormity of His work staggers us, and so it should! It reflects the majesty and the glory that He has. It is a picture that He gives us of His greatness. It is spoken without words, as the psalm goes on to say, and in a way that everyone can see—in a way that transcends language because it is instilled in and expressed through the creation itself.

When I spoke about "containing the light by the constraints of the physical laws" I was speaking from a perspective that has come up before: In the beginning the "formless and void" primordial substance did not necessarily obey the current physical laws. Thus as God proceeded in the creation steps He might have instilled those natures into the objects that He was forming as He formed them, thus "enclosing" their behavior within the boundaries or constraints of those laws. Current cosmological theories speak of the same thing; that is, they speak of the establishing of the "four basic forces" at the time of the Big Bang or immediately thereafter. Such a step is vital to establishing the creation so that it behaves in an orderly way, like the cosmos that we are so familiar with today.

Let us think again about the image that we had of the original unformed substance which at the first God called "the heaven(s) and the earth." We stated that initially He also created space and time. That statement is coming from our current physics which sees the universe as a space-time continuum. If you thought of that first matter as a (possibly) spherical ball of water many light years in diameter you might have formed a picture in your mind of a huge ball of water hanging in space with the earth at the center. If so then the implicit idea of the "heaven(s)" that you had was what we now call space, the very same space that surrounded that huge sphere of liquid.

Did that mental image of space extend out in an unlimited way in your imagination? The universe today seems to extend without limit, but when God created it in the beginning, unlike now, it might have been limited. I say this because He "stretched out" the heavens at some point, as we noted; that is, He actually stretched out the fabric of space itself. When this verse (1:6) speaks of the Lord forming an expanse in the midst of the waters, in the midst of the great "deep" of the primordial substance, it seems to be speaking of making an open area that lies just above the earth and which leaves some of the waters below it still over the surface of the earth, with the rest of the waters suspended above the open area. But the rest of the space "above" the large sphere of water has not yet been stretched out. The ball of water is a bit larger, and the space in which it resides is a little bit bigger. But it has not yet been stretched out to its present vastness.

In the next steps of creation God will form the upper waters into the celestial objects while He simultaneously "stretches out" the space where they reside to enlarge it into the huge cosmos that we see today. That is, space itself will be stretched to become larger. This concept of stretching space is found in cosmological theories today and is what the General Theory of Relativity says would result in a massive time dilation between the earth and the cosmos. Augustine explains:

> So then, that formless material which God made from nothing was first called "heaven and earth" where it said: *In the beginning God made heaven and earth* (Gn 1:1), not because that is what it already was [i.e., not because it already was the heavens that we know now], but because it was able to be that–the making of heaven, you see, is also described a little later on. It's as if, when we examine the seed of a tree, we were to say that the roots are there, and the trunk and the branches and the fruit and the leaves, not because they are in fact already there, but because they are going to come from there. That's how it says, *In the beginning God made heaven and earth,* as a kind of seed of heaven and earth, when the material of heaven and earth was still all unsorted; but because it was quite certain that heaven and earth were going to come from there, the material itself was also already called heaven and earth.[526]

When He creates the atmospheric expanse God is configuring the world to have the shape and the behavioral characteristics that are familiar to us. As He does this He is redefining for us the components of the reconfigured cosmos: The expanse He just formed is the area that we know as our atmosphere. Thus the "heaven(s)" of the original unformed and void substance have been opened up somewhat by the formation of that expanse, and eventually they will be stretched out even further—very much further.

Another Scripture indicates that there are water reserves above the heavens.

> Praise Him, highest heavens, and the waters that are above the heavens. Let them praise the name of the LORD, for He commanded, and they were created. He has also established them forever and ever; He has made a decree which will not pass away. (Psalm 148:4–6)

Some scientists think the heaven this verse is referring to is the atmospheric heaven, for there is reason to believe that the initial atmospheric configuration of earth included a layer of water vapor which was high enough up that it was not part of the hydrologic cycle of the earth; that is, it did not participate in the weather patterns of the earth. Such a layer would have resulted in a more even spreading out of the heating effect of the sun, and would have given the earth a uniformly warm climate without sharply defined cold and warm fronts, and so also without destructive weather patterns. Normally the atmosphere of the earth cannot hold enough water to rain for forty days and forty nights, so they also speculate that the rain that fell during the Deluge resulted from the collapse of that layer of water vapor above the atmosphere (and/or from the spurting forth of the water from the "fountains of the great deep" as they burst open). That water vapor was never restored because it does not participate in the cycle of evaporation, cloud formation, and rain that constitutes the regular earth climate. That is why we do not observe it today. Possibly!

But the "waters above the heavens" referred to by psalm 148 are permanent, and since they are undetectable they must be above the stary, or the "second," heaven. These must be left over from "the waters above the expanse" that God used to form the celestial objects. I wonder if there are large lakes and oceans in the glorious heaven of God.

Although the Holy Spirit is not explicitly mentioned in this step of creation, in Job 26:13 it says, "By His breath [Spirit] the heavens are cleared [lit., are made beautiful]." So the activity of creating this open area was accomplished by utilizing the power of the Holy Spirit. So the command to make the heavenly expanse was issued by the Father and enacted by the Son by using the power of the Holy Spirit.

The Fathers' Ideas and Modern Theories of Origins:
Augustine understood the creation acts not as having produced a world that operated by constant on-going miracles of God—that is, not by the continual contravening of the regular natures of created elements—but as having produced a world whose on-going operation was the result of the ordinances instilled in the nature of things that He had made during the six days (or in that one "Day" before time began). The world functioned according to the created natures that we can observe when we study it. We hold many different ideas today, but we still understand the on-going operation of the world as from the outworking of consistent physical laws—laws that are reflective of the nature of matter.

Augustine distinguished the days of creation from the times that we now live in. The creation acts were unique divine commands by which He brought everything into existence and formed all things, and which eventually ceased at the end of the six days. The present ordinances that govern the heaven and the earth were established at that time and still remain today. So creation was a unique and supernatural event while the present time is mostly, except for a few special divine interventions, operating under the established ordinances. He never imagined that the creation itself happened as the outworking of the presently established regulations, for the world was only placed under those regulations after God completed the creation at the end of the sixth day.[527]

The philosophical view which asserts that the present ordinances have always been in effect is called uniformitarianism. This is the basis of the world view within which all the modern naturalistic theories of origins are formulated. This philosophical assumption is fundamentally opposed to the Bible because it rules out God. Whatever we think God is, He is not a natural cause and He is not part of the physical realm. He is outside of nature—He is supernatural. And He is not implicated in the constant changes that are the regular functions of the creation—He is said to be transcendent and He never changes.

If we choose not to allow a supernatural explanation for the origin of the world, then we must assume that the processes that produced the present form of the world took very long times to achieve their ends. No human being can imagine in their mind what "billions of years" would mean, but as research has continued many naturalistic theories have been proposed to explain how the basic structures of the world came to be over many billions of years by the outworking of the same natural laws that we see in operation around us today. Those structures (the stars, the earth and moon, the sun, etc.) are precisely the same ones that Genesis attributes to the supernatural creative acts of God. All of those naturalistic theories have been shown to be inadequate and impossible, as we will see.

I want to consider the cosmological world view that was held by the ancients. It is very instructive. Today it is clear to us that the world view undergirding their thinking was in some ways deficient. We have taken our understanding of the world around us quite for granted, as if it is completely accurate, but our cosmology is also deficient. Only the Bible is not deficient. Although all humanly devised world views have problems, we will notice repeatedly that the Bible is not implicated in any erroneous world views. Written as they were by God, the Scriptures rise far above world view and present to us the eternal truth of God. They were given to us in human language and were translated and interpreted by men immersed in a deficient world view, yet they do not partake of that deficiency. This is a spectacular testimony to their divine inspiration.

When the cosmology of the ancients collapsed and was replaced by the present pseudo-scientific world view there was a cultural earthquake in Europe and in Christianity. The time of human "enlightenment" affected people's ability to believe in the Scriptures, even though when properly understood the Scriptures were not affected by the intellectual revolution that resulted from the changing of the times. All mankind is grass, and all the works of his hands are like the flower of the fields. The grass withers and the flower fades, but the word of our God endures forever (see Isaiah 40:6–8).

From our perspective we also are immersed in a certain cosmological view of the world. In the modern world view we imagine the universe to be randomly formed, meaningless, and as having come about by the outworking of natural processes which operated under the present physical laws. This gradual development took place over many billions of years. It is tempting to read this world view back into Genesis just as the ancient Jews injected their view of things into their translation of Genesis into Greek. That would be a huge mistake! Rather, in due time the sacred Scriptures will correct the deficiencies in our present world view, which at this time men are too proud to acknowledge.

Genesis presents us with a supernatural view of the creation of the universe. While this age says that the stars evolved from the condensation of vast gaseous clouds over eons of time, the Bible says that God created them and placed them in the expanse of heaven. He did this with the ease and majesty that is appropriate to Him Who is the Creator and Who is not limited by our frailties. All the creative works that *'elohiym* did were enacted instantaneously, for the matter created by Him cannot resist His almighty word.

Where the theories of our time present the earth and its atmosphere as developing out of material that was in orbit around the sun long after the sun was in existence, the Bible presents it to us as the supernatural work of God Who spoke the earth into existence, and then stretched out the atmospheric and starry heavens by the word of His command. The earth was the foundation upon which He built the universe, and human beings were what He made this creation for—as a place of preparation for His sons and daughters.

Underneath all of this, whatever God is, He cannot be a natural cause. The first cause of creation was not a natural process operating under the currently known physical laws. It was instead the imposition of the will and the word of an extra-natural (i.e., supernatural) being on the natural realm that first willed it into existence and then configured it to be the way it appears to us today. The universe is not causally self-contained. It was caused both in its substance and in its structural forms by a supernatural being Who is Himself eternal and uncaused, Who resides outside of the natural realm, Who is transcendent. Thus we must resist the idea of re-thinking our understanding of Genesis to agree with the current world view. It cannot be done, for our present world view is also deficient.

We are immersed in a culture that saturates us with "scientific" words, concepts, and perspectives, and it can seem to us as if our society's scientific view of the world is the ultimate truth and that the theories of origins also partake of scientific certainty and will never pass away. But the truth is that our culture will pass away just like all others. Yes indeed: All mankind is grass and all the works of his hands are as the flower of the field. The grass withers and the flower fades but the word of our God endures forever.

When you see *Star Trek* and they imagine for us what the future will be—the warp-speed space ships darting throughout the Milky Way, the many different man-like species from other "solar systems" that each have "evolved" separately into their diverse semi-humanoid forms, their godless cultures rife with the same sinful lust and hatred that is in our culture now—remember what the Bible says. Such ideas are modern "false prophecies" that present us with an illusion about the future of mankind—one that will never be. God has other plans for the human race. He explains them to us in the Book of Revelation.

Closely related to the idea of our world view is how we tend to look at and think about the ancients. They had a different cosmology than we do, but they did not believe what the Bible says about creation because of their cosmology. They believed because the Bible is the Word of God, and God cannot lie or be mistaken. As noted, it does not partake of the errors of any cosmological theory—even though those who read the Bible read it and understand it from within a deficient cosmological framework. Instead, it is a supernatural book, written by the Lord God to teach us exactly how He created everything, accurate in what it tells us, and expressed in a way that a person of normal intelligence can grasp.

We should believe the Bible—especially Genesis—for the same reason, i.e., because it is the Word of God and its truth rests on His nature as being faithful and wise and true. As we read it we might inject a more highly-developed scientific perspective into the way that we read it and understand it—but we should not allow pseudo-scientific theories to insert themselves into our interpretation of the book of Genesis, for such theories were crafted in direct opposition to the basic parameters of our Christian faith and world view.

Day 3:
Genesis 1:9—Then God said, "Let the waters below the heavens be gathered into one place, and let the dry land appear"; and it was so.

Genesis 1:10—God called the dry land earth, and the gathering of the waters He called seas; and God saw that it was good.

The phrase "and it was so" is the Hebrew word *ken* which means so, thus, just so. There are certain things we can note about the phrase "and it was so" in this and other statements in the creation account: It can be viewed as an acknowledgement of the command that the Father has given—an affirmation given in reply by the Son. When the Father issues a command the Son often replies by this phrase to indicate that He has or is about to obey the command. We are being shown a conversation within the Trinity. This bidding by the Father is not followed by the statement "then God made the seas and the dry land" as in other cases. Thus we must infer that Jesus actually performed His bidding from the general fact that "through Him [Jesus] all things were made" (John 1:3).

These verses explain the formation of the oceans and continents. Because the waters are said to have been "gathered together" to "let the dry land appear" it is now revealed that from the beginning there was land under the waters of the great deep. Since the waters are said to be gathered into one place it is logical that the land also was all in one place. The subsequent steps of creation, the making of vegetation, animals, and man, took place on that one large mass of land.

Observations from Geology:
Geologists have uncovered evidence that the continents were together, almost like the pieces of a giant puzzle, and formed one large continent which they call Pangaea. The evidence for this is varied and persuasive. At a later time they were driven apart into their present state. I assume that this separation occurred during the Deluge. Frozen plants of a tropical nature lie buried underneath the permanent ice sheet of Antarctica, so even that frozen wasteland was once bathed in a warm climate. Thus the continent of Pangaea must have been situated in a temperate zone and was designed to be comfortably inhabited.

The origin of the continents and the oceans is a mysterious riddle to science—as is the origin of the atmosphere of the earth. No satisfactory explanation has ever been offered. This is because scientists are looking for a naturalistic explanation for the formation of these structures. But the earth does not contain in itself a built-in inclination to organize into large land masses and seas, nor to give rise to our life-sustaining atmosphere. The processes that formed these things had to be initiated by a force that is outside of the natural realm. They were caused by God, who is supernatural and transcendent.

The creation was not the only supernatural intervention that formed the continents as they are today. There is worldwide evidence for the Deluge at the time of Noah. Sedimentary deposits covering many thousands of square miles of the earth are found on every one of the continents. These layers of the geologic column were clearly deposited by the waters of a flood. Because of the vast extent of the deposits it was a flood of gigantic proportions, unlike anything in historic times. Because there are multiple layers of such deposits and there is no indication of large amounts of time (such as extensive erosion) between the layers, the deposits are best seen as having been laid down in a short time. Because these sedimentary deposits are found throughout the world, on every continent, they are best understood as having been formed by one worldwide event. This is strong evidence for the Flood of Noah as described in Genesis. This data has come to light largely as a result of extensive geologic mapping by oil companies in recent decades.[528] It does not fit with the idea that these strata were laid down one-by-one over millions of years.

At this point in the creation God has an unfinished heavenly area and an unfinished earthly area that He must adorn so as to complete His creation.

Genesis 1:11—Then God said, "Let the earth sprout vegetation, plants yielding seed, *and* fruit trees on the earth bearing fruit after their kind with seed in them"; and it was so.

Genesis 1:12—The earth brought forth vegetation, plants yielding seed after their kind, and trees bearing fruit with seed in them, after their kind; and God saw that it was good.

Genesis 1:13—There was evening and there was morning, a third day.

At the conclusion of the various days of creation it never says, "there was darkness and there was light" but rather "there was evening and there was morning." This is because the statements are referring specifically to the earth and its cycle of days. The creation account is timed by the rotation of the earth and by the cycle of nights and days that are produced in that rotation. There was light in His creation when it was night on the earth; and there was still darkness at places in His creation when it was daylight on the earth.

Augustine continues his commentary by noting the instantaneous effect of the creative commands of day three:
> After the earth and sea were made and named and approved of (which as I have said often enough is not to be taken as involving intervals of time, in case the inexpressible ease with which God works should be limited by some kind of slowness) . . .[529]

In day 3, verses 9–13 of the creation account, we are again being given a glimpse into the interchange within the Trinity and the roles that the three persons were playing during the creation. The Holy Spirit was sent by the Father (verse 2b) to provide power for the creation. When the Father issues a command to create, the Son uses the Spirit to carry out His command, affirming it with the words "and it was so". "Truly, truly, I say to you, the Son can do nothing of Himself, unless it is something He sees the Father doing; for whatever the Father does, these things the Son also does in like manner" (John 5:19). Once a creative act is completed then the Father affirms the work of the Son and the Holy Spirit and pronounces it as "good." Thus we are being allowed to see the inner relationships of the Trinity. This gives us a peek into how the three worked together in the creation, allowing us to understand that work as a mutual effort among the Father, the Son, and the Holy Spirit.

As a final thought on the passage of time during the first three days, on which we have touched somewhat before, I want to present one more quotation. We remarked on, and many Fathers asked, how, in the absence of the sun and the moon, there could be the alternation of day and night that is described. This is closely related to the question of how God separated the light from the darkness, another mystery in its own right. This is not something we can understand, as Augustine noted, for the physical laws were not in effect and the way things worked then is a mystery known only to God. However there are some assertions we can make about the first three days.

The Coptic commentator Didymus the Blind directly addressed one issue relating to the duration of the first three days.
> [S]ome people beyond the pale of religion have asked in an attempt to test us, "Why on earth in your view were the days mentioned when the sun was not yet in existence?" For one thing, you could say to them that all this is to be interpreted in an anagogical sense; teaching through symbols is not out of the question for us. On the other hand, since it is normal for someone dealing with them to uphold even the literal sense, come now, let us take up a few details in regard to this. *Day* has two senses, temporal duration and light of the air about us; when it is said, "And on the third day," there is reference to the number of the day, not the day's brightness or gloom, whereas if you were to say that today is a gloomy day, you would not be

> speaking with reference to its number. So if the divine word says that a first and second and third day existed before the creation of the sun and the other lights, we should consider the extent of temporal duration. To the person having difficulties with the divine Scripture the reply should be given that seventy-two hours, as it were, elapsed between the creation of the firmament and that of the lights, which is not surprising. Far from making the day, in fact, the sun indicates it, no more than anyone would say that instruments mechanically constructed make the hours: they only indicate them. So the sun and the moon indicate the times; they do not make them. It is one thing to indicate, another to make, the result being that there is nothing illogical in such a lengthy period intervening between the creation of the sun and the other lights which, had there been something to indicate it, would have been a period of three days.[530]

Thus we can at least assert that the duration of time expressed by each of the three first days was the same duration that we now associate with the passage of one of our days. This agrees with the views of many other expositors, but Didymus says it most directly and clearly. Just because we cannot understand how the alternation between day and night happened we do not have to give up our understanding of the duration of time that must have passed during the course of that mysterious alternation. Because Didymus looks at the heavenly bodies as indicating the light—not as making it—his remarks fit in with our observations from day one that there will be light in the New Jerusalem, but without attributing the source of that light to the sun and moon. In the new creation the heavenly indicators will have a different function.[531]

Remember that when God first created the primordial substance, because it was truly physical matter in some form, its eventual tendency would be to behave according to the natural laws that we see in effect around us now. These physical laws reflect the nature of created substance. However, because God was continually operating on that matter to form it into the structures that we see around us now, those tendencies either were not yet instilled into matter or were constantly being contravened; that is, extra-natural, or super-natural, forces were in play that caused the matter to organize into what we see around us, and while that was going on the present laws were not in effect.

Thus the way in which the creation happened cannot be deduced from the way the world is now functioning. The present consistent physical ordinances were established by God only at the end of the sixth day when His creative works had been completed. God was in direct control of those processes and whatever God is, He is not a part of the natural realm and His actions are not "natural" causes. God is "super" natural.

As for understanding this more deeply, or expecting to have full understanding about how God divided the light from the darkness or the nature of the first three days, here are some words that the Lord spoke to Job after he had prayed for an audience with the Lord God because of his sufferings. These put this issue into perspective for us.
> Who is this that darkens counsel by words without knowledge? Now gird up your loins like a man, and I will ask you, and you instruct Me! . . . Have you ever in your life commanded the morning, and caused the dawn to know its place? . . . Where is the way to the dwelling of light? And darkness, where is its place? . . . Where is the way that the light is divided? (Job 38:2–3, 12, 19, 24)

How can any person grasp the mysterious way this world was upheld before the Lord established the ordinances that govern it, before He enclosed light within the laws that direct it? The "six days of awe" are beyond the understanding of Job and of all humans. There are some things about the creation of this universe that we will never understand. Today we often hear, or implicitly assume, that the reason why ancient men could not understand the creation and the world around them was because they were "primitive," and the obvious reason why we can and do understand things is because we are not so primitive. We do indeed know more about the working of this world than the ancients.

But when it comes to the subject of origins the reason the ancients could not understand it was more basic. It was because they were human—because they were creatures and not the Creator. That same limitation still applies to us today. If we kid ourselves by not acknowledging our human state and its implied limitations—if we refuse to acknowledge this built-in truth about ourselves, then we are falling into a kind of pride that the ancients called "hubris." It is a danger that stems from the many accomplishments that God has granted to us in the past few centuries—accomplishments that are a gift to us, but which were never intended to dazzle us with our own intelligence. The limits of true science are to discover and apply usefully the principles of operation that govern the functioning of all things in the world around us. Science cannot tell us about the unseen distant past.

Day 4:

Genesis 1:14—Then God said, "Let there be lights [or light bearers] **in the expanse of the heavens to separate the day from the night, and let them be for signs and for seasons and for days and years.**

LXX—And God said: Let lamps be made in the *solid structure* of heaven, in order to shine upon the earth and to divide between day and night, and to be for signs and for times and for days and for years,

Genesis 1:15—and let them be for lights in the expanse of the heavens to give light on the earth"; and it was so.

LXX—and to be for brilliance in the *solid structure* of heaven, in order to shine upon the earth. And thus it was made.

Genesis 1:16—God made the two great lights, the greater light to govern the day, and the lesser light to govern the night; *He made* the stars also.

LXX—And God made two lamps, the greater lamp the beginning of the day, and the lesser lamp the beginning of the night.

Genesis 1:17—God placed them in the expanse of the heavens to give light on the earth

LXX—And God placed them in the *solid structure* of heaven, in order to shine upon the earth.

Genesis 1:18—and to govern the day and the night, and to separate the light from the darkness; and God saw that it was good.

LXX—And let them preside over day and night and divide between day and night.

Genesis 1:19—There was evening and there was morning, a fourth day.

Here we must point out that the wording of these verses makes the understanding of the Hebrew word *raqiya`* as "expanse" rather than as "solid structure" most reasonable.

If it is understood as a solid structure then placing stars in the *raqiya`* might imply God embedded them in something solid. But some of them move with respect to the others. How could the planets or "wanderers" move? But understanding this word to mean an expanse with qualities both of flexibility and hardness, as we discussed, allows us to make much more sense of these verses. Augustine noticed this problem:

> Question: weather this [these verses of scripture] was only said about the fixed stars or also about the wandering ones [i.e., the planets]? But the two lamps, the greater and the lesser, are counted among the wandering stars; so how are they all made in the solid structure, when all the wanderers have each their own proper sphere or circle?[532]

The purpose of these lights is to "give light on the earth" thus replacing the light source of the first three days. They also serve as our built-in calendar and watch. People tell time and determine the passage of seasons and years by them. God placed them in the heavens to govern the day and the night which He had already established.

God did not name these luminaries. He referred to them simply as "the greater light" and "the lesser light." This detail is one piece of evidence that this account is very ancient indeed, preceding all known civilizations. All ancient peoples had names for the sun and the moon and would have inserted those names into this account if the creation story had been produced in the context of their civilization.

In these verses we see God the Father commanding that the lights be made (1:14–15) and we see the Son carrying out that command (1:16–18). Psalm 33:6 says "by the breath of His mouth were the host [of heaven] made," so we understand that the Son used the power of the Holy Spirit to accomplish these mighty deeds, the Spirit that was dispatched with the Father's initial creative act of willing at the beginning of the creation. In this case the affirmation of obedience by the Son (1:15) comes before He completes the tasks of the fourth day.

A Critique of Modern Cosmology:
Comparing Creation to Naturalistic Theories—The Big Bang:[533 see note]

Now that the cosmos has been completed let us look at present-day cosmological ideas and compare their theory with what we have just read. I want to explain historically how the present theory of origins was developed.

The key observed phenomenon that ignited cosmological theories of origins was what is called the Doppler effect. This is an observed shift in the light from distant objects in the universe towards the red end of the spectrum. This has been interpreted to mean those objects are moving away from us. The red shift (the Doppler effect) is greater in some objects and less in other objects, and the amount of shift is greater for those objects that are further away from us. This observation implies that the universe is expanding.

If the universe is expanding then if we go back in time far enough we must reach a time when all matter was together in one place. Observations and calculations have shown that about 13.787 billion years ago all matter must have been concentrated in one place. It has been expanding from that place since then. Thus the universe began when a large collection of matter that was in one place began to expand. That initial expansion is what cosmologists call the Big Bang.

From this straightforward observation—the fact that the universe is expanding—we are able to explain scientifically how the universe began. The assumption that God was not involved has been easily inserted into the theory because we assume that the physical laws have been in effect consistently throughout. This assumption is called uniformitarianism. That assumption means that God was not involved because He is not a natural cause. Here is a more detailed explanation of what had to have happened.

1. A quantum fluctuation in nothingness produced a singularity of enormous density. That is how the basic substance of the universe came to be. Of course, such a happening would contradict the law of the conservation of matter and energy, which states that the total amount of matter and energy is fixed. No new matter/energy is ever formed and none is ever destroyed. This is one huge problem with insisting on a naturalistic explanation for the universe. (The Bible says God willed the basic substance of the cosmos to exist in the beginning. His name is "I Am," and it is His nature to exist. His choice to create is the reason why there is something rather than nothing.)
2. The cosmological theories assert that the expanding universe was the result of an initial "Big Bang" which was comprised of primordial sub-nuclear substance; that is, the matter that was formed within that singularity, that primordial stuff, expanded. Of course such an expansion would violate the law of gravity because the hypothetical singularity where all of the original matter was concentrated would be the biggest and deepest black hole possible, and thus would draw all things into itself. Thus it could never expand outward. (The Bible asserts that God stretched out the heavens.)
3. As the expansion progressed the temperatures dropped, and the sub-nuclear particles condensed into electrons, protons, and other basic particles. These in turn spontaneously formed the atoms that make up all matter. Of course, the expansion had to proceed within strict parameters—not expanding too slowly or too quickly—so the primordial matter did not collapse again, and so it did not fly apart so quickly that the atoms could not form. Scientists have computed the likelihood of the expansion falling within those limits to be less than one in 10 to the 50th power (1 followed by fifty zeros). Very unlikely!
4. Scientists realized that the only elements that would be formed in this way would be hydrogen, a tiny bit of helium, and perhaps an infinitesimal amount of beryllium and lithium. Therefore they hypothesized that giant stars formed rapidly (called population III stars), which fused the lighter elements into heavier ones and quickly exploded. The debris of those stars re-condensed to make population II stars, which fused the nuclei of the largest atoms and then also exploded. That is how the heavier elements in the universe were formed. All this happened as the expansion continued. Then population I stars like our sun developed over billions of years. The heavier elements make up the planets and asteroids. This cannot even begin to be proven and, by any reasonable judgment, is an infinitely unlikely scenario.

As we look through the Hubble we can see as far as 13.2 billion light years away,[534] which means we are looking 13.2 billion light years into the past—less than 600 million years after the hypothetical Big Bang. If there was a Big Bang then we should be seeing the universe as it was in its initial stages of development soon after the Big Bang. But what we see at that great distance is galaxies with stars in them, like what we see in galaxies near us, not the universe in its "early" stage of development.

5. One population I star, as it condensed from a large hydrogen cloud, left a thin disk of debris around it which condensed into planets and moons—our solar system. The atmosphere of earth came from the ejected gasses of volcanoes, and the continents and the basins of the oceans were formed by tectonic plate movements over millions of years. Ideas about the formation of the earth and its atmosphere are completely hypothetical, unproven in any way, and under constant debate.

According to the book of Genesis God willed into existence the primordial substance of the universe—some solid matter and a lot of water covering it. He energized that first substance (created light) and separated the light from the darkness by a method that we cannot visualize. He then opened up a space in the water and moved most of it up high enough to make an open area that was as large as earth's atmosphere. On the earth He moved aside the water to make seas and uncover the dry land. Then He formed the upper waters into the objects in the heavens, including the sun, moon, and stars that man can see. As He did this He stretched out the upper area to be the size that it now is; that is, as big as we now know the universe to be. This supernatural account of how the cosmos came to be is admittedly just that—supernatural.

The account of modern philosopher-scientists purports to proceed according to natural laws yet at every step is "impossible" (in violation of known laws), highly unlikely, and/or unprovable. It only appeals to us today because of the inclination that we have to accept scientific reasons for all things. That is because science—true science—has reshaped our lives, i.e., recent technological, medical, and engineering inventions have completely determined the tenor of our society. Therefore a theory that sounds like science and that claims to proceed from a scientific basis has inherent convincing power in our minds.

One fundamental biased assumption scientists made when they formulated the Big Bang was that the present scientific laws had always been in effect; that is, the way to explain the world is through the outworking of completely natural processes. Such an assumption explicitly rules out a supernatural explanation. Thus it rules out God as having had any part in the process. That basic assumption is why their theories have been shown to be impossible at every step. The universe is a supernatural phenomenon just as Scripture says. The explanation of all things must be sought within a super naturalistic world view. This thinking is not Christian bias; it is plain objective logical necessity.

So their theory—the best guess of the brightest minds of our day—is impossible. There never was a Big Bang. It is a myth. But their theory does prove one thing: It proves that there can be no explanation for how this universe came to exist that follows a naturalistic scenario; that is, one that proceeds according to the inherent nature of the physical realm and without external "supernatural" intervention. The Big Bang Theory proves to us that something like the Genesis account is the only way to understand how the cosmos came to be. The universe is a supernatural object. It surely does "declare the glory of God." Naturalistic explanations fail, so a supernatural explanation is the only possibility.

Contrasting these two approaches to explaining the origin of world around us:
- The natural realm exists because of properties that are inherent in it. No, it exists by the will of God Who summoned it into existence, Who by His nature must exist. He, in His overflowing goodness, chose to create. That is why this world exists.
- The world came to be as it is by the nature of matter, which possesses the inherent inclination to self-organize into the structures around us. No, the world was formed into its present configuration by commands of God, Who is outside the natural realm.
- The universe took billions of years to arrive at its present state. No, the commands of God resulted in an instantaneous response from the created realm, for it owes its very existence to Him and cannot resist His will or His word for even a moment.

- The times of creation in the past are like today and we can understand the processes of creation by extending present processes into the distant past. No, the processes of creation were known only to God—days of awe and mystery partially shrouded from us by Him. The present ordinances came into effect only at the end of the six days.
- The Bible, especially Genesis, is a collection of ancient myths that primitive people, who did not understand the world as clearly as we do, wrote to explain the mystery of existence. No, the Bible was inspired by God and thus is completely true. (In fact, as we assert, it was written by men who were directly involved in the events that are related within its pages, and their accounts were edited and organized by Moses to make Genesis.)

Because Genesis is true, the creation of all things happened just a few thousand years ago, as indicated by the genealogies of Genesis. Every ancient writer believed this. Their issue with the timing of the Genesis account was only this: was all or part of the creation carried out in an instant in eternity, or did all of the times of the six days pass as time does today?

Creation and the Cosmic Configuration:
Cosmology also speaks volumes to us about the meaning of life and our place in creation. We have noted that the goal and working assumption of all science is to explain the world only as the outworking of natural causes operating under the immutable physical laws. In effect this takes God out of the picture because He is not part of the natural realm. He is supernatural and transcendent. Cosmology rests on one additional theoretical assumption called the Cosmological Principle. Here is how one researcher describes this principle:

> The contemporary cosmological models are based on the cosmological principle, which states that the Universe, smoothed over large enough scales, is essentially homogeneous and isotropic. Isotropy means given [any observation point,] the Universe looks the same in every direction. Homogeneity states that matter and radiation are uniformly distributed throughout the Universe . . . The Copernican principle states that there is no specially favored position in the Universe.[535]

This principle is naturally associated with the theories of origins that view our universe as formed by blind forces operating in random ways over long periods of time. This kind of assumption will lead to cosmological models that are formulated in such terms. This is another underlying assumption that leaves no room for purpose or meaning in one's view of the universe, of the earth, or of one's individual life. We are not special in any way and our home the earth has no special position in the vast scheme of the universe.

Carl Sagan is famously quoted as saying:
> Where are we? Who are we? We find that we live on an insignificant planet of a humdrum star lost between two spiral arms in the outskirts of a galaxy which is a member of a sparse cluster of galaxies, tucked away in some forgotten corner of a universe in which there are far more galaxies than people.[536]

This is a perfect expression of the Cosmological Principle, and also an expression of his atheistic world view. In this section I want to assemble definitive cosmological evidence showing this view of the universe to be utterly unscientific and wrong.

Since the 1970's evidence has been accumulating which indicates that we on this planet are in **the** uniquely special and privileged position within the universe. Astronomers have been systematically mapping out the universe for many decades, and actual observations do not support the idea that we are a chance happening in a far corner of the cosmos.

Physicist Y. P. Varshni, from analyzing the distribution of quasars in the cosmos, stated:
> [In this paper] it is shown that the cosmological interpretation of red shift in the spectra of quasars leads to yet another paradoxical result: namely, that the earth is the center of the Universe.[537] [see note]

> **[By the "cosmological interpretation of red shifts" he means assuming a redshift in the spectrum of light from a celestial body is due to its rapid motion away from us, which motion is the result of the expansion of the universe that is happening because of the Big Bang. Additionally, red shifts give us the distance of objects from the earth, since the speed of recession of a celestial object (calculated from its redshift) has been found to be a function of how far away from us it is. Thus the amount of red shift gives its recession velocity and also gives its distance from us.]**

What observational evidence led Dr. Varshni to make this claim? He was analyzing 384 quasars which had been found in the systematic, decades-long, mapping of the heavens.

Dr. Varshni displays the red shift and corresponding distance from earth of each quasar in a simple table. He then observes that the quasars fall neatly into 57 groups based on their distances from the earth. He summarizes his findings:
> In other words, assuming the cosmological red-shift hypothesis, the quasars in the 57 groups in Table I are arranged on 57 spherical shells with Earth as the center.[538]

Dr. Varshni then calculates for us the probability that this could be just chance:
> From the multiplicative law of probability, the probability of these 57 sets of coincidences occurring in this system of 384 QSOs ~ 3×10^{-85}.[539] **[QSO: quasi-stellar object or quasar]**

That probability is approximately 3 chances in 10,000,00 . . . ,000 (85 zeroes in the number).

For some time cosmologists have dithered and stewed about how they can interpret this observation in a way that does not place the earth at the center of the universe, and this area of cosmology in general is one huge unsolved mystery, as seen by the many articles and diverse ideas on the subject. (See the endnote on the first quotation from Dr. Varshni.)

But does the Genesis creation account fit with these observations? As we have shown, in the biblical account of creation God "stretched out" the heavens on the fourth day. All primordial matter was originally surrounding the earth (the deep). So it is very plausible that the cosmos would be configured with the earth at the center. It is not at all Inconceivable that the quasars would be arranged in concentric shells around a centrally located earth. It would be the result of God's action of creating them as He stretched out the firmament in every direction, formed the celestial bodies, and placed them within it.

There are several other striking violations of the Cosmological Principle that have been observed and catalogued by astronomers in recent years, and some of them also place the earth at a special position in the creation—once again, at the center of the cosmos.
- We are (providentially) located in the cosmos so that we have a chance to observe it in several directions. This makes our careful study of the universe possible.
- Analysis of Cosmic Microwave Background Radiation (CMBR) reveals temperature variations that align with the plane of the earth-sun orbit, with the equinoxes of the earth, and with the plane of the earth's equator. These alignments are confirmed to a high degree of certainty. CMBR reaches the earth from the farthest sectors of the detectible universe. These results indicate the earth is located at a central position in the cosmos and that our orientation is influencing in some way even the most distant regions of the universe.[540] [see note] Once again, the scientific community is baffled and even refers to one of these symmetries as the "axis of evil."

So in no way do actual observations correlate with the statement of Carl Sagan. There is clear purpose revealed in these findings, a purpose that places the earth in a special and privileged position within the grand scheme of the creation. They place the earth at the center of the entire universe. They do not correlate with the Big Bang Theory or with the Cosmological Principle. They also indicate that our understanding of celestial mechanics (the science of how and why the heavenly bodies move as they do) must be modified.

Celestial Mechanics:

We have noted just a few of many cosmic configurations that militate against the present "standard model" of the universe, the Big Bang Theory. But Dr. Varshni also notes that such discoveries will compel scientists to rethink their understanding of how the universe operates. The forces that govern the motion of the heavenly bodies, as we understand them today, are significantly deficient. I want to examine some of these more serious problems.

As astronomers look out into the cosmos they can tell that certain galaxies are rotating at a rate that should be causing them to fly apart; that is, the gravitational attraction which would result from the calculated mass of the galaxies is not sufficient to hold them together. This widely observed fact has forced cosmologists to postulate that there is a large amount of unseen matter associated with the galaxies. They call this "Dark Matter." However no one can imagine what dark matter is or why we cannot detect it in any way. This points to a serious deficiency in our understanding of the forces that govern the universe.

Astronomical observations tell us that not only is the cosmos expanding, it is expanding at an ever-increasing rate. The universe is accelerating outward. Such an acceleration requires massive amounts of energy, but no such source of energy can be found. Thus cosmologists must postulate that a massive force called "Dark Energy" is responsible for this outward acceleration of the galaxies. No one knows what dark energy is. Once again this points to a serious deficiency in our understanding of celestial mechanics.

It has also been noted that the present universe, basically homogeneous and in thermal equilibrium, could not have attained this homogeneity unless there was a short time for rapid inflation near the beginning of the Big Bang. Cosmologists postulate that inflation began at 10^{-36} seconds after the Big Bang and continued until about 10^{-33} or 10^{-32} seconds after the Big Bang, during which (infinitesimal) time the universe expanded suddenly to 10^{54} times its size, then slowed down again. The acceleration of the universe due to dark energy began about nine billion years later, or about four billion years ago.[541] [see note] Again, this special construct points to a serious deficiency in present day celestial mechanics. I might note that these observational anomalies are not for celestial objects that are near the earth but are observations in deep space, many light years from us. It is as if the laws of physics are different that far away, as if new and unknown forces come into play.

These difficulties in understanding and explaining the observed universe are in addition to the many difficulties that we noted earlier, where at each stage of the Big Bang scenario the postulated cosmic development was impossible or infinitely unlikely. Such a pervasive problem indicates that a radical error has been made. Radical: from the Latin *radix*, the root of a matter. So let us step back a bit and consider how historically we arrived at our present theories of cosmogeny, to see if we can determine how we got into the tangle of ideas that we call the Big Bang Theory.

Historical Overview of Cosmological Thought:

About five centuries ago the geocentric cosmology of the Middle Ages came under attack when that model of the solar system was challenged by Galileo and Copernicus. When Newton provided a mathematically based explanation for the motion of the planets around the sun, the heliocentric view of the solar system became firmly rooted in people's minds. Thus a smaller earth surely revolved around a larger sun, as did the other planets, and the earth was seen as just another planet, the one on which we happen to live, rather than as the cornerstone of God's creation and as the central purpose of His creative works. From this basic change in perspective mankind also was implicitly demoted in the cosmic plan, so there were profound philosophical/theological ramifications to the new cosmology.

The new cosmology was intrinsically an assertion of human reason over Christian revelation. As mankind sought to find its way in a new cosmic order, and as the methodology of science arose, mankind began more and more to view true knowledge and understanding as the product of human effort and human thinking, rather than as coming from divine revelation. Geocentrism was seen as an ancient and primitive idea, associated with the religiously dominated cultures of less advanced times. The world was ripe for rationalistic ideas.

By the late 1800's science had discovered the laws of electricity and magnetism and had put in place a basic idea of the earth and the solar system. The cosmos was seen as an ether field that surrounded all celestial bodies and conducted light. Then scientists tried to measure experimentally the earth's movement through the ether as it orbited around the sun. In 1887, in what would turn out to be the most significant experiment in the history of science, Albert A. Michelson and Edward Morley attempted to measure the movement of the earth.[542] The experiment revealed, to the consternation of the world's scientific community, that earth was not moving around the sun at 30 km/sec as expected, but was essentially stationary in space.[543] The experiment was repeated many times by many scientists—even into the 1930's—but always with the same results.[544] The implication: the observed relative motion of the sun and planets in the solar system had to be explained by starting with the "fact" that the earth was not traveling around the sun; therefore what was observed in the heavens could only be accounted for by saying that the sun was going around the earth. But such a decision would cause science to revert back to a geocentric view of the solar system like what had been put forth by Tycho Brahe.[545] That was seen as intolerable.[546]

What exactly did the Michelson-Morley experiment measure? The basic idea was that, as the earth traveled about the sun, light from the earth that was directed along the path of the earth's motion would travel more slowly than light that was directed perpendicular to the path of its orbit. The light waves sent out in the direction of the earth's motion would be "scrunched up" and would travel through the ether more slowly. However the effect was not observed—not nearly enough to account for the speed of the earth if it orbited the sun. There was supposed to be a significant "ether drag," but very little was observed.

To compound this problem, two other related experiments were conducted to measure the rotation of the earth in space.[547] These experiments did indeed show that there was an "ether drag," and thus the absence of any measurable effect in the Michelson-Morley experiment was highlighted even more. The conclusion from all three experiments was: The earth is not revolving about the sun, but is fixed in the cosmic ether field containing the sun, the planets, and the stars; and either the earth is rotating on its axis or the entire field of the cosmos and its supporting ether medium are rotating about a non-rotating earth. (It is not possible to tell from this or any experiment whether the earth is stationary, or the entire field of the cosmos is stationary; only that one rotates with respect to the other.) This was the awkward position of the scientific community early in the twentieth century.

Into this distressing situation came Einstein and his Special Relativity Theory. Einstein put forth his theory in 1905. It stated that the reason the Michelson-Morley experiment did not measure a difference in the speed of light along the path of the earth's orbit was because any object that moved would become shorter in the direction it was moving. As it moved faster it would shorten by a greater amount. Thus the equipment used in the Michelson-Morley experiment became shorter in the direction of the earth's motion and so did not measure the decrease in the speed of light that had taken place. Rather, the speed of light as measured from any perspective—from any frame of reference—would always be the same. At the time, this unintuitive perspective for viewing the world around us seemed preferable to a return to the geocentric view of the solar system.

In order to assert this Einstein also had to assert that as objects moved their passage of time as measured by others slowed down. The absolute upper limit of all velocity was the speed of light, or when length was shortened to zero and time stopped completely. Thus at this point in history science departed from an experimentally-based discipline that took reality at face value, and instead chose a view of the world that proceeded along lines that were determined by people's philosophical preferences—views which incorporated more esoteric ways of understanding the world. The Special and the General Theory of Relativity are the basis for how scientists interpret what they see as they look out of their telescopes at the universe. Yet experiments had indicated that parts of relativity theory were suspect.

But was it possible that this radical departure from how we think about the world around us was needful? After all, science is not only about observing the heavens, but also about explaining the observed motions of the heavenly bodies. It is not just about what we see out in the universe, but also about the dynamics that explain why bodies move as they do, about what we see and about how we explain it, about observation and also about celestial mechanics and the dynamic forces that govern the celestial bodies. Here is what I mean: We might reasonably ask, if we were to revert to a geocentric view of the solar system, then what would happen to Newton's mathematical explanation for the motion of the sun and the planets, based as it was on his theory of gravity as a universal attracting force? And Einstein built upon Newton's calculations, extending them to more general situations.

The truth is Newton clearly explained that the motion of the heavens in the Tycho-Brahe geocentric model could also be explained mathematically. He would just have to recognize certain other forces which would then come into play (these are called the Coriolis force, the Centrifugal force, and the Euler force) and incorporate them into his equations of motion. Einstein also acknowledged this possibility, as did many other physicists throughout the decades,[548] but this option was rejected anyway. It was rejected on philosophical grounds, and in direct defiance of the obvious interpretation of the results of the Michelson-Morley experiment, because it would immediately lead to a geocentric model of the universe.

What I am saying here is that, not only could what we see in the motion of the planets of the solar system be interpreted by a model that was geocentric as readily as one that was heliocentric, but also that dynamic forces to explain the observed motions of the heavenly bodies can be postulated just as well for either model of the solar system. The decision on which view to accept has been made on philosophical grounds and not on experimentally based grounds; in fact, the decision to go along our present direction was made in the teeth of experimental results. It was not experimentally mandated; rather, it was contraindicated, since the one thing heliocentrism could not explain was the lack of "ether drag," as indicated by the various abortive attempts to measure the speed of the earth as it orbited the sun.

But the earth is the foundation of God's entire creation. If men misunderstand the motion of our planet then they will carry that mistake into their understanding of the entire cosmos. That is exactly what happened.

In the late 1920's Hubble first observed the redshift in the light reaching us from the distant galaxies as viewed in every direction from the earth. This omnidirectional observation, if given its most natural interpretation, would imply that the earth was situated at the center of the cosmos and that everything was receding from us in all directions—assuming that the meaning of the redshift is that the galaxies are in fact receding away from the earth. But Hubble considered that interpretation of the redshift as unacceptable.[549] Hubble and his successors devised the idea that the universe was 4-dimensional, and our 3-dimensional world lay on the surface of a 4-dimensional expanding sphere. Thus every position on the sphere would observe the same thing that we see from earth; that is, the entire universe would be seen as receding away from any point. Thus the earth was not in any special place in the grand scheme of things. Thus the Copernican Principle, which stated that the earth was not the center of the solar system, was extended into the Cosmological Principle, which asserted that the earth (and humanity) occupied no special or privileged place in the cosmos. Hubble's idea of the expanding universe became the foundational insight that undergirds the Big Bang Theory, and the Cosmological Principle became the basis for how scientists look at and understand the cosmos. That is how cosmology got to where it is today.

So how we interpret what we see as we look out into the heavens MIGHT have proceeded along geocentric lines, but did not for philosophical reasons—reasons rooted in how our understanding of physics evolved, in the arguments between the Church/Bible and certain early astronomers, in the antagonism between religion and human speculations which these produced, and in the resulting philosophical biases of scientists that developed as centuries passed. Today many astronomical observations seem to indicate that the ancient geocentric view of the heavens is correct, and modern cosmological theories are in shambles—both when trying to explain the configurations of distant heavenly bodies and when trying to explain the dynamic forces that govern the motion of those bodies. Cosmology has taken a wrong turn, and the above insights seem to be pointing us to how and when that happened.

So let me assert something here—something that is "radical" in that it pierces to the root of modern cosmology. I propose that a geocentric model of the universe and of the solar system, along with the celestial mechanics that attend that model of the cosmos, probably would be able to explain what we are seeing as we look out into the universe.[550] All of the observed anomalies that I have listed probably would be explained, and the problems with celestial mechanics that I have enumerated would likely find reasonable solutions. This is radical, but the problems with celestial mechanics are radical, calling for "thinking outside the box." This would also put astronomy back on an experimental, not a philosophical, footing.

Theologically, this change in world view would restore human beings to our rightful position at the center of God's plan of creation. It would return to us the fundamental meaning of our life, putting in perspective this life in view of eternity. It would allow us to see the Scriptures as the inspired, infallible, inerrant word of God.[551] **It would undergird the truth of Genesis, since the creation account in the Bible specifically lays the foundation for a geocentric view of the world.** It would break the iron fist of scientific naturalism that has such a tight grip on most intellectual and academic disciplines today. It would instead restore divine wisdom to its rightful place as the light that must guide the human race, rather than only the human intellect divorced from and in defiance of biblical truth.[552] [see note]

One other little detail: Einstein's General Theory of Relativity asserts that the speed of light is not constant, but that it varies when light is traveling through force fields. Huge forces (that is, the Centrifugal and Coriolis forces from a rotating universe, which dramatically increase the further the distance is from earth) hold the heavens in place in the celestial mechanics of geocentric cosmology. So once light was far enough from the earth—outside the solar system—it would travel MUCH faster. So the question of how light from distant regions of the cosmos has reached the earth in less than 6,000 years would become a non-issue.[553]

Finally, I want to mention a term that crops up in cosmology from time to time. The term is "Boltzmann's Brain."[554] This is the solipsistic dead-end of godless speculation about the origin of our cosmos. Because of the obvious fine tuning of the universe,[555] (a diverse set of dovetailing circumstances about reality that allows intelligent creatures to exist) it is observed that it would be more likely for a single brain to spontaneously pop into existence in a void, complete with false memories of having existed in a universe just like our own, than for this finely-tuned cosmos to have come about without an Intelligent Purposeful Designer and to have been so constituted that it could support the normal development of such a brain.

The fine tuning of the universe also spawned the idea that our cosmos is part of a "multiverse" that contains an infinite number of universes, and that ours just happens to be the one in which we find ourselves because it happens by chance to be capable of supporting intelligent life. This is the ultimate result of adhering to the Cosmological Principle and of continuing down the path of godless theorizing. Clearly this world and our existence have meaning and purpose, and that truth must, by its very nature, be rooted in the high and holy ways of our Creator. Our minds and spirits need this truth for us to be stable, sane individuals.

Day 5:
Genesis 1:20—Then God said, "Let the waters teem with swarms of living creatures, and let birds fly above the earth in the open expanse of the heavens."

Vetus—And God said: Let the waters produce reptiles of live souls and flying things over the earth along the *solid structure* of heaven. *And it was made thus*.

Genesis 1:21— God created the great sea monsters and every living creature that moves, with which the waters swarmed after their kind, and every winged bird after its kind; and God saw that it was good.

Genesis 1:22—God blessed them, saying, "Be fruitful and multiply, and fill the waters in the seas, and let birds multiply on the earth."

Vetus—And God blessed them saying: Increase and multiply and fill the waters in the sea; and let flying things multiply over the earth. *And thus it was made.*

From verse twenty-two Augustine concluded that the days of Genesis (at least some of them) were not normal days because after God blessed the creatures He had just created to their fecundity, it then says, "and thus it was made." Thus he notes that the full import of what God did was to create the animals, bless them, command them to multiply, and then to fill the earth and waters. Only after that was the fifth day ended. But it is clear that animal propagation takes time: First there is fertilization, then gestation, then birth. The breeding of each new generation would take many days. Many generations would be required before the blessing could have its full effect and before the earth and the waters could be filled. But the account concludes by saying "and thus it was made," and only then does it say in the next verse that the fifth day was completed. Because of this he concluded that the fifth day of creation was not a regular day.[556] This is in his unfinished commentary, but in his full work decades later the phrase "and thus it was made" is omitted.

Indeed, this deduction is based on an interpretation that is peculiar to his translation. In the Hebrew Bible the statement "and thus it was made" is missing. The Hebrew text says only that the Lord created the first pair (or perhaps multiple pairs) of each kind of animal and blessed them and then the fifth day ended. The Hebrew text does not say that they bred and filled the earth (as "and thus it was made" would imply) before the fifth day ended. This difference in the text allows for the regular passage of time—for very many centuries—before the blessing achieves its total effect and before the various kinds of animals actually do fill the earth. Therefore the blessing of God need not be fulfilled during the fifth day as Augustine understood from his translation.

The Original State of the Biosphere:
This raises an important point about the creation of both the plants and the animals. We know that there was only one pair of human beings created at the beginning, and we all have descended from that first pair. It seems that something similar must be for the plants, fish, and animals. I say this because God blessed the animals and commanded them to be fruitful and multiply and fill the earth. That sounds as if the full population of animals was not created, but only developed over time, as we noted. However, God did say "let the waters teem with" and this seems to imply that schools of some fish were created from the start. He said, "let the birds fly" and even this *might* indicate that He created more than one pair of some birds—those that like to flock, for example. This might also be true of some species of fish and not others, for some like to school but not all.

Thus the initial population of the earth, both in the sea and in the air, might have been many pairs of certain birds and fishes, but not as many as would have been necessary to fill all the earth; indeed, not nearly that many. Also from the wording of verses 11-12 it is not clear how thickly the vegetation was created at the beginning. When I plant a stand of vegetation I plant them far apart so they can grow and fill in the bare spots. The command of God for the vegetation says that they were created with seeds and fruit, so I assume the plants were ready to propagate. But was the initial earth lush everywhere with dense vegetation? I would imagine that it was not, but it grew into that over time.

So here is my picture of the biosphere of the earth after the creation: There were many plants of all kinds, each mature and bearing seeds and fruit, but they were not densely planted. There was an abundance of open places for them to expand and grow into in due time. Thus the original appearance of the vegetation on the earth was sparse in some places. There were birds and fish of all kinds. There were large schools of some fishes, more of some kinds than others, and there were birds of all the different species in varying quantities, with more of some kinds than others, but in no way did the population of birds fill the earth—nor did the population of fishes fill the sea. It would take many years for the various kinds of growing things to fill the world—but they would, for God directly blessed the fish and birds. That blessing will also carry over to the land animals of the sixth day.

Again we have the command of God to create issued by the Father (verse 20) and then the actual fulfillment of that command executed by the Son (verse 21). But there is no "and it was so" in this verse. This is a special turning point in the creation as can be understood from several points. The word "create" in verse twenty-one is the Hebrew word *bara'* that was used in verse one to indicate the *ex nihilo* creation of the formless substance. This is the second time in the narrative that this word is used. This surely indicates that at this juncture there is more to what God is doing than just fashioning or forming the primeval substance that He previously called into existence from nothing.

These creatures have the breath of life in them. The plants that God formed along with the land and oceans on the surface of the earth on the third day did not possess this property "life." Animal life has a special essence inherent in it, something that is more than just the sum of its physical components. The use of *bara'* in this verse indicates the forming or shaping of new substances or circumstances. These creatures have life in them (Hebrew *nephesh*), which is translated as "soul" in most places in the Bible. This is not an immortal soul like humans have, but it is special. It partakes of a reality that was not included in the primordial substance that God created in the beginning. We can only conclude that it touches on a spiritual reality that is interconnected with the physical realm in some way that is not revealed to us. But only the Father creates *ex nihilo*.

That is why we should understand that the Father takes a personal role in this creative activity—this step involves more than just forming a structure. Something is created *ex nihilo*. God confirms this new step in His creative action, and indicates the dignity of the animals, by blessing them before He commands them to be fruitful and to multiply. This is the first blessing that God gives during His creative work. These creative actions must have been fulfilled partially by the Father Who is the preeminent creator. This is why the phrase "and it was so" is not present. There was no affirmation of this command by the Son because He could not carry it out by Himself. The Father used the Spirit in His *ex nihilo* work of creating animal souls, and the Son used Him in forming their bodies.

Because the Son formed the animal bodies God did affirm it ("and God saw it was good"); that is, He affirmed the part that the Son performed. Then God blessed the work of the fifth day. We see that the wording of this verse indicates in two ways that something new is being created: The lack of an affirming "and it was so" by the Son, and the presence of the word *bara'* for "created" in verse 21.

There is a contrast between the creation of animals and the creation of man. Although both have souls we see from these verses that animals were made both body and soul in one step. When their bodies die so do their souls. There was a connection created between the physical and "soulish" realm, which is activated when animals reproduce, that forms their soul along with their body. It is a created, mechanistic connection.

We will see that God personally creates each human soul and that humans (body and soul) are made in two steps, although we are a perfectly coordinated unity. When our bodies die our souls remain. This simple truth undergirds our hope for resurrection and eternal life.

After Their Kind:
These land animals, which renew themselves by seminal propagation, are all stated to reproduce "after their kind" even as was stated for the plants on day three. Thus each kind of creature is stated to have the ability only to propagate a new generation that is like itself. Genesis is not compatible with the theory of evolution which states that living forms gradually evolve from simple to more complex types, eventually producing all the various kinds of living things by unlimited variation in form. That view of origins asserts that a one-celled protozoan chanced to develop from non-living material and happened to evolve over a long time into all other life forms.[557 see note]

Paul implicitly refers to the biblical fact that "like begets like" in his discussion about the resurrection body that we will each be given. He talks about what the resurrection body might be like, comparing it to the sowing and subsequent sprouting of a seed into a plant:
> [A]nd that which you sow, you do not sow the body which is to be, but a bare grain, perhaps of wheat or of something else. But God gives it a body just as He wished, and to each of the seeds a body of its own. (1 Corinthians 15:37–38)

Thus each seed sprouts a body of its own, depending on what kind of seed it is. It will sprout "after its own kind." The type of plant that it produces depends upon the genetic code programmed into it by God when He initially created it during the six days.

A Critique of Biological Evolution:
Let us examine evolution theory in a little detail. The idea behind the theory of biological evolution can be summarized as follows:[558 see note]
> There is a principle within nature that affects living things. As living things reproduce, the successive generations vary from their ancestors. Over time these variations sometimes produce new and more resilient creatures, and the older varieties are eliminated by natural selection because they are not as adept at life. The principle of automatically developing increased complexity also applies to organic molecules, which over time have evolved into simple living things, and these simple life forms have gradually become more complex and have diversified into the plethora of living things that we see around us today. This adaptability and unrestricted changeability of life is a fact—the fact of evolution. This is the "molecule to man" theory.
>
> There is a simple observation about the world around us that undergirds this theory. We can easily see that all living things do produce different varieties in their offspring. This clearly indicates that life in its myriad forms has a certain amount of plasticity built into it. Over enough time this plasticity will produce completely new types of life, new species. When this theory of life was originally posited the hypothetical carrier of genetic change was called a gemmule. That was the name given to the part in living things that carried the genetic history into successive generations as reproduction took place, and which resulted in a slightly different and better organism. This theory was to be verifiable quite easily by looking at the fossil record. We should be able to see the changes in life forms preserved as fossils. The gradual development of life should be recorded in stone for us to read.

This was the theory as it was postulated more than a century and a half ago. What have we observed about the world of living things since then?

For over a century an earnest but futile search for the transitional forms was conducted in the fossil record. In 1972 Stephen Jay Gould and Niles Eldredge published a landmark paper called *Punctuated Equilibrium* that observed that stasis (no change in species) was the universal norm in the fossil record and therefore we should take the view that changes in species happen suddenly, and that short times of rapid development punctuate the stasis that species normally exhibit. This theory is widely accepted today in various forms. It indicates that the fossil record did not display the developmental changes in living things that was expected based on the evolutionary principle hypothesized as inherent in all living things. *Punctuated Equilibrium* is itself just another kind of naturalistic theory which purports to explain the origin of life, and it would seem to be even more problematic. What would cause the long periods of stasis and then sudden bursts of change? Whatever problems this theory may have, its formulation and acceptance show that many scientists have given up the search for transitional forms.

In the late 1800s Gregor Mendel formulated his theory of genetic inheritance. This was expanded on in the early 1900s by Thomas Hunt Morgan. The brunt of their work shows that there is a "genetic pool" of traits that each "kind" of living organism carries within its chromosomes. The traits that are passed along to an offspring from each of its parents at reproduction are taken from this pool of traits, a pool that is fixed for each organism type. Thus we will see variations in organisms from generation to generation, but the amount of change that is possible is limited. Each organism can only pass on traits that are in its genetic pool. Life has a certain amount of plasticity, but it is strictly limited. This explains the different varieties that we see in offspring but prohibits true evolution from one form of life into another. The word "gemmule" as it was originally hypothesized has become obsolete.

It seems to me that if the infinite plasticity of living things were a fact, then what we should observe around us would not be a plethora of well-defined but distinct species, but we would rather see a continuum of living things without well-defined boundaries separating them into identifiable species or types of life forms.

This leads us to another assumption inherent in the theory of evolution: the chemical basis of life must be relatively simple. This is important because living things evolved out of basic molecules by chance. The chemical basis of life must be fairly simple in order for this to have happened. In 1953 Francis Crick and James Watson discovered the structure of DNA. I was a little boy then and reveled in each scientific achievement, from rocks to rockets, from genomes to galaxies. When this was announced there was an unusual reaction of heated accusations from certain scientists. I remember it because I had never before heard such pejorative speech between scientists reported in the newspapers. The accusations lasted for a few weeks and then died out without a trace, and the dispute was never resolved. When I was young I did not understand why this dispute and heated reaction occurred, but I surely do now. The incredibly complex structure of DNA makes it prohibitively unlikely that it could ever have arisen from simpler molecules by random chance. But the DNA discovery was and is undisputable today. Later on Crick and Leslie Orgel proposed that life on earth may have been planted here by an advanced civilization from another world. This was proposed because it could not have arisen by chance. The theory was named Panspermia.[559]

Michael J. Behe, professor of Biochemistry at Lehigh University, living several decades after Crick's discovery and deeply involved in continuing research to uncover the mysteries of life locked within the intricacies of the cell, comments on the complexity of the biochemical basis of life and its implications for evolutionary theory:

> Understanding how something works is not the same as understanding how it came to be. For example, the motions of the planets in the solar system can be predicted with tremendous accuracy; however, the origin of the solar system (the question of how the sun, planets, and their moons formed in the first place) is still controversial. Science may eventually solve the riddle. Still, the point remains that understanding the origin of something is different from understanding its day-to-day workings.

> Science's mastery of nature has led many people to presume that it can—indeed, must—also explain the origin of nature and life. Darwin's proposal that life can be explained by natural selection acting on variation has been overwhelmingly accepted in educated circles for more than a century, even though the basic mechanisms of life remained utterly mysterious until several decades ago. Modern science has learned that, ultimately, life is a molecular phenomenon: All organisms are made of molecules that act as the nuts and bolts, gears and pulleys of biological systems. Certainly there are complex biological features (such as the circulation of blood) that emerge at higher levels, but the gritty details of life are the province of biomolecules.[560]

How does this affect the theory of evolution in its attempt to explain the origin of life? Such an intricate biomolecular mechanism could not have arisen by chance. Behe continues:

> [T]he science of biochemistry, which studies those molecules, has as its mission the exploration of the very foundation of life. Since the mid-1950s biochemistry has painstakingly elucidated the workings of life at the molecular level. Darwin was ignorant of the reason for variation within a species (one of the requirements of his theory), but biochemistry has identified the molecular basis for it. Nineteenth-century science could not even guess at the mechanism of vision, immunity, or movement, but modern biochemistry has identified the molecules that allow those and other functions. It was once expected that the basis of life would be exceedingly simple. That expectation has been smashed. Vision, motion, and other biological functions have proven to be no less sophisticated than television cameras and automobiles. Science has made enormous progress in understanding how the chemistry of life works, but the elegance and complexity of biological systems at the molecular level have paralyzed science's attempt to explain their origins. There has been virtually no attempt to account for the origin of specific, complex biomolecular systems, much less any progress. Many scientists have gamely asserted that explanations are already in hand, or will be sooner or later, but no support for such assertions can be found in the professional science literature. More importantly, there are compelling reasons—based on the structure of the systems themselves—to think that a Darwinian explanation for the mechanisms of life will forever prove elusive.[561]

Scientists have tried to produce evolutionary changes by controlled breeding of species. Fruit flies are ideal since they reproduce quickly with new generations about once a day. Many thousands of generations of fruit flies have been bred under the most stressful conditions: radiation, ultraviolent light, various chemicals, etc. All these were attempts to induce mutations in their genes, to cause a new organism to arise. The result after many thousands of generations is many dead or mangled fruit flies but not a new kind of insect. No evolution has ever resulted under any circumstances—not in this experiment, in any other experiment, or by any observation in the natural world.

Today we realize that any trait that a species possesses is actually tied to a complex combination of interconnected genetic configurations embedded in the structure of their genome. A change in that trait is connected to intertwining changes in biochemical structures that would have to be modified in a coordinated way to effect the macro-sized change in the organism. Such interrelated changes are essentially impossible, and this is an even deeper reason why evolutionary transformations never happen; this is why the genetic pool is fixed for any given "kind" of living organism.

> Here is an apt illustration of this conundrum as faced by the evolutionist: What if we were trying to "evolve" an old 4x3 TV into a more advanced flat-screen TV? Well, just stretch it out to have a 16x9 ratio and flatten the bulge in the picture tube. But that is not it at all. Inside the TV we must change the mechanism that sprays those electrons onto the screen—in fact it no longer "sprays" anything. The entire mechanism is revamped to something completely different. The screen is not just reshaped, but also has a revised mechanism for emitting picture images. The

way that the signal is interpreted from the remote broadcasting station has been changed, and the way it is mapped onto the screen employs a different set of protocols for handling that interface. The simple external changes, so easy to conceptualize at first, are linked to an interconnected set of complex internal structures that all must be changed in a coordinated way to create the new and better TV. This could never happen by chance. However the chemical basis of life is magnitudes more intricate and complicated than the structure of the television set. This is directly connected to what Michael J. Behe was saying.

The conclusion about biological evolution is immediate. There is no "principle" within living things that can produce better offspring, or that can produce gradual, *unrestricted* changes to living organisms as one generation after another is born; instead the amount of change possible for a given kind of living thing is limited to choosing characteristics from its given fixed genetic pool. Each basic kind of living thing has its own peculiar and unique chemical makeup at the cellular level—its own genetic pool of characteristics.

Thus all basic "kinds" of animals must have been originally created by God. The many variations that have arisen within each kind over the generations have never produced a new "kind" of living thing. This reinforces the third principle of origins as stated above. Because the Lord God has told us that He created living animals on the fifth and sixth days of creation we should realize that we cannot expect a naturalistic theory of origins to explain life. We should see the flexibility of living things and their ability to change somewhat as the generations pass—but only within certain fixed bounds—as the Lord's providential provision for their continued existence under diverse conditions on earth.

Augustine points out that today living things, such as a tree for instance, grow from a seed or a clipping by gradual growth and development. But in the initial creation,
> He made them in the way in which He created all things simultaneously, and finished them on day number six . . . not as a series one after another in time, but as a series to be known in due order in their causes. From these works He rested on the seventh day . . . [but] without setting up any further creature, but steering and guiding by His regulatory action all things made simultaneously, He continues to work without ceasing [as stated by Jesus "My Father works even today" (John 5:17)].[562]

Thus he draws a sharp distinction (common with the ancients) between works of the six days of creation—the unique processes that God used to initially create all things during the six days—and the on-going processes that are now in effect. The ordinances that characterize the present world, which we understand and study scientifically—the laws that now maintain the creation—were only brought into effect at the end of the six days.

When you ponder the simple—but clear and reasonable—objections that I have listed to the present-day naturalistic theories of origins, it might make you ask why those theories still stand. The objections that I raise, though they are simple, penetrate to the root of their respective scientific disciplines—but it is difficult to change your world view. Such ideas are rooted in 400-year-long history of philosophical/intellectual flight from God, a movement hailed as "liberation from the bondage of ignorance"—an idea that feeds upon and bolsters human intellectual pride. Thus they have ensnared men of great intellectual achievement.

Nevertheless the theories that seem so solidly in place and impregnable are on the verge of collapse. It is only a matter of time before they are openly discredited. That is why it is especially foolish to base any of our biblical interpretations on such flimsy claims. They are like the flower of the field. They truly are fading and passing away (Isaiah 40:8). What would we expect from an idea that contradicts God's word and that places mankind in the position of the Creator? They are doomed to destruction.

Genetics and the Future of Biological Life Forms on Earth:
Twenty-first century genetics has fatally undermined the biological theory of origins that is so prevalent today and has also painted a clear picture of the future of living things.

A dear friend and his wife, whom I had not seen for forty years, were visiting me. He was a life-long atheist and a professor of microbiology at a certain university. Someone asked him about the complexity of the genome and its implications for evolutionary theory. My friend said with a light wave of his hand, "Aw, they'll figure it out. It's just a matter of time." Of course, this was an act of faith on his part. But it was also very revealing. By this reply he confirmed that the problem was a very real present concern, but he also expressed his unwavering belief that "they" would resolve it—science would explain all.

What exactly is the content of the "faith" that my friend so easily espoused? According to Dr. John Sanford the Primary Axiom of biological evolution can be stated as:
> **Life is life because random mutations at the molecular level are filtered through a reproductive sieve acting on the level of the whole organism.**[563]

He explains that an axiom is not testable, but is accepted as true by faith because "it seems to be obviously true to all people." This is the faith my friend holds to. Expanding it a bit, this is a short statement encoding the idea that mutation (at the molecular level) operated on by natural (unguided, blind, random) selection at the level of the whole organism, has produced the plethora of living forms, as well as the chemistry that supports their complex genetic machinery. So life is the product of a long series of accidental mutations at the chemical level, sifted out at the level of the whole organism by a random selection process.

Let us examine the chemistry that supports living things. The chemical basis of life is its genome, which is a detailed instruction manual for constructing the total organism. It is located in the nucleus of the organism's cells. When parents produce offspring the entire manual is copied and given to the next generation. A mutation is a copying error. It is a mistake that happens at the biochemical level within the cell nucleus. Unless some other factor is in operation mutations will accumulate within the biochemical mechanism of the species. Over generations it will degenerate, become less viable, and eventually die out.

Now let us look at the blind, random, selection process that is called "natural selection." Natural selection operates at the level of the whole organism, within large populations of animals. The function of natural selection is to "sift out" weaker organisms from the total population and keep the individuals that are stronger and more able to reproduce. Any organism carrying harmful mutations will not be as viable; that is, it will not be as strong or as likely to survive and reproduce. So any organism that has **measurably** lessened functionality because of a harmful mutation will gradually be "sifted out" by the blind and randomly operating process of natural selection. And any animal that has a **measurably** increased functionality because it carries a beneficial mutation will be selected for. This describes how beneficial mutations are carried forward, along with the organisms which carry them, and how harmful ones are left behind, along with the organisms that had the sad misfortune to carry them. This is the mechanism that drives evolution.[564]

However the great majority of mutations have only a small effect on their carrier, one that is **not noticeable** at the level of the total organism, one which will not affect viability for the organism in any **measurable** way, and which therefore will not be selected for or against by natural selection. These minute changes, for better or worse, are invisible to natural selection.[565] Thus they will remain in the population and will be dispersed throughout it by interbreeding over successive generations. Such mutations will accumulate in the total population and effect a gradual diminishment or increase in the viability of the species.

The above logic, along with the following discoveries, show that evolution is impossible.
- Almost all mutations are deleterious,[566] although only slightly so. It is questionable whether even one beneficial mutation has ever been documented. All mutations destroy information, they do not create new information. They muddy or confuse the instructions in the genome that will assemble the next generation, they do not generate new/better instructions for making new/more efficient organisms. Also, slightly beneficial mutations, those which do not produce a significantly more viable animal, will not be selected for by natural selection, for the same reason that slightly harmful mutations are not selected against—they are "invisible" at the level of the total organism. They do not affect its viability appreciably and so do not give the organism that is carrying them a plus or minus in the fight for survival. In order for evolution to operate, a **measurably** beneficial mutation would have to occur. This type of mutation has been carefully watched for by the evolutionary community at large for more than 100 years,[567] and no such mutation has ever been documented.
- The mutation rate for human beings is in the range of hundreds of times higher than would be allowable for the population to not degenerate over time.[568]

When we consider these simple facts, which have come to light in the last 20-25 years of research, it becomes forcefully apparent that species are not evolving, but rather that they are slowly and inexorably degenerating. The gradual accumulation of many small but deleterious mutations within the genome of each living thing will lead to a slow decline in viability, and will eventually drive all species to extinction. This process is slow, but not on the order of millions of years; rather, on the order of just thousands of years.[569] The human species, and all life forms, were created some thousands of years ago and are gradually degenerating and will cease to be viable in some thousands of years more.

The Primary Axiom was supposed to be "obvious to all." But was it truly obvious, even before the latest discoveries were made public? Dr. Sanford observes:
> **Isn't it remarkable that the Primary Axiom of biological evolution essentially claims that typographical errors and limited selective copying within an instruction manual can transform a [one-celled organism] into a [human being] in the absence of any intelligence, purpose, or design? Do you find this concept credible?** It becomes even more startling when we realize that the [human being] was in no way specified under the Primary Axiom, not even in the mind of God. It truly "just happened" by accident [bold in the original].[570]

The act of faith that my friend and his cohorts have made runs counter to our first intuition, and research shows that it also runs counter to the scientific discoveries of the twenty-first century. Instead we are faced with the inexorable degeneration of the human genome; indeed, we are looking at the gradual degeneration of the instruction manuals for all living things. The word used to describe this is a very appropriate one—genetic entropy.

Man will eventually be forced to abandon his philosophical biases and acknowledge reality. As my friend said, "Aw they'll figure it out. It's just a matter of time."

<u>A Spiritual Perspective on the Issue of Evolution in our Day</u>:
When I was a little boy growing up in the 1950's I reveled in everything scientific. I filled my mind with stories about scientific discoveries on every topic. The "space race" was the

biggest news in those days. I cut out stories from the newspapers in Fort Wayne, Indiana and taped them to my bedroom walls. They were covered with newspaper articles. When Crick's discovery of the structure of DNA was announced, and when the many heated denunciations from other scientists followed, those stories also went up on my walls. As a child I did not understand the reason for their heated reactions, but I was fascinated because I had never before heard such pejorative statements from scientists. I waited for a resolution, but the accusations died out and nothing came of the issue.

Today I understand the shock and disappointment generated in evolutionary circles by that discovery. Evolutionists **might** have reconsidered their position at that point. The rational response would have been to back off on their assertions. But the attempt to explain the origins of human life was never merely an intellectual and/or scientific effort. But nstead people redoubled their intensity and made every effort to push their thinking on others at every level of education. It was not science. It was and is spiritual warfare. It was and is a world view traceable directly back to rationalist philosophical assumptions.

What I am doing in this book is very simple. I am removing the Sword that the Lord has given the Church from the sheath where we have been carefully protecting it. It gleams very brightly and has two sharp edges. There is not one nick or dulled place on it. The Sword of the Spirit is the Word of God. We have been given this one weapon with which to conduct our battles in situations like this. This is the Sword that the Fathers used to bring down the edifice of Greek speculative knowledge in their day, and it is the one and only weapon that God has for us today. Jesus called this Sword "Truth" (John 17:17).

A Story to Illustrate our Situation:
Here is a simple story, a kind of parable, to illustrate the situation that we are in today with respect to these theories. A few decades ago there was a TV show in which the audience members had a chance to vote on who was "correct" in some kind of debate. Let us assume that they witnessed a debate between Mortimer Schnurrr—an imaginary person who definitely is not the sharpest knife in the drawer—and Albert Einstein. They were to debate on a certain subject in mathematics. Who do you think would win that debate? Do you think it would be Albert or Mortimer? Is there any doubt? But I will now add one more detail about the debate. Mortimer will hold to the position that two plus two is four, and Albert will hold that two plus two is five. Now who will win? Let me expand on this light-hearted hypothetical scenario in a little more detail.

Here is how the debate will go. Mortimer will stand up there and pull out two oranges from his right pocket, then two from his left, hold them up and say, "Duh! See? Two in my left hand and two in my right. Now I put dem together and I get four oranges. Dat's my proof." Then he might repeat it a few times using ping-pong balls and marbles. Then he would sit down saying, "It's simple."

Now Albert gets up. "Very nice, Mort. But it is simplistic of you, not really just simple." Then he would go to the blackboard and fill it with multi-dimensional tensors and partial differential equations, all the while talking and explaining how and why appearances are "relative" to various circumstances and cannot be relied upon, and how physics and astronomy have shown . . . etc. At the end he would sit down with a flourish and say, "it is not as simple a matter as we have always thought." Who would be the winner now? Who would get the votes?

The answer is not so obvious! Each person in the audience would have to go through a thought process something like this: "Well, I know what Mortimer is talking about—what I always experience—but Albert is such a brain, and he is so confident. I don't understand what he is saying, but his reasons are so impressive." Each personal vote would come down to this issue: Do I trust what my own mind says is correct, or do I abdicate my powers of thinking and let Albert think for me? Does my "common sense" prevail, or am I willing to believe that behind the veil of what seems obvious there is a deeper truth that eludes all but the very learned? It is not at all obvious who would win that vote.

And this is exactly the situation you are in as you listen to me explain these quite simple things about cosmology, geology, and biology. I am Mortimer Schnurrr, and the present scientific establishment is Albert Einstein. Who do you vote for? All I ask is that you use the brain that God gave you and think for yourself. Do not let all of the abstruse and incomprehensible arguments of "experts" sway your thought process. In our culture the scientific experts have the "spirit of the age," which is scientific naturalism, undergirding everything that they say. But their theories are not science and they are not true.

The idea that underlays evolution is simple: successive generations of living things differ from their ancestors by a certain amount. Over many generations these differences will accumulate and eventually a completely new and better kind of animal will arise. However that idea did not hold up. The expected transitional forms were not in the fossil record and life was not chemically simple. The idea that underlays the Big Bang is simple: the universe is expanding and so it must have all been in one place in the distant past and expanded into its present form. But the details of how the elements of the universe and the stars could have formed cannot be worked out. No scenario about the distant past is possible. Those simple ideas, once the details of reality became known, were unworkable.

In this way scientists who have doggedly pursued those original hypotheses to their final conclusions have come up against an insurmountable barrier. It can be stated in very simple words: the natural realm cannot spontaneously produce the universe that we see around us, and it cannot produce the life forms that we see. Some force outside of the natural realm must have been in operation to bring things to their present state. That is what God was doing during the six days.

The "Scientific Mystique" of Our Age:
There is a mysterious aura about science that has developed and grown during the past few centuries. Mankind has always known that our world was governed by stable "laws" that upheld its consistent functioning. But in the past we could not identify and describe those laws. Recently we have precisely identified them and have expressed them in the language of mathematics. We can now predict exactly how material reality will behave. In our day we have used this understanding to arrive at engineering, technological, and medical achievements that have completely transformed human life on this planet. These achievements have also transformed how men and women think about the world around them and how they see their place in it—and how they think about the origin of things.

In the past the Christian culture of the west acknowledged that the governing principles of the universe had come into effect at the end of the six days of creation. Thus implicitly they could not be used to explain the origin of all things because they were not in effect when God put the universe together. However, because of the astounding success that we have had in constructing our present scientific-technological society, it is difficult for men today to imagine that there ever was a time in the past when the present laws were not in effect and governing the material world as they presently do. They are seen as inviolable. This is the "scientific mystique." We cannot believe that the laws themselves were ordained by God at some point in the past when He completed the creation.

We insist on asserting that "everything has a scientific explanation;" that is, everything is explainable by reference to the laws of science only; that is, everything has a fully naturalistic explanation. Because God is not part of the natural realm, because He is super-natural, He can never be the reason for or the cause of anything. This is not science. It is an act of faith. It is the "scientific mystique" that gives rise to such attitudes and beliefs. This attitude implicitly places mankind at the apex of all knowledge and makes us the judge of all things—and it makes the scientific methodology the criterion of all truth. These ideas can be traced straight back to the Rationalism of Descartes and to the "Enlightenment."

The "mystique" is what undergirds the theory of evolution and the Big Bang, not hard facts. The facts are totally against those theories. They have been disproven. But it is quite difficult for people to change their basic assumptions or abandon their world view. Thus our entire culture is shaped by theories that cannot actually be true, that are impossible.

Philosophical Bias in Scientific Theories:
The situation today can be described as follows: The various theories of origins that are prevalent today in our culture arose from a certain philosophical perspective. They were put forth before any solid research had been done to either verify them or falsify them. But today these theories are universally claimed to be scientific fact and are widely accepted as such. Yet at this time observation and research have "caught up" with these theories.

In geology, Charles Lyell published his theory that the geologic formations of the earth were formed over millions of years.[571] But later exploration by companies in search of oil and other valuable deposits revealed vast sedimentary formations covering thousands of square miles that were deposited layer upon layer with no indication of great ages separating the layers. Careful examination did not support the theory that they had been laid down over millions of years, but that one single huge Flood deposited them at one time. Then careful studies in radiometric dating showed that many carboniferous substances within the layers were merely thousands of years old, not millions or billions as Lyell had postulated.

In the area of biology and the Theory of Evolution, Charles Darwin formulated his theory to explain the origin of life before the fossil record had been carefully studied and before the chemical basis of life was understood. So he formulated his theory in the dark. But the fossil record does not contain the transitional forms that Darwin predicted, and the chemical basis of life is not "simple" as his immediate successors imagined. Once these two areas of study caught up with his theory—once the observational data from careful research came in—he was discredited. It became obvious that the fossil record did not support biological evolution as he had postulated, and that the unexpectedly intricate chemical basis of life could not have arisen from the outworking of blind random forces.

But more than that, the proposed mechanism of evolution—mutations at the biochemical level operated upon by natural selection at the level of the total organism—was revealed to be unworkable. Instead life is gradually wearing out, devolving from its original created state because of the accumulation of damaging mutations in the genome. Thus Evolution is impossible, and the theory is exposed as having come from a fatal philosophical bias.

In the field of Cosmology, the Standard Model—the Big Bang—was formulated before the key observations of the cosmos that we related earlier had been made, and before the results had been analyzed. The theory was based on the simple fact that the universe was expanding and thus must have been together at one place initially, from which it expanded. This might have been correlated with the creation account in Genesis, but instead people chose a random, purposeless, naturalistic framework for their theory. This was a decision based on the philosophical preferences of those who formulated it. We chose to explain the world without God. When the observations and research finally came in the theory based on that assumption was discredited and could not stand.

But more than that, as observational data accumulated it became clear that the dynamic forces that had been postulated to hold the world together simply could not explain what we were seeing in deep space. The decision to ignore key experimental results and to go with a cosmic model based on extremely unintuitive understandings of the world around us led to insurmountable difficulties. Today the Standard Model (the Big Bang Theory) is under attack from hundreds of scientists around the globe.

In the same way, men formulated the JEPD Theory for the authorship of Genesis (and of the whole Pentateuch) before archeology uncovered the writings of the ancient Middle East—writings that gave us a direct understanding of the style and techniques that those ancient peoples used when they wrote. Once those discoveries were made public, then an explanation of how Genesis came to be written down became possible. That theory, **The Genesis Documents**, is the central thesis of this book. But the idea that Genesis had been written down over many centuries by multiple unknown authors, and that it was just the distillation of an ancient myth from primitive cultures—that it was in fact just the Hebrew rendition of that ancient creation myth—was no longer reasonable. Thus the JEPD Theory was exposed as coming from an anti-supernaturalistic, anti-biblical, philosophical bias.

This exhibits a pattern across several diverse areas of study, and we need to understand why theories like these were developed. I will put forth the following historical hypothesis:

First is the undermining of the geocentric world view, which had profound implications for how mankind viewed its relationship to God and its place in the creation. It took the earth out of the center of His creative effort and it took mankind out of its place as the purpose of His creation and as the precious object of His love and affection, created in His image and likeness. It demoted us to being merely a corollary in the mindless and meaningless unfolding of a vast and purposeless cosmos. It plunged us into despair and precipitated a cultural earthquake in Christendom. In this an anti-God, anti-Christian foundation was laid.

Second is the disenchantment with the faith that arose out of the corruption of the Church and the acrimony of the reformation. The glorious hope of eternal life with a loving God, Who had created us and Who had a wonderful plan for our lives, seemed to be too much to believe in or to hope for. Into this emptiness of spirit a despair and hatred of God arose in Europe which spawned many anti-God philosophical notions. The key entry point for a demonic deception were the ideas put forth by Descartes, which led to Rationalism. Men believed they were on their own in a dark and hostile world, that they had to determine the meaning of life for themselves. Such ideas became the foundation for the pseudo-scientific theories we see around us. Thus the leading European thinkers of the last few centuries, men without hope in God, formulated theories that had no place in them for God.[572]

In many ways these theories are arresting and captivating to our minds and our hearts. I know that I was utterly captivated, especially by the cosmological theories. Many people are being deceived by the world view that they present. These are not foolish, sinister, or immoral people. They are just seeking some understanding of the world around them.

But changing such beliefs is difficult because they are the foundation of our view of life, of its meaning, and of our place in the grand scheme of things. When our Lord showed Adam the creation tablet and explained to him how everything came to be, he was laying a basic foundation of truth, meaning, and purpose in his mind and heart. Alternate ideas such as those floating around today have put in place a contrary foundation.

Thus the basic Christian/Biblical world view is at stake in these matters, the Ancient Faith—the faith that was received from Jesus and the Apostles. Genesis is not the center of the Christian faith, Jesus is that. But Genesis is the rational and intellectual foundation upon which Christianity rests. Each of these theories impacts the book of Genesis, whether by undermining it with erroneous explanations of how it came to be written down, or by directly contradicting what it so clearly asserts. Genesis is the lightening rod in this spiritual battle.

We know that God and His Word will prevail in the end. Isaiah says it like this:
> All mankind is grass and all the works of his hands are like the flower of the field. The grass withers and the flower fades, but the word of our God endures forever. (from Isaiah 40:6-8)

In this passage God might have likened the "works of our hands" to a cedar of Lebanon, or to an oak of Bashan, but he did not. Instead He chose to liken them to a flower, which is beautiful and striking today, but is gone without a trace in a short time. God does love us, but He knows that we are but a vapor and all our imposing intellectual constructions, which we erect in defiance of Him, are destined to pass away in a relatively short time. We can now see the Truth that is being brought to light. The victory of God's Word is near.

We are in an apocalyptic situation. Daniel describes a time of intense spiritual conflict in which the evil one and his protégé oppress and trample the saints for a time. But then,
> The Ancient of days came, and judgment was given to the saints of the most High; and the time came when the saints possessed the kingdom. (Daniel 7:22)

> And the kingdom and dominion, and the greatness of the kingdom under the whole heaven, shall be given to the people of the saints of the most High, whose kingdom is an everlasting kingdom, and all dominions shall serve and obey Him. (Daniel 7:27).

I think that is what is coming—a divine intervention on behalf of the saints of the most High that will reveal the errors in modern theories and establish the reign of God on this earth.

Genesis 1:23—There was evening and there was morning, a fifth day.

Day 6:
Genesis 1:24—Then God said, "Let the earth bring forth living creatures after their kind: cattle and creeping things and beasts of the earth after their kind"; and it was so.

Genesis 1:25—God made the beasts of the earth after their kind and the cattle after their kind and everything that creeps on the ground after its kind; and God saw that it was good.

Again the Father commands that a step in the creation be done and the Son executes His command. "For by Him all things were created, both in the heavens and on earth, visible and invisible, whether thrones or dominions or rulers or authorities—all things have been created through Him and for Him" (Colossians 1:16). The phrase "through Him" indicates a cooperative venture between Jesus and the Father. The phrase "for Him" indicates that the creation was a kind of gift that the Father gave to the Son. Thus the word elucidates, "Then I was by him, *as* one brought up *with him*: and I was daily *his* delight, rejoicing always before him; rejoicing in the habitable parts of the earth; and my delights were with the sons of men" (Proverbs 8:30–31). So Jesus loved His gift! In the end He will return the perfected creation back to His Father (1 Corinthians 15:28).

Since the principle of conscious life, of living breathing animals, had been established and blessed on day five, it was not necessary to bless them or to command them to multiply again. Also a direct blessing might have been avoided because of the serpent. The word *bara'* is not used because the works of this day are a variation on the theme that was introduced the previous day and not another *ex nihilo* creation. Thus we see the phrase "and it was so" appearing; that is, the Son affirming the Father's command and carrying it out completely.

The change in the order in which the animals were bidden to be created in verse twenty-four (cattle, creeping things, beasts) and the order in which they were created in verse twenty-five (beasts, cattle, creeping things) may be a way of indicating that they were all created simultaneously. The participation of the Spirit in the creation of animal life is explicitly stated in Psalm 104:30 which speaking of animals says, "You send forth Your Spirit, they are created."

Again, I think God created a limited number of each kind of land animal, more of some (those that live in herds) and fewer of others, but not nearly enough to fill the earth. The subsequent centuries would allow all of them to multiply and fill the earth. When the time for the Flood comes Noah is told to take just one pair of each kind of animal onto the ark (except for the clean animals). If it was possible to replenish the earth from one pair of each type of animal after the Flood then it was also possible to start at the beginning with just one pair of each kind. If we also allow for the possibility of more pairs of some kinds, that is probably more than was needed.

There is an easily missed but important distinction between the creation of the animals of the sixth day and the creation of the birds and sea creatures of the fifth day. On the sixth day our Lord said "let the earth **bring forth**," but in the commands of the previous day God said "let the waters teem with" and "let birds fly above." So does His command of the sixth day indicate that the earth itself brings forth the creatures of the sixth day? St. Basil the Great answers this question, for it was an issue in his day just as it is an issue in our day. If one speaks of "mother earth," in what sense is the earth a mother?

> "Let the earth bring forth living creatures." Is the earth, then, possessed of life? And do the mad-minded Manicheans hold the vantage point, since they put a soul in the earth? No, when He said: "Let it bring forth," it did not produce what was stored up in it, but He who gave the command also bestowed upon it the power to bring forth. Neither did the earth, when it heard, "Let it bring forth vegetation and the fruit trees," produce plants which it had hidden in it; nor did it send up to the surface the palm or the oak or the cypress which had been hidden somewhere down below in its womb. On the contrary, it is the divine Word that is the origin of things made. "Let the earth bring forth;" not, let it put forth what it has, but, let it acquire what it does not have, since God is enduing it with the power of active force. And now, in the same way, "Let the earth bring forth the living creature," not that stored up in it, but that given to it by God through His command.[573]

Thus the earthly realm does not have within itself the power to generate vegetation, and it does not have the inherent power to bring forth animal life. Rather it is the Word of God that has creative power and that operated upon matter to cause it to bring forth life. It is the difference between the natural realm having within itself the power to create, and the Lord God alone having that power and creating or molding the created realm.

This is the consistent point of view of all the Fathers on creation, as we have noted. This point of view is emphatically affirmed by the futile attempts of men to prove evolutionary theories, as we explained, and especially by their inability to cause life to spontaneously arise in the laboratory. The Son brought forth life from the earth by using the power of the Holy Spirit that was granted to Him by the command that the Father issued.

Then we ask, why did God phrase this command as "let the earth bring forth?" It was to delineate the clearest boundary between animal life and human life, between the soul of animals and the soul of man. This is reflective of our divergent destinies in His divine plan.

> Why does the earth bring forth a living creature? In order that you may learn the difference between the soul of a beast and that of a man. A little later you will come to know how the soul of man was formed; now, hear about the soul of the irrational animals. Since, as it is written, the life of every creature is its blood, and the blood, when congealed, is wont to change into flesh, and the flesh, when corrupted, decomposes into earth, reasonably, the soul of animals is something earthy. Therefore, "Let the earth bring forth a living creature." See the relation of soul to blood, of blood to flesh, of flesh to earth; and again, after having resolved it into its elements, return through the same steps from earth to flesh, from flesh to blood, from blood to soul, and you will find that the soul of beasts is earth. Do not think that it is antecedent to the essence of their bodies or that it remains after the dissolution of the flesh. Shun the idle talk of the proud philosophers, who are not ashamed to regard their own soul and that of dogs as similar, who say that they were at some time women, or bushes, or fish of the sea.[574]

We noted above that animals are made, body and soul, by one command. We will see that we are made, body and soul, in a two-step process, by two acts of God. The soul of animals is intrinsically linked to their earthly vessel. Humans, both body and soul, are destined for heavenly glory. This earthly life is only a place of preparation for eternity.

In general, the life of animals is only on earth. The creative action that made them—both body and soul—was a single command. The life of mankind, although beginning on this earth, is destined for the heaven of God, and the command that made us was two: first the formation of the body from the earth, then the breathing in of the soul. However, there is still some element of the animal soul that required a creative act and that merited the use of the word *bara'* to prepare the way for their formation. This points to a mysterious interconnection between the physical realm and the non-physical that comes into play with the creation of sentient life that has a soul—even if it is animal soul.

Thus before the earth could "bring forth" these animals there had to be associated non-physical substance, created by the *bara'* action of the fifth day, from which Jesus formed the souls of the animals on the sixth day (like for the birds and the fish on the fifth day).

This is the end of God's work of creating things and animals. God has only to create man. So God takes this occasion to observe that what He has done is good, to state His approval of what He has made thus far. This is the second time (see also 1:10) that God observes that His work is good in the middle of a day's work of creating. The Lord rounds this corner and makes this observation before He continues on to complete His work of the sixth day.

The Creation of Man:

We noted that the creation was made for Jesus, but it was also made for man.

> [T]he human being is the creature more important than all the other visible beings, and for this creature all the others have been produced–sky, earth, sea, sun, moon, stars, the reptiles, the cattle, all the brute beasts. Why is it, you ask, that if this creature is more important than all these, it is brought forth after them? A good question. Let me draw a comparison with a king on the point of entering a city on a visit: his bodyguard has to be sent on ahead to have the palace in readiness, and thus the king may enter his palace. Well now, in just the same way in this case the Creator, as though on the point of installing some king and ruler over everything on earth, first erected the whole of this scenery, and then brought forth the one destined to preside over it, showing us through the created things themselves what importance he gave to this creature.[575]

Genesis 1:26—Then God said: Let Us make [*asah*] **man in Our image, according to Our likeness, and let them rule over the fish of the sea and over the birds of the sky and over the cattle and over all the earth, and over every creeping thing that creeps on the earth."**

Genesis 1:27—God created [*bara'*] **man in His own image, in the image of God He created [*bara'*] him; male and female He created** [*bara'*] **them.**

Genesis 1:28—God blessed them; and God said to them, "Be fruitful and multiply, and fill the earth, and subdue it; and rule over the fish of the sea and over the birds of the sky and over every living thing that moves on the earth."

Although it is not explicit in these particular verses we know that the Holy Spirit was also active in the creation of man, as with all things, for Job says, "The Spirit of God has made me" (Job 33:4). In Job 33:6 Elihu responds to Job and says, "I also am formed out of clay." We are made out of clay, **by** His Spirit, but not **from** His Spirit, i.e., our souls, although immortal, do not share in God's essence, in His uncreated divinity. But God still proposes to make us in His image and likeness. It is only stated here that He made us in His image, but in 5:1 it is stated that He made us in His likeness as well. Thus of all creatures, human beings alone possess a double similarity to the Lord God—a tremendous dignity.

Chrysostom comments on the meaning of the Divine deliberation before the critical step of creating man—that this was a divine counsel between the Father and the Son:

> What then do they say these people [i.e., the Jews] who still have a veil lying over their hearts and refuse to understand what is contained in these words? Oh what stupidity! What idiocy! What reason do you have for saying, human being that you are, that an angel is party to the counsels of the Lord, creatures sharing the Creator's thought? Not for angels is it to be party to the counsels of the Lord, but to stand in waiting and fulfil sacred ministry . . . So who is this to whom he says, "Let us make a human being?" Who else is it than the Angel of Great Counsel, Wonderful Counsellor, Figure of Authority, Prince of Peace, Father of the age to come, Only-begotten Son of God, like the Father in being, through whom all things were created? To him is said, "Let us make a human being in our image and likeness."[576]

Basil sees humanity's dignity expressed in the deliberation and joint work of our creation.

> Light came to be . . . heaven came to be . . . without deliberation. Sea and boundless ocean . . . fish of all kinds . . . He spoke and they came into being. [But] there is deliberation concerning the human. He did not say, as with the others, "Let there be a human being." Learn well your own dignity . . . Did He lose his skill, and did he deliberate in anxiety as he created in his masterpiece completion and perfection and exactitude? Or rather, did he intend to show you that you are perfect before God?[577]

Augustine also comments on the implied special work that God was about to perform in creating man, and the cooperative role of the Father and the Son revealed throughout all the steps of creation:

> In other cases God said "let it be made, and it was made" while here God said "let us make" so that in this way too the Holy Spirit wished to suggest the superiority of human nature. To whom, although does He say "let us make" if not to the One to whom He said in the other cases "Let it be made." "For all things were made through Him and without Him was nothing made" (John 1:3). But why do we suppose it was said in one way "let it be made" if not to mean that He should make it at the Father's bidding; and in the other "Let us make" if not to mean that they should both make together? Or else, everything the Father makes He makes through the Son, and that is why it now says "let us make" so that we human beings, on whose account scripture itself was made, might have it demonstrated in our very selves that what the Son makes on the Father's instructions the Father Himself also makes.[578]

Thus when we read the previous biddings, "let it be," and the words "and it was so," and the statement "and God made," we are being given a picture of how the Trinity worked as one to create all things. There is not a rigid formula in these statements, as if they always must appear and must be in the same order. We are being given **glimpses** of what is happening within the Trinity as the creation progresses. The phrasing in earlier steps of creation presented to us a less explicitly personal way in which the Father was acting, but still the Trinity was fully involved. But in the creation of man the Father and the Son explicitly work together as one to create us in their mutual image and likeness.

Once again—for the third time—the word *bara'* is used as the Father and Son together create man as stated in verse 27. This indicates that another new *ex nihilo* creative act is being described, and this is the reason why the Father must be personally involved. The human soul, like animal soul, is more than just the interconnection of the complex chemical structures that undergird the life of our bodies. But unlike animal souls, human souls also share in His divine "image and likeness" and are intrinsically destined to exist forever. Human souls partake of a reality that is more than, and that extends beyond, the merely physical realities. Human souls are not composed of the primordial substance that God called into existence in the beginning. Thus the word *bara'* is used again.

In this step of the account the Lord Himself is creating the non-physical human soul that is part of the spiritual realm of being. As He did with animals, God establishes a functionality that spans the physical and spiritual realms. But that functionality does not reside in any created thing. Rather, when two human beings cooperate to conceive then God Himself creates the human soul that corresponds to that new body. The privilege of making new life in cooperation with the Lord God is part of our human nature, as God's command to multiply asserts. Thus human beings are a functioning bridge between the two realms of existence, a bridge that involves personal interaction with God. This connection **in God** between the spiritual and physical realms is an inseparable part of the nature of man.

On the Creation of Human Souls:
The Catholic Church has an official position on the creation of the human soul.

> But the Catholic Church teaches neither that souls were made simultaneously, nor from one another, but that they are infused into bodies which have been inseminated and formed through coition, and they are created at the moment of their infusion . . .
>
> In *On Ecclesiastical Dogmas*: "We do not say that human souls existed from the beginning among the other intellectual natures, or that they were created all at once, as Origen falsely

> states. Neither are souls inseminated with the body through coition, as the Luciferians, and Cyril, and some presumptuous Latins affirm. We say that the body alone is inseminated by the conjugal union, but that the Creator alone knows the creation of the soul. It is by His judgment that the body is composed, brought together, and formed in the womb; once the body is formed, the soul is created and infused, so that in the womb lives a human being composed of body and soul, and a living person comes from the womb, filled with human substance."[579]

Psalm 33:15 says, "He who fashions the hearts of them all." We see this as implying that God creates each human soul individually and that He creates it from nothing. Thus God personally forms each human soul, just as He did with Adam and Eve at the beginning. We hold that God does not form the soul from preexisting substance, but "creates" it. We can see this as asserting the permanent connection between the non-physical and the physical realms **in the Lord God Himself** that was established in human nature.

For animals, the soul material was created once, and a connection was established in the creation between the soulish and the physical realms. When an animal is conceived the connection is activated and a corresponding soul is made from the soul substance. When an animal dies its soul dies with it and its existence, which was destined to be only on the earth, ends. But for human beings the connection between the physical and spiritual realms is not built into the creation but functions through the direct personal action of the Lord God. He personally creates each human soul to go into the newly formed human body that came about by coition. When a human body dies the soul continues to live, for that person by nature was destined to live forever and will eventually have a spiritual body that is immortal. Human life and destiny are not bound only to this earth.

The Unique Nature of Man:
It is clear that we of all creatures are situated at the conjunction of the physical and the spiritual parts of God's creation and are rational like God. Thus we have been prepared to rule all things. The conjunction of the physical and the spiritual is also built into the reproductive process and is activated by men and women through the sexual act.

Human sexual acts, especially when they result in a conception, partake of both spheres of reality and tap into a process that our Lord has built into His creation that brings to bear both divine-spiritual and human-physical forces, which combine to create a new human being. Because we were designed this way initially, we will continue to have gender in the resurrection, even though we will not marry or be given in marriage.

Thus our masculinity and femininity must be the reflection of a more pervasive aspect of our humanity, used now in procreation and as an impetus to deeper giving and selfless love in the marriage relationship, but also indicative of His eternal purposes for us. This is reflected in the fact that the Church is called the bride of Christ. Human relationships in this life prefigure, foreshadow, and prepare us for the relationship with God for which we were predestined. Gender reaches to the core of our humanity and is sacred, pointing to the ultimate fulfillment of our humanity with God in eternity. We will continue to have a male and a female gender in eternity. We won't be sexually active, but we will be male and female, for that is how He created us in the beginning.

What is the root of sexuality? It is not intercourse, but a deep desire for fellowship with another. It is the root in human nature that impels us toward another person, to take delight in them. It is that impulse that sees the other person as precious, that seeks for them the best, and that wants their happiness and welfare above all. It is selfless love, putting the other first—and taking delight in so doing. The impulse to love another and to take delight in others is foundational to human nature. It can be blunted and/or distorted by sin—by selfishness, envy, lust, covetousness, pride, fear, suspicion. When it is not thus constrained it blossoms into a plethora of fruitful and blessed relationships.

Thus sexuality is supposed to be a foundation of human society, injecting peace and joy into our lives. At the core of human nature there is a parity and a contrast between the masculine and feminine that drives this dynamic in human relationships. Therefore, the multidimensionality of human relationships that is found at the various levels of human society has this gender dynamic at its very foundation. Masculinity and femininity are at the root of the marriage relationship—the foundation of family and of all human society.

The gender dynamic, which God built into human beings, finds its first expression in the relationship between the husband and wife. This is the first love in human culture. God has made us so that from this basic relationship of love we can join with Him to create new human life. This is the generative foundation of humanity.

Many human relationships are not symmetrical because of the presence of gender. A brother and sister have a non-symmetrical relationship, unlike that between two sisters or two brothers. The gender contrast is what allows for the plethora of different types of relationships that comprise families and extended families. Within these multidimensional relationships the Lord God reveals Himself to human beings in His multifaceted glory and splendor. Our sexuality (not sex, but gender) is intrinsic to this societal structure. Without it the multidimensional relationships collapse. In this way we are unlike angels.

Therefore, unlike some of the Fathers, I do not think that God made us to fill the place of the fallen angels. Angels and men were created differently and have different roles and purposes in God's creation.

Angels do not have gender. Thus their society is much more one-dimensional. Angels participate in sonship, servanthood, and the camaraderie of brothers. It could also be that, because of the different orders of angels, they have relationships of authority and submission. It seems that the company of the angels was created without their being able to generate themselves, for each was directly created by the Lord God. They are sons of the Father and brothers of the Son. It is only through human beings that the fuller glory of God can be manifested.

Thus Abba's purpose is
> To bring to light what is the administration of the mystery which for ages has been hidden in God who created all things; so that the manifold wisdom of God might now be made known through the church to the rulers and the authorities in the heavenly *places. This was* in accordance with the eternal purpose which He carried out in Christ Jesus our Lord. (Ephesians 3:9–11)

Therefore the heavenly watchers are looking to observe His plans as they unfold in the pages of human history on this earth.

But some angels did not easily accept this disparity of nature with human beings, or our planned leadership role in the creation. They looked upon us from their heavenly place with envy and disgust.

The Envy of Satan:

Angels were certainly given a role in this world from the beginning. Exactly what that is we cannot be sure. They might be viewed as "keepers of the divine order," both in the cosmos and in human society. Some angels deal with cosmic realities and others are concerned with the society of men. We might say that they play a role in maintaining the order of God's creation, almost as if the laws or ordinances that govern reality are not merely abstract principles, as we tend to think of when studying physics or other natural sciences, but that the governing laws are associated with powerful beings who consciously work to establish and maintain universal harmony and order. They function as servants. But man, not angels, was created to rule the creation of God.

Here is an example. A man owns a business and has many hired employees that work for him to help him run the business. They are very knowledgeable and well trained in their work. But he has a young son whom he wants to bring into the family business. In time he wants to elevate him to the role of boss—over the employees that he has hired and who have given him their faithful service. In order to prepare him for that role he institutes a training program and asks the employees to help the son to learn all about the business from their very knowledgeable and hands-on perspective. But when they have completed their task, the son will be elevated over them and will become their boss. This is the way the creation is with angels (employees) and human beings. God plans to elevate man to rule over His creation.

It starts with Jesus Christ.
> *I pray that* the eyes of your heart may be enlightened, so that you will know what is the hope of His calling, what are the riches of the glory of His inheritance in the saints, and what is the surpassing greatness of His power toward us who believe. *These are* in accordance with the working of the strength of His might which He brought about in Christ, when He raised Him from the dead and seated Him at His right hand in the heavenly *places*, far above all rule and authority and power and dominion, and every name that is named, not only in this age but also in the one to come. And He put all things in subjection under His feet, and gave Him as head over all things to the church, which is His body, the fullness of Him who fills all in all. (Ephesians 1:18–23)

Jesus plans to share His place of universal authority with all those who comprise His body.
> He who overcomes, I will grant to him to sit down with Me on My throne, as I also overcame and sat down with My Father on His throne. (Revelation 3:21)

> He who overcomes, and he who keeps My deeds until the end, TO HIM I WILL GIVE AUTHORITY OVER THE NATIONS; AND HE SHALL RULE THEM WITH A ROD OF IRON, AS THE VESSELS OF THE POTTER ARE BROKEN TO PIECES, as I also have received *authority* from My Father; (Revelation 2:26–27)

This plan was not lately decided. It was the plan of God from the creation of the world. This is the pattern of life that He planned for man from the beginning. But some of the angels did not like this plan. So some of the keepers of the divine order have rebelled and are now our mortal enemies. And they have seduced us into rebelling with them.

When we sinned and fell away from God we became unfit for this role, for this glorious destiny. So first He had to redeem us, and ultimately He plans to restore us.
> In Him we have redemption through His blood, the forgiveness of our trespasses, according to the riches of His grace which He lavished on us. In all wisdom and insight He made known to us the mystery of His will, according to His kind intention which He purposed in Him with a view to an administration suitable to the fullness of the times, *that is*, the summing up of all things in Christ, things in the heavens and things on the earth. In Him also we have obtained an inheritance, having been predestined according to His purpose who works all things after the counsel of His will. (Ephesians 1:7–11)

By the blood of Jesus we are forgiven, cleansed, and made partakers with him in this glorious inheritance. This allows us reentrance into the eternal purposes of God that we forfeited in Eden. We can see that plan stated in germinal form in our creation.

God gave human beings the mandate to subdue the earth and rule over it and all the creatures in it (1:28). We who share in the fullness of His creation, both physical and spiritual, are most suited to rule over it. Whatever initial role angels had in this world it was the intention of the Lord God to eventually elevate us to the place of full dominion. As we propagated and became more numerous we were to take over the governance of this world completely, each generation helping and training the next, developing in wisdom and responsibility. Perhaps the angels, as "ministers to the heirs of salvation" (Hebrews 1:14), were to help us to ascend into this role. But as they contemplated this turn of events, some of the angels did not want to accept this. They were envious of us and they rebelled against God and determined to fight against His plan and purposes.

> For God created man to be immortal, and made him to be an image of his own eternity. Nevertheless through the envy of the devil came death into the world. (Wisdom of Solomon 2:23–24)

So it was probably at this point in the creation that certain of the "morning stars" and the "sons of God" became our adversaries. They were too proud to become our servants, so when they understood this part of His plan they refused to go along.

Those angels who did not sin are very interested in His glorious plan—to redeem us and restore us and then to finally establish His ultimate world order—a purpose that has been sidelined and delayed by the sin of men and angels, but that has not been obliterated.

> To me, the very least of all saints, this grace was given, to preach to the Gentiles the unfathomable riches of Christ, and to bring to light what is the administration of the mystery which for ages has been hidden in God who created all things; so that the manifold wisdom of God might now be made known through the church to the rulers and the authorities in the heavenly *places. This was* in accordance with the eternal purpose which He carried out in Christ Jesus our Lord. (Ephesians 3:8–11)

They are interested in it not just as observers, but also as participants, because they too have a role in this glorious plan—a plan that cannot come to completion until mankind is ready to take its place in the scheme of things. This glorious mystery becomes visible, in outline form at least, in this age of the world; that is, as Christ is revealed and as His body the Church takes shape. His eternal plan is now unfolding at last. It involves both Jews and gentiles joined together in the body of Christ as one new redeemed man.

Reflections on the Creation Scenario:
The creation scenario that we have been following answers a few detailed questions that Augustine posed but could not answer adequately. We can offer simple answers to these questions from our way of viewing the creation. I will base my answers on the internal logic of the creation narrative that we have uncovered.

- The reason why there is no "and it was so" after the decision to create man is that both the Father and the Son were involved in that unique work and there was no need for an affirmation by the Son of what the Father had commanded—just as there was no such statement after the command to create life on the fifth day. In the work of the fifth day the Father stepped in to assist in a crucial part of that work. In that case the Father and the Son worked sequentially to accomplish the final act of creating the first living animals; that is, the Father created the non-physical "animal soul material" and then the Son formed their natures out of the already-existing physical-spiritual substances. On the sixth day the Father and Son explicitly work together to create human beings. So the Son does not need to affirm the Father's command. They mutually use the Holy Spirit in the task of making us—our souls created *ex nihilo* and our bodies formed from existing matter.

- The reason why there is no "and God saw that it was good" after the creation of man is that each time that statement is made it was the Father affirming that what the Son had done was excellent. When they both explicitly act together such an affirmation is not necessary. Here the Father is not just performing a part of the creation, as He did for the Son on day five by making soul material for consciously aware animals, but He is fully involved in the work of making man. On day five the Son did a portion of the work by himself so there was an affirmation by the Father. But the creation of man is a fully shared work between the Father and the Son.
- However the Father does affirm at the end that the completed creation is "very good." This is most appropriate because the totality of creation is not just individual pieces, not just the various parts. It is comprised of all parts working together as they were created to do. There is a unity and a harmony to the completed creation.[580] This harmony is more than just each individual part being "good" by itself. Rather, it is itself a good thing, and is an indication of the wisdom, forethought, and design that went into the creation.

Made in His Image and Likeness:

Augustine says that the words "in Our image and likeness" refer to the rational soul of mankind, which sets us apart from the entire animal kingdom and qualifies us for fellowship with God. He sees the likeness of God as first and foremost possessed by the Son of God who is in the express image of His person (Hebrews 1:3). We are in His likeness in that we participate partially in that likeness which the Son of God has in its fullness.[581] Chrysostom sees our "likeness" as a reference to the authorization that God gave us to rule over creation.[582] He makes this connection because of the phrase "and let them rule" that follows immediately after.[583] Basil connects the two concepts and says that our authorization to rule derives from our rationality.[584] Thus they and many other early thinkers maintain that God has no form or shape in whose image we can be.[585]

But using the Hebrew Scriptures we see that *tselem* means *image* as of an idol or as an image that is stamped on a coin or on a personal seal that people would carry to sign documents; Hebrew *demuth* means *likeness* and is used in other verses in the Scriptures. Some examples from the Hebrew Scriptures:

To what *likeness* will you compare God? (Isaiah 40:18)

In Ezekiel chapter 1, in His vision of the throne of God, he repeatedly uses the word:

The *likeness* of a wheel within a wheel. The *likeness* of a man sitting upon the throne
The *likeness* of the firmament above the four beings who stand about the throne
The *likeness* of a throne above the heads of those four beings

On the repeated use of "likeness" by Ezekiel, Saadia ben Joseph Goah, the 10th century Egyptian-born scholar and founder of Hebrew linguistics and theology, says this vision revealed to Ezekiel a noble form above that of the angels, but by the "likeness" we must understand a vivid picture of God that still does not capture His full essence.

[T]his form [the apparition that Ezekiel saw] was something specially created. Similarly the throne and the firmament, as well as it bearers, were all of them produced for the first time by the Creator out of fire for the purpose of assuring His prophet that it was He that had revealed His word to him . . . It is a form nobler than that of the angels, magnificent in character, resplendent with light, which is called *the glory of the Lord*. It is this form, too, that one of the

> prophets described as follows: *I beheld till thrones were placed, and one that was the ancient of days did sit* (Dan. 7:9), and the sages characterized as *sekhinah* [shekinah].[586]

The apostle John also says, "No one has seen God at any time; the only begotten God who is in the bosom of the Father, he has explained *him*" (John 1:18).[587 see note]

Finally, *demuth* has been connected to the ancient notion of being a deputized governor with the responsibility to act on behalf of the one who was granting the authority. This was discovered in the Ebla tablets. In the Genesis account this implies that God granted us authority as His representative over all creation, as Chrysostom and Basil asserted, even though they did not have the advantage of an archeological discovery to guide them. Thus "image and likeness" means that we look like Him but not perfectly, and we act as deputies with His authority in our dominion over creation.

We might also note that in Revelation 11:18 when the seventh trumpet is blown—when the time comes to "reward His servants . . . both great and small, and to destroy those who destroy the earth"—that the worthless deputies (*demuth*) who have exercised their dominion over creation badly will not fare well. They will certainly be held accountable for their destructive decisions toward God's creation.

The section that follows is not in agreement with most of the Fathers of the Church, but Irenaeus is one who would probably find it quite acceptable. However I share it because I believe it is important. I am writing it based on what I see as the proper understanding of a number of Scriptures. These passages point to the nature and meaning of gender, the meaning and purpose of authority and submission in human society, and the nature of God. They give us insight into the nature of man, woman, and human life, and also point to the nature of our final state of consummate glory in His presence. This way of looking at God flows naturally from our understanding of how the accounts of Genesis arose—as first-hand personal accounts of human interactions with God.

These considerations are where I get my comments on the form of God. (see also the section "Meditation on Human Nature," part of the comments on 2:21–23)

<u>Male and Female</u>:
God created us male and female. This is such a fundamental reality of life that we can only consider it with difficulty. Why did God do such a thing? Think about how much of human existence is bound up with and influenced by this simple truth. It is situated at the foundation of family life and determines both its structure and its basic nature. The variety of human relationships that exists within a family and within the broader society of humanity is rooted in our division into two genders. So the multidimensional character of human relationships that circumscribe the experience of what it means to be human flows from the family and from the fact that we are made with two genders. The totality of the experience of being human is rooted in our creation as male and female.

Augustine writes on the creation of woman and the purpose that God had in so doing.
> If the question is asked, though, for what purpose it was necessary for this help [Eve, the "helper" suitable to Adam] to be made, no more likely answer suggests itself than that it was for the sake of procreating children . . . [W]hat could have prevented their also being wedded and bedded *without spot or wrinkle* (Ephesians 5:27) in Paradise, God granting this right to them if they lived faithfully in justice and served Him obediently in holiness, so that without any restless fever of lust, without any labor and pain in childbirth, offspring would be brought forth from their sowing.[588]

But he does not consider the nature of our family life on earth or the necessary logical consequences that follow on being created as "male and female." He says this,

> Or if it was not for help in producing children that a wife was made for the man, then what other help was she made for? If it was to till the earth together with him, there was as yet no hard toil to need such assistance; and if there had been the need, a male would have made a better help. The same can be said about companionship, should he grow tired of solitude. How much more agreeably, after all, for conviviality and conversation would two male friends live together on equal terms than man and wife? While if it was expedient that one should be in charge and the other comply, to avoid a clash of wills disturbing the household, such an arrangement would have been ensured by one being made first, the other later, especially if the latter were created from the former, as the female was.[589]

Thus he does not see that human nature is incomplete without both men and women; he fails to consider the significance of the fact that God created us "male and female," and that He created both of us in His likeness and in His image. Therefore he does not consider the basic nature of human life as God intended it to be, both on this earth and in eternity. Thus he ignores a clear indicator of what God is like, as deduced from what human beings are like and from the fact that we are created in His image and likeness. Thus he ignores the fact that human society is founded from and upon the husband-and-wife relationship and on the structure of the family. Thus he sees only one dimension to the division of humanity into male and female and that is the need to reproduce.

Augustine's statement about male companionship being more agreeable than female completely misses the happiness and love that should always characterize marriage. And when has our glorious loving heavenly Father ever created with only one purpose in mind? The importance of family in the shaping of a child and in teaching the young what it means to love and be loved—earthly preparation for the relationships of heaven—this perspective is missing. Does Augustine actually believe that women are given to us merely to bear children, but not also to be the heart and center of family life and the transmitters of human nature to the next generation when it is in its youngest and most impressionable years? How could we be human without females? What would be left? Without women "life" would not be human life at all; the entire nature of our existence would be dulled; the nature of humanity could never survive intact. I want to address these issues and the meaning of human society, beginning with the family.

Authority and Submission:
Human family life and social organization rely on one further reality that is vital to the nature of man as created in His image and His likeness. The Trinity is a social unit with authority and submission, and thus authority and submission are also intrinsic to human society. What is the right understanding of human nature as it touches on the exercise of authority and on how it should operate within the family and the broader society?

Here is a comment about authority and submission by Chrysostom:
> Listen to Paul's words: "It is not proper for a man to cover his head, being image and glory of God, whereas the woman is man's glory." One is in command, the other is subordinate, just as God had also said to woman from the beginning, "your yearning will be for your husband, and he will be your master."[590]

His quote "your yearning shall be . . ." is part of the Lord's judgment because of the fall, so it almost sounds as if Chrysostom thinks that the subordination of woman to man is the result of the fall. But Jesus was obedient to the Father from before all ages, and thus the exercise of authority—and obedience to it—is intrinsic to interpersonal relationships. It is authority and obedience together that undergird Trinitarian relationships. Both men and women are created in the image and likeness of God. Therefore this statement of Chrysostom must be modified by that observation because the exercise of authority as well as submission to that authority, since fully present within the Godhead, are both equally expressions of the nature of God within us. They both were present from the creation.

Thus neither man's exercise of authority nor woman's submission to it is in any way a measure of inferiority in dignity or worth, nor is the submission of woman to man a result of the fall. Rather there is a difference in the way that men and women are to function in family relationships. "The husband is the head of the wife, even as the head of Christ is God" (Ephesians 5:23, 1 Corinthians 11:3).[591] The creation of man and woman in His image and likeness does not at all preclude relationships of authority and submission; in fact, it requires it. Every human society is intrinsically hierarchical and must always be dependent both on the exercise of authority and on submission to it. A family must have authority to function well, as is so for every human grouping. This is a reflection of the eternal life of the Trinity, a life to which we are all destined in the end.

Therefore what resulted in the fall was not that woman was placed under man, but that the relationship between man and woman was distorted and the exercise of authority became a kind of domination. Authority was always supposed to be exercised, but in the original very good creation it was not intended to be heavy-handed or overbearing. The fall resulted in a perversion in the husband-wife relationship. Both men and women became selfish, bitter, vindictive, lustful, etc. Thus both authority and submission were distorted.

Men became self-seeking and overbearing in their authority, and women became fearful and manipulative in their relationships to men. We must consider what a husband and wife relationship was actually intended to be in order to understand what human nature was supposed to be in God's original perfect plan.

There is a lovely truth about authority and submission that we fail to understand or we distort because of our sinful state. Within the Trinity authority and obedience are always expressed with servant-hearted love. Jesus demonstrated this for his disciples after the last supper when He took off His outer garments, girded Himself, and washed their feet. Consider how aghast the disciples were at this action! That was because the divinely ordained meaning and use of authority was very far from their experience. Thus what Jesus did seemed incongruous, even outrageous to them. Assertions about submission and authority must include this vital truth or else they will certainly be misunderstood.

From our perspective as fallen creatures we tend to think about authority along military lines, with the command and the obedient salute. This is not the way of God. The statement that God made to Eve after the fall, which Chrysostom quoted, referred to conditions in the husband-wife relationship that were a result of the fall. In Jesus these should never be the experienced reality, for in Him all curses are cancelled—and in the consummation of all things they will be unheard of. Our present perceptions about the exercise of authority and about submission to it have been contaminated by the fall.

How do authority and obedience work between the Father and the Son in the Trinity? If you say "I do not know" then you are in the same place that I am and in the same place as all human beings. If sin had not entered the picture then this reality would have been reflected in the husband-and-wife relationship in the family—and thereafter in a myriad of ways throughout human society.

But sin has distorted our humanity—on the personal level, on the familial level, and on the broader societal level. Thus there are obstacles to really knowing Him as we were intended to—as we were created to know Him in the beginning. Although I acknowledge these obstacles, the authority-submission dynamic, like sexuality, is intrinsic to humanity.

So a second dynamic in human relationships, besides male and female, is authority and obedience, foundational to all lasting human groupings, intrinsic to human nature because it was first of all intrinsic to divine nature, and human beings are created in His likeness and image. Authority and obedience instill order and structure into human society.

When gender differences and authority are functioning correctly in human society and human relationships, the result is first of all a family that is functional (as opposed to one that is dysfunctional) where a lovely variety of interrelationships exist and operate, and which catch up the people in many satisfying and fulfilling ways. This was the plan of God for human life from the beginning, from the first moment of His very good creation.

Families themselves extend inevitably to tribes, where a broader variety of relationships are formed that again incorporate gender differences and the exercise of authority in various ways. Tribes extend to peoples and these groupings extend to ethnic groups or nations or cultures. This is the schematic of human society on earth. Interwoven within all these relationships are people who still possess their gender, both men and women, and where the exercise of authority (and submission to it) undergirds societal structures at all of the various levels. God made us to be this way. Our identity is only to be found and expressed within a social matrix of relationships such as this. This is the basis for the dominion mandate that assigns to us the role of overseer in creation.

He made us male and female, and gender itself is intrinsic to humanity. He established authority and submission from the first, a reflection of the life of the Trinity. Thus both will be carried into the consummation of all things. Both will play an essential role in our relationship with the Lord throughout eternity. In eternity we will come to know God and He will reveal Himself to us and draw us into the relationships of the Trinity.

The self-disclosure of God to human beings happens to us not only as single individuals but as members of a social structure, especially as members of a family. It is within familial relationships that God will act and reveal Himself to us throughout eternity. However, no family could be complete without both women and men. And no family can operate correctly without authority and obedience. Both are necessary components in God's eternal plan. We were always thus from the first moment of our creation.

Thus He made us both male and female and we will always be such. And He made authority and obedience foundational to all human social structures. As noted, this is the basis for the multidimensionality of our human social order. But God is not content to only create us, watch us as we develop into this multidimensional interrelated social order, and bless us from afar. He intends to enter into our human relationships with us.

God is our brother, our spouse, our kinsman, our father. The Lord God Himself takes His place and plays His role in this social structure. He is Jesus the bridegroom and the older brother. God is Abba, the Father of all, the source of authority, protection, security, order, meaning, and purpose. The life of heaven is a society of human beings with the Lord Himself participating with us—or rather, with humans participating with Him, for it is an extension of the nature of the Triune God Who has existed from all eternity, with human beings drawn into it and sharing in the life of the Trinity, the society of God.

This truth means that God is not someone alien to us. We were created in His image and likeness, and the pattern of life that we have described is the fulfillment of our destiny as

His children. The Father is Abba (Daddy, Papa)—and He is near to us. Heaven is a place that no eye has seen, no ear heard, and no sense of it has entered into the heart of man. Yes, the life of heaven is inconceivable to us. But the reason why we cannot conceive of it is not because the categories of heavenly life and existence are alien to our humanity. The categories of thought and life that describe heaven are the same ones that describe the relationships of the family and the broader society of man.

Then why is heaven beyond our understanding and experience? Because human sin has distorted our understanding of what it means to be a human being, because it has distorted our understanding of what it means for the family to operate correctly, and because it has distorted human relationships at every level of society. It has also made it impossible for us to relate to God. Heaven is a life different from this life not in nature but in its quality of relationships. And in heaven Jesus and Abba will participate with us in society, fulfilling social roles like those that we are familiar with from our human life on earth, but transcendently exceeding what humans can be—even then, when we will be in our sinless human nature. He will be with us, among us, and infinitely beyond us as well.

Another way to express what I am saying: The categories of thought which we use to talk about the eternal realities should be the same as the categories of thought that we use to talk about human life and familial relationships. However, in this life what we are living and experiencing is but an ephemeral shadow of what He has prepared for us in His presence. He shows us the shadow, and we make our choice: embrace it and say yes to it, or reject it and destroy it. The earthly choice we make amidst the shadows of the eternal realities He will confirm with an eternal "Amen"—to our blessing or our loss.

Thus the realities are present to us even in this life, for this life is the place of human preparation for eternity. It is on this earth and in this life that we must make our decision. In order for this life to present us with an accurate picture of the life of heaven and of participation in the Trinity, so that we can make a true choice, the basic realities of human life must be similar to those of heaven. If this were not so then we would not be able to reject or accept those realities. We would not be held accountable in eternity for a choice made by us in a situation where we were kept ignorant of the reality that we were being asked to decide about.

The earthly human realities and the heavenly realities are rooted in the fundamental nature of human beings, and of God in whose image and likeness we are created. The Father, whom the Spirit instructs us to call "Abba," is at the core of all of these realities. He is The One to Whom we can relate in a most familial way. God has a heart capable of responding to people and to situations just like we do. **In addition, God possesses a human form so that we can relate to Him in a family way. We will show this to be so.** Let us review the logic of these considerations: God created us both male and female. He made authority and submission intrinsic to human nature and human relationships.

From these two realities, gender and authority, flow the basic structure of human life— of all human relationships in the family and throughout human society. God intends to participate with human beings in such relationships, for in that way He makes Himself known to us. He intended this for human life on earth, as a way to prepare us for life with Him in eternity, but the sin of Adam and Eve, and the universal human participation in that rebellion threw up an obstacle to it. Heavenly life will involve divine participation with man in society. In order to participate with us in this way God must have a human heart which responds to situations with grief, joy, anger, sorrow, love, repulsion, etc. God must also have a body of light that is in our form so that we can relate to Him meaningfully. When we arrive in heaven the infinitely satisfying and fulfilling relationship to God that is life in heaven will be fulfilled by the Lord God, Who will be seen and related to in our human form.

The Form of God:
The tendency of the Fathers was to assert that God has no shape, form, or color since He is pure spirit. Thus being "in His image and likeness" cannot mean that we actually look like Him. Cyril of Alexandria explains forcefully the view held by most of the ancients.

> Men of good sense who focus their minds' eyes sharply on the attributes of the ineffable Godhead, see it as existing beyond every created thing, transcending all acuity of intellect, being wholly outside bodily appearance and, as all-wise Paul says, "dwelling in light unapproachable." But if the light surrounding it is unapproachable, how can one gaze on it? . . . Deity, then, is wholly incorporeal, without dimensions or size and not bounded by shape. How could one who is like this in his own nature be thought to consist of parts and limbs? . . . So one must not conceive of eyes or ears, or indeed hands, feet and wings as belonging to God, even though one elects to conceive of such things not as they exist in palpable, gross, bodies but as existing in fine-drawn immateriality and in correspondence with God's nature; it is utterly silly to entertain such an idea . . . If divine Scripture mentions parts or limbs in telling us of his attributes, it is to be interpreted as speaking to us in terms of what we know and are. . . Our poverty of mind and speech is the real cause and occasion . . . of inspired Scripture's addressing us about God in bodily terms.[592]

Ephrem the Syrian echoes the same sentiments in his poetic verses.

> Let us give thanks to (God) who has clothed Himself in the names of the (body's) various parts. (Scripture) refers to His "ears," to teach us that He listens to us; it speaks of His "eyes," to show that He sees us. It was just the names of such things that He put on, and—although in His true Being there is no wrath or regret—yet He put on these terms because of our weakness . . . We should realize that, had He not put on the names of such things, it would not have been possible for Him to speak with us humans . . . It is our terms that He has put on—though He did not literally do so. He then took them off—without actually doing so: when wearing them, He was at the same time stripped of them. He puts on one when it is beneficial, then strips it off in exchange for another; the fact that He strips off and puts on all sorts of metaphors tells us that the metaphor does not apply to His Being; because that Being is hidden, He has depicted it by means of what is visible.[593] [see note]

This concept also might have been helped along by a peculiarity of the LXX translation. The LXX relates how God proposes to make us in His "image **and** likeness" (1:26) but that He actually only makes us in His image. This is because 1:27 says only that we are made in His image; and again in verse 5:1 it says that we are made in His image. However in the Hebrew text Genesis 5:1 says that we are made in His likeness. Thus the Hebrew Scriptures assert that we actually were created in His image **and** His likeness. This is more than a technical point. Some Fathers speculated that the fullest human likeness to God would be attained only in the consummation, asserting it to be only an eschatological reality.[594] [see note] The seriousness of this confusion is stressed by a question posed to Cyril of Alexandria by several other Christian leaders of his day.

> Are "in God's image" and "in God's likeness" different or the same thing? [Some] say that we received the "image" immediately on creation but not the "likeness," for it is reserved for us till the world to come. Which is why (it is asserted) it is written, "When Christ appears we shall be like him" and again it is said "Let us make man in our image and likeness;" and after his creation it is said "And God made man and made him in his own image," making no mention here of the likeness, to demonstrate (it is said) that we have not received it but that it is reserved for us in that blessed life.[595]

Cyril gives his straightforward answer.

> If holy writ asserted at some point that God made man in his own image and did not mention "likeness" we should appreciate that it was sufficient to say "image" because it means the same thing as "likeness." It is out of the question to say that the latter is reserved for us in the world to come. If God said "Let us make man in our image and likeness" who will rashly assert that man has been made in God's image but not yet in his likeness?[596]

Cyril notes that the Scriptures employ two words to assert our similarity to God, but that fact does not impress him. The result of the translation difference in the LXX is to affect our understanding of just how much we are like God, and just how much He is like us. The Hebrew Scriptures assert that we were created from the beginning in His image **and** His likeness. No wonder the Godhead carefully deliberated over the creation of man! We are doubly like Him! This is important because how much we are like God and how much He is like us affects how He can and will participate with us in human relationships; that is, it affects how we understand the final state of Glory that awaits us with Him in heaven.

Because of the archeological insight that the accounts of Genesis are personal records of the lives of the first men and women, we should think carefully about the way that God is described as interacting with human beings. This is not, as some Fathers imagined, the careful exposition of a later inspired writer; rather, these stories are the direct first-hand experience of Adam, Noah, the sons of Noah, Shem, Abraham, Isaac, and Jacob. They say that God interacted with them in a form like their own. This should inspire us as we read their accounts—it should instill in us a more directly personal concept of Who God is and of what our interactions with him would be if we were not immersed in sin—if we did not have a nature that is inherently opposed to Him on every level. The concept that the Lord will interact with us from within a form that is like ours once sin has been dealt with is simply to take their accounts at face value. How else, once we understand how they were written, could we take them?

There are many Old Testament Scriptures that show us Jesus the Son of God before He became incarnate as a man. He was active in the Old Testament and is often portrayed as having a human form. In Genesis 18 He ate with Abraham before the destruction of Sodom. And in Genesis 16:6ff the Angel of the Lord looked after Hager as she fled from Sarah, and Hagar saw Him. In Genesis 28:13 He appeared to Jacob at the top of the ladder as he fled to Paddan-Aram. These and many other pre-incarnate appearances of Jesus are commented on by Cyprian in *Testimonies against the Jews*, by Novatian in his *Treatise on the Trinity*, chapters XVII-XX, and by others.

This kind of interaction is not found only in Genesis. The Lord appeared to Gideon as recorded in Judges chapter 6. There our Lord assured Gideon that, although he had seen the Lord, he would not die (Judges 6:22–23). Thus before He was born as a man He was in the human form and was carefully watching over mankind. In 1 Corinthians 15 Paul says there is a natural body and there is a spiritual body; that is, a body that is animated by a soul and a body that is animated by a spirit. Jesus had a spiritual form of pure and holy light, and it was like our human form even before He was incarnate.

In the consummation we will have spiritual bodies; that is, bodies activated by the spirit. A body that is activated by the spirit expresses the attitudes and character of that spirit. A pure and godly spirit will have a body that is lovely and that expresses in a beautiful way their human nature the way that God created him or her to be. A spirit that is enslaved to sin will show forth a body that is grotesque and monstrous. This is true for men and for angels, for the fallen angels and for the holy angels.[597]

I think this simple definition expresses something of the mysterious connection between the physical and the spiritual realms, especially as it relates to human nature and to our creation in His image and likeness. Jesus took on a natural human body. In Him the fullness of the Godhead was pleased to dwell in bodily form. In the glorified state, when He assumed His spiritual body, He expressed fully the perfect nature of God through His glorified human body. The spiritual nature of God is perfectly expressed through the human form in the person of Jesus. But the risen Jesus had a glorified body just like we will have.

The Form of our Glorified Bodies and the Form of our Earthly Bodies:
I want to ask one simple question: Is the form of our present earthly bodies the same as the form of our glorified bodies? Will we change in form when we rise again? Or will we be recognizably human, even as we are now? It would seem that we will be somewhat different because we will not **need** to eat as we do now. Thus we probably will not digest food in the same way that we do now, and we will not eliminate. We will not have sexual relations either, like God's angels. So will all of our internal and external features remain? This is something that no one can answer. But we will be immortal, unable to die.

And we will be human; truly, fully human, even as God intended for us from the time that he first created us. That implies that we will still possess the human form. Yes, we will look like human beings. Why? We can say this because Jesus is the prototype for resurrected humanity. And Jesus, in His resurrected body, definitely had a human form. He looked like a human being, and he interacted with others like a human being.

This means that the form of our resurrected bodies will be very much like the form that our bodies have now. We will not be amorphous spirits. We will not look like an animal or some other creature. We will present ourselves to the senses like a person. This is the way that God created us, so this is what it means to be "in His image and likeness."

Yet, there is a radical transformation that takes place when an earthly body, one that is designed to live and function on this earth, is transformed into a glorified body, one that is designed to live and function in the heavenly realm. "If there is a natural body there is also a spiritual (*pneumatikos*) body" (1 Corinthians 15:44). The sense of *pneumatikos* as it is used with "body" in this verse is: "a body that is animated and controlled only by the rational soul and by means of which the rational life, or life of the spirit is lived." This explanation is from Thayer's Greek lexicon, and it is the way that Augustine understood and explained this phrase as well.

Spiritual bodies are not governed by physical laws such as gravity or electromagnetic forces but by spiritual laws operating through the ones to whom the bodies belong. In the resurrection human beings will have spiritual bodies, like the angels already have. The form of a spiritual body is determined by the one to whom it belongs, and it reflects their spiritual state. Christians who are "born again" are being transformed from one degree of glory to another as they walk along with the Lord God. They are predestined to be conformed to the image of Jesus Christ—the risen and glorified Jesus Christ. We will be like Him. This is a necessity so that we can "see Him as He is." In order to commune with the Lord in heaven we need to have a spiritual body. The form of that body will be like the form of our present body, and it will also be identical to the form of the resurrected body of Jesus. But Jesus had a form even before He became a man.

<u>The Word always had a Form</u>:
> "Jesus Christ, although He existed in the **form** of God, did not regard equality with God a thing to be grasped, but emptied Himself, taking the **form** of a bond-servant, *and* being made in the **likeness** of men" (Philippians 2:6–7).

God has a form. Jesus had a form before He became incarnate, God's form. The word for form that is used here is *morphe* in the Greek. Jesus was in the form of God but then took on the form of man. *Morphe* is the form by which an object strikes the vision, or the external appearance of a thing, but faithfully representing its inner nature. It stands in contrast to the Greek word *schēma* that is used for the word "likeness," as that which is intrinsic and essential contrasts with that which is outward, circumstantial, or accidental.

So *morphe* indicates an external appearance that is accurately indicative of the internal nature of what is seen. Jesus was in the form of God, took our form, and was made in our likeness; that is, He adopted our human way of living—our figure, our bearing, our actions, and our manner of life. So God does have a form, a form that appropriately indicates His internal nature as God. Jesus was in that form and He adopted our form. When He adopted our form it appropriately indicated His nature as man. But He did not stop being God at that point. His inner nature was also still God. The form of man was at least compatible with His divinity. It was not inconsistent with the nature of God.

When Jesus adopted our *morphe* or form it still was reflective of His inner nature; that is, His nature as **both** God and man. When He appeared in the burning bush to Moses that form was not indicative of His inner nature. He assumed that appearance for a specific reason. But the form of a man is indicative of His inner nature. Jesus left off His intrinsically immortal Trinitarian existence, assumed our mortal appearance, and participated in our human "*schēma*" in that He needed to eat, to breathe, to receive comfort, etc. This was because He became physically and emotionally limited and vulnerable just as we are.

So Jesus gave up the circumstances of divine existence and took upon Himself our human condition and circumstances with all of their earthly weakness and dependency. When Jesus rose from the dead and assumed His glorified body He retained our human form. The form of our bodies, whether natural and earthly or glorified and heavenly, is the same, so He still had the human form. But the form of God that Jesus had before the incarnation He has today now that He is seated on the Father's throne. His divine form was not lost. He has it still, or He has it back again. Therefore Jesus has both the human form and the Divine form. So they are the same. When He emptied Himself and accepted our human circumstances, except for sin, He could do so because the two forms are the same.

The form of Jesus before He became man is described for us in numerous Old Testament apparitions, as referred to above. It was like our glorified human form, at least in most ways. His divine essence was faithfully reflected in that form, but was not totally revealed in the visions that are described. But Jesus is the exact image of the Father (Hebrews 1:2).

These considerations seem to indicate that both the Son and the Father have a form that is like ours. This agrees with the fact that they were both speaking when they said, "Let Us make man in Our image and according to Our likeness."

God, in His eternal nature, possesses a form that expresses the perfection of His nature, but without a corporeal structure. He is form without body. Our human body has a form like His form so we are in His image and likeness.

We have been created and made in the eternal and unchangeable form of God Himself—both formed (*asah*) and created (*bara'*) in the everlasting form of the Eternal Creator.

No one knows anything about what God looks like except from what we are told in the Scriptures. The statements to the effect that God is a spirit and therefore must "have no form or shape or color" are rooted in philosophical notions rather than in the Scriptures. Whenever I read these statements they are never accompanied by Scripture verses to back them up. Can a spirit have a form? I think that it can. It can reveal itself in various different forms. The native form for the pre-incarnate Lord was the human form.

The risen Lord Jesus became a "life-giving spirit" (1 Corinthians 15:45). Yet He was still in the form of man (Philippians 2:7) and will always be both fully God and fully man. Thus a spiritual body certainly does have a form because the spiritual body of Jesus still has our human form. God usually and normally employs His human form when relating to us.

Chrysostom says, in regard to those who take the language describing the creation of man from the dust of the earth so very concretely:
> [L]et us follow the direction of Sacred Scripture in the interpretation it gives of itself, provided we don't get completely absorbed in the concreteness of the words, but realize that our limitations are the reason for the concreteness of the language. Human senses, you see, would never be able to grasp what is said if they had not the benefit of such great considerateness. So recognizing our limitations, and the fact that what is said refers to God, let us accept the words as equivalent to speaking about God; let us not reduce the divine to the shape of bodies and the structure of limbs, but understand the whole narrative in a manner appropriate to God.[598]

Is it out of "consideration" for our human limitations that God speaks to us in this way? Assertions like this affect our understanding of what the final state of glory with Him will be like. How will God treat us in eternity, in the New Jerusalem, when we are with Him? Will He, out of consideration for our human limitations, present Himself to us in human form so that we can relate to Him in our humanity? Or did He not instead create us to be in an intimate union with him from the beginning, and thus we will see Him "as He is" (1 John 3:2), which would be the fulfillment of His purpose in creating us?

Yes, our life with Him in heaven is the fulfillment of His eternal purposes for us because before the creation He predestined us to be before Him in love as His sons (Ephesians 1:4–5) and made us to "see His face" (Revelation 22:4). Thus our Lord does not need to "accommodate" Himself to us at all. Eventually He will "dwell with us" (Revelation 21:3).

Our human nature requires no special "accommodation" from His *morphe*, for from the moment of creation we were designed to be with Him. Once we are cleansed of sin and in our glorified body we leave the *schema* of earthly life and take on His divine *schema*. We will commune with Him for all eternity, sharing in the life of the Trinity as Jesus does.

Chrysostom continues,
> For the deity is simple, free of parts and shape; should we form an impression from ourselves and want to ascribe an arrangement of limbs to God, we would be in danger of falling into the irreverence pagans are guilty of.[599]

But from what Scriptures does Chrysostom derive the emphatic assertions that he makes about God; that is, that He is "simple, free of parts and shape?"

The concept of "simple, free of parts and shape" is a philosophical concept which finds no substantiation in the Word of God. The idea is contrary to the word *morphe*, which means shape! As for falling into the irreverence of the pagans, the goal of Christian theology is not to avoid any points of agreement with philosophies and ideologies other than our own—it is to arrive at an accurate and faithful knowledge of God so that we can worship Him "in spirit and in truth." Of course God surely possesses none of the moral weaknesses of the pagan myths, but having a human form is not a weakness.

There is a well-known story about Augustine and a small boy that illustrates the fact that human speculation and philosophy cannot reason to the nature of God. Augustine was walking along a beach contemplating the mystery of the Trinity. He came upon a young boy playing on the beach. He hollowed out a hole in the sand, scooped up water from the sea, and poured it into the hole. Augustine asked him, "What are you doing?" "I am going to put the ocean into this hole." "That is impossible! The ocean cannot fit into the hole you have made." The little boy replied, "Neither can you fit the Trinity into a human mind." Then the boy disappeared, for he was actually an angel.

Therefore I posit this: How well do the various philosophically based assertions relating to the nature of God actually capture His essence? Can they stake claim to any more accuracy, do you think, than a picture that a small boy might scratch in the dust of the ground with a stick? What we know or understand about God is exactly and only what He has been pleased to reveal to us in His word, what we can deduce logically from those biblical accounts, and what we can see by contemplating Jesus Who is the exact image of the Father.

I trust that my suggestions are in no way irreverent toward my Creator. For indeed, I do realize that when God picks up the dust of the earth His hands do more than mine could ever do. "God's molding . . . and His creative activity fashioned all things in depth, working from within."[600] He touches not only the particles of dust but also the molecular and sub-atomic structures that comprise dust. His molding of the dust into a man was accomplished at a level of intricacy and detail that I cannot even imagine. He is still the Lord God, the Creator of all things, and not merely a man. And when the Lord breathes into Adam the breath of life His breath is not just the wind being exhaled from His lungs. It is infused with the Spirit of Life that proceeds from His divine being. God performs His acts while operating through a form that is like our human form, but the effects of God's works are clothed in glory and are of a nature to which no mere man could ever attain.

Thus when I ascribe a human form to God I do not detract from the fact that He alone is uniquely and forever the Creator. I uphold His majesty and glory, even though He does accomplish His divine acts while working from within a form that is like our human frame. Remember that the creator Himself decided to make us in His image and His likeness. It was the sovereign decision that He made—a fact that undergirds the dignity of human beings and explains the careful deliberation that preceded the creation of man, as well as the joint effort that was involved in that final mutual creative work of God.

Our human form is directly connected to our soul, which seat of consciousness receives and interprets the sensory input from our sight, hearing, touch, taste, and smell. When our soul is separated from our body, will it no longer receive input? Will it then exist in a dark isolation? No, the soul will still accept input via the same five senses. The self-consciousness of the soul will continue, and it will still "see," "hear," "feel," etc. Because of the continuity of consciousness that we will maintain, the sense of the soul will still be active, and we will still exist in some form. That form will be "like" our bodily form.

Purely spiritual bodies also have a form. The angels have a form, and the Lord God has a form even without having a body. This is why the Scriptures speak of them and Him as "seeing" and "walking" and "hearing" etc. This is why the Father is seen as having a hand (Revelation 5:1). The Lord God interacts with His creation just as we do. This means that He also has a form like ours which can support His various ways of perceiving and relating to this world that He has made. This fact is also necessarily true about Him because that is what will allow us to relate to Him in a direct and familial way throughout eternity.

The Fathers constantly struggled with how the two realms of reality were interconnected; that is, the physical and the spiritual. I am trying to explain something about this without resorting to the categories of Greek philosophical thought like they did. I accept the truth of the scriptural descriptions as they are given to us, rather than trying to reinterpret them by using categories and concepts derived from Greek philosophy. Thus I assert the Lord God has a form. Intelligence and Divinity have a form, always had a form, even from before the foundation of the world. And that form is the human form. That is the dignity of man that is expressed in the statement that He created us "in His image and likeness."

Seeing God:
When He brings us before Him we will see Him in the form that He actually has; that is, "we shall see Him as He is" (1 John 3:2). This will be possible because "we will be like Him" (1 John 3:2). We were created in His image **and** His likeness from the beginning explicitly for that purpose. At that time the "image and likeness" to Him in which we all were created will be perfected—not that we will possess His divine nature, but that we will have attained to His original intention for us—free from sin and in glorified bodies. The idea of seeing God accompanies the fact that He has a form like our own.

When I speak of "seeing the Father" I do not want to bypass any contrary verses in the Scriptures, so I will quote and explain two key ones here. "No man has seen God at any time. The only begotten, Who is in the bosom of the Father, has made Him known" (John 1:18). That is true; we have not seen the Father—yet. Certainly, what we know of Him is only what we learn from Jesus or what we can deduce by thinking about Jesus.

"Who alone possesses immortality and dwells in unapproachable light, whom no man has seen or can see" (1 Timothy 6:16). That is true, we have not seen Him nor can we see Him—in these bodies. He is unapproachable because in our sinful state we cannot bear His goodness and love. But many Scriptures indicate that in the consummation we will see Him, and we will relate to Him directly and intimately in familial relationships.

Here are a few such verses. The idea of seeing God is not only in the New Testament.
> As for me, I shall behold Your face in righteousness. I will be satisfied with [or: *with* beholding] Your likeness [*těmuwnah*] when I awake. (Psalm 17:15)

Thus being in His likeness and/or beholding His likeness in the final state of glory was the hope of David as well. The word for likeness, *těmuwnah* in Hebrew, means *form*, *image*, *representation*, or *semblance*.

And in his psalms David says:

> For You will not abandon my soul to Sheol, nor will You allow Your Holy One to undergo decay. You will make known to me the path of life. In Your presence is fullness of joy. In Your right hand there are pleasures forever. (Psalm 16:10–11)
>
> The upright will behold His face. (Psalm 11:7)

The often-quoted statement that "no man can see My face and live" (Exodus 33:20) is not a statement that reflects the initial innocent nature of man nor the ultimate purpose of God for mankind; rather, it is the result of mankind's fall into sin, and it will be overcome in the final redemption. Not seeing His face is a sad commentary on the effect of our fall into sin and degradation. But God intends to save us from our fall and restore us to His presence—to our destined place before Him. We will dwell with Him and see His face.

What more can be said about the One Who is ultimately most responsible for the entire creation? No man has seen God, but the Son has made Him known (John 1:18). Jesus is the "express image" of the Father, bearing the very stamp of His image within Himself (Hebrews 1:3). The fact is that no one can know anything about what the Father looks like except by reading about Him in the inspired Scriptures, or by gazing at Jesus (John 14:9). We cannot know what a spiritual being looks like by reasoning. But Isaiah saw Him sitting on His throne (Isaiah 6:1–3), Ezekiel saw Him on His throne (Ezekiel 1:26), Daniel saw Him (Daniel 7:13), and John saw Him sitting on His throne (Revelation 4:3, 4:10)—and also saw His right hand which held a scroll (Revelation 5:1).

Even though we claim that biblical visions can never contain or express the full essence of the Father (John 1:18), we still must realize that they give some indication of what it would be like to directly see God. In heaven the angels constantly see the Father's face (Matthew 18:10). In the end we will be His sons and see His face (Revelation 21:7:, 22:4).

This intimacy is the essence of heaven—not just the glorious surroundings by which the New Jerusalem is described. The whole force of Revelation chapters 21 and 22 is the familial intimacy that we will have with Abba. Direct relational intimacy like that is the fulfillment of our purpose, the reason why we were created, and the plan of God from before the foundation of the world; that is, that we be His sons and daughters and live before Him in love (Ephesians 1:4). In order for this to happen He also must have a form that we can see and relate to as human beings once we are in glorified bodies.

The Spirit that He has placed in us cries out "Abba, Father" (Romans 8:15, Galatians 4:6; see also Mark 14:36). In the end our heart's cry for union will be fulfilled. Here is a simple story that explains the import of the word *Abba*.

> In the Jewish sector of Jerusalem a woman and her three-year-old son are standing out in the narrow street straining to see her husband as he comes home from work. Suddenly the little boy cries out "Abba! Abba!" and rushes through the crowded and narrow street to his father who holds out his arms to him, picks him up, and places him on his shoulder. The little boy puts his arms around his daddy's head, holds on and says "Abba! Abba is home!"

This tender and intimate scene pictures for us the meaning of the word that His Spirit cries from within our hearts. There truly is an Abba-shaped emptiness within us, and no philosophical notion or abstract concept will fill it. Our human hearts, our very nature as rooted in the first moment of our creation from the dust of the earth, cry out for the One Who created us—One Whom we can see, can touch, can hold—and Who can hold us in love. In the promise of the final resurrection of our bodies is the testimony that God must have a human form for us to relate to when our fully sinless humanity is restored.

That relationship is heaven. The problem with the various philosophical disclaimers of this simple fact, although they often proceed from piety and reverence, is that they all distance heaven from us to such an extent that we can no longer believe that it will be the fulfillment of our human heart's desire, the realization of the deepest longings of our nature. The following observations imply that God has a form like our own:

- Jesus had the "form" of God and then took on our human *form*. In each case the use of the word *morphe* indicates that the "form" expressed accurately the inner nature of Jesus. But the Eternal Son of God kept our human form at His resurrection. He now has both the form of man and the form of God. The two are the same.
- We are created in His image and likeness, both men and women, with authority and submission built into our relationships. This creates a multidimensional social structure that will be the structure of life in heaven.
- God will participate with us in that social structure. That structure is actually how we participate in the life of the Trinity.
- God will interact with us and reveal Himself to us as our Brother, Father, Spouse, Lord, Kinsman, and Friend. These familial relationships will transpire via a human form.
- The fact that "the Word became flesh and dwelt among us" is powerful evidence that God intends for us to relate to Him in the same way that the Incarnate Word does once we have glorified bodies like His. Jesus did not lose His eternal relationship with the Father when He assumed human form. He is "the first among many brothers," and intends for us to enter into the same relationship with the Father that He always had. Jesus still has that intimate loving relationship with the Father, still is "in the bosom of the Father." He created us for the same glory. The Incarnation has not distanced Jesus from the Father in any way. Instead it must draw us into an intimate personal relationship with Him that is like what Jesus has always had from all eternity.

The Incarnation is irrefutable evidence of the nature of our predestined relationship with the Father, for our glorified bodies will be like His resurrection body. Our relationship will be like the relationship that Jesus has always had. The word *Abba* that wells up in us by the inspiration of the Holy Spirit is a heart-image of what that will mean.

Chrysostom and the other Fathers sometimes seem to ignore, or perhaps to downgrade, women in their commentaries on the Scriptures. I think the primary root cause of this is not a misogynist attitude but rather an overly philosophical view of God and a failure in understanding the familial nature of our humanity, and therefore the familial nature of our heavenly destiny. Once we realize that heaven is a huge loving family, then the vital role that women must play is instantly evident. A family without Mom and without sisters is sterile and unappealing. The final reward that God has for us, His ultimate plan for our salvation, includes men and women imbedded in family relationships—including familial authority. In the beginning He created us as male and female with the man as the head of the woman. To depart from that idea results in the distortion of our understanding of ourselves, of our understanding of the meaning of the love of God, of our understanding of human nature, and of our understanding of the glory of heaven.

A Further Consideration of Heavenly Glory in His Presence:
In the Bible the human race is divided into families, tribes, peoples, tongues, and ethnic groups. The division into tongues is a result of the judgment of God at Babel and so will

not be represented in heaven. The other four groupings present us with a series of ever-enlarging hierarchically ordered matrices within which individual human beings live. This is not the individualistic picture that is held up to us in our society. Ideally people should identify with and take their identity from such human groupings. This is the social order of heaven. In his cynical play *No Exit* Sartre has his protagonist concluding his part with the statement, "Hell is . . . other people!"[601] The truth is exactly the opposite. Heaven must involve other people—people sanctified and totally cleansed of their envy, spite, lust, fear, suspicion, jealousy, and covetousness—all that is endemic to our fallen nature.

In heaven we will experience the joy of human relationships properly ordered by selfless servant-hearted love—topped with the same kind of relationship with the Lord Himself, Who will dwell in our midst as a servant and as a brother. "Blessed are those slaves whom the master will find on the alert when he comes; truly I say to you, that he will gird himself *to serve*, and He will have them recline *at the table*, and will come up and wait on them" (Luke 12:37). Such grace and kindness toward us who believe—to us who have been raised up and seated in the heavenlies with Christ Jesus—by the ones Who created all things and then redeemed us at such a great cost to themselves, is beyond our ability to comprehend. In the ages to come the Father will shower us with the surpassing riches of His grace and kindness—including especially Himself (Ephesians 2:6–7). This is heaven.

If we do not have in our mind and our heart a clear picture of the essential meaning and purpose of our human existence, of how God made us to be and of how in the end we will live and love in His presence, then we will not understand the defining parameters that circumscribe our existence: What is humanity, what is gender, what is authority for, what was human life meant to be? The fact is, we were created in His image and His likeness, and in heaven He will be "like" we are. The only Begotten Son, Who is in the bosom of the Father, is about the task of making Him known to us—and of leading us into the bosom of the Father to be with Him there, as He was even from before the foundation of the world (John 17:24). We were created in His image and likeness for this glory.

Thus in the end we will see Him as He truly is (1 John 3:2); that is, "in proportion as" (*kathos*) He is, or "according as" He is. Now we see Him "in a mirror," or even in a riddle or in an enigma (1 Corinthians 13:12), but then we will see Him "face to face." Now we know Him in part but then we will know Him even as He knows us; that is, we will become acquainted with Him and will know Him thoroughly and accurately. The knowledge of Him will grow in us as we live with Him, and as we share the life of the Trinity as it has existed from before all ages. These many and various considerations indicate that in the consummation we will see Him in a form that presents itself to us as the human form—for in fact that is how He actually is. He will not be accommodating Himself to us; rather, He created us in His image and likeness for the purpose of direct fellowship with Himself.

Genesis Implies This View of God:
The Fathers of the Church were not immersed in the pseudo-scientific and naturalistic world view that so overwhelms our age, but they were deeply influenced by the thinking of the philosophers. They imported philosophical ideas and categories of thought into their understanding of God and of man. These ideas, when mingled with the account of origins that the Bible presents to us, resulted in a certain distortion. The understanding of God and of man was most adversely affected. This is what I have pointed out here. I can do this because we now have a clearer understanding of how Genesis was written.

Because we now know that the narratives of Genesis are first-hand personal accounts by men who lived in ancient times, what they relate cannot be taken in an allegorical way. Such modes of expression developed later on as the science of writing proliferated into many literary styles. Thus while many Fathers of the Church[602] understood the sections of Genesis that talk about God walking in the garden and talking to Adam and Eve, or to Abraham or other people, as necessarily to be taken in some kind of a non-literal way, we now see them as a personal account of what actually happened to the one writing the story. Thus God actually did walk in the garden, and He actually did talk to Adam and Abraham and others in the biblical accounts. Thus He does have a human form and He does intend to relate to us through that form. That was His original intention.

This way of interpreting the Scriptures is necessary in order to preserve the basic integrity of the account as it is written. It also removes from us the subjectivity inherent in deciding when something that is beyond our own experience is "according to reason" and when it is not. Because this is what the person who lived through the events says happened to them, we know it is plain truth. As I pointed out in the arguments above, saying that God has a form like ours is completely consistent with many other biblical passages, contradicts none at all, and exposes the philosophical bias underlying the reasoning of many of the early Fathers—philosophical reasoning that is not supported by the Bible and that is actually foreign to it.

Thus this viewpoint is fatal to some of the philosophical constructs to which Augustine and the other Fathers had recourse when they interpreted Genesis. It is no longer logical to assume that angels perceive things instantly. They are not "amorphous" spirits but also have a form and interact in a way that is like our interactions. The idea of one "Day" in eternity when God instantaneously created all things before the minds of the angels no longer makes sense. Our understanding of how Genesis was written clarifies for us what the Creator is like and also what His actions were like as He created all things.

A Perspective on God and on our Life on the Earth:
So now we can look at God this way: God the Father and God the Son have a form like the human form—composed of pure spiritual light (1 John 1:5), which are immortal by nature—that must exist by nature. The Holy Spirit is the divine "aura" that emanates from them and that extends to all parts of existence—to all places and to all times—and that makes them present to all of their creation. In this way all three persons of the Trinity are always everywhere and are always all-knowing and almighty. Because earthly life was designed to be a place for man to be prepared to enter fully into God's presence, the revelation of God that we experience is subdued; thus we are functioning in His creation and in His constant presence, but we are not fully aware of His majesty, and we are not confronted with His glory—yet. We are being prepared for that. It is our final destiny.

God is unchanging in certain fundamental ways. He is always good, loving, just, merciful, faithful, and true. These qualities are joined in the essential nature of God, and He never acts in a way that is contrary to His essential nature. He can never deny Himself, which is what it would mean if He ever acted outside of these virtuous ways. These qualities all fit together in the perfect holiness of God. In such ways as these God never changes. His form is the perfect expression of these qualities without a body. It is like the human form.

But God is not static. He does change in certain ways. At one time He chose to create. At that time there was a council in the Trinity and a decision was made that the Son had to die for the sins of mankind. This was part of the planning that the Father and the Son did when the Father and the Son planned the ages of the world (Hebrews 1:2). After that planning session the Trinity actually created all things, including the angelic hosts. That is why the wicked angels did not understand about the cross (1 Corinthians 2:6–8). It was because they were not part of the planning session that was conducted before all ages.

Earthly reality, as distinct from eternal spiritual reality which it mirrors, was necessary so that this life could be a place of preparation for mankind. It is amidst the subdued and partially shielded realities that we live and make our choice. It is amidst the shadows of the eternal realities that we choose to receive Him or to reject Him. Once we leave this place of preparation our choice becomes confirmed and finalized. God knew that some angels would fall and turn irrevocably against Him. He made the lake of fire for them. He knew that we would be tempted by that clever evil being and would also fall. But He also knew that our choices in this life were not irrevocable. Thus He formulated a plan to redeem us from our error and to save us from captivity to the evil fallen angels.

Originally there was nothing within mankind—nothing in our created nature—that was hostile to Him or opposed to Him. Sin changed all that and now we have to deal with that difficult fact in all that we do. Therefore the subdued presence of God and our sin-induced distortion of reality make it difficult for us to relate to Him or to know Him as He is, but it also allows us time to correct our errors before our final and irrevocable choice. This is because we are living and choosing amidst the shadows of the ultimate realities, and we are not confronted with the final realities themselves—not in this life—not yet.

When God created He determined to reveal Himself through the events of history. Thus He shows Himself angry at times—when the perverse actions of mankind warrant such a response from One Who is utterly good and holy. He rejoices when we make good and right choices. He responds in these ways even though He knew from eternity that we would behave thus. His responses are always a reflection of His unchanging nature of perfect love and justice. He never changes, and His many responses to the varied facts of history reveal His constant unchanging nature in a multiplicity of ways. At the time of the Deluge He was rightly grieved at the tragic situation on earth and wished He had never made us, rather than having to destroy almost every human being on earth. In the end, when we depart this place of preparation for eternity, He will reveal Himself to us in a face-to-face, direct, personal relationship that will never end.

In response to the descriptions of God that many of the Fathers made, and to balance the way they speak of Him, I assert this: When we get to heaven we will relate directly to the Father—to our Abba. We will look into His eyes. He will put His arms around us and kiss us tenderly (Song 1:2)[603]. We will behold the One Who knew us and loved us from before the foundation of the world. We will know His approval, love, acceptance, and affirmation in all of our being. We will have come home to the place where we truly belong. We will be full participants in the life of the Trinity, in the relationship that was the purpose He had for us from before all time. We will exult as His beloved children. Abstract metaphysical assertions about the Trinity might still be true, but this will certainly be true as well. This relationship with the Father **is** heaven. The uncreated Creator is also our Abba.

If we look at the Lord God in this way then we can understand that He is transcendent because He is outside of the physical realm, but He is immanent because He is in every place at all times. He is near to us, just as far away as a word of prayer. In Him we live and move and have our being, and He upholds all things by the word of His power.

How the Creation Looked at the End of the Six Days:
God blessed us and commanded us to multiply and fill the earth. This is the identical blessing that He gave to "the great sea monsters and every living creature that moves, with which the waters swarmed . . . and every winged bird" (1:21) that He created. That blessing was imparted immediately after they were created, just as it was imparted to humans immediately after we were created. It was stated in this way: "Be fruitful and multiply, and fill the waters in the seas, and let birds multiply on the earth" (1:22). We know that at the end of the sixth day there was only one human pair on the earth and that all men and women have descended from that first couple. Therefore, we should assume that at the beginning God created one pair of each kind of living creature, or at least that He created limited numbers of each kind of creature, as we discussed before, and that over the intervening years and centuries all creatures have multiplied and filled the earth, just as people have done.

The development of the earth's biosphere into its present luxurious state probably also happened over many years. We can look at the initial state of the creation of the plants as follows: they were distributed throughout the entire earth (1:30) but were more sparsely planted than now and destined to grow into their full luscious greenery over time. But the creation was complete in that each type of tree and plant was present; that is, in the same way that each type of animal was present, but only in a limited quantity. We will discover that the Garden of Eden was probably an exception to this principle of being "sparsely planted." It was the one place of luxurious greenery on the new earth. God planted it.

Genesis 1:29—Then God said, "Behold, I have given you every plant yielding seed that is on the surface of all the earth, and every tree which has fruit yielding seed; it shall be food for you;

Genesis 130—and to every beast of the earth and to every bird of the sky and to everything that moves on the earth which has life, *I have given* every green plant for food"; and it was so.

Genesis 1:31—God saw all that He had made, and behold, it was very good. And there was evening and there was morning, the sixth day.

From the beginning it appears that both we and the animals were vegetarians. God gave plants to the animals, and He gave seed/fruit-bearing trees and seed-bearing plants to us. This agrees with the view of natural peace and harmony that characterized the original creation and that describes the kingdom that will eventually be established[604] on earth:
> And the wolf will dwell with the lamb, and the leopard will lie down with the young goat, and the calf and the young lion and the fatling together; and a little boy will lead them. Also the cow and the bear will graze, their young will lie down together, and the lion will eat straw like the ox. The nursing child will play by the hole of the cobra, and the weaned child will put his hand on the viper's den. They will not hurt or destroy in all My holy mountain, for the earth will be full of the knowledge of the LORD As the waters cover the sea. (Isaiah 11:6–8)

This will happen when Israel is restored to a new kind of intimacy with Jehovah, and when even animals will no longer be hunted.

> "It will come about in that day," declares the LORD, "That you will call Me Ishi [my husband] and will no longer call Me Baali [my master]. For I will remove the names of the Baals from her mouth, so that they will be mentioned by their names no more. In that day I will also make a covenant for them with the beasts of the field, the birds of the sky and the creeping things of the ground. And I will abolish the bow, the sword and war from the land, and will make them lie down in safety. I will betroth you to Me forever; yes, I will betroth you to Me in righteousness and in justice, in lovingkindness and in compassion, and I will betroth you to Me in faithfulness. Then you will know the LORD." (Hosea 2:16–20)

Thus the present dispensation is sandwiched between times when the purposes of God for His creation are lived out without bloodshed—without violently shedding the blood even of animals. The present state of affairs where the animals fear us is an anomaly. The peaceful interaction of men and animals that is hinted at is a necessary backdrop to the account of life in the Garden of Eden that we will see in chapter 2. There was no death in His initial very good creation, for the plants were never thought of as "alive" in that sense. They are complex replicating machines that God prepared for us and the animals for food. They take into themselves various earthly elements and by the power of sunlight transform them into complex biochemical structures that our bodies ingest and assimilate easily. Humans were given the "higher" and "tastier" seed and fruit bearing plants and trees.

When did the present predatory nature of some animals develop? It was certainly after the fall but it might not have happened all at once. Perhaps after the Flood there was a further change in animal behavior, when man was authorized to eat animal flesh. We cannot tell.[605] As for the fangs and other physical features that some animals show along with their predatory behavior, we can look at these as having developed from recessive characteristics that became more dominant as the years wore on and the environment on earth worsened after the fall and after the Flood. That is a guess. We do not know.

Because the vegetation was "on the surface of all the earth" we can assume that there were no deserts, high uninhabitable mountain recesses, or frozen arctic wastelands. The original earth was designed for man to live in. The prohibitively high mountains were formed at the time of the Deluge. The uniformly temperate climate on the earth was also changed after that catastrophe. That was also when the deserts and cold areas formed. The inhospitable areas of the earth are the result of a judgment from God. Bede says:

> The world inhabited by those who existed before the Flood is the very same world in which the human race now lives, but it is nonetheless properly said to be the "ancient world," as if it were another because, as is found written in the following parts of the epistle "the world that then was, being overflowed with water, perished" (2 Peter 3:6), namely, both the heavens that existed formerly (cf. 2 Peter 3:5) (that is, all the spaces of this present stormy atmosphere) were destroyed by the height of the increasing waters and the land, too, was changed to another appearance by the destructive waters. For although some mountains and valleys are believed to have been in existence from the beginning, yet they were not the same size as they are now seen to be throughout the entire world. Perhaps this could be denied except that even now we see the appearance of the land changed every year by the eroding waters. This action is believed to have been all the greater then in proportion to the stronger and longer-lasting force of the waters that surged up over and washed away the land.[606]

Because God pronounced His completed creation as "very good" we can assume that there was no animal or human death anywhere on earth. But if we accept the explanation for fossil remains that geologists offer today, then they bear certain testimony to the presence of death on a massive scale centuries before the advent of man. They should be seen rather as the result of the great Flood of Noah that destroyed all living things, at which time many animals were caught up in the waters and buried in the ground.

It is also impossible to reconcile the genealogies of Genesis with the eons claimed for the geologic ages. Those ages are delineated by the various layers of the fossil bearing rocks. If the fossil deposits are interpreted as geologists do today, then there must have been death even before Adam and Eve sinned, and even for millions of years before they lived. The world would necessarily be millions of years old, not just thousands.

But the promised age of glory that we hope for is in some sense a restoration of what man lost in the beginning. If animal death were universal before Adam and Eve then how can there be a time of peace and harmony to look forward to? How can there ever be a time when the glory of God is clear and manifest on this earth? The future time of harmony and peace within the entire natural realm is the restoration of the creation to a state like what was in the beginning.

If there was not a time of peace and harmony at the first, then what about the future? We must understand that the creation was made subject to futility because of the sin of Adam, that the present state of things in human life and in the creation at large was imposed on this world by God as a result of sin. All of the creation will be freed from its bondage to corruption when Jesus returns and the "sons of God" are revealed (Romans 8:20–23). This is an integral part of our blessed hope.

Genesis 2:1— Thus the heavens and the earth were completed and all their hosts.

Let us review how the Trinity carried out the creation. God decided to create during a council held before the foundation of the world. He did not create either from constraint or out of any need on His own part, but rather out of His own good and excellent pleasure. The Father freely chose to create, and for this reason He is worthy to receive glory and honor and power (Revelation 5:11). He chose to share His abundance and His fullness with us.

- The Father created the primordial substance *ex nihilo* by an act of His will. He also dispatched the Holy Spirit, which hovered over that substance waiting to carry out the creation steps. This decision to create is not revocable. Matter will always exist. This world will be the abode (in its reconstituted form) for men for all eternity.
- In a series of steps the Father issued commands to the Son to create.
- The Son carried out each of the commands of the Father by using the power of the Holy Spirit.
- The Son never creates ex nihilo, but He created (that is, He formed) all things by His wisdom.

We can view the events of the six days as the Father granting all power to His beloved Son—the power of the Holy Spirit—to make all things. The Father's creation decrees are irrevocable for it is written, in speaking of the creation of the heavens and their hosts, "He has also established them forever and ever; He has made a decree that will not pass away" (Psalm 148:6). Therefore Jesus still possesses the complete Holy Spirit power—total authorization over all creation. Jesus said, "All power in heaven and earth has been given unto me" (Matthew 28:18). We know that the fullness of the spirit has been given to the Son, for the Father has given Him the Spirit "without measure," and the Father "has given all things into His hands" (John 3:34–35). These statements refer not only to the power to redeem us but also to initially make all things and to eventually reconstitute them.

God did not create the world and send it away to exist on its own. The Father continues to uphold the existence of the universe and Jesus continues to hold all things together, maintaining their form. If the Father rescinded His initial decision then there would no longer be anything. If Jesus ceased upholding things (or holding things together) the world would revert back into the formlessness of the initial primordial substance; that is, Jesus "upholds all things by the word of His power" and their forms would dissolve if He ceased. As the Father will never change His mind about creating, so His authorization that allows the Son to reconstitute all things will never be revoked.

God created this world for us to live in, and we are destined to live forever. Therefore it should not be surprising that our dwelling place should also be destined to exist forever.

Also, the divine support of creation is why the world operates in a consistent and rational way. The world is orderly and logical because the Lord is rational and logical, and He is upholding it consistently—not because we happen to have evolved in a "bubble" where the initial Big Bang produced physical laws by chance that are capable of supporting the development and continued existence of intelligent beings.[g] We who are created in His image and likeness can understand and appreciate the logic and order of the universe—a cosmos that is reflective of His nature and glory. Thus scientists of past centuries said that they were "thinking God's thoughts after Him."

Proverbs relates to us the acts of Wisdom before time and during the creation:
> The LORD possessed me at the beginning of His way, before His works of old. From everlasting I was established [or consecrated], from the beginning, from the earliest times of the earth. When there were no depths I was brought forth, when there were no springs abounding with water. Before the mountains were settled, before the hills I was brought forth; while He had not yet made the earth and the fields, nor the first dust of the world. When He established the heavens, I was there, when He inscribed a circle on the face of the deep, when He made firm the skies above, when the springs of the deep became fixed, when He set for the sea its boundary so that the water would not transgress His command, when He marked out the foundations of the earth; *then I was beside Him, as a master workman*; and I was daily *His* delight, rejoicing always before Him, rejoicing in the world, His earth, And *having* my delight in the sons of men (italics added). (Proverbs 8:22–31)

Wisdom is the personification of Jesus the Word (1 Corinthians 1:24, Colossians 2:3). It appears that He was working with the Father as a master craftsman in the creation. It was His delight to create the world and all that is in it. We might think of the authorization of the Father as granting Jesus the basic power to perform certain tasks, but Jesus retained the option to make things according to His creative desires. The bidding of the Father left Him complete leeway to make as He wished. This world is His sand box!

The Son functions as the Artist and Master Craftsman Who fashioned all things from the substance that the Father summoned into existence.
> I was beside Him, *as* a master workman. (Proverbs 8:30)

Thus all things were made by Him, so that without Him was not anything made that has been made. Thus in Him all things hang together. Thus He upholds the universe (in its form and its structures, which have all been fashioned by Him) by His word of power. He accomplishes His work by using the authorizations that the Father granted to Him during the six days of creation. Like the basic substance, these decrees will never be rescinded. They authorize the Son to fashion and refashion all things as He sees fit.

---

[g] See Appendix II for an overview of the secular theories of origins.

This division of the roles in creation is like what was expressed by Methodius of Olympus.[607]

At the appointed future time Jesus will reconfigure the material and the spiritual realms as prophesied in His holy word. When the end of the world comes and it is time for the creation of the "new heavens and the new earth" (see Revelation 21:1ff), that work will not be accomplished by another command from the Father. It will be enacted by the Son by using the same everlasting authorization that He received at the creation. This has granted Him the permanent power to form and to reconstitute all things as He wills.

Once Jesus has reconstituted all things into their final and permanent state He will deliver the consummated creation over to God the Father (1 Corinthians 15:24).

The plans that Jesus has for reconstituting the creation are revealed to us in the Scriptures. The consummation, which will happen at an undisclosed future time, will be destructive because of the sin of man and the consequent curse that has been levied on the creation, and because of the divine intention to completely scour away all effects of sin. Otherwise it could be accomplished without damaging things:
> But by His word the present heavens and earth are being reserved for fire, kept for the day of judgment and destruction of ungodly men. (2 Peter 3:7)

The earth will be burnt up:
> But the day of the Lord will come like a thief, in which the heavens will pass away with a roar and the elements will be destroyed with intense heat, and the earth and its works will be burned up. (2 Peter 3:10)

The heavens will also vanish.
> The heavens will be destroyed by burning, and the elements will melt with intense heat! (2 Peter 3:12)

Then there will be new heavens and a new earth:
> But according to His promise we are looking for new heavens and a new earth, in which righteousness dwells. (2 Peter 3:12)

Here are some passages that amplify this idea for us:
> Then I saw a great white throne and Him who sat upon it, from whose presence earth and heaven fled away, and no place was found for them . . . for the first heaven and the first earth passed away, and there is no longer *any* sea. (Revelation 20:11, 21)
> Of old You founded the earth, and the heavens are the work of Your hands. Even they will perish, but You endure; and all of them will wear out like a garment; like clothing You will change them and they will be changed. But You are the same, and Your years will not come to an end. (Psalm 102:25–27)

> Heaven and earth will pass away, but My words will not pass away. (Matthew 24:35)

> Then I saw a new heaven and a new earth. (Revelation 21:1)

> "For just as the new heavens and the new earth which I make will endure before Me," declares the LORD, "so your offspring and your name will endure." (Isaiah 66:22)

These verses indicate that the reconstituting of the creation might take place at the sub-nuclear level. The very "elements" will be "dissolved" for they are all under the curse at this time on account of our sin (Genesis 3:17, 8:21). So they must be purified by fire before they can become the final and permanent creation that the Bible calls the new heaven and the new earth. **This is one reason for thinking that radioactivity began when Jesus cursed the ground for Adam's sake. The fact that things must be reconstituted at the sub-nuclear level indicates that the curse originally affected the creation even at that level.**

I conclude day six, the time of the creative acts of God, with this observation based on the creation account that we have just studied:

The doctrine of the Trinity perfectly retro fits the account of creation, undergirding its divine inspiration even before God explicitly revealed His Trinitarian nature to mankind.

Day 7:

Genesis 2:2—By the seventh day God completed His work which He had done, and He rested on the seventh day from all His work which He had done.

Genesis 2:3—Then God blessed the seventh day and sanctified it, because in it He rested from all His work which God had created [bara'] **and made** [asah].

These verses contain repeated assertions that the creative work of God ended when the six days were completed. Therefore, the processes by which He created all things are no longer in effect. Instead at this time "He upholds all things by the word of His power" (Hebrews 1:3). This truth is expressed in the first law of thermodynamics: Today nothing is being created or destroyed. The sum total of all matter and energy is unchanging. No physical creation *ex nihilo* (*bara'*) is going on. The act by which He created the substance of things was a one-time decision. The specific acts of forming (*asah*) the basic structures of this world that Jesus performed as the works of the six days are also completed. That means, in particular, that no new life forms are being created (formed). But God can and still does sometimes intervene miraculously in the course of this world.

On the seventh day God rested. The Hebrew word for rest is *Shabath* which is the word that the Jewish people use today for their day of rest. It means to *cease*, *desist*, or *rest*. In understanding that God "rested" we should in no way think that this indicates that He became worn out or tired. The nature of His creative works, inexpressibly majestic and instantaneous—carried out with the ease of a spoken word—could hardly allow for such a view. Rather, we should understand that He simply ceased from what He had been doing for, "the everlasting God, the Lord, the Creator of the ends of the earth does not become weary or tired" (Isaiah 40:28). As Augustine explains,

> Before we attempt as best we can, and to the extent that we are assisted by him, to reach that far with our understanding, we must first purge from our minds the materialistic ideas about this that people sometimes express. Is it right and lawful, I mean, to say or to think that God found his work hard going when he created the things that have been described above, when *he spoke and they were made* (Ps 148:5)? In that way, surely, not even human beings would find it hard going, if something were made the moment they said it was to be made. Yes, it is true that human words are uttered aloud by sounds in such a way that a long speech will tire one; still, when the words spoken are as few as we read, where it is written that God said "Let light be made, let a solid structure be made," and all the rest until the end of his works, which he finished on the sixth day, it would be the height of absurdity, utter nonsense, to think that this was hard, laborious toil even for a human being, let alone for God.[608]

The "rest" that is expressed at this juncture is related to the Sabbath rest that He enjoined upon Israel in the Law. God wrote the commandments on tablets of stone with His own fingers. The "creation tablet" is not the only Scripture that was personally written by God:

> When He had finished speaking with him upon Mount Sinai, He gave Moses the two tablets of the testimony, tablets of stone, written by the finger of God. (Exodus 31:18)

Here is the Sabbath commandment that God wrote with His own finger:

> Remember the Sabbath day, to keep it holy. Six days you shall labor and do all your work, but the seventh day is a Sabbath of the LORD your God; *in it* you shall not do any work, you or your son or your daughter, your male or your female servant or your cattle or your sojourner who stays with you. For in six days the LORD made the heavens and the earth, the sea and all that is in them, and rested on the seventh day; therefore the LORD blessed the Sabbath day and made it holy. (Exodus 20:8–11)

In this commandment **only** are we commanded to "remember" since it commemorates the supernatural 6-day creation account, which people are prone to forget, ignore, or deny. The Sabbath itself is still vital to us today. If we neglect the Sabbath rest, then our lives become overly focused on work, and family life and the home become diminished. This is especially hard on the woman since her domain of responsibility is the home. With a society like ours where men often work outside of the home her very worth and purpose is lost. We need to protect our weekly leisure time for the sake of our personal mental health, to preserve the meaning of our lives, and for our psychological well-being—to keep the proper perspective on home and family life and to avoid becoming "workaholics."

Genesis 2:4—This is the account [*toledot*] **of the heavens and the earth when they were created.**

This is the "signature" line, implying that no human being was responsible for the content of this account. The Lord God is the only person Who could possibly know about the events in this tablet, and He wrote it. He wrote it when "God rested from all of His work" (Genesis 2:3, the date line). That would be the seventh day.

Some have asserted that the seventh day is still going on because in the account it is not concluded by the words "and it was evening and morning, the seventh day" like all of the other day are concluded. But because God wrote the account during the seventh day it ends in the midst of that day. The seventh day had not yet ended. Also the word for rest is in the past tense. It does not say that God "is resting" from all His work. Therefore the seventh day is not still going on. All of the days referred to in the account of creation were normal 24-hour days. None were long periods of time, even the seventh day.

God blessed the seventh day because on it He rested. However this age of the world is not under His blessing. It is under His curse because of the sin of Adam and Eve, and man makes his way by working in the sweat of his brow. Because the seventh day was blessed it cannot be understood as extending into this present time, which is under the curse. However every curse is canceled in Christ. That is the reason we should seek to enter into the rest that we are granted in Him. Although this rest is for all to enter into, not all do so. It must be entered into through faith (Hebrews 4:1ff).

The Sabbath commandment from God's writing in Exodus 20:8–11 confirms the creation account in summary form and gives us a hint of why, when His creative commands were instantly enacted, God still made all things over a period of six days. It was to serve as a pattern for us, who would need to rest. It was also how the Father shared the creative effort with His Son. They worked together in steps that extended for six days, then rested.

Concluding Observations about the Creation Account:

Modern Perspectives on the Creation Account:
Recall that the creation account was not written from within any human culture, and it in no way partakes of ancient pagan mythology. The Lord God wrote the creation account to be simple so that all could understand it, but it is not simplistic; thus it is accurate in all it says. The New Testament reveals a deeper understanding of it, highlighting its divine inspiration.

Some critics claim the Fathers believed Genesis because they were ignorant of science—a misleading and even irrelevant charge. Yes, the Fathers believed it—not because they were ignorant or simple-minded; rather because it was the inspired, infallible, inerrant

Word of God. They realized that it could never be fully comprehended—not because they were scientifically uneducated; rather because they were human and the creation of all things is, by its very nature, beyond the comprehension of human beings. This is in stark contrast to the presumption of Rationalism that all knowledge is attainable via the naturalistic investigations of mankind, using the powers of his own mind, which is the final judge and arbiter of all truth.

The world view of the ancients might have been deficient in some ways, but that was not the reason why they thought the creation account of Genesis was true; and when aspects of that world view collapsed the assertions of Scripture did not fall with them because they were and remain the eternal, unchanging Word of God—written from outside all cultures and dependent upon none—and in their assertions of truth they stand far above and beyond all incidental human cultural circumstances.

Today when we dismiss the Genesis account of creation it is not really because we have advanced scientifically beyond it. We reject it out of the illusion that we now have a human explanation that is correct with which to replace it; that is, we imagine that we have risen—not just beyond an ancient less-advanced culture, but beyond the human condition that is and has always been the lot of mankind, and that illusion prevents us from accepting the divine account of the creation of all things. That deception comes from hubris.

The fundamental fallacy is that the discoveries that man has made, which show us how to make mechanical devices, grant us medical cures, and generally make our life more pleasant in many ways—that the method of investigation that underlies all these various discoveries—can be extended to explain to us how events happened in the distant past. Thus we have arrived at a set of theories that are said to be scientific and that reveal to us how things began. **But these theories are not science and they are not true.** They are a deception that essentially denies the basic parameters that circumscribe human nature. They extend our role in the creation beyond the purposes for which God made us. Their effect is to put us in the place of God.

Summary of the Genesis Creation Scenario:
In a brief moment of His eternal existence God willed into being the primordial matter of the universe—some solid matter, with volumes of water covering it. He energized that substance to make light and then divided the light from the darkness in some way that we cannot visualize. He opened up a space in the water and moved most of it up sufficiently high to make an open area that was as large as earth's atmosphere. He providentially established the life-supporting atmosphere that all things need to survive. On the earth He moved aside the water to make seas and dry land and caused vegetation to begin to grow on the land. He then formed the upper waters into the heavenly objects, including the sun, moon, and stars that man can see. As He did this He stretched out the upper expanse to be the size that it now is—larger than we can ever observe or discover—as an expression of His surpassing glory (Psalm 19:1). On the earth He created the birds, fish, and land animals. Then He created man. That took Him six days—also known as 144 hours.

At that point the present consistent physical laws came into effect. We know this is how it happened because God has told us. God wrote His account of the creation near the end of the first week and gave it to Adam. He has providentially preserved it for us to this day—the first writing in the history of the world—communicating to us the basic truth about Himself and the creation, telling us that He created everything out of nothing and explaining to us exactly how He did it. This is the undergirding truth of human existence.

The internal logic of the creation account, showing the consistent way that the Father and the Son interacted, is powerful confirmation of the correctness of the Christian Faith and of its fresh insights into the Jewish Scriptures. It is also a good reason for believing that it was written by God. The logic of the story could not have come from any human source for it reflects the Trinitarian nature of God before that truth was explicitly revealed by Jesus.

Also, is intertwined with the fact that the Father possesses the power of existence—that He by His own choice always wills to exist. Thus it is the nature of God to exist, and it is His sovereign choice always to be. God has chosen to grant a share in that being to the created realm. Thus all the creative acts were enacted instantaneously because matter, which owes its very existence to Him, could never resist His will or His commands.

Why the Creation Account Is Important to Mankind and to Christianity:
The truth of supernatural creation is most vital. The concept is inextricably interwoven with the perspective that creation occurred a few thousand years ago as the genealogies of Genesis teach. This is the teaching of Scripture, the Ancient Faith, the faith of all the holy ones of old. It is the foundation of the Christian world view. Our understanding of the meaning of human life rests on it. Our understanding of God and man rests on it.

The Genesis account of creation is humanity's fundamental connection to God; that is, it explains to us Who He is and what it means to say that He created all things—and what it means to say that He created us. If we lose this truth, then we inevitably fall away from Him in certain important ways. We lose our direct connection to Him and are left with a feeling of meaninglessness and purposelessness in our lives. We retain little sense of being accountable for how we live because we are distanced from Him. The world itself becomes an alien and hostile place, devoid of His providential love and care, and without a purpose or goal.

The Genesis creation account directly contradicts the "spirit of the age" in which we are living. That opposing spirit has given rise to a conflicting world view in which we are all immersed. It is another spirit, not the Holy Spirit. The two concepts of origins cannot be reconciled. As Christians we must cling firmly to His word at this time in history.

There is nothing more spiritually stultifying than the secular theories of origins. And to think I was actually enamored with them when I was young! Appendix II has a summary of those pseudoscientific philosophical fantasies.

Adam

Here is the beginning and the end of the text of the second set of tablets:

2 ⁴ᵇwhen they were created, in the day that the LORD God made earth and heaven. ⁵ Now no shrub of the field was yet in the earth, and no plant of the field had yet sprouted, for the LORD God had not sent rain upon the earth, and there was no man to cultivate the ground. ⁶ But a mist used to rise from the earth and water the whole surface of the ground . . .

5 ¹ This is the book of the generations of Adam. [In the day when God created man He made him in the likeness of God. (This phrase begins the next tablet, that of Noah.)]

Archeological Considerations:

This text is the story of the creation of man and woman, the story of the temptation and fall, the story of Cain and Abel, the story of the development of human civilization apart from God, and a peek into the successive generations of the godly line of patriarchs—all told from Adam's perspective. Note the <u>marks of antiquity</u> Wiseman points out in the text.

> The second tablet or series of tablets extends from 2:5–5:2 and contains an account of the beginning of man upon the earth, the Garden of Eden, the Fall, and the murder of Abel. This tablet also bears the clearest marks of extreme antiquity and simplicity, which could never have come from a late hand. For instance, <u>the test of obedience is the eating or refraining from eating the fruit of a tree</u>. <u>The tempter is referred to after the Fall as "a serpent in the dust," a form never afterwards used in the Old Testament</u>. Again, it is one that no late writer was likely to employ. Then there are <u>expressions such as "sin crouching at the door"</u> in connection with the story of the offering made by Cain. Also there is the remark of Lamech, "<u>I have slain a young man to my wounding and a young man to my hurt</u>," pointing to contemporary archaic events of which no explanation is given. Again the record shows evidence of being a personal one, "<u>I heard Thy voice in the garden and I was afraid . . . I hid myself</u>." I suggest that no late writer would have used such intimate phrases as "<u>the Lord God walking in the Garden in the cool of the day</u>." The Jew had been taught a most reverential conception of God, as One infinitely eternal and supreme, the Maker of the heavens and the earth. Even unto Moses God did not appear except in majesty and awe. The expression "cool of the day" is most natural in the Near East; for the greater part of the year it experiences intense heat throughout midday, while in the evening a cool wind blows. Often in Iraq I have heard that expression used to indicate the time immediately after the sun has gone down and the evening wind begins to blow. [Underlining mine]

> The one person who knew all the facts about the Fall is stated to be the source from which the account came. This second tablet takes the story up to the birth of the sons of Lamech. Soon after this Adam died; the concluding words of the tablet are, "This is the book of the origins of Adam."[609]

Relation to the Creation Account and Introductory Remarks:

The way that we view this tablet in its relation to the previous tablet has been a source of controversy among Christian scholars for centuries. During ancient times there was a question in some minds of when the account passed into earthly time; that is, when did the narrative pass from events that happen in an instant in eternity to events that take place during earth time as we experience it? In more modern times those who hold the tradition received from the ancients—that Moses wrote the Genesis account—see this story as a continuation of the previous tablet. Others insist that certain internal details of the story indicate that it must have been written by a separate author and that two accounts of creation were merged from diverse traditions at a later date. The second view rejects the traditional idea that Moses was the final editor of Genesis and asserts that there were several redactors involved over the centuries that produced our account.

From our perspective, noting the way in which Moses edited and combined the ancient records that he had at his disposal, we say this: Moses was the "final redactor" of the Genesis account. The first tablet was written by the Lord Who created all things. The second tablet, the one which we are considering in this chapter, was written by Adam.

This second tablet begins by describing the world that presented itself to Adam at the moments immediately after He first became aware of his existence, right after the Lord God breathed into him the breath of life. The words written in this tablet are his personal impressions, plus the thoughts and ideas that He gleaned from interacting with those close to him. According to this account we know that Adam interacted with only a few people: The Lord God, who interacted with him in the garden; his wife Eve whom the Lord God gave to him; his children and their further descendants. Thus in this personal account we are reading his description of things as they were at the beginning of the human race as he would have gleaned them from these few close sources.

The first account was written by God at the very end of His creative works, but this story was written by Adam. Both describe events that happened in time as we know it, not in eternity, or instantaneously. But there is a paradigm shift in perspective. The shift is from the perspective of the Holy One, the Most High, the Eternal Creator, to the perspective of the man whom He created at the first—from the divine to the human perspective.

Augustine observed that in the transition from the creation account of tablet one to this account we are transitioning from events that happened as the outworking of completely supernatural processes—whose mysterious timing is intertwined with the humanly incomprehensible times of the six days (whether they are thought of as six days or as one magnificent Day in eternity), to events that are happening in order and according to the sequence of things that unfold in history through intervals of time—things that are unfolded in time like the events that characterize our daily human perceptions.[610] There is validity to his observations because we are now reading the account of Adam the first man and are transitioning to his human perspective in this account. However, we see no need to posit a change in how the actual passage of time takes place.

The name that God employed to refer to Himself in the first account was the name of the great and awesome One Who summoned all things into existence from non-being and Who formed all existing structures into their present configurations. In this account He is seen as the One Who speaks to Adam, lovingly and graciously provides for his very existence and sustenance, and providentially cares for and teaches him. Intrinsic to His self-revelation to Adam is His giving Adam a name by which the man can call on Him and by which He is to be known. That name was "I AM" or "I am that I am." "Lord" or "Lord God" is the name by which Adam refers to Him in his personal account of things.

The fact that God has a name is a very significant point. Today we are not only created by Him but also redeemed by Him. His name to us is "Jesus" which ultimately means "The Lord God saves." At the time of the creation He was not yet known as a redeemer or as a savior. He was known only by His great and awesome work of creating and by His daily providential care for the man. But implicitly man was accountable to the One Who created him. These truths are reflected in the name used to refer to God in this account by Adam—in His name "Lord God."

Thus this does indeed represent a second account of the beginning of things, from the Lord's story to Adam's. This is a partial account, as is appropriate not to the One Who actually called forth all that exists, but as is appropriate to one who was himself called into existence in his proper order within the great panoply of all things. Adam will tell us how he perceived the world from the time of his first breath—when he became a living soul.

When we comment on Adam's opening words—"when they were created, in the day that the Lord God made earth and heaven"—which tell us when the first section of Adam's account took place, we should see that he is intentionally following up on the account in the first tablet by saying when the account of his tablet begins—it begins during the time when God was making all things. The account of Adam begins with his story of how he and Eve came to be. Their creation happened during day six, as part of the creation of all things. Again, both creation stories relate events that happened in time, not in eternity.

The account of the Garden of Eden is vital to the Christian perspective on life. It is the necessary backdrop to our basic assertions that "God is good" and "God loves us" and "God is kindly intentioned toward us." The hundreds of statements to this effect that are found in the Old and New Testaments lose their convictive force without this clear picture of what the beginning of the human race looked like.

Today we live in such a dark and hopeless world! It is vital to our faith—it is vital to our understanding of the nature of God—for us to know that at the beginning human life definitely was not this way. This perspective necessarily implies that human life has undergone a radical change from what God originally intended it to be. The reason for the change must be clearly understood as well. This account is by Adam, the first member of our race, the one who experienced the initial events of human history, and the one who lived through them. Adam wrote this account under divine leading so that we could know these things.

Suppose that we evolved from bands of "hunter gatherers" thousands of years ago. We had, by the testimony of those who concoct such stories, a harsh and difficult life then. Once we figured out how to domesticate certain animals instead of having to chase and hunt them, and once we learned how to grow crops instead of having to find them as we traveled "on the go," then we were able to settle down and build civilizations. This idea merely projects our present life circumstances—difficult and competitive as they are—into the distant unseen past. It also implies that the same conditions that govern human life now—our sin nature and all that is implied by that—were also in effect back then; that is, we "inherited" our human state from our animal ancestors. Behind that scenario lurks the assumption that "kill or be killed" and "survival of the fittest" was and remains today as the basic rule of life. This leaves no room for the goodness of God.

The history of Adam is vital for counteracting that hideous picture of human life and the cruel and unfeeling idea of God that it implies. God is good. In the beginning He placed us in a situation that was pleasant and fulfilling—both physically, in that all of our needs were taken care of, and spiritually, because our intimate connection with Him was the source of joy, inner peace, meaning, and purpose. Human existence today is generally bereft of such consolation. Adam assures mankind that it was the inevitable result of a terrible choice that he made, that we have landed in our present sorry state.

We are now living a "sub-human" life, one that has been stripped of the essential good qualities that characterized it at the beginning. The entire creation is groaning under the effects of that terrible choice as well. Before that choice mankind was living in an intimate direct relationship with God. He was also our Lord as the name given to Him by Adam implies. The loss of that relationship is the essential fact that we glean from the history of Adam. The loss of that relationship is the foundational reason why we and the entire creation are in the state that we see around us now. The initial state of peace and joy that Adam testifies to in his story is the basic historical fact upon which we base our hope for the future. The final glory and blessing to which we look forward is a reflection of, a bringing to perfection of, and the consummation of the good, wholesome, blessed state in which God originally made us—and is redemption from our present darkness.

Adam himself assures us that God was and is good, that His intentions toward us were and are only good, and that the difficulties that we are now experiencing are because he rejected Him as Lord. Today we, his descendants, are still in rebellion against Him. We are in complicity with the wrong decision that Adam made at the beginning of human life.

There is no date line to tell us when Adam completed his account. The phrase "in the day when God created man" (5:1b) is probably the first line of Noah's account because date lines generally precede the signature lines. But Adam's account divides easily into five sections. We can assign a date when Adam wrote each section, estimating based on the contents of each section. Thus we can obtain a rough hypothetical chronology. The five sections in Adam's tablet are:

- Genesis 2:5–Genesis 2:25: This is the account of the creation of Adam and Eve and the Garden of Eden, and of their placement therein. Adam wrote this story early on, perhaps after a couple of months. After he was created there was a period of time when he and Eve lived in the garden and enjoyed their life there.[611] In that simple and innocent life the Lord visited them from time-to-time, as described in 3:8, but they were not frightened of Him. They easily and unselfconsciously related to Him.

  I assume that it was during this time of delight and innocence, after perhaps two or three months, that Adam wrote this part of his story. My reason: Because he could write, why would he not write the account of his first days in the garden? I imagine that the Lord God even encouraged him to write his first impressions for the sake of his later descendants. At that time the Lord God did not permit Satan to tempt them.

- Genesis 3:1–3:24: The account of the temptation and the fall. As Adam and Eve lived their blissful lives and interacted with the Lord some of the heavenly watchers became envious of them. After a certain time of stabilization for Adam and Eve God permitted the Devil to approach them with a test. The writing of this part took place after the fall, while Adam and Eve were living outside the garden, after they settled into their new lifestyle—a life without their natural, easy, and intimate relationship with the Lord God. The name "Eve" suggests that children had already been born.

- Genesis 4:1–4:15: The account of Cain and Abel. From the account we cannot tell for certain that Cain was the first person to be born, but it seems likely that he was the first **male** child to be born. Eve's exclamation of delight "with the help of the Lord I have gotten a man child" indicates this, for I assume she was happy because the prophecy of the coming "seed of the woman" named a man as the promised one to correct the terrible situation into which they had gotten themselves. The account of

Cain and Abel happened after Adam and Eve had birthed many children, for Cain was fearful that "anyone who sees me will kill me" and this fear indicates that there had to be a number of other grown people around—enough to give him someone to fear. I will assume that Adam added this part of his story sometime after the murder of Abel and the judgment and banishment of Cain by the Lord God.

- Genesis 4:16–4:24: Cain's genealogy to the seventh generation (including Cain). This part of Adam's story was written after the banishment of Cain. The generations stretch over many centuries. The long duration that the genealogy of Cain covers, stretching as we will show, into the old age of Adam, is strong evidence that Adam, whose name is appended to the account, actually would have had to endure for many centuries to record it. Thus the presence of the genealogy of Cain—written no doubt out of Adam and Eve's continuing love and concern for their erring son—also shows that a lifetime of 930 years for Adam is reasonable.
- Genesis 4:25–4:26: The godly line of patriarchs starting with Seth, written late in life.

The detailed descriptions of these events had to be written by one who was there. Adam wrote them, as a general time frame, at the dawn of human history.

The Content of these Tablets Span the Life of Adam:
Let us compare the genealogies of Seth (from this table) and Cain (from the table on the next page) to estimate the full span of time covered by the genealogy of Cain.

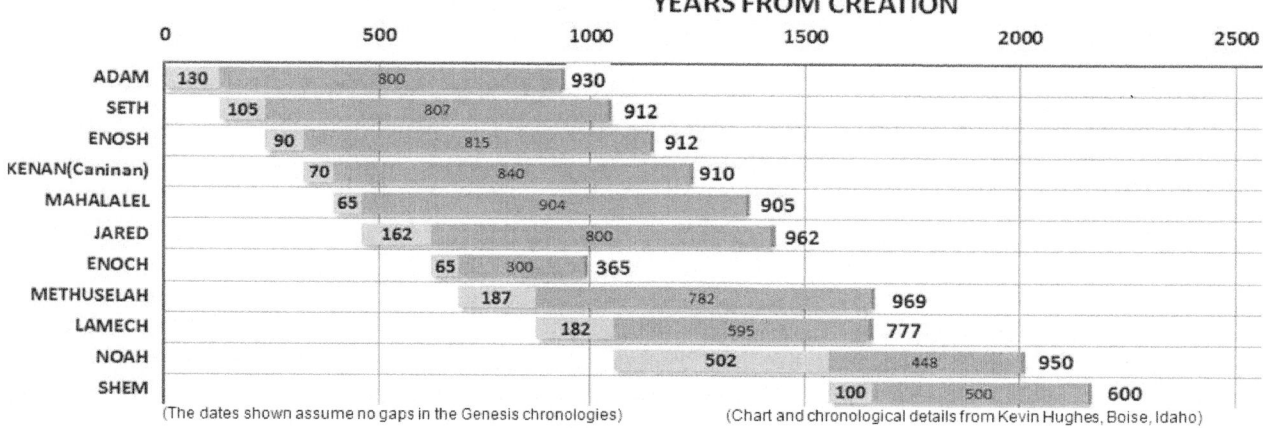

(The dates shown assume no gaps in the Genesis chronologies)   (Chart and chronological details from Kevin Hughes, Boise, Idaho)

From this chart, which pictures for us the generations that descended from Seth, we see that Adam lived just long enough to see Lamech born. Lamech was the father of Noah. Note that the seventh generation in the line of godly patriarchs, including Seth, would be Methuselah, and his life overlapped Adam by over 200 years. But his son Lamech was born when Adam was near death. It is logical to assume therefore that in the genealogy of Cain the seventh generation as recorded by Adam would have fallen in his old age.

Now looking at the genealogy that Adam recorded for Cain in chapter 4 of Genesis it is written: Cain, Enoch, Irad, Mehujael, Methusheal, Lamech—and Lamech's four children: Jabal, Jubal, Tubal-cain, and Naamah. This covers seven generations (including Cain) so that the four grown children of Lamech were the seventh generation in Cain's line.

Thus the fact that the genealogical list for Cain ends when it does gives credence to the assertion that Adam did indeed compile this list, ending his record keeping when he was an old man. The chronological considerations for these statements follow.

> This shows how the dates listed for Seth's descendants fit into the Old Testament and secular chronology.
>
> The dates for Cain's offspring are only estimated of course.

Seth's Line	Date Born[h]	Cain's Line
Enosh	3724 BC	Enoch
Kenan	3634 BC	Irad
Mahalalel	3564 BC	Mehujael
Jared	3499 BC	Methusheal
Enoch	3337 BC	Lamech
Methuselah	3272 BC	Four children

Adam was 687 years old when Methuselah was born. Cain was almost 130 years older than Seth, so Adam was about 557 years old when Lamech's children were born. Their inventions—keeping livestock, using musical instruments, and working in iron and bronze—would come later, in their adulthood. Adam's observation of these achievements, that they had determined the course of later generations, would extend later still, even into Adam's old age. (Archeology verifies writing existed by 3300 BC. Adam, who died in 3029 BC, could have written his story even in that case. However, we assert that writing was in use from the beginning, but has not been discovered because extensive civilizations did not arise until human beings multiplied enough to become quite numerous on the earth.)

Other Archeological and Historical Considerations:

A Jewish tradition[612 see note] says that Naamah, daughter of Lamech in the line of Cain, was the wife of Noah. By comparison of the genealogical lists for Cain and his descendants with the genealogical lists for Seth and his descendants we see that she must have been born about 3272 BC—approximately the same time as Methuselah, since she was of his generation—but Noah was born 2903 BC, well over 350 years later than she was. How could Adam, when he wrote his story, have known that she would be the wife of someone that was not born yet—who would not be born until more than a century after Adam's death? It does make one wonder though—why did Adam single her out in the genealogy? Was she a great queen or an important personage in her day? Her brother Tubal-Cain was a forger of implements of bronze and iron, and her half-brother Jubal invented musical instruments. Her other half-brother Jabal dwelled in tents and kept livestock, which was significant enough to merit mention by Adam. It appears that each of these new skills was a key step in the formation of the first pre-Flood civilization.

Archeologists have made some interesting discoveries at Ur-Nammu in Mesopotamia:

> In 1929 Sir Leonard Woolley instructed his workmen to dig a deep pit in a selected part of the city. In doing this they unexpectedly found a remarkable change in the character of the soil, for clean water-laid clay suddenly commenced. The Arab workmen reported it and were told to continue digging down. After a depth of eight feet this clean water-laid clay eased as suddenly as it had commenced, for below it broken pottery was found and other evidences of the existence of a village before the layer of clay became deposited. The place where this discovery occurred was down through strata which covered the sloping face of a mound and the thickness of the water-laid clay varied across it from eight to eleven feet in depth. The water necessary to lay such a great thickness of deposit must have been so considerable that Sir Leonard Wooley came to the conclusion that the only possible explanation of his discovery was that they had found definite evidence of the effects of the Flood. In the season 1929-30 he dug down through the Flood level into virgin soil, and in 1934 he sank another pit some distance away, again through the water-laid clay of the Flood, discovering some statues and pottery in the pre-Flood level. At the conclusion of this last season's work, he told me

---

[h] See Appendix I for an explanation of how the dates are determined from Scripture and secular history.

that his findings regarding the Flood had been abundantly confirmed. I have examined this Flood earth. The complete absence of salt prevalent in other levels, its exceptional nature, the sudden beginning and as abrupt cessation, then the recommencement of broken pottery and bones beneath it, are certainly most remarkable evidence of a Flood.[613]

Once the Flood level had been determined it was also possible to estimate the dates of many of the older discoveries at that site.

> Beginning in the year 1927, at a level which he later dated 3500 BC, Sir Leonard Woolley unearthed a large cemetery, and many grim discoveries suggested deaths which had probably been violent. In it, however, were many fine examples of the type of golden headdress worn by women of those times, also numerous bead necklaces. One of the most spectacular finds was that of a golden helmet of Mes-kalam-dug, whom Sir Leonard placed as having lived about 3500 BC.[614]

Perhaps what Adam was impressed with, and what he noted in his brief history of the sons of Cain, was that they had begun to form what we would now call "civilization." We take this for granted as what people do when they get together. But that early in man's history it must have been an admirable and fascinating thing to see. It would have been comparable in those days to the development of our modern technological society, and it might have produced the same awe toward "man and his limitless creativity and skill."

Textual and Theological Considerations:
Genesis 2:4a—In the day that the LORD God made earth and heaven.

This time phrase was greatly misleading to Augustine who attempted to use it to date the account of the creation of the plants to the eternal "Day" when the creation of all things happened together at once. Here is the misleading translation of this and the following words from which Augustine was working:

> When the day was made God made heaven and earth, and all the greenery of the field before it was on the earth, and all the hay of the field before it sprang up.

Augustine saw this as an assertion about the concurrent timing of creation events:
- when the day was made (that would be the first day, when God made the light)
- when God made the heaven and the earth (that also would be the first day)
- when God made the greenery of the field before it was in the earth
  (How could God make the greenery of the field before it was in the earth?)
- when he made the hay before it sprang up
  (How could God make the hay before it sprang up?)

God made the day, the heavens and the earth, the greenery, and the hay on that one "Day" in eternity. That is one reason why, as he understood these words, God had to have made everything together simultaneously, and it had to be in eternity on that one "Day." That also explained how God made the greenery before it was in the field and how He made the hay before it sprang up! It was all made in that one great "Day" in its primary causes. Then it actually began to grow once the transition from eternity to earth time happened. This reinforced for Augustine the idea that everything had been created simultaneously together, and confirmed his erroneous translation of Sirach 18:1 where it said that "God made all things together simultaneously." He asserted that these things, and all things, were made in their "potentialities" on that one great "Day."[615]

The King James translation of these verses is like Augustine's.

> These *are* the generations of the heavens and of the earth when they were created, in the day that the LORD God made the earth and the heavens, and every plant of the field before it was

> in the earth, and every herb of the field before it grew: for the LORD God had not caused it to rain upon the earth, and *there was* not a man to till the ground. (Genesis 2:4–5)

With Wiseman's insights in view we translate from the Hebrew as:

> This is the account of the heavens and the earth [end of first tablet] when they were created. In the day that the LORD God made earth and heaven [catch-phrase connecting to first tablet at 1:1]. Now no shrub of the field was yet in the earth, and no plant of the field had yet sprouted, for the LORD God had not sent rain upon the earth, and there was no man to cultivate the ground. (Genesis 2:4–5)

We realize that the "catch phrase" makes for clumsy wording, but archeology points to this translation of the Hebrew, similar to the NASB translation.

Despite the textual restrictions under which he was laboring, Augustine recognized this section of Genesis as the transition from when all things were made in an instant, to the time when events passed by in the sequence of time that we are familiar with as human beings—as a transition from an era in which the passage of time was incomprehensible to us as humans, to an era in which the passage of time was like we now understand it in daily human experience.[616] Thus Augustine had a deep insight into the significance of this section of Genesis, that it was indeed a turning point in the creation narrative, that it transitioned us from God's time frame to our human time frame—or rather, as we assert, it marked a transition from the divine perspective to the human perspective. Additionally the JEPD Theory sees this verse as a point of transition in the authorship of the account of Genesis based on the change in the name that is used to refer to God.

We understand 2:4b to be a "catch-line" by Adam that connects his account in this tablet with the previous account and also situates the account of the creation of man within the overall account of the creation as given by the Lord God. It marks a transition from the divine perspective to the human perspective, as Augustine observed. It also indicates a change in authorship—from God to Adam—like the JEPD Theory asserts. At this point Adam is intentionally continuing the Lord's account of the creation by appending to it the record of his personal experience as a participant. This is the account of one who was a part of the creation instead of the account written by the One Who created all things.

<u>More on the Change in Divine Name from Elohim to Jehovah Elohim:</u>
Augustine notices the change in the name of God that takes place and attributes the use of the divine name "The Lord God" to the fact that the inspired author wants us to realize how important it is that we accept God as our own lord and master, rather than presuming to live our lives according to our own wisdom and purpose. This is the basic message of the account of Adam in the garden. The change in the name used to refer to God is also a key observation within the JEPD Theory of the composition of Genesis.

In this work we see this change as indicative of not only a change in authorship but also of a transition in perspective from the divine to human, agreeably with what Augustine noted. God first reveals Himself to us within His own writing as the One Who summoned all things into existence. But then He reveals Himself as the One Who created mankind and Who loves and cares for us by providing for us a lovely place of delightful existence where we can come to know Him from our limited human perspective. The name that He gives to Adam for calling upon Him is indicative of His divine nature, but it also reflects how Adam knows God in relationship to himself. He knows God as the One Who speaks with him on a regular basis, teaches him, cares for him, and to Whom he is responsible.

This tablet is signed, "the **book** of the generations of Adam" (Genesis 5:1). Therefore, we know that Adam could write. We should understand that as Adam wrote this account He was being guided by the Holy Spirit. The Spirit revealed to him exactly what to write, gave him the right perspective on those things, and made sure that he used the proper words to express accurately the truths that the Lord God intended for all the successive generations of man to accurately understand.

Genesis 2:5—Now no shrub of the field was yet in the earth, and no plant of the field had yet sprouted, for the LORD God had not sent rain upon the earth, and there was no man to cultivate [Lit:, work or serve] **the ground.**

As we consider this account remember that Adam (and Eve) did not have a background in "civilization" like we do. They had just awakened to life and awareness in a new world. Adam was eventually placed in the garden by the Lord God to till it (Genesis 2:15), and he has been doing that for some period of time, learning about horticulture, watching all his different plants grow as he tends them and as the rains water them. Now it is time for him to write the account of how his life started—and how Eve's life started as well.

I want to supplement the above translation of this particular verse, for there is a further implication within its words. Both the KJV and the Douay-Rheims translate this verse with this sense: "every plant of the field before it sprung up (or before it was in the earth, KJV), and every herb of the ground before it grew." How could God create them before they sprung up? Here Adam is explaining that at the beginning of the creation God made these things by supernatural means; they did not arise or "spring up" in accordance with the normal course of nature, sprouting and growing by taking their nourishment from the ground over time; instead they were produced directly by supernatural means. He says there was no rain to gradually cause growth, and there was no man to till the soil and to cause them to grow. All of the "normal" or "natural" means of plant development were missing. These are the supplemental implications of this verse.

Now to comment on what is given in our text, the NASB translation, also very helpful in how it translates this verse.

When Adam awoke he saw that the earth was somewhat barren. This was because, as we noted in our comments on the tablet of the Lord, the entire biosphere was created in a way that included every type of plant and animal, but with each type represented in a limited quantity. The earth was not yet filled with the various types of plants or animals. The Fathers observed that Adam was made from a "virgin earth," one that had never seen death or struggle under sin, just as Christ, the second Adam, was made from a sinless virgin.[617] It was also true that the earth had not yet been used to produce any vegetation. In fact, the area of the earth where Adam was created, from which the Lord God formed his body, did not even have any plant roots or seeds in it. It was pure soil. This also fits the idea of virgin earth. Thus it was virginal both in the moral sense of being untouched by sin or death, and in the physical sense of not having been used for production in any way. This was the soil from which Adam was made by the Lord God.

It was Adam's understanding from God's command—and from his experience in the first few months of his existence—that man was to help the earth enter into its fully luscious state by his work of tilling the soil. That process also required rain to make things grow. Neither of those things had happened at the time when he was created on the sixth day; that is, no farmer and no rain—yet. Adam is describing two things for us: the first vegetation did not arise by the means that would be familiar to all of his descendants throughout subsequent ages of the earth, and the earth at the beginning was barren, or at least was sparsely planted—especially at the location where he was created.

In Augustine's view this was a way of saying that at this initial point in time the normal processes of plant growth that involved being watered by rain and cultivated by men, and which over intervals of time resulted in the growth of vegetation—all such time bound processes—had not yet begun.

Sometimes people have taken the statement of "no rain" to mean that it never rained before the Flood, perhaps because of different atmospheric conditions then. But Adam specifically mentions "rain," and Adam died well before the Flood. Thus it seems better to assume that the absence of rain was specific only to the very beginning of his time in Paradise. Yet it would seem that any rain which fell would not be accompanied by the violent and destructive winds that can accompany it today. The reason why the rain was not violent was because of the layer of water vapor that (we assume) was above the layers of atmosphere and was not part of the hydrologic cycle. Such an atmospheric canopy would tend to distribute the suns warming effect more evenly over the one huge continent. There would be no cold/warm fronts to collide and produce violent storms, so a more uniformly temperate and peaceful climate would characterize the entire earth.

My father used to talk of something called a "farmer's rain" in which the rain fell as small drops with little or no wind, and which continued for a long time. It produced a thorough soaking of the ground without damaging the vegetation. It would seem that this kind of life-giving rain would be expected in the original "very good" creation. Adam must have experienced this as time went on, since he mentions it by name, but he notes here that no such rain had yet fallen.

This point in the Genesis narrative is quite significant. The JEPD Theory sees this verse as the beginning of a "second creation story." The idea is that there were two ancient creation myths that were melded together and that they overlap and contradict a bit at this point. Such an interpretation of the Genesis narrative is utterly foreign to all ancient commentators. They all saw this point as the beginning of a more detailed description of the creation, a description that added more details about the creation of woman and of man that showed something of their interrelation in the total creation and included the description of the garden into which the Lord God placed mankind at the beginning.

The Geography of the Newly Created World:
Genesis 2:6—But a mist [or flow] **used to rise from the earth and water the whole surface of the ground.**

This flow of water appears to be a kind of artesian well that was bubbling up out of the earth. Psalm 136:6 says, "to Him Who spread out the earth above the waters." This can be understood to mean that in the beginning the earth was resting upon a network of interconnecting subterranean waters that rose up and watered the whole earth. This was the way that God first created things. These subterranean waters interconnected with the "great deep." At the time of the Flood all the fountains of the great deep burst forth, all the floodgates of the heavens were opened up, and the earth was flooded.

This description of the initial geography of the earth helps explain the unique nature of the Deluge. The layer of water above the atmosphere fell down while the waters of the subterranean deeps gushed up, and the entire earth was flooded. Remember that at this time there were no extremely high mountains as now. That one-time catastrophic event is what destroyed the "world at that time" (2 Peter 3:6). The present geography of our world is greatly different: there are very few underground or artesian wells, no water layer above the atmospheric heavens, the land is now divided into several parts, there are high mountains, there are violent wind/rainstorms, there are extreme temperatures that at times and places are not suitable for men to live in comfortably, and there are vast areas of erosion and desert where man always finds it difficult to live. However the initial geography of the earth was designed so that men could live in all of it comfortably. This is the description of the world that was in the beginning that Adam wrote for us, the world as it was when man was created.

More on Augustine's Thinking:
Before entering into the description of the creation of man as Adam describes it to us I want to review the way that Augustine approaches the next part of the creation account. He faces a problem because he asserts that the work of the six days was accomplished in the single great "Day" before time began to pass as humans perceive such passage, and before human existence was possible, for things were happening in an instant. Yet in the passage that we are studying it is obvious that Adam is alive and interacting with his environment as time passes according to regular human perception.

The account of Genesis 2 gives more details about the creation of man and woman that is briefly described in chapter 1, verses 25-27. It tells us that between the creation of man and the creation of woman a number of events transpired: The man was placed in Paradise, he was shown the animals and named them, God formed Eve from his side, and Adam hailed Eve with delight when God brought her to him. These things seem to be happening in human time as we know and experience it.

It was the common faith of the ancients that the creative commands of God were carried out immediately. That is, when God commanded then the created realm necessarily had to respond to His will at once. This understanding flowed from the fact that this world owes its very existence to Him and thus it cannot resist Him for even an instant. But the idea that a lengthy sequence of actions, such as the entire creation account or a major section of it, might have been enacted instantaneously was NOT the common faith of the ancient Church. Origen, Didymus the Blind, and Augustine expressed such ideas, but the common patristic view was that creation was spread over six normal days.

The view that the creation scenario, or some major part of it, happened in an instant is inextricably interwoven with a theory about the spiritual realm of existence. In that view of things God and the angels, as spiritual beings, perceived and came to know things in an instant. They existed in an eternal ever-present "NOW" and did not experience the passage of time the way that we do on this earth.

Those ancient commentators who believed that the creation scenario transpired in one instant in eternity had to decide when the events of the creation account transitioned from eternity to "time as we experience it." In our explanation of the Ancient Faith we noted that for Didymus the Blind this occurred when Adam and Eve were expelled from Eden. This was because he believed that Eden was in a spiritual plane rather than being on this earth. We inferred that Origen likely thought in a similar way. But Augustine asserted that Eden was a place on this earth. Accordingly, he set the boundary between divine and human time at Genesis 2:6, "But there went up a mist from the earth." From that verse on the account is in human time according to his thinking. Again, he set it at that point because He asserted that Eden was a physical place on this earth and not a mystical place that existed in some spiritual plane. Most of the Fathers of the Church did not insert the complication of this temporal transition into the Genesis account, and neither do we.

But Augustine encountered a major problem with reconciling the account of Paradise as given in Genesis chapter 2 with the account of the creation in Genesis chapter 1:26–7, which said that man was created in the one "Day" when light was made in the intelligent creation of the angels. So how did he arrive at a suitable joint understanding of Genesis 1:26–27, which he said happened in an instant in eternity, and the present passage, which shows Adam as he moves and talks and responds with human speech? For he is acting within the events described in Genesis 1:26–27 which happened in an instant!

After much lengthy discussion of the various ways of understanding things Augustine says, in referring to the creative words of God in 1:26–27:
> These words of His were uttered before any sound waves in the air, before any voices from lips or clouds, uttered in that supreme Wisdom of His, through Whom all things were made, uttered not as if to be dinned by human ears, but to insert into things already made the causes of things still to be made. With them He was making by His almighty power things still in the future, and was establishing as it were in the seed or root of all times the man still to be formed in his own due time. This was when He was establishing the point from which the ages, established by Him Who is before all ages, were to begin.[618]

But Augustine also maintains that these events in chapter 2 happened in time; that is, in the time that we perceive as human beings—the time of our human experience.
> However easy, after all, a human being may think it is for God to have done all this simultaneously with the rest, we know with absolute certainty that the words of a human being can only be uttered aloud over intervals of time. When we hear the man's words, therefore, when he was giving names either to the animals or to the woman, or when he also went on to say, *For this reason a man shall leave his father and mother and be joined to his wife, and they shall be two in one flesh* (Genesis 2:24), whatever syllables this was uttered with, not even any two of them could have been spoken simultaneously.[619]

It is with much painstaking care and intricate reasoning that Augustine pursues his idea that "all things were made together simultaneously." In this pursuit he repeatedly returns to that erroneous Scripture from Sirach 18:1, and refers to the misunderstood passage that we discussed from Genesis 2:4.
> When the day was made God made heaven and earth, and all the greenery of the field before it was on the earth, and all the hay of the field before it sprang up.

Through all this Augustine constantly upholds the absolute truthfulness of all of Scripture because he sees it as the Word of God. All of the Church Fathers saw Scripture as true in this way. Pope Leo XIII explains the significance of this in *Providentissimus Deus*:

> [T]he Holy Fathers, we say, are of supreme authority, whenever they all interpret in one and the same manner any text of the Bible, as pertaining to the doctrine of faith or morals; for their unanimity clearly evinces that such interpretation has come down from the Apostles as a matter of Catholic faith. (Paragraph 14.39)
>
> But it is absolutely wrong and forbidden, either to narrow inspiration to certain parts only of Holy Scripture, or to admit that the sacred writer has erred. For the system of those who, in order to rid themselves of . . . difficulties, do not hesitate to concede that divine inspiration regards the things of faith and morals, and nothing beyond, because (as they wrongly think) in a question of the truth or falsehood of a passage, we should consider not so much what God has said as the reason and purpose which He had in mind in saying it–this system cannot be tolerated. For all the books which the Church receives as sacred and canonical, are written wholly and entirely, with all their parts, at the dictation of the Holy Ghost . . . Such has always been the persuasion of the Fathers. (Paragraph 20.56–57)

With this in mind notice the simplicity, directness of logic, clarity, and consistency of the approach to the Genesis account that we are taking in this work. Once we assert that the philosophical concept of God, angels, and the spiritual realm is non-biblical and we reject it, then there is no need to agonize over when the transition from eternity to "time as we know it" happens in the creation account. And there is no need to posit that there are two diverse creation narratives being joined together. This is simply the transition from the narrative that God wrote to the one that Adam wrote.

The Creation of Adam:
Genesis 2:7—Then the LORD God formed man of dust from the ground, and breathed into his nostrils the breath of life; and man became a living being [or soul].

This description of the creation of man supplements the account in Genesis 1:26–27. This account of his creation had to have been given to Adam during his personal talks with the Lord God. It was additional details on just how it had been accomplished. It gave Adam much-needed information on how it was that he suddenly woke up on earth. In Genesis 1:26–27 we were told that the Father and the Son created men and women in Their image and likeness. Here we see that after forming his body Abba breathed into Adam and he became a living soul. This clearly shows the participation of the Spirit in creating man. Thus Job 33:4 says, "The Spirit of God has made me."

This also indicates that the soul of man was not made from the primordial substance that God instantly called into existence "in the beginning." Its creation involved something non-physical. Thus the use of the word *bara'* in the account of the creation of man and woman in the first chapter was revealing. It indicated a special circumstance—a newly created substance—that was being brought forth at that stage. Not only did God make a substance that does not partake of the physical realm, but concurrently He established a relationship between the physical and non-physical realms. That connection was made in and through human nature, which spans both the physical and the spiritual realms of existence, and which brings them together in the persons of men and women. Also, in conjunction with the verses that follow, this text shows that Adam and Eve were not created at the same moment on the sixth day. At first only Adam was formed.

These thoughts point to the additional realm of existence, the spiritual or non-physical realm of existence, with which the Genesis account of creation is not directly concerned. That realm of existence includes the angels, as we noted, as well as our human souls, and also the souls of animals. Animal souls also partake of that realm of existence but do not partake of the rationality that is common to God, angels, and men—and thus they also can die and cease to exist—something that can never happen to human souls or to angels. The property of necessary unending existence is a corollary of the fact that both angels and men are created to fellowship with God. Remember that the word that created animals was one word. Thus their souls and their bodies are not separable as are the bodies and souls of human beings. When the body of an animal dies so also does their soul. Human beings were created in two stages—first body, then soul.

We might add that the reason why the creation account even alludes by inference to this non-physical realm of existence, since it is properly only dealing with the creation of the "heavens and the earth," is that the creation of man and of sentient life necessarily spans both realms and thus any way of completely describing their creation must also touch on the non-physical aspect of their being. Again, although the human being was created as a unified whole, body and soul, the parts were created in two steps, allowing for the death of the body while preserving the soul. **This is needful for our resurrection**. For animals, body and soul live and die together, having been created by God with a single word of command. Thus for animals the death of the body is the end of existence.

The statement that "God saw it was good" does not apply to Adam because Eve had not yet been created, and after making Adam but before making Eve God will observe, "It is **not good** for man to be alone." At this point we are in the midst of the creative acts of day six as described in the Lord's account in verses 1:26–30. The creation of mankind is not yet complete, and His work is not yet what He pronounces as "very good" in verse 31.

Meditation on The Creation of the Soul:
When the Lord God breathed into the man that He had formed and "the man became a living soul" how should we understand the "breathing" that God did? Because we are created substance and only God is uncreated substance we cannot say that the breath (or the soul) that God breathed into us was a part of His own substance; that is, our souls do not partake of the substance of the Holy Spirit, for we are not divine.

Instead we can understand it by considering how we ourselves exhale breath. The air that comes out of our lungs does not partake of our substance but still impacts other things and causes a change in them. When God breathed His Holy Spirit into the man and thereby gave him life it was not the substance of the Holy Spirit that became the soul of the man, but something that the Holy Spirit imparted to him that was separate from its own substance. God made Adam's soul from nothing.

We have observed that the word *bara'* is used just three times in the creation account: In the beginning, to describe the calling into being of the primordial unformed material of which the entire material universe is comprised; in 1:21 where God creates the animals that have non-rational souls; and in 1:27 where God creates mankind in His image. In our comments on the creation we noted that these last two references to *bara'* indicated that there was another creative act involved in each of these steps; that is, calling into existence something that partook of a being that extended beyond the physical realm and that was not part of the original primordial substance that He called into being in the beginning. This was a different, separate, non-physical realm of existence.

In verse 1:21 the Father called into existence the non-material substance from which was formed into the non-rational souls of the animals. The Father had to be the One Who called that substance into being, for He was always involved in every true act of "creating from nothing." But the Son used that substance to form the souls of the various animals and birds on the fifth and the sixth days. In 1:27 the Father was active in summoning into existence the non-material human soul. The Father and the Son worked together to form (*asah*) the body of the man (1:26), after which both together breathed into Him the spirit of life (Zechariah 12:1) by using the agency of the Holy Spirit. This is how man became a living soul. His soul was created from nothing, as the use of the word *bara'* indicates and as the logic of the interaction between the Father and Son also indicates. All human souls are created from nothing before they are instilled into the newly formed embryo.

Propagation Is Part of Human Nature:
Both man and animals possess the ability to propagate; that is, part of what God made when He formed us, part of what we are, includes the power to make more of ourselves. This seems obvious to us, but it is a power that the angels apparently were not granted. Instead the angelic hosts were all created directly by God. Thus the methodology for creating new human life is an integral part of human nature—it is connected to the fact that He made us male and female and that He blessed us and commanded us to be fruitful, to multiply, and to fill the earth. This implies that the Lord God established a functioning connection between the material realm of which our bodies partake and the non-material realm of which our souls partake. The connection is activated in and by God each time He forms a unique living human soul; that is, each time there is a sexual act that results in a conception in the physical realm. The Lord built this "channel of reproduction" into us from the beginning. By nature we receive and pass on life within a family unit, which reflects the nature of God and the reality that we were created in His image and likeness. Thus God Himself is personally involved in the creation of each soul. The creation of each new human life is a cooperative venture between God and man. Only Adam and Eve were directly created by God. He formed the first family directly by His own hands.

Just to reiterate this truth again: The soul of Eve was directly created by God as was that of Adam. It was uniquely created by God before the "channel of reproduction" was established for the human race. Eve did not derive her soul from Adam—only her flesh and bones. Adam said, "this is now flesh of my flesh and bone of my bones" but he did not say "this is soul of my soul." After Eve was made, all later human beings have come into this world via the "channel of reproduction" that was fashioned by God at the same time that the man and the woman were created, and which He established in their very humanity. All successive human souls were patterned after those of Adam and Eve for they all are designed by God to correspond to the human body into which they are to be placed, and the bodies of all human beings are genetically derived from their parents, and ultimately from Adam and Eve. Thus there is a continuity and unity to human nature.

However, God has a direct personal involvement in the creation of each human soul, for in his psalm recalling the creation David refers to God as:
> He who fashions the hearts of them all. (Psalm 33:15)

And when Zechariah recalls the great creative acts of God during the six days he says,
> *Thus* declares the LORD who stretches out the heavens, lays the foundation of the earth, and forms the spirit of man within him. (Zechariah 12:1)

Therefore the channel of reproduction makes mankind co-creators with the Lord God of new human life—a great and awesome power because people are created in His image and likeness. This is a privilege that even angels do not have.

Let us reiterate this again. God foresaw the totality of human history. Every generation was in His mind before He started to create. He reserved for Himself personally the act of forming each individual soul. He granted to us the privilege of cooperating with Him in this holy work by contributing our unique personal characteristics to our children through what we give them by physical inheritance. But the soul and the body are inextricably intertwined as a marvelous unity. Thus we contribute greatly to who the next generation is. This is the purpose and meaning of human sexuality. Families reflect the nature of God. Human nature, made in His image and likeness, is passed on via sex and family. The bitter spite and envy of Satan has led him to twist and debase this in every way possible.

When sinful human beings approach God the result, because of our fallen human nature, is that the interchange is distorted. One very intimate connection that we have with the Lord God is through the channel of reproduction when we work with Him to create new human life. Sin has deeply distorted this cooperative effort. Thus when two sinful people join to make a new human being the result, because the very process of procreation has been distorted, is another fallen sinful person. Because of this the pollution of humanity at the source has resulted in the pollution of all human beings throughout history. This universal reality is what we refer to as "original sin" or "the sin nature."

Two Insights from Genetics:
The discovery of the biochemical complexity of life was a devastating blow to the theory of evolution, but it completely confirmed the Christian understanding that life begins at conception. The connection between the physical realm and the spiritual realm that the Lord God established with the creation of Adam and Eve is still working. Thus the soul will be produced in conjunction with the physical apparatus. The soul is what makes the person into the unique individual that he or she is. Thus it should spring into existence at the moment when the physical body has differentiated itself enough that a unique new person can be identified. From simple genetics we now know that this happens at the moment of conception—at the moment of mitosis when the man's sperm and the woman's egg combine to form the genetically new and unique physical composition of their offspring. Logically, this has to be the moment when the connection between the physical and the spiritual realms activate, and the Lord instills the soul in the child. In other words, we would reasonably affirm that the soul is formed at the moment of conception. Modern science has removed all previous ambiguity about when human life begins, and therefore all doubt about the morality of abortion at any point during a pregnancy.

If the chemical basis of life had been found to be relatively simple as evolutionary theory had predicted, then the moment of conception could never have been the moment when the soul was infused because that tiny, simple, biochemical structure could never have specified the unique physical characteristics of a new human life. The soul would have had to be instilled into that growing fetus later on in its embryonic development, after its body had grown and developed in its complexity to the point where its unique individual physical characteristics were fully specified within the fetus. In medieval times this was a common way of thinking for Christians (although abortion was still forcefully condemned), but modern science has clarified this. The soul is instilled—and life begins—at conception.

Therefore, as a direct corollary to the incredible complexity of life at the biomolecular level we know that the unique genetic makeup of each human being is fully determined at the moment of conception, and thus that would be the expected moment when the soul would be created and infused by Abba—and that is also the moment when a new human being comes into existence. Thus human life begins at conception.

Another ancient controversy is resolved for us by our understanding from Genetics. In the early centuries of Christianity one argument against the resurrection of the body that the Fathers had to contend with was raised by unbelievers who observed that a human body might contain matter that had been part of another human body at a previous date.

> These persons [those who deny the resurrection of the body], to wit, say that many bodies of those who have come to an unhappy death in shipwrecks and rivers have become food for fishes, and many of those who perish in war, or who from some other sad cause or state of things are deprived of burial, lie exposed to become the food of any animals which may chance to light upon them. Since, then, bodies are thus consumed, and the members and parts composing them are broken up and distributed among a great multitude of animals, and by means of nutrition become incorporated with the bodies of those that are nourished by them,—in the first place, they say, their separation from these is impossible; and besides this, in the second place, they adduce another circumstance more difficult still. When animals of the kind suitable for human food, which have fed on the bodies of men, pass through their stomach, and become incorporated with the bodies of those who have partaken of them, it is an absolute necessity, they say, that the parts of the bodies of men which have served as nourishment to the animals which have partaken of them should pass into other bodies of men, since the animals which meanwhile have been nourished by them convey the nutriment derived from those by whom they were nourished into those men of whom they become the nutriment. Then to this they tragically add the devouring of offspring perpetrated by people in famine and madness, and the children eaten by their own parents through the contrivance of enemies, and the celebrated Median feast, and the tragic banquet of Thyestes; and they add, moreover, other such like unheard-of occurrences which have taken place among Greeks and barbarians: and from these things they establish, as they suppose, the impossibility of the resurrection, on the ground that the same parts cannot rise again with one set of bodies, and with another as well; for that either the bodies of the former possessors cannot be reconstituted, the parts which composed them having passed into others, or that, these having been restored to the former, the bodies of the last possessors will come short.[620]

From medical science we know that the entire substance of our body is recycled every seven years or so. Thus our bodies are not composed of certain unalterably fixed atoms or elements. But rather, as genetics teaches us, the unique nature of each human body is determined by its personal genetic configuration, which parameters are established at the moment of its conception. These parameters are the personal contributions which it derives from its mother and its father in a unique combination at mitosis. Thus for the Lord God to raise a human body He would only need to know the unique genetic make-up of that individual and He could reconstruct their body according to that pattern. God could use any particles that He wanted, and it would not matter.

In the early centuries of Christianity this argument against the resurrection must have seemed to be almost insurmountable. How could God raise our bodies, even if He were to gather the scattered elements from far and wide, if two different bodies partook of their existence by making use of the same elements? How could they be part of two different resurrected bodies? It must have seemed to be an unanswerable objection.

Yet Athenagoras took up the challenge and wrote his defense of the resurrection. Today with our understanding of genetics this entire argument against the resurrection of the body dissolves into nothing. A seemingly insurmountable argument from ancient times is now seen as a trivial non-issue. **We should remember this if/when we encounter similar seemingly "unanswerable" arguments against basic Christian truth in our day.**

Adam's Account:
These additional details about the creation of mankind, over and above those given by the creator in His general creation account, are from the person who lived through the creation event, who was personally involved in it. The dominion mandate that God gave to mankind—as recorded in the first tablet—is not mentioned here. At first Adam was only concerned with the small task of keeping and living in the garden. But eventually he would move into the Lord God's larger role for mankind in the creation. God must have used the first tablet to explain to him the broader creation and the role of mankind within it. Thus the Lord God explained to Adam that he and his descendants were destined to inhabit the entire earth and to extend their cultivation efforts to every part of it.

The Garden of Eden:
Genesis 2:8—The LORD God planted a garden toward the east, in Eden; and there He placed the man whom He had formed.

Genesis 2:9—Out of the ground the LORD God caused to grow every tree that is pleasing to the sight and good for food; the tree of life also in the midst of the garden, and the tree of the knowledge of good and evil.

Eden means "pleasure" or "delight." In Hebrew the verb "planted" could just as well be translated as "had planted." Adam is describing the one area on the earth for which the sprouting of day three resulted in plant life that was rich and dense. All the animals were here, this is where the two special trees were, and this was where the man was to live. In time they would spread out and fill the earth as God commanded.

Did the animals also eat of the tree of life? No, recall they ate common plants. Even today animals have instinctual leadings to eat something that is appropriate for them and avoid what is not. God gave them this inherent wisdom and it remains in many ways, even after the fall. Before the fall it would not have been proper for them to eat of the three of life. It was a special tree for Adam and Eve. The tree of the knowledge of good and evil, as Eve observed, was pleasing to look at and good for food; that is, for human consumption. But again, the animals would not have eaten it.

Let us tie this into the creation account of the third day when the plants were made, and the fifth and sixth days when the animal life was made. We noted that populations were limited, and the earth was not fully covered with vegetation. However, the garden seems to have been a luscious fully developed environment. And it was into this lovely area that the Lord God placed man. From this statement I imagine that, although God had created the vegetation on the third day, in the beginning the garden was the only location on the earth where it was luxurious and fully ready to support human and animal life.

God had placed all of the various animal species that He had created in this lovely area. They were not yet full populations, as we noted, and so they were not scattered over the entire earth. They were living in the garden where the plant life was mature enough to support them. This beautiful place is where God placed the man as well.

Genesis 2:10—Now a river flowed out of Eden to water the garden; and from there it divided and became four rivers.

Genesis 2:11—The name of the first is Pishon; it flows around the whole land of Havilah, where there is gold.

Genesis 2:12—The gold of that land is good; the bdellium and the onyx stone are there.

Genesis 2:13—The name of the second river is Gihon; it flows around the whole land of Cush.

Genesis 2:14—The name of the third river is Tigris; it flows east of Assyria. And the fourth river is the Euphrates.

This is a more detailed description of the geography of the Garden of Eden. We should see the garden as a very large area on the earth, not like we normally think of a garden today. It was a broad area where our first parents could roam about. It was watered by a large artesian well that split into four branches. This is like the geographical details of the rest of the earth that Adam mentioned briefly in 2:6, but it appears to involve a much larger volume of water. So Adam wrote this account after he had explored for a while.

If we try, from this description, to identify this place on the earth today it will be a futile effort. The ancient world was destroyed by the Flood. The names that are given in this account to the rivers and the lands were their right names at that time long ago. But there is no indication that anyone has ever found a trace of Eden or of any of its features in this present world. When the Deluge struck all the fountains of the great deep burst forth and all of the underground structures that supported these rivers were destroyed. The geographical features of the ancient world were also destroyed.

After the Flood when men began to resettle the earth they saw certain rivers and places that reminded them of the long-lost antediluvian world and they named them after those places in the old world. We do this often. There are multiple places and cities in the Americas that people named after places in the old country, either because of nostalgia or because they reminded people in some way of their long-lost home. Thus the present rivers and places that bear the ancient names from before the Deluge are not the ones that existed in Eden, because all of those geographical features were destroyed at the time of the Flood.

I want to explain further what I am saying about the destructive work of the Deluge. The contribution of geology to this has been the discovery of vast sedimentary deposits that are found on all of the continents. These are often thousands of feet thick and extend over thousands of miles. The volume of water that would have been required to deposit such vast sedimentary beds, and its destructive power as it surged over the land, are therefore revealed. These extensive geological deposits were unknown to the ancients.

Thus, after arguing at length for the physical historical reality of the garden[621], Augustine says that certain rivers in his time were the remnants of the garden. But the ancient reality described by Adam in his account was totally destroyed, so the angel that guards the way to the tree of life is out of a job today! The Deluge completely reshaped the geography of the world so that when Peter says "the world that then was perished being overrun by the waters of the Flood" we now should understand him to be referring not only to the life forms but also to the geographical and atmospheric configuration of that ancient world. This additional fact helps us to accept the historical reality of Eden, for it is described to us in such a way that we can see that it clearly is not on this earth today; in fact, it would seem unlikely that even a remnant of the lovely first dwelling place of man would be found any more. Yes, Eden was on this earth, not on a spiritual plane!

When Sir Leonard Wooley discovered a very thick layer of mud in his digs in the Middle East he recognized it as the certain sign of the Deluge. But when similar deposits were not forthcoming in other areas of the world he concluded that the Deluge must have been a local flood—a conclusion that can never be reconciled with the Genesis account, and an assertion that stands against the universal unbroken testimony and belief of all of the Fathers. But the problem is that naturalistic science has jumped in and reinterpreted the sedimentary deposits in a way that excluded connecting them with the Flood; that is, they are seen as the result of millions of years of death as species evolved and died.

However, the world view of this interpretation is dependent on evolution, which has been shown to be genetically impossible. Thus we can and should see these deposits, which present incontrovertible proof that every part of the earth was inundated at some time in the past, as clear evidence of the Deluge—and as a solemn testimony to the worldwide destruction that accompanied that event. These deposits are also an important piece of information for understanding details about the Flood of Noah; that is, how the Flood affected various areas of the earth, and how the providence of God was active for Noah.

What we can see from these facts—the contrast between the layer of mud in the Middle East and the fossil-bearing deposits that abound in other parts of the world—is that in the Middle East the Flood seems to have been less destructive than in other areas of the world. This is because the thick layer of mud does not speak of the violent destruction of life on a massive scale in the same way that the fossil deposits do. In the area of the Middle East the movement of the continents as they separated was a distant event, as were most of the catastrophic geological effects that accompanied that drift. In the "middle of the land" there was relative safety. This somewhat more tranquil and less destructive action of the Flood in the area of the Middle East can be seen as a divinely providential way of preserving Noah and the ark. Tectonic action powerful enough to catch up and deposit the volume of sediments that we see in many places of the world would have destroyed the ark.

Are Eden and the glory of Paradise lost to mankind forever? Not at all. God is merciful. The picture of the river that originated in Eden is similar to two eschatological pictures of Paradise given to us in Scripture.

- In Ezekiel chapters 40-48 the prophet describes a vision of the future kingdom glory to which Israel can look forward. In chapter 47 of that vision he describes a river that flows out from under the threshold of the temple toward the east. That river of water gets deeper and wider as it goes toward the Dead Sea. Along its banks grow many healthful trees, and in its water fish thrive.
- In Revelation chapter 21-22 there is a description of the New Jerusalem. There John saw the river of the water of life flowing out from the throne of God and the Lamb. It went through the city and had the tree of life growing on either side of it. The original

Paradise that was on earth was lost when Adam and Eve sinned, but one aspect of the promise of redemption is the assurance that it will yet be fully restored.

These pictures remind us vividly of the original plan that God had when He created us, and promise us that His lovely plan will still be brought to perfect fulfillment. The hope has not been lost even though the struggle sometimes makes it difficult to see.

After this short digression to give us a description of the geography of the garden Adam returns to describe his placement in the garden and the two special trees that were in the midst of the garden.

Human Life in Eden:
Genesis 2:15—Then the LORD God took the man and put him into the garden of Eden to cultivate it and keep it.

Genesis 2:16—The LORD God commanded the man, saying, "From any tree of the garden you may eat freely;

Genesis 2:17—but from the tree of the knowledge of good and evil you shall not eat, for in the day that you eat from it you will surely die.

God placed Adam in the garden to cultivate it and to keep it. "Keep" (Hebrew: *shamar*) has connotations of preserve and beware. Adam was warned of a possible marauder.

Adam ascribed the relatively stark appearance of the rest of the earth to the absence of a human cultivator because in his mind the proper appearance of any stand of vegetation could only be maintained by human care. The first job assigned to man was farming and cultivation of the land—and protecting the garden as well. The workman deserves his wages, and therefore Adam could eat of any tree in the garden, except for the tree of the knowledge of good and evil. In the day that he ate of that tree he would surely die.

The Nature of God from His Interaction with Adam and Eve:
In the account of Adam we are given repeated pictures of the Lord God interacting with him and with Eve in a direct personal way. The implication of these accounts is that He looks like a person and we can relate to Him in that way. Thus He is not a vast spiritual power that is so far distant from us that we could never approach Him or interact with Him. Both God the Son and God the Father should be seen as in our human form, but the only one that any person has ever seen is the Son. This direct intimate interaction of man and God was the plan for life from the beginning. Our hope of participating in the divine life was lost in the fall, which resulted in the degradation of our humanity. The effects of that progressed as the years and centuries wore on. The continual trend of our personal, familial, and societal behavior toward a less godly tone offended the goodness and sweetness of the Lord God and distanced us from Him ever more and more.

The Holy Spirit is not in human form. We should see Him as an all-present pervasive spiritual power that we can communicate with in our heart and mind, and Who wants to draw us into the presence of the Father and the Son. The Spirit is the One Who fills the description that certain of the Fathers of the Church applied to all three persons of the Holy Trinity. When we are "right with God" it means that we are so constituted in our person that we can be drawn by the Holy Spirit into the presence of the Father and the

Son without destroying us—which is eternal life. That is, there is nothing within us that is fundamentally opposed to God. Of course sin has changed our human nature, both in body and in soul, so that we are opposed to Him by nature. Salvation must involve the complete reconstituting of our humanity so that we can be in His presence. This is why, as Jesus said, we must be "born again" in order to enter into the kingdom of God.

But Adam and Eve were not fallen and sinful. Thus we are reading the only account by any human being that describes the way that God related to man, and how they related to Him, before the fall. We are also going to read about the change that the fall caused.

Meditation on the Spiritual State of Adam and Eve and our State:
In what state was Adam (and therefore also Eve) created? What does it mean that He "became a living soul" (Genesis 2:7)? Paul says, when speaking of our bodies and their resurrection, "It is sown a natural body; it is raised a spiritual body. If there is a natural body, there is also a spiritual body. So it is written 'The first man Adam became a living being [or soul]; the last Adam became a life-giving spirit'" (1 Corinthians 15:44–45).

The natural body is the body that we have as a result of having been born on this earth. The spiritual body is what we will receive as a result of having been either raptured or raised from the dead when Jesus returns at the last trumpet. Jesus will "transform the body of our humble state into conformity with the body of His glory, by the exertion of the power that He has even to subject all things to Himself" (Philippians 3:21). Jesus received that power from the creation decrees issued by the Father during the six days.

As to the state of Adam before the fall: Because death entered the world through sin, Adam was not destined to die. Because Adam was able to sin and thus to die, he was not fully immortal. He was potentially immortal. Because Adam was able to not die he was not completely mortal. He was potentially mortal. The reality that he "hung in the balance" is what is meant when we say that he was in a state of preparation for union with the immortal God, but that he had not yet attained that state. When Adam sinned his spirit died and his body became certainly mortal, destined to die. That condition was passed on to all of his descendants. Thus we all are certain to die. We are mortal. Our body is dead because of sin (Romans 8:10) just as Adam's became dead because of sin, as the Lord God said, "In the day that you eat thereof you shall surely die" (Genesis 2:17). The dead bodies of human beings can only reproduce more dead bodies. People with a fallen human nature will always reproduce a person who also has a fallen human nature.

We must also conclude that the entire creation was changed as the result of the sin of Adam for that is when death entered the world, and that is also when this creation was made subject to futility (Romans 8:19–22). Thus human death, animal death, and the various physical disorders entered the world as the result of the sin of Adam. Adam died judicially on the day that he sinned, but the carrying out of his sentence was mercifully postponed for the sake of all those whom God intended to create and to save.

Adam was alive in his inner man and fully able to commune with the Lord. His corpus was potentially immortal and it was in harmony with his inner man and fully supportive of his intimate union with God. When he sinned this changed immediately. He lost that constant communion with God and was plunged into the emptiness that characterizes the psychological state of all men and women today. His body became "dead" like ours; that is, opposed to communion with God. I say "dead" and not just "mortal" because it was not only destined to die, which would be mortal, but it was opposed to communion with God, and such communion is eternal life (John 17:3). So the sin of Adam had two immediate consequences: Severing the relationship with God in which he had been created, and changing his body to be "dead" in that it became mortal and destined to die and in that it became opposed to communion with God and thus cut off from Him.

As a result of the sin of Adam the natural body that we all possess as his descendants has been rendered "dead." Thus Paul says, "our body is dead because of sin" (Romans 8:10). It is not said to be "mortal" because of sin, but actually "dead" or under the certain judgment of death from God. This is the consequence of the sin of Adam. Also the inner man that we are born with is bereft of the constant intimate communion with God that Adam had before the fall. The separation of our inner man from God and the death of our body are interconnected because we are a unified whole. Today we are separated from God just as Adam was after the fall—unless we have been "born again."

Of course Adam knew and remembered what communion with God had been like. We do not because we have never experienced it. But when people are born again that communion is reestablished within them. "The spirit is alive because of righteousness [i.e., the righteousness of Jesus]" (Romans 8:10). But our life is subject to spiritual attack because we are still dwelling within a body that is "dead," subject habitually to sinful impulses, and opposed to the new life that has been infused into the inner man.

We are enjoined, "in reference to your former manner of life . . . lay aside the old self, which is being corrupted in accordance with the lusts of deceit" (Ephesians 4:22). Thus when we are born again we retain the body that we inherited from Adam, which body is mortal and "dead," but we are given a new inner man. In the resurrection our "body of death" will be replaced with a spiritual body which is modeled after the resurrection body of Jesus, Who is the new Adam.

If Adam had not sinned then eventually he would have been offered a share in the divine nature (born again) and then given a body like the body of the risen Lord. Adam would have been clothed upon with immortality, clothed from a state of potential immortality—not from a state of mortality and certain death like us. At the time when Adam's period of preparation for union with God—and of preparation for participating in the life of the Trinity—was complete, he would have ascended into his eternal inheritance and into his eternal destiny. We will still arrive at the same destination but by a more arduous route because of sin. Sin has not changed God's ultimate purposes for mankind.

Did the deathless state of Adam and Eve hinge on their eating of the fruit of the tree of life? In a lengthy discussion of these issues Augustine says that he believes that the immortality of Adam and Eve was the result of their right to eat from that tree, which was revoked when they fell.[622] I think that the immortality of Adam and Eve did not depend on their eating from the tree of life for three reasons:
1. If Adam had not eaten of that tree but also had not sinned, then he would not have died because death came into the world through sin, not through failure to eat from a certain tree. His body would not have stopped living.

2. Not only was Adam deathless, but the animal kingdom was deathless. Did animals also eat of the tree of life to maintain their life? Certainly not! They did not need to die at first because death had not yet entered the world. It was their nature to not die, just as it was the nature of Adam. When man sinned death became a reality for all (Romans 5:12), and futility was enjoined on the entire creation (Romans 8:19–22). Thus the state of the entire creation was changed radically because of sin.

   Considerations like this, to which I have repeatedly referred, grant us a glimmer of how much the world we know today must differ from the world that God originally created—the lovely place that was free from all death. It was the nature of the entire created order, and of man as a part of that created order, not to die. Normal life would not have resulted in aging, sickness, feebleness, or death. Of course, if people were to refuse to eat then they would eventually die; and if people were to take violent action against others and kill them then they would die. But all such perverted activities were not a part of the original very good, sinless creation.
3. In the consummation the tree of life appears again. In Revelation 22:2 and 2:7 the tree of life is given to the redeemed to eat. However in heaven we are all immortal by nature and do not need to eat anything to live. Thus eating of that tree is an additional blessing that we are granted in heaven. It was like that in Eden. It did not cause or maintain life but enhanced the daily lives of Adam and Eve in some way.

Therefore we will try to explain the purpose and function of the tree of life in God's plan for humanity. In fact, we will discuss both of the two special trees that were in the garden, and will theorize about how they will function in the consummation as well.

The Two Special Trees in Eden:

The Tree of Life:
Augustine quotes Proverbs 3:18, "Wisdom is a tree of life to all who embrace her," to say the tree signified Jesus, Who is the Wisdom of God. He argues that eating from the tree was like partaking of a kind of sacrament for Adam and Eve.[623] But we can assert more. There is more to life than the preservation or the enhancement of our physical well-being. What living thing does not grow? To live is to expand into new avenues and truth. Thus there is more to life than not dying. There is a quality to life that gives glory and peace, which connects people to their purpose for living, to the most deeply meaningful aspect of existence.

The tree of life was designed first of all to enhance and further the overall life of Adam and Eve, to prepare them for participation in the life of the Trinity—not by granting to them unending physical life, for death came into the world through sin. Thus if Adam and Eve had never eaten of it, but still had not sinned, then they would not have died.

The tree did grant them wisdom. Wisdom in biblical usage denotes a kind of knowledge that enables people to live successfully; that is, a kind of knowledge that has practical implications in how we live out our lives—in relationship to God, to the loved ones in our family, and to the broader society. The tree was connected to wisdom, to knowing how to successfully conduct our affairs on earth as people became more numerous.

Human life on this earth was supposed to grow and deepen as more people were born and as human society and culture developed. This tree was the channel through which divine life was to be injected into human society, granting us wisdom to form our lives, our families, and all of civilization in a way that honored God, reflected His divine nature, and drew all men and women to Him. Thus we were to grow up in every way into Him Who is the creator and Lord, the One in whose image we were created. In every way; that is, in our individual persons, in our families, and eventually—as men and women became more numerous—in all of human society. This growth would require wisdom, humility, love, trust, and all godly and divine attributes. Eating from the tree was a way for His life, in myriad forms, to enter into men.

What exactly were Adam and Eve to experience when they ate the fruit from this tree? The tree of life was meant to give to human beings a tangible experiential entrance into the character and nature of God. It was a way for Adam and Eve to grow in the likeness of God by the direct infusion of His grace and nature. It served to transform them from one degree of glory to another. The fruit of this tree granted to them an experiential taste of the goodness of God that drew them more deeply into His life by making them love Him and long for more of Him. This tree was for them like the movement of the Holy Spirit in our hearts today.

Adam and Eve did not have the sacraments to serve as channels of His grace, and they did not have the Bible to read, or inspiring preaching to listen to. But by eating from this tree the divine life that they shared with God would be deepened. The "means of grace" that God has given to us today are suited to men and women who are sinners by nature and are living in mortal bodies; that is, they nourish our inner man but do not flow over into our bodies—except incidentally. This is appropriate to this sinful age, for today our bodies are "dead" because of sin and thus ought not to have their existence unduly prolonged by any means. Such an effect would be contrary to the just judgment of God for sinful man—the judgment of death.

But the first provision for helping man to grow in God's divine life was perfectly suited to innocent and sinless men and women—people who were destined to live forever. One effect of eating from the tree of life was that it also affected the bodies of Adam and Eve by strengthening them and enhancing their physical vitality, just as it did their souls. This is because their body and their soul were united in life and immortality at that time. We still see this happen today. When a person's spiritual life is strong and their relationship with God is growing then it can also tend to augment the health of their body. God made us to be a spiritual-physical unity.

But what about eating normal food? Adam and Eve did have to eat and drink like we do. If they never ate or never drank they would have died. But refusing to eat or drink would have been perverse. So eating and drinking and eliminating were a part of their human life just as it is for us. God said, "Any tree of the garden you may eat" (Genesis 2:16). Their earthly life was intermingled with the life of the rest of the biosphere that God had created. All living things, by their very nature, had to take in nourishment and eliminate waste in order for their life to be sustained. Life in Eden was not some supernatural and other-worldly existence, but it was so designed as to be free from death.

However, the tree of life was a source of life and well-being for Adam and Eve that was not merely a part of the biosphere. It was a source of spiritual life for Adam and Eve. It was special in that it fed their inner man. Eating from the tree was not mandatory, but of course it would have been a normal part of their day-to-day lives, just as was any other eating and drinking. It was a special privilege that God gave to them that enhanced their life on earth, both soul and body. We must realize that Church and prayer are a provision for fallen man. God planned other things for mankind in the beginning, other ways to relate to Him and to grow in His likeness.

There is a tree of life in the New Jerusalem. There it functions in a way that is proper to people who are truly immortal. Again, it will nourish their bodies and their souls. Eating from it will be a privilege and not a necessity, for in Revelation 2:7 Jesus says that to the one who overcomes He will "grant" to eat from the tree of life which is in the Paradise of God; that is, in the heavenly city in the New Jerusalem.

In Revelation 21:5 it says that the leaves of that tree are for the healing of the nations. What kind of "healing" will be needed in heaven? To understand this we must realize that when we die we do not somehow turn into a different person. There is a continuity of personality that we maintain as we enter into eternal life. That also means that we carry certain scars and hurts from this life as well. Not just personal hurts but societal injustices that have grieved our souls and violated our sense of justice. We are saved and we are filled with His presence, but only over time are we healed and restored by the influx of divine life and blessing that flows from Him. The healing that the leaves of this tree grant to us is not just or primarily for our individual person. The effect of sin, as we have noted, is to distort us at every level of human life—at the individual level, at the familial level where families are "dysfunctional," and at the tribal and national level also. The leaves of the tree in the Paradise of God are for healing and restoring to humanity the godly wholeness that He always planned for human societies.

Here is a concrete example of what the heavenly "healing of the nations" means. When this country was settled and we pushed aside the Indians, there was grief and pain not only on a personal level, but entire Indian tribes and societies were destroyed. This type of disaster was not unique to the settling of America. When Caesar invaded Gaul and the Romans established their rule there, native peoples were squelched. Whenever a territory that is inhabited experiences the influx of new peoples the effect tends to be the same. There is a clash of cultures, and hostility and destruction follow in the wake of the immigration. This is because of sin, and because we lack the Godly wisdom that would have been ours from the tree of life in Eden. That was lost to man because of sin.

In the final consummation this healing power will be restored to the human race—when the divinely-ordered pattern of life is reestablished for mankind. The healing that is necessary is at the broader societal level—the healing of the nations; that is, entire cultures and societies must be restored, and their grievous lacerations healed.

Remember that heaven consists of multiple levels of human relations expressed within a social matrix of families, tribes, peoples, and nations or ethnic groups (Greek *ethnos*). The healing and restoration will happen at every level of society—a restoration that will repair the human family that was broken by sin at the fall and that developed without the blessing and wisdom that should have come from the tree of life that was in the garden. Any member of a mistreated and oppressed minority understands what I mean.

To reiterate, the tree in Eden was for helping us to grow into perfection at every level of society, and it provided the wisdom that was necessary for that perfect godly growth—but it was not for healing, because in Eden there was not yet any sin, and thus no such healing was needed.

There is a provision for healing that will be granted to men on this earth during the reign of Jesus in the kingdom age. This is envisioned by Ezekiel. In Ezekiel 47:12 we see many kinds of trees growing up along the bank of the river that flows from underneath the temple in Jerusalem. These trees are not said to be a tree of life, for in that age of the earth the inhabitants of the world are still sinners who live in mortal bodies, and God will not grant the tree of life to them—for the same reason that He removed it from Adam and Eve after the fall. But the leaves of those trees are "for healing." This is a function that is similar to the function of the tree of life that is in the New Jerusalem, but not associated with the deathless state of being that characterizes heaven.

As we noted, the various provisions that God gives to mankind are perfectly suited, in each instance, to the state of life of mankind at that time.

The Tree of the Knowledge of Good and Evil:
The purpose of the tree of the knowledge of good and evil, and the purpose of the command attached to it, was to prepare human beings to live in a society where relationships were founded on authority and obedience. It was to teach mankind obedience.

In attempting to understand the purpose and meaning of this tree we should look at two New Testament passages that reveal to us the overarching purpose for which God created human beings.
> He chose us in Him before the foundation of the world, that we would be holy and blameless before Him. In love He predestined us to adoption as sons through Jesus Christ to Himself, according to the kind intention of His will, to the praise of the glory of His grace, which He freely bestowed on us in the Beloved. (Ephesians 1:4–6)

Before He created anything Abba predestined men to be holy and blameless before Him and to be adopted as His sons. This act of kindness was His own free choice and is the outworking of His grace freely bestowed on us in Christ. For this reason He is worthy of all praise. This purpose is completely shared by Jesus the Son of God.
> Father, I desire that they also, whom You have given Me, be with Me where I am, so that they may see My glory which You have given Me, for You loved Me before the foundation of the world. (John 17:24)

It should be clear from the account of man's life in Eden that we were not already in that final state of perfection and union with God when He made us. However, we were created in a state of friendship with God and with a basically good disposition toward our Creator. Nevertheless we would have to freely choose to be with God for all eternity. Man had to be "prepared" to enter into the final state of glory as His children. Our eternal relationship with God was to be like that of His only Begotten. The initial lesson of obedience and filial trust was being taught in germinal form by the condition of human life established on the earth by the Lord God. Life on earth was a time of preparation for an eternity with Him. It was a preparation for our full participation in the loving relationships of the Trinity.

Again, the command was given to train mankind to understand experientially and enter into a relationship governed by authority and obedience. The Trinity is a society where such relationships have always been in existence. Jesus stated, "I do exactly as the

Father commanded Me" (John 14:31; see also John 6:38). God the Father is the head of Christ (1 Corinthians 11:3). If we are to participate in the Trinitarian society then we must be formed in obedience just like Jesus the Son.

Our training was to be conducted within the loving relationships of the Trinity, with the love of God in our hearts. This assurance and comfort would make our training and growing up in Him a pleasure and a joy. All human society—the basic family unit, every business affiliation, all governmental organizations, all military units, and all social units, no matter what their nature or purpose, possess a hierarchical structure that is based on authority and obedience. Without it no grouping can function. This is a reflection of the life of the Trinity and of the fact that we are created in His image and likeness.

The tree of the knowledge of good and evil, and the commandment attached to it, were designed as the initial primordial situation or "test" for training men and women for their participation in the life of the Trinity. If they were to relate to God as He was, then they had to relate to Him as their Lord. Today when we accept Him then it must be as our Lord and Savior, for that is what He is. If we deny Him that place in our lives then we deny Him—period. When we do that then we reject Him. Adam and Eve had not sinned and did not need a savior in the way we do. To them He was Lord, a fact reflected in the name Adam uses for Him in his account. The tree of the knowledge of good and evil was God's way of allowing them to freely accept Him as He truly was—as their Lord. Adam and Eve failed the test. They chose not to obey Him. They rejected Him as their Lord.

Why did God choose a tree from the garden and the simple command to not eat from it to teach Adam and Eve about obedience at the beginning of human history? Their world was a very simple and uncomplicated place. He chose something with which they were very familiar and comfortable in order to put the lesson before them. Here is an example from life today. If you wanted to train your young children how to handle a computer would you immediately begin by teaching them how to program in machine language? No, you would show them a keyboard and a mouse, have them look at the screen, play with the keyboard and mouse, discover how it connected to what he or she saw on the screen, etc. You want to connect the function and the use of the computer to realities that they were closely associated with and could easily understand from their personal experience. God wanted to teach Adam and Eve about obedience.

With that in mind let us think about the tree of the knowledge of good and evil. In this we see the ultimate plan of God for man as it was initially introduced to us. Against this background we can understand the simple commandment that the Lord God enjoined upon Adam: Do not eat of the tree of the knowledge of good and evil. This initial test was drawn from the simple environment into which Adam and Eve had been created. It was imbedded in the fabric of their lives in the garden. It was not grievous, burdensome, or complex. It was easy to understand. I am sure that in their inner persons they totally understood it and were able to obey it without any confusion or stress.
> This is eternal life that they may know You, the only true God, and Jesus Christ whom You have sent. (John 17:3)

If you eat then you will die. To eat of that tree was to sever the relationship of trust and obedience that was just beginning to grow. That would immediately separate man from the source of his life. He would die spiritually immediately.

The tree of the knowledge of good and evil was not itself a bad thing, for God saw all that He had made, and it was "very good." As Eve observed, it was pleasing to the eye and good for making one wise. It was also a good thing because the purpose of God that was behind it was good. His only intention was to instruct us in obedience and the divine life. God was about the task of drawing people into His divine life for all eternity.

Only the disobeying of the commandment not to eat of the tree was evil. As always, that proceeded from the heart of man (Matthew 18:18–20). It is clear from the account that the reason why our first parents ate from this tree was in order to not be under the authority of the Lord God. It was not an innocent act. It was deliberate disobedience in a situation where they had been provided with every conceivable good and pleasant thing, and where they understood the terms of the command.

Let us look again at the warning that the Lord attached to the tree. We can gain a deeper insight into the command and the result of disobeying it. When the Lord God gave Adam the commandment not to eat from this tree He said that "in the day that you eat of it you shall surely die" (2:17). In Hebrew this is more exactly rendered as
> In the day that you eat of it dying you shall die.

The emphasis that we translate into English by use of the adverb "surely" is, in the original Hebrew, expressed via a repetition of the word that means "to die," first in the present tense and then in the future tense. This could hint that two deaths are in view.

From our perspective, considering what Jesus taught us about the two deaths, we could look at this as saying, you die spiritually and you will die physically. Thus, if Adam were to eat of this tree then he would die spiritually immediately, in that the filial bond with the Lord God in which he had been created would be severed immediately, and he would eventually have to die physically. Physical death would come as a judicial decision from the Lord God. That decision was perfectly just because the bodies of Adam and Eve had become bastions of opposition to God and had become enemies of their own best interest. From our perspective, given the further revelation of what Jesus has told us about the two deaths, this is how that first warning of God should be understood.[624]

The Creation of Eve:
Genesis 2:18—Then the LORD God said, "It is not good for the man to be alone; I will make him a helper suitable for [lit., corresponding to] **him."**

Genesis 2:19—Out of the ground the LORD God formed every beast of the field and every bird of the sky, and brought *them* to the man to see what he would call them; and whatever the man called a living creature, that was its name.

Genesis 2:20—The man gave names to all the cattle, and to the birds of the sky, and to every beast of the field, but for Adam there was not found a helper suitable for him.

Apparently Adam was quite content, but the Lord God knew that he was not in a state of full blessing. The conditions needed to prepare him for his eternal place with God were not complete. It was the Lord who said, "It is not good for the man to be alone". "Helper" is `ezer (2:18), most often used of God as the helper of His people when they are in distress, indicating powerful help. Then followed a simple ploy by the Lord to make the man realize that he alone of all the creatures was without another of his kind. God brought each kind of animal before Adam and allowed him to name them (2:19–20). The verb "formed" in verse 2:19 can also, perhaps preferably, be translated as "had formed." The animals which God "had made," which were all living in the garden, were brought before Adam for him to see and to name. Ambrose observes the simple effect that must have had.

> [T]here is a reason why everything was brought to Adam. In this way he would be able to see that nature in every aspect is constituted of two sexes: male and female. Following these observations, he would become aware that association with a woman was a necessity of his lot.[625]

Because God said, "it is not good" we know that the creation of Eve took place before the end of the sixth day when all was pronounced "very good." Her formation from the side of Adam happened in the middle of the sixth day, during verses 1:26 and 1:27, as this comment by the Lord God shows. These events all happened during the sixth day.

Some have wondered how Adam could have participated in this activity in any reasonable length of time. I have two personal examples to share that illustrate this.

- When I was saved Jesus stood before me while I was seated in my chair at the prayer meeting. His love went through me and I instantly saw my life before me with all my insufficient actions. I saw it in a flash. I knew how I had been living. The totality of my life was before me in a moment. God can deal with us thusly.
- On another occasion I was thinking about the present distress of the world and I thought how nice it would have been to live at a time that was not so dark and full of strife. I told the Lord that and instantly He showed me the panorama of human history with its constant darkness of one type or another. There had never been a time of peace and security. I saw the sweep of Church history in a flash. One of the dark errors that I saw was called Docetism. I didn't even know what it was, but it was darkness!

The fact that Adam could actually examine and name each of these indicates the clarity of mind that he had, his insight into the nature of things, the extent of his intelligence and understanding due to the infused knowledge with which God had created him. Adam was not a primitive person; rather, he was quick-witted and intelligent. His mind, unclouded by sin and the disordered passions that arise therefrom, was very sharp.

God was showing Adam these animals with His own purposes in mind. He wanted him to see the creation over which He had placed Adam, and He wanted him to understand that it was not yet complete. This was specifically a buildup to introduce the woman that He was about to give to Adam. She would be a very important gift, a vital piece of His plan for human life. This preparation for her introduction was necessary.

God performed a similar service for John in Revelation chapter 5. There a vital scroll is revealed in the right hand of God. It was of supreme importance that the scroll be opened. But who could open it? An angel asked in a loud voice, "Who is worthy to open the scroll and to break its seals?" Initially no one was found who was worthy. This caused John enormous distress and he wept bitterly. Then God revealed the Lamb Who was slain, Who is the key to the completion of human history and to the fulfillment of human destiny. In the same way, God was preparing Adam for that part of the creation that would be most important to him. Adam saw no one "like" himself, which observation prepared him to receive with exultant joy the great gift that God was about to prepare for him—a gift that he did not even know that he needed.

Genesis 2:21—So the LORD God caused a deep sleep to fall upon the man, and he slept; then He took one of his ribs and closed up the flesh at that place.

Genesis 2:22—The LORD God fashioned [lit., built] **into a woman the rib which He had taken from the man, and brought her to the man.**

Genesis 2:23—The man said, "This is now bone of my bones and flesh of my flesh; she [lit., this one] **shall be called woman** [Hebrew: 'ishshah] **because she was taken out of man** [Hebrew: 'iysh].

With this build up, God put Adam to sleep, performed an operation on him, created the woman, and brought her to him. The word for "rib" can mean "side" as well, although it is usually understood to mean rib when referring to a person. Some have asked why a man does not have fewer ribs on one side or have fewer ribs than a woman. The effect of such an operation would not be passed on to the next generation. Similarly, if I had a leg amputated that surgical change would not be passed on to my children.

The creation of Eve from the side of Adam is a statement about the unity of nature that we share as man and woman, a unity that is rooted in our initial creation. It does not appear as if such special unity of nature applies to any of the animals that God created.

> Not without significance, too, is the fact that woman was made out of the rib of Adam. She was not made of the same earth with which he was formed, in order that we might realize that the physical nature of both man and woman is identical and that there was one source for the propagation of the human race . . . God willed that human nature be established as one. Thus from the very inception of the human stock He eliminated the possibility that many disparate natures should arise.[626]

This is a more detailed account of how God created man and woman, a process that in chapter 1, in God's account of creation, was described in less detail. Here Adam gives us additional details. Eve, the most precious thing in Eden, most merited protecting. Note that Adam was created outside of Eden—in the rough, in the outback—and was placed into the garden. But Eve was created within the lovely environs of the garden, which Adam was told to "keep." In this way the Lord God emphasized to Adam her precious value, for He could have made her outside of Eden just as He had made Adam.

The part of Adam's body that was used by the Lord God to form Eve is also significant. It was not his feet, lest she be thought of as his slave. It was not his head, lest she be thought of as his master. It was from a place near or right at his heart, so that she must be thought of as his companion, his helpmate, his sweetheart, his beloved. In view of the panoply of animals that God had shown to Adam in leading up to His gift of Eve, it is also sure that Adam perceived that, as no animal was an appropriate partner for him, so the woman was perfectly suited to fill that missing niche.

The words of Adam when he saw Eve expressed great delight. Adam loved the woman that the Lord God had made to be his helpmate. Adam gave her a name just as he had given names to all of the other creatures. It is noteworthy that Adam did not say, "this is flesh of my flesh and bone of my bone **and soul of my soul**." He might have said this in his prophetic exclamation if it had been true. But it was not. This indicates that the soul of Eve was not created from the soul of Adam, but was created directly by the Lord, just as was the soul of Adam. Eve derived her physical body from Adam, but not her soul.

This pattern is followed for all later generations of human beings, those brought into the world via the usual channels of reproduction. That is, all children derive their physical makeup from their parents, but their souls are directly made by God. Isaiah 57:16 refers to, "The souls which I [the Lord] have made," and Numbers 16:22 calls God, "the God of the spirits of all flesh." Thus there is a connection between the physical and the spiritual realms—the one that the Lord established when He created Adam. One aspect of that connection is the channel of reproduction by which new human life is created. Using the channel to create human life is the joint responsibility of God and man. Thus we work with the Lord to bring new human beings into this world. It is a cooperative effort. That is how God designed humanity from the beginning when He created us male and female.

Meditation on Human Nature:
I want to set before us the Scriptures that relate to the original creation of mankind.

> Then God said, "Let Us make (`asah) man in Our image, according to Our likeness . . ." God created (bara') man in His own image, in the image of God He created (bara') him; male and female He created (bara') them. (Genesis 1:26–27)

> Then the LORD God formed (yatsar) man of dust from the ground, and breathed into his nostrils the breath of life; and man became a living being. (Genesis 2:7)

> In the day when God created (bara') man, He made (`asah) him in the likeness of God. He created (bara') them male and female, and He blessed them and named them Man in the day when they were created (bara'). (Genesis 5:1–2)

Recall that in the context of the creation account bara' means to make out of nothing. The Father was preeminently responsible for this activity. This action is described by the word bara' and refers to our soul. The words `asah and yatsar mean to form, and they both presuppose that the basic substance has been created which is to be worked on and formed. The act of forming during creation was usually the work of the Son, but in the creation of man it was the joint work of the Father and the Son (1:26). In 2:7 we see that they also used the Spirit in their work. The work of forming can refer to both the soul and the body of man. Note: our **bodies** have been formed in Their image and likeness (1:26–27).

When God brought Eve to Adam he said, "This is now bone of my bones and flesh of my flesh" (Genesis 2:23), but he did not say, "this is soul of my soul." This indicates that the body of Eve was derived from the body of Adam, but her soul was not. Eve's inner person was created directly by God, made from nothing by a creative act on His part. Note that we are in His image both in our body and our soul, in the totality of our humanity.

Since the time of Adam and Eve all human beings have been created by a cooperative act between God and a male-female pair. Their bodies are patterned after the bodies of their parents, deriving their unique personal physical characteristics from a combination of their parent's genetic characteristics. The soul of each person is created by God by an act of creation from nothing. Yet, in other passages the Bible uses yatsar (form) to refer to this creative act. For example, "God Who forms (yatsar) the spirit of man within him," (Zechariah 12:1), and "He who fashions (yatsar) the hearts of them all" (Psalm 33:15). Genesis 1:27 implies that "both" do the making, so I think the Father creates the human soul material and both make or fashion it; that is, both form us in our unique personalities.

By inheritance continuity is maintained throughout the generations. All human beings share a common "human nature" that is ultimately derived from our first parents. We are linked together, both body and soul. Although the soul is created separately by God, it corresponds to the body in which it is placed by God, and that body is inherited from our own parents, eventually from Adam and Eve, and ultimately from Adam. The definition of "human being" might be stated as follows: Physically, the nature of all human beings was determined when God created Adam. The spiritual nature of each human being is determined when God creates a soul to be infused into their physical body.

To be human is to be descended from our parents—and ultimately from Adam and Eve—via reproduction. The reproductive act grants each person a unique personal physical makeup that is derived from their immediate parents but that is ultimately linked to and derived from Adam and Eve. God creates in each person an appropriate soul from nothing that corresponds to the body of the person.

Observe the following things about the creation of man and woman: When the word *bara'* (1:27, 5:1, 2) is used in describing the creation of human beings it always refers to the soul and it is preeminently the work of the Father. Although all three persons of the Trinity are always involved in whatever one does, it still is preeminently the work of the Father to create out of nothing. Our souls are created and formed in the image of God.

But in the creation account the verbs for "form" also refer to the making of the bodies of Adam and Eve. They were created *(bara')* in the image of God and they were formed (`*asah, yatsar*) in the image of God (1:27, 2:7) and in the likeness of God (5:1). Their souls were created (*bara'*) in the image of God and their bodies and souls were formed (`*asah*) in the image and likeness of God. Thus they carried a double similarity to God in their physical makeup. The simple fact that their physical makeup is spoken of as having been "formed" in the image and likeness of God—the fact that the word used is "formed"—indicates that God has a form. This also agrees with our observations at Genesis 1:26–27 about our double similarity to God.

Allegorical Meaning of the Creation of Woman:
Genesis 2:24—For this reason a man shall leave his father and his mother and be joined to his wife and they shall become one flesh.

This statement at this point should be understood as a prophetic insight. Adam saw or understood the importance and significance of the woman. It was the occasion for him to have and to express an insight into the foundational truth about human life on earth; that is, he stated that marriage and sexual union was the plan of God for mankind. In this way we would be allowed to participate with God in making new human life. Thus I do not think that this statement is a comment added by Moses when he put together the account from the Genesis Documents that were before him. It was a prophetic insight given to the first man at the beginning of the human race, to express for all generations to come the divine plan for mankind. Again, Adam was a brilliant man, with a clear mind that was unfettered by sin or its consequences. He clearly perceived God's intentions.

An exclamation like this, written for people to read for all generations, is most naturally understood as the personal account of the one who lived through it, for who else would have been there to hear it? That is, it is Adam, the first human being, who is writing this for us—for all human beings throughout history. The Lord recalled this special moment to Adam's mind and inspired him to include this when he was writing.

This is the time, at the beginning of the creation, when marriage was created and when the husband/wife bond was declared to be unbreakable. This is a foundational pillar in the divine plan for human life on this earth. Jesus quoted this very verse in answer to a question about divorce. He taught us directly that the marriage bond was indissoluble in God's plan even from the beginning of the creation, for God Himself joins husband and wife together (Mark 10:2–9). Paul teaches that the bond of believers with Jesus is like this bond. We become one body with the Lord, which is a great mystery (Ephesians 5:25ff). Thus the permanence and indissolubility of the marriage bond is a reflection of the eternal nature of our relationship with the Lord God.

Jesus is the new Adam or the last (final) Adam.
> The first MAN, Adam, BECAME A LIVING SOUL. The last Adam *became* a life-giving spirit. However, the spiritual is not first, but the natural; then the spiritual. The first man is from the earth, earthy; the second man is from heaven. As is the earthy, so also are those who are earthy; and as is the heavenly, so also are those who are heavenly. Just as we have borne the image of the earthy, we will also bear the image of the heavenly. (1 Corinthians 15:45–49)

The Church, the bride of Christ, was created from the side of Jesus as He slept the sleep of death on the cross. This happened on Friday, the sixth day of the week, when the centurion pierced His side and blood and water flowed out, as John himself saw and to which he personally bore testimony (John 19:34). This is the reason why Paul refers to the creation of Eve from the side of Adam to explain our relationship with Jesus. Adam was man ('iysh) and his wife was woman ('ishshah). Jesus is the new 'iysh and His bride the Church is the new 'ishshah; that is, the new man and the new woman.

Paul states in 1 Corinthians 6:16 that one who joins himself to a prostitute becomes one flesh with her. That is, a bond is established thereby, just by the sexual act itself, which clearly indicates the spiritual nature of sex. Such disordered sex, like any sexual activity, establishes within the person engaged in it a linkage. In our culture today many men and women are in bondage to disordered sexual desires that have ensnared them through misuse of their sexual powers, or because they were the victims of predatory sexual acts inflicted upon them by another. It is common knowledge within the Body of Christ that if someone comes to the Lord with such a past history then the attainment of true freedom often involves several steps: repentance and renunciation of the past wrong, prayer for deliverance from the past bondage, and a certain time of careful walking apart from that darkness, until finally a true measure of freedom is reached. Human sexuality reaches to the deepest part of our human nature, and damage there is profound and lasting.

The Hebrew word for Adam ('adam) is the root word from which the Hebrew word for the ground ('adamah) is derived. Thus Adam (i.e., mankind) was formed from the ground. At first God created us from the earth and gave us a life on this earth. But He created us in two steps—first from the ground and second by His own breath. Thus, in contrast to animals, His ultimate plan for mankind extends beyond the shadow realities that we live within on this earthly plane of existence. Even after the fall God held out to Adam and Eve the hope of redemption and the ultimate restoration to that destiny.

We who have been redeemed by His blood are a new creation, a new kind of people that God is making who are destined to fulfill His purposes for mankind by living eternally in

His presence. Even the Church's relationship to Jesus as His bride is a kind of prophecy of something in eternity, for in the consummation we will be His wife (Revelation 19:7).

Both of these earthly realities (marriage and the Church) foreshadow an ultimate reality—the eternal destiny that the Lord God planned for men and women—the destiny that will be realized in the Trinitarian life of heaven, in the beatific vision. The woman is necessary for the man, and the man is vital to her, for their relationship in marriage prefigures and prepares us for the glory of living as the sons and daughters of God and as the eternal spouse of His beloved Son. The saved will enter into this reality fully, both body and spirit, when the dead are raised incorruptible and we are all changed (1 Corinthians 15:52), when the Lord transforms our humble body to be like His glorious body (Philippians 2:21).

This is our destiny in the new Adam. This was our destiny from the beginning of the creation, from when He formed Adam and Eve out of the dust of the earth. It was His plan for mankind even from before the foundation of the world. We were always destined to be members of His heavenly family, His daughters and sons, His beloved wife. This is the purpose for which He created us (Ephesians 1:4–5).

Marriage is a covenant and all such human relationships are sacred because they are a passageway into the ultimate plans and purposes of God for mankind.
> My lovingkindness I will keep for him forever,
> and My covenant shall be confirmed to him. (Psalm 89:28)

Love, by its very nature, is made to last forever. Interwoven into its pillars are steadfast lovingkindness and faithfulness. Love never ends. Our life with Him will never end. We are made to live forever and to participate in unending relationships. From the nature of man and of woman, and from the understanding of marriage and family, we understand the nature of mankind, the meaning of our relationship with God, and the nature of our final destiny together in heaven. No wonder the woman was considered to be such an important part of the creation. Thus God carefully built up to the introduction of Eve.

The Innocence of Adam and Eve in the Beginning:
Genesis 2:25—And the man and his wife were both naked and were not ashamed.

In this initial created state the innocence of our first parents precluded any shame due to concupiscence springing from their nakedness. In the beginning men and women were not subject to the law of sin and death that Paul describes in Romans 7:23, "But I see a different law in the members of my body, waging war against the law of my mind and making me a prisoner of the law of sin which is in my members." Any bondage that we experience in our sexual feelings, and any resultant misuse of our sexuality, is one effect of the severed bond with God under which we all groan.

In reading the account of Adam and Eve we must avoid interpreting their actions and/or their words through the lens of our own daily lives. Adam and Eve were newly created. They had no other people to bounce their thoughts off of. They had no background in civilization and no outside communication. They had each other and they had the Lord God. Their world was circumscribed by the animals and the trees of Paradise. Thus it would not have seemed odd if an animal talked to them like the serpent did. The terms of their obedience to God were simple and were drawn directly from objects with which they were familiar in their world—the trees, what they ate or did not eat, and the simple, joyful, and unselfconscious life that they lived in Eden as they explored and became ever more familiar with their fresh existence. The story that Adam wrote is an expression of that original innocent life. We must see it as produced from such a perspective. As noted in the archeological considerations, this account would never have arisen within a later culture. It is pristine, without cultural indicators, from the dawn of history.

Adam and Eve were created in a bond of union with God that satisfied them completely. He is our heart's desire and the only fulfillment that our human nature wants or needs. Adam and Eve were not ashamed because there was no reason to be ashamed. They were created in perfect innocence, in a state where their human nature was satisfied with what it truly needed and longed for. But today we are alienated from God by our sin and by the spirits that have deceived mankind in this darkness. In this state we grasp futilely for any glimmer of the satisfaction that God intended to flood into our being from Him. Sin is a deception, vainly placing a created thing where only God belongs.

> You have rejected all those who wander from Your statutes, for their deceitfulness is useless [lit., falsehood]. (Psalm 119:118)

All ungodly impulses—sexual, covetous longings, envy, fear, etc.—were unknown. All needs were satisfied in their relationship with the Lord. The disordered lives that we experience in this world are the result of our severed relationship with God—a breaking away and a distancing that occurred at the time of the fall and that was inherited by all successive generations. Men and women were initially created free from such bondage.

The account to this point was probably written by Adam early on, before the temptation and fall, perhaps a few of months after the creation, after they became familiar with Eden.

How Human Life Would Have Progressed on Earth if Adam and Eve Had Not Sinned:

Adam and Eve would have had children and populated the earth, just as the Lord God commanded. As the centuries progressed, how would this state of affairs come to a consummation? We noted that Adam and Eve were not created in the final state of perfection but were being prepared for that state by their time on earth. If they did not have to die to go to heaven then what would have happened? Augustine comments on the succession of generations and the birth of children as the ages progressed:

> This [begetting of successive generations] would not be in order that children might take the place of their parents when they died; the parents, rather, would remain in their primes and receive bodily vigor from the tree of life which had been planted there, while their offspring would be brought up to the same perfect adult state until some definite number of human beings had been reached. Then, if they all lived lives of justice and obedience, the change would be brought about by which their merely "ensouled" animal bodies [by this he is referring to the natural bodies Paul mentions in 1 Corinthians 15:35–49] would be converted without dying into something of a different kind, and be entirely at the beck and call of the spirit governing them [This is what Paul refers to as the spiritual body], and with only the spirit quickening them would live without having to be sustained by any bodily nourishment; their bodies would in fact be called spiritual. This could have happened, if the transgression of the commandment had not earned the punishment of death.[627]

Augustine continues to discuss this transformation:

> [I]f it was right and proper for parents to give way to their children by departing this life, so that in this way the whole human race could mount up to a definite predetermined number through a succession of generations, it would also have been possible for human beings, after breeding children and justly carrying out their duties, to be transferred to better things by some kind of change other than death. This could either be that supreme change by which on getting

> back their bodies they will become *like the angels in heaven* (Matthew 22:30); or else, if this may only be properly granted to all mankind together at the end of the world, it would be by some kind of lesser change, which for all that would still bring about a better condition than either this body has, or even the bodies of the two who were created at the beginning, the man's from the mud of the earth, the woman's from the man's flesh.[628]

Thus we see that Augustine by this reasoning implicitly states that the final state of glory that we seek now would also have been granted to men and women if we had not fallen from His grace. The purpose and destiny of mankind has not changed because of the fall, only the getting to it has changed—and the path has now become more precarious because of sin and Satan.

Thus Augustine allows that all men and women might have stayed in their bodies, which were potentially mortal and potentially immortal, until the entire creation was perfected. Then together all people would have been taken into their final union with God.

But the purpose for which God created man was not to live on this earth, even when it was lovely and sinless, but to be in direct glorified communion with Him. Thus when a person had completed their time of preparation they would have been glorified. Also, it makes no sense to allow for some kind of partially glorified intermediate state for them, and for the same reason; that is, when their time of preparation was complete then they were ready to enter into the glory of heaven and direct fellowship with God. Therefore I think that the best way to understand this process is to say that Adam and Eve and all other generations of men and women, as they completed their time of preparation, would have eventually been given glorified bodies and been taken into heaven.[629 [see note]]

At the ultimate consummation, when the predestined number of the redeemed was attained unto, then would the Lord have transformed the creation into its perfected state and things would have looked like what is presented to us in Revelation 21 and 22. In that state God Himself dwells with man, the entire creation is transformed, and heaven and earth are united in a single unified continuum.

But if there had been no sin then that final transformation of the creation would have been without violence because it would not have involved the disintegration of this creation and the reconstituting of all things. Such an extraordinary and violent change will now be necessary to remove every trace of sin from His world. Thus the resulting new creation is now referred to as "the new heaven and the new earth" (Revelation 21:1). If there had been no sin, then it probably would have been referred to as the "perfecting" or "glorifying" of the original heavens and earth.

Thus we can say that men and women would have lived on this earth until their time of preparation for fellowship with the Lord was completed, until their living had fulfilled its God-given purpose of preparing them for ultimate union with Him, and then they would have been given a share in His divine nature and "raptured" or "glorified."

Because it was God's stated purpose for men and women to exercise dominion over His creation, I assume that they would have continued to do that in their glorified state. The wisdom and power available to them in the glorified state would have enabled them to exercise their dominion in a more effective way. They would have assumed a role over the angels, who were "filling in" until mankind could be "grown into" exercising its predestined dominion. We would have gradually taken over and exercised dominion over the entire earth from the heavenly angelic powers.

The significance of exercising our role as glorified saints from heaven instead of as men and women in potentially mortal bodies upon this earth can be partially understood if we compare the ministry of our Lord Jesus as He exercised it in Old Testament times with how He exercises it after His death, resurrection, and ascension into heaven. His work in Old Testament times was limited to appearances and words of instruction as given to His people in various and sundry ways. But after His glorification He sent the Holy Spirit to enhance His ministry with heavenly power. Millions have been blessed thereby.

This might be a skewed example, because the people who would have ascended into heaven would not have been the Lord of the whole universe. But their position of power and perfection, and their access to the eternal heavenly realities would have given them an immense amount to offer to those who still lived on earth. We are used to living in this dark and fallen world with demonic forces in the heavenlies that influence mankind in the most destructive ways. To imagine spiritual powers that are working only for our best interest is a huge change in perspective, but just such a wonderful reality was the original perfect plan of our Lord for human life. The glorified men and women, having been trained in obedience, would have exercised their heavenly ministry over the earth under the direction and lordship of the Creator and Lord of all.

Unlike today, the division between the heavenly and the earthly realms would not have been so sharply delineated. The separation from heaven that we live in today is greatly attributed to the sin that characterizes our human life on earth. In the absence of such sin glorified men and women would have still maintained some fellowship with those whom they left behind on earth. Therefore, their glorification would not have been a cause for grief to either those who were left behind or to those who were glorified. The veil between this life and the next would not have been like it is today. The glorified men and women would have been able to help those who still lived on the earth to fulfill their goals and grow to spiritual readiness. They would have been like "tutelary spirits" ruling over the earth, fellowshipping with God in heaven and with mankind on earth.

When saints die today, why don't they receive their glorified bodies and enter into the glorious heavenly ministry that we described for Adam and Eve and all those who had completed their time of preparation for entrance into the glory of God? Why do we just "go to heaven," but we do not assume our glorified bodies and serve as "tutelary spirits" over the earth? Why must we wait until the Lord returns to receive our glorified bodies?

Because during this age Satan and his fallen demonic powers are still in the heavenlies. The envy of the Devil at this glorious plan for human beings was the reason why he fell in the beginning. He has not yet been dislodged from his heavenly place. We now fight against principalities and powers and the spirits of wickedness in the heavenlies. At the end of this age the Lord will dethrone Satan and the other fallen angels in the heavens (see Revelation 12:7–12), and that will make room for His people to reign over the earth as He originally intended. When man fell then Satan was granted a kind of foothold in human life on this earth. If we had not fallen he could have been banished, but now that cannot happen until the demands of divine justice are met in the affairs of men on earth.

Let us consider for a moment the things that Jesus did for us at His coming to earth.
- He paid the price for our sins so that we could be forgiven; that is, He reconciled the world to God.
- He broke the power of Satan in our lives and gave us freedom from his dominion.
- He made us partakers of the divine nature and heirs of eternal life.
- He brought us into the family of God and placed His divine life in us. (See John 5:21, and 5:26–27)

The first two things were directed at undoing (in part, not totally) the effects of the fall in us. But the second two things go beyond restoring what was lost by Adam and Eve. When we receive Jesus we are not just forgiven, we are born again. We are in a better position with God now than Adam and Eve ever were in that we are living in the time when He has implemented the next step in His plan for mankind, and we are the beneficiaries of that.

Ambrose refers to the verse "Your life is hidden in Christ with God" (Colossians 3:3) and then explains the state of Adam and Eve before the fall—in a way not as blessed as we.
> Man, therefore, was, figuratively speaking, either in the shadow of life—because our life on earth is but a shadow—or man had life, as it were, in pledge, for he had been breathed on by God. He had, therefore, a pledge of immortality, but while in the shadow of life he was unable, by the usual channels of sense, to see and attain the hidden life of Christ with God. Although not yet a sinner, he was not possessed of an incorrupt and inviolable nature. Of course, one who [only] afterwards lapsed into sin was far from being as yet in the category of sinner. Hence, he was in the shadow of life, whereas sinners are in the shadow of death.[630]

The Lord always had a plan for bringing mankind into His incorruptible Trinitarian life in heaven—a series of steps for bringing human beings into His divine life. The Father and Jesus planned these steps when they made the ages (Hebrews 1:2). When Jesus came as a man He implemented the next phase of God's plan for mankind—granting a share in His divine life to men on earth. At the same time that Jesus inaugurated that phase of the plan with people on earth—when He marked out believers to be given the eternal life of heaven—He also forgave their sins and gave them power over Satan.

Thus even if we had not fallen, at the right time in history Jesus would have become man. When it was time to inaugurate the next phase of the divine plan on earth then He would have been born. He would not have had to die for our sins, but He still would have elevated mankind into participation in the divine nature and the divine life. It was always God's plan to share in our earthly human life in order to elevate us to His heavenly divine life.

He would have grown up and lived on this earth until it was time for Him to ascend into heaven with a glorified body. He also would have cast Satan and the fallen angels into the lake of fire. Jesus is the judge of all, and the fallen angels are His servants and must answer to Him and only to Him. Because we were granted dominion over creation we could banish Satan; that is, we could forbid him to act in any way in human affairs on the earth, but his final judgment belonged only to the Lord (John 5:22).

Thus the coming of the Word as a human being was absolutely necessary in God's plan, for the Incarnation was always the method by which the divine life was to be made fully accessible to humans on earth before we ascended into heaven. This was a phase in God's plan to bring us into His Trinitarian life in heaven. God would condescend to share our life so that we could share His and ascend. Once the Word took His place at the right hand of God then other people could have ascended into heaven to take their places.

In this world, Jesus came first to give us eternal life in our inner man. He will return to grant eternal life to or bodies; that is, when He returns He will bring about the resurrection of the dead and the redemption of our bodies. This two-fold work of salvation was only because of death, which resulted in the eventual separation of the body and the soul. If Adam had not sinned then there would have been no death and Jesus would have come into this world only once. At that time people would have been offered a share in divine life. Eventually He would have also given them a glorified body to accompany that inner transformation. Then men would have been able to ascend into heaven to be with the Lord God.

People who were "born again" in that sinless world would have received their glorified body without ever passing through death. As noted, those who were glorified could still have fellowshipped with others on this earth and would have passed easily between the sphere of life on earth and the life of the New Jerusalem. The boundary between life on earth and life in heaven would not have been as definitive and impassible as it is now. This present age of the world, which we know as the Church age, when people are born into eternal life but die without receiving their glorified bodies, would never have existed.

It seems likely that if Adam and Eve had not fallen into sin then His advent on earth would have been quite early in human history because other men and women would not have been able to precede Him in having glorified bodies, and because we were not created to live on this earth for too long—only long enough to prepare us for living in His presence.

So the consequences of the fall were staggering. But Jesus still promises "To him who overcomes I will grant to sit down with Me on my throne, even as I also overcame and sat down with My Father on His throne" (Revelation 3:21). This is still His plan for mankind, and it will be implemented in the fullness of time. When at last we reign in glory, we will reign with Him and under Him. In the meantime divine justice demands that Satan and his angels be granted a foothold in the life of men and women on this earth. The spiritual territory lost in the fall must be recovered by men before the evil one is removed from the earthly scene. This is an aspect of the "mystery of iniquity" (2 Thessalonians 2:17).

Details about the Ages to Come:
I also want to point out one other thing that Augustine mentioned. When women and men received their glorified bodies then they would not **need** to eat. I agree with that, but it is still true that the tree of life will be available to men and women in the ultimate consummation (Revelation 22:2). Rather, Jesus says that we will have the **right** to eat from it (Revelation 2:7). Recall that the tree of life in the garden was perfectly suited to men and women who were living in sinless bodies that were not condemned to death, that were potentially immortal. But those bodies did need food and water. In that way they were similar to the bodies that we have. Eating from the tree of life in the garden was a privilege God granted to them to bless their total human person, body and soul.

The tree of life in heaven will be perfectly suited to our immortal state. What does that imply? In heaven the bodies that people have will be fully immortal. That means that the function of food will not be the same as it is for our present mortal bodies, or how it was for the bodies of Adam and Eve before the fall. When we eat food in these bodies some of it is digested and becomes a part of our body; that is, some of it is transformed into our human body. The rest passes out into the drain. In heaven "normal" food will no longer be necessary. In the consummation, in our immortal bodies that cannot die (Luke 20:36), we will no longer need normal food to nourish our bodies. Therefore, the purpose of eating and ingesting food will change. We will no longer eat physical food.

We will no longer eat normal food, but the tree of life is not normal. The tree of life will still nourish our inner man to transform us into His likeness ever more. Both the tree of life and the river of the water of life have their effect in our inner man. But will they also affect our immortal bodies? Because we are a perfect unity of body and spirit they will also affect our body in a way that corresponds to how they act in our inner man. When we eat from the tree of life or drink from the living water in the heavenly city we will be transformed from one degree of glory to another. We become more like the Lord as we eat of it. It is nourishment that promotes our spiritual growth and maturity. It enters into us and our spiritual nature is enhanced by it. This is a growth process that affects both our inner man and our body. But no part of it passes through us. In the consummation we do not procreate and we do not eliminate. There are no remains from the food or water of heaven. The tree of life and the river of living water are gifts granted to the immortal redeemed in heaven which are perfectly suited to their state of immortality.

The life of God that He shares with us comes to us through all our human senses. We see Him and are transformed into His image. We hear Him speak and are edified by the words. We eat from the tree and drink from the water (and we surely take in their aroma as well) and are spiritually edified by both of those gifts. We touch Him and we directly interact with Him and are glorified by that exchange. All of these are ways that we grow in every way into Him. This is a quality of living things—they constantly grow. We grow eternally in heaven because we are heirs to eternal life.

In summary, if Adam and Eve had not sinned then they would have lived a life of growth in the knowledge of God until such time as they were ready and prepared to ascend into heaven and be in direct communion with Him. While being in union with Him they would have served as tutelary spirits over the earth and the rest of mankind that were not yet glorified. The demonic enemies, having been repulsed by human beings, would have been judged quickly, and people would not have had to continue to contend with them throughout history. In the fullness of time, when the complete number of the predestined population of human beings had been reached, God would have smoothly transformed this heaven and earth into its permanent and eternal state, and all mankind would have entered the final consummation. There would have been no death, hell, sin, or suffering. That was the original very good plan of our God.

How the Rest of Creation Would Have Progressed If There Had Been No Sin:
The animals procreate today to maintain their numbers which are constantly being lost to death by predatory influences and by old age. This would not have happened in the original very good creation; that is, neither predatory actions nor old age would have depleted the population of animals. Therefore, they would have multiplied and filled the earth, as the Lord commanded them, and then would have stopped reproducing.

This seems strange to us today, because our view of "nature" is distorted. Mankind, for whom sexuality is disordered, often uses sex as a tool for recreation or as a way to play around. It is disconnected from its first and primary function, which was reproduction. In the animal kingdom sex still retains its created connection to reproduction. No animal uses sex for recreational purposes. All animals mate in order to produce more of their own species. This obvious connection was instilled into their nature by the Creator. He is able to regulate it to whatever ends are appropriate, and He would have done exactly that as necessary—in the absence of the destructive results of the fall.

The physical order of creation, the inanimate world of matter, would have continued in a state of harmony. The fountains of the great deep and the waters above the heavens would have remained and continued to provide for the health and life of the biosphere of the earth—for all of the creatures that God had created to live on earth. There would have been no destructive weather patterns, no death or corruption, and no hurtful part in His very good creation. "They will neither harm nor destroy on all my holy mountain, for the earth will be filled with the knowledge of the LORD as the waters cover the sea" (Isaiah 11:9). At the time when the total predestined number of people had been born and lived on earth the final transformation into immortality would have taken place and all mankind would have been in union with the Lord God, sharing Trinitarian life with Him as He had planned. This pattern of life will yet be attained.

An Interpretation Based on the Documentary Hypothesis:

Now let us look at the Garden of Eden passage from the viewpoint of a person who is a devout orthodox Roman Catholic, and examine his ideas. In his book *Free from All Error* Fr. William G. Most gives an explanation of this passage for us. First Fr. Most discusses what the genre of Genesis is; that means, what style or class of writing do we encounter as we are reading the opening chapters of Genesis? The genre he assigns to the first several chapters of Genesis is *myth*.

When you and I hear the word *myth* we think of a story that is not really true, which immediately puts us on the defensive. But then Fr. Most explains that the designation *myth* does not indicate that the story has a content that is not true, but that it is just an ancient way of telling a story. This almost makes the word *myth* digestible! But what significance does that word really carry?

In the beginning of the chapter on the "genre" of Genesis, Fr. Most observes that in his encyclical *Divino Afflante Spiritu* (1943) Pope Pius XII deplored the excessively loose application of genres to Genesis and insisted that the first eleven chapters do pertain to the genre of history, although perhaps not bearing the same style of expression as the Greek or Latin historians or that of modern historians. Thus Fr. Most lists the historical facts that the Genesis account contains. This is stated from his point of view that the first eleven chapters of Genesis are of the genre *myth*.

> Those chapters of Genesis pertain to history in that they do relate events that really happened. They present facts within the special framework of a story, however. We might even call it a stage setting. Hence Genesis 1–11 is historical in that it tells what really happened, chiefly these: God made all things; in some special way, He made the first human pair; He gave them some command (we do not know what the command was—the garden and the fruit are part of the stage setting); they violated the command and fell from favor.[631]

It should be obvious to everyone reading this book that in comparison to how all of the holy men and women of old viewed Genesis, this is a "less inspired" view of the creation account. It uses the genre *myth* to reduce the details of the account of creation to an elaborate "stage setting" and then states a few general ideas from the account as the sum total of what it has to say to us.

If the word *myth* were actually used in a different way, in a way that allowed for the truth of the passage under consideration while merely understanding it as using an ancient mode of expression, then it would be a fine word. But in its actual application it always means a "story" that is not really true.

Designating the ancient accounts of Genesis as *myth* has drastically modified the understanding of how the text of the passages must be understood when we read it. No father of the Church ever approached this text of Genesis, or the text of any biblical passage, in that way; that is, by assuming it was a mass of details that were not true but were there just to "set the stage" for the story. The genre of *myth* is used in a way that is contrary to the Ancient Faith. Thus the Documentary Hypothesis in no way supports the Ancient Faith of the Church.

Every holy woman and man of God in the history of the Church would blanch at such a denuding of the Genesis story. The ancients spent their lives defending the truth of the text of Scripture, defending it from every aberrant philosophical and religious notion—including the idea that things might have developed over a long period of time through natural processes—and now their successors are reduced to this? However, from the viewpoint of a *myth* Fr. Most then confidently asserts that the Bible is still "free from all error." But what meaning is left in his assertion? How little he actually says with such a weakened claim! The belief in the "inerrancy of Scripture" has been lowered in meaning. Speaking about Genesis in this way is, in my opinion, a kind of "double speak."

However, Fr. Most is definitely much less corrosive in his approach than are many who espouse the JEPD Theory as the way to understand how Genesis was written. Some see little or no truth at all in the Genesis account—not even the basic facts that Fr. Most holds to. All of that is what Pope Pius XII was referring to when he "deplored" the loose application of the concept of genre to Genesis.[632] [see note]

The idea behind the assertion that the Genesis accounts should be classified as the genre *myth* is this: In the prehistory of mankind, when we roamed the earth as bands of "hunter-gathers," when the tribe sat around the campfire at night and told stories about their mysterious past, when the "holy man" would arise and explain to the primitives how they had come to live on earth—then were born the mythological and legendary tales about human origins that we see in many of the ancient cultures.

These are what the anthropologists heard as they interviewed the "primitive" tribes that they encountered as they investigated the various peoples who were scattered over the whole earth. Genesis is only one such mythological tale—the one that the Hebrews adopted. If you happen to maintain a shred of your Christian faith then you assert that, while the Hebrews assembled their particular version of mankind's past, and while they intermingled with other primitives and mixed and matched stories with them, then God actually intervened in some way so as to plant a bit of His divine wisdom into their particular account. This is the reconstruction of ancient human "pre-history" that underlies the designation of the genre of *myth* to the Genesis accounts of the creation of the world and the early history of man.

But the Bible says that no word of prophecy ever came about by the will of man, but holy men of old spoke as they were carried along by the Holy Spirit. God did not make use of pagans to write His account of the origin of things. He always maintained a holy man of His choosing through whom He worked to inspire His truth to be written down. It was Adam who wrote the account that we are reading. It is his personal record of how the earliest years of mankind transpired. It is in no way a myth.

As we shall see, all of the accounts in the book of Genesis were written by men who were directly involved in the events that are recorded. They were moved by the Holy Spirit to write their accounts. And because the telling of history is prone to being "slanted" by the one who writes it, they were inspired by the Holy Spirit to write down things from God's point of view, recording exactly what He wanted to be kept as the record of mankind's past, so that we have His mind on this subject. The records are "free from all error" for that reason. This is the Ancient Faith!

The stories that we read from other ancient peoples—which deal with the same subjects that Genesis deals with—those stories are properly designated as *myths*. They are the confused and fragmented stories of people who were lost in the darkness of separation from God and who forgot the true story of their origins over the centuries. They retain a small glimmer, at best, of the full truth of human origins that is related to us in Genesis.

In considering the text of the Bible, whether it is Genesis or another passage, the men of old believed that what they read was true. The Documentary Hypothesis and any type of classification of Scripture as *myth* will not help us understand Scripture. It will dismiss major details of the text as part of the "stage setting" or as a "story teller's setup." This way of approaching the Bible does not explain Scripture; rather, it explains it away.

There are two major factors that influence people in the Church today to approach the Genesis account in this way:
- The belief that scientists have proven their theories of origins, such as the theory of biological evolution or the Big Bang, or that they have come very close, and so we must understand the Bible in a way that allows us to agree with them. Thus we are drawn to a "loose" application of genre and to an interpretation that can be "massaged" to go along with whatever new scientific ideas come into vogue. Believing Genesis is actually true is not allowed in that view.
- The belief that archeological studies have shown that Genesis (and much of the Bible) is a collection of *myths* derived from similar mythical stories from ancient pagan cultures of the Middle East, and that they have little or no truth value to them. Thus they see the accounts in Genesis as adapted from ancient pagan mythological legends and "purified" in some way, but as still sharing the genre of those accounts. They are still just *myths*. Therefore when we read those books any truth that they contain must be carefully distilled from the account. They can never be taken at face value. If the ancients had thought of the Genesis account of Adam and Eve in this way then they could never have reasoned about this and other creation passages to arrive at the theology that supports Christianity today.

Previous examples have shown how absurd it is to assert that the Genesis account of creation was adapted from any pagan myth. It was clear as we compared them that the

Genesis record was a complete and straightforward historical account, while the other accounts were fragmentary and intermingled with mythological details. The true account of creation was preserved in Genesis and the other accounts were diluted—debauched because of the descent of those cultures into the errors of pagan idolatry.

But how, more precisely, do these present scientific ideas influence our interpretation of Genesis? When a modern interpreter reads the first few chapters of Genesis he **knows** that the text cannot be true as written. So it is necessary to "get behind" the text and to explain its real meaning. Closely connected to discovering its "real" meaning is the need to understand how the text came to be written in the first place. Therefore, the notion of understanding the text as having arisen from a combination of mythological stories has appeal to the person who reads the creation account with that previous mindset.

I know that is what happens because that is exactly how I used to read Genesis. And as I read it I did not understand it because I also knew it was true! Thus the preconceived notion that it cannot be true as written, when mingled with the notion that it must be true, kept me from understanding the text. It placed a veil over my understanding when I read it. The reason for the veil was that I was always looking for the "real" meaning of the text. What was it really saying, since it could not actually be true in a plain sense?

Of course I did not have any understanding of the concept of "genre" at that time, so I could not lay any such pseudo-explanations upon the text. Thus its meaning remained opaque. But after I had my divine revelation about the present-day theories of origins the veil was no longer there. As I read Genesis I understood it clearly. It meant exactly what it said and it said exactly what it meant to say. And the Holy Spirit directly affirmed the full truth of what I was reading to me as I read it. I did not need to "get behind" the apparent meaning of the text to find its "real" meaning.

The holy men and women of previous centuries did not feel the need to "get behind" the text of Genesis and figure out its true meaning either. Any meaning that the text had was to be discovered only by understanding the words that were written there, and by connecting them to any related Scripture passages in order to gain a fuller insight into their significance. Thus the text of Genesis, like the text of all of the biblical books, was accepted as having been given to mankind from God and as being true. This is the Ancient Faith. This is the faith that our minds, when our thinking has been distorted by the pseudo-scientific theories of origins that are so prevalent, cannot accept anymore. The application of the idea of "genre" to the text of Genesis appeals to such minds. That is why it is so widely accepted today.

As I consider the JEPD Theory it seems to me to be cumbersome, composed of diverse ideas and constructs, and extremely unlikely. The Wiseman idea is simple and is fully confirmed by the text of Genesis. However, it fits only in a super naturalistic world view.

The average reader, who sees an explanation of Genesis from a "lessened inspiration" point of view, where it is "explained away" by the JEPD Theory, is unable to discern what is going on. Such a reader always assumes that the commentator has a deep and far-reaching understanding of how ancient writings were created, based on his reading of volumes of ancient Sumerian and other Middle Eastern literature—a background which the reader has no knowledge about and whose conclusions he or she cannot challenge in any way. And thus the reader is buffaloed into accepting the conclusion that, indeed, Genesis has been "explained away" by these deep and profound discoveries. The spirit of the age—that is, Scientific Naturalism, the Cartesian-Darwinian narrative—rises up to insulate their minds so they cannot understand and accept the truth of the Scriptures.

In truth, such commentators approach the text of Genesis with a fatal bias that has little to do with their profound understanding of ancient forms of literature and that has a lot to do with their previously established mindset—a perspective that was established not by their understanding of ancient literature but by their acquiescence with the spirit of the age rooted in secular theories of origins. However, we can all easily see that such a technique—no matter what the scholarship behind it and despite the previous mindset of the interpreter—destroys the Ancient Faith and undermines the truth of the Bible.

The miraculous revelation that God gave me over thirty years ago—before I understood anything about the JEPD Theory and before I had been exposed to any logic based on "genre"—and the clear understanding of Genesis that He gave me as a consequence of that revelation is the definitive condemnation of such modern scholarship and its aberrant assertions.

I show this to my readers so that they can see what modern Bible scholarship has done to the understanding of Scripture, especially to the first chapters of Genesis, and judge for themselves if this is in accord with the Ancient Faith of the Church—and also if it is in accord with what Pope Leo XIII stated in his encyclical *Providentissimus Deus* where he reminds us that the unanimous belief of the Fathers is definitive with matters of faith and doctrine. This is because their unanimity is a sure sign that they are expressing the one faith that was given to the Church by Jesus and the Apostles.

I summarize these points of comparison between the Documentary Hypothesis and The Genesis Documents as follows:

- The JEPD Theory arises from the evolutionary world view—from the assumption that mankind arose from primitive bands of people who were inferior to us (not as evolved), ignorant, and superstitious. They did not understand the physical laws that govern the world and thus were prone to accept "super naturalistic" ideas and explanations for the world around them.

  The Genesis Documents theory assumes that God created man in His image and likeness and that man was intelligent from the beginning. Then God chose holy men to hear His decrees and to write down the details of how the human race started—and how it misfired at the beginning.

- The JEPD Theory is set squarely within the world view of the Cartesian-Darwinian narrative, and in every way reflects the preconceptions of that world view.

  The Genesis Documents theory is set squarely within the biblical world view and in every way reflects the preconceptions of that world view.

- The JEPD Theory, when it is presented to a Christian, weakens and undermines their faith in God and in His word. I know because whenever I used to read such ideas I was disturbed by them. They undermine our faith!

  The Genesis Documents theory, when presented to a Christian, strengthens and undergirds faith in God and His word, and creates a sense of closeness to Him.

- The JEPD Theory denies the truth of Scripture and denies its divine inspiration.

   The Genesis Documents theory explains exactly how God inspired holy men of old and how He chose them to hear His decrees and to understand His mind on the events that shaped human history at the beginning.
- The JEPD Theory is opposed to the Ancient Faith. It implicates biblical thinking in the present pseudo-scientific cosmological/anthropological theories. The same mistake was made before. The Jews who translated the Hebrew Bible into Greek assumed the cosmology of the ancient world. When it was disproven the Bible was also seen as dubious or untrue. Let us not make that mistake again.

   The Genesis Documents theory is fully consistent with and fully supportive of the Ancient Faith of the Church. It does not implicate us in any "scientific" world view.

Thus the Genesis Documents theory is the first and only actual explanation of how God inspired the holy men of old to write Genesis—an explanation that is consistent with, and that is set squarely within, the traditional, orthodox, Christian, supernatural world view.

The insistence of all the ancients on the full truth of Genesis cannot be emphasized too strongly. For instance, it is with earnest and diligent efforts that Augustine pursued his attempt to understand the historical events that are described in the creation account, being diligently careful not to allow any verse of Scripture to fall to the ground. Every verse had to be absolutely true. Thus he reiterated the conflicts and the troubles that he had gone through in attempting to arrive at a comprehensive view of the creation—one that faithfully took into account all of the Scriptures that related to it in any way.

Augustine spoke to his readers and mentioned all the different considerations that anyone must weigh if they were to attempt the task of fully explaining the creation as it is presented to us in all of Scripture. Here I repeat the issues that he raised, reiterating again the struggles that he had so laboriously gone through before. These are listed in his book *The Literal Meaning of Genesis*.[633]

1. How could the flying things and beasts have been made on the fifth day and also be made and brought to Adam (presumably just created) on the sixth day?
2. How could the trees have been planted in Paradise on the sixth day but also have been made on the third day?
3. How is it that God made all things over a period of six days when Genesis 2:4–5 says, *when the day was made, God made heaven and earth and all the greenery of the field?* (This is his translation from the Vetus Latina Bible.)
4. How also does He say in Genesis 2:5 that He made *all the greenery of the field* **before it was upon the earth**, and all the hay of the field **before it sprang up**? (Again, this is his translation of this verse from the Vetus Latina.)
5. One must also remember the verse in Sirach 18:1 which states, *The One Who lives forever created all things simultaneously at once.* This is his translation of that verse—a completely faulty translation, but the only one available to him.
6. One must show how God rested from all His works on the sixth day (Genesis 2:2) and how He is working still today (John 5:17).[634]
7. One must consider how things were said to have been finished and also to have just been begun. This comes from his translation of Genesis 2:1–3 in the Vetus:
   And heaven and earth and all of their furniture were finished. And God rested on the seventh day from all his works, which He had made. And God blessed the

> *seventh day and sanctified it, because on it He rested from all his works, which God had begun to do.*[635]

Such painstaking care to the exact details of every verse of biblical text shows that his repeated assertions that every word of Scripture is true—that this is the only faith of the Church, that no jot or tittle can fall to the ground—was his constant working assumption.

Augustine recognizes the complications in what he has said and reiterates again that he would welcome a better approach if anyone could produce it. He concludes,

> It was by all these evidences, you see, of the divine scripture, **of which none doubt the veracity but unbelievers or the ungodly**, [emphasis added] that we were led to the necessity of saying that God from the start of the ages first created all things simultaneously together, some already in their established natures, some in their pre-established causes. Thus the Almighty made not only things actually present but also things that were to come in the future, and rested from them as made, so that from then on as he administered and regulated them he would also create the series of times and of time-bound things. And so he had both finished them because of the limit set to all the different kinds of things, and begun them because of the extension of the ages into the future. Thus he could rest because they were finished, and could be working until now because they were begun. **But if there is a better way in which this can all be understood, not only shall I make no objection, I shall also be positively in its favor** [emphasis added].[636]

In contrast to the approach to interpreting Genesis that is contained in the Documentary Hypothesis, what I present in this book—the recognition that Moses compiled Genesis from first-hand accounts written by those who were involved in the events that Genesis describes—fully supports the Ancient Faith of the Church, i.e., the belief that the Genesis accounts are reliable and true in all details.

Brothers and sisters, I am confident when I say that as Augustine views from heaven this work that I write for you, he is delighted to see the simple and clear answers that it contains and the cohesive understanding of the creation account that it presents. It resolves *all* of his difficult questions. On the other hand, when he reads an approach to understanding Genesis like that presented by Fr. Most he must be sick at heart! They both are in heaven now. I wonder what kind of conversations they have had on this.

Answers to All of the Issues that Plagued Augustine:
Having explicitly listed the foundational issues that Augustine dealt with in his work of explaining the creation account of Genesis, I want to review all of the answers that we have discovered to his conundrums. These are rooted in the faulty translations that he was working with as well as certain philosophical assumptions that he carried into his work.

Here is what I mean about his assumptions: Recall that Augustine was part of the North African group of Origen and Didymus the Blind, and that they influenced his thinking by making use of a philosophical framework that explained the creation scenario, or a part of it, as the instantaneous effect of the will of God. This concept was an integral part of the thinking that Augustine began with as he approached the creation account. Add to that his idea that angels, as spiritual beings, understood things instantaneously. Add to that his view of spiritual personalities as pure intellect, separating them from humanity so far that we could never relate to them directly, and we have the intellectual backdrop for Augustine's explanation of the creation account in Genesis.

Then add to these ideas the fact that he inherited a number of translation peculiarities in his Greek manuscript of Genesis. Here are our responses to his conundrums.

- How could the flying things and beasts have been made on the fifth day and also be made and brought to Adam on the sixth day? Genesis 2:19 says, "Out of the ground the LORD God formed every beast of the field and every bird of the sky, and brought *them* to the man to see what he would call them" (Genesis 2:19).

  In the Hebrew a permissible and even a preferable translation of "formed" would be "had formed." The Lord God "had formed" them on the fifth day and brought them to Adam on the sixth day to see what he would name them. Presumably this verb tense option was not allowable in the Greek translation that was in use by Augustine. We explained this in the course of our comments on Genesis 2:19. We also noted that these animals had been created in limited quantities and that they all were living in Eden, the only place on earth with fully developed vegetation that could support them. Thus they were close at hand and could easily be brought before him in the garden.

- How were the trees planted in Paradise on the sixth day but yet were made on the third day? In the Greek translation that Augustine was using it says, "He still cast up from the earth every tree that had a beautiful look about it and was good for eating" (Genesis 2:9).

  The Hebrew text says, "The LORD God **planted** a garden toward the east, in Eden; and there He placed the man whom He had formed. Out of the ground the LORD God caused to grow every tree that is pleasing to the sight and good for food; the tree of life also in the midst of the garden, and the tree of the knowledge of good and evil" (Genesis 2:8–9). Once again, the tense of the Hebrew word "planted" is best translated as past perfect. It can and should be understood as saying He "had planted" the garden. This completely mature biosphere is where the animals were, and this is where He placed the man as well as the animals—the one special place He had made on the third day.

- How could things be made over a period of six days when Genesis 2:4b–5 says, "When the day was made God made heaven and earth and all the greenery of the field before it was on the earth and all the hay of the field before it sprang up?" This seems to imply that the trees and vegetation were made "when the day was made" and "before they were in the field."

  We carefully explained this verse (and Augustine, as we noted, even agreed with us.) The first plants were created before they "sprung up" in that the normal growth of plants that we observe now did not apply to the first created vegetation. It was supernaturally produced, immediately, without rain or human cultivation. It might be that Augustine raises this issue to bolster a position he has taken for other reasons.

- The answer to the most pressing issue that Augustine was dealing with in the total biblical scenario of creation was the verse from Sirach 18:1,
  The One Who lives forever created all things simultaneously at once.

  The correct translation of this verse from Sirach is, "He Who lives forever created all things in common (or without exception.)" Perhaps more accurately it might be translated as, "He Who lives forever created the whole universe."

- One must show how God rested from all His works on the sixth day (Genesis 2:2) and how He is working still today (John 5:17).

Augustine actually did explain this himself[637] where he said that God created all things, and at the end of the six days He rested from all His work of creating. That does not mean that He rested from all that He does, for He is still "upholding the universe by the word of His power" (Hebrews 1:3) and He is still continuing to work today to maintain all things in existence or else they would immediately fall back into the nothingness from which He summoned them. This is a statement that the unique time of creation was ended. At that point, at the end of the sixth day, God ceased from His specific work of creating.

- How could things be said to have been finished and yet to have been just begun?
  And heaven and earth and all of their furniture were finished. And God rested on the seventh day from all his works, which He had made. And God blessed the seventh day and sanctified it, because on it He rested from all his works, which God had begun to do.

Once again, the translation of Genesis 2:1–3 that Augustine was using is in error. The Hebrew text reads as follows:

By the seventh day God completed His work which He had done, and He rested on the seventh day from all His work which He had done. Then God blessed the seventh day and sanctified it, because in it He rested from all His work which God had created and made." (Genesis 2:2–3)

It says nothing about the work that God had "begun to do." Again this is a problem that he tried to solve by saying that God made everything instantaneously, and He did rest from that eternal work, but then He made things in six days and so He just began to do them. Thus he sees 2:1–3 as referring to the moment after the instant of eternal creation but before the actual six days, during which time things were being unfolded for the human mind to understand. This complicated explanation, which is so difficult for a person to comprehend, is unnecessary once the translation errors are corrected. The works from which God is resting are the unique creative works that He was doing during the six days, as a straightforward reading of the text implies. Other works of God continue on into the present time.

In this way we have treated each of the translation issues that plagued Augustine, and we have also provided a simple and straightforward way of understanding the text of Genesis. Our reading rescues the text from the tortuous explanation that was forced upon Augustine by the plethora of mistranslations in his Greek texts, and is far superior to the JEPD Theory which asserts that ancient redactors were trying to mix together two different creation accounts and their clumsy efforts finally gave us what we have now.

But we have also rescued the entire book of Genesis from involvement in the various philosophical formulations about the nature of God and the entire spiritual realm which sees spiritual personalities as without form and existing and acting in eternity in various instantaneous ways that are far removed from human concepts. That view of the spiritual realities is not rooted in Scripture. It must not be imposed on Genesis or injected into our understanding of it. Such were the underlying philosophical assumptions upon which Augustine was erecting his theory about the creation account.

Conclusion of Our Comparison with the JEPD Theory:

We are about to read how the serpent at the beginning called into question to Eve the truth of what God had said. "Did God really say that you cannot eat from any tree of the garden?" "Can you really be sure that a being like God has spoken to you in a clear and definitive way that precludes any thoughtful reconsideration on your part? Did you really understand it correctly? Isn't there broad leeway for interpreting His words, or for understanding how they apply to this specific situation? In fact, they are not true at all! Here is another, different, and better way to look at your situation."

We are in a position today that is like Eve's position as she dealt with the serpent. If we allow for the Word of God to be called into question by this method of interpretation—that is, by categorizing it as belonging to the genre of myth—then we are allowing it to be made subordinate to human theories, assumptions, interpretations, and ideologies. If we do that, then we are judging the Word from our human cultural perspective.

It is indeed a good idea to try to comprehend the mind and heart of the ancients, if we can do it, and thus to more clearly understand the Word of God as it was delivered in the context of their lives. However we must always remember that it was delivered to them by God—that it arose not from the will of man but as men were carried along by the Holy Spirit. Thus it cannot be only the outgrowth of their ancient culture.

The Bible must always remain the inspired, infallible, inerrant Word of God. As such it also remains absolutely true throughout all ages. For all mankind is grass, and all the works of his hands are like the flower of the field. Yes, the grass withers and the flower fades, but the Word of our God endures forever (from Isaiah 40:6–8). Therefore heaven and earth will pass away, but God's word will never pass away (Matthew 24:35).

An Explanation of the Human Condition from Scientific Naturalism:

Much of modern psychology is rooted in the assumption that man evolved from animals and that much of what humans experience in the way of emotional and psychological disturbances is ultimately to be understood and explained as latent animal instincts seeking expression within the structure of modern human civilization—but as unable to be acknowledged, and therefore as repressed. For example, our disordered sexuality is seen as the animalistic desire to mate that we inherited from the pre-hominid creatures from which we have evolved.

But how can the carefully regulated sexuality of animals, which is always directed to reproduction, ever have developed into sexual urges like human beings experience—disconnected as they are from the desire to reproduce, but directed simply to their own expression, for their own sake. Sex has become a form of recreation, or an activity that is engaged in as a form of self-expression or self-gratification. It is never that for animals.

Christianity itself is "explained away" by naturalistic psychology. In his book *The Future of an Illusion* Sigmund Freud explains for his readers the origin, development, and future of religion. He characterizes religion as an illusion and as a universal obsessive neurosis—the most stubborn and persistent of all neuroses. He explains it as a complex psychological projection, the profound longing for the fulfillment of ancient, powerful, repressed human desires. It is seen as compensation for childhood longings that persist into adulthood, as a neurosis that develops as children mature and lose the protection and comfort of the father whom they had in their youth. In the attempt to deal with the reality of adult life they adopt a new father figure who can never be displaced.

The infantile need for paternal comfort, which Freud refers to as the "father complex," is transferred in adulthood to the imaginary God figure. This is the source of the phenomenon that we call religion. Freud understands the basic nature of the Christian experience—that we have been adopted into the family of God and received as His precious sons and daughters, but he twists this fact, reinterpreting it as a tragic emotional weakness within believers, and most fundamentally, as an illusion. In this way he takes our most basic human need—the need for God, and the emptiness of our life apart from Him—and makes it a kind of emotional sickness. Thus he tragically fails to accurately diagnose the basic truth of our human condition. We are lost sinners who are separated from God and who desperately need to be reconciled to Him.

The bitterness that characterized the latter portion of Freud's life may account for this totally negative assessment, since this explanation of the Christian life of faith falls short in so many ways. It seems incredible that anybody could accept such a baseless and dismissive explanation of something that has been the foundation of our culture for centuries, as if the life-transforming power of the Holy Spirit and its effects in individuals and in society could be reduced to a weak and childish neurosis. In this perverse view the glorious loving lives of thousands of selfless saints, the written testimonials of their transformed lives, the schools, hospitals, orphanages, and all their many works of piety and devotion, are reduced to the outworking of an illusion and a psychological disorder. As absurd as this is, the ghost of his theory still lingers within society today.

But naturalistic assumptions also come to bear on this issue. The rejection of all revealed knowledge and the need to create a naturalistic explanation for all things has led our culture to question and reject the testimony of hundreds of millions of living Christians and to discount, dismiss, and reinterpret the last two thousand years of western civilization. Something like this perverse explanation must be accepted in order for naturalistic humanism to remain as a viable world view, because human beings are by their nature composed of a non-physical component—the soul. And Christianity and the lives of Christians are a testimony to the soul of man and to the existence of a realm of being that is outside of this physical world. Thus our faith must be "explained away."

Therefore this view of human nature contains a fundamental rejection of the idea of a "soul" as we understand it in Christianity; that is, as a spiritual, non-physical, part of our nature that is the seat of intelligence, virtue, and love, and which allows mankind to be in communion with the Lord God—and which can be and has been corrupted by sin that has cut us off from Him. If followed or acted upon, either in one's personal life or in the development of a system of thought, the Freudian belief system will block humans from entering into their eternal purpose; that is, an intimate trusting personal relationship with the Lord God. It will cause men to fear and despise "religion" as a crutch for the weak.

There is a common underlying world view to the Big Bang Theory, biological evolution, and the Freudian analysis of the Christian spirituality and the human condition. In each case the explanation that is offered is based on the assumption that "the universe is all there is and all there ever was." That is, these theories attempt to explain supernatural phenomena in purely naturalistic terms.

The origin of the universe was a supernatural event. It was the result of the direct actions of God to summon the basic material of this world into existence and then to shape it into the structures that we see in the universe around us. But men deny the supernatural and supply us with a purely naturalistic way of looking at the process instead. The various living things were created—each type—by the direct action of God, but biological evolution insists upon a long sequence of natural causes to explain life and human life. The human being with its consciousness and will is a clear testimony to the non-physical part of our humanity. But men explain awareness, intelligence, and free will as merely a complex biochemically based logical decision chain.

The multitude of science fiction shows that portray consciousness as a very complex computational operation bear testimony to this idea. The *Terminator* movies explain to us that a very advanced computer chip allowed for the self-complexification of the programed logic of Skynet so that eventually it became self-aware and decided to eradicate human beings. The *Star Trek* series *Voyager* portrays a holographic medical doctor that eventually becomes a living and aware individual. Thus the human soul is seen as the product of extremely complex computational decision-making logic, a purely mechanistic and naturalistic phenomenon, instead of a non-material entity.

Finally, the glorious story of Christian life during this age of the world is reduced to a neurotic psychological projection that is merely a sickness and a subjective illusion that resides within the human mind and heart of the weak.

All of these explanations are utterly inadequate and false. Together these give us a very clear picture of the spirit of the age in which we live. This spirit has a name: Scientific Naturalism. It is not science, it is not natural, and it is not the truth. That spirit is the same one that opposes itself to the proper understanding of Genesis.

The Hope of the Human Race:
There is a need for mankind to see a larger and more expansive picture of human life than what we have on this earth. In order for life to have meaning we must envision the future of our race in some way. In Christian thinking the vision of the future that gives us a concrete expectation is the "blessed hope." This hope, as portrayed for us in detail by the prophetic Scriptures, is the specific future that God has planned for us.

In the world of scientific naturalism there is no hope of individual immortality, but there is a hope held out to us for the future of our race. That hope is expressed in the various science fiction works that are so popular today. We are told that in the future we will fly throughout the universe, interact with and join with or conquer many other races of beings, and expand our species throughout the limitless regions of the cosmos.

Without some kind of picture of the future we cannot live our present daily lives, but instead we are overcome with despair. The Christian "blessed hope," in all of its details, is not an illusion; however, the future that we see portrayed for us in the various works of science fiction is an illusion! No such future will ever come to pass for the human race. The entire world view within which science fiction stories are cast is itself an illusion and a deception.

Our blessed hope involves more than merely freedom from the confines of this planet; it involves liberation from the confines of our sinful and fallen condition—sad realities that materialistic ideologies can neither understand nor accept. Our hope involves glorious communion with the One Who created us in the beginning.

The dreams of scientific naturalism are bound to this world in their thinking and in their aspirations. But our predestined future is to be completely delivered from our sin nature and to dwell before God as His beloved children. Every earth-bound or materialistically oriented view of reality fails to accurately assess our present condition or understand its essential nature—and inevitably obscures the purpose and meaning of our existence. We were created to be with God by sharing in the life of the Trinity. This life is only the time of preparation for what He ultimately has in mind for us.

The Temptation and Fall:
Before commenting on the fall of man we should reconsider, as best we can from our present perspective, from where we have fallen. The previous passages of Genesis have painted for us a picture of unselfconscious innocence and communion with God—the original state of the human race. Our first parents were not destined to die, and had no fear of death or God's judgment. In this state our first parents were unaware of what any other psychological state might feel like. Man was created to be in such a union with the Lord God. It is the only possible state in which true peace and joy can be sustained.

This state of being is the perfect fulfillment of what we now know as the foundational law of God: Thou shalt love the Lord your God with all of your heart, with all of your mind, and with all of your strength. Yet they had no such commandment, for it was built into them when they were created. They did not need a commandment, for that was added at a later time for those who were law-breakers (1 Timothy 1:9), to guide them into the way of life because they no longer were conscious of the innate knowledge that they should have inherited from their first parents.

Adam and Eve were in true personal contact with all that is good, but they knew not that which was evil. The tree of the knowledge of good and evil was necessary for their growth in understanding, a vital ingredient in God's plan to educate them and to mature them in His way of life and His wisdom. At this initial time in their lives it served as an instrument of instruction in obedience and trust, both of which were the most basic attributes needed to establish them as His son and daughter. We cannot see how God would have used that tree later on in their lives if they had obeyed at the beginning.

How did God speak to Adam in this initial time of man? Did He speak in his inner man or did He speak through the air? Most importantly, was He actually present to them when He spoke? Since He spoke to both Adam and Eve together (3:9ff) in a three-way conversation I believe that He stood before them and spoke to them as one person to another, either reproducing the understanding of His words in both of their minds or as seems most likely, using audible speech sounds. But in either case, from the description that Adam gives, the Lord God must have stood before them in Eden.

Direct personal communication with mankind was His way in the beginning.

How could Adam understand what evil or death were since he had never experienced either? He understood them to be the opposite of, or the total absence of, the good and sweet life that he was experiencing. The Lord God was and is completely able to make us understand Him. Therefore the command and the warning of the Lord God were communicated to him clearly and without ambiguity. He understood the terms of His life in the garden. Therefore, how could he ever choose to disobey unless he was persuaded somehow that he would not lose the sweet life that he had been given? This is what the serpent set out to do.

In the account of the temptation, the fall, and the consequent curses which are placed on mankind we see not only the disobedience of man but also his on-going ensnaring by Satan. These always go together in this world. If the angels had not fallen, then human disobedience might not have had such drastic consequences. Life on earth is a grand love story set in the midst of a life-and-death cosmic battle. Sin always opens us up to demonic influence. Satan knew this and sought to subject us to his deceptions, for at the beginning he could not paint perverted images in their minds or act inwardly upon their hearts. His temptations were only ideas proposed to their minds for consideration.

In addition, because of the nature of sin Jesus said, "anyone who sins is a slave to sin." Sin is a deep pit with steep and slippery sides. If we plunge into it then climbing out is quite difficult. Sin changes the nature of the human condition from a stance of being friendly toward God to one of being hostile toward Him. This is the nature of Satan, to be sure, but more fundamentally it is the nature of evil. Satan is like this because he is irrevocably evil. Sin corrupts our will so that we cannot pull away from it, and it darkens our minds so that we cannot understand clearly the condition that we are in. Our sin is a deception that tends to lead us to justify it instead of repenting of it so as to turn away from it. In this sense sin is captivity to Satan at the deepest levels of our being.

Today there is no part of our human nature that remains unaffected by sin. Thus we cannot deliver ourselves from captivity to it. To rebel against the One Who is all-good, Who is the source of all that is true and beautiful is, by its very nature, to place ourselves within the realm of all that is opposed to good. Again, it is the nature of good as well as of evil that such an act would ensnare us. Thus the effect of the sin of Adam and Eve cannot be undone simply by an "I'm sorry," for such words do not come heartily from the lips of one who is subjected to evil. A new state of existence was introduced by the fall, one in which men were made distant from and hostile to God. Now Satan has a foothold in each of us.

<u>The Sin of Adam and Eve</u>:
Why would the Lord God allow a world in which sin has a place, since He is perfectly good, and ultimately all things must reflect His goodness and wisdom? They must necessarily be directed to His glory, and they inexorably must lead to an accurate manifestation of who He is as pure, selfless, love and overflowing goodness. So why did God allow Adam to sin? And once he sinned, why did He decree that the effects of his sin would fall on his descendants?

Man was created in God's image and likeness so that we might ultimately share in His divine life with Him. Therefore we had to have a truly free will in choosing God and His ways, or in rejecting them. Love must be freely given and freely entered into. And His divine Trinitarian life is family life. Being human includes the power to beget children, assuring the continuity of human nature. And family life reflects and prepares us for His divine life. These could not be weakened or undermined. Rather, in Abba's wisdom and goodness He decreed from before all time—as He planned the ages with His Only Begotten—that we would inevitably share in the first Adam's fall, but also be the recipients of His great mercy through the second Adam.

A divine decree of universal sin does not contradict the glory of God because the most perfect possible expression of goodness and love is manifested in the gift that He gives to humans who are most undeserving, who are alienated from Him by their hatred of Him. God showed His love for us in that while we were yet sinners Christ died for us (Romans 5:8). Sin was the occasion for the ones whom He had created to see His overflowing goodness and love manifested, transcendentally exceeding all human love. God concluded all under disobedience that He might show mercy to all (Romans 11:32), and God confined all under sin that the gift of eternal life might be given to those who believe in His Only Begotten Son (Galatians 3:22).

God configured the spiritual realities so that only in His Beloved Son could men find eternal life. This decree is to His glory, to that of His Beloved Son, and to ours as His precious children. Oh the depth of the riches both of the wisdom and the knowledge of God (Romans 11:23)!

Now let us turn to the concrete drama of the fall, the particular circumstances in the lives of Adam and Eve, that display for us the initial enactment of God's eternal decision to allow sin.

Genesis 3:1—Now the serpent was more crafty than any beast of the field which the LORD God had made. And he said to the woman, "Indeed, has God [Elohiym] **said, 'You shall not eat from any tree of the garden'?"**

Genesis 3:2—The woman said to the serpent, "From the fruit of the trees of the garden we may eat;

Genesis 3:3—but from the fruit of the tree which is in the middle of the garden, God [Elohiym] **has said, 'You shall not eat from it or touch it, or you will die.'"**

Genesis 3:4—The serpent said to the woman, "You surely will not die!

Genesis 3:5—For God [Elohiym] **knows that in the day you eat from it your eyes will be opened, and you will be like God** [or gods: Elohiym]**, knowing good and evil."**

Genesis 3:6—When the woman saw that the tree was good for food, and that it was a delight to the eyes, and that the tree was desirable to make one wise, she took from its fruit and ate; and she gave also to her husband with her, and he ate.

Genesis 3:7—Then the eyes of them both were opened, and they knew that they were naked; and they sewed fig leaves together, and made themselves loin coverings.

Eve probably did not receive the command to "not eat" from God, for the Lord God gave Adam this command before she was made from his side. Also, Eve does not call the tree by the name "the tree of the knowledge of good and evil," which is the name that the Lord God gave it when he spoke the command to Adam. So Adam must have relayed the word of command to Eve, and he might not have conveyed to her the full story. Also, because here she goes beyond the command and adds, *neither shall you touch it*, either the original explanation (coming to her through Adam) was faulty or she is exaggerating the command because she is already seeking a reason to not obey it. Thus we must consider that in her act of disobedience Eve might have been directly disobeying her husband, but perhaps was only indirectly disobeying the Lord God. I wonder what Adam was doing while this interchange was taking place, for it says that he was with her.[638 see note] Finally, because Eve did not seem to know the name of the "tree in the middle of the garden," she might also have not had full understanding of its purpose, which was to teach them obedience. I assume that a brilliant man like Adam had such knowledge from His conversations with the Lord God. But did he take the time to convey all of this to his companion Eve? The text hints that he did not.

The name of God that the serpent uses in these verses, "has **God** said" is not *Yĕhovah Elohiym*, the personal name of God that Adam uses throughout most of this account. It is merely *Elohiym*, the name that God used for Himself in the creation story. This is not an accident, but an indication that the serpent in no way accepts God as his Lord and Master. That same is true in verse 3:5 where he says, "for God doth know" and, "You shall be as Gods." It is also true that when Eve answers him, "God hath said, 'you shall not eat of it'" in verse 3:3 that she employs the more distant name for God as well. In all other uses in this chapter the name used for God is *Yĕhovah Elohiym*.

This is an indication that in these acts the serpent, who is distant from the Lord God, is leading Eve to distance herself from Him as well—and she is being so led. These verses recount how Eve left off her life of submission to the Lord God and asserted her own will against Him. This interchange can be simply assessed as follows: Is *Elohiym*, the One Who created all things, also *Yĕhovah*, our personal Lord and Master? The choice is hers and ours. The decree of God to allow sin did not take away free will.

The answer to this question is not an abstract proposition. The answer is expressed in the concrete response that Eve was to make to the serpent's suggestion. If Eve rejects God as her Lord and Master then she rejects Him—period—for that is Who He is, Who he created her to relate to Him as, and Who He always must be in relation to her. If she denies Him that role in her life then she denies herself any way of relating to Him. Adam was not directly active in this conversation. He was with Eve and eventually acquiesced with her in what she said and in her act of disobedience. But why did he remain silent? Why did he not say something to help his wife withstand the assault of the enemy's lies? Adam was warned when he was placed in the garden: Keep it, be vigilant!

The serpent was "more crafty." The Hebrew word is `*aruwm* which indicates a kind of sly or shrewd smartness. This kind of wisdom or knowledge is not admirable or virtuous. The serpent possessed this dark quality because in this scene it was being used and empowered by a hostile spiritual intelligence that was very clever and very wicked.

The serpent spoke. To us it seems strange that any animal could speak, but to Adam and Eve at the dawn of human history no conventions, expectations, and understandings of what was normal had been established in their minds. In the beginning all animals were friendly with man and intermixed with Adam and Eve without fear. The Devil, not without the permission of God, chose the serpent as the instrument by which he would approach and talk to Eve. The particular choice of the serpent to be used by the Devil, as this passage relates, became the standard way to refer to him throughout Scripture.

We also might ask just how the serpent spoke. The mouth and tongue of a serpent are not suited to producing the sounds of human speech. We are not told how this happened but only that the Devil used the serpent and spoke through it. The Evil One who was empowering the serpent may have spoken to Eve in the same way that God spoke to them; that is, by forming various ideas in her mind as words, which she realized were coming from the serpent that was situated directly before her. Thus there might possibly have been no physical sounds entering the ears of Adam and Eve.

When I was in fourth grade and had just finished speaking with my teacher about the Big Bang Theory, then last of all she said to me, "Mike, I don't know about those theories but I know the Bible is God's word and so it must be true," I left her to go outside and play with the other children and this idea came into my mind: "So—they're both true. They each say the same thing but in different ways." I remember the sentence and its content. At that time I did not realize where that idea came from. It found a ready place in my mind because I did not want to let go of the Big Bang. I was ripe to hear and receive his lie.

That erroneous idea stayed with me until I was in my thirties and the Lord "blew it away" while I was standing in the parking lot off Hoover Street in Ann Arbor, Michigan. When my teacher replied to me in that simple conversation I remember the effect of her words. They went into my heart and I affirmed them completely. But the idea that came to my mind as I left her presence was **not** from the Lord! The effect of that idea was to obscure and muddle my thinking and to cast confusion on the whole conversation. It blunted the heart-felt affirmation that I had made to what she had told me. It was the serpent speaking to me. He was taking the Word of God from my heart—or, at least, he was burying it beneath an incomprehensible syncretism.

The serpent in Paradise was quite able to converse with Eve in a similar deceptive way. Eve took in the carefully crafted and coherent sequence of thoughts and ideas that came into her mind as the serpent stood before her and rightly ascribed the ideas to it. Both Adam and Eve "heard" these words. The Lord did not permit the serpent to speak to and tempt Eve without the knowledge of Adam, who was charged with "keeping" her.

Why did God allow Adam and Eve to be tested? To produce steadfastness (James 1:3). We see God using the Devil as an instrument to test His people throughout history.

> It is a principle of God's dealings with us that our relationships with Him are not secure until we have passed through certain tests which He has appointed. This applies to both angels and human beings. Untested relationships are like unrefined gold. They are not acceptable in heaven. For this reason Jesus said to the Christians in Laodicea: "I counsel you to buy from Me gold refined in the fire" (Revelation 3:18). In other words, "Your claim to be My people is not valid until you have passed the test." Gold of that quality is not cheap. We have to buy it. There is a price to pay! (From an instructional letter entitled *Angels* by Derek Prince)

Thus God allows men to be tested in order to establish the authenticity and sincerity of their commitment to Him. He wants those who fellowship with Him to be whole-heartedly given to Him, just as He is totally given to us. Adam and Eve were ripe for deception.

Even Jesus had to undergo such a test at the beginning of His ministry. We are told that "the Spirit drove Him" into the desert where He was tempted by the Devil. But we also must understand that Jesus rebuffed Satan and finally defeated him at the cross.

> When He had disarmed the rulers and authorities, He made a public display of them, having triumphed over them through Him [or through it, i.e., the cross]. (Colossians 2:15)

And Jesus shares that victory with us, for the Scriptures tell us that soon God will crush Satan beneath our feet (Romans 16:20).

The simple carefree state of our first parents would seem to preclude the possibility of their being tempted to reach for even more. St. John Chrysostom remarks:

> Consider, I ask you, the transcendence of their blessed condition, how they were superior to all bodily concerns, how they lived on earth as if they were in heaven, and though in fact possessing a body they did not feel the limitations of their bodies. After all, they had no need of shelter or habitation, clothing or anything of that kind. It was not idly or to no purpose that Sacred Scripture indicated this to us; it was that we might learn of this carefree condition of theirs, their trouble-free life and angelic condition, as you might say.[639]

It would require a very careful approach to the man and woman to lead them away from the Lord by inducing them to disobey Him. Thus the Scripture says that the serpent was craftier than all the beasts of the field (3:1) in this wicked design. His plan was to induce doubt in the woman first. She was more vulnerable. Then use her to get at the man.

Why did the Devil want to rob Adam and Eve of their happy life in the garden? Why bother them or seek to upset them? He was motivated by envy as he watched them, as the time passed, and they reveled in Paradise and interacted with God so easily.

> When the devil, as you remember, evil spirit and enemy of our nature as he is, saw the first human being living in the garden, how his life was carefree and how he lived on earth in bodily form yet like an angel, he wanted to trip him up and dislodge him with the hope of greater promises, and so he cheated him of the possession of what he had.[640] [see note]

He succeeded by holding out to them a promise of even greater things. The fact that they could be successfully tempted by such an offer shows that they were incomplete in their wisdom and in their virtue. Temptation reveals our steadfastness or our lack of it. Before they fell by disobedience our first parents were already prone to pride. They carried an attitude of self-seeking and self-aggrandizement in them—at least in germinal form—that the tempter could play on by his promises. He led them by stages.

He began by a statement that indicated his concern for them, asking them, perhaps with some solicitude, if they could eat of the trees of the garden (3:1). In this way he was expressing concern for them and presenting himself to them as a friend. He was using this opening line to enter into their fellowship and gain their implicit trust. Once he had gained a place in their simple society of two people then he could inject new and dangerous ideas into their minds. They did not realize the insidious intentions that he had in his own mind as he initiated this conversation. In this way he was subtle, tricky, and double-dealing with them. Speech and the tongue are very powerful.

Here is what I mean about the power of speech, especially when it is coming from one whom we trust and regard as an insider, as "one of us." When I was on a team that was charged with implementing a huge computer system for the University of Michigan our team was a very close and tight-knit group of people. One person became unhappy with the way the team was being run. They began to speak in slanderous and negative ways. Simple morning conversations developed a tone that was undermining the entire team and the direction that the leadership was trying to establish. The speech of that person was poison. It was difficult to listen without being drawn into the attitude and point of view that they had. I began to avoid conversations with them because I felt the tug of discontent that they were expressing. I trusted them and they had a place in my mind and heart that was influential with me. I felt as if I was "supposed" to go along with their statements just to be a nice guy. That was the influence that they wielded.

James says this about speech:
> [T]he tongue is set among our members as that which defiles the entire body, and sets on fire the course of *our* life, and is set on fire by hell . . . *It is* a restless evil *and* full of deadly poison . . . But if you have bitter jealousy and selfish ambition in your heart, do not be arrogant and *so* lie against the truth. This wisdom is not that which comes down from above, but is earthly, natural, demonic. For where jealousy and selfish ambition exist, there is disorder and every evil thing. But the wisdom from above is first pure, then peaceable, gentle, reasonable, full of mercy and good fruits, unwavering, without hypocrisy. (James 3:6, 7, 14–16)

Ambrose meditates on this wicked attribute of our adversary.
> [The Devil] is believed to be a deadly, double-tongued serpent, doing [his] work by saying one thing with the tongue and by harboring other thoughts in his mind.[641]

Adam and Eve were not acquainted with this type of speech; that is, duplicitous speech that has the motive of selfish ambition and jealousy behind it—hypocritical speech. James identifies this type of speech as "earthly, natural, demonic." The devil began his speech with Eve in this way: First insinuate himself into their little circle as a trusted confidant and friend. Gain influence with them, then speak poison.

Thus I believe that there was more to the total conversation than we have been given, but let us now return to what is related to us. Once the devil had asked about the trees of the garden and broached the subject with Eve in an innocent way, she explained that they could eat of all of the trees except for the one tree in the middle of the garden (3:2–3). If they ate of that one tree then they would die. At this point the devil lied to Eve and spoke a direct contradiction to what God had told them:

> You surely shall not die (3:4). [or more exactly, it is not true that "dying you shall die."]

She should have known that believing God had to be the right thing to do, but she had never encountered a blatant lie before. She was befuddled and did not know what to do. Where was her protector while this was transpiring? He was with her. Why was he silent?

After that the Devil spoke to her something that was still true, but which was misleading in the present situation. It brought Eve to the point of questioning God.

> For God knows that in the day you eat from it your eyes shall be opened and you will be like God, knowing good and evil (3:5).

Still using the word *Elohiym* for God the serpent now informs Eve that she will "become like God" if she eats of the tree. To someone who might not have known the name of the tree, as her previous words hinted, this was quite a revelation. Since the word used for "God" in this verse is *Elohiym*, it is also just possible that he was telling her that she would gain insight and wisdom like the angels (also referred to by this name *Elohiym*) if she did in fact eat of it. In other words, God was keeping her and her husband in a lower state than was possible for them by keeping them from eating from this tree. This was a lie that was easier to accept because it was accompanied by the new information which was connected to the actual name of the tree—new information for her. Whatever was the content of his deceptive assertion (being like God Himself, or being like an angel), it surely did promise her some kind of elevation to a new level of existence. Inherent in this claim or promise, in either case, was a kind of accusation against God and a claim that He had not yet given her (and her husband) all that they were potentially capable of.

Realize that Adam and Eve were not in a final state of perfection, so there was indeed a much more fulfilling destiny that awaited them in the plan of God, and there was a kind of incompleteness within them, a revelation still to be attained. They were being prepared. It was true that this tree was intended to teach Adam and Eve about good and evil, and it would be an eye-opening experience for them. Following upon his foundational lie the effect of this second (partially true) statement was to present to Eve the idea of eating from the tree immediately. The implication was that God was withholding something good from her—something that would enhance her greatly—something that He had not fully explained to her. She looked at the tree and noticed three attributes about it (3:6):

- It was nice to look at—the lust of the eyes.
- It bore fruit that was edible—the lust of the flesh.
- It **seemed to her** as if the fruit would indeed make her wise—the pride of life.

The last point was a judgement on the part of the woman. Thus Eve decided to eat the fruit. Then she gave some to her husband who was with her and he ate also (3:6).

Why did Adam also eat and disobey the direct command of God? Eve had just been tricked or deceived. But Adam was not (1 Timothy 2:14). I think he might have looked at her with care and concern, fearful of what might befall her if she were separated from him and estranged from his company. He loved her and did not want to be distanced from her. So he followed her in her transgression. No conversation between Adam and Eve is given to us but we know that there was one because when God pronounced His judgment He said to Adam, "Because you have listened to the voice of your wife." Thus we know that there was a conversation between Them. He was not deceived; rather he was persuaded. Adam listened to his wife rather than to God. And he apparently had not told his wife the whole story about the foundational truth of their existence. Why?

Notice that when Eve ate no special result is recorded, although she had disobeyed her husband. But when Adam ate it is written that, "the eyes of both of them were opened and they knew that they were naked, and they sewed fig leaves together to make themselves loin coverings" (3:7). Sin entered the world through the disobedience of one man (Romans 5:12) and not through the disobedience of the first human couple.

Adam was responsible for the fall of mankind, for he was the spiritual leader. In the final crisis he did not obey God. But leading up to that, it appears that he did not fully explain to Eve the basic underlying parameters of their life in the garden, including the meaning and purpose of the "tree in the middle of the garden." He did not intervene in the conversation Eve had with the serpent. And he did not take heed of the implicit warning from the Lord God to "beware" or "be on guard" (*shamar*) when He had first placed him in the garden.

This principle of authority and responsibility permeates our daily lives constantly. I used to design and build computer systems for the University of Michigan, feeding into those systems that printed paychecks for people. If I had announced one day that we would no longer print paychecks for the employees at the University of Michigan it would have caused a small uproar but would not have affected too much else—except perhaps my enduring employment! But if my boss's boss, who was responsible for all the computer support for the administrative offices of the university, had announced that very same thing it would have been devastating. She was in charge of all such processes. I was not. My aberrant behavior would have been sticky, but hers would mean the end of financial support for thousands. This is because she was in charge.

So when Eve ate of the tree her bond with Adam was damaged, and her bond with God surely suffered. Eve must have known immediately that something was not right, but instead of warning Adam she drew him after her. Yet Adam was the person who was in charge and who was responsible directly to God. When he ate then his bond with God was severed and that affected both of them. They both experienced that tragic reality immediately. The decision that Adam made brought a disaster upon the entire human race. The misbehavior of Eve certainly was horrid, but it did not carry the same weight and implications as Adam's. Through one **man** sin entered the world (Romans 5:12).

The account implies that Adam and Eve had a conversation that is not related to us, for God said to Adam, "because you have **listened to the voice of your wife**" (Genesis 3:17), not just "because you took the fruit from her." We can imagine fancifully what might have happened.

> As soon as Eve eats of the fruit she has misgivings about what she has done. She says to Adam, "Well . . . I am OK, am I not?" He replies, "No, it cannot be right." "But it tastes fine. Why are you looking at me like that? Try some yourself and see." "No." "Why? Don't you trust me? Do you think that I am so different now that I have eaten of this one fruit?" "No." "But you don't trust me, do you? You don't love me anymore. I can see it in your face. You don't!" "That isn't so, Eve." But Eve begins to cry. Adam weakens and says, "OK, I'll try it too."

Ambrose theorizes that, because Eve ate from the tree of the knowledge of good and Evil, she acquired the knowledge of evil through her act of disobedience. Then she led her spouse into the same error knowingly and deliberately.

> After eating she acquired a knowledge of evil. She ought not, therefore, have made her husband a partaker of the evil of which she was conscious; neither should she have caused her own husband to violate the divine command. She sinned, therefore, with forethought, and knowingly made her husband a participant in her wrongdoing . . . many, however, are of the opinion that she should be excused for the reason that, because she loved her husband, she was afraid that she would be separated from him.[642]

Why are we not told about the broader scenario that took place? Eve obviously did say something to convince Adam. It is because whatever did happen, and whatever was said, Adam was totally responsible for disobeying God and eating the fruit. We must see that when Eve ate the fruit her relationship with Adam was immediately damaged. Possibly that could have been repaired without great distress—possibly. But when Adam ate the fruit his relationship with the Lord God was ruined. That had far-reaching consequences for the entire human race—for Adam, for Eve, and for all their descendants throughout the ages. As the head of the whole human race, Adam was responsible to God.

We are all suffering under the effects of Adam's disastrous choice. Thus when the Lord God led Adam to write the account He purposely omitted any such interchange with Eve because it would distract from the spiritual reality of what was happening. Adam was totally responsible for what he did, and through him—and only through him—humanity's bond with the Lord was severed and sin entered into the world. Through one **man** . . .

We must understand the situation that Adam and Eve were in at the dawn of human history. This one commandment was given to teach them about obedience. It was not given to teach them to do what seemed best in their own eyes. Without a command "to do or not do" something there could be no obedience. If their entire life were to be lived according to their own best judgment and their own choices then there would be no way for them to connect to the One Who by His very nature was in authority over them.

The filial bond with authority had to involve a command that would be obeyed because, and only because, it was given as a command. If it simply affirmed to them what their own judgment or desire already told them, then it would have been incapable of drawing them out of themselves and turning them to God. Obedience is the path that leads us to God because He is our Creator and the ultimate authority in our life—and the source of all purpose and direction. Not slavish obedience, but obedience that proceeds from a filial bond of love, respect, and trust. The command was necessary to prepare them for union with Him. Their disobedience necessarily erected a barrier between them and God because it denied to Him His rightful place in their lives as their beloved Lord.

When it says "the eyes of both of them were opened" we must not think that before then they had closed eyes. This statement is describing a kind of spiritual enlightenment that came over them. But it was not a spiritual experience that was rooted in God. They did become like "gods," like intellectual natures, seeing what before they did not know. But the Devil had his way with them at that point and he was the one who "opened their eyes." He is the one who brought them into an experiential knowledge of evil. This new kind of understanding was not what they had imagined. This was an initiation into the spirit and mind of the evil one. It captured them and enslaved them. They were no longer living in innocence. They were no longer free. They had become enslaved to one who was their mortal enemy. Satan had gained a foothold in the life of human beings on this earth.

The two disciples on the road to Emmaus were being instructed by the risen Lord Jesus when they experienced an "opening of their eyes" while our Lord broke bread with them (Luke 24:31). It meant that suddenly they realized something that previously had been eluding their understanding. The new spiritual state into which Adam and Eve had been propelled created a mindset in them—and it instigated new feelings and attitudes in their hearts—that made it impossible for them to continue in the presence of God. It separated them from Him immediately. It made them fear Him and distrust Him.

This spiritual change entered into them through the one who was the spiritual leader. It overtook them through Adam. This change was not revocable; that is, it was constituted in such a way that they could not extricate their personality from their new condition. Every part of their humanity was catapulted into a new mindset that separated them from the Lord God. They reacted by sewing fig leaves together as a covering—a poor solution for thoughtful people to choose. It must have been carried out precipitously, to counter the sudden powerful urges that swept over them. It was done in a panic.

Severus of Antioch meditates on the precipitous slope that the human race was placed on after the fall:

> After the expulsion from the blessed life in the Paradise *of Eden*, when the sentence concerning sin had gone forth *and it had been said* to Adam "dust thou art and to dust shalt thou go *back*," like a wheel running *rapidly* downwards all our race was *hastening and* being driven to utter destruction; and it had not the power to *turn and* look towards heaven; and there was no plan or device which could draw *and drag* upwards those who *had been hurled downwards and* had fallen.[643]

We will observe the degeneration of individual human beings and of human society as we move through Genesis. The course of human history had been changed downward forever by the decision in Eden. No human decision or effort could reverse the trend. A direct action of God was the only hope for men and women.

Genesis 3:8—They heard the sound of the LORD God walking in the garden in the cool of the day, and the man and his wife hid themselves from the presence of the LORD God among the trees of the garden.

Genesis 3:9—Then the LORD God called to the man, and said to him, "Where are you?"

Genesis 3:10—He said, "I heard the sound of You in the garden, and I was afraid because I was naked; so I hid myself."

Genesis 3:11—And He said, "Who told you that you were naked? Have you eaten from the tree of which I commanded you not to eat?"

Genesis 3:12—The man said, "The woman whom You gave *to be* with me, she gave me from the tree, and I ate."

Genesis 3:13—Then the LORD God said to the woman, "What is this you have done?" And the woman said, "The serpent deceived me, and I ate."

Many early writers see this part of the account, speaking of the Lord God with physical words like "walking" and "speaking," as not to be taken literally because, they assert, He has not a human form. But I see this as the personal account of Adam and as such it is his description of how the Lord God related to them from the first. It is accurate just as Adam wrote it. The Lord God came to them in just the way that Adam is describing.

From this part of the story I think it is most reasonable to assume that Adam and Eve had been living in Eden for a while—perhaps several months—when this happened. Enough time for them to establish a pattern and routine to their lives and to their relationship with the Lord God. During that time the Lord God would visit them and commune with them from time to time, as now. But their attitude toward God after their act of disobedience had been radically altered. A fearful wounded conscience led them to hide from Him.

What happened to Adam and Eve spiritually as they ate of the tree God had forbidden? It appears that their filial bond with the Lord God was severed when they ate the fruit of the tree. They did in fact die spiritually as the Lord God had said. The result was that their psychological state was transformed from one of natural and unselfconscious joy coming from their bond of fellowship with Him to one of alienation and emptiness. The need to fill that emptiness was immediate—a longing and desire that compelled them as nothing else had ever done. This subjugated them and enslaved them by demanding to be fulfilled. This was something they had never before experienced. It was the initiation into the mindset and the heart of the devil.

They immediately descended into the psychology of the human race that is now the universal experience of all people. They felt selfishness. They felt lust. They felt fear. They felt greed. Their nakedness became a source of shame for them, stirring up within them unholy and self-serving longings. They needed to cover themselves up to protect themselves from each other. And when God came to them they would not accept responsibility for their sin!

In this state they were prey to Satan and his demons, unprotected by their Bulwark and their Shield. Surely they did know evil as the serpent had said. And it was surely God's plan to eventually teach them all of these things, but not by severing them from Himself, not by subjugating them to evil, not by immersing them in it and allowing them to drown in it. Because of the ever-present demonic powers, the nature of the fall became more tragic and the fate of the human race became more precarious. They were not only cut off from God and slaves to sin, but they were vulnerable to one who was very cunning, committed to sin completely, the enemy of God, and their personal enemy.

How did the Lord God discover that this had happened? Of course He knew all this from before the foundation of the world. But when He chose to create, He also chose to enter into His creation and participate in it. He made this choice in order to fellowship with us in whom He delighted. This was most clearly manifested in the Incarnation. So the Lord God allows the events of history to unfold and participates in them in various ways. He thus comes to "know" about people and events in a way that corresponds to our human state, through actual experience embedded in the unfolding history of the world of men.

Thus the Lord God walked in the garden in the cool of the day looking for His usual time of fellowship with His creatures in which He took such delight—perhaps also like a kind physician coming now to heal the ones who were sick and injured. But the man and the woman were afraid of Him and hid when He called to them (3:8–9). And then the truth came out. They could only be concerned about their nakedness for one reason. "Have you eaten from the tree of which I commanded you not to eat" (3:11)? Yes, that was it. Thus He diagnosed the problem at its root and spoke it out so that all would know.

I wonder what would have happened if, after their sin, they had each acknowledged the part that they had played in it and had asked for forgiveness. But it is the nature of sin that it is like a psychological black hole. It draws us into itself by marshalling all of our personal faculties to reinforce and support itself. Thus sin makes us long to justify what we have done to others. It blinds our minds and sets our emotions against the reality and the truth of what we have done.

God is the fountainhead of all truth and goodness and when we are cut off from Him we have no such qualities remaining within ourselves. Instead they drain out of us and leave us in a self-fortified and reinforced state of denial. "The woman you gave to me . . ." and, "the serpent deceived me . . ." (3:12–13). It is the nature of sin that it changes us in some way, even at the root of our humanity. Thus the external effects of sin have to be profound, affecting all aspects of human life on earth.

Thus God was about to change the parameters of human existence on earth for all time. That is what His judgments are about. The most tragic change in our human lives was an inevitable distancing of the Lord God from mankind and from each level of our deteriorating human culture—personal, familial, and societal.

The True Nature of Sin:
Before we study the response of our Lord to the sin of Adam and Eve I want to carefully consider what sin is. We cannot appreciate the justice, mercy, love, and compassion of God as He responds to what his children have done unless we accurately understand the reality of sin, what its true nature actually is.

There was a book on psychology and human behavior entitled *Games People Play* by a psychiatrist named Eric Berne that describes certain peculiar and inauthentic ways of relating to each other that people can and do adopt. It indicates that, for a variety of reasons, people sometimes deceive themselves and each other by assuming artificial roles as they relate to each other. This posturing before each other makes relationships both difficult to deal with constructively and deeply unsatisfying. We must understand that the Lord is utterly genuine and that He never plays relational games. God is Truth. When we come near to Him, with no interposed veil, there will be no playing of games.

In our minds we sometimes think that when a person who is a "sinner" comes before the judgment seat of God the conversation might go something like this:
    Person: Oh, I . . . uh . . . I know I didn't . . . er . . . exactly measure up, but I truly am sorry. Will you forgive me and give me a chance to make it up to you, to change?
    God: No! You had your chance. Now you must pay. Depart from Me into the eternal fire!

This is utterly the wrong scenario. God is always loving and just and merciful. He wants all men to be saved and to come to the knowledge of the truth. Then you might ask, and quite reasonably, how is it that anyone ever gets sent to hell? In fact, how can it be that anyone ever comes under judgment in any way?

This is where we must understand the nature of sin. When Adam and Eve sinned they cut themselves off from God, Who is the source of all that is good (Mark 10:18). Their hearts were emptied of the presence and consolation of His Holy Spirit. They quickly descended into a state of pride, fear, shame, bitterness, covetousness, lust, and a certain kind of mean-spirited selfishness. Today we commonly hide these disgusting character faults by playing games with each other. This allows us to cover up our desperate emptiness. Note that this understanding of sin highlights the grace of God, Who loves us even in this sad state.

It was the reality of sin from the beginning that it denied and refused to acknowledge its own true nature. God always tried to call us from our sin, but we turned aside from Him.

> And now listen and I will tell you something which no one has yet expressed with complete clarity. The Divine scripture says: *God said to Adam: Adam, where art thou?* (Genesis 3:9). Why did the Creator of all things say this? Of course, it was in order to dispose Adam to come to his senses, to acknowledge his sin and repent . . . As it were he said to Adam, "Adam, enter into yourself, acknowledge your nakedness and understand what a garment and what a glory you have lost. Adam where are you?" In a certain way, as it were, He awakens him and says, "O Adam, come to yourself and confess with humility your sin. Come out of the place where you are hiding . . . Say: 'I have sinned.'"

> But he [Adam] did not say this (or rather, I the wretched one do not say this, because this is [also] my own passion) . . . For Adam was deceived and truly thought that God did not know about his sin, saying to himself as it were: "I will say that I am naked. God, not knowing the reason for this, will ask, 'How did you become naked?' And I will reply to him, 'I do not know.' Thus I will deceive Him and again receive my previous covering. And even if I do not receive this, at least He will not banish me now from Paradise . . ." This is what Adam thought, as now also many people think—and first of all I myself—when we hide our sins . . .

> [So] he [Adam] did not say this [I have sinned, please forgive me.], did not humble himself, did not become contrite. His heart was hardened, just as mine is, the wretched one. But if he had said this he would have remained in Paradise . . .

> Adam refused to acknowledge his sin and did not repent even when he was accused by God; for he said, *The woman that Thou gavest to be with me—she deceived me* (Genesis 3:12) . . . O woe to his blinded soul! Saying this, he as it were said to God: "Thou Thyself art guilty, because the woman whom Thou gavest me hast deceived me." This very same thing I myself now suffer, wretched and miserable, when I do not desire to be humbled, and to say with my whole soul that I am guilty. [So I also blame others.] Woe to my poor soul which speaks such words filled with sin! O most shameless and irrational soul!644

What we see in Adam and Eve at the beginning, blaming God instead of admitting their sin, is still the universal norm for people today. Much of human society is constructed in such a way that it provides people with ways of living out their lives without being forced (very often) to confront the deep insecurities and vanity that lie within. When we come before God that charade will immediately come to an end. He sees right through us, to the very core of our being. No such game playing will be possible when we are in His presence.

God will judge the secrets of men through Jesus Christ (Romans 2:16) and He will bring to light what is hidden and judge even the innermost motives of our hearts (1 Corinthians 4:5). Thus the fundamental realities of our existence will immediately come to the fore.

Consider what sin has done to us! The Bible says that fallen human beings are enemies of God (Romans 1:30), stubborn in their sin (Romans 2:5), alienated from the Lord by the hostility of their minds (Colossians 1:21), that they do not love God (John 5:42), are liars and estranged from Him even from their birth, and they are deaf to the truth no matter how lovingly or skillfully it is presented to them (Psalm 58:2–5). These attributes of our fallen human nature are common to all people no matter how intelligent or soft-spoken we are, no matter how cultured or sophisticated we are, no matter how educated or eloquent we are. We shift blame from ourselves to our parents, our culture, our circumstances, to God.

The veneer of human culture and civilization will be left behind as we approach the judgment seat of God, and these sinful qualities will emerge as we stand before Him. This is what the fall has done to us. This is what happened to mankind when we were cut off from Him and removed from His presence. This is the true nature of sin.

So how does this affect our picture of what happens when a sinner approaches the throne of God? Remember in *The Lord of the Rings*, that sad character named Gollum? He hated bright places, ate raw food, and squirmed in misery when he had to associate with kind and gracious people. There was something in him that abhorred all that is good and right and noble and true. Think of how he whined and shrieked when Frodo and Sam put that elvish rope on him! That is the way the sinner will be when he or she stands before the judgment seat of God—screaming, cursing, bucking like a wild beast, unreasoning, and violent. Will we feel remorse, shame, grief, and disgust at ourselves? Yes, but that is not all we will feel. We will hate God and refuse to repent anyway! We will not want to be judged, but we will still hate and reject the Holy One and His ways. There is no place of peace for such people. Their very humanity has been destroyed. They have lost their soul.

Add to this picture the statement of Jesus that "anyone who sins is a slave to sin" and we see that, once people have died, once they have exited from this earthly life and thus have departed from the place where life decisions are made—once they have left behind the place of preparation (this earthly life) that God created in order for them to prepare for the glory of His unveiled presence—then they must understand that there will never be another chance to change or to repent. The sinners who are still in their sin nature, who have never been born again, will be trapped in their sin. It is and always will be their chosen way of thinking and choosing and relating to others—including to God.

Sin captivates men and women at the core of their humanity. People who are caught in sin cannot change because they do not want to change, because they refuse to change. In this state lost sinners are under the condemnation of Satan; that is, they think of God as a hard and condemning judge who has levied upon them the guilt and weight of their many sins, and who totally disapproves of them. This is the demonic deception that the enemy lays upon their heart. This is the psychological black hole, the spiritual bottomless pit, into which they have fallen—this is the paradigm shift of Eden still actively in charge in their heart. No human work can change such people or lift them from such a mental state. The love and merciful forgiveness of God was their only hope, and when they die in their sin it means that they have rejected that gracious offer.

Sin destroys our souls; that is, it destroys that which makes us human; that is, it leaves us an empty, corroded, ruined vessel that can never fulfill the purpose for which we were created—to be in an intimate, direct, loving relationship with the Lord God Who created us. Those eternally trapped in sin are no longer human. They have lost their humanity, their soul. That is what sin does to people, and this truth is what guides every judgment and decision that our Lord makes as He carefully determines what must happen to men and women now that they have fallen under the dominion of Satan and sin.

This solemn truth is what our Lord sees and understands perfectly clearly as He lovingly promises to send a redeemer to save us. Adam and Eve do not understand this, and even we who are thousands of years further along in human history, who have the advantage of being able to look back over the course of human history and see the darkness that has always characterized human life on this earth, who have the light of His word illuminating our minds and hearts—even we do not understand sin and its effects on mankind. Only our Lord does. These facts about sin are why Jesus said, "you must be born again."

With this sobering reality before us, let us continue on with our reading of what happened to Adam and Eve after the fall, and how our Lord passed His judgments.

Genesis 3:14—The LORD God said to the serpent, "Because you have done this, cursed are you more than all cattle, and more than every beast of the field; On your belly you will go, and dust you will eat all the days of your life;

Genesis 3:15—And I will put enmity between you and the woman, and between your seed and her seed; he shall bruise [or crush] you on the head, and you shall bruise him on the heel.

Genesis 3:16—To the woman He said, "I will greatly multiply your pain in childbirth [lit., your pain and conception]. **In pain you will bring forth children; yet your desire will be for your husband, and he will rule over you."**

Genesis 3:17—Then to Adam He said, "Because you have listened to the voice of your wife, and have eaten from the tree about which I commanded you, saying, 'You shall not eat from it'; cursed is the ground because of you; in toil [or sorrow] you will eat of it all the days of your life.

Genesis 3:18—Both thorns and thistles it shall grow for you; and you will eat the plants of the field;

Genesis 3:19—By the sweat of your face you will eat bread, till you return to the ground, because from it you were taken; for you are dust, and to dust you shall return.

The Lord did not ask the serpent why he had done this thing, because the serpent was behaving according to his nature when he spoke his lie (John 8:44). But God did not create Adam and Eve with such a perverse nature, and only at this moment had they changed. They fell from their position of grace. Why, He asked? Why? At this point the Lord God pronounced the curses with which we are so familiar, setting the terms of human life on earth for the rest of history, laying down the parameters to guide fallen human beings in their sin-ridden lives until His promised redemption (3:14–19).

How did the thorns and thistles suddenly become a factor in Adam's work of cultivating the ground? Did God cause the plants to change in some way, or were they always in existence but certain varieties became more prevalent? The original creation had nothing about it that was harmful or that dealt death or injury. The plants may have had certain recessive characteristics that God allowed to become dominant. The same reasoning must apply to the more violent and destructive animal characteristics—predatory habits of living and of hunting other animals—as well as the physical apparatus that made such behavior possible. God changed the creation because of the sin of Adam.

How does God Himself respond to the sin of mankind? We must understand that He is pure and selfless love at all times. But He is also perfect justice. To set our attitude in this matter I want to recall an incident in the life of David. In 2 Samuel 12, Nathan is sent to David to rebuke him for his sin with Bathsheba. David had committed adultery with her and gotten her pregnant, then had killed her husband Uriah as part of his attempt to cover it up. Nathan spoke to David for God:

> "It is I who anointed you king over Israel, and it is I who delivered you from the hand of Saul. I also gave you your master's house and your master's wives into your care, and I gave you the house of Israel and Judah; and if *that had been* too little, I would have added to you many more things like these! Why have you despised the word of the LORD by doing evil in His sight? You have struck down Uriah the Hittite with the sword, have taken his wife to be your wife, and have killed him with the sword of the sons of Ammon. Now therefore, the sword shall never depart from your house, because you have despised Me and have taken the wife of Uriah the Hittite to be your wife." Thus says the LORD, "Behold, I will raise up evil against you from your own household; I will even take your wives before your eyes and give *them* to your companion, and he will lie with your wives in broad daylight. Indeed you did it secretly, but I will do this thing before all Israel, and under the sun." (2 Samuel 12:7–12)

This was extremely serious. The consequences of David's sin were far-reaching and very tragic. This was the justice of God. But the passage goes on:

> Then David said to Nathan, "I have sinned against the LORD." And Nathan said to David, "The LORD also has taken away your sin; you shall not die. However, because by this deed you have given occasion to the enemies of the LORD to blaspheme, the child also that is born to you shall surely die." (2 Samuel 12:13–14)

David acknowledged his sin, confessed it and repented of it, and the Lord forgave Him. That meant that the breach between God and David was healed and their relationship was restored. But the adverse consequences of his actions remained. The disorder that would afflict his household was the direct result of the shameful deeds that he had done, probably giving his sons a picture of life that scandalized them and carried into their own lives. The Lord allowed this disordered behavior to happen, not covering them with His righteousness, and publicly showing this to all. In addition, because of the larger scandal to His own holy name, a scandal that gave occasion to His enemies to blaspheme, God also decreed that the child would not live.

Thus we see that God forgives, in that the eternal purpose that He had for the person when He created them is not lost—so the person is not eternally condemned—but there are inescapable consequences that must ensue because of the sin. Even though Adam and Eve hid from their full guilt and responsibility at first, God still did eventually bring them to repentance, and He did forgive them. But the consequences of what they had done were severe and far-reaching. They could not foresee them, and we today do not understand them all either. The curses were the inevitable result of the sin of Adam.

In levying the curses, the Lord explained to them, in germinal form, the consequences that had to follow as a result of what they had done. The far-reaching consequences of their sin explain why we today cannot even imagine what life was like at the beginning. God is merciful and God is also just, never compromising the majesty of His law.

Therefore, as we look at these curses we must not read back into them the motives by which we in our sinful natures might be guided. The Lord our God is pure, selfless, self-sacrificing love. He is also perfect justice. He is never vindictive, He never loses His patience, and He never becomes irritable or short with His creatures. Now He was going to fulfill His word to Adam—the word that He had spoken to Him when He gave him the commandment—and Adam and Eve would have to die. This was not vindictive on His part. This was the most gracious and loving way that He could have dealt with them after the tragedy that they had enacted. The curses are utterly just and necessary.

The first curse was directed at the one who was the deceiver and instigator of the sin. It pinpoints the serpent, or rather the Devil who used him, as the root cause of the tragedy.
> Perhaps, however, someone may say: if the devil worked through the serpent to deliver his advice, why was such punishment inflicted on that reptile? This happened as an example of God's loving kindness beyond all telling: just as a loving father punishes the man who killed his own son, and destroys the sword and dagger by which he committed the murder, smashing them into many pieces, in just the same way the good God, too, sentenced this creature to an eternal punishment, when like some sword, he served the purpose of the devil's villainy so that we might reason from this evident and visible punishment to the depths of dishonor in which the devil also found himself. After all, if this creature who played the part of an instrument suffered such frustration, what kind of punishment is it likely that the devil received?[645]

Jesus said that eternal fire was not made for man but for the wicked angels. "Depart from me accursed ones, into the eternal fire which has been prepared for the Devil and his angels" (Matthew 25:41). That judgment was not yet visible to men, so for the time the serpent's punishment would serve as a sign and reminder of what was yet to come.

The serpent would henceforth be without legs, cursed to crawl on the ground (3:14–15). God established that visible punishment for the serpent because His eternal judgment on Satan was waiting until the end of the age. In the meantime the visible change in the serpent was a sign to all of His judicial decision. The Lord God also established enmity between the serpent's seed and the seed of the woman. This means that the serpent will have progeny of his own on earth, those who continue to be deceived by him and follow in his ways. But God also spoke of "the seed of the woman," who would stand in enmity to the seed of the serpent and who would crush the head of the serpent.

Therefore in this curse there is the promise of redemption. The serpent would bruise "the seed" on the heel, but the seed would crush the serpent's head. The crushing of the head indicates a total and definitive victory over the serpent and his seed. The "striking at his heel" that the serpent would inflict in return indicates a blow that would not be fatal.

The serpent had deceived her in this instance, so God decreed that in the end her offspring would conquer him and his seed (see Romans 16:20). In justice this was necessary in order to right her wrong. In this curse we see the divine intention to eventually correct this problem completely. This is merciful love and justice together. The initial divine promise of redemption, spoken at the moment when sin first entered the world, pinpoints the foundational nature of sin as deception by and subjection to the serpent. All other aspects of sin flow out of this basic reality. We are enslaved by the Devil.

The Nature of Salvation:
We have considered the nature of sin. Now we will consider the nature of the salvation that our Lord foretold to Adam and Eve, and that He has now brought to light.

First we must understand why God would ever decide to redeem mankind. Especially in the face of our hardness of heart and our refusal to acknowledge our sin and repent of it. It is only and exactly because of His unfathomable goodness and love.
> The Only-begotten Son and Word of the Unoriginate Father descended from the heavens to earth, and not only became man like them [Adam and Eve], but even was pleased to endure a violent and shameful death; then He descended into hell [where the souls were before Christ died for our sins], brought them up from there and restored them . . . And [then] what did He do? Behold how great is God's Love of mankind! . . . He did not bring them again into the same Paradise from which they had been banished, but He raised them up to the heaven of heavens; and when He sat down at the right hand of His God and Father, He sat them down together with Him. Just think what great honor He gave to Adam who by nature was His slave . . . See to what a height our Master Christ raised him up . . . O the ocean of Love for mankind which is beyond words, and mercy which cannot be traced out![646]

At its core salvation is the goodness and love of God. His goodness is manifested in the way He relates to human beings who are hardened in their fallen and sinful state. So how is the love and goodness of God displayed in His saving actions?

It is a common principle that the first time the Bible mentions something, because God is the author of what we are reading, it gives us the foundational insight into the matter. In the curse that our Lord directs toward the serpent, and therefore toward the Devil who used him, He says, "the Seed of the woman will crush your head." This indicates to us the foundational nature of the redemption that He was planning, and that He has now accomplished through His cross. It is a question of power and of ownership!

At its core, redemption is God, who is more powerful than Satan, ruining him, freeing us from his dominion, and restoring us to Himself—to the plan and purpose that He always had for us. The issue at the core of salvation is this: When we die, to whom do we belong? Do we belong to Satan, or to God? There is a mystery in what transpires at the moment when we die—when we finally pass from this life, which is the place of our preparation for eternity, into eternity itself. This moment is dramatized vividly in a delightful story by C. S. Lewis. This is an excerpt from *The Screwtape Letters* in which a senior tempter devil Screwtape writes to his understudy Wormwood after he has allowed his charge to die in the grace of the Lord God, thus losing him to hell forever.
> You have let a soul slip through your fingers. The howl of sharpened famine for that loss reechoes at this moment through all the levels of the Kingdom of Noise down to the very Throne [of hell] itself. It makes me mad to think of it. How well I know what happened at the instant when they snatched him from you! There was a sudden clearing of his eyes (was there not?) as he saw you for the first time, and recognized the part you had had in him and knew that you had it no longer. Just think (and let it be the beginning of your agony) what he felt at that moment; as if a scab had fallen from an old sore, as if he were emerging from a hideous, shell-like tetter, as if he shuffled off for good and all a defiled, wet, clinging garment. By Hell, it is misery enough to see them in their mortal days taking off dirtied and uncomfortable clothes and splashing in hot water and giving little grunts of pleasure—stretching their eased limbs! What, then of this final stripping, this complete cleansing?[647]

Thus as we shed our body we leave this place of preparation; we pull back the veil of this life, and confront the eternal realities of our existence. Then we see the issues that we have only known through the shadows. And, most importantly, we see Him.

> The more one thinks about it, the worse it becomes . . . As he saw you, he also saw Them. I know how it was . . . You reeled back dizzy and blinded, [you were] more hurt by them than he had ever been by bombs . . . He saw not only Them; he saw Him. This animal, this thing begotten in a bed, could look on Him. What is blinding, suffocating fire to you is now cool light to him, is clarity itself, and wears the form of a man . . . All the delight of sense or heart or intellect with which you could once have tempted him, even the delights of virtue itself, now seem to him in comparison but as the half-nauseous attractions of a raddled harlot would seem to a man who hears that his true beloved whom he has loved all his life and whom he had believed to be dead is alive and even now at his door. He is caught up into that world where pain and pleasure take on transfinite values and where all our arithmetic is dismayed. Once more, the inexplicable meets us. Next to the curse of useless tempters like yourself, the greatest curse upon us is the failure of our Intelligence Department. If we could only find out what He is really up to! Alas, alas, that knowledge, in itself so hateful and mawkish a thing, should yet be necessary for Power![648]

In the end redemption is God, by His power, snatching us from the dominion and control of one who is too strong for us. All who call on the name of the Lord will be saved, for His power is greater than that of our enemy—and He is faithful to receive all who come to Him. The dark and unyielding pride that besets us, the captivating power of sin that has its hold on us, is at its root a captivity of our minds and our wills to Satan. He owns us at a deep level of our being and we are incapable of breaking free by our own power.

The nature of sin is ultimately to be understood as slavery to a spiritual being that will never let go of us by his free will. He is captive to destructive hatred and bitterness, and he will only release us if he is compelled to do so. And the fundamental nature of salvation, at its root, is power from on high that the Devil cannot comprehend and that overcomes him and snatches us from his grasp. He only knows that he hates God and that he is utterly undone by the presence of his mortal enemy. He wants us to end up in exactly the same condition.

The lake of fire was not made for men, but for Satan and his demons (Matthew 25:41)—but those who belong to him, who are held captive by him, must share in his horrible fate because they are constitutionally opposed to God. This opposition is a dark, willful, continuous animosity toward and rejection of God.

A Reply to Origen on Universal Salvation:
In his work *The Principles* Origen discusses the nature of spiritual beings and shows that fallen angels were not created as evil, but that they truly did make a choice against the Lord God and thus fell into separation from Him. Because they are not evil from the fundamental nature of their creation but by a choice they made, he says that in the end all creatures, even Satan, will finally be restored to God. Of course he has been roundly opposed and condemned for taking this position, and rightly so. It is contrary to many Scriptures. But how did he ever fall into such an error? Here are the words of Origen as he argues for the eventual salvation of the Devil:

> The end of the world, then, and the final consummation, will take place when everyone shall be subjected to punishment for his sins; a time which God alone knows, when He will bestow on each one what he deserves. ***We think, indeed, that the goodness of God, through His Christ, may recall all His creatures to one end, even His enemies being conquered and subdued.*** For thus says holy Scripture, "The LORD said to My Lord, Sit Thou at My right hand, until I make Thine enemies Thy footstool." And if the meaning of the prophet's language here be less clear, we may ascertain it from the Apostle Paul, who speaks more openly, thus: "For Christ must reign until He has put all

> enemies under His feet." But if even that unreserved declaration of the apostle does not sufficiently inform us what is meant by "enemies being placed under His feet," listen to what he says in the following words, "For all things must be put under Him." What, then, is this "putting under" by which all things must be made subject to Christ? I am of the opinion that it is this very subjection by which we also wish to be subject to Him, by which the apostles also were subject, and all the saints who have been followers of Christ. For the name "subjection," by which we are subject to Christ, indicates that the salvation which proceeds from Him belongs to His subjects, agreeably to the declaration of David, "Shall not my soul be subject unto God? From Him cometh my salvation" (emphasis added).[649]

Of course Origen is completely correct in understanding the infinite goodness of God. And He surely does use even the evil one for the ultimate good of His chosen ones. It is from considering this that he concludes that in the end all creatures must be saved.

But he fails to understand the nature of sin, which is what we have been considering. Sin is the corruption of the intellect and the will of intelligent created beings that sets them against God and opposes them to Him. Sin results in a separation from God that is irrevocable in its final stages because the very wills of such beings are so corrupted that they refuse to change, and their intellect refuses to acknowledge the truth.

Thus the only way for God to save such beings would be for Him to take away their free will; that is, to unmake them; for love is, by its very nature, freely given and freely received. To take away the free will of one of His creatures would be to destroy them by undermining their basic created nature. Thus it is the irrevocable conclusion that those who become trapped in their rebellion against Him are eternally lost. They see the angels and the Lamb in His goodness (Revelation 14:10) and are tormented at their own loss, but they cannot and will not repent so as to join them in their glory.

This is all the more confusing, from our perspective, because in this life—which is by its nature a place of preparation for union with God in eternity—we never see the final state of one who has totally rejected God. We only see glimmers of what sin really is—only half-hearted efforts at the utterly irrevocable state of destruction into which the Devil and his angels have fallen, and into which men also fall if they are enslaved by him at death. In his ponderings Origen does not accurately consider or understand the nature of sin. That is why he fell into the error of believing in universal salvation.

God understood the awesome truth of eternal damnation before He chose to create the universe. He knew that, because of the nature of love—because of His holiness and His nature as pure selfless love—if He created beings that were truly in His image and likeness, beings that were fit and able by their nature to commune with Him, then they necessarily would have to possess the freedom and power to reject Him.

God knew that if his creatures made such a decision then He would have to allow them to make it; that is, He would necessarily have to respect their choice, even though the consequences would be their eternal and irrevocable separation from Him. That would be an infinitely miserable state for them to wind up in. But if they chose to accept Him and to enter into fellowship with Him, then they would be able to share in His divine life—the life of the Trinity—for all time. The stakes of creation could not be higher!

In His goodness and His wisdom God chose to create this world with its many intelligent creatures. He chose to offer the infinite grace of His life of joy and happiness to many others. This was the choice that our all-wise and perfectly good God made when He chose to create. He determined that the simpering self-pity of hell would not hold hostage the joy and glory of heaven. The destructive choice of the sinful lost would not be allowed to cancel out and prevent the splendor of the saved.

As God contemplated this choice He knew that He would have to bear in Himself the brunt of His decision; that He would carry the weight of joy for the saved and the weight of grief over the lost. The uncompromising reality of His compassion and lovingkindness is eternally expressed for all to see in the wounds of His beloved Son, Who shares with the Father in everything that He does and feels. Oh Lord, Your compassion and Your lovingkindness have been from everlasting (Psalm 25:6)!

God is definitely not unfeeling about this tragic situation. He has a heart like ours that understands most clearly the consequences of His decision to create. Thus He and His Son decided that Jesus would die for our sins on the cross. That selfless and self-sacrificing decision was made before they ever chose to create (1 Peter 1:19–21). God made every effort that was within His divine power to save us from that final awful fate. But creatures created with the potential to fellowship with Him and share His divine life must also have free wills. Even God cannot undo that truth, rooted as it is in His nature and in the nature of those made to His image and likeness.

The Fundamental Issue of Salvation:
The issue that underlies salvation is simple: when we die, do we belong to Jesus? If we belong to Jesus, then we will have a new human nature that loves God and is eager to enter into His eternal plans with Him. If we do not belong to Jesus, then we will still be in our sinful human nature. We will have irreconcilable issues with God. We will object to His creative decisions and to Him personally. We will not be able to find any place of peace, hope, or joy. We will not "fit in" anywhere. We will be left without a purpose and without a reason to exist. But we will exist.

Better for such people if they had never been born! They will blame God for creating them, since He knew that they would end up like this, but they will know inexorably that their fate is the result of a choice that they made and that they are still making.

The misery of existence with no hope of fulfillment! There will be exactly one just end for them, one fate that suits them perfectly, and that will be the lake of fire. The lake of fire is the logical and inevitable end that must fall upon such people because of several realities: the nature of God, the fact that they were created in His image and likeness to be with Him forever, the fact that they have freely and irrevocably rejected Him, the fact that by nature they must exist forever, and the fact that some just and right end must be accorded for them. It is the only arrangement that can be made for such people.

Perspectives on the Fall and the Promise of a Savior:
Adam and Eve did not have the perspective of centuries of history and biblical revelation. We understand that the seed of the woman is Jesus the promised redeemer. Adam and Eve did not understand this. They almost certainly thought that the woman God was talking about was Eve. Thus they hoped in a soon fulfillment of His promise of a release from the state of sorrow, suffering, and alienation they were experiencing.

When Eve gave birth to Cain she said, "with the help of the Lord I have brought forth a man child." She must have thought, or at least hoped, that Cain was the promised seed who would conquer the serpent. The word "Cain" is related to the word for "spear" indicating their hope that perhaps he would be the promised deliverer.

Adam and Eve did not understand the profound implications of the act of disobedience they had committed. They did not understand the doctrine of original sin, or the fact that the state they had fallen into would be passed on to the next generation of women and men. They could not foresee that all of human society would degenerate as a result of their sin because it would be passed on to all generations to come. They surely did not understand how difficult it would be for the seed to be born as a human being in the midst of a race of fallen and sinful people.

In order for the "seed" to redeem mankind it would have to not be subject to the diverse consequences of the fall. But those had been decreed to be passed on to the children of Adam and Eve, and would afflict all subsequent generations of human beings. At that time in the history of the human race, only the Lord God understood these truths.

The Far-Reaching Effects of the Fall:
Let us consider the effects of the fall in view of the unique nature of man as both body and soul made in the image and likeness of God. When man fell then the bridge in creation between the spiritual world and the physical world was corrupted. We tend to see this world as merely a physical reality, but from the beginning the creation was both spiritual and physical, a unified whole. Angels were also granted a role in creation, but subordinate to mankind. Satan could not execute his perverse deeds against our will. But when man fell we became subject to Satan and divine justice demanded that he be granted a foothold in the lives of mankind and in the broader creation as well.

Since man had been given the power to create new human life, this powerful channel, a key link between the spiritual and the physical realms, was polluted as well. The bodies of Adam and Eve were dead because of sin (Romans 8:10). Their dead bodies could not produce anything but more dead bodies. Their state of death would be passed on to their children. Thus Satan gained a foothold in the affairs and lives of all generations.

The pristine working of the creation was disjointed because the one who was placed as ruler over it was corrupted. God in wisdom and justice permitted Satan to exercise a foothold in creation, and it also came under bondage to him. God decreed this because as sinners we are prone to reject God and to take this world and this life as the final purpose and meaning of our existence. Mankind had to be deflected away from such self-deception. The promised redemption would not be implemented until the full effect of the fall was made clear to mankind. Then release would be granted to man and also to the creation (Romans 8:19–23). The curses that were spoken at this point by the Lord God were designed to offer man an initial explanation of what the fall meant.

The birthing of children would be much more painful (3:16) as a reminder that the channel between the spiritual and physical realms was polluted. New human life could no longer be born into this world in an innocent state. Adam and Eve did not yet understand this. Some have thought that the birthing of children as conceived by sexual intercourse was designed by the Lord as His way of producing the human race once the fall happened, and that if the fall had not happened then we would have produced new human beings in some other way. But the fact that He "increased" the pain associated with bearing children indicates that the plan for the woman to bear children had been in place before.

Thus sex was designed by the Lord God and is good because it was part of His original "very good" creation. It is not something that God implemented because of the fall. But we have become sinful, and now tend to pollute or misuse it. The idea that sex became the chosen way to create new human beings only after the fall is linked to the idea that Eden was in a spiritual plane and not on this earth, and that human life before the fall was like that of angels. I do not think that Adam's story upholds that idea.

The relationship between the woman and her husband was also distorted to "grasping vs domineering." She would long for him, but he would be inclined to exercise his authority over her in an overbearing way. The determination of her will would now be yielded to her husband, a more strict and grievous obedience than before when authority was more gracious. And she would no longer be submissive to him the way God planned in the beginning. This was because no human being could now function in a truly loving and gracious way. The loss of fellowship with the Lord God meant that human relationships were being used by desperate people to fill a void that only the Lord God could fill.

All human relationships today tend to be polluted by selfish motives. This is reflected in the marriage relationship most clearly because that is the place that most completely mirrors mankind's relationship with God. The twist in this central relationship within the family, the fundamental building block of society, radiates outward to cause problems in all human relationships and all of society. The redemption that is coming must redeem individual human beings first of all, then human relationships, and then all of civilization.

The ground that was so malleable when Adam tilled it previously would no longer be so. All labor would be a difficulty and a burden (3:17–19). Before he ate the best fruits, but now he would often have to eat plants like the animals! (compare Genesis 1:29,30 at the original creation, with Genesis 3:18, at the curse.) Man's dominion over the creation would be twisted. No good thing would be accomplished without a fight, and even then it would only be a mixed and partial blessing. Creation itself had been adversely affected by the fall and would also have to be redeemed; that is, the freeing of the creation would have to wait until the resurrection from the dead and the glorification of living believers. Until that time every good and spiritual work would inevitably involve spiritual warfare.

This was a direct result of the choice that Adam had made to disobey God (3:17). We see that it would never do for fallen and sinful men and women to preside over a world that was pristine and perfect. This was the perfect justice of God toward Adam, always reminding him, and also us his descendants, of the state that we are in because of the sin that separates us from Him, but not directly condemning us to eternal punishment, for God wants all men to be saved and to come to the knowledge of the truth. He made life on earth seriously flawed so that we would remember and long for Him, rather than easily falling into seeing this life as our ultimate purpose for living.

Most grievous, our relationship with God was damaged. And our relationships with each other became infested with sinful and carnal motivations.

The animal kingdom was estranged from man. Think how comforting a dog can be. A dog can actually help a person be more peaceful and less stressed. What would it have been like to have more friendly relations with other animals and birds? It is a comfort to experience our essential unity with the rest of the fleshly creatures that live with us on earth. Now we are alienated from them instead. In addition, creation itself was placed under the curse and began to disintegrate. When mankind fell then all of creation fell with us—the physical apparatus around us began to malfunction in various ways.

Finally, Adam and Eve had to die physically. The bodies of men and women, we now understand, are bastions of opposition to God. Thus we understand that we now live in a "body of sin" (Romans 6:6) and a "body of death" (Romans 8:23). Therefore, our body is condemned to eventually wear out, stop working, and return to the dust from which it was made (3:19). Therefore, "it is appointed for men to die once" (Hebrews 9:27). This inevitable future is the strongest possible motivation to long for God and His eternal life.

This was not the way that God had originally designed things to work, but the original pattern of life that God had designed for human beings on earth was no longer feasible, for mankind could no longer ascend up to God when their time of preparation on earth was completed, as had been the plan. This was not possible with our "bodies of sin."

In order for mankind to attain unto the final state of union with God, the inner man would have to be reborn with a new life, and the sinful flesh would have to be disposed of in some way—or be transformed into a new and different kind of human body. We now understand that the redemption was to come many centuries in the future. This world was never intended to be a permanent residence for people. All of these facts imply that once we became sinners then we would have to die physically. Additionally it is no great blessing to stay in this sinful body and this frustrating world forever. (Philippians 1:23)

Also, God had to create the netherworld and Hades (or Sheol) where the souls of sinful men could reside when they died until the final judgment, since they could not come into His presence. When the Seed eventually came, those who had hoped in Him would be freed from that dim place and could finally enter the presence of God in heaven.

Life on earth became difficult and burdensome. While physical death was a frightening and unnatural thing, it was necessary, and it was better than living forever in our bodies of sin. Thus even that curse, as difficult as it was, reflected the faithfulness, mercy, and love of God and His ultimate desire to eventually bring us into His presence as His beloved children. But the path to that glorious end has become much more difficult.

Thus we see that the curses were divine pronouncements that set new parameters for the lives of men and women on earth in the ages to come. Life had to change radically in order to justly and mercifully deal with the situation that the man and woman had fallen into—a situation that they did not understand and that we still understand only feebly. The curses were just and merciful, loving and wise, and the best and necessary answer to our sin. God, Who implemented the physical and spiritual laws, changed them by His sovereign decree to the working of His purposes. What we see as immutable laws are a divine decree, a simple choice He made. The final purpose of God for man remained—to share in His Trinitarian life forever—but attaining it had become much more perilous.

An enemy had asserted itself against us and would not be disposed of until we had regained the position that he had removed from our reach. It was necessary for our earthly human life to be a battle against that enemy. Still, the Lord God promised us victory, and in that promise He indicated both the nature of the struggle and the nature of our victory: enmity between the seed of the woman and the seed of the serpent—pain and hurt to the seed of the woman—death and ultimate loss for the serpent and his seed. Praise the Lord that the Seed will share His victory over the serpent with us for, "The God of peace will soon crush Satan under your feet" (Romans 16:20).

God's Special Concern for Women:

Adam was totally responsible for the fall, but what Eve did was reprehensible. When she first ate of the tree she had to have known something was wrong, but her first act, instead of warning her husband not to eat, was to persuade him to join her. It was the first time a woman exercised authority over a man—an abuse of the power of her role as helper (`ezer). Paul refers to this when he says:

> A woman must quietly receive instruction with entire submissiveness. But I do not allow a woman to teach or exercise authority over a man, but to remain quiet. For it was Adam who was first created, *and* then Eve. And *it was* not Adam *who* was deceived, but the woman being deceived, fell into transgression. (1 Timothy 2:11–14)

Man was in authority from the beginning because he was created first. But the normal was inverted. "Exercise authority" is one word *authenteō*, in the Greek. It means "to exercise authority on one's own account," "to domineer over," "to usurp authority," or just "to have dominion." It denotes one who acts on his or her own authority as an absolute master. "Quietly" and "Remain quiet" are *hēsychia* in the Greek. It is the description of one who stays at home doing his own work, not officiously meddling with the affairs of others. To attain and maintain order in the Church the original disordered use of authority must not be repeated. Jesus does not want the disorder that was introduced in the man-woman relationship at the time of the fall to be carried into the governance of His Church. This decree does not mean that women have no place of authority in the Church, for there are deaconesses and other positions of leadership that are appropriate. But we must maintain in the Church the properly exercised authority and submission that was part of the original very good creation before the fall, before sin distorted the man-woman relationship.

God does not want anyone to be under a dark cloud in heaven, so in grace He has granted women a special place in the redemption. It is His gracious empowerment that allows us to participate in His works, and He determined that a woman would make the key choice that allowed the Savior to become man. It has been a long tradition among Christians to honor women because of Mary. Women expressed love and faith toward Jesus more so than the Apostles, and they did not abandon Him at the crucifixion as the men did. Severus of Antioch notes the special role granted to women in the resurrection events and sees the kindness of God in these acts. They reverse the covetous glance of Eve in Eden.

> It was before the eyes of a woman which look perversely and are prone to the lapses of transgression, which from love of pleasure looked at the tree in Paradise of *the fruit of* which the law of God forbad *any man* to eat, that the angel who sat before the holy life-giving grave said, "Come *and* see the place in which the Lord was laid." Women, who brought about the fall for us, them he *now* commanded to *go at once and* announce the resurrection *of our Savior*. They who cast the *bitter* seeds of sorrow *and a curse* into the world, *they* first heard from him that had risen the word "Rejoice."[650]

This is the justice and the grace of God, making right the imbalance and the wrong that had been done, removing all shame from women, and restoring them to equal dignity with men. God grants all of His children the grace to be fully restored and placed in honor before Him.

Genesis 3:20—Now the man called his wife's name Eve [living or life], because she was the mother of all *the* living.

Adam gave his wife another name besides 'ishshah, or woman. That name had been given to her because she was "flesh of his flesh and bone of his bone" and thus was his wife, one flesh with him. The new name "Eve" indicated her unique place in the history of mankind as the one from whom all the living would come. She was not called "Eve" because she was his wife, but because she was to be the mother of all the living. The new name indicated her role in human history rather than her relationship to Adam. Her new name could only have been bestowed after children came along, so this section of Adam's account had to have been written a while after the creation.

Genesis 3:21—The LORD **God made garments of skin for Adam and his wife, and clothed them**.

The garments of skin were a covering for their nakedness and shame. They were much more effective than the fig leaves they had made for themselves. God did not want them to be ashamed, nor to be subject to their baser passions, which would distract them from the life of godliness. Adam and Eve were unable to clothe themselves adequately.

In order for God to clothe Adam and Eve with skins of animals, some animals would have to die. This was the first sacrifice for sin in human history. The result of the sacrifice was to provide Adam and Eve with a covering for their nakedness and to help restrain their sinfulness. It is likely that the Lord God taught them sacrificial offering as a way of being acceptable to Him and approaching Him in a limited fashion. He taught them this at the same time that He taught them about clothing. God did not just make garments for them, He actually clothed them. This is more intimate, like a parent putting winter leggings on a child before sending them out in the cold. In every way God provided a covering for them.

This first sacrifice for sin prefigures every sacrifice that the Bible enjoins upon us for sin, especially the one ultimate sacrifice that Jesus made when He died on the cross for our sins. The result of that sacrifice was to grant to us to be clothed in fine linen, clean and white, which is the righteous acts of saints (Revelation 19:8), and to give us a new nature that is not bound by sin. It causes us to be born again, and enables us to stand before Him on the great day of His judgment, rather than being ashamed at His coming (1 John 2:28). It means that, instead of shying away from Him like Adam and Eve did, we will look upon His face with love. We will be ready to enter into His presence forever.

The sacrifice of Jesus recreates us and gives us a new nature so that we are ready to accept the glorious predestined purpose for which God first made us. Thus clothing has become the biblical symbol for righteousness. Sacrifice always involves the death of an innocent and the shedding of its blood for us—a representation of the fact that whatever prepares the way for us to approach God can never be something that proceeds from our own selves, but must involve the death and shedding of the blood of another.

A provision was made for Adam and Eve first of all, but it also became an image of how successive generations of men and women could approach Him. It provided for their personal forgiveness and it also showed the way for all men and women to be forgiven and restored to Him as the generations wore on.

Notice that when God made garments for each of them—for Adam and for Eve—it was His divine choice on how to deal with concupiscence. He also "clothed them" which has a personal and more intimate signification to it. The Lord God still loved Adam and Eve and was carefully preparing them for their difficult life outside of the garden.

We might note here that only man needs clothing to survive. We would need it even if it were not for the purpose of decency. We could not survive in most earthly climates if we did not have clothes. They protect us from the cold and from the sun. But animals seem to have their own built-in clothing. They survive, and even thrive, with no additional coverings. God clothed Adam and Eve because He knew our bodies needed coverings.

Genesis 3:22—Then the LORD God said, "Behold, the man has become like one of Us, knowing good and evil; and now, he might stretch out his hand, and take also from the tree of life, and eat, and live forever"

Genesis 3:23—Therefore the LORD God sent him out from the garden of Eden, to cultivate the ground from which he was taken.

Genesis 3:24—So He drove the man out; and at the east of the garden of Eden He stationed the cherubim and the flaming sword which turned every direction to guard the way to the tree of life.

Here again we see a conversation that was happening within the Trinity, "The man has become like one of Us" (3:22). At this time the Lord God reflected on this sorrowful turn of events and let Adam know His thoughts. Adam then wrote this for us so that we might understand the mind of God on this most critical turning point in human history. A spirit of prophecy was granted to the men who wrote the Scriptures, to write the mind of God.

Adam and Eve had indeed come to know both good and evil, as the serpent had said, in accordance with the name of the tree from which they had eaten. But the kind of knowledge that they had gained was not what the Lord God had desired for them, for it was a kind of knowledge that subjugated them to evil rather than granting them a wise understanding of it and a mastery over it. In their fallen state, with the bodies of sin that they now inhabited, they could never come into the presence of God. This was the ultimate tragedy of their sin. The loss of Eden has grieved man throughout history.[651] [see note]

The Lord God said that we are to be "wise as serpents but innocent as doves" (Matthew 10:16). We are to be wise enough to understand evil and not be taken in by it, but innocent as far as any participation in it or tainting by it. We are to be wise and understanding about the light, and innocent and unknowledgeable about the darkness.

Unfortunately Adam and Eve were learning about evil by being immersed in it and by being overcome by it. So what the serpent had said was "true" in a certain way, but it was very deceptive. Our Lord wanted Adam and Eve to learn about the devil and his subtle stratagems from their encounter with him at the tree. He did not want them to be overcome by him and his evil. The tree was predestined to be the place and the issue of trial and testing for them. God wanted them to emerge as overcomers.

The angel sent by God with a sword assured that Adam and Eve could not live too long. Because the angel that blocked the way to the tree of life was situated at the east of Eden it seems that the man and the woman were banished to a place that was east of the garden. God blocked the way to the tree of life so that man could not eat of it and continue to live, restoring his body indefinitely and thereby postponing death. The course of life must be allowed to come to its natural and inevitable end (3:22–24).

The word for "forever" in verse 22 is `owlam, which can possibly mean "for a long time" as well as "forever." When Adam and Eve were in potentially immortal bodies, eating of this tree was appropriate. In mortal bodies it would extend their life contrary to the judgment of God—either forever or for a very long time. Death is a punishment for our sin, and thus it is not something over which God has allowed us to have power.

The tree of life was no longer in accord with His purposes for mankind, so God denied them access to it. In fact it was no longer possible for human beings to enter Paradise independently from God's plan for them. It was the initial plan of creation for human beings to dwell in that place, but now it was denied to them. The sword that turned in every direction makes me think of trying to walk where an airplane propeller is spinning rapidly. It would cut one to pieces.

God sent Adam out to till the ground from which he was taken. From the account that Adam gave of his creation, we read that the Lord God planted a garden "eastward" in Eden. Thus the actual location of his creation was west of the garden. Now he is being banished to the east of the garden. Thus the phrase, "the land from which he was taken" must not mean the exact physical location of his creation but merely the earth from which he had been formed, the less-luscious place outside of the area of the garden.

The beautiful and luscious state of the garden was unlike that of the ground from which Adam had been formed, and unlike the rest of the earth. The state of things where Adam had first been formed had been somewhat barren (2:5). He was formed "in the rough." That appearance resulted from the fact that in its initial created state the vegetation did not completely fill the earth. From now on Adam would have to dwell outside the area of the earth where things were fully developed. He would have to eat the "plants of the field" (3:18), which were formerly designated for the animals, and would have to expend effort to produce food to eat. This would cause him to "sweat" (3:19). Sweat was a sign of the fall and a direct result of it.

Sweat:
The word "sweat" is only used in three places in the Bible. Here is the first and defining place, where it is connected to the curse that resulted from the original sin of man. The second place is in Ezekiel 44:18, in the description of the garments that the priests shall wear when they sacrifice before the Lord God in the temple during the millennium. God commands that they not wear anything that makes them sweat. This is surely because He does not want any sign of the fall or the curse to be brought before Him when priests are offering a sacrifice to Him.

The third time that sweat is mentioned is in Luke 22:44, in the agony of Jesus in the garden. There Jesus is being shown the full extent of what would be required of Him in the coming sacrifice that He must make of Himself when He was to die for our sins and be made a curse for us. Yes, He was the "lamb foreordained," and He knew He had come to die for our sins. But the reality had to be presented to Him in His humanity, and He had to accept it as man. This preview of the reality of His sacrifice caused Him to sweat profusely, with the sweat falling to the ground like drops of blood in His agony. Thus "sweat" is only used in the Bible in conjunction with the curse due to sin, and the most dramatic instance of its use is in reference to the final price paid for sin.

The previous section of the narrative of Adam, which explained the fall of man for us, was probably written by him a while after the events that it describes, before the events with Cain and Able took place. I believe the Lord God was leading Adam to write these accounts for the sake of posterity. The Bible says:

> Knowing this first; that no prophecy of the scripture is of any private interpretation. For the prophecy came not in old time by the will of man: but holy men of God spake *as they were moved* by the Holy Ghost. (2 Peter 1:20–21, KJV)

Thus the Lord God moved holy men in ancient times to write the Bible. That is why we should assume that the Lord God was leading Adam to write each part of this account.

<u>Echoes of Eden in Society Today</u>:
The account of the fall reveals the failures of Adam and of Eve. Adam was created as the protector of Eden, and especially of Eve. He failed in that respect. Eve may also have acted without consulting him on this very important issue when she could have done so. Thus she also failed in her own way. Therefore Eve was deceived by the serpent and fell into sin. Adam was not deceived but was persuaded by Eve, and then he also fell into sin. Thus Eve usurped authority and Adam failed to exercise it. The whole human race has suffered.

The nature of man as created in the image and likeness of God implies that the husband is intended to exercise loving servant-hearted authority in the home, like the Father's authority in the Trinity (1 Corinthians 11:3). The woman is to respect and obey her husband. This is how Jesus relates to the Father. We are being prepared to share in God's divine life.

> Wives, *be subject* to your own husbands, as to the Lord. For the husband is the head of the wife, as Christ also is the head of the church . . . Husbands, love your wives, just as Christ also loved the church and gave Himself up for her . . . So husbands ought also to love their own wives as their own bodies. He who loves his own wife loves himself, for no one ever hated his own flesh, but nourishes and cherishes it, just as Christ also *does* the church . . . Each individual among you also is to love his own wife even as himself, and the wife must *see to it* that she respects her husband. (Ephesians 5:22–33)

The husband is to love his wife even as he loves himself, even sacrificing himself for her, for the two are one flesh (Ephesians 5:31). This is how Jesus loves His Church.

> Wives . . . [Let your adornment be] the hidden person of the heart, with the imperishable quality of a gentle and quiet spirit, which is precious in the sight of God . . . Husbands in the same way live with *your wives* in an understanding way, as with someone weaker, since she is a woman; and show her honor as a fellow heir of the grace of life, so that your prayers will not be hindered. (1 Peter 3:1–7)

Husbands be considerate of your wives. Remember they are co-heirs with you of eternal life. Even though they do not have the same power (the phrase "as with someone weaker" refers to the divinely ordered submission of wives in marriage), men must not use authority for their selfish advantage! That perversion, which was introduced by the fall, must not be allowed to continue. Wives, cultivate a quiet and gentle spirit with your husband, obeying in a sweet and loving way, not striving with him for control. Return to the respect and honor that was the norm before the fall, a spirit that is opposite to "usurping authority," and one that surely describes the way in which Jesus has obeyed the Father from before all ages.

> Older women likewise are to be reverent in their behavior, not malicious gossips nor enslaved to much wine, teaching what is good, so that they may encourage the young women to love their husbands, to love their children, *to be* sensible, pure, workers at home, kind, being subject to their own husbands, so that the word of God will not be dishonored. (Titus 2:3–5)

> Therefore, I want younger *widows* to get married, bear children, keep house, *and* give the enemy no occasion for reproach. (1 Timothy 5:14)

Women primarily work in the home caring for children and being subject to their husbands. Older women are to model this for young ladies and to teach them. This is the right witness to those around us in the world, and it gives no chance for the enemy to reproach us.

In our culture it is considered demeaning for a woman to actually obey her husband. People are suspicious of authority and characterize it as overbearing and heavy-handed. A woman's true fulfillment is said to be in a career outside of the home. If she cannot hold a position of authority then she is being oppressed. And ravishing, sexy looks are most highly prized. The present idea that "anything a man can do a woman should also do" is perverse. It creates a confusing picture of masculinity and femininity for children as they grow up. It is part of the chaos that develops in a society that has rejected God as creator (Romans 1:28–32). Clearly our society is in direct rebellion against God in how it thinks about men, women, authority, submission, and family. These disordered social ideals are also directly connected to the pervasive sexual sin that has flooded into our culture. They are echoes of the fall in Eden.

Life Outside of Eden:
Genesis 4:1—Now the man had relations with his wife Eve, and she conceived and gave birth to Cain, and she said, "I have gotten a man-child with *the help of* the LORD."

In looking at the immediate aftermath of the fall we have not assumed that Adam and Eve initially had the same centuries-long view of the curse and the promised redemption as we do today. The seed of the woman was to be a man, and the woman was almost certainly assumed to be Eve! When they conceived and Eve brought forth a man "with *the help of* the Lord" (4:1) they reasonably assumed, from their perspective and with the hope that they carried in their hearts, that Cain was the promised seed.

The meaning of the name "Cain" in Hebrew might not be utterly certain, but it is identical to the Hebrew word *qyn* or *qayin* which means "possession," and is related to the word for spear. This may mean that they named him in anticipation of, and in the hope that, he would be a powerful fighter—the one to crush the head of the serpent. If we follow up with this line of reasoning, then we must realize that Cain grew up with a tremendous burden of expectation placed on his shoulders. This was a lot to live with. Adam and Eve did not understand that their sinful state would be passed on to their children. They did not understand that the channels of reproduction had also been polluted by the fall.

Genesis 4:2—Again, she gave birth to his brother Abel. And Abel was a keeper of flocks, but Cain was a tiller of the ground.

Abel's name in Hebrew is *hebel* or *hehbel* ("breath"), similar to the Hebrew word *heh'vel* meaning "vanity," perhaps because life was already experienced as a burden by his parents, who must have pined over the loss of their beautiful garden and the joy of their intimacy with the Lord God. Life "under the sun" is "vanity" (Ecclesiastes 1:1–3), a sorrowful insight into the human condition after the fall. No one else could understand what they had lost. In fact, from the fall until this present time all people have been living subhuman lives, but most never realize that.

The two brothers each had their own skills as they grew up—Cain was a farmer and Abel kept flocks. We must realize, from subsequent verses, that Adam and Eve had other sons and daughters as well. Thus Cain and Abel might have had wives. From this account we do not know that Abel was the second child born, or even that Cain was the first. I will speak as if he was. Cain was probably the first son to be born because of the words of Eve at his birth and the implied fulfillment of hope that they expressed.

In listing their occupations—Abel kept flocks and Cain farmed—the younger is mentioned first. This may indicate that, although he was not the firstborn, he was first in virtue. If Adam and Eve recognized Able for such excellence it would have been a reason for strife with Cain and would have produced envy in him.

Genesis 4:3—So it came about in the course of time [lit., at the end of days] **that Cain brought an offering to the LORD of the fruit of the ground.**

Genesis 4:4—Abel, on his part also brought of the firstlings of his flock and of their fat portions. And the LORD had regard for Abel and for his offering;

Genesis 4:5—but for Cain and for his offering He had no regard. So Cain became very angry and his countenance fell.

Genesis 4:6—Then the LORD said to Cain, "Why are you angry? And why has your countenance fallen?

Genesis 4:7—If you do well, will not *your countenance* be lifted up [or: surely you will be accepted]**? And if you do not do well, sin is crouching at the door; and its desire is for you, but you must master it.**

The young men brought sacrifices to the Lord God, as they were no doubt instructed to do by Adam. This was performed "at the end of days" (the literal translation of "in the course of time"), which probably means on the seventh day—on the Sabbath day (4:3). Adam and Eve had been taught by the Lord God to offer a sacrifice that shed blood, for no man could approach the Lord God by any other means (Psalm 50:5).

But Cain instead brought some of the produce from his garden, while Abel brought the sacrificial animal (4:3–4). This is an example of, "acceptance with God via the works of our hands" vs., "acceptance with God via the shed blood of a sacrificial substitute." Hebrews 11:4 says, "By faith Abel offered to God a better sacrifice than Cain." This implies that Abel not only followed the prescribed form for sacrifice, but he also offered it with faith in God. It also implies that Cain did not offer his sacrifice with faith. Faith and obedience go together. Abel had both and his brother Cain had neither.

But there is more to what the brothers offered. Able brought the firstborn of his flock and fatty portions. This was the best that he could offer. Cain brought some of his produce, but it is not stated that it was the best of it—it was not the "first fruits" of the land. This implies a careless and presumptuous attitude on his part (recall Esau) as if he did not attribute all that he had and all of his prosperity to God. This reveals the lack of faith on his part. I think this, more than the materials that he sacrificed, is what grieved God.

God accepted Abel, but not Cain (4:5), for without faith it is impossible to please God. Still, God encouraged Cain. "If you do well, will you not be accepted?" This rejection of his sacrifice was certainly aimed at instructing Cain in the proper attitude of heart as he approached the Lord God. He was trying to instruct Cain, but a heart of envy and pride prevented Cain from hearing or understanding what the Lord God was saying to him. "My dear child, this is between you and Me. Abel has nothing to do with this matter."

Perhaps the older brother thought it was his necessary role as the "promised seed" to win acceptance with God, and thereby to earn some reprieve from Him for his parents, his siblings, and the whole world. Such an attitude would make a faithful approach to God impossible, for faith is, by its very nature, oriented toward the other person (in this case, the Lord God) and contains the hopeful expectation that they will respond graciously. It is not faith to approach others with the idea that we are performing the required duties and that they must receive us on that account. Cain felt that Abel was upstaging him.

When his hopes were thwarted Cain was devastated (4:5). I can picture him walking around with his head low, sad and weighed down with the sense of failure. It might be that such feelings had never before alighted on the firstborn from the womb. Weighty feelings like that are hard for anyone to bear, and Cain was not used to living under such a burden of condemnation. I am sure that the Devil was oppressing him and making the matter worse in his mind and heart. The Lord God saw what was happening to him and spoke to him to encourage him and point him in the right direction. He also warned him about his anger and the sin that was waiting to pounce on him (4:6–7).

This story shows us that the Lord continued to have contact with mankind even after the fall, and that He spoke to them. How could Cain have known that he was not accepted with the Lord—and how could Abel have known he was accepted—if the Lord was not communicating with people on a regular basis? This shows that as mankind descended more and more deeply into sin we continued to distance ourselves from the Lord ever more. But at this time men were still close enough to Him to have regular relationships with Him and to communicate with Him. Thus the Lord sought out Cain and spoke to him about the difficulty that he was experiencing. That sin of yours "longs for you" (4:7). It longs to overpower and to control you. It has a kind of perverse will of its own because within it is the same evil that was in the serpent. Our Lord repeatedly tried to help Cain through this difficult time in his life. But even the Lord God does not always get His way.

Think of times when the Lord has spoken to you about something serious and difficult in your life—how special it was and how powerfully it affected you. The Lord was very concerned about the trauma that Cain was experiencing. He did not allow him to stew in his sense of failure but went to him, foreseeing the tragedy that was looming. Cain did not understand the power of the spiritual forces that were brewing inside him. He had always wanted to be a good man, the one that everyone looked up to, the firstborn son. He felt the burden of "great expectations" upon him. And Abel stood personally in his way. Cain did not master the sin—the envy and sibling rivalry—that was crouching at the door.

Genesis 4:8—Cain told [or: spoke to] **Abel his brother. And it came about when they were in the field, that Cain rose up against Abel his brother and killed him.**

Cain did not listen, and instead was driven to murder his brother out of envy and pride— a picture instilled into human relationships of the sin of the one who had fallen from grace himself in the heavenlies, who was a murderer from the beginning (John 8:44), who had deceived mankind, and who now held them under his dominion. God spoke to Cain about his difficulty, but Cain never repented of his error. A sin left undealt with grows deeper and becomes darker. Think of the horror that Adam and Eve felt at the discovery of what had happened! They deeply loved Cain and considered him to be very special and precious.

Genesis 4:9—Then the LORD said to Cain, "Where is Abel your brother?" And he said, "I do not know. Am I my brother's keeper?"

Genesis 4:10—He said, "What have you done? The voice of your brother's blood is crying to Me from the ground.

Genesis 4:11—Now you are cursed from the ground, which has opened its mouth to receive your brother's blood from your hand.

Genesis 4:12—When you cultivate the ground, it will no longer yield its strength to you; you will be a vagrant and a wanderer on the earth.

Adam and Eve would have had no idea how to handle this situation. They were totally unequipped, so the Lord God stepped in and spoke to Cain. Here we see Cain denying any knowledge at all of what happened, an even worse response than Adam and Eve had given to the Lord after their sin. The Lord had to confront him with the facts directly, "The ground has opened its mouth to receive your brother's blood from your hand" (4:11). Hebrews 12:24 refers to, "the sprinkled blood [of Jesus], which speaks better than *the blood* of Abel." As Jesus was being crucified He said, "Father, forgive them, for they do not know what they are doing" (Luke 23:34). So when the Lord said, "The voice of your brother's blood is crying out to Me from the ground" we can assume that as Cain was killing Abel, his brother was calling out to the Lord for vengeance.

But the first thing God said to Cain was "Where is thy brother Abel?" He knew, but He was trying to solicit an admission of wrongdoing from Cain, to allow him to express remorse and to repent. But again, Cain was evasive with God. Like his mother and father when they sinned, he did not want to acknowledge his error openly.

The Lord judged Cain by removing from him the abundant produce that he had been taking from the ground. This was because that ground had been defiled with the blood of his brother Abel (4:11). But it also served to force him to acknowledge the One from Whom his abundance had come—something that was lacking in his sacrifice, and which grieved the Lord. Then God banished him to a life of wandering (4:12). This sentence took away from Cain the livelihood that had sustained him. It also distanced him from the rest of mankind. This might have been to protect others from his violent tendencies, or to protect him from their revenge.

Genesis 4:13—Cain said to the LORD, "My punishment is too great to bear!

Genesis 4:14—Behold, You have driven me this day from the face of the ground; and from Your face I will be hidden, and I will be a vagrant and a wanderer on the earth, and whoever finds me will kill me.

Cain understood that this would mean separation for him from his parents and from the Lord. But was his understanding accurate? Was not the Lord God seeking to call him to repentance? It is not clear from this verse that the Lord God banished Cain from His presence as well—or if Cain thought that, as a wanderer, he would no longer be able to return to sacrifice to the Lord and to commune with Him as before.

I say this because the entrance to Eden—where the cherubim were situated—might also have been the place of access to the Lord God, the place where people went to offer sacrifice to Him and to speak with Him. This sacrificial way of approaching God was not the way He designed it to be in the beginning, but for sinful and fallen man it was the best that could be arranged. The whole human race was being distanced from God.

Thus because Cain was compelled to leave the geographical area of Eden, he also might never again speak to the Lord God. One way or another, sin always separates us from the Lord. This was a further step away from God for Cain. All mankind was to follow in time. Cain was worried that others might kill him in retaliation for his deed, possibly a real concern, but I think Cain was deceived about God at this time. He probably thought God hated him and was taking revenge on him for his wrongdoing.

Genesis 4:15—So the LORD said to him, "Therefore whoever kills Cain, vengeance will be taken on him sevenfold." And the LORD appointed a sign for [or: put a mark on] **Cain, so that no one finding him would slay him.**

But God was solicitous of Cain and would not allow anyone to kill him in reprisal. At this time in history God had not established civil government to deal with evil committed by one person against another. Banishment was the solution that God chose, for He would not allow Cain to continue in fellowship with other men and women.

This statement from Cain shows that there were already many other sons and daughters born to Adam and Eve, and that they were outraged when they learned what Cain had done. But the population of the earth was still very small, and the best solution was to separate Cain from other men and women to prevent further bloodshed.

We are not told what sign or mark the Lord put on Cain, but it did dissuade other people from killing him by giving notice that whoever killed him would be avenged seven times over. This shows that the heart of mankind at that time could, under provocation, turn ugly and vindictive, and that it could only be controlled by the presence of a threat. God banished Cain to separate him from others, and marked him to protect him from others.

The Banishment of Cain:
Genesis 4:16—Then Cain went out from the presence of the LORD, and settled in the land of Nod [that is, wandering], **east of Eden.**

It is not clear how Cain made a living after his banishment. But when he left he took his wife along, and they were successful in starting a new life east of Eden—but separated by some distance from the rest of the human race, and also from the Lord God. It was said that God expelled Adam and Eve from the garden, implying something that was against their wishes. But here it is not stated that God expelled Cain or forced him to go away, despite his claims. It just says that Cain went out from the presence of the Lord.

Perhaps his pride was still in control, and his anger was against the Lord as well. He left of his own accord. Perhaps his grievous sin had caused him to accept a faulty understanding of what God and other people wanted from him. Cain was under heavy condemnation because of what he had done. Sin was distorting his thinking, and it was profoundly affecting his relationship with God and his very perception of God.

Cain never gives any indication that he dealt rightly with the situation that he was in. The understanding that he was now cut off from the face of God did not move him. The Lord God will forgive sin and iniquity, as He explained to Moses when He gave Him the law (Exodus 34:6), but Cain did not repent. He did not seem to realize the nature of his wrong, so he could truly repent of it. He had a kind of knowledge of evil in that he was immersed in it, but he did not understand its inevitable implications or see it in a way that allowed him to gain mastery over it. It was separating him from his family and from the Lord. Sin was reigning over him (Romans 5:14). It blinded him. He did not have the spiritual illumination he needed to understand his condition and to get extricated from it.

I am sure that Adam and Eve still loved Cain, and this incident must have been for them a sad and grievous awakening to the far-reaching implication of their own disobedience years before. For one thing it was clear that sin had been passed on to their children, perhaps in an even more virulent form, like a cancer that was growing. They also might have come to understand that the channel through which new human life entered the world was polluted, so how could it ever be cleansed of its defilement? How could the promised seed ever be born? Their children were just as guilty before God as the two of them were, and the next generation did not even understand their state before God.

The human race was descending into spiritual darkness. The redemption would not be accomplished as simply or as quickly as they had first hoped. It also might have led them to think about the naïve expectations they had levied upon Cain. Now they were essentially bereft of two of their sons and were left without hope of the promise.

This is the end of the third section that Adam wrote. I assume that God prompted him to write it soon after He had dealt with Cain.

The Civilization of Cain and his Descendants:
Genesis 4:17—Cain had relations with his wife and she conceived, and gave birth to Enoch; and he built a city, and called the name of the city Enoch, after the name of his son.

Genesis 4:18—Now to Enoch was born Irad, and Irad became the father of Mehujael, and Mehujael became the father of Methushael, and Methushael became the father of Lamech.

Genesis 4:19—Lamech took to himself two wives: the name of the one was Adah, and the name of the other, Zillah.

Genesis 4:20—Adah gave birth to Jabal; he was the father of those who dwell in tents and *have* livestock.

Genesis 4:21—His brother's name was Jubal; he was the father of all those who play the lyre and pipe.

Genesis 4:22—As for Zillah, she also gave birth to Tubal-cain, the forger of all implements of bronze and iron; and the sister of Tubal-cain was Naamah.

Genesis 4:23—Lamech said to his wives, "Adah and Zillah, listen to my voice, you wives of Lamech, give heed to my speech, for I have killed a man for wounding me; and a boy for striking me;

Genesis 4:24—If Cain is avenged sevenfold, then Lamech seventy-sevenfold.

This genealogy of Cain is given to us by Adam. This indicates that, despite the fact that his son had been banished, Adam kept in touch with him until he was very old. This must have been compiled by Adam as the years wore on. Adam still loved Cain.

The society of men and women during the early years of earth was quite different from the large and established civilization that we take for granted today. Still, the growth in population that must have taken place is astounding. I assume this fact as the direct result of the initial blessing that God gave to mankind when He told us to be fruitful, multiply, and fill the earth. I am going to assume that the result of that directive, and the blessing of God that accompanied it, was an initial surge of human birth that gradually tapered off over the centuries to the more normal levels of population growth.

If we assume that the human population grew at a rate of about 10% per year for the first century or so, then decreased to 5% and then to 3% in the following centuries, then the human population of the early years of mankind would look like this:

Years after Creation	Growth Rate	Population	
0		2	
50	10%	235	(The story of Cain about here?)
100	10%	27,561	
150	5%	316,951	
200	3%	1,389,513	
250	3%	6,091,624	
300	3%	26,705,683	

Of course we have no way of knowing the exact growth rates, but I am assuming that the blessing of God resulted in an initial growth spurt of some kind, which then tapered off; that is, His original command to "be fruitful and multiply and fill the earth" should have actually produced a population explosion at the beginning of the human race.

This indicates that well before Adam died the population of the earth could have been in the hundreds of millions. This is a direct result of the health and longevity of people at the beginning, which was the direct outcome of God's original directive to mankind.

As we look at the genealogy of Cain as recorded for us by Adam, we must realize that as he was compiling these records the population of the earth was exploding. After just a few hundred years large population groups of people would have been forming and Adam would have been witnessing the birth of culture and civilization. That seems to be what he was recording for us as he carefully kept tabs on his long-lost son Cain. The meanings of the names of the descendants of Cain are thought-provoking.

- Enoch or *Chanowk* means "dedicated" and is from the word *chanak* meaning to "train up, dedicate, or inaugurate." The descendants of Cain were making a new start apart from the rest of the family and apart from God.
- Irad or `Iyrad means "fleet" and is from the same word as `Arad or a wild ass. This is from an unused root meaning to "sequester itself" or "fugitive." The separation from man and from God was deeply felt as successive generations were born.
- Mehujael is *Měchuwya'el* meaning "smitten by God." This is from *machah* meaning "to blot out or to put out or destroy," and *"el"* meaning God. The people in this line felt the curse of Cain on them to the third and fourth generation (Exodus 34:7).

- Methusael or *Mĕthuwsha'el* means "who is of God;" that is, a man who is of God. This was the fourth or the fifth generation depending on whether or not you count Cain. This person's name indicates a turn in the spiritual tone. Perhaps with him the curse on Cain began to lift.
- Lamech or *Lemek* means "powerful." Lamech was the first recorded bigamist in history. Lamech was a man who was violent, misusing the tools of brass and iron that his son Tubalcain invented to slay people, and then threatening massive retaliation against anyone who tried to punish him in return.
- Adah or `*Adah* means "ornament."
- Zilla or *Tsillah* means "shade or shadow," perhaps related to the idea that life is of a transitory nature.
- Adah's first son was Jabal or *Yabal* meaning "stream, watercourse," similar to Jubal.
- Adah's second son was Jubal or *Yuwbal*, meaning "stream" or "moist country." Both names are derived from *yabal* which means "to bring, lead, carry, or conduct."
- Zillah's son was Tubalcain or *Tuwbal Qayin*, meaning "you will be brought of Cain."
- Zillah's daughter and the sister of Tubalcain was Naamah or *Na`amah*. Her name means "loveliness."

There is no clear indication that the Lord God was welcome within this social order or that the men and women descended from Cain sought Him or called out to Him. It seems to be a world of people with little mention of God in the picture—like American culture today.

This fourth section of Adam's narrative, as we have shown, extended into the later years of his life—probably until Adam was well over 800 years old.

The Beginning of the Patriarchal Line:
The fifth section of the history of Adam follows. This short section was written last of all, after the godly line of men had extended itself for many generations—probably to the time of Methuselah. I say this because the genealogy of Cain extended until the time of that patriarch. I assume Adam's account was written in the order that we have received it.

Genesis 4:25—Adam had relations with his wife again; and she gave birth to a son, and named him Seth, for, *she said*, "God has appointed me another offspring in place of Abel, for Cain killed him."

Noah explains that Seth was born when Adam was 130 years old. Thus the story of the two brothers Cain and Abel had to have taken place before then, very early in the history of mankind, yet after there were enough people around for Cain to fear for his life. I was estimating when I placed the story of Cain and Abel at about 50 years after the creation.

The name Seth or *Sheth* means "compensation" and comes from *shiyth* which means to put, set, or appoint. Eve saw the birth of Seth as compensation for Abel, but not for Cain. Adam and Eve gave birth to many sons and daughters, but as the subsequent narrative indicates, the general social trend was away from God. Thus not every one of the children of Adam and Eve were a replacement for Abel, whose deeds were righteous—which is why Cain murdered him (1 John 3:12). Cain's envy was probably because in his godliness Abel was displacing him from his presumed place of honor as the one who would stand before God for the whole family.

This statement about the birth of Seth indicates that he was the direct descendant of his parents Adam and Eve; that is, there were not many unmentioned generations between Seth and Adam. The same thing can be said of the description of the birth of Enosh as the direct descendant of Seth. In general, when the genealogies state that "so-and-so begat so-and-so" we should assume that direct sonship is intended. The idea that there might be many missing generations in the genealogies of Genesis is not reasonable.

As Adam and Eve brought forth their children they were looking for one who would carry on the godly line, because Abel had been marked for that and had been killed. Noah says that Seth was begotten in the image and the likeness of Adam (see 5:3). "Image and likeness" in that statement could mean that Seth also shared the spiritual perspective of Adam and Eve—the realization that life on earth was not what God had intended it to be, and that the only hope was the promised "seed of the woman" that God had predicted would come to crush the head of the serpent.

Therefore Seth was a man of faith and spiritual vision. It is likely that God specifically gave him to Eve as a divinely provided person to carry on the hope of the human race.

> [H]is mother in giving her son this name did so with thanks, attributing the birth of a son not to nature or to the process of birth but to the power of God. This it was [i.e., divine power], you see, that fertilized nature for giving birth . . . I mean, she spoke as if to say, He has raised up this child for me in place of the fallen one . . . Do you see the woman's gratitude? Do you see the Lord's loving kindness? How he envisaged speedy consolation for them? Let us all imitate this, and attribute everything to grace from on high. You see, even if nature takes its course, it does so, not by its own power but in response to the direction of the Creator.[652]

Referring to the growth chart we made we can see there would have been thousands of people on earth by the time Seth was born.

The fact that the birth of Seth is recorded after the genealogy of Cain indicates that Adam did not write the fifth and last section of his account until much later in his life. His decision to write about Seth was made late in his life. Adam did not keep a record of the genealogy of the godly line as he did for Cain and his line. This omission was not because they were unimportant but because they were keeping their own records. The genealogy of the godly line from creation to the Deluge is found in the account of Noah. Adam gives us additional supplemental family information, not the official genealogy.

Thus this omission by Adam indicates that the practice of the godly line of patriarchs from the earliest time was to keep records of their generations. Adam did not need to keep their family register because that task was understood to be the on-going duty of successive generations. In the account of Noah we will see the family register from Seth through Noah and his sons. But Adam does tell us enough that we can see the effects of the fall on the immediately following generations. His short statements give us an insight into the reaction of godly men and women to what had happened in the fall—a contrast to Cain and his line where no concern for the human condition is manifested.

Genesis 4:26—To Seth, to him also a son was born; and he called his name Enosh. Then *men* began to call upon the name of the LORD.

Seth had a son whom he named Enosh or *'enowsh* meaning "man or mankind," but especially "mortal man." The word comes from *'anash* meaning "incurable, desperate, or desperately wicked." The likely meaning of that name is "man frail and miserable." Recalling the name Abel (vanity), this name reflects the same insight into the sorrowful life of fallen mankind.

At this time men began to call on the Lord. All who call on the Lord will be saved, so this is a good thing to do. This probably indicates the beginning of religious services, where men came together to seek Him. Religious services arose out of the knowledge of the desperate situation that mankind was in. There was a growing realization among those of the "godly" line that the human race was in a place with no possible solution in sight. It was also true that as human culture developed, it turned away from God ever more, and He was not seen or heard from with the same regularity as in the beginning.

Religious services were not the way that man was supposed to relate to God in the beginning. Our life was supposed to be intertwined with the Lord God, and he intended to be involved in our daily individual, familial, and social lives in a regular on-going way. Religious services are an artificial way that we use now to turn to Him and to call upon Him from our sinful state. Life was supposed to develop on earth in a way, and according to a pattern, that included Him in every way. This was reflected in germinal form in the relationships that He had with Adam and Eve in the garden.

After the fall, fellowship with God continued in a modified form through the sacrifices that men brought to Him. The sacrifices allowed sinful men and women to approach Him because they prefigured the one perfect sacrifice that was to come, which would re-establish the broken bond between God and man. But as life progressed, and as society expanded, and as human civilization developed, men developed patterns of life that were not amenable to God. We grew away from Him and distanced ourselves from Him. Thus religious services became the way that people who knew their need for Him could turn to Him and invite Him into their sinful and broken lives.

> Not forsaking our own assembling together, as is the habit of some, but encouraging *one another*, and all the more as you see the day drawing near. (Hebrews 10:25)

Not only did human civilization not develop along the lines that God had intended from the beginning, but there was also satanic influence in it—the dark spiritual influence—that tended to direct mankind away from Him. We had an enemy, one who was too powerful and too clever for us. Mankind was in bondage to sin. This was because of our fallen nature and because of the enemy who now had a foothold in human life. Thus within the nested matrices of relationships at the familial and societal level, each fallen individual contributed his or her own personal measure of sin and guilt that gave growth to the ever-increasing gap between God and human beings.

At the same time that this reality was impressed on Seth, Enosh, and their descendants, Cain and his descendants were becoming numerous and building a city on earth. Adam never forgot about Cain, as his lengthy genealogy of his descendants indicates.

In his story of Cain's family (4:16–24) Adam records the many achievements they had, continuing to the seventh generation. With this short story we see the beginnings of human civilization apart from God. It was apart from God because they had no realization of what righteousness is—and God is a moral and righteous being. They were immersed in sin but could not or would not acknowledge that it was truly evil, that it was preventing them from entering into the purpose for which they had been created—communion with the Lord. The understanding of good and evil was distorted, and people were immersed in living in and for this world. This happened in the generations leading up to Lamech and his children. This shows us the first instances of human civilizations on this fallen earth. The cultures of these ancient peoples have been unearthed by archeologists.

Because the godly line was carefully recording its genealogy for posterity, Adam did not need to add his own writing on top of theirs. The absence of a full godly genealogy in the account of Adam is an indication that the godly line was aware of the need for records to be handed on to future generations. And they were keeping their own records. They were aware of this because the Lord God was leading them to keep these records.

The patriarchal genealogy is given by Noah in the next series of tablets. Noah received it from his ancestors and included it in his story. Thus when Adam and Eve saw that Seth was the divine provision to carry on the godly line, it was not necessary for Adam to record the genealogy of Seth and those who were born after him. Seth and his descendants were keeping the "official" family genealogical records. Nevertheless, the presence of Seth and Enosh in Adam's story and in Noah's serves to connect them—not as catch-lines might do, but by the fact that their content overlaps somewhat. Adam chose to write this last section very late in his life. Why do this? He wanted to include vital information about the generations that followed him that was not in the official genealogical record kept by the godly line of patriarchs. First, Seth—born 130 years after the creation—was a gift from God. Second, observations about the vanity of life and the decision to "call on the name of the Lord" were important insights on the human condition from the godly patriarchal line.

In Adam's story that we have just studied, we have seen from his early perspective the immediate descent of mankind into darkness and away from the Lord God after the fall. Adam did not understand the effect of the fall as clearly as Noah could many years later when it was more pronounced. The testimony of Noah given in the next tablet allows us to see the picture of the fall of man from about 700 years after Adam.

The Signature of Adam:
Genesis 5:1a—This is the book of the generations of Adam. In the day when God created man.

Here we see the signature of Adam indicating that he was the person who wrote these accounts. The inclusion of the word "book," which really means a "written record," is a testimony to the fact that writing was known and used at that early time in human history and civilization. The date attached to this set of writings is "in the day when God created man," or at the dawn of history. These records are the earliest accounts of what human beings and God did when the human race was just getting started.

All of the details of this account were readily available to Adam. And only he could know about and record what we have just read about the beginning of the human race, our fall from grace, and the subsequent disorders that befell mankind as a result of that disaster. The genealogy of Cain ends when Adam was a very old man, just before he died at the age of 930. If the age of Adam as recorded in this section were inflated and not really 930 years, as some have suggested, then the lengthy genealogy of Cain could not have been part of the personal story of Adam.

In every way; in the genealogy of Cain, in the marks of antiquity noticed by Dr. Wiseman, and in all of the details of this section of Genesis, we see a story that bears the marks of having been written at the beginning of human history by a man named Adam who lived to well over 800 years. Once the information in the patriarchal genealogy is taken into account, then the age of Adam, specified as 930 years, becomes most reasonable. This is a strong confirmation that the last line of Adam's account is indeed his signature line, written by that man when he completed his story late in his life.

We have just read the personal account of Adam, who was at the origin of the human race. Adam was privy to the events of the early details of the human race. God also revealed to him His thoughts and decisions as He patiently dealt with mankind throughout those events. Adam was God's chosen instrument to record for us the story of the beginning of the human race. Thus we must see Genesis as a testimony to the reality of God and to His direct actions within our world—not only in what it says, but in itself. This section of Genesis bears the marks of a document written by Adam, and because of that it can only be correctly understood within the Christian-biblical-supernatural world view. It could never have been written as the product of regular human social and religious movements. It had to have been produced in the way that we are describing. Thus it is reflective of the direct action of God, both in what it says and in what it is.

Adam's Account and the Account of Noah:
Adam wrote the last section of his account in his later years, after the genealogy of Cain had been written. Let us assume that he wrote the account of Seth and Enosh when he was about 850 years old. In that case the genealogy of the godly line of patriarchs was at the point where Methuselah was over 150 years old but Lamech was not yet born. The genealogy of the godly line included the following patriarchs who had already been born: Adam, Seth, Enosh, Kenan, Mahalalel, Jared, Enoch, and Methuselah.

Therefore, when Adam added his account of Seth and Enosh he was adding a section to the end of his account that overlapped the next account with two names, and he was adding that information at the same time that the genealogical record of the patriarchal line was being written by his descendants. The last part of his account and the earlier part of the genealogy of Noah were written at the same time.

What Adam wrote was not a "catch-line," because adding a catch-line is done by the person who writes the later account, to consciously connect it to a previous account. But the events within the two accounts are connected. When Noah received the patriarchal genealogy from his family a few generations later and added his personal story to complete his writing, then the two accounts reinforced and complimented each other.

The Importance of Adam's Story:
In Adam's story of origins we see the goodness of God. Look at the lovely way that He created us in the beginning! We see His power and His incomprehensible love for us. We understand His high and glorious purpose for mankind, and thus the reason He created us. Only in the totality of the biblical revelation can we understand this. Only in the biblical world view can we understand the blessed hope for which we were created.

Only in Adam's story of the creation of man can we understand the original state of mankind from which we have fallen. What was lost was known to Adam and Eve, but none of their children ever experienced what it was. If we completely forget the height from which we have fallen, then we can never imagine the hope to which we are called. And if we do not understand the original state of mankind as God planned it and created it, then we will never understand the state that we are in now.

We are so used to the mindset of bitterness, vindictiveness, fear, lust, covetousness, anger, and pride that we can forget the hope of glory God has for us. The story of how He created us and how we were at the beginning helps us understand why we are so tragically broken now. We have fallen from something that was the fulfillment of all of our hearts' desires. The emptiness that characterizes our human state—that has written the vain history of mankind throughout the ages—cannot be comprehended unless we accept the truth of how we began, what His plan was for us, and what we have lost.

Our entire view of reality is at stake in the way that we understand the earliest accounts in the book of Genesis. How we view the salvation that Jesus Christ won for us at such an enormous price is dependent on whether we believe Genesis, or we minimize its truth and thereby lose the fullness of it. What are at stake are the Ancient Faith, the entire Christian world view, and our connections to our origins and our purpose for existing.

If we depart from the historical truths expressed in Genesis, carefully preserved by God throughout the ages, then we lose this precious deposit of faith. The beliefs of those who would undermine the historicity of the Genesis account of creation and the fall by making the stories into a mythological tale derived from pagan legends and compiled at a later date greatly diminishes this truth in our minds and hearts. The competing claims of the secular scientific theories of origins can lead us to compromise and dilute the vital truths of our origins that were providentially preserved for us in the Genesis tablets and then compiled by Moses. How the Church responds to these challenges will either keep the Ancient Faith clear and whole or will weaken and blur the Christian doctrine of salvation.

This viewpoint affects how we think about the problems that we face in our daily lives—the personal problems as well as the societal problems. We must know that the various problems that we face, and that we have faced historically through the ages, are not the result of a wrong form of government, a poorly designed economic system, a lack of the necessary education, or the fact that men—rather than women—have been running this world. We can juggle all of these factors as much as we want, but the fact is, it is human nature itself that is the "problem." We are sinners, cut off from God, alienated from the One for Whom we were created—empty, lost, hurting, afraid, and without hope.

This is the solemn truth of our human condition. Juggling the governmental, economic, educational, or other systems of our lives will never restore what has been lost. The call of communism, feminism, nationalism, democracy, monarchy, intellectualism, science, and every possible human invention or "advancement" is just a siren call away from the basic reality in which we find ourselves—a reality that is testified to most eloquently and clearly by the story that Adam tells us about the foundational events of our race.

In this dark world there still remains one—and only one—ray of light; and one—and only one—hope for human beings. That hope and light is "the Seed of the woman." If God had judged that our situation was beyond hope, that it could not be overcome, He would have un-made us when we first sinned—indeed, in His prescience He would never have created us at all. But He knows that there is hope and glory waiting for us in His plan. That hope was firmly established before the foundation of the world when the Son, in loving obedience to His Father, agreed to be the Lamb who would be slain for our sins.

The difficult conditions that characterize human life on earth were never intended by the Lord God. The oppression that we commonly experience as a result of demonic forces that oppose us was never a part of His original very good creation. The alienation and sorrow that is such a common experience in our daily relationships was not His will.

That is not to imply that He did not foresee this situation arising. Of course He did. And it does not mean that He did not want it so that He prevented it. It was His permissive will that He allowed this to happen. But in His omnipotence and His omniscience He has a perfect plan that will be sovereignly fulfilled through the circumstances of human history, even through the darkest times; in fact, even because of those darkest times.

In all of these events we must remember the glory of God, His infinite goodness, grace, and love that is being manifested both to us who are being saved and to the holy angels in heaven, who long to peer into these matters. These dark events constitute the divine medium through which His creatures will perceive His true nature—His innermost heart of pure and selfless love. This is how He reveals Himself to us and brings us to Himself.

But the goodness of God is not self-centered, for it is His glory to give to His creatures. It is certain that He has joy and glory for us in and through this darkness. God chooses to share His divine life with us, making us partakers of His own nature, members of His very household. Every family in heaven and on earth takes its name, its innermost character, from Him (Ephesians 3:15). God is the author of family life. It proceeds directly from His nature as a Trinitarian being. He intends to share that with us for all eternity.

Yes, in all of these things He intends that we be more than conquerors through Him Who loved us. This is the message of hope for the world, and it only makes sense when it is situated squarely within the total Christian world view—when it is understood in the light of the stories of the creation of the world and of the first Adam. For in him all die, but in Christ are all made alive again. How can we appreciate what the second Adam has done for us unless we understand and accept what the first Adam did—and unless we understand and accept that we all are complicit with him in his disobedience, enslaved to sin, and in need of a savior?

Jesus is the Lamb foreknown before the foundation of the world (see 1 Peter 1:19–20). In speaking of Jesus as the "Lamb" God is referring to His sacrificial death for our sins. Thus before God chose to create He knew and prepared for the fall and all its consequences.

In His goodness He foreordained glory and final victory for His chosen people. Our Lord decreed that through the glorious cross of Jesus Christ, through the blood that He shed for us, and through His sacred wounds that plead for us without ceasing, we would come to know and experience personally the infinite lovingkindness of the One Who created us for His glory out of the unfathomable depths of His goodness and His love.

This is what God, to His eternal glory and praise, planned before the ages, before He ever chose to create us, and this is why He allowed the fall and its consequent darkness.

Noah

Here is the beginning and end of the text of the third set of tablets:

5 ² He created them male and female, and He blessed them and named them Man in the day when they were created. ³ When Adam had lived one hundred and thirty years, he became the father of *a son* in his own likeness, according to his image, and named him Seth. ⁴ Then the days of Adam after he became the father of Seth were eight hundred years, and he had *other* sons and daughters . . .

6 . . . ⁷ The LORD said, "I will blot out man whom I have created from the face of the land, from man to animals to creeping things and to birds of the sky; for I am sorry that I have made them." ⁸ But Noah found favor in the eyes of the LORD. ⁹ᵃ These are [*the records of*] the generations of Noah.

Archeological Considerations:

> Noah's tablet comprises 5:2–6:9 and commences with a genealogical register of the patriarchs connecting him with Adam. This list is followed by a statement concerning the corruption extant in his day, together with an explanation of the cause of it. "These are the origins of Noah." It is a small tablet of narrative writing added to a genealogical list.[653]

Connections to the First Two Tablets:

The existence of the catch-line "In the day when they [i.e., mankind] were created," connects this tablet with the second tablet. In explaining the origin of his name Noah shows that he also had Adam's tablet because as he explains the meaning of his name he refers to the curse that God placed on the land as a result of the fall, as described by Adam, "Now he called his name Noah, saying, 'This one will give us rest from our work and from the toil of our hands *arising* from the **ground which the LORD has cursed**'" (Genesis 5:29, referring to 3:17). Thus we know also from this statement that the tablets had been passed on to successive generations. These connections within Noah's account indicate that he was knowingly maintaining a cumulative record of human history by adding to what he had received from earlier generations. Noah received the genealogical list in 5:3–5:31 from Lamech, Methuselah, and his earlier ancestors. The task of maintaining the register was given to Seth and Enosh by Adam, and this was how it was passed down through successive generations to Noah.

> Several cuneiform tablets bearing some resemblance to this chapter have been found; they refer to ten men who "ruled before the Flood." Noah's tablet is simple and straightforward compared with these, and the ages given are not a tenth of those stated in the Babylonian tablets.[654]

The account of 5:32–6:9 is Noah's personal story of the corruption in his day—the demonically exacerbated societal disorders that erupted during the final 120 years before the Deluge. Because Noah lived for 350 years after the Flood he was able to help collect later records as well. Note these important insights by Wiseman:

> His [Noah's] sons, we are informed in Genesis, wrote the account of the Flood, while Shem wrote the genealogical list which now occupies chapter 10, as well as the brief description of the building of the Tower of Babel. Thus we see how Noah, possessing the tablets relating to the Flood, these, including his own [plus] Genesis 10 and the Tower of Babel, would naturally pass down to Abraham, with the genealogical tablet written by his father Terah. Thus to him were committed these ancient "oracles of God" (that is Genesis 1-11:27.)

> This does not by any means imply that copies were not made by other members of these families. There is every reason to believe that they were made. A scrutiny of the later copies of these copies, which excavators have dug up, however, reveal that they had become hopelessly corrupted very early by the introduction of dozens of contemporary gods into the Creation tablets, and a similar distortion befell the Flood tablets. **On the other hand, all scholars would recognize that the records preserved for us in Genesis are pure and free from all these corruptions.** (emphasis added)[655]

The continuity of the biblical record is attested by the "catch-lines" throughout:
> [We have seen] the archaeological evidence suggesting that the . . . series of tablets relating the story of the Fall was joined to [the] recording of the story of Creation . . . We have also seen the way that the sons of Noah joined their accounts of the Flood to their copy of Noah's tablet by a repetition of certain words, and [that] Shem connected his tablets with the previous tablets.[656]

Thus a unity of thought and purpose was maintained by the successive patriarchs, for each had the previous records before him and pointedly joined his own story to theirs.

Theological Considerations:

The Genealogy from Adam to Noah:

Genesis 5:3—When Adam had lived one hundred and thirty years, he became the father of *a son* in his own likeness, according to his image, and named him Seth.

Genesis 5:4—Then the days of Adam after he became the father of Seth were eight hundred years, and he had *other* sons and daughters.

Genesis 5:5—So all the days that Adam lived were nine hundred and thirty years, and he died.

Notice that the first generation after Adam in the patriarchal line, Adam's son Seth, is mentioned in a special way. It is said that, "Adam begot a son in his own likeness and according to his own image" (5:3). Adam was initially created in the image and likeness of God (1:26–27, 5:1). This statement indicates that a certain image was being passed along to successive generations. But since Adam was fallen, so his son was also fallen. This was one lesson that was distilled from the story of Adam. The fallen state was passed on to his children—and to all successive generations.

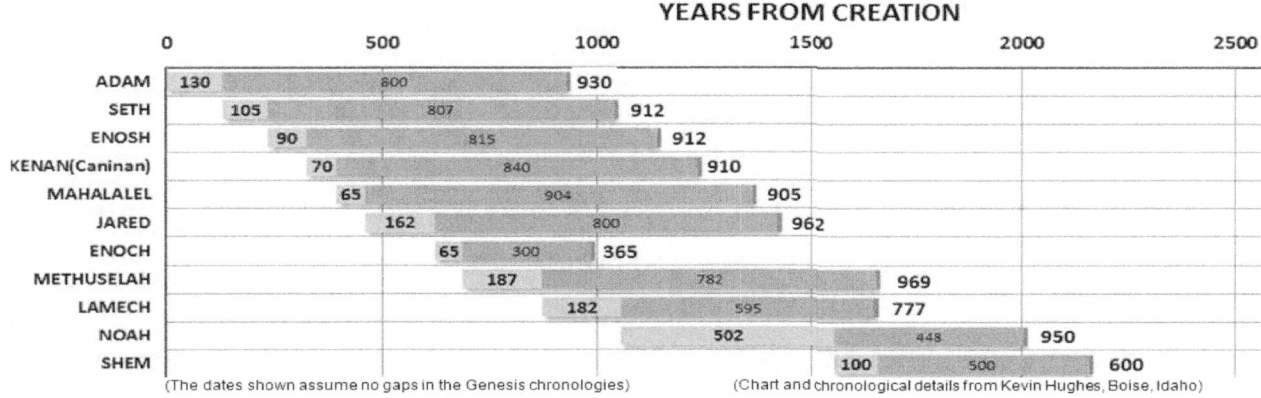

(The dates shown assume no gaps in the Genesis chronologies) (Chart and chronological details from Kevin Hughes, Boise, Idaho)

Genealogies are part of sacred Scripture and are worthy of careful consideration. The names often have significance beyond what we are accustomed to ascribing to them.
> [I]n these mere names a great wealth of thought lies hidden. That is to say, they reveal in this case not simply the piety of the parents but also the great concern they had for their children, and how from the very beginning they instructed the children born to them through the names they gave them to cling to virtue. They didn't give names casually and by chance, like people today, who say, the child is to be called after his grandfather or great grandfather. The ancients, on the contrary, didn't act that way; instead, they took great pains to give such names to their children as not merely led to virtue those receiving them but proved instructive in complete wisdom for everybody else and for later generations too.[657]

These meaningful names indicate that each patriarch was raised up by God, like Seth, and his parents knew and named him accordingly. God was carefully tending the godly line.

Genesis 5:6—Seth lived one hundred and five years, and became the father of Enosh.

Genesis 5:7—Then Seth lived eight hundred and seven years after he became the father of Enosh, and he had *other* sons and daughters.

Genesis 5:8—So all the days of Seth were nine hundred and twelve years, and he died.

Genesis 5:9—Enosh lived ninety years, and became the father of Kenan.

Genesis 5:10—Then Enosh lived eight hundred and fifteen years after he became the father of Kenan, and he had *other* sons and daughters.

Genesis 5:11—So all the days of Enosh were nine hundred and five years, and he died.

The name Kenan or *Qeynan* means "possession." It is related to a word *qen* that means "nest" (as fixed), as of a bird, sometimes containing the young; or "cell," as in Noah's ark.

The successive generations in this line of patriarchs are not necessarily the firstborn of their fathers, but those whom God raised up in each generation to carry on the godly line. Seth, the "appointed" one, had been a divine gift, as Eve noted, and they waited many years for him. The growth of the population of the earth resulted from the fact that people lived a long time and had many other children, as stated repeatedly in this register.

Genesis 5:12—Kenan lived seventy years, and became the father of Mahalalel.

Genesis 5:13—Then Kenan lived eight hundred and forty years after he became the father of Mahalalel, and he had *other* sons and daughters.

Genesis 5:14—So all the days of Kenan were nine hundred and ten years, and he died.

The name Mahalalel or *Mahalal'el* means "praise of God."

Genesis 5:15—Mahalalel lived sixty-five years, and became the father of Jared.

Genesis 5:16—Then Mahalalel lived eight hundred and thirty years after he became the father of Jared, and he had *other* sons and daughters.

Genesis 5:17—So all the days of Mahalalel were eight hundred and ninety-five years, and he died.

The name Jared or Yered means "descent." It comes from *yarad* meaning, "to come or go down, to decline, to descend, to sink." Was the human race declining or sinking morally into a quagmire? It would seem so from what Noah tells us about the people in his day.

Genesis 5:18—Jared lived one hundred and sixty-two years, and became the father of Enoch.

Genesis 5:19—Then Jared lived eight hundred years after he became the father of Enoch, and he had *other* sons and daughters.

Genesis 5:20—So all the days of Jared were nine hundred and sixty-two years, and he died.

The name Enoch or *Chanowk* means "dedicated." It comes from *chanak* which means, "to train, dedicate, or inaugurate." It really was a new beginning when he was born. Enoch was the seventh generation from Adam and was born at least a century after the sons of Cain's violent descendent Lamech.

Genesis 5:21—Enoch lived sixty-five years, and became the father of Methuselah.

Genesis 5:22—Enoch walked with God three hundred years after he became the father of Methuselah, and he had *other* sons and daughters.

Genesis 5:23—So all the days of Enoch were three hundred and sixty-five years.

Genesis 5:24—Enoch walked with God; and he was not, for God took him.

It is twice stated that, "Enoch walked with God." The first mention is after the birth of his son Methuselah when he walked with God for 300 years. He was taken by God, a sign that the original plan of God was still not dead in the midst of the extreme ungodliness of his day. Recall that it was the original plan of God that, after the preparation of a man or woman was completed, they would be taken by God into the heavens to dwell with Him in glory. Since the fall no human being had fulfilled that destiny. It might be that the birth of Methuselah was an important turning point in Enoch's life, turning him from the generation of wickedness in which he was immersed and to the Lord God.

> After having Methuselah, the text says, remember, "Enoch pleased God," and it was for no short period that he followed this virtuous way but, as the text tells us, he lasted two hundred years [note: the LXX differs from the Masoretic text by 100 years]. Since, after the fall of the first formed, a human being was found to ascend the very heights of virtue and to revoke the sin of our first parents through his own acceptable way of life, see the exceeding love of the good God. When he found someone capable of revoking Adam's sin, he showed through his very actions that it was not out of a desire to inflict death on our race for transgression of the command that he had condemned the person who had been given the command; he took him away during his lifetime to another place.[658]

The name of his son Methuselah or *Měthuwshelach* means most directly "man of the dart." It comes from *math* or *mat* meaning "man," especially a "man capable of combat." *Shelach* means a "sword, weapon, or dart" (sent against an enemy). Some interpreters translate his name as, "when he is dead it will be sent [i.e., the dart or missile will be sent]." It is true that the year that Methuselah died (at age 969) the Flood was sent upon the earth, for it came when Noah was 600 years old, and Noah was 369 years younger than his grandfather (i.e., 187+182). Perhaps his name reflected a prophetic insight that Enoch had from the Lord about the coming Deluge. Enoch is directly stated to have received a revelation of the second coming of our Lord.

> Enoch, *in* the seventh *generation* from Adam, prophesied, saying, "Behold, the Lord came with many thousands of His holy ones, to execute judgment upon all, and to convict all the ungodly of all their ungodly deeds which they have done in an ungodly way, and of all the harsh things which ungodly sinners have spoken against Him." (Jude 14–15)

Thus from the possible meaning of his son's name ("when he is dead it will be sent") we see that Enoch also might have received a prophetic message about the coming Deluge and then named his son as a divine warning to remain as a testimony after he left. Did Enoch realize that he was going to be taken and leave his son as a prophetic warning?

The second time it says that, "Enoch walked with God" is just before he was taken by God. This is commented on in the New Testament:

> By faith Enoch was taken up so that he would not see death; AND HE WAS NOT FOUND BECAUSE GOD TOOK HIM UP; for he obtained the witness that before his being taken up he was pleasing to God. (Hebrews 11:5)

Thus we see that he was a faithful man, walking with God in the midst of a generation of wicked people. Suppose that he did carry a direct warning about the coming judgment to his generation. It is sobering to note that almost no one listened to the testimony of Enoch. Only Noah was found righteous before God (7:1), and only he and his family were saved through the Deluge. But we should not miss the fact that the testimony of Enoch was underscored by the Lord God when He took him. This might not have had an effect on the general population of his day, but it must have had a profound effect on his great-grandson Noah who was a "preacher of righteousness" (2 Peter 2:5) in his generation, and who kept this fact for posterity. It might have strengthened his faith so that he was able to carry through and build the ark to save his family—and the entire human race.

The mercy of God in the midst of the wickedness was revealed in the taking of Enoch. He was hinting to the people of that time what His original plan for mankind had been, quietly reminding them of the glory that He had intended before the fall. The wages of sin is death (Romans 6:23), so Enoch must have been fully cleansed of sin to be thus blessed.

> Hence once again obscurely, so to say, and imperceptibly he wants the sentence he had passed on Adam to be revoked. But he doesn't make it obvious, so that fear may have the effect of bringing people to their senses. Consequently, he took away Enoch, who pleased him. If, however, someone were anxious to be meddlesome and ask, Where did he take him? Has he continued to live till the present? Let that person learn not to follow human reasoning or to pry into God's doings but to believe what is said. In other words, whenever God reveals anything, we shouldn't question what is said but rather treat with the highest regard the words spoken by God, even if they do not correspond to the things that lie before us plain to see. I mean, the fact that God took him away to another place Sacred Scripture has told us, as well as the fact that God took him during his lifetime without his having experienced death; rather, through the personal satisfaction he found in God's eyes he proved superior to the sentence passed on the race of human beings. But where he took him, or what kind of life he lives now, these further details were not given.[659]

Genesis 5:25—Methuselah lived one hundred and eighty-seven years, and became the father of Lamech.

Genesis 5:26—Methuselah lived seven hundred and eighty-two years after he became the father of Lamech, and he had *other* sons and daughters.

Genesis 5:27—So all the days of Methuselah were nine hundred and sixty-nine years, and he died.

The long life that Methuselah had, the longest recorded in the Bible, ended in the same year that the Flood came. His long life is a sign to us of the longsuffering and patience of God that granted the men and women of the pre-Flood times every chance to repent and to turn from their wickedness.

> The patience of God kept waiting in the days of Noah, during the construction of the ark, in which a few, that is, eight persons, were brought safely through *the* water. (1 Peter 3:20)

Jesus said "as it was in the days of Noah, so will it be in the days of the coming of the Son of Man" (Matthew 24:37). If you ever wonder why our society is allowed by God to continue in its present state of rebellion against Him, then this is an indication of how He responds to our human sinfulness. He is longsuffering and He is patient.

Genesis 5:28—Lamech lived one hundred and eighty-two years, and became the father of a son.

Genesis 5:29—Now he called his name Noah, saying, "This one will give us rest [lit., comfort us] from our work and from the toil of our hands *arising* from the ground which the LORD **has cursed."**

Genesis 5:30—Then Lamech lived five hundred and ninety-five years after he became the father of Noah, and he had *other* sons and daughters.

Genesis 5:31—So all the days of Lamech were seven hundred and seventy-seven years, and he died.

The name Noah or *Noach* means "rest" or "resting place." Noah did provide a place of safety and rest on the ark for both men and animals during the Deluge. The statement by his father Lamech (Lamech or *Lemek* means "powerful") about the name of Noah and his special destiny shows that men had the gift of prophecy from God during those days.

> See once again in the name of Lamech's newborn child the greatness of the mysteries, the extraordinary nature of the prophecy, and the good God's unspeakable love. I mean, when by his own prescience he foresees the future, and descries the increase in human beings' wickedness, he foretells by means of the child's name the evils that will come upon all the race of human beings, in the hope that, provided they respond to fear, come to their senses and eschew wickedness, they may choose virtue instead. See also the Lord's longsuffering, how long before the event he makes his prophecy so as to demonstrate his characteristic love and deprive of any excuse those destined to suffer the punishment.[660]

God will also be patient and longsuffering with mankind at the end of this age.

The Flood was a judgment on evil men. All the godly patriarchs from before the Flood who preceded Noah died before it came. So Noah did not need to take any of them on the ark. Only he and his immediate family went into the ark. It might have been a sign to Noah that the Deluge was immanent when his grandfather Methuselah died, based on the prophetic name given to him by his godly ancestor Enoch. But no one else heeded the sign.

The Corruption of Mankind on the Earth:

What follows is the testimony of Noah about the corruption of his day. This testimony explains to us why God had to bring the Flood upon the earth and destroy all men.

Genesis 5:32—Noah was five hundred years old, and Noah became the father of Shem, Ham, and Japheth.

Here is a good perspective on the spiritual forces at work in human society at the time of Noah. Evil catches up and ensnares societies. This is important because Jesus said, "For the coming of the Son of Man will be just like the days of Noah" (Matthew 24:37).

> Neither fear of punishment nor the extent of God's longsuffering won them away from their evil behavior; instead, once they had plunged into the abyss and had been blinded in their mind's eye, they no longer had the will to be rescued, immersed as they were in evil desire as if in some intoxication-just as some sage has said, "When the godless fall to the depths of evil, they lose all sense of respect." It is a terrible thing, you see, dearly beloved, a terrible thing to fall into the clutches of the devil. I mean, the soul then, as though caught in a net, and like a boar trapped in the mire, is likewise caught up in pleasure and, swept along by its evil habits, it loses all sense of the foul odor of its sins. Consequently, we must be awake and on our guard so as never to allow the evil demon any entrance at the outset, lest he cloud our reasoning, blind the sharp vision of our mind, and thus as if robbing us of sunlight render us unable to see the rays of the Sun of Justice and cause us to fall into the abyss—something that befell those people at that time.[661]

Just as individuals become enslaved to sin, so any human society, once it plunges into a downward spiral away from God, cannot and will not stop its descent. It becomes insensitive to evil. That is why the only response that God can make is judgment. This is why people are so insensitive to the wickedness in which we have become ensnared as a society in our day, and why they are so immune to the message of the gospel.

Genesis 6:1—Now it came about, when men began to multiply on the face of the land, and daughters were born to them,

Genesis 6:2—that the sons of God saw that the daughters of men were beautiful; and they took wives for themselves, whomever they chose.

Genesis 6:3—Then the LORD said, "My Spirit shall not strive with [or rule in] man forever, because he also is flesh; nevertheless [or therefore] **his days shall be one hundred and twenty years."**

Genesis 6:4—The Nephilim were on the earth in those days, and also afterward, when the sons of God came into the daughters of men, and they bore *children* to them. Those were the mighty men who *were* of old, men of renown.

In just four verses Noah gives us a description of the conditions that prevailed in human society before the Deluge. This passage has been a source of consternation and debate among Bible commentators. Many see it as describing the intermarrying of the godly line of Seth [sons of God] with the daughters of Cain, and by that all of society was corrupted. The Bible exhorts us to "not be unequally yoked" with unbelievers, for that is a major factor in causing believers to stumble in their walk with the Lord God. Thus as the godly line of men—born of the patriarchs mentioned in the previous genealogy—saw the lovely women that there were among the descendants of Cain, then they were lured into marrying them. In this way the godly line was seduced and the entire antediluvian civilization lost its moral footing and became corrupt and filled with violence.

But the Hebrew word translated "sons of God" always denotes spiritual beings in the Old Testament. They (and Adam, Luke 3:38) are likely so called because they had no parents, but were directly created by God. Also, the Nephilim were "giants," as shown by other Scripture passages. So there is another way of viewing this passage. But before we look at that I want to show you an interpretation of this passage based on the JEPD Theory.

An Interpretation of the Nephilim from the Documentary Hypothesis:
I want to briefly summarize the thoughts of Fr. Most on this passage. These are taken from sources that are available in his on-line library in the sections entitled *Commentary on Genesis* and *Angels*. Here is a summary:

> [In Genesis 6:1–4] we read that the "sons of God" saw the daughters of men, became amorous, had children. The children were the *Nephilim*, which some translate as giants. Were the sons of God angels? Some of the early Fathers of the Church seem to have thought so. Thus St. Justin Martyr, around 150 A.D. in his Second Apology 2.5 wrote: "The angels transgressed this arrangement and were caught by love of women and begot children who are those that are called demons." **St. Justin clearly did not know about the principles of literary genre. In fact, those principles were not known until our own century. So he could make a mistake like this. Again, the lack of knowledge about genres led to these mistakes.** We still must ask: What really is the genre of that mysterious passage in Genesis 6? We need to look at the larger picture. The sacred writer wanted to show the steady decline of the human race until it became so wicked as to call for the deluge. As in the case of the creation account, where he used a story that may have been already in circulation, he found this strange tale. He did not *assert*

that it was historical—but it did serve well his purpose of painting the steady decline of the human race before the flood. (emphasis added) (*Angels*)

> [on Genesis 6:1–4] Many Fathers in the first 4 centuries thought angels had bodies, and so these lines meant real children of angels: St. Justin, Athenagoras, Clement of Alexandria, Tertullian, St. Irenaeus, St. Cyprian, St. Augustine . . . Then Julius Africanus proposed they were children of Seth. But today we consider it a fragment, within the mythic genre . . . which the inspired writer used, without *asserting* its truth, to show the decline of the race leading to the deluge. On Feb. 13, 1905, the Pontifical Biblical Commission said we may consider the possibility of implicit citations if there are solid reasons, and if it does not contradict the Church. Our case meets those standards. Cf. EB 160 and 181-86. (*Commentary on Genesis*)

Thus once again the use of "genre" is the vehicle by which the truth of this passage is diminished, and its meaning is not even considered. Some Fathers thought this passage was referring to intermarriage between the godly line and the line of Cain, and some saw it as describing the incursion of demonic possession into the human race, leading it into a debauchery that required a judgment on the scale of the universal Flood. But no father, indeed no commentator in the first sixteen centuries of the Church, ever hinted that this passage was anything other than a sober description of an actual historic event that they then tried to understand by analyzing the words of the text. In my opinion this application of an "implicit citation" does contradict the Church.

All that is left of this text, according to Fr. Most is the bland assertion that something happened before the Flood that caused a divine judgment. This is combined with his statement about the intention of the sacred writer—to show the moral decline of the human race, with no intention of saying what really happened—and so that writer chose this "strange tale" that was already floating around, as his vehicle for this assertion. This way of understanding the text before us is beyond credence. This cannot be how it was written! As for the Flood, was it even a universal worldwide flood that ensued? Fr. Most does not say but is reduced to considering to what extent the biblical account of the Flood was derived from other Middle Eastern flood stories (*Commentary on Genesis*).

At this point I want to quote in some detail from *Divino afflante Spiritu* by Pope Pius XII, extracting sections that encourage the application of ancient languages, archeology, history, philology, and other sciences to better understand the sacred writings. We are to seek first of all the literal meaning of the text, then the spiritual meaning if there is one to be found. We are to compare it with other texts, seek out the meaning of words, refer to the works of the Fathers with their uniquely inspired and penetrating insights, and thus explain difficult passages (e.g., the first chapters of Genesis) that eluded the Fathers. This we hope to do by taking on the actual mind and spirit of the biblical writers.

> Being thoroughly prepared by the knowledge of the ancient languages and by the aids afforded by the art of criticism, let the Catholic exegete undertake the task, of all those imposed on him the greatest, that namely of discovering and expounding the genuine meaning of the Sacred Books. In the performance of this task let the interpreters bear in mind that their foremost and greatest endeavor should be to discern and define clearly that sense of the biblical words which is called literal. Aided by the context and by comparison with similar passages, let them therefore by means of their knowledge of languages search out with all diligence the literal meaning of the words. (Paragraph 23)

> The commentators of the Sacred Letters . . . [w]ith special zeal should . . . apply themselves, not only to expounding exclusively these matters which belong to the historical, archaeological, philological and other auxiliary sciences . . . but, having duly referred to these . . . they should set forth in particular the theological doctrine in faith and morals of the individual books or texts. (Paragraph 24)

> Now Our Divine Savior Himself points out to us and teaches us this same sense [the spiritual sense of scripture] in the Holy Gospel; the Apostles also, following the example of the Master, profess it in their spoken and written words; the unchanging tradition of the Church approves it; and finally the most ancient usage of the liturgy proclaims it. (Paragraph 26)
>
> In the accomplishment of this task the Catholic exegete will find invaluable help in an assiduous study of those works, in which the Holy Fathers, the Doctors of the Church, and the renowned interpreters of past ages have explained the Sacred Books. For . . . they are distinguished by a certain subtle insight into heavenly things and by a marvelous keenness of intellect, which enables them to penetrate to the very innermost meaning of the divine word. (Paragraph 28)
>
> Moreover we may rightly and deservedly hope that our time also can contribute something towards the deeper and more accurate interpretation of Sacred Scripture. For not a few things, especially in matters pertaining to history, were scarcely at all or not fully explained by the commentators of past ages, since they lacked almost all the information which was needed for their clearer exposition. How difficult for the Fathers themselves, and indeed well-nigh unintelligible, were certain passages is shown, among other things, by the oft-repeated efforts of many of them to explain the first chapters of Genesis. (Paragraph 31)
>
> [To understand the ancient writers of the East we must] go back wholly in spirit to those remote centuries of the East and with the aid of history, archeology, ethnology, and other sciences, accurately determine what modes of writing, so to speak, the authors of that ancient period would be likely to use, and in fact did use. (Paragraph 35)

When Pope Pius XII wrote this it was not his intention that we should demolish the text of Scripture as Fr. Most has done. This was the farthest thing from his mind! We are to elucidate the text, not explain it away. We are to approach it, as the Fathers did, as if it is completely true and trustworthy, seeking the deeper meaning that places it within the overall context of all Scripture and within the context of the times in which it was written. In that way we seek to clarify the literal meaning of the text. Then we are to discern the spiritual meaning of the text, as appropriate. We are not to treat it as some kind of imaginative story-telling escapade. Such a dismissive approach to interpreting the holy Scriptures is contrary to the Ancient Faith of the Church.

Another Interpretation of the Nephilim in Genesis 6:1–4:

The following understanding of Genesis 6:1–4 (and 6:5–7) disagrees with many Bible expositors. The reasons for this are varied and diverse, but in some ways they are perhaps similar to the reasons why a few people in the early Church rejected the idea that Paradise (the Garden of Eden) was actually the beautiful physical place that is described in chapter 2; that is, that it actually had lovely trees and artesian wells and rivers with two special trees in it as well—the tree of life and the tree of the knowledge of good and evil. These things seemed to some people to be incredible when considered as actual physical realities, and so they assumed that the accounts were allegorical and were depicting certain spiritual realities, or that Paradise was not on this earth at all, but that it existed on a spiritual plane. This was because of certain basic ideas that they had about God, the spiritual realm, the moral realm, etc.

In like manner, the verses that we will be considering, if we understand them as I am about to do, will violate basic preconceptions that some people have about the nature of angels, the kind of body that they have, how they can or might interact with people, etc. But the interpretation I give of this passage is in my opinion the most deeply integrated into the total biblical revelation. In addition, it is the most reasonable way to interpret the passage once we understand that we are reading Noah's personal first-hand description of what happened in society in his day. Yet I acknowledge that it was a minority position in ancient times, and it still is today.

I am putting this interpretation forward because I think it is important to see and to understand. Here is the interpretation I propose: fallen angels took women as wives, had intercourse with them, and begat the Nephilim (giants). This transgression caused the judgment of the Deluge.

With the words of Pius XII clearly in mind, let us do a careful analysis of this passage of Genesis and see what interpretation it should have. First, I note that many ancient writers held to the view I am about to espouse, but Sulpicius Severus expresses it most clearly.

> At that time, when the human race was already flourishing, the angels, whose abode was in heaven, eagerly indulged their illicit appetites because they had been ensnared by the appearance of beautiful maidens. They relinquished their own natures and origins, abandoning the higher realms where they resided, and entered into mortal marriages. These angels, gradually spreading harmful morals, corrupted the human offspring, and from their intercourse, the giants are said to have been brought forth. The intermingling of two different natures produced monsters.[662 see note]

Second, let us set the genre of our passage. This is a personal historical account by Noah, describing the dark events that he saw around him before the Flood, conditions that were directly responsible for the judgment of the Deluge. Thus we can be sure it describes to us exactly what was happening in human society at that time. That situation was the key factor in the widespread wickedness of his day. This way of seeing the text, where we accept it as a truthful description of the past, was the approach of all the Fathers. If we see it as a personal, first-hand account, then the possibility that a later inspired author was recounting something mysterious in allegorical or parabolic speech is unlikely.

Now let us do a word study and a comparison with other Bible passages. The key term that is translated "sons of God" (Hebrew: *ben 'elohiym*) is used in several places in the Bible and always applies to angels or spiritual beings. Here are all of those passages:

> Now there was a day when the **sons of God** came to present themselves before the LORD, and Satan also came among them. (Job 1:6)

> Again there was a day when the **sons of God** came to present themselves before the LORD, and Satan also came among them to present himself before the LORD. (Job 2:1)

> When the morning stars sang together and all the **sons of God** shouted for joy. (Job 38:7)

The following passages use a similar phrase that also denotes angels or spiritual beings:

> Ascribe to the LORD, O **sons of the mighty** [lit., sons of God, Hebrew: *ben 'el*], Ascribe to the LORD glory and strength. (Psalm 29:1)

> For who in the skies is comparable to the LORD? Who among the **sons of the mighty** [lit., sons of God, Hebrew: *ben 'el*] is like the LORD. (Psalm 89:6)

> "Look! I see four men loosed *and* walking *about* in the midst of the fire without harm, and the appearance of the fourth is like a **son of *the* gods** [Aramaic: *bar 'elahh*]!" (Daniel 3:25)

In the New Testament the events of Genesis 6:1–4 are referred to in several places:

> For Christ also died for sins once for all, *the* just for *the* unjust, so that He might bring us to God, having been put to death in the flesh, but made alive in the spirit; in which [that is, in the spirit but not in His resurrection body yet. He had not yet risen.] also He went and made proclamation to the spirits *now* in prison, who once were disobedient, when the patience of God kept waiting in the days of Noah, during the construction of the ark, in which a few, that is, eight persons, were brought safely through *the* water. (1 Peter 3:18–20)

The word used in this passage for "spirits" usually applies to angelic beings when used in the plural. These were disobedient in the time of Noah and did not keep their proper domain when they chose to intermarry with human beings. The word "proclamation" is not the proclamation of the gospel but is rather a proclamation issued by a conquering king to establish his hegemony over those whom he has conquered. Jesus defeated all demonic powers and was making sure that they knew it. Thus, every knee shall bow to Him, whether on earth or, like these lost spirits, under the earth.

> God did not spare angels when they sinned, but cast them into hell [Greek: *tartarus*] and committed them to pits of darkness, reserved for judgment; and did not spare the ancient world, but preserved Noah, a preacher of righteousness, with seven others, when He brought a flood upon the world of the ungodly. (2 Peter 2:4–5)

Some fallen angels are still allowed to roam about and, like roaring lions, seek someone to devour (1 Peter 5:8). But others are chained in the abyss which in Greek thought was called *Tartarus* (translated as "hell"). According to the Greek way of thinking Tartarus is situated as far below the rest of Hades as that "place of the dead" is below the earth. In their minds it was seen to be the place where very wicked people were sent after death.

Because Peter uses the word "Tartarus" we know that it exists, but there are no human beings there. It is a deep pit where certain wicked angels are being imprisoned until it is time for their judgment. The ones that disobeyed at the time of the Flood, as the passage in Genesis 6 describes, are chained in that dark and horrible place waiting for the day of judgment. Thus they are prevented from interacting with humanity in any way today.

> And angels who did not keep their own domain, but abandoned their proper abode, He has kept in eternal bonds under darkness for the judgment of the great day. (Jude 6)

The term "domain" is the Greek work "*arche*" which is translated as "principality" in the seven other places that it is used in the New Testament (Romans 3:38, Ephesians 1:21, 3:10, 6:12, Colossians 1:16, 2:10, and Titus 3:1). They abandoned their angelic state.

The other key word in this passage, on which its interpretation must certainly depend, is the word *Nephilim.* Many versions of the Bible translate this as "giants," but the NASB transliterates it from the Hebrew word *něphiyl* as *Nephilim*. Further insight into the nature of the *Nephilim* as "giants" is afforded to us by a short comment in verse 4 "and also afterward" (6:4) that was probably inserted by Noah when he translated the antediluvian tablets several centuries after the Flood. I say "inserted later" because it is not stated as a prophecy, but as if it was an observed fact. This ancient passage directly concerned the Israelites at the time of the Exodus. Here is the account from Exodus that relates the situation of the Jews to this passage in Genesis:

> So they gave out to the sons of Israel a bad report of the land which they had spied out, saying, "The land through which we have gone in spying it out is a land that devours its inhabitants; and all the people whom we saw in it are men of *great* size. There also we saw the Nephilim (**the sons of Anak are part of the Nephilim**); and we became like grasshoppers in our own sight, and so we were in their sight." (emphasis mine) (Numbers 13:33)

This description from the spies as they returned from Canaan, and the terrified reaction of Israel at this report—so fearful that they could not enter into the promised land in that generation—shows that the *Nephilim* were truly of great stature. Here they are identified as the "sons of Anak" or the Anakim. There were other giants in the land of Canaan at that time, called by other names in Scripture. In speaking of the land of Moab,

> The Emim lived there formerly, a people as great, numerous, and tall as the Anakim. Like the Anakim, they are also regarded as Rephaim, but the Moabites call them Emim.
> (Deuteronomy 2:10–11)

And in speaking of the land of Ammon,

> It is also regarded as the land of the Rephaim, *for* Rephaim formerly lived in it, but the Ammonites call them Zamzummin, a people as great, numerous, and tall as the Anakim.
> (Deuteronomy 2:20–21)

These names are connected together in Genesis in the account of the battle campaign that Chedorlaomer waged against the kings of Sodom and Gomorrah.

> Twelve years they had served Chedorlaomer, but the thirteenth year they rebelled. In the fourteenth year Chedorlaomer and the kings that were with him, came and defeated the Rephaim in Ashteroth-karnaim and the Zuzim in Ham and the Emim in Shaveh-kiriathaim.
> (Genesis 14:4–5)

Because the war that Chedorlaomer waged was against the people of great stature (the "giants") and also against the kings of Sodom and Gomorrah at the same time, it might be that the giants were associated in some way with those wicked cities.

The Hebrew word *nĕphiyl* is translated as "giants or bullies or tyrants" in Strong's, and in Gesenius' Hebrew-Chaldee Lexicon it says,
> Giants, Genesis 6:4, Numbers 13:33. I prefer the Hebrew interpreters who say it means falling on, attacking. Those who use it to interpret the fall of angels were accustomed to render it as fallers, rebels, apostates.

The word derives from *naphal* meaning "to fall or to fall down" as in a violent death.

With that information and the passages that use the word before us, let us continue. All of these eruptions of "giants" were in the land of Canaan. This might have been like the pre-Flood days of Noah, with evil men mingling with fallen angels in a similar way. This can also guide us in understanding why the Lord God commanded Israel to completely eradicate the Canaanites and their civilization.[663] The same kind of demonic activity and the same associated sexual perversions were breaking out there as had been before the Flood. And the same intolerable situation had arisen, perhaps in a less widespread way, in which "fallen ones" were born—creatures that were constitutionally unable and unwilling to be in the presence of God—monsters that should never have existed at all.

This intolerable wickedness is why, when the Lord God spoke to Abraham about his descendants possessing the land, He said that it would be in the fourth generation after entering Egypt, at the time when the "iniquity of the Amorites was complete" (Genesis 15:16). Today the "sons of God" are locked up in the abyss until the end of the age when it will be time for them to be judged (Jude 6). Thus this cannot happen in our time.

The textual reasons for assuming this point of view are extensive, as we have seen, but there are also objections to understanding the passage as outlined. This interpretation issue is part of a broader consideration; that is, how we think about the spiritual realities. How can angels, which are "pure spirits," ever desire or participate in things having to do with corporeal bodies? Cyril of Alexandria explains this as he comments on how he understands the "sons of God," which cannot be angels according to his thinking.
> For my part, I would say, and indeed affirm, that all manner of disordered thinking would suit these beings, but to allow this as an explanation of this event would be to take things far beyond what is reasonable, and would, in my view, be quite out of place. For our aim is to be disposed to examine the truth of each thing that is written, and not at all to give undue consideration to the disorders of a horde of demons . . . Indeed, almost every passion that is in the world comes through . . . [the flesh], as was stated by the wise disciple with respect to "everything in the world, the lust of the flesh, the lust of the eyes, and the pride of life." The intense and powerful lusts of this kind easily entangle us, so that our minds become fixed upon wanting and doing the things of the flesh. There is no argument, however, that could induce us to desire those things outside the body which are contrary to nature.
>
> How then could it not amount to folly to say that spirits, which are distinct from and high above flesh, desire fleshly things? What manner of natural inclination could there be, or what kind of principle could provoke them to act as we ourselves most certainly do, that they should long after those things that arouse the passions . . . Moreover, it can seem that, together with these other things, they might even have a morbid craving for pleasures that are contrary to nature. However, when the divine Scripture speaks of how the sons of God came together with women, they brought forth those called *giants*, that is, extraordinary, wondrous beings, though they were rational humans nevertheless. What then ought one to think with regard to this? It was not, in fact, through spirits separated from flesh that the conception of humans in the women came about. Yet some do speak rashly about the matter and misrepresent it, and by means of what they imagine to be persuasive arguments they erroneously make it mean what is impossible. For they say that the evil demons

> came into men and brought about conception through them. But we shall find their opinion to be extremely incongruous and full of ignorance. For how is that we should accept what the divine Scripture has not stated and reckon it as being among those things that are true?[664]

In this way Cyril dismisses even the possibility that the phrase the "sons of God" might be referring to fallen angelic beings.

Yet we have seen that the pre-incarnate Christ was in a human form, and according to certain visions many angels appeared and interacted with human beings in that form. (Daniel 10:18, 12:5-7 and many passages in Revelation, the annunciation to Mary, etc.) We know God did not create all spiritual beings in the human form (Revelation 4:6–8). But if we understand the Genesis accounts as first-hand personal records, then they are telling us that some angels interact with humans, appearing to us in the human form.

When it comes to specifically sexual interaction people also raise an objection based on what Jesus said about the state of those human beings who attain unto the resurrection.
> For in the resurrection they neither marry nor are given in marriage, but are like angels in heaven. (Matthew 22:30)

This has indicated to some that angels cannot have sex. But we have seen that human gender has an eternal purpose to it that transcends earthly reproductive functions—for it will be a gateway into intimacy with the Lord God. In the resurrection mankind will not cease to be a sexual being, for this is an essential facet of our humanity as created in the beginning. Thus the relationship that resurrected saints have, and that angels have, with God satisfies something within us that is related to sexuality. It touches something at the core of our being, and at the core of angelic natures, at which sexuality only hints. Both angels and men have the same basic need for the fulfillment that can only come to us through a direct intimate relationship with the Lord God. Sex touches upon this area.

Therefore, we can see the quotation of Jesus not as contradicting this view but as actually enhancing it. Here is why: Some of the fallen angels who had lost their fellowship with Him and were denied that satisfaction involved themselves with human women in order to fill their emptiness. It is not that they were created as sexual beings, but that they sought out something similar—but which was contrary to their created nature. In so doing they left their "first estate" or their "own domain." They saw the channel between the spiritual and the physical realms that was established for creating new human life and used it to their own ends, and in the process created offspring that were not human but also not angelic. They were a monstrous mixture that stood outside of the creative intentions of the Lord God.

The offspring of these unions were gigantic in size, domineering and bullying, opposed to the Lord from their conception, and unable to please him. The term used to describe them was "*Nephilim*" which means "fallen ones." These were constitutionally unable and unwilling to fellowship with the Lord God, being formed in direct opposition to His plans and purposes. They truly were monsters. This was an intolerable situation for the Lord and brought about His plan to judge the world in a short time. "[Man's] days will be 120 years" (Genesis 6:3). The angels were never supposed to affect human life on earth by participating in our human relationships. This crossing of the created order was utterly perverse in itself. The sex that was a part of that transgression was totally disordered, as were the offspring that resulted from those unions.

There are further connections in Scripture when we understand the passage in the way I am suggesting. We have noted that the fallen angels that were involved in this demonic infestation are presently being kept in a deep pit called *tartarus*. They must stay there until the judgment of the great day. In the Book of Revelation a passage that has been difficult and obscure now becomes quite clear.

> Then the fifth angel sounded, and I saw a star from heaven which had fallen to the earth; and the key of the bottomless pit was given to him. He opened the bottomless pit, and smoke went up out of the pit, like the smoke of a great furnace; and the sun and the air were darkened by the smoke of the pit. Then out of the smoke came locusts upon the earth, and power was given them, as the scorpions of the earth have power. They were told not to hurt the grass of the earth, nor any green thing, nor any tree, but only the men who do not have the seal of God on their foreheads. And they were not permitted to kill anyone, but to torment for five months; and their torment was like the torment of a scorpion when it stings a man. And in those days men will seek death and will not find it; they will long to die, and death flees from them. The appearance of the locusts was like horses prepared for battle; and on their heads appeared to be crowns like gold, and their faces were like the faces of men. They had hair like the hair of women, and their teeth were like *the teeth* of lions. They had breastplates like breastplates of iron; and the sound of their wings was like the sound of chariots, of many horses rushing to battle. They have tails like scorpions, and stings; and in their tails is their power to hurt men for five months. They have as king over them, the angel of the abyss; his name in Hebrew is Abaddon, and in the Greek he has the name Apollyon. (Revelation 9:1–11)

John saw of the release of these pent-up demons at the end of this age in preparation for their judgment, as Jude said. This is part of the general judgment of all fallen angels that happens at that time. Thus our passage has far-reaching connections in Scripture.

How can we best understand the vision from John? I repeat a prior explanation.

> If there is a natural body, there is also a spiritual (*pneumatikos*) body. (1 Corinthians 15:44)

The sense of *pneumatikos* as it is used with "body" in this verse is this: "a body that is animated and controlled only by the rational soul and by means of which the rational life, or life of the spirit is lived." This explanation is from Thayer's Greek lexicon, and this is also the way that Augustine understood and explained this phrase. Spiritual bodies are not governed by physical laws such as gravity or electromagnetic forces, but by spiritual laws operating through the ones to whom the bodies belong. In the resurrection human beings will have spiritual bodies, as angels already have. The form of a spiritual body is determined by the one to whom it belongs. It is a reflection of their spiritual state.[665] People who are "born again" are being transformed from one degree of glory to another as they commune with the Lord God, and are predestined to be conformed to the image of Jesus Christ. The fallen ones in this vision have bodies with twisted hideously monstrous forms, a reflection of their perverse spiritual state.[666]

We noted that angels were made by God with their own role in the creation, perhaps to be understood as keepers of the divine order. The ones who transgressed as in our text were obviously angels that were concerned with the order of human society rather than the cosmic order. Their monstrous and hideous forms, as described by John in his vision centuries later, shows their twistedness due to their fall from grace.

In 1 Corinthians 11:2–16 Paul discusses order within the Church during worship. The basic point of that passage is to emphasize to the Corinthians—to remind them—of the created order that puts man in headship over the woman and Christ in headship over the man. Veils were a sign to the angels. Thus the angels must be watching us when we worship. Proper order during worship is important to the angels that are present, for they are observing redeemed women and men fulfill the destiny for which God originally created them. The manifold wisdom of God is being made known through the Church to the heavenly beings (Ephesians 3:10). This is an important aspect of worship and is one reason why head coverings are good for women to use.

On the other hand, it might grant a foothold to the fallen angels to allow women without head coverings, perhaps recalling the ugly event that is portrayed in our passage. I am not saying Genesis 6:1–4 provides us with the proper way to understand the phrase "because of the angels" (11:10), but I am claiming that proper societal order is important to angels when the people of God worship, and improper order in worship could incite the wicked angels, or offer them a foothold in people's lives. It could grieve the holy angels at the same time.

I see two reasons why 1 Corinthians 11:2–16 is difficult for us to understand today. We have deemphasized the importance and role of angels in the world and Church because we have not understood Genesis 6:1–4 correctly. When at last the book of Enoch was definitively rejected as canonical, then expositors assumed that Genesis 6:1–4 was no longer to be understood as referring to angels. Also we are in an age and in a culture that looks down upon the idea of the man exercising headship over his wife in marriage. Thus this passage seems opaque and obnoxious to us.

The general effect of the imprisonment of these particular demons in the deep pit called *tartarus* is to induce the other demons to keep their evil works within bounds. An insight into this truth can be seen in the story of the demons who infested the demoniac of the Gerasenes (Luke 8:26–39, Mark 5:1–20). They had greatly afflicted that sorry man and when Jesus was casting them out they begged Him not to send them into the abyss (Luke 8:31). The word for abyss (Greek: *abyssos*) is the same word used in Revelation 9 for the pit from which the demons are released by the one who was given the key.

The Gerasene demons did not want to go to that place of isolation and darkness—away from all life and with no company except other chained demons. The effect of confining the demons from before the Flood in a deep pit was to keep other wicked spiritual beings in line. When mankind fell Satan was granted a certain foothold and a certain place of testing in the affairs of mankind. The justice of God demanded this for a time in human history. But the demons that "left their first estate" and attempted to insert themselves into human history as participants in our affairs had crossed the line and exceeded their boundaries. They went beyond what divine justice had permitted to them.

The demons of the Gerasenes had also gone far in their abuse of that man and feared that they had also exceeded their boundaries. They begged Jesus not to banish them into that pit as well. This shows us one underlying reason why we do not see these extraordinary abuses happening on the earth today. The punishment of confinement in that pit was what put the fear into all the wicked spirits. Why do people believe the death penalty would not have a restraining effect on evil?

These many connections to this interpretation of Genesis 6:1–4 explain why I said it is the view that is "most fully integrated into the total biblical revelation." As noted, many will not accept what I am proposing because of various preconceptions about the spiritual realities. I am not criticizing such attitudes. I am just observing the reasons why people sometimes take the positions that they do on such "controversial" subjects. It is not always directly related to the Bible passage in question, but might stem from more far-flung reasons.

The interpretation of Genesis 6:1–4 that I offer also explains the observation recorded by Noah when he translated his account in his old age: "and also afterwards" (Genesis 6:4). It was at least three hundred years after the Flood when he wrote that simple warning. It was written because he saw the same phenomenon that was widespread before the Flood breaking out once again within the civilizations of the Canaanites. Israel had to face that situation when they attempted to enter the promised land at the time of the Exodus. God eventually dealt with it—locking up those demons in the bottomless pit of *tartarus*—stopping their perverse and disordered angelic interference in human affairs.

The earthly theater is for humans, and those demons had exceeded their divinely allotted place of influence in human history. Satan was permitted a certain prescribed foothold in human life for a season. After that period demons will be locked in the bottomless pit so that they can no longer deceive the nations (Revelation 20:1–3). This interpretation of Genesis 6:1–4 draws together all these diverse but interrelated passages, allowing us to construct the broader scenario into which they all fit cohesively.

Spiritual Application:
For the spiritual application of this passage we must look at the rest of what Noah says, which reveals to us the response of the Lord God to this situation as He explained it to Noah at that dark time in human history.

Genesis 6:5—Then the LORD saw that the wickedness of man was great on the earth, and that every intent of the thoughts of his heart was only evil continually.

Genesis 6:6—The LORD was sorry that He had made man on the earth, and He was grieved in His heart.

Genesis 6:7—The LORD said, "I will blot out man whom I have created from the face of the land, from man to animals to creeping things and to birds of the sky; for I am sorry that I have made them."

These verses reveal to us the relationship that Noah had with God. The Lord God was willing to speak to him directly at this time, and He communicated His mind to him. In the degradation of human society that was rampant, God spoke directly to Noah. He may not have come to him in person as He had done in Eden in the beginning, but He spoke to his chosen one to reveal His mind to him at this critical juncture in human history. So the person who was originally inspired at the time this account was written was Noah. A long time later, around nine hundred years later, God moved Moses to include Noah's account in the book of Genesis. That is what it means to say that God inspired the book of Genesis. That is how the inspiration happened historically. It was in two steps.

Again, the word *nĕphiyl* implies tyrannical behavior. So the giants were violent in their behavior and were bullies! We all know what it is like to have someone who is bigger than us attack us either physically or verbally. It is difficult to endure, and it distorts our relationships and undermines our self-worth. The *nĕphiyl* introduced a more violent and vicious tone into human life. They did great and daring exploits, but they lorded it over others. Human society became vicious and violent. This was in addition to the sexual disorder and perversion that the angels brought into society. Jude follows his statement about the angels that were imprisoned for this perverted activity, saying,
> Sodom and Gomorrah and the cities around them, since they in the same way as these [the wicked angels] indulged in gross immorality and went after strange flesh, are exhibited as an example in undergoing the punishment of eternal fire. (Jude 7)

This clearly shows that sexual perversion was part of the twisted social disorder that the angels brought with them. Peter speaks of Noah and the "angels that sinned" and follows with:
> He condemned the cities of Sodom and Gomorrah to destruction by reducing *them* to ashes, having made them an example to those who would live ungodly *lives* thereafter. (2 Peter 2:6)

Thus he also associates the situation in Genesis 6:1–4 with the perversion of Sodom. The connection that we noted in the war of Chedorlaomer between the giants, which were the offspring of sexual disorder, and the two wicked cities is confirmed by these passages.

Jesus also connects the time of Noah before the Flood with the time of Lot in Sodom, and both of those times with His second coming.
> And just as it happened in the days of Noah, so it will be also in the days of the Son of Man: they were eating, they were drinking, they were marrying, they were being given in marriage, until the day that Noah entered the ark, and the flood came and destroyed them all. It was the same as happened in the days of Lot: they were eating, they were drinking, they were buying, they were selling, they were planting, they were building; but on the day that Lot went out from Sodom it rained fire and brimstone from heaven and destroyed them all. It will be just the same on the day that the Son of Man is revealed. (Luke 17:26–30)

Thus the conclusion is inescapable: There was rampant sexual disorder in the times before the Flood—disorder of a kind that crossed the boundary into something that was against the natural. And unnatural sexual disorder was present in Sodom at the time of Lot. The same kind of thing will be present in society just before His return. In the two past instances the social perversions were suddenly terminated by an act of judgment from God that the wicked did not foresee. The second coming will fall upon the wicked at the end of this age in the same sudden and unexpected way. Only those who waited on God and feared Him were delivered from the stroke of divine judgment that fell in the time of Noah and the time of Lot—and that is just the way it will be at the end of this age.

If we look around us today, the situation that has developed in western culture over the past thirty or forty years is very similar to what is described in the historical cases that Jesus referred to. In the last few decades sexual disorders, including unnatural sexual expressions, have exploded into our society. Violence has increased dramatically, both on an international scale and in local areas. Murder and other violent crimes, public indecency, scandalous activities of various kinds—all have become common place. At the same time people are leaving their religious duties and falling away from God, and many atheistic and idolatrous ideologies are spreading in our culture. The lessons of Genesis chapter 6 are important and apply directly to us today.

Does this interpretation meet all of the expectations that Pope Pius XII mentioned in his encyclical—encouraging the use of ancient forms of writing, the Fathers, word studies, and connecting passages in biblical interpretation? Does it give us a deeper insight into the passage, and set it squarely within the broader Scriptures? Does it connect to other biblical passages to provide a solid moral and spiritual message for today? I think that it does. How does the interpretation from the Documentary Hypothesis compare?

The truth of the Flood is vital today because we are living in times that are spiritually akin to the days of Noah. The devastating judgment that followed the mass apostasy of the days of Noah is vital because we are seeing apostasy reenacted today before our eyes. It is important to realize that the unbelief toward this event that we see around us is part of the ungodly spirit that is afflicting people in our world and is part of the reason that it is so difficult for mankind to repent today. People are caught up in a cultural as well as a spiritual deception and they cannot see their way out of it. The truth of God's word must not be compromised by the Church at this time. This is for our own sake as well as for the sake of the general population of the world around us.

The JEPD Theory, also called the Documentary Hypothesis, is another attempt to offer a naturalistic explanation for a supernatural phenomenon. The Bible is a supernatural book because it did not arise by the will of man but rather from holy men of old who were carried along by the Holy Spirit and thus wrote it. This fact is fully acknowledged in the theory of The Genesis Documents as put forth in this book. But the JEPD Theory makes the book of Genesis the outcome of a long series of human choices that happened over many centuries as various unknown "redactors" added sections to it and reworked texts to mold them into what we have today. The entire process as described is devoid of the direct leading and inspiration of the Holy Spirit. Once again we can see the influence of the spirit of this age as it attempts to explain a supernatural revelation from God as the product of this-worldly human activities spread over many centuries.

Conclusion to the Account of Noah:

Consider the phrases that are used to describe the state of the human race in the days of Noah, just 1,600+ years after the creation and the fall: "every intent of his heart was only evil continually," and "the wickedness of man was great" (6:5). "The earth was corrupt in the sight of God," and "the earth was filled with violence," and "all flesh had corrupted their way upon the earth" (6:11–13). This after-effect of the fall could not have been imagined by Adam and Eve in their day. It is difficult for us to imagine it today, even as we see a similar time of darkness coming upon us.

As in what happened after the sin of Adam, the punishment that God decreed for man on account of this debauchery was also decreed for the animals and the birds. That is, the entire creation would suffer. So God snuffed out the existence of "everything that had in it the breath of life." This is the second curse on the creation because of man.

Genesis 6:8—But Noah found favor in the eyes of the LORD.

Genesis 6:9a—These are *the records of* the generations of Noah.

The pronouncement of the coming judgment on man ("120 years") was at the beginning of the period of time during which Noah constructed the ark. His account describes events that were situated approximately between that decree from God and the Deluge. But as time went on Noah must have realized how blessed he was to be preserved through the time of judgment. The last statement that Noah wrote was that he found favor with God. It was only the grace of God that preserved him and his family, as he testifies with his last sentence. Then Noah signed the document.

Noah was in a perfect position to know about and record all of the facts in this account. The information he gives are: the genealogy of his family, the details about human society during his lifetime—especially as they were in the century or so before the Flood—and the messages that the Lord God spoke to him about His decision to deal with the situation. It is impossible that someone living after the time of Noah could have written this account in such a way and then affixed his signature. These simple details, derived directly from the contents of the text, are confirmation that Noah wrote this account.

Noah's account reveals to us just how far human culture can fall. It shows the irresistible power of evil over mankind once it is established in society. This same phenomenon will be exhibited at the end of this present age. Peter tells us,
> In the last days mockers will come with *their* mocking, following after their own lusts, and saying, "Where is the promise of His coming? For *ever* since the fathers fell asleep, all continues just as it was from the beginning of creation." For when they maintain this, it escapes their notice that by the word of God *the* heavens existed long ago and *the* earth was formed out of water and by water, through which the world at that time was destroyed, being flooded with water. (2 Peter 3:3–6)

Interlude: Creation Theory

In this section I want to acquaint the reader with a perspective on geological history that is compatible with an understanding of Genesis as historically accurate. It is known among those who are advocates of "scientific creationism" and who want to offer an alternative way of viewing the unseen past of the earth and of human history that is in agreement with the Scriptures—a view not situated within or dependent upon the presuppositions of scientific naturalism. This is an extension of ideas we have already touched on in our commentary.

> It is my belief that no humanly devised theory of origins can possibly be accurate for certain, and all hypothetical reconstructions of the past are necessarily just that: Nice perhaps, but hypothetical reconstructions. No imagined theory of men even comes close to accounting for the plethora of observations that we have now accumulated, whether that theory is a "secular" one or one that is scripturally based. But the approach given here is definitely as valid and reasonable as any that has been proposed, and in my opinion it is actually a far superior way of viewing the history of the earth. This perspective on the history of the earth will help us better understand the account of the Flood.

This theory is adapted from a foundational work in the creationist movement. That work is *The Genesis Flood: The Biblical Record and Its Scientific Implications* by Henry M. Morris and John C. Whitcomb.[667] I recommend this work as a careful and exhaustive book that discusses all of the ramifications of believing in the historicity of a worldwide Flood as described in the book of Genesis. It discusses the difficulty that arises as we consider how Noah and his family could have kept such a zoo on the ark, the size of the ark, its construction, biological and geological implications of the Flood, and especially what the antediluvian world must have been like, based on the earlier texts of Genesis. In this chapter we will begin with their picture of the "world that was at that time and that was destroyed." I am taking this description (somewhat) from chapter VI of their book which is titled "A Scriptural Framework for Historical Geology."

Overview of the Originally Created Earth:
The view of earth history that supports the truth of the Bible, especially Genesis, is quite lovely and simple. The original earth was founded upon the waters of the great deep. Adam describes this in his account of the Garden of Eden. Thus springs of water were flowing beneath the earth and an extensive interconnected network of artesian springs watered the earth. The earth was a single large land mass, as hinted at by the biblical account of creation, and it was situated in the temperate and tropical zones of the earth. Thus Antarctica was also a warm and hospitable place for it was not at the south pole. There may have been hills and lower mountains, but not the massive towering peaks that we now see in the world. There were no desert waste areas and no cold or barren areas. The entire surface of the earth was friendly to and inhabitable by man.

Above the present atmosphere of the earth, and not implicated in the weather patterns of the planet, was a layer of water vapor—the waters above the heavens—that covered the earth and surrounded it like a blanket. This layer of the atmosphere was in the form of vapor and thus was transparent. It produced many beneficial effects on the earth.
- The climate was uniformly warm.
- There were no conflicting cold and warm fronts because of the layer of water in the atmosphere, and thus there were no violent or destructive storms.
- The climate was uniformly comfortable for human beings.

- The atmospheric pressure was higher because of the additional layer of water that overlaid the rest of the atmosphere of the earth. Thus birds could fly more easily and animals could breathe more easily.
- There was a higher concentration of CO_2 in the atmosphere that augmented plant growth and that produced an additional warming effect as well.

At the time of the Flood of Noah the fountains of the great deep were broken up and the upper layer of the atmosphere condensed and fell as rain. This signaled the destruction of the large continental land mass and its inundation with water. The land broke up and spread apart to form the present continents. Only Noah and those with him in the ark survived that catastrophe. The world that existed before the Flood was completely lost and the present earth and atmosphere differs from it in many radical ways. The life that we live on this earth has been changed beyond recognition. The patterns of climate, the mountain ranges that divide the land masses on earth, the deserts and the uninhabitably cold areas of the earth, the places of desolate erosion such as in the southwestern United States, are all signs of the devastating after-effects of the Flood of Noah.

This view of the history of the earth rests upon the reinterpretation of the fossil beds that are so prevalent today. Instead of being formed over many millions of years we see them as having been formed at the time of the Deluge of Noah when all the animals were caught up in the waters of the Flood and were killed—buried within the tumultuous slurry of water, earth, and vegetation that was stirred up by the violence of the Deluge.

This view of ancient earth is the backdrop to the account of Eden. This chapter presents a perspective of historical geology that supports and explains this view of earth history.

I want to begin this section with a comment from the Venerable Bede on 2 Peter 2:5. I do this because it is important to know that what we are about to read is an extension of the thought of holy men of ages past, not some new or radical idea.

> This is the very same world in which the human race now lives which those who existed before the flood inhabited but it is nonetheless properly said to be the primordial world, as if it were another, because, as is found written in the following parts of this Letter, *that world which existed then was deluged with water and perished* [2 Peter 3:6], namely, both the heavens that existed formerly [2 Peter 3:5] (that is, all the spaces of this present stormy atmosphere) had been destroyed by the height of the increasing waters and the land, too, had been changed to another appearance by the destructive waters. For although some mountains and valleys are believed to have been in existence from the beginning, yet they were not the same size as they are now seen to be throughout the entire world. Perhaps this could be denied except even now we see the appearance of the land changed every year by the eroding waters. This action is believed to have been all the greater then in proportion to the stronger and longer-lasting force of the waters that surged up over and washed away the land.[668]

Now let us proceed with the presentation of modern creationists, describing in detail the five geological ages identified from the text of Scripture and supported by observation:[i]

1. The initial act of creation that happened on day one: The waters covered the primeval earth, and all was shrouded in a thick darkness. The creation happened instantaneously, as He spoke His word. This occurred when God laid the foundations of the earth—its

---

[i] You can contrast the theory outlined in this chapter with the secular theory of origins in Appendix II.

core, and its mantle. Despite the expansive claims of some scientists, there are events in the distant unseen past that are permanently beyond the reach of human scientific investigative efforts. The creation of the cosmos, whose full extent is not even knowable, is one example that we have noted in our comments on the creation tablet. The formation of the earth's core and mantle are another example.

> Thus says the LORD, "If the heavens above can be measured and the foundations of the earth searched out below, then I will also cast off all the offspring of Israel for all that they have done," declares the LORD. (Jeremiah 31:37)

Here are some geological facts that we can apply to our understanding of this creative act.

> It [the creation of the core and mantle of the earth] was a once-for-all event, never repeated and not observed by man. Therefore the only real knowledge of the mode of origin must be by means of divine revelation . . .
>
> The earth has a radius of about 3,959 miles. Of this only the top 20 to 25 miles, down to the so-called "Mohorovocic Discontinuity" [sic] (after the scientist who first found evidence of its existence in 1909), comprises the crust. Below this is the mantle, extending to a depth of about 1,800 miles, and the core, whose radius therefore is about 2,160 miles. Obviously, man can learn little or nothing by direct observation about the deep interior of the earth. Most of what is believed about the nature of the mantle and core, as well as the deeper crust, is inferred from characteristics of seismic waves. It has long been supposed that the core consists primarily of molten iron, mixed with nickel; but a prominent alternative theory supposes that the extremely high pressures in that region cause whatever matter is there to assume an entirely different physical state from that of ordinary matter. The mantle seems to consist of several indistinctly defined layers of rock, also of uncertain composition. The rocks in this zone seem most probably to be predominantly silicates, rich in iron and magnesium, but this is uncertain, as is the question of the exact physical state of the materials. Deep-focus earthquakes originate in the mantle, and the earth's magnetic field probably originates from phenomena in the core. Two other facts about the interior regions, about which there is little question, are that the densities of the materials increase with depth and that the temperature increases with depth to a certain point and then apparently remains essentially constant throughout the core at a temperature of the order of magnitude of 2,500° C. Presumably these characteristics must date either from the initial creation or from the six-day period of creative activity.
>
> The core and mantle are probably essentially the same today as when first created. The materials of the crust, on the other hand, give much evidence of intricate and extensive changes. There is a possibility that the afore-mentioned Mohorovocic [sic] Discontinuity marks the lower limit of the orogenic [i.e., mountain and continent building] activity of the third day of creation. It is a worldwide discontinuity and so must have a global cause. However its nature is still uncertain."[669]

2. The succeeding days of creation:
   - On the second day the Lord divided the waters by establishing an expanse that separated them. It is best to understand the "waters above" as more than just the atmospheric water that we know of today. There was an area above the expanse, another layer of the upper atmosphere, where God had placed a wide band of water vapor. This was the creative act of God at the beginning, and these waters were never replenished as are the current atmospheric vapors. The "waters above" did not participate in the hydrologic cycle that we now have on earth. These waters were in the form of water vapor, and therefore were transparent. It is worthy of note that this would mean that the atmospheric pressure of the pre-Flood world was substantially more than it is now. This canopy of water vapor would have acted as

a kind of blanket over the earth to produce more uniformly warm temperatures in all regions by distributing the sun's heat evenly and thereby reducing the movement of warm and cold fronts.

The climate on the earth would have been uniformly temperate—free from the cycle of violent and destructive wind/rainstorms characterizing the weather patterns on earth today. Such storms are produced when warm and cold fronts clash.

A denser atmosphere would have made it easier for birds to fly and for all plants and animals to absorb oxygen. It is universally observed that fossil remains throughout the world indicate that warm climates were experienced over the earth in the times when those fossils were formed. Even Antarctica has warm-weather fossils buried underneath its massive ice sheet. In addition the pre-Flood world maintained a higher concentration of carbon dioxide in the atmosphere, thus producing a much more luxuriant plant growth than now, augmenting heat-retention in the biosphere of the earth, and stabilizing the uniformly warm climate.

- On the third day God caused the earth to move up in some areas and to sink down in other areas, moved aside of the waters of the deep, and caused the dry land to appear. This was when God formed the crust of the earth, i.e., the upper layer of the earth that is situated above the Mohorovocic Discontinuity. This layer shows the marks of the primeval activity that created the continents. There is deformation, pressure, metamorphism, etc. Vegetation was created on that day, so God must have created large areas of fertile soil in which plants could grow.

The "waters below" were more than just the seas and rivers as now. There were the "fountains of the great deep" that produced artesian wells on the earth and that watered the plants of the earth. These were subterranean water sources on which the ancient world's geological system depended, and upon which the earth was situated before the Flood of Noah. The earth was established on the waters.

Many radioisotope measurements give ages for the earth in the hundreds of millions and billions of years. However, the RATE project (**R**adioisotopes and the **A**ge of **t**he **E**arth) has found worldwide measurements of carbon 14 that indicate ages of thousands of years in all coal and diamonds on the earth. They have also found indications of past accelerated radioactive decay in rocks, significant discrepancies in the age measurements that are obtained by these methods, and other strong consistent indications that the crust of the earth is in the area of 6,000 years old. Scientists can offer no comprehensive explanation for the mixed results; that is, for thousands of years vs. millions or billions of years.[670]

- On the fourth day God stretched out the heavens and placed the sun and the moon in place. This began the light energy that has fed the earth's biological systems from then until this day. The rhythm of the tides began.
- Many other detailed creative acts must have taken place during this period, but they are not recorded in Scripture. God was preparing the earth for the advent of human beings—the place where they would be prepared to join the Lord God in His heavenly dwelling for all eternity in fulfillment of mankind's original purpose as stated in God's word. We can highlight the fundamentally unique characteristic of the six days of creation in scientific terms as follows:

> The most important thing to recognize in connection with the events recorded in

Genesis 1 as taking place during the six days of creation is that these were days of *creation*. The two most basic and certain of all laws of modern physical science are the first two laws of thermodynamics. The first law of thermodynamics is the law of energy conservation, affirming that although energy can be converted from one form to another, the total amount remains unchanged. Energy is neither being created nor destroyed at the present time. The second law states that, although the total amount [of energy] remains unchanged, there is always a tendency for it to become less available for useful work. That is, in any closed mechanical system in which work is being accomplished through energy conversions, the entropy increases, where entropy is essentially a mathematical formulation of the non-availability of the energy of the system.

It is not too much to say that these two laws provide the very foundation upon which the great superstructure of modern science and technology has been erected. All the various geological processes as well as all other physical and biological processes operate in accordance with these principles. In none of them is any energy or matter (matter may be regarded as one form of energy) being created. But during the six days of creation, both matter and energy *were* being created. Still more significantly, this newly-created matter and energy were being organized into increasingly complex and highly energized systems, in exact contradistinction to the universal tendency toward disorganization and de-energization experienced at the present time.[671]

Today all processes in the world are moving toward a greater randomness, disorder, and disorganization. The universe is "running down" today.

But during the period of Creation, God was introducing order and organization and energization into the universe in a very high degree, even to life itself! *It is thus quite plain that the processes used by God in creation were utterly different from the processes which now operate in the universe!* [emphasis in the original] The Creation was a unique period, entirely incommensurate with this present world. This is plainly emphasized and reemphasized in the divine revelation which God has given us concerning Creation, which concludes with these words:[672]

. . . the heavens and the earth were **completed** . . . By the seventh day God **completed** His work which He **had done**, and He **rested** on the seventh day from all His work which He **had done**. Then God blessed the seventh day and sanctified it, because in it He **rested** from all His work which God **had created and made**. (Genesis 2:1–3)

This principle of increasing disorder, or increasing entropy, contrasts with the assumed theory of evolution, which says that there is a principle within matter that causes biological systems to organize themselves into ever more complex configurations. This explains the problems observed with evolution that we listed when we were commenting on it with the days of creation. If evolution were true, then it would contradict the second law of thermodynamics.

The second law of thermodynamics is the fundamental reason that the complexity of life observed at the biochemical level could never have arisen without a direct creative act of God. Cataloging life's detailed intricacies at the molecular level of life allows us to apply the second law of thermodynamics to the evolutionary model of the origins of life. The result is that it is seen to be impossible. Order of that type cannot spring out of the randomness that universally characterizes the physical world. A few evolutionists do recognize this problem and try to answer it in some way, but unsuccessfully. Most of the thinkers in those areas of study simply ignore it.

Finally we must understand that any act of true creation will produce material objects that have "the appearance of age" when viewed from the mindset of contemporary science. This is because when scientists look at any material object they presume that it arose from "natural processes" as they are now understood and observed, and thus it must be very old. For example, when Adam was formed from the dust of the earth, if a doctor were to examine him then he would appear to be in his twenties or thirties and educated (since he could read and write). Yet he would be only a few minutes old. It is the same with other material objects such as the earth, mountains or streams, etc. The "appearance of age" comes from the fact that God actually did supernaturally create the object, but the observer is assuming that it was formed by long-standing natural processes.

3. The antediluvian era: When Adam sinned the curse brought corruption and death into the world. This certainly marked the point when the creation was placed in bondage to corruption and decay. This means that the physical laws must have changed in some way as creation groaned under the change. This **may** have been when the second law of thermodynamics became such a universal reality in the natural world. As we noted previously, this **may** also have been when radioactive decay began with a burst, an event whose effects as observed today are mysteriously mixed.

4. The Deluge: This happened when the Lord God caused the water vapor canopy to condense and the "floodgates of the heavens were opened" and it rained for forty days. Worldwide torrential rain of this duration would not be supportable by the condensation of water vapor that is now carried in the atmosphere of the earth. The collapse of the canopy was a unique one-time event in the history of the earth.

At the same time all the "fountains of the great deep burst open" and the earth was inundated both from above and from below. The hydrologic and the atmospheric systems of the pre-Flood earth were destroyed as the Flood progressed and covered the entire earth for over a year. This process affected both the "heavens and the earth that then was" for one year and finally destroyed them forever (2 Peter 3:6).

The single large continent on the earth was split apart, the underlying water reservoirs burst forth, and the sections hydroplaned apart on the waters. The fragments became the continental land masses that we now have on earth. The sudden "bursting forth of the fountains of the great deep" was necessarily accompanied by a significant amount of volcanic activity and earthquakes. These continued in gradually abating severity as the crust of the earth sought a new equilibrium.

As the Flood reached its end the buckling of the crust of the earth resulting from the continental movement slowed. This caused the mountains to grow higher and the waters flowed off of the earth (Psalm 104:6–8). As the waters receded the land reappeared. During this time Noah's ark came to rest on the mountains of Ararat.

5. The postdiluvian period: As the after-effects of the Flood wore on over the years we gradually settled into patterns of weather and climate that were suitable to the changed geology that the Flood brought on the earth, and we entered into the world with which we are familiar today. Some significant geological changes can be noted:

When the fountains of the great deep were broken up, massive tectonic upheavals resulting in many volcanic eruptions spewed dust particles into the air and lowered the temperature of the atmosphere. The ocean waters were still warm so there was an increase of evaporation and precipitation. Heavy snow falls formed glaciers and an ice age for about 500 years. Ocean levels were significantly lower than today because of the amount of water trapped in the glaciers. Thus ice and land bridges formed in the Bering Straits and between Asia and Australia.

Upheavals in the crust of the earth also caused tectonic plate movements and the buckling of the crust of the earth. Thus the mountain ranges that formed were much larger than those from before the Flood.

New climate and new weather patterns stabilized as the centuries passed. Temperatures were no longer uniformly warm, and the climate regularly included violent destructive wind and rain storms as warm and cold fronts clashed.

The sudden death and burial in the ice and snow of the Mammoths, with many having undigested food still in their stomachs, is one of many indications of the sudden and catastrophic advent of the Deluge.

The huge fossil bed deposits that cover large areas of the earth are another indication of the great number of animals that were swept away with the Flood. No similar fossil deposits are being formed at the present time. In order for them to form the creatures in them would have to be caught up in a mixture of water and earth and buried suddenly, before they have time to decay and revert to their basic elements. The fossils show the violent nature of the events that entombed them. Fossil bearing rocks cover most of the crust of the earth, and processes like what formed them are not in evidence in our day. Because they are found in almost all areas of the globe they testify to a past unique event—the Deluge, which was of world-wide extent.

The present coal beds were formed when large amounts of the lush antediluvian forests were washed away and buried suddenly. These were compressed under layers of rock and eventually became our coal and oil deposits.

> [T]he vast coal measures . . . [and] tremendous numbers of coal beds . . . exist all around the world and in most parts of the geologic column, implying unimaginably great accumulations of metamorphosed vegetable matter . . . The physical evidence plainly and emphatically demonstrates the fact that the coal seams are water-laid deposits, in which great agglomerations of plants were rafted down on the surface of the Deluge rivers, then conveyed back and forth on the shifting currents until finally brought to rest in some basin of deposition, to be followed by a reacting current from another direction bearing nonorganic materials perhaps, then another current with a load of plant debris, and so on.[673]

These and the other present geologic and climatic features of the earth are attributable to the work of God in creation, to the Deluge, or to the various uniformitarian processes that were established and have been in effect since the great Flood.

There is a huge cadre of people who deny and fight against these ideas today. Remember the warning that Peter gave to us in 2 Peter 3:3–6. There will be mockers in the last days who deny the creation and the Flood. We understand that this has happened because of the spirit of "scientific naturalism" in society. Peter gave us an elementary explanation of "why" men would do this. It would be because they assumed that "all things have continued as they were since the creation." This is a good statement of the uniformitarian assumption and belief.

Geological Indications of a Universal Flood as Described in Genesis:

The course of intellectual thought in the past few centuries has led mankind to view the world and man in a way that fundamentally diverges from all previous generations. We have come to believe that because we have discovered the patterns of behavior that govern matter then we also might be privy to matter's ultimate origin. No one would believe that the complex patterns we see in the world around us have arisen by random chance, but people still think—given all the natural laws we have discovered—that if the universe were given enough time it would produce what we see around us. This is not quite the same as believing in random chance. It is rather a kind of faith in the power of the orderly system that we have discovered—faith in the intrinsic nature of the material realm—that it will self-order and self-create if we can just give it enough time. This view of the world *a priori* excludes the action of God in the process. According to the rules of the game He is not allowed to play; instead the assumption that the physical laws have been operating uniformly forever is its one absolutely indispensable postulate. The major goal of science in the past two centuries has been to formulate an overall comprehensive explanation of physical reality, and to deduce how it originally came to be—without God. This end has eluded even the brightest minds, although some scientists in their secular faith have claimed that it has been attained. We must realize that this goal is rooted in a world view that fundamentally opposes Christian faith, for we assert that God created all things and formed them into the basic configurations that we see about us today. This is the Ancient Faith.

- Worldwide distribution of flood traditions
- Worldwide occurrence of water-laid sediments and sedimentary rocks
- Marine fossils on crests of mountains
- Evidence of former worldwide warm climate
- Necessity of catastrophic burial and rapid lithification of fossil deposits in order for them to not decay. When animals die now they are not covered by sediment in time to be preserved
- Recent origin of many datable geological processes
- Worldwide distribution of all types of fossils
- Uniform physical appearance of rocks from different "ages"
- Frequent mixing of fossils from different "ages"
- Near-random deposition of formational sequences
- Equivalence of total organic material in present world and fossil world
- Wide distribution of recent volcanic rocks
- Evidence of recent drastic rise in sea level
- Worldwide occurrence of raised shore lines and river terraces
- Universal occurrence of rivers in valleys too large for the present stream
- Sudden extinction of dinosaurs and other prehistoric animals
- Rapid onset of glacial period
- Existence of polystrate fossils (fossils that cross multiple layers of strata)
- Preservation of tracks and other ephemeral markings throughout geologic column
- Worldwide occurrence of sedimentary fossil "graveyards" in rocks of all "ages"
- Absence of any physical evidence of chronologic boundary between rocks of successive "ages"
- Occurrence of all rock types (shale, limestone, granite, etc.) in all "ages"
- Lack of correlation of most radiometric "ages" with assumed paleontological "ages"
- Absence of meteorites in geological column
- Absence of hail imprints in geological column despite abundance of fossil ripple marks and raindrop imprints
- Hydraulic evidence of rapid deposition of each stratum and of continuous formation of every sequence of strata, with no worldwide time gap between any another above it

(Adapted from Appendix 6 of the Defender's Study Bible)

The Deluge

Here is the beginning and the end of the text of the fourth set of tablets:

6 ⁹ᵇ Noah was a righteous man blameless in his time; Noah walked with God. ¹⁰ Noah became the father of three sons: Shem, Ham, and Japheth. ¹¹ Now the earth was corrupt in the sight of God, and the earth was filled with violence. ¹² God looked on the earth, and behold, it was corrupt; for all flesh had corrupted their way upon the earth. ¹³ Then God said to Noah . . .

9 ²⁸ Noah lived three hundred and fifty years after the flood. ²⁹ So all the days of Noah were nine hundred and fifty years, and he died.

10 ¹ Now these are *the records of* the generations of Shem, Ham, and Japheth, the sons of Noah;

Archeological Considerations:
These are the archeological comments on this section:

> The next series of tablets form 6:9-10:1. We are still in an ancient realm of thought. It commences in a Babylonian scene but ends outside that country. Although for the first time we have moved beyond the confines of the ancient Mesopotamian plain, the writer does not take us to Palestine but to Ararat. We also have the use of that exceptional word "gopher" wood in connection with the construction of the ark. This is most archaic, and the word is never used again. The tablets end with the statement, "These are the origins (or family histories) of the sons of Noah." They are almost wholly taken up with the account of the Flood. This story has received considerable attention from modern scholars who assert that it was borrowed from Babylonia. They have made much of "two accounts" or "three accounts" interwoven into the narrative. Jean Astruc, when he came to analyze this story, insisted that it contained three accounts. He instanced such passages as these in Genesis 7:
>
> > 18 And the waters prevailed, and were increased greatly upon the earth.
> > 19 And the waters prevailed exceedingly upon the earth.
> > 20 Fifteen cubits upward did the waters prevail.
>
> Also,   21 And all flesh died that moved upon the face of the earth.
> > 22 All in whose nostrils was the breath of life and all that was in the dry land died.
> > 23 And every living substance was destroyed.
>
> It is sufficient here to note two most significant facts. First, the conclusion of the tablet informs us that more than one person is connected with the writing of the narrative, for it is the history of the three *sons* of Noah. Next, that an examination of it reveals every indication that it was written by several eye-witnesses of the tragedy.⁶⁷⁴

The unique feature of this section of Genesis, having been written by three men instead of one, is worth further thought. When the tablets came into Moses' hands, were these three accounts separated, and did he then combine them, or were they already intermingled as one account? Because of the care that he took to preserve diverse native features of the various accounts, as we have already observed, it is most likely that he carefully preserved this account just as he received it; therefore, it was written originally in this intermingled way. This indicates that the three sons of Noah wrote the account when they were together and, for the story of the Flood and its preparations from 6:11 through 8:19, this could only have been while they were living together in close quarters, either while building the ark, or while living on the ark. So we should look at the sections of this account as having been written in the following way:

- The preparations for the Flood (6:11 through 6:22): This was written while they lived near each other, helping their father with the construction of the ark and the preparations for the coming Deluge. All three sons contributed to this part.
- The account of the Flood (7:1 through 8:19): This part also has several accounts intermingled in it. It was written by the sons while they were together on the ark. Each son added a bit to the story as the events of the Flood progressed.

- The part after the Flood (8:20 through 9:27): This was written by the three sons of Noah while they still were living near each other and near their father. After their families grew in number, they scattered and were living farther apart so that one unified account was no longer feasible and thus their joint account ended. The following account of Shem pointedly picks up at the point where the sons part.
- The final short ending (9:28 through 10:1) was written by the sons long after they had parted. It was 350 years after the Flood, and this is the account of the death of Noah. It was the ancient custom for sons to reconvene to bury their father, as we shall see also for the death of Abraham and the death of Isaac.

We can see that the account of the three sons is a record of events that progresses in a chronological fashion; that is, it never turns back on itself to describe events of an earlier moment. When Shem begins his account it reverts back to a time before the end of this account, then progresses forward chronologically once again. This is true for each of the accounts that comprise Genesis. This makes sense because each section of Genesis is a personal account of events that the author or authors were directly involved in.

This simple fact, observed from the text of Genesis, is another indication of the validity of our identification of the "generations" lines as signature lines indicating the end of an account. Then a new account begins. Each section contains exactly the information that would have been known to the person who is named in the "generations" line, and each section proceeds in a chronological way, as if the person were telling his story. When one section is ended then the next section might skip many years or centuries, or it might back up chronologically to begin its own story, but then that account progresses in a chronological way once again.

Historical Considerations:

In commenting on this account I want to focus on the problems that have been brought up about the feasibility of such an undertaking as building the ark.[j] I also want to list the sequence and timing of the events described, which can be discerned through the "multiple accounts," since those accounts are supplemental and complementary, rather than contradictory. This will emphasize the accuracy of the biblical account, even down to the most exacting details.

Genesis 6:9b—Noah was a righteous man, blameless in his time; Noah walked with God.

It is significant that the first thing that the sons relate about their father is he was totally upright and blameless among all the people of his day, and he walked with God. This is a statement that is like what was said of Enoch. That holy one was taken by God for his faith; this one will be delivered, along with his immediate family, for his faithfulness.

Genesis 6:10—Noah became the father of three sons: Shem, Ham, and Japheth.

This simple statement connects this account with that of Noah by restating the fact that Noah was their father. See 5:32 for Noah's statement that he begat three sons. So the sons have Noah's account and are pointedly adding their account to it. We should see 6:9

---

[j] For a defense of all the practical details of building and living on the ark, which are beyond the scope of my work, see *Noah's Ark: A Feasibility Study*, by John Woodmorappe. In his work every objection that I have ever heard of or thought of is carefully considered and answered.

and 6:10 as introducing the account of the three sons and as backtracking to cover some of the same information that was given by Noah in his account. The following verses are an expansion by the sons on the short description of what God said to Noah in 6:5–8 about His sorrow over man, His decision to judge human beings, and His favor on Noah.

I do not think we can identify any additional "catch-lines" in this section. However, the account of the sons and that of their father Noah certainly do overlap in their content.

The Divine Assessment Revealed to the Sons of Noah:
Genesis 6:11—Now the earth was corrupt in the sight of God, and the earth was filled with violence.

Genesis 6:12—God looked on the earth, and behold, it was corrupt; for all flesh had corrupted their way upon the earth.

We can think of these two verses as saying essentially the same thing and therefore as written by two different sons of Noah. This surely indicates that the Lord God was speaking opening to Noah and also to his sons as the time of the Flood drew near. Thus they all heard the divine assessment of the state of human society and two sons were impressed enough to write down what God had told them. God might have spoken to all of the men so that they were all impelled to undertake together the enormous project of building the ark. It prepared them to hear what God told Noah in the next verse.

Moses chose to keep these "duplicates" in his edited version out of reverence for the ancient writings. Also a story that is told by three witnesses is more convincing than a story that is told by only one. This is an awesome account! It is divinely providential that it is related to us by three witnesses. But today people still do not believe it.

Genesis 6:13—Then God said to Noah, "The end of all flesh has come before Me; for the earth is filled with violence because of them; and behold, I am about to destroy them with the earth.

Genesis 6:14—Make for yourself an ark of gopher wood; you shall make the ark with rooms, and shall cover it inside and out with pitch.

The faith that would have been needed to accept and carry out this command! Such a huge project would have taken the men many years to complete. These verses must have been spoken by the Lord around the same time that Noah wrote the description of his times that we read in 6:1–4 and the response of the Lord as recorded by him in 6:5–8.

> By faith Noah, being warned *by God* about things not yet seen, in reverence prepared an ark for the salvation of his household, by which he condemned the world, and became an heir of the righteousness which is according to faith. (Hebrews 11:7)

> Not that he did the condemning but that the Lord declares the condemnation by comparison; that is to say, those who enjoyed the same advantages as the good man did not share with him the same path of virtue. So it was through the faith that he exemplified that he condemned those who exemplified lack of faith, failing to believe the forewarning.[675]

The Lord spoke openly to Noah and his sons about the situation, and also expressed His favor toward Noah (6:8). That is a reason why the sons began their account with praise of their father. Because of his uprightness of life and heart they were going to be saved.

This proceeded directly from his faith and reverence toward God (Hebrews 11:7). Thus at this time the Lord was speaking openly and clearly both to Noah and to at least two of his sons. Noah and his sons were providentially in the right place spiritually so that they could hear God and respond to Him, as opposed to the general populace that was caught up in their sin. This allowed them to be used by God at this critical time in history.

The Building of the Ark:[676] [see note on the discovery of the ark by Edward E. Crawford]

Genesis 6:15—This is how you shall make it: the length of the ark three hundred cubits, its breadth fifty cubits, and its height thirty cubits.

Genesis 6:16—You shall make a window for the ark, and finish it to a cubit from the top; and set the door of the ark in the side of it; you shall make it with lower, second, and third decks.

God followed up with precise instructions for building the ark. We do not know what gopher wood was. Was it a certain type of tree? Was it wood that had been treated in a special way, perhaps like Womanized lumber is today? The Hebrew *gopher* comes from an unused root that probably means "to house in." Gesenius says it refers to pitch trees or resinous trees such as pine, fir, cypress or cedar. Such trees are commonly used in building ships. But this may be setting the meaning of the word from its contextual use rather than from some known etymological derivation. The command of God was to cover the ark with pitch—not petroleum-based before the Flood, for there were no oil deposits; so tree resin perhaps—obviously to water-proof it and protect it from any deterioration due to prolonged contact with water. The top cubit of the ark held windows for circulation.

The ark was to have rooms in it and to have three decks. The size was enormous. If a cubit was just eighteen inches, then the dimensions were 450 feet long, 75 feet wide, and 45 feet high, and Crawford's dimensions are over twice that big! [677] From the science of naval architecture we know that a vessel of those proportions is well suited for floating in a stable manner and is almost impossible to capsize. Because God decreed that man's days would be 120 years (6:3) we can deduce that building the ark took about that long.

In other words, all of these warnings and divine statements that assessed the state of mankind, and the instructions to Noah to build the ark, began to come from God to Noah about 120 years before the Deluge. When his sons were born and grew up they were caught up into the project of building the ark, and God also spoke to them to encourage them and to assure their continued joint effort to complete the huge project. Starting 120 years before the Flood gave Noah time to complete the massive project, especially once his sons joined him in the effort. Note that God told Noah to make the ark "for yourself." He already knew that only Noah and his family would be saved on it.

Genesis 6:17—Behold, I, even I am bringing the flood of water upon the earth, to destroy all flesh in which is the breath of life, from under heaven; everything that is on the earth shall perish.

Along with the instructions for building the ark God explains the method He has chosen for judging the earth: A gigantic Flood will come that will destroy not only the people but also all animals and birds—everything that breaths air—the very creatures that God had created on days five and six of the creation week. In this statement God makes it clear that He is personally bringing the Flood upon the earth, "Behold I, even I . . ."

Even the traditional size ark was large enough to carry all of those animals. The ark had three decks in it (6:16). The total capacity of such a vessel is 1,518,750 cubic feet, the equivalent of about 568 standard boxcars. About 240 animals the size of a sheep could be carried in a standard box car. So how many types of animals are there in the world? After referring to the statistics of leading taxonomist Ernst Mayr and eliminating species of fishes and other marine animals we can estimate the numbers in this way:

> For all practical purposes, one could say that, at the outside, there was need for no more than 35,000 individual invertebrate animals on the ark. [This is because] [t]he total number of so-called species of animals, birds, reptiles, and amphibians listed by Mayr is 17,600, but undoubtedly the number of original "kinds" was less than this. [We can assume] the average size of these animals to be about that of a sheep (there are only a very few really large animals, of course, and those could have been represented on the ark by young ones). [The authors then go on to calculate the capacity of the arc for holding animals.][678]

The calculations show that these could be fit in less than 150 box cars with space left over. The ark described had a capacity of almost four times that amount. But there is more to be considered when we think about how many present animal species are varieties from the original "kinds" that existed at the time of the Flood.

> A hundred years of further study in the science of zoology has brought to light some interesting facts concerning the amazing potentialities for diversification which the Creator has placed within the Genesis kinds. These "kinds" have never evolved or merged into each other by crossing over the divinely-established lines of demarcation; but they have been diversified into so many varieties and sub-varieties (like the races and families of humanity) that even the greatest taxonomists have been staggered at the task of enumerating and classifying them.

> Frank Lewis Marsh has [explained] how some of the typical *baramins* (from *bara*-"created," and min-"kind") might have become diversified before and after the Flood. He points out that over 500 varieties of the sweet pea have been developed from a single type since the year l700; and that over 200 distinct varieties of dogs, as different from each other as the dachshund and the collie, have developed from a very few wild dogs. In further discussing the matter, Dr. Marsh writes:

>> "In the field of zoology a very good illustration of descent with variation is furnished by the domestic pigeon. The diversity in form and temperament to be found among strains of pigeons would stagger our belief in their common origin if we did not know that they have all been developed from the wild rock pigeon of European coasts, *Columbia Livia*. It is extremely interesting to see the variations from the ancestral form which are exhibited in such strains as the pouter, the leghorn runt, the fantail, the tumbler, the owl, the turbit, the swallow, the carrier, the nun, the jacobin, and the homer. Different 'species' names and possibly even different 'generic' names would certainly be assigned to some of these if it were not known that they are merely strains of a common stock."[679]

Thus we can state that the present population of animals almost certainly includes many diversified varieties from a much smaller population of original created kinds.

And we must not lose sight of the fact that there was a strong supernatural element in the preservation of the animals through the Flood. God brought them to Noah (6:20). Thus it is reasonable that God also provided for their survival on board the ark by allowing them to hibernate for much of the time. In this way they needed less food and care from the humans on the ark, and the preservation of the animals became a more manageable task for them to perform. The calculations given assume the traditional smaller size for the arc. If the dimensions from Crawford's find are used then the ark is over 6 times more spacious.

Genesis 6:18—But I will establish My covenant with you; and you shall enter the ark—you and your sons and your wife, and your sons' wives with you.

At this same time God assures Noah and his family that He will protect and preserve them through this catastrophe. They will enter the ark, which is being built with the very intention of saving them and the many different types of animals from extinction.

Advance Preparations for the Flood:
The pre-Flood world was significantly different from this world in its geography, geology, and climate. The different climatic zones that we now have were not present on the earth before the Flood. There was a uniformly warmer climate which meant that the animals of each kind were scattered throughout the world, including near where the ark was being built. There was only one huge continent, not the scattered land masses that we now have with the various continents. Thus it was possible for pairs of all kinds of animals to be gathered in a relatively short time frame.

Genesis 6:19—And of every living thing of all flesh, you shall bring two of every *kind* into the ark, to keep *them* alive with you; they shall be male and female.

Genesis 6:20—Of the birds after their kind, and of the animals after their kind, of every creeping thing of the ground after its kind, two of every *kind* will come to you to keep *them* alive.

Genesis 6:21—As for you, take for yourself some of all food which is edible, and gather *it* to yourself; and it shall be for food for you and for them.

Genesis 6:22—Thus Noah did; according to all that God had commanded him, so he did.

Two of each kind of animal were to be taken aboard (6:19–20). This was the command of the Lord that started Noah gathering the animals for boarding onto the ark. God said that He wanted Noah to do this "to keep them alive" (6:19). God also said that they would "come to you to keep them alive" (6:20). This indicates that our Lord was actively working with the animals to choose the pairs which he wanted to survive, and that He brought them to Noah. This command applies to the diverse animals that were living in the world but were not necessarily closely associated with man. The animals referred to here were not necessarily "clean" animals; that is, not those suitable for offering to God in a sacrifice. They also did not necessarily live in close proximity with people. These animals God brought to Noah to keep in preparation for the coming disaster.

Food was to be taken for the people and for the animals (6:21). These preparations would have taken a long time and so must have been given well in advance of the Flood. Noah obeyed God in all of these things. All of these commands were given as advance preparations for the Flood, not immediately before it.

Immediate Preparations for the Flood:
Genesis 7:1—Then the LORD said to Noah, "Enter the ark, you and all your household, for you *alone* I have seen *to be* righteous before Me in this time.

Genesis 7:2—You shall take with you of every clean animal by sevens, a male and his female; and of the animals that are not clean two, a male and his female;

Genesis 7:3—also of the birds of the sky, by sevens, male and female, to keep offspring alive on the face of all the earth.

Genesis 7:4—For after seven more days, I will send rain on the earth forty days and forty nights; and I will blot out from the face of the land every living thing that I have made.

The immediate command to enter the ark was issued just seven days before the Flood began (7:4). At this time Noah was commanded to take seven pairs of clean animals. We might understand this command as referring to the animals that were more closely associated with humans as well as suitable for sacrifice. There is no indication here that they would come to Noah, but rather that he was to take seven pairs of each kind (literally: seven seven) of each if they were "clean" and still just one pair if not, and also seven pairs of the birds of the air, if they were clean. So he must have taken seven pairs of doves, for example, but not seven pairs of ravens; and he would have taken seven pairs of cows, but not seven pairs of hogs.

The Lord explains that these actions are required because in just seven days He would send rain and blot out all living things from the earth. This is not a natural phenomenon. Again the Lord states that the Flood is His direct action and that it will kill all living things.

The Lord is speaking to Noah and telling him these things. It is not possible that Noah only thought or surmised or assumed that the Flood was over the entire earth, because God told him directly that it was a worldwide judgment. It could not have been a local Flood that Noah simply assumed was worldwide.

Genesis 7:5—Noah did according to all that the LORD had commanded him.

Just as Noah had obeyed the advance directives from God, so now he also obeyed the immediate instructions that led directly up to the Flood.

Genesis 7:6—Now Noah was six hundred years old when the flood of water came upon the earth.

These final instructions and the boarding of the ark and the advent of the Deluge all happened in the 600th year of Noah's life and about 1656 years after the creation.

Genesis 7:7—Then Noah and his sons and his wife and his sons' wives with him entered the ark because of the water of the flood.

Genesis 7:8—Of clean animals and animals that are not clean and birds and everything that creeps on the ground,

Genesis 7:9—there went into the ark to Noah by twos, male and female, as God had commanded Noah.

Genesis 7:10—It came about after the seven days, that the water of the flood came upon the earth.

Genesis 7:11—In the six hundredth year of Noah's life, in the second month, on the seventeenth day of the month, on the same day all the fountains of the great deep burst open, and the floodgates of the sky were opened.

Genesis 7:12—The rain fell upon the earth for forty days and forty nights.

These verses might be looked at as written by another son. This is a second account of the final preparations before the Flood. In this account we are told that animals went into the ark two by two, both the clean and the unclean. This means that there were seven pairs of clean animals loaded onto the ark at this time. This also implies that the animals that were unclean and that had been sent to Noah earlier by God, since they only now went onto the ark, must have been kept by Noah for a time. Thus he might have had animal pens and enclosures where he kept them in readiness for these final steps of preparation.

Again we are told that Noah was 600 years old when everything was loaded into the ark and the Deluge came. This time the exact date of the Flood is given, even to the very day. Again we are told that the rains lasted for forty days and forty nights. In the previous account we were only told that the Lord *said* there would be rain for that time. Now it is reported to have actually happened. Thus it would seem that the son who wrote the previous account wrote it before the forty days and nights had passed, but this son wrote his account while they were on the ark and after the rains had stopped. He was keeping very precise and exact records of the event.

Genesis 7:13—On the very same day Noah and Shem and Ham and Japheth, the sons of Noah, and Noah's wife and the three wives of his sons with them, entered the ark,

Genesis 7:14—they and every beast after its kind, and all the cattle after their kind, and every creeping thing that creeps on the earth after its kind, and every bird after its kind, all sorts of birds.

Genesis 7:15—So they went into the ark to Noah, by twos of all flesh in which was the breath of life.

Genesis 7:16—Those that entered, male and female of all flesh, entered as God had commanded him; and the LORD closed *it* behind him.

This may be yet another account of the time immediately before the Flood, but written by the third son of Noah. It repeats some of the previous information. It appears that after Noah had loaded all the animals into the ark, last of all he and his family entered in on the seventh day and then the Lord shut them in the ark. On that very day the Flood came upon the earth. These accounts explain to us very precise and exact details about the preparations of Noah and his sons for the Flood. They are not contradictory, but rather supplement each other.

Other Accounts of the Flood:[k]
Before we comment on the biblical Flood account, let us look at some pagan accounts of the Flood. These are said by some to be what the biblical account was "derived" from.

In the Gilgamesh Epic Gilgamesh finds Utanapishtim who tells him about the flood.

Ea, a clever prince among the gods, told Utanapishtim to stop what he was doing and build a boat to house all living things. Its dimensions must be equal, length and width: 120 cubits by 120 cubits. Its height was also 120 cubits. [How could it float if it had these dimensions?] It had six decks, seven total levels. The inside was divided into nine compartments. Three times 3,600 units of raw bitumen were used in its making. He stored up two times 3,600 casks of oil, butchered many oxen and sheep. The workmen consumed ale, beer, oil, and wine like river water and partied like a New Year's festival. And he began to oil the boat.

---

[k] For information on a few of the more than 500 ancient accounts of the Flood, see:
James Churchward, *The Lost Continent of Mu* and *The Children of Mu*;
Charles Martin, *Flood Legends: Global Clues of a Common Event*; and
Sir James George Frazer, *Folk-Lore in the Old Testament: Studies in Comparative Religion Legend and Law.*

He completed it by sunset and it was launched, with difficulty, using a runway of poles. It sank two-thirds of the way into the water. He loaded everything he had on it: All his silver and gold, and all the animals he had, and all of his relatives. He also put aboard all the animals of the field and had the craftsmen who helped build it go up. He went in and sealed the entry as the god Shamash had commanded him to do. For the caulking of the boat, to Puzuramurri, the boatman, he gave the palace together with its contents.

At dawn a black cloud arose, the gods set the land ablaze with their torches, the land shattered like a pot, and the south wind blew submerging the mountain in water and overwhelming the people like an attack. No one could even see his fellow men in the torrent. Even the gods were frightened by the flood. Retreating and ascending to the heaven of Anu, they cowered like dogs by the outer wall. Ishtar shrieked and they all wept at the destruction of the people, wishing that they had not ordered the catastrophe. The rain continued for six days and seven nights. On the seventh day the sea grew calm.

Utanapishtim looked at the calm that had set in, opened a vent, and fresh air fell on his nose. He fell to his knees and wept. He saw a region of land twelve leagues away. The boat lodged firm on Mt. Nimush for seven days when he sent forth a dove but it returned because there was no place for it to perch. He sent forth a swallow and it also came back. He sent forth a raven and it saw the waters slither back. It ate, scratched, and bobbed, but it did not return to him.

Then he sent out everything in all directions and sacrificed, offering incense in front of the mountain-ziggurat.[680]

The Karina (or Kalina) people of South America have this Flood story:
Long age the sky god Kaputano came to the kingdom of the Karina and warned them of a flood to come, but only eight people listened to him. The rest scoffed at the idea. Then he helped those eight people build a great canoe and gather two of each animal and seeds of all types of plants. As soon as all were on board the sky darkened and it rained for many days. All animals and the unbelieving people drowned. The whole world was covered.

Many days later, when the waters began to recede and the land began to dry, the four couples exited the canoe. They looked at their world. It was void and empty, with nothing to be seen. The people were devastated and asked Kaputano how they were to go on living? It was impossible. So out of love for his children Kaputano recreated the earth making rivers, lakes, trees, etc. for the Karina.[681]

The Kaska Indians of British Colombia combine their Flood story with their Babel story:
There once was a flood that covered the whole earth. The sky grew very dark and the winds became very severe and many people took to canoes or rafts. But the wind separated the people. When the waters finally receded the people had come to land far from each other, so they decided to live where they each had landed. But after a long time as they made contact with each other again they discovered that they all spoke different languages. This is why there are so many tribes and so many languages.[682]

The Montagnais People of Hudson Bay have this Flood story:
A race of giants was destroying the earth and God was angry with them for doing so [Notice that giants were the cause of the judgment of God.] Thus He commanded one man to build a very large canoe. He obeyed, and as soon as it was completed the water rose until no land could be seen in any direction. The man got bored with the scenery and so he told an otter to dive down and see what he could find. The otter brought up a piece of earth and the man breathed on it and it grew. The man laid it on the water and kept it from sinking and it became an island. He placed reindeer on the island and they made a quick circuit around it. Since it was still small the man kept blowing on it and it enlarged and grew and lakes and rivers and mountains were formed on it and the man left the canoe and lived on it.[683]

A more Bible-like account of the Flood was found on an ancient tablet from the Middle East.

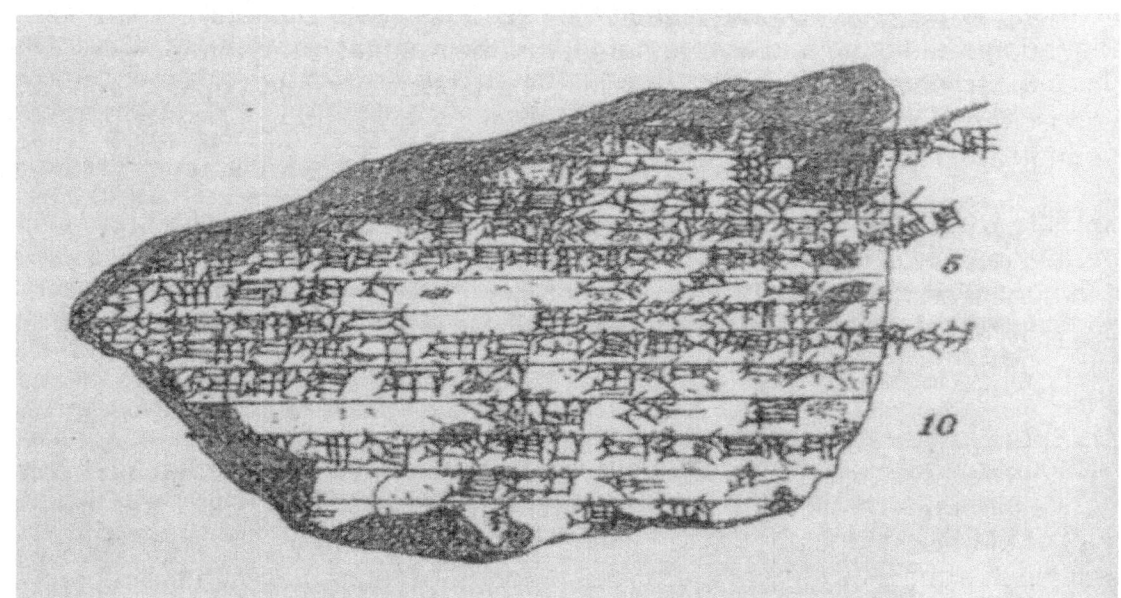

A fragmented tablet found by Hermann Hilprecht at Nippur in 1910, originally dated to 2187-2005, BC but now dated to 2000-1900 BC, and translated by him says this:[684] [see note]

Line #, text from Nippur tablet		Corresponding biblical text
2	...I will loosen	All the fountains of the great deep were broken up and the windows of heaven were opened
3	it shall sweep (or "take") away all men together	Behold, I will destroy them with the earth
4	...life (?) before the deluge cometh forth	But with thee I shall establish my covenant
5	[...over] as many as there are I will bring overflow, destruction, annihilation	And behold, I do bring the deluge upon the earth, to destroy all flesh, wherein is the breath of life, from under heaven; everything that is on the earth shall perish
6	...build a great ship and	Make thee an ark
7	...total height shall be its structure	And thus shall you make it ... and thirty cubits its height
8	It shall be a houseboat* carrying what has been saved of life	A roof shalt thou make to the ark, in its (entire) length thou shalt cover it; and the door of the ark shall be set in the side thereof; (with) lower, second, and third stories shalt thou make it
9	with a strong roof cover it	
10	[the boat] which thou shalt make ... into it [br]ing the beasts of the field, the birds of heaven,	And from every living thing, from all flesh, two from everything shalt thou bring into the ark, to keep them alive with thee; they shall be male and female,
11	...instead of a number	(two) from the birds instead of a number thereof; (two) from the beasts instead of a number thereof; (two) from everything creeping on the ground instead of a number thereof;**
12	and family	And thou shalt come into the ark; thou and thy sons and thy wife and thy sons' wives with thee

*The word for "houseboat" in this text is similar to the Semitic word for "ark."
    **The translation of Genesis is quoted from the book. It sometimes varies from standard text. The bracketed text was interpolated by Hilprecht, and the rest is directly from the tablet. In his book Hilprecht asserts that this earliest account of the Deluge must have been carried into Canaan when Abraham left Ur (see p. 62 of his book).

As we read the Genesis account of the Flood we must realize that all of the above stories are legendary, fantastic, and/or fragmentary in their content, but the Genesis account is told in a sober way with complete details. The biblical account could never have been derived from pagan myths; rather, all such stories are fractured and distorted remnants of the original and true account that is preserved for us in the Bible.

In the Bible we are in possession of the account that was written by first-hand witnesses of the Deluge. It was written by the only ones who could have known the facts—those who went through it and survived it! This account also fits in with the broader story of creation, the fall, and mankind's descent into the debauchery that brought the Flood. Therefore the broader biblical record is intact, consistent, and accurate.

Description of the Deluge—Psalm 29:
The account of the Flood that we have before us should be seen as having been written by the sons of Noah while they were on the ark together. This is the first-hand running account of the Flood. Included is the timing of the Flood events as recorded by the three sons of Noah from within the ark. Each son added his statements to the record and that is why there are some statements that overlap in what they say.

Before we look at the description of the Flood that Moses has left for us I want to pause and consider what happened to the documents that he used to write this account. They were certainly not just tossed out once he completed editing them and creating what we are reading. They must have been kept and remained the heritage of Israel for centuries. It is also plausible to assume that there were other ancient documents that Moses did not use in his writings but that were preserved for many centuries.

One of those documents might have been written by Noah or his sons giving more details about the Flood. I suggest that such a document, describing in detail the onset of the Flood, including a vison of the heavenly scene that accompanied it, was the basis and inspiration for the poetic description of the Flood in the following psalm that David wrote:
>Ascribe to the LORD, O sons of the mighty, ascribe to the LORD glory and strength.
>Ascribe to the LORD the glory due to His name. Worship the LORD in holy array.
>The voice of the LORD is upon the waters. The God of glory thunders.
>The LORD is over many waters. The voice of the LORD is powerful.
>The voice of the LORD is majestic. The voice of the LORD breaks the cedars.
>Yes, the LORD breaks in pieces the cedars of Lebanon. He makes Lebanon skip like a calf, and Sirion like a young wild ox. The voice of the LORD hews out flames of fire.
>The voice of the LORD shakes the wilderness. The LORD shakes the wilderness of Kadesh.
>The voice of the LORD makes the deer to calve and strips the forests bare and in His temple everything says, "Glory!"
>The LORD sat *as King* at the flood. Yes, the LORD sits as King forever. The LORD will give strength to His people. The LORD will bless His people with peace. (Psalm 29)

This psalm describes the onset of the Deluge as it swept over the earth and ravished the trees and forests. It sees the angels of heaven praising God and ascribing to Him glory and honor as He brings the destructive waters over the earth. The deafening noise of the surging waves is actually His powerful voice that convulses the earth. Flames of fire leap from the ground as the crust of the earth fractures and the fountains of the great deep burst forth. As the waters rise and the Flood covers everything the scene quiets down and the Lord reigns over the earth.[685]

Only the people in the ark remained, and the animals that were with them. The family in the ark saw this happen as the Flood began. This sight, accompanied as it was by the music of the heavenly choir, is what gave them the courage and fortitude to survive for over a year on the ark. They realized that the Flood was not merely an outburst of earthly destruction, but that it was the opening of the heavens upon the earth, the majestic intervention of God, and the glorious expression of His righteous indignation.

This psalm is a picture of what happened when "the fountains of the great deep burst forth" (7:11). This gives a graphic picture of how "the Flood came and took them all away" (Matthew 24:39). This was the scene in the area of the Middle East where the ark was floating—the area of the world where the Deluge was less severe out of mercy for those who were to survive in the ark! In other areas of the world the Flood crushed the land and volcanoes burst forth, billions of tons of sediment were stirred up and redeposited, and the geography of the earth was changed forever. The ancient world that was back then perished as it was overrun by the waters of the Deluge. With this picture before us let us turn to the sober description of the Flood that Moses gives us.

Genesis 7:17—Then the flood came upon the earth for forty days, and the water increased and lifted up the ark, so that it rose above the earth.

Genesis 7:18—The water prevailed and increased greatly upon the earth, and the ark floated on the surface of the water.

Genesis 7:19—The water prevailed more and more upon the earth, so that all the high mountains everywhere under the heavens were covered.

Genesis 7:20—The water prevailed fifteen cubits higher, and the mountains were covered.

Genesis 7:21—All flesh that moved on the earth perished, birds and cattle and beasts and every swarming thing that swarms upon the earth, and all mankind;

Genesis 7:22—of all that was on the dry land, all in whose nostrils was the breath of the spirit of life, died.

Genesis 7:23—Thus He blotted out every living thing [lit., all existence] that was upon the face of the land, from man to animals to creeping things and to birds of the sky, and they were blotted out from the earth; and only Noah was left, together with those that were with him in the ark.

Genesis 7:24—The water prevailed upon the earth one hundred and fifty days.

There are some key words used in these verses. "Increased" (7:17) is the Hebrew word *rabah* meaning "to increase in whatever respect." When used in reference to people it means "to become numerous or multiply," and when referring to things it means "to grow great or become much." The word that is constantly translated as "prevail" (7:18), (7:19), (7:20), (7:24) is the Hebrew word *gabar* which means "to prevail, have strength, be strong, be powerful, be mighty, or be great." Perhaps the waters came back again and again in waves that continually swept over the land in ever increasing height and power.

The waters became great and lifted up the ark and it was carried by the waters above the earth (7:17). Then the waters continued to prevail (be mighty, have strength) and continued to increase (become more) greatly after that and carried the ark up with them

(7:18). The water prevailed more and more (so they were more and more powerful still) so that they covered all the mountains under the heavens (7:19). Remember, this is the first-hand account by the only ones who survived this catastrophe.

The waters prevailed fifteen cubits higher and the mountains were covered (7:20). This statement could mean that it required fifteen cubits more of water to reach and submerge the tops of the highest mountains. In other words, as the ark was carried higher and higher by the waters (7:18) that it took fifteen more cubits of water to cover the mountains. But it is usually taken to mean that, after all the mountains had been covered (7:19), then the waters continued to rise until they were covered by fifteen cubits more of water. The reason for this understanding is the progressive nature of what is being related in these verses. Thus, to continue the narrative as the events progressed, after the mountains were covered (7:19) then the waters continued to rise over the mountain tops for another fifteen cubits. The best way to understand what is being said is that the waters prevailed another fifteen cubits over the mountains (7:20).

Another reason to understand it this way is that it says that every living thing was destroyed. If the waters had reached only to the tops of the highest mountains then perhaps a few enterprising souls might have climbed up those high hills (remember that before the Flood there were no gigantic and high mountains like there are now) and perhaps have survived. However, it emphatically and repeatedly says everyone perished in the Flood except for those on the ark with Noah (7:21–23). These three emphatic and repetitive statements might have been written by each of the three sons of Noah. They were each so very impressed by what they were seeing.

Also, there was a moral necessity behind this total extinction. Chrysostom explains:
> On this point, I ask you, dearly beloved, recall what was spoken by the Lord when he said, "My spirit is not to remain with these human beings on account of their being carnal," and again, "The earth was corrupt, and was filled with lawlessness," and "The Lord saw that the earth was utterly corrupt because all flesh had corrupted their ways upon earth." Accordingly, the world needed a complete cleansing; every stain had to be expunged from it, all leaven of the previous wickedness had to be sifted out and no trace of evil left; instead, a certain renovation had to be effected, like some skilled craftsman taking a vase that had aged with time and rusted away, so to say, and putting it into the kiln to ensure the removal of all the rust, thus reshaping and refashioning it and returning it to its pristine form. In the same way our Lord too cleansed the whole world by the deluge and, so to say, freed human beings from their wickedness, their defilement, and all their corruption, leaving the world more resplendent and once more revealing the brightness of its countenance, and not permitting even a trace of the previous ugliness to persist.[686]

How did they know that it was fifteen cubits higher, since it would have been difficult to measure the amount of rise in water level, because there was nothing against which to measure it? Did they plumb the water from the ark to see exactly how far down the ground was? How could they have been sure they were positioned above the highest peak(s) when they made such a measurement, or was there a quality about the Flood that allowed them to estimate the continual influx of water and estimate the full effect of the continual surge? We are not told how the sons of Noah determined exactly the "fifteen cubits more" by which the mountains were covered. The waters continued to prevail (be great, have strength) over the earth for one hundred fifty days.

Through all of this disaster the brothers maintained an exact chronology of the Flood. We will follow their revealing and detailed chronology.

17th day of the 2nd month:	The Flood began on the 17th day of the second month. Rain fell and the floodgates of the great deep burst forth. Rain fell for 40 days and nights. Water covered the earth to 15 cubits above the mountains. The waters continued to cover the earth for 150 days.

Genesis 8:1—But God remembered Noah and all the beasts and all the cattle that were with him in the ark; and God caused a wind to pass over the earth, and the water subsided.

Noah and his family must have felt incredibly alone and isolated in the ark, terrified by the violent and destructive rains and the waters surging up from the great deep, tossed to and fro with no avenue to peace and a feeling of security. They were the only people left in the world—the world population of hundreds of millions or even billions had been completely eradicated. How long would they be able to endure living like this? Did the glory of a heavenly choir singing praises to God (as in Psalm 29) help to sustain them?

> Whenever, on the other hand, I ponder this just man's existence in the ark, I am struck with amazement, and once more attribute it all to God's loving kindness: unless that had strengthened his resolve and had rendered difficult things easy, how would he have been able, tell me, to bear being locked in there like that as though in some dungeon or prison? How could he, tell me, have put up with the awful crashing of the waves . . . I mean, finding himself on the ark as though in prison, as I was just saying, he gazed hither and yon, unable to see the sky and having nowhere to direct his eyes, forced to remain inside, with nothing at all to look at that could afford him any comfort . . . [F]or a whole year he dwelt in the strange and unusual prison without even being able to breathe the fresh air. How could he, after all, with the ark closed in on all sides? How did he put up with it? How did he last? I mean, even if their bodies had been made of iron and steel, how could they have survived without fresh air, without the breeze . . . without being able to feast their eyes on a glimpse of the sky or the range of colored flowers growing on land . . . Leaving that aside, how did this good man with his sons and their wives manage to abide living with animals and brute beasts and all the rest? How did he put up with the stench . . . . [He did it] in no other way than by the grace from above that makes all things possible. I mean, was it not due to grace from above that the ark was tossed this way and that without being submerged in such a force of water . . . So, whenever God does something, dearly beloved, don't insist on inquiring with your human reasoning into whatever he has done: it surpasses our understanding, and the human mind could not succeed in measuring up to it or grasping the secret of what has been created by him. Hence, after hearing that God has so directed, we ought believe and obey what is said by him. After all, being Creator of our nature he transforms and reshapes everything according to his own decision . . . Faith, you see, was responsible for the building of the ark, for his putting up with his quarters without resentment, tolerating the hardships of existence with animals and all the wild beasts.[687]

But God mercifully remembered them. He caused the waters to subside. At that same time the sons of Noah say that God sent a great wind over the earth (8:1). The canopy layer had collapsed, and the uniformly warm and temperate atmosphere of the antediluvian world was transitioning into the present stormy climate with which we are familiar. The earth was experiencing a major shift in its atmosphere. In a world covered with water, and with no surface obstacles to curtail it, a wind of historic proportions roared over the waters. Before the Flood no violent winds or weather patterns had ever arisen. This would have been the first time that the brothers had witnessed a meteorological phenomenon anything like this, so they recorded it; that is, a very strong wind. It came at the same time that the waters began to abate.

Genesis 8:2—Also the fountains of the deep and the floodgates of the sky were closed, and the rain from the sky was restrained;

From these statements and others like them we must realize that from within the ark the sons were able to perceive some of what was happening outside. They knew when the rains fell and when they stopped, and when the fountains of the great deep began to erupt and when they stopped. They could tell from the way the ark was tossed to and fro, or the way that it was no longer being tossed, when the fountains of the great deep began to erupt and when they were shut off. That is how they were able to record all of these detailed facts as the Deluge progressed.

Genesis 8:3—and the water receded steadily from the earth, and at the end of one hundred and fifty days the water decreased.

Genesis 8:4—In the seventh month, on the seventeenth day of the month, the ark rested upon the mountains of Ararat.

It must have been a source of hope and encouragement to those on the ark to feel, day by day, the slow decline of the waters, and then to eventually feel the ark resting on the solid ground of a mountain top. The brothers had been recording the day and night cycles from within the ark. It was the 150th day of the Flood, and the 17th day of the 7th month when the ark touched down.

Considering How the Brothers Could Have Known the Passage of Months:
Because the time from the 2nd month 17th day to the 7th month 17th day was reckoned as 150 days it is likely that the months as they were reckoned before the Flood had 30 days. When the brothers recorded this fact (that the period of 150 days extended from the 17th day of the 2nd month to the 17th day of the 7th month) they were inside the ark and in constantly stormy weather, unable to see the moon and observe it as it went through its monthly cycles. All they could do was mark the passage of the days. This was all the information they had as they recorded the dates given to us in the Genesis record.

Thus they knew that 150 days had passed, but they had to **assume** that it brought them to the 17th day of the seventh month. That assumption was based on their knowledge of how long the lunar cycles had been before the Flood. But after they disembarked they saw the unexpected position of the moon—that it had advanced to several days ahead of what they expected. Then the sons had to change the way they reckoned calendar dates. All people had to devise new calendar systems. At that time they started to use the current reckoning that the lunar cycle was about 29½ days long instead of thirty days long. But during the Flood, while inside the ark, the sons calculated that the 150th day was the 17th day of the 7th month. This detail reveals to us the antediluvian lunar cycle.

All calendars in the Middle East were lunar in ancient times, and the cycle of the moon must have been 30 days before the time of the Flood. Very many ancient peoples make reference to a calendar of 360 days per year with 12 months in it of 30 days each. This is probably a memory from before the Flood. This means that part of what happened during the great Deluge as, "the heavens and the earth that then were perished," was that the lunar orbital cycle was disturbed, and possibly the relative motions of the earth and sun. This time of 150 days counts just the first day and not the last day in this interval of time. As we follow the dates given in this account we will assume that the dates recorded by the sons of Noah from within the ark are reflective of their antediluvian observations that the months had 30 days in them; that is, that the lunar cycle took 30 days.

The Ark Touches Down:
When the ark finally touched down on solid ground it is recorded that it was on the "mountains of Ararat." How did they know the name of the place where they landed? They could not see anything—even if they were able to peek out of the ark through the window that was a cubit from the top of the ark (6:16)—for the tops of the mountains would not become visible for several more months (8:5).

The name Ararat means "curse of trembling" according to the *Hitchcock Bible Dictionary*. It might also mean something like "the curse reversed." The Hebrew word *Ararat* is of foreign origin, and we cannot give a positive etymology for it. The sons did not call the mountain Ararat because it was familiar to them but because of how they experienced touching down on it. Thus their touching down felt very rough.

We can make some observations about the difficulties that they were experiencing when the ark finally rested on solid ground. During the Flood, the earth was in turmoil. The continents were separating and the fountains of the great deep had been recently broken up and the land was seeking a new equilibrium. Before the Flood, the brothers had never experienced an earthquake, for the earth had not been disturbed from the way that God had first created it. When the ark touched down the shaking of the earth as it was seeking a new equilibrium was unsettling and frightening. The sons recorded it in the name that they gave to the mountain: "curse of trembling."

Therefore the sons of Noah did not name the mountain "Ararat" because they realized that they had come to rest on a familiar peak that they had known before. The entire geography of the earth was reshaped by the Flood and no identifiable features remained. The name was rather a description of what they experienced, and today it has "stuck" and is the name by which we refer to that mountain and to the surrounding area.

Genesis 8:5—The water decreased steadily until the tenth month; in the tenth month, on the first day of the month, the tops of the mountains became visible.[688]

Assuming 30-day months this would be an additional 74 days that elapsed. This counts the starting point of this interval but not the end point because that will be counted in the next time interval. That was how I treated the initial time interval of 150 days, and that is how I will treat the subsequent time intervals as well. During this time Noah and his family were in the ark and feeling the seismic tremors constantly. It must have been unsettling. Finally on the 1st day of the 10th month it is reported that they could see land.

Genesis 8:6—Then it came about at the end of forty days, that Noah opened the window of the ark which he had made;

Genesis 8:7—and he sent out a raven, and it flew here and there until the water was dried up from the earth.

Forty days more brought them to the 11th day of the 11th month if we count as the sons of Noah would have done by their reckoning from within the ark. Noah sent out a raven. Because the raven is a scavenger it probably was able to find something to eat. It did not return to Noah in the ark but continued to fly around outside of the ark until the waters were fully dried up.

In the events that follow, note the caution with which Noah moves ahead. Remember that they have come to rest on the mountain that they named the "curse of trembling." At this time the waters are abating, the ground is rising, and the present mountains are being formed. The earth is not stable at all. The tremors that the family felt on the mountain of Ararat were accompanied by severe and far-reaching geologic changes on the earth. A psalm describes this for us. Once again we might see the source of these verses as documents—not used by Moses in the Flood account but preserved from the ancients—describing the geological changes accompanying the termination of the Flood.

> You covered it with the deep as with a garment; The waters were standing above the mountains. At Your rebuke they fled, at the sound of Your thunder they hurried away. The mountains rose; the valleys sank down to the place which You established for them. You set a boundary that they may not pass over, so that they will not return to cover the earth. (Psalm 104:6–9)

This time was not an easy or peaceful time for Noah and his family. That is why he is proceeding with care and is feeling his way slowly, step by step. There were still many ominous climactic and geological happenings. Besides the tremors, the sun was still hidden by clouds and thunder was prevalent.

Genesis 8:8—Then he sent out a dove from him, to see if the water was abated from the face of the land;

Genesis 8:9—but the dove found no resting place for the sole of her foot, so she returned to him into the ark, for the water was on the surface of all the earth. Then he put out his hand and took her, and brought her into the ark to himself.

Noah sent the first dove out after waiting seven days; that is, seven days after he had sent out the raven. This seems to be the right understanding of this verse because in 8:10 it says "he waited yet another seven days" before he again sent out the dove. With that understanding, the date when the dove was sent out this first time was the 18th day of the 11th month. The dove must have flown around for a while and returned to the ark in just a short time. There was no place for it to alight.

Genesis 8:10—So he waited yet another seven days; and again he sent out the dove from the ark.

Genesis 8:11—The dove came to him toward evening, and behold, in her beak was a freshly picked olive leaf. So Noah knew that the water was abated from the earth.

The second time Noah sent out the dove it was gone for much longer. It returned to him near the end of the day and it had a freshly picked olive leaf in its beak. This was surely a providentially granted sign that somewhere out there the waters had abated and the vegetation had started to grow again. This was on the 25th day of the 11th month, if we again reckon as the brothers would have, without yet being able to see the moon.

Genesis 8:12—Then he waited yet another seven days, and sent out the dove; but she did not return to him again.

This third time the dove did not return to Noah. It had found places to live and food to eat. This also was a sign to Noah that the Flood waters were receding more and more. This was on the 2nd day of the 12th month. Noah and his family continued to carefully watch as the water level fell.

Genesis 8:13—Now it came about in the six hundred and first year, in the first *month*, on the first of the month, the water was dried up from the earth. Then Noah removed the covering of the ark, and looked, and behold, the surface of the ground was dried up.

The time is now the 1st day of the 1st month of the next year. It is twenty-nine days after the dove was sent out and it did not return. At this point the land was dry. Noah finally removed the covering of the ark and took a good look at the area around him. It was dry. These phrases might have been written by two of his sons, each repeating in their own words the wonderful fact that the terrible Deluge was over. Noah did not leave the safety of the ark until he was certain. It is not stated what the "covering" of the ark was. It was different from the window near the top and from the door in the side of the ark.

Genesis 8:14—In the second month, on the twenty-seventh day of the month, the earth was dry.

Genesis 8:15—Then God spoke to Noah, saying,

Genesis 8:16—Go out of the ark, you and your wife and your sons and your sons' wives with you.

Genesis 8:17—Bring out with you every living thing of all flesh that is with you, birds and animals and every creeping thing that creeps on the earth, that they may breed abundantly on the earth, and be fruitful and multiply on the earth.

Genesis 8:18—So Noah went out, and his sons and his wife and his sons' wives with him.

Genesis 8:19—Every beast, every creeping thing, and every bird, everything that moves on the earth, went out by their families from the ark.

On the 27th day of the 2nd month the land was dry. It was still dry. At this point the Lord God spoke to Noah and told him to leave the ark with his family and all of the animals. This was the sign that Noah was waiting for—the word from God that it was now safe to leave the ark. This was 56 days later still. The total time that Noah and his family had been in the ark, counted in days, assuming that the dates given to us by the sons of Noah were based on their antediluvian perspective that each month had thirty days, was: 150+74+40+7+7+7+29+56=370 days.

Here is a bit more about the 360-day year that we have been following in this part of the narrative. Today we have a solar year of 365 or 366 days with months that range in duration from 28 days to 31 days.   This was unheard of in ancient times. All Middle Eastern calendars were lunar; that is, they marked the months according to the cycle of lunar phases. Thus twelve months accounted for about 354 days and they inserted an extra month as needed to make the years come out correctly. They were still concerned with the annual passage of the seasons and so inserted an extra month as necessary.

This ancient practice probably goes back to Genesis 1:14 where it explains that when God created the heavenly lights He appointed them to mark the seasons and days and years. The moon currently circles the earth in about 29½ days. If it had been this way at the time of the Flood then the number of days from the 17th day of the 2nd month to the 17th day of the 7th month would have been 147 or 148 days, in accordance with the length of the present lunar cycle of 29½ days, but could not have been 150 days.

The calendar of 360 days each year and 30 days each month is of interest biblically because the prophetic books of Daniel and Revelation both use it as the chronological calendar for the end-times. Daniel also uses it in the prophecy of the seventy weeks that is given in Daniel 9:24–27. Thus this calendar has relevance to Bible prophecy.[1]

Events Immediately after the Flood—The Promise to Noah:

Genesis 8:20—Then Noah built an altar to the LORD, and took of every clean animal and of every clean bird and offered burnt offerings on the altar.

Genesis 8:21—The LORD smelled the soothing aroma; and the LORD said to Himself, "I will never again curse the ground on account of man, for the intent of man's heart is evil from his youth; and I will never again destroy every living thing, as I have done.

Genesis 8:22—While the earth remains, seedtime and harvest, and cold and heat, and summer and winter, and day and night shall not cease.

This promise is very clear and is strongly worded. It is recalled by Isaiah as part of a promise that the Lord was making to Israel about the kingdom blessings that He would bestow on them and would never withdraw.
> For this is like the days of Noah to Me, when I swore that the waters of Noah would not flood the earth again; so I have sworn that I will not be angry with you nor will I rebuke you. (Isaiah 54:9)

The first thing that Noah did was to thank God for their miraculous preservation through the Deluge. They looked at the earth and saw the universal destruction that surrounded them. The small amount of vegetation that was beginning to grow was all that remained from the luscious growth of trees and plants that covered the earth before the Flood. No people anywhere; no animals; no birds. Noah offered a sacrifice of every clean animal. This confirms that he must have taken seven pairs of all such animals onto the ark. It allowed Noah to sacrifice one of them to God without making that species extinct.

Crawford's Archeological Evidence for the Sacrifice of Noah:

Proto-Sumerian inscriptions were found on a stone in the Ahora Gorge on Mt. Ararat by Edward E. Crawford in 1983. The fact that they are less stylized than proto-Sumerian pictographs found to the south and in Mesopotamia, plus the irregular size and manner in which the pictographs are arranged in relation to each other, indicate that the Ahora inscriptions are older. Below is his schematic of the stone that he found in a cave on Ararat with its pictographs. He also explains the meaning of the symbols. (see photo next page)
> Reading counter-clockwise and primarily from right to left, following the direction of the foot:
> > God's sacrificial offering of the ox (and possibly of sheep and other animals) [is or gives rise to] the covenant of the bright bow [or the rainbow]: let man and woman go forth and procreate. (Or, go forth and procreate.)[689]

This stone was inscribed by Noah when he offered a sacrifice to God after the Flood, before he left Ararat. It explains that the Lord received it (8:20–22), then established the covenant of the rainbow with Noah and his sons (9:9–17), and then gave them the command to go forth and multiply (9:1, 9:7). Therefore this discovery is important verification of the Flood account.

---

[1] For a more thorough discussion of this calendar as it applies to Bible prophecy see this author's work *Consummation: A Theology of the End-Times*, chapter "The Chronology of God's Program for Israel."

This find also shows that before the Flood writing was pictographic, not cuneiform. So the first four sets of tablets were originally written in pictographs; that is, the tablets written by God, Adam, Noah, and the sons of Noah. As we shall hypothesize later, these four sets of tablets were translated into cuneiform by Noah (and probably also by Shem) after Babel.[m]

Here I show once again the stone with the "Ahora Covenant Inscription" on it that Crawford discovered, along with his explanations/interpretations of the pictographs.[690]

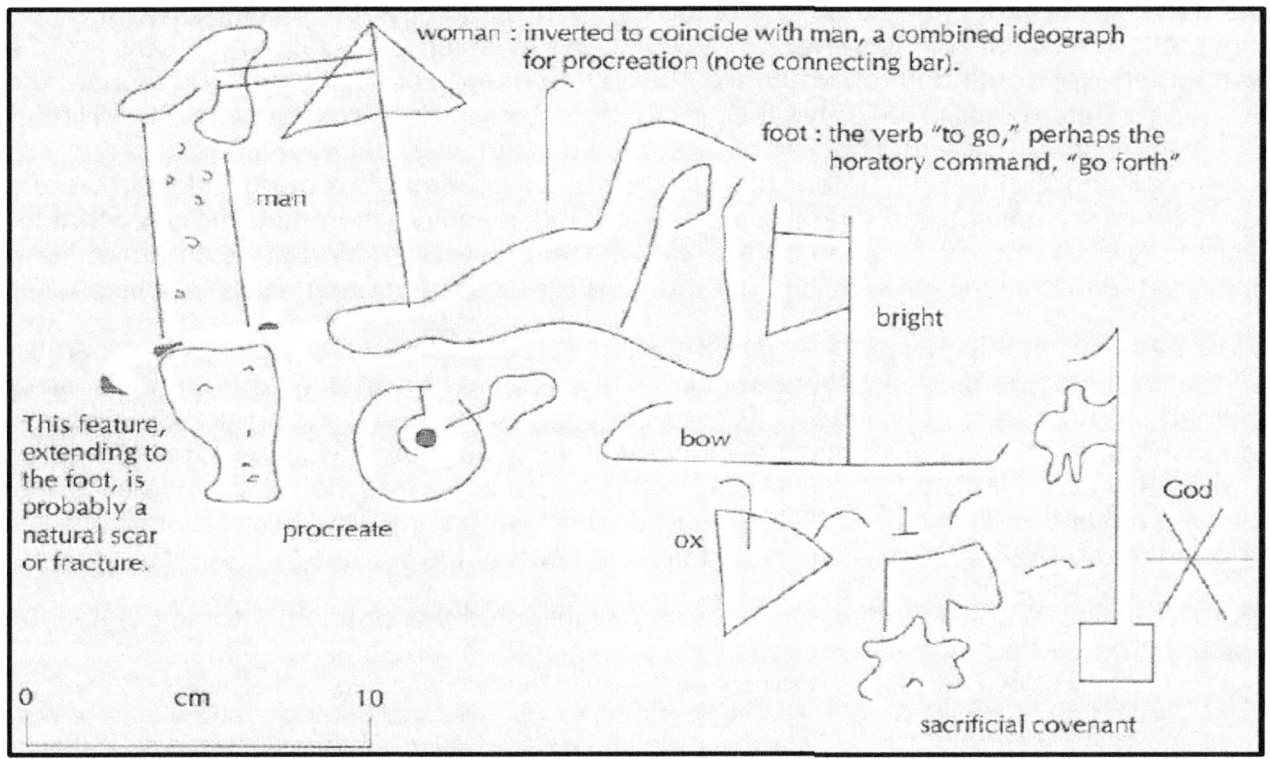

The Promises God made to Noah Extend to all Mankind:
The Lord God made promises to Noah and to his family—promises that surely must have been a great comfort to them. He would never again curse the ground because of the sinfulness of human beings, and He would never again destroy all flesh. The reason was that "man's heart is evil from his youth." This was the major lesson that men learned from the antediluvian age; that is, when Adam and Eve sinned it was not immediately apparent to them just how profound the ramifications would be because of their fall. At first they even thought that Cain might be the promised seed. But eventually they saw that their sin was a progressive cancer that had been passed on through the generations.

As human history developed mankind's distance from God became much more profound than they could have imagined at first. When the Lord God made this statement He was explaining the doctrine that we now know of as original sin. Once the Lord God confirmed this foundational fact to mankind He revealed His judicial decision based on that fact:
   I will never again destroy every living thing, as I have done (8:21).
God had twice before cursed the ground because of the sin of mankind: Right after Adam and Eve had sinned and then in bringing the Deluge. Each of these events changed the conditions of life on this earth forever. God would not do that again. The response of the Lord to our sinful state would be mercy and forbearance.

---

[m] See the chapter "Babel" for a detailed explanation of how, when, and why I surmise this to be the case.

The promise of "the seed of the woman" still remained and mankind still had hope. God also promised that the earth would continue to have days and seasons and would continue to produce food to sustain men and women. Human life on earth would continue as long as the earth remained. God is very gracious and patient. This divine forbearance will continue as long as the earth does, as some of the Fathers observed.[691]

Original Sin and the Birth of the Messiah:
As we come to understand the force of the sin nature and how it is passed on to the next generation we must ask ourselves: How could the Messiah ever be born, or how could a redeemer ever come from a human womb? Every person born of woman is by nature a sinner, by nature hostile to God in their mind, by nature inclined to turn away from Him as life progresses. The very channel of reproduction, the way that new life is created, has been polluted by the fall. Before the fall the sexual organs of woman and man were a glory for us. They showed forth the majesty of God in His creation, and the glory that He shared with us in allowing us to participate with Him in the creation of new human life—life created in conjunction with Him and bearing His and our mutual image and likeness.

Now the sight of this glory incites us to twisted and disordered lust, so that the memory of that first glory is blurred beyond recall. The meaning of sexuality and the purpose of human life has been obfuscated. The mystery is how a human being could be born—one who truly shares our humanity—but who is not caught in the web of that sin which universally characterizes our existence. How can he enter into the life that we all share, be with us, and walk in our midst as one of us, and yet be unsullied by our condition? All that Adam and Eve knew was he would be "the seed of the woman."

For Augustine, a consideration of Hebrews 7 highlighted this problem and pinpointed the issue for him. Melchizedek received tithes from Abraham and blessed him:
> [He] collected a tenth from Abraham and blessed the one who had the promises. But without any dispute the lesser is blessed by the greater. In this case [the case of the tribe of Levi] mortal men receive tithes, but in that case one *receives them*, of whom it is witnessed that he lives on. And, so to speak, through Abraham even Levi, who received tithes, paid tithes, for he was still in the loins of his father when Melchizedek met him. (Hebrews 7:6–10)

Levi paid tithes to Melchizedek and was blessed by him because he was in the loins of Abraham. This shows that the priesthood of Melchizedek was greater than that of Levi, and that Melchizedek was greater than Levi—for the greater receives tithes from the lesser and the greater blesses the lesser. But Christ was also in the loins of Abraham.

So how can the fulfillment pay tithes to that which is merely its foreshadowing? How can the fullness pay tithes to the one who is only in part? The "woman" who was to bear the Seed was in the loins of Father Abraham, and so was Jesus, the Seed—but Jesus was not there in the same way that Levi was. Let us consider in what way the presence of Jesus in Abraham's loins was different from the way that Levi was present. The answer to this question will help us to understand how the Seed could be born of a woman.

Of course all would agree that Christ was in the loins of Abraham according to His flesh. And if new human life derives from its parents both its body and its soul, then Levi was in the loins of Abraham both in his body and in his soul, whereas Christ was there only in His body, for His soul was supernaturally instilled in Him by God at the moment when "the Word became flesh and dwelt among us" (John 1:14). But we established that the soul of every new human being is instilled by God in the embryo at the moment of their conception—and that the soul is not derived from the bodies of the parents—so Levi also was in the loins of Abraham only according to the flesh, as was Jesus the Christ. (see my comments on *The Creation of Man*, Genesis 1:26–28). So again we ask: In what way was Levi in the loins of Abraham that Christ was not?

Augustine considers this question[692] and observes that the method by which Levi came into this world—the method established by the Lord God at the creation of mankind—was not the same way in which Christ came into the world. Levi came into this world by means of those human members which fight against the law of God and which are prisoners of the law of sin (Romans 7:23); that is, by those members which are polluted by concupiscence. But Christ came into the world by another means which in no way partakes of the sinful impulses of our fallen nature. The way in which He differed from Levi was in the method of His entry into our human state—a key difference which allowed Him to participate in our human condition in every way except for sin. The method of entrance into human life is implicit in the human condition and is part of what was with Levi in the loins of Abraham. That method was not present with Christ in the loins of Abraham. Augustine refers to this "method of reproduction" as "the divine formula for human life" and we have referred to it as the "channel of reproduction."

The substance of our bodies and of Christ's body derives from the same material; that is, He truly did have a human nature, derived ultimately from Adam, like our own. However, the formula of generation for Christ was different. He did not assume our nature via the channel of reproduction—or via the divine formula—that was established at creation.

> So that one [Levi] then was tithed in Abraham who, though only there as regards the flesh [that is, not also as regards his soul], was still in his loins in the same way as Abraham had been in his father's (loins), that is, who was born of his father Abraham in the same way as Abraham was born of his father [that is, by the regular divine formula from the creation] . . . Not also tithed there, however, was that other one [Christ], whose flesh drew from there [that is, from the loins of Abraham] not the inflammation of the wound but [only] the material for healing it [and thus the inflammation was bound up in the method of procreation that God had instituted when He created man and woman]. That tithing after all was about prefiguring the healing, so while that which was to be cured was tithed in the flesh of Abraham, that by which it was to be cured was not. The very flesh indeed, not just of Abraham but of that first and earth-made man, had in it . . . the wound from the transgression in the law of the members fighting back against the law of the mind, which through all the flesh propagated from there is, so to say, encoded in the seminal formula; [that is, the sin nature is propagated through the "formula" or method of reproduction] and the medicine for the wound in what, without any lustful activity, was taken from there of the Virgin in its bodily material alone by means of a [separate and unique] divine formula for its conception and formation—this for the sake of sharing in death without iniquity, and of providing an instance of resurrection without falsity.[693]

The Centrality of the Mystery of the Incarnation:

The Ancient Faith is very "reasonable" in that we can indeed reason about its truths and we can reason from them to certain other facts. But at its core the Ancient Faith is still "faith." It is not a kind of philosophy or merely a body of logical interrelated facts. It was originally revealed to us by God. It was not "figured out" by brilliant, or even by inspired human beings. Its transmission to mankind, its entrance into the sphere of knowledge on this earth, was a supernatural act of God. It is and must always remain "the faith that was delivered once and for all to the saints" (Jude 1:3). At its core the faith embodies certain imponderable mysteries that cannot be explained by even the most erudite. The attempt to do so—to resolve or to fully explain rationally those core mysteries—is a source of error and heresy. Similarly, the inclination to dismiss those mysteries or to downplay them, to make them more understandable or acceptable, is another dynamic that leads to error.

In simple words, the channel of reproduction was polluted by the fall and in this way all humans were polluted by the fall. Christ truly and fully partook of our human flesh, but because His method of entry into this life was accomplished according to a different and divinely-provided formula—because He did not assume our human condition by means of the normal channel of reproduction—He also did not assume the sin nature of man.

Thus Jesus could die for the sins of mankind according to the mercy of God and be raised up again without violating the justice of God. This is why the "seed of the woman" came into the world, and this is how He was able to come into the world; that is, by reasoning from Hebrews 7 we understand that the special way in which Christ was in the loins of Abraham, different from Levi, was this: the method by which He assumed our humanity was different. The channel of reproduction that produced Him was unique and different —although the flesh that He bore was the same as our flesh; that is, it truly was from Adam. This is vital, for to redeem us and give us a share in the divine nature He first had to share in our human nature. This reasoning pinpoints for us the distinctive aspect about the birth of Christ that accounts for His sinlessness as well—His method of entry into this world—the formula by which He assumed human nature, was different from ours. I want to conclude this part of our discussion by saying that I think that Jesus tithed Melchizedek because it was not a sin to do so and He was like us in every way but sin. It is similar to how He paid the temple tax, as described in Mathew 17:24–27.

Let us go beyond Augustine's thinking and peer a bit more deeply into this glorious mystery. I want to ask one more question: What is it about the formula of procreation that makes it the carrier of the sin nature? Or else, what is it about the unique and divinely provided formula for generating Jesus that shielded Him so that He did not assume our sin nature when He became a human? Augustine's comments on Hebrews 7 highlight for us certain things about the way in which the humanity of Jesus was like ours but still was truly unique.

First we can assert that human flesh, our physical body, **was not** sinful in the beginning, because the flesh that Jesus bore was the same as our flesh; that is, He was fully human and shared fully in our humanity. But something about the human condition **is** corrupted, and that fallen condition is connected to the reproductive process in a way that assures that newly born human beings are inducted into our fallen state. Second, when we say that the channel of reproduction has been polluted we do not mean that sex is sinful. The marriage bed is undefiled, but God will judge adulterers (Hebrews 13:4). Sex is not sinful because from the beginning God instilled the ability to make new life into our human nature. This wonderful privilege that He gave us has also become corrupted by the fall, and that is why we pass our fallen sinful condition on to successive generations. But **how** does our sinful condition, our sin nature, get passed on to successive human generations via the channel of reproduction? I want to present two perspectives on this question.

1. The sin nature is handed on **by the man** during the act of procreation. This is hinted at because God's word says, "Through one **man** sin entered into the world . . . and so death passed to all because all have sinned" (Romans 5:12). Therefore, when God introduced His new formula for generating Jesus' embryo He was formed free of sin.

   It was onto this pure and sinless flesh, conceived in a woman without the participation of any man, that God engrafted His Eternal Word. With all other births the usual divine activity creates a unique soul and inserts it into a body. That person possesses a sin nature that is derived from its parents—derived not only from their flesh, but from of the method by which they generated that new body, and specifically because of what the man brought to the process of generation.

This reasoning does not take into account the continuity of human nature and the fact that Jesus would have received sinful flesh, and the sin nature, from His mother.

2. In the second way of thinking the sin nature is seen as being transmitted by a more widespread condition—the fallen state of the human race as a whole is the cause of the pollution. **The fallen condition is shared by the man and the woman**, and so the pollution within the channel of reproduction cannot be healed by removing only the man from the process of reproduction. The woman also brings pollution into the act of reproducing new human life (her own sinful flesh), so the divinely-provided method for bringing Christ into the world could not shield Him from our fallen nature unless the woman chosen to be the carrier of the "Seed" were also removed from the process of reproduction that produces the Seed—an impossibility in view of the prophecy that identifies Him as "the seed of the woman"—or unless she (her flesh) were sinless.

Therefore, to bring into our human condition a sinless person, someone Who shares in our human flesh and in all of the conditions of human existence—except for sin—the woman who bears the seed would have to be prepared beforehand by being cleansed from sin. If initially born without the sin nature this is called the Immaculate Conception. Or she could have been cleansed at the time of the annunciation when "the Holy Spirit came upon her." Then, "the power of the Most High overshadowed" her and she conceived Jesus in her womb without the agency of a man. In this way the human flesh from which the body of Jesus was formed would have been sinless. Every servant of God is purified by Him when he or she is chosen for a task. Bearing the Son of God required a complete cleansing of Mary's humanity from sin.

Mary's sinlessness was the necessary prerequisite to the Incarnation because the sin nature would have been passed on to Jesus unless she was sinless. Concupiscence is not in the sex act but *per se*, but rather is the basic reality of our human condition, tainting everything we do. The corruption of the channel of reproduction is the result of this fact, coming from both the man and the woman. Thus the Incarnation of the Eternal Word was a two-step process: First a miraculous step that brought forth a sinless woman; second a miraculous step in which she was impregnated without the agency of a man. The woman who was chosen to bear the Seed had to be prepared.

Therefore, God, understanding that it was time for the Seed to be born, prepared a woman to carry within her that Seed—a woman who was cleansed, utterly pure, and sinless—*theotokos*, the God-bearer. On her part the woman acquiesced by submitting to the will of God throughout her life—in contrast to Eve in Eden. This was the justice of God—contradicting the effects of the rebellion of Eve by means of the obedience of Mary, a new Eve, and propitiating for the sin of Adam by the death of Jesus Christ. Thus in this view the prophecy of the redeemer being "the seed of the woman" implies a prior cleansing of the woman so she could bear Him. The idea that Mary was cleansed somehow is in Augustine, John of Damascus, Fulgentius, etc. It is quoted in the *Sentences*.[694] [see note]

I add this: Heaven admits no sin, so Elijah and Enoch, being taken by God, must have been cleansed of their sin to be taken into heaven. They were born as sinners, but were cleansed at some point. So Mary also might have been thus cleansed when "the Holy Spirit came upon her" at the time of the annunciation. However, it is a principle of God that untested virtue, that which has not been fully tried in the crucible of daily life, is not acceptable before the throne of God in heaven. If Mary was cleansed at the time of the annunciation then her sinlessness was untried, like unrefined gold. Because this sinless virtue was what was given to the Savior, and because the salvation of all men depended upon it, this would not seem to be a viable option. The sinless flesh that Jesus received most surely had to have been tried and tested beforehand, just like all other virtue.[695]

Another reason the Roman Catholic Church asserted in 1854 that the cleansing of Mary had to have happened before the annunciation—even at her conception—is that the salvation of the entire world rested on her response to the angel, and God did not want that response to depend on a sinful human being. In fact, God wanted a whole-hearted "yes" and only a sinless person could give that, because sin always limits our ability to respond to Him—to conform to and affirm His purposes.

On the other hand many Bible verses directly state the universal sinfulness of all men and women! The Bible specifically states that, "**all** have sinned and fall short of the glory of God" (Romans 3:23); and, "**all** we like sheep have gone astray, we have turned **everyone** to his own way, but the Lord laid on Him the iniquity of us **all**" (Isaiah 53:6); and from the apostle John, with whom Mary lived after Jesus died, "If we say that we have no sin, we are deceiving ourselves and the truth is not in us" (1 John 1:8). Given these and other affirmations of the universality of sin, how could Mary have been born sinless? Also if Mary was born sinless then the mystery of how a sinless person could ever be born is just pushed back by one generation; that is, how did Mary herself, if she had been thus prepared, escape being born with the sin nature, since she surely was born according to the regular divine formula and via the regular channel of reproduction.

It seems simpler to some, and more directly scriptural, to hold on to the biblical assertions about universal sinfulness and, if needed, to allow the mystery of the Incarnation to be exactly that—an impenetrable mystery that we can never explain in any way. If God did work a miracle in her conception, then why couldn't He have just worked the same miracle at the conception of Jesus? Then He would have been born without the sin nature even though His mother was a sinner. But if God changed Mary's flesh as He took it from her, then how was it actually the flesh of Mary? And how was it tried and refined in daily life? This presents the same problem as assuming Mary was cleansed at the annunciation.

Thus God surely did not do the Incarnation that way. Mary was in the loins of Abraham in precisely the same way as Levi was, and she certainly paid tithes to Melchizedek just as Levi did. But for God to bring about the Incarnation, preparing Mary before the time of the annunciation was the only way for Jesus to be born of tested, sinless, human flesh. So Mary is God's gift to all of us. She is our mother-in-grace, the new Eve, and the mother of all those who are alive via the second birth. Every child wants to view his or her mother as a pure, virtuous, lady, above all reproach. Mary is that gift of love to all of us.

> My soul magnifies the Lord, and my spirit has rejoiced in God my Savior. For He has had regard for the humble state of His handmaid. For behold, from this time on all generations will count me blessed. For the Mighty One has done great things for me; and holy is His name. (Luke 1:46–49)

Here are the consequences of not believing that Mary was prepared. In his excellent study bible, in a footnote on Luke 1:31, Dr. Morris meditates on the miraculous birth of Jesus.

> The . . . conception [of Jesus] was . . . uniquely miraculous in that no man was involved. "that holy thing" was placed directly in Mary's womb by God "the Holy Ghost" (Luke 1:35) and thus was uniquely "the seed" of the woman (Genesis 3:15). Just as the body of the first Adam was directly formed by God with no genetic connection to either father or mother, so the body of "the last Adam" (1

> Corinthians 15:45) was directly formed by God (Hebrews 10:5), with no genetic connection to either parent. [contrast with Augustine] Since the very "ground" was brought under God's curse because of sin (Genesis 3:17), all the elements of the ground (i.e., "the dust of the earth"), out of which the bodies of Adam and Eve and all their descendants had been formed, were contaminated with the "bondage of corruption" (or decay—Romans 8:21–22). This was just as true of Mary's body as of Joseph's, so there could have been no natural genetic connection of Jesus' body to that of Mary any more than to that of Joseph's. The "holy thing" placed in Mary's body by the Holy Spirit could have been nothing less than a special creation—just as was the body of Adam. Otherwise, like all men born of women, Jesus would have inherited . . . the sin-nature of Adam and Eve . . . Jesus was the only begotten Son of God, as well as the son of Mary, but He was not the son of God and Mary.[696]

Dr. Morris also states this when discussing the fact that Jesus was "made" of the seed of David as stated in Romans 1:3 (and also in Galatians 4:4). He explains further:

> The central truth of Christianity is the incarnation of God in human flesh, in the person of His Son, the Lord Jesus Christ. He was a true man "made of the seed of David," as foretold by the prophets; His birth was completely natural from the point of conception [that is, He was conceived in a human womb like all human beings], but His conception was altogether miraculous. He had no human father . . . and His mother remained a virgin until after He was born. Mary herself was a descendant of David, and He grew in her womb for nine months, so He was indeed "made" of one who was of the seed of David . . . [But] His conception necessarily involved the special creation of the cell placed by the Holy Spirit in Mary's womb. "A Body thou hast prepared me" (Hebrews 10:5) . . . He was indeed "made of the seed of David according to the flesh," although the specifications for the "making" of His body were contained in the DNA code programmed by God in the created cell.[697]

But there is a serious problem with this explanation. It makes Mary a kind of "surrogate mother" who loaned out her womb to be the gestation place for the Son of God. He was not part of our human race, but rather He began a new and separate race. Thus his work was not to redeem our fallen race from its sinful state, but rather to replace it with another race of beings that were similar to but distinct from the race of Adam. This would also mean that Jesus was not truly "the seed of the woman" at all, contrary to what is stated in the prophecy (Genesis 3:15). It would also mean that Jesus was not really the seed of David and He was not the seed of Abraham or of Adam. By such logic Jesus would not have been in the loins of Abraham at all. He was not truly fully human![698 [see note]]

The reasoning that Henry Morris uses to explain why Jesus could not have been made of the actual flesh of Mary, that He could not have had a true genetic connection to her, is compelling indeed, but the conclusion that we must come to is not the one at which he arrives. The most logical conclusion is this: The woman who gave birth to the Seed had to be specially prepared by God. Then "the holy thing" that was conceived in her womb could actually be made of her flesh. Thus it had a true genetic connection to her, to her father David, to Abraham, and to Adam. It was truly human just as we all are. So Jesus had to have a genetic connection to Mary. He had to receive His flesh from her, and it could not have been modified as it came from her by having her sin removed from it or it would not have actually been her flesh; and it had to have been tried in daily human life as well. Finally, overcoming Satan via the very human stock that he overwhelmed in the beginning (not via a new human race) was the best way—was the only way—for the justice of God to be fully satisfied. This solution alone can fully restore humanity.

Thus the new life that we receive from Him through faith when we are born again is truly divine life and remains truly human life—the same human life that has been shared by all of the descendants of Adam and Eve since the beginning of the world. It is not a different life that arises from a different but parallel race of beings, but it is the human life and the human nature that God first created when he made Adam and Eve at the beginning—it is a redeemed fully human life and a purified sinless fully human nature. Therefore our Lord repeatedly refers to Himself as "the son of man," like us in all ways except sin.

This doctrine is the essential truth of Christianity. Whatever way we theologize about it we must arrive at the conclusion that Jesus was truly fully God and truly fully man. If we fail in either of those points then the act of redemption is powerless. The vital nature of this truth has been tenaciously fought for throughout the ages. Blessed Theophylact of Ochrid is adamant as he comments on the annunciation to Mary by the angel Gabriel.

> *Therefore that Holy Thing Which is* **begotten** *of thee shall be called the Son of God* (Luke 1:35). It was not that the virgin did not believe, that she said, *How shall this be?* Rather, it was because she was wise and astute, and sought to understand the manner in which this would take place. For nothing like this had ever happened before [note Jeremiah 31:22, *For the Lord has created a new thing in the earth—a woman shall encompass a man.*] This is why the angel forgives her and does not chastise her as he did Zacharias, but instead explains to her how it would come about . . . *The Holy Spirit*, he says, *shall come upon thee*, rendering thy womb fertile, and creating flesh for the Word Which is one in essence with the Father . . . The Lord, in creating flesh for Himself and fashioning the icon of a man, first drew the shadow of the image in the womb of the Virgin, incorporating flesh from the blood of the Ever Virgin, and then little by little gave it form. But this is unclear. [There is an impenetrable mystery about this.] . . . Listen to what the angel says: *Therefore also that Holy Thing Which is begotten of thee*, in other words, that Holy Thing Which is growing within your womb in extraordinary manner, and does not at once exist in completed form. Here the mouth of Nestorius is sealed. For that man said that the Son of God did not take flesh by dwelling in the womb of the Virgin, but that a mere man was born of Mary, and only later was this man "accompanied" by God. [Note: Nestorius rejected the title *Theotokos*, the "bringer forth of God," for Mary.] Let Nestorius hear, therefore, that that *Holy Thing* Which is being begotten in the womb is the Son of God. That which was carried in the womb and the Son of God are not two separate entities, but the one and the same, the Son of the Virgin and the Son of God. [bold on begotten in Luke 1:35 is mine][699]

The force of this passage turns on the word *gennaō* that is translated as "begotten." It is not the same word that is used in Galatians 4:4 and Romans 1:3, which is translated as "made;" that is, "made of a woman" and "made of the seed of David." The word used in this part of Luke truly means **begotten** and is used, for example, in the genealogies of Matthew. The "Holy Thing" truly was constructed from the human flesh of Mary. Thus it was truly fully human, sharing in the common inherited human nature of all people. But, in the impenetrable mystery of the Incarnation, it was also truly and fully God, and it was so from the beginning; that is, from the very first moment of its conception.

This is the glorious and breath-taking fulfillment of the prophecy that our Lord spoke to Eve after the fall. At that time our first parents knew only that the coming deliverer would be "the seed of the woman." But how could that seed not also be contaminated with the effects of the fall that tainted all human beings? Finally we see the fulfillment. Not only would the Seed be preserved from sin, but he would be God the Creator Himself! What a glorious, humble, and completely unimaginable fulfillment! No one before the time had ever thought of such a response from the Lord God. But now that it has been revealed to us the Church is adamant about preserving the full glory of this holy truth.

Mary and the Hypostatic Union:
Who was the first person in the new dispensation to understand this great truth? The passage in consideration from Luke 1 gives us a clear indication that it was Mary. How fitting it was that, before the Holy One involved her in His glorious plan of redemption, He would reveal to her the nature of the drama in which she was being asked to play a part.

And, behold, thou shalt conceive in thy womb, and bring forth a son, and shall call His name Jesus. He shall be great, and shall be called the Son of the Most High: and the Lord God shall give unto Him the throne of His father David: and He shall reign over the house of Jacob forever; and of His kingdom there shall be no end (Luke 1:31–32). Here we see that Mary is given to understand that the child she is to bear will be the long-awaited promised seed of David (2 Samuel 7:11–16). Thus he will be a human being, the descendant of David. It says that He will be called the "Son of the Most High," but that term was loosely applied to the rulers of Israel, and it did not convey to Mary the full implication of His divinity. But Mary providentially asked the question, *How can this be?*

Now the angel speaks again, and the second time there can be no failure to understand the import of his words. *The Holy Spirit shall come upon thee, and the power of the Most High shall overshadow thee:* **therefore** *also the Holy Thing Which is begotten of thee shall be called the Son of God* (Luke 1:35). Now it is very clear. The child she will bear will be fully God as well! At this point, when Mary finally understands exactly what part she is being asked to play, she says, *Be it done unto me according to thy word.* Mary was the first person to understand the glorious reality of the Hypostatic Union, the wonderful way in which God determined to fulfill His prophetic promise of deliverance for mankind.

Again, the mystery that Jesus is truly fully God and truly fully man is the most vital and central of all Christian doctrines. When the prophecy of the "seed of the woman" was given to Adam and Eve they could not have realized the awesome implications of that promise. Eventually, as the true nature of sin became clear, and as its universal extent became evident, it seemed impossible for a person to fully share in our humanity—to be born of woman—and yet to avoid being contaminated with our sinfulness. How could he not inherit our sinful condition? Thus the advent of the seed was a divine mystery. But when the fullness of time came and God sent His own Son into the world—when it became clear that the Seed was actually fully God as well as fully man—then a second wonderful mystery presented itself. How can any person be both God and man? And so the advent of the Seed is now presented to the Church as a glorious double mystery—first His sinless humanity, and then over and above that, His full divinity. Both of these beautiful truths must be accepted by faith, for they are incomprehensible in their entirety.[700] [see note]

The truth of His full divinity is vital, for those who believe in Him are made "partakers of the divine nature" (2 Peter 1:4) just as He condescended to share, both body and soul, in our human nature. Our participation in His divine nature is the way that we will enter into the life of the Trinity, the way that we will fulfill our predestined purpose to be before Him as His sons (Ephesians 1:5), the way that we will see His face in glory (Revelation 22:4), the way that we will be conformed to His image so that He might be the first among many brethren (Romans 8:29). By sharing our humanity and yet also being fully God He makes a way for human beings to enter into the divine life and fellowship that He had planned to give freely to us (John 5:26–27, 5:21) even from before all time.

Yes, the plan to share in our humanity and for us to share His divinity was the plan of God from before the creation of the world. Because of sin, which God foresaw and planned for, the glory of "the Word becoming flesh" also had to involve yet another miracle—the miracle of being preserved from the sinful state of all human beings. Then that sinless one had to pay the penalty of sin for all other human beings. Because He is also the "Lamb foreordained from before the foundation of the world" (1 Peter 1:20) we know that God foresaw the fall of man and planned for it before He ever began to create.

Let us summarize the various issues that arise as we try to understand how the Incarnation was accomplished by God, how any man born of a woman could be sinless, how the body of Jesus could have been prepared for Him (Hebrews 10:5; Psalm 39:7, LXX):
- The unity and continuity of human nature was a fundamental aspect of the design of God when He created mankind. We are all descended from Adam and we all share his humanity. This assures that God has made of one blood all those who dwell upon the earth (Acts 17:26). Jesus was truly fully human, sharing in the human nature of Adam, just as we all do. Thus He must have had a direct genetic connection to Mary, David, Abraham, and Adam. In addition, the justice of God is perfectly satisfied only if the same flesh that was defeated by Satan in Eden is used to defeat him in the final Consummation. This assures us that humanity will be fully restored in the end.
- Jesus received His flesh from Mary, so at the time that he received it, it must have been sinless. But virtue that is not tested in the crucible of daily life is not acceptable before the throne of God. If the flesh of Mary was sinful but was cleansed at the moment of the Incarnation as it was taken from her—but without also cleansing her—then the flesh that Jesus received would not actually be her flesh and would never have been tried in the crucible of life. Additionally, if Mary herself was cleansed at the time of the annunciation, just before the Lord was begotten of her, then His sinless flesh would never have been tried in life. It would be like unrefined gold. How could the salvation of the entire human race be based on untested virtue?
- Add to this the fact that God states repeatedly in His word that all have sinned.

It is clear from the considerations we have listed here, with the various options examined, that the Incarnation is a great mystery of the faith. The one doctrine in Christian history to offer a partial insight into this foundational mystery of the faith is the decree of the Immaculate Conception. The theology of this doctrine is not widely known, so I will outline it here. The decree *Ineffabilis Deus* (God Ineffable) was issued by Pope Pius IX on December 8, 1854. Here are a few key sentences from that decree:

> God Ineffable—whose ways are mercy and truth, whose will is omnipotence itself, and whose wisdom "reaches from end to end mightily, and orders all things sweetly"—having foreseen from all eternity the lamentable wretchedness of the entire human race which would result from the sin of Adam, decreed, by a plan hidden from the centuries, to complete the first work of his goodness by a mystery yet more wondrously sublime through the Incarnation of the Word. . .. From the very beginning, and before time began, the eternal Father chose and prepared for his only-begotten Son a Mother in whom the Son of God would become incarnate and from whom, in the blessed fullness of time, he would be born into this world. . .. God, by one and the same decree, had established the origin of Mary and the Incarnation of Divine Wisdom.

The basic presupposition of the doctrine is that the Incarnation was not decreed because of sin, but rather was an essential aspect of the divine plan for creation that preceded and was independent of the fall of man and of the wicked angels.[701] Thus before the foundation of the world, as the Father and the Son were planning the ages, they decided that the Word would become flesh. At that same time—as part of that same decision—it was determined (predestined) that the Word would become incarnate via a chosen woman from whom He would receive His human flesh. Mary was decreed at the same time as the Incarnation, and irrespective of and prior to the fall. She was prepared beforehand. The sinlessness of Mary was a prerequisite of the fact the Jesus would receive His flesh from her.

But it was also foreseen that man would fall into sin. Thus the Word was foreordained to be a lamb of sacrifice to redeem us. As a result of that foresight our Lord concluded the whole human race under sin so that He might have mercy on all (Romans 11:32, Galatians 3:22). The decree to confine the entire human race under sin so that Jesus could redeem us all came after the decision that the Word would become flesh.

Thus Mary was preserved beforehand from the universal sin that would engulf those who were "in Adam," and which would result in the fact that "in Adam all die." For this reason the biblical assertions about the universal sinfulness of the human race, which apply to all who are "in Adam," do not apply to Mary, who was previously decreed to be a sinless virgin without any hint of the stain of sin. She was "in Adam," but she was not included in the decree to conclude all under sin. Instead, Mary was predestined to become the sinless companion of the New Adam, a sinless Eve, a pure and spotless mother for all the redeemed. This is how, after over 1,800 years of mulling over the conundrum of the Incarnation, the Church decided on and decreed this one insight into that glorious mystery.

Finally, to assure the full humanity of the God-man Jesus Christ, His soul was created *ex nihilo* by Abba and fashioned by Abba and the Word as are all human souls, then joined (an impenetrable mystery) with the divinity of the Word. It was without sin in correspondence to the conceptus that was in Mary as it was joined to it in the womb. This is the way of all human souls, for all are created in correspondence to the human body to which God joins them. The correspondence between body and soul assures the unity and integrity of each human person, even though he/she is created from two separable parts. However all other human souls share in the sin nature, for they correspond to the "body of sin" inherited from their mother and father. But the soul of the Word was made to correspond to the sinless conceptus in the womb of Mary. In this way the Word, Who was and remained fully God, also became fully human, both body and soul, and was totally sinless. The "Holy Thing" that was begotten in Mary was fully man and fully God, both body and soul. Mary was *Theotokos*, "the one who brought forth God." We must always preserve the fullness of this glorious truth in whatever way we seek to explain or understand it, even as it is and must always remain mostly shrouded in mystery.[702 see note for summary conclusions]

There are several other mysteries that the Ancient Faith—the Christian world view—has inextricably interwoven within it:
- The mystery of human nature as created—body and soul, male and female—in the image and likeness of God.
- The mystery of sin or the "mystery or iniquity" that has befallen mankind because of the transgression of our first parents.
- The mystery of salvation and the new birth that we experience when we trust Jesus to save us and we are born again; that is, the mystery of how sin is overcome.

Undergirding these uniquely Christian mysteries are other universal mysteries shrouding the creation, so that the world—and mankind itself—are not fully comprehensible.[703 see note]
- Why is there something rather than nothing?
- What is this world in which we live and how is it held together? What is the meaning of existence? What is the basic nature of being? Penetrating beneath the various physical laws that have been discovered and that order creation, why are they there? What links them together and makes the world function in an orderly and consistent way? For example, what is gravity so that one body attracts another that is distant from it even when there is no connection between them? How do the various forces that hold the world together work? These mysteries are meant to lead us to the Creator.

The initial answer to these questions has been revealed to us, locked up in the nature of God, the self-existent, necessary One Who has always existed, and His explanation to us of how He created all things according to His wisdom and power. This explains to us the personal nature of the answer to our questions—and it tells us something about God—but it still leaves God Himself as the ultimate mystery. Who is He, and what is He like?

Life on earth is a place of preparation for seeing Him face-to-face in glory. We must be given a share in His divinity in order to participate with Him in His life. That is the way in which He intends to fulfill our innermost longings and to answer all of the imponderable mysteries that undergird creation and human existence. The ultimate answers to these mysteries will be unfolded to us in eternity as we share in the life of the Trinity.

The Incarnation embodies the central truths about God and existence, mankind and sin, salvation and eternal life. Through this glorious revealed mystery God will accomplish all of His purposes for His creation and for mankind.

When God established death as the universal and necessary result and sign of sin, then by implication when the Seed arrived one thing that He would have to do was conquer death. That would be the certain proof that He had conquered sin. To visibly conquer death the seed could either live on forever or He could die and rise again. If He lived forever then He personally would have conquered death, but his arrival among us and his life on earth would not have brought reconciliation and life to the rest of the human race.

But the promise of the Seed was given to the human race as our hope. Therefore, He would have to die (John 12:24), though He was not subject to death by nature—since He would be sinless and immune to death. Nevertheless He would have to die because it would be His assigned role in history. By dying even though He was sinless His death could be reckoned as the act that fulfilled divine justice for all men. Then He could rise again from the dead and by that definitive act prove His victory over death—and also over sin. Then He would have the right to grant forgiveness and eternal life to men.

But sin does not just affect individual human beings or human society. Sin began as the rebellion of a key spiritual power that had been given a foundational role in the creation. Yet man was granted dominion over creation. When the federal head of the human race fell—when Adam rebelled against God—the effects of sin rippled through all of creation because mankind became subject to that fallen spiritual being. Thus dealing with sin involves judging the fallen angels and restoring all things as well as forgiving mankind.

The restoration of this creation must involve the revelation of the "mystery of iniquity" (2 Thessalonians 2:7) that encompasses all of these things. Then it can be dealt with in the sight of all men. This is much more than any mere man could do, even if he were sinless. That is why the Seed had to be the Creator Himself. The Lord came to earth to forgive and save men, destroy Satan's works, and "restore all things" (Acts 3:19–20).

The death, resurrection, and ascension of the Seed revealed to us certain fundamental spiritual realities that undergird human existence. Death is a consequence of sin, which was and is a personal rejection of our Creator, and which separates us from Him. The universal reality of sin is rooted in the sin of Adam in Eden, the context within which the coming of the Seed was announced. By dying for our sins the Seed set in place a path of repentance, forgiveness, reconciliation, and restoration of our relationship with God, and opened again to us the doorway to eternal life. The fact of reconciliation with God through faith in Jesus is the uniform experience of Christians throughout this age. The

Holy Spirit that Jesus sent upon the Church at Pentecost revealed this to us. This reality is set squarely within the context of Adam and Eve in Eden. So we know the account of the creation and the fall is also true. Therefore human theories or ideologies which claim they are not true are deceptive lies. When we investigate such theories we can see that they are not science and they are not true. This is one basic theme in this book.

Sin and Sanctification:
Once we understand that the fall of Adam has resulted in a distortion of our humanity—a twisting of our human nature away from its original creation in the image and likeness of God—then we must also realize that, now that the promised Seed of the woman has come, if we accept His forgiveness and enter into the salvation that He has prepared for us, then we are returning to the plan that God intended for us when He first created us. This is exactly how we experience it when we come to our Lord for forgiveness and for deliverance from the power of sin. It is truly a release from bondage, the untying of a Gordian knot that has been lodged in our souls, a return to a place that we experience as blessed, as home, as where we always belonged. It is the experiential entrance into a psychological and spiritual state that feels right and completely natural.

It is the restoration, to a partial degree, of the initial state of innocence and holy union with our Creator, a foretaste of heaven and of the ultimate glory that awaits us in that final consummation, a restoration to what we were always intended to be. How truly Jesus spoke when He said, "anyone who sins is a slave to sin" (John 8:34), but "if the Son sets you free you will be free indeed" (John 8:36). This is how our "inner man" is restored. Our bodily restoration must await the resurrection of the body and/or the rapture of the Church.

However, if we evolved from animals then our "sinful" impulses are merely the left over beastly instincts that must be curbed and "held down" so that civilization can go on and so that men can coexist in some semblance of peace and order. Then sanctification is merely the power to shackle those aberrant impulses, and the experience of it must be a feeling of repression. In such a case sanctification is actually unnatural, and living the Christian life on this earth is a constant tug-of-war between the demands of the broader society or the Church and the normative desires of our human nature.

With such a world view people see God as the ultimate authoritarian power, the one to whom we are all accountable under threat of damnation, the one who is the basic glue that keeps society from coming unraveled. In such a view it is hard to truly long for righteousness because we have no picture of the glorious freedom that awaits us when we walk in the Spirit and do not gratify the desires of the flesh.

The evolutionary world view also makes God responsible for our sorry state because He brought us into being through a lengthy chain of natural processes that have resulted in our formation, and our sinful state of being is not the result of specific decisions we have made to disobey Him; rather, things just developed this way and here we are. Thus the "gospel" demands that we deny our inherited inclinations and obey His laws instead, and if we do not succeed in that unnatural task then He condemns us.

But the truth is this: Adam and Eve departed from God by a direct, willful choice. By so doing they distanced themselves from Him and fell into captivity to their own sinful lusts. From that original decision the reproductive process that made new human beings was also corrupted, and we, their descendants, were born in a state that inclined us to reject

God and His ways. In truth, every human being in history has followed that inclination and has personally turned from God and rejected Him. The way back must involve an admission of our lost and sinful state. On His part, God has, at the greatest possible cost to Himself, made a way back to Him for those who are willing to repent and call on Him.

A personal decision to reject Him calls for a personal decision to accept Him again. The Lord is willing if we are. The reward for such repentance is that we are restored to true humanity; that we repair what was distorted by the fall; that we save our souls; that we are prepared to reenter the plan that God had for us from the beginning of the creation; that we are reconciled to God; that we take up again our predestined purpose, to be in an intimate, direct, personal relationship with Him for all eternity when we leave this life.

God Re-establishes Mankind after the Deluge:
Genesis 9:1—And God blessed Noah and his sons and said to them, "Be fruitful and multiply, and fill the earth.

Genesis 9:2—The fear of you and the terror of you will be on every beast of the earth and on every bird of the sky; with everything that creeps on the ground, and all the fish of the sea, into your hand they are given.

Genesis 9:3—Every moving thing that is alive shall be food for you; I give all to you, as *I gave* the green plant.

Genesis 9:4—Only you shall not eat flesh with its life, *that is*, its blood.

At this point God actively blessed Noah and his sons and reiterated to them the initial command from Eden: Be fruitful, multiply, and fill the earth. Thus we should expect another population explosion. He then set the conditions of life in the post-Flood world: All animals would be food for man and the fear of man would be upon them. This was a distinction from the original creation where both men and animals were vegetarians. Only one restriction was placed on this: Do not eat the flesh with the blood in it.

We might understand the rationale behind this one new commandment as follows: The blood is seen as the life of a creature and mankind is not to take in animal life. It is not in accord with the dignity with which the Lord God created him, which was in His own image and likeness. To drink the blood of a creature is to take their life into us. From the start man was meant to share God's life, not that of the animals.

Genesis 9:5—Surely I will require your lifeblood; from every beast I will require it. And from *every* man, from every man's brother I will require the life of man.

Genesis 9:6—Whoever sheds man's blood, by man his blood shall be shed, for in the image of God He made man.

This commandment was given to man after the Flood. It was certainly wrong to take man's life before the Flood, as the story of Cain and Abel so clearly revealed. Such truths were written into the heart of Man from the creation. Now, in view of the fact of our evil inclinations even from birth, this simple truth has been obscured. Many such simple truths have been lost. So God gives us an explicit commandment. Do not murder (9:5–6). This underscores the dignity of man as created in the image and likeness of God.

There was a punishment attached to this command: Anyone who kills someone else must be killed. The penalty was attached for the same reason as the commandment itself;

because mankind had become evil and only a threat could dissuade us from ignoring the command. This was exactly the opposite of what God told Cain after he had killed Abel. Cain was not to be avenged. The command that God gave to Noah was the basis for human governmental authority. It authorized the civil authorities to enforce laws that protect those people under their jurisdiction from the chaos of sin. Our constitution was established with this in mind. The preamble says:

> We the people of the United States, in order to form a more perfect union, establish justice, insure domestic tranquility, provide for the common defense, promote the general welfare, and secure the blessings of liberty to ourselves and our posterity, do ordain and establish this Constitution for the United States of America.

The entire fabric of social order begins with "establishing justice" and "insuring domestic tranquility." Governments exist primarily for this reason.

Genesis 9:7—As for you, be fruitful and multiply; populate the earth abundantly and multiply in it.

This is a repetition of a previous (9:1) blessing from God. Right after the Flood the three sons of Noah were still living close together and these blessings are for all of them. The population explosion that logically should follow upon this, and the extended long lives of men with many children, is necessary in order to get the human race going again and to repopulate the earth. This is still the writing of more than one son, and this reiterated blessing at this time emphasizes that this is the will of God for all of them.

Based on this blessing we will do an estimated population projection for the human race for the time immediately after the Flood, and extending until the confusion of tongues at Babel. (But Later on we will be told that Noah did not father any children after the Deluge. And why, after that divine blessing, did Noah not have children? An incident in the account of the three sons hints at why. Something happened that defiled his wife.)

This account of the time immediately after the Flood states explicitly that God spoke to and blessed Noah and his sons. Thus it would not be surprising to find that each of the sons of Noah wrote something describing this time. In the entire text from 8:15 where God spoke to Noah through 9:19 we are probably seeing three accounts intermingled. Moses kept the ancient account intact and did not remove any overlapping narratives. This agrees with the fact that for a time after the Flood the three sons were still living near each other.

Genesis 9:8—Then God spoke to Noah and to his sons with him, saying,

Genesis 9:9—Now behold, I Myself do establish My covenant with you, and with your descendants after you.

Genesis 9:10—and with every living creature that is with you, the birds, the cattle, and every beast of the earth with you; of all that comes out of the ark, even every beast of the earth.

Genesis 9:11—I establish My covenant with you; and all flesh shall never again be cut off by the water of the flood, neither shall there again be a flood to destroy the earth.

The covenant God establishes here is the one He promised Noah before the Flood (6:18). In this account we see that the Lord God made promises not only to Noah and his sons, but He also made a promise to the animals that came out of the ark. He promised never again to destroy the earth with a universal Flood. Because God punished the entire earth and the animals for the sin of mankind, now He makes a promise to them also.

These verses are said to have been addressed to Noah and to his three sons. Therefore, I do not see the repetition in these verses as the work of several men but as the exact way that the Lord spoke to them as a group. The repetition serves to emphasize to us the solemn nature of the agreement that God made with human beings, with the animals, and even with the earth itself after the Flood. These are the conditions under which we have lived on this earth throughout the 4,000+ years of history since then.

This is not just a promise; it is a covenant, a sacred, legally binding agreement. When God chose to relate to man throughout history—as He condescended to insert Himself into human lives in this way—He at times has made such agreements. Covenants are the most solemn form of agreement, and He is utterly faithful and true to His word.

However, I believe that the following lines do involve the testimony of multiple sons. God spoke clearly to each of the three sons, and each testified to what he heard the Lord say. Thus the following verses about the rainbow are probably the writing of two or more of the sons of Noah.

Genesis 9:12—God said, "This is the sign of the covenant which I am making between Me and you and every living creature that is with you, for all successive generations.

Genesis 9:13—I set My bow in the cloud, and it shall be for a sign of a covenant between Me and the earth.

Genesis 9:14—It shall come about, when I bring a cloud over the earth, that the bow will be seen in the cloud,

Genesis 9:15—and I will remember My covenant, which is between Me and you and every living creature of all flesh; and never again shall the water become a flood to destroy all flesh.

Genesis 9:16—When the bow is in the cloud, then I will look upon it, to remember the everlasting covenant between God and every living creature of all flesh that is on the earth.

Genesis 9:17—And God said to Noah, "This is the sign of the covenant which I have established between Me and all flesh that is on the earth."

In order to underscore His kindly intentions toward man, the Lord God gave a sign for all men to see that would remind them and Him of the covenant He was making with Noah, his descendants after him, and with all flesh on earth. The rainbow was clear and visible for all of mankind to see. Before the Flood, rain was mild and always a blessing. During this age of the world storms sometimes rage violently, but the Lord God will never allow them to cause the universal destruction of all living things.

It might even have been that the rainbow was not known before the Flood because rain was not accompanied with violent storms as it can be at times today. If the rainbow was a known phenomenon, then it certainly was not invested with the significance that God gave to it here. The sun shining onto and reflecting off of the clouds is a reminder that

He will not allow a Deluge to happen again. This is an excellent choice as a sign for this covenant because it serves to reassure men and women whenever violent storms come.

Life after the Deluge:
The century that followed the Flood saw a new beginning for human life on earth. Their first century of expansion was punctuated by one singular event in human history: the confusion of tongues at Babel and the scattering of mankind over the earth. This event was the direct act of God, and it gave rise to the languages, nations, and cultures of the world of men today.

The historical data that is available to us from the few centuries that followed the Flood is sparse and fragmented. Archeology has attempted to piece it together, but always from a perspective that is firmly rooted in the evolutionary world view and with a chronology that is derived from that belief system. From the biblical perspective we have three stories that tell us about this chaotic and obscure time in human history:
- The last part of the history of the sons of Noah—Shem, Ham, and Japheth. This covers a short time immediately after the Flood when the sons of Noah and their families are living near one another geographically. This is why they continue to write more on their common document. When the population grows larger and people move apart from one another then their common testimony ends.
- The account of Shem follows their account and begins with the migration of the human race eastward. Its purpose is to explain to us the confusion of tongues and the scattering that happened at Babel. This was meant to be a continuation of the history compiled by the three brothers. But from various considerations we will see that it was written long after the scattering at Babel, specifically in order to give us an explanation of that foundational historical event.
- The history of Terah, which was written to connect the times immediately after the Flood and the scattering at Babel to the age of the patriarch's and the divine promise.

The Final Section of the Joint Account of the Three Sons:
Only eight human beings were alive on earth after the Flood and after God spoke to Noah and his sons and blessed them. Unlike the time of Adam and Eve at the creation, they are fallen human beings who are not in full fellowship with the Lord God—men and women who are empty-hearted and sinful because of that fact. The story of Ham and Canaan that is presented in the account that follows is not very pretty, but it gives us another picture of the degeneration that engulfed humanity because of the fall.

Genesis 9:18—Now the sons of Noah who came out of the ark were Shem and Ham and Japheth; and Ham was the father of Canaan.

Genesis 9:19—These three *were* the sons of Noah, and from these the whole earth was populated.

These lines state in an unequivocal way that:
- The sons of Noah who came out of the ark, those who survived the Flood, were Shem, Ham, and Japheth. And Ham was the father of Canaan.
- The entire earth was repopulated by the three sons of Noah; that is, Noah did not beget any more children after the Flood.

Both of these statements assert that Noah was not the father of Canaan. This simple fact is very important in the story that is to be developed next. This is the only story after the Flood that the sons relate. It must have been very important to the family.

Genesis 9:20—Then Noah began farming and planted a vineyard.

Genesis 9:21—He drank of the wine and became drunk, and uncovered himself inside his tent.

Genesis 9:22—Ham, the father of Canaan, saw the nakedness of his father, and told his two brothers outside.

Genesis 9:23—But Shem and Japheth took a garment and laid it upon both their shoulders and walked backward and covered the nakedness of their father; and their faces were turned away, so that they did not see their father's nakedness.

Genesis 9:24—When Noah awoke from his wine, he knew what his youngest son had done to him.

Genesis 9:25—So he said, "cursed be Canaan; a servant of servants he shall be to his brothers."

The meaning of this story turns on the way we understand certain phrases that are used: "Noah . . . uncovered himself in his tent" and "Ham . . . saw the nakedness of his father." It sounds from the plain reading of the text as if Noah was drunk and naked in his tent, and his son Ham saw him in that exposed condition and told his brothers about it. That was his offense. But in later verses of the Pentateuch Moses uses very similar phrases to refer to "having sexual relations" in various disordered ways. Here are some examples:

> If *there is* a man who lies with his father's wife, he has uncovered his father's nakedness; both of them shall surely be put to death. (Leviticus 20:11)
>
> If *there is* a man who takes his sister, his father's daughter or his mother's daughter, so that he sees her nakedness and she sees his nakedness . . . He has uncovered his sister's nakedness. (Leviticus 20:17)
>
> You shall also not uncover the nakedness of your mother's sister or of your father's sister, for such a one has made naked his blood relative; they will bear their guilt. (Leviticus 20:19)
>
> If *there is* a man who lies with his uncle's wife he has uncovered his uncle's nakedness; they will bear their sin. They will die childless. (Leviticus 20:20)
>
> If *there is* a man who takes his brother's wife, it is abhorrent; he has uncovered his brother's nakedness. They will be childless. (Leviticus 20:21)

A long list of prohibitions against sexual relations that would disorder the God-ordained pattern of family and society are listed in Leviticus 18:6–20, and consistently the phrase describing the offense is this: "uncovering your (uncle's, father's, brother's, sister's, etc.) nakedness." The term speaks of the nakedness of that person or, if she is a married woman, about the nakedness of her husband; that is, a married woman's nakedness is also her husband's nakedness. The term always refers to having intimate relations with a person within the immediate family. To rephrase the above passage with this in mind:

> Then Noah began farming and planted a vineyard. He drank of the wine and became drunk, ~~and uncovered himself~~ [this may mean he not only took off his own garments, but also that he undressed his wife (for she is his nakedness)] inside his tent. Ham, the father of Canaan, ~~saw the nakedness of his father~~ [saw Noah's wife, his mother, naked, not only his father], and told his two brothers outside. But Shem and Japheth took a garment and laid it upon both their shoulders and walked

backward and ~~covered the nakedness of their father~~ [covered their mother as well]; and their faces were turned away, so that they did not see ~~their father's nakedness~~ [they did not see Noah or their mother lying naked in her tent]. When Noah awoke from his wine, he knew what his youngest son had done to him. So he said,
"Cursed be Canaan; A servant of servants he shall be to his brothers."

Look at it like this: Noah and his wife were drunk and naked and might have intended to have relations, but fell asleep instead. Ham came in, found them in that condition, and talked about it. The other brothers did not look at their mother in that way but covered her modestly and left. But in fact Ham did more than just look. Now I am going to insert something into this story that I know is not explicitly stated, but that makes it much more logical. As a result of what Ham did the wife of Noah got pregnant.

Ham had sexual relations with his own mother at that time. Perhaps he did not admit that to his brothers, and he said that he just looked. But eventually she became pregnant and then the whole truth came out. Their disordered union produced the child Canaan. When Noah's wife became pregnant the realization of what had happened impressed itself upon Noah and upon everyone else. There was no way to hide it in their tiny group.

Canaan was a baby without social standing. Did he inherit from Noah, from Ham, from anyone? His father was also his half-brother. His mother was also his grandmother. He was an anomaly in all family relationships. He did not fit into any social structure. He was cursed! Therefore Noah pronounced a curse upon him. He would be a servant of servants to his brothers—not really having the status of a son in any way. Noah was the senior patriarch and the head of the family of mankind, and he had spoken.

This "augmentation" of the story is hinted at in certain ways within the account itself.
> Now the sons of Noah who came out of the ark were Shem and Ham and Japheth; and Ham was the father of Canaan. These three *were* the sons of Noah, and from these the whole earth was populated. (Genesis 9:18–19)

The statement that "Ham was the father of Canaan" asserts and emphasizes that Ham begot him. This phrase might be inserted because he was born of Noah's wife. The statement that "from these the whole world was populated" again emphasizes that Noah did not have any children after the Flood. Only his sons begat children after the Flood. Again in the story it is "Ham, the father of Canaan" that saw the nakedness of his father. It was not just Ham, but "Ham, the father of Canaan" who saw the nakedness.

These extra emphatic inserts lead us to the conclusion that the family judged that Ham had transgressed and fathered this child through his mother. It appears that he never admitted his deed to the family, and so the story was written in this way, insinuating but not explicitly airing the dark family secret.

Noah was so angry that he refused to adopt Canaan as his own, and he did not have any more children. Thus Canaan was left dangling in the early pre-Flood social order. He was no one's son. The two verses that introduced this story, 9:18 and 9:19, were the writing of Shem and/or Japheth (but not Ham) as they related the story for posterity.

This disordered sexuality immediately after the Flood reminds us of the tragic family life that Lot had after he fled from Sodom and Gomorrah. Something like this happened to Lot and his daughters when they initiated sexual relations with him in order to conceive.

Living in a society where family life and sexuality is out of order can have deep-seated effects on the children. Sometimes they cannot leave it behind. It follows after them and establishes continuity into successive generations, and this is what appears to have happened to one of the sons of Noah. Who knows what disorders were prevalent in the antediluvian society that the Lord saw fit to eradicate so completely?

Some observations on the timing of this episode: We cannot determine chronology by looking at the genealogies in chapter ten and noting that Canaan was Ham's fourth son because those genealogies do not include every offspring of the sons. The genealogies that Shem gives us in chapter ten are specifically crafted to identify those descendants of the three sons who became the progenitors of the nations of the world. Therefore, they are incomplete and cannot tell us how many children Ham had before Canaan was born. All we can say is that this unfortunate incident happened before the three brothers moved apart so far that they discontinued their joint account.

Here is a projection of population growth after the Flood as the years wore on, based on what we did for the beginning of the human race (see comments on 4:24). I will also do an estimate for when the incident with Canaan might have taken place.

Estimated Post-Flood Population Projection:
Because God again directed mankind to be fruitful and to multiply, and because He also blessed the sons of Noah from whom the population of the earth was derived (9:1, 9:7, 9:19), we should assume that there was another population explosion just as there was after the initial creation of man. If we do a population projection like we did for the time immediately after the creation, then the expected population of the earth until 100 years after the Flood—at the time when the confusion of tongues happened at Babel—is given in the following chart. I assume three couples to reproduce instead of just one.

Years after Deluge	Growth Rate	Population	
0		8	(but Noah had no children after the Flood)
15	10%	27	(time of the incident with Ham and Canaan?)
50	10%	705	(Shem, Ham, Japheth joint account ends?)
100	10%	82,685	(time of confusion of tongues at Babel)

This is the estimated population of the earth after the Flood and leading up to the time when the confusion of tongues took place. This gives us an idea of what the world of man looked like at that pivotal period in history. I am sticking the incident with Ham and Canaan at some guessed time, and I am also guessing at when the brothers parted.

Genesis 9:26—He also said, "Blessed be the LORD, the God of Shem; and let Canaan be his servant.

Genesis 9:27—May God enlarge Japheth, and let him dwell in the tents of Shem; and let Canaan be his servant.

Let us look at Noah's original patriarchal curse on Canaan once again:
> Cursed be Canaan; A servant of servants he shall be to his brothers. (Genesis 9:25)

In the curse of 9:25, Canaan was to be the servant of his brothers; that is, of Put, Cush, and Mizraim (10:6). This removed him from any status in the fellowship with his peers. Thus in the little society of men and women that was developing after the Flood he had no dignified status or place. He was to be a servant in the social order of his childhood.

We tend to assume that all of the curses that Noah levied on Canaan were pronounced at the same time, that verses 9:26 and 9:27 happened at the same time as 9:25. But the first curse on Canaan in 9:25 was levied as soon as he was born, or even before. And it probably was later that Noah gave a blessing to his two sons Shem and Japheth, and in this statement we see that he marks Canaan as a servant to them as well.

The blessings given here, and thus the second curse against Canaan that accompanies them, might well have been given when the family was larger and the brothers parted with their respective descendants to start new lives. If we understand the timing in this logical way then it means that Noah extended the curse on Canaan to include his relationships with his uncles and their own children, who were his cousins. But Noah must have seen something developing in the line of Canaan to make him repeat and extend his curse on that ill-born child after he was an adult and had children of his own.

The Family of Noah Parts:[704]
It is logical that Noah would bless his sons as they separated from him, and it is logical even more because this is the end of the joint account of the three sons. At this time of parting Noah blessed Shem and Japheth, but he still did not bless his son Ham. Instead he extended the curse on Canaan. We should assume that this was because he could see that Canaan and his descendants were already developing along ungodly lines.

When the family parted they migrated east and settled in Shinar, as Shem relates (11:2). This would mean that as the family grew larger and parted—as they began to form the city-states of Mesopotamia—Canaan, and also probably his descendants, would still have been kept in the status of servants in the households of the other sons. Archeology reveals to us that the primitive civilizations of the cities of Mesopotamia did indeed have slaves. The slaves would work for a family for a few years and then were released; that is, it was a transient and mild form of servanthood that was practiced in those societies.

Again, Noah blesses his two sons Shem and Japheth, but not his son Ham, most likely because the descendants of Canaan were already displaying some kind of disordered sexuality. Canaan was the progenitor of the Canaanites who lived in the land that God was giving to the Israelites at the time of the Exodus. By that later time the nations that had descended from Canaan had become very wicked and corrupt. These are the nations whom God commanded the Israelites to completely eradicate. The Exodus was the time when the iniquity of the Amorites (who were among the sons of Canaan) was finally complete (Genesis 15:16). This is the people who had the giants living in their midst—the product of further disordered sexuality similar to what had been common before the Flood—which had been instrumental in instigating the societal conditions that forced God to bring the Flood on the whole human race.

Several centuries later the problems that had surfaced in the family before the three sons separated had grown much worse. They were exhibited in the depravity of Sodom and Gomorrah and all of the Canaanite nations. All such perversions finally came to a head at the time of the Exodus, when the "iniquity of the Amorites was complete" (Genesis 15:16). At that time God ordered Israel to exterminate those peoples completely.

Again, we see that Noah explicitly blesses Shem and Japheth, but does not bless Ham at all—but he does not curse him either. After the Flood God Himself had blessed the three sons of Noah (9:1), so it is reasonable that Noah would not want to contradict that blessing by speaking badly of his third son. But he adds no further blessing to him.

The curse on Canaan might seem cruel or undeserved, but we should view it as Noah's way of placing this ill-begotten person in an appropriate place in the social order. He did not fit properly into any family tree. The curse determined he would hold the role of servant to the rest of the family. This assigned him a place, but not a place of dignity or honor.

It is important to note that the curse did not originally extend to his descendants. The second curse was probably based on problems observed a generation later. Finally, the descendants of Canaan were seen as wicked in the days of Moses—not because of their fathers, but because of the cruel, perverted nature of their own culture, a depravity which was the result of wicked choices that they themselves had made. God ordered them to be eradicated because of their own wickedness. Nevertheless, it might well have been that the son of Ham took upon himself the sin of his father and passed it to his own children. As the generations passed, the disorder deepened and again displayed what had been prevalent in human society before the Flood. Noah saw this in his son Ham, saw it also in Canaan and his immediate descendants, and twice spoke a curse against it.

Every human civilization today has deep taboos against incest—against sexual relations between a parent and his or her child. This story, including the curse of Noah, set at the second origin of human history, and thus etched in the cultural memory of all peoples, is probably a major reason for this universal reality.

It is also worthy of note that even at this early time Noah referred to "the God of Shem" when he conferred his blessing on his other two sons. Even as the sons parted Shem was marked as a godly son in some special way. These two blessings, and also the curse on Canaan, must have been spoken while the brothers and the whole family were still living close together, before the social structure had become so large that they had to move apart. Thus all three sons were still involved in the writing of this story.

Genesis 9:28—Noah lived three hundred and fifty years after the flood.

Genesis 9:29—So all the days of Noah were nine hundred and fifty years, and he died.

Genesis 10:1a—Now these are *the records of* the generations of Shem, Ham, and Japheth, the sons of Noah.

The last verses written in the history of the three brothers was the record of the death of their father Noah. This did not happen until several centuries after the episode with Ham and Canaan, and thus it took place after the family had split up. But the brothers must have come back together to bury their father, for these two final repetitive verses appear to have been written by two different sons of Noah. It was a common ancient practice for sons to come together to bury their father. The same custom is seen with Ishmael and Isaac at the death of Abraham, and with Esau and Jacob at the death of Isaac. At the time that they buried Noah the three sons signed their account.

The Long Lives of the Patriarchs:
Why did the people live so long before the Flood? It was not a result of the tree of life, because they had no access to it. Adam and Eve **might** have eaten from it before they sinned, but no one else could have—and Adam did not live any longer than most of his immediate descendants. Only after the Flood did life spans begin to decrease. After the scattering at Babel they decreased yet again. Perhaps longer lives were a way God that provided for the multiplication and spread of humanity over the whole earth. Once the population was large enough, God allowed a decrease in vigor and vitality, so we died more quickly. Under the curse of death and sorrow, life was not the blessing that it would have been before the fall. Death is a hated enemy, but fallen human life is itself a mere vanity.

Looking at this from a scientific perspective instead of a theological/spiritual perspective, note that, if radioactive decay began after the fall, then deleterious mutations would have begun to accumulate in the human genome. After the Flood the human gene pool was greatly narrowed, so genetic entropy began to show its effect—lessened vitality and shortened life spans.

Concluding Remarks on the Flood Account:
The Flood account is best seen as an accurate historical record of the Flood for a variety of interlocking and convincing reasons.
- The account is detailed and complete. It is not written as a mythological story but as a sober historical record of events. The wording leads us to understand it in this way.
- The account is chronologically ordered, making it more reasonable that it is the story of a sequence of events—a story that was written in the order that it unfolded by men who were intimately familiar with and involved in those events. The only people who could actually know about those events were the survivors of that catastrophe.
- Based on the duplicate statements within the account it appears to be the work of three men. This has been noted by many commentators and agrees with the fact that the authors that are named are three: Shem, Ham, and Japheth.
- The joint account ends with Noah blessing his sons, an event that logically would have occurred as the family separated and some or most of them moved apart. Thus any further continuous joint writing would have been impractical.
- The account of Shem begins after this account ends. It explains "Now the whole earth spoke the same language and the same words. It came about as they journeyed east that they found a plain in the land of Shinar and settled there" (Genesis 11:1–2). Thus this is where the family of Noah moved to, and where they initially settled down, as they became too numerous to remain in one place—and also, we may assume, at the command of God. For the Lord had said to them after the Flood "Be fruitful and multiply, and fill the earth." At Shinar mankind decided not to fill the earth but to stay in one area. Shem records this rebellion for us—about a century after the Flood.
- The historical accuracy of the Flood account, attested to in every way by the text of Genesis, shows that the prevailing theories of origins cannot be accurate. Geological theories uniformly ignore the Flood and pretend that it never happened. Instead they consistently try to account for the evidences of the Flood in some naturalistic way.

Noah was deeply impressed with the tragic conditions of his day—conditions that were the immediate reason for the judgment of the Flood. The perversions of the men and women of his day were carried across the Flood and were displayed by his son Ham in the way he begat Canaan. Noah was aghast at this wicked deed. As Canaan grew up—as the family parted ways—Noah again was dismayed at the way that Canaan and his descendants were developing. That is why he again marked him as a servant of his uncles and their families. When Noah, in his old age, translated his own tablet from pictographic to cuneiform, he again warned of this danger. The phrase "and also afterward" in 6:4 pointed to what was developing among the descendants of Canaan. It was like before the Flood.

Spiritual Connection to the Story of Creation:
We have seen that the account of the Flood as given in Genesis attests to an early human history that is completely at odds with the scientific-naturalistic theories of our day. But the account of the Flood is spiritually connected to the story of creation. Peter connects them when he comments on the unbelief that will arise at the end of the age, when men will deny the truth of both of these facts for a certain common underlying reason:

> [I]n the last days mockers will come . . . saying, "Where is the promise of His coming? For *ever* since the fathers fell asleep, all continues just as it was from the beginning of creation." For when they maintain this, it escapes their notice that by the word of God *the* heavens existed long ago and *the* earth was formed out of water and by water, through which the world at that time was destroyed, being flooded with water. But by His word the present heavens and earth are being reserved for fire, kept for the day of judgment and destruction of ungodly men. (2 Peter 3:3–7)

Thus Peter connects the two skeptical attitudes and shows the common reason for that disbelief. It is the perspective that "all things have continued as they were from the time of the fathers." This is essentially what philosopher-scientists say today when they assert that the physical laws—which mankind has discovered and has come to understand—have been in effect without interruption throughout all of the past. Thus, in their view and according to their theories, the origin of things must be explained by the ages-long working out of natural processes operating under those immutable laws. This attitude essentially rules God out of the picture because whatever our understanding of Him is, He is not a natural cause. He is outside the natural realm—supernatural, transcendent.

Secular Theories of Origins:
In pursuing this idea and in marshalling their "evidence" to support it, people have built a huge edifice of human speculation and reasoning. This body of "evidence," slanted as it is against the supernatural, is leading people to think that there is no God—or that He is extremely distant and not intimately concerned about human life on this earth—or that the biblical account of the Flood cannot be trusted. From the perspective of this world view the account of the creation, the fall, and the degeneration of mankind—and the eventual divine judgment of the Flood—are all considered to be fanciful myths carefully formulated by people who were not as "advanced" as we are and thus were not as able to understand the true nature of the world. We today are much too mature to take them at face value. If we are unbelievers then we dismiss them with contempt or perhaps some amusement. If we are believers then we reinterpret them in some way to arrive at the real "spiritual" truth that lies within them, but we do not accept them as the truth about our origins.

As we have departed from the Ancient Faith we have failed to realize something about the theories of origins that permeate our culture and deeply shape our thinking and our world view: they are not really science at all! They tell us stories about the origin of the universe, the earth, and life that cannot possibly be verified by the scientific method and that are internally inconsistent and inadequate. In fact, they are scientifically impossible! Thus we have replaced the Ancient Faith with a different faith—one based on the wisdom of man. Our new belief exalts mankind to the pinnacle of creation as the leading edge of evolutionary development. Yet ironically it also debases us, deprives us of the image of God, views us as formed in the image of primates, and robs us of our divine origin and destiny.

The Forward-Looking Purposes of God in the Deluge:
The events before the Flood showed that a humanity that had rejected God and that was subject to demonic deception, if allowed to be united in the earth, would turn against the Lord. The division of the land into continents and the formation of impassable areas of land such as mountains and deserts can be seen as God's providential preparation of the post-Flood earth as a safe location for fallen humanity. After the Flood it was vital for mankind to spread out over the earth before the land bridges to Australia and America were lost to the rising seas. Then the barriers would keep mankind from a united culture that would lead all people to reject God. These were the spiritual reasons for the judgment of Babel. The geography of the post-Flood earth was designed to inhibit fallen humanity from being fully united. This has been effective throughout history until the present time, when the barriers have been overcome by modern modes of travel and communication.

Lyrical Verses on The Tower of Babel

The righteous Noah became a new beginning, a second Adam . . .

The phrase 'Be fruitful and multiply' that was said [by the Lord God] showed its strength . . .
    and the crowds and people of humanity began to increase.
They went out and found a land that had been laid waste by the floods,
    an entire world that was devoid of heirs . . .

When the people went out to settle
    rebellion showed her nature among the generations.
The people clapped their hands with one mind
    to begin the wicked deed with a hardened heart . . .

Let each of us persist and not be scattered throughout the lands . . .

Let us build a city that will not be vanquished by a deluge.
Let us erect a building that not even floods will overwhelm.
Let us make a citadel . . .

Let us build and raise up to the heavens by our workmanship
    a great fortress in the awesome name of might.
Let us ascend and be neighbors with the sun in its high place,
    and our dwelling place will be close to it.
Let us ascend and stand on the path where the moon crosses,
    and let us gaze upon the change of the seasons as they turn.
Come, let us attain the stars of light in their paths,
    And come, let us make for ourselves a name that is more distinguished than theirs . . .

Let us build a castle that is the beginning and the end,
    which there has been nothing like it on earth nor will there be.
Come, let us make for ourselves a city that reaches even to the heavens,
    And let us dwell there in a place that is above destruction . . .

Let us go beyond the clouds and settle above them . . .

They rebelled against the Lord and did not understand
    that their deed could not be accomplished.
They embarked on a great work that had no reward
    And a harsh labor in infamy that could not be finished . . .

A hardened heart assured them at the beginning,
    but judgment shamed them toward the end.
They approached the act of rebellion with a blind understanding,
    filled with pride concerning the mighty construction.

Justice, however, allowed them to begin
    so that it might bring them down through that work by way of punishment.
It bound the wild animals as with a yoke
    so that they would become wearied through that work because of their presumptuousness.
He beat them with the great work as if with a rod,
    that Wise One who knows how to beat kindly.[705]

—Jacob of Sarug, 6th century

Babel

Here is the beginning and the end of the text of the fifth set of tablets:

10 ¹ᵇ and sons were born to them after the flood. ² The sons of Japheth *were* Gomer and Magog and Madai and Javan and Tubal and Meshech and Tiras. ³ The sons of Gomer *were* Ashkenaz and Riphath and Togarmah . . .

11 ⁸ So the LORD scattered them abroad from there over the face of the whole earth; and they stopped building the city. ⁹ Therefore its name was called Babel, because there the LORD confused the language of the whole earth; and from there the LORD scattered them abroad over the face of the whole earth. ¹⁰ᵃ These are *the records of* the generations of Shem.

Archeological Considerations:

> Tablet (series) 5 (10:2-11:10) [was] written or owned by Shem. He writes of the birth and the formation into clans of the fifth generation after him. We know that he outlived the last generation recorded in this tablet, that is, the sons of Joktan.[706]

> The fifth series of tablets . . . includes the famous tenth chapter—the account of the origins of the clans which became nations. Embedded in this chapter is a brief statement regarding Nimrod. In the earlier verses of the eleventh chapter we have an account of the building of the Tower of Babel and the scattering of the peoples. Of these records it is written, "These are the histories of Shem." We have already referred to the significance of the seemingly abrupt ending of his genealogical list with the "sons of Joktan," and the repetition and its completion in Terah's tablet. This tablet of Shem's is an outline of developments during the 500 years after the Flood.[707]

Historical Considerations:

Historical Background for the Account of Shem: Only a small number of the cities of ancient Shinar shown here existed in the period when the story of Shem took place. Each of them was what we would call a small town, with perhaps one to ten thousand people. Thus the total population of all the cities might have been about 50,000 people, with perhaps a few tens of thousands more scat- tered about. This was the extent of the post-Flood human culture at the time of Babel. After the Deluge God repeated His initial directive to be fruitful, multiply, and fill the earth. Then He blessed mankind again (9:1). The directive and blessing were given to Noah and to his sons. So we can assume there was another population growth spurt like what happened in the beginning with Adam and Eve.

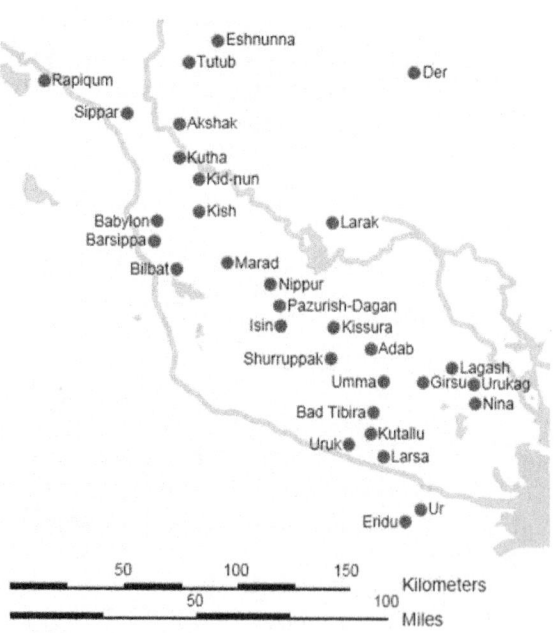

Ciudades_de_Sumeris.svg Cratesderivative work: Phirosiberia (talk)

We did a population projection for the time immediately after the Flood (see the population projection just before the comments on Genesis 9:26) and we estimated that by the time of the confusion of languages at Babel, around 100 years after the Deluge, the projected population of the earth would have been 82,685 people. This was the approximate size of the family of mankind at the time of Babel.

Introduction and Overview of Shem's Account:

The account of Shem has two main sections: The table of nations (chapter 10), and the account of the confusion of tongues (chapter 11:1-10). These two sections are written in reverse order; that is, chapter 10 historically follows chapter 11. Why is that? I think that the full significance of the confusion at Babel, and the need to relate it, was not immediately obvious. It was seen as necessary to relate this pivotal event only after its consequences became clear. First Shem recorded the dispersion of mankind in the table of nations. But how and when did Shem write the table of the nations—the descendants of this brothers? Shem was not in direct daily contact with his brothers and their extended families. The account of the three sons ended when the family became large enough to split up, when Noah blessed the sons as they spread out to fill the entire earth as God has commanded.

To understand how Shem gathered the information in the table of nations, since he was not in direct contact with the broader human race, I make an important observation about the culture of ancient times: It was the ancient custom for sons to come back together to bury their father, as will be observed with the death of Abraham, when Ishmael and Isaac together buried him, and with the death of Isaac, when Esau and Jacob together buried him. After the death of Abraham, Isaac (his chronicler) records information about the family of Ishmael—information that he surely had obtained from his far-flung brother at the time of their father's death. Likewise, after the death of Isaac, Jacob lists genealogical information for his brother Esau—information that he obtained from him when they came together to bury their father. We should see the same thing as happening for Noah and his sons.

Thus when Noah died we should assume that the three sons came together to bury him. That is also when the three sons of Noah completed their joint account and signed it, and that is also when they exchanged information about their respective families. By that time it became much clearer how significant the confusion of tongues at Babel had been. It had resulted in the scattering of mankind over the entire earth and the formation of many new languages and new nations. Shem used the genealogical information obtained from his brothers to write the table of nations. He must have written that down soon after his brothers departed after burying Noah, or a little more than 350 years after the Flood.

But Babel, the actual event, the source of the confusion of tongues, seems to have happened earlier, only 101 years after the Deluge. We can deduce this because of one verse in the genealogy of Shem.
> Two sons were born to Eber; the name of the one *was* Peleg, **for in his days the earth was divided**; and his brother's name *was* Joktan. (Genesis 10:25) (bold mine)

From the genealogical records of Terah we know that Peleg was born 101 years after the Flood. This tells us that the confusion of tongues that divided the earth came upon men at that time. Contrast with 11:1, where the whole earth used the same language. Thus Noah died 249 years after Babel. So the table of nations was written long after Babel, and the account of Babel was written even after that. Why did Shem write the account of Babel?

Shem eventually wrote the story of Babel to explain the key event that had sparked the history-changing division of the human race. He begins by explaining, "The whole earth used the same language and the same words. It came about as they journeyed east, that they found a plain in the land of Shinar and settled there." (11:1,2). This is the event that ended the previous account—the joint account of the three sons. They parted, and at least some of them journeyed east and settled in Shinar, and they all had one language.

We tend to imagine that the confusion of tongues was one sudden and short-term event, and that the people immediately picked up and scattered. It is much more reasonable to see it as something that began suddenly, but which continued for many years, even for many decades. The scattering that it caused also happened over a long time. The full implications of what had happened did not immediately become obvious. As confusion over the multiplication of languages was sorted out people formed groups by language and migrated away over a long period of time. Each of the sons watched as his descendants scattered to distant realms, and each recorded who left—who was the head of each group. That is the way that they each compiled the genealogical data that Shem used.

Note that Shem's table of nations does not give the complete genealogies of the sons of Noah. Consider these explanatory statements of Shem:

For Japheth: From these the **coastlands of the nations were separated** into their lands, everyone **according to his language**, according to their families, **into their nations**. (Genesis 10:5)

For Ham: . . . the sons of Ham, according to their families, **according to their languages**, by their lands, **by their nations**. (Genesis 10:20)

For Shem: . . . the sons of Shem, according to their families, **according to their languages**, by their lands, **according to their nations**. (Genesis 10:31)

Summary: These are the families of the sons of Noah, according to their genealogies, **by their nations**; and **out of these the nations were separated on the earth** after the flood. (Genesis 10:32)

They are crafted, as Shem explains, to identify exactly those groupings that correspond to a language and a nation, and to name the leaders of each of those groupings. The reason why Shem wrote this account was to describe and explain the division of the human race into nations that spoke different languages. The death of Noah was 249 years after Babel. That is when the three brothers shared this information. It had been gathered by each of them over a length of time—over many years, many decades. When they shared it, then the enormity of the event became clear. Then it became necessary to write it all down— the description of what happened, and the ultimate cause of the event.

The account of Shem was written to explain to us how and from whom the nations of the world originated, and the "sons" that are mentioned in the genealogies are those who became the progenitors of the various nations and language groups that spread out from Babel to populate the earth. We take "many languages" and "diverse nations" for granted, but before Babel that was unheard of on the earth.

Thus each of the sons of Noah had many more sons and daughters born to them, for the human race was expanding rapidly as the result of the blessing that God had given to them after the Flood. But they are not listed because they were not directly caught up in the confusion of tongues. Also, from the wording we can see that Noah and his sons were not caught up in the confusion of the tongues. They continued to speak the original language of mankind from before the Flood. We should see this as divine providence that allowed the patriarchs to work together as they continued to serve the Lord faithfully.

Let us expand a bit on this thinking. Let us count the languages that were on the earth as a result of Babel. As noted, Noah, Shem, Ham, and Japheth were not dispersed, and did not have their language confused.

Looking at the family of Japheth: Ashkenaz, Riphth, Rophath, and Togrmah had their language changed. But did Gomer also have his changed, or is he in this listing only to explain who his sons are who were so affected? This is not completely clear. Magog has no sons shown, so we can assume that he is in the list because his language was changed. The same for his brothers Madai, Tubal, Meshech, and Tiras. But Javan, who has four of his sons listed, might not have had his tongue changed.

Japheth	Gomer	Ashkenaz
		Riphath
		Rophath
		Togarmah
	Magog	
	Madai	
	Javan	Elishah
		Tarshish
		Kittim
		Dodanim
	Tubal	
	Meshech	
	Tiras	

Thus how many descendants of Japheth were affected by the confusion of Babel? If we count every descendant of Japheth, then 15 people in all were affected, and 15 new languages and nations arose from his descendants. If we do not count the intermediate generations that are listed then there were only 13 new languages and nations that immediately arose from his descendants as a result of the confusion at Babel.

Shem	Elam				
	Asshur				
	Arpachshad	Shelah	Eber	Peleg	
				Joktan	Almodad
					Sheleph
					Hazarmaveth
					Jerah
					Hadoram
					Uzal
					Diklah
					Obal
					Abimael
					Sheba
					Ophir
					Havilah
					Jobab
	Lud				
	Aram	Uz			
		Hul			
		Gether			
		Mash			

Looking at Shem's genealogy we get either 26 new languages that arose from his family of descendants, or we get only 21 new languages, because Arpachshad, Shelah, Eber, Joktan, and Aram would not be counted. They would only be listed so their descendants could be properly identified.

Looking at Ham's genealogy and applying the same logic we see that, if we count all of his descendants, then 30 new languages arose from them. But if we do not count the intermediate generations—those who are perhaps in the listing only because they have children who were affected by Babel, but who were not affected themselves—then we get only 26 new languages that arose from the descendants of Ham. This is because Cush,

Raamah, Mizraim, and Canaan would be considered to be in the listing only so that certain of their descendants could be properly listed and identified.

Ham	Cush	Seba	
		Havilah	
		Sabtah	
		Raamah	Sheba
			Dedan
		Sabteca	
		Nimrod	
	Mizraim	Ludim	
		Anamim	
		Lehabim	
		Naphtuhim	
		Pathusim	
		Casluhim (Philistines)	
		Caphtorim	
	Put		
	Canaan	Sidon	
		Heth (the Hittites)	
		Jebusite	
		Amorite	
		Girgashite	
		Hivite (Kadmonites)	
		Arkite (12 miles north of Tripoli in Syria)	
		Sinite (Lebenon)	
		Arvadite	
		Zemarite (Lebanon)	
		Hamathite (north Palestine)	

The situation might also have been a mixture of cases, where some intermediate people did have their languages changed and some did not. The text of chapter ten is not clear on this point. So we can say that between 60 total languages (13+26+21), and 71 total languages (15+30+26), resulted from the confusion of tongues at Babel.

Surely the purposes of God were to force the scattering of people throughout the earth, as He first commanded. But He providentially allowed Noah and Shem to keep their tongue so that they could continue His work. I would also assume that rest of the Godly line was not affected by the confusion of tongues—the line from Shem through Peleg (Arpachshad, Shelah, Eber, and Peleg) retained the original language, for the same reason—so they could work together because they were the chosen godly line of patriarchs.

Therefore, this modifies our estimates of the total number of languages from the confusion at Babel because the number from Shem and his descendants is lessened. Thus the line including Arpachshad, Shelah, Eber, and Peleg kept their original language. So the low estimate of 60 is lessened by one to 59 (Peleg does not count as a new language, because he kept his original tongue), and the high estimate of 71 is lessened by four to 67, since all four of these men were not affected by Babel, but kept their original language. So to reiterate, there were between 59 and 67 total languages (and nations) that resulted from the confusion at Babel. One of them was the original tongue of the human race.

<u>Timing and Duration of the Scattering:</u>
The command of the Lord God, "be fruitful, multiply . . ." in 9:1 and 9:7 implies that people married and had children early in their lives. Thus the three generations after Ham and the two after Japheth that had their tongues confused were, at the time of the confusion, already adults. Each became the head of a linguistic and national group.

For Shem that is not the case at all. According to the genealogy of Terah, Eber begat Peleg when he was thirty-four years old (11:16). However Peleg's brother Joktan had thirteen sons who were heads of tribes that developed distinct languages and that became distinct nations. Even if Joktan was the first born of Eber, and if he was born when Eber was only twenty, he would have been just fourteen when Peleg was born, when the tongues were divided. He could hardly have been much older than that. Thus Joktan's children were not even born when the confusion of Babel struck the human race.

This gives yet another reason to believe that the division of tongues took place over many decades, perhaps even over a century or more. As the time wore on, and as the confusion of tongues continued to progress, even over several decades or longer, thirteen sons that eventually became the leaders of a language group and nation were born to Joktan. Once we understand the duration for the scattering we realize that Joktan might even have been a younger brother of Peleg. Note that Peleg has no descendants listed, indicating that his children, who were in the godly line of patriarchs, were not affected by the confusion of tongues. They kept Peleg's tongue, man's original language. That line of descendants, going down all the way to Terah and Abram, kept the original language of the human race.

It seems reasonable that Shem could list his descendants as far as the fifth generation for two reasons: First, they were his descendants, with whom he had a closer contact than the descendants of his brothers; second, his descendants all settled in the general area of the Middle East, where they were close enough for him maintain some contact, even after the scattering began.

Summary of these introductory observations:
- Babel came upon mankind at the time of Peleg, about 101 years after the Flood.
- The far-reaching consequences of that judgment became obvious only after many years. It was finally emphasized when the sons of Noah gathered to bury their father 249 years after Babel.
- After the burial of Noah Shem wrote down the information in chapter 10 of Genesis.
- Soon after that he wrote the account of Babel to explain the dispersion of mankind and the creation of many languages and nations.

Finally, the confusion of tongues that began at Babel was an astounding phenomenon as it descended upon the human race. For over seventeen centuries there had been just one human tongue. Suddenly many began to develop. This tendency is still present within the human family, as linguists know very well. It brought a time of chaos, confusion, and rapid change upon the human race. The confusion at Babel was a judgment by God that worked out several discernable divine purposes.
- Compel mankind to spread out and fill the earth in accordance with His mandate at the time of the creation, which was repeated immediately after the Flood (9:1).
- Assure that a world-wide pagan culture could not develop on earth that would completely eclipse knowledge of Him and obviate His purposes for mankind.
- Protecting God's chosen patriarchal line by not confusing their tongue so that they could continue to communicate with each other and pass on the divine revelation that they carried within them to subsequent generations. It was not God's intention to allow the knowledge of the Creation and the early history of the human race to be lost in the chaos of those times.

The Table of Nations:
Genesis 10:1b—and sons were born to them [the sons of Noah] **after the flood.**

We should assume that each of the sons of Noah had many sons and daughters born to them, for the human race was expanding rapidly as the result of the blessing that God had given to them after the Flood—many more than are mentioned in these genealogies.

Genesis 10:2—The sons of Japheth *were* **Gomer and Magog and Madai and Javan and Tubal and Meshech and Tiras.**

Genesis 10:3—The sons of Gomer *were* **Ashkenaz and Riphath and Togarmah.**

Genesis 10:4—The sons of Javan *were* **Elishah and Tarshish, Kittim and Dodanim.**

Genesis 10:5—From these the coastlands of the nations were separated into their lands, everyone according to his language, according to their families, into their nations.

Genesis 10:2–5 gives us two generations after Japheth—whom the Greek people know as *Japetus* or *Iapetos*—whom they call "the founder of the human race." He is probably their ancestor and the ancestor of all peoples who settled around the area near Greece. This is a skeleton list of the Indo-European peoples who were descended from Japheth. Most of these names have likely identifications in those countries.

Genesis 10:6—The sons of Ham *were* **Cush and Mizraim and Put and Canaan.**

Genesis 10:7—The sons of Cush *were* **Seba and Havilah and Sabtah and Raamah and Sabteca; and the sons of Raamah** *were* **Sheba and Dedan.**

Genesis 10:8—Now Cush became the father of Nimrod; he became a mighty one on the earth.

Genesis 10:9—He was a mighty hunter before the LORD**; therefore it is said, "Like Nimrod a mighty hunter before the L**ORD**."**

Genesis 10:10—The beginning of his kingdom was Babel and Erech and Accad and Calneh, in the land of Shinar [that is, Mesopotamia. See map below, p. 475.].

Genesis 10:11—From that land he went forth into Assyria, and built Nineveh and Rehoboth-Ir and Calah,

Genesis 10:12—and Resen between Nineveh and Calah; that is the great city.

Genesis 10:13—Mizraim became the father of Ludim and Anamim and Lehabim and Naphtuhim

Genesis 10:14—and Pathrusim and Casluhim (from which came the Philistines) and Caphtorim.

Some of the sons of Ham, other than the sons of Canaan, settled in North Africa and eventually spread out eastward through Asia. Thus Cush is Ethiopia, Put is Libya, Mizraim is Egypt, and the first five sons of Cush settled in Arabia. From Egypt the sons of Mizraim migrated south to populate the continent of Africa. The sons of Canaan all settled in the Middle East, and the cities that Nimrod founded are all located in Babylon. He is an important figure in the story of Babel and the scattering of man over the earth.

Certain names in the genealogy of Ham may have been updated later by Moses. For example, the Casluhim are said to have been ancestors of the Philistines (10:14). This might have been an editorial insert by Moses with the purpose of explaining to Israel the origin of their major enemy. He might have updated the genealogy of Canaan in this way to make certain connections for the Israelites as they were coming out of Egypt.

Genesis 10:15—Canaan became the father of Sidon, his firstborn, and Heth

Genesis 10:16—and the Jebusite and the Amorite and the Girgashite

Genesis 10:17—and the Hivite and the Arkite and the Sinite

Genesis 10:18—and the Arvadite and the Zemarite and the Hamathite; and afterward the families of the Canaanite were spread abroad.

Genesis 10:19—The territory of the Canaanite extended from Sidon as you go toward Gerar, as far as Gaza; as you go toward Sodom and Gomorrah and Admah and Zeboiim, as far as Lasha.

Genesis 10:20—These are the sons of Ham, according to their families, according to their languages, by their lands, by their nations.

Because Shem wrote his story later on in his life—several centuries after the Flood—it can reference cities of the plains (Sodom, Gomorrah . . .) that did not arise until quite a while after Babel. The descendants of Ham that came from Canaan, including those who lived in those cities, remained in the area of the Middle East. Those cities were destroyed and so had passed out of memory by the time of the Exodus. Thus the time Shem's account was written must have been two to four centuries after the Flood. Although some tribal names may be newer, perhaps updated by Moses, the description of the area where they settled is ancient, written by Shem. This timing for the writing of Shem's account is consistent with what we discussed earlier—that he wrote it after the death of Noah.

Genesis 10:21—Also to Shem, the father of all the children of Eber, *and* the older brother of Japheth, children were born.

Genesis 10:22—The sons of Shem *were* Elam and Asshur and Arpachshad and Lud and Aram.

Genesis 10:23—The sons of Aram *were* Uz and Hul and Gether and Mash.

Genesis 10:24—Arpachshad became the father of Shelah; and Shelah became the father of Eber.

Genesis 10:25—Two sons were born to Eber; the name of the one *was* Peleg, for in his days the earth was divided; and his brother's name *was* Joktan.

As noted, in the days of Peleg, or about 101 years after the Flood, the newly developing civilization on earth was divided by the confusion of tongues. The name Peleg means "division." From this important name, included perhaps to give us this information, we can see the timing of this event—the approximate date for the confusion of tongues at Babel.

See the matrix of people and their associated birth dates below.

Genesis 10:26—Joktan became the father of Almodad and Sheleph and Hazarmaveth and Jerah

Genesis 10:27—and Hadoram and Uzal and Diklah

Genesis 10:28—and Obal and Abimael and Sheba

Genesis 10:29—and Ophir and Havilah and Jobab; all these were the sons of Joktan.

Genesis 10:30—Now their settlement extended from Mesha as you go toward Sephar, the hill country of the east.

Genesis 10:31—These are the sons of Shem, according to their families, according to their languages, by their lands, according to their nations.

Eber was the eponymous progenitor of the Hebrews. Thus they were the descendants of the one who had not departed from the Lord God. God was "the God of Shem" as Noah had stated, and he was also the God of Abraham, Isaac, and Jacob. Shem lived for 500 years after the Flood, and must have known and associated with both Abraham and Isaac. By the time Shem wrote his account he knew Terah was in the godly line.

Shem lists five generations (not just three) of his own descendants in Genesis 10:22–31, and twenty-six descendants in all are named. Many of these settled in the areas stretching from the region of Mesha—a place in southeast Arabia or present-day Yemen—to Sephar, a mountain in the east, in the southwest area of Arabia, near the southern part of Yemen, known as the hill country of the east (as in Genesis 10:30). Terah's genealogy connects the Hebrews who left Egypt at the Exodus to Shem via Eber.

Genesis 10:32—These are the families of the sons of Noah, according to their genealogies, by their nations; and out of these the nations were separated on the earth after the flood.

The word "separated" in Hebrew is *parad*, meaning to separate, or divide; to break through or to spread or separate (oneself). As noted, the name Peleg is the Hebrew word *peleg*, meaning division. This similarity is why we link his birth to the confusion of tongues.

This concluding comment to the "table of nations" summarizes the intent of Shem as he wrote this chapter. It was to identify the progenitors of the various languages and national groups that were formed as a result of the confusion at Babel. From the closing statements of the genealogies of each of the brothers (10:4, 20, 31) we should understand that the nations arose because when people were scattered those of like tongue settled in the same area. Then they grew into a nation. As we saw, there were between 59 and 67 total tongues or languages that resulted from the confusion at Babel.

But a proliferation of languages has continued into present times. The 7,000+ languages in existence today arose as those tongues changed and diversified. Languages are grouped by linguists into from 45 to 140 "language families." The initial division that Shem described may have been speaking of certain basic "language families" that were established at Babel, from which all human languages have "devolved."

I say "devolved" because all languages inevitably simplify structurally and grammatically over time. Note that this observed fact is not consistent with the idea that human beings and human society evolved from a primitive state, for ancient languages were not primitive. They were very sophisticated. Also, within the evolutionary worldview, we might ask why multiple languages ever would have developed? For example, any two chimpanzees from whatever diverse places, families, or tribes, if brought together, can communicate with each other. Why can't human beings? What happened to produce multiple languages? In evolutionary thinking we might ask, what survival advantage did it provide to people?

Chronological Matrix—Adam to Exodus:
This matrix is derived from the chronological chart created by Kevin Hughes.[n]

Bible Dates:	From Creation (FC)—From Before Flood Began (BFB)—or After Flood Began (AFB)					
	Born (BC)	Born (FC)	Died (BC)	Died (FC)	Born (BFB/AFB)	Died (BFB/AFB)
Adam	3959	0	3029	930	1656 BFB	726 BFB
Seth	3829	130	2917	1042	1526 BFB	614 BFB
Enosh	3724	235	2812	1147	1421 BFB	509 BFB
Kenan	3634	325	2724	1235	1331 BFB	421 BFB
Mahalalel	3564	395	2659	1300	1261 BFB	356 BFB
Jared	3499	460	2537	1422	1196 BFB	234 BFB
Enoch	3337	622	2972	987 *	1034 BFB	669 BFB *
Methuselah	3272	687	2303	1656	969 BFB	0
Lamech	3085	874	2308	1651	782 BFB	5 BFB
Noah	2903	1056	1953	2006	600 BFB	350 AFB
Shem	2401	1558	1801	2158	98 BFB	502 AFB
Flood	2303	1656	2302	1657	0	1 AFB
Arpachshad	2301	1658	1863	2096	2 AFB	440 AFB
Shelah	2266	1693	1833	2126	37 AFB	470 AFB
Eber	2236	1723	1772	2187	67 AFB	531 AFB
Peleg/**Babel**	2202	1757	1963	1996	101 AFB	340 AFB
Reu	2172	1787	1933	2026	131 AFB	370 AFB
Serug	2140	1819	1910	2049	163 AFB	393 AFB
Nahor	2110	1849	1962	1997	193 AFB	301 AFB
Terah	2081	1878	1876	2083	222 AFB	427 AFB
Abram	1951	2008	1776	2183	352 AFB	527 AFB
Isaac	1851	2108	1671	2288	452 AFB	632 AFB
Jacob	1791	2168	1644	2315	512 AFB	659 AFB
Levi	1726 est.	2233 est.	1589 est.	2370 est.	577 AFB est.	714 AFB est.
Kohath	1665 est.	2294 est.	1532 est.	2417 est.	638 AFB est.	771 AFB est.
In Egypt	1661	2298	1446	2513	642 AFB	857 AFB
Amram	1595 est.	2364 est.	1455 est.	2501 est.	708 AFB est.	845 AFB est.
Moses	1526	2433	1406	2553	777 AFB	897 AFB
Exodus	1446	2513			857 AFB	
Other Dates:						
Israel went into Egypt at age 130, or in 1661 BC; * Enoch did not die but was taken by God.						

Babel:
Shem next explains, from a revelation the Lord gave him, how and why the various nations and languages of the world developed.

Genesis 11:1—Now the whole earth used the same language and the same words.

Genesis 11:2—It came about as they journeyed east, that they found a plain in the land of Shinar and settled there.

---

[n] See Appendix I for his chart and a discussion of biblical chronology.

When the family of Noah left the ark they all spoke the same language. According to Shem this continued even after they separated and journeyed eastward. Eventually they came to the land of Shinar. This explains how the joint tablet of the three brothers came to an end. It ended when people migrated east to the region between the rivers. This separated the family. That was the time when Noah blessed his sons (9:26, 9:27).

This means that immediately after the Flood people settled in the area west of Shinar, in what is now the Arabian desert, or perhaps even in or near Israel. The area to which they migrated is known to archeology as the ancient city-states of Babylon (or Sumer), and it was previously mentioned in the Bible as the cities that Nimrod established. Those cities were Babel, Erech, Accad, and Calneh in the land of Shinar, and later Nineveh, Rehoboth-Ir, Calah, and Resen (10:10–12).

(Ownership/proprietary rights unknown/unavailable)

This complex of cities formed the first civilization of mankind after the Flood. There have been many archeological digs in this area, as we have noted previously, and the digs show that those city-states were explicitly pagan. Many of the ancient cities had a temple complex that dominated the economic, governmental, educational, religious, and cultural life of the inhabitants. How did they get to be that way? After the Flood Noah and his three sons knew the Lord and had first-hand knowledge of what had happened when the antediluvian society departed from His ways. Shem explains their thinking.

Genesis 11:3—They said to one another, "Come, let us make bricks and burn *them* thoroughly." And they used brick for stone, and they used tar for mortar.

Genesis 11:4—They said, "Come, let us build for ourselves a city, and a tower whose top *will reach* into heaven, and let us make for ourselves a name, otherwise we will be scattered abroad over the face of the whole earth.

From archeology and Jewish tradition it seems that Nimrod was the leader of a rebellion that caught up most of the people in his day. The name Nimrod means "rebellion" or "the valiant." He established an explicitly pagan social order which apparently also refused to "fill the earth" as the Lord God had commanded (9:1). This distanced mankind from the Lord God and threatened to engulf all of humanity in a culture that had rejected Him and had lost the knowledge of God. Still, God had promised not to destroy all flesh again.

Genesis 11:5—The LORD came down to see the city and the tower which the sons of men had built.

Genesis 11:6—The LORD said, "Behold, they are one people, and they all have the same language. And this is what they began to do, and now nothing which they purpose to do will be impossible for them.

Genesis 11:7—Come, let Us go down and there confuse their language, so that they will not understand one another's speech.

Genesis 11:8—So the LORD scattered them abroad from there over the face of the whole earth; and they stopped building the city.

Genesis 11:9—Therefore its name was called Babel, because there the LORD confused the language of the whole earth; and from there the LORD scattered them abroad over the face of the whole earth.

How could anyone know what God said in response to the building of the Tower of Babel? Hosea 12:10 says that God spoke to the prophets, gave them visions, and told mankind parables through them. The person to whom God spoke these particular words was Shem, and Moses preserved his story for us as he transcribed it from the ancient tablets.
> When He saw the wickedness developing and the disease intensifying, He did not allow it to reach its goal; instead He revealed His characteristic goodness and, like an excellent doctor who sees the complaint becoming aggravated and the ulcer turning incurable, He performs an immediate excision so as to remove completely the source of the complaint. So He does not destroy or curse, as He promised. But He sees the problem will end in great trouble for all so He acts in a way to thwart their efforts completely. **Think how this and similar statements about the words and intentions of God given to us in the early chapters of Genesis imply a prophetic spirit in the patriarchs**. [bold added][708]

But the full import of the confusion that God performed (11:6, 7) did not become clear to Shem until years later because the judgment developed over a period of many decades. At that later time, after the scattering ran its course, Shem wrote and signed his account.

Genesis 11:10a—These are *the records of* the generations of Shem.

God revealed to Shem His response when mankind explicitly rejected His commandment. Thus Shem understood the nature of what happened at Babel, but until he met with his two brothers to bury his father Noah—when he received from each of them their family registers that explained how the confusion of tongues had affected their descendants—he did not write his account. It was of great importance that this pivotal event in human history be recorded, for it tells us how languages and nations arose. God had spoken to Adam, Noah, and other holy men at critical points in human history, whenever a divine decision was revealed to direct mankind. At this time He spoke to Shem.

The explicitly rebellious historical context within which this account is situated must have been well known in the time of Shem. But we need archeology to dig it out from the sands of the Middle East so that we can understand it today. It seems that one big reason why God confused the tongues at Babel and thus scattered mankind abroad over the face of the whole earth was this: He wanted to prevent a worldwide pagan culture from engulfing all of mankind. He intended to preserve some faithful men for His own purposes. This is another reason why Noah, Shem, and the godly line were left unaffected by Babel.

Eventually God would choose a man who would be faithful to Him and walk in His ways. Abram would be called to further the divine purposes for mankind and reintroduce to all nations the knowledge of the One True God that was about to be lost forever. God would not allow mankind to lose His revelation about its origin and early history.

Archeological findings from the plain of Shinar and its cities abundantly support the story of the Tower of Babel in general terms. But to arrive at an accurate overall picture of what was happening and at the precise reason why the Lord God levied the confusion of tongues is elusive if we use archeology alone. Therefore, some illuminating historical facts can come from archeology, but our theological understanding must come from the Bible—from God's prophet Shem, to whom He revealed His mind. The following historical material has been condensed and summarized from an article that appeared on ChristianAnswers.net.[709]

> Religious structures called ziggurats were common at the time of the biblical tower of Babel. It may have been that they were built as a stairway to be used by the gods as they traversed from earth to heaven and back. They contained food for the god and a place to rest as he went on these journeys. The stairs provided him entrance to the divine dwelling place. The towers were a gateway for the gods to use, probably not for human beings to use.

> The building materials that were specified for the construction of the towers were not the usual materials that were used for the other buildings in those ancient cities. Sun-dried mud bricks were used for the more "common" city buildings, while burnt bricks covered with bitumen were reserved for the towers. The tower and other public buildings were usually located together and served as a major focus of wealth and culture for the city. An example of this is found at Nippur where this complex of buildings constituted the east half of the city, a large area of almost 80 acres.

> From the various names that were ascribed to the ziggurat and that identified its purpose, two names stand out as seeming to indicate that it was the dwelling of their god or gods. Four other names point toward a possible understanding that the ziggurat was considered to be a passageway between heaven and earth, or between heaven and the netherworld.

> An ancient Babylonian myth supported the idea that the ziggurat was a gateway for the gods. The myth is the story of Nergal and Ereshkigal and of their wedding in the netherworld.
>
>> Ereshkigal was the goddess of the "Land of No Return" and Nergal was the god of "War and Disease." But according to the "cosmic laws" the dwellers in the heavens were forbidden from descending to the netherworld and the dwellers in the netherworld could not ascend to the heavens. When the celestial gods held a banquet (to celebrate their wedding perhaps?) how could Ereshkigal take part in it and eat of the delicacies? Namtar, a name meaning "fate" in Sumerian, the faithful servant of Ereshkigal, was sent by the goddess to represent her and to receive her portion from the banquet. Namtar uses the stairway to move back and forth between the heavens and the netherworld as this story progresses.

> As the civilization of the city states progressed, the gods that they honored took on the image and likeness of men. They shared human weaknesses and foibles and were brought down to the level of man in the estimation of the populace. This was in contrast to the Lord God Who had created man in His image, and Who sought to elevate us into communion with Him. If the ancients began with this twisted idea then what would they do next? Thus the Lord God interrupted the development of that worldwide pagan civilization lest it completely obscure mankind's knowledge of Him and of His purposes for us, as before the flood!

The Development of Human Civilization after the Flood and after Babel:
Let us connect the pieces of the story of the post-Flood civilization to make it coherent. After the Flood Noah and his sons journeyed from Ararat to the area of the Middle East that is now Israel or the Arabian Desert. The incident with Canaan and Ham happened there a couple of decades after the Flood. Until the second generation they stayed there, until the human population grew somewhat, until the days of Shelah and Nimrod, about fifty years after the Flood. Then the family migrated eastward to the plains of Shinar, in the Tigris and Euphrates valley. This occurred when Nimrod was young. As civilization in the area of Shinar progressed, Nimrod became a leader and chose to build the first empire of the post-Flood age, founding it on two basic principles:
- Do not spread all over the earth as God has commanded. Instead stay together in this fertile place and I will be your leader and protector.
- Establish/invent a pantheon of imaginary gods to replace the Lord God. If we honor and remember Him then my authority and my influence will be undercut.

In pursuing these goals he was making himself a great and mighty man on the earth, an emperor among men. He had "help" from demonic hosts who wanted to lead mankind away from the knowledge of God and into the darkness of illusory pagan religious belief. Their help was a key factor in Nimrod's success. God used Babel to thwart these goals.

The empire that developed certainly did offer a measure of fame and success to those who were instrumental in founding it. It also afforded worship to the demons who aided in the deception. A human civilization that diverted man's attention from God and focused instead on human exaltation and demon worship appealed to the corrupt leaders and to the demons. But it also led its inhabitants into separation from God and into a lifestyle that kept them from preparing for eternity with Him—as was His plan.

People who lived according to this cultural model could never enter the destiny for which God had created them. God allowed this to continue for a few decades, until about 101 years after the Flood. At that time the Lord God intervened, confused the tongues, and scattered mankind over the face of the earth. Eber begot a son at that time, so he named him "Peleg" ("division") because of the division of humanity that the confusion caused.

Here are some observations about the post-Flood genealogies: After the confusion of tongues the ages of the patriarchs dropped quickly. Here is the pattern:

Noah, who lived for 600 years before the Flood:	Lived for 950 years
Shem, who lived for 100 years before the Flood:	Lived for 600 years
Arpachshad, Shelah, Eber born before Babel:	Lived 400+ years
Peleg, Reu, Serug born after Babel:	Lived 200+ years

Then the ages of the humans gradually decreased until they fell in line with ages today.

Other Events after Babel:

We have already discussed how and when Shem wrote his account. Now I want to piece together the events that led up to the completion of the joint account of the three brothers and the writing of the account of Terah, which happened about the same time. As we do this we will use the chronological information that is found in the matrix of dates that we compiled from the charts of Mr. Hughes. Here are a few dates to which we will refer:

Event:	Date AFB (after Flood began)	Date BC
Peleg dies	340	1963 BC
Noah dies	350	1953 BC
Abram born	352	1951 BC
Reu dies	370	1933 BC
Serug dies	393	1910 BC
Terah dies	427	1876 BC
Abram leaves for Canaan	427 or soon after	1876 BC or soon after
Isaac born	452	1851 BC
Shem dies	502	1801 BC
Eber dies	531	1772 BC

First of all I am going to reiterate one observation about the times that we are considering. God did not intend for mankind to lose His revelation about the origin of mankind when He confused the tongues. His purposes were quite the opposite. So we must assume that the patriarchs, those from the chosen line, kept in touch with each other as generations passed. Continuing communication was possible because the confusion of tongues and the scattering that affected the descendants of the sons of Noah did not touch them.

Noah recognized Shem as the "godly son" soon after the Flood, as his blessing of Shem indicated. Since Noah himself was a godly man it is reasonable that as he grew older he stayed near Shem because they had work to do. Noah and Shem had two precious things to pass on to later generations:
- The knowledge of the One True God
- The ancestral tablets that we know as the early sections of the book of Genesis, the precious heritage of the origin and early history of the human race

Age of Shem and His Brothers:
The genealogical record departs from the usual formula when it tells us how Noah begat his three sons. He was 500 years old and he begat the three brothers. However, they are not all the same age. 10:21 says "Shem the brother of Japheth the elder," or, as our translation says, "the elder brother of Japheth," possibly because the Hebrew text is ambiguous. But the records of Terah say, "Shem was 100 years old and begat Arpachshad two years after the Flood" (11:10); that is, as with Noah, "after the Flood began." Thus we know that Shem was not the oldest of the brothers because he was born 98 years before the Flood began, or when Noah was 502 years old. So when the record says that Noah begat Shem, Ham, and Japheth (listing them in that order) it is not an indication of the order in which the sons were born.

Abram:
Let us look ahead a bit. "Terah begat Abram, Nahor, and Haran" (11:27). And "The days of Terah were 205 years" (11:32). And speaking about Abram, Stephen says in his defense before the Sanhedrin, "And when his father was dead He [God] moved him into the promised land" (Acts 7:4). "Abram was 75 years old when he departed from Haran" (Genesis 12:4). Therefore, Abram was not the firstborn of Terah either. He was not born until his father was at least 130 years old. Here is the timing of Abram's life as shown in the matrix of dates derived from the diagram of Kevin Hughes:

Event:	Date After the Flood Began	Date BC
Abram born	352	1951 BC
Terah dies	427	1876 BC
Abram leaves for Canaan	427 or soon after	1876 BC or soon after

The Death of Noah and the Completion of the Account of the Three Sons:
Noah was living close to Shem, who must have informed the other brothers of the death of their father. This was possible because the three sons had not had their tongues confused and had not been scattered far and wide like their descendants. They were not in regular daily contact, but they also were not completely cut off from each other.

The three brothers came back together to bury their father. That is how and when the tablet of the sons of Noah was completed.

> Noah lived three hundred and fifty years after the flood. So all the days of Noah were nine hundred and fifty years, and he died. Now these are *the records of* the generations of Shem, Ham, and Japheth, the sons of Noah (Genesis 9:28–10:1a)

Noah lived 950 years, was 600 when the Flood began, and lived 350 years "after the Flood." Thus dates "after the Flood" are measured from after the Flood began, not after it ended.

The Writing of the Account of Terah:
The impetus from the Lord to migrate was driving people throughout the habitable earth. As the language groups departed the sons of Noah watched their children leave with their

families and noted who was at the head of each group. The records that Shem compiled from the three sons reflect the genealogical precision—and also the parental solicitude—of the brothers during these separations, during the time of difficulty and societal chaos.

Shem and Noah and Terah maintained contact with each other. When Noah died in 1951 BC and Abram was born in 1953 BC, Shem and Terah still maintained contact. Early in his life, while his family still lived in Ur, Abram received the call from God (Acts 7:2), and this was surely understood by the patriarchs as the decision of God for carrying on His work. The entire family of Terah was aware of this, and all knew the Lord, although some eventually also served other gods (Joshua 24:2).

It was within this historical, cultural, and familial setting that Terah started to compile his short genealogical record, reaching from Shem down to his three sons Abram, Nahor, and Haran. However, it was not possible for him to record the deaths of four of his ancestors because the lifespans were decreasing (unexpectedly) so rapidly after Babel that he died before four of his ancestors did. Here is the chronology of their deaths:
- Shem (75 years after Terah died)
- Arpachshad (13 years after Terah died)
- Shelah (39 years after Terah died)
- Eber (104 years after Terah died)

Therefore these final details, the death dates of these four patriarchs, were completed by Abram, or actually by Isaac—who was the chronicler for Abram—as life went on in Canaan, and as they heard the news from the family that was still living in the area of Haran. Thus Terah's history is unique among the tablets for several reasons:
- He is the bridge between the most ancient times when God was dealing with the human race as a whole, and the time when God began to work with one person to further His plan of redemption.
- This was a time of chaos in the world because of the confusion of tongues, the loss of cultural cohesion, and the scattering of people to distant areas of the earth. This is also when the city-states of Babylon arose and developed cuneiform writing.
- Many patriarchs were alive at the time that Terah lived, and thus many of them could have, and probably did, know each other.
- The life spans of men were decreasing very quickly, **an unforeseen happening**.
- Terah's tablet is the only one that contained information that he could not have obtained— the death dates of four of his ancestors, all of whom outlived him.
- Therefore, it appears that the history of Terah was a coordinated effort. It was completed by Abram and/or Isaac, a necessity because Terah died before many of his ancestors.

The Faith of Abram:
We often refer to the "faith of Abraham" as something exemplary. But the holy Scriptures say that faith comes by hearing, and hearing by the Word of God. If Abraham showed great faith then he must have heard the Word of God in order for him to be able to have and exercise faith in it. The precious truths about creation, the fall, the promise by God of a redeemer, the tragedy of the Deluge, the confusion of tongues, and the scattering of mankind over the face of the earth—all of these events laid the foundation for the time of Abraham and for his call by God. They also constituted the content of his faith.

Abraham had to know of these things so that, when the call of God came to him, he could understand it and respond to it in faith. Thus the idea that Noah and Shem were close to Terah and his family is most reasonable and is even necessary for the continuance of the faith. The idea of a patriarchal library, carefully put together by Noah and Shem from the ancient tablets, is most reasonable. Their careful explanation of these things to the next generation, both verbally and in written form, was not only reasonable but was surely an obedient response by these men to the express leading of God.

The Creation of the Genesis Documents:
The evidence for the original authorship of the preceding sections of Genesis—that they were written by the various ancient men that are named in their signature lines—has, by any fair estimation, been very convincing, and it will continue to be more evident as we look at the historical records that follow. Also, the time after Babel was a critical turning point in human history. Cuneiform writing was invented as the city-states of Mesopotamia formed after Babel. It became the standard method/style of written communication among Middle Eastern peoples even before the time of the Old Babylonian era (2000 BC), **and it remained the script of the educated throughout patriarchal and Old Testament times.**

But the discovery of the stone on Ararat that contains the "Ahora Covenant Inscription" indicates that right after the Flood, when God made the covenant with Noah and his sons, writing was still pictographic. This form of writing continued until the rise of the city-states of Mesopotamia after Babel. Therefore the following accounts were written in pictographs:
- The creation account written by the Lord
- Adams tablets about the earliest formative events of human history
- Noah's tablets comprised of the pre-Flood genealogy and his account of the dark times before the Flood.
- The account of the Flood and the few decades after it by the three sons of Noah

Therefore the most ancient writings had to have been translated into a more modern script at some point. Now I want to develop a reasonable reconstruction of that event—of the translation of the tablets into the script (but not the language) that would be carried forward into the time of Abraham, Isaac, and Jacob, and which would eventually be used by Moses in the creation of the book of Genesis as we now have it. Noah died in 1953 BC, after the time when Cuneiform writing was in use. Noah was the one, likely with the help of his son Shem, who had to translate those tablets into a script that could be read by the later generations of patriarchs. The right moment for that to happen would be a few centuries after the Flood, after the confusion of tongues at Babel, after the scattering that followed Babel was complete, after the rise of the Babylonian city-states and the invention of cuneiform writing, and after the literary techniques of the Babylonian scribes were in place. Thus the translation took place in the time of Noah's old age, probably around 2000 BC or soon thereafter. The place was Ur of Haran, where the family of Terah lived.

Noah must have decided to create a library of patriarchal documents, translating the older tablets into cuneiform, retaining the language of Terah and his family (the original language of man) so that the tablets could be read by them. Semitic languages were spoken in Ur. Thus the family of Terah spoke a form of ancient proto-Hebrew. Noah and Shem wrote their translations using the methods and techniques of the scribes of ancient Mesopotamia, creating **The Genesis Documents** which would be carried by Abraham, Isaac, and Jacob for several centuries. Eventually Jacob would carry them into Egypt.

By that time Noah had noticed a recurrence of the pre-Flood perversions developing in the society of the Canaanites. The action of Ham had been so despicable! The reason for the curse Noah placed on Canaan—and then on his descendants as the family separated after the Flood—had now escalated into a widespread characteristic in the civilizations of the children of Canaan. Thus Noah added this simple warning to his tablet:
> There were giants in the land in those days, **and also after that**, when the sons of God came into the children of men, and they bore children unto them. (Genesis 6:4)

This is my hypothesis: That these ancient tablets had to be translated after the Flood, and that Noah and Shem were the ones to do it; and that Noah saw the developing problem in the Canaanite culture from early on, and at that time he carefully warned his descendants about it because it had been the main reason for the judgment of the Deluge.

The timing again: Noah and Shem translated the tablets before the knowledge of pictographic writing was lost to the patriarchal line, after cuneiform gained widespread acceptance, and after the chaos from Babel had settled down. At that time—when post-Babel cultures stabilized (Old Babylonian era), when mankind was developing libraries of written records and the literary techniques of Mesopotamian scribes had been established, when Noah was quite old—then the translation of the pre-Flood tablets was undertaken. Both Noah and Shem knew how to read pictographic writing. The task of translating the ancient records and converting them to cuneiform using the then-standard Babylonian methods and techniques fell to them.

In all of this we must also acknowledge the hand of the Lord God. Surely God directed Noah and Shem in their work after the Flood and after Babel. Surely they knew that He wanted the information about the human race from before the Flood to be preserved. It is reasonable to presume that God also clearly identified Terah and his family as the next in the patriarchal line—it was His choice and only His. He led Shem to collect the necessary data and complete his account so that a critical piece of human history from the most chaotic and confusing of times would be preserved for us. And finally, he chose Abram.

Scattering Details:

Other Ancient Accounts of the Confusion of Tongues:
Abraham was not the only one to know about, remember, and record the story of Babel. Many ancient stories from around the world tell of a time when the peoples of the earth all spoke the same language, and explain that it was confused by "the gods."

> **There is a Sumerian myth called *Enmerkar and the Lord of Aratta*.** Part of it goes like this:
> Once upon a time there was no snake, there was no scorpion, there was no hyena, there was no lion, there was no wild dog, no wolf, there was no fear, no terror, and Man had no rival. In those days, the lands of Subur [a political entity in northern Mesopotamia] (and) Hamazi, Harmony-tongued Sumer, the great land of the decrees of prince ship, Uri, the land having all that is appropriate, the land Martu [biblical connection: the Amorites lived there], resting in security, the whole universe, the people in unison to Enlil, everyone in one tongue [spoke]. (Then) Enki, the lord of abundance (whose) commands are trustworthy, the lord of wisdom, who understands the land, the leader of the gods, endowed with wisdom, the lord of Eridu changed their speech in their mouths, (brought) contention into it, into the speech of man that (until then) had been one. Then Enmerkar of Uruk who was building a massive ziggurat in Eridu, prayed to the god Enki to restore the linguistic unity of all the peoples; i.e., Subur, Hamazi, Sumer, Akkad . . . asking that they be allowed to address Enlil together in the same tongue once again.[710]

> **There is an account of the Tower of Babel incident from the indigenous Mexican people.**
> And after that as men multiplied on the earth they constructed a very high and strong tower in order to protect themselves against the possibility that the second world [this means the post-flood world] should be destroyed. At a crucial time their languages were changed, and they scattered to different parts of the world because they could no longer understand one another.[711]

There was a story from the Native American Toltec people stating that after the flood men erected a great tower to protect themselves from a possible second flood. But their tongues were confused and then they went to separate parts of the earth.[712]

The Choctaw Indians have this legend: Aba the good spirit created many men all of whom spoke the Choctaw language. They wondered what the clouds and blue expanse above might be, and eventually began building a mound to reach the sky. That night a wind blew it down. They persisted and the next night a wind blew again and knocked it down and they awoke to discover they spoke different languages. Then men scattered in all directions.[713]

In French Polynesia: (on the island Hao) there is a story of the three sons of Rata [a person from their mythology] who with their parents were the sole survivors of a great flood. They tried to erect a building to reach the sky. The creator god Vatea became very angry, chased them away, destroyed the building, and changed their tongues so they could not understand each other.[714]

The Admiralty Islands: (South Pacific) the story is that a tower was being built to heaven but a man named Po Awi forbade them to continue. Then their tongues were confused and they scattered far and wide.

The Mikirs: (a Tibeto-Burman tribe of Assam) tell of a tower to heaven that was constructed but the project ended as the tongues were confused and all were scattered.[715]

What additional details can we assemble about how the sons of Noah and their families scattered across the earth after Babel? This is not stated in Scripture, and what meager secular records we have come from certain Church Fathers, from documents and maps of ancient times, and from Josephus and other historians. These must be pieced together to give us partial information. Here are a few sparse examples:

> Gomer founded the Gomerites or Galatians, called the Galls by the Greeks. Meshech or Mosech founded the Masocheni, called the Cappadocians by the Greeks. Kittim or Cethimus, settled on the island of Cethima, now called Cyprus. The inhabitants of Lybia were called Phutites after their founder Phut or Put. Elam founded the Elamites, the progenitors of ancient Persia.

Generalizations are not reliable but, **Probably** the north Asian and European areas were settled mostly by the sons of Japheth. **Probably** the areas of Africa and southern Asia were settled mostly by the sons of Ham. **Probably** the small area of rectangular shape around the Middle East was settled by the sons of Shem and the Canaanites.

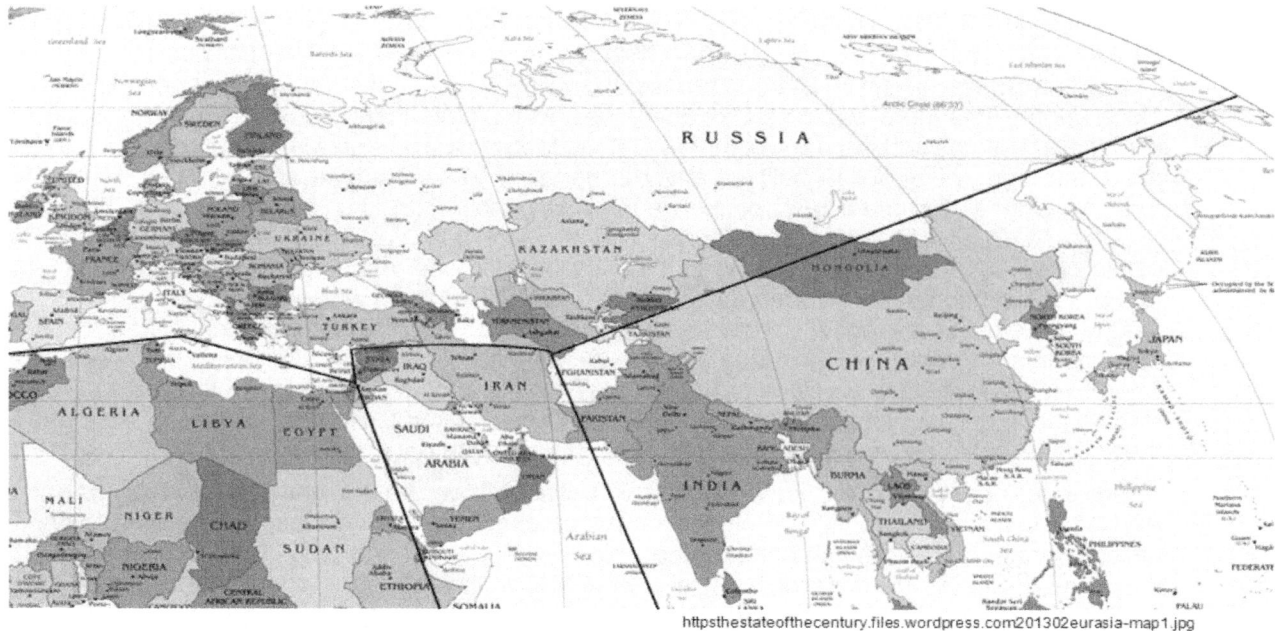

httpsthestateofthecentury.files.wordpress.com201302eurasia-map1.jpg

The worldwide migration of people from Babel was complex and intermingled. What we know is based on fragmented records from diverse peoples. Research is necessary to assemble the pieces, and the picture may never be complete.° But it is clear that men did eventually cross the Bering Straits and settle in North and South America. This probably happened after the Deluge and during the ice age, while the Bering Straits were still covered with ice. People migrated from Babel on foot over land and also by boat across the sea.

Some Native American migration stories agree with the idea that people came to America in these ways. These would probably be the descendants of Ham.[716]

> **The Kiche Indians** (also called Quiche) who were associated with the Mayan civilization tell of a time when the sun was weak and its rays dull. There are references to crossing great waters covered by shining sand, perhaps referring to ice and snow.
>
> Likewise **the Aztec** migration story talks of the Indians coming from a place called Aztlan by rowing in boats. At the time when they crossed the waters there were four tribes.
>
> **The Leni-Lenape** Indians, from the east coast of North America, tell of a distant time when they crossed the frozen sea, frozen over the deep waters of the great ocean, to reach a new land. According to their story this happened after the great flood.

Theological Considerations and Perspectives:

How could the people of the earth have departed from God so quickly? Before the Flood there were over 16 centuries for human culture to develop in defiance of our creator. In the end, for perhaps 120 years, there was also a strong release of demonic influence into the society of men that propelled the wickedness of men to the point of forcing the Lord to intervene with His judgment. After the Flood the sudden turn to paganism must be seen not only as human perversity but also as the result of significant influence again by demonic powers. People were geographically more centralized, and the time frame was shorter. It took just over 100 years before our Lord moved again to curb the trend of mankind. He confounded the tongues before the situation got as bad as it had been before the Flood.

The rapid decline in the spirituality of that culture is not at all difficult to understand if we look at the decline of godliness in our time. In my own lifetime I have seen an ostensibly Christian culture in America transformed into a culture that is hostile to Christ and to His people. When I was in grade school in the 1950s there was no thought in any mind to:
- Forbid the teaching of creation in public schools
- Teach sexual immorality (so-called "sex education") in public schools
- Call laws against pornography "too vague" and declare them unconstitutional
- Forbid prayer in school
- Declare abortion to be a "right" and
- Declare homosexual unions to be a "right"
- Argue for the legalization of intoxicating drugs
- Promote gambling throughout society

The dark themes that have emerged in our entertainment, the violence that is prevalent throughout our society, etc.—these have all been widely lamented by many but still defy every human solution. These problems are not limited to America; rather they are a worldwide phenomenon. People know that these many things are not right, but fail in search of any remedy. This is a sure sign that behind all of this is a significant effort by the enemy to destroy humanity.

° Bodie Hodge, *Tower of Babel: The Cultural History of our Ancestors*, chapters 17–18 has more details.

> For still our ancient foe
> Doth seek to work us woe.
> His craft and power are great
> And armed with cruel hate.
> On earth is not his equal.

When the post-Flood civilization departed so radically from the Lord we seldom think about how it must have grieved Him. This was certainly the result of wrong choices by human beings, but it was also the result of the influence of demonic powers. This is the second recorded incident in Genesis where spiritual powers were influencing the course of human civilization in a major and obvious way.

The Antediluvian Demonic Powers:
We analyzed the forces that were at work in human society before the Flood and observed that they carried over into Canaanite civilization even after the Flood. Noah warned men that the disorder of Ham and Canaan was widespread within the descendants of Canaan after the Flood, and the *Nephilim* that had arisen before the Flood, at the final stage of the decline of the antediluvian culture, were also observed in the post-Flood Canaanite culture. These still inhabited the "promised land" at the time of the Exodus. Finally, at the time of the Exodus, "the iniquity of the Amorite was complete" (Genesis 15:16).

At the time of the Exodus Moses was more than just a chronicler of history—he was the prophet of God given to Israel to explain to them the meaning of what had been written by the patriarchs and apply it to understanding the time of the Exodus. It was time to levy judgment on the inhabitants of the land of Canaan. Fortunately today the spiritual powers involved in the antediluvian tragedy have been "bound in darkness waiting for the great day of His judgment" (Jude 6). But Revelation 9:1–11 tells us that there is a time coming when those spiritual powers will no longer be held captive in Tartarus.

The Spirits behind Babel:
And what of the evil spirits that instigated the rebellion at Babel? The Book of Revelation reveals that these powers are also bound at this time, and envisions their final release for judgment. The following vision reveals to us the release of the spirits that have been bound at the river Euphrates, which will be let loose at the sixth trumpet of Revelation:

> Then the sixth angel sounded, and I heard a voice from the four horns of the golden altar which is before God, one saying to the sixth angel who had the trumpet, "Release the four angels who are bound at the great river Euphrates." And the four angels, who had been prepared for the hour and day and month and year, were released, so that they would kill a third of mankind. The number of the armies of the horsemen was two hundred million; I heard the number of them. (Revelation 9:13–16)

The demons bound at the river Euphrates and waiting to be released at the end of this age are the same demons that led the people of Babel astray—that instigated them to reject God so quickly and to depart into paganism. Those demons were bound when the scattering took place. At the end of this age they will again be unleashed on the world—when the wickedness of human beings will have again become "complete," and when once again mankind is united as one. Then both the wicked people and those perverted demons will be finally judged. The monstrous beings in this vision once were beautiful angelic powers, created to live in harmony with human beings and to help them fulfill the plans and purposes of God. How they are fallen and revealed as odious at the end of the age![p]

---

[p] For details of how God will deal with all of the fallen angels at the end of this age see this author's book *Consummation: A Theology of the End-Times*, especially the chapter on the "Seven Trumpets."

The wickedness of these fallen angels is revealed in the distorted forms of their bodies. It is utterly monstrous, a reflection of their twisted and perverted spiritual state.

The Patriarchal Library at the Beginning of Historical Times:

Let us review the patriarchal library that Abram had as he prepared to leave Haran, and also the understanding that had been imparted to him by Shem. Abram carried with him the following tablets, written in accord with the literary methods and conventions of his time:

- The Lord's tablets, written initially in pictograph but translated by Noah and/or Shem into a cuneiform script that was understandable to him and to his family.
- Adam's tablets, written initially in pictograph but translated by Noah and/or Shem into a cuneiform script that was understandable to Abram and his family.
- Noah's tablets, written initially in pictograph, but translated by Noah and/or Shem into a cuneiform script that would be understandable to the successive generations.
- The tablets of the sons of Noah, written initially in pictograph, translated by Noah and/or Shem into cuneiform in accord with the techniques of the post-Babel city-states.
- The tablets of Shem, written in cuneiform script.
- The incomplete tablets of Terah. This was the official genealogical register of the post-Deluge patriarchs. It extended from Shem down to Terah's generation and to his sons Abram, Nahor, and Haran. It was written in the cuneiform script of his day.

It was while living in Ur that Abram first heard the call of God on his life. Then Shem was able to prepare him for the life to which God was calling him. The translation of the older tablets happened while the family of Terah lived in Ur of the Chaldees or in Haran.

So Abram was instructed by Shem, and he had the tablets to refer to. From the warning of Noah (Genesis 6:4) Abram knew that the land he was being called into was inhabited by the Canaanites and that they had already become depraved and godless. He knew that the disorders that had been prevalent before the Deluge, and which had resulted in the judgment of the Flood, were present again in their society. He had every reason to be worried about leaving his father's family; that is, his brothers and their wives.

People who knew the Lord God and who honored Him were few and far between. This simple fact is often overlooked as we read and comment on the life of Abraham. He was definitely fearful of the people among whom he was being sent. This explains many of his actions, and it also makes it clear why the Lord told him early on, "Do not fear, Abram, I am a shield for you" (Genesis 15:1). This was after he dared to rescue Lot.

Therefore God's solemn covenant promise, to give the land of the Canaanites to Abram's descendants when "the iniquity of the Amorites was complete," (see Genesis 15:12–21) was a wonderful and comforting word. In the meantime Abram saw the land into which he was called by God as a foreign and hostile place where he was "sojourning" or visiting or just passing through—a land that was not his home.

Finally, we sometimes think of Abram's delay in leaving Terah as a kind of "slowness" in his response of faith. But it was necessary that he take with him the precious tablets, and they would not come to him until his father Terah died and passed them along. Thus the death of Terah was a key turning point in the outworking of the call of God on his life. Lot, whose father had also died, shared Abram's faith and left with him.

Summary and Perspective on the First Eleven Chapters of Genesis:
These eleven chapters describe for us the common history that is shared by all mankind.
- The creation account tells us who God is. It reveals the most foundational truth to us about Him: His power and majesty, His glory and wisdom. The account of creation is our fundamental connection to Him, defining Him to us. The creation was a work that only God could do—it was proper to God alone. He was the only One Who knew how it was accomplished. Thus the first section of Genesis was written by God.
- The beginning of the human race—the first and defining events of humanity, which include our creation by God and placement in a pleasant situation where all of our needs were met; our willful disobedience of God and His subsequent judgment; the understanding of sin and its consequences; the fundamental nature of sin as captivity to a hostile and malevolent being who is bent on our destruction; the promise by the Lord God of a savior who would crush the enemy's head and free us from his power. These events are related to us by Adam, the progenitor of the human race.
- The devastating effects of sin on human society—how far down mankind can sink if immersed in sin. This account, situated about 1600 years after the initial fall, reveals to us the captivity to lawlessness that characterizes a society that has followed in the path of rejecting God. Such a society cannot and will not turn back to Him. Such a society is, on the corporate level, just as captive to Satan as any individual. The only response that God can make is judgment. This truth is revealed to us by Noah.
- The Deluge—the single most destructive and earth-reshaping event in history—the response of God to the universal rebellion and departure from him that characterized human civilization in the time of Noah. God's merciful treatment of people afterward is also described, for "man's heart is evil from his youth." These events, which explain original sin, are described to us by the sons of Noah: Shem, Ham, and Japheth.
- The division of the human race into nations and languages—the event that explains how the present age of the world has come to be. Again, this occurred as the result of a rapid departure of the human race from the Lord God soon after the Flood. The development of the human race into families after the Flood, its rebellion against the Lord God, and the confusion of tongues and the scattering over the whole earth that followed, are related to us by Shem, who lived through those events.

Because we can identify the authors of each of these sections of Genesis, and because each author is the most appropriate person to give testimony to us about the events that they relate, we can be confident that the early chapters of Genesis are accurate history; that is, first-hand personal accounts of events in which the author was directly involved.

These formative early events shaped the world of mankind and produced the world of many nations and languages—scattered over the whole earth—that men inhabit today. This was the cultural milieu within which God began His specific program of bringing forth the "Seed of the woman" who would be the savior of the human race. He would do this by choosing one man and his descendants, and by working with them.

These events also produced the geographical configuration of the earth, erecting natural barriers to a fully unified humanity, which had degenerated to the point of being extremely prone to being misled by demonic deception. The oceans, mountains, and other dividing barriers should be seen as divinely providential until the "Seed" returns at last to lead us.

Terah the Father of Abraham

The History of Terah, the sixth set of tablets:

> **11** [10b] Shem was one hundred years old, and became the father of Arpachshad two years after the flood; [11] and Shem lived five hundred years after he became the father of Arpachshad, and he had *other* sons and daughters. [12] Arpachshad lived thirty-five years, and became the father of Shelah; [13] and Arpachshad lived four hundred and three years after he became the father of Shelah, and he had *other* sons and daughters. [14] Shelah lived thirty years, and became the father of Eber; [15] and Shelah lived four hundred and three years after he became the father of Eber, and he had *other* sons and daughters. [16] Eber lived thirty-four years, and became the father of Peleg; [17] and Eber lived four hundred and thirty years after he became the father of Peleg, and he had *other* sons and daughters. [18] Peleg lived thirty years, and became the father of Reu; [19] and Peleg lived two hundred and nine years after he became the father of Reu, and he had *other* sons and daughters. [20] Reu lived thirty-two years, and became the father of Serug; [21] and Reu lived two hundred and seven years after he became the father of Serug, and he had *other* sons and daughters. [22] Serug lived thirty years, and became the father of Nahor; [23] and Serug lived two hundred years after he became the father of Nahor, and he had *other* sons and daughters. [24] Nahor lived twenty-nine years, and became the father of Terah; [25] and Nahor lived one hundred and nineteen years after he became the father of Terah, and he had *other* sons and daughters. [26] Terah lived seventy years, and became the father of Abram, Nahor and Haran. [27] Now these are *the records of* the generations of Terah.

Archeological Considerations:

> Tablet 6 (11:10-27) written or owned by Terah. Terah's genealogical list registers the death of his father Nahor, while he himself lived on until his son Abraham was seventy-five years old. Had Terah lived another eleven years he would have been able to record the birth of Ishmael, and if for another twenty-five years it would have been possible for him to add, "and Abraham begat Isaac." But the history contained in this tablet ends immediately before his own death.[717]

Genealogical lists like this were common in the ancient Middle East.

> Several such genealogical lists from Babylon are in existence, written long before Terah's.[718]

Speaking of the continuity of the Genesis history,

> **We would claim that the archaeological evidence suggests that a tablet such as Terah's was written in the ordinary cuneiform script used at Ur of the Chaldees. But the earlier tablets were probably written in a more ancient script, and these would possibly be transcribed into the current language of the day.** Abraham, coming into possession of these precious documents telling of the God of his fathers (the one God, the Creator of the heavens and the earth), was called by God to leave Ur for Canaan. The most sacred possession that he would carry with him was these tablets. **Some uncertainty still exists about the language spoken in Palestine at the time of Abraham's arrival there; though we know that 600 years later correspondence with both Babylonia and Egypt was still conducted in cuneiform script . . . the script of the educated. There can be little doubt that Isaac and Jacob would have used this script when writing their tablets.**[719] (bold mine)

The time of Terah and Shem is a critical time of transition from the ancient script of pre-cuneiform (that is, pictograph) writing to cuneiform writing, which would be the script of the patriarchs from Shem on, and which also would have been well known by the educated of Egypt at the time of Moses. Moses himself was educated in all of the learning of Egypt and would have known the script of the tablets as well as the techniques of the ancient scribes that were used in signing, connecting, and dating them. Those same methods had been employed by Noah and Shem when translating the tablets. Thus Noah, Shem, and Moses shared a common literary tradition.

The time of Terah was critical in history for two more reasons:
- It followed after the confusion of the tongues at Babel and the time of the scattering of people over the whole face of the earth. One purpose of Babel was to blunt the power of a united pagan culture that could have overwhelmed mankind and eclipsed the truth about God for all people. Thus in the scattering and its aftermath we can assume that God so arranged events that the godly line of patriarchs would not lose contact with each other and would not lose the tablets that had been passed down through Noah and Shem. Their tongues were not confused.
- The life spans of the patriarchs were decreasing so quickly that Terah knew of the death of Peleg, Rue, Serug, and Nahor but did not live to see the death of their ancestors Shem, Arpachshad, Shelah, and Eber. Isaac lived to see the death of the last four patriarchs but never knew the first four. **No one person** lived over a time frame long enough to write the totality of the genealogy that included the post-Flood line of patriarchs. Thus we must assume that after the death of Terah his history was augmented with the death dates for Shem, Arpachshad, Shelah, and Eber. Isaac wrote the next history, lived through their deaths, and must have added that information to Terah's history when he appended his account, the seventh group of tablets, onto that of Terah.

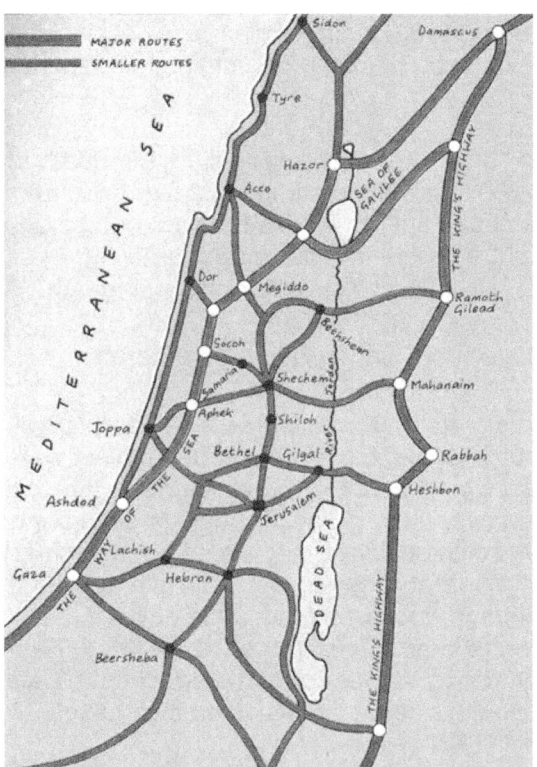

From: *Bible Mapbook* by Simon Jenkins

As we look at the histories of Terah, Isaac, and Jacob, we are entering ancient times that are also known to us through secular historical sources. I want to comment on these sections using these historical sources as supplemental information. I will include various geographical, chronological, and historical data. The map at left shows the known ancient travel routes in the area of Israel.[720] This will help us as we discuss the movements of the patriarchs by placing before us the most commonly used highways of the ancient peoples.

The fact that many such land routes existed is a strong indication that travel and communication were a normal reality of life. It is possible that not all of the routes shown existed for all of the times that we will be commenting on, but most of them were in use throughout the times of the patriarchs. Communication within family groupings that were separated was quite possible and was even a common thing in patriarchal times.[721]

The sections that follow will comment on many stories recorded by the patriarchs, showing the consistency of their records even when examined in minutest detail. Because the stories hold up under such scrutiny, we have solid evidence that they are personal and first-hand accounts of their times, preserved accurately and intact.

Historical Considerations:
When Terah was seventy years old he begat his three sons: Abram, Nahor, and Haran. The Lord first called Abram while he was still in Ur of the Chaldees.

In his defense before the Sanhedrin Stephen reviewed these events and said,

> "Hear me, brethren and fathers! The God of glory appeared to our father Abraham when he was in Mesopotamia, **before he lived in Haran**, and said to him, 'LEAVE YOUR COUNTRY AND YOUR RELATIVES, AND COME INTO THE LAND THAT I WILL SHOW YOU.' Then he left the land of the Chaldeans and settled in Haran. From there, after his father died, *God* had him move to this country in which you are now living. (Acts 7:2–4)

Stephen may have gotten this fact from Genesis 12:1. Abram is still in Haran and it says that God *had* called Abram. So God spoke to Abram when he was still with his family in Ur, well before he left them to follow God's call. The importance of this fact is that it says that the entire family of Terah knew of his divine call and had some kind of faith in God. That is why they all left Ur and moved to Haran. When it became time for Abraham to choose a wife for Isaac he chose her from within the family.

Haran died while Terah was still in Ur (11:28), and then his family moved to the city of Haran (different word than the son). In the map[722] below this route is marked as 1. Perhaps they left Ur in order to distance them-selves more from the pagan way of life there. Abram left his family in Haran after his father Terah died (Acts 7:4), departing when he was seventy-five.

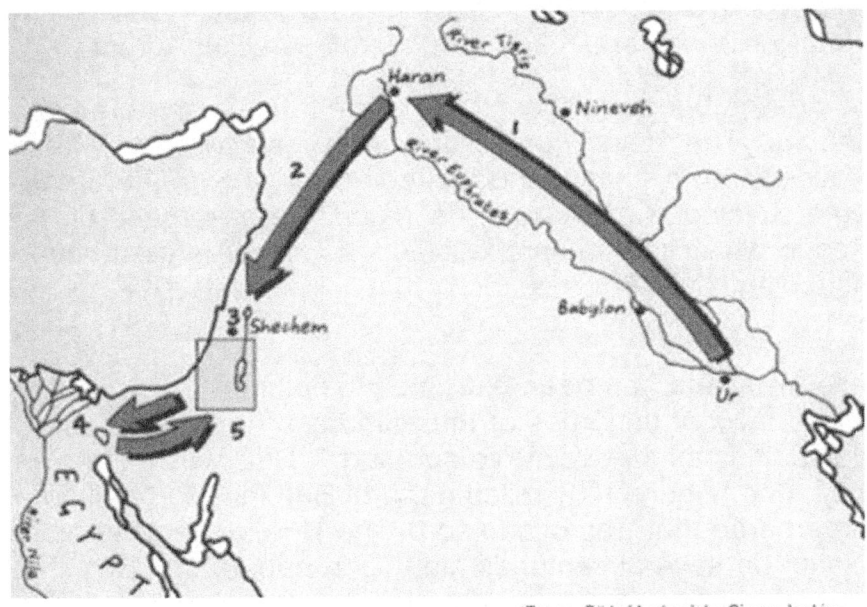

From: *Bible Mapbook* by Simon Jenkins

So Abram went forth as the LORD had spoken to him; and Lot went with him. Now Abram was seventy-five years old when he departed from Haran. (Genesis 12:4)

The journey of Abram to Shechem is marked as 2. Therefore Terah was 205 minus 75 or 130 years old when Abram was born.

Terah did not finish his tablet until near his death, and Abram wanted to take it with him when he left. As the one chosen by God Abram would inherit the tablets. So he waited until his father died before leaving for the land of Canaan. It was also the custom for sons to "bury their father" and that may have been another reason why he waited to depart.

The call of Abram seems to have affected the entire family of his father, and this may also have been connected to the influence of Shem and/or Noah in their family. The godly line continued through Terah and his family when Shem or Noah passed on the tablets (and faith in God) to them. The truth that Noah spoke was confirmed to Abram by the personal appearance of God to him (Acts 7:2), and by the direct call that he received at that time. Abram believed God, obeyed Him, and departed from the pagan cities of Mesopotamia for the land that God had promised to show to him (12:1). Abram took with him all of his possessions when he left—and that would have included The **Genesis Documents** that he had received from his father Terah when he died. Abram had been called by the Lord God to continue the godly line and he obeyed—and he took the written history of the beginning of the human race with him when he left Haran.

> Abram took Sarai his wife and Lot his nephew, and all their possessions which they had accumulated, and the persons which they had acquired in Haran, and they set out for the land of Canaan; thus they came to the land of Canaan. (Genesis 12:5)

The godly line stayed very close together. Nahor married Milcah the daughter of his brother Haran. Abraham also married his half-sister, as he explained to Abimelech:

> Besides, she actually is my sister, the daughter of my father, but not the daughter of my mother, and she became my wife. (Genesis 20:12)

Marriage to close relatives in those days was permitted because deleterious mutations had not yet accumulated in the human genome and weakened humanity physically.

It was very important that those of faith maintain supportive relationships with each other. Marriage was the most important expression of this reality. The entire family understood this truth at that time. We can assume that the patriarchs continued to communicate with each other in some way, and we will see that later passages of Genesis support this. But we must also understand that even Terah and his family were only partially true to God, for they also served other gods (Joshua 24:2). This is a solemn testimony to the power of the unified pagan culture of Babylon to subvert men and draw them away from Him. Idolatry is like a leaven that spreads inexorably. Calling and preserving a people that are totally His was one major purpose of God with Abram.

The Terah tablet and his time are the bridge between very ancient times and the times of known history and the patriarchs. The remaining sections of Genesis, written by Isaac and Jacob, are supported by significant historical and archeological finds in the area of the Middle East. The following archeological data gives us important background on the customs and laws of the times in which the patriarchs lived. It will serve as a helpful introduction to the history of Isaac and the history of Jacob that follow next.

The Nuzi Tablets:[723]

This find of over 6,000 cuneiform tablets has been extremely helpful in understanding and illuminating the customs and laws of the times of the patriarchs. For this reason I want to take time to review these finds as they relate to our study. Nuzi was an ancient Mesopotamian city in Iraq about one hundred fifty miles north of Bagdad. In patriarchal times Nuzi and Haran were in an area that was occupied by the Hurrian people whose laws and customs were dominant for several centuries starting in about 2000 BC. The Nuzi tablets reveal the customs of that area of the world during those ancient times.

The most important effect Nuzi has on Scripture studies is to place the patriarchal accounts that we are reading squarely within the times and cultures indicated by the biblical records themselves, and according to the biblical chronology. This is important because certain secular scholars today assert that these accounts were written much later by an unknown redactor. Here are a few of the topics discussed in the tablets:

Adoption: If a man had no children then it was customary for him to adopt someone to carry on his name and to inherit his property. This is probably reflected in the statement of Abram to the Lord in Genesis 15:2, that Eliezer of Damascus would be his heir. The Old Testament gives no indication that such customs were in effect later on in the times of ancient Israel. This is a strong indication of the ancient origin of this passage.

Birthrights: It was allowed for a man to sell his birthright as Esau did to Jacob when he was hungry (Genesis 25:31).

Enrolling a Wife as a Sister: A number of legal contracts were found indicating that a sister was of higher social standing than a wife, and that a wife was sometimes honored by her husband by being accorded that position. This custom was well known in those areas where Abram had lived, but it was not understood in Egypt or Gerar. Thus there was a misunderstanding between Pharaoh and Abram (Genesis 12:10–20), between Abimelech and Abraham (Genesis 20:1–18), and finally between Abimelech and Isaac (Genesis 26:6–11). Those two kings considered Abraham and Isaac guilty of deceit.

Although it does seem to involve a deception made out of fear, it appears to also be a case of misunderstanding of customs as well. Centuries later in Israel the custom of enrolling a wife as a sister was as unknown as it had been to those two kings in the time of the patriarchs. The underlying social contract for enrolling a woman as a sister and the high status that it then accorded to her was also unknown. Thus it is hard to imagine that this story could have been composed by a later redactor.

Barren Wives: The law of barren wives stated that, because a male child was vital to the family line, if a wife did not bear children—especially a son—for her husband, then it was allowable practice for her to provide him with a servant-wife as a surrogate for that purpose. This is also known from the Code of Hammurabi. But in that code (#144) only a priestess has such a right, and even then the child is not her own but the servant's.

In the story of Jacob's marriage to Leah and Rachel (Genesis 29:15–29) it was believed that the giving of maids by Laban to each of his daughters did not fit into this episode but had to be a later interpolation by a redactor, probably from the **P** document. But the Nuzi documents make it clear that the giving of a maid to a daughter when she married was a normal part of the marriage, written into the contract. Many of the documents of marriage specified a maid by name. Perhaps this was looked upon as an "insurance policy" in case the daughter was barren or did not happen to give her husband a son.

Teraphim: These are called "household gods" or just "gods" in the Old Testament. This helps us understand the story of Jacob fleeing from Laban after serving him for twenty years (Genesis 31:1–55). The Nuzi tablets indicate that if Jacob could produce the household gods of Laban after he died then it would confirm that he had been appointed heir to his estate; that is, this could be a way for Jacob to cut the sons of Laban out of their family inheritance—dealing deceitfully with them as he had done with his brother Esau. This law was in the background of that entire incident and explains the actions of Rachel, the heated reactions of her father and brothers, and the insistence by Jacob that they bury the gods once he discovered that Rachel had stolen them. This is a powerful indication that the story was originally set in patriarchal times in Mesopotamia.

The Role of a Father and Weddings: It was the duty of the father to find a suitable wife for his son. This must be in the background of the story of Abraham sending his servant to find a wife for Isaac (Genesis 24:1–67). When a wedding contract was drawn up the father of the bride was to receive a payment for the loss of his daughter. It was customary that work could be done in payment for the daughter. These are reflected in the marriage arrangements made for Rebekah (Genesis 24) and for Leah and Rachel (Genesis 29:15–29). Also, the oral will of a father was unchangeable, as reflected in the irrevocable blessing that Jacob deceptively stole from Esau (Genesis 27:1–40).

Abraham and Isaac

(Text omitted for this seventh set of tablets because of length; Genesis 11:27b–25:19a)

Archeological Considerations:

In the story attributed to Isaac we note this:

> The latest chronological statement (25:1-4) refers to the birth of Abraham's great-grandsons, and of their growth into clans. Ishmael died forty-eight years and Isaac one hundred five years after Abraham. As Abraham would seem to have married Keturah soon after Sarah's death (which occurred thirty-eight years before Abraham died), this period of thirty-eight years added to the remaining one hundred five years of Isaac's life, is a most reasonable period to assign for the birth of Abraham's great-grand-sons by Keturah. This indicates that the history recorded in these tablets ceases just before the death of Isaac, whose name is given as the last writer, for Isaac survived Ishmael by fifty-seven years and records his death.[724]

We should also note that the account of Isaac ends with the genealogy of Ishmael, received from him by Isaac when they came together to bury their father Abraham. The next section, starting in Genesis 25:19b, is the story of Jacob. Up to that point the story told by Isaac had been in chronological order. But at 25:20 the narrative backtracks somewhat as Jacob relates events from his perspective. This break in the chronology of the accounts and the reversion to an earlier time is a clear clue to the fact that a new author has taken over the telling of the story.

Now we return to the analysis given by Wiseman of the account written by Isaac:

> Abraham alone could have recounted most of the incidents, but it would appear that his sons wrote them down, or at least, the copies which we believe that Moses had before him belonged to them. The whole story shows a great familiarity with details. For instance, the visit of the three men recorded in the eighteenth chapter:
>> As he sat in the tent door *in the heat of the day,* and he lift up his eyes and looked, and, three men stood over against him; and when he saw them he ran to meet them from the tent door, and bowed himself to the earth . . . And he hastened into the tent unto Sarah, and said, "Make ready quickly three measures of fine meal . . ." And Abraham ran to the herd and fetched a calf tender and good and gave it unto his servant and he hastened to dress it . . . and set it before them; *and he stood by them under the trees,* and they did eat.
>
> The remainder is an intimate personal account of Abraham's prayer for Sodom. After its overthrow we read, *"And Abraham got up early in the morning to the place where he had stood before the Lord,* and he looked toward Sodom and Gomorrah and toward the land of the plain, and beheld and lo, the smoke of the country went up as the smoke of a furnace" (19:27-28). The style is just what we would expect of Abraham relating the incidents to Isaac who is stated to have owned the tablets containing these events.[725]

The Contents of Isaac's Story:

This tablet (11:27–25:12) contains almost all of what we know about Abraham. He related this to Isaac his son who recorded it for the family. Isaac's history follows.

Genesis 11:27b—Terah became the father of Abram, Nahor and Haran; and Haran became the father of Lot.

This first phrase of Isaac repeats the information at the end of the generations of Terah as a way of connecting this account with his. The patriarchs intentionally created a cumulative history of mankind and of the workings of God in human history. Isaac adds that Haran became the father of Lot. This is probably because Lot was to be important in the life of Abram, whose life story Isaac is about to relate.

Genesis 11:28—Haran died in the presence of his father Terah in the land of his birth, in Ur of the Chaldeans.

This explains how and why Lot would accompany Abram as he left to answer the call that God had placed on his life. Abram was his closest family. Lot undoubtedly shared the faith of Abraham and identified, even if only in a partial way, with the call that he had received from God.

Genesis 11:29—Abram and Nahor took wives for themselves. The name of Abram's wife was Sarai; and the name of Nahor's wife was Milcah, the daughter of Haran, the father of Milcah and Iscah.

The other two brothers married while the family was still in Ur. Their wives were taken from within the immediate family. Nahor married the daughter of Haran, his deceased brother. Abram married Sarai, whom we find out was the daughter of his father Terah, but by another woman than his own mother (20:12). So Terah had at least two wives.

At this time there were no laws against marrying such close relatives, and to marry in this way, to marry one who shared faith in the one true God, was an important way of keeping the faith in the midst of a perverse culture of almost total idolatry.

Genesis 11:30—Sarai was barren; she had no child.

This simple statement—Sarai was barren and had no child—made at this earliest time in the narrative, is an indication of the extreme importance that was attached to children. The command to multiply and fill the earth, and the huge blessing that attended it, was strong and greatly influenced people. The earth was still not very heavily populated in Abram's day.

Genesis 11:31—Terah took Abram his son, and Lot the son of Haran, his grandson, and Sarai his daughter-in-law, his son Abram's wife; and they went out together from Ur of the Chaldeans in order to enter the land of Canaan; and they went as far as Haran, and settled there.

Genesis 11:32—The days of Terah were two hundred and five years; and Terah died in Haran.

As noted in previous discussions, the call that God gave to Abram was first delivered to him while he was still in Ur of the Chaldees. From (11:31) we see that the call affected the entire family. They all intended to go to Canaan. Only Nahor remained in Ur. But the family only went as far as Haran, and stopped there. We do not know how long they were in Haran, or why they stopped there, but Terah died in Haran. It may be that they settled there because he was already ill.

After his father died Abram decisively responded to the call of God. He left Haran and entered the immoral and frightening land of Canaan.

Genesis 12:1—Now the LORD said [in the KJV this is translated as "had said"] to Abram, "Go [lit.: go for yourself] forth from your country, and from your relatives and from your father's house, to the land which I will show you;

The call of Abram from God was not an easy call to obey! It meant leaving his country and his family. He was to be totally dependent on the Lord God to guide, protect, and sustain him among those who were godless and immoral, about whom he had been forewarned by Noah.

Genesis 12:2—And I will make you a great nation, and I will bless you, and make your name great; and so you shall be a blessing;

Genesis 12:2—"And I will bless those who bless you, and the one who curses you I will curse. And in you all the families of the earth will be blessed."

Despite the seeming peril of His call on Abram, God's promise is what actually prevailed for him in his life. He was protected and blessed, many were blessed through him in his lifetime, and many more have been blessed through him in the centuries since.

Genesis 12:4—So Abram went forth as the LORD had spoken to him; and Lot went with him. Now Abram was seventy-five years old when he departed from Haran.

<u>Abraham Enters the Land of Canaan</u>
(Genesis 12:5–13:18; Date: BC 1876ff):
When he was seventy-five Abram arrived at Shechem in Canaan. God appeared to him and promised the land to his descendants. In Galatians 3:17 Paul explains that 430 years later God gave the law at Mt. Sinai (Exodus 19:1ff).

Abram traveled south to Bethel, built an altar to the Lord, and then traveled further south until a famine forced him to move into Egypt. Abram worried about his welfare in this situation for he was in a pagan nation of strange ungodly men. He was still learning how to trust God in these situations, so he asked Sarai to say that she was his sister.

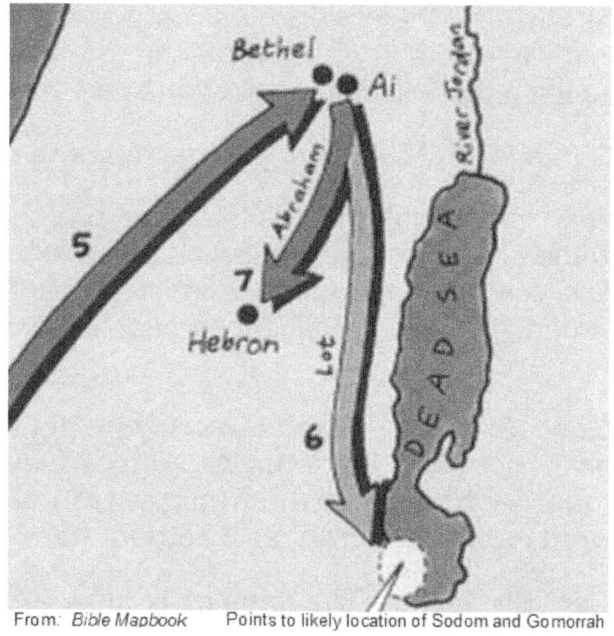

From: *Bible Mapbook*   Points to likely location of Sodom and Gomorrah

Knowing the Hurrian customs of that day, it is likely that he had previously enrolled her as his sister. After leaving Egypt Abram and Lot returned to Bethel (see route 5 on the map[726]) where they parted. Lot chose the area of Sodom and Gomorrah (route 6) and Abram stayed in Canaan, settled at Hebron in the plain of Mamre (see route 7), and built an altar to God. God spoke to him again at that time and promised him the land and very many descendants. God called Abram while he was still in Ur, quite a while before he finally responded fully to the call. In the many intervening years there is no record of God speaking to him. But once Abram obeyed God and moved to Canaan, then the Lord continued to speak to him and to lead him in a regular way.

There are offhand remarks in 12:6 that "the Canaanite was then in the land" and in 13:7 that "the Canaanite and the Perizzite were then in the land." These have been taken to indicate a much later writing of this passage. Recall that Moses is writing this account as the Israelites are about to enter the land. At that time Scripture says,
> Amalek is living in the land of the Negev and the Hittites and the Jebusites and the Amorites are living in the hill country, and the Canaanites are living by the sea and by the side of the Jordan (Numbers 13:29).

Thus in Abram's day the Canaanites were living in the mountainous regions near Bethel and Shechem and they must have migrated by the time of the Exodus over 430 years later. Moses is explaining this to the Jews of his day. It was very important because of the degradation that had taken place within the Canaanite civilization by that time.

Abram Rescues Lot and the Kings of Sodom (Genesis 14:1–14:24):
Abram's nephew Lot had pitched his tent toward Sodom and Gomorrah. The two cities were very corrupt by that time (13:13). Lot and the kings of five cities were taken captive by a contingent of four kings who attacked the cities of the plain and carried them off. This is the war that was conducted against the giants in Canaan, as we noted in our comments on 6:1–4. Abram rescued them for Lot's sake but refused any reward from the kings of Sodom, "lest it be said that the kings of Sodom made Abram rich" (14:22–23). The corruption of Sodom and Gomorrah was surely in accord with Noah's warning. Abram is referred to as a Hebrew, so the sons of Eber must have been known in those areas.

Archeological Considerations: In this passage there is another offhand reference that is taken by some to indicate a later date of writing for Genesis, for it says that "Abram pursued them unto Dan" (14:14). This tiny remark is the kind of thing that some scholars have seized upon to make their case that much of Genesis must have been assembled at a later date. A plausible explanation for this name is that the use of the term "Dan" is an update from a later century.[727] But it is also possible that we will find a reference to this place showing it was already named "Dan" at the time of the Exodus.
> Contemporary scholars assume that it refers to the town of Dan taken in the days of the Judges. This assumption cannot be proved or pressed; the scholars of ancient days would know as well as the critics of today the date when Laish was named "Dan." Such repetition of simple names is constantly occurring in ancient tablets, and no Assyrian scholar would jump to the conclusion that there was necessarily a contradiction. In all probability the reference was to an ancient town of this name in existence long before the person or town of Laish was taken by the tribe of Dan.[728]

But consider the many explanatory remarks in this passage:
> Moses explains that the ancient city "Bela" is what the Israelites knew as "Zoar" at the time of the Exodus (14:2); the ugly salt sea once was a lovely valley, the "vale of Siddim" (14:3); "Kadesh" used to be "En-Mishpat" in Abram's day (14:7); "Hobah" is north of Damascus (14:15); and "the valley of Shaveh" is also called "the king's valley" (14:17). Such explanations of ancient names and places show that Moses wrote this account while working from a record from the time of the patriarchs. He was carefully bringing it up to date for the Jews of his time so they could understand what had been written on the tablets centuries before. These ancient names are never used anywhere else in the Bible. No later redactor would have written thus.[729]

God Confirms the Covenant to Abram (Genesis 15:1–21):
Abram was left in the land in a possibly vulnerable position, for the five kings might have returned to wreak vengeance on him at any time. The Lord spoke to him in a vision and

said, "I am thy shield and thy exceedingly great reward" (15:1). At that time Abram pointed out that he still had no children and that, in accordance with the customs described in the Nuzi tablets, Eliezer of Damascus would be his heir. However the Lord again promised him descendants like the stars of heaven. At this point the Lord made a unilateral covenant with Abram, passing through the midst of the divided bodies of a heifer, a goat, a ram, a turtledove, and a pigeon. God put Abram into a deep dark sleep and told him his descendants would be strangers in a foreign land for 400 years, would serve the inhabitants of the land, and would be afflicted. They would only inherit their own land, Canaan, when the wickedness of its current inhabitants was "complete." The Lord did not identify the land where Abram's descendants would be for the 400-year period.

Passing through cut-up animals to confirm a covenant was known in Israel centuries later.
> I will give the men who have transgressed My covenant, who have not fulfilled the words of the covenant which they made before Me, *when* they cut the calf in two and passed between its parts . . . into the hand of those who seek their life. (Jeremiah 34:18, 20)

The Birth of Ishmael (Genesis 16:1–16; 1865 BC):
Sarai gave Hagar to Abram because she herself had borne him no children. Hagar bore Ishmael. Strife developed when Hagar became haughty and Sarai became abusive. Hagar fled, but the Lord called her back to the family. Abram was eighty-six years old at the time Hagar bore Ishmael. In reading this account we should keep in mind the known law of those times as explained in the Code of Hammurabi:
- If a man take a wife and this woman give her husband a servant-wife, and she bear him children, but this man wishes to take another wife, this shall not be permitted to him; he shall not take a second wife (Statute 144).
- If a man take a wife, and she bear him no children, and he intend to take another wife: if he take this second wife, and bring her into the house, this second wife shall not be allowed equality with his wife (Statute 145).
- If a man take a wife and she give this man a maid-servant as wife and she bear him children, and then this maid assume equality with the wife: because she has borne him children her master shall not sell her for money, but he may keep her as a slave, reckoning her among the maid-servants (Statute 146).

These indicate that certain laws and customs of the day circumscribed the way in which a man might treat his wife and her maid in special difficult situations. A man was not to take a second wife if his first wife provided him with children, even if it was by giving him her maid (144). If he does take a second wife because his first wife was barren, even if the second wife then bears him children, he cannot thereby demote his first wife (145).

Hagar was to assume equal status with his wife Sarai (146) once she bore Abram children; that is, she could not be sold as a slave, although Abram might still keep her as a servant in his house. This custom of giving a servant wife is also described in the Nuzi tablets. But the divine promise was made to Abram through Sarai (17:19). This was a unique and exceptional situation. The later law of Deuteronomy does not address this situation in any way. This account is set squarely in the time of the patriarchs, and the tension and dynamics of the relationships are best understood in that social context. This story could not have been written by a later redactor.

Arpachshad Dies (1863 BC): Arpachshad was an ancestral patriarch of Terah.

Archeological Considerations:[730] In explaining the well "Beer-lahai-roi" as being "between

Kadesh and Bered" we see again how Moses explains the location of the ancient places for the Israelites of his day. This location is not known to us today. Beer-lahai-roi means "well of the life of vision." It is where Hagar saw God and her life was preserved.

The Covenant of Circumcision (Genesis 17:1–27; 1852 BC):
When Abram was 99 years old, twenty-four years after he had left Haran, the Lord appeared to him at Mamre, established the covenant of circumcision with him, and changed his name to Abraham. He changed Sarai's name to Sarah and promised the two of them a son. Abraham laughed because he would be 100 and Sarah would be 90. He asked God to bless his son Ishmael. God promised that He would bless Ishmael, but that His original purpose for Abraham was not thereby fulfilled. The fulfillment of the promise was still in the future and would come about through a son to be born to him and to Sarah. They were to name that promised son Isaac, which means "laughter." Abraham obeyed by circumcising himself and all the males in his family.

Confirmation of the Birth of Isaac (Genesis 18:1–15; 1852 BC):
The Lord and two angels appeared to Abraham again, promised a son to him and to Sarah "at the time of life" (18:10). Sarah laughed when she heard this just as Abraham had done. The Lord was accompanied by two angels at this time. It seems most clear that "the Lord" in this passage is the pre-incarnate Jesus Christ.

These two accounts of the Lord announcing the birth of Isaac, not just as the son of Abraham but also of Sarah, have been called duplicates by some. I do not see why they say that. It seems that in the first account the Lord is announcing the birth of Isaac to Abraham, and Sarah does not overhear it at all. In the second account the Lord arranges for Sarah to hear His promise herself. When they hear the news each of them laughs at the idea that they could bear a son together. Therefore the name "Isaac" (which means "laughter") is most appropriate.

The Destruction of Sodom and Gomorrah (Genesis 18:16–19:29; 1852 BC):
The Lord and the angels walked on toward Sodom and Gomorrah and Abraham walked with them. God revealed His plans to destroy the cities of the plain because of the outcry that had come up to him of their extreme wickedness. Abraham stood before the Lord and interceded for them while the two angels went on to investigate the cities personally. Abraham bargained at length for the cities, asking eventually that if even ten righteous could be found in them, then surely the Lord should not destroy them. The Lord conceded to the logic of Abraham and honored his request.

Meanwhile the two angels found Lot and his family in the city. The ensuing tragedy of the angels' treatment by all the men of Sodom (19:4) showed the universal wickedness of the people in those cities. Thus the Lord destroyed Sodom and Gomorrah, for not even ten righteous could be found there. But He saved Lot from destruction in that catastrophe. Isaac must have gotten some of these details from his uncle Lot.

In this account, written by Isaac as it was told to him by his father Abraham, we see the Lord God interacting with Abraham and we see the two angels interacting with him, and also with the people in Sodom and Gomorrah. It is best to see this story as a revelation to us of the angelic nature and the divine pre-incarnate nature. It clearly indicates that angels can and sometimes do interact with human beings on this earth, speaking with us as we do with each other. If we view angels as Augustine suggested, as formless spiritual beings who know things in an instantaneous way, then how does that idea fit with this account that we get from Abraham? The word says, when speaking of the fascination that angels have with human history, especially the history of salvation,

> As to this salvation, the prophets who prophesied of the grace that *would come* to you made careful searches and inquiries, seeking to know what person or time the Spirit of Christ within them was indicating as He predicted the sufferings of Christ and the glories to follow. It was revealed to them that they were not serving themselves, but you, in these things which now have been announced to you through those who preached the gospel to you by the Holy Spirit sent from heaven—things into which angels long to look [or: gain a clear glimpse]. (1 Peter 1:10–12)

And Paul explains their watchful oversight of our lives is

> so that the manifold wisdom of God might now be made known through the church to the rulers and the authorities in the heavenly *places*. (Ephesians 3:10)

It is best to see the angels as coming to know things through the on-going events of history on this earth, just as we do. They come to know of them by observation, but we come to understand them both by reflecting on them when they are past and by participating in them as they transpire. Even the Lord God chooses to participate in our earthly lives at times, and He sometimes allows His angelic servants to do the same.

The many accounts of Scripture reveal this to us quite clearly and imply that angels do not come to know or understand things instantaneously. This appearance is not an "accommodation" of eternal spiritual beings to our human condition. The Lord God also speaks to his angelic servants in heaven in conversational interchanges:

> Again there was a day when the sons of God came to present themselves before the LORD, and Satan also came among them to present himself before the LORD. The LORD said to Satan, "Where have you come from?" Then Satan answered the LORD and said, "From roaming about on the earth and walking around on it." The LORD said to Satan, "Have you considered My servant Job? For there is no one like him on the earth, a blameless and upright man fearing God and turning away from evil. And he still holds fast his integrity, although you incited Me against him to ruin him without cause." Satan answered the LORD and said, "Skin for skin! Yes, all that a man has he will give for his life. However, put forth Your hand now, and touch his bone and his flesh; he will curse You to Your face." So the LORD said to Satan, "Behold, he is in your power, only spare his life." (Job 2:1–6)

It is not best to describe these recorded events by making use of the dismissive term "anthropomorphism," for we should see these accounts as telling us about the personal experience of Abraham and other Old Testament men and women, or at least as divine revelation given to them about heavenly realities. When God, in the fullness of time, chose to personally make His tabernacle with human beings, He condescended to enter our realm of existence by being born of a woman, even as we all were, and to live and interact with us on our human plane, even accepting the humiliating death on the cross in order to reclaim eternal life for us all. He had been in the "form of God," but took on Himself the "form of a man" yet He still remained God. He has now become a life-giving spirit, but He is still fully a man and will always be thus.

Chrysostom speaks of this particular appearance of the Lord God to Abraham, pointing out the unique language that Scripture uses in introducing it.

> "The Lord God appeared to Abram," the text says, "and said to him." Wasn't I right in saying at the outset that a great treasure is contained in these brief words? I mean, notice at once the strange and unusual opening of the expression: "The Lord God appeared to Abram," it says. This is the first time

> we find this stated in Scripture, "he appeared." Neither in the case of Adam, nor Abel, nor Noe [Noah], nor anyone else did Sacred Scripture employ this expression. So why is the expression, "he appeared," used? And how is it that elsewhere Scripture says, "No one will see God and live"? How, then, would we interpret the words of Scripture, "He appeared"? How did he appear to the just man? Surely he didn't see his true being? No-God forbid. What, then? He was seen in the way he alone knows and in the manner possible for Abram to see. In his inventiveness, you see, our wise and loving Lord, showing considerateness for our human nature, reveals himself to those who worthily prepare themselves in advance. He explains this through the sacred author in the words, "I gave many visions and took shape in the works of the inspired authors." Isaiah in his turn saw him seated, something that is inapplicable to God, since he doesn't sit down—how could he, after all, with his unique nature being incorporeal and indefectible? Daniel too saw him, as the Ancient of Days; Zechariah had a different vision of him, and Ezekiel in turn a different one. This is the reason, therefore, that he said, "I gave many visions," that is, I appeared in a way suited to each one.[731]

Chrysostom goes on to observe that God had uprooted Abraham from his home and had sent him into a far country that was populated with godless and hostile people. And still the promise of offspring had not been fulfilled. Thus He appeared to Abraham in this way to reassure and strengthen him and to give Him the courage to continue in faith.[732]

Surely this is true. Abraham was the friend of God (James 2:23), and God spoke to him just as He had interacted with Adam and Eve in Eden. So God is not a formless spirit. His nature is such that He and we are by design intended to interrelate directly.[733]

Chrysostom is correct in what he says, that we cannot see God as He is in our fallen and sinful state. But we will see Him directly when we have our body of glory—a body that is like His own resurrection body. God is far removed from us, not because He is by nature existing in a form that is completely different from ours, but because, in our fallen state, we cannot bear to receive the direct infusion of His love and goodness.

Our prideful nature cannot bear the manifest experience of the holiness and sweetness of the Lord God. That is what separates us from Him, and that has nothing to do with a difference in form. It is a difference that proceeds not from our original created nature but from the distortion of that nature that resulted from the fall. In our original purpose we were created to see Him as He is and to dwell before Him, seeing His face, relating to Him as His beloved sons and daughters. In this vision, and in other appearances that the Scriptures report to us, the Lord God is pulling back the veil a bit to let us glimpse Him, but not in His full and manifest glory. His overwhelming splendor is veiled but a brighter shadow of His essence is allowed to appear to us. Thus our sinful nature is not assaulted by His radiance. In the fullness of His plan of salvation however, our sinful nature is to be replaced. Our inner man will be regenerated at the moment of salvation, and our body of sin will die and be resurrected, or it will be transformed at the rapture

> so that Christ may dwell in our hearts through faith; *and* that we, being rooted and grounded in love, may be able to comprehend with all the saints what is the breadth and length and height and depth, and to know the love of Christ which surpasses knowledge, that we may be filled up to all the fullness of God. (Ephesians 3:17–19)

<u>The Origin of Moab and Ammon</u> (Genesis 19:30–38; 1852–1 BC):
After Sodom fell the daughters of Lot had children by their father. These two unnatural unions produced the nations of Moab and Ammon. This is another example, like the birth of Canaan, of how children are adversely affected when they are raised in a culture of great decadence and sexual disorder. Children are so very easily influenced!

Some have suggested that Moses inserted this comment at the time of the Exodus as an explanation to the Israelites. By that time these nations would have been fully formed. But Isaac did not write his history until after the death of Ishmael, and he was thirteen or fourteen years old at this time. Since Ishmael died at age 137 (25:17) that would be well over a century later. Isaac himself was not yet born at this time and would live for 180 years (35:28). It is surely possible that the people descended from these unions could have begun to emerge as identifiable nations by the time that Isaac was writing his history, almost two centuries later.

Abraham in Gerar with Abimelech (Genesis 20:1–18):
Abraham journeyed south to Gerar. But he feared for his safety since Sarah was still a beautiful woman. Again he asked her to say that she was his sister. Abimelech the king took her into his harem. Again the Lord God spoke to the king and told him to restore her to Abraham, and he did so. Again Abraham gained wealth from this transaction—the king gave him sheep, oxen, menservants, maidservants, and finally a thousand pieces of silver. In this account it is also made clear that there was an agreement between Abraham and Sarah dating back to when they left their family in Haran. Accordingly she was to claim that she was his sister wherever they went.

Once the king understood this he gave Abraham freedom to dwell wherever he wanted in the land. It must have been common for the powerful to take beautiful women from other men to be their wives, killing or enslaving the men at the same time. According to the customs recorded on the Nuzi tablets we know that among other things a wife might be adopted as a sister by her husband. Therefore, she could be accorded a higher esteem and social status. This might be part of the background of these stories and would help explain why Abraham and Isaac spoke of their wives as their sisters. In a society where women were not held in high esteem, being able to produce a contract of adoption as a sister might have offered them a measure of protection. Abram and Sarai could have drawn this up before they left Haran.

The Birth of Isaac and the Expulsion of Ishmael (Genesis 21:1–21; 1846 BC):
Isaac was born as God predicted. Abraham was 100 years old and Sarah was 90 (17:17) when it happened, and the way it happened is a certain testimony to the power and the providence of God. This birth was miraculous. Isaac grew and was weaned, so Abraham gave a great feast at that time. According to Jewish rabbinical traditions, weaning could take place anywhere between 18 months and 12 years of age. Another Jewish tradition says Ishmael was cast out when Isaac was five years old.[734] I assume Isaac was five.

Ishmael saw that his privileged place in the family was threatened by Isaac, and he had a very bad response. Paul says that Ishmael "persecuted" Isaac (Galatians 4:29). Sarah saw this, realized that he was a threat to Isaac in more ways than one, and demanded that he and his mother Hagar be forced to leave. This might have been a resurfacing of the old resentment between Hagar and Sarah from before Ishmael had been born, but it is also a fact that women have keen perceptions about these things. Abraham was grieved at her demands, but the Lord agreed with Sarah. The customs of the times, according to the Nuzi tablets and the Code of Hammurabi, forbad this harsh treatment of a servant-wife. This must have made the decision even more difficult for Abraham.

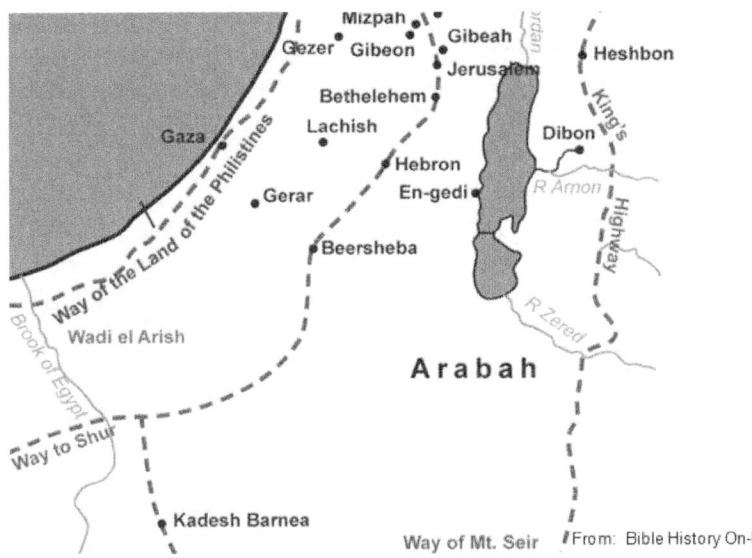

God promised Abraham that He would make a great nation out of Ishmael because he was the seed of Abraham. This was surely His faithfulness to the prayer of Abraham for his first son (17:18), for at that time the Lord God had promised to bless Ishmael (17:20). However "the" promise of God would come through Isaac, as the Lord had stated before (17:19).

Thus Abraham did what was necessary, even though it was difficult for him. Early in the morning he rose up, gave Hagar a bottle of water and some bread, and sent her and Ishmael away. If this was difficult for him to do, it would surely have been devastating for Hagar and for Ishmael. No wonder he grew up and was "a wild man, his hand against every man and every man against him" as the Lord God had told Hagar when he was younger (16:12). This ordeal would have been enough to destroy Ishmael's very will to live but the Lord helped him and Hagar by intervening. Isaac received this story from Ishmael as part of his brother's family record.

Hagar and Ishmael wandered in the wilderness of Beersheba. It does not say that they went south out of Hebron, so Abraham seems still to have been dwelling in Gerar and not to have returned to Hebron after his dealings with Abimelech. This would have been a desolate area for them to wander in. They may have not seen anyone or have been unable to get help from those whom they did encounter. Thus they were left without resources. But the Lord God intervened, led them to a well of water, and gave them the strength to go on with life. Ishmael was 19 when this happened.

Ishmael went southeast from there and dwelt in the wilderness of Paran (21:21). In time Hagar found him an Egyptian wife, and he settled in Paran, further south than the map shows, in the northern part of the Arabian Peninsula. This story must have been related to Isaac by Ishmael sometime later. Perhaps that happened when they met to bury their father Abraham (25:9). However, it could have been part of an on-going interchange that they maintained. Apparently they still kept in touch as the years went on after that, for Isaac records Ishmael's death. After all, they still shared faith in the One True God.

Continuing Interaction between Abraham and Abimelech (Genesis 21:22–34):
By this time Abimelech realized that God was blessing Abraham. After all, God had closed the wombs in his house because of the incident with Sarah and then had opened them up when Abraham prayed for him. Thus he made a covenant with him for "God is with thee" (21:22). After this Abraham sojourned in the land of the Philistines for a long time (21:34). It appears that Abraham moved to Gerar before Isaac was born, that Isaac was born there, and that he stayed there until after Ishmael was banished. Thus the birth of Isaac, his weaning, and the banishment of Ishmael all happened in the midst of a lengthy series of

interchanges between Abraham and Abimelech that took place after Abraham moved from Hebron to Gerar. Some think the name for the residents of the land, Philistines, might be a later update to the text.[735] I think it is more likely that our secular history is inaccurate.

Abraham Is Asked to Sacrifice Isaac (Genesis 22:1–19):
Once Ishmael had departed and Isaac was Abraham's only remaining son, with all of God's promises wrapped up in him, the Lord asked Abraham to sacrifice Isaac to Him. This is the first time that the word "love" is used in Genesis. It is the love of a father for his only son at the moment when he realizes that he must sacrifice him by his own hand: "Take now thy son, thine only son Isaac, whom you love . . ." This is a picture of the decision made in eternity, before the foundation of the world, when the Father and His beloved Son decided that Jesus would have to be sacrificed for our sins. That was the initial love of all creation, the foundation upon which it was predicated.

A key verse in this story is Abraham's reply to Isaac when he asks him where the lamb is for the sacrifice. Abraham says, "God will provide Himself a lamb for the offering." It is not stated that "God Himself will provide . . ." but that "God will provide Himself . . ." This may indicate that in the midst of these events the Lord God gave Abraham an insight into the coming sacrifice of His only Son for the sins of mankind. (also note John 8:56)

Sometimes it is necessary that we give the most precious things that we have into the hands of the Lord. In this way we avoid making them an idol and place all things in proper perspective in our lives, and thus the Lord God can bless us more abundantly. After this Abraham went to Beersheba to live (22:19).

Shelah Dies (1833 BC): Shelah was one of the long-lived ancestral patriarchs of Terah.

Abraham Receives Word of Nahor's Growing Family (Genesis 22:20–24):
This communication was vital. It offered Abraham a way to find a wife for his son Isaac; one who was not an unbeliever from among the Canaanites. Here is the family of Nahor as told to Abraham.

Nahor and Milcah his wife	Huz	
	Buz	
	Kemuel	Aram
	Chesed	
	Hazo	
	Pildash	
	Jidlaph	
	Bethuel	Rebekah
Nahor and Reumah his concubine	Tabah	
	Gaham	
	Thahash	
	Maachah	

The news from the family of Nahor must have been welcome to Abraham and Isaac because it was so important to them for Isaac to marry a believing wife. The information from Haran certainly shows that the families were able to keep in touch. We will see that Isaac and also Jacob waited to get married until a godly wife could be found for them. But Esau married Canaanite women. God-centered values were eroding. The sons of Jacob married at younger ages and often wed women from the land of Canaan.

The Death of Sarah (Genesis 23:1–20) (1814 BC):
Sarah died at the age of 127 (23:1). Abraham sought for and was granted a place that was appropriate to bury his wife from among the sons of Heth. Because Isaac was born when

Sarah was 90 years old (21:5, 17:17), he was 37 years old and still was not married when she died.

Archeological Considerations: In describing where this cave is, Moses explains to the Jews of the time of the Exodus that it was called "Kiriath-Arba," which is "Hebron," and is in the land of Canaan (23:2). No later writer would have had to explain that Hebron was in the land of Canaan. This was an explanation appropriate to the time of the Exodus, given to the Jews of that time by Moses, explaining for them exactly what had been written in their ancient historical tablets, in anticipation of their entering into the land in the near future. In a similar vein the note Moses adds in (23:19), "the cave of the field of Machpelah before Mamre (the same is Hebron in the land of Canaan)," is specifically suited to the generation that is about to enter the land.

> This quote is of special interest as it was necessary to give not only its modern name but even to say that Hebron was in the land of Canaan. This surely indicates that the note was added at a very early date and before the children of Israel had entered the land. No one in later times would need to be told where Hebron was. The children of Israel must have known it quite well after its capture in Joshua's day, when the city was given to Caleb for an inheritance. It then became one of the "cities of refuge" and as such must have been familiar throughout the land. Besides all this, David was king in Hebron for seven years. On the other hand, it would be necessary for a people not yet entered into the land to be told, not only the name of the place where the founders of the race had lived but where this place was situated.
>
> We get a similar note in 23:19: "the cave of the field of Machpelah before Mamre (the same is Hebron in the land of Canaan)." Abraham, Isaac, and Jacob had been buried in this cave of Machpelah; consequently it would have been well known to their contemporaries. But it must be remembered that the whole of the nation excepting Joshua and Caleb had died in the time which had elapsed between leaving Sinai and entering into the land of Canaan. I submit that once the children of Israel had settled in the land, there would be no need of a note to explain where the founders of their race, Abraham, Isaac, and Jacob had been buried. I suggest that these explanations were written for those who were about to enter into the land of Canaan. This supports the view that these notes were written by Moses who died on the margin of the land, immediately before the Israelites had entered into it.[736]

Isaac Marries Rebekah (Genesis 24:1–67) (1811 BC):
This detailed account of how Isaac and Rebekah found each other has illuminating statements in it. Abraham was getting old and well stricken with age (24:1). Isaac was 40 years old when he married Rebekah (25:20). In the Nuzi tablets it is stated that one of the major responsibilities of a father toward his son was to find him a wife. Thus Abraham may have felt that it was incumbent upon him to initiate the proceedings that are recorded in this chapter, lest perhaps he die before fulfilling his duty. On the other hand, he was not so old that he could not marry again, as the next section shows. We no longer understand what happened to people when they got so old. We have no first-hand experience in understanding what happens during such long life spans.

The strong emphasis on how Abraham made his servant swear that he would look for a wife only from his kindred and not from the daughters of Canaan shows what a serious matter this was for Abraham. The providential way that the servant came upon Rebekah at the well was also understood by Abraham's servant, by Laban, and by Bethuel as the hand of God (24:50). The way the servant found Rebekah, an immediate response to the prayer of his heart, is emphasized by its repetition. This is a beautiful story of God's providential care in bringing about their marriage—a marriage union that was foundational in the establishment of the nation of Israel.

It is written that Rebecca was a virgin **and** that no man had known her—a repetitious statement. Origen picks up on this and says,
> I have often said already that in these stories history is not being narrated, but mysteries are interwoven. I think, therefore, that something such as this is indicated in this story.
>
> Just as Christ is said to be the husband of the soul, to whom the soul is married when it comes to faith, so also, contrary to this, he who also is called "an enemy" when "he oversows tares among the wheat" is called the husband to whom the soul is married when it turns away to faithlessness. It is not sufficient, therefore, for the soul to be pure in body; it is necessary also that this most wicked man "has not known it." For it can happen that someone may possess virginity in body, and knowing that most wicked man, the devil, and receiving darts of concupiscence from him in the heart destroy the purity of the soul. Because, therefore, Rebecca was a virgin holy in body and spirit, for this reason the Scripture doubles her praise and says: "She was a virgin; a man had not known her."[737]

The negotiations to give a daughter in marriage were normally conducted by her father. Thus Bethuel is involved. But a brother like Laban could also be involved, normally only if the father was dead or incapacitated. If the brother was involved, then the woman had the right to refuse the arrangement. Since Abraham did not have Isaac until late in his life we see that Nahor has children and grandchildren by this time, and the servant is negotiating for Isaac to marry his second cousin. The dowry that Abraham offered was clearly substantial (24:10, 24:35), giving the family of Nahor great impetus to approve the wedding. Rebekah would be well cared for.

Finally once the family verified that Rebekah was willing to accept the wedding proposal, the family blessed her and sent her off to a new life with Abraham and Isaac. In accordance with custom they also sent her nurse, whom we find out later is named Deborah (35:8) and who would be a long-time companion for Rebekah. There is a tradition that Rebecca was only ten years old[738] when she went to Isaac.

When Rebekah arrived in Beersheba, Isaac was in the fields meditating, and he saw her coming. When they were introduced he loved her, brought her into Sarah's tent, took her as his wife, and was comforted over the loss of his mother.

<u>From Abraham's Marriage to Keturah until his Death</u> (Genesis 25:1–10):

After this Abraham married Keturah (meaning "perfumed" or "sweet-smelling incense") and she bore more sons to him. She is his wife (25:1), and also his concubine (see 1 Chronicles 1:32). And 25:6 says he sent "the sons of his concubines" into the "east country." Perhaps she was a concubine who then became his wife. The family tree of Abraham and Keturah is shown here.

Abraham and His concubine Keturah	Zimran		
	Jokshan	Sheba	
		Dedan	Asshurim
			Letushim
			Leummim
	Medan		
	Midian	Ephah	
		Epher	
		Hanoch	
		Abidah	
		Eldaah	
	Ishbak		
	Shuah		

Isaac married Rebecca when he was 40, thus when Abraham was 140 years old. Because Abraham died at age 175 he had almost 35 years after Isaac married to build his family

505

with Keturah. Isaac lived a total of 180 years (35:28); i.e., for almost 140 years after his father married Keturah. It is therefore very reasonable for him to record the descendants of Abraham by Keturah down to the third generation after his father, and to record the fact that they eventually settled in the east because the genealogy of Abraham and Keturah would extend into Isaac's old age. So the account that bears Isaac's name reaches to his later years.

Midian was the ancestor of Jethro, the father-in-law of Moses. Jethro lived in northwest Arabia. The Midianites and the Ishmaelites intermarried and became one group at the time that Joseph was sold into slavery (see Genesis 37:27 and 37:28; 37:36 and 39:1), another example of those of faith intermarrying. Abraham gave gifts to each of the sons he had by his concubine and he sent them away to the "east country." But he gave all that he had unto Isaac. Abraham lived for 175 years and he died. He was buried by his sons Isaac and Ishmael in the cave where he had buried Sarah.

Archeological Consideration:[739] In Genesis 25:6 the text says Abraham sent his sons by Keturah to the "east country." This would be an unlikely reference for that area if it were written by a later redactor. A more informative name, perhaps Arabia, would be a likely choice. The nameless geographical designation is more appropriate to the time of the patriarchs when the names for the area were not yet established.

Shem Dies (1801 BC):
Abraham Dies (1776 BC):
Eber Dies (1772 BC): This was 19 years after the birth of Esau and Jacob. Eber was the last remaining ancestral patriarch of Terah. His death was recorded by Isaac, not in his own story but in that of Terah. He had to complete the genealogical register of his grandfather Terah who died, because of the rapid decrease in life spans after the Flood and after Babel, many years before four of his ancestors.

Genesis 25:11—It came about after the death of Abraham that God blessed his son Isaac; and Isaac lived by Beer-lahai-roi.

This "date line" indicates when Isaac wrote his account. It was written after the death of Abraham, while he was dwelling near the well Beer-lahai-roi.

The Generations of Ishmael (Genesis 25:12–18):
Next the generations of Ishmael are listed by Isaac. Ishmael lived for 137 years and died in 1728 BC. Because Isaac was 14 years his junior, he was 123 years old when Ishmael died. This was 57 years before Isaac died at the age of 180.

Isaac could have learned of this family genealogy from his older brother when they came together to bury their father Abraham. In fact, I think it is reasonable to believe that they were in contact occasionally because, as we shall see, Esau went to the family of Ishmael to take a wife.

Ishmael	Nebaioth
	Kedar
	Adbeel
	Mibsam
	Mishma
	Dumah
	Massa
	Hadad
	Tema
	Jetur
	Naphish
	Kedemah

The Signature of Isaac:
Genesis 25:19a—Now these are *the records of* the generations of Isaac, Abraham's son

This is the story of Isaac, relating what he heard from Abraham his father and from Ishmael his older brother. Every fact that he records would have been easily known to Isaac. As noted, it is likely that the statement that "Isaac dwelt by the well Lahai-Roi [or Beer-La-Hai-Roi, for "Beer" in Hebrew means "well"]" (25:11) is a "date line" for his history; that is, he wrote it while he was living in Hebron after the death of his father Abraham.

It seems that the commissioning of the family history, or the personal writing of it—whatever the case may be—was often an undertaking of the latter years of a patriarch's life, after the death of his father. Upon the death of his father he inherited the family history tablets and then added his own personal account to them. After Isaac and Ishmael came back together to bury their Father, Ishmael related some of his family stories to Isaac, possibly even in written form. Isaac then included them in his own history.

Again in this case of the record written by Isaac, we see that the events of this tablet end just before the death of Isaac, thus giving strong internal evidence that he was the author and that he completed this account of the ancient times of his father Abraham at a time that was in his later years, as the "date line" indicates. Notice also that all of the information in this narrative was readily available to Isaac. The story of the expulsion of Ishmael could easily have been received from him when the brothers came together to bury their father Abraham or could even have been communicated to Isaac earlier as part of an on-going relationship. At the funeral he also received from Ishmael the records of descent for his family. Both of these are included in his account, which he wrote after Abraham died and while he was under the blessing of God and "dwelt by the well La-Hai-Roi."

Notice also that the account that Isaac wrote is in chronological sequence; that is, it is the story of the various events that he and his father Abraham lived through, in their order of occurrence. This also is a testimony that this entire account was written by one person.

This account would have originally been written in the scholarly language of Isaac's day—cuneiform. Isaac either wrote it himself or employed a scribe to write it for him. In either case, we can reasonably presume that it would have been written in accordance with the scribal methods and practices of that time. We can see this clearly as we read it. Moses preserved those elements for us as he transcribed Isaac's account into Genesis. He did that intentionally, so that his readers would understand the authority behind this writing, that it originated with an eyewitness of unimpeachable character—Isaac.

When we begin the next section, the history written by Jacob, the Genesis story returns to a time before the end of this account. In other words, there is a chronological break where the new account begins. Jacob turns time back a few years and tells us several events about his own birth and the birth of his brother Esau that Isaac did not mention—from his own perspective. Then the account of Jacob is related to us as a chronological record of events. This is more evidence that what we are reading in Genesis is the concatenation of two accounts: the first by Isaac, and the second by his son Jacob. The two accounts were later edited and put together by Moses when he wrote Genesis.

Jacob

(Text omitted for this eighth set of tablets because of length; Genesis 25:19b-37:2a)

<u>Archeological Considerations</u>:

> Jacob is the central figure in the record, and the latest chronological statement in them is that of the death of Isaac. Immediately before the ending formula, "these are the origins of Jacob," we read, "and Jacob dwelt in the land of his father's sojourning, in the land of Canaan." This sentence has seemed so isolated that it has been regarded by many to have little relation to the context, yet . . . it is evidence of the date when and where the tablets were written. Within a few years Jacob had moved down to Egypt. This sentence indicates where he was living when he closed his record. For although he tells us of the death of Isaac, he says nothing whatever of the sale of Joseph into slavery, which occurred eleven years before Isaac's death. [Mike Gladieux—Note: I will deal with this issue more completely and accurately in the commentary.] Neither does he tell of Joseph's interpretation of the butler's dream or of any other event in Egypt. Until Jacob went down to Egypt (ten years after he had buried his father), thus leaving "the land of his father's sojourning," he could not know anything whatever about these things. Thus the record of Jacob closes precisely at the period indicated in the sentence in 37:1. He had gone back to the south country, Hebron (where his father lived), only ten years [Correction: Jacob was 87 when he arrived at Hebron, as we shall see, so this would be 33 years before Isaac dies.] before Isaac had died, and he records his death. Within ten years of this latter event, Jacob was himself living in Egypt. So this previously obscure verse of Genesis 37 clearly indicates not only that Jacob wrote the tablets but when and where they were written.[740]

Thus the record given to us from Jacob is dated by him. It was written between the time when he buried his father Isaac and when he went into Egypt, while he was dwelling at Hebron. Isaac died at the age of 180, in 1671 BC—632 years after the Flood. Jacob was 120 years old when Isaac died, 10 years before he went into Egypt at age 130. We will explain why Jacob's record says nothing about the disappearance of his son Joseph.

We should also see that the patriarchs Abraham, Isaac, and Jacob were of a status such that recording their family history was well within their means. We should expect that they could write it themselves or, as is perhaps more likely, that they would employ a scribe to do the recording for them, thus assuring that it reflected the literary techniques of their day. As such it would be clearly understood by any educated reader.

> The greater part of the story concerns Jacob, and more than half of it refers to his journey to and from Paddan-aram and his life there. He alone could have recorded the events occurring during this period of his life.

> It is necessary to bear in mind the place occupied by the patriarchs in the affairs of the time. For instance, Abraham comes into contact with Pharaoh and the princes when he goes into Egypt. In his day Egypt was a mighty power, and he must have had a status that made him a person of prominence in that country, for it was not merely an oriental mode of speech that made the sons of Heth say, "Hear us, my lord: thou art a mighty prince amongst us." We are told that he had "menservants and maidservants," and that "Abram was very rich in cattle, in silver and in gold," and that "their substance was great." So great a person was he, that when he returned to Canaan, he could say to Lot, notwithstanding the presence of the Canaanites in the land, "Let there be no strife, I pray thee, between my herdsmen and thy herdsmen, for we are brethren. *Is not the whole land before thee?* Separate thyself, I pray thee, from me: if thou wilt take the left hand, then I will go to the right, or if thou take the right hand then I will go to the left." (13:8-12).[741]

Thus Abraham (or Isaac) was financially able to hire a scribe to write his family history. This is likely what happened, and so the scribal literary methods of Mesopotamia were followed.

In such a manner the choice was made where he would live, and thus the scene is set for the next chapter where he meets the four kings, among them one so mighty as Amraphel, King of Shinar. When these four kings from the East easily overcame the five petty city-state kings of Transjordan, we read that, when Abraham heard that his brother Lot had been taken captive, he led forth his trained men born in his own house, three hundred and eighteen, and pursued them as far as Dan . . . and smote them and brought back all the goods, and also brought again his brother Lot, and his goods, and the women also, and the people . . . And Abraham said unto the King of Sodom, I have lift up my hand unto the Lord God Most High, possessor of heaven and earth, that I will not take a thread or a shoe latchet or aught that is thine, lest thou should say I have made Abraham rich. [Genesis 14:14–23]

In a like manner Isaac and Jacob are depicted as possessing considerable status in their day, and they are quite capable of writing or employing scribes to write the tablets containing narratives from which Moses compiled the account.[742]

Indeed, all of the patriarchs were able to have their family histories transcribed for them.

The Contents of Jacob's Story:

The Birth of Jacob and Esau (Genesis 25:20–34) (1791 BC):
Isaac was 40 when he married Rebekah, the daughter of Bethuel the Syrian of Paddan-Aram and the sister of Laban the Syrian (25:20). Rebekah did not bear children at first, and so Isaac entreated the Lord on behalf of his wife Rebekah and then she conceived. When she felt the struggle within her body during pregnancy she sought the Lord and He told her that two nations were in her womb, and two types of people. The one would be stronger than the other and the older would serve the younger.

Isaac was 60 when they were born (25:26). Esau was born first and was hairy and red. Jacob came out next and his hand took hold of Esau's heel. Their names mean "hairy" (Esau) and "he grasps the heel" or "usurper" (Jacob). Esau was a skilled hunter. Jacob was not. Isaac loved Esau the most and Rebekah loved Jacob. When the boys were older Jacob bargained with Esau: his birthright (as the oldest son) for a bowl of stew. Although selling a birthright was known in the customs of the day, the cheap price he settled for shows how little Esau thought of what he stood to inherit from his fathers. It probably meant that he would no longer inherit the family historical records, The Genesis Documents.

Dealings with the Philistines (Genesis 26:1–33):
There was a famine in the land, so Isaac moved to Gerar, to Abimelech, the king of the Philistines. There God appeared to him and told him not to go to Egypt and promised to give the land to his descendants, as He had sworn to Abraham. Isaac also played false with the king by claiming that Rebekah was his sister rather than his wife. As we noted from the Nuzi tablets it may also have been Isaac's life-long plan to protect Rebekah by providing her with additional status as his sister. This way of relating must have been inherited from Abraham who, as we noted, probably had made such an agreement with Sarah when they left Haran (20:13). Some believe the name "Philistine" might be seen as a twelfth-century update to the text.[743] But secular history might be missing some facts.

Two Rulers Named Abimelech:
The name "Abimelech" can be a title like Pharaoh. In Psalm 34 it is applied to the king of Gath whose name was Achish (see 1 Samuel 27:2–3). God protected Isaac from the king, and he stayed in Gerar for a time prospering greatly. But the Philistines grew envious, and finally Abimelech asked him to leave. Isaac moved to the valley of Gerar and re-dug two wells that had originally been dug in the days of Abraham. When the Philistines strove

with his servants over those wells too, Isaac moved to Beersheba. That night the Lord appeared to him and said, "Fear not for I am with you and will bless you."

Isaac was afraid because of the envious hostility of the Philistines. The Lord's reassurance must have encouraged him and he built an altar to God. Then Abimelech came to make a "non-aggression" pact with Isaac, confirming God's promise. Beersheba received its name from this pact between Abimelech and Isaac since the word "shebah" means "oath" or "seven" ("well of the oath"). Moses does not give us an older name for this place.

Esau and Jacob as Adults (Genesis 26:34–27:46) (1751 BC and following):
When Esau was 40 years old (1751 BC, 26:34–35) he married two women from the land of Canaan, and they brought grief to Isaac and Rebekah. Evidently Esau did not want to wait for the "right" woman that his parents would pick for him. Thus Isaac was 100 years old when Esau married.

Later on Isaac lost his sight. He must have felt that he was going to die soon, so he called Esau with the intention of blessing him as the eldest son and as the one who was his favorite. But Rebekah heard Isaac instructing Esau and led Jacob to deceive Isaac into blessing him instead. Through this ruse Jacob usurped his brother's blessing and caused Esau to hate him deeply. Esau planned to kill Jacob as soon as Isaac died. Rebekah heard of this and complained to Isaac about the Canaanite wives of Esau, to carefully pave the way for Jacob to leave for Paddan-Aram. She said if Jacob also took such a woman as a wife then her life would be worthless. This laid the groundwork for sending Jacob to her family in Paddan-Aram to seek a wife there—away from Esau.

Underlying this story is the custom that the oral will of a father was unchangeable. Thus Esau's loss was irreversible, and this trick was very hurtful to him.

There appear to be two stories of Jacob's departure for Paddan-Aram. In 27:41–27:45 we have Jacob's account of his leaving. Because of his reaction of anger when Jacob usurped his blessing, Esau determined to kill him after Isaac passed away. Rachel heard of this and sent Jacob away. In 27:46-28:9 we have the story of Jacob's departure from Esau's point of view. He did not hear his mother Rebekah when she told Jacob to leave for Paddan-Aram. He did hear her reiterate to Isaac how disgusted she was with the Canaanite wives that he had married. He heard her ask Isaac to send Jacob to her family to find a wife from among them (27:46).

These stories indicate that Rebekah was a subtle and conniving woman in how she dealt with her family—both with Isaac and with her sons. Esau took a cue from what his mother had said about his wives and married another wife from Ishmael's daughters. This happened after Jacob had left for Paddan-Aram. Later on Esau decided that his flocks and Jacob's flocks had become too large to share the same space and he moved to the hill country of Seir. This is also reflected in his genealogies in chapter 36. The account written by Jacob of his departure to Paddan-Aram recommences in 28:10 ff.

It has been suggested that the presence of these two separate accounts with styles that are somewhat different is an indication that Genesis was written at a later date by an unknown compiler using several traditions as his source. But there is a much simpler and more logical way to understand it. Jacob received stories from Esau when they met to bury their father Isaac (or at other times in their lives when they met for some reason) and inserted them into his account of the family history. In general it seems likely that separated family members kept in touch in some way. This is indicated by the narrative, which often records communications and travel between family members, and by the plethora of known trade routes that existed in patriarchal times.

The timing of Jacob's departure can be narrowed by noting that Ishmael died at age 137 and he was fourteen years older than Isaac. When Esau was forty, when he married his Canaanite wives, Isaac was 100 and Ishmael was 114. When Esau went to Ishmael to marry one of his daughters Esau could not have been more than 63 years old or Ishmael would have been dead, and the account indicates otherwise (28:9). But Esau had to be somewhat older than 40. This still leaves great leeway for the ages of the two brothers during these episodes. Thus, as noted in chapter two, the precise chronology of Jacob's family life is not given in Genesis. I am going to assume they were 47 when Jacob left.

Jacob Sent to Paddan-Aram (Genesis 28:1–9) (1744 BC, Jacob is 47, estimated):
The date of Jacob's leaving for Paddan-Aram is estimated from the chronology of the later years of his life and the lives of his sons. (This will become clear as the story progresses because we will see that he begins his family about seven years after he arrives in Paddan-Aram.) Therefore Isaac called Jacob to himself and truly blessed him with the blessing of Abraham—the inheritance of the land for him and his seed. It must have finally become evident to him that Jacob was the one to whom the promise was to pass. This realization dawned as both sons got older and their basic character was revealed.

When Jacob left Rebekah said she would send for him after the anger of Esau had abated and it was safe for him to return. Again this shows that there was regular communication between separated branches of the family. There is a Jewish tradition that she sent people to Paddan-Aram to check on Jacob.[744] Rebekah's expectations and plans did not fully materialize, and Jacob stayed in Paddan-Aram for twenty years.

During this time Esau saw that Jacob had obeyed his parents and also understood how badly they both felt about his own Canaanite wives. So he took a wife from the Ishmaelites whose name was Mahalath, the sister of Nebaioth. Ishmael died at the age of 137 (25:17) in 1728 BC. Jacob departed in 1744 BC, or sixteen years before his death. Therefore by the time Esau married Mahalath, Ishmael would have been quite old and perhaps was in ill health. Normally the father would make the marriage arrangements for his daughter, but his age might have precluded this, for this was less than sixteen years before his death. Thus his oldest son Nebaioth made them for his sister, and that is why his name is mentioned here. Sometime after this marriage and the birth of their son Reuel, Esau moved away to the hill country of Seir because the land was not large enough for his flocks and Jacob's flocks (36:6–7). Jacob and Esau both had large herds and many possessions by this time. Thus we see that Jacob left his possessions behind when he traveled to Paddan-Aram. He truly must have feared for his life because of his brother's anger. The fact that Esau could go to Ishmael to get a wife shows once again that the extended family continued to keep in touch and maintain communication with each other.

Jacob Journeys to Paddan-Aram (Genesis 28:10–22) (1744 BC, Jacob is 47):
On his journey Jacob rested one night and the Lord appeared to him in a dream standing above a ladder reaching from earth to heaven that had angels ascending and descending

upon it. In the dream God promised the land to Jacob and his descendants and promised to make his descendants of great number. God said that all the families of the world would be blessed in them. Jacob made a vow that if God would protect him and would bring him back home in safety, then He would be his God. This was a significant dream for Jacob, indicating God's hand of protection upon him personally. It must have been a great comfort to Jacob, since this was a time of uncertainty and fleeing from his brother. Jacob named the place "Bethel" in memory of this incident. Bethel means "house of God." Jacob would never forget the place or the time of his personal encounter with God that happened there. Years later, after returning to the land, he stopped there to seek God.

Jacob in Paddan-Aram (Genesis 29:1–31:21; from 1744 BC to 1724 BC):
Jacob providentially met Rachel at a well where they watered the animals. This must have reminded him of the way that his father connected with Rebekah, and he wept as he realized how God must have directed his steps in a similar way. Jacob dwelt with Laban, and after a month Laban asked him what wages he would like for working for him. Jacob already loved Rachel and asked for her hand in marriage. He agreed to work seven years for her. This type of agreement, that the father of the daughter must be recompensed for his loss, was customary in that day. It was also common for the groom to pay the cost in labor.

The shepherding contract that Jacob made with Laban was according to the customs of the times and shows that this story cannot be from a writer of a later era. That is, the shepherd normally bore the cost of losses in the herd; the other contractual terms described were normative for that period. However, it was not usual for the owner of the herd to change the wages or contract terms, so the reproach of Laban from Jacob for this is most reasonable. Even the practice of selective breeding is known to have been widespread at that time in the Middle East. Thus in many of its details this story bears the marks of the known customs of the times in which it is set.[745] These customs were unknown a few centuries later so they pinpoint the time this account was written.

Because the father was making the marriage arrangements, there is no indication in this story that either of the daughters had the option of declining. After seven years there was a marriage, but Laban tricked Jacob and gave him Leah instead. "It is not our custom for the younger to marry before the older." Jacob actually wed both sisters in the period of two weeks, but still had to work another seven years for Rachel. The family also gave maids to their daughters when they got married. Leah's maid was Zilpah and Rachel's maid was Bilhah. Taking sisters and their maids was a known custom of that ancient time. However, later Moses forbade marrying a woman and her sister lest it "vex her" (Leviticus 18:18). Again, these details indicate that this story, set squarely within the customs of those times, was not written at a later date by an unknown redactor.

Jacob shows the rivalry of the sisters as his wives. Their giving of their handmaids to him as concubines indicates the painfulness of the overall family situation. During the next seven years Jacob had eleven sons and one daughter through these four women.

At the end of fourteen years he sought to return to Beersheba and his parents, but Laban prevailed upon him to stay. But after six more years jealousy developed in Laban and his sons because of the prosperity of Jacob. The Lord God spoke to Jacob, telling him to return to Canaan. Jacob left suddenly, without saying good-by. He had been in Paddan-Aram for a total of twenty years.

Rachel took along the household gods from her father without Jacob's knowledge. From the Nuzi tablets we know that possession of these gods gave one the right to inherit upon the death of the father. This adds a further insight into the way that Laban and his sons reacted to the sudden departure of Jacob—the household gods had been taken and the family inheritance of his own sons was in jeopardy!

This was the family tree of Jacob when he departed from Paddan-Aram in 1724 BC. It shows the estimated ages of his first eleven children.

Leah sons:	Reuben (12)	
	Simeon (11)	
	Levi (10)	(Jacob was 56 and had been with Laban for nine years when Levi was born)
	Judah (10)	
Bilhah sons:	Dan (10)	Rachel's maid
	Naphtali (9)	
Zilpah sons:	Gad (9)	Leah's maid
	Asher (8)	
Leah sons:	Issachar (8)	
	Zebulun (7)	
	Dinah the daughter (7)	
Rachel son:	Joseph (6)	

Jacob and Laban at Mount Gilead (Genesis 31:22–31:55; 1724 BC):
Mount Gilead is in the area of modern-day northeast Jordan. Laban pursued and caught up to Jacob there, but the Lord warned Laban not to say or do anything against him.

Jacob had served Laban for twenty years in all. Rachel had taken the household gods with them and Laban accused Jacob of this deed, but he denied it. Laban demanded a thorough search for the missing gods, and when he could not find them he still insisted that they make a solemn compact not to advance past Gilead to harm one another.

Considering the significance of having the household gods and how Laban had treated Jacob—in the estimation of his wives, he had cheated him—perhaps Rachel's deed was her way of gaining some recompense for their family. This custom also explains why Laban pursued so hotly with his kinsmen—to protect the inheritance of his sons. That is why he searched for them and why, when he did not find them, he wanted to make a compact with Jacob that he never return to Paddan-Aram to "do harm to him."

These details also indicate that this account, peppered with the customs prevalent in that era, as we now know from the Nuzi tablets, was written by Jacob, not at a later time. The compact between Jacob and Laban was made before the "God of Abraham and the God of Nahor," showing that both Nahor and Abraham knew and feared God. Two generations after Abraham and Nahor the family members still believed in the God of creation, the God whom Jacob referred to as "the fear of Isaac." They set up a heap of stones there as a memorial of their covenant. Laban called this place Jegar-sahadutha which is Aramaic for "heap of testimony" and Jacob called it Galeed which is Hebrew for "heap of witness."

Jacob Reconciles with Esau (Genesis 32:1–33:20):
As Jacob entered the promised land, the angels of God met him. He sent messengers to Esau to make peace with him. When they returned saying that Esau was coming with 400 men Jacob feared greatly. While at Penuel he beseeched the Lord to protect him, reminding Him of His promises to him when he had first gone to Paddan-Aram. Then he sent abundant gifts ahead to Esau. And Jacob wrestled with a man all that

evening as he waited there alone. And the man, the Angel of the Lord, blessed Jacob, gave him the name "Israel," and touched his thigh—which caused him to limp henceforth. Moses inserted this explanation: Therefore from that time the sons of Israel did not eat the sinew of the socket of the thigh—in memory of the time when God touched Israel in that place. The name "Israel" may mean "prevailing prince with God."

Jacob and Esau met with cordialities and made peace at this time. Esau returned to the hill country of Seir amicably, and Jacob went to Shechem to settle down. Because it says Esau "returned to Seir" we know that he had already moved there before this time; that is, before Jacob's return to Canaan.

In his genealogy of Esau Jacob says that Esau moved to Seir after he had married Basemath, Ishmael's daughter, the sister of Nebaioth (36:6) and had fathered Reuel by her. He also said that the reason why Esau moved was because the land could not contain all of their flocks (36:7). Thus the move by Esau happened after the departure of Jacob for Paddan-Aram, after Jacob was asked by his parents to go there to find a wife. It happened at a time that was later enough that the herds Jacob left behind had become quite large.

The Defilement of Dinah at Shechem (Genesis 34:1–35:22a) (about 1713 BC):
We will see that Joseph being sold into Egypt (37:2–36) at age 17 happened while Jacob was in Hebron (37:14), a few months after Dinah is raped. So at this time Joseph is 16 or 17 and Dinah is 17 or 18. Thus this incident takes place about 11 years after Jacob left Paddan-Aram, or about 1713 BC.

Jacob's daughter was defiled by Shechem, the son of Hamor the Hivite, a prince of the land. This led to deceit and bloodshed by Simeon and Levi who killed the entire male population of the city and looted it. They were 21/22 years old when they perpetrated this atrocity—hot-headed young men. They killed the men of Shechem while they were in pain from having been circumcised and were unable to fight back. The two brothers took their wives, children, and possessions—and reclaimed their sister. This brutal act of retaliation grieved Jacob, and he considered that his life might be in jeopardy from the other Canaanites. Then the Lord told Jacob to go to Bethel. Jacob must have recalled his flight from Esau, when his life was also in jeopardy, and he had left his flocks behind.

Jacob told those in his house to put away their foreign gods and purify themselves. Thus some in his household held idolatrous practices or beliefs. Perhaps this was the newly captured wives and children of Shechem. It seems likely that their introduction into his house would cause problems as time went on. The spoils from the butchery by his sons were no asset to the family. When Abraham rescued Lot and the kings of Sodom he refused any reward. Again we are told that Jacob called this place Bethel, or "House of God" (35:15). Again the Lord tells Jacob that His name shall be called "Israel" (35:10).

In all of his relationships—with Esau, with Laban and his brothers, with the inhabitants of the land of Canaan—it is striking how much deceit and strife there was in the life of Jacob and his family. The customs and the lack of moral principles—the godlessness of the surrounding culture—was deeply affecting Jacob, and especially his sons. It was a moral necessity that God remove them from this environment.

As Jacob traveled there was great terror upon the cities in the area and they did not pursue him. We should see this as divine protection. Jacob was probably fleeing quickly and in fear of reprisal. At Bethel God again appeared to Jacob and promised to him the blessings of Abraham. This must have been to comfort him in the midst of his heartaches.

Deborah, Rebekah's nurse, died while the family was at Bethel. Recall the tradition[746] that Rebekah sent a contingent to Paddan-Aram to inquire about Jacob while he was there and that Deborah her nurse was among them. When the group returned to Isaac and Rebekah Deborah stayed with Jacob. She was still in his company at this time, and she died at Bethel. If she had been twenty years old when Isaac married Rebecca (in 1811 BC) then at the time of her death she would have been 118 years old.

From Bethel Jacob journeyed toward Ephrath (also known as Bethlehem). While on this trip Rachel died giving birth to Benjamin. Jacob erected a pillar to her that was still visible "to this day" (35:20), as Moses explained to the children of Israel.

Jacob then pitched his tent at Eder. There Reuben entered his tent and lay with Bilhah. There is a tradition that after Rachel died Jacob stayed in the tent of her maid Bilhah.[747] Reuben was jealous for his mother Zilpah, so went into Bilhah and defiled her. This act, whatever reasons are attached to it, is yet another sign of the tragic disorder in the family of Jacob. The following events happened in a rapid succession: Dinah was raped; two of Jacob's sons killed the men of Shechem; Deborah died; Rachel died; Reuben defiled Bilhah. And next we will see that Joseph was sold into slavery by his brothers and that Judah begets three sons by a Canaanite woman and the Lord has to kill two of them for of their wickedness. This is family disorder on a massive scale. With these such things going on, Jacob needed the Lord to comfort him in some way—to properly maintain his perspective on God. And this is why the family needed to get out of the land of Canaan.

The Family of Jacob (Genesis 35:22b–26):
At this point we are given a list of the twelve sons of Jacob.
> Now there were twelve sons of Jacob—the sons of Leah: Reuben, Jacob's firstborn, then Simeon and Levi and Judah and Issachar and Zebulun; the sons of Rachel: Joseph and Benjamin; and the sons of Bilhah, Rachel's maid: Dan and Naphtali; and the sons of Zilpah, Leah's maid: Gad and Asher. These are the sons of Jacob who were born to him in Paddan-aram. (Genesis 35:22b–26)

This is the only time while Jacob is in Canaan when all his sons are with him. Benjamin had just been born and Joseph had not yet been sold into slavery. We should see this insert as the work of Moses who removed from the account of Jacob all references to the disappearance of Joseph because they were factually incorrect and inserted this.

Jacob surely grieved over the loss of Joseph, but his sons deceived him about the true circumstances of that disappearance. His personal history must have reflected this and was removed by Moses, who instead gives us this summary list of his sons.

It appears that this was a life-long deception within the family, even carrying into the land of Egypt after Jacob wrote his personal life story, even to his death in Egypt. The book of Genesis never states that Jacob knew the truth about how or why Joseph disappeared. He believed what his sons had told him. The truth only comes out in the stories of the sons of Jacob, and these were written by them in Egypt after the death of Jacob.

Archeological Considerations:[748] Moses has to explain to the Jews at the time of the Exodus that Ephrath is Bethlehem. This would not be a necessary explanation if this account had been written by a later redactor since all later generations of Israelites knew that town very well. This indicates again that Moses was working from an older document and updating the place names for the benefit of the Jews of his time.

Jacob at Hebron (Genesis 35:27–37:2a; 1713 BC):
Finally Jacob came to dwell with his father Isaac at Mamre of Kiriath-arba, which is also called Hebron, where Abraham and Isaac had sojourned. Jacob was 78 years old when he came to Hebron. From here he sent Joseph to Shechem to see his brothers (37:14).

This is when Joseph was lost, but Jacob would never understand the true reason why. He would not see him again until he entered the land of Egypt at the age of 130 (47:9). Again, the absence of any reference to the loss of Joseph in the story by Jacob is due to the editing of the accounts by Moses. The truth about what happened is revealed in the stories of the sons of Jacob. Thus Moses removed the account Jacob wrote that was based on the deceptive lies told to him by his sons. However, throughout the full history of the family of Jacob the moral lapses of the sons are not covered up—a testimony to the candid truthfulness and accuracy of the scriptural account.

While Jacob was in Hebron Isaac died at age 180 and was buried by his sons Esau and Jacob (35:29). Jacob was 120 years old when Isaac died, ten years before he was to go into Egypt. Joseph had been missing for thirty-two years by the time Isaac died. The chronology of the loss of Joseph will be made clear when we read the accounts of the sons of Jacob. At the time of Isaac's death Jacob inherited all his possessions, including the patriarchal tablets. Esau had forfeited this privilege by selling his birthright.

During the ten years at Hebron after the death of Isaac Jacob wrote his history to append to the other tablets. He could have written it himself or he may have hired a scribe. The date of the writing immediately precedes his signature.
> Now Jacob lived in the land where his father had sojourned, in the land of Canaan. These are *the records of* the generations of Jacob. (Genesis 37:1–2a)

Perspective:
Throughout the lives of the patriarchs God has been carefully watching over them, keeping them from the debauched influence of the pagan culture in which they were immersed. Both Isaac and Jacob waited to marry until they could find believing wives. Esau did not, and neither did the twelve sons of Jacob. They married early, and some married Canaanites. In so many ways the moral fabric of the family life of Jacob was deteriorating rapidly! The famine that drove them into Egypt should be seen as a providential act of God that kept them from totally losing their faith in Him.

The Family Trees of Esau (Genesis 36:1–43):
The family of Esau, those whom he begot while he was still living in Hebron with Jacob and his parents—before Jacob left for Paddan-Aram—would have been known to Jacob for decades. It is described in the first genealogy of Esau (36:1–8).

Esau with his wife Adah	Eliphaz
Esau with his wife Oholibamah	Jeush
	Jalam
	Korah
Esau with his wife Basemath	Reuel

These were the children born to Esau while he was still living in the land of Canaan (36:5). Jacob explains that Esau left Hebron when their flocks became too large for the land to support them both. At that time Esau took his possessions and moved to the land of Edom. That was sometime after Jacob left for Paddan-Aram. Esau gave this information about his life in Canaan after Jacob left for Paddan-Aram to Jacob when the brothers met—some of it when Jacob reentered the land and some when they met to bury Isaac.

When Jacob and Esau came together to bury their father Isaac, Jacob would have obtained updated records from Esau about his family, including the time when he had been living in Edom, in the hill country of Seir. Jacob inserted that information into his family history next (36:9–19).

Esau/Adah	Eliphaz	Teman
		Omar
		Zepho
		Gatam
		Kenaz
		Amalek (by Timna)
Esau/Basemath	Reuel	Nahath
		Zerah
		Shammah
		Mizrah
Esau/Oholibamah	Jeush	
	Jalam	
	Korah	

Seir	Lotan (whose sister Timna married Eliphaz)	Hori
		Hemam
	Shobal	Alvan
		Manahath
		Ebal
		Shepho
		Onam
	Zibeon	Aiah
	(This is the Anah who found hot springs)	Anah
	Anah	Dishon
	(This is Anah's daughter)	Oholibamah
	Dishon	Hemdan
		Eshban
		Ithran
		Cheran
	Ezer	Bilhan
		Zaavan
		Akan
	Dishan	Uz
		Aran

The third genealogy that Jacob includes is the genealogy for Seir the Horite who lived in the land of Edom. He must have developed a close relationship with Esau, and that is why Esau shared this information with Jacob—and that is why Jacob included his family tree (36:20–30). It seems probable that the descendants of Esau and those of Seir the Horite intermarried as time went on.

A listing of the kings of Edom is given next (36:31–39) and are identified as "the kings that reigned in the land of Edom before any king reigned over the children of Israel" (36:31). This listing extends past the time of Jacob to the time when the children of Israel were living in Egypt. It must have been compiled by Jacob's sons while they were in Egypt and inserted by Moses at the time of the Exodus. By then the king of Egypt had begun to reign over the sons of Israel. The Israelites kept in touch with Esau while in Egypt, just as they had before—until they were taken as slaves! The record-keeping stopped when the oppression began. They could no longer keep in touch with Edom. "These are the kings who reigned in the land of Edom **before any king reigned over the sons of Israel**" (36:31).

> Bela son of Beor reigned in the city of Dinhabah,
>   and he died and then
> Jobab son of Zerah became king in his place,
>   and he died and then
> Husham of the land of the Temanites became king in his place,
>   and he died and then
> Hadad son of Bedad (who defeated Midian in the field of Moab) who reigned from Avith
>   and he died and then
> Samlah of Masrekah became king in his place,
>   and he died and then
> Shaul of Rehoboth on the Euphrates river became king in his place,
>   and he died and then
> Baal-hanan son of Achbor became king in his place,
>   and he died and then
> Hadar became king in his place and his city was Pau.
>   His wife was Mahatabel daughter of Matred daughter of Mezahab

Some have asserted that this list of eight Edomite kings was a much later insert; coming after the kingship of Israel was instituted at the time of Saul. If it is to stretch to the time of Saul, after 1100 BC, then it would cover over 600 years. This is unlikely. But if it only stretches to sometime while the sons of Jacob were living in Egypt, until the time when the Egyptians began to oppress them, then it would cover a more reasonable duration.

Here is the chronology of that scenario: Esau moved to Seir after Jacob went to Paddan-Aram and before he returned to Canaan, so between 1744 and 1724 BC, say about 1735 BC. The "reigning of a king over Israel" began when Moses was a baby or a bit earlier, so about 100 years before the Exodus, when a king "who knew not Joseph" (Exodus 1:8) came to power. Thus Egypt began to oppress Israel, about 1550 BC. Thus this listing would need to cover 185 years, a very reasonable time span for a listing of eight kings.

This same list is in Chronicles where it adds, "Then Hadad died" (1 Chronicles 1:51). That implies that he had not yet died at the time the account in Genesis was written, i.e., when the oppression of Israel began and their dealings with Edom stopped—because all of the previous kings' deaths are listed. Yet this is considered by higher critical scholars as the definitive proof that Genesis was written at a later date than Moses.

The last genealogy given (36:40–43) is a list of chiefs descended from Esau in the land of Edom. It was also probably compiled by the sons of Jacob while they were in Egypt and was inserted by Moses at the time of the Exodus. These extensive records indicate how close the sons of Jacob felt to their brothers the Edomites, and why it hurt them so badly when Edom refused them passage through their land (Numbers 20:14–21).

> chief Timna, chief Alvah, chief Jetheth, chief Oholibamah, chief Elah, chief Pinon, chief Kenaz, chief Teman, chief Mibzar, chief Magdiel, chief Iram

This should be looked at as a listing of later chiefs of Edom who ruled from the time of Jacob and Esau, perhaps also until the oppression of Israel began, and were identifiable as having descended from Esau. "These are the names of the chiefs descended from Esau, according to their families and their localities, by their names" (36:40).

These passages indicate that Jacob received quite a bit of family information from his brother Esau and that the sons of Jacob kept it and valued their relationship with Edom. Some of this family information was from the time when Jacob and Esau lived near their parents at Beersheba before Jacob left to take a wife in Paddan-Aram; some of it was from when they reconciled after Jacob reentered the land 20 years later; and the rest of it was from when they came together to bury their father Isaac—or perhaps from other unrecorded contacts between the brothers. Finally, the sons of Jacob maintained contact with the sons of Esau for many years while they were in Egypt—only losing that contact when at last the oppression by the Egyptian kings cut it off.

When Israel escaped from under the oppression of Egypt, as they were migrating to their promised inheritance, Edom should have rejoiced with them and helped the children of Jacob who had finally escaped from bondage, but they refused (Numbers 20:14–21).

The Conclusion of Jacob's Account:

Jacob lived in the land where his fathers sojourned, in the land of Canaan (37:1). This is the "date line" for the history of Jacob, saying that he wrote it when he was dwelling at Hebron, after he returned from Paddan-Aram with his wives and family, after his father Isaac died, before he went into Egypt. The date of writing was between 1671 BC and 1661 BC. Jacob inherited the family tablets from Isaac and appended his own story to the records.

This is the story written by Jacob of his life and the life of his family, told chronologically. To ascribe it to him is most reasonable. The understanding of the signature "these are the generations of" (37:2) as his personal signature line fits the accounts of Genesis perfectly. The testimony is never contra-indicated by the text. This is overwhelming evidence that this section was written by Jacob.

As we would expect, since Jacob wrote this during the ten years after the death of Isaac and before going into Egypt, there is no mention by Jacob of Egypt or of his reunion with Joseph. Jacob's account of the disappearance of Joseph is missing because it had been removed by Moses when he edited the accounts in Egypt. Instead Moses inserted the listing of the sons of Jacob into Jacob's record and reported to us the correct account of the disappearance of Joseph as recorded by the sons of Jacob.

As part of this commentary on Jacob I have explained the reasons why certain inserts into this record were made by Moses. In particular, information about later descendants of their brother Esau was compiled in Egypt by the sons of Jacob. It was important information which fit naturally after the genealogies of Esau that Jacob had included in his personal account. Thus Moses appended it when he edited the original accounts while creating the book of Genesis as we now have it. Other than these additions the information in these records is exactly what Jacob could have known from his own perspective.

The Sons of Jacob

(Text omitted for this ninth set of tablets because of length; Genesis 37:2b–50:26):

<u>Archeological Considerations</u>:

> The early chapters of Genesis contain Babylonian words; in fact, it is said by some linguistic experts that the whole environment of these chapters is Babylonian. As these chapters claim to have been written down by persons then living in that country, this is what we would expect. It is a strong indication that they were written at a very early date . . . The only definitely Babylonian words are to be found in the earlier chapters of Genesis and not in the latter part of the book or in the rest of the Pentateuch.[749]

This observation about identifying place names and personal names of the previous 36 chapters of Genesis is additional evidence in support of the fact that those accounts were written by the men whose names appear in the signature lines, and they were written while those men were living in ancient Mesopotamia. Now for this section:

> When the narrative reaches the point at which Joseph arrives in Egypt, the whole environment changes. We find definite Egyptian names such as "Potiphar, the captain of the guard" (37:36) or "Zaphnathpaaneah and Asenath" (41:45). A. S. Yahuda's testimony regarding this is weighty. **[Abraham Shalom Yahuda** (1877–1951), a renowned Jewish scholar, teacher, writer, linguist] We find ourselves removed from the simple country life of the patriarchs in Palestine and introduced to the customs of a Pharaoh and the constitution of a kingdom. We are told of the particular method by which the land was granted to the Egyptian priests (47:22); that Joseph has a gold chain about his neck and that runners who went before his chariot demand homage to him as to the highest official of the court (41:42). When Joseph's brethren come down to Egypt he does not eat with them, "because the Egyptians might not eat bread with Hebrews, for that is an abomination to the Egyptians"–a statement which I submit would never have been written at a time later than Moses. Finally, we are told how the bodies of Jacob and Joseph were embalmed in accordance with the normal Egyptian custom, and of the forty days that this process occupied. The person who wrote these chapters was intimately acquainted with Egyptian life and thought.[750]

From these considerations and from the content of this final section of Genesis we can see that in Genesis 37 through 50 we are reading a story written in the land of Egypt and written by the sons of Jacob. As we read the last 14 chapters of Genesis we are leaving ancient Mesopotamia and are immersing ourselves in the land and the customs of Egypt.

This account will not end with any statement such as "these are the generations of" because it was not written on clay tablets but is rather a collection of stories written by the sons of Jacob after they had settled in Egypt. It was written on the medium of choice in Egypt— papyrus scrolls. These accounts are not necessarily in chronological order, for they are the work of many, and some events they relate took place in Canaan and some in Egypt. They were written by the descendants of Jacob, and they will clarify many details for us about his wanderings in Canaan and will fill in certain chronological details that were not discernable from Jacob's story. They will also tell us the candid and sorry story of what actually happened to Joseph and how he came to be in Egypt.

- The first section is the account of the selling of Joseph into Egypt, written by one or more of his brothers (37:2–37:36).
- Next is Judah's story, written about his early family life in Canaan (38:1–38:30).
- The rest of the account (38:31–50:26) must have been written by Joseph while he was in Egypt, and by later generations—perhaps by his sons—who recorded his death and burial and his solemn prophetic charge to carry his bones back to Canaan when the Lord finally visited the sons of Jacob to fulfill His ancient promise to them and to their fathers the patriarchs (50:24–25).

The Narratives:

Joseph is Sold into Slavery in Egypt (Genesis 37:2–37:36; 1713 BC):
These events took place while the family was living at Hebron (37:14). Joseph was 17 (37:2) and pastured the flocks with his brothers. When the family was at Hebron Jacob sent him to Shechem to check on the welfare of the flock and the brothers. The flocks were probably that far away because they had left them behind while fleeing in haste from the Canaanites. Thus this episode can be seen as taking place very soon after the family arrived at Hebron. Joseph eventually went as far as Dotham seeking them. It was a few miles north by northeast from Shechem. This is the physical location from which he was sold into Egypt by his brothers. Dotham was near the major trade route called "the way of the sea," shown on the map of ancient routes at the beginning of Terah's history. A caravan of traders coming from Gilead (from the north), was heading along the trade route to Egypt. The brothers sold Joseph to them. Only Joseph and his brothers could have known these details. They wrote this story after settling in Egypt.

Consideration of Joseph's Dreams:
Joseph had two dreams. In the second he dreamed that the sun and the moon and eleven stars were bowing down to him. Jacob interpreted this as Rachel, himself, and his eleven sons bowing down to him. This interpretation makes the most sense after Benjamin has been born. But it also would make the most sense if Rachel were still alive—which she was not. There is no time when both were alive since she died giving birth to him.

The timing of this episode also gives us the timing of the rape of Dinah, for if Joseph was 16/17 then Dinah was 17/18, thus the date of (about) 1713 BC for when she was raped.

Judah and His Canaanite Family (Genesis 38:1–30):

This story mentions a number of place names, all near Hebron. They include Adullam (where an Adullamite friend of Judah lived); Chezib (also called Achzib); Enaim (also called Enam); Timnah. All of these places are found on the map of Israel near Hebron. This episode takes place when Jacob is in Hebron with Isaac. It must have been written by Judah since only he would have known the information in this story.

The timing: "And it came about at that time . . ." (38:1). The time referred to, as stated in the previous verse, is when Joseph was being "sold in Egypt to Potiphar" (37:36), after his betrayal. Moses must have seen this as a key chronological indicator as he edited and combined the narratives from the sons of Jacob that he had before him. Thus he carefully retained it.

This is the setting for this story: Jacob traveled from Bethel to Ephrath to Eder (that is, Migdal Eder, Tower of the flock, which is very near to Bethlehem). (The Talmud[751] says that any animals raised in the area of the tower were subject to being taken for temple sacrifices at Jerusalem. This prefigures Jesus, the Lamb of God, Who was born in that location.[q]) There he pitched his tent. While there Judah made friends with a man from

---

[q] There is an often-missed messianic prophecy in Micah 4:8 referring to this tower, which was called Ophel.

Adullam named Hirah. When the family left there and settled in Hebron, Judah departed to tend the flocks in Shechem and visited Adullam again (38:1). At that time he started an affair with the daughter of Shua. Judah was 19 or 20 years old. From the affair Shua bore Judah three sons in rapid succession. By the age of 22 he had become the father of Er, Onan, and Shelah. His last son was born at Chezib (Achzib) so Judah must have married the daughter of Shua and lived there with her at that time, which was in 1711 BC. This was not a godly union, and the fruit of this marriage was not godly sons.

When Er was old enough to get married (perhaps 17, in 1694 BC) Judah gave Tamar to him. But he was wicked and the Lord slew him. According to the Nuzi tablets the Levirate law to "beget descendants for your brother" was widely known at the time—a custom among the Canaanites as well as among Jacob's family. So Judah gave Onan to Tamar in accordance with this acknowledged custom, but Onan refused his Levirate duty and the Lord slew him as well. Shelah was only 15 and Judah used his young age as an excuse to not give him to Tamar immediately, fearing that the Lord might also slay him. After a few years it became clear that Judah was defaulting on his duty to Tamar, so she sat by the gates of Enaim—on the road from Achzib to Timnah. She lured Judah as he passed by and had relations with him. (She obviously understood his moral fiber well.) This was circa 1692 BC. She gave birth to Perez and Zerah in about 1691 BC.

Joseph in Egypt (Genesis 39:1–47:26):
Joseph was sold into slavery in 1713 BC. Joseph displayed wonderful character, in contrast to Judah, and had many skills besides. After serving capably and faithfully in many capacities and finally correctly interpreting Pharaoh's dreams, he was elevated to second in power in Egypt. He was 30 years old (41:46) so the date was 1700 BC.

Joseph advised Pharaoh to appoint someone "discerning and wise and set him over the land of Egypt" (41:33). He advised Pharaoh to appoint overseers in charge of the land—to extract one fifth of the land's produce during the seven years of plenty and to gather, store, preserve, and protect the accumulated grain in anticipation of the coming years of famine (41:34–36). That was a huge task! Pharaoh was impressed with Joseph and so entrusted him with this vital endeavor. Once Joseph was appointed as the man in charge of this effort, Pharaoh gave him a wife. Then Joseph went through all the land of Egypt (41:46). The preparations for the seven years of plenty and famine must have taken a long time. I allowed 30 years for this activity when I choose/set Jacob to leave for Padam Aram in 1744 BC at age 47. Also, Jacob's family needs time to grow to 70 people.

I assume this reasonable time frame to give adequate time for the family of Jacob to grow because, while Joseph was building grain storage bins in Egypt and formulating the overall plan to fill them in anticipation of the coming famine, the family of Jacob was expanding in Canaan. The final result of Joseph's work was that so much grain was collected and saved that it became impossible even to keep records of all of it (41:49). Archeology has found the remains of these ancient storage bins in Egypt.
> In ancient Egypt the dry climate allowed farmers to effectively store their grain. Storage was in brick or dried-clay enclosures, silos. These have been excavated at Tell Edfu. Grain was considered to be a form of currency, it seems. Thus if pharaoh controlled these he would have been very wealthy. These surely are what Joseph used, constructing huge numbers of them throughout the land, in every city under Pharaoh's command. The executing of this massive project would have taken

---

It is also mentioned in 2 Kings 5:24, Isaiah 32:14, 2 Chronicles 27:3 and 33:14, and Nehemiah 11:21.

many years. Joseph may have invented these. Likely the practice associated with them— giving twenty percent to Pharaoh—persisted for many years, perhaps as part of pharaoh's government run insurance program to guard against another terrible famine.[752]

Another interesting and relevant discovery:

An ancient tablet was discovered in Yemen in the nineteenth century that described an event in that land: Seven years of abundance followed by years of famine. The years of famine were not specifically numbered.[753] The age of the tablet cannot be determined for sure. Could this refer to the same famine as at this time in Egypt?

After 30 years of preparation Joseph was 60 and Jacob was one 121. The year was 1670 BC. In Canaan the family of Jacob had expanded to cover several generations and included 70 souls according to Genesis (according to Acts 7:14 there were 5 more). When the seven years of plenty began, and before the famine set in, Joseph had begotten two sons, Ephraim and Manasseh. Egypt was the only place that had an abundance of food stored-up.

Then two years of famine set in (45:6) and the sons of Jacob came to Egypt to buy grain. And eventually their father Jacob moved to Egypt (45:11). The date was 1661 BC. Jacob was 130 years old (47:9) when he and his family entered Egypt and Joseph was 69.

Entering Egypt:
The famine that forced the family of Jacob to seek grain from Egypt was certainly God's careful design. It allowed Jacob to be reunited to his son Joseph, it allowed the family to be healed of its grievous relationship wounds, and it removed the degenerating family of Jacob from the corrosive environment of Canaan. It was absolutely necessary.

When Abram left his family in Ur we noted that one of the major purposes of God in calling him was to establish a people for Himself—a chosen people that would be His and only His. Consider the three generations that followed Abraham. Isaac and Jacob were each careful to marry godly wives, and each were specifically given to God. Think of the time at Bethel when God appeared to Jacob, and the many times He spoke to him and called him by name and even gave him a new name, Israel.

But we cannot say the same for the sons of Jacob. The moral deterioration of the family is clear. Not one of them is said to have married a godly wife. Their behavior, other than that of Joseph, was despicable. And they envied and hated Joseph, in part because he was a godly man. Just as Nahor's descendants acknowledged other gods (consider the Teraphim that were the focus of the controversy in Genesis 31 when Laban pursued Jacob as he fled), so also now the sons of Jacob were turning away from the God of Abraham, Isaac, and Jacob. Oh yes, they still acknowledged Him as God, but they also looked to other gods as well. They had divided hearts. Thus God dealt forcefully with the family of Jacob in many ways, and finally sent them into Egypt to protect them from themselves and from the devastating effects of the Canaanite culture. I see the move of Jacob into Egypt as providential in many ways, providing an environment where Israel could grow into a great nation. But, as we have seen, when they finally left they still had a divided heart.

The family tree of Jacob, showing all 70 known members (There are 5 more that are not mentioned in Genesis according to Acts 7:14) when he entered Egypt, with their ages in parentheses, is given on the next page. This family tree includes Jacob and Joseph, as well as Ephraim and Manasseh the two sons of Joseph that were born to him in Egypt.

Jacob (130) by Leah	Reuben (75)	Hanoch	This is the genealogy of Jacob's family at the time of their entrance into Egypt. There were seventy people in all. Their approximate ages are shown in parentheses.
		Pallu	
		Hezron	
		Carmi	
	Simeon (74)	Jemuel	
		Jamin	
		Ohad	
		Jachin	
		Zohar	
		Shaul (born of a Canaanite woman)	
	Levi (73)	Gershon	
		Kohath	
		Merari	
	Judah (72)	Er (died in Canaan)	
		Onan (died in Canaan)	
		Shelah	
		Perez	Hezron
			Hamul
		Zelah	
	Issachar (71)	Tola	
		Puvvah	
		Iob	
		Shimron	
	Zebulun (70)	Sered	
		Elon	
		Jahleel	
	Dinah (70)	(their sister)	
Jacob by Zilpah	Gad (71)	Ziphion	
		Haggi	
		Shuni	
		Ezbon	
		Eri	
		Arodi	
		Areli	
	Asher (70)	Imnah	
		Ishvah	
		Ishvi	
		Beria	Heber
			Malchiel
		Serah (their sister)	
Jacob by Rachel	Joseph (69)	Manasseh (estimated to be 38)	
		Ephraim	
	Benjamin (62)	Bela	
		Becher	
		Ashbel	
		Gera	
		Naaman	
		Ehi	
		Rosh	
		Muppim	
		Huppim	
		Ard	
Jacob by Bilhah	Dan (73)	Hushim	
	Naphatli (72)	Jahzeel	
		Guni	
		Jezer	
		Shillem	

Additional Considerations:
There are several stories about the sons of Jacob as they were growing up in Canaan. They all present a very ugly picture of their character.
- They murdered the men of Shechem and took their families and possessions.
- One of them slept with their father's concubine.
- They were jealous and plotted to kill their own brother. Finally they sold him into slavery and lied to their father to cover up their filthy deed.
- Judah slept with a Canaanite woman, married her, and raised wicked sons. The Lord had to directly intervene in his family.

The effects of growing up in a society that was far from the Lord were causing them to forsake godliness. Something had to be done to remove them from that environment until the "wickedness of the Amorite was complete" (15:16). The land of Goshen was an excellent place for the family of Jacob to grow into a small nation. It was a fertile land, cut off somewhat from the general population of Egypt. It was like a womb where Israel could grow into a people that the Lord could use for His holy purposes.

The time in Egypt was providentially planned. The famine was designed by the Lord God to draw Jacob and his family into Egypt until they could grow into a nation.

There is another important factor that came into play at the time Israel entered into Egypt. The character of Joseph contrasts with the lust and violence of his brothers. A spoiled, self-centered little boy had grown into a skilled, humble man. Instead of seeking revenge against his brothers he forgave them and protected them and their families. They were terrified of him, and not without reason! From their perspective it would seem that he might utterly destroy them for what they had done. But he did the exact opposite.

When Joseph spoke of the events of his childhood in Canaan he saw them through the lens of God's divine plan. "You meant it for evil, but God meant it for good—to save many people today" (50:20). Let us look at the gracious act that transformed a bickering carnal tribe of Arameans into a loving cohesive family from which a nation would be born:

> Then Joseph said to his brothers, "Please come closer to me." And they came closer. And he said, "I am your brother Joseph, whom you sold into Egypt. Now do not be grieved or angry with yourselves, because you sold me here, for God sent me before you to preserve life. For the famine *has been* in the land these two years and there are still five years in which there will be neither plowing nor harvesting. God sent me before you to preserve for you a remnant in the earth, and to keep you alive by a great deliverance. (Genesis 45:4–7)

If the time of Israel in Egypt is viewed as the period of the gestation of the nation in the womb of Goshen, then this moment is the conception of the nation of Israel, the time when a soul was instilled into her, giving the family cohesiveness and transforming it into a people. The bond created allowed them to maintain their identity throughout the time in Egypt.

Moses:
Archeology indicates that The Genesis Documents were written by the men named in the signature lines and passed on through successive generations. They were intentionally linked together by the "catch-lines" scattered throughout them and were intended to be read and understood as a unified work. They became the heritage of the patriarchal line from Adam and Noah, continuing through Shem, Abraham, Isaac, and Jacob. At the time that Israel entered Egypt they were carried by Jacob and his family. They were preserved

and added to by his descendants as the stay in Egypt wore on. Their last additions were on papyrus, the writing medium of Egypt. The history of mankind and the history of their own patriarchs was the heritage of the sons of Israel that was preserved on those tablets. At the time of the Exodus Moses read them and he believed in God.

> In Egypt [the tablets] became the heritage of Joseph and the family then developing into a nation. They would naturally pass into the hands of Moses, not necessarily the actual originals (though stone and baked clay are the most imperishable forms of writing material known) but true copies of [them]. An educated Egyptian of his day would be able to read cuneiform writing with as much facility as a classical scholar today is able to read Greek or Latin. At the time of Moses this cuneiform writing was the current diplomatic script, and the dispatches received at the Egyptian Foreign Office, from eastern lands, were in this script. The hundreds of Tel-el-Amarna tablets are examples of such correspondence. Moses, learned in the arts of the Egyptians, would readily be able to read and, if necessary, to translate them.[754]

Moses Edited the Account of Jacob:

We see that Joseph was betrayed and sold into Egypt by his brothers, but it is not clear from the book of Genesis that Jacob ever realized how his older sons had mistreated Joseph. There is no statement indicating that he knew, and no mention of any rebuke that he gave to his sons either for the way they had treated his "special" son or for the extended grief that they had put him through. It is very possible that, for the 17 years of his stay in Egypt, no one ever told Jacob how Joseph got into Egypt, other than perhaps that he was captured by the Ishmaelites, carried to Egypt, and sold as a slave.

When Jacob died the brothers came to Joseph to plead for their lives. Recall how Esau had vowed to kill Jacob after Isaac died, in revenge for the way that Jacob had connived and cheated him. The sons of Jacob feared that Joseph would behave in that way—that his "forgiveness" was only for Jacob's benefit, and that he would carry out his vengeance upon their families now that their father was dead (see Genesis 50:15–18).

I think that their story about Jacob asking Joseph to forgive them for the way that they treated him was a contrived story. Joseph wept, assured them he did not seek revenge, and confirmed that his forgiveness had been from the heart and would not be revoked.

Again, there is no reason from the stories themselves to assert with certainty that Jacob ever realized the horrible dark truth about his sons and his family as they were growing up in Canaan. The stories of the sons of Jacob were all written after the death of Jacob. At that time the full truth was written down for all their descendants to see.

The account Jacob wrote about the disappearance of Joseph was incorrect because he surely did not know the truth before he went into Egypt, and in fact he probably never knew, even later, what really happened. Thus his personal account was inaccurate.

Recalling again Genesis 35:22–26, the list of Jacob's sons. I reiterate that when the full accounts were read by Moses, he then inserted that list of the sons of Jacob into Jacob's account and removed his story about the loss of Joseph. The entire incident, as it was told by Jacob, was inaccurate. Moses decided to remove the account that Jacob wrote and to include the full account of all the events as told by the sons of Jacob in their stories. I think that we must credit Moses with this careful job of editing the accounts at this point in order to present the full, accurate, and consistent picture to his readers.

Moses Providentially Called and Chosen by God:

As the divinely scheduled time for the Exodus neared, God raised up a servant to do His will in the midst of Egypt and the sons of Jacob. Moses was carefully educated in all of the knowledge of the Egyptians, even in the house of Pharaoh. But he also knew of his Hebrew heritage. He read the tablets that related human history from Adam to Jacob. He understood and believed them. He was looking for the reward that God had promised to Adam and Eve after the fall (Hebrews 11:24–29). He was looking for the Messiah, the Seed of the woman. In his heart, he was a son of Levi.

He was providentially banished from Egypt for 40 years until God spoke to him directly and called him to his task. He learned first-hand about the peoples, cultures, history, and geography of the Middle East. When the Lord called Moses He spoke to him as to one who would know Him from what He had read in the tablets.

> I am the God of your father, the God of Abraham . . . of Isaac . . . of Jacob. (Exodus 3:6)

Again the Lord God spoke to Moses as He commissioned Him:

> God spoke further to Moses and said to him, "I am the LORD; and I appeared to Abraham, Isaac, and Jacob, as God Almighty, but *by* My name, LORD, I did not make Myself known to them. I also established My covenant with them, to give them the land of Canaan, the land in which they sojourned. Furthermore I have heard the groaning of the sons of Israel, because the Egyptians are holding them in bondage, and I have remembered My covenant. Say, therefore, to the sons of Israel, 'I am the LORD, and I will bring you out from under the burdens of the Egyptians, and I will deliver you from their bondage. I will also redeem you with an outstretched arm and with great judgments.'" (Exodus 6:2–6)

The phrase "*by* My name, LORD, I did not make Myself known to them" can and should be translated as a question: "*by* My name, LORD, did I not make Myself known to them?" This is permitted in the Hebrew and is preferable considering the message contained in the tablets and the immediate context of this exchange.[755] God was saying to Moses, You know who I am! I am the same God that you read about in the Hebrew tablets. Go! Tell them that is who I am. I am about to deliver them. They will believe.

From Jacob to the Exodus:

In Exodus 6:16–18 we have the genealogy of Levi that leads from the time when Jacob entered Egypt to the time of Moses and the Exodus. The numbers in parentheses are the ages of the persons when they died. We do not know for sure how old they were when they had their children. The total time span from when Jacob entered Egypt to the time of the Exodus is known, but the length of each generation must be estimated. They were to leave in the fourth generation Genesis (15:16). Four generations are listed for Levi.

Levi (137)	Gershon	Libni	
		Shimi	
	Kohath (133)	Amram (137)	Aaron
			Moses (120)
		Izhar	
		Hebron	
		Uzziel	
	Merari	Mahali	
		Mushi	

Now let us see how and why Israel entered Egypt in 1661 BC and left 215 years later in 1446 BC. Let us see how the dates of our chronology are connected to secular history.

Reiterating a few Chronological Details in Summary Form:
We need to make a few chronological connections within this account. In 1876 BC God made His promise to Abram to give him the land of Canaan. Galatians 3:17 says that this was 430 years before giving the law, which happened at Mt. Sinai at the time of the Exodus. This fits with the idea that the Exodus was in 1446 BC. Before the birth of Isaac the Lord told Abram that his descendants would be oppressed in a land that was not theirs, and then they would enter into the land that was theirs, when the wickedness of the inhabitants of that land was "complete." The "oppression of Abraham's descendants" could be reckoned to begin when Isaac was weaned at age five, when he was mocked and persecuted by Ishmael. That date was 1846 BC. The oppression ended in 1446 BC with the Exodus. Thus there were 185 years of oppression in Canaan (from 1846 BC to 1661 BC, or 185 years) and 215 years of oppression in the land of Egypt (from 1661 BC to 1446 BC) for a total of 400 years—just as the Lord had told Abraham. The descendants of Abraham "sojourned" as "oppressed aliens" during those 400 years, and that type of mistreatment was a common experience throughout the time when they were in Canaan and Egypt.

As the Israelites were leaving Egypt Moses wrote,
> Now the time that the sons of Israel lived in Egypt was four hundred and thirty years. (Exodus 12:40)

So did the Israelites dwell in Egypt for 430 years? Galatians (3:17) and rabbinic tradition hold that there were 430 total years from God's covenant with Abraham in Genesis 15 unto the departure from Egypt, which only leaves 215 years for Israel to live in Egypt. There are sound reasons for this tradition. Another translation of the above verse is:
> Now the time of [or the sojourning of] the sons of Israel, who dwelt in Egypt, was four hundred and thirty years. (see also the KJV)

Israel had been sojourning for 430 years in all—215 in the land of Canaan, and 215 in Egypt—and now they were coming out of Egypt as free men and going into the land that God had promised to the patriarchs, to live without being oppressed any more. They had only been "visiting" in those places. Their home, the land promised to them by the God of Abraham, Isaac, and Jacob, was only now being granted to them. This was because by this time the wickedness of the Amorites was finally complete (Genesis 15:16).

But there is a missing piece: How do we tie these dates into secular time? The Exodus was 480 years before Solomon began to build the house of the Lord in the fourth year of his reign (1 Kings 6:1). Solomon's reign is a period that can be determined from secular history. His reign was from 970 BC to 931 BC.[r] The temple was started in the fourth year of his reign or in 966 BC. The Exodus was in 966+480 or 1446 BC. This is the way that Bible chronology can be linked to known historical dates. Thus we see how the accounts of Isaac and Jacob, in all of their exacting details, fit into known historical chronology.

The Population Growth of Israel in Egypt:
There is one other detail that I want to address. Would a small group of perhaps fifty family units become a nation with a large population in 215 years? About 600,000 men of age 20 or more left Egypt in the Exodus. Certain verses in the Bible are important as we do the calculations of Israel's population growth in Egypt. Here is one:
> But the sons of Israel were fruitful and increased greatly, and multiplied, and became exceedingly mighty, so that the land was filled with them. (Exodus 1:7)

---

[r] See Chapter 2 and Appendix I for more details of this determination, taken from Edwin Thiele's chronology.

Here is another from when Joseph spoke to his brothers urging them to come to Egypt:
> I will give you the best of the land of Egypt and you will eat the fat of the land. (Genesis 45:18)

And this promise to Jacob from the Lord God, given as he was on the way to Egypt:
> He said, "I am God, the God of your father; do not be afraid to go down to Egypt, for I will make you a great nation there." (Genesis 46:3)

And this explanation by Joseph to his father Jacob that shepherds were loathsome to the Egyptians and thus they would live in Goshen. The implication is that Goshen was somewhat isolated from the rest of Egypt, and that they could dwell there in peace and thus not be totally overwhelmed by the culture of Egypt nor be assimilated into Egypt.
> When Pharaoh calls you and says, "What is your occupation?" you shall say, "Your servants have been keepers of livestock from our youth even until now, both we and our fathers," that you may live in the land of Goshen; for every shepherd is loathsome to the Egyptians. (Genesis 46:33–34)

And this decision by Pharaoh when Jacob stood before him.
> Then Pharaoh said to Joseph, "The land of Egypt is at your disposal; settle your father and your brothers in the best of the land, let them live in the land of Goshen." (Genesis 47:5–6)

And again:
> So Joseph settled his father and his brothers and gave them a possession in the land of Egypt, in the best of the land, in the land of Rameses, as Pharaoh had ordered. (Genesis 47:11)

All of this was the result of what God had said to Jacob earlier when he was at Bethel.
> Then God appeared to Jacob again when he came from Paddan-aram, and He blessed him. God said to him, "Your name is Jacob. You shall no longer be called Jacob, but Israel shall be your name." Thus He called him Israel. God also said to him, "I am God Almighty. **Be fruitful and multiply.** A nation and a company of nations shall come from you, and kings shall come forth from you." (Genesis 35:9–11)

Israel had ideal conditions while they dwelt in the fertile and abundant land of Goshen. Israel was protected from undue Egyptian dominance or influence. Israel was under the blessing of God. Thus the family multiplied rapidly and grew quickly—so much so that they were seen as a threat to the Egyptians with whom they were living. When I estimate their size at the time of the Exodus I will assume their population grew at a high rate—a rate that was near the top of the expected growth rate for populations.

The Population of Israel at the Exodus:
Here is one simple calculation starting with fifty family units with one adult male in each:
- 50 family units had to become 600,000 family units (adult males)
- If there were always exactly four generations as in Moses' genealogy then that the number of family units had to grow by a factor of 23 with the passing of each generation.
- 50 * 23 * 23 * 23 = 608,350 family units.

This means that families had to be huge—or that the genealogy of Moses presented to us, with just four generations from Jacob to himself, was not the norm for all family lines in Israel. If children got married at 19 or 20 years old, so that there were ten or twelve generations from Jacob to the Exodus, then families would have to contain about five children to arrive at the population shown. There must have been more generations with fewer children per family or fewer generations with more children per family. Likely there was some combination of these situations among the Israelites.

There is a way to estimate population growth using known statistics that bypasses the need to determine exactly how many generations there were and how many children each family had. Such things are imponderable. Statistics show[756] that the increase in population can be as high as 4.8% per year for a period of time—when the conditions are optimal for a people group. Let us assume that Goshen and Egypt were near optimal conditions for the sons of Jacob. I say this because of all the verses that indicate that Goshen was a rich and very fertile location in Egypt, and because after 215 years the inhabitants of Egypt were extremely concerned about the drastic increase in the Hebrew population—so much so that they plotted to murder the male Hebrew children who were born in an attempt to blunt the population spurt. Exodus tells us this:

> Joseph died, and all his brothers and all that generation. But the sons of Israel were fruitful and increased greatly, and multiplied, and became exceedingly mighty, so that the land was filled with them. Now a new king arose over Egypt, who did not know Joseph. He said to his people, "Behold, the people of the sons of Israel are more and mightier than we. Come, let us deal wisely with them, or else they will multiply and in the event of war, they will also join themselves to those who hate us, and fight against us and depart from the land." (Exodus 1:6–10)

Therefore, I am going to assume that the population growth of Israel during those 215 years was quite high because of the many scriptural testimonies indicating the optimal conditions in Goshen and the blessing that was upon Jacob and his sons. There were 69 men to begin with. If we assume an annual growth rate of 4.6% per year for the descendants of Jacob, then at the time of the Exodus the population of males would be:

> 1,142,070 (total number of males, not including the women, after 215 years)

This is much larger than the population of 603,550 (Numbers 1:45) that left Egypt, which only counted males of 20 years and older who were able to fight in war. Israel might have outnumbered the Egyptians at the time of the Exodus!

We did calculations earlier showing the population growth of the human race early on. Those long-lived patriarchs must have had very many children during their lives. The ancestors of Moses lived a very long time—all of them over 130 years. So either they had huge families, or some generational lines—some ancestral paths from the time of Jacob until the Exodus—comprised more than four generations. However, since God told Abram that his descendants would return to the land of Canaan in the "fourth generation" (Genesis 15:16), we assume that the third-generation descendants of Jacob, all of his children and grandchildren, died before the Exodus.

Another point: If we assume that the sons of Jacob were in Egypt for 430 years, then the expected population at the time of the Exodus, even with a much lower growth rate assumed, would be much too large. Thus the 215 years that Israel dwelt in Egypt is also a very reasonable duration when considered from the perspective of population growth. This shows most reasonably how the small family of Jacob that entered Egypt became a mighty nation with millions of people (including women) in the space of 215 years.

Connection to the Rest of the Pentateuch:
Moses connects Genesis to Exodus through the first verse of Exodus which begins,
> Now these are the names of the sons of Israel. (Exodus 1:1).

This verse begins a few sentences that list the sons of Jacob that came into Egypt, and that describe the total family population that had come from Jacob's loins and that entered with them. This verse is similar to a signature line, although it is not. It sounds like "this is the history of the sons of Israel." Thus we might view the first few verses of Exodus as both beginning Exodus and as connecting that book with the final fourteen chapters of the book of Genesis. Indeed for a variety of reasons we should see the first five books of the Bible as one unified work written by Moses.

The Genesis Documents:

The original personal accounts from which Genesis was composed were written by: God; Adam; Noah; The sons of Noah; Shem; Terah; Isaac; Jacob; The sons of Jacob. The first four accounts were originally in pictograph writing and were translated by Noah and Shem after the Flood and Babel, in the period from 2000 BC to 1950 BC, in and around the area of ancient Ur. That translation process produced a set of tablets in cuneiform that was the beginning of a patriarchal library. Added to the library right away were the account of Babel by Shem and the short genealogical register of Terah. Abram possessed these tablets when he left Ur to answer the call of God after his father Terah died—the beginning of a patriarchal library, the earliest history of their family and of the family of man.

Isaac and Jacob added their own accounts to the library while they were living in the land of Canaan, and Jacob carried the complete set of documents into Egypt in 1661 BC when the great famine was upon the world.

While Joseph was in Egypt, even before his family joined him, he was employed by Pharaoh to prepare for the seven years of famine. He knew Egyptian Hieroglyphics well because that was the written form of communication within the land of Egypt. But under inspiration from the Lord he invented a simple written language whose characters were derived from Egyptian Hieroglyphics, but whose comprehensibility was based neither in pictographic nor in logographic methods, but which was rooted in symbolizing the relatively few vowel sounds that comprised his Semitic language. That written language with its relatively few symbols was linked directly to the Semitic language that he spoke when he had lived with his family in Canaan. When his family joined him in Egypt Joseph taught them that simple to learn and simple to use written script, crafted specifically to their own language—the first alphabetic script in history. It was the script that we know today as **proto-Sinaitic**.

The last personal accounts that we see in Genesis, chapters 37 through 50, were written by the sons of Jacob after Jacob died. They were written on papyrus, the medium of choice in Egypt, either in the cuneiform script of their ancestors or in the alphabetic script, **proto-Sinaitic**, that Joseph had taught them. This explains how, when, where, and by whom each section of Genesis was originally written. This explains how the total set of **The Genesis Documents** originally came to be written down.

About two centuries after the great famine Moses saw and read the history of his Hebrew family because the complete set of **The Genesis Documents** was there before him for him to read. He believed what he read and became zealous for the Israelites, who were being unfairly treated by their Egyptian oppressors. At that time God heard the cries of His people in Egypt and called Moses to lead the Israelites to freedom from their overlords. At that time, and in conjunction with the great move of God that led to the establishment of the nation of Israel, Moses wrote the last four books of the Pentateuch in the **proto-Sinaitic script**. They detailed his personal struggle in leading the Hebrew people out of Egypt to the border of the promised land. Those books were written either by Moses or by a designated scribe under his direct supervision, first-hand personal accounts of the Exodus and the desert wanderings.

About that same time Moses also wrote Genesis using **The Genesis Documents** from his Hebrew ancestors as sources. Moses transcribed the book of Genesis into the script that was familiar to his fellow Hebrews, the **proto-Sinaitic** script. He intentionally transliterated the methods and techniques of Babylon into Genesis because the Hebrews knew and understood those literary techniques. In that way he testified to them of its reliability, not because that book contained his personal first-hand experiences but because the accounts in that book were first-hand personal family records of the earliest ancestors of his people and of the entire human race. Therefore they represented an historical record that was vital to the Hebrews and to all people. God inspired him to organize the accounts, to edit them, and to put them down in an orderly form for all of posterity.

Those records also served as the perfect logical introduction to the other four books that Moses was writing because they explained the origin of the world, the origin of the human race, and the origin of the Hebrew people—and because they also explained how the Hebrews first came to reside in the land of Egypt. Therefore Genesis became the first book in the five-volume set that Moses was to write. This is how, when, why, and by whom Genesis—the book as we have it today—came to be written down.

Thus we assert that that Moses wrote Genesis, and this is how he did it.

Concluding Thoughts:
When Moses wrote Genesis it was well over 500 years since the literary style of the Middle Eastern writers had arisen—a style that employed colophons, catch-lines, signature lines, etc. It would be more than 1,000 years longer before the changing of times in the Middle East caused the common understanding of these literary methods to be lost to Israel and to mankind. Thus the message of Genesis was clearly proclaimed—and the basic reasons for its reliability were firmly rooted in Jewish thought—for over a millennium. The logic that undergirded their faith was impeccable. Genesis consisted of the personal accounts of men who had lived through the tremendous formative events from the dawn of human history. What could be more authoritative and more surely true? The ancient Jews knew that.

The destruction of the literary milieu in which Genesis had arisen caused the underlying reasons for its certain truth and reliability to be obscured and become opaque. Therefore the magnificent demonstration of the accuracy of the Genesis record, and the irresistible conclusion that it must be the true story of the origin of the world and of mankind, were lost for over two millennia. People continued to believe Genesis, but the full reasons for doing so were not understood. Today we can see once again the basic reasons why it was thought to be the completely true Word of God—and why we can confidently assert once again that it is the true account of the origin of the world and of the human race.

When Moses wrote Genesis, just how much did he "edit" or modify the original Genesis documents which were the source of his information? The most ancient documents, the ones from Babel, the Flood, and before the Flood, were fully intact and there is no reason to think that he changed their content. He might have omitted some parts that seemed redundant or that covered tangential subjects. Some of the accounts were large enough that they surely could not have fit onto a single clay tablet. The stories of Adam and the three sons of Noah are examples. Multi-tablet documents had special connecting data.

When copying such tablets to papyrus, the medium of the Egyptians, it would have been superfluous and even confusing to include such information from the tablets. It was not part of the account itself, but was only a way of clearly organizing it that was dependent upon the medium in which it was recorded—the medium of clay tablets. We can assume that Moses edited out such elements as inter-tablet connecting phrases and numbering.

Because Moses was "educated in all the learning of the Egyptians" (Acts 7:22), he must have understood such things. We know from archeology that it was common for the wise men of Egypt to transcribe documents from the medium of clay tablets, which was in wide use throughout the ancient world, onto their own medium of papyrus. Thus Moses simply followed the customary techniques of the learned of his day. Therefore I believe that the contents of the oldest tablets were preserved by Moses without change. When we read Genesis we are reading the earliest accounts as they were written by God, Adam, Noah, the sons of Noah, Shem (perhaps with people-name updates, as noted above), and Terah.

Some of the accounts must have stretched over many tablets. Again, the way to view the process of their conversion to papyrus is that Moses preserved those accounts intact, but removed the inter-tablet connectors and indicators that were specific to the medium of the clay tablets on which they were written.

However Jacob's story had to be fundamentally wrong in how it described the loss of his son Joseph because Jacob's sons had deceived him on this matter.

As Moses read the account of Jacob, plus the accounts of his sons which had been written after the death of Jacob and that related the whole dirty truth, he needed to make a decision about how to edit the accounts to present to his readers an accurate picture of what had actually happened. He decided to remove the incorrect story from the account of Jacob and replace it with a statement about the twelve sons of Jacob (Genesis 35:22–25). He placed this near the end of Jacob's story, just before the date line and the signature line. But Moses kept the account as it was explained in detail by the sons of Jacob. He also included other stories about the times of Joseph in Egypt, plus accounts that explained certain details about the lives of the sons of Jacob while the family was still living in the land of Canaan. These illustrated the increasing immorality of the descendants of Jacob under the influence of the Canaanite culture as the years wore on.

So Moses wrote Genesis, and this is how he did it. This is a more detailed reconstruction of how Moses edited the accounts that he received on tablets of clay as he transferred them to papyrus at the time of the Exodus, and how he produced the book of Genesis as we now have it. This shows us why Genesis is a reliable and accurate account of the first events of the human race. It is reliable because it is a series of first-hand accounts.

The accounts of Genesis are personal accounts written by those who lived through—and were intimately involved in—the initial events of human history. And what could be more reliable than a personal first-hand record of your own family's history? The interconnected and cumulative accounts of the patriarchs were transferred to papyrus intact by Moses. This provides us with a firm basis for asserting the accuracy of the first eleven chapters of Genesis as well as the reliability of the chapters that follow. This revelation comes to us at a time in the world when people are more incredulous toward the Bible than in any previous age, and when they are especially skeptical toward the book of Genesis. This is providential, and it should be seen as such by believers.

In the next section I want to summarize the conclusions we have reached in this book and then summarize the underlying historical reasons for the unbelief that afflicts our age.

Summary and Final Conclusion

What we have Discovered:
Here are the main points/insights we have established about Genesis in this work:[757]
- Genesis 1:1–37:2 was originally written on tablets of clay or stone in an ancient script in the land of Mesopotamia.
- It was written in those lands by the line of patriarchs stretching from Adam through Jacob, as named in the signature lines. The first tablet was written by the Lord God.
- The last fourteen chapters were originally written by the sons of Jacob in Egypt.
- The narratives were accumulated by the patriarchs as the generations passed, and they consciously linked the narratives together and realized that they were compiling a cumulative unified history. Because of the detailed consistency and cohesion of the total account, this is a much better theory than the idea that various unknown clumsy redactors pieced together diverse accounts and left repetitions.
- Moses received the narratives and, under divine inspiration and guidance, edited them into the account that we now have—the book of Genesis. He did this at the time of the Exodus. In order to identify his sources Moses preserved signature lines at the time he edited the documents. He also kept catch-lines to show the unity of the accounts. He also kept date lines for they are important time indicators. Moses wrote the entire Pentateuch, not just Genesis, in the proto-Sinaitic script.
- Genesis is the logical and necessary introduction to and basis for the accounts contained in the other four books of the Pentateuch. Together they form a single unified work best seen as written by Moses at the time of the Exodus.

These assertions are attested to by archeological, historical critical, geographical, historical, and chronological details so varied and so numerous that they exclude any other possible explanation for the composition of Genesis. Many of the details that we have observed could not have been planned or designed. These details include the following facts:
- In each section of Genesis the information that is presented is exactly what the imputed author would have been able to know and exactly what he would have had access to in his day.
- The chronology of the accounts, both within each individual account and between accounts, is fully supported by the chronological data that the accounts contain. That is, the ages of the patriarchs are supported by the fact that the information they record reaches to near the end of their lives. This supports the specific ages that are imputed to them and gives us strong reasons to accept the long life spans that are recorded for them. It also indicates that at the beginning of the human race our condition on this earth was radically different from now, when the typical life span is 70-90 years, even with the best medical support.
- The geographical places are given using their most ancient names. The travels and events that happened are logically interrelated and reflect the customs and lifestyles of those ancient times, as verified by archeology.
- Other details about life in ancient times are supportive of the accounts, indicating their ancient origin: The names of ancient places and people mentioned, other fragmented accounts of the Flood and of the confusion of tongues, the reasonableness of the size and dimensions of the ark, the description of the phenomena during the Flood, and the interwoven moral lessons that are consistent with all of Christian revelation.

Additional information, with more detailed assertions about the previous general points:
- Archeological discoveries were made after the formulation of the "higher critical" theories for the composition of Genesis. These give us the ancient cultural and geographical settings of the various sections of Genesis, and these discoveries agree with the contents of the book, section by section.
- Genesis implies that rapid cultural and societal development took place at the beginning of the human race. Archeology also supports this, and gives us abundant evidence that writing, art, commerce, and government were common attributes of the earliest civilizations of man in the Middle East, going back at least to 3300 BC.
- The contents of even the earliest chapters of Genesis claim to have been written. This adds weight to their basic accuracy and their historical character.
- The structure of Genesis and archeological discoveries indicate that the sections of the book, both the narratives and the genealogies, were originally written on tablets of clay or stone. They reflect the literary methods of ancient Babylon and the cultures of the Middle East: colophons, ownership lines, catch-lines, titling, and dating are still in evidence in the text, even though edited by Moses later on.
- In no instance is the content of any tablet beyond the personal knowledge of the presumed author of the section that bears his name. This is strong evidence—from the text itself—that it was written by the person named. (Note the one tablet that we discussed, Terah's tablet, is a special case for certain death dates only.)
- Additionally each person's account ends at the time of the writing of that account, if a date is given for the writing, or at least before the death of that person if no date is given.
- The presence of Babylonian words in the text of the earlier chapters of the book, and of many Egyptian words in the last fourteen chapters of the book, supply us with collaborating evidence for the geographical location of their original writing.
- The first tablet looks as if it was written at the dawn of human history. It was laid down before there were countries, before the sun and moon had been named, and before polytheism had developed.
- Scripture never asserts that the accounts were handed down orally, but instead claims that they were written.
- Many references are made to towns that had ceased to exist or had been given different names by the time of the final composition. These names and their explanations fit the circumstances of Moses and the time of the Exodus, as the children of Israel were about to enter the promised land. This indicates that Moses wrote the version that we presently have, and that he had reference to earlier manuscripts from which he took his material.
- The fact that Genesis still contains archaic expressions and still shows traces of the literary practices of ancient Mesopotamia is also a testimony to the reverence and care that Moses took in using the records from which he compiled Genesis.
- The other accounts of the Flood and of creation are clearly corrupted forms of the Genesis accounts—fragmentary in nature and distorted by pagan influences. The Genesis narratives are definitely not a "purified" version of the creation and the Flood that were derived from the "older and previous" Babylonian accounts. Genesis is the previous and old account, preserved for us intact. The other accounts are more recent and are corruptions of it.

- Archeology completely undermines the theory that Genesis is a collection of myths and legends. Many evidences of persons once thought to be mythological have been found by archeology showing that they were historical people.
- The difficulties alleged against Genesis by "higher critics" vanish quite naturally when it is understood that the narratives and genealogies were first written on tablets in an ancient script, by the persons whose names they bear, and that the book was compiled by Moses. Any differences of phraseology and style are just what we should expect in these circumstances. The "repetition of the same event," of which many modern scholars speak, is shown to harmonize exactly with the arrangement of the tablets from which the book was composed and to conform to ancient Sumerian usage.[758]
- With the explanation of the connecting "catch-lines" of Genesis, the assertion that Genesis is the interweaving of "multiple accounts taken from a variety of authors" is specific only to the account of the Flood and the events just after it and immediately preceding it, which events were recorded by three individuals. In fact this "several authors" phenomenon ends at the signature line of the tablet of Noah's sons.
- The outstanding examples brought forward by critics to suggest a later date for its composition (later than the time of the Exodus) are thereby shown to prove the very opposite.
- The material in each section, by the nature of its content, is historical rather than allegorical or mythological. Thus the genre of Genesis is most reasonably set as "historical narrative." This is in clear contrast to all comparable pagan stories of the same era. The other accounts are always exaggerated, fantastic in their claims, or unrealistic in their descriptions and are mere fragments of a larger total account.
- The accounts, though they sometimes tell of awesome events, do so with sober, descriptive words that bear the mark of being a personal account of what was directly seen or known.
- When the stories are checked to their minutest detail they still remain consistent and fully accurate. It is impossible to imagine that someone from a later time could have created the stories in the way that these are written. It is hard to imagine that someone, writing at a later date, could have composed stories that match the facts of ancient history, geography, culture, and chronology so well.
- When taken together the sections form a clear developing story that none of the authors of any section could have understood or anticipated. But the cumulative effect of the historical accounts is to present us with a consistent interlocking set of stories that only God Himself could have masterminded.
- When taken as a whole the many sections are clearly seen to provide us with a comprehensive picture of the origins of the human race and of all creation—facts that are vital to the Christian faith and vital to Christian theology. These accounts provide us with precious insights into the purposes of the Lord God for creating us.
- Therefore, the book of Genesis is a divinely-inspired historical account of the origins of the human race and of the whole world, written under His providential guidance by His chosen servants the patriarchs, who had first-hand knowledge of the events—and which has been carefully preserved for us throughout the ages.
- Because the composition of the book of Genesis has eluded us until this time, diverse theories have been proposed to explain how it came to be written down. Some have

served to undermine the reliability of the book and to impugn its historical accuracy. This in turn has shaken the foundations of Christian theology, removing from us the biblical world view that is essential to the proper understanding of all Scripture. Now that the composition of the book has become clear, all of these variant theories can be laid to rest. The Ancient Faith is firmly supported, and we have a solid basis for evaluating/rejecting the many theories of origins that call into question the biblical view of history and of human life. We can do apologetics again.
- The writers of the New Testament books base many important theological discussions, explanations, and arguments on the narratives of Genesis. These would be without a firm foundation if the stories in Genesis were not historically accurate.
- Jesus testifies to the historicity and accuracy of many of the details of Genesis.
- The accounts of Genesis are chronologically consistent, historically reasonable, and, in many instances, verifiable. They are geographically sound and accurate. They fit logically into the secular history of the ancient Middle East.

> It would seem that the key to its composition [i.e., the composition of Genesis] has previously remained unrecognized, and therefore unused. While prevailing theories have been unable to unlock the door to its literary structure, it is submitted that the following explanation does:
>
> *The book of Genesis was originally written on tablets in the ancient script of the time by the patriarchs who were intimately concerned with the events related, and whose names are clearly stated. Moreover, Moses, the compiler and editor of the book, as we now have it, plainly directs attention to the source of his information.*
>
> **—D. J. Wiseman: *Ancient Records and the Structure of Genesis***

The facts listed above are the details of this generally observed truth:
> The form of writing common to the ancient Middle East during the years from at least as early as 2000 BC and extending to between 300 BC and 200 BC, as has been clearly seen in tens of thousands of cuneiform tablets from those times, is reflected in the book of Genesis. An understanding of this style of writing shows that Genesis is composed of the personal accounts of the men whose names are seen in the phrases "these are the generations of . . ." The authors of the parts of Genesis, in sequence, would seem to be: God, Adam, Noah, the sons of Noah, Shem, Terah, Isaac, Jacob, and the sons of Jacob. This simple observation about the authorship of the book of Genesis, when examined in detail, agrees with every word of every section of the book. This is overwhelming confirmation of the truth of this fact and also confirms the chronology of Genesis, the ages of the patriarchs, and the basic accuracy and reliability of the entire book. All of this flows naturally from the text of Genesis itself once a person makes this simple observation.

Therefore the truth and accuracy of the first book of the Bible is established from evidence internal to the book itself. The ancients in Israel knew and understood the customs of the scribes from centuries before them. Thus they did not attribute the information in Genesis to Moses primarily, but they did acknowledge that Moses was responsible for writing the book. Rediscovering this fact in the midst of the present-day controversy about how the world and the human race came to be undergirds the Ancient Faith, both in the Mosaic authorship of Genesis and in the historical reliability of the book.

Genesis and the Spirit of the Age—The Modern Controversy:

In every age men and women are deeply influenced by the spirit that rules the hearts and minds of their culture. All who would serve the Lord must identify and understand the spirit that is "the prince of the power of the air" and which is leading men to walk "according to the course of this world." This is the first, indispensable step to becoming free of its influence so that the child of God can understand His holy word and obey it. This is especially true today because we live in a powerful worldwide culture—one that has rebounded from a previously Christian culture and that has forcefully rejected much of it. We are now living in a post-Christian age that is philosophically hostile to Christianity and to the Bible.

Let us do an overview of the path that western intellectual thought traversed to arrive at the assumptions and attitudes that underlie the post-Christian culture in which we live.

The Best Hope the Pre-Christian World had to Offer to Mankind:

The transformation in thought that began in Europe about five centuries ago left behind ancient Stoic cosmology as well as Christian ethics and salvation. The Greeks viewed the world as a perfectly harmonious rational, living, system—a cosmos. The world had a kind of logic inherent within it, a *logos* that made it comprehensible to men. Salvation or the overcoming of death was accomplished through carefully understanding this system and our proper place in it, and then living our lives in accord with this understanding.

The world was thought of as an eternal, divine organism, and each man, as a part of the whole, derived his eternity or immortality from assuming his proper place within it.

Death was seen as the transition from personal existence to an eternal but impersonal state of being. Truly ethical behavior, in accord with the cosmic order of things, was the way to find one's proper place in the universe, to connect with what was real, eternal, and divine, and to achieve a kind of immortality—thus to attain a measure of freedom from death and its terrors. The "philo-sopher" or "lover of wisdom," by contemplating the deeper truths of reality, by engaging his entire being and not just his reason, sought union with that one truly real and eternal thing, the perfect orderly cosmic truth.

The Advent of Christianity:

When the Christian gospel was preached to the Greeks it stood in stark contrast to the Stoic philosophy of the Greek and Roman world. In Christianity the impersonal *logos* of the Greeks was incarnated in the person of Jesus Christ, the Creator of all things, Who became a man like us. The cosmos was not alive but the One Who created it was the source of all life—He was Himself the Life of men and women.

Because the creator of the world was rational, and because we were made in His image and likeness, we also were rational and could come to understand His creation. Yet it was not our understanding of the cosmic order that saved us; rather, it was a direct personal relationship of love and trust with the incarnate Logos that saved us. Faith replaced wisdom as the vehicle of personal salvation, and salvation itself was seen not merely as attaining our impersonal place within the cosmic whole but as our fully conscious personal existence in His presence for all eternity, an inheritance in His kingdom as His own precious child. This was a spiritual existence but would eventually result, through the resurrection of the body, in a totally human immortal life.

Death was seen as a temporary, necessary evil we must endure because of personal sin, but which was conquered by the Logos through His own full participation in the human condition—including His death—and was attested to by His personal resurrection. To attempt to attain immortality in any way by one's own reason or works was itself a sin—the refusal to trust in the Lord's divine provision—and was doomed to failure. The hubris of the Greeks was denounced. Christianity contradicted Greek philosophical thought.

The contemplation of the true and real remained in Christianity; however the object of the act of contemplation was understood to be the Creator, not His creation.

The Post-Christian Era:
We might summarize this as "the rise of Godless humanism." Noted philosopher and author Luc Ferry eloquently describes the cultural earthquake initiated in Europe about 500 years ago:

> The modern world arose out of the collapse of ancient cosmology and a new questioning of religious authority, and eventually a scientific revolution unprecedented in the history of humanity, which occurred in Europe over the course of one hundred and fifty years. To my knowledge, no other civilization has undergone such a radical upheaval in the fabric of its culture.

> This upheaval began with the publication of Copernicus's work *On the Revolutions of the Heavenly Bodies* in 1543, continued with that of Newton's *Principia Mathematica* in 1687, and took in Descartes' *Principles of Philosophy* (1644) and Galileo's *Dialogue Concerning the Two Chief World Systems* (1632). These four dates and these four authors were to mark the history of thought as no other thinkers before them. A new era was established, which, in many respects, we still inhabit today. It was not only man who "lost his place" in the world, as is often said, but the *cosmos* itself—the enclosed and harmonious frame of human existence since antiquity—quite simply evaporated; leaving the intellects of the time in a state of confusion it is virtually impossible for us to imagine today. Modern physics annihilated the foundations of the ancient world-picture—through its assertion, for example, that the world is not round, enclosed, hierarchical and divinely ordered, but rather is an infinite chaos devoid of sense; a field of forces and objects jostling for place without harmony and [this also] weakened considerably the foundations of Christian religion.[759]

The bitterness of the Christian reformation served to further disillusion men, alienating them from the Church and from God, and the Rationalism of Descartes found acceptance from many eager and disillusioned minds and spread rapidly into all areas of thought. The contemplation of a true and beautiful cosmos lost all appeal. It was now up to man to find his way and place in a new world that was infinite and chaotic. In the face of a meaningless chaos how could human beings find order and make sense of the physical world? How could they find the principles of cause and effect that connected all events meaningfully and that governed reality? The burning issue was no longer contemplating an existing orderliness. Rather, it was seeking to discover logical connections beneath the apparent chaos of all being, the true relationships of causality that directed the world—but from an attitude of radical skepticism toward the past. It was an intellectual explosion that viewed itself as escaping from a previous ignorance that had been confining and restrictive.

It was also the transition from a merely passive kind of knowledge to an active knowledge, from assumption to construction. It was the birth of the scientific method, and it arose to undergird all modern inquiry into the world around us. It was necessary for people, by means of their intellectual labor, to make sense of a world that had lost its meaning and its order. This revised understanding of knowledge put mankind at the center of thought and of meaning—in the place of divinity. Humanism as we know it today was born.

In this struggle for purpose, truth itself was redefined. The *cogito ergo sum* of Descartes was the result of an exercise of radical doubt as man searched for anything that was surely true. The introspective nature of Descartes' answer served to identify truth as a subjective reality, something certain in the mind in the new age of chaos and uncertainty. This eventually became the standard for the modern thinkers; that is, henceforth all received ideas were rejected and people called into question all inherited beliefs and preconceptions—those from tradition, from revelation, or from whatever source.

The goal of humanity's new thinking, spearheaded by the scientific method, was to cast skeptical doubt on all previous beliefs and establish a comprehensive understanding of the world and of itself by discovering the causal associations inherent in the physical universe around us, using only our own observational powers to guide us—and to count as true and viable only the facts that could be established by this methodology. All had to be explained as the outworking of natural processes following the newly discovered laws of science. The explanation for how this world came into existence, and for how life—and even human life—had come to be, had to be sought only within this framework.

Our present-day theories explaining human behavior and the origin of all things are the result of careful theoretical constructions built by those who adhere to the assumption that the entire physical world is causally self-contained—that everything can and must be explained as the outworking of completely naturalistic processes operating under the observed physical laws. The total reality of the cosmos and of mankind, including their ultimate origin, can and must be explained in this way.

In this view of the cosmos the physical laws are sacrosanct—they are never violated. Within this system of belief the cosmological, geological, and biological theories that purport to explain the origin of the cosmos, of the earth, and of life—including human life—are vital ingredients, as are theories that naturalistically explain the phenomenon of human beings. Without them the edifice of humanistic thought collapses because its foundational assumptions are disproven.

That is the reason certain modern theories and ideas are so resilient in our society—not because of any compelling evidence that supports them. Western European culture has gone through a paradigm shift in its thinking over the last few centuries, a shift to a world view that supports such theories and that has an inherent bias toward them—a view of the world that leaves no room for God or for the supernatural.

<u>The Ancient Faith and Apologetics</u>:
This shift in thinking has affected every area of human scholarship and we are unable to argue against it by any means at our disposal. Thus, there are people in every area of study who argue that the Christian and biblical world view is incorrect—in cosmology, geology, biology, archeology, psychology, history, etc.—and they are aggressive in their stance.[760] [see note] Such is our position as believers in this world today. Augustine said that, even if we cannot prove their unbiblical theories to be untrue, we still must believe firmly that they are false.

In this work I offer us a firm foundation upon which to base our faith. As the men of old said when looking for a firm foundation for their belief, "Nowhere better, as yet, than in the Holy Scriptures."[761] The evidences and the logic for the patriarchal authorship of Genesis, as presented in this work, are powerful, for we can see how the first eleven chapters of Genesis were written by the Lord, Adam, Noah, the sons of Noah, Shem, and Terah.

A Brief Personal Story:
About thirty-five years ago when I was unexpectedly assaulted by the hostile voice of scientific naturalism—before I had any understanding of the breadth of these issues—I asked the Father this question,

> **Father, there has to be an apologetic for this. It has to be simple, straightforward, and clear—and I need to know it.**

He has given me that answer. The "apologetic" is quite easy to understand, it is very straightforward, and it is utterly clear. Anyone can easily see it just by reading the book of Genesis—once they know enough to recognize the personal signature lines for what they are. Once they understand that simple fact, then the truth and accuracy of the book is a logical conclusion. I offer this to you as the basis of your faith in this dark age, until He returns to rescue His Church and to judge this world.

Remember the unanswered question that Jesus posed:
> **However, when the Son of Man comes, will He find the faith on the earth? (Luke 18:8)**

We all want that answer to be, "Yes, Lord."

The Unavoidable Choice that Stands Before us:
This book is addressed to all of the churches in the world today and it sets before all Christians a certain choice.

The issue this book highlights is quite simple, so let us not confuse it in any way. I am pointing out to my readers that inexorably Christians have a decision set before them at this time in history. I am *not* proposing that people choose between Greek Orthodox Christianity and Western or European Christianity. I am *not* suggesting that we choose between Roman Catholicism and Protestantism. I am *not* setting before my readers a choice about whether they want to be liberal Christians or conservative Christians. I am not proposing that any of us must make any such partisan choices.

In this book I have clearly portrayed for you what the Ancient Faith was and is. I have clearly displayed to you what ALL previous generations of Christians believed. I have described the Cartesian-Darwinian Narrative (aka scientific naturalism), explained how it happened to arise in our day, and put forth its basic points of contrast with the Ancient Faith. So I have set before you the fundamental Christian world view, and the opposing world view of scientific naturalism. I have set before you two faiths—faith in God and His holy word, and faith in brilliant human beings and their clever theories.

Now I propose—I must point out to you—that inevitably you have to make a choice. Will you trust God and stand with all the holy men and women of old? Do you believe in the faith that was delivered once and for all to the saints? What is your answer?

If the churches on this earth do not stand with God and His word, then the Ancient Faith is dead, the Christian world view has been discarded, and the Bible must be seen as full of serious and fundamental errors by which all the holy men of old were deceived. Yet I have displayed before you certain simple, straightforward, and clear reasons why the book of Genesis is true—reasons that have come to light at this critical time in the history of the Church. And these simple facts undermine the world view of scientific naturalism.

So once again I pose to you a simple question:

When the Son of Man returns will He find The Ancient Faith on the earth?

Appendix I – Old Testament Chronology

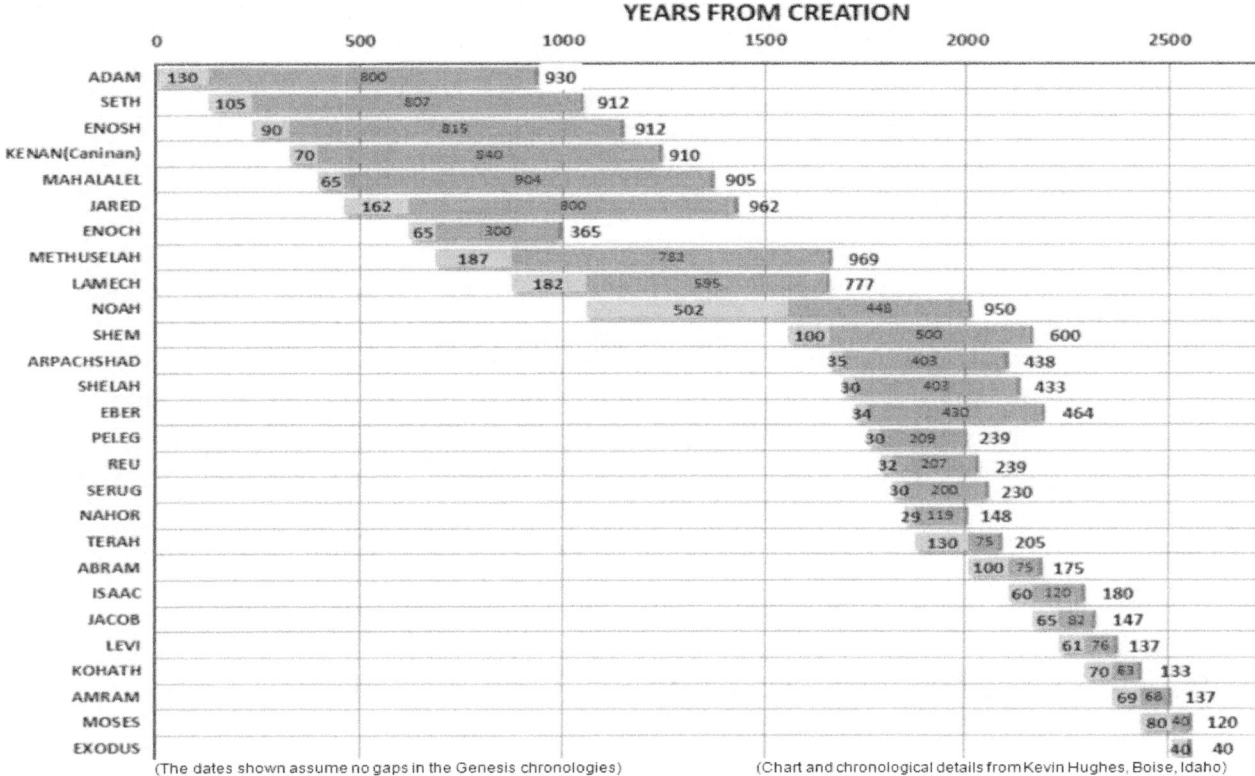

(The dates shown assume no gaps in the Genesis chronologies)   (Chart and chronological details from Kevin Hughes, Boise, Idaho)

The chart is reproduced here for reference. Here are some details from Kevin Hughes explaining a little bit about how the dates are computed within the Bible and then are connected to other dates in history.

Time from the Abrahamic Covenant to the Exodus: (See Chart)

Abram had just departed from Haran and was 75 when God gave him the covenant as described in Genesis 12:1-4. In Galatians 3:16–17 Paul says that this was 430 years before the law was given at the time of the Exodus.

Abraham was 100 when Isaac was born so Isaac was born 25 years after the promise was given to Abram by God.

Isaac was 60 years old when Jacob was born so Jacob was born 25+60 or 85 years after the promise was given to Abram by God.

Jacob was 65 years old when Levi was born, so Levi was born 85+65 or 150 years after the promise was given to Abram by God.

Levi was 61 years old when Kohath was born, so Kohath was born 150+61 or 211 years after the promise was given to Abram by God.

Kohath was 70 when Amram was born so Amram was born 211+70 or 281 years after the promise was given to Abram by God.

Amram was 69 years old when Moses was born so Moses was born 281+69 or 350 years after the promise was given to Abram by God.

Moses was 80 years old at the time of the Exodus, so the Exodus was 350+80 or 430 years after the promise was given to Abram by God.

At the time of the Exodus Moses and the Israelites went to Mount Horeb, and there God gave them the Law. It was 430 years from the events of Genesis twelve until the giving of the law. According to Exodus 19:1 it was in "the third month after the sons of Israel came out of Egypt" that the law was given.

Note: We know that this time period was 430 years because Paul confirms this to us in Galatians. It is helpful that we were given this confirming piece of chronological data in the New Testament. From the fact of 430 years we have to estimate the age of Jacob when Levi was born, the age of Levi when Kohath was born, the age of Kohath when Amram was born, and the age of Amram when Moses was born. All we know from the Scripture is that the time period in question totals to 430 years and that Abraham was 100 when Isaac was born, Isaac was 60 when Jacob was born, and Moses was 80 at the time of the Exodus. The rest of this chronology must be filled in by making some reasonable estimates of the ages of the patriarchs of the intervening generations at the time of the births of their sons.

Time from the Abrahamic Covenant to Entering Egypt:

Abram was 75 when the covenant was given to him by God as described in Genesis 12:1-4.

Abram was 100 when Isaac was born, so Isaac was born 25 years after the covenant was given to Abram by God.

Isaac was 60 years old when Jacob was born, so Jacob was born 25+60 or 85 years after the covenant was given to Abram by God.

Jacob was 130 years old when he entered Egypt (Genesis 47:9). So it was 130+85 or 215 years from the covenant that God made with Abram until the Israelites entered Egypt.

Time from Entering Egypt to the Exodus:

Thus the time of the sojourning of Israel in Egypt was 430-215 or 215 years. In this time of just over two centuries the family of Jacob became a nation. This period is where we estimate the ages of certain patriarchs at the births of their sons.

Linking the Biblical Chronology to Known Historical Dates:

From the chronological chart of Old Testament birth and death times in the section titled "Babel" we see that it was 2513 years from creation to the Exodus. There is one additional important chronological link to later events in biblical history:

> Now it came about in the four hundred and eightieth year after the sons of Israel came out of the land of Egypt, in the fourth year of Solomon's reign over Israel, in the month of Ziv which is the second month that he began to build the house of the LORD. (1 Kings 6:1)

Thus the fourth year of the reign of Solomon was 480+2513=2993, or 2,993 years after the creation of the world.

<u>Finally a Link to Secular Dates</u>: The reign of Solomon, according to the most widely used chronology based on the work of Edwin R. Thiele (1895-1986), was from 970 BC to 931 BC. Thus the fourth year of his reign was 970-4=966 BC, or 966 years before Christ. Thus the date of creation can be set at 2993+966=3959 BC, or three thousand nine hundred fifty-nine years before the birth of Christ.

> Thiele's chronology is accepted in several recent study Bibles and is the chronology used for the Hebrew monarchs in the *Cambridge Ancient History* (T. C. Mitchell, "Israel and Judah until the Revolt of Jehu (931-841 B.C.)" CAH 3, Part 1, p. 445). Thiele's chronology with some slight modifications by Leslie McFall, ("*A Translation Guide to the Chronological Data in Kings and Chronicles*," Bibliotheca Sacra 148 [1991], pp. 3-45) is accepted in Jack Finegan's influential *Handbook of Biblical Chronology*, rev. ed. (Peabody, MA: Hendrickson, 1998), p. 249.
>
> The chronology of the Davidic dynasty (to which King Solomon belongs) can be checked against datable Babylonian and Assyrian records at a few points, and these correspondences have allowed archeologists to date its kings in a modern framework. In a similar vein certain links to ancient Egyptian chronology and the reigns of various pharaohs have been useful in establishing additional chronological connections to the Old Testament.
>
> **Edwin R. Thiele** (1895–1986) was an American Seventh-day Adventist missionary in China, an editor, archaeologist, writer, and Old Testament professor. He is best known for his chronological studies of the Hebrew kingdom period. A native of Chicago, Illinois he graduated from Emmanuel Missionary College (which became Andrews University in 1960) in 1918 with a bachelor's degree in ancient languages. After two years of work as the home missionary secretary for the East Michigan Conference of Seventh-day Adventists, he left in 1920 for mission service in China. During almost twelve years of work in China, he was an editor and manager for the Signs of the Times Publishing House in Shanghai. Soon after returning to the United States Thiele received a master's degree in archaeology from the University of Chicago in 1937. At that point he joined the religion faculty of Emmanuel Missionary College and continued on with his doctoral work at the University of Chicago. He obtained a PhD degree in biblical archaeology in 1943. His doctoral dissertation, later published in 1951 as *The Mysterious Numbers of the Hebrew Kings*, is widely regarded as the definitive work on the chronology of Hebrew kings. He traveled extensively throughout the Middle East during the course of his research.

> <u>Comparison with Ussher's date of 4004 BC for the Creation of the world</u>: The difference is with the date that is established for the beginning of the construction of the temple of Solomon. Once that date is set then the rest of the chronology, being internal to the Bible, is set to within a few years. A minor technical consideration here or there could make a couple of years difference.
>
> Ussher did not have archeology to help him in his work *The Annals of the World*. He said: From the Babylonian captivity in 586 BC count 390 years (Ezekiel 4:4–5) = 976; then -1 year to 975 since the 390 years began with 586, not after. Then add 40 years (Ezekiel 4:7) to get 1015 BC. Three years later, or 1012 BC, Solomon began the temple. (see p. 67 of *The Annals of the World* for this.)
>
> Thiele (i.e., our chronology) derived his dates from Assyrian chronology/archeological discoveries relating to Daian-Ashur and the Battle of Qarqar (853 BC). He saw 78 years from then to 930 (or 931) BC (the end of Solomon's reign) and subtracted 36 years to get the year 966 for the year that Solomon began building the temple instead of Ussher's date of 1012, 46 years different.

Appendix II – The Modern Theory of Origins

The idea that earth and its living organisms have come about via processes that took place within a "deep time" scale emerged from systems of thought associated with both Copernicus and Darwin. Our understanding of the vast processes that gave birth to the cosmos and that describe its evolution is the foundation for explaining the ancient history of earth and the living systems that have emerged on it.[762]

Cosmological Perspective:

The foundational observation on which we base our theory about the origin of the world is that structures in space are moving away from us. We note the "Doppler effect" or the shift of the spectra from distant objects in space toward the red end of the light scale. The amount of the redshift seems to be a function of the distance of the object from us. Since all objects in deep space are receding from us, if we trace their path back through time into the distant past we deduce that at one time all matter must have been together in space. The substance of the universe, at some point in the distant past, was all concentrated in one place and has expanded from there to form the cosmos that we now observe. This simple fact is the basis for our cosmological theory known as the Big Bang. We need only assume that the present physical processes and laws have been functioning in a continuous and uninterrupted manner for many billions of years.

In the beginning there was nothing. Over 13.787 billion years ago, a quantum fluctuation in nothingness, which happened for no reason, produced a multi-dimensional (a ten- or eleven-dimensional) singularity of infinite density which began to expand, along with the space that contained it, for no reason, like a bubble—the Big Bang. (There can be as many as eleven dimensions to any bubble of the "multiverse," each bubble floating in a larger arena called hyperspace. Each bubble is its own universe. Our universe is one of those bubbles.) At the moment of the Big Bang the physical laws, constants, and mathematical relationships of the universe were also brought into existence. The four forces of the universe were combined into a "super force" in the first instant. At about 10^{-43} seconds after the Big Bang all but three space dimensions stopped expanding. As the universe expanded further, gravity broke off from the "super force" first. Less than one second later the "super force" spontaneously decayed into the three remaining forces. This is the time when the foundational laws of physics spontaneously came into effect.

About three minutes after the Big Bang the expanding universe had cooled to about one billion degrees—cool enough for the nuclei of atoms to form. Hydrogen atoms formed and a small percentage of the hydrogen atoms combined together to make helium.

Less than one billion years later the quickly expanding cloud of hydrogen gas began to "condense" and the first stars were formed. These were the "population III" stars. The initial stars were supergiants that burned up quickly (in ten million years or so) and then exploded and spread their remains throughout the universe. This star debris contained the heavier elements like carbon, oxygen, nitrogen, etc. From the ashes of these stars the next generation of stars formed. These were the "population II" stars. They eventually exploded as well. From the ashes of the "population II" stars, which were even richer in heavy elements than the ashes of "population III" stars, the "population I" stars formed, along with all of the planets and the objects that contain the heaviest elements.

After ~billion years matter and gravity worked together to bring about the formation of a "population I" star that we know as our sun. A cloud of gaseous hydrogen (like in Orion) collapsed due to a pressure change in the center of the cloud, or perhaps as the result of a disturbance from a nearby star that went supernova and sent waves through space that squeezed the cloud of gas. The collapse resulted in the formation of a hot, pressurized central mass of hydrogen gas that erupted into a fusion reaction and became the sun. A residual ring of dust particles was left orbiting the sun.

The ring of dust remaining from the formation of the sun condensed into the planets of our solar system. This happened as particles began to clump together into larger and larger combinations as they were drawn together by gravity. In a few million years chunks ~1000 meters in diameter formed. These are called planetesimals. They continued to join into larger objects about the size of the moon called protoplanets. This process (accretion) of forming into larger-sized bodies ended ~4 billion years ago with a "late heavy bombardment" where smaller objects from the solar system kept pelting the larger bodies that we know as the planets. One of these planets was the earth.

At that time, while the earth was molten and the solid crust was very thin, a large body—perhaps the size of Mars—struck the earth and broke off a large amount of material from it, producing a disk of particles that orbited around the earth. These eventually adhered together and formed the moon. It has been proposed that the moon was gravitationally extracted from the Pacific Ocean and that the earth eventually redistributed its remaining mass into the oceanic and continental crusts.

Developments on Earth:

The processes that play their part in the vast cosmic scheme also shape our planet. As we look at our earth we must ask how the atmosphere, continents, oceans, and the other major geological features came into their present configuration. How did they form?

Perhaps the earth's original atmosphere was just hydrogen and helium, the main gases in the planetary disk that formed around the sun, which evaporated into space because the earth's gravity could not hold them. The next atmosphere formed mainly from gases that were ejected by volcanoes as the earth slowly cooled from its original molten form. It was composed of hydrogen sulfide, methane, ammonia, and one hundred times more carbon dioxide than is now present. Eventually the present atmosphere was formed in a way that cannot be seen at this time.

During the "Archean Eon" the first continents began to coagulate at the earth's surface. How they got there is one of the longest standing, most debated questions for geoscientists. According to the deep melt hypothesis the early continents formed within the mantle of the earth when one tectonic plate plunged more deeply into the mantle under another plate. However, some think the early continents just oozed out at the surface of the earth, from processes completely within the crust. Another idea is the continent accretion theory in which the continents have always been stationary, with the gradual addition of new material around a central nucleus. Another theory, called the continental assimilation hypothesis, says that the ocean areas accumulate the denser elements and then subside to form basins. Another hypothesis asserts that the present continents split apart as the earth expanded, noting that the continents could overspread a sphere half the surface area of the present earth. Accepted theory today points to continental drift and seafloor spreading as a result of plate tectonics.

Continuing the explanation: On the surface of our planet hundreds of smaller pieces of crust called tectonic plates were floating in the mantle of the earth. During the "Archean Eon" they collided with each other with great force and fused together. After 1½ billion years about ¼th of the earth's crust had been formed. Mountains formed at the edges of the tectonic plates as they collided, and lava also flowed there as a result of the heat and pressure. The lava hardened and "glued together" the plates to form a single large continent. Then that "super continent" eventually split apart into the several continents that we now have. The original "super continent" is sometimes called Pangaea or Pangea. It is assumed that Pangea existed approximately 300 million years ago in the late Paleozoic and early Mesozoic eras. That is, it was formed from earlier continental units, from the fusing of the tectonic plates. Eventually Pangea broke up. This breaking apart started about 175 million years ago, eventually forming the continents that we now know. The continental crust contains rocks measured to be about four billion years old.

When the surface of the earth was still very hot there was constant heavy rain from thick clouds in the atmosphere. The rain fell and then evaporated again because of the heat of the crust. This cycle continued for millions of years until the earth cooled down. Then the heavy constant rains began to fill the low-lying areas of the crust. As the continents drifted apart, the deep basins that were formed filled with water and became the oceans. This happened between 500 million and 1 billion years ago.

Once water formed in volume on the surface of the earth most carbon dioxide in the atmosphere dissolved into the oceans. Eventually a variety of chemical reactions took place in the water that produced living cells, the first life forms. This could happen because earth has just the right set of environmental factors: right atmosphere, right geological processes at work, right temperature, right amount of light, etc. The earliest evidence of life is the fossilized mats of cyanobacteria called stromatolites, believed to be about 3.4 billion years old. They had to be preceded by other simpler life forms, so life in its simplest form must have begun about 3.8 billion years ago, at the time before the oceans were even formed. The first living things, perhaps what we would now call "replicating molecules," were subject to the force of Darwinian evolution and developed into the myriad of living things that we see around us today, including human beings.

Now—13.787 billion years after the Big Bang—our universe, our "bubble," is 156 billion light years across and is filled with stars. On our planet a plethora of carbon-based life forms exist, and human beings are one of them.

Focus on the Advent of Man:
Over tens of thousands of years the slow development of gradually evolving hominid life forms produced a more intelligent species that organized its life into small tribes roaming the earth and supporting their existence by hunting other animals and by foraging off the land whatever they could find. A certain critical point was reached when that species evolved to a sufficient level of intelligence—an evolutionary development precipitating the formation of the first human civilizations. That moment in the history of life marked the emergence of the first intelligent life form and the establishment by that life form of primitive social units. The first human cities came into existence.

It was the "Neolithic Transition," a time in the history of human development that coincided with the geologic epoch called the Holocene. It was about 10000 BC. This time marked the transition for ancient man from living as a "hunter gatherer" to a more domesticated and agricultural type of life—the life of a farmer. This transition was what allowed for the birth of modern man and the development of the first civilizations. This is the reason this change in life-style was so important.

Men made their living by hunting wild animals for food, moving constantly as they followed the herds from here to there. As they traveled they would also gather wild berries, nuts, and green seeds for food. This difficult life style meant that men could not know where their next meal was coming from. Then men discovered they could plant and harvest grain that they found growing wild. They also figured out how to tame wild animals such as goats and sheep and to raise them for food—it was the beginning of domesticated animals. Humans no longer had to hunt for food since they could grow it themselves. They found that their crops grew better in Mesopotamia than anywhere else, so they stopped moving around and settled there. In the Sumerian cities of the Middle East we can see the first fully developed example of what is called the Neolithic Complex. This emerged about 5500 BC in what we also call the Bronze Age. The oldest archeological digs are dated to about this time.[s]

The major accomplishment of these societies was making agriculture more efficient. They did this by learning to control the rivers' waters with levees, gated locks, and dams. This made agricultural practices more reliable and productive and lessened their dependence on the whims of weather. People invented the plow, the wheel, cuneiform writing, weaving of cloth, and the calendar with twelve months of thirty days each.

As agricultural skills became more efficient, it was no longer necessary for everybody to farm in order to produce enough food to survive. Some farmed, some did other things; for example, music, fishing, religion, dancing, writing, storytelling, pottery, art, law and government, etc. People gathered in small villages that supported their common life. They developed different social roles as society became more complex. These villages developed into the city-states of ancient Mesopotamia: Mari, Sippar, Nippur, Nineveh, Assur, Babylon, Uruk, etc. This was the beginning of modern civilization.

As we study these ancient civilizations we must comprehend the broad scope of history from which they emerged; that is, we must situate the chronology of their development squarely within the expansive sweep of the history of all life, of the earth and its physical systems, and of the entire universe. Only by comprehending the development of human life and civilization in this way do we understand our current human cultures properly.

Only in this way can we see the proper place for government and power, sexuality and reproduction, family life and the broader society, religion and myth and spirituality—and ultimately the meaning of all existence; that is, that mysterious emerging of spirit and self-awareness from the chaos of non-being that has finally resulted in the generation of intelligent and conscious creatures—human beings.

---

[s] Example: The dig at Tepe Gawra, Iraq is dated back to at least 5500 BC by secular scholars. Christians need to re-examine the archeological data for this site and formulate an accurate chronology for it. It must be part of a comprehensive biblically based chronology for the entire ancient Middle East. It should also include Egypt.

Appendix III – The Documentary Hypothesis

Moses did not write much of the Pentateuch. We understand it to have been written by various post-Mosaic authors. These can be detected by the variations in their usage of different words within the books. We call these ancient writers the **J**ehovist, **E**lohist, **P**riestly, and **D**euteronomist authors of Genesis.

We base our assertion on four basic observations about the text of Genesis:
- There is variation in the Divine Names in Genesis.
- There are variations in the style of the writer and in his diction; that is, in the choice of words and phrases that he uses as he writes.
- There are parallel or duplicate accounts of events in Scripture.
- If you pull out one "source" from the entire body of the text, then the story it tells flows in a coherent and continuous way.

Some sections of Genesis use the name "Jehovah" for the Lord more often than they use "Elohim." Other passages use the name "Elohim" more frequently. This indicates different authorship for the two sections. Perhaps a half dozen people proposed ideas like this in the 1700s and 1800s. Then in the 1870s Karl Graf and Julius Wellhausen said that the priestly legislation of the middle books of the Pentateuch was added at a later time because they were not known in pre-exilic times. They asserted this based on their reading of the historical and prophetical books of the Old Testament. This later-written part of the Pentateuch was designated by the letter **P** in their theory. Upholding the theory of Wellhausen was the idea that the evolving religious culture of Israel was associated with a gradual growth in the power and influence of the priesthood.

The first five books are arranged in their authorship basically as follows:
- The oldest part of the Pentateuch was written from the Jehovist document from about 950 BC and the Elohist document from about 850 BC. The Jehovist then compiled his work from these two sources about 650 BC. Anthropomorphism is common in this tradition. It has many narratives in it explaining the meaning and purpose of human life on earth. It emphasizes the covenant promises of God to Abraham, their fulfillment by Him, and the high destiny of Israel.
- In the time of King Josiah Deuteronomy was written and included in the Pentateuch. It was addressed to the exiles in Babylon exhorting them to repent and to cry out to God. It explained to them that the reason for the captivity was that they did not live up to the law of the Lord. They had flagged in their loyalty to Him for centuries.
- The Priestly legislation from the Elohist tradition was written mostly by Ezra or by Jewish priests in Babylon and was completed by about 500 BC. It stresses the importance of the priesthood, contains many genealogies, numbers, dates, and laws. In this stream of writing God is seen as distant from men and not prone to being merciful. He is interested in religious ritual and obedience to His laws and focuses on the temple and various rituals associated with it.

In about 200 BC a later redactor revised and edited the whole work into the form that we have today. This explains the basic internal consistency of the work.[t]

---

[t] A comprehensive reply to all "higher critical" claims about the Bible must be developed by Christians.

End Notes

The Ancient Faith

[1] Philip Jenkins, *The Lost History of Christianity: The Thousand–Year Golden Age of the Church in the Middle East, Africa, and Asia–and How it Died* (New York: HarperCollins Publishers, 2008).

[2] Augustine, *Responses to Miscellaneous Questions*, vol. 12, In *The Works of Augustine: A Translation for the 21st Century* (New York: New York City Press, 2002). Response to Question 65.

[3] The LXX was translated, according to Anatolius of Alexandria (3rd century) as stated in his Paschal Cannon and in section III, during the reign of Ptolemy Philadelphus and his father. This is understood to be Ptolemy II Philadelphus who reigned from 309 BC to 246 BC.
See also Eusebius of Caesarea, *Preparation for the Gospel*, 8, Preface–5, vol. 1, trans. Edwin Hamilton Gifford (Grand Rapids, MI: Baker Book House, 1981), pp. 377–385.

[4] For a more complete analysis of Augustine's commentary *The Literal Meaning of Genesis*, see this article: https://www.kolbecenter.org/st-augustine-rediscovered-a-defense-of-the-literal-interpretation-of-st-augustines-writings-on-the-sacred-history-of-genesis/

[5] Didymus the Blind, *Commentary on Genesis*, 1, vol. 132, In The Fathers of the Church, The Catholic University of America Press, 1986, pp. 43–44.

[6] See also Basil of Caesarea, for example. *On the Human Condition*, 2, 8–11, trans. Nonna Verna Harrison, (Crestwood, NY: St. Vladimir's Seminary Press, 2005), pp. 54–58.
Basil mentions the numbers 6, 7, and 8 and discusses their meaning in Scripture. Interestingly, he sees Enoch, the seventh from Adam, as a mystery of the church, which will be "snatched away." But Moses is the seventh from Abraham and was given the law. As Lamech was avenged seventy times seven times (Genesis 4:24) so also Jesus instructs Peter to forgive seventy times seven times (Matthew 18:21–22). And the eighth day is the day of judgment.

[7] Ibid., pp. 47–48.

[8] Augustine, *The City of God*, 11,9, vol. 7, in *The Works of Augustine; A translation for the 21st Century* (New York: New York City Press, 2002).

[9] Augustine, *The Literal Meaning of Genesis*, vol. 13, in *The Works of Augustine; A translation for the 21st Century* (New York: New York City Press, 2002). Summarized from Book 2, 16–18.

[10] Ibid., 2,19.

[11] Ibid., 4, 1.

[12] Ibid., 7, 40–42.

[13] Ibid.

[14] Ibid., 2, 19.

[15] Ibid., 3, 31.

[16] Ibid., 3, 36–37.

[17] Ibid., 4, 43.

[18] Ibid., 4, 44.

[19] Ibid., 4, 45.

[20] Ibid., 4, 52.

[21] Augustine, *The City of God*, 15, 10–14.

[22] Augustine, *The Literal Meaning of Genesis*, 6, 2–3.

[23] Ibid., 6, 4.

[24] Ibid., 4, 53.

[25] Ibid., 4, 56.

[26] Ibid., 4, 45.

[27] Augustine, *The City of God*, 12, 11.

[28] Ibid., 12, 12.

[29] Ibid., 11, 6–7.

[30] Origen, *Commentary on Genesis*, introduction, vol. 71, in *The Fathers of the Church* (Washington, DC: The Catholic University of America Press, 1986), p. 8.

[31] Ibid., p. 10.

[32] Ibid., p. 24.

[33] Origen, *Commentary on Genesis, fragment from Book 3*, trans. Joseph W. Trigg, in *Origen*, ed. Carol Harrison (London: Routledge, 1998), pp. 86–102.

[34] Origen, *De Principiis*, vol. 4, in *Fathers of the Third Century: Tertullian, Part Fourth; Minucius Felix; Commodian; Origen, Parts First and Second*, eds. A. Roberts, J. Donaldson, and A. C. Coxe, trans. F. Crombie (Buffalo, NY: Christian Literature Company, 1885), pp. 346-347. See 3, 5, 5–8; 3, 6, 1–9.

[35] Sulpicius Severus, *First Dialogue*, 7, vol. 7, in *The Fathers of the Church* (Washington, DC: The Catholic University of America Press, 1986), pp. 169–170.

[36] Origen, *Origen against Celsus*, 4, 38, vol. 4, in *Fathers of the Third Century: Tertullian, Part Fourth; Minucius Felix; Commodian; Origen, Parts First and Second*, eds. A. Roberts, J. Donaldson, & A. C. Coxe, trans. F. Crombie (Buffalo, NY: Christian Literature Company, 1885), p. 514.

[37] Ibid., 4, 39. P. 515.

[38] Ibid., 4, 41, p. 516. See also his more complete commentary on the Flood in Origen, *Commentary on Genesis*, "Homily 2," pp. 72ff.

[39] Ibid., 4, 44, p. 517.

[40] Ibid.

[41] Origen, *Commentary on Genesis*, "Homily 1," 1, p. 47.

[42] Ibid., p. 48.
[43] Ibid., 2, pp. 48–49.
[44] Ibid., 3, pp. 51–52.
[45] Ibid., 8, p. 57.
[46] Ibid., 9, p. 58.
[47] Ibid., 10, p. 59.
[48] Ibid., 11, p. 60.
[49] Ibid., 13, p. 63.
[50] Ibid., p. 65.
[51] Ibid., 14, p. 67.
[52] Ibid., 16, p. 69.
[53] Ibid., 17, pp. 69–70.
[54] Origen. (1885). *De Principiis*, 3, 5, 1, p. 341.
[55] Origen, *Commentary on Genesis*, "Homily 15," 5, p. 211.
[56] Didymus the Blind, *Commentary on Genesis*, 2, p. 84.
[57] Ibid., 2, pp. 84-113.
[58] Ibid., Preface, 8.
[59] Ibid., Preface, 4.
[60] Ibid., Preface, 7.
[61] Ibid., 3, 5, 3.
[62] Origen. (1885). *Origen against Celsus*, 1, 19, p. 395.
[63] Origen, *Commentary on Genesis*, "Homily 2," 1, p. 72.
[64] Ibid., 1, pp. 73–74.
[65] Ibid., 1, pp. 74–75.
[66] Ibid., 3-5, pp. 77–85.
[67] Ibid., 6, p. 85.
[68] Augustine, *The Literal Meaning of Genesis*, 8, 1
[69] Ibid., 8, 2.
[70] Ibid., 8, 4.
[71] Ibid., 8, 5.
[72] Clement of Rome, *The First Epistle of Clement to the Corinthians*, 4, vol. 1, in *The Apostolic Fathers with Justin Martyr and Irenaeus*, eds. A. Roberts, J. Donaldson, and A. C. Coxe (Buffalo, NY: Christian Literature Company, 1885), p. 6.
[73] Papias, *Fragments of Papias*, Fragment 10, vol. 1, in *The Apostolic Fathers with Justin Martyr and Irenaeus*, eds. A. Roberts, J. Donaldson, and A. C. Coxe (Buffalo, NY: Christian Literature Company 1885), p. 155.
[74] Mathetes, *The Epistle of Mathetes to Diognetus*, vol. 1, in *The Apostolic Fathers with Justin Martyr and Irenaeus*, eds. A. Roberts, J. Donaldson, and A. C. Coxe (Buffalo, NY: Christian Literature Company, 1885), pp. 29–30.
[75] The Pastor of Hermas, *Commandments*, 1, vol. 2, in *Fathers of the Second Century: Hermas, Tatian, Athenagoras, Theophilus, and Clement of Alexandria (Entire)*, eds. A. Roberts, J. Donaldson, and A. C. Coxe, trans. F. Crombie (Buffalo, NY: Christian Literature Company 1885), p. 20.
[76] Justin Martyr, *The Second Apology of Justin*, 7, vol. 1, in *The Apostolic Fathers with Justin Martyr and Irenaeus*, eds. A. Roberts, J. Donaldson, and A. C. Coxe (Buffalo, NY: Christian Literature Company, 1885), p. 188.
[77] Justin Martyr, *Apology 2*, 6, *Writings of Saint Justin Martyr*, vol. 6, in *The Fathers of the Church*, ed. Thomas B. Falls (Overbrook, PA: St. Charles Seminary, 1948), p. 125.
[78] Justin Martyr, *Apology 1*, 10, *Writings of Saint Justin Martyr*, p. 42.
[79] Tatian, *Address of Tatian to the Greeks*, 4, vol. 2, in *Fathers of the Second Century: Hermas, Tatian, Athenagoras, Theophilus, and Clement of Alexandria (Entire)*, eds. A. Roberts, J. Donaldson, and A. C. Coxe, trans. J. E. Ryland (Buffalo, NY: Christian Literature Company, 1885), p. 66.
[80] Ibid., 5, p. 67.
[81] Ibid., 12, p. 70.
[82] Ibid., 20, p. 74.
[83] Theophilus of Antioch, "Theophilus to Autolycus," 2, 9, vol. 2, in *Fathers of the Second Century: Hermas, Tatian, Athenagoras, Theophilus, and Clement of Alexandria (Entire)*, eds. A. Roberts, J. Donaldson, and A. C. Coxe, trans. M. Dods (Buffalo, NY: Christian Literature Company, 1885), p. 97.
[84] Ibid., 2,10, pp. 97–98.
[85] Ibid., 2, 12, p. 99.
[86] Ibid., 2, 22, p. 101.
[87] Ibid., 2, 21, p. 103.
[88] Ibid., 2, 23, p. 103.
[89] Ibid., 2, 24, p. 104.
[90] Ibid., 3, 28, p. 121.
[91] Eusebius Pamphilus, *Eusebius' Ecclesiastical History*, 6, 31, trans C. F. Cruise (New York: Merchant Books, 2011), p. 235.
[92] Dionysius of Alexandria, *The Extant Fragments of the Five Books of the Chronography of Julius Africanus*, 1, vol. 6, in *Fathers of the Third Century: Gregory Thaumaturgus, Dionysius the Great, Julius Africanus, Anatolius and Minor Writers, Methodius, Arnobius*, eds. A. Roberts, J. Donaldson, and A. C. Coxe, trans. S. D. F. Salmond, (Buffalo, NY: Christian Literature Company, 1886), p. 131.
[93] Ibid., 18, vol.6, p. 138.
[94] Eusebius Pamphilus, *Eusebius' Ecclesiastical History*, 6, 31, p. 235.

[95] Minucius Felix, *Octavius*, 18, 7, in *Tertullian Apologetical Works and Felix Minucius Octavius*, vol. 10, *The Fathers of The Church*, trans. Rudolph Arbesmann, Emily Joseph Daly, and Edwin A. Quain (Washington, DC: Catholic University of America Press, 1950), p. 353.

[96] Cyprian of Carthage, *On the Mortality*, 17, vol. 5, in *Fathers of the Third Century: Hippolytus, Cyprian, Novatian, Appendix*, eds. A. Roberts, J. Donaldson, and A. C. Coxe, trans. R. E. Wallis (Buffalo, NY: Christian Literature Company, 1886), p. 473.

[97] Ibid., 23., p. 474.

[98] Irenaeus of Lyons, *Irenaeus against Heresies*, 5, 28, 3, vol. 1, in *The Apostolic Fathers with Justin Martyr and Irenaeus*, eds. A. Roberts, J. Donaldson, and A. C. Coxe (Buffalo, NY: Christian Literature Company, 1885), p. 557.

[99] Ibid., 3, 23, 3, vol. 1, p. 315.

[100] Ibid., 4, 20, 6, p. 489.

[101] Ibid., 5, 6, 1, pp. 531–532.

[102] Irenaeus of Lyons, *The Demonstration of the Apostolic Preaching*, 4, J. Armitage Robinson, Society for Promoting Christian Knowledge (New York: Macmillan, 1920), p. 73.

[103] Ibid., 5, pp. 73–74.

[104] Ibid., 11, pp. 80–81.

[105] Ibid., 12, pp. 81–82.

[106] Ibid., 15, p. 83.

[107] Hippolytus of Rome, *The Commentary of Holy Hippolytus of Rome on Genesis*, vol. 5, in *Fathers of The Third Century: Hippolytus, Cyprian, Novatian, Appendix*, eds. A. Roberts, J. Donaldson, and A. C. Coxe, trans. S. D. F. Salmond (Buffalo, NY: Christian Literature Company, 1886), p. 163.

[108] Hippolytus of Rome, *Against the Heresy of One Noetus*, 10, vol. 5, in *Fathers of the Third Century: Hippolytus, Cyprian, Novatian, Appendix*, eds. A. Roberts, J. Donaldson, and A. C. Coxe, trans. S. D. F. Salmond (Buffalo, NY: Christian Literature Company, 1886), p. 227.

[109] Hippolytus of Rome, *The Refutation of All Heresies*, 10, 26, vol. 5, in *Fathers of the Third Century: Hippolytus, Cyprian, Novatian, Appendix*, eds. A. Roberts, J. Donaldson, and A. C. Coxe, trans. J. H. MacMahon (Buffalo, NY: Christian Literature Company, 1886), p. 149.

[110] Ibid., 10, 29, p. 151.

[111] Hippolytus of Rome, *The Commentary of Holy Hippolytus of Rome on Genesis*, p. 168.

[112] Hippolytus of Rome, *Fragments from Commentaries on Various Books of Scripture*, vol. 5, in *Fathers of the Third Century: Hippolytus, Cyprian, Novatian, Appendix*, eds. A. Roberts, J. Donaldson, and A. C. Coxe, trans. S. D. F. Salmond (Buffalo, NY: Christian Literature Company, 1886), p. 179.

[113] Tertullian, *A Treatise on the Soul*, 37, vol. 3, eds. A. Roberts, J. Donaldson and A. C. Coxe, trans. P. Holmes, in *Latin Christianity: Its Founder, Tertullian* (Buffalo, NY: Christian Literature Company, 1885), p. 218.

[114] Tertullian, *The Apology*, 17, vol. 3, in *Latin Christianity: Its Founder, Tertullian*, eds. A. Roberts, J. Donaldson, and A. C. Coxe, trans. S. Thelwall (Buffalo, NY: Christian Literature Company, 1885), p. 31.

[115] A Partial listing of the early thinkers who espoused this idea can be seen in *Creationism and the Early Church* by Robert I. Bradshaw, available on-line for download. He states, "The belief that the world would last 7,000 years appears to have been almost universally accepted by the early church." (see section on "The Days of Creation", p. 1.) His table on page 2 lists the following early Fathers who espoused this idea: Pseudo Barnabas, Irenaeus, Supliicius Severus, Gaudentius of Brescia, Hippolytus, Julius Africanus, Hilary of Poitiers, Lactantius, Firmicus Maternus, and Tyconius. I believe this idea was common but perhaps not universal as he asserts. Still, his list is not exhaustive. Many others said this in their writings. We saw that Tertullian alluded to this belief. A less well known person which I have not otherwise quoted is:
Gregory the Illuminator, *The Teaching of Saint Gregory: An Early Armenian Catechism*, trans. Robert W. Thomson (Cambridge, Mass: Harvard University Press, 1970), section 366, pp. 74–75; sections 668-670, pp. 166-167. (He brought the gospel to the Armenians in Eastern Turkey around AD 300.) In addition, we can quote this well-known father:
John Damascene, On the Orthodox Faith, 2,1 refers to "the seven ages of the world" which will be followed by an eighth age. This seems, in his view, to follow the general resurrection of all men.

[116] Clement of Alexandria, *The Miscellanies*, 6, 16, vol. 2, in *The Writings of Clement of Alexandria, Anti-Nicene Christian Library, Translations of the Writings of the Fathers*, eds. A. Roberts, J. Donaldson, trans. William Wilson (Edinburgh: T & T Clark, 1867), p. 512.

[117] Ibid., p. 513.

[118] Clement of Alexandria, *The Stromata, or Miscellanies*, 1, 21, vol. 2, in *Fathers of the Second Century: Hermas, Tatian, Athenagoras, Theophilus, and Clement of Alexandria (Entire)*, eds. A. Roberts, J. Donaldson, & A. C. Coxe (Buffalo, NY: Christian Literature Company, 1885), p. 332.

[119] Tatian, *Address of Tatian to the Greeks*, 31, 36–41, pp. 76, 77, 80–81

[120] Theophilus of Antioch, *Theophilus to Autolycus*, 1, 4, p. 90.

[121] Athenagoras, *A Plea for the Christians*, 10, vol. 2, in *Fathers of the Second Century: Hermas, Tatian, Athenagoras, Theophilus, and Clement of Alexandria (Entire)*, eds. A. Roberts, J. Donaldson, and A. C. Coxe, trans. B. P. Pratten (Buffalo, NY: Christian Literature Company, 1885), p. 133.

[122] Dionysius of Alexandria, *On the Books of Nature against the Epicureans*, 2, 1, vol. 14, in *Anti-Nicene Christian Library: The Writings of Gregory Thaumaturgus, Dionysius of Alexandria, and Archelaus*, eds. A. Roberts, J. Donaldson (Edinburgh: T. & T. Clark, 1871).

[123] Ibid., 2, 2.

[124] Ibid., 2, 3.

[125] Victorinus of Pettau, *On the Creation of the World*, vol. 7, in *Fathers of the Third and Fourth Centuries:*

[125] *Lactantius, Venantius, Asterius, Victorinus, Dionysius, Apostolic Teaching and Constitutions, Homily, and Liturgies*, A. Roberts, J. Donaldson, and A. C. Coxe, trans. R. E. Wallis (Buffalo, NY: Christian Literature Company, 1886), p. 341.

[126] Methodius of Olympus, *The Banquet of the Ten Virgins*, Discourse 8—Thekla, 11, vol. 6, in *Fathers of the Third Century: Gregory Thaumaturgus, Dionysius the Great, Julius Africanus, Anatolius and Minor Writers, Methodius, Arnobius*, eds. A. Roberts, J. Donaldson, and A. C. Coxe, trans. W. R. Clark (Buffalo, NY: Christian Literature Company, 1886), p. 339.

[127] Ibid., Discourse 2—Theophila, 1 and 7, p. 313 and 316.

[128] Methodius of Olympus, *Fragments*, 7, vol. 6, in *Fathers of the Third Century: Gregory Thaumaturgus, Dionysius the Great, Julius Africanus, Anatolius and Minor Writers, Methodius, Arnobius*, eds. A. Roberts, J. Donaldson, and A. C. Coxe, trans. W. R. Clark (Buffalo, NY: Christian Literature Company, 1886), p. 381.

[129] Lactantius, *The Divine Institutes*, 7, 14, vol. 7, in *Fathers of the Third and Fourth Centuries: Lactantius, Venantius, Asterius, Victorinus, Dionysius, Apostolic Teaching and Constitutions, Homily, and Liturgies*, eds. A. Roberts, J. Donaldson, and A. C. Coxe, trans. W. Fletcher (Buffalo, NY: Christian Literature Company, 1886), p. 211.

[130] Ibid., 2, 14, p. 63.

[131] Eusebius of Caesarea, *Preparation for the Gospel*, 7, 11, vol. 1, pp. 342-343.

[132] Ibid., 7, 13, vol. 1, p. 349.

[133] Ibid., p. 350.

[134] Aphrahat, *The Demonstrations of Aphrahat the Persian Sage*, 23, 44, trans. Adam Lehto, (Piscataway, NJ: Georgias Press, 2010), p. 510.

[135] Ibid., 23, 45–46, pp. 510–512.

[136] Ibid., 23, 69, pp. 530–531.

[137] Ephrem the Syrian, *Commentary on Genesis*, prologue, 2, trans. Edward G. Matthews and Joseph P. Amar, ed. Kathleen McVey (The Catholic University of America Press: Washington DC, 1994), pp. 67–68.

[138] Ibid., 5, p. 69.

[139] Ibid., 1, 1–3; 8, p. 74–76, 80.

[140] St Ephrem, *Hymns on Paradise*, introduction, trans. By Sebastian Brock (Crestwood, NY: St. Vladimir's Seminary Press, 1990), pp. 49–74. The introduction has much valuable explanatory background information. See also Gregory of Nazianzus where he lists the canonical books, omitting Revelation: Gregory of Nazianzus, "On the genuine books of divinely inspired Scripture", in *Poems on Scripture*, I.1.2, trans. Brian Dunkle (Yonkers, NY: St. Vladimir's Seminary Press, 2012), pp. 37; 39.

[141] Ibid., 1, 4, pp. 78–79.

[142] Ibid., 11, 7–8, p. 156.

[143] Ibid., 1, 10, p. 81.

[144] Ibid., 1, 12–13, p. 82.

[145] Ibid., 3, 1, pp. 90–91.

[146] Ibid., 3, 14, p. 95.

[147] Ibid., 3, 13, p. 95.

[148] Hilary of Poitiers, *Commentary on Matthew*, 20, 6, vol. 125, trans. D. H. Williams, in *The Fathers of the Church, A New Translation*, ed. David G. Hunter, (Washington, D.C.: The Catholic University of America Press, 2012), p. 211.

[149] Cyril of Jerusalem, *The Catechetical Lectures of S. Cyril, Archbishop of Jerusalem*, 12, 5, trans. by members of the English Church (Oxford: Bibliolife, LLC, 1839), p. 125.

[150] Basil the Great, *Exegetical Homilies (on the Hexaemeron)*, "Homily 1," 6, vol. 46, in *The Fathers of the Church* (Washington, DC: The Catholic University of America Press, 1986).

[151] This is the Latin Church version. The Latin Church added the phrase "and the Son" (filioque) amidst Much controversy a few centuries later. The Eastern Orthodox Churches never acquiesced with this, and at last a schism occurred in 1054 that has not been healed to this day.

[152] Gregory or Nazianzus, *On his own Verses*, Poem 2.1.39, 1–24, in *On God and Man, The Theological Poetry of St Gregory of Nazianzus*, trans. Peter Gilbert (Crestwood, NY: St. Vladimir's Seminary Press, 2001), pp. 153–154.

[153] Ibid., *In Praise of Virginity*, Poem 1.2.1, 56–81, pp. 90–91.

[154] Ibid., *On the Soul*, Poem 1.1.8, 55–91, pp. 64–66.

[155] Gregory of Nyssa, *On the Making of Man*, Prologue, vol. 6, in *A Select Library of Nicene and Post-Nicene Fathers of the Christian Church*, eds. Phillip Schaff and Henry Wace, trans. Rev. H. A. Wilson (Grand Rapids, MI: Wm. B. Eerdmans Publishing Company, 1994), p. 387.

[156] Ibid., 3, 1, p. 390.

[157] Ibid., 16, 3–4, p. 404.

[158] Ibid., 16, 10, p. 405.

[159] Ibid., 17, 1–5, pp. 406–407.

[160] Athanasius of Alexandria, *Against the Heathen*, 3, 46, 3–8, vol. 4, in *St. Athanasius: Select Works and Letters*, eds. P. Shcaff and H. Wacw, trans. A. T. Robertson (New York: Christian Literature Company, 1892), pp. 28–29.

[161] Athanasius of Alexandria, *On the Incarnation of the Word*, 1–5, vol. 4, in *St. Athanasius: Select Works and Letters*, eds. P. Shcaff and H. Wacw, trans. A. T. Robertson (New York: Christian Literature Company, 1892), pp. 36–39.

[162] Macarius the Great, *Fifty Spiritual Homilies of Macarius the Egyptian*, 12, 6; 8, A. J. Mason, eds. W. J. Sparrow Simpson and W. K. Lowther Clarke (New York: Macmillan, 1921), pp. 91–92.

[163] Ibid., 12, 1, p. 89.

[164] Ibid., 26, 9.

[165] Ambrose of Milan, *Hexameron*, 8, vol. 42, in *The Fathers of the Church*, trans. John J. Savage (Washington, DC: The Catholic University of America Press, 1961), pp. 7–8.

[166] Macarius the Great, *Fifty Spiritual Homilies of Macarius the Egyptian*, 19–20, pp. 18–19.

[167] Ibid., 22, pp. 20–21.
[168] Ibid.
[169] We tend to think that such issues are certainly and solidly understood and settled today in physics and cosmology, but that definitely is not the case. And this issue of "just what is or what causes inertia in a body, and what is or what causes gravity" is an openly debated issue. And it deeply affects our view of cosmology. As one example, physicists assert, and reasonably so, that motion is relative; that is, a body that is in motion is said to to be in motion when it is compared to other bodies—it is moving with respect to them. However, acceleration or the increase in motion does not seem to be relative. The famous "bucket experiment" of Newton, where he caused a bucket of water to rotate, showed that the water climbed up the sides of the bucket whether the bucket was also rotating or not. The inertia of the water was not relative to the surrounding bucket. But the physicist Ernst Mach seems to have claimed that inertia WAS relative—not to nearby objects but to the huge masses of the distant stars. He claimed that there is a physical law that relates the motion of the distant stars to the simple inertial frame of the water. He suggests that there is a physical law that makes the water exhibit centrifugal force—that the distant masses influence inertia locally, that local physical laws are determined by the large-scale structure of the universe. Distant masses, even though very distant, do not lose their local influence via a kind of "inverse square" law as in Newton's laws of gravity. They keep their influence, which is a function of their total mass, irrespective of their distance. The interested reader can look at this book: *Mach's Principle: From Newton's Bucket to Quantum Gravity*, Juliann Barbour and Herbert Pfister, editors, (Boston: Birkhauser, 1995). Look at the first 57 pages as the authors discuss the acceptance or dissonance accorded to Mach's Principle by physicists. Clearly there is no unanimity. This was a hard idea for scientists to accept, but it seemed necessary to some, including Einstein in his General Theory of Relativity. Mach hated his own idea. "[the] only salvation [from the problem of centrifugal forces] was to bring the centrifugal appearances into relation with the fixed stars, and, in fact, Mach also accepts this in the last (7th) edition of his mechanics . . . he was forced to do it, even though this also obviously contradicted his sensibilities." (p. 27.) Indeed, a short note from Ernst Mach's son Ludwig states that his father found the idea "especially tormenting." (p. 27.) [We will discuss this more as we comment on the creation and on how Genesis affects our view of cosmology.]
[170] Ibid., 6, 9, p. 232.
[171] Ambrose of Milan, *Paradise*, 1–25, vol. 42, in *The Fathers of the Church*, trans. John J. Savage (Washington, DC: The Catholic University of America Press, 1961), pp. 287–303.
[172] Ibid., 51, p. 329.
[173] Firmicus Maternus, *The Error of the Pagan Religions*, 25, 3, trans. Clarence A. Forbes, (New York: Newman Press, 1970), p. 101.
[174] Tyconius, *Tyconius: The Book of Rules*, 5 Times, trans. William S. Babcock (Atlanta, Georgia: Scholars Press, 1989), pp. 89; 91.
[175] Paulus Orosius, *Seven Books against the Pagans*, 1, vol. 50, trans. Roy J. Deferrari, in *The Fathers of the Church a New Translation* (Washington, DC: The Catholic University of America Press, 1964), pp. 5–6.
[176] Ibid., p. 21.
[177] Epiphanius of Cyprus, *Ancoratus*, 55, 1–3, vol. 71, in *The Fathers of the Church*, (Washington, DC: The Catholic University of America Press, 1986), p. 138.
[178] Epiphanius of Salamis, *The Panarion of Epiphanius of Salamis*, 1,1,1, eds. Einar Thomassen and Johannes van Oort, trans Frank Williams (Leiden, The Netherlands: Kroninklijke Brill NV, 2009), p. 15.
[179] Ibid., p. 15.
[180] Ibid., 1, 1, 2, p. 19.
[181] Jerome, *Saint Jerome's Hebrew Questions on Genesis*, 1:1, eds. Henry Chadwick and Andrew Louth, trans. C. T. R. Hayward (Oxford: Oxford University Press, 1995), p. 30.
[182] Ibid., 1:2, p. 30.
[183] Ibid., 6:2–6:4, pp. 36–37.
[184] Saint Jerome, *Ad Titum*, 1, 134–135, in *S. Hieronymi presbyteri opera. / Pars I, Opera exegetica. 8, Commentarii in Epistulas Pauli apostoli ad Titum et ad Philemonem*, (Turnhout: Brepolis, 2003), p. 10.
[185] Jerome, *Commentary on Titus*,1, 2–4, in *St. Jerome's Commentaries on Galatians, Titus, and Philemon*, trans. Thomas P. Scheck (Notre Dame, IN: University of Notre Dame, 2010), pp. 284–285.
[186] Jerome also has a chronology, appending dates to that of Eusebius and thus affirming his belief in his work. See *A Translation of Jerome's Chronicon with Historical Summary*, trans Malcolm Drew Donaldson, 1996
[187] Of course, Peter says that Jesus was "foreordained before the foundation of the world" (1 Peter 1:20).
[188] Jerome, *Saint Jerome's Hebrew Questions on Genesis*, 5:25–5:31, pp. 35–36.
[189] Nemesius of Emesa, *Of the Nature of Man*, ed. William Telfer, in *Cyril of Jerusalem and Nemesius of Edesa*, 5 (Louisville, KY: Westminster John Knox Press, 2006), pp. 238–239.
The personal information about Nemesius can be found in the translator's introduction, pp. 206ff.
[190] Ibid., 7, p. 244.
[191] Sulpicius Severus, *Chronicles*, 1, preface, 1, trans., intro. and notes Richard J. Goodrich, in *Sulpicius Severus the Complete Works* (New York: The Newman Press, 2015), p. 67.
[192] Ibid., 1, 1, 1, p. 68.
[193] Ibid., 1, 2, 2, p. 69.
[194] Ibid., 1, 4, 1, p. 70.
[195] Cyril of Alexandria, *Glaphyra on Genesis*, 1, trans. Nicholas Lunn, intro. and notes Gregory Hillis, unedited, unpublished manuscript (Washington, DC: The Catholic University of America Press, forthcoming)
[196] Ibid., 1, "Concerning Adam", 2.
[197] Ibid.
[198] Ibid.

[199] Ibid.
[200] Ibid., 1, 5.
[201] Ibid., 1, 3.
[202] Ibid., 1, 5.
[203] Ibid., 1, "Concerning Cain and Abel," 1.
[204] Theodoret of Cyrus, *The Questions on the Octateuch*, Preface, vol. 1, trans. Robert C. Hill (Washington, DC: The Catholic University of America Press, 2007), p. 5.
[205] Ibid., 19, 2, p. 47.
[206] Ibid., 20, 2, p. 53.
[207] Ibid., 49, p. 105.
[208] Ibid., 6, p. 21.
[209] Jacob of Sarug, *Jacob of Sarug's Homilies on the Six Days of Creation: The First Day*, 65–70, trans. Edward G. Matthews Jr. (Piscataway, NJ: Georgia Press, 2009), p. 14.
[210] Ibid., 133–138, p. 22.
[211] Ibid., 345–347, pp. 44; 46.
[212] Ibid., 379–388, p. 48.
[213] Jacob of Sarug, *Jacob of Sarug's Homilies on the Six Days of Creation: The Second Day*, 535–546, trans. Edward G. Matthews Jr. (Piscataway, NJ: Georgia Press, 2016), p. 8.
[214] Fulgentius of Ruspe, *To Peter on the Faith*, 5, vol. 95, in *The Fathers of the Church*, trans. Robert B. Eno (Washington, DC: The Catholic University of America Press, 1997), p. 63.
[215] Ibid., 25, 28, 29, 32, pp. 75, 77, 78, 80.
[216] Ibid., 68, p. 99.
[217] Ibid., 37, p. 83.
[218] Fulgentius the Mythographer, *On the Ages of the World and on Man*, in *Fulgentius the Mythographer*, trans. Leslie George Whitbread (Columbus, Ohio: Ohio State University Press, 1971), Prologue, p. 189.
[219] Gregory of Tours, *History of the Franks*, 1, preface, trans Ernest Brehaut, ed. W. T. H. Jackson (New York: Colombia University Press, 1965), pp. 6–7.
[220] Ibid., 1, 4, p. 8.
[221] Isidore of Seville, *Chronica Maiora*, available on-line. See, for example: http://www.tertullian.org/fathers/isidore_chronicon_01_trans.htm.
[222] Isaac the Syrian, *The Ascetical Homilies of Saint Isaac the Syrian*, 54, trans. Holy Transfiguration Monastery (Boston, MA: Holy Transfiguration Monastery, 1984), p. 406.
[223] Ibid., pp. 407–408.
[224] Anastasius of Sanai, *Anastasios of Sanai Questions and Answers*, 23, trans. Joseph A. Munitiz (Turnhout, Belgium: Brepols Publishers, 2011), pp. 103–104.
[225] Anastasius of Sinai, *Hexaemeron*, 1, 6, 2, trans. Clement A. Kuehn and John D. Baggerly S. J., ed. Edward G. Farrugia, S. J. (Roma IT: Pontifico Istituto Orientale, 2008), p. 19.
[226] Ibid., 1, 6, 2, p. 19.
[227] Ibid., 3, 2, 1, p. 63. Anastasius repeats his firm belief in the literal understanding of the six days often throughout his work. Another example: 4, 1, p. 95, and also thereafter. He might be carefully distancing himself from Origen, for he refers to the denunciation of Origen. (Issued by the Second Council of Constantinople in 553, and then **specifically** upheld by the Third Council of Constantinople in 680-681.) He strongly expresses his approval of it. Since his own commentary has much allegorical thinking in it, he might be protecting himself from possible similar accusations. By asserting the literal understanding of the six days of creation and only then expressing many allegorical interpretations of them he falls in line with many before him.
[228] Ibid, 1, 7, 3-4, p. 25.
[229] Ibid., 1, 8, 1-2, p. 27.
[230] Ibid., 5, 2, 1, p. 151; 7 (alpha), 1, 3, p. 209; 12, 2, 1, p. 399.
[231] Venerable Bede, *The Book on Times*. In *Bede on the Nature of Things and On Times*, trans. Calvin B. Kendall and Faith Wallace (Liverpool, UK: Liverpool University Press, 2010), pp. 107, 117–118.
[232] Venerable Bede, *On Genesis*, 1, in *In Principio*, trans. Calvin B. Kendall (Liverpool UK: Liverpool University Press, 2008), p. 68.
[233] Venerable Bede, *On the Nature of Things*, in *Bede on the Nature of Things and On Times*, trans. Calvin B. Kendall and Faith Wallace (Liverpool, UK: Liverpool University Press, 2010), pp. 74–75.
[234] John of Damascus, *Orthodox Faith*, vol. 37, In *The Fathers of the Church* (Washington, DC: The Catholic University of America Press, 1986), selections from 2, 2, p. 205 and 2, 5, p. 210 and 2, 11, pp. 230, 232. See also 2, 5–12 for an extended discussion of the creation, including heaven, paradise, man, etc.
[235] George Synkellos, *The Chronography of George Synkellos*, Introduction, trans. William Adler and Paul Tuffin (Oxford: Oxford University Press, 2002), pp. xxix–xxx.
[236] Ibid., 1, pp. 1–2.
[237] Ibid., 4, p. 5.
[238] Ibid., 4–5, pp. 6–8.
[239] Ibid., 4, p. 6.
[240] Ibid., 96–100, pp. 120–124.
[241] Symeon the New Theologian, *The First-Created Man*, 45, 1, trans. Fr. Seraphim Rose (Platina, CA: St. Hermon of Alaska Brotherhood, 2001), p. 87.
[242] Ibid., pp. 89–90.
[243] Ibid., p. 90.
[244] Ibid., p. 88.

[245] Peter Abelard, *An Exposition on the Six-Day Work*, Preface, trans. Wanda Zemler-Cizewski (Turnhout, Belgium: Brepols Publishers, 2011), pp. 31–32.
[246] Ibid., 17–21, pp. 35–36.
[247] Ibid., 21, p. 36.
[248] Ibid., 43–60, pp. 41–45.
[249] Ibid., 76–128, pp. 47–56.
[250] Ibid., 114–115, pp. 53–54.
[251] Ibid., 117, p. 54.
[252] Ibid., 118–119, pp. 54–55.
[253] Ibid., 255–258, pp. 77–78.
[254] Bernard of Clairvaux, *The Sentences of Bernard of Clairvaux*, 3, 78–79, in *Bernard of Clairvaux, the Parables*, trans. Francis R. Swietek and John R. Sommerfeldt, ed. Maureen M. O'Brien (Kalamazoo, MI: Cistercian Publications, 2000), pp. 260–261.
[255] Hugh of St. Victor, *On the Three Days*, 2, 1, in *Trinity and Creation*, eds. Boyd Taylor Coolman and Dale M. Coulter, trans. Hugh Feiss (Hyde Park, NY: New City Press, 2011), p. 62.
[256] Hugh of St. Victor, *Sentences on Divinity*, 1, in *Trinity and Creation*, trans. Christopher P. Evans, p. 130.
[257] Ibid., pp. 138–139.
[258] Ibid., p. 132.
[259] Ibid., p. 134.
[260] Ibid., p. 139.
[261] Peter Lombard, *The Sentences, Book 1*, Prologue, 1, trans. Warren Becket Soule, (Ave Maria, FL: Sapientia Press of Ave Maria University, 2016), p. 3.
[262] Ibid., Prologue, 2, p. 3.
[263] Ibid., Prologue, 3, pp. 3–4.
[264] Ibid., Prologue, 4, p. 4.
[265] Ibid., 3, 2, p. 23.
[266] Ibid., 3, 3, p. 24.
[267] Peter Lombard, *The Sentences*, translator's introduction, vol. 3, trans. Giulio Silano, (Toronto, ON: Pontifical Institute of Mediaeval Studies, 2008), p. vii.
   Note: Put "Guilio Silano" in your search engine and look at the diverse reviews has he received from his many students at the university in Toronto. It is ***very*** interesting. The website is: http://www.ratemyprofessors.com/ShowRatings.jsp?tid=234511.
[268] Ibid., translator's introduction, vol. 2, p. ii.
[269] Ibid.,
   1. 1, 2, pp. 3–4.
   2. 1, 4, 3, p. 5.
   3. 1, 5, pp. 6–7.
   4. 2, 1, 3, p. 9.
   5. 2, 4, 1–3, p. 11.
   6. 3, 2, 1–5, pp. 13–14.
   7. 3, 4, 9–11, pp. 17–18.
   8. 4, 1, 4, p. 20.
   9. 6, 3, p. 25.
   10. 6, 4, pp. 25–26.
   11. 7, 8, 1–3, pp. 31–32.
   12. 8, 1, 1–3, pp. 33–34.
   13. 8, 2, 1, p. 35.
   14. 8, 3, pp. 36–37.
[270] Ibid.,
   1. 12, 1, 2, p. 49.
   2. 12, 2, p. 50.
   3. 12, 3, 1–2, pp. 50–51.
   4. 12, 3, 3, p. 51.
   5. 13, 2, 1–3, p. 54.
   6. 13, 4, 1–2, p. 55.
   7. 13, 6, p. 57.
   8. 13, 7, 1–5, pp. 57–58.
   9. 14, 5, 1–2, p. 60.
[271] Ibid.,
   1. 16, 2, p. 68.
   2. 16, 3, 5, p. 70.
   3. 17, 1, 1–3, pp. 71–72.
   4. 17, 1, 5, p. 72.
   5. 17, 2, 4, pp. 73.
   6. 17, 3, 2, pp. 73–74.
   7. 17, 5, 2–4, pp. 74–75.
   8. 17, 6, 1–2, p. 75.
   9. 18, 7, 1, pp. 80–81.
   10. 18, 7, 2–4, p. 81.

    11. 19, 1, 1–3, pp. 81–82 and 19, 3, 1–2, p. 83.
    12. 20, 1, 1–3, pp. 86–87.
    13. 20, 3, 1–2, p. 88.

[272] Robert Grosseteste, *Robert Grosseteste on the Six days of Creation*, 1, 7, 1, trans. C. F. J. Martin, (Oxford: Oxford University Press, 1996), p. 55.
[273] Ibid., 2, 5, 1, pp. 88–89.
[274] Ibid., 4, 13, 1, p. 148.
[275] Ibid., 5, 12, 2, pp. 173–174.
[276] Ibid., 8, 13, 4, p. 242.
[277] Ibid., 9, 3, 1–2, pp. 275–276.
[278] Bonaventure, *Bonaventure Tests in translation Series: Breviloquium*, 1, 1, vol. 9, trans. Dominic Monti, (Bonaventure, NY: Franciscan Institute Publications, 2005), p. 59.
[279] Ibid., 2,1, p. 62–63.
[280] Ibid., 2, 5, pp. 65–66.
[281] Ibid., 5,2, p. 72.
[282] Thomas Aquinas, *Quaestiones Disputatae de Potentia Dei*, q. 3, 1, http://dhspriory.org/thomas/, trans. by the English Dominican Fathers (Westminster, Maryland: The Newman Press, 1952)
[283] Ibid., q. 4, 2.
[284] Roger Bacon, *The Opus Majus of Roger Bacon*, 4, vol. 1, trans. Robert Belle Burke, (Philadelphia: University of Pennsylvania Press, 1928), pp. 208–209.
[285] See this Wikipedia article for an overview of this effort. Look in the section "Abrahamic Religions" for many examples of people who used either the LXX or the Masoretic text for their calculations. https://en.wikipedia.org/wiki/Dating_creation. Or search for "Dating Creation" to get the same web site.
[286] Gregory of Palamas, *The One Hundred and Fifty Chapters*, 16–18, trans. Robert E. Sinkewicz, C. S. B., (Toronto, Canada: Pontifical Institute of Mediaeval Studies, 1988), pp. 99, 101.
[287] Ibid., 21, pp. 103, 105.
[288] Gregory of Palamas, *St. Gregory Palamas the Homilies*, 6, 7, trans. Christopher Veniamin, (Waymart, PA: Mount Thabor Publishing, 2009), p. 44.
[289] Ibid., 6, 10, pp. 45–46.
[290] Saadia Gaon, *The Book of Beliefs and Opinions*, "Treatise 1," Exordium, trans. Samuel Rosenblatt (New Haven, CT: Yale University Press, 1948).
[291] Ibid., "Treatise 1," 1.
[292] Ibid., "Treatise 1," 4.
[293] Augustine, *The Literal Meaning of Genesis*, 1 39.
[294] Ibid., 1, 40.
[295] Ibid.
[296] Ibid., 1, 41.
[297] Augustine, *The City of God*, 11, 6.
[298] Ibid.
[299] Ibid., 11, 7.
[300] Origen. (1885). *De Principiis*, 4, 16, p. 365. (Translation from the Greek)
[301] Nemesius of Emesa, *Of the Nature of Man*, 2–4, pp. 228–235.
[302] Basil of Caesarea, *The Hexaemeron*, "Homily 1," 1.
[303] The encyclical of Pope Leo XIII was considered the most sublime and exquisite guidance for the Church in how to approach and understand the inspiration and truth of the Bible. It was exalted over and was followed up on by subsequent popes. As we saw in the dedication of this book, in 1907 Pope Pius X issued *Lamentabili Sane* to combat the effects of Modernism. In 1915 Pope Benedict XV wrote *Spiritus Parachetus* in honor of St. Jerome, whom he called "the greatest doctor divinely given to her [the Church] for the understanding of the Bible." In that encyclical the pope repeatedly asserts the inerrancy of the Scriptures, referring to Jerome's way of looking at them as exemplary and referring back to Leo's wonderful encyclical. (See specially sections 8 through 30 for this.) In 1943 Pope Pius XII wrote *Divino Afflante Spiritu* and again praised Leo for his encyclical and again affirmed its correctness and its importance. And he again asserted forcefully the inerrancy of the Scriptures. Thus a 1950 edition of the Douay Rheims Bible states plainly in the footnote to Genesis 1:1 that Catholics are not allowed to see the creation account as a myth or a legend, and the 1962 Confraternity Bible in its introduction to Genesis asserts its Mosaic authorship.

  In contrast to this we see today that in the Roman Catholic Church there is no emphasis at all on the truth or inerrancy of the Bible. The authorship of almost every book is called into question. This is the fruit of the "higher critical" school of thought that is so prevalent. (This same school of thought also finds reasons why the biblical proscriptions against homosexuality are not to be taken at face value.) In particular, the 1966 edition of the Jerusalem Bible asserts that the Pentateuch was written over the course of many centuries by multiple authors. And today the Church asserts that the creation account in Genesis is a myth, one of many ancient Middle Eastern creation myths, the Hebrew version of that myth. (The critical turning point in the understanding of Genesis in the Roman Catholic Church might have come with the "Letter of the Secretary of the Biblical Commission to Cardinal Suhard, Archbishop of Paris, January 16, 1948" entitled *Critical Questions on the Pentateuch*.) How can one letter sway the church in view of fifty years of strong papal teaching to the contrary?

  Finally, it is worth nothing that this same path was taken within almost every Protestant tradition several decades earlier. The ultimate result was that many traditions split into the "liberal" churches and the more "conservative" churches—the evangelical and fundamental churches.

[304] Basil of Caesarea, *On the Human Condition*, "Homily Explaining that God Is Not the Cause of Evil," 2, p. 66.

305 Augustine, *The City of God*, 11, 4.
306 Severian of Gabala, *Homilies in Creation and Fall*, "Homily 1," in *Ancient Christian Texts, Commentaries on Genesis 1–3*, eds. Thomas C. Oden and Gerald L. Bray (Downers Grove, IL: Intervarsity Press, 2010), p. 24.
307 Heinrich Denzinger, *Compendium of Creeds, Definitions, and Declarations on Matters of Faith and Morals*, ed. Peter Hunermann for the Latin–English edition, 43rd edition, (San Francisco, CA: Ignatius Press, 2012), p. 687. **3394–3397; Response of the Biblical Commission, June 27, 1906**: *The Mosaic Authorship of the Pentateuch* **3395** *Question 3*: Can it be granted, without prejudice to the Mosaic authenticity of the Pentateuch, that Moses for the composition of the work made use of sources, namely, written documents or oral tradition, from which, according to the particular goal set before him and under the influence of divine inspiration, he made some borrowings, and these, arranged word for word according to sense or amplified, he inserted into the work itself? *Response*: Yes. [Obviously, this particular question/response on "sources" applies most especially to Genesis.]

Biblical Archeology and the Pentateuch
308 Dr. Douglas Petrovich, *The Battle for the History of the Bible*. This is from the fourth in a series of lectures that he gave, focused mainly on the development of alphabetic consonantal Semitic scripts. These lectures can be accessed at the following site: https://patterns of evidence.com.
309 Pope Leo XIII, *Providentissimus Deus*, 10
310 What follows is taken from *The Fall of Darwin's Last Icon and the Failure of the Cartesian-Darwinian Narrative* by John Wynne, (Restoring Truth Ministries, LLC, 2020), pp. 1–270.
311 Jacques Maritan, *The Dream of Descartes*, (Dallas, TX: Taylor Publishing Company, 1969), trans. by Mabelle L. Andison, p. 168.
312 Ibid., pp. 172–173.
313 Ibid., p. 174.
314 Ibid., p. 177.
315 Ibid., p. 178.
316 Ibid., p. 179.
317 Kathleen M. Kenyon, *Digging up Jericho*, (London: Ernest Benn Limited, 1957), pp. 28–30.
318 John J. Bimson, *Redating the Exodus and Conquest*, (Sheffield, England: The Almond Press, 1981)
What I present in this picture of scholarly thinking is only a relatively small part, the present state, of theories. To gain an overview/perspective on the past history of such theories/ideas the reader needs only look at his "Introduction" (pp. 13–28). This will give the reader a picture of the constantly shifting panoply of ideas and chronological assertions that has plagued (and still plagues) the field of archeological studies as it relates to Egypt, the Middle East, and Israel.
319 J. Maxwell Miller and John H. Hayes, *A History of Ancient Israel and Judah*, (Philadelphia, Pennsylvania: Westminster Press, 1986), p. 74.
320 Ibid., pp. 74,75.
321 Ibid., p. 76.
322 Ibid.
323 Ibid.
324 Ibid., p. 77.
325 Ibid., p. 77.
326 Ibid.
327 Ibid., p. 78.
328 Ibid., pp. 77–79.
329 James K. Hoffmeier, *Israel in Egypt—Evidence for the Authenticity of the Exodus Tradition*, (New York, NY: Oxford University Press, 1996), p. 43.
330 Ibid., pp. 25–26.
331 Ibid., pp. 52–56, note especially "Conclusion," p. 68.
332 Ibid., pp. 77–98.
333 Ibid., pp. 135–155.
334 K. A. Kitchen, *On the Reliability of the Old Testament*, (Grand Rapids, MI: William B. Eerdmans, 2003), p. 207.
335 Ibid, *On the Reliability of the Old Testament*, chapters 5, 6, pp. 159–312.
336 Ibid, p. 167.
337 Ibid, p. 167.
338 Ibid., pp. 174–175.
339 Ibid, p. 175. See also p. 191–192 for a similar naturalistic explanation of the earth swallowing up Korah and his rebels.
340 Ibid., p. 182ff.
341 Ibid., pp. 199–220.
342 Some epigraphers do not consider pictographic writing to be a fully developed form of writing, and some consider it to be an early form of cuneiform. For these reasons cuneiform is sometimes said to be the earliest form of writing.
Leonard Cotrell, *Reading the Past*, (London: J. M. Dent & Sons, Ltd, 172), pp. 8,9.
Dominique Charpin, *Reading and Writing in Babylon*, (Cambridge: Harvard University Press, 2010), trans. Jane Marie Todd, pp. 8, 9.
Jean-Jacques Glassner, *The Invention of Cuneiform*, (Baltiore, MD: The John Hopkins University Press, 2000), trans. Zainab Bahrani, Marc Van de Mieroop, pp. 3,4.
Florian Coulmas, *The Writing Systems of the World*, (Oxford: Basil Blackwell, Ltd., 1990), p. 23ff., p. 38ff.
343 This entire section follows a pattern that is similar to what the reader can see/listen to at "Patterns Of Evidence," at the website https://www.revelationmedia.com/. At that site you can watch several related videos and lectures that present this material. The credit they deserve is that they sifted through the confusing mess and chaos of Egyptian and Middle Eastern archeology to bring forth these key discoveries and present them clearly. Of special benefit

are the following: *The Exodus, The Moses Controversy, The David Rohl Lectures, The Douglas Petrovich Lectures.*

[344] Ibid., pp. 39–43ff. Dr. Rohl gives a nice summary of the chronological thinking behind the dates of Israel's kings. But see also the note a few lines below on the opinion and reasoning of Kitchen, who espouses a date of 1250 BC for the Exodus.

[345] Edwin R. Thiele, *The Mysterious Numbers of the Hebrew Kings*, (Grand Rapids, MI: The Zondervan Corporation, 1983), p. 15.

[346] Ibid., p. 23.

[347] Ibid., p. 25.

[348] Ibid., *Redating the Exodus and Conquest*, p. 75.

[349] Ibid., *Digging up Jericho*, pp. 257–258.

[350] David Rohl, *Exodus—Myth or History*, (St. Louis Park, MN: Thinking Man Media, 2015), pp. 334–335.

[351] Ibid., pp. 55, 56.

[352] Ibid., *Exodus—Myth or History*, pp. 22–26.

[353] Ibid., *Israel in Egypt—Evidence for the Authenticity of the Exodus Tradition*, pp.27–31.

[354] Ibid., *Exodus—Myth or History*, pp. 26–27.

[355] Ibid., pp. 61–69.

[356] Ibid., p. 69.

[357] Ibid., pp. 71–85. Dr. Rohl has an extended discussion of chronology ending with this astronomical correlation.

[358] Ibid., p. 77.

[359] Ibid.

[360] Ibid., *Exodus—Myth or History*, p. 78.

[361] Ibid., p. 121. See also:
Manfred Bietak, *Avaris, the Capital of the Hyksos—Recent Excavations at Tell el-Daba*,
(London: British Museum Press, 1996), pp. 3ff.

[362] Ibid., *Exodus—Myth or History*, p. 122.

[363] Ibid., *Exodus—Myth or History*, p. 122. See also,
Avaris, the Capital of the Hyksos—Recent Excavations at Tell el-Daba, pp. 19–20

[364] Ibid., *Exodus—Myth or History*, p. 122.

[365] Ibid., p. 133ff.

[366] Ibid., p. 135. The records of servants at a Theban estate show at least 50% had Semitic names. This was in Upper Egypt (that is, further south). Thus the Hebrews from the Nile delta truly had spread throughout the land.
For a description of this papyrus and other records of Asiatic servants in the 12th Dynasty see: A. R. David,
The Pyramid Builders of Ancient Egypt—A Modern Investigation of Pharaoh's Workforce,
(London: Routledge and Kegan Paul, 196), pp. 189–194.

[367] Ibid., p. 127.

[368] Ibid., pp. 106–130, 133.

[369] Ibid., *Avaris, the Capital of the Hyksos—Recent Excavations at Tell el-Daba*, pp. 20–21. Manfred only mentions it in passing and does not describe all of its features. But the next source from his expedition does. (See next note.)

[370] Ibid., p. 116. Dr. Rohl has reproduced this from:
R. Schiestl: 'The Cemeteries of F/I in the Strata d/2 (H) and d/1 (G/4), late 12th Dynasty and early 13th Dynasty' at
http://www.auaris.at/html/stratum_f1_en.html.

[371] Ibid., pp. 153–156.
See also this website for Kahun: Kahun - CreationWiki, the encyclopedia of creation science
Also, David Down, *Unwrapping the Pharaohs: How Egyptian Archaeology Confirms the Biblical Timeline*,
(Green Forest, Arizona: Master Books, A Division of New Leaf Publishing Group, 2007)

[372] Ibid., *The Pyramid Builders of Ancient Egypt*, pp. 194, 199. See also,
David Down, *Unwrapping the Pharaohs: How Egyptian Archaeology Confirms the Biblical Timeline*, p. 86.
This author also notes primitive scratchings on pottery as perhaps indicating the beginning of alphabetic writing.

[373] Ibid., *Exodus—Myth or History*. Quotes from Ipuwer are from pp. 150–152 and from Miriam Lichtheim below.

[374] Miriam Lichtheim, *Ancient Egyptian Literature*, (Oakland, CA: University of California Press, 2019), Vol. 1, p. 156.
This distinctive saying, so descriptive of Moses, is on page 156.
[Note: page numbers vary with the printing. Look for *Admonitions* by name or for Ipuwer to find this text.]

[375] Ibid., p. 151.

[376] Ibid. The quotes given here appear in fragments. I separate the fragments by "..." These sayings are scattered throughout the text and must be looked for in pieces. In *Exodus—Myth or History* Dr. Rohl gives them as a unified quote.

[377] Ibid. The quotes given here appear in fragments. I separate the fragments by "..." These sayings are scattered throughout the text and must be looked for in pieces. In *Exodus—Myth or History* Dr. Rohl gives them as a unified quote.

[378] Ibid. This key verse is on page 159.

[379] Ibid., *Exodus—Myth or* History, p. 152.

[380] Ibid., *Ancient Egyptian Literature*, Vol. 1, pp. 149–150. This is taken from her introductory remarks.

[381] Ibid. The quotes given here appear in fragments. I separate the fragments by "..." These sayings are scattered throughout the text and must be looked for in pieces. In *Exodus—Myth or History* Dr. Rohl gives them as a unified quote.

[382] Ibid., *Exodus—Myth or* History, pp. 152–153.

[383] Ibid., p. 153.

[384] John Garstang, *The Fate of Jericho Revealed by the Spade*. "The bronze age city of Jericho perished by earthquake and fire about 1400 BC." Definite conclusions, after four years of excavation, and new discoveries on a famous site. The Illustrated London News, vol. 183, no. 4939, Dec 16, 1933.

[385] Kathleen M. Kenyon, *Excavations at Jericho, Volume III, The Architecture and Stratigraphy of the Tell* (Text),
Ed. Thomas A. Holland, (London: British School of Archeology in Jerusalem, 1981), p. 109.

[386] Ibid., *Excavations at Jericho, Volume III*, Figure 4, just before p. 1.

[387] Ibid., *Exodus—Myth or* History, p. 276.
[388] Ibid., *Excavations at Jericho, Volume III*, p. 110.
[389] Ibid., *Exodus—Myth or* History, p. 277.
[390] Ibid., *Excavations at Jericho, Volume III*, p. 370.
[391] Ibid., *Exodus—Myth or* History, p. 278.
[392] Ibid.
[393] Ibid., pp. 281–282
[394] Ibid., pp. 287–290.
[395] Ibid., p. 362.
[396] Ibid.
[397] Ibid., *Redating the Exodus and Conquest*, pp. 188-210, 216.
[398] Ibid., *Digging up Jericho*, p. 260.
[399] Ibid., p. 262.
[400] Ibid., *On the Reliability of the Old Testament*, p. 187.
[401] Ibid., *Redating the Exodus and Conquest*. The quote, summarizing his points, is from pp 107 and 111. But see his extensive discussion, which covers the entire chapter, pp. 106–136.
[402] Ibid., *Excavations at Jericho, Volume I*, pp. 264, 267, 268.
[403] Ibid., *Excavations at Jericho*, Appendix C, p. 501.
[404] Andrew J. Shortland and C. Bronk Ramsey eds., *Radiocarbon and the Chronologies of Ancient Egypt*, M. Bietak, Antagonisms in Historical and Radiocarbon Chronology, (Oxford, UK: Oxbow Books, 2013), p. 77.
[405] Ibid., p. 79.
[406] Ibid., p. 81ff.
[407] From Dr. Petrovich Lectures, Lecture #4, *The World's Oldest Alphabet is Hebrew*. You can view this on the Patterns of Evidence website.
[408] Ibid.
[409] W. M. Flinders Petrie, *Researches in Sinai*, (New York: E. P. Dutton and Company, 1906), pp. 131-132.
[410] Joseph Naveh, *Early History of the Alphabet—An Introduction to West Semitic Epigraph and Palaeography*, (Jerusalem: The Magnes Press, The Hebrew University, 1982), pp. 23ff.
[411] Douglas Petrovich, *The World's Oldest Alphabet—Hebrew as the Language of the Proto-Consonantal Script*, (Jerusalem, Israel: Carta Jerusalem, 2016), Preface, p. x.
[412] Ibid., pp. 101–117.
[413] Ibid., pp. 140–153.
[414] Ibid., pp. 172–182.
[415] Ibid., pp. 158–172.
[416] Ibid., pp. 15–29.
[417] Stephania Pignattari, *Amenemhat IV and the End of the Twelfth Dynasty*, (Oxford: BAR Publishing, 2018), p. 2.
[418] Sir Alan Henderson Gardiner, *The Inscriptions of Sinai*, (London: Oxford University Press, 1955), Vol. 2, p. 206.
[419] Ibid., *Exodus—Myth or History*, p. 229.
[420] Ibid., *Early History of the Alphabet—An Introduction to West Semitic Epigraph and Palaeography*, p. 26.
[421] This has not yet been published in journals. It is described here:
ABR Researchers Discover the Oldest Known Proto-Hebrew Inscription Ever Found - Associates for Biblical Research (biblearchaeology.org)
[422] This has not yet been published in journals. It I described here:
Ancient Inscription Found from Conquest of Canaan | Patterns of Evidence
[423] Using Dr. Rohl's data and the Bible we get: 19th year of Amenemhat III is the last year of abundance. His 21st year is the 2nd year of the famine, and also the year Jacob entered Egypt. If the Exodus was in 1446 BC and the Sojourn lasted 215 years, then Jacob entered Egypt in 1661 BC, the 21st year of Amenemhat. So that pharaoh's first year had to be 1681 BC, not 1678 BC. And his father Senuseret III began his reign 20 years earlier, or 1701 BC. This adjustment of the dates by three years is commanded by the total logic of what Dr. Rohl and the Bible say when the two sources are combined to make a unified narrative. I use these adjusted/corrected dates to construct my chronology.
[424] Ibid., *Exodus—Myth or History*, pp. 93–102.
[425] Ibid., p. 97.
[426] Douglas Petrovich, Origins of the Hebrews, (Nashville, TN: New Creation, 2021), pp. 99ff.
[427] Ibid., p. 99.
[428] Ibid., p. 101.
[429] See the table of dates going back to the creation in the chapter "Babel" in this book.
Also see Appendix I and chapter 2 for a brief discussion of chronology.
[430] Ibid., p. 97.
[431] Ibid., p. 53.
[432] Ibid., pp. 26ff.
[433] David M. Rohl, *The Lost Testament—From Eden to Exile: The Five-Thousand-Year History of the People of the Bible*, (London, UK: Random House UK Ltd, 2002), p. 221.
[434] K. A. Kitchen, *On the Reliability of the Old Testament*, (Grand Rapids, MI: William B. Eerdmans, 2003), pp. 329–330. Also see the footnote in *The New Defender's Study Bible* on Exodus 6:3, pp 134–5.
[435] Henry Denzinger, *Compendium of Creeds, Definitions, and Declarations on Matters of Faith and Morals*, forty-third edition, San Francisco, CA: Ignatius Press, 2012), p. 687.
Response of the Biblical Commission, June 27, 1906; # 3396.

The Genesis Documents
436 Ean-Jacques Glassner, *The Invention of Cuneiform Writing in Sumer*, trans. & ed. Zainab Bahrani and Marc Van de Mieroop, (Baltimore, MD: The Johns Hopkins University Press, 2003), Introduction, p. 1.
437 Leonard Cottrell, *Reading the Past—The Story of Deciphering Ancient Languages*, (London: J. M. Dent & Sons, Ltd., 1972), pp. 4–8.
438 Ibid., *The Invention of Cuneiform Writing in Sumer*, selected from pp. 49,50.
439 P. J. Wiseman, *Ancient Records and the Structure of Genesis: A Case for Literary Unity*, ed. D. J. Wiseman (Nashville, TN: Thomas Nelson, 1985), p. 48.
440 Ibid., *The Invention of Cuneiform Writing in Sumer*, p. 52.
441 Ibid., pp. 56, 57.
442 C. B. F. Walker, *Reading the Past—Cuneiform*, (Berkley, CA: University of California Press, 1988), p. 38.
443 Ibid., p. 33.
444 Ibid., p. 17.
445 Edward E. Crawford, "Proto-Sumerian Inscriptions in the Ahora Gorge of Buyuk Agri (Greater Mt. Ararat), Turkey," in *Research & Exploration, A Scholarly Publication of the National Geographic Society*, published quarterly, vol. 10, Autumn of 1994, p. 484.
446 Ibid.
447 Ibid., pp. 19-20.
448 Ibid., pp. 54-55.
449 Dr. Clifford Wilson, *Visual Highlights of the Bible* (Boronia, Australia: Pacific Christian Ministries, 1993), p. 13.
450 P. J. Wiseman, *Ancient Records and the Structure of Genesis*, pp. 57-58.
451 Erle Leichty, *The Colophon*, in *Studies Presented to A. Leo Oppenheim*. eds. Robert D. Biggs and John A. Brinkman (Chicago: Oriental Institute, 1964), p. 147.
452 Ibid., p. 150.
453 Ibid., p. 147.
454 Christine Proust, *Reading Colophons from Mesopotamian Clay-Tablets Dealing with Mathematics*, in *NTM Zeitschrift fur Geschichte der Wissenschaften, Technik und Medizin*, 20, no. 3, (2012): 123–156. See the beginning section, p. 123.
455 Erle Leichty, *The Colophon*, pp. 147–148.
456 James Strong, *Enhanced Strong's Lexicon* (Elmira, Ont: Woodside Bible Fellowship, 1995).
457 R. Laird Harris, Gleason L. Archer Jr., and Bruce K. Waltke, eds., *Theological Wordbook of the Old Testament* (Chicago: Moody Press, 1999), pp. 378–379.
458 Francis Brown, Samuel Rolles Driver, and Charles Augustus Briggs, *Enhanced Brown-Driver-Briggs Hebrew and English Lexicon* (Oxford: Clarendon Press, 1977), p. 410.
459 Ludwig Koehler et al., *The Hebrew and Aramaic Lexicon of the Old Testament*, trans. M. E. J. Richardson (New York: E.J. Brill, 1994–2000), pp. 1699–1700.
460 P. J. Wiseman, *Ancient Records and the Structure of Genesis*, p. 62.
461 Ibid., pp. 54-55.
462 Erle Leichty, *The Colophon*, p. 148.
463 P. J. Wiseman, *Ancient Records and the Structure of Genesis*, pp. 81–83.
464 Ibid.,
465 Ibid., pp. 82–83.
466 Ibid., p. 67.
467 Ibid., p. 69.
468 Christine Proust, *Reading Colophons from Mesopotamian Clay-Tablets Dealing with Mathematics* See the beginning section, p. 124.
469 Ibid., note 16, p. 153.
470 Ibid.
471 T. Rice Holmes, *Caesar's Conquest of Gaul—An Historical Narrative*, Second Edition (London, Macmillan and Co., Limited, 190), Chapter II, pp. 26, 27.
472 P. J. Wiseman, *Ancient Records and the Structure of Genesis*, p. 112.
473 Ibid., pp. 88–90.
474 Ibid., pp. 115–116.
475 Ibid., pp. 89–90.
476 *The Jerusalem Bible* (Garden City, NY: Doubleday, 1970), p. 3.

The Creation
477 P. J. Wiseman, *Ancient Records and the Structure of Genesis*, p. 88.
478 Ibid., pp. 88-89
479 Ibid., p. 89.
480 Ibid., p. 90.
481 Dr. Clifford D. Wilson, *Visual Highlights of the Bible* (Victoria, Aust: Pacific Christian Ministries, 1993), vol.1, p 13.
482 See http://www.sacred-texts.com/nam/mmp/mmp08.htm.
483 See http://www.sacred-texts.com/nam/mmp/mmp06.htm.
484 Ibid.
485 See http://www.read-legends-and-myths.com/aztec-creation-myth.html.
See also another summary at: http://indigenouspeople.net/aztecs.htm.

486 See http://www.bigmyth.com/myths/english/2_inca_full.htm.
487 See http://indigenouspeople.net/commcrea.htm.
488 See http://www.bigorrin.org/archive31.htm.
489 There is a delightful website that admirably shows us the enormous size of our universe. No human being could ever figure out how it came to be. The size of the cosmos is unknown and is forever beyond our finding out! Search for "The Scale of the Universe 2" or go to this location directly: http://www.htwins.net/scale2/
490 St. John Chrysostom, *Homilies on Genesis*, "Homily 14," 2, vol. 74, in *The Fathers of the Church*, (Washington, DC: The Catholic University of America Press, 1986)
491 Ibid., "Homily 2," 4.
492 Saadia Gaon, *The Book of Beliefs and Opinions*, "Treatise 1," Exordium.
493 Basil the Great, "Homily 1," 2, in *Exegetical Homilies (on the Hexaemeron)*, p. 53.
494 *Catechism of the Catholic Church*, Sections 290-292.
495 Basil the Great, "Homily 1," 6, in *Exegetical Homilies (on the Hexaemeron)*.
496 Heinrich Denzinger, *Compendium of Creeds, Definitions, and Declarations on Matters of Faith and Morals*, **800**, p 266. Here is the relevant text of the declaration:
> We firmly believe and confess without reservation that there is only one true God, eternal, infinite, and unchangeable, incomprehensible, almighty, and ineffable, the Father, the Son, and the Holy Spirit; three Persons, indeed, but one essence, substance, or nature entirely simple. The Father is from no one, the Son from the Father only, and the Holy Spirit equally from both. Without beginning, always, and without end, the Father begets, the Son is born, and the Holy Spirit proceeds. They are of the same substance and fully equal, equally almighty, and equally eternal. **(They are) the one principle of the universe, the creator of all things, visible and invisible, spiritual and corporeal, who by his almighty power from the beginning of time made at once out of nothing both orders of creatures, the spiritual and the corporeal, that is, the angelic and the earthly, and then the human creature**, who, as it were, shares in both orders, being composed of spirit and body. For the devil and the other demons were indeed created by God naturally good, but they became evil by their own doing. As for man, he sinned at the suggestion of the devil.

497 Ibid., "Homily 1," 5.
498 Ibid., "Homily 1," 4.
499 Dr. Don DeYoung, *Thousands, Not Billions* (Green Forest, AR: Master Books, 2005).
500 Paul Geim, Geoscience Research Institute Origins 51, 2001, pp. 6-30. This article can be found on-line here: https://grisda.org/origins-51006
Or search for "Geoscience Research Institute Origins 51, 2001"
501 Dr. Don DeYoung, *Thousands . . . not Billions*, (Master Books, Inc., Green Forest, AR: 2005) The author describes the project, the gathering and testing of the samples, and the incontrovertible results.
502 Contested Bones, Christopher Rupe and Dr. John Sanford (FMS Publications, 2017), p. 264.
503 Steven A. Austin, "Excess Argon within Mineral Concentrates from the New Dacite Lava Dome at Mount St. Helens Volcano," Creation Ex Nihilo Technical Journal, Vol. 10, no. 3 (1996): p. 335-343.) This article is on-line here: https://www.icr.org/i/pdf/technical/Excess-Argon-New-Lava-Dome-at-Mount-St-Helens.pdf
Or search for "Excess Argon within Mineral Concentrates from the New Dacite Lava Dome at Mount St. Helens Volcano"
504 Dr. Andrew A. Snelling, "The Cause of Anomalous Potassium-argon 'Ages' for recent Andesite Flows at Mt. Ngauruhoe, New Zealand, and the Implication for Potassium-argon 'dating,'" in Robert E. Walsh, editor, *Proceedings of the Fourth International Conference on Creationism* (Pittsburgh, PA: Creation Science Fellowship, 1998), p. 503-525. This can be found on-line by searching for the title or by going to this site: https://www.semanticscholar.org/paper/The-Cause-of-Anomalous-Potassium-Argon-%E2%80%9CAges%E2%80%9D-for-Snelling/a85f02167455024c6e8cb5b4e611022c62eef44f
Or you can just search for the full title.
505 Dalrymple, G.B., $^{40}Ar/^{36}Ar$ Analyses of Historic Lava Flows, Earth and Planetary Science Letters, 6 (1969), pp. 47-55 This full paper can be requested at this site: https://www.researchgate.net/publication/223024476_Argon_isotopic_composition_of_some_Hawaiian_historical_lavas
506 Dr. Don DeYoung, *Thousands . . . Not Billions*, (Master Books, Inc., Green Forest, AR: 2005), p. 126.
507 See a fuller explanation of the group's presentation at this website: Dinosaurs and C-14 - Ancient America. See a sampling of the many C-14 anomalies that form the broader picture of a massive dating problem here: C-14 Dating (sciencevsevolution.org).
Even these many issues are only a small part of the widespread tests indicating a young age for the crust of the earth—test results from various types of tests, and coming from many researchers.
508 Thank you to colleague Pamela Ackers who supplied me with these communications, since Hugh Miller died recently.
509 Many have pondered throughout the ages if or why the specific sacrifice of the cross was necessary. (See Peter Lombard, *The Sentences*, 20, 1–2, vol. 3. Lombard quotes Augustine, *On the Trinity*, 13, 10 n13, for his thoughts.)
510 Jerome, *Saint Jerome's Hebrew Questions on Genesis*, 1:2, p. 30. (see quotation from Jerome in "The Ancient Faith")
511 Augustine, *The Literal Meaning of Genesis*, 1, 9.
512 St. John Chrysostom, *Homilies on Genesis*, "Homily 5," 9.
513 Ibid., "Homily 5," 11.
514 Basil the Great, *Exegetical Homilies (on the Hexaemeron)*, "Homily 3," 2.
515 St. John Chrysostom, *Homilies on Genesis*, "Homily 6," 12.
516 Thomas Aquinas, http://dhspriory.org/thomas/, q. 67.
517 Ibid.
518 St. John Chrysostom, *Homilies on Genesis*, "Homily 3," 6.
519 Augustine, *Unfinished Literal Commentary on Genesis*, 28.
520 Augustine, *The City of God*, 11, 7.

521 Ibid.
522 I have found ten verses in Scripture where the Hebrew word *natah* is used to state the Lord "stretched out" the heavens. This Hebrew word is translated as "stretch out" in all ten of these verses (NASB). Note: *natah* can also mean "pitch" (referring to a tent) or "turn, pervert" (as in moral deflection).
  The 10 verses are: Isaiah 40:22, Isaiah 42:5, Isaiah 44:24, Isaiah 45:12, Isaiah 51:13
  Job 9:8, Psalm 104:2, Jeremiah 10:12, Jeremiah 51:15, Zechariah 12:1
  Additionally in Isaiah 40:22 the Hebrew word *mathach* is translated as "spread [the heavens] out."
  Finally in Isaiah 48:13 the Hebrew word *taphach* is translated as "spread out [the heavens]."
523 For a rather technical set of papers on this see: http://www.planckvacuum.com/. But also notice another paper that dismisses this idea as fanciful and unworkable: http://www.ptep-online.com/2006/PP-06-13.PDF. In cosmology the "Planck epoch" is the earliest stage of the Big Bang, before the duration of time that passed was equal to the Planck time, or approximately 10^{-43} seconds after the Big Bang began, before the period of inflation.
524 Ibid., 11, 29.
525 Hippolytus of Rome, *Fragments from Commentaries on Various Books of Scripture*, p. 163.
526 Augustine, *On Genesis: A Refutation of the Manichees*, 1, 11, in *The Works of Augustine; A Translation for the 21st Century*, Part 1, vol. 13 (Hyde Park, NY: New York City Press, 2002).
527 Augustine, *The Literal Meaning of Genesis*, 5, 40–46.
528 An excellent treatment of this evidence can be found in *Carved in Stone: Geological Evidence of the Worldwide Flood* By Timothy Clarey, published in 2020 by The Institute for Creation Research. A simple introduction to these concepts is found on pp 51ff. More details, including primary source references, are abundantly preset throughout the work.
529 Augustine, *Unfinished Literal Commentary on Genesis*, 34.
530 Didymus the Blind, *Commentary on Genesis*, 1, pp. 35–36.
531 But see also Augustine's discussion of this point in *On Genesis: A Refutation of the Manichees*, 1, 20.
532 Augustine, *Unfinished Literal Commentary on Genesis*, 37.
533 Increasing numbers of secular scientists are publicly rejecting the Big Bang as impossible/untenable.
  An open statement to this effect, signed by hundreds of such authorities, can be found at: http://blog.lege.net/cosmology/cosmologystatement_org.html. Some statements made there:

  - The Big Bang today relies on a growing number of hypothetical entities, things that we have never observed—inflation, dark matter and dark energy are the most prominent examples.

    But the big bang theory can't survive without these fudge factors. Without the hypothetical inflation field, the big bang does not predict the smooth, isotropic cosmic background radiation that is observed, because there would be no way for parts of the universe that are now more than a few degrees away in the sky to come to the same temperature and thus emit the same amount of microwave radiation.

    Without some kind of dark matter, unlike any that we have observed on Earth despite 20 years of experiments, big-bang theory makes contradictory predictions for the density of matter in the universe. Inflation requires a density 20 times larger than that implied by big bang nucleosynthesis, the theory's explanation of the origin of the light elements. And without dark energy, the theory predicts that the universe is only about 8 billion years old, which is billions of years younger than the age of many stars in our galaxy.

  - What is more, the Big Bang Theory can boast of no quantitative predictions that have subsequently been validated by observation. The successes claimed by the theory's supporters consist of its ability to retrospectively fit observations with a steadily increasing array of adjustable parameters, just as the old Earth-centered cosmology of Ptolemy needed layer upon layer of epicycles.

  Of course, these scientists want research funding to go toward other models that **might** explain the naturalistic origin of the universe. But at this time no other conceivable naturalistic explanation exists.
534 The picture of "the deep space field" at 13.2 billion light years away is available on-line. Just do a search for "Hubble deep space field" and it will come up. The successor to the Hubble and a greatly improved version of it, the James Webb Space Telescope, is due to be launched in 2021 (not 2018 as hoped).
535 Song Chen, *Large Scale Structures and Radio Galaxy Survey*, Supervisor: Prof. Dr. Dominik J. Schwarz, Faculty of Physics, University of Bielfeld, September, 2105, § 1.1 Homogeneity and Isotropy, p. 1.
536 Carl Sagan, *Cosmos*, (New York, NY: Random House, 1980), p. 193.
537 Y. P. Varshni, *The Red Shift Hypothesis for Quasars: Is the Earth the Center of the Universe?*, September, 1975, Department of Physics, University of Ottawa, Canada, p. 4.
  See also this related paper:
  Note: THESE TWO PAPERS ARE ACCESSIBLE ON-LINE, NOT JUST IN SCIENTIFIC JOURNALS
  Ashok K. Singal, *Is there a violation of the Copernican principle in radio sky?*, Indian Space Research Organization, Bengaluru, India, May 2013.
    Cosmic Microwave Background Radiation (CMBR) observations from the WMAP satellite have shown some unexpected anisotropies, which surprisingly seem to be aligned with the ecliptic [1,2]. This alignment has been dubbed the "axis of evil" with very damaging implications for the standard model of cosmology[3]. <u>The latest data from the Planck satellite have confirmed the presence of these anisotropies</u>[4]. Here we report even larger anisotropies in the sky distributions of powerful extended quasars and some other sub-classes of radio galaxies in the 3CRR catalogue, one of the oldest and most intensively studies sample of strong radio sources[5,6,7]. The anisotropies lie about a plane passing through the two equinoxes and the north celestial pole (NCP). We can rule out at a 99.995% confidence level the hypothesis that these asymmetries are merely due to statistical fluctuations . . . **Two pertinent questions then arise. First, why should there be such large anisotropies present in the sky distribution of some of the most distant discrete sources implying inhomogeneities in the universe at very large scales** (covering a fraction of the universe)? **What is intriguing even further is why such anisotropies should lie about a great circle decided purely**

by the orientation of earth's rotation axis and/or the axis of its revolution around the sun? **It looks as if these axes have a preferential placement in the larger scheme of things,** implying an apparent breakdown of the Copernican principle or its more generalization, cosmological principle, upon which all modern cosmological theories are based. (p. 1.)

See also this related paper:

Ashok K. Singal, *A large anisotropy in the sky distribution of 3CRR quasars and other radio galaxies*, Astronomy and Research Division, Physical Research Laboratory, Navravgpuru, Ahmedabad–380 009, India, Astrophysics and Space Science, Vol. 357, May 2015.

EXAMPLES OF OTHER RELATED ARTICLES, BY TITLE ONLY, AVAILABLE ON-LINE INCLUDE:
A review of redshift and its interpretation in cosmology and astrophysics, not dated but 2008 or later.
Lecture 20: The Redshift Controversy, The University of California, Irvine, CA, not dated.
Quasars and Galactic Nuclei, a Half-Century Agitated Story, September 2006.
Cosmology and Cosmogony in a Cyclic Universe, January 2008.
The Cosmological Constant and the Redshift of Quasars, not dated but 1992 or later.
The Reciprocal System of physical theory: Quasars—Three Years Later, September 2012.
Research on candidates for non-cosmological redshifts, September 2005.
The Shell Model of the Universe: A Universe Generated from Multiple Big Bangs, February 2016.

[538] Y. P. Varshni, *The Red Shift Hypothesis for Quasars: Is the Earth the Center of the Universe?*, p. 8.

[539] Ibid., p. 4.

[540] The discussion of this topic spans many technical papers. Here are a few:

ALL OF THESE PAPERS ARE ACCESSIBLE ON-LINE, NOT JUST IN SCIENTIFIC JOURNALS
Schwarz, Dominik & Starkman, Glenn & Huterer, etc al., *Is the Low-ℓ Microwave Background Cosmic?*
In Physical Review Letters, December 2004

The large-angle (low-ℓ) correlations of the Cosmic Microwave Background exhibit several statistically significant anomalies compared to the standard inflationary cosmology [i.e., Big Bang]. We show that the quadrupole plane and the three octopole planes are far more aligned than previously thought (99.9% C.L.). Three of these planes are orthogonal to the ecliptic at 99.1% C.L., and the normal to these planes are aligned at 99.6% C.L. with the direction of the cosmological dipole and with the equinoxes. (p. 1.) [Note: "C.L." means "confidence level."]

We find it hard to believe that these correlations are just statistical fluctuations around standard inflationary cosmology's prediction of statistically isotropic Gaussian random aℓms [Gaussian random distributions] . . . The correlation of the normals with the ecliptic poles suggest an unknown source or sink of CMB radiation or an unrecognized systematic. (p. 5.)

Prabhakar Tiwari, Rahul Kothari, et al., *Dipole anisotropy in sky brightness and source count distribution in radio NVSS data*, in Astro Particle Physics, 2014-06-004.

Our results suggest that the Universe is intrinsically anisotropic [a violation of the Cosmological Principal] with the axis of anisotropy axis pointing roughly towards the CMBR dipole direction., p. 1.

Glenn D. Starkmen, Craig J. Copi, Dragan Huterer, Dominik Schwarz, et al., *The Oddly Quiet Universe: How The CMB Challenges Cosmology's Standard Model*, Adapted from a talk given by one of us at the SEENET-2011 meeting in August 2001 on the Serbian bank of the Danube River.
[SEENET: Southeastern European Network in Mathematical and Theoretical Physics]

In the rest of this paper we will investigate the large angle properties of the CMB. We will discover that if one uses the full-sky ILC map [Internal Linear Combination, from the Wilkinson Microwave Anisotropy Probe, WMAP] then one finds very odd correlations in the map, that correlate unexpectedly to the Solar System . . . Looking into this anomaly more deeply we will find that it remains robust through all seven years of published WMAP data, and furthermore that it is very difficult to explain within the context of the canonical Inflationary Lambda Cold Dark Model of cosmology. (p. 2.)

[That is, it does not fit the Big Bang Theory with dark matter and dark energy included in it.]

Future results from the Planck satellite may show these large-angle/low-ℓ anomalies to be nothing more than systematic errors in the measurements or analysis of the WMAP (and the COBE) team, but unless and until they do these anomalies remain the outstanding point of disagreement between the standard cosmological model and observations., p. 12.

[Note: the Planck satellite confirmed the anisotropies and emphasized them in greater detail. See the acknowledgement of this in the underlined comments by Ashok K. Singal a few notes above.]

These results are examined, explained, and illustrated nicely and non-technically in the following work:
Robert A. Sungenis, *Geocentrism 101: An Introduction into the Science of Geocentric Cosmology, 4th Edition*, 2013. See chapter 20, p. 191ff.

[541] This goes along with the idea that the observable universe is part of a much larger universe, much of which lies beyond the limits of our observation because those far distant galaxies are receding at speeds faster than light, and thus light from them never reaches us. This "limit of observability" is called the horizon of the universe. It is like the horizon of the earth that makes ships far out to sea invisible because they are below earth's curvature. Scientists note that microwave photons from opposite sectors of the cosmos appear to be in thermal equilibrium, or at almost the same temperature. This implies that the universe has come to this state of equilibrium through interactions between different regions. Unfortunately in the Big Bang theory this is not possible for there was no moment during the Big Bang before those photons were emitted when those regions could have interacted, because of the size of the cosmic horizon. Light does not travel fast enough to provide the needed communication between these distant sectors of the universe. This would prevent the smoothing of the universe, or the homogeneity, that we observe. Thus the Big Bang could not predict the origin of the basic observed homogeneous structure of the cosmos. Scientists do not want to replace the Big Bang Theory totally, but they need to add on the period of inflation quite early in the

process. It comes to an end at 10^{-32} seconds and is followed by the more conventional expansion we observe now. Note that the numbers I give (10^{-32}, 10^{54}, etc.) differ depending on which source you read on this subject.

[542] The name of the paper that Michelson-Morley wrote is: *On the Relative Motion of the Earth and the Luminiferous Ether*. It can be found on-line by entering the title in any search engine. In the section labeled [314] it states:
"It appears, from all that precedes, reasonably certain that if there be any relative motion between the earth and The luminiferous ether, it must be small."
Also noted is that the experimenters removed the possibility that the solar system is moving through the ether, which might have been countering the motion of the earth around the sun. To rule this out they repeated the experiment at three-month intervals, when the earth would be moving in its orbit around the sun in different directions.

Their experiment was preceded by an experiment by George Airy in 1881 that also indicated a fixed earth. His title: *On the Supposed Alteration in the Amount of Astronomical Aberration of Light, Produced by the Passage of Light through a Considerable Thickness of Refracting Medium* is partially available on-line.

[543] The experiment showed a small amount of either drag, about 5% of what was expected. This small positive result is best explained by the fact that the rotating universe that is geometrically centered on the sun has the center of its mass at the position of the earth, so it will sometimes make the ether register this small "ether drift." But for sure the earth could not be revolving around the sun as had been expected by every scientist in the world.

[544] See Robert A. Sungenis, Ph.D., *Geocentrism 101: An Introduction to the Science of Geocentric Cosmology*, see p. 147, where he lists many of the eminent men who worked with interferometers and did similar experiments.

[545] In the Tycho Brahe view of the solar system, the sun revolves around the earth, but the universe of stars revolves around the sun as it orbits the earth. Therefore the sun is the geometric center of the universe, but the earth is the center of mass for the universe. From our vantage point on earth these motions would look exactly like what we observe as we peer out into the heavens, just as the heliocentric view of the cosmos describes what we are seeing. In other words, both models describe the heavenly motions perfectly. So considering observational data only, either model could be correct.

An interesting historical tidbit: In the 11th century Hildegard of Bingen, a German Benedictine abbess, writer, mystic, visionary, philosopher and composer described her visions of the solar system. They perfectly match the Tycho Brahe model, the only geocentric model of the heavens that accurately describes the motion of the heavenly bodies as seen from earth. In 2012 she was declared a saint and a doctor of the Church by Pope Benedict XVI. (See Helmut Posch, *The True Conception of the World according to Hildegard Von Bingen*, trans. Dean H. Kenyon.)

[546] See W. G. V. Rosser, *An Introduction to the Theory of Relativity*, (London: Butterworth & Co., 1964), pp 57–60. He explains the consternation of the scientific community at the results of the scientific community, the various proposed explanations that were offered and their inadequacies, **the loathing of people to accept the conclusion that the earth was fixed in the ether field, in "an omnipotent position,"** and the eventual acceptance of Special Relativity as the final conclusion from the experiment, as its most preferable explanation.

[547] A. A. Michelson, *The Effect of the Earth's Rotation on the Velocity of Light*, April 1925. This can be found on-line By searching by title. Or, it is at: http://articles.adsabs.harvard.edu/full/seri/ApJ../0061//0000145.000.html
On the third page of the paper, in describing the set-up of the experiment, he states:
In general the two sets of fringes will not coincide in position, entirely aside from any question of ether drift or the earth's rotation, unless the two direct images and the two reflected images of the source are exactly superposed. The central fringes of the set formed by the mirrors of the short circuit will be halfway between the direct and reflected images of the source, and the central fringe of the long line would be halfway between the direct and reflected images if there were no difference due to the earth's rotation.
On the second last page of the paper, listed as page 143, they state:
The displacement of the fringes due to the earth's rotation was measured on many different days, with complete readjustments of the mirrors, with the reflected image sometimes on the right and sometimes on the left of the transmitted image, and by different observers. The deflections were averaged usually in sets of twenty, in the order in which they were taken. The resulting means are given in table I. The entire set of two hundred and sixty-nine determinations and their distribution about the mean value is shown graphically in Figure 3. The final displacement, expressed as a fraction of a fringe, is $0.230 \pm .005$ obs. $0.236 \pm .002$ calc.
In view of the difficulty of the observations, this must be taken to mean that the observed and calculated shifts Agree within the limits of observational error.
Note: There were 269 trials performed in this experiment, which showed with a 98% certainty that there is a relative rotation between earth and space. Also, this experiment was based on the same empirical principle as the 1887 experiment by Michelson-Morley; that is, that ether exists and causes impedance on the speed of light, which therefore verifies that the 1887 experiment did NOT produce a revolution about the sun and the 1925 experiment certainly DID show a relative rotation between earth and space. Since heliocentrism needs both a revolution of the earth around the sun and a rotation of the earth in space the two experiments combined falsify heliocentrism.

Georges Sagnac, his 1913 paper in French is nicely commented on in English by Robert Sungenis, PhD., in *Geocentrism 101, An Introduction into the Science of Geocentric Cosmology*. He quotes Sagnac on his results:
"In clear conception it ought to be regarded as a direct manifestation of the luminous ether. . . ." (p. 150.)
But the scientific community continues to re-explain this effect, which is necessary for GPS satellites to operate in a correct and accurate manner, in relativistic terms. The confusion from this attempt is shown by the fact that over a dozen different explanations have been offered for using Sagnac. Einstein stated that the existence of the ether drag was certain proof that his theory was wrong. Also, search for this pdf paper: *Sagnac Effect in GPS* for yet one more non-relativistic explanation. Sagnac interpreted his results himself as due to the ether, as the quotation shows.

[548] These forces are the product of a rotating universe, as acknowledged by science. (See Wikipedia "Centrifugal force," the subsection "Force" for an explanation. In a rotating cosmos these are NOT fictitious forces.) The Coriolis force is twice the magnitude of the centrifugal force, so we obtain a net centripetal force on all celestial objects, which is just enough to maintain their respective positions in the rotating universe without being forced outward or sideways. This is

why the dynamics of the geocentric model will produce the same effect in the motion of the heavenly bodies as what we observe now. But in the geocentric model, when we get far from the earth into deep space, the rotating and accelerating galaxies would have additional forces to help explain their (presently incomprehensible) motions.

Following are quotes from Einstein, a modern author Julian B. Barbour, Einstein again, another modern author Steven Weinberg, Isaac Newton, and another modern author Max Born.

Albert Einstein and Leopold Infeld, *The Evolution of Physics: The growth of Ideas from Early Concepts to Relativity and Quanta*, (New York: Simon and Schuster, 1961), p. 212. In speaking of how we can view the heavens in either a heliocentric or geocentric manner, not considering the necessary dynamic forces involved, Einstein says:
> The struggle, so violent in the early days of science, between the views of Ptolemy and Copernicus would then be quite meaningless. Either coordinate system could be used with equal justification. The two sentences: 'the sun is at rest and the Earth moves,' or 'the sun moves and the Earth is at rest,' would simply mean two different conventions concerning two different coordinate systems.

The dynamic forces referred to in the following are the Euler, Coriolis, and Centrifugal forces of the Geocentric Model. These men are not just speaking about redescribing the heavenly motions from a different coordinate system, but are proposing new forces to explain the motion of the heavenly bodies that would arise in a geocentric model of the world.

Julian B. Barbour and Herbert Pfister, eds., *Mach's Principle: From Newton's Bucket to Quantum Gravity*, (Boston: Birkhauser, 1995), p. 69. He cites a 1914 paper by Einstein, trans. Carl Hoefer. In it Einstein says, in reference to the dynamic forces that would be needed to explain the motion of the heavenly bodies in a geocentric model of the universe. Here Einstein also takes up the idea of Ernst Mach that distant stars influence local forces. In this case, and in these other quotes, Mach's Principle is directly linked to the geocentric model of the universe.
> We need not necessarily trace the existence of these centrifugal forces back to an absolute movement of K' [Earth]; we can instead just as well trace them back to the rotational movement of the distant ponderable masses [the stars] in relation to K' [Earth] whereby we treat K' [Earth] as 'at rest.'

Steven Weinberg, *To Explain the World: The Discovery of Modern Science*, (London: Allen Lane, an imprint of Penguin Books, 2015), pp. 251–252. The author says the following when discussing the dynamic forces that are associated with the geocentric model of the cosmos:
> The success of Newton's treatment of the motion of planets and comets shows that the inertial frames in the neighborhood of the solar system are those in which the Sun rather than the Earth is at rest (or moving with constant velocity). According to general relativity, this is because that is the frame of reference in which the matter of distant galaxies is not revolving around the solar system. In this sense, Newton's theory provided a solid basis for preferring the Copernican theory to that of Tycho. But in general relativity we can use any frame of reference we like, not just inertial frames. If we were to adopt a frame of reference like Tycho's in which the Earth is at rest, then the distant galaxies would seem to be executing circular turns once a year, and **in general relativity this enormous motion would create forces akin to gravitation, which would act on the Sun and planets and give them the motions of the Tychonic theory.** Newton seems to have had a hint of this. In an unpublished "Proposition 43" that did not make it into the *Principia,* Newton acknowledged that Tycho's theory could be true if some other force besides ordinary gravitation acted on the Sun and planets. [Bolding mine]

Here is Newton's Proposition 43, explaining the dynamic forces involved in a geocentric cosmology. This is from: Robert A. Sungenis, Ph.D., *Geocentrism 101: An Introduction to the Science of Geocentric Cosmology*, p. 48.

Dr. Sungenis gives us Proposition 43 from Newton, which "was originally planned to be added to page 510." It is:
> In order for the Earth to be at rest in the center of the system of the Sun, Planets, and Comets, there is required both universal gravity and another force in addition that acts on all bodies equally according to the quantity of matter in each of them and is equal and opposite to the accelerative gravity with which the Earth tends to the Sun . . . For, such a force, acting on all bodies equally and along parallel lines, does not change their position among themselves, and permits bodies to move among themselves through the force of universal gravity in the same way as if it were not acting on them. Since this force is equal and opposite to its gravity toward the Sun, the Earth can truly remain in equilibrium between these two forces and be at rest. And thus celestial bodies can move around the Earth at rest, as in the Tychonic system.

Max Born, *Einstein's Theory of Relativity*, (New York: Dover Publications, Inc., 1965), pp. 344–346.
> Furthermore [in General Relativity], we are quite free to refer the laws of physics not to the ordinary system of coordinates. . . . The general form of all physical laws remains always the same. . . . This invariance of the laws alone contains the difference between the new and the old dynamics.
>
> In the general theory of relativity . . . the ordinary geometrical and mechanical formulae hold in . . . any other (say rotating) system of reference . . . . Thus we may return to Ptolemy's point of view of a "motionless earth." This would mean that we use a system of reference rigidly fixed to the earth in which all stars are performing a rotational motion with the same angular velocity around the earth's axis. It is not sufficient simply to transform the usual metric . . . to this rotating system; **one has to show that the transformed metric can be regarded as produced, according to Einstein's field equations, by rotating distant masses. This has been done by [Walter] Thirring. He calculated the field due to a rotating, hollow, thick-walled sphere and proved that inside the cavity it behaved as if there were centrifugal and other inertial forces usually attributed to absolute space.** [For a review of Thirring's work see Robert Sungenis Ph.D., and Robert Bennett, Ph.D., *Galileo was Wrong, the Church was Right*, Vol. 2, pp. 116–119] [Continuing the quotation of Dr. Born, he says:]
>
> Thus from Einstein's point of view Ptolemy and Copernicus are equally right. What point of view is chosen is a matter of expediency. . . . But it is meaningless to call the gravitational fields that occur when a different system of reference is chosen "fictitious" in contrast with the" real" fields produced by near masses . . . . A gravitational field is neither" real" nor" fictitious" in itself. It has no meaning at all independent of the choice of coordinates. . . . **Nor are the fields distinguished by the fact that some are directly produced by masses while others**

are not; in the one case it is particularly the near masses that produce an effect; <u>in the other it is the distant masses of the cosmos</u>.

In *Relativity: The Special and General Theory*, (Gloucester, Mass.: Peter Smith, 1959), trans. Robert W. Lawson. Einstein explains his general principle of relativity as including "all bodies of reference . . . whatever be their state of motion." (p. 72.) Einstein explains why both uniform motion and acceleration must be "relative" in pages 78–83. It is because inertial and gravitational mass are necessarily equivalent. This extended relativity can only be accomplished by using Mach's ideas of the distant stars as related to nearby bodies and as causing their inertia. Thus these "fictitious" forces must exist and be actively involved in upholding the working of a geocentric model Of the cosmos. [All bolding and underlining in this end note are mine]

[549] Edwin Powel Hubble, *The Observational Approach to Cosmology*, (Oxford: Clarendon Press, 1937)

Such a condition would imply that we occupy a unique position in the universe, analogous, in a sense, to the ancient conception of a central earth. The hypothesis cannot be disproved, **but it is unwelcome and would be accepted only as a last resort in order to save phenomena**. (p. 50) [bold mine]

But the unwelcome supposition of a favoured location [of the earth at the center of the cosmos] **must be avoided at all costs.** (p. 51) [bold mine]

[550] For instance, a rotating universe has angular momentum, which cannot be decreased, only transferred within itself, from one object to another. A spiral galaxy created spinning by God would be able to take in the angular momentum. This is probably what is holding together the spiral galaxies as they rotate, as observed in the depths of space.

[551] If we view the Scriptures as speaking of things as they actually are, as the church believed in the Middle Ages, (and not as speaking just of appearances) as was explained when opposing the heliocentric theories of Copernicus and Galileo, then many Scriptures outside of the creation account state that the earth is fixed and unmovable. This implies that the earth does not go around the sun, and so the sun must go around the earth. Some examples: Joshua 10:10–14, the account of how the sun and moon stood still in the sky. The earth did not stop rotating, rather the heavenly bodies stopped their motion. Habakkuk 3:11 refers to this event and reiterates that the heavenly bodies stood still. 2 Kings 20:9–12 is the account of the sign given to Hezekiah that he would indeed be healed by the Lord. It says that Isaiah cried to the Lord and He brought the shadow back ten steps, by which it had gone down on the Stairway of Ahaz. Isaiah 38:8 says, "So the sun turned back on the dial the ten steps by which it had declined." In 2 Chronicles 32:31 it seems as if the rulers of Babylon sent envoys to Hezekiah to inquire about this wonder, and thus they must have seen it from hundreds of miles away in their own country. 1 Chronicles 16:30 says "The earth stands firm, never to be moved." Psalm 93:1 says, "The world is established, it will never be moved." Psalm 96:10 says the same thing. Psalm 75:3 speaks of the earth tottering (at the time of God's judgment) but it is the Lord Who keeps steady its pillars (apparently under all other conditions). Psalm 104:4 says that God set the earth on its foundations and it will never be shaken. Psalm 119:90 says God established the earth and it stands fast. Ecclesiastes 1:4–7 says the earth remains forever, but the sun rises, goes down, and hastens to the place where it rises.

Thus, although no experiment can determine if the earth is fixed and the heavens rotate around the axis of the earth, **or** the heavens are fixed, and the earth rotates, the Scriptures tell us which it is that is the truth. If we accept the Bible as true and build our cosmological theories on that, then we will arrive at an accurate picture of the world and cosmos. **The Bible gives us the one basic fact that we need to know what is real: The earth is fixed. It does not move. From this one fact we can deduce, from our observations of the heavens, the Tycho-Brahe geocentric model of the cosmos, then the existence of ether and the existence of the Coriolis and Euler forces that hold the cosmos together.**

[552] Once again, this has been rejected for a variety of reasons including: The repugnance that scientists have for allowing that the distant stars influence the physical laws of motion locally; the philosophical revolution implied in the geocentric implications of this alternative—the fact that this would dethrone purely humanistic science in our culture and compel people to acknowledge the absolute truth of God's word in the Bible, with the many cascading implications that such a change implies to all human life on earth. Here are a few quotes from *Mach's Principle* as the editors discuss the ideas of relative vs. absolute motion. In reference to Newton's bucket experiment he says: ". . . it seems possible to know that a body is accelerating without any concern for whether it accelerates with respect to other bodies around it. This outcome contradicts the doctrine of the relativity of motion as applied to acceleration. For about a century now the most popular escape from this unwelcome refutation has been the following simple idea. Relativists point out that experiments such as Newton's reveal only that inertial forces are not noticeably related to motion with respect to *nearby* bodies. That, however, does not rule out the possibility that inertial forces are caused by acceleration with respect to more distant bodies. If this were the case, then inertial forces would not reveal an absolute acceleration but merely an acceleration relative to these distant masses. The core idea is that the inertial forces acting on an accelerating body arise from an interaction between that body And other bodies. The idea is not so much the proposal of a definite, new physical law; rather, it is the prescription that such a law should be found. . . . **It must be such that more distant masses play the decisive role in fixing the inertial forces on a given body, for example.**" (pp. 9–10.) [Bolding mine]

From an August Foppl paper, *On Absolute and Relative Motion*, we get an explanation of **why this is so important**: **The most acute observations on the physical significance of the law of inertia and the related concept of absolute motion are due to Mach. According to him, in mechanics, just as in geometry, the assumption of an absolute space and, with it, an absolute motion in the strict sense is not permitted.** Every motion is only comprehensible as a relative motion, and what one normally calls absolute motion is only motion relative to a reference system, a so-called inertial system, which is required by the law of inertia and has its orientation determined in accordance with some law by the masses of the universe (Weltsystem). Most authors are today in essential agreement with this point of view . . .

Experience teaches us first that the inertial system required by the law of inertia can be taken to coincide with the heaven of the fixed stars to an accuracy adequate for practical purposes. **It is also possible to choose a reference system differently, for example, fixed relative to the earth, in order to describe the phenomena of motion. However, it is then necessary** to apply to every material point the Coriolis additional forces of relative motion if one is to predict the motions correctly. One can therefore say that the inertial system is distinguished from any other reference system by the fact that in it one can dispense with the adoption of the additional forces. (*Mach's Principle*, pp. 120–121) [Bolding mine]

So, how we understand inertia sets our view of celestial mechanics and how we interpret what we see in the cosmos.

[553] A rotating universe is a non-inertial frame, so the speed of light is not constant, as Einstein and all scientists agree.

Albert Einstein, *Relativity: The Special and General Theory*, p. 89. After stating that light rays must be bent in a gravitational field, Einstein states:
In the second place our result shows that, according to the general theory of relativity, the law of the constancy of the velocity of light *in vacuo*, which constitutes one of the two fundamental assumptions in the special theory of relativity and to which we have already frequently referred, cannot claim any unlimited validity. A curvature of rays of light can only take place when the velocity of propagation of light varies with position.

W. G. V. Rosser, *An Introduction to the Theory of Relativity*, p. 460. He says:
[In the case of a universe rotating about the earth] the distant stars would have . . . velocities exceeding. . . the terrestrial value of the velocity of light. At first sight this appears to be a contradiction of the conclusion . . . that the velocities of all material bodies must be less than c. However, . . . according to the general theory [of relativity] . . . this is not true when gravitational fields are present. . . . If [they] are present the velocities of either material bodies or of light can assume any numerical value depending on the strength of the gravitational field. If one considers [earth] as being at rest, the centrifugal gravitational field assumes enormous values at large distances, and it is consistent with the theory of general relativity for the velocities of distant bodies to exceed 3×10^8 m/sec [the velocity of light] under these conditions.

Here is an analogy with sound waves as they travel through mediums of differing density or hardness.
In air: 343 m/sec; in water: 1482 m/sec; in rolled aluminum: 5000 m/sec; in beryllium: 12870 m/sec., etc. These values and many others for different mediums can be found in these two locations on the web:
https://www.engineeringtoolbox.com/speed-sound-d_82.html
https://www.engineeringtoolbox.com/sound-speed-solids-d_713.html
Although it is not agreed just what "the ether" or "space" or "the gravitational field" is that fills the cosmos, we can say that the enormous forces of the geocentric universe in regions more and more distant from earth would constrict it, modify its density or firmness, and thus greatly increase the transmission speed of light in those distant reaches of space. Newton showed that the speed of sound = (elastic modulus/density)$^{1/2}$. (H. G. V. Rosser, *The Theory of Relativity*, p.26.)

Light traveling at these higher speeds allows the universe to be interconnected in a way that removes the "horizon" problem and that also allows us, God's children, to actually see His glory, since the heavens declare His glory to us. Also, it can explain how, when we look through the Hubble telescope at galaxies that are supposedly 13.2 billion light years away (so that we are supposedly seeing them as they were 13.2 billion years ago) they look just like the stars and galaxies that are near to us. Currently this is a problem because the life span of our sun is less than 11 billion years. Thus how could stars have looked like our sun and other nearby stars over 13 billion years ago if the universe and all of its stars were formed at about the same time? The universe should look younger if we are viewing it as of 13.2 billion years ago. But if that light only took a short time to get to us then we are not looking into the distant past and the observational anomaly disappears.

[554] In the late 1800's Ludwig Boltzmann put forth a theory that tried to account for the presence of intelligent creatures like ourselves in a universe that was not as random or chaotic as might be expected from considerations from the field of thermodynamics. He suggested that the universe might spontaneously fluctuate into a more ordered state. One criticism of this idea was that it would be more likely for independent brains to simply assemble spontaneously. This idea resurfaced in the early 21st century when some cosmologists noted that Boltzmann Brains are statistically more likely to exist than "real" people like ourselves in this "real" universe. Thus perhaps we do not exist, but are merely Boltzmann Brains that have the thoughts that we exist within ourselves. I think that people do not actually believe this, but use the concept to speak of the unlikelihood of various cosmic theories in the "multiverse" context.

[555] People in the Intelligent Design movement like Hugh Ross explain the many "just right" parameters that make life possible in this universe. The exact strength of the various forces that hold atoms and molecules together, the relative size of subnuclear particles, the strength of gravity, the gravitational constant, Planck's constant, the Cosmological constant, the Hubble constant, the expansion rate of the universe, etc. etc. etc. For all of these and many other parameters to have just the right values is so very unlikely. These values all must be what they are or very close to their value (within a narrow range) in order for life to have developed ("evolved").

[556] Augustine, *Unfinished Literal Commentary on Genesis*, 51.

[557] The principle of "like begets like" can be seen as rooted in the nature of God, where the generate and the ingenerate are of the same nature (as opposed to the created and the uncreated which do not share the same nature.) This idea bears some further thought. The various created natures, once they have been brought into existence by God, generate offspring of like nature. See the discussion in Gregory Nazianzan for this idea as it applies to the Trinity and the nature of God.

Gregory Nazianzan, *Oration 29: On the Son*, 29, 10ff., in *Faith Gives Fullness to Reasoning—The Five Theological Orations of Gregory Nazianzen*, trans. Lionel Wickham and Frederick Williams (Leiden: E. J. Brill, 1991), pp. 251ff. However, such reasoning must be cautiously developed, for one complaint of Gregory is that his opponents are making observations about the created order and indiscriminately extending ideas and reasoning that applies properly to them to the Trinity and the nature of God. Gregory argues elsewhere that the attempt to understand what is given to us as revealed truth, but which still is a mystery, will become a source of error for us if we insist on understanding it by the use of our intellect and thereby attempt to resolve or explain the mystery. We must humbly accept the mysteries of the faith for what they are—mysteries beyond our full comprehension. This certainly must apply to the Trinity and to any reasoning by which we might try to understand it.

[558] Hundreds of scientists have questioned or repudiated the evolutionary theory of Darwin. A list of many scientists who have publically expressed some serious reservations about it for various reasons is here:

http://www.discovery.org/scripts/viewDB/filesDB-download.php?command=download&id=660.
[559] A Hollywood movie produced in the year 2000 called "Mission to Mars" dramatizes this idea nicely.
[560] Michael J. Behe, *Darwin's Black Box* (New York: Touchtone Books, 1996).
[561] Ibid.
[562] Augustine, *The Literal Meaning of Genesis*, 5, 46.
[563] John C. Sanford, *Genetic Entropy*, Fourth Edition, (FMS Publications, 2014), p. 5.
All of the discoveries and concepts in this short section are explained at length in this book.
Dr. Sanford includes full references to all of the technical papers that develop these ideas.
[564] Ibid., pp. 6ff. Dr. Sanford uses the analogy of an instruction manual for assembling a little red wagon.
[565] Ibid., pp. 33–35. Estimates are that 1 in 10 to 1 in 50 have a measurable effect at the level of the phenome.
[566] Ibid., pp. 17ff.
[567] Ibid. p. 17.
[568] Ibid., pp. 37–38; 75–175 mutations/generation actual; .1 estimated maximum allowable for continued viability, p. 195.
Or see Kondrashov's Numbers p. 209., which give only 300–900 times too high.
Or see Muller's Fear, p. 194., which gives us about 1,000 times too high (100 mutations per generation vs .1 allowable).
[569] Ibid., p. 71. See also these articles indicating that creationists realized this fact as long as a decade ago:
Brian Thomas, "Human Mutation Clock Confirms Creation," article on ICR.org dated 10-31-2012.
Brian Thomas, "The Human Mutation Clock is Ticking," article on OCR.org dated 07-07-2011.
Brian Thomas, "New Genomes Project Data Indicate a Young Human Race," article on ICR.org dated 11-09-2010.
[570] Ibid., p. 9.
[571] Charles Lyell, *Principles of Geology*, published in the 1830's. He assumed that the major geological features of the earth were formed by the same processes that we see around us now. This idea was called Uniformitarianism. It stands in opposition to Catastrophism, which attributes these features to unique catastrophic events that are not going on at this time. Clearly, the Bible depicts a number of catastrophic events in the past that brought the earth to its present state: the creation, and the Deluge of Noah in particular. If we assert Uniformitarianism as the only explanation allowed for the earth and its major geological features, then we rule out divine actions completely. So Lyell's approach asserts as it's *a priori* assumption a point of view that is contrary to the Scriptures.
[572] For an excellent overview, with enough detail to give the reader many concrete historical insights into what was happening, see the following excellent book: *The Fall of Darwin's Last Icon and the Failure of the Cartesian-Darwinian Narrative*, by John M. Wynne. The first ten chapters explain how we got where we are today, where almost every academic discipline is dominated by assumptions contrary to Christian teaching on origins and human nature.
[573] Basil the Great, *Exegetical Homilies (on the Hexaemeron)*, "Homily 8," 1.
[574] Ibid., "Homily 8," 2.
[575] St. John Chrysostom, *Homilies on Genesis*, "Homily 8," 4–5.
[576] Ibid., "Homily 8," 6–8.
[577] Basil of Caesarea, *On the Human Condition*, 1, 3, pp. 32–33.
[578] Augustine, *Unfinished Literal Commentary on Genesis*, 56.
[579] Peter Lombard, The Sentences, 18, 7, 1–4, vol. 2, pp. 80–81.
[580] See Augustine's discussion of this in *On Genesis: A Refutation of the Manichees*, 1, 32.
[581] Ibid., 1, 60.
[582] St. John Chrysostom, *Homilies on Genesis*, "Homily 8," 9.
[583] But see a lengthy discussion in Anastasius, Hexaemeron, 6, 6, 1 through 6, 6, 5, pp. 195-199, where he argues against the position of Chrysostom.
[584] Basil of Caesarea, *On the Human Condition*, 1, 7–8, pp. 35–37.
Basil says: "Let us make the human being according to our image." It speaks of the inner man; that is, let us give him the superiority of reason. "And let them rule." . . . as soon as you are made you are also made ruler . . . [You] received it from God, not written on wooden tablets, nor on perishable leaves wasted on moths, but your nature has the divine voice inscribed in it . . . [W]here the power to rule is there is the image of God.
[585] Ibid., 5–6, pp.34–35. See also Augustine's comments in *On Genesis: A Refutation of the Manichees*, 1, 27ff.
[586] Saadia Gaon, *The Book of Beliefs and Opinions*, "Treatise 2," 10.
[587] See also Gregory Nazianzan, *Oration 28: On the Doctrine of God*, 28, 17–20, pp. 233–235.
Gregory discusses the apparitions of God that were granted to various men throughout the ages and asserts that these visions, whatever they were, did not fully reveal to them His true nature or essence.
[588] Augustine, *The Literal Meaning of Genesis*, 9, 5–6.
[589] Ibid., 9, 9.
[590] St. John Chrysostom, *Homilies on Genesis*, "Homily 8," 10.
[591] Pope Leo XIII, *Arcanum Divinae [On Christian Marriage]* (1880), teaching on the sanctity of marriage, emphasizes this. See especially Sections 11 and 26, and also 9 and 10.
[592] Cyril of Alexandria, *Select Letters*, 9, 1, ed. Lionel R. Wickham, trans. Lionel R. Wickham (London: Oxford University Press, 1983), pp. 185, 187.
[593] Ephrem the Syrian, *Select Poems*, 2, 1; 2; 3, trans. Sebastian P. Brock and George A. Kiraz, eds. Daniel C. Peterson, Carl W. Griffin, Kristian S. Heal (Provo, Utah: Brigham Young University Press, 2006), pp. 19, 21.
So many of the Fathers speak this way. See also Gregory of Nyssa, *The Life of Moses*, 2, 221–255, trans. Abraham J. Malherbe and Everett Ferguson (NY: Paulist Press, 1978), pp. 112–120.
Gregory is forced to interpret the vision of Moses on the mountain, where he is allowed to see "the back of God," in a non-literal fashion. In his thinking God cannot have a front or a back because that would mean He has a shape or a form, for such pertains only to bodies, and God is not such.
Origen reiterates this often in *Against Celsus*. For example, 4, 30, p. 509.
[594] Didymus the Blind, *Commentary on Genesis*, 1, esp. pp. 63–66.

See also Basil of Caesarea, *On the Human Condition*, 1, 15–17, pp. 43–45.
    He asserts that we "grow into" the likeness of God by "putting on Jesus Christ" and by thereby growing into or maturing into His likeness. In this way God allows us to play a part in just how thoroughly we are "like" Him, to our praise and recompense before Him in heaven.
    See also Anastasius, *Hexaemeron*, 6, 4, 5, where he asserts that we were created in the image of God but attain His likeness only by choosing the good and rejecting the evil. "But that which is in the likeness is something related to our free will."

[595] Ibid., 9, 3, p. 193.
[596] Ibid., 9, 3, p. 195.
[597] Peter Lombard, *The Sentences*, 8, 1, 1–3, pp. 33–34.
    He discusses the bodies that angels have and the change that come upon the bodies of the fallen angels as punishment for their rebellion.
[598] St. John Chrysostom, *Homilies on Genesis*, "Homily 12," 8–9.
[599] Ibid., "Homily 12," 9.
[600] Basil of Caesarea, *On the Human Condition*, 2, 14, p. 60.
[601] Jean Paul Sartre, *No Exit*, in *"No Exit" and Three Other Plays*, trans. Stuart Gilbert (New York: Vintage International, 1989), p. 45.
[602] But not all. See the quotation from Irenaeus on man being created in the image of God, both body and Soul, for example. It is in the section of this book "The Ancient Faith."
[603] In Judaism the Song of Songs is seen as a picture of the love relationship between God and Israel.
[604] See Irenaeus of Lyons, *The Demonstration of the Apostolic Preaching*, 61, pp. 124–125 where he sees the violence and animosity of the animal kingdom being removed when Jesus returns, and where he likens that to the harmony that will be established between various different men at the same time. Both are the result of the removal of the curse of sin from parts of God's creation.
[605] See also the discussion on this point by Augustine in *On Genesis: A Refutation of the Manichees*, 1, 19. There he asserts that the dangerous or harmful aspects of the creation were the result of the curse that God placed on the ground because of the sin of Adam.
[606] Venerable Bede, *Commentary on 2 Peter*, in *Commentary on the Seven Catholic Epistles*, trans. Dom David Hurst, Cistercian Studies Series, 82 (Kalamazoo, MI: Cistercian Publications WMU, 1985)
[607] Methodius of Olympus, *Fragments*, 7, vol. 6, p. 381. One of the quotes of Methodius that summarizes his thoughts on this subject is in this work. It is in the chapter "The Ancient Faith."
[608] Augustine, *The Literal Meaning of Genesis*, 4, 15.

Adam

[609] P. J. Wiseman, *Ancient Records and the Structure of Genesis*, pp. 90-91.
[610] Augustine, *The Literal Meaning of Genesis*, 5, 45–46.
[611] Many of the ancients asserted (with no particular scriptural authority to back it up) that Adam sinned early on, perhaps even on the day that he was created and placed in Paradise. See for example George Synkellos, *The Chronography of George Synkellos*, 4, p. 5. He also quotes from St. John Chrysostom, *Commentary on the Gospel of Matthew*, Homily 59.I, commenting on Matthew 18:7.
    I hold to the idea that Adam and Eve had a period of time to get used to and enjoy their blessed state, a kind of honeymoon, before the Lord God allowed them to be tested. This view also fits with the fact that Adam wrote the first part his account during that period of time, before he fell.
[612] *The Book of Jasher*. See the text of this medieval book (probably from the seventeenth century) on-line at http://www.sacred-texts.com/chr/apo/jasher/index.htm. The story of Naamah is in 2:23ff and 5:14–17. In that account Naamah is born when her parents are very old, so she would be about the same age as Noah.
[613] P. J. Wiseman, *Ancient Records and the Structure of Genesis*, pp. 34-35.
[614] Ibid., p. 35.
[615] Augustine, *The Literal Meaning of Genesis*, 5, 1–16.
[616] Ibid., 5, 17–19.
[617] The earth was in a virginal state when the first Adam was formed from it, just as the second Adam was formed from a virgin. We see this idea, for example, in Irenaeus of Lyons, *The Demonstration of the Apostolic Preaching*, 32, p. 99.
[618] Augustine, *The Literal Meaning of Genesis*, 6, 13.
[619] Ibid., 6, 4.
[620] Athenagoras, *On the Resurrection of the Dead*, 4, vol. 2, in *Fathers of the Second Century: Hermas, Tatian, Athenagoras, Theophilus, and Clement of Alexandria (Entire)*, eds. A. Roberts, J. Donaldson, and A. C. Coxe, trans. B. P. Pratten (Buffalo, NY: Christian Literature Company, 1885), p. 151.
[621] Augustine, *The Literal Meaning of Genesis*, 8, 1–13.
[622] Ibid., 6, 31–39.
[623] Ibid., 8, 8–11.
[624] Symeon the New Theologian, *The First-Created Man*, 1, 2, pp. 44, 45.
    See his discussion of the two deaths and how they came upon Adam when he fell.
[625] Ambrose of Milan, *Paradise*, 49, p. 328.
[626] Ibid., 48, p. 327.
[627] Symeon the New Theologian, *The First-Created Man*, 9, 6.
[628] Ibid., 9, 10.
[629] But Elijah and Enoch were taken into heaven and could not have had glorified bodies at that time because Jesus is the first born from the dead, the first to receive a glorified body. So when they were taken into heaven they had to have sin-free bodies like Adam and Eve had at the beginning. When Jesus rose from the dead

then Enoch presumably received a glorified body, like the saints who were raised up at His resurrection to be "first fruits" with Jesus (Matthew 27:52–53). But Elijah has not yet received his glorified body because he must come back (along with Moses whose body God took after he died (Jude 9)) at the end of this age.) At that time they will preach until the beast kills them, and then will be raised back up (Revelation 11:7–12). They could not be killed if they already had their glorified bodies, for those bodies are unable to die.
   See my other book *Consummation: A Theology of the End-Times*, especially the chapter "Two Witnesses" for a discussion of both Moses and Elijah on this point.

630 Ambrose of Milan, *Paradise*, 29, pp. 306–307.
631 William G. Most, *Free from All Error* (Libertyville, IL: Prow Books/Franciscan Marytown Press, 1985), p. 63.
632 This location on Wikipedia has an example of the thinking that I am referring to: https://en.wikipedia.org/wiki/Genesis_creation_narrative.
Or do a search for "Genesis creation narrative" to get the same Wikipedia entry.
   The author tells us how the Genesis account was borrowed from the Mesopotamian mythology and adapted to the monotheistic beliefs of the Hebrews. These assertions are made but no evidence is given to substantiate the claim. The reader is left to assume that behind the claims is a deep understanding of ancient Middle Eastern literature, but no concrete information is shared with the reader. Thus no personal understanding is imparted to the reader, who must simply trust the claims of the author. Intermingled with their claims is the equally unsupported assertion that the Genesis creation account was not written by Moses at all, but by several later redactors.
   Finally, the author refers to two enigmatic passages (Psalm 74:13–14, Isaiah 51:9–10) and claims that these connect to ancient mythological phrases in a Canaanite myth. This is not convincing evidence in support of his expansive claims.
   Another example of this thinking can be found in Wikipedia here: https://en.wikipedia.org/wiki/Chronology_of_the_Bible.
Or do a search for "Chronology of the Bible" to get the same Wikipedia entry. The thinking there is of the same ilk—Genesis is just a myth. As you read this article you can see that the author calls into question the historicity of much of the Old Testament. How very far this thinking departs from the Ancient Faith!
633 Augustine, *The Literal Meaning of Genesis*, 7, 40–42.
634 Ibid., 4, 22.
635 Ibid., 4, 1.
636 Ibid., 7, 42.
637 Ibid., 4, 22.
638 There is an ancient lithograph called "The Adam and Eve Seal", museum number 89326 (or ME89326) that is in the British Museum. It is dated to between 2100 BC and 2200 BC. You can see it here: http://www.britishmuseum.org/research/collection_online/collection_object_details.aspx?objectId=368842&partId=1. Or just do a search for ME89326 or for "British Museum – Adam and Eve Seal" to see it. Here is another link to a clearer picture of the seal: http://adamandeveakkadianseal.blogspot.com/.
Or do a search for: "Akkadian Temptation Seal showing Adam and Eve" to see more.
639 St. John Chrysostom, *Homilies on Genesis*, "Homily 16," 2.
640 Ibid., "Homily 1."
   Also see Ambrose of Milan, *Paradise*, 54, pp. 332–334. He muses on the motives of the Devil. These are just two examples of the many Fathers who attribute envy to the Devil as his motive for tempting Adam and Eve and seeking to rob them of their joy. Usually they quote a verse from the Wisdom of Solomon, "Through the envy of the Devil death came into the world" (2:24).
641 Ambrose of Milan, *Paradise*, 55, p. 334.
642 Ibid., 34, pp. 312–313.
643 Severus of Antioch, *The Hymns of Severus and Others in the Syriac Version of Paul of Edessa as Revised by James of Edessa*, fasc. 13, vol. 6, trans. E. W. Brooks, in Patrologia Orientalis (Paris: 1909), pp. 55–56.
644 Symeon the New Theologian, *The First-Created Man*, 66, 1, pp. 108–110.
645 St. John Chrysostom, *Homilies on Genesis*, "Homily 17," 24.
646 Symeon the New Theologian, *The First-Created Man*, 66, 1, pp. 113–114.
647 C. S. Lewis, *The Screwtape Letters and Screwtape Proposes a Toast* (London: Macmillan, 1970), p. 146.
648 Ibid. pp. 146–149.
649 Origen. (1885). *De Principiis*, 1, 6, 1. See also 1, 5, 2–5 for a preparatory discussion of how the holy angels and the fallen angels arrived at their present conditions. They were not created good or evil, so that their wickedness cannot be ascribed to their creator, but they each made a choice. Because the fallen angels are evil by a choice that they made, he concludes that they might be recalled again to what is good. This is the conclusion that he arrives at in De Principiis.
650 Severus of Antioch, *The Hymns of Severus and Others in the Syriac Version of Paul of Edessa as Revised by James of Edessa*, fasc. 78, pp. 120–121.
651 There is an ancient lithograph of the expulsion of Adam and Eve from the garden. It was discovered in the 1930's by E. A. Speiser of the University of Pennsylvania at Tepe Gawdra. It is dated to several thousand years before Christ. You can search for "TepeGawraMound" and look at "Bible Archeology: Adam and Eve in the Garden of Eden," http://www.bible-archaeology.info/adam.htm.
652 St. John Chrysostom, *Homilies on Genesis*, "Homily 21," 8.

Noah
653 P. J. Wiseman, *Ancient Records and the Structure of Genesis*, p. 90.
654 Ibid., p. 103.

655 Ibid.
656 Ibid., pp. 103-104.
657 St. John Chrysostom, *Homilies on Genesis*, "Homily 21," 10.
658 Ibid., "Homily 21," 13.
659 Ibid., "Homily 21," 14.
660 Ibid., "Homily 21," 15.
661 Ibid., "Homily 22," 12.
662 Sulpicius Severus, *Chronicle*, 1, 3, pp. 68–69. Some of the others who ascribed to this position but did not develop the concepts in such detail, perhaps just referring to the "angels who sinned" include:
 Justin Martyr, *The Second Apology of Justin*, 5, p. 188;
 Athenagoras, *A Plea for the Christians*, 24, p. 133;
 Tertullian, *On Idolatry*, 9, p. 31;
 Irenaeus of Lyons, *Irenaeus against Heresies*, 4, 36, 4, p. 315;
 Irenaeus of Lyons, *The Demonstration of the Apostolic Preaching*, 18, p. 85.
 Clement of Alexandria, *The Miscellanies*, 5, 1, pp. 446–447.
 Origen, *Against Celsus*, 5, 55–56, pp. 567–568. (Origen, as usual, allows that this might be allegorical)
 Fulgentius the Mythographer, *On the Ages of the World and of Man*, 2, p. 191.
 Eusebius of Caesarea, *Preparation for the Gospel*, 7, 8, vol. 1, pp. 309, 310.
  Eusebius actually states that the wicked race of giants before the Flood "who were carrying on with ungodly and impious efforts their wars with God which are still so celebrated" had "sprung from some condition mightier than man's nature, or in whatever way endowed" and thus he leaves open the exact identification of the beings from which the giants took their origin.
 Lactantius, *The Epitome of the Divine Institutes*, 27, pp. 231–232;
 Cyprian of Carthage, *On the Dress of Virgins*, 14, vol. 5, in *Fathers of the Third Century: Hippolytus, Cyprian, Novatian, Appendix*, eds. A. Roberts, J. Donaldson, and A. C. Coxe, trans. R. E. Wallis (Buffalo, NY: Christian Literature Company, 1886), p. 434.
 Didymus the Blind, *Commentary on Genesis*, 6.
  There is a discussion of options on pp. 142–147.
 Jerome, *Saint Jerome's Hebrew Questions on Genesis*, 6:2–6:4, pp. 36–37.
  I quoted parts of this in the section "The Ancient Faith." This gives a glimpse of Jerome's ideas.
 Augustine, *The City of God*, 15, 9. Father Most seems to think that Augustine understood Genesis 6:1–4 as referring to angels, perhaps because in this place in his *City* he argues for the past existence of giants. But I doubt that Augustine would have accepted that interpretation because of his basic stance towards the spiritual realm. Thus he would not, it seems to me, have believed that angels could ever have interacted sexually with human beings because of his understanding of what the spiritual realm was and what it meant to say that they were spirits.
663 Israel did not obey God at the time of Joshua, but probably the final destruction of the giants, and of all their descendants, is recorded in 2 Samuel 21:18–22.
664 Cyril of Alexandria, *Glaphyra on Genesis*, 2, "Concerning Noah and the Ark," 2.
665 Peter Lombard, *The Sentences*, 8, 1, 1–3, pp. 33–34.
 I refer the reader to this section of *The Sentences* where he discusses the nature of the spiritual body of the angels and what happened to the bodies of the wicked angels when they fell.
666 For a humorous example of this see C.S. Lewis, *The Screwtape Letters and Screwtape Proposes a Toast*, p. 103. The senior tempter devil Screwtape, in the midst of a particularly heated bout of frenzied wickedness while writing to his protégé Wormwood, suddenly transforms into a giant cockroach.

Interlude: Creation Theory
667 John C. Whitcomb and Henry M. Morris, *The Genesis Flood: The Biblical Record and Its Scientific Implications* (Phillipsburg, NJ: Presbyterian and Reformed Publishing Company, 1961).
668 Venerable Bede, *Commentary on 2 Peter*, p. 137.
669 John C. Whitcomb and Henry M. Morris, *The Genesis Flood: The Biblical Record and Its Scientific Implications*, pp. 219-220.
670 See DeYoung, *Thousands, Not Billions*.
671 John C. Whitcomb and Henry M. Morris, *The Genesis Flood: The Biblical Record and Its Scientific Implications*, *The Genesis Flood*, pp. 222-223.
672 Ibid., p. 223.
673 Ibid., p. 277.

The Deluge
674 P. J. Wiseman, *Ancient Records and the Structure of Genesis*, pp. 92–93.
675 St. John Chrysostom, *Homilies on Genesis*, "Homily 25," 15.
676 Photographic evidence from three different satellites shows that the ark rests on Mt. Ararat at an elevation of about 14,765 feet. It is located at these exact coordinates:
  N 39 degrees, 43 minutes, 7.6 seconds   E 44 degrees, 17 minutes, 38.7 minutes
 For all the details of this discovery see this website:
https://www.scribd.com/document/26969803/Evidence-Noah-s-Ark-Located-Noah-Real-or-Myth-Noah-s-Ark-Found
The ark was discovered by Edward E. Crawford. He was inspired to look at this location as he read Genesis 8:5 "the tops of the mountains became visible" and eventually deduced that, given the geography of Ararat, the only possible place on the mountain where the receding waters would have produced this sight for Noah and his family was at this approximate

location. Further careful investigation showed the ark's precise spot as given above. At this time the Turkish government will not allow long-time investigation or digging at the site of the ark.

677 Crawford's find indicates that the pre-Flood cubit was MUCH larger. The Ark that has been found buried under the ice (via satellite photos on three occasions) has the following dimensions: 1145 feet long, 190 feet wide. Its expected height is thus about 127 feet. The straight lines of the object show clearly that its relative dimensions are exactly as described in Genesis, but the "cubit" used by Noah before the Flood must have been almost 46 inches long!

Here is a short word study on "cubit" (Hebrew 'ammah). It is a prolonged form of the Hebrew "ām" meaning mother and, while father is the provider, mother is the measurer. So the base word indicates "measure" and the word translated "cubit" could mean simply "measure," in which case the text indicates the ark was 300 measures long, 50 measures wide, and 30 measures high. The actual size of the ark buried under the ice indicates that the pre-Flood "measure" or "cubit", had to be much longer. So the actual volume of the ark is over 16 times what is traditionally understood! Do not be too surprised. The assumption the pre-Flood cubit was about the same as the post-Flood cubit was reasonable but not definitive. Now that the ark has been found we know the pre-Flood "cubit" or "measure" was much larger.

678 John C. Whitcomb and Henry M. Morris, *The Genesis Flood: The Biblical Record and Its Scientific Implications*, The Genesis Flood, p. 69.

679 Ibid., pp. 66–67.

680 Eleventh tablet of the *Gilgamesh Epic*.

681 Charles Martin, *Flood Legends: Global Clues of a Common Event* (Green Forest, AR: Master Books, 2009), pp. 128–129.

682 Ibid., pp. 134–135.

683 Ibid.

684 H. V. Hilprecht, *The Earliest Version of the Babylonian Deluge History and The Temple Library of Nippur* (Philadelphia, PA: University of Pennsylvania, 1910), pp. 35-40 and 64-65. This tablet can be seen (but not its translation) at the CDLI (Cuneiform Digital Library Initiative) on-line. It can be found by entering "CBS 13532" in the search field "Collection #".

685 Also note the graphic description that David gives of his deliverance from Saul in Psalm 18:7–16. This is best understood as a description of the onset of the Deluge. Perhaps such documents from the time of Noah were still in existence at the time of David, from which he took his imagery.

686 St. John Chrysostom, *Homilies on Genesis*, "Homily 25," 19.

687 Ibid., "Homily 25," 13–15.

688 It was this verse that provided the clue to Crawford as to the possible location of the ark. Very few places on Ararat would have allowed Noah to see this sight as the waters receded. This fact limited the possible places to search for the ark and eventually led Crawford to it.

689 Edward E. Crawford, "Proto-Sumerian Inscriptions in the Ahora Gorge of Buyuk Agri (Greater Mt. Ararat), Turkey," in *Research & Exploration, A Scholarly Publication of the National Geographic Society*, published quarterly, vol. 10, Autumn of 1994, p. 484.

690 Ibid.

691 St. John Chrysostom, *Homilies on Genesis*, "Homily 27," 10, for example.

692 Augustine, *The Literal Meaning of Genesis*, 10, 34–37.

693 Ibid., 10, 36.

694 Peter Lombard, *The Sentences*, 3, 1, 1–4 and 3, 2, vol. 3, pp. 9–10.

As a help, I list the relevant verses in the writings of the Fathers that Peter Lombard quotes from:
John of Damascus, *The Orthodox Faith*, 3, 2.
[After reviewing the Scripture of Luke on the annunciation he gives the orthodox understanding.]
So then, after the assent of the holy Virgin, the Holy Spirit descended on her, according to the word of the Lord which the angel spoke, **purifying her** [So she was a sinner but was cleansed when "the Holy Spirit came upon her."], and granting her power to receive the divinity of the Word, and likewise power to bring forth. And then was she overshadowed by the enhypostatic Wisdom and Power of the most high God, the Son of God Who is of like essence with the Father as of Divine seed, and from her holy and most pure blood He formed flesh animated with reason and thought, the first-fruits of our compound [i. e., body and soul] nature: not by procreation but by creation through the Holy Spirit: not developing the fashion of the body by gradual additions but perfecting it at once, He Himself, the very Word of God, standing to the flesh in the relation of subsistence.

Fulgentius of Ruspe, *To Peter on the Faith*, 2, 15 and 2, 17.
Therefore, believe that Christ, the Son of God, i.e., one of the persons of the Trinity, is true God, so that you do not doubt that his divinity has been born of the nature of the Father. And so, also, believe that he is truly human, so that you do not think that his flesh is of a celestial, or heavenly, or some other kind of, nature, but that **his is the flesh of every human being, i.e., that which God himself fashioned for the first human being** from the earth and fashions for other human beings, whom he creates through human reproduction. But, although the flesh of Christ is of one and the same nature as that of all human beings, still, that which God the Word deigned to unite to himself from the virgin Mary, **conceived without sin**, was born without sin.

Thus the sin and the punishment for the sin which through the crime of a corrupted woman entered the world, is taken away from the world through birth from an inviolate virgin. And, because in the condition of the human race [brought about] by a woman made from a male only, it came about that we were held in custody by the chains of death; in the redemption of the human race, the divine goodness accomplished that through a man who was born from a woman only, life was restored to human beings.

Augustine, *On Nature and Grace*, 36, n42. After listing many whom Pelagius called sinless (with whom he disagrees) Augustine says: "[Referring to the Virgin Mary as one possible exception] . . . out of respect for the Lord, I wish to raise no question at all when the discussion concerns sins–for whence do we know what **an abundance of grace for entirely overcoming sin was conferred on her** who had the merit to conceive and bear him who undoubtedly was without sin?"

Augustine, *On the Trinity*, 13, 18, n23. Augustine says: "**For God was certainly able to assume human nature elsewhere than from the race of Adam**, who by his sin bound the human race, in which He might be the Mediator between God and man, just as He did not create the first man whom He created from the race of anyone else. He could, therefore, create another man in this manner or in any manner that He pleased, by whom the conqueror of the first man would be conquered. **But God judged it better, both to assume human nature from the race itself that was conquered, through which He would conquer the enemy of the human race, and yet to take it from a virgin, whose conception the spirit, not the flesh, the faith, not passion, preceded.**

[Augustine continues on to explain what he means by spirit, not flesh, faith, not passion.]

"**Nor did the concupiscence of the flesh intervene, by which all others are propagated and conceived who contract original sin; since concupiscence was wholly absent, the holy virginity was fecundated by believing, not by lying together, so that what was born from the stock of the first man drew its origin only from the race, not from the sin also**. For a nature was born that was not corrupted by the contagion of transgression, but was the only remedy for all such vices. For a man was born, I say, having no sin and not to have any sin at all, through whom those who were to be liberated from sin and who could not be born without sin would be born again." [This goes with his idea that sexual reproduction is the transmitter of the sin nature] [He then explains why (disordered) sexuality could have had no part in the conception of Jesus.] "For although conjugal chastity can make good use of the carnal concupiscence which is in the genital members, yet it has involuntary movements, which prove either that it could not exist at all in paradise before sin, or if it did exist, that it was not then such that it should sometimes resist the will. But now we feel it to be such that it fights against the law of the mind and arouses the desires of intercourse, even if there is no question of begetting; if it yields, then it is satisfied by sinning; if it does not yield, then it is restrained by withholding its consent; who can doubt that these two things were alien from paradise before sin? For neither did that honesty do anything indecent, nor did that felicity tolerate anything unquiet. **It must needs be, therefore, that no carnal concupiscence should be at all present there when the offspring of the Virgin was conceived, in whom the author of death would find nothing worthy of death, and yet would slay Him, only to be conquered by the author of life.**"

[695] We noted this in our reflections on Genesis 3:1–7 where we asked the question, "Why did God allow Adam and Eve to be tested?" There we referenced the basic principle that untested virtue is like unrefined gold or silver, and as such is not acceptable before the throne of God in heaven. This was stated most clearly and succinctly by Derek Prince in his instructional letter entitled *Angels*. We restate his explanation here:

> It is a principle of God's dealings with us that our relationships with Him are not secure until we have passed through certain tests which He has appointed. This applies to both angels and human beings. Untested relationships are like unrefined gold. They are not acceptable in heaven. For this reason Jesus said to the Christians in Laodicea: "I counsel you to buy from Me gold refined in the fire" (Revelation 3:18). In other words, "Your claim to be My people is not valid until you have passed the test." Gold of that quality is not cheap. We have to buy it. There is a price to pay!

If God allowed the first Eve and the first Adam to be tested, how could he not allow the "New Eve" to be similarly tested? He allowed the "New Adam" to be tested. (see Matthew 4:1–11)

[696] See *The New Defender's Study Bible*, ed. Henry Morris (New York: World Publishing, 2005), footnote on Luke 1:31, p. 1497.

[697] Ibid., footnote on Romans 1:3, p. 1698.

[698] Peter Lombard, *The Sentences*, 12, 2, 1–2, pp. 47–48.
He discusses whether "God could have taken on another human nature, or other than from the stock of Adam." He quotes Augustine, *On the Trinity*, 13. He could have done such, but that "He judged it better to take human form through which to conquer the enemy of humankind from the very stock that had been conquered."
This is an excellent example of divine justice in my opinion. Justice: restoring what has been damaged or lost; that is, putting it back into proper order so that it can function as it was intended to from the beginning.

[699] Blessed Theophylact, *Blessed Theophylact's Explanation of the New Testament*, 1, vol. 3. Trans Fr. Christopher Stade (House Springs, MO: Chrysostom Press, 2007), pp. 16–18.

[700] See a discussion of the persistent and varied errors in this regard as discussed by John Cassian in his *Conferences. The Seven Books of John Cassian on the Incarnation of the Lord, against Nestorius*, 1, 5, Vol. 11, in *Sulpitius Severus, Vincent of Lerins, John Cassian*, eds P. Schaff and H. Wace, trans. E. C. S. Gibson (New York: Christian Literature Company, 1894), pp. 554–555.
In this section he carefully states the received orthodox understanding of the Incarnation and asserts that it is "ours to believe, His [God's] to understand" and that "We should not then in our feeble minds make guesses" about how this might have happened.

See also Fulgentius of Ruspe, *To Peter on the Faith*, 21–22, for a discussion of the great mystery of our faith in how "The Word became flesh." He explains the Incarnation to Peter before he traveled to Jerusalem as a protection for him so that his faith might not be corrupted in any way. Our Lord first prepared a humble handmaid then condescended to take His humanity from her, just as He received His divinity from the Father and from His own eternal nature as God. This was necessary, as he explains, so that His sacrifice could result in the complete forgiveness of our sins.

[701] Jean-Francois Bonnefoy, O. F. M., *The Immaculate Conception in the Divine Plan*, trans. from French by Michael D. Meilach, O. F. M. (Patterson, NJ: St. Anthony Press, 1967), pp. 24–31, 51–59.
This book contains an excellent explanation of the thinking that undergirds this decree. It also mentions the various diverse ideas within Catholic Tradition that attributed some sort of sin to Mary (*debitum* peccati, see pp. 39–51), no doubt because of the biblical verses asserting the universality of sin noted in our discussion.

[702] So we can theorize in two basic ways how Jesus avoided the universal human condition of the sin nature:
- It can be explained by the fact that no man was involved in His conception.

- It can be asserted that, because His flesh still came from Mary, that she must have been cleansed beforehand; that is, she was prepared. This could have been at her conception or when "the Holy Spirit came upon her." Then when "the Most High overshadowed her so that the holy thing **begotten** in her would be called the Son of God" the embryo was constructed out of human flesh that had been preserved from or cleansed from all sin.

Here are some scriptural connections with the last theory:
- Both Enoch and Elijah were "taken" by God, and presumably were taken to heaven. They could not have entered heaven with a sin nature. So they had to be cleansed of their sin nature at some point in their ministry on earth before being taken, just like Mary was. But they could not have been given glorified bodies when they were taken because Jesus is "the first born from the dead" and so is the first to receive a glorified body. They had to have been given sin-free bodies like those of Adam and Eve before they sinned.
- Mary was cleansed in the same way, but was not immediately taken. She was destined to bear the Son of God and that was why she was cleansed of or preserved from sin.
- But death comes to us because of sin (Romans 6:23) and since Mary was sin-free she would not have died. Thus she also was taken into heaven after her work on earth was completed. This is the Roman Catholic doctrine of the Assumption of Mary. She was given a glorified body.
- At this time there are a number of people besides Jesus in heaven with their bodies. Among them are the resurrection saints that were the "first fruits" along with Jesus when He ascended into heaven on the Sunday after His resurrection—who also have glorified bodies like our Lord (Matthew 27:52–53). Then there are Mary, Enoch, and Elijah. Moses is also in heaven in his body because God wanted his body for a special reason (Jude 9). See my book *Consummation: A Theology of the End-Times*, especially the chapter "Two Witnesses" for a discussion of Moses and Elijah on this point.
- At the end of this age the entire body of church believers will be "changed" (1 Corinthians 15:51–52) and will be cleansed from their sin nature. After that they will be "caught up . . . in the clouds to meet the Lord in the air" (1 Thessalonians 4:17), and will have glorified bodies. Thus, in some sense, Mary was a forerunner of the raptured end-times saints.

[703] Gregory Nazianzen, *Oration 28: On the Doctrine of God*, 28, 22–31, pp. 237–244.
Gregory has an extended meditation on the many mysteries of man and beast. His awe at the handiwork of the Creator leads him to awe at the Artist Himself. This is the proper spiritual stance for us, rather than insipid assertions about "mother nature" and "the inevitable result of millions of years of evolution." The attribution of God's wonders to such mindless chance are the final stage of deteriorated reasoning that our futile and vain culture has produced. It distances us from God by denying His glorious acts.

[704] According to Flavius Josephus, in the *Antiquities of the Jews*, an ancient town named Seron or "place of dispersion" in Armenia is where the family of Noah is said to have parted sometime after the Flood.

[705] Jacob of Sarug, *Jacob of Sarug's Homily on the Tower of Babel*, pp. 81, 87, 90–92, 95–98, 101, 103–104, 106, 113–120, 123–126, 129, 135–138, 145–154, trans. Aaron Michael Butts, ed. George A. Kiraz (Piscataway, NJ: Georgias Press, 2009), pp. 16, 18, 20, 22.

Babel

[706] P. J. Wiseman, *Ancient Records and the Structure of Genesis*, p. 71.

[707] Ibid., p. 93.

[708] St. John Chrysostom, *Homilies on Genesis*, "Homily 30," 11.

[709] John H. Walton, *The Mesopotamian Background of the Tower Account and Its Implications*, in *Bulletin for Biblical Research* 5 (1995): 155-75.

[710] See https://en.wikipedia.org/wiki/Enmerkar_and_the_Lord_of_Aratta.

[711] Don Fernando de Alva Ixtlilxochitl, *Obras Historicas*, vol. 1 (Mexico City: Editora Nacional, 1959), pp. 11–13. A rough translation/paraphrase, but it catches the meaning.

[712] See https://rperon1017blog.wordpress.com/2015/01/21/flood-stories-the-toltec-aztecs-and-chinese/. This also includes their memory of the great Flood.

[713] See http://www.firstpeople.us/FP-Html-Legends/TheTowerofBabel-Choctaw.html.

[714] Robert W. Williamson, *Religious and Cosmic Beliefs of Central Polynesia*, vol. 1 (Cambridge UK: Cambridge University Press, 1933), p. 94.

[715] Sir James George Frazer, *Folk-Lore in the Old Testament: Studies in Comparative Religion Legend and Law*, vol.1 (London: Macmillan, 1919), pp. 383–384.

[716] See on-line at this location under the section entitled "American Migrations": http://www.meta-religion.com/World_Religions/Ancient_religions/central_america/myths_of_the_maya.htm#.VmnMw5ZliLk.

Terah the Father of Abraham

[717] P. J. Wiseman, *Ancient Records and the Structure of Genesis*, pp. 71-72.

[718] Ibid., p. 93.

[719] Ibid.

[720] Simon Jenkins, *Bible Mapbook* (Oxford: Lion Publishing, 1985), p. 15.

[721] K. A. Kitchen, *On the Reliability of the Old Testament*, (Grand Rapids, MI: William B. Eerdmans, 2003). See pp. 316–318 for a discussion of the wide scope of travel in patriarchal times, showing how people could move freely in the area of Mesopotamia during the Old Babylonian period.

[722] Simon Jenkins, *Bible Mapbook*, p. 19.

[723] For a discussion of customs of adoption and proxy wives in patriarchal times see also K. A. Kitchen, *On the Reliability of the Old Testament*, pp. 324–328.

Abraham and Isaac
[724] P. J. Wiseman, *Ancient Records and the Structure of Genesis*, p. 72.
[725] Ibid., pp. 94–95.
[726] Simon Jenkins, *Bible Mapbook*, p. 19.
[727] K. A. Kitchen, *On the Reliability of the Old Testament*, p. 335.
   He opines that this was an update of the twelfth century or later. That is, it is an anachronism, like naming The city the Hebrews built for Pharaoh "Ramesses" instead of "Avaris," which had become an obsolete word.
[728] P. J. Wiseman, *Ancient Records and the Structure of Genesis*, p. 120.
[729] Ibid., p. 77.
[730] Ibid.
[731] St. John Chrysostom, *Homilies on Genesis*, "Homily 32," Section 4.
[732] Ibid., "Homily 32," 5.
[733] See Irenaeus of Lyons, *The Demonstration of the Apostolic Preaching*, 44, p. 109. There Irenaeus explicitly identifies the visitors that spoke with Abraham as two angels and the Son of God.
[734] *The Book of Jasher*, 21:13.
[735] K. A. Kitchen, *On the Reliability of the Old Testament*, pp. 339–340.
   He opines that this was an update of the twelfth century or later. That is, it is an anachronism.
[736] P. J. Wiseman, *Ancient Records and the Structure of Genesis*, pp. 77–78.
[737] Origen, *Commentary on Genesis*, "Homily 10," Section 4, p. 164.
[738] *The Book of Jasher*, 24:40.
[739] Ibid.

Jacob
[740] Ibid., pp. 72–73.
[741] Ibid.
[742] Ibid., pp. 95–96.
[743] K. A. Kitchen, *On the Reliability of the Old Testament*, pp. 339–340.
   He opines that this was an update of the 12th century or later. That is, it is an anachronism.
[744] *The Book of Jasher*, 31:22–30.
[745] K. A. Kitchen, *On the Reliability of the Old Testament*, pp. 337–338.
[746] *The Book of Jasher*, 31:22–30.
[747] Ibid., 36:13–14.
[748] P. J. Wiseman, *Ancient Records and the Structure of Genesis*, p. 77.

The Sons of Jacob
[749] Ibid., pp. 75–76.
[750] Ibid.
[751] *Babylonian Talmud, Book 2: Tracts Erubin, Shekalim, Rosh Hashana*, trans and ed. by Michael L. Rodkinson, (New York: Talmud Society, 1918). For chapter 7, see http://www.sacred-texts.com/jud/t02/shk11.htm.
[752] See this site for a description of the grain silos used in ancient Egypt around estimated dates 1630-1520 BC. Archaeologists find silos and administration center from early Egyptian city (uchicago.edu)
[753] The tablet was translated by Rev. Charles Forster, see the footnote in *The New Defender's Study Bible* on Genesis 41:54, p. 110. See also http://www.reshafim.org.il/ad/egypt/timelines/topics/harvesting_grain.htm.
[754] P. J. Wiseman, *Ancient Records and the Structure of Genesis*, p. 105.
[755] K. A. Kitchen, *On the Reliability of the Old Testament*, pp. 329-330.
   Also see the footnote in *The New Defender's Study Bible* on Exodus 6:3, pp 134–5.
[756] See http://geography.about.com/od/populationgeography/a/populationgrow.htm.

Summary and Final Conclusion
[757] P. J. Wiseman, *Ancient Records and the Structure of Genesis*, pp. 143-148. I have extracted some of this information and added other information as the content of this concluding chapter.
[758] Ibid., pp. 146-147.
[759] Luc Ferry, *A Brief History of Thought*, trans. Thoe Cuffe (New York: Harper Perennial, 2003), pp. 93-94.
[760] A few days after my supernatural revelation about the theories of origins I asked a friend who was three days away from his PhD in biochemistry at the University of Michigan about the complexity of life. I mentioned some **creationist** ideas and he said "Oh my teachers call those guys buffoons." I said, "I didn't care about the accusations, I just wonder if they are right" "Oh, my profs make cartoons of such people." "But are they correct?" "Mike, they **ridicule** those men and their ideas!" "But is life too complex to have arisen by chance?" With that he stomped away in a huff. As he left the Lord stood next to me and these words came into my mind: "They call it academic freedom." They were from our Lord, His way of introducing me early on to the spiritual battle that is in progress at all levels of our educational and legal system. To understand the bigotry in academia against biblical concepts, especially as they relate to evolution, the courageous reader can see:
   Jerry Bergmen, *The Slaughter of the Dissidents* (Southworth, WA: Leafcutter Press, 2009)
   Jerry Bergman, *Silencing the Darwin Skeptics* (Southworth, WA: Leafcutter Press, 2009)
   Jerry Bergman, *Censoring the Darwin Skeptics* (Southworth, WA: Leafcutter Press, 2009)
[761] Augustine, *The City of God*, 11, 4.

Appendix II – The Modern Theory of Origins
[762] The interested reader might look at this excellent and easily accessible discussion of "deep time."
   Michael J. Oard, The Deep Time Deception, (Powder Springs, GA: Creation Book Publishers, 2019)

Printed in Great Britain
by Amazon